The Complete Dictionary of
Opera & Operetta

The Complete Dictionary of OPERA & OPERETTA

James Anderson

Previously titled
The Harper Dictionary of Opera and Operetta

WINGS BOOKS

New York • Avenel, New Jersey

Copyright © 1989 by Bloomsbury Publishing, Ltd.

This 1993 edition is published by Wings Books,
distributed by Outlet Book Company, Inc., a Random House Company,
40 Engelhard Avenue, Avenel, New Jersey 07001,
by arrangement with HarperCollins Publishers, Inc.

Random House
New York • Toronto • London • Sydney • Auckland

Printed and bound in the United States of America

Library of Congress Cataloging-in-Publication Data

Anderson, James.
    [Bloomsbury dictionary of opera and operetta]
    The complete dictionary of opera & operetta /
        James Anderson.
        p.   cm.
    Originally published: Bloomsbury dictionary of opera and
        operetta.
    London : Bloomsbury pub., 1989. With new introd.
    ISBN 0-517-09156-9
    1. Opera—Dictionaries.   2. Operetta—Dictionaries.
        I. Title.
    II. Title: Complete dictionary of opera and operetta.
    [ML102.O6A6   1993]
    782.1'03—dc20   93-14823
                                               CIP
                                               MN

ISBN 0-517-09156-9

8 7 6 5 4 3 2 1

CONTENTS

INTRODUCTION

This book was undertaken partly as an act of self-defence: for many years friends had been urging me to put my knowledge of music to some practical use. This book is the result of that urging, and I hope that it will stop them nagging me. My initial feeling on undertaking a project of this scale on so demanding and wide-ranging a subject, was one of awe at the work of predecessors in the field, particularly the *Complete Opera Book* of Kobbé (recently revised by Lord Harewood), the Oxford *Dictionary of Opera* by Harold Rosenthal and John Warrack and the *Metropolitan Encyclopedia of Opera* edited by David Hamilton. As does everybody writing on opera, I owe an enormous debt to them for the vast amount of factual information which they have made available.

Although such outstanding works were already in existence, I was persuaded to write another for a number of reasons. Firstly, I have tried to provide a reference guide that is fully up-to-date. This wish is reflected in my attempt to respond to contemporary trends in operatic performance and in public taste. I have endeavoured to take account of such recent developments as the major renewal of interest in early opera (especially the works of Rameau, Lully, Cavalli and Charpentier), of the continuing and still-growing interest in the Italian bel canto and Czech repertories, and the recent revival of interest in the operas of individual composers such as Haydn, Zemlinsky and Massenet.

In addition, I have attempted (as is reflected in the book's title) to give a comprehensive coverage to operetta, a field which seems to receive short shrift in many reference works, despite its great popularity. I have, as well, provided a representative selection of material on the most significant modern operas which are, naturally, not dealt with in older reference works. I have thus included the recent works of Musgrave, Reimann, Maxwell Davies and Glass, as well as covering the remarkable operatic flowering currently taking place in Finland. I have also tried to write this book with a younger audience in mind: to this end, I have included more composers, more operas and more contemporary performers at the expense of many singers from the past who have no meaning for audiences of the late 1980s who have never heard of them. That said, such singers, where of particular note, or historical interest, are here.

My own personal experience of reference works of any kind (an experience which I should imagine is shared by most people) is that they are frequently difficult to use, have print which requires a microsope, are full of mystifying abbreviations, are opaque and, in general forbidding; in short I often cannot find what I want even if it is actually there somewhere. Bearing this in mind, I have endeavoured at all times to make this dictionary "user friendly", to use a current expression. As a general rule, this means that entries are placed where I believe that the average user would look for them; where there might be confusion, they are cross-referenced. I have laid down a few ground rules for where things should go, which I hope will assist the reader. Rules were, of course, made to be broken, and I have not followed them slavishly where common sense or logic dictated otherwise.

Perhaps the most important of these ground rules is the thorny old question of languages, about which I have decided as follows. When the original language concerned is French, German, Italian or Spanish, the entry is listed under its original language and the titles of operas are given in translation in brackets afterwards. For the reader's convenience, some operas which are frequently referred to by their English translation are cross-referenced (for example, *The Merry Widow*: see *Die Lustige Witwe*). When any other language (such as Russian or Czech) is concerned, the entry is listed under its English translation unless the original is so near to English as to render a translation superfluous (for example, *Kát'a Kabanová*). In a few cases where logic dictates, I have ignored this rule: to have listed Moniuszko's best-known work as *Helen* rather than *Halka* would have been ludicrous. A special note about operas written by Italian composers to French libretti: all references to them are listed under their original French. This applies particularly to Rossini's *Guillaume Tell* and *Le Comte Ory*, Cherubini's *Médée*, Donizetti's *La Favorite* and *La Fille du Régiment* and Verdi's *Les Vêpres Siciliennes*. Again, common sense has dictated one exception: Verdi's *Don Carlos* is almost universally know and performed in Italian, and to refer to it in French would be simply perverse.

I have also laid down an immutable rule on names which contain prefixes such as van, von, de and so on. It would never occur to anybody to look up Ludwig van Beethoven or Carl Maria von Weber under letter V, so why (as I discovered in one publication) is one expected to look up Richard van Allan under V? In this dictionary, all names with a prefix are listed under the letter of the main surname.

Opera is now one of the most rapidly growing entertainments as far as popularity is concerned. The packed houses, the enthusiasm, and the average age of audiences at the London Coliseum confirm this, as do the full houses and enthusiastic reception given outside London to Britain's regional opera companies. Certainly, it is a dramatic form for which I personally have a great love. I am a passionate believer in music-drama, even though few composers other than Mozart, Verdi and Wagner have ever truly achieved it. An "irrational and exotic entertainment", as the redoubtable Dr Johnson described it, I do *not* believe opera to be, even if the exercise of providing over 520 plot summaries for this dictionary has led me to think that Mark Twain was not entirely exaggerating when he said that anything too stupid to be said was sung. Opera is a living, developing art form and, indeed, one in which its earliest masterpieces still have a striking relevance today, as audiences at Monteverdi's operas often discover. Opera is nearly 400 years old and still going strong, ever appealing to a new audience. I offer this book as a small contribution to today's audiences, in the hope that it may help them a little towards a further enjoyment and understanding of opera.

James Anderson
London, 1989.

ACKNOWLEDGMENTS

I should like to take this opportunity to thank the many people, both personal friends and professional musicians, who have given me advice and encouragement during the two years I have spent writing this book. Many individual musicians and musical organisations have provided me with information, advice and invaluable comment. I am particularly indebted to Ronald Corp of the BBC, to William Elvin of the Luzern Stadttheater, to Findlay Wilson, to Eilene and Terence Hilton (on whose dining-room table a fair proportion of this was written), to the press office of the English National Opera, to the unfailingly helpful staff of Putney Music Library, and to Thomas Randle for kindly giving his permission to be shown on the book's front cover.

To my immediate family I owe an enormous debt of thanks for their never-flagging support and encouragement, even after the project had gone on so long as to have driven them mad. To my friends I also owe a big debt of thanks for their constant encouragement, even if the book's subject matter did not particularly interest them. For their support and enthusiasm, my special thanks to John Spencer, Robert Taylor, Greg Johnson, Todd Legrée, Nicholas Shakespeare and Mark Barnett. Finally, I must thank in particular the staff of St Thomas's Hospital (especially Dr Jan Welch, Brenda Jones, Dr Michael O'Docherty and Dr Alan Tang) for keeping me going; without them the project would not have seen the light of day.

James Anderson
London, 1989.

ABBREVIATIONS

b	born	Op	opus number (Mozart,
bar	baritone		Schubert and Weber have K, D
b-bar	bass-baritone		and J numbers)
BBC	British Broadcasting	perf	performed; performance
	Corporation	R	commercially recorded
cap	seating capacity	sop	soprano
cont	contralto	ten	tenor
c-ten	counter-tenor	TV	television
d	died	U	unfinished
Exc	excerpts	*	See separate entry
libr	libretto		
NBC	National Broadcasting		
	Company		

Nationalities:

Arg	Argentinian	Jam	Jamaican
Aus	Austrian	Jap	Japanese
Aust	Australian	Mart	Martiniquan
Belg	Belgian/Flemish	Mex	Mexican
Br	British/Welsh/Scottish	Neth	Dutch
Braz	Brazilian	Nor	Norwegian
Bulg	Bulgarian	NZ	New Zealand
Can	Canadian	Per	Peruvian
Chil	Chilean	Pol	Polish
Cz	Czechoslovakian/Bohemian	Port	Portuguese
Den	Danish	PR	Puerto Rican
Est	Estonian	Rom	Romanian
Fin	Finnish	Russ	Russian
Fr	French	Sp	Spanish
Ger	German	Swe	Swedish
Gk	Greek	Swit	Swiss
Hung	Hungarian	Turk	Turkish
Ind	Indian	Ukr	Ukranian
Ire	Irish	US	American
Isr	Israeli	Yug	Yugoslavian/Croatian/Serbian
It	Italian		

Alphabetisation:

Titles which begin with a definite or indefinite article are listed under the letter of the first main word. Names which contain a prefix (de, von) are listed under the letter of the main surname.

A, An

Titles beginning with the English indefinite article are listed under the letter of the first main word; for example, the entry for *A Tale of Two Cities* is under T.

Aachen Opera

(Aix-la-Chapelle when it was part of France). The present opera house (cap. 944) in this city in North Rhine Westphalia was opened in 1951. One of the most important provincial German houses, it has acquired a reputation for fostering major talent. Musical directors have included Fritz Busch, Herbert von Karajan, Wolfgang Sawallisch and Gabriel Chmura.

Abbado, Claudio *(b 1933)*

Italian conductor, particularly associated with Rossini, Verdi and Moussorgsky operas. Also a champion of contemporary Italian composers, such as Nono, he conducted the first performance of Giacomo Manzoni's *Atomtod*. He is one of the outstanding opera conductors of recent times, whose performances are notable for their muscular attack, their strong dramatic tension and their scrupulous observance of the composer's intentions. He was musical director of La Scala, Milan (1971–86), and the Vienna State Opera (1986–). His nephew Roberto Abbado is becoming a well-known conductor in his own right.

Abencérages, Les
or L'Etandard de Grenade

(*The Standard of Grenada*)
Opera in three acts by Cherubini. 1st perf. Paris, 6 April 1813; libr. by Victor Joseph Etienne de Jouy, after Jean-Pierre Florian's *Gonzalve de Cordove*. It is about the victories and final defeat in 1492 of Almansor, the last of the Moorish Abenceragi warriors. Very successful in its time, it is nowadays only rarely performed.

Abduction from the Seraglio, The

See Entführung aus dem Serail, Die

Abigaille

Soprano role in Verdi's *Nabucco*. She is Nabucco's elder but illegitimate daughter.

Ábrányi, Emil *(1882–1970)*

Hungarian composer and conductor. He was musical director of the Cologne Opera (1904–6) and the Hanover State Opera (1907–11). He wrote a number of operas, all now long forgotten, including *Monna Vanna* (1907; libr. after Maurice Maeterlinck), *Paolo and Francesca* (1912; libr. after Dante's *La Divina Commedia*), *Don Quixote* (1917; libr. after Miguel Cervantes) and *A Tamás Templom Karnagya* (1947), about J. S. Bach. His father Emil (1851–1920) was a librettist and translator whose texts included several for his son.

Abreise, Die *(The Departure)*

Comic opera in one act by d'Albert. 1st perf. Frankfurt, 20 Oct 1898; libr. by Ferdinand von Sporck after August von Steinentsech. Principal roles: Luise (sop), Trott (ten), Gilfen (bar).

D'Albert's only opera other than *Tiefland* to have survived, it is still occasionally performed in Germany.

Plot: Trott tries to persuade Gilfen to set out on a journey so that he can make advances to Gilfen's neglected wife Luise. However, it is Trott who is dispatched and Gilfen's jealousy reawakens his own love for his wife. [R]

Abscheulicher!

Soprano aria for Leonore in Act I of Beethoven's *Fidelio*.

Abu Hassan

Comic opera in one act by Weber (J106). 1st perf. Munich, 4 June 1811; libr. by Franz Karl Hiemer after *The Thousand and One Nights*. Principal roles: Fatime (sop), Abu Hassan (ten), Omar (bass). The most successful of Weber's early Singspiels, it is a delightful and charming little piece which is still quite often performed.

Plot: In legendary Bagdad, the poet Abu Hassan and his wife Fatime each pretend that the other is dead, so as to collect the funeral money which will pay their debts. When the deception is revealed, the Caliph forgives their audacity and their creditor Omar is disgraced for having tried to purchase Fatime's love. [R]

Ach, ich fühl's

Soprano aria for Pamina in Act II of Mozart's *Die Zauberflöte*.

Ach ich liebte

Soprano aria for Constanze in Act I of Mozart's *Die Entführung aus dem Serail*.

Ach so fromm (often sung in Italian as 'M'appari')

Tenor aria for Lionel in Act III of Flotow's *Martha*. It was not in the original score and Flotow inserted it from his earlier *L'Ame en Peine*.

Achilles

The Homeric Greek hero appears in several operas, including: (1) Tenor role in Tippett's *King Priam*. (2) Tenor role in Offenbach's *La Belle Hélène*. (3) Soprano trouser-role in Handel's *Deidamia*. (4) Baritone role in Schoeck's *Penthesilea*.

Acis and Galatea

Masque in two acts by Handel. 1st perf. Cannons (Edgware), 1718; 1st public perf. London, 10 June 1732; libr. by John Gay and others, after Ovid's *Metamorphoses*. Principal roles: Galatea (sop), Acis (ten), Polyphemus (bass), Damon (ten). It is notable both for the skill with which Handel adapts his style to the requirements of the English masque, and for its delightful sense of characterisation: the giant is represented by the piccolo, the smallest instrument in the orchestra. One of Handel's most popular stage works, it is still regularly performed.

Plot: Galatea laments the absence of her husband Acis. He returns followed by the giant Polyphemus, who also loves Galatea. Polyphemus crushes Acis under a rock, but Galatea uses her divine powers to transform him into a spring. [R]

Ackermann, Otto *(1909–60)*

Swiss conductor, associated with the German repertory, especially Mozart and J. Strauss. He was musical director of the Cologne Opera (1953–8) and the Zürich Opernhaus (1958–60).

Ackté, Aïno *(1876–1944)*

Finnish soprano, acclaimed in Wagner and Strauss roles. She had a pure, radiant voice of considerable power and a strong stage presence. She was director of the Finnish National Opera (1938–9), of which she had been a co-founder in 1911. She wrote the libretto for Merikanto's *Juha* and two volumes of autobiography, *The Book of My Recollections* (1925) and *My Life as an Artist* (1935). Her sister Irma Tervani (1887–1936) was a successful mezzo.

Adalgisa
Soprano role in Bellini's *Norma*. She is Norma's confidante and rival for Pollione's love. The role is frequently sung by a mezzo.

Adam, Adolphe *(1803–56)*
French composer. His first stage work *Pierre et Catherine* (Paris, 22 Jan 1829) was followed by 23 other *opéra-comiques*, notable for their grace and tunefulness. The most important include *Le Chalet* (Paris, 25 Sept 1834; libr. Eugène Scribe and Anne-Honoré Joseph de Mélesville, after Goethe's *Jery und Bately*), *Le Postillon de Longjumeau**, by far his most successful and enduring work, *Lambert Simnel* (Paris, 14 Sept 1843; libr. Scribe and Mélesville), a completion of an unfinished work by Monpou, *Le Toréador* (Paris, 18 May 1849; libr. Thomas Sauvage), *Giralda* (Paris, 20 July 1850; libr. Scribe), *La Poupée de Nuremberg* (Paris, 21 Feb 1852; libr. Adolphe de Leuven and Arthur de Beauplan, after E. T. A. Hoffmann's *Der Sandmann*), the successful *Si J'Etais Roi**, *Le Muletier de Tolède* (Paris, 16 Dec 1854; libr. Louis François Clairville and Adolphe Philippe d'Ennery) and *Falstaff* (Paris, 18 Jan 1856; libr. de Leuven and Jules-Henri Vernoy de Saint-Georges after Shakespeare's *The Merry Wives of Windsor*). His autobiography *Souvenirs d'un Musicien* was published in 1857.

Adam, Theo *(b 1926)*
German bass-baritone, associated with Wagnerian roles, especially Wotan. An intelligent singing-actor with a powerful if not intrinsically beautiful voice, he has also had success in contemporary operas, creating Prospero in Berio's *Un Rè in Ascolto*.

Adamastor
Baritone aria for Nélusko in Act III of Meyerbeer's *L'Africaine*.

Adami, Giuseppe *(1878–1946)*
Italian librettist and critic. He provided texts for Alfano (the unfinished *I Cavalieri e la Bella*), Puccini (*La Rondine*, *Il Tabarro* and *Turandot*), Vittadini (*Anima Allegra*, *Nazareth*, *La Sagredo* and *Fiametta e l'Avaro*) and Zandonai (*La Via della Finestra*).

Adams, Donald *(b 1929)*
British bass-baritone, associated with Sullivan and other buffo roles. He spent many years with the D'Oyly Carte Opera Company, becoming one of the best-loved Gilbert and Sullivan artists. He later enjoyed a second, highly successful career in opera. An outstanding singing-actor, he has a good voice and superb diction and timing. He married the soprano Muriel Harding.

Addio, addio speranza ad anima
Soprano/tenor duet for Gilda and the Duke of Mantua in Act I of Verdi's *Rigoletto*.

Addio del passato
Soprano aria for Violetta in Act III of Verdi's *La Traviata*.

Addio fiorito assil
Tenor aria for Pinkerton in Act II of
Puccini's *Madama Butterfly*.

Adelaide
See New Opera South Australia

Adelaide
Mezzo role in Strauss's *Arabella*. She is
Count Waldner's wife.

Adelaide di Borgogna
Opera in two acts by Rossini. 1st perf.
Rome, 27 Dec 1817; libr. by Giovanni
Schmidt. Principal roles: Adelaide (sop),
Adalberto (ten), Ottone (mezzo),
Berengario (bass). Unsuccessful at its
première, it is virtually never
performed.

Adele
Soprano role in: (1) Rossini's *Le Comte
Ory* (she is the countess who is the
object of Ory's amorous intentions). (2)
J. Strauss's *Die Fledermaus* (she is
Rosalinde's parlourmaid). (3) Bellini's *Il
Pirata* (she is Imogene's companion).

Adelson e Salvini
Opera in three acts by Bellini. 1st perf.
Naples, 12 Jan 1825; libr. by Andrea
Leone Tottola. Principal roles: Nelly
(sop), Salvini (ten), Adelson (bar),
Fanny (mezzo), Struley (bass), Bonifacio
(bass). Bellini's first opera, in a style
heavily influenced by Rossini, it is all
but forgotten.
    Plot: The painter Salvini loves Nelly,
the fiancée of his Irish patron Lord
Adelson. He foils an attempt by her
uncle Struley to abduct her, but hearing
a shot believes that she has been killed.
He is dissuaded from suicide when he
discovers that she is still alive. Cured of
his infatuation, he becomes engaged to
his pupil Fanny while Adelson marries
Nelly.

Adieu Mignon
Tenor aria for Wilhelm in Act II of
Thomas' *Mignon*.

Adieu, notre petite table
Soprano aria for Manon in Act II of
Massenet's *Manon*.

Adina
Soprano role in Donizetti's *L'Elisir
d'Amore*. She is a capricious landowner
loved by Nemorino.

Adler, Kurt Herbert *(1905–88)*
Austrian conductor, resident in the USA
from 1938. He had a wide-ranging
repertory and was musical director of
the San Francisco Opera Association
(1953–81).

Admeto, Rè di Tessaglia
(*Admetus, King of Thessaly*)
Opera in three acts by Handel. 1st perf.
London, 31 Jan 1727; libr., possibly by
Nicola Francesco Haym, after Aurelio
Aureli's *L'Antigona Delusa da Alceste*.
Principal roles: Admetus (c-ten), Alceste
(sop), Antigone (sop), Hercules (bass),
Apollo (bass), Orindo (mezzo),
Trasimede (c-ten). Telling much the
same story as Gluck's *Alceste*, it is only
rarely performed. [R]

Admetus
Tenor role in Gluck's and Lully's
Alceste. He is King of Thessaly.

Administrator
See panel on page 5

Adolar
Tenor role in Weber's *Euryanthe*. He is
a knight in love with Euryanthe.

ADMINISTRATOR

The administrator of an opera house has responsibility for both the day-to-day functioning of the theatre and long-term planning. The post is not the same as either artistic director or musical director, though they have occasionally been combined. The administrator is called *Intendant* in Germany and Austria, General Manager in the USA and *Sovrintendente* in Italy.

Below are listed the 15 administrators with entries in this dictionary (with their nationalities).

Arlen, Stephen (Br.)	Carvalho, Léon (Fr.)	Harris, Sir Augustus (Br.)
Barbaia, Domenico (It.)	Fox, Carol (US)	Liebermann, Rolf (Swit.)
Baylis, Lilian (Br.)	Gatti-Casazza, Giulio (It.)	Merelli, Bartolomeo (It.)
Bing, Sir Rudolf (Aus.)	Gentele, Göran (Swe.)	Tooley, Sir John (Br.)
Carte, Richard d'Oyly (Br.)	Harewood, Earl of (Br.)	Webster, Sir David (Br.)

Adriana Lecouvreur
Opera in four acts by Cilea. 1st perf. Milan, 6 Nov 1902; libr. by Arturo Colautti, after Eugène Scribe and Ernest Legouvé's *Adrienne Lecouvreur*. Principal roles: Adriana (sop), Maurizio (ten), Michonnet (bar), Prince and Princess de Bouillon (bass and mezzo), Abbé de Chazeuil (ten). Much the most successful and enduring of Cilea's operas, it tells of the historical Comédie-Française actress Adrienne Lecouvreur (1692–1730).

Plot: Paris 1730. Adriana is in love with Maurizio, Count of Saxony, who for political reasons is having a liaison with the Princess de Bouillon. Adriana saves her rival from a compromising situation, but later insults her under the cover of a recitation of Racine. The Princess sends Adriana a bunch of poisoned violets which she smells. She dies in Maurizio's arms watched by the stage manager Michonnet, who also loves her. [R]

Aegisthus
Tenor role in Strauss's *Elektra*. He is Clytemnestra's foppish lover.

Aeneas
The Virgilian hero appears in several operas, including: (1) Tenor role in Berlioz's *Les Troyens*. (2) Baritone role in Purcell's *Dido and Aeneas*.

Aeschylus
See panel on page 6

Africaine, L' (*The African Girl*)
Opera in five acts by Meyerbeer. 1st perf. Paris, 28 April 1865; libr. by Eugène Scribe. Principal roles: Sélika (mezzo), Vasco da Gama (ten), Nélusko (bar), Inès (sop), Don Pédro (bass), Don Alvar (ten), High Priest (bar). Meyerbeer's last opera, produced posthumously, it is one of the longest operas ever written. It was enormously popular throughout the second half of

AESCHYLUS

The works of the Greek playwright Aeschylus (525–456 BC), the earliest dramatist whose work survives, have inspired some 30 operas. Below are listed, by play, those operas by composers with entries in this dictionary.

Agamemnon

Brian	*Agamemnon*	1957
Hamilton	*Agamemnon*	1969

The Choephori

Milhaud	*Les Choéphores*	1919

Oresteian Trilogy

Taneyev	*Oresteia*	1895

Prometheus

Fauré	*Prométhée*	1900
Wagner-Régeny	*Prometheus*	1959
Hanuš	*The Torch of Prometheus*	1963
Orff	*Prometheus*	1966

the 19th century but is now only infrequently performed.

Plot: Vasco da Gama returns to Lisbon from an expedition to Africa with two native captives, Nélusko and Sélika. He is accused of heresy and imprisoned with them. In his absence, his beloved Inès has been promised to Don Pédro. She and Sélika, who also loves Vasco, conspire for his release. Vasco returns to Africa with Sélika, but cannot forget Inès. Sélika releases him to return to Inès and despite Nélusko's offer of love, she commits suicide under the poisonous Manchineel tree.

Agamemnon

The Homeric Greek king appears in several operas, including: (1) Baritone role in Gluck's *Iphigénie en Aulide*. (2) Bass-baritone role in Offenbach's *La Belle Hélène*. (3) Bass role in Taneyev's *Oresteia*.

Agathe

Soprano role in Weber's *Der Freischütz*. Cuno's daughter, she is in love with Max.

Agnes von Hohenstaufen

Opera in three acts by Spontini. 1st perf. Berlin, 12 June 1829; libr. by Ernst Raupach. Principal roles: Agnes (sop), Henry of Brunswick (ten), Henry VI (bass), King of France (bar). Spontini's last opera, it was very successful in its time but is now infrequently performed.

Plot: Mainz. It tells of the love of Agnes, daughter of the Countess Ermengard, for Henry of Brunswick, son of the rebel Duke of Saxony. The Emperor Henry VI and the King of France (disguised as the Duke of Burgundy) intrigue to prevent the lovers from marrying.

Agrippina

Opera in three acts by Handel. 1st perf. Venice, 26 Dec 1709; libr. by Vincenzo Grimani. Principal roles: Agrippina (sop), Poppea (sop), Ottone (mezzo), Nerone (sop), Pallante (bass), Narciso (mezzo), Claudio (bass). It is the earliest of Handel's operas still occasionally performed.

Plot: In the absence of her husband, the Emperor Claudius, Agrippina intrigues to ensure the succession of her son Nerone. Following Claudius's unexpected return, she poisons his mind against Ottone whom he has chosen to succeed him. Exploiting the fact that both Claudius and Nerone love her, Ottone's fiancée Poppea sets out to thwart Agrippina. Compromising both of them, she obtains Claudius's permission to marry Ottone, who renounces the succession for her sake. Agrippina extricates herself and sees Nerone declared Claudius's heir.

Ägyptische Helena, Die (The Egyptian Helen)

Opera in two acts by Strauss (Op 75). 1st perf. Dresden, 6 June 1928; libr. by Hugo von Hofmannsthal, after Euripides's *Helen in Egypt* and other classical legends. Revised version 1st perf. Salzburg, 14 Aug 1933. Principal roles: Helen (sop), Menelaus (ten), Altair (bar), Aithra (sop), Da-Ud (ten). Never one of Strauss's more popular works, it is only infrequently performed.

Plot: Egypt after the Trojan War. Menelaus intends to kill his wife Helen because of the slaughter she has caused, but the sorceress Aithra persuades him that she was never in Troy and gives Helen a potion to forget past evils. They are sent to a land that knows nothing of the Trojan War, where the desert chieftain Altair and his son Da-Ud both fall in love with Helen.

Menelaus kills Da-Ud. He and Helen take an antidote to the potion of forgetfulness and their life begins afresh after Aithra has intervened to thwart the vengeance of Altair. [R]

Ah chi mi dice mai

Soprano aria for Donna Elvira in Act I of Mozart's *Don Giovanni*.

Ah! fors'è lui

Soprano aria for Violetta in Act I of Verdi's *La Traviata*. Its cabaletta is the famous 'Sempre libera'.

Ah, fuyez douce image

Tenor aria for Des Grieux in Act III of Massenet's *Manon*.

Ah je ris

Soprano aria (the Jewel Song) for Marguerite in Act III of Gounod's *Faust*.

Ah la faveur

Soprano/mezzo/tenor trio for Countess Adèle, Isolier and Ory in Act II of Rossini's *Le Comte Ory*. It is one of the most beautiful individual numbers Rossini wrote.

Ah, la paterna mano

Tenor aria for Macduff in Act IV of Verdi's *Macbeth*.

Ah mes amis

Tenor aria for Tonie in Act I of Donizetti's *La Fille du Régiment*. Its cabaletta 'Pour mon âme' contains nine written high Cs.

Ah! non credea mirarti

Soprano aria for Amina in Act II of Bellini's *La Sonnambula*. The sleepwalking scene, its cabaletta 'Ah!

non giunge', is the final scene of the opera.

Ah que j'aime les militaires

Soprano aria for the Grand-Duchess in Act I of Offenbach's *La Grande-Duchesse de Gérolstein*.

Ahronovich, Yuri *(b 1932)*

Russian conductor, particularly acclaimed in the Russian repertory. He is an exciting orchestral conductor, but his operatic appearances have been infrequent. He left the USSR in 1972 and is now an Israeli citizen.

Ah! se tu dormi

Soprano aria for Giulietta in Act II of Vaccai's *Giulietta e Romeo*. During the 19th century, it was often inserted into the final scene of Bellini's *I Capuleti e i Montecchi*.

Ah si, ben mio

Tenor aria for Manrico in Act III of Verdi's *Il Trovatore*. Its cabaletta is the notorious 'Di quella pira'.

Aida

Opera in four acts by Verdi. 1st perf. Cairo, 24 Dec 1871; libr. by Antonio Ghislanzoni and Camille du Locle, after Pietro Metastasio's *Nitteti* and a synopsis by the Egyptologist Auguste Mariette Bey. Principal roles: Aida (sop), Radamès (ten), Amneris (mezzo), Amonasro (bar), Ramphis (bass), King of Egypt (bass), High Priestess (sop). Telling of the conflict between love and patriotism in the Egypt of the Pharaohs, it was an instant success and has remained one of the most enduringly popular operas ever written. Marking the transition between Verdi's middle and late periods, it is notable for its orchestral and harmonic richness, its magnificent choral scenes and for Verdi's psychological penetration in his depiction of the jealous Amneris. The opera was not, as is so often thought, commissioned to celebrate the opening of the Suez Canal. For the Milan première, Verdi wrote an overture that was cut before the first performance; it has not been performed in the theatre but has been recorded.

Plot: Aida, an Ethiopian slave to Amneris, daughter of Pharaoh, is emotionally torn by her love for the general Radamès when he is named as commander of a campaign against Ethiopia. Amneris is also in love with Radamès and tricks Aida into revealing her feelings. The victorious Radamès returns in triumph and is rewarded with Amneris's hand. Disguised among the prisoners is Aida's father Amonasro, the Ethiopian King. He persuades his daughter to wheedle out of Radamès the route of the next army campaign. Radamès's inadvertent betrayal is overheard and Ramphis and the priests condemn him to be buried alive. Aida joins him in the tomb. [R]

Aida trumpet

An instrument invented by Verdi for the Triumph Scene in *Aida*. It is much longer than a normal orchestral trumpet. The score requires six, three in A♭ and three in B.

Aiglon, L' *(The Eaglet)*

Opera in five acts by Honegger (who wrote the three inner acts) and Ibert (who wrote the outer acts). 1st perf. Monte Carlo, 11 March 1937; libr. by Henri Cain, after Edmond Rostand. Principal roles: Aiglon (sop), Flambeau (bass), Metternich (bar), Frédéric (ten), Marmont (bass), Thérèse (mezzo). The finest of the three operas on which Ibert and Honegger collaborated, it was reasonably successful at its appearance but is nowadays almost never performed.

Ai nostri monti

Mezzo/tenor duet for Azucena and Manrico in Act IV of Verdi's *Il Trovatore*.

Aio nell'Imbarazzo, L' (*The Embarrassed Tutor*)

Comic opera in two acts by Donizetti. 1st perf. Rome, 4 Feb 1824; libr. by Jacopo Ferretti, after G. Guiraud. Revised version *Don Gregorio*, 1st perf. Naples, 1826. Principal roles: Gregorio (bass), Enrico (ten), Gilda (sop), Don Giulio (bar). An entertaining little piece in Rossinian style, it is the earliest of Donizetti's operas still occasionally performed. [R]

Air

The term has two meanings in opera: (1) The French term for aria. (2) A term used in ballad operas to indicate the source of a melody; for example, 'Since laws were made' in Act III of *The Beggar's Opera* carries the superscription 'Air: Green Sleeves'.

Aix-en-Provence Festival

An annual summer opera festival in France founded in 1948 by Gabriel Dussurget and André Bigonnet. Performances are given at the open-air theatre (cap. 1700) in the Archbishop's palace, which was designed by A. M. Cassandre. The repertory is notable for its Mozart and Rossini productions. Musical directors have included Hans Rosbaud.

Akhnaten

Opera in three acts by Glass. 1st perf. Stuttgart, 24 March 1984; libr. by the composer, after Shalom Goldman. Principal roles: Akhnaten (c-ten), Tye (sop), Nefertiti (mezzo), Aye (bass), High Priest (ten), Horemhab (bar). The third of Glass's minimalist stage works, it concerns the 'heretic' Pharaoh Akhnaten (*d* c1358 BC), sometimes regarded as the first monotheist. One of the most successful operas of the 1980s, it has been widely performed.

Plot: Akhnaten abandons polygamy for the love of his beautiful wife Nefertiti and builds a city in honour of his new god, the Aten. Failing to produce a male heir and oblivious to the sufferings of his people, he sees his family carried off and his temple to the Aten destroyed. Egypt's immemorial old order is restored. [R]

Albanese, Licia (*b 1913*)

Italian soprano, associated with Verdi and Puccini roles, especially Cio-Cio-San. She was an intense singer with a beautiful voice which she used with a fine technique.

Albani, Dame Emma (*b Marie Louise Lajeunesse*) (*1847–1930*)

Canadian soprano. One of the greatest sopranos of the late 19th century, she was particularly admired in Wagnerian roles. Her autobiography *Forty Years of Song* was published in 1911.

Albéniz, Isaac (*1860–1909*)

Spanish composer. He wrote several stage works, now largely forgotten. They include *The Magic Opal* (London, 19 Jan 1893; libr. Arthur Law), the zarzuela *San Antonio de Flórida* (Madrid 26 Oct 1894; libr. E. Sierra), *Enrico Clifford* (Barcelona, 8 May 1895; libr. Francis Burdett Money-Coutts), *Pepita Jiménez* (Barcelona, 5 Jan 1896; libr. Money-Coutts), his most successful work, and the unperformed *Merlin* (1906; libr. Money-Coutts, after Thomas Mallory's *Morte d'Arthur*), part of a projected Arthurian trilogy.

Alberich

Baritone role in Wagner's *Das Rheingold*, *Siegfried* and *Götterdämmerung*. The leader of the Nibelung dwarfs, he steals the gold from the Rhine and fashions the Ring by his renunciation of love.

Albert

Baritone role in Massenet's *Werther*. He is Charlotte's fiancé.

Albert, Eugen d' *(1864–1932)*

Scottish-born German composer and pianist. His first opera *Der Rubin* (Karlsruhe, 12 Oct 1893; libr. composer, after Christian Friedrich Hebbel) was followed by 19 others, of which only the comedy *Die Abreise** and the verismo-style *Tiefland** are still remembered. Of the rest *Flauto Solo* (Prague, 12 Nov 1905; libr. Ernst von Wolzogen) and *Die Toten Augen* (*The Blind Eyes*, Dresden, 5 March 1916; libr. M. Henry) enjoyed brief successes.

Albert Herring

Comic opera in three acts by Britten (Op 39). 1st perf. Glyndebourne, 20 June 1947; libr. by Eric Crozier, after Guy de Maupassant's *Le Rosier de Madame Husson*. Principal roles: Albert (ten), Lady Billows (sop), Sid (bar), Nancy (mezzo), Florence Pike (mezzo), Sptd Budd (bass), Mr Gedge (bar), Miss Wordsworth (sop), Mr Upfold (ten), Mrs Herring (mezzo), Emmie (sop). One of Britten's most popular operas, it contains a magnificent gallery of local characters from Britten's native Suffolk.

Plot: Loxford, East Suffolk, 1900. Lady Billows and a committee of local notables are unable to find a suitably chaste girl to crown as Queen of the May so they decide on a May King, the virtuous Albert Herring. At his coronation, Sid and Nancy spike his lemonade; emboldened, he sets out with his prize money to sample the delights of alcohol and female companionship, blaming his mother for a repressive upbringing. The dignatories are scandalised, but Albert's friends cheer his emancipation. [R]

Albiani, Paolo

Baritone role in Verdi's *Simon Boccanegra*. A goldsmith, he engineers Simon's election as Doge but then plots against him.

Albinoni, Tomaso *(1671–1750)*

Italian composer. He wrote over 40 operas, including *Astarto* (Venice 1708; libr. Apostolo Zeno and Pietro Pariati) and *Il Nascimento dell'Aurora* (*c*1716) [R]. Only the comedy *Pimpinone** is remembered today.

Alboni, Marietta *(b Maria Anna Marizia) (1823–94)*

Italian contralto, particularly associated with the French and Italian repertories. One of the greatest contraltos of all time, she possessed a range so wide that she was able to sing Don Carlo in the first London performance of *Ernani* when baritones had refused to sing it. She created the title-role in Auber's *Zerline*.

Albrecht, Gerd *(b 1935)*

German conductor, particularly associated with Wagner, Strauss and Zemlinsky operas. He was musical director of the Lübeck Opera (1963–6), the Kassel Staatstheater (1966–72) and the Hamburg State Opera (1988–). He conducted the first performances of Fortner's *Elisabeth Tudor* and Reimann's *Troades*.

Alceste

Works of this title based on Euripides's *Alkestis* include:

(1) Opera in prologue and five acts by Lully. Subtitled *Le Triomphe d'Alcide*. 1st perf. Paris, 10 Jan 1674; libr. by Philippe Quinault. Principal roles: Alceste (sop), Admetus (ten), Alcide (bar), Céphise (sop), Apollo (ten), Charon (bass). Sometimes regarded as Lully's finest opera, it has been his most regularly performed work in recent years and was described by Madame de Sévigné as 'a prodigy of beauty'.

Plot: King Admetus must die unless someone can be found who will take his place. His wife Alceste volunteers and dies in his stead. She is brought back from Hades by Alcide (Hercules). [R]

(2) Opera in three acts by Gluck. 1st perf. Vienna, 26 Dec 1767; libr. by Ranieri de' Calzabigi. Revised version 1st perf. Paris, 23 April 1776; libr. revised by Bailli Leblanc du Roullet. Principal roles: Alceste (sop), Admetus (ten), High Priest (bar), Oracle (bass), Apollo (ten), Hercules (bar). One of Gluck's greatest works, the famous preface to the score – one of the most important documents in the history of opera – contains Gluck's insistence that opera should be serious music-drama and not the elaborate and artificial concert-in-costume which it had become. The most important of Gluck's 'reform' operas, it remains regularly performed and is a seminal work in the development of opera.

Plot: The oracle decrees that the ill king, Admetus, must die unless someone will take his place, and his wife Alceste offers herself. When Admetus recovers, he doesn't wish to live without Alceste and joins her at the entrance to Hades. Determined to save his king, Hercules comes to defy the rulers of Hades. Apollo raises Hercules to godhood for his actions, and decrees that Alceste and Admetus shall live to serve as an example of perfect conjugal love. [R]

Alcina

Opera in three acts by Handel. 1st perf. London, 16 April 1735; libr. by Antonio Marchi, after Lodovico Ariosto's *Orlando Furioso*. Principal roles: Alcina (sop), Ruggiero (c-ten), Bradamante (mezzo), Morgana (sop), Oronte (ten), Melisso (bass). Handel's last fully successful Italian opera for London, it has in recent years become one of his most frequently performed works.

Plot: Alcina the enchantress rules over the magic island where she lives with her sister, Morgana, and her general, Oronte. She has transformed the many knights who have come to court her into curious inhuman creatures but she has allowed her current suitor, Ruggiero, to remain a man. Utterly infatuated with Alcina, Ruggiero has quite forgotten his fiancée, Bradamante who, disguised as her own brother, Ricciardo, journeys to find her missing lover. Bradamante and her guardian, Melisso, with whom she is travelling, are shipwrecked on Alcina's island. A series of complications and misunderstandings follow: Morgana falls for 'Ricciardo', rejecting Oronte; infuriated, Oronte tells the besotted Ruggiero that Alcina has fallen in love with 'Ricciardo'; and Bradamante and Melisso try in vain to convince Ruggiero that his supposed rival is really his own fiancée. Eventually, all is resolved: Alcina's powers are destroyed, the captured knights are restored to human form, and Ruggiero returns to Bradamante. [R]

Alcindoro

Bass comprimario role in Puccini's *La*

Bohème. He is Musetta's elderly admirer.

Alda, Frances *(b Davies) (1883–1952)*

New Zealand soprano, famous for her explosive temper and her involvement in several law suits. Particularly associated with the French and Italian repertories, she also created Roxane in Damrosch's *Cyrano de Bergerac* and the title-roles in Herbert's *Madeleine* and Hadley's *Cleopatra's Night*. Married for a time to the administrator Giulio Gatti-Casazza*. Her autobiography, *Men, Women and Tenors*, was published in 1937.

Aldeburgh Festival

An annual summer music festival in Suffolk, founded in 1948 by Britten, Eric Crozier and Peter Pears. It is largely devoted to the music of Britten and other English composers. Since 1970, opera has been given in the Maltings (cap. 840), in nearby Snape, redesigned by Ove Arup after the original building burnt down in 1969 after the opening night of the Festival. Artistic directors have included Britten and Mstislav Rostropovich.

Al dolce guidami

Soprano aria (the Mad Scene) for Anna in Act II of Donizetti's *Anna Bolena*. The melody is derived from 'Home, sweet home' from Bishop's *Clari*, and Bishop brought an action against Donizetti for 'piracy and breach of copyright'. Its cabaletta, 'Coppia iniqua' is the final scene of the opera.

Aleko

Opera in one act by Rachmaninov. 1st perf. Moscow, 27 April 1893; libr. by Vladimir Nemirovich-Danchenko, after Alexander Pushkin's poem, *The Gypsies*. Principal roles: Aleko (bass), Zemfira (sop), Young Gypsy (ten), Gypsy Chief (bass). Rachmaninov's first opera, written as a student graduation exercise, it is very seldom performed outside Russia.

Plot: Aleko gives up a quiet life to join a band of gypsies. When his lover, Zemfira, grows bored with him and plans to run off with one of the gypsies, Aleko kills her and is abandoned by the others. [R]

Alerta! Alerta!

Bass aria for Ferrando in Act I of Verdi's *Il Trovatore*. One of the longest bass arias ever written.

Alessandro *(Alexander)*

Opera in three acts by Handel. 1st perf. London, 5 May 1726; libr. by Paolo Antonio Rolli after Ortensio Mauro's *La Superbia d'Alessandro*. Principal roles: Alessandro (c-ten), Rossane (sop), Lisaura (sop), Clito (bass), Leonato (ten). Telling of Alexander the Great, it is only very rarely performed. [R]

Alessandro nell'Indie

(Alexander in India)

Opera seria. Libr. by Pietro Metastasio. It is one of the most frequently set of the Metastasian texts, including by the following composers with entries in this dictionary: (1) Opera by Uttini. 1st perf. Genoa, 1743. (2) Opera by Jommelli. 1st perf. Stuttgart, 11 Feb 1760. (3) Opera in three acts by J. C. Bach. 1st perf. Naples, 20 Jan 1762. (4) Opera by Sacchini. 1st perf. Venice, 1763. (5) Opera in three acts by Anfossi. 1st perf. Rome, 1772. (6) Opera in three acts by Paisiello. 1st perf. Modena, 26 Dec 1773. (7) Opera in three acts by Cimarosa. 1st perf. Rome, 1781. (8) Opera in two acts by Cherubini. 1st perf. Mantua, 1784. (9) Opera in two acts by Pacini. 1st perf.

Naples, 29 Sept 1824. Libr. revised by Andrea Leone Tottola.

Alessandro Stradella

Opera in three acts by Flotow. 1st perf. Hamburg, 30 Dec 1844; libr. by Friedrich Wilhelm Riese, after P. A. A. Pittaud de Forges and P. Duport. Principal roles: Stradella (ten), Leonore (sop), Bassi (bass). Dealing with supposed events in the colourful life of the composer Stradella*, it is Flotow's only opera apart from *Martha* that is in any way remembered, and that mainly for the tenor's prayer 'Jungfrau Maria'.

Plot: Venice and Rome, c 1670. Leonore, ward of Bassi, is carried off by Stradella at a Venetian Carnival and taken to Rome. They are pursued by Bassi's hired assassins, but the composer wins them (and later Bassi) over with his musical genius.

Alexei

(1) Title role (tenor) in Prokofiev's *The Gambler*. (2) An aviator (baritone) in Prokofiev's *The Story of a Real Man*.

Alfano, Franco *(1876–1954)*

Italian composer. He wrote 11 operas, firstly in verismo and later in romantic style. Some are occasionally performed in Italy, but almost never elsewhere. The works are the unperformed *Miranda* (1896), *La Fonte di Enschir* (Breslau 1898; libr. Luigi Illica), the successful *Risurezzione**, *Il Principe Zilah* (Genoa 1909; libr. Illica), the unfinished *I Cavalieri e la Bella* (1910; libr. Giuseppe Adami and T. Moniccelli), *L'Ombra di Don Giovanni* (1914; libr. L. Moschino, after Prosper Mérimée's *Les Âmes du Purgatoire*; revised version *Don Juan de Mañara*, Florence 1941), *La Leggenda di Sakùntala* (Bologna 1921; libr. composer, after Kalidasa), *Madonna Imperia* (Turin 5 May 1927; libr.

Arturo Rossato, after Honoré de Balzac's *Contes Drôlatiques*), *L'Ultimo Lord* (Naples 1930; libr. Rossato and U. Falena), *Cyrano de Bergerac**, possibly his finest work, and *Il Dottor Antonio* (Rome 1949; libr. Mario Ghisalberti, after Giovanni Ruffini). Outside Italy, Alfano is best known for having completed Puccini's *Turandot*.

Alfio

Baritone role in Mascagni's *Cavalleria Rusticana*. A carter, he is Lola's husband.

Alfonso

(1) Baritone role in Mozart's *Così fan Tutte*. He is a cynical bachelor. (2) Bass role in Donizetti's *Lucrezia Borgia*. Lucrezia's husband, he is the historical Alfonso d'Este (1476–1534), Duke of Ferrara. (3) Baritone role in Donizetti's *La Favorite*. He is King Alfonso IX of Castile. (4) Tenor role in Hérold's *Zampa*. He is Camilla's fiancé. (5) Tenor role in Korngold's *Violanta*. He is the seducer of Violanta's sister. (6) Baritone role in Donizetti's *Torquato Tasso*. (7) Tenor role in Schubert's *Alfonso und Estrella*. He is Troila's son. (8) Tenor role in Auber's *La Muette de Portici*. He is the viceroy of Naples.

Alfonso und Estrella

Opera in three acts by Schubert (D 732). 1st perf. Weimar, 24 June 1854 (composed 1822); libr. by Franz von Schober. Principal roles: Alfonso (ten), Estrella (sop), Troila (bar), Mauregato (bar), Adolfo (b-bar). It is Schubert's only through-composed opera, containing neither dialogue nor recitativo secco. Despite its weak libretto, it is arguably Schubert's finest and most important opera, containing some of his greatest music. Quite unaccountably, it is almost never performed.

Plot: Troila, King of Leon, his throne usurped by Mauregato, lives with his son Alfonso in an arcadian valley, filled with wisdom and kindness. Alfonso meets and falls in love with Mauregato's daughter, Estrella. Her rejected suitor Adolfo attempts to overthrow Mauregato, but is vanquished by Alfonso. Troila and Mauregato are reconciled in the face of a common enemy, and Alfonso weds Estrella. [R]

Alfred

(1) Tenor role in J. Strauss's *Die Fledermaus*. He is an Italian tenor in love with Rosalinde. (2) Tenor role in Liebermann's *Leonore 40/45*. He is a German soldier. (3) Baritone role in Einem's *Der Besuch der Alten Dame*. He is Claire's former lover. (4) Baritone role in Offenbach's *La Vie Parisienne*. He is the head waiter.

Alfredo

Tenor role in Verdi's *La Traviata*. Giorgio Germont's son, he is in love with Violetta.

Ali

Bass role in Rossini's *L'Italiana in Algeri*. He is captain of the Algerian corsairs.

Alice

(1) Soprano role in Verdi's *Falstaff*. Ford's wife, she is Nannetta's mother. (2) Soprano role in Meyerbeer's *Robert le Diable*. She is Bertram's sister. (3) Mezzo role in Goehr's *Arden Must Die*. (4) Soprano role in Rossini's *Le Comte Ory*. She is a peasant girl.

Alidoro

Bass role in Rossini's *La Cenerentola*.

A philosopher, and teacher to Don Ramiro, he takes the place of the traditional fairy godmother.

Alkmene

Opera in three acts by Klebe. 1st perf. Berlin, 25 Sept 1961; libr. by the composer, after Heinrich Wilhelm von Kleist. Principal roles: Alkmene (sop), Jupiter (bass), Amphitryon (ten), Cleanthis (sop), Sosias (bar), Mercury (bass). Klebe's most successful work, it tells how Jupiter assumes the form of the Theban general Amphitryon in order to pursue his conquest of Alkmene.

Allan, Richard van (b Alan Jones) (b 1935)

British bass, particularly associated with Britten and Mozart roles, notably Leporello and Don Alfonso. One of the most outstanding contemporary British singing-actors, with a repertory of over 100 roles, he is equally at home in serious or comic roles. He created Col. Jowler in Maw's *The Rising of the Moon*. Director of the National Opera Studio (1986–).

Alla vita

Baritone aria for Renato in Act I of Verdi's *Un Ballo in Maschera*.

Allen, Thomas (b 1944)

British baritone, particularly associated with Mozart roles and with Billy Budd and Pelléas. Possessing a beautiful voice, used with outstanding intelligence and musicianship, he is one of the finest British singing-actors of the postwar era. He created Valerio in Musgrave's *The Voice of Ariadne*.

All'idea

Tenor/baritone duet for Count

Almaviva and Figaro in Act I of
Rossini's *Il Barbiere di Siviglia*.

Almächt ger Vater
Tenor aria for Rienzi in Act V of
Wagner's *Rienzi*.

Almaviva, Count
The amorous nobleman of
Beaumarchais' plays appears as: (1)
Tenor role in Rossini's and Paisiello's *Il
Barbiere di Siviglia*. (2) Baritone role in
Mozart's *Le Nozze di Figaro*.

Almaviva, Countess
Soprano role in Mozart's *Le Nozze di
Figaro*. She is Dr Bartolo's former
ward.

Almeida, António de *(c 1702–55)*
Portuguese composer. He wrote many
operas, now largely forgotten, including
La Pazienza di Socrate (Lisbon 1733;
libr. Nicolò Minato), *La Spinalba*
(Lisbon 1739) and *L'Ippolito* (Lisbon 4
Dec 1752; libr. A. Tedeschi).

Almira
Opera in three acts by Handel. 1st perf.
Hamburg, 8 Jan 1705; libr. by
Friedrich C. Feustking, after Giulio
Pancieri. Handel's first opera and now
totally forgotten, it includes 15 arias in
Italian and a further 41 in German.

Alpaerts, Flor *(1876–1954)*
Belgian composer and conductor. He
wrote one opera *Shylock* (Antwerp 22
Dec 1913; libr. after Shakespeare's *The
Merchant of Venice*). He was director
of the Antwerp Conservatory (1933–41).

Alt (German for 'high')
The German term for the contralto
voice.

Alte Stürme, Der
Mezzo/baritone scene for Fricka and
Wotan in Act II of Wagner's *Die
Walküre*.

Altistin
German term for a contralto singer.

Alto (Italian for 'high')
Applied to two voice types: (1) Female:
a contralto or low mezzo. (2) Male: a
bass or baritone singing falsetto. The
term is also often used in reference to a
counter-tenor, but this is not strictly
correct.

Altoum
Tenor comprimario role in Puccini's
Turandot and bass role in Busoni's
version. He is the aged Emperor of
China.

Altra notte, L'
Soprano aria for Margherita in Act III
of Boito's *Mefistofele*.

Alva, Luigi *(b Luis) (b 1927)*
Peruvian tenor, particularly associated
with Mozart, Rossini and lighter
Donizetti roles. One of the leading
tenore di grazias of the postwar era,
with a fine technique and excellent
diction, he was also an accomplished
comic actor. He created roles in R.
Malipiero's *La Donna è Mobile* and
Chailly's *Una Domanda di Matrimonio*.
In 1981, he founded Peru's opera
company, Fundación para Arte Lirica,
of which he is producer and artistic
director.

Alvaro, Don
(1) Tenor role in Verdi's *La Forza del
Destino*. A Peruvian with Inca blood,
he is Leonora's lover. (2) Baritone role
in Rossini's *Il Viaggio a Reims*.

(3) Tenor role in Gomes's *Il Guarany*.
(4) Tenor role in Spontini's *Fernand Cortez*.

Alvise

Bass role in Ponchielli's *La Gioconda*. He is a nobleman married to Laura.

Alwa

Tenor role in Berg's *Lulu*. Dr Schön's son, he is one of Lulu's lovers.

Alwyn, William *(1905–85)*

British composer. His five operas include *The Libertine* (1971) and *Miss Julie* (BBC radio 1977; libr. after August Strindberg) [R].

Alyabyev, Alexander *(1787–1851)*

Russian composer. His study of folk music and his knowledge of Caucasian and Oriental subjects (mostly acquired during a period of political exile) helped shape the development of Russian opera, of which he was possibly the most important composer before Glinka. His works, nowadays all but forgotten, include the comedy *The Moonlit Night* (*Lunnaya Noch*, 1823), *The Tempest* (*Burya*, 1835; libr. after Shakespeare), *The Enchanted Night* (*Volshebnaya Noch*, 1839; libr. A. F. Weltman, after Shakespeare's *A Midsummer Night's Dream*), *The Fisherman and the Water-Nymph* (*Rybak i Rusalka*, Moscow 1965; composed 1843) and *Ammalet-Bek* (1847).

Alzira

Opera in prologue and two acts by Verdi. 1st perf. Naples, 12 Aug 1845; libr. by Salvatore Cammarano, after Voltaire's *Alzire, ou les Américains*. Principal roles: Alzira (sop), Zamoro (ten), Gusmano (bar), Ataliba (bass).

Perhaps Verdi's least successful opera (he himself described it as '*bruta*'), it is only very rarely performed.

Plot: In mid-16th century Peru, Inca chief Zamoro returns to his tribe after being tortured by the Christians. He discovers that his beloved, Alzira, has been abducted by the Christian governor Gusmano, who attempts to arrange peace with the Incas and keep Alzira for himself. Zamoro is recaptured, and to gain his release Alzira agrees to marry Gusmano. Disguised, Zamoro appears at the wedding and kills Gusmano. [R]

Amadis

Opera in prologue and five acts by Lully. 1st perf. Paris, 18 Jan 1684; libr. by Philippe Quinault, after García Ordóñez de Montalvo's *Amadis de Gaule*. Principal roles: Amadis (ten), Oriane (sop). It is an important work historically, being the first French opera to be based on a subject other than classical mythology. Drawn from a 14th-century chivalric romance, it tells of Amadis's reunion with his real parents, his receipt of knighthood, the tests of his courage and his love for and reconciliation with a princess.

Amahl and the Night Visitors

Opera in one act by Menotti. 1st perf. NBC TV, 24 Dec 1951; 1st stage perf. Indiana, 21 Feb 1952; libr. by the composer, inspired by Hieronymus Bosch's painting *The Adoration of the Magi*. Principal roles: Amahl (treble), Mother (mezzo), Melchior (bar), Kaspar (ten), Balthazar (bass). The first opera written specifically for television, it has always been one of Menotti's most popular works.

Plot: The crippled boy, Amahl, lives in poverty with his mother. They are visited by the Magi on their way to see the infant Jesus and, during the night, the mother succumbs to temptation and steals some of their gold. She is caught, but explains that the money is for her boy; the Magi tell her to keep it, since Jesus will build his kingdom on love. Amahl offers his crutch as a gift to Christ and discovers that he can walk unaided. His mother allows him to accompany the Magi on their journey. [R]

Amalia
Soprano role in Verdi's *I Masnadieri*. She is in love with Carlo.

Amara, Lucine *(b Armaganian) (b 1927)*
American soprano, particularly identified with the Italian repertory. A versatile singer with a fine voice, she was largely based at the Metropolitan Opera, New York.

Amato, Pasquale *(1878–1942)*
Italian baritone, especially associated with the Italian repertory. Possessor of a rich and vibrant voice and exemplary diction, he created Jack Rance in *La Fanciulla del West*, Napoleon in Giordano's *Madame Sans-Gêne* and the title role in Damrosch's *Cyrano de Bergerac*.

Ambo nati
Baritone aria for Antonio in Act I of Donizetti's *Linda di Chamounix*.

Amelia
Soprano role in: (1) Verdi's *Un Ballo in Maschera*. Renato's wife, she is loved by Gustavus. (2) Verdi's *Simon Boccanegra*. In reality Boccanegra's daughter Maria, she has been brought up as Amelia Grimaldi. (3) Donizetti's *Elisabetta al Castello di Kenilworth*. She is the historical Amy Robsart. (4)

Donizetti's *Le Duc d'Albe*. She is Egmont's daughter.

Amelia al Ballo *(Amelia Goes to the Ball)*
Comic opera in one act by Menotti. 1st perf. Philadelphia, 1 Apr 1937; libr. by the composer. Principal roles: Amelia (sop), Husband (bar), Lover (ten), Friend (mezzo), Police Chief (bass). Menotti's first opera, it is a satire on the female attitude to social priorities.
  Plot: Amelia, leaving to attend a ball, is detained by a showdown between her husband and her lover. She strikes the husband, leaving him unconscious, has the lover arrested, and proceeds to the ball with the police chief. [R]

Ameling, Elly *(b 1938)*
Dutch soprano. Best known as one of the finest contemporary lieder singers, her operatic appearances have sadly been very rare, and restricted to an occasional Mozart performance.

America
See United States of America

American opera composers
See Antheil; Barber; Beeson; Bernstein; Blitzstein; Converse; Copland; Damrosch; Floyd; Foss; Friml; Gershwin; Giannini; Glass; Gruenberg; Hadley; Hanson; Herbert; Herrmann; Joplin; Kurka; Levy; Moore; Nabokov; Pasatieri; Romberg; Schuller; Sessions; Sousa; Still; Talbot; Taylor; Thomson; Ward
  Other national opera composers include John Adams, Ernest Bacon (b 1898), William Bergsma (b 1921), Eugene Macdonald Bonner (b 1899), Paul Bowles (b 1911), George Bristow

(1825–98), Benjamin Carr (1768–1831), whose *The Archers* (New York 18 April 1796; libr. William Dunlap) was the first American opera, John Eaton (b 1935), William Henry Fry (1813–64), Horatio William Parker (1863–1919) and Bernard Rogers (1893–1968).

American Opera Society

Founded in 1951 by Allen Sven Oxenburg and operating until 1970, it was devoted to giving concert performances of little-known operas. Most of these were held at Carnegie Hall, New York, with top international casts.

Amerò sarò costante, L'

Soprano aria for Amintas in Act II of Mozart's *Il Re Pastore*.

Amfiparnasso, L' (roughly *The Lower Slopes of Parnassus*)

Comedy in prologue and three acts by Vecchi. 1st perf. (?) Modena, 1594; libr. by the composer and, it is thought, Giulio Cesare Croce. One of the most important 'proto-operas', it is a madrigal cycle for five voices and is one of the earliest attempts to combine farce with music. Its plot, comprising various episodes related to love, as well as its character types and use of dialect, derive from the Commedia dell'Arte tradition. The piece has occasionally been staged as an opera in modern times. [R]

Amfortas

Baritone role in Wagner's *Parsifal*. Titurel's son, he is the guardian of the Holy Grail.

Amico Fritz, L' (*Friend Fritz*)

Opera in three acts by Mascagni. 1st perf. Rome, 31 Oct 1891; libr. by Nicola Daspuro after Emile Erckmann and Alexandre Chatrian's *L'Ami Fritz*. Principal roles: Fritz (ten), Suzel (sop), David (bar), Beppe (mezzo). Mascagni's most successful work other than *Cavalleria Rusticana*, it is a pastoral comedy.

Plot: In Alsace during the late 19th century, Fritz, a wealthy middle-aged landowner, has a bet with the Rabbi David that he will always remain a bachelor. However, David notices that Fritz is captivated by Suzel, the daughter of one of his tenants. When David mischievously tells Fritz that he has found Suzel a young husband, Fritz is so upset that he leaves without a word to the young woman, who is in love with him. Despairing, she appeals to him to save her from the so-called marriage and he finally confesses that he loves her. David has won the bet and he donates his winnings – a vineyard – to Suzel. [R]

Amina

Soprano role in Bellini's *La Sonnambula*. Teresa's foster-daughter, she is the sleepwalking girl of the opera's title.

Amis, l'amour tendre

Tenor aria for Hoffmann in the Giulietta Act of Offenbach's *Les Contes d'Hoffmann*.

Amneris

Mezzo role in Verdi's *Aida*. Pharaoh's daughter, she loves Radamès.

Amonasro

Baritone role in Verdi's *Aida*. Aida's father, he is the Ethiopian king.

Amore dei Tre Re, L' (*The Love of Three Kings*)

Opera in three acts by Montemezzi. 1st

perf. Milan, 10 April 1913; libr. by Sem Benelli after his own verse play. Principal roles: Archibaldo (bass), Fiora (sop), Manfredo (bar), Avito (ten), Flaminio (ten). A hauntingly beautiful work, this is Montemezzi's masterpiece and one of the finest of all 20th-century Italian operas. It is especially notable for its magnificent orchestration and for the remarkable characterisation of the old, blind king.

Plot: 10th-century Italy. The Italian princess Fiora, originally betrothed to Avito, has been forced to marry Manfredo, son of the old, blind barbarian king Archibaldo. Already suspecting her of infidelity, Archibaldo chances on her and her lover declaring their feelings, but Avito escapes. Archibaldo strangles Fiora, who refuses to reveal her lover's identity, so Archibaldo lays a trap by smearing Fiora's lips with poison. Avito kisses her lips and dies, but Manfredo, who has forgiven her and no longer wishes to live, does the same. Archibaldo finding the body he thinks is Fiora's lover discovers that he has also killed his son. Everything is now the darkness to which the old king has so long been accustomed. [R]

Amore Medico, L' (Love the Doctor)

Comic opera in two acts by Wolf-Ferrari. 1st perf. Dresden, 4 Dec 1913; libr. by Enrico Golisciani after Molière's L'Amour Médecin. Principal roles: Lucinda (sop), Clitandro (ten), Arnolfo (bar). An elegant example of Wolf-Ferrari's neo-classical comic style, it was successful at its appearance but is now rarely performed.

Plot: The outskirts of 17th-century Paris. Arnolfo has forbidden his lovesick daughter Lucinda to marry. However, her secret lover, Clitandro, disguises himself as a doctor and prescribes a mock marriage as the cure

for her condition. It is, needless to say, a real marriage to which Arnolfo eventually gives his blessing.

Amor ti vieta

Tenor aria for Loris in Act III of Giordano's Fedora.

Amour est un oiseau rebelle, L'

Mezzo aria (the Habañera) for Carmen in Act I of Bizet's Carmen. It is adapted from the song El Arregilito by the Spanish composer Sebastián Yradier (1809–65).

Amsterdam

See Netherlands Opera

Am stillen Herd

Tenor aria for Walther von Stolzing in Act I of Wagner's Die Meistersinger von Nürnberg.

Anacréon

Works of this title about the mythical Greek hero include:

(1) Opera-ballet in one act by Rameau. 1st perf. Fontainebleau, 23 Oct 1754; libr. by Louis de Cahusac. Principal roles: Anacréon (bar), Cupid (sop), Agathocle (mezzo), Priestess (sop). [R]

(2) Opera-ballet in two acts by Cherubini, subtitled L'Amour Fugitif. 1st perf. Paris, 4 Oct 1803; libr. by R. Mendouze. Successful in its time, only its fine overture is at all remembered today.

Anch'io dischiuso

Soprano aria for Abigaille in Act II of Verdi's Nabucco.

Ancona, Mario (1860–1931)

Italian baritone, associated with the

Italian repertory. One of the leading baritones of the early 20th century, he had a beautiful voice, used with elegance and a superb technique. He created Silvio in *Pagliacci*.

Anders, Peter *(1908–54)*

German tenor. Possessing a beautiful voice used with fine musicianship, he began as a lyric tenor and was especially successful in Mozart roles. After the war, he undertook heroic roles with equal success. He was killed in a car accident.

Andersen, Hans Christian

See panel on page 21

Anderson, June *(b 1950)*

American soprano, notable in French and Italian coloratura roles. Possessing a beautiful voice which is both large and extraordinarily agile, coupled with a superb technique, she is possibly the finest coloratura to have emerged since Joan Sutherland.

Anderson, Marian *(b 1902)*

American contralto with a large, rich voice. In 1955, she became the first black singer ever to appear at the Metropolitan Opera, New York (as Ulrica). Described by Toscanini as "the voice that comes once in a hundred years", her operatic appearances were very rare.

Andrea Chénier

Opera in four acts by Giordano. 1st perf. Milan, 28 Mar 1896; libr. by Luigi Illica. Principal roles: Chénier (ten), Madeleine (sop), Carlo Gérard (bar), Bersi (mezzo), Countess de Coigny (mezzo), Madelon (mezzo). Giordano's most successful and enduring work, it is historically based on the life of the French poet André Chénier (1762–94).

Plot: Paris during the French Revolution. At a party the poet Chénier rebukes the wealthy Madeleine de Coigny for scorning love. They meet again after the Revolution and fall in love. Gérard, who had loved Madeleine when he was a servant in the Coigny household, is now a revolutionary leader and denounces Chénier. To save Chénier, Madeleine offers herself to Gérard, who repents and intervenes on her lover's behalf – in vain, for Chénier is condemned to death. Madeleine bribes the jailer to let her change places with a condemned female prisoner, and she and Chénier go to death together. [R]

Andrei

(1) Baritone role in Prokofiev's *War and Peace*. He is a prince loved by Natasha. (2) Tenor role in Tchaikovsky's *Mazeppa*. He is in love with Maria. (3) Tenor role in Moussorgsky's *Khovanschina*. He is Ivan Khovansky's son. (4) Bass role in Prokofiev's *The Story of a Real Man*.

Andres

(1) Baritone role in Offenbach's *La Périchole*. He is the viceroy of Peru. (2) Tenor role in Berg's *Wozzeck*. He is Wozzeck's companion. (3) Tenor comprimario role in Offenbach's *Les Contes d'Hoffmann*. He is the stage-door keeper of the opera house.

Anelli, Angelo *(1761–1820)*

Italian librettist, sometimes writing under the pseudonyms Nicolò Liprandi and Marco Landi. One of the best Italian librettists of his day, excelling in comedy, he provided texts for Cimarosa, Coccia, Gazzaniga, Guglielmi, Martín y Soler, Mayr, Pacini, Paer, Pavesi, Portugal, Rossini

HANS CHRISTIAN ANDERSEN

The Danish writer Hans Christian Andersen (1805–75) was himself keenly interested in opera: he had originally hoped to be an actor or a singer and worked at the Theatre Royal, Copenhagen. He wrote a number of opera libretti, including *The Watersprites* (*Nokken*, 1835) and *The Wedding on Lake Como* (*Bryllupet ved Como Soen*, 1849, after Alessandro Manzoni's *I Promessi Sposi*) for Franz Gläser and adaptations of Sir Walter Scott's *Kenilworth* (*Festen paa Kenilworth*, 1836) for Christoph Weyse and *The Bride of Lammermoor* (*Bruden fra Lammermoor*, 1832) for Bredal. Over 50 operas have been based on his fairy tales. Below are listed, by work, those operas by composers with entries in this dictionary.

The Emperor's New Clothes

Wagner-Régeny	*Der Nachte König*	1928

The Garden of Paradise

Bruneau	*Le Jardin du Paradis*	1923

Little Christina

Leoni	*Ib and Little Christina*	1901

The Magic Violin

Egk	*Die Zaubergiege*	1935

The Match Girl

Enna	*The Little Match Girl*	1897
Veretti	*Una Favola di Andersen*	1934

The Nightingale

Enna	*The Nightingale*	1912
Stravinsky	*The Nightingale*	1914

The Prince and the Swineherd

Rota	*Il Principe Porcaro*	1925

The Princess and the Pea

Enna	*The Princess and the Pea*	1900

The Travelling Companion

Stanford	*The Travelling Companion*	1925

(*L'Italiana in Algeri*) and Zingarelli amongst others.

Anfossi, Pasquale (1727–97)
Italian composer. He wrote some 70 operas, beginning with *La Serva Spiritosa* (Rome 1763). Many of his operas enjoyed considerable success in their day, but all of them are now forgotten. His most important works

include *L'Incognita Perseguitata* (Rome 1773; libr. after Carlo Goldoni), his most successful work, *La Finta Giardiniera* (Rome 1774; libr. Marco Coltellini), *L'Avaro* (Venice 1775; libr. Giovanni Bertati), *La Vera Costanza* (Rome 1776; libr. Francisco Puttini) and *Il Curioso Indiscreto* (Rome 1777; libr. Bertati).

Angeles, Victoria de los *(b López Chima) (b 1923)*

Spanish soprano, particularly identified with Italian and French lyric roles. An artist of outstanding musicianship, she possessed one of the loveliest voices of the immediate postwar era. Her affecting stage presence and her warm personality have made her a great favourite with audiences everywhere, in recital as well as opera.

Angélique

Comic opera in one act by Ibert. 1st perf. Paris, 28 July 1927; libr. by Nino. Principal roles: Angélique (sop), Boniface (ten), Charlot (bar). Ibert's most successful work, it tells of a shopkeeper who is persuaded by his friend that the only way to get rid of his ill-natured and sharp-tongued wife is to put her up for sale.

Angelotti, Cesare

Bass role in Puccini's *Tosca*. He is an escaped political prisoner. In history, he was Liberio Angelucci, Consul of the short-lived Roman Republic.

Anges du Paradis

Tenor aria for Vincent in Act III of Gounod's *Mireille*.

Ange si pure *(often sung in Italian as 'Spirto gentil')*

Tenor aria for Fernand in Act IV of Donizetti's *La Favorite*.

Aniara

Opera in two acts by Blomdahl. 1st perf. Stockholm, 31 May 1959; libr. by Erik Lindegren after an epic poem by Harry Martinson. Principal roles: Daisy Doodle (sop), Blind Poetess (sop), Mimarobe (bar), Blind Man (ten). Employing electronic music, it has proved one of the most successful postwar operas and has been widely performed.

Plot: A spaceship is carrying refugees from an Earth devastated by a nuclear holocaust to a settlement on Mars. The ship collides with an asteroid and is knocked off course and is doomed to journey in space through eternity. [R]

Anima del Filosofo, L'

See Orfeo ed Euridice (Haydn)

Ankerström

The adviser to Gustavus III of Sweden, he appears as: (1) Baritone role in Verdi's *Un Ballo in Maschera*. Amelia's husband, he is Renato in the Boston setting. (2) Baritone role in Auber's *Gustave III*. (3) Bass role in Werle's *Tintomara*. In history, Jakob Johan Ankerström was indeed Gustavus's assassin, but he did not know him personally.

Anna

(1) Mezzo role in Berlioz's *Les Troyens*. She is Dido's sister. (2) Soprano role in Donizetti's *Anna Bolena*. She is the historical Anne Boleyn (c 1507–36), second wife of Henry VIII. (3) Soprano role in Catalani's *Loreley*. She is Walther's fiancée. (4) Soprano role in Puccini's *Le Villi*. She is Robert's fiancée. (5) Soprano role in Sallinen's *The Horseman*. (6) Soprano role in Strauss's *Intermezzo*. (7) Soprano role in Boïeldieu's *La Dame Blanche*. She is Gaveston's ward. (8) Soprano role in

Rossini's *Maometto II*. (9) Soprano role in Zandonai's *I Cavalieri di Ekebù*. (10) Soprano role in Marschner's *Hans Heiling*. (11) Mezzo comprimario role in Donizetti's *Maria Stuarda*. She is Hannah Kennedy, Mary's companion. (12) Soprano comprimario role in Verdi's *Nabucco*. She is Zaccaria's sister.

Anna, Donna

Soprano role in Mozart's *Don Giovanni* and Dargomijsky's *The Stone Guest*. She is the Commendatore's daughter.

Anna Bolena (*Anne Boleyn*)

Opera in two acts by Donizetti. 1st perf. Milan, 26 Dec 1830; libr. by Felice Romani partly after Alessandro Pepoli's play and Ippolito Pindemonte's *Enrico VIII*. Principal roles: Anne Boleyn (sop), Jane Seymour (mezzo), Henry VIII (bass), Richard Percy (ten), Smeton (mezzo), Rochfort (bass), Harvey (ten). Donizetti's 33rd opera, it was his first major success and established his European reputation. One of the composer's finest works, both musically and dramatically, it has been a key work in the postwar Donizetti revival, particularly the 1957 La Scala production with Maria Callas.

Plot: Windsor, 1536. Henry has tired of his queen Anne and transferred his attentions to her lady-in-waiting Jane Seymour. Hoping to compromise the queen he recalls her first love, Richard Percy, from exile, but it is, in fact, through the unintended indiscretion of the page Smeton, that Henry is able to order her trial for adultery. Learning that Jane is her rival, Anne forgives her and, despite Jane's pleas to Henry for mercy, she is condemned to death. She loses her reason, but on hearing the music of

Henry's new wedding she recovers her senses and forgives the pair. [R]

Ännchen

Soprano role in Weber's *Der Freischütz*. She is Agathe's cousin.

Annina

(1) Soprano role in J. Strauss's *Eine Nacht in Venedig*. She is Barbara's friend. (2) Mezzo role in Strauss's *Der Rosenkavalier*. Valzacchi's colleague, she is an Italian schemer. (3) Mezzo comprimario role in Verdi's *La Traviata*. She is Violetta's maid.

Annius

Mezzo trouser-role in Mozart's *La Clemenza di Tito*. He is loved by Servilia.

Annunzio, Gabriele d'

See panel on page 24

Ansermet, Ernest (*1883–1969*)

Swiss conductor, particularly identified with the French repertory. Founder of L'Orchestre de la Suisse Romande, he was musical director of the Grand Théâtre, Geneva (1962–69). He conducted the first performances of *The Rape of Lucretia*, *Renard* and Martin's *Der Sturm*, *La Mystère de la Nativité* and *Monsieur de Pourceaugnac*.

Antheil, George (*1900–59*)

American composer. His operas, written in a variety of styles, are the jazz-influenced *Transatlantic* (Frankfurt 25 May 1930; libr. composer), *Helen Retires* (New York 28 Feb 1934; libr. J. Erskine), *Volpone* (Los Angeles 9 Jan 1953; libr. A. Perry, after Ben Jonson), *The Brothers* (Denver 28 July 1954;

GABRIELE D'ANNUNZIO

The Italian playwright and patriot Gabriele d'Annunzio (1863–1938) has an important place in operatic history. He was a close associate of Pizzetti and wrote the libretto for his *Fedra*, as well as that for Mascagni's *Parisina*. With Pizzetti, Casella and Malipiero, he was editor of the *Roccolta Nazionale della Musica Italiana*. An opponent of verismo and a qualified admirer of Wagner, he was an encourager of classical and pre-classical opera. The constitution which he drew up during his military occupation of Fiume contained two clauses giving music a central position in the life of the state. His plays have inspired a number of operas. Those by composers with entries in this dictionary are given below by play.

La Fiaccola Sotto il Moggio

Pizzetti	*Gigliola*	1915 (U)

La Figlia di Iorio

Franchetti	*La Figlia di Iorio*	1906
Pizzetti	*La Figlia di Iorio*	1954

Francesca da Rimini

Zandonai	*Francesca da Rimini*	1914

La Nave

Montemezzi	*La Nave*	1918

Il Sogno d'un Tramonto

Malipiero	*Il Sogno d'un Tramonto*	1913

libr. composer), *Venus in Africa* (1954) and *The Wish* (Louisville, 2 April 1955; libr. composer). A colourful figure, he wrote detective stories, a syndicated agony column and his autobiography, *Bad Boy of Music*, which was published in 1945.

Antigone

Works of this title based on Sophocles's play include:

(1) Opera in three acts by Traetta. 1st perf. St Petersburg, 11 Nov 1772; libr. by Marco Coltellini.

(2) Opera in three acts by Honegger. 1st perf. Brussels, 28 Dec 1927; libr. by Jean Cocteau. Principal roles: Antigone (mezzo), Ismène (sop), Hémon (bar), Créon (bar), Tirésias (bass). The familiar story tells how Antigone defies Créon's ban on the burial of her brother and how she dies with her lover Hémon, Créon's son. Although it contains much fine music, it is rarely performed.

(3) Opera in one act by Orff. 1st perf. Salzburg, 9 Aug 1949. A setting of Friedrich Hölderlin's translation. Principal roles: Antigonae (sop), Creon (bar), Haemon (ten), Tiresias (ten), Eurydice (mezzo), Messenger (bass). An austere and powerful setting, it consists

of heightened declamation of the text over a percussive and largely rhythmical accompaniment. It is only infrequently performed. [R]

Antonia

Soprano role in Offenbach's *Les Contes d'Hoffmann*. She is a consumptive singer.

Antonida

Soprano role in Glinka's *A Life for the Tsar*. She is in love with Sobinin.

Antonio

(1) Baritone role in Donizetti's *Linda di Chamounix*. He is Maddalena's husband. (2) Baritone role in Lehár's *Giuditta*. (3) Tenor role in Prokofiev's *The Duenna*. (4) Bass role in Mascagni's *Lodoletta*. (5) Bass role in Gomes's *Il Guarany*. He is Cecilia's father. (6) Bass role in Mozart's *Le Nozze di Figaro*. Susanna's uncle, he is a drunken gardener. (7) Baritone role in Sullivan's *The Gondoliers*. He is a Venetian gondolier. (8) Tenor comprimario role in Rossini's *La Gazza Ladra*. He is the jailer.

Antony and Cleopatra

Opera in three acts by Barber. (Op 40). 1st perf. New York, 16 Sept 1966; libr. by Franco Zeffirelli (later revised by Gian-Carlo Menotti) after Shakespeare's play. Principal roles: Cleopatra (sop), Antony (b-bar), Augustus Caesar (ten), Iras (mezzo), Enobarbus (bass). Commissioned to open the new Metropolitan Opera House, it was not successful, but was subsequently revised by the composer, and revived with better fortune.

Plot: Antony leaves his mistress Cleopatra, Queen of Egypt, and returns to Rome, where he is forced to marry Caesar's sister Octavia. When he returns to Cleopatra, Caesar goes to war against him. Defeated, Antony commits suicide and dies in Cleopatra's arms. The Queen, to avoid being paraded in Caesar's triumph, commits suicide by means of being bitten by an asp.

Antwerp

See Royal Flemish Opera

Anvil Chorus

Chorus of gypsies ('Vedi le fosche') in Act II of Verdi's *Il Trovatore*, during which on-stage anvils are struck rhythmically.

Apollo

The Graeco-Roman god appears in many operas, including: (1) Baritone role in Gluck's and tenor role in Lully's *Alceste*. (2) Tenor role in Mozart's *Apollo et Hyacinthus*. (3) Counter-tenor role in Britten's *Death in Venice*. (4) Tenor role in Handel's *Semele*. (5) Baritone role in Rameau's *Les Boréades*. (6) Tenor role in Strauss's *Daphne*. (7) Bass role in Handel's *Admeto*. (8) Baritone role in Taneyev's *Oresteia*. (9) Tenor role in Boughton's *Alkestis*.

Apollo et Hyacinthus

Intermezzo in one act by Mozart (K 38). 1st perf. Salzburg, 13 May 1767; libr. (in Latin) by Rufinus Widl. Principal roles: Melia (sop), Oebalus (ten), Apollo (ten), Zephirus (ten), Hyacinthus (mezzo). Mozart's second stage work, written at the age of 11, it comprises a prologue and nine musical numbers, originally designed for insertion into Widl's *Clementia Croesi*. It is still occasionally performed. [R]

Appia, Adolphe (1862–1928)

Swiss designer. Sometimes regarded as the father of modern operatic staging, he was a pupil of Liszt and a fanatical admirer of Wagner. Horrified by the old-fashioned naturalism of Bayreuth, he advocated three-dimensional, sculptural stagings with abstract scenery. Regarding lighting as "the supreme scene painter, the interpreter, the most significant plastic medium on stage", his sets were always grey, awaiting light to give them colour. His actual theatre work was limited, but included principally a controversial *Tristan und Isolde* at La Scala in 1923 and a *Ring* in Basel which was abandoned halfway through. His theories, expounded in two books *La Mise-en-Scène du Drame Wagnérien* (1895) and *Die Musik und die Inszenierung* (1899), exerted a powerful influence on 20th-century designers and producers such as Max Reinhardt, Stanislavsky, Josef Svoboda and, particularly, Wieland Wagner.

Appoggiatura (Italian for 'leaning')
A vocal ornament or 'grace note', mainly used in the 18th century, consisting of an unharmonised auxiliary note falling (or, less frequently, rising) to an adjacent note which is harmonised or which is implied to be so.

Aprite un po'
Bass-baritone aria for Figaro in Act IV of Mozart's *Le Nozze di Figaro*.

Arabella
Opera in three acts by Strauss. (Op 79). 1st perf. Dresden, 1 July 1933; libr. by Hugo von Hofmannsthal. Principal roles: Arabella (sop), Mandryka (bar), Zdenka (sop), Matteo (ten), Count Waldner (bass), Adelaide (mezzo), Count Elemer (ten), Fiakermilli (sop), Count Dominik (bar), Count Lamoral (bass). One of Strauss's lushest neo-classical scores, it was an immediate success and has always been one of his most popular operas.

Plot: Vienna, 1860. Pressed by his creditors, Count Waldner needs to arrange a financially satisfactory marriage for his elder daughter Arabella and has sent her picture to a rich but elderly friend. It is, however, the friend's son, Mandryka, who arrives, wanting to marry Arabella. The two meet at a ball and fall in love. Arabella parts from her other suitors, particularly the officer Matteo, who is desolated. Arabella's sister Zdenka, brought up as a boy as an economy measure, is secretly in love with Matteo. She promises him a meeting with Arabella, and gives him a letter and a key. Mandryka overhears and, thinking himself betrayed, flirts with the regimental mascot Fiakermilli. Confusion reigns until Zdenka explains that the key was to her own room, whereupon Matteo transfers his affections to her, while Arabella and Mandryka are engaged. [R]

Aragall, Giacomo (b Jaime) (b 1940)
Spanish tenor, particularly associated with Verdi and Puccini roles and with the French repertory. He possesses an extremely pleasing and easily-produced voice, used with fine musicianship, and has a handsome stage presence.

Araiza, Francisco (b 1950)
Mexican tenor, particularly associated with Mozart, Rossini and Donizetti roles. One of the most stylish and musicianly lyric tenors to have emerged in recent years.

Arbace
Tenor role in Mozart's *Idomeneo*. He is Idomeneo's counsellor.

Arcadians, The

Operetta in three acts by Monckton
and Talbot. 1st perf. London, April
1909; libr. by Mark Ambient, A. M.
Thompson, Robert Courtenidge and
Arthur Wimperis. Perhaps the finest
non-Sullivan British operetta apart from
Merrie England, it was sensationally
successful at its appearance and is still
sometimes performed, despite its dated
quality. [R Exc]

Archibaldo

Bass role in Montemezzi's *L'Amore dei
Tre Re*. Manfredo's father, he is the
old, blind king of Altura.

Arden Must Die

Opera in two acts by Goehr (Op 21).
1st perf. Hamburg (as *Arden Muss
Sterben*), 5 Mar 1967; libr. by Erich
Fried after *Arden of Faversham*.
Principal roles: Arden (bar), Alice
(mezzo), Mosbie (ten), Mrs Bradshaw
(mezzo), Franklin (bass), Susan (sop),
Michael (ten), Reede (bass). Goehr's
most important opera, it is a black
comedy, dealing with the attempts,
instigated by his wife, to kill Arden.

Arditi, Luigi *(1822–1903)*

Italian conductor and composer.
Largely based in London, he was one
of the leading operatic conductors of
the 19th century, particularly of the
Italian repertory. Best known as a song
composer, he also wrote three operas: *I
Briganti* (1841), *Il Corsaro* (Havana
1847; libr. after Lord Byron's *The
Corsair*) and *La Spia* (New York
1856). His autobiography, *My
Reminiscences*, was published in 1896.

Ardon gl'incesi

Soprano aria (the Mad Scene) for Lucia
in Act III of Donizetti's *Lucia di*

Lammermoor, one of the most famous
and demanding soprano scenes in all
opera. The long central duet between
voice and flute before the cabaletta
'Spargi d'amaro pianto' is *not* in the
original score. The original obbligato
instruments were glass harmonica and
glockenspiel, but Donizetti was forced
to abandon them as impracticable and
replaced them with the flute.

Arensky, Anton *(1861–1906)*

Russian composer. His first opera *A
Dream on the Volga* (*Son na Volge*,
Moscow 2 Jan 1891; libr. after
Alexander Nikolayevich Ostrovsky)
enjoyed very considerable success. This
was not shared by his two subsequent
operas *Rafael* (Moscow 18 May 1894;
libr. A. Kryukov) and *Nal and
Damayanti* (Moscow 22 Jan 1904; libr.
Modest Tchaikovsky after Vasily
Zhukovsky). He was also a
distinguished teacher, whose pupils
included Rachmaninov and Scriabin.

Argentina

See Teatro Colón, Buenos Aires

Argentinian opera composers

See Beruti; Castro; Gaito;
Ginastera; Panizza

Other national opera composers
include Felipe Boero (1884–1958),
Enrique Mario Casella (1891–1948),
Arnoldo d'Espósito (1907–45), Gilardo
Gilardi (1889–1963), Valdo
Sciammerella (*b* 1924), Alfredo L.
Schiuma (1885–1963) and Héctor
Iglésias Villoud (*b* 1913).

Argomento (Italian for 'argument')

A term describing the summary of the
plot that precedes the text in the
printed libretto of an opera.

Aria (Italian for 'air')
A musical number for solo singers.
Until the end of the 17th century, the
term was used for a piece with any
number of soloists, but since then it has
denoted a piece for a single soloist. The
aria developed from the early recitative-
style operas as a point of heightened
emotional and musical tension, and
soon became a fully self-contained
number. It reached its first period of
rigid formality during the late Baroque,
with the da capo* form (A – B – A
decorated). Gluck and Mozart loosened
the rigidity, but by the early 19th
century a second formal structure had
developed in Italy. This was the 'aria
and cabaletta*', which comprised a
lyrical (usually slow) aria, followed by
a contrasting (usually fast) two-verse
cabaletta, in which singers displayed
their virtuosity by decorating the second
verse. The form was dramatically
suffocating, and it was left to Verdi
and Wagner to loosen the structure
once more, and eventually almost to
dispense with arias altogether.

Many different types of aria, usually
relating to specific dramatic situations,
came into being, especially in 18th-
century opera seria. They included Aria
di Infuriata (for anger), Aria di
Sentimento, Aria di Lamento and many
others (including the six following
entries). They refer more to the
sentiment of an aria rather than to any
specific structure.

See also Air; Aria del Sorbetto;
Aria di Baule; Aria di Bravura;
Aria di Catalogo; Aria di
Imitazione; Aria di Sortita; Arie;
Arie Antiche; Arietta; Arioso;
Aubade; Auftrittslied; Ballad;
Berceuse; Brindisi; Cabaletta;
Canzona; Canzonetta; Cavatina;
Da capo; Dal segno; Lamento;
Lied; Metaphor Aria; Romanza;
Serenade; Vengeance Aria

Aria del Sorbetto (Italian for
'sorbet air')
An aria in an early 19th-century Italian
opera for a secondary character, during
which the audience would often leave
their seats to buy their ices and chat
with their friends. An example is
Berta's 'Il vecchioto' in *Il Barbiere di
Siviglia*. Nowadays, the audience is
expected to listen to them.

Aria di Baule (Italian for 'trunk
air')
An individual singer's favourite aria,
which they would carry around with
them in their luggage and insert into
whatever opera they happened to be
appearing in at the time. In the 19th
century, many great singers indulged in
this, but nowadays the practice is
frowned upon.

Aria di Bravura (Italian for
'swagger air')
An aria specifically designed to show
off a singer's virtuosity. Typically, such
arias were of great technical difficulty,
involving wide intervals, long runs and
elaborate coloratura.

Aria di Catalogo (Italian for
'catalogue air')
An aria in an 18th- or early 19th-
century Italian comic opera, in which
the singer reels off a long list of names,
places or items, usually at high speed
(see: Patter). Had Rossini carried out
his famous offer to set a laundry list to
music it would have been an aria di
catalogo. Perhaps the most famous
example is Leporello's Catalogue Aria
in *Don Giovanni*, although it is
atypical. Possibly the finest examples
are by Donizetti: Dulcamara's

proclamation of his wares in *L'Elisir d'Amore* and, particularly, Enrico's unbelievable prescription in *Il Campanello*, which is so long and goes so fast that Donizetti recommends the singer to take the words on stage with him! Non-Italian composers also used the form occasionally, for example Sullivan with Col Calverley's 'If you want a receipt' in *Patience*.

Aria di Imitazione (Italian for 'imitation air')

Two types of aria: (1) In which the voice and/or the orchestra imitate the sounds of nature. (2) In which the singer imitates the sounds of the orchestra. Much the most famous example is Cimarosa's *Il Maestro di Cappella*.

Aria di Sortita (Italian for 'departure air')

An aria for a character about to leave the stage. Very popular in the 18th century.

Ariadne auf Naxos

Opera in prologue and one act by Richard Strauss (Op 60). 1st perf. (second part only) Stuttgart, 25 Oct 1912. Revised version 1st perf. Vienna, 4 Oct 1916; libr. by Hugo von Hofmannsthal after Molière's *Le Bourgeois Gentilhomme*. Principal roles: Prima Donna/Ariadne (sop), Zerbinetta (sop), Composer (mezzo), Tenor/Bacchus (ten), Music Master (bar), Harlequin (bar), Major-Domo (speaker), Dancing Master (ten), Truffaldino (bass), Brighella (ten), Scaramuccio (ten), Naiad (sop), Dryad (mezzo), Echo (sop). A popular and highly sophisticated work in Strauss's neo-Mozartian vein, it gave him the opportunity to put on the stage some of his ideas concerning music and drama.

Plot: In the prologue, a wealthy gentleman has hired a Commedia dell'Arte troupe, led by Zerbinetta, and an opera company to provide entertainment for his guests. The Major-Domo informs the two groups that time limitations mean that they must perform their offerings simultaneously. Despite the protests of the Composer, cuts are made in the opera, 'Ariadne', which the comedians plan to enliven. In the opera, set on a desert island, Ariadne bemoans the fact that Theseus has abandoned her, and resists all attempts by the comedians to cheer her up. Bacchus arrives and Ariadne believes him to be the god of death. He persuades her that life is just beginning and they depart together with the approval of Zerbinetta. [R]

Ariane et Barbe-Bleue (*Ariane and Bluebeard*)

Opera in three acts by Dukas. 1st perf. Paris, 10 May 1907; libr. by Maurice Maeterlinck. Principal roles: Ariane (mezzo), Bluebeard (bar), Nurse (mezzo), Ygraine (sop), Selysette (mezzo), Mélisande (sop), Bellangère (sop). Dukas' only opera, it is rarely performed.

Plot: At his castle, Bluebeard gives his wife Ariane six silver keys and one of gold but forbids her to use them. The silver keys open doors to Bluebeard's treasure, the golden a door to a staircase, which she opens. Hearing the wailing of women, she discovers Bluebeard's former wives imprisoned. Bluebeard tries to drag her away, but later, when he is away, she and her nurse unlock the prison vault. Bluebeard is captured by peasants, but Ariane releases him and, freeing the captive women, encourages them to emerge into a world of hope. They hesitate and remain in the castle. [R]

Arianna (*Ariadne*)
Works of this title include:
(1) Opera in prologue and eight
scenes by Monteverdi. 1st perf.
Mantua, 28 May 1608; libr. by Ottavio
Rinuccini. Virtually all of the music is
lost, the famous lament being the only
substantial portion to survive.
(2) Opera in three acts by Handel.
1st perf. London, 26 Jan 1734; libr. by
Francis Colman, after Pietro Pariati's
Arianna e Teseo. It is only very rarely
performed.

Arie (German for 'air')
The German term for aria.

Arié, Raphael (*1920–88*)
Bulgarian bass, particularly associated
with the Italian repertory. A rich-voiced
singer with a good stage presence, he
created Truelove in *The Rake's
Progress*.

Arie Antiche (Italian for 'ancient
airs')
Songs and arias by 17th- and early
18th-century composers (mainly Italian),
a group of which often opens a solo
recital by a singer. These often include
operatic arias, of which two popular
examples are 'O cessate di piagarmi'
from A. Scarlatti's *Il Pompeo* and 'Nel
cor più' from Paisiello's *La Molinara*.

Arietta (Italian for 'little air')
A short aria, such as 'Quand'ero
paggio' in Verdi's *Falstaff*.

Ariodant
Opera in three acts by Méhul. 1st perf.
Paris, 11 Oct 1799; libr. by François
Benoît Hoffmann, after Lodovico
Ariosto's *Orlando Furioso*. Successful in
its time but now forgotten.

Ariodante
Opera in three acts by Handel. 1st perf.
London, 8 Jan 1735; libr. by Antonio
Salvi, after Lodovico Ariosto's *Orlando
Furioso*. Principal roles: Ariodante
(mezzo), Ginevra (sop), Polinesso
(c-ten), Lurcanio (ten), Dalinda (sop),
King (bass), Odoardo (ten). In recent
years it has been one of the most
frequently performed of Handel's
operas.
    Plot: Ariodante is betrothed to
Ginevra, daughter of the King of
Scotland, but has a rival in Polinesso,
Duke of Albany. Polinesso uses the
maid Dalinda to help him contrive false
evidence that Ginevra is not chaste.
Ginevra is saved from execution by a
dying confession from Polinesso and the
return of Ariodante, who had been
thought dead. [R]

Arioso
Something which is mid-way between
an aria and plain recitative, lacking the
formal structure of an aria. It is
epitomised in early opera by
Monteverdi and in the 19th century by
Wagner and Moussorgsky.

Arkel
Bass role in Debussy's *Pelléas et
Mélisande*. He is the old, blind king of
Allemonde.

Arkhipova, Irina (*b 1925*)
Russian mezzo who enjoyed a
remarkably long career, particularly in
the Russian repertory and with Verdi
roles. One of the greatest mezzos of the
postwar period, she possessed a rich
and beautiful voice, used with
outstanding musicianship, and she had
a keen dramatic sense. She created
Klavdiya in *The Story of a Real Man*,
Nilovna in Khrennikov's *The Mother*

and Varvara in Shchedrin's *Not Love Alone.*

Arlecchino (*Harlequin*)

Comic opera in prologue, one act and epilogue by Busoni (Op 50). 1st perf. Zürich, 11 May 1917; libr. by the composer. Principal roles: Arlecchino (speaker), Matteo (bass), Abbot Cospicuo (bar), Columbina (mezzo), Dr Bombasto (bass), Leandro (ten). Dealing with the traditional Commedia dell'Arte figures, it is Busoni's most accessible opera and is still performed from time to time.

Plot: Bergamo, 18th century. Arlecchino flirts with the mute Annunziata in front of her husband, Matteo the tailor, trying various ploys to get rid of him. His disgusted wife Columbina berates him and he leaves her in the hands of Leandro, a bombastic cavalier much given to operatic outbursts in Italian. Arlecchino injures Leandro in a duel, and while Columbina takes him to hospital, Arlecchino elopes with Annunziata. Matteo returns blissfully unaware of the goings-on, and calmly continues with his sewing and his reading of Dante. [R]

Arlen, Stephen (*1913–72*)

British administrator. As administrator of Sadler's Wells Opera from 1966, he planned and began both the company's move from Sadler's Wells Theatre to the London Coliseum and the project of an English-language *Ring*. He persisted despite bitter opposition and prophecies of doom, but tragically did not live to see the triumphant success of both ventures.

Arlesiana, L' (*The Girl From Arles*)

Opera in three (originally four) acts by Cilea. 1st perf. Milan, 27 Nov 1897; Libr. by Leopoldo Marenco, after

Alphonse Daudet's *L'Arlésienne.* Revised version 1st perf. Milan, 22 Oct 1898. Principal roles: Federico (ten), Rosa Mamai (mezzo), Vivetta (sop), Metifio (bar), Baldassare (bass), L'Innocente (mezzo). Cilea's only opera apart from *Adriana Lecouvreur* still to be remembered.

Plot: In Provence, Rosa Mamai's son, Federico, is in love with a girl from Arles, while his mother's godchild, Vivetta, is in love with him. Rosa and Vivetta produce some letters which reveal that Federico's girl has been the mistress of Metifio. Federico decides to forget her and marry Vivetta, but Metifio rouses him to a jealous rage and he finally kills himself in despair. [R]

Arme Heinrich, Der (*Poor Henry*)

Opera in three acts by Pfitzner. 1st perf. Mainz, 2 April 1895; libr. by James Grun, after a medieval legend. Pfitzner's only opera, apart from *Palestrina*, still remembered.

Armenian opera composers

See **Chukhadjian**

Other national opera composers include Artemy Ayvazian (*b* 1902), Alexander Spendiarov (b Spendiarian) (1871–1928), Aro Stepanian (1897–1966) and Armen Tigranian (1879–1950). *See also* **Turkish opera composers**

Armida

Works of this title based on Torquato Tasso's *Gerusalemme Liberata* include:

(1) Opera by Graun. 1st perf. Berlin, 27 Mar 1751; libr. by Villati.

(2) Opera by Traetta. 1st perf. Vienna, 3 Jan 1761; libr. by G. Durrazzo.

(3) Opera in three acts by Anfossi.

1st perf. Turin, 1770; libr. by Jacopo Durandi.

(4) Opera by Jommelli. 1st perf. Naples, 30 May 1770; libr. by F. S. de Rogati.

(5) Opera in three acts by Salieri. 1st perf. Vienna, 2 June 1771; libr. by Marco Coltellini.

(6) Opera by Sacchini. 1st perf. Milan, 1772; libr. by Giovanni da Gamerra. Revised version *Renaud* 1st perf. Paris, 28 Feb 1783; libr. revised by J. Leboeuf and Abbé Simon Joseph de Pellegrin. Principal roles: Renaud (ten), Armide (sop), Hidraot (bar), Adraste (bar), Antiope (sop). One of Sacchini's finest operas, now all but forgotten.

(7) Opera in three acts by Naumann. 1st perf. Padua, 13 June 1773; libr. by Giovanni Bertati.

(8) Opera in three acts by Haydn. 1st perf. Esterháza, 26 Feb 1784; libr. by Jacopo Durandi. Principal roles: Armida (sop), Rinaldo (ten), Zelmira (sop), Idreno (bass), Ubaldo (ten), Clotarco (ten). After a long period of complete neglect, it has received an occasional performance in recent years. [R]

(9) Opera by Zingarelli. 1st perf. Rome, 1786; libr. by Jacopo Durandi.

(10) Opera in three acts by Rossini. 1st perf. Naples, 11 Nov 1817; libr. by Giovanni Schmidt. Principal roles: Armida (sop), Rinaldo (ten). Although never one of Rossini's most successful works, it is still occasionally performed.

Plot: The sorceress Armida, unable to vanquish the heart of Rinaldo, spirits him away to an enchanted island and falls in love with him. He reciprocates her passion until he realises that he has been enslaved by magic, whereupon he rejects her.

(11) Opera in four acts by Dvořák (Op 115). 1st perf. Prague, 25 March 1904; libr. by Jaroslav Vrchlický. Dvořák's last opera, it is almost never performed.

Armide

Opera in five acts by Gluck. 1st perf. Paris, 23 Sept 1777; libr. by Philippe Quinault, after Torquato Tasso's *Gerusalemme Liberata*. Principal roles: Armide (sop), Renaud (ten), Phénice (mezzo), Sidone (sop), Hidraot (b-bar), Ubalde (bar). Although it contains much fine music, it is one of the least often performed of Gluck's mature works.

Plot: During the First Crusade, Hidraot King of Damascus and the sorceress Armide plan to kill Renaud, general of the victorious crusaders, but Armide falls in love with him. Renaud, ensnared by her magic, is rescued by his fellow knights. [R]

Armide et Renaud

Opera in five acts by Lully. 1st perf. Paris, 15 Feb 1686; libr. by Philippe Quinault, after Torquato Tasso's *Gerusalemme Liberata*. One of Lully's finest operas and still occasionally performed. [R Exc]

Arminio

Opera in three acts by Handel. 1st perf. London, 12 Jan 1737; libr. by Antonio Salvi. Never one of Handel's more successful works, it is very rarely performed.

Armstrong, Richard *(b 1943)*

British conductor, particularly associated with the Italian and Czech repertories. He was musical director of the Welsh National Opera (1973–86).

Arne, Thomas *(1710–78)*

British composer. His many stage works, in various forms, include *Rosamond* (London 7 March 1733; libr. Joseph Addison), the masque *Comus* (London 4 March 1738; libr. J. Dalton, after John Milton) [R], *The*

Judgement of Paris (London 1 Aug 1740; libr. William Congreve), the masque *Alfred* (Clivedon 1 Aug 1740; libr. J. Thomson and D. Mallet), in which 'Rule Britannia' appears, *Artaxerxes**, *Thomas and Sally**, the ballad opera *Love in a Village* (London 8 Dec 1762; libr. Isaac Bickerstaffe), *Olimpiade* (London 27 Apr 1764; libr. G. G. Bottarelli, after Pietro Metastasio) and *The Cooper* (London 9 June 1772; libr. composer after Audinot and F. A. Quétant's *Le Tonnelier*) [R]. He made a crucial contribution to the development of British opera, but nowadays his works are very infrequently performed. His illegitimate son Michael (1740–86) was also a composer of several stage works.

Arnold

Tenor role in Rossini's *Guillaume Tell*. Melcthal's son, he is a Swiss patriot in love with Mathilde.

Arnold, Malcolm *(b 1921)*

British composer. He has written two operas: *The Dancing Master* (1951) and *The Open Window* (1956).

Arnould, Sophie *(1740–1802)*

French soprano. The leading soprano at the Paris Opéra (1757–78), she was said to have had a fine if not over-large voice and to have been a passionate actress. Excelling in Rameau and Monsigny, she also created for Gluck the title role in *Iphigénie en Aulide* and Eurydice in the revised French version of *Orfeo ed Euridice*. A famous wit and conversationalist, much sought after in high society, Madame de Pompadour said of her "with such talents you may become a princess". A famous portrait of her by Jean Baptiste Greuze is in the Wallace collection, and Pierné's opera *Sophie Arnould* is based on incidents in her life.

Aroldo *(Harold)*

Opera in four acts by Verdi. 1st perf. Rimini, 16 Aug 1857; libr. by Francesco Maria Piave. The revised version of *Stiffelio**. Principal roles: Aroldo (ten), Mina (sop), Egberto (bar), Briano (bass). It contains a considerable amount of new music, including the whole of Act IV. Since the rediscovery of its orchestral score, *Stiffelio* has nearly always been performed in preference to *Aroldo*.

Plot: Britain, 1189–92. The Saxon warrior, Aroldo, returns from the Crusades to discover that his wife Mina has been seduced by the knight Godvino. Mina's father, Egberto, avenges his own honour by killing Godvino, while Aroldo divorces Mina. She swears eternal love for Aroldo, but he becomes a hermit on the edge of Loch Lomond. When Mina and Egberto are cast ashore there by a storm, husband and wife are reunited. [R]

Arriaga y Balzola, Juan *(1806–26)*

Spanish composer whose tragically early death cut short a career of great promise. He wrote one opera: *Los Esclavos Felices* (*The Happy Slaves*, Bilbao 1820; libr. Comella y Comella).

Arrieta y Corera, Emilio *(1823–94)*

Spanish composer. He wrote a number of operas, including *Ildegonda* (Milan 1845) and *La Conquista di Granada* (1850), but he is chiefly remembered as a zarzuela composer. He wrote over 50 works in this genre, some of which are still performed in Spain. The most successful were *El Dominó Azul* (1853) and *Marina* (1855), which was later revised as an opera (Madrid 16 April 1871).

Arroyo, Martina *(b 1936)*

American soprano, particularly identified with Verdi roles. She possessed a rich and beautiful voice of considerable power, which she used with fine musicianship. Her substantial physique proved an occasional handicap on stage.

Arsace

(1) Mezzo trouser-role in Rossini's *Semiramide*. He turns out to be Semiramide's long-lost son. (2) Counter-tenor role in Handel's *Tamerlano*. (3) Mezzo trouser-role in Handel's *Berenice*. (4) Castrato role in Rossini's *Aureliano in Palmira*. One of the last roles written for a castrato.

Arsena

Soprano role in J. Strauss's *Der Zigeunerbaron*. She is Zsupán's daughter.

Artaserse *(Artaxerxes)*

Opera seria; libr. by Pietro Metastasio. Perhaps the most popular of all the Metastasian texts, it was set at least 50 times. Settings by composers with entries in this dictionary include: (1) Opera in three acts by Hasse. 1st perf. Venice, Feb 1730. (2) Opera in three acts by Gluck. 1st perf. Milan, 26 Dec 1741. Gluck's first opera. (3) Opera by Graun. 1st perf. Berlin, 2 Dec 1743. (4) Opera by Duni. 1st perf. Florence, 1744. (5) Opera by Jommelli. 1st perf. Rome, 4 Feb 1749. (6) Opera in three acts by J. C. Bach. 1st perf. Turin, 26 Dec 1760. (7) Opera in three acts by Paisiello. 1st perf. Modena, 26 Dec 1771. (8) Opera in three acts by Cimarosa. 1st perf. Turin, 26 Dec 1784. (9) Opera in two acts by Anfossi. 1st perf. Rome, 1788. (10) Opera by Zingarelli. 1st perf. Trieste, 19 March 1789. (11) Opera in three acts by Isouard. 1st perf. Livorno, 1794.

Artaxerxes

Opera in three acts by Arne. 1st perf. London, 2 Feb 1762; libr. by the composer, after Pietro Metastasio's *Artaserse*. Possibly Arne's finest full-scale opera, it is nowadays all but forgotten.

Artists in opera

The lives of a number of painters, sculptors and metalsmiths have been the subject of operatic treatment. Amongst the artists who appear as operatic characters are: (1) Benvenuto Cellini in Berlioz's *Benvenuto Cellini*. (2) Paul Gaugin in Gardner's *The Moon and Sixpence*. (3) Goya in Menotti's *Goya*. (4) Matthias Grünwald in Hindemith's *Mathis der Maler*. (5) Michelangelo in F. Ricci's *Luigi Rolla e Michelangelo*. (6) Raphael in Arensky's *Rafael*. (7) Rembrandt in Klenau's *Rembrandt van Rijn*. (8) Salvator Rosa in Gomes's *Salvator Rosa*. (9) Andrea del Sarto in Lesur's *Andrea del Sarto*. (10) Titian in Kubelík's *Cornelia Faroli*.

Arts Florissants, Les

A vocal and instrumental ensemble founded in Paris in 1979 by the American conductor and musicologist William Christie *(b 1944)*, which takes its name from a work by M.-A. Charpentier. It is devoted to the performance of works by 17th- and early 18th-century composers, especially Monteverdi, Lully, Charpentier and Rameau, and has been responsible for the performance and recording of many early French operas.

Arturo

(1) Tenor role in Bellini's *I Puritani*. He is Lord Arthur Talbot, a Cavalier in love with Elvira. (2) Tenor role in

34

Bellini's *La Straniera*. He is in love with Alaide. (3) Mezzo trouser-role in Donizetti's *Rosmonda d'Inghilterra*. (4) Tenor comprimario role in Donizetti's *Lucia di Lammermoor*. He is Lord Arthur Bucklaw, whom Lucia is forced to marry.

Arundell, Dennis *(1898–1988)*
British producer, actor, writer and composer. He directed many notable productions for Sadler's Wells Opera in the immediate postwar period, particularly *Der Fliegende Holländer*, as well as directing the first performances of *Irmelin* and *The Pilgrim's Progress*. He wrote three books on musical topics: on Purcell, on Sadler's Wells and his witty *The Critic at the Opera* (1957). He also wrote two operas: *Ghost of Abel* and *A Midsummer Night's Dream* (1930; libr. after Shakespeare).

Arvidson, Madame
Contralto role in Verdi's *Un Ballo in Maschera*. Ulrica in the Boston setting, she is a fortune-teller.

Ascanio
Mezzo trouser-role in Berlioz's *Benvenuto Cellini*. He is Cellini's apprentice. He is also the subject of Saint-Saëns' *Ascanio*.

Ascanio in Alba
Opera in two acts by Mozart (K 111). 1st perf. Milan, 17 Oct 1771; libr. by Giuseppe Parini. Principal roles: Ascanio (sop), Silvia (sop), Venus (sop), Aceste (ten). One of Mozart's earliest operas, it prompted Hasse (whose own last opera had had its first performance the previous day) to remark "this boy will make us all be forgotten". Rarely performed nowadays.
   Plot: Ascanio has been promised the Arcadian nymph Silvia by his grandmother Venus. Happily, he turns out to be the young man whom Silvia has loved in her dreams. [R]

Aschenbach, Gustav von
Tenor role in Britten's *Death in Venice*. He is a writer whose love for a beautiful boy leads to his death.

Asile héréditaire
Tenor aria for Arnold in Act IV of Rossini's *Guillaume Tell*. One of the most fearsomely difficult heroic tenor arias ever written.

Assassinio nella Cattedrale, L' *(Murder in the Cathedral)*
Opera in two acts by Pizzetti. 1st perf. Milan, 1 March 1958; libr. by the composer and Alberto Castelli, after T. S. Eliot's play. Principal roles: Thomas (bass), four Knights, four Tempters. Dealing with the murder of Archbishop Thomas à Becket in 1170, it is one of Pizzetti's finest works and has been widely performed.

Assedio di Corinto, L'
See Maometto II; Le Siège de Corinthe

Assisa a pie d'un salice
Soprano aria (the Willow Song) for Desdemona in Act III of Rossini's *Otello*.

Assur
Bass role in Rossini's *Semiramide*. He is Semiramide's lover.

Astrologer
(1) Tenor role in Rimsky-Korsakov's *The Golden Cockerel*. It is one of the highest tenor roles ever written. (2) Baritone role in Britten's *The Burning Fiery Furnace*.

Astuzie Femminili, Le (*Female Wiles*)

Comic opera in two acts by Cimarosa. 1st perf. Naples, 16 Aug 1794; libr. by Giovanni Palomba. Principal roles: Bellina (sop), Leonora (mezzo), Giampolo (bass), Dr Romualdo (bass), Filandro (ten). Cimarosa's only full-length work apart from *Il Matrimonio Segreto* still to be at all remembered.

Plot: According to her father's will, Rome's wealthiest heiress, Bellina, has to marry the elderly Bergamo merchant Giampolo. Her tutor Romualdo (although engaged to her governess Leonora) also wants to marry her; she herself loves Filandro and they run away together. Returning in the guise of Cossack officers, the lovers succeed in a subterfuge to marry.

Atalanta

Opera in three acts by Handel. 1st perf. London, 12 May 1736; librettist unknown, after Belisario Valeriani's *La Caccia in Etolia*. Principal roles: Atalanta (sop), Meleagro (sop), Irene (mezzo), Nicandro (bass), Mercury (bass), Aminta (ten). Written to celebrate the wedding of Frederick, Prince of Wales and Princess Augusta of Saxe-Gotha, it tells of the love of a huntress-nymph for a shepherd-king. It is infrequently performed. [R]

Atanasov, Georgy (*1882–1931*)

Bulgarian composer and conductor. The effective founder of Bulgarian opera, always known as 'The Maestro', many of his operas are still performed in Bulgaria, but are unknown elsewhere. His stage works include the children's opera *For the Birds* (*Za Ptichy*, 1909), the historical *Borislav* (1911; libr. after I. Wasov), two further children's operas *The Fountain of Samodiva* (*Samodiskoto Izvorche*, 1911) and *The Golden Girl* (*Zlatnoto Momiche*, 1915),

Moralisti (1916), which is the first Bulgarian operetta, *Gergana* (1917; libr. after P. Slaweikov), *The Abandoned Mill* (*Zapustyalata Vodenitsa*, 1923), *The Flower* (*Tsveta*, 1925), *Kosara* (1927) and *Altsek* (1930).

A te, o cara

Tenor aria for Arturo in Act I of Bellini's *I Puritani*.

Athalia

Secular oratorio in three parts by Handel. 1st perf. Oxford, 10 July 1733; libr. by Samuel Humphreys, after Jean-Baptiste Racine's *Athalie*. Principal roles: Athalia (sop), Josabeth (sop), Joad (c-ten), Abner (bass), Mathan (ten). Although it is not strictly speaking an opera, it has occasionally been staged. [R]

Athanaël

Baritone role in Massenet's *Thaïs*. A Coenobite monk, he attempts to redeem the courtesan Thaïs but ends up falling in love with her.

Athens

See Greek National Opera

Atherton, David (*b 1944*)

British conductor, particularly associated with 20th-century works. He was a co-founder of the London Sinfonietta, and at his Covent Garden debut was the youngest conductor ever to have appeared in the house. He conducted the first performances of Henze's *We Come to the River*, Birtwistle's *Punch and Judy* and Crosse's *The Grace of Todd*.

Atlántida, L' (*Atlantis*)

Scenic oratorio in prologue and three parts by de Falla. 1st perf. Milan, 18 June 1962; libr. (in Catalan) by the composer, after Mosén Jacinto Verdaguer and other sources. Principal roles: Queen Isabella (sop), Pyrene (mezzo), Narrator (bar), Archangel (ten). A vast Spanish epic, calling for enormous resources, it was left unfinished at the composer's death and was completed by Ernesto Halffter.

Plot: Covering a wide range of Spanish myth and history, it includes the immersion of Atlantis, the rescue of Spain by Hercules from the monster Geryon, and the discovery of the New World by Columbus. [R]

Atlantov, Vladimir *(b 1939)*

Russian tenor with a dark and powerful voice, he is particularly identified with Otello and the heavier Russian roles, but his technique is such that he also sings more lyrical roles successfully. The leading contemporary Russian tenor.

Attaque du Moulin, L' *(The Attack on the Mill)*

Opera in four acts by Bruneau. 1st perf. Paris, 23 Nov 1893; libr. by Louis Gallet, after Emile Zola's *Les Soirées de Médan*. Principal roles: Merlier (bar), Françoise (sop), Dominique (ten). An anti-war protest, based on an incident in the Franco-Prussian War, it is Bruneau's most successful work, but is nowadays almost never performed.

Plot: The betrothal of the Flemish peasant Dominique to Françoise, daughter of the miller Merlier, is interrupted by the sounds of war. The Germans attack the mill and seize Dominique who is condemned to be shot at dawn. He escapes by stabbing a sentry. Merlier is taken out and shot in his place, but almost at once, Dominique – who has joined the French forces – arrives with a squadron proclaiming 'Victory'.

Atterberg, Kurt *(1887–1974)*

Swedish composer. His five operas, which met with some success in Sweden but which have not been performed elsewhere, are *Harvard the Harper* (*Härvard Harpolekare*, Stockholm 1919), *The River Horse* (*Bäckahästen*, Stockholm 1925), *The Burning Land* (*Fanal*, Stockholm 1934; libr. after Heinrich Heine's *Der Schlem von Bergen*), *Alladin* (Stockholm 18 April 1941) and *Stormen* (Stockholm 1948; libr. after Shakespeare's *The Tempest*).

At the Boar's Head

Comic opera in one act by Holst (Op 42). 1st perf. Manchester, 3 April 1925; libr. by the composer, after Shakespeare's *King Henry IV*. Principal roles: Falstaff (bass), Prince Hal (ten), Dol Tearsheet (mezzo), Mistress Quickly (sop), Pistol (bar). Following Shakespeare closely, it is one of Holst's finest stage works, but rarely performed. [R]

Attila

Opera in prologue and three acts by Verdi. 1st perf. Venice, 17 March 1846; libr. by Temistocle Solera, after Zacharias Werner's *Attila, König der Hunnen*. Principal roles: Attila (bass), Odabella (sop), Ezio (bar), Foresto (ten), Leone (bass). One of Verdi's most vigorous early works, it has been regularly performed in recent years.

Plot: Italy, 452. Attila has invaded Italy and conquered Aquileia. The captured Odabella pretends loyalty to Attila but secretly plans revenge for the death of her father and persuades her lover Foresto to help her. Ignoring the warning of an omen, Attila entertains the Romans to a feast where Odabella saves him from being poisoned by Foresto so that she can kill him herself. She persuades Attila to spare Foresto and he promises to marry her. Foresto and the Roman general Ezio now doubt Odabella, but when Attila joins them she stabs him to death. [R]

Aubade

A French term meaning a song for the morning (as opposed to a serenade, which is a song for the evening). In opera, the term is best known as a reference to Mylio's 'Vainement ma bien-aimée' in Lalo's *Le Roi d'Ys*.

Auber, Daniel François Esprit (1782–1871)

French composer. He wrote 46 operas, one of them in collaboration with Boïeldieu and one with Halévy. The large majority are opéra-comiques, notable for their elegance and sparkling melodies. Many were great successes in their day, but with the exception of *Fra Diavolo**, his most popular work, most of them, other than their several overtures, are now forgotten. The most important include *Leicester* (Paris 25 Jan 1823; libr. Eugène Scribe and Anne-Honoré Joseph de Mélesville, after Sir Walter Scott's *Kenilworth*), *Gustave III* (Paris 27 Feb 1833; libr. Scribe), *Le Cheval de Bronze**, *L'Ambassadrice* (Paris 21 Dec 1836; libr. Scribe), *Le Domino Noir**, *Les Lacs des Fées* (Paris 1 April 1839; libr. Scribe and Mélesville), *Zanetta* (Paris 18 May 1840; libr. Scribe and Jules-Henri Vernoy de Saint-Georges), *Les Diamants de la Couronne**, *L'Enfant Prodigue* (Paris 6 Dec 1850; libr. Scribe), *Zerline* (Paris 16 May 1851; libr. Scribe), *Marco Spada* (Paris 21 Dec 1852; libr. Scribe and Germain Delavigne), which was later revised as a ballet, and *Manon Lescaut**. In an altogether different category is the magnificent *La Muette de Portici** (or *Masaniello*), which is in effect the first French grand opera.

Auber's contemporaries, particularly Wagner, thought highly of him; Rossini (referring to his diminutive stature) called him "a small musician but a great music-maker". An almost pathologically shy man, he was a respected director of the Paris Conservatory (1842–70).

Auden, W. H. (1907–73)

British poet and librettist. He provided texts for Britten (*Paul Bunyan*), Henze (*Elegie für Junge Liebende* and *The Bassarids*), Nabokov (*Love's Labour's Lost*) and Stravinsky (*The Rake's Progress*). All but the first were written in collaboration with Chester Kallman.

Audran, Edmond (1840–1901)

French composer. He wrote some 20 operettas, of which the most important are *La Mascotte**, his most successful work, *Gilette de Narbonne* (Paris 11 Nov 1882; libr. Henri Charles Chivot and Alfred Duru, after Shakespeare's *All's Well That Ends Well*) and *La Poupée* (Paris 21 Oct 1896; libr. Maurice Ordonneau, after E. T. A. Hoffmann's *Der Sandmann*). He also wrote one opera *Photis* (1896), which was never published.

Au fond du temple saint

Tenor/baritone duet for Nadir and Zurga in Act I of Bizet's *Les Pêcheurs de Perles*. Perhaps the most famous duet in all opera.

Aufstieg und Fall der Stadt Mahagonny (*Rise and Fall of the City of Mahagonny*)

Opera in three acts by Weill. 1st perf. Leipzig, 9 March 1930; libr. by Bertolt Brecht. Principal roles: Jenny (sop), Jimmy Mahoney (ten), Trinity Moses (bar), Mrs Begbick (sop), Jake (ten). One of the most popular of all Weill's works, it is an expansion of his earlier *Mahagonny Singspiel**.

Plot: The escaped convicts Mrs Begbick, Trinity Moses and Jake establish Mahagonny where pleasure will hold sway. To the city come Jenny and her fellow whores, as well as Jimmy and his friends from Alaska. After a close shave with a hurricane, Jimmy decrees anarchy, and the inhabitants have unlimited licence to enjoy themselves. The only condition to be outlawed is that of shortage of money. When Jimmy cannot pay for his drinks, he is arrested, tried and executed. Inflation and disorder cause the citizenry to demonstrate, and Mahagonny burns. [R]

Auftrittslied (German for 'entry song')

The name given to an aria, usually in a singspiel, in which a character introduces himself to the audience on his first appearance. A famous example is Papageno's 'Der Vogelfänger bin ich ja' in *Die Zauberflöte*.

Augér, Arleen *(b 1939)*

American soprano, particularly associated with Mozart and Handel roles. She possesses a pleasing and agile voice used with a fine technique and great musicianship.

Augsburg Stadttheater

The present opera house (cap. 1,010) in this city in Bavaria opened in 1877. Destroyed by bombs in 1944, it reopened in 1956. Musical directors have included Heinz Wallberg, István Kertesz and Gabor Otväs.

Au Mont Ida

Tenor aria for Paris in Act I of Offenbach's *La Belle Hélène*.

A un dottor

Bass aria for Dr Bartolo in Act I of Rossini's *Il Barbiere di Siviglia*. It is occasionally replaced by a less demanding alternative, 'Manca un foglio', which was composed by Pietro Romani (1791–1877).

Auntie

Mezzo role in Britten's *Peter Grimes*. She manages the pub, where her nieces are the principal attractions.

Aura amorosa, Un

Tenor aria for Ferrando in Act I of Mozart's *Così fan Tutte*.

Aureliano in Palmira

Opera in two acts by Rossini. 1st perf. Milan, 26 Dec 1813; libr. by Luigi Romanelli. About the Roman Emperor Lucius Domitius Aurelianus (215–75), it is one of Rossini's least successful works and is nowadays almost never performed. The overture is well-known as Rossini re-used it for both *Elisabetta Regina d'Inghilterra* and *Il Barbiere di Siviglia*.

Auric, Georges *(1899–1983)*

French composer and administrator. A member of the group 'Les Six', he wrote one opera *Sous le Masque* (1927; libr. Laloy). He was administrator of the Opéra-Comique, Paris (1962–8).

Austin, Frederic *(1872–1952)*

British baritone. One of the leading British singers of the inter-war period, his 1920 edition of *The Beggar's Opera* enjoyed the longest run in operatic history. He was artistic director of the British National Opera Company from 1924. His son Richard (1903–89) was a conductor.

Austral, Florence (b Mary Wilson) (1894–1968)
Australian soprano. Possessing a rich and warm voice, she was one of the leading Wagnerian sopranos of the inter-war period.

Australia
See Australian Opera; New Opera South Australia; Sydney Opera House

Australian Opera
Australia's principal opera company, it was founded in 1956 as the Elizabethan Trust, acquiring its present name in 1969. Now based at the Sydney Opera House*, musical directors have been Karl Rankl, Carlo Felice Cillario, Edward Downes, Richard Bonynge and Moffatt Oxenbould.

Australian opera composers
See Benjamin; Williamson
   Other national opera composers include John Antill (b 1904) and Richard Meale (b 1932).

Austria
See Bregenz Festival; Graz Opernhaus; Linz Landestheater; Salzburg Festival; Theater an der Wien, Vienna; Tirolese Landestheater, Innsbruck; Vienna Chamber Opera; Vienna State Opera; Vienna Volksoper

Austrian opera composers
See Berg; Biber; Dittersdorf; Einem; Fall; Fux; Haydn; M. Haydn; Heuberger; Holzbauer; Hummel; Kauer; Kienzl; Korngold; Křenek; Mahler; Millöcker; Mozart; Müller;

Reznìček; Schmidt; Schönberg; Schubert; Seyfried; Stolz; O. Straus; J. Strauss; Suppé; Süssmayr; Wellesz; Zeller; Zemlinsky; Ziehrer

Auto da Fé Scene
Act III Scene II of Verdi's Don Carlos. The grand public scene which includes a ballet and ends with the burning of the heretics.

Avant de quitter ces lieux
Baritone aria for Valentin in Act II of Gounod's Faust.

Ave Maria
Soprano aria for: (1) Desdemona in Act IV of Verdi's Otello. (2) Giselda in Act II of Verdi's I Lombardi.

Ave Signor
Chorus of the heavenly host in the prologue of Boito's Mefistofele.

Avito
Tenor role in Montemezzi's L'Amore dei Tre Re. He is a prince in love with Fiora.

Azerbaijani opera composers
See Hadjibeyov
   Other national opera composers include Fikret Amirov (1922–84), Afrasiyab Badalbeyli (b 1907), Kara Kareyev (b 1918), Abdul Muslim Mahomeyev (1885–1937) and Boris Zaidman (b 1908).

Azione sacra (Italian for 'sacred action')
A term occasionally used to describe an Italian opera on a religious subject, such as Refice's Cecilia.

Azucena

Mezzo role in Verdi's *Il Trovatore*. An old gypsy, she is presumed to be Manrico's mother.

B

Baba the Turk
Mezzo role in Stravinsky's *The Rake's Progress*. She is the bearded lady.

Baccaloni, Salvatore *(1909–69)*
Italian bass, particularly associated with Italian buffo roles. Possessing a rich voice and abundant, if occasionally rather broad, comic talents, he is often regarded as the greatest buffo artist of the 20th century. His most famous roles were Don Pasquale and Dr Bartolo.

Bacchus
Tenor role in Strauss' *Ariadne auf Naxos*. The Tenor of the Prologue, he rescues the abandoned Ariadne.

Bach, Johann Christian
(1735–82)
German composer. Youngest son of Johann Sebastian Bach, he spent much time in Britain and is sometimes referred to as the 'English Bach'. He wrote 12 operas, all on tragic subjects and notable for their grace, delicate orchestration, and their introduction of German techniques into the Italian opera seria style. His works, which had some influence on Mozart and which are today surprisingly neglected, are *Artaserse* (Turin 26 Dec 1760; libr. Pietro Metastasio), *Catone in Utica* (Naples 4 Nov 1761; libr. Metastasio), *Alessandro nell'Indie* (Naples 20 Jan 1762; libr. Metastasio), *Orione* (London 19 Feb 1763; libr. G.G. Bottarelli), *Zanaida* (London 7 May 1763; libr. Bottarelli), *Adriano in Siria* (London 26 Jan 1765; libr. Metastasio), *Carattaco* (London 14 Feb 1767), *Gioas Rè di Giuda* (London 22 March 1770; libr. Metastasio), *Temistocle* (Mannheim 4 Nov 1772; libr. M. Verazi, after Metastasio), *Lucio Silla* (Mannheim 4 Nov 1774; libr. Verazi, after Giovanni da Gamerra), *La Clemenza di Scipione* (London 4 April 1778; libr. composer), perhaps his finest and most successful work, and *Amadis des Gaules* (Paris 14 Dec 1779; libr. de Vismes, after Philippe Quinault). His brother, Johann Christian Friedrich (1732–95), also wrote some operas.

Bacquier, Gabriel *(b 1924)*
French baritone, closely connected with the Italian and French repertories. He had an incisive voice, used with style and musicianship, and was a fine singing-actor equally at home in serious or comic roles. He created Abdul in Menotti's *The Last Savage* and the title role in Lesur's *Andrea del Sarto*.

Bailey, Norman *(b 1933)*
British baritone who made a notable reputation in Wagnerian roles (especially Wotan, Hans Sachs and the Dutchman) and with Giorgio Germont and Kutuzov in *War and Peace*. One of the outstanding postwar British operatic artists, he possesses superb diction, a rich and grainy voice used with unfailing intelligence and musicianship, and he is a singing-actor of remarkable insight and humanity.

Baillie, Dame Isobel *(b Bella)* *(1895–1983)*

British soprano. One of the leading British concert artists of her time, her operatic appearances were very rare. Her autobiography *Never Sing Louder Than Lovely* was published in 1982.

Baker, Dame Janet *(b 1933)*

British mezzo, particularly distinguished by her Mozart, Handel and Monteverdi roles and with the title role in *Maria Stuarda*. Often regarded as the finest British mezzo of the postwar era, she possesses a voice of great beauty and considerable power which she has used with intelligence and outstanding musicianship, and has been a compelling singing-actress. Also associated with British opera, she created Kate Julian in *Owen Wingrave* and Cressida in the revised version of *Troilus and Cressida*. She retired from the stage in 1982 and her account of her final operatic year, *Full Circle*, was published in 1983.

Baku Opera and Ballet Theatre

Built in 1911 and reconstructed in 1938 (cap. 1,281), it is the principal opera house in Soviet Azerbaijan. It maintains separate Russian and Azerbaijani sections.

Balassa, Sándor *(b 1935)*

Hungarian composer. He has written one opera, *The Man Outside* (1977; libr. after Borchert) [R].

Balducci

Bass role in Berlioz's *Benvenuto Cellini*. Teresa's father, he is the Papal Treasurer.

Balen, Il

Baritone aria for Conte di Luna in Act II of Verdi's *Il Trovatore*.

Balfe, Michael *(1808–70)*

Irish composer and baritone. Following a short but successful singing career, he turned to composition, making a crucial contribution to the development of British opera and becoming its most important composer of the first half of the 19th century. His operas, nearly all forgotten, are notable for their graceful and tuneful melodies. His 26 stage works, beginning with *I Rivali di Se Stesso* (Palermo 1829), include *The Siege of Rochelle* (London 29 Oct 1835; libr. Edward Fitzball, after Madame de Genlis), which established his British reputation, *The Maid of Artois* (London 27 May 1836; libr. Alfred Bunn), *Catherine Grey* (London 27 May 1837; libr. G. Linley), which is the first British opera without spoken dialogue, *Joan of Arc* (London 30 Nov 1837; libr. Fitzball after Friedrich von Schiller's *Die Jungfrau von Orleans*), *Falstaff* (London 19 July 1838; libr. S. Maggione, after Shakespeare's *The Merry Wives of Windsor*), *The Bohemian Girl**, by far his most successful and enduring work, *The Daughter of St Mark* (London 27 Nov 1844; libr. Bunn, after Jules-Henri Vernoy de Saint-Georges), the highly successful *The Rose of Castille* (London 29 Oct 1857; libr. Augustus Harris and Edmund Falconer), *Satanella* (London 14 May 1858; libr. Harris and Falconer), which was long popular, *The Armourer of Nantes* (London 12 Feb 1863; libr. J.V. Bridgeman, after Victor Hugo's *Marie Tudor*) and *Il Talismano*, originally written as *The Knight of the Leopard* (London 11 June 1874; libr. A. Mathison, after Scott's *The Talisman*), which was produced posthumously. He married the Hungarian soprano Lina Roser.

Ballad

Strictly speaking, the term means an old song, such as a folk song, which tells a story. It thus came to refer to a self-contained narrative song. Although the most famous operatic ballad is Senta's Ballad in *Der Fliegende Holländer*, they are most often found in French opera. The term is also used to refer to the sentimental songs so popular in English drawing rooms in Victorian times of which there are a number in opera, particularly by Sullivan.

Ballad of Baby Doe, The

Opera in two acts by Moore. 1st perf. Central City, 7 July 1956; libr. by John Latouche. Principal roles: Baby Doe (sop), Tabor (bar), Augusta (mezzo), Mama McCourt (mezzo), Wm. J. Bryan (bass). One of the most successful modern American operas and arguably Moore's finest work, it incorporates American folk melodies. Set during the Colorado gold rush, it recounts the life of the historical Baby Doe Tabor (1854–1935).

Plot: America, 1880–99. Elizabeth 'Baby' Doe has left her husband. She goes to Colorado and falls in love with Horace Tabor, a wealthy man 30 years older than her. Horace divorces his wife Augusta and marries Baby, but the new Mrs Tabor is not accepted in society. Augusta warns Tabor that the price of silver is about to collapse, but he ignores her and is ruined. When he dies, Baby retreats to his Matchless Mine, which she has sworn never to sell, to remain there for the rest of her life. [R]

Ballad opera

An 18th-century English theatrical form, which consisted of a play interspersed with songs whose music was arranged from popular melodies by various composers. Nearly always of a comic nature, it usually ridiculed the excesses of contemporary opera and contained political satire. Much the most famous is *The Beggar's Opera*, but there are also fine examples by Arne, while Allan Ramsay's *The Gentle Shepherd* (Edinburgh 29 Jan 1729) enjoyed great success in Scotland. In the 20th century, the term has occasionally been used by composers to describe a pastoral piece in simple style, such as Vaughan Williams's *Hugh the Drover*.

Ballet

In early operas, particularly in France, dance was an integral part of the drama (as it had been in Greek drama which early opera sought to recreate). Only in the early 18th century did opera and ballet become two totally independent art forms. Subsequently, dance has formed an important part of the operatic tradition of only two countries. In Russia, 19th-century nationalist composers (particularly Borodin, Tchaikovsky and Rimsky-Korsakov) made extensive use of traditional national and regional dances. In France, the rigid structure of 19th-century grand opera at the Paris Opéra demanded a ballet in Act III. This is epitomised in the works of Meyerbeer, but the best examples are actually by Italian composers: Verdi in *Les Vêpres Siciliennes* and *Macbeth* and Rossini in *Guillaume Tell*. Famous operatic dances are listed under their various titles, as also are specific dance types.

Ballo delle Ingrate, Il (*The Dance of the Ungrateful Women*)

Opera-ballet by Monteverdi. 1st perf. Mantua, 4 June 1608; libr. by Ottavio

Rinuccini. Principal roles: Pluto (bass), Venus (mezzo), Cupid (sop). Really a 'proto-opera' and a forerunner of Lully's early works, it has been regularly performed in recent years. [R]

Ballo in Maschera, Un (A Masked Ball)

Opera in three acts by Verdi. 1st perf. Rome, 17 Feb 1859; libr. by Antonio Somma, after Eugène Scribe's libretto for Auber's *Gustave III ou Le Bal Masqué*. Principal roles (with the Swedish names first): Gustavus/Riccardo (ten), Amelia (sop), Ankerström/Renato (bar), Oscar (sop), Madame Arvidson/Ulrica (cont), Count Ribbing/Samuel (bass), Count Horn/Tom (bass), Christian/Silvano (bar). One of Verdi's finest and richest middle-period works, distinguished by a precisely balanced score, it deals with supposed events surrounding the assassination of Gustavus III of Sweden. Censorship troubles forced Verdi to transpose the action to 17th-century Boston, with Gustavus becoming the English governor Richard Earl of Warwick. Most modern productions revert to the Swedish setting.

Plot: Stockholm, 1792. Gustavus is in love with Amelia, the wife of his friend and adviser Ankerström. He is warned by the fortune-teller Madame Arvidson that he will be killed by the next man to shake his hand. In the event, that is Ankerström. Amelia returns Gustavus's love and Arvidson tells her of a magic herb which will cure her of her feelings. As Amelia is gathering the herbs near the scaffold, she is joined by Gustavus and, later, Ankerström. When the latter discovers that the veiled woman he had agreed to escort back to town is his own wife, he joins Counts Ribbing and Horn in their conspiracy to kill Gustavus. He is chosen for the act and at a masked ball discovers Gustavus's identity from the page, Oscar, and shoots him. Gustavus dies declaring Amelia's innocence and forgiveness to his enemies. [R]

Balstrode

Baritone role in Britten's *Peter Grimes*. He is a retired sea captain.

Baltimore Civic Opera

Originally founded in 1932 as an opera workshop, the company became fully professional in 1950, with Rosa Ponselle as artistic director.

Baltsa, Agnes (b 1944)

Greek mezzo and a particularly fine interpreter of Rossini, Mozart, Strauss and Verdi. An impressive singing-actress and possessor of a rich and flexible voice, she is one of the finest mezzos to have emerged in recent years.

Bampton, Rose (b 1909)

American mezzo, later a soprano. A musicianly and sympathetic singer, largely based at the Metropolitan Opera, New York, she enjoyed a successful career as a mezzo, mainly in the Italian repertory, before changing to soprano in 1937 and achieving success in Wagnerian roles. Her husband Wilfrid Pelletier (1896–1982) was a successful conductor.

Banda (Italian for 'band')

The off-stage instrumental ensemble in a 19th-century Italian opera, usually comprising wind and brass only. An example of its use is the arrival of King Duncan in Verdi's *Macbeth*.

Banfield, Raffaello de (b 1922)

Italian composer and administrator. His most important opera is *Lord Byron's Love Letter* (1955; libr. Tennessee Williams). Artistic director of the

Teatro Communale Giuseppe Verdi, Trieste (1972–).

Bánk Bán

Opera in three acts by Erkel. 1st perf. Budapest, 9 March 1861; libr. by Béni Egressy, after József Katona's play. Principal roles: Bánk Bán (ten), Melinda (sop), Otto (ten), Petur Bán (bass), Queen Gertrude (mezzo), King Endre (bar). Erkel's most successful opera, it is a strongly nationalist work. Still very popular in Hungary, it is rarely performed elsewhere.

Plot: 13th-century Hungary. In the absence of her warring husband, Gertrude oppresses the country. Her brother Otto tries to seduce Bánk Bán's wife Melinda. Bánk is troubled by the sad state of the country and goes to confront Gertrude. She attempts to stab him, but he seizes the weapon and kills her. Melinda goes mad and drowns herself. King Endre orders Bánk to be tried, but at this moment servants bring in Melinda's body. Bánk tells Endre that he is avenged for Gertrude's death. [R]

Bantock, Sir Granville (1868–1946)

British composer. He wrote two operas, the first Caedmar (1893; libr. F. Corder) being a student work. The Seal Woman (Birmingham 28 Sept 1924; libr. Marjory Kennedy-Fraser) reflected his long-standing interest in Hebridean folklore. It was successful in its time but is now forgotten.

Banquo

Bass role in Verdi's Macbeth and tenor role in Bloch's version. He is Macbeth's co-general.

Bär, Olaf (b 1958)

German baritone, particularly associated with Mozart and Strauss roles. His attractive voice, used with outstanding intelligence and musicianship, and his good stage presence, make him one of the finest artists to have emerged in the late 1980s.

Barak

Baritone role in: (1) Strauss' Die Frau ohne Schatten. He is a dyer.
(2) Busoni's Turandot. He is Calaf's servant.

Baranović, Krešimir (1894–1975)

Yugoslavian conductor and composer. Particularly associated with the Russian repertory, he was musical director of the Zagreb Opera (1915–25), the Belgrade Opera (1927–9) and the Bratislava Opera (1945–6). He wrote two operas: Shaven and Shorn (Striženo-Košeno, Zagreb 1932; libr. G. Krklec), a nationalist work incorporating folk material, and the comedy The Bride of Cetingrad (Nevjesta od Cetingrada, Belgrade 1952, composed 1942; libr. M. Fotez, after the novel Turci Idu).

Barbaia, Domenico (1778–1841)

Italian impresario and administrator. One of the most colourful figures in operatic history, he began life as a waiter, inventing the barbaiata – chocolate or coffee with a head of whipped cream. Turning to opera management, he ran the Teatro San Carlo, Naples, almost continuously from 1809 to 1840. In the 1820s, he also ran the Theater an der Wien and the Kärntnertortheater in Vienna, and both La Scala and the Teatro Canobbiana in Milan. Possessing a remarkable nose for talent, he commissioned many of the finest works of Rossini and Donizetti as well as Mayr's Medea in Corinto and Weber's Euryanthe. He lived for some time with the soprano Isabella Colbran* until Rossini relieved him of her. He appears as a character in Auber's *La Sirène*, and was the inspiration for Luca's novel *Der Impresario*.

Barbarina
Soprano role in Mozart's *Le Nozze di Figaro*. She is Antonio's daughter.

Barbe-Bleue *(Bluebeard)*
Operetta in three acts by Offenbach. 1st perf. Paris, 5 Feb 1866; libr. by Henri Meilhac and Ludovic Halévy. Principal roles: Bluebeard (ten), King Bobèche (ten), Boulotte (sop), Clementine (mezzo). Although never one of his most popular works, Offenbach's irreverent view of the Bluebeard legend is still performed from time to time. [R]

Barber, Samuel *(b 1910)*
American composer. He has written three operas, in a readily accessible late romantic style. They are *Vanessa**, the mini-opera *A Hand of Bridge** and *Antony and Cleopatra**. His aunt was the mezzo Louise Homer*.

Barber of Seville, The
See Barbiere di Siviglia, II

Barbier, Jules *(1822–1901)*
French librettist. He wrote a large number of libretti, usually in collaboration with Michel Carré*, including texts for Gounod (*Le Médecin Malgré Lui, Faust, Roméo et Juliette, La Colombe, Polyeucte* and *Philémon et Baucis*), Massé (*Les Noces de Jeanette, Pygmalion, Paul et Virginie* and *Galathée*), Meyerbeer (*Dinorah*), Offenbach (*Les Contes d'Hoffmann*), Reyer (*La Statue*), Saint-Saëns (*Le Timbre d'Argent*) and Thomas (*Mignon,*

Psyché, Hamlet and *Françoise de Rimini*).

Barbiere di Siviglia, II *(The Barber of Seville)*
or L'Inutile Precauzione *(The Useless Precaution)*
Works of this title based on Pierre Augustin Caron de Beaumarchais' *Le Barbier de Séville* include:

(1) Opera in four acts by Paisiello. 1st perf. St. Petersburg, 26 Sept 1782; libr. by Giuseppe Petrosellini. Principal roles: Figaro (bar), Rosina (sop), Count Almaviva (ten), Dr Bartolo (b-bar), Don Basilio (bass). Enormously popular until eclipsed by Rossini's version, it is still occasionally performed. However, its merits deserve more frequent hearings: the trio for Bartolo and his sneezing and yawning servants is one of the gems of opera buffa. [R]

(2) Opera in two acts by Rossini. 1st perf. (as *Almaviva*) Rome, 20 Feb 1816; libr. by Cesare Sterbini. Principal roles: Figaro (bar), Count Almaviva (ten), Rosina (mezzo), Dr Bartolo (bass), Don Basilio (bass), Berta (sop). Its première was one of the most famous fiascos in operatic history, but the work soon established itself and it has arguably remained the most popular of all comic operas.

Plot: 18th-century Seville. Rosina is kept under lock and key by her crusty old guardian Bartolo, who intends to marry her with the aid of the unscrupulous priest Don Basilio, Rosina's music teacher. Count Almaviva, disguised as Lindoro, a student, woos her with the aid of the cunning local barber and general busybody, Figaro. Almaviva gains entry to the house, first as a drunken officer and secondly as a priest, managing to cause total confusion each time, but also to speak to Rosina. Figaro and Almaviva plan Rosina's escape and after various confusions and

47

misunderstandings, the lovers are united. [R]

Barbieri, Fedora *(b 1920)*

Italian mezzo, particularly associated with the Italian repertory. Possessing a powerful and exciting voice, she was the leading Italian mezzo of the 1950s. Her repertory ran to over 100 roles, and she continued singing into her mid-60s. She created Dariola in Alfano's *Don Juan de Mañara* and the Wife in Chailly's *L'Idiota*.

Barbieri, Francisco Asenjo *(1823–94)*

Spanish composer. The leading exponent of the zarzuela revival of the mid-19th century, he wrote 77 stage works. The most successful included *Jugar con Fuego* (*Playing With Fire*, Madrid 6 Oct 1851; libr. V. de la Vega), *Pan y Toros* (*Bread and Bulls*, Madrid 22 Dec 1864; libr. Picón) and *El Barbarillo de Lavapiés* (Madrid 19 Dec 1874; libr. Lara) [R].

Barbier von Bagdad, Der

Opera in two acts by Cornelius. 1st perf. Weimar, 15 Dec 1858; libr. by the composer, after *The Tale of the Tailor* in *The Thousand and One Nights*. Principal roles: Abul Hassan Ali Ebn Bekar (bass), Nureddin (ten), Margiana (sop), Caliph (bar), Bostana (mezzo), Cadi (ten). By far Cornelius's most successful work, it is a delightful piece which is still regularly performed in Germany but only seldom elsewhere.

Plot: Nureddin is madly in love with the Cadi's daughter Margiana. A meeting is arranged by Bostana, who stipulates the involvement of the barber Abul Hassan to prepare Nureddin. Unfortunately, the barber's unstoppable vocal flow almost causes Nureddin to miss the rendezvous, to which Abul insists on accompanying him. However

when the lovers' meeting is interrupted and Nureddin is shut into a stifling chest, the barber's resourcefulness is instrumental in reviving him. Eventually the Cadi agrees to the lovers' marriage. [R]

Barbirolli, Sir John *(1899–1970)*

British conductor. He conducted a number of operas, mainly Italian, during the early part of his career, but sadly none (apart from two recordings) after 1954.

Barcarolle

A French word, used internationally, but derived from the Italian *barcaruola*, meaning a boat song (particularly of Venetian gondoliers). In 6/8 time and with alternating weak and strong beats, the rhythm is suggestive of the motion of a boat. There are many examples in opera, much the most famous being 'Belle nuit, o nuit d'amour' in Offenbach's *Les Contes d'Hoffmann*.

Barcelona

See Teatro Liceo, Barcelona

Bardolph

Tenor role in Verdi's *Falstaff*. He is a follower of Falstaff.

Barenboim, Daniel *(b 1942)*

Argentine-born Israeli conductor and pianist. His operatic appearances, infrequent until recently, have included a number of notable Mozart performances. Appointed musical director of the new Opéra Bastille, Paris but dismissed in Jan 1989 because of artistic disagreement. He was married to the cellist Jacqueline du Pré.

Bari

See Teatro Petruzzelli, Bari

Baritone
See panel on pages 50–51. See also
Bass-baritone; Basse-taille;
Martin; Verdi baritone

Barnaba
Baritone role in Ponchielli's *La Gioconda*. He is a spy for the Inquisition.

Barnett, John *(b Beer) (1802–90)*
British composer. Although none of his works are now remembered, he played an important part in the development of British opera. *The Mountain Sylph* (London 25 Aug 1834; libr. J. T. Thackeray), his finest work which was long popular, is the first significant British romantic opera. In his later, less distinguished, works such as *Fair Rosamond* (London 28 Feb 1837; libr. C. Z. Barnett and F. Shannon) and *Farinelli* (London 8 Feb 1839; libr. Barnett) he returned to simpler, ballad opera style.

Baroque
A term which music has borrowed from architecture, where it means construction which is elaborate, twisting and heavy. In music, it describes the style of the late 17th and early 18th centuries; broadly speaking, from Lully to Handel in opera.

Barraud, Henry *(b 1900)*
French composer. His four operas, which have had some success in France, are *La Farce de Maître Pathelin* (Paris 1948, composed 1937; libr. G. Cohen), *Numance* (Paris 1955, composed 1950; libr. Salvador de Madariaga, after Miguel Cervantes' *La Numancia*), the comedy *Lavinia* (Aix-en-Provence 1961, composed 1958; libr. Félicien Marceau) and the radio opera *La Fée aux Miettes* (1967; libr. after C. Nodier). He was

musical director of Radio France (1937–44).

Barstow, Josephine *(b 1940)*
British soprano. A splendid interpreter of Verdi, Janáček and of contemporary opera roles, her voice is good but not outstanding; however, she is a powerful and intense singing-actress. She created Denise in *The Knot Garden*, Gayle in *The Ice Break*, the Young Woman in Henze's *We Come to the River*, Marguerite in Crosse's *The Story of Vasco* and Benigna in Penderecki's *Die Schwarze Maske*. Married to the producer Ande Anderson.

Bartered Bride, The *(Prodaná Nevěsta)*
Comic opera in three acts by Smetana. 1st perf. Prague, 30 May 1866; libr. by Karel Sabina. Revised version (without spoken dialogue) 1st perf. Prague, 25 Sept 1870. Principal roles: Mařenka (sop), Jeník (ten), Kecal (bass), Vašek (ten), Krušina (bar), Ludmila (mezzo), Circus Master (ten), Tobias Mícha (bass), Esmeralda (sop), Háta (mezzo). Smetana's most successful work and the most popular of all Czech operas, it combines much traditional Czech material with its charm and humour, and is one of the very few intensely nationalist operas to have transcended national boundaries.
  Plot: The peasant girl Mařenka is in love with the handsome but poor Jeník, whose family origins are unknown in the village. Working with the persuasive and grasping marriage broker, Kecal, Mařenka's parents are adamant that she must marry the son of a wealthy man and agree to Vašek, the son of Tobias Mícha. Furious, Mařenka seeks out Vašek, whom she has never seen – and who turns out to be somewhat of a simpleton with a nervous stammer – and, pretending to be someone else,

BARITONE

Baritone is the middle of the three natural male vocal ranges, between tenor and bass. Its tonal quality is nearer to bass than to tenor. The word baritone derives from the Greek βαρύτονος, meaning 'heavy-tone'. Baritone became generally regarded as a separate vocal range only at the beginning of the 19th century; until then, all non-tenors were called basses of one type or another. Many different subdivisions of the baritone voice have evolved, particularly in France and Germany. They often overlap and do not correspond precisely from one country to another. They are seldom used by composers, but are useful as an indication of the character of a role, if rather less so for its exact tessitura. The main French, German and Italian categories are as follows:

	Name	Range	Example
France	basse-taille	g to f	Theseus in Hippolyte et Aricie
	bariton	C to a♭'	Athanaël in Thaïs
	Martin	C to a'	Pelléas in Pelléas et Mélisande
Germany	Bass-bariton	A♭ to f	Wotan in Das Rheingold
	Spielbariton	A♭ to g	title role in Don Giovanni
	Heldenbariton	C to a♭'	Jokanaan in Salome
	Hoher Bariton	C to a♭'	Sir Ruthven in Der Vampyr
	Kavalierbariton	C to a♭'	Count in Capriccio
Italy	baritono cantante	C to g	title role in Belisario
	baritono brillante	C to a♭'	Dr Malatesta in Don Pasquale
	Verdi baritone	C to a'	di Luna in Il Trovatore

discourages him from marrying her. Meanwhile, Kecal persuades Jeník to relinquish Mařenka in exchange for a generous payment; he agrees on condition that Mařenka marries 'the eldest son of Tobias Mícha'. Both Mařenka's wiles and Jeník's apparent disregard for her lead to numerous misunderstandings until it is revealed that Jeník is, in fact, the eldest son of Tobias Mícha, long supposed dead. Vašek joins the travelling circus, the marriage broker is outraged at losing his money and his contract, and the lovers are betrothed amidst general rejoicing. [R]

Bartók, Béla *(1881–1945)*
Hungarian composer. One of the most

important composers of the 20th century, he wrote only one opera, the symbolist *Duke Bluebeard's Castle**.

Bartoletti, Bruno *(b 1926)*
Italian conductor, particularly associated with the Italian repertory and with contemporary operas. He was musical director of the Rome Opera (1965–9) and the Chicago Lyric Opera (1964–). He conducted the first performances of Rocca's *Antiche Iscrizioni*, Malipiero's *Il Figliuol Prodigo* and *Venere Prigioniera*, Mortari's *La Scuola delle Mogli* and Ginastera's *Don Rodrigo*.

Bartolo, Dr
The pompous physician of

Below are listed the 106 baritones with entries in this dictionary. Their nationalities are given in brackets afterwards.

Adam, Theo (Ger)
Allen, Thomas (Br)
Amato, Pasquale (It)
Ancona, Mario (It)
Austin, Frederic (Br)
Bacquier, Gabriel (Fr)
Bailey, Norman (Br)
Bär, Olaf (Ger)
Bastianini, Ettore (It)
Battistini, Mattia (It)
Bechi, Gino (It)
Berry, Walter (Aus)
Blanc, Ernest (Fr)
Bockelmann, Rudolf (Ger)
Bösch, Christian (Aus)
Bruscantini, Sesto (It)
Bruson, Renato (It)
Capecchi, Renato (It)
Cappuccilli, Piero (It)
Dam, José van (Belg)
Domgraf-Fassbaender, Willi (Ger)
Evans, Sir Geraint (Br)
Faure, Jean-Baptiste (Fr)
Fischer-Dieskau, Dietrich (Ger)
Forsell, John (Swe)
Frantz, Ferdinand (Ger)
Fugère, Lucien (Fr)
Galeffi, Carlo (It)
García, Manuel (Sp)
Glossop, Peter (Br)
Gobbi, Tito (It)
Gramm, Donald (US)
Guelfi, Giangiacomo (It)
Hagegård, Håkan (Swe)
Hammond-Stroud, Derek (Br)

Hemsley, Thomas (Br)
Herincx, Raimund (Br)
Hotter, Hans (Ger)
Hynninen, Jorma (Fin)
Inghillieri, Giovanni (It)
Jerger, Alfred (Aus)
Kéléman, Zoltán (Hung)
Kraus, Otakar (Cz)
Krause, Tom (Fin)
Kunz, Erich (Aus)
Kusche, Benno (Ger)
Leiferkus, Sergei (Russ)
Lisitsian, Pavel (Russ)
London, George (US)
Luca, Giuseppe de (It)
Luxon, Benjamin (Br)
McIntyre, Donald (NZ)
MacNeil, Cornell (US)
Manuguerra, Matteo (Fr)
Marcoux, Vanni (Fr)
Martin, Jean-Blaise (Fr)
Massard, Robert (Fr)
Maurel, Victor (Fr)
Mazurok, Yuri (Russ)
Merrill, Robert (US)
Milnes, Sherrill (US)
Neidlinger, Gustav (Ger)
Nimsgern, Siegmund (Ger)
Nissen, Hans Hermann (Ger)
Noble, Dennis (Br)
Noble, John (Br)
Nucci, Leo (It)
Panerai, Rolando (It)
Paskalis, Kostas (Gk)
Pini-Corsi, Antonio (It)

Prey, Hermann (Ger)
Quilico, Louis (Can)
Reardon, John (US)
Reich, Günter (Ger)
Roar, Leif (Den)
Ronconi, Giorgio (It)
Rothmüller, Marko (Yug)
Ruffo, Titta (It)
Santley, Sir Charles (Br)
Schlusnus, Heinrich (Ger)
Schöffler, Paul (Ger)
Schorr, Friedrich (Hung)
Scotti, Antonio (It)
Sereni, Mario (It)
Shilling, Eric (Br)
Shirley-Quirk, John (Br)
Silveri, Paolo (It)
Singher, Martial (Fr)
Souzay, Gérard (Fr)
Stabile, Mariano (It)
Stewart, Thomas (US)
Stracciari, Riccardo (It)
Taddei, Giuseppe (It)
Tagliabue, Carlo (It)
Tamburini, Antonio (It)
Tibbett, Lawrence (US)
Trimarchi, Domenico (It)
Uhde, Hermann (Ger)
Uppman, Theodore (US)
Valdegno, Giuseppe (It)
Varesi, Felice (It)
Wächter, Eberhard (Aus)
Warren, Leonard (US)
Weikl, Bernd (Aus)
Wixell, Ingvar (Swe)
Zancanaro, Giorgio (It)

Beaumarchais' plays appears as a bass role in Rossini's and Paisiello's *Il Barbiere di Siviglia* and Mozart's *Le Nozze di Figaro*.

Basel Stadttheater

The opera house (cap. 1,150) in Basel, Switzerland, opened on 20 Sept 1909. Musical directors have included Silvio

Varviso, Armin Jordan and Michael Boder.

Basilio, Don

The intriguing priest in Beaumarchais' plays appears as: (1) Bass role in Rossini's and Paisiello's *Il Barbiere di Siviglia*. (2) Tenor role in Mozart's *Le Nozze di Figaro*.

Basoche, La

Operetta in three acts by Messager. 1st perf. Paris, 30 May 1890; libr. by Albert Carré. Principal roles: Clément Marot (ten), Colette (sop), Marie (mezzo), Duc de Longueville (bar). One of Messager's most successful works, it tells of a student elected 'King of the Basoche' (a students' guild) who is mistaken for King Louis XII. [R Exc]

Bass

See panel on pages 52–3. See also Bass-baritone; Basso-buffo

Bassarids, The

Opera in one act, with intermezzo, by Henze. 1st perf. (as *Die Bassariden*) Salzburg, 6 Aug 1966; libr. by W. H.

BASS

Bass is the lowest male vocal range. The word derives from the Italian *Basso* ('low'). Many different subdivisions of the bass voice have evolved, particularly in France and Germany. They often overlap and do not correspond precisely from one country to another. They are seldom used by composers, but are useful as an indication of the character of a role, if rather less so for its exact tessitura. The main French, German, Italian and Russian categories are as follows:

	Name	Range	Example
France	basse-bouffe	F to f	Agamemnon in *La Belle Hélène*
	basse de caractère	G to e	Méphistophélès in *Faust*
	basse noble or basse chantante	F to f	Bertram in *Robert le Diable*
Germany	basse-contre	E♭ to d	Pluto in *Hippolyte et Aricie*
	Bass-bariton	A♭ to f	Wotan in *Das Rheingold*
	hoher Bass	G to f	Caspar in *Der Freischütz*
	komischer Bass	F to f	Osmin in *Die Entführung aus dem Serail*
Italy	tiefer Bass	E to e	Sarastro in *Die Zauberflöte*
	basso cantante	F to f	King Philip in *Don Carlos*
	basso-buffo	F to f	Don Magnifico in *La Cenerentola*
	basso profondo	D to e	Grand Inquisitor in *Don Carlos*
Russia	bass	E to f	title role in *Boris Godunov*
	low bass	G' to e	Farlaf in *Ruslan and Ludmila*

Below are listed the 75 basses with entries in this dictionary. Their nationalities are given in brackets afterwards.

Adams, Donald (Br)
Allan, Richard van (Br)
Arié, Raphael (Bulg)
Baccaloni, Salvatore (It)
Böhme, Kurt (Ger)
Borg, Kim (Fin)
Brannigan, Owen (Br)
Burchuladze, Paata (Russ)
Chaliapin, Fyodor (Russ)
Christoff, Boris (Bulg)
Corena, Fernando (Swit)
Czerwenka, Oskar (Aus)
Dara, Enzo (It)
Díaz, Justino (PR)
Edelmann, Otto (Aus)
Estes, Simon (US)
Flagello, Ezio (US)
Franklin, David (Br)
Frick, Gottlob (Ger)
Galli, Filippo (It)
Ghaiurov, Nicolai (Bulg)
Ghiuselev, Nicola (Bulg)
Greindl, Josef (Ger)
Haken, Eduard (Cz)
Haugland, Aage (Den)
Hines, Jerome (US)

Howell, Gwynne (Br)
Journet, Marcel (Fr)
Jungwirth, Manfred (Aus)
Kipnis, Alexander (Ukr)
Lablache, Luigi (It)
Langdon, Michael (Br)
Lazzari, Virgilio (It)
Lloyd, Robert (Br)
Manners, Charles (Ire)
Mayr, Richard (Aus)
Moll, Kurt (Ger)
Montarsolo, Paolo (It)
Morris, James (US)
Navarini, Francesco (It)
Neri, Giulio (It)
Nesterenko, Yevgeny
  (Russ)
Pasero, Tancredi (It)
Petrov, Ivan (Russ)
Petrov, Osip (Russ)
Pinza, Ezio (It)
Plançon, Pol (Fr)
Plishka, Paul (US)
Raimondi, Ruggero (It)
Ramey, Samuel (US)
Reizen, Mark (Russ)

Reszke, Edouard de (Pol)
Ridderbusch, Karl (Ger)
Robinson, Forbes (Br)
Rossi-Lemeni, Nicola (It)
Rouleau, Joseph (Can)
Salminen, Matti (Fin)
Siepi, Cesare (It)
Sotin, Hans (Ger)
Soyer, Roger (Fr)
Tajo, Italo (It)
Talvela, Martti (Fin)
Tomlinson, John (Br)
Tozzi, Giorgio (US)
Treigle, Norman (US)
Uhde, Hermann (Ger)
Vedernikov, Alexander
  (Russ)
Vieuille, Félix (Fr)
Vinco, Ivo (It)
Wallace, Ian (Br)
Ward, David (Br)
Weber, Ludwig (Ger)
White, Willard (Jam)
Zaccaria, Nicola (Gk)
Zítek, Vilém (Cz)

Auden and Chester Kallman, after Euripides' *The Bacchae*. Principal roles: Pentheus (bar), Dionysus (ten), Agave (mezzo), Tiresias (ten), Autonoë (sop), Cadmus (bass), Captain of the Guard (bar), Beroë (mezzo). Structured on the lines of a symphony, this is one of the most powerful of postwar operas, and arguably Henze's masterpiece. In the contrasting intermezzo, four of the characters enact the Judgement of Calliope.

Plot: Thebes. In a story of the conflict between social repression and sexual liberation, King Pentheus attempts to suppress the worship of Dionysus. Eventually, he is torn to pieces by a group of the god's frenzied worshippers, which includes his mother, Agave.

Bass-baritone

A loose term which describes a voice or a role (such as the Dutchman) which contains both bass and baritone elements.

Basse-taille

A term used in France in the 17th and 18th centuries to describe a low tenor (who would nowadays be called a baritone).

Basso-buffo

An Italian term which describes a role (such as Bartolo or Dulcamara) of a comic nature which usually requires a voice with a facility in patter. It is called *basse-bouffe* in France. Famous basso-buffos have included Salvatore Baccaloni and Fernando Corena.

Basso continuo

See Continuo

Bastianini, Ettore *(1922–67)*

Italian baritone, particularly associated with the Italian repertory. Beginning as a bass, he turned to baritone roles in 1952 and developed a rich, dark and velvety voice which he used with a fine technique. His tragically early death from cancer removed one of the finest Verdi baritones of the postwar era.

Bastien und Bastienne

Comic opera in one act by Mozart (K 50). 1st perf. Vienna, Sept 1786; libr. by Friedrich Wilhelm Weiskern, after Charles-Simon Favart's *Les Amours de Bastien et Bastienne* (a parody of Rousseau's *Le Devin du Village*). Principal roles: Bastien (ten), Bastienne (sop), Colas (bass). One of Mozart's earliest works, written at the age of 12, it is musically astonishingly assured. It is still quite often performed.

Plot: Bastienne, believing that Bastien no longer loves her, seeks the help of the soothsayer Colas to win him back. Colas advises her to pretend indifference towards Bastien, at the same time informing Bastien that her ardour has cooled. The ploy succeeds: Bastien woos Bastienne with renewed passion and wins his suit. [R]

Battaglia di Legnano, La *(The Battle of Legnano)*

Opera in three acts by Verdi. 1st perf. Rome, 27 Jan 1849; libr. by Salvatore Cammarano, after Joseph Méry's *La Battaille de Toulouse*. Principal roles: Arrigo (ten), Lida (sop), Rolando (bar), Federico (bass). A strongly nationalist work, recounting the defeat of the Emperor Frederick Barbarossa by the Lombard League in 1176, it was Verdi's gift to the Risorgimento, which was at that time attempting to expel the Austrians from Lombardy, and it disturbed the censors. It is still occasionally performed.

Plot: Milan and Como, 1176. Arrigo returns wounded from war to discover that his beloved, Lida, has married Rolando, a Milanese army captain. Federico invades Italy and Arrigo joins the Knights of Death, who vow to die in the defence of Milan. Lida tries to dissuade him and the two are discovered together by Rolando, who denounces them. Arrigo kills Federico but is himself fatally wounded. He dies swearing to Rolando that Lida's honour is intact. [R]

Batti, batti

Soprano aria for Zerlina in Act I of Mozart's *Don Giovanni.*

Battistini, Mattia *(1856–1928)*

Italian baritone, particularly known for Verdi and Donizetti roles. One of the greatest baritones of all time, he possessed a voice of great beauty and flexibility, used with style and a matchless technique. His range was so wide that Massenet adapted the role of Werther for him. He enjoyed an exceptionally long career, singing well into his 70s, and was the one great singer of the late bel canto period who lived to preserve his singing on record.

Battle, Kathleen *(b 1948)*

American soprano, distinguished for her Mozart roles and some coloratura roles

such as Zerbinetta. She possesses a
ravishing voice and a fine technique,
and has an enchanting stage presence.
One of the finest operatic artists to
have emerged in the 1980s.

Bavarian State Opera
One of Germany's most important
companies, it is based at the
Nationaltheater (cap. 2,100) in Munich,
which originally opened in 1818 and
was rebuilt in 1963. The annual season
runs from September to July and the
repertory is notable for its strong
Wagner and Strauss tradition. Musical
directors have included Hans von
Bülow, Franz Wüllner, Hermann Levi,
Felix Mottl, Bruno Walter, Hans
Knappertsbusch, Clemens Krauss,
Ferdinand Leitner, Sir Georg Solti,
Rudolf Kempe, Ferenc Fricsay, Joseph
Keilberth and Wolfgang Sawallisch.

Baylis, Lilian *(1874–1937)*
British administrator. As manager of
London's Old Vic Theatre from 1898
to 1937 and by her reopening of
Sadler's Wells Theatre in 1931 (where
she presented opera in English with
British singers), she laid the foundations
from which grew Britain's two great
national companies: the Royal Ballet
and the English National Opera.

Bayreuth Festival
The annual summer festival at this
German town is devoted to the operas
of Wagner. Performances are given at
the Festspielhaus (cap. 1,800), which
opened on 13 August 1876. Because of
financial problems there were no
further performances until 1882, when
Parsifal received its première. Since
then, there have been performances
each year except during World War II.
Designed by Wagner himself, it
resembles a classical amphitheatre and
has a superb acoustic owing to the fact

that the orchestra is covered. The hard
benches which serve as seating have
been a trial for audiences for over a
century! Control of the festival has
always remained in the hands of the
Wagner family: the artistic directors
have been Cosima Wagner (1883–
1908), Siegfried Wagner (1908–30),
Winifred Wagner (1931–44), Wieland
and Wolfgang Wagner (1951–66) and
Wolfgang Wagner (1966–).

Bear, The
Comic opera in one act by Walton. 1st
perf. Aldeburgh, 3 June 1967; libr. by
Paul Dehn, after Anton Chekhov's play.
Principal roles: Madame Popova
(mezzo), Smirnov (bar), Luka (bass).
Walton's second opera, it is an amusing
comedy involving affectionate parodies
of several contemporary composers,
including Britten.
    Plot: Russia, 1890. Madame Popova,
in mourning, and the boorish Smirnov,
a creditor of her late husband, quarrel
violently and decide to fight a duel.
Whilst he is instructing the widow in
the use of firearms, he falls in love with
her. [R]

Beaton, Sir Cecil *(1904–79)*
British designer and photographer. His
widespread theatrical work included the
designs for three notable productions at
the Metropolitan Opera, New York:
Vanessa, *La Traviata* and *Turandot*. He
also designed a *Turandot* for Covent
Garden.

Beatrice di Tenda
Opera in two acts by Bellini. 1st perf.
Venice, 16 March 1833; libr. by Felice
Romani after Carlo Tebaldi Fores'
novel. Principal roles: Beatrice (sop),
Filippo (bar), Orombello (ten), Agnese
(mezzo). Bellini's penultimate opera, it
was a failure at its première and,
although one of the composer's finest

works, it has been infrequently performed ever since.

Plot: Milan, 1418. Having gained his dukedom by marriage to Beatrice, whose subjects he rules by oppression, Filippo Visconti tires of his wife and falls in love with Agnese del Maino. Beatrice has rejected the advances of Orombello, whom Agnese secretly loves but whom she eventually betrays to the Duke. Under torture, Orombello falsely testifies against Beatrice but, although he recants, the Duke remains obdurate in condemning his wife to death. As she is led to her execution, Beatrice forgives the now distraught and repentant Agnese. [R]

Béatrice et Bénédict

Opera in two acts by Berlioz. 1st perf. Baden-Baden, 9 Aug 1862; libr. by the composer, after Shakespeare's *Much Ado About Nothing*. Principal roles: Béatrice (mezzo), Bénédict (ten), Héro (sop), Ursule (mezzo), Claudio (bar), Somarone (b-bar), Don Pédro (bass). Berlioz's last opera, it follows Shakespeare's comedy quite closely, but omits the darker Don John sub-plot and replaces Verges and Dogberry with the pedantic Kapellmeister Somarone. Never one of Berlioz's more popular works, it is infrequently performed.

Plot: Claudio is warmly welcomed home from the wars by his beloved Héro, while his friend Bénédict invites only disdain from Béatrice. Bénédict is as scornful of marriage as Béatrice is of him, and they develop a relationship composed of verbal sparring. They eventually capitulate to the growing feelings of love for one another, and marry in a double wedding with Claudio and Héro. [R]

Beatrix Cenci

Opera in two acts by Ginastera. (Op 38). 1st perf. New York, 14 March 1973; libr. by Alberto Girri and William Shand, after Stendhal's *Chroniques Italiennes* and Percy Bysshe Shelley's *The Cenci*. Principal roles: Beatrix (sop), Count Francesco (b-bar), Lucrecia (mezzo), Orsino (ten), Bernardo (treble). Possible Ginastera's finest opera, it tells of the gory events surrounding the execution of a 22-year-old girl in Rome in 1599 for complicity in the murder of her father.

Beaumarchais
See panel on page 57

Bécaud, Gilbert *(b 1927)*
French composer. Best known as a prolific song composer, he has also written one opera, the successful *L'Opéra d'Aran* (1962) [R].

Bechi, Gino *(b 1913)*
Italian baritone, particularly associated with Verdi roles. One of the leading baritones of his period, and an admired singing-actor, he created roles in Rocca's *Monte Ivnor* and Alfano's *Don Juan de Mañara*.

Beckmesser, Sixtus
Baritone role in Wagner's *Die Meistersinger von Nürnberg*. The pedantic town clerk, he is a caricature of the critic Eduard Hanslick*.

Bedford, Steuart *(b 1939)*
British conductor, particularly associated with Mozart operas and with the English repertory. Musical director of the English Music Theatre, he conducted the first performance of *Death in Venice*. Married for a time to the soprano Norma Burrowes*.

BEAUMARCHAIS

The French playwright, adventurer and musician Pierre Augustin Caron de Beaumarchais (1732–99) occupies an important place in operatic history. He wrote a number of libretti, of which the most important is Salieri's *Tarare* (1787), whose second edition contains a preface discussing opera's musico-dramatic parameters and claiming that greater weight should be given to the words. His trilogy of Figaro plays has attracted more composers than almost any other one literary subject. Those operas by composers with entries in this dictionary are listed below. Beaumarchais is also the subject of an operetta by a minor composer.

Le Barbier de Séville

F. Benda	*Der Barbier von Sevilla*	1776
Paisiello	*Il Barbiere di Siviglia*	1782
Isouard	*Il Barbiere di Siviglia*	1796
Rossini	*Il Barbiere di Siviglia*	1816
Giménez	*El Barbero de Sevilla*	1901

La Folle Journée or Le Mariage de Figaro

Mozart	*Le Nozze di Figaro*	1786
Dittersdorf	*Die Hochzeit des Figaro*	1789
Portugal	*Le Nozze di Figaro*	1799
L. Ricci	*Le Nozze di Figaro*	1838

La Mère Coupable

Milhaud	*La Mère Coupable*	1966

Operas not based directly on the trilogy but using their characters are:

Paer	*Il Nuovo Figaro*	1794
Morlacchi	*Il Nuovo Barbiere di Siviglia*	1816
Carafa	*Les Deux Figaros*	1827
Rossi	*La Figlia di Figaro*	1846
Cagnoni	*Il Testamento di Figaro*	1848
Massenet	*Chérubin*	1905
Klebe	*Figaro Lässt sich Scheiden*	1964

Beecham, Sir Thomas (*1879–1961*)
British conductor. His repertory was vast, but he was particularly associated with Mozart operas and with Delius, of whose music he was a tireless champion. Dictatorial, controversial, and possessing a brilliant (if often cruel) wit, he was one of the greatest of

all British conductors. His interpretations, although often idiosyncratic, were always illuminating. He founded the Beecham Opera Company* and was musical director of Covent Garden (1932–9). He conducted the first performances of *Irmelin* and Holbrooke's *The Children of Don*. His autobiography, *A Mingled Chime*, was published in 1944.

Beecham Opera Company

Founded by Sir Thomas Beecham, the company operated from 1915 until 1920, when financial difficulties forced it into liquidation. It was then reorganised as the British National Opera Company*.

Beeson, Jack *(b 1921)*

American composer. He has written a number of operas on American subjects, which have had considerable success in the USA but have not been performed elsewhere. The most important are *Jonah* (1950; libr. composer after P. Goodman), *Hello Out There* (New York 1954; libr. composer, after William Saroyan) [R], *The Sweet Bye and Bye* (New York Nov 1957; libr. Kenward Elmslie) [R], *Lizzie Borden* (New York 25 March 1965; libr. Elmslie, after Richard Plant) [R], his most successful work, *My Heart's in the Highlands* (1970; libr. composer, after Saroyan) and *Captain Jinks of the Horse Marines* (Kansas City 20 Sept 1975; libr. Sheldon Harnick, after Clyde Fitch) [R].

Beethoven, Ludwig van *(1770–1827)*

German composer. His only completed opera is *Fidelio** (originally given as *Leonore*), in which Beethoven's genius and burning humanity transform the simple structures of Singspiel into powerful drama and one of the greatest of pleas for liberty. He toyed with many other operatic projects, but only two – *Macbeth* and Emanuel Schikaneder's *Vestas Feuer* (1803) – ever progressed even to the stage of preliminary sketches. Nevertheless, Beethoven's contribution to opera is vast – out of all proportion to the quantity which he wrote.

Beggar's Opera, The

Ballad opera in three acts arranged by Pepusch. 1st perf. London, 29 Jan 1728; libr. by John Gay. Principal roles: Macheath (bar), Lucy (sop), Polly (sop), Peachum (bass), Lockit (bar), Mrs Peachum (mezzo). By far the most successful of all ballad operas, it satirises both music (the conventions of Italian opera and the rivalries of prima donnas) and politics – Macheath is a caricature of Horace Walpole. Innumerable editions of the work have been made in the 20th century, including those by Frederic Austin (whose initial run of 1,463 performances from June 1920 was the longest run in operatic history), Britten, Brecht and Weill (see *Die Dreigroschenoper*), Edward J. Dent, Blitzstein, Manfred Bukofzer, and Bliss (for the 1953 film starring Laurence Olivier).

Plot: The highwayman Macheath, a womaniser, has seduced both Polly, daughter of the criminal Peachum, and Lucy, daughter of the jailer Lockit. In Newgate prison after he has been arrested at his favourite bordello, Lucy and Polly vie for his affections and vow to die with him. The beggar of the work's title (a speaking role) intervenes, and, with the threat of Macheath's execution removed, ensures a happy ending. [R]

Beginnings of a Romance, The *(Počátek Románu)*

Opera in one act by Janáček. 1st perf. Brno, 10 Feb 1894 (composed 1891);

libr. by Jaroslav Tichý, after Gabriela Preissová. Janáček's second opera, almost never performed, is a light comedy in traditional Czech style. Janáček later destroyed some of the music; it was reconstructed by Břetislav Bakala.

Begnis, Giuseppina Ronzi de (1800–53)

Italian soprano. One of the leading lyric sopranos of her time, she created for Donizetti Elizabeth I in *Roberto Devereux*, the title roles in *Maria Stuarda* and *Gemma di Vergy* and roles in *Fausta* and *Sancia di Castiglia*. Her husband, Giuseppe (1793–1849), was a leading buffo who created Dandini in *La Cenerentola*.

Behrens, Hildegard (b 1937)

German soprano, especially prominent in Wagner and Strauss roles. Her bright, powerful and intelligently used voice make her one of the finest contemporary Brünnhildes and Elektras. She is also a vivid singing-actress.

Bei Männern

Soprano/baritone duet for Pamina and Papageno in Act I of Mozart's *Die Zauberflöte*.

Bel canto (Italian for 'beautiful singing')

An imprecise term meaning the art of singing in the Italian style: with beauty, elegance, flexibility, an assured technique, and a certain bravura, often in coloratura. The term is also used to refer to the type of operas written in Italy in the first half of the 19th century (by Rossini, Bellini, Donizetti, Mercadante and Pacini). It is fashionable to maintain that the art of bel canto is long dead; the singing of artists of the stature of Alfredo Kraus, Marilyn Horne, Joan Sutherland or Renato Bruson would suggest otherwise.

Belcore

Baritone role in Donizetti's *L'Elisir d'Amore*. He is the bumptious sergeant who takes a fancy to Adina.

Bel dì, Un

Soprano aria for Cio-Cio-San in Act I of Puccini's *Madama Butterfly* (often referred to by its English translation 'One fine day').

Belgian opera composers

See Alpaerts; Blockx; Franck; Gossec; Grétry; Ysaÿe

Other national opera composers include Jean Absil (1893–1974), Auguste de Boeck (1865–1937), Jan van der Eeden (1842–1913), Léon Jongen (1885–1969), Henri Pousseur (b 1929), Eugène Samuel-Holeman (1863–1944) and Victor Vreuls (1876–1944).

See also Flemish opera composers

Belgium

See Grand Théâtre, Liège; Royal Flemish Opera; Royal Opera, Ghent; Théâtre Royal de la Monnaie, Brussels

Belgrade Opera

The company was founded in 1920 and soon achieved the high artistic standards which it has maintained ever since. Performances are given at the National Theatre, and the repertory offers a preponderance of Slavonic works. Musical directors have included Stanislav Binički, Stevan Hristić, Krešimir Baranović and Oskar Danon.

Belisario

Opera in three acts by Donizetti. 1st perf. Venice, 4 Feb 1836; libr. by Salvatore Cammarano, after Jean-François Marmontel's *Bélisaire*. Principal roles: Belisario (bar), Antonina (sop), Irene (mezzo), Alamiro (ten), Justiniano (bass), Eutropio (ten). Telling of Justinian's general Belisarius (*c* 505–65), it is one of Donizetti's finest operas and is fairly often performed in Italy.

Plot: The Emperor Justinian's general, Belisarius, enjoys a triumphal homecoming to Constantinople after vanquishing the Bulgarians. His wife, Antonina, however, believes him to have murdered their son which, added to the fact that she is in love with Eutropio, captain of the imperial guard, leads her to manufacture false evidence that he is planning to kill the Emperor. Charged with this crime, he is blinded and exiled and departs with his daughter Irene. Alamiro, his son, is in fact alive, and they are reunited. Alamiro helps Justinian's troops to victory but Belisarius is fatally wounded. Before he dies, Antonina reveals the truth to the horrified court.

Bella

Soprano role in Tippett's *The Midsummer Marriage*. King Fisher's secretary, she is Jack's girlfriend.

Bella figlia dell'amore

Soprano/mezzo/tenor/baritone quartet for Gilda, Maddalena, the Duke of Mantua and Rigoletto in Act III of Verdi's *Rigoletto*. One of the greatest ensembles in all opera, Verdi himself admitted that he never expected to surpass it.

Bella siccome un angelo

Baritone aria for Dr Malatesta in Act I of Donizetti's *Don Pasquale*.

Belle Hélène, La (*Beautiful Helen*)

Operetta in three acts by Offenbach. 1st perf. Paris, 17 Dec 1864; libr. by Henri Meilhac and Ludovic Halévy. Principal roles: Helen (sop), Paris (ten), Agamemnon (b-bar), Menelaus (ten), Calchas (bar), Orestes (mezzo), Achilles (ten), Ajax I and II (ten and bar). An hilarious send-up of the classical legend of Helen of Troy, it provided Offenbach with a superb vehicle for his favourite occupation: satirising Second Empire society whilst simultaneously debunking mythological personages. It also contains some splendid musical satire. Triumphantly successful at its appearance, it remains one of the most popular of all operettas.

Plot: Sparta. Queen Helen and her ladies pray to Venus to send them lovers. The Goddess obliges with Paris, to the delight of the beautiful Helen, who is bored with her wimpish husband Menelaus. She attempts the experiment of yielding to Paris emotionally whilst resisting him rationally, an enjoyable experience which also pleases the young blade, Orestes, since her example now renders all the wives of Greece unfaithful. Agamemnon and the high priest Calchas are horrified by the lax state of affairs and round on Menelaus for his inadequacy. Paris disguises himself as a priest of Venus and tells the people that the only way for normality to return is for Helen to leave with him to worship Venus on his island. Helen finds this arrangement eminently satisfactory. [R]

Belle insecte à l'aile adorée

Soprano/bass-baritone duet (the Fly Duet) for Eurydice and Jupiter in Act III of Offenbach's *Orphée aux Enfers*.

Belle nuit, o nuit d'amour

Soprano/mezzo duet (the Barcarolle) for

two voices on the lagoon in the Giulietta Act of Offenbach's *Les Contes d'Hoffmann*. It is often sung by Giulietta and Nicklaus. One of the most famous melodies in all opera, Offenbach incorporated it from his earlier *Das Rhein Nixen*.

Bellezza, Vincenzo *(1888–1964)*

Italian conductor, mainly of the Italian repertory. Working principally at the Teatro Colón, Buenos Aires, the Rome Opera and the Metropolitan Opera, New York, he was one of the leading Italian conductors of the inter-war period.

Bellincioni, Gemma *(1864–1950)*

Italian soprano, particularly remembered for Italian verismo roles and for the role of Salome. An emotionally intense singing-actress, she created Santuzza in *Cavalleria Rusticana* and the title role in *Fedora*. Her autobiography, *Io e il Palcoscenico*, was published in 1920. Her husband Roberto Stagno (1840–97) was a successful tenor who created Turiddù in *Cavalleria Rusticana*. Their daughter Bianca (1888–1980) was a soprano.

Bellini, Vincenzo *(1801–35)*

Italian composer. His 10 operas, nearly all of which have libretti by Felice Romani, mark a move away from the florid style of Rossini to something simpler, more lyrical and more intense. His melodies are notable for their great beauty and their long, arching phrases, and are the very epitome of the romantic period in opera. His first two works, *Adelson e Salvini** and *Bianca e Fernando**, are unremarkable and are heavily influenced by Rossini. However, *Il Pirata**, which established his

reputation, marks a new departure in Italian opera. *La Straniera** and *Zaira** are less impressive, but *I Capuleti e i Montecchi** marks a further advance. His *Ernani* (libr. Romani, after Victor Hugo's *Hernani*) was abandoned halfway through because of censorship problems, and he turned instead to the pastoral *La Sonnambula**, one of his most popular works. This was followed by his masterpiece *Norma**. The fine *Beatrice di Tenda** has never achieved the success it deserves, but his last opera *I Puritani** was a triumph.

Bellini's genius was almost exclusively musical: it has to be admitted that his melodies, for all their elegiac beauty, often have minimal relevance to the dramatic situation, and there is little true dramatic insight in any of his operas. The exception to this is *Norma*, which despite its almost total lack of 'action', is intensely powerful and dramatic; here the music not only reflects the dramatic situation, but also heightens it, encouraging reflection on what Bellini might have achieved had he not died so tragically young. His music was highly esteemed by his contemporaries, particularly by Wagner, Berlioz and Donizetti, and exercised a powerful influence on many composers, especially Chopin.

Bell Song

Soprano aria ('Où va la jeune Hindoue?') for Lakmé in Act II of Delibes' *Lakmé*.

Belmonte

Tenor role in Mozart's *Die Entführung aus dem Serail*. He is in love with Constanze.

Bel raggio lusinghier

Soprano aria for Semiramide in Act I of Rossini's *Semiramide*.

Belshazzar

Dramatic oratorio in three parts by Handel. 1st perf. London 27 March 1745; libr. by Charles Jennens, after the Old Testament. Principal roles: Belshazzar (ten), Nitocris (sop), Daniel (c-ten), Cyrus (mezzo), Gobrias (bass). Telling the famous biblical story of Belshazzar's Feast, this is not strictly speaking an opera, but it has often been staged. [R]

Beňačková, Gabriela *(b 1947)*

Czech soprano, chiefly associated with the Czech repertory. Warm-voiced, and with an affecting stage presence, she is one of the finest Czech singers of recent years.

Benda, Jiří Antonín *(1722–95)*

Bohemian composer. He wrote a number of operas and Singspiels, of which the most successful were *Der Dorfjahrmarkt* (Gotha 10 Feb 1775; libr. F. W. Gotter) and *Romeo und Julia* (Gotha 25 Sept 1776; libr. Gotter, after Shakespeare). Benda is chiefly remembered, however, for his four melodramas (which he called duodramas): spoken texts to an orchestral accompaniment. The finest were *Ariadne auf Naxos* (Gotha 27 Jan 1775; libr. J. C. Brandes) and *Medea* (Leipzig 17 May 1775; libr. Gotter). They made a considerable impression on his contemporaries, including Mozart, and influenced several later Czech composers, particularly Fibich. His nephew Friedrich (1745–1814) was also a composer who wrote a number of Singspiels. The most successful was *Das Blumenmädchen* (Berlin 16 July 1806; libr. F. Rochlitz).

Bendl, Karel *(1839–97)*

Czech composer and conductor. He wrote 12 operas in a wide variety of styles, the musical qualities of which make the oblivion into which they have fallen difficult to understand. The Meyerbeerian *Lejla* (Prague 4 Jan 1868; libr. Eliška Krásnohorská, after Edward Bulwer Lytton) was successful, and *Břetislav* (Prague 18 Sept 1870; libr. Krásnohorská) established his reputation. His subsequent works include *The Indian Princess* (*Indická Princezna*, Prague 26 Aug 1877; libr. A. Pulda), which is the first Czech operetta, the verismo *The Montenegrins* (*Černohorci*, Prague 11 Oct 1881; libr. Josef Otakar Veselý), *The Old Bridegroom* (*Starý Ženich*, 1882, composed 1874; libr. Karel Sabina), which was considered too similar to Smetana's *The Bartered Bride*, the comedy *Karel Škréta* (Prague 11 Dec 1883; libr. Krásnohorská), the tragedy *The Child of Tabor* (*Dítě Tábora*, Prague 13 March 1888; libr. Krásnohorská) and the verismo *Máti Míla* (Prague 25 June 1895; libr. A. Delmar and V. J. Novotný).

Benedict, Sir Julius *(1804–85)*

German-born British composer and conductor. He wrote eight operas, in all of which the influence of Weber is strong. His first three operas, *Giacinta ed Ernesto* (Naples 1829; libr. L. Riciutti), *I Portoghesi in Goa* (Stuttgart 28 June 1830; libr. V. Torelli) and *Un Anno ed un Giorno* (Naples 19 Oct 1836; libr. D. Andreotti) were unsuccessful. After settling in Britain, he played an important part in the development of native British opera. *The Gypsy's Warning* (London 19 April 1838; libr. G. Linley and R. B. Peake) was followed by *The Brides of Venice* (London 22 April 1844; libr. Alfred Bunn), *The Crusaders* (London 26 Feb 1846; libr. Bunn), *The Lily of Killarney**, by far his most successful and enduring work, and *The Bride of Song* (London 3 Dec 1864; libr. H. B. Farnie).

Benelli, Ugo

Italian tenor, particularly associated with Rossini and Donizetti roles. One of the leading tenore di grazias of the 1960s, he was also an accomplished comic actor.

Beneš

Bass role in: (1) Smetana's *Dalibor*. He is the jailer. (2) Smetana's *The Devil's Wall*. He is the Devil disguised as a hermit.

Benjamin, Arthur *(1893–1960)*

Australian composer. He wrote five operas, all of which enjoyed some success. They are the comedy *The Devil Take Her* (London Dec 1931; libr. A. Collard and J. B. Gordon), *Prima Donna**, *A Tale of Two Cities**, *Mañana* (BBC radio 1 Feb 1956; libr. Carol Brahms and G. Foa), and *Tartuffe* (London 30 Nov 1964; libr. Cedric Cliffe, after Molière), of which only the vocal score had been completed at his death.

Bennett, Richard Rodney *(b 1936)*

British composer. He has written five operas in a fluent and readily accessible style. They are *The Ledge* (London 12 Sept 1951; libr. Adrian Mitchell), *The Mines of Sulphur**, his most successful work, *A Penny For a Song* (London 31 Nov 1967; libr. Colin Graham, after John Whiting's play), the children's opera *All the King's Men* (Coventry 28 March 1969; libr. Beverley Cross) [R] and *Victory* (London 13 April 1970; libr. Cross, after Joseph Conrad).

Benois, Alexandre *(b Alexander Nikolayovich) (1870–1960)*

Russian designer. Principally associated with Sergei Diaghilev's Russian Ballet, he also designed a number of operas.

His vivid sense of colour and his taste for the spectacular and fantastical were best exemplified in his Paris designs for *The Golden Cockerel* in 1927. His *Memoires* were published in 1964. His son Nicola (*b* 1901) was also a distinguished designer. He was chief designer at the Rome Opera (1927–32) and La Scala, Milan (1936–70). He married the soprano Disma de Cecco.

Benoit

Bass comprimario role in Puccini's *La Bohème*. He is the bohemians' landlord.

Benvenuto Cellini

Opera in two acts by Berlioz (Op 23). 1st perf. Paris, 10 Sept 1838; libr. by Léon de Wailly and Auguste Barbier, after Cellini's autobiography. Principal roles: Cellini (ten), Teresa (sop), Fieramosca (bar), Ascanio (mezzo), Balducci (bass), Cardinal Salviati or Pope Clement VII (bass), Pompeo (bar). Berlioz's first completed opera, and based on events in the life of the goldsmith Benvenuto Cellini (1500–71), it was a failure at its appearance and it is only in recent years that it has been much performed. The concert overture *Le Carnival Romain* is drawn from music from the opera.

Plot: The sculptors Cellini and Fieramosca are rivals both in their art and for the love of Teresa, daughter of the papal treasurer Balducci. A fight develops during Carnival in which Cellini, disguised as a friar and planning to elope with Teresa, kills Pompeo. The Cardinal comes to Cellini's studio, where Teresa has been brought by Ascanio, the sculptor's apprentice, and insists that a statue which he has commissioned is completed by midnight. If Cellini fails, he will hand him over to the law for murder and abduction. Despite a strike organised by Fieramosca, Cellini, using

every piece of precious metal he has,
succeeds, with Ascanio's help, in casting
his Perseus and so is pardoned. [R]

Beppe
(1) Tenor role in Leoncavallo's
Pagliacci. He is a member of Canio's
troupe. (2) Mezzo trouser-role in
Mascagni's *L'Amico Fritz*. He is a
young gypsy. (3) Tenor role in
Donizetti's *Rita*. He is Rita's first
husband.

Berbié, Jane *(b Jeanne Marie Louise Bergougne) (b 1934)*
French mezzo, particularly associated
with the French repertory and with
Mozart roles. She had a fine voice and
an assured technique, and was an
accomplished comic actress.

Berceuse
A French term for a lullaby or cradle
song. The most famous operatic
example is that for the tenor in
Godard's *Jocelyn*.

Berenice
Works of this title about the legendary
Egyptian queen include:
(1) Opera by D. Scarlatti and
Porpora. 1st perf. Rome, 1718; libr. by
Antonio Salvi.
(2) Opera in three acts by Handel.
1st perf. London, 18 May 1737; libr.
by Antonio Salvi. Principal roles:
Berenice (sop), Selene (mezzo), Arsace
(mezzo), Alessandro (sop), Demetrio
(mezzo). Unsuccessful at its appearance,
it is infrequently performed.
Plot: Berenice is under pressure from
Rome to marry Alessandro, but is in
love with Demetrio, who himself loves
her sister Selene. Berenice orders Selene
to marry Arsace. Demetrio believes
Selene faithless and conspires with the
enemy, for which Berenice has him
condemned to death. However,

impressed with Alessandro's nobility,
she agrees to marry him, pardons
Demetrio and allows him to marry
Selene.
(3) Opera by Zingarelli. 1st perf.
Rome, 12 Nov 1811; libr. by Jacopo
Ferretti, after Apostolo Zeno's *Lucio
Vero*. Zingarelli's most successful opera,
it is now forgotten.

Berg, Alban *(1885–1935)*
Austrian composer. Strongly influenced
by Schönberg, he wrote two operas,
*Wozzeck** and the unfinished *Lulu**.
Both deal with the plight, and the
exploitation, of the dregs of humanity,
and are among the greatest, most
powerful and most disturbing of all
20th-century operas.

Bergamo
See Teatro Donizetti, Bergamo

Berganza, Teresa *(b Vargas) (b 1935)*
Spanish mezzo, noted for Rossini and
Mozart roles and identified with
Carmen and the Spanish repertory
(incuding zarzuela). Possessing a rich
and alluring voice of great range and
agility, together with an outstanding
technique, she was one of the leading
mezzos of the postwar era. Married to
the composer and pianist Félix Lavilla.

Berger, Erna *(b 1900)*
German soprano, excelling in Mozart
roles, especially the Queen of the
Night. She had a beautiful voice which
retained its fresh, girlish quality
throughout her career. Also a noted
teacher, her pupils included Rita
Streich.

Bergonzi, Carlo *(b 1924)*
Italian tenor, mainly interpreting the
Italian repertory, especially Verdi.

Beginning as a baritone, he retrained himself as a tenor in 1951. One of the greatest tenors of the 20th century (despite a total inability to act), he possessed a smooth and gloriously toned voice, used with impeccable taste and style. His recording of Verdi's complete tenor arias was an extraordinary achievement which is likely to remain unique. He created the title role in Napoli's *Masaniello*.

Berio, Luciano *(b 1925)*

Italian composer. One of the leading contemporary avant-garde composers, his stage works include *Opera* (Santa Fe 12 Aug 1970; libr. composer and Umberto Eco), *Amores* (1972) and *Un Rè in Ascolto* (Salzburg 7 Aug 1984; libr. Italo Calvino). Artistic director of the Maggio Musicale Fiorentino (1984–). His wife Cathy Berberian (1925–83) was a successful soprano, who specialised in early and contemporary works.

Berkeley, Sir Lennox *(1903–89)*

British composer. He wrote five operas, which have been rarely performed. They are *Nelson* (London 22 Sept 1954; libr. Alan Pryce-Jones), the comedy *A Dinner Engagement**, his most successful work, *Ruth* (London 2 Oct 1956; libr. Eric Crozier, after the Old Testament), *The Castaway* (Aldeburgh 1967; libr. Paul Dehn) and the unfinished *Faldon Park* (1980).

Berlin

See Berlin State Opera; Deutsche Oper, Berlin; Komische Oper, Berlin

Berlin State Opera

Originally called the Königliche Oper, the theatre was destroyed in World War II and rebuilt (cap. 1,452) only in 1954, reopening in September 1955. Now East Germany's principal opera house, it pursues a traditional repertory policy. The annual season runs from September to July. Musical directors have included Leo Blech, Erich Kleiber, Wilhelm Furtwängler, Clemens Krauss, Robert Heger, Franz Konwitschny and Otmar Suitner.

Berlioz, Héctor *(1803–69)*

French composer and critic. One of the greatest, most original and innovative composers of the 19th century (often said to be the inventor of the modern orchestra), Berlioz had little luck with his operas in his own lifetime. His first, *Estelle et Némorin* (1823) is lost, and *Les Francs Juges* (1826; libr. Humbert Ferrand) was abandoned; only the well-known overture survives. His first completed opera *Benvenuto Cellini** was a failure despite its magnificent music. *La Damnation de Faust**, described by Berlioz as a 'dramatic legend' is, despite its elements of great theatricality, not really an opera, although it has often been staged. His operatic masterpiece (and perhaps his greatest piece of music) is the vast *Les Troyens**, but he saw only half of it performed in his lifetime: it had to wait until 1969 for its first uncut performance in French. His last opera, the Shakespearean *Béatrice et Bénédict**, had only moderate success.

Only in the last 30 years have Berlioz's dramatic works been appreciated at their true value, especially *Les Troyens*. All of his operas are now regularly performed, particularly in Britain as a result of the tireless championing of them by Sir Colin Davis, perhaps the greatest modern interpreter of Berlioz's music. The composer's fascinating *Mémoires* were published in 1870.

Bernauerin, Die: ein Bayrisches Stück (*The Bernauer Girl: a Bavarian Tale*)

Opera in two acts by Orff. 1st perf. Stuttgart, 15 June 1947; libr. (in Bavarian dialect) by the composer, after a 17th-century ballad. More of a play with music than an opera, it focuses on the destruction of love by demonic forces. Rarely performed. [R]

Berners, Lord (*b Sir Gerald Hugh Tyrwhitt-Wilson*) (*1883–1950*)

British composer, diplomat, writer and painter. Best known as a ballet composer, his music exhibits the same wit and irony as his writings. He wrote one opera, *La Carrosse du Saint Sacrement* (Paris 1924; libr. after Prosper Mérimée's play).

Berne Stadttheater

The opera house (cap. 1,000) in the capital of Switzerland opened on 25 Sept 1903. Musical directors have included Klaus Weise.

Bernstein, Leonard (*b 1918*)

American conductor and composer. One of the leading conductors of the postwar period, with a wide-ranging repertory, his operatic appearances have been infrequent. Apart from *West Side Story* (New York 26 Sept 1957; libr. Stephen Sondheim) [R] and other musicals, his operatic stage works are the duodrama *Trouble in Tahiti**, the operetta *Candide** and the opera *A Quiet Place**.

Berry, Walter (*b 1929*)

Austrian baritone, particularly associated with Mozart and Strauss roles and with Wozzeck. His fine, expressive voice was matched by a strong stage presence. He created roles in Egk's *Irische Legende*, Einem's *Der Prozess* and Liebermann's *Penelope*. Married for a time to the mezzo Christa Ludwig*.

Berta

Soprano role in Rossini's *Il Barbiere di Siviglia*. She is Dr Bartolo's housekeeper. The role is often sung by a mezzo.

Bertati, Giovanni (*1735–1815*)

Italian poet and librettist. He wrote some 70 libretti, the best being comedies notable for their sharp social comment. He provided texts for Anfossi, Cimarosa (*Il Matrimonio Segreto*), Galuppi, Gazzaniga (*Don Giovanni*), Guglielmi, Mayr, Naumann, Paer, Paisiello, Portugal, Sacchini, Salieri, Spontini, Traetta, Winter, Zingarelli and others.

Bertini, Gary (*b 1927*)

Russian-born Israeli conductor and composer, particularly associated with Rossini operas and with contemporary works. He founded the Israel Chamber Ensemble in 1966, and conducted the first performances of Tal's *Masada 967*, *Ashmedai* and *Die Versuchung*. Musical director of the Frankfurt Opera (1988–).

Beruti, Arturo (*1862–1938*)

Argentinian composer. He wrote eight operas, some of which are still performed in Argentina. They are *Vendetta* (1892), *Evangelina* (1893), *Taras Bulba* (1895; libr. after Nikolai Gogol), *Pampa* (1897; libr. after Eduardo Gutiérrez's *Juan Moreira*), which is the first Argentine national opera, *Yupanki* (1899; libr. Enrique Larreta), *Khrysé* (1903), *Horrida Nox* (1908) and *Los Héroes* (Buenos Aires 1919).

Berwald, Franz *(1796–1868)*
Swedish composer. Although best
known as a symphonic composer, he
also wrote a number of stage works,
most of them largely forgotten. His first
work was an unfinished opera *Gustaf
Vasa* (1827; libr. after J. H. Kellgren).
His first completed work was *Estrella
di Soria* (Stockholm 9 April 1862,
composed 1840; libr. Otto Prechtler),
whose overture is still remembered. It
was followed by two operettas, *I Enter
the Monastery* (*Jag Går i Kloster*,
Stockholm 2 Dec 1843; libr. composer
and H. Satherberg) and *The Modiste*
(*Modehandlerskan*, Stockholm 26
March 1845; libr. composer). Two
further operas followed: *Ein Ländliches
Verlobungfest in Schweden* (*A Swedish
Country Betrothal*, Vienna 26 Jan
1847; libr. Prechtler) and *The Queen of
Golconda**.

Bess
Soprano role in Gershwin's *Porgy and
Bess*. She is Crown's and later Porgy's
woman.

Besuch der Alten Dame, Der
(*The Visit of the Old Lady*)
Opera in three acts by Einem (Op 35).
1st perf. Vienna, 23 May 1971; libr. by
Friedrich Dürrenmatt, after his play.
Principal roles: Claire Zachanassian
(mezzo), Alfred (bar), Mayor (ten).
Perhaps Einem's most successful work,
it has been widely performed.
   Plot: The once poor Klara Wäscher,
returns to her home town of Güllen as
Claire Zachanassian, the world's
wealthiest woman. She meets Alfred,
her former lover and father of her
illegitimate child, who abandoned her,
and offers the town a fortune in return
for his death. He is killed, but the
cause of death is given as heart failure.
Claire claims the body and hands the
mayor the cheque, while the people of

Güllen express their satisfaction at
seeing justice done.

Betly or **La Capanna
Suizzera** (*The Swiss Cabin*)
Opera in one act by Donizetti. 1st perf.
Naples, 24 Aug 1836; libr. by the
composer after Eugène Scribe and
Anne-Honoré Joseph de Mélesville's
libretto for Adam's *Le Chalet*, itself
based on Goethe's *Jery und Bately*. A
delightful little work, it is still
occasionally performed.

Betrothal in a Monastery
See Duenna, The

Bettelstudent, Der (*The Beggar
Student*)
Operetta in three acts by Millöcker. 1st
perf. Vienna, 6 Dec 1882; libr. by F.
Zell (Camillo Walzel) and Richard
Genée after Victorien Sardou's *Les
Noces de Fernand*. Principal roles:
Simon (ten), Laura (sop), Palmatica
(mezzo), Bronislawa (sop), Col
Ollendorf (bass), Enterich (bar), Jan
(ten). Millöcker's most successful and
enduring work, it received over 5,000
performances in Germany alone in its
first 25 years of life and is still
regularly performed. [R]

Bianca
(1) Mezzo role in Britten's *The Rape of
Lucretia*. She is Lucretia's nurse.
(2) Soprano role in Bellini's *Bianca e
Fernando*. She is Filippo's sister.
(3) Mezzo role in Zemlinsky's *Eine
Florentinische Tragödie*. She is Simone's
wife. (4) Soprano role in Donizetti's
Ugo Conte di Parigi. She is the king's
fiancée. (5) Soprano role in Musgrave's
The Voice of Ariadne.

Bianca e Fernando
Opera in two acts by Bellini. 1st perf.

(as *Bianca e Gernando*) Naples, 30
May 1826; libr. by Domenico
Gilardoni after Carlo Roti's play.
Revised version, 1st perf. Genoa, 7
April 1828; libr. revised by Felice
Romani. Principal roles: Bianca (sop),
Fernando (ten), Filippo (bar), Carlo (b-
bar). Bellini's second opera, Rossinian
in style, and now almost never
performed.

Plot: Fernando, son of Duke Carlo
d'Agrigento (imprisoned by the usurper
Filippo), visits the court of his enemy in
disguise. Together with his sister
Bianca, whom Filippo wishes to marry,
he gains access to his father's dungeon
just as the people of Agrigento rise
against Filippo.

Biber, Heinrich Johann *(1644–1704)*

Austrian composer and violinist. He
wrote two operas: *Chi la Dura la Vince*
(1687; libr. Francesco Maria Raffaelini)
and the lost *Alessandro in Pietra* (1689;
libr. Raffaelini).

Bielefeld Stadttheater

The opera house (cap. 890) in this
German town opened in 1904. Musical
directors have included Bernhard Conz
and Rainer Koch.

Billows, Lady

Soprano role in Britten's *Albert
Herring*. She is the local aristocrat.

Billy Budd

Works based on Herman Melville's
Billy Budd, Sailor include:

(1) Opera in one act by Ghedini. 1st
perf. Venice, 8 Sept 1949; libr. by
Quasimodo.

(2) Opera in two (originally four)
acts by Britten (Op 50). 1st perf.
London, 1 Dec 1951; libr. by E. M.
Forster and Eric Crozier. Revised
version, 1st perf. BBC TV, 13 Nov

1960. Principal roles: Billy Budd (bar),
Capt Vere (ten), John Claggart (bass),
Mr Redburn (bar), Mr Flint (bass),
Dansker (bass), Novice (ten), Mr
Ratcliffe (bass), Squeak (ten), Donald
(bar), Red Whiskers (ten). Notable for
its all-male cast and its atmospheric
orchestration, it explores Britten's
favourite theme of the corruption of
innocence and is one of the finest of all
postwar operas.

Plot: H.M.S. Indomitable, 1797. The
tale unfolds in the form of a
recollection by Captain Vere, haunted
by the past. Young and handsome Billy
Budd, an indentured sailor, is liked by
all except the master-at-arms Claggart,
who envies his popularity and is
disturbed by his goodness. Claggart
systematically persecutes him, tries to
incite him to mutiny, and finally
accuses him in the presence of Captain
Vere. Billy, suffering from a stammer, is
unable to speak in his defence and
strikes out at Claggart, who dies from
the blow. Although Vere is deeply
troubled in his conscience, he has to
obey the law: a drumhead court
convicts Billy, and he is hanged from
the yardarm. [R]

Bing, Sir Rudolf *(b 1902)*

Austrian administrator (a British citizen
since 1946). He was general manager
of the Glyndebourne Festival (1936–
46), director of the Edinburgh Festival
(1947–49), of which he was a co-
founder, and general manager of the
Metropolitan Opera, New York (1950–
72). His autobiography, *5,000 Nights
at the Opera*, was published in 1972.

Birtwistle, Sir Harrison *(b 1934)*

British composer. One of the most
talented and original contemporary
British opera composers, several of his
stage works have met with considerable

success. *Punch and Judy** was followed by the macabre cabaret-style *Down By the Greenwood Side* (Brighton 8 May 1969; libr. M. Nyman), *The Mask of Orpheus* (London 21 May 1986, composed 1977; libr. Peter Zinovieff) and *Yan Tan Tethera* (London 1986).

Bis (Latin for 'twice')
Audiences in European opera houses shout 'bis' when they want an encore.

Bishop, Sir Henry *(1786–1855)*
British composer and conductor. He is credited with having written 57 operas, but the vast majority consist of little more than musical numbers inserted into a play. Shallow and sentimental, his stage works are justifiably forgotten. His most important opera was *Aladdin* (London 29 April 1826; libr. G. Soane). He was musical director of Covent Garden (1810–24) where he was responsible for the rearrangement and mutilation of many major operas. His wife Ann Riviere (1810–84) was a successful soprano who led a colourful life and created a role in Mercadante's *Il Vascello di Gama*.

Biterolf
Bass role in Wagner's *Tannhäuser*. He is a minstrel knight.

Bizet, Georges *(1838–75)*
French composer. One of the greatest French opera composers, although slow to reach his full potential. It is not exactly certain how many operas he actually wrote as several remain unperformed, lost or incomplete. His first opera was *La Maison du Docteur* (libr. Henry Boitteaux) which has never been published. His earliest extant work is the delightful *Le Docteur Miracle**, joint winner with Lecocq of a competition organised by Offenbach for a one-act opéra-comique. This was

followed by the comedy *Don Procopio* (Monte Carlo 10 March 1906, composed 1859; libr. Carlo Cambaggio). Of greater substance is his one grand opera *Ivan IV**, which was not performed until 1946; Bizet incorporated parts of it into later works. His first real success was the gloriously melodious *Les Pêcheurs de Perles**, where his dramatic gifts are first apparent. These gifts are still further evident in the unjustly neglected *La Jolie Fille de Perth**. The incomplete *La Coupe du Roi de Thulé* (1868; libr. Louis Gallet and Edouard Blau) survives only in fragments; scholars believe that it might have been one of his greatest works. Three opéra-comiques followed, all of which are lost except for fragments of the second: *Calendal* (1870; libr. P. Fernier), *Clarissa Harlowe* (1871; libr. Philippe Gille, after Samuel Richardson) and *Grisélidis* (1871; libr. Victorien Sardou). His next work, *Djamileh**, was a failure and was followed by the operetta *Don Rodrigue* (1873; libr. Blau and Gallet, after G. de Castro's *La Jeunesse du Cid*) of which only a fragment survives.

Much of Bizet's operatic failure can be attributed to poor libretti or to subjects which failed to fire his imagination sufficiently. Finally, for his last opera he found both the right subject and a superb libretto in *Carmen**. Although it failed at its première, it soon came to be regarded by both public and musicians alike as one of the greatest of all music-dramas; Tchaikovsky was not far out when he predicted that in ten years it would be the most popular of all operas. Bizet also completed the unfinished *Noé* by his father-in-law Halévy.

Bjoner, Ingrid *(b 1927)*
Norwegian soprano, particularly associated with Wagner and Strauss

roles. She possessed a radiant voice of great beauty and considerable power, which she combined with a fine stage presence.

Björling, Jussi *(b Johan)* *(1911–60)*

Swedish tenor who sang the Italian, French and Russian repertories. He possessed a voice of rare warmth and sweetness, considered one of the finest of the 20th century, which he used with matchless style and technique and with impeccable good taste. Married to the soprano Anna-Lisa Berg. His son Rolf *(b 1937)* was also a tenor.

Blacher, Boris *(1903–75)*

German composer and librettist. One of the leading postwar German opera composers, many of his stage works have met with success in Germany but are little known elsewhere. His operas are: *Fürstin Tarakanova* (Wuppertal 5 Feb 1941; libr. K. O. Koch), the chamber opera *Die Flut* (*The Tide*, Berlin Radio 20 Dec 1946; libr. Heinz von Cramer), the scenic oratorios *Romeo und Julia* (Berlin Radio 1947; libr. after Shakespeare) and *Der Grossinquisitor* (Berlin 1947; libr. L. Borchard, after Fyodor Dostoyevsky's *The Brothers Karamazov*), *Die Nachtschwalbe* (*The Night Swallow*, Leipzig 22 Feb 1948; libr. F. Wolf), *Preussisches Märchen* (*Prussian Tale*, Berlin 23 Sept 1952; libr. von Cramer, after Carl Zuckmayer's *Der Hauptmann von Köpenick*), *Abstrakt Oper No 1* (Frankfurt Radio 28 June 1953; libr. Werner Egk), *Rosamunde Floris* (Berlin 21 Sept 1960; libr. after Georg Kaiser's play), *Zwischenfälle bei einer Nottlandung* (*Incidents at a Forced Landing*, Hamburg 4 Feb 1966; libr. von Cramer), *Zweihunderttausend Taler**, *Yvonne, Prinzessin von Burgund* (Wuppertal 15 Sept 1973; libr. after

Gombrowicz) and *Das Geheimnis des Entwendeten Briefes* (Berlin 2 Feb 1975; libr. H. Brauer, after Edgar Allan Poe's *The Purloined Letter*). He also wrote the libretti for Einem's *Dantons Tod*, *Der Zerrissene*, *Der Prozess* and *Kabale und Liebe*.

Blachut, Beno *(1913–85)*

Czech tenor, particularly associated with the Czech repertory. One of the finest tenors of his time, he never achieved the international recognition which should have been his. Later in his career, he excelled in comic character roles.

Blake, David *(b 1936)*

British composer. He has written two operas: the epic *Toussaint* (London 1977; libr. Anthony Ward, after C. L. R. James's *The Black Jacobins: Toussaint l'Ouverture and the San Domingo Revolution*) and the comedy of manners *The Plumber's Gift* (London 25 May 1989; libr. John Birtwhistle).

Blanc, Ernest *(b 1923)*

French baritone, closely identified with the French repertory. He possessed a rich and attractive voice, marred only by a tendency to sing flat. His international career was limited by his disinclination to leave France.

Blavet, Michel *(1700–68)*

French composer. He wrote two operas: the pastiche intermezzo *Le Jaloux Corrigé* (Château-de-Berney 18 Nov 1752; libr. G. Collé) [R] and *La Fête de Cythère* (Château-de-Berney 19 Nov 1753; libr. A. de Laurès).

Bleat

Also known as the Goat's Trill, it is called *Trillo Caprino* in Italy,

Bockstriller in Germany, *Trino de Cabra* in Spain and *Chevrotement* in France. It is a vocal device consisting of the rapid repeating of a single note with varied pressures of the breath. It is usually found in early opera, but Wagner calls for it in the final scene of *Die Meistersinger von Nürnberg*.

Blech, Leo *(1871–1958)*

German conductor and composer. An outstanding Wagnerian interpreter, he was also associated with Verdi, and with *Carmen* which he conducted over 600 times. He was musical director of the Berlin State Opera (1913–23 and 1926–37). He also composed several operas, of which the most successful were *Das War Ich* (Dresden 1902), *Alpenkönig und Menschenfeind* (Dresden 1903) and the comedy *Versiegelt* (Hamburg 4 Nov 1908; libr. Richard Batka and Pordes-Milo, after Rauppach).

Blegen, Judith *(b 1941)*

American soprano, particularly remembered for Mozart and Menotti roles. She uses her appealing voice intelligently and has a delightful stage presence.

Blind, Dr

Tenor comprimario role in J. Strauss' *Die Fledermaus*. He is Eisenstein's stammering lawyer.

Bliss, Sir Arthur *(1891–1975)*

British composer. He wrote two operas: *The Olympians** and the television opera *Tobias and the Angel* (BBC TV 1960; libr. Christopher Hassall). He also prepared an edition of *The Beggar's Opera* for the 1953 film starring Laurence Olivier. His autobiography, *As I Remember*, was published in 1970.

Blitzstein, Marc *(1905–64)*

American composer. Starting as a disciple of Schönberg, he soon abandoned his experimental style in favour of a direct and easily accessible vein in which he could communicate his left-wing political views to the widest possible audience. His first opera was the satirical one-act *Triple Sec* (1930; libr. R. Jeans). His first major stage work was *The Cradle Will Rock* (New York 3 Jan 1938; libr. composer), which was originally banned by the US government because of its advocacy of social revolution. His next opera *No For an Answer* (1941; libr. composer) was also banned for similar reasons. His last work, less overtly political, was the successful *Regina* (New York 31 Oct 1949; libr. composer, after Lillian Hellman's *The Little Foxes*) [R]. He also produced an adaptation of Weill's *Die Dreigroschenoper* in 1954, which enjoyed great success.

Bloch, Ernest *(1880–1959)*

Swiss composer. Best known as an orchestral composer, he also wrote one opera, the unjustly neglected *Macbeth**.

Blockx, Jan *(1851–1912)*

Flemish composer. He wrote seven operas, several of which enjoyed considerable success in their time, but which are now largely forgotten. The comedy *To Forget Something* (*Iets Vergeten*, Antwerp 19 Feb 1877; libr. V. de la Montagne) was followed by *Maître Martin* (Brussels 30 Nov 1892; libr. E. Landoy, after E. T. A. Hoffmann's *Meister Martin*) and *The Princess of the Inn* (*Herbergprinses*, Antwerp 10 Oct 1896; libr. Nestor de Tière), his most successful work. There followed *Thyl Uilenspiegel* (Brussels 12 Jan 1900; libr. Henri Cain and L. Solvay), the successful *The Bride of the*

Sea (*De Bruid der Zee*, Antwerp 30 Nov 1901; libr. de Tière), *The Chapel* (*De Kapel*, Antwerp 7 Nov 1903; libr. de Tière) and *Baldie* (Antwerp 25 Jan 1908; libr. de Tière; revised version *Liefdelied*, Antwerp 6 Jan 1912).

Blodek, Vilém *(1834–74)*

Czech composer and flautist. He is chiefly remembered for the enormously successful comedy *In a Well**. The historico-romantic *Zítek* (Prague 3 Oct 1934, composed 1869; libr. Karel Sabina) [R Exc] was left unfinished at his death.

Blomdahl, Karl-Birger *(1916–68)*

Swedish composer. He wrote three operas, of which *Aniara** has proved to be one of the most successful of modern operas. The other two are *Herr von Hancken* (Stockholm 1965; libr. Erik Lindegren after H. Bergman) and the unfinished *The Tale of the Big Computer* (*Sagan om den Stora Datan*). He was musical director of Swedish Radio (1965–68).

Blönchen (or Blonde)

Soprano role in Mozart's *Die Entführung aus dem Serail*. She is Constanze's English maid.

Blood Wedding *(Vérnász)*

Opera in three acts by Szokolay (Op 19). 1st perf. Budapest, 1964; libr. after Federico García Lorca's *Bodas de Sangre*. A powerful work which has been widely performed, it is perhaps the finest modern Hungarian opera. [R]

Blow, John *(1649–1708)*

British composer. His one stage work *Venus and Adonis** is the earliest English opera.

Bluebeard's Castle

See Duke Bluebeard's Castle

Boatswain's Mate, The

Opera in one act by Ethel Smyth. 1st perf. London, 28 Jan 1916; libr. by the composer, after W. W. Jacobs' *Captains All*. Principal roles: Harry Benn (ten), Mrs Waters (sop), Ned Travers (bar). Smyth's most successful opera, it was long popular, but is now all but forgotten.

Plot: Mrs Waters, the landlady of 'The Beehive', rejects the marriage proposal of the ex-boatswain Harry. His friend Ned Travers pretends to be a burglar so that Harry can impress Mrs Waters by playing the hero. Mrs Waters captures Ned and to teach Harry a lesson tells him that she has shot the intruder. Harry gives himself up and the affair is sorted out, with Mrs Waters taking a fancy to Ned.

Bobinet

Baritone role in Offenbach's *La Vie Parisienne*. He is one of the two rakes in love with Métella.

Boccaccio

Operetta in three acts by Suppé. 1st perf. Vienna, 1 Feb 1879; libr. by F. Zell (Camillo Walzel) and Richard Genée. Principal roles: Boccaccio (bar), Fiametta (sop), Beatrice (sop), Lotteringhi (ten), Leonetto (bar), Isabella (mezzo), Pietro (ten), Petronella (sop), Scalza (bass). Suppé's finest work, it is based on the life of the Italian poet Giovanni Boccaccio (1313–75). An immediate success, it is still regularly performed. [R]

Bocca chiusa (Italian for 'closed mouth')

Humming. A vocal technique used predominantly for teaching purposes to encourage breath preservation. Its most famous operatic usages are the Humming Chorus in Puccini's *Madama Butterfly* and the off-stage chorus in the storm music in the last act of Verdi's *Rigoletto*.

Boccherini, Luigi *(1743–1805)*

Italian composer and cellist. Although best known as an orchestral composer, he also wrote one stage work, the zarzuela *La Clementina* (1786; libr. Ramón de la Cruz).

Bockelmann, Rudolf *(1892–1958)*

German baritone, noted for Wagnerian roles, especially Wotan and Hans Sachs. An outstanding heldenbariton, he was widely regarded in the inter-war period as Friedrich Schorr's only rival. He created Orestes in Křenek's *Leben des Orest*. His Nazi sympathies brought his career to an abrupt halt in 1945.

Bohème, La

Works based on Henri Murger's *Scènes de la Vie de Bohème* include:

(1) Opera in four acts by Puccini. 1st perf. Turin, 1 Feb 1896; libr. by Luigi Illica and Giuseppe Giacosa. Principal roles: Mimì (sop), Rodolfo (ten), Marcello (bar), Musetta (sop), Colline (bass), Schaunard (bar), Benoit (bass), Alcindoro (bass). An immediate success, it has remained one of the most popular of all operas.

Plot: the young bohemians Rodolfo, Schaunard, Marcello and Colline live in penury in a garret owned by Benoit. Rodolfo meets and falls in love with the poor seamstress Mimì. Marcello gets back together with his old flame Musetta, who tricks her elderly admirer Alcindoro into paying their bill at the Café Momus. Rodolfo's jealousy is too much for Mimì, and they agree to part

– in fact, he cannot bear to watch her suffering in their miserable conditions. In the winter, Mimì appears at the garret desperately ill with consumption. Rodolfo's friends rush out to pawn their few paltry belongings to buy Mimì medicine and, her greatest wish, a warm muff. They return to find her dying in Rodolfo's arms. [R]

(2) Opera in four acts by Leoncavallo. 1st perf. Venice, 6 May 1897; libr. by the composer. Principal roles: Mimì (sop), Marcello (ten), Musetta (mezzo), Rodolfo (bar), Schaunard (bar), Barbemuche (bass). Following Murger much more closely than Puccini's version, it is one of Leoncavallo's finest works, but was almost entirely eclipsed from the start by the huge success of Puccini's setting. It deserves more than the occasional performance which it currently receives. [R]

Bohemian Girl, The

Opera in three acts by Balfe. 1st perf. London, 27 Nov 1843; libr. by Alfred Bunn, after Jules-Henri Vernoy de Saint-Georges' ballet-pantomime *The Gypsy*, itself based on Miguel Cervantes' *La Gitanilla*. Principal roles: Arline (sop), Thaddeus (ten), Count Arnheim (bar), Gypsy Queen (mezzo), Devilshoof (bass). Balfe's finest work, it was the most successful British opera of the 19th century and retained its popularity for nearly 100 years. Infrequently performed nowadays.

Plot: 19th-century Hungary. The noble Polish refugee Thaddeus loves Arline, who has been raised by a gypsy band. Accused of theft, Arline is brought for judgement to Count Arnheim, who recognises her as his long-lost daughter. In spite of the machinations of the vengeful Gypsy Queen to prevent it, Arline and Thaddeus marry.

Böhm, Karl *(1894–1981)*
Austrian conductor. One of the greatest conductors of the 20th century, and a major interpreter of Mozart, Wagner and Richard Strauss, he was musical director of the Darmstadt Opera (1927–31), the Hamburg State Opera (1931–33), the Dresden State Opera (1934–42) and the Vienna State Opera (1942–44 and 1954–55). He conducted the first performances of *Daphne*, *Die Schweigsame Frau* and Einem's *Der Prozess*.

Böhme, Kurt *(1908–89)*
German bass. One of the finest Wagnerian performers of the immediate postwar era, he was equally successful in comic roles, particularly Baron Ochs. He created Vanuzzi in *Die Schweigsame Frau*, Odysseus in Liebermann's *Penelope*, Aleel in Egk's *Irische Legende* and, for Sutermeister, Capulet in *Romeo und Julia* and Prospero in *Die Zauberinsel*.

Boïeldieu, Adrien *(1775–1834)*
French composer. He wrote 32 operas (including one each in collaboration with Cherubini, Hérold and Auber). His early works are pleasing but derivative, but in his later operas, which were much admired by Weber and Wagner, he developed a distinctive romantic style. His operas are notable for their charming melodies and their fine orchestration. His first opera *La Fille Coupable* (Rouen 2 Nov 1793; libr. J. F. A. Boïeldieu) was a success. The most important of his later works were *Zoraime et Zulnar* (Paris 10 May 1798; libr. Claude Godard d'Aucour de Saint-Just), the very successful *Le Calife de Bagdad**, *Ma Tante Aurore* (Paris 13 Jan 1803; libr. Charles de Longchamps) [R], *Aline Reine de Golconde* (St Petersburg 17 March 1804; libr. J. Vial and E. de Favières),

Télémaque (St Petersburg 28 Dec 1806; libr. P. Dercy), *Jean de Paris**, *Angéla* (Paris 13 June 1814; libr. C. Montcloux d'Epinay), his masterpiece *La Dame Blanche** and *Les Deux Nuits* (Paris 20 May 1829; libr. Eugène Scribe), which contains a chorus filched by Wagner for the Bridal Chorus in *Lohengrin*. His son Adrien-Louis-Victor (1816–83) was also a composer, whose most successful opera was *Marguerite* (Paris 18 June 1838; libr. Scribe).

Boito, Arrigo *(b Enrico) (1842–1918)*
Italian composer, poet, librettist and critic. One of the most remarkable and versatile figures in operatic history, he had imbibed transalpine culture, was an early admirer of Wagner, and a leading member of the Scapigliatura, a Milanese movement for the reform of Italian art. As a composer, his fame rests chiefly on the extraordinary *Mefistofele**. Few operas were (or have remained) so controversial: dismissed out of hand by some critics, regarded by others as one of the finest and most highminded Italian works since those of Gluck. In it, Boito attempted a synthesis of Italian lyricism and German philosophy and drama; the result is like no other opera. He worked intermittently on his second opera *Nerone** for some 40 years, but it was still incomplete at his death and was prepared for performance by Toscanini and Vincenzo Tommasini.

Boito was one of the very few truly great librettists, his best work being done for Verdi. In his youthful days he had denigrated Verdi in an *Ode to Italian Art* which had deeply hurt the composer. Later, Boito came to revere Verdi and the quarrel was patched up. Their remarkable partnership produced the revised *Simon Boccanegra* (Boito wrote the Council Chamber Scene) and Verdi's last two Shakespearean masterpieces, *Otello* and *Falstaff*. The libretto for *Falstaff* is sometimes regarded as the finest which any composer has ever been given. He also began work on a *King Lear* libretto for Verdi, but the project failed to materialise. As well as those for his own operas, Boito also provided texts for Catalani (*La Falce*), his close friend Faccio (*Amleto*), Mancinelli (*Ero e Leandro*) and Ponchielli (*La Gioconda*). Boito was for many years the companion of the actress Eleanora Duse.

Bolero

A Spanish dance, usually accompanied by voices, with a triplet on the second half of the first beat of the bar. The best-known operatic number in Bolero rhythm is Hélène's aria in Act V of Verdi's *Les Vêpres Siciliennes*.

Boles, Bob

Tenor role in Britten's *Peter Grimes*. He is a bigoted Methodist preacher.

Bolivar

Opera in three acts by Milhaud (Op 236). 1st perf. Paris, 12 May 1950 (composed 1943); libr. by Madelaine Milhaud and Jules Supervielle. Principal roles: Bolivar (bar), Manuela (sop), Maria-Teresa (sop), Nicador (ten), Bovès (bass), Precipitation (mezzo). Dealing with events in the life of the South American liberator Simón Bolívar (1783–1830), it was received with respect rather than enthusiasm at its première and has since been only very rarely performed.

Bologna

See Teatro Communale, Bologna

Bolshoi Opera

The present theatre (cap. 2,100) in Moscow was designed by Alberto Cavos and opened in 1856, replacing a previous theatre of the same name (which means 'Grand'), opened on 18 Jan 1825 but burnt down in 1853. Now the USSR's principal opera house, its repertory and stagings are conservative, but its musical standards are very high. The annual season runs from September to July. Musical directors have included Gennadi Rozhdestvensky, Mark Ermler and Yuri Simonov.

Bomarzo

Opera in two acts by Ginastera (Op 34). 1st perf. Washington, 19 May 1967; libr. by Manuel Mujíca Laínez, after his novel. Principal roles: Pier Francesco (ten), Silvio da Narni (bar), Diana (mezzo), Pantasilea (mezzo), Giulia Farnese (mezzo), Maerbale (bar), Girolamo (bar), Gian Corrado (bass), Niccolo (ten). One of the most controversial of all modern operas, it has enjoyed a *succès de scandale* in many countries, but was banned as immoral in Ginastera's native Argentina by President Onganía's government. An erotic and hallucinatory work, it is notable for the scene in which the chorus intones the word 'love' in 40 different languages.

Plot: 16th-century Italy. The astrologer Silvio da Narni gives Pier Francesco Orsini, Duke of Bomarzo, a potion meant to secure him immortality. It is in fact a fatal poison. Pier Francesco relives the secret, sordid and erotic episodes of his life and then dies.

Bonci, Alessandro *(1870–1940)*

Italian tenor, largely singing the lighter roles in the Italian repertory. Possessor of an elegant and stylish voice, he was the first tenor to introduce the laughs into Gustavus' 'È scherzo od è follia' in Verdi's *Un Ballo in Maschera*.

Bondeville, Emmanuel *(b 1898)*
French composer and administrator. His
three operas have met with considerable
success in France. They are *L'Ecole des
Maris* (Paris 1935; libr. after Molière)
[R Exc], *Madame Bovary* (Paris 1951;
libr. after Gustave Flaubert) and
Antoine et Cléopâtre (1972; libr.
composer, after Victor Hugo's
translation of Shakespeare's *Antony and
Cleopatra*). He was director of the
Opéra-Comique, Paris (1948–51) and
the Paris Opéra (1951–59).

Bonisolli, Franco *(b 1938)*
Italian tenor, particularly associated
with heavier Italian roles such as
Manrico and Calaf. An exciting but not
exactly subtle tenore di forza.

Bonn Stadttheater
The opera house (cap. 896) in the
capital of West Germany opened in
1965. Musical directors have included
Peter Maag and Dennis Russell Davis.

Bononcini, Giovanni Battista
(1670–1747)
Italian composer and cellist. He
composed some 20 operas, many of
which were first performed in London,
where the rivalry between himself and
Handel was the main feature of
operatic life at the time. The rivalry
included a jointly-written opera *Muzio
Scevola* (London 15 April 1721; libr.
Paolo Antonio Rolli, after Silvio
Stampiglia), which has an act each by
Bononcini, Handel and Amadei. His
works, now largely forgotten, include
Griselda*, perhaps his finest, *Farnace*
(London 27 Nov 1723; libr. after L.
Morani), *Calfurnia* (London 18 April
1724; libr. Nicola Francesco Haym,
after G. Braccioli) and *Astianatte*
(London 6 May 1727; libr. after
Antonio Salvi). His brother Antonio

Maria (1677–1726) also composed
several operas. *Camilla* (1696), usually
attributed to him, is actually by
Giovanni.

Bonynge, Richard *(b 1930)*
Australian conductor, pianist and
musicologist, particularly associated
with early 19th-century Italian and
French operas. A distinguished
musicologist but as a conductor little
more than an accompanist, he was
musical director of the Vancouver
Opera Association (1973–78) and the
Australian Opera (1976–85). Married
to the soprano Joan Sutherland*.

Bonze
Bass role in: (1) Puccini's *Madama
Butterfly*. He is Cio-Cio-San's uncle.
(2) Stravinsky's *The Nightingale*.

Booing
This is a regrettably prevalent feature
of operatic performances, especially on
the continent (in Italy the audience
usually hisses). People try to justify the
practice on the grounds that the
audience has paid for its seats and is
thus entitled to register its disapproval.
However, no arguments can disguise
booing as anything other than what it
is: bad manners.

Bordeaux
See Grand Théâtre, Bordeaux

Bordoni, Faustina
See under Hasse, Johann

Boréades, Les or **Abaris**
Unfinished opera in five acts by
Rameau. 1st perf. London, 19 April
1975 (composed 1764); libr. possibly
by Louis de Cahusac. Principal roles:
Alphise (sop), Abaris (ten), Calisis (ten),
Borilée (bar), Adamas (bar), Sémir

(sop). Rameau's last opera, it was edited for performance by John Eliot Gardiner. [R]

Borg, Kim *(b 1919)*
Finnish bass (and also a qualified engineer), who also sang baritone roles. Particularly associated with Mozart roles, he was a fine singing-actor with an effective if not intrinsically beautiful voice. He created a role in Schuller's *The Visitation.*

Borgatti, Giuseppe *(1871–1950)*
Italian tenor, particularly associated with Wagnerian roles. Italy's first and finest heldentenor, he created the title-role in *Andrea Chénier.* His autobiography, *La Mia Vita d'Artista,* was published in 1927.

Borgioli, Dino *(1891–1960)*
Italian tenor, particularly associated with Mozart and Donizetti roles. He was one of the most stylish and musicianly lyric tenors of the inter-war period.

Bori, Lucrezia *(b Lucrecia Borja y González de Riancho) (1887–1960)*
Spanish soprano, particularly associated with the Italian and French repertories. One of the most stylish and elegant singers of the inter-war period, her lovely voice was matched by her looks and her considerable dramatic ability.

Boris
(1) Tenor role in Janáček's *Káťa Kabanová.* Dikoi's nephew, he is in love with Káťa. (2) Bass role in Moussorgsky's *Boris Godunov.* He is the Tsar of Russia. (3) Bass role in Shostakovich's *Lady Macbeth of Mtsensk.* He is Katerina's father-in-law.

Boris Godunov
Opera in prologue and four acts by Moussorgsky. 1st perf. Leningrad, 16 Feb 1928 (composed 1869); libr. by the composer after Alexander Pushkin's *The Comedy of the Distress of the Muscovite State* and Nikolai Mikhailovich Karamzin's *History of the Russian Empire.* Revised version, 1st perf. St Petersburg, 17 Feb 1873. Revised edition by Rimsky-Korsakov, 1st perf. St Petersburg 10 Dec 1896. Further version edited by Shostakovich, 1st perf. Leningrad, 4 Nov 1959. Principal roles: Boris (bass), Grigori/False Dimitri (ten), Pimyen (bass), Marina (mezzo), Varlaam (bass), Prince Shuisky (ten), Rangoni (bar), Schelkhalov (bar), Hostess (mezzo), Simpleton (ten), Fyodor (mezzo) Misail (ten), Nurse (mezzo), Xenia (sop). Moussorgsky's masterpiece, set in the reign of Tsar Boris (1598–1605), and his only completed opera, this vast, sprawling tapestry of Russian life – whose central character is, in fact, the Russian people rather than Boris – is the epitome of Russian opera. Neither the fact that it obeys none of the rules of dramatic structure, nor that the self-taught Moussorgsky commits what the academic world of music would regard as mistakes is in any way relevant: it is a work of genius, and the opera has a vision and sense of purpose unequalled by almost any other composer. In recent years, Rimsky-Korsakov has come in for much criticism for his 'tidying-up' of the score. History should, however, be grateful to him: without his having made the music more easily digestible for conservative-minded audiences, the work would have remained largely unperformed. Nowadays, the original version is nearly always preferred, usually in the critical edition prepared by David Lloyd-Jones. The work's influence on

the subsequent development of opera, not just in Russia, has been vast, and at last its acknowledgment as one of the greatest of all operas seems assured.

Plot: Russia and Poland, 1598–1605. Exhorted by the police, the Russian people entreat Boris to accept the vacant throne. At his coronation he experiences pangs of conscience, since he had the young Tsarevich Dimitri murdered. In the Chudov Monastery, the old chronicler Pimyen tells the young novice Grigori of these events, and Grigori vows to avenge the Tsarevich. He runs away from the monastery, joining the itinerant monks Varlaam and Misail and, at an inn, escapes from the police and crosses the Lithuanian frontier. The scheming Prince Shuisky, Boris' adviser, exacerbates the Tsar's guilt and he begins to hallucinate. Grigori has gone to Poland and declared himself to be the Tsarevich Dimitri. Urged on by the Jesuit Rangoni, who wishes to convert Russia to Catholicism, the princess Marina accepts Grigori's love. The tormented Boris is told by Pimyen of a miracle at the Tsarevich's tomb. This news induces a seizure in Boris who, naming his son Fyodor as his successor, dies begging God's forgiveness. In the Kromy Forest, Varlaam and Misail incite the mob in support of Grigori, who invites all to join him on the march to Moscow. The Simpleton is left alone to bewail the fate of Russia. The original version did not include the Polish or Kromy Forest Scenes, but did include a scene before the death of Boris in St Basil's Cathedral square in which Boris is confronted by the Simpleton, who refuses to pray for him. [R original and Rimsky versions].

Borkh, Inge (b Ingeborg Simon) (b 1917)

Swiss soprano, particularly associated with Strauss roles and with Lady Macbeth and Turandot. A magnificent singing-actress, she possessed a powerful and incisive voice. She created Cathleen in Egk's *Irische Legende*. In 1977 she returned to her original career as a straight actress.

Borodin, Alexander (1833–77)

Russian composer (and also a distinguished research chemist). Like the other members of the Mighty Handful, he was an amateur and was largely self-taught musically. Of his four operas, only the first was actually completed: *The Bogatyirs* (Moscow 18 Nov 1867; libr. Viktor Krylov), which is a pastiche based on a number of other composers' music. *Mlada* (1872; libr. Krylov, after S. A. Gedeonov) is an unfinished collective opera-ballet, written with Cui, Moussorgsky and Rimsky-Korsakov, for which Borodin was responsible for Act IV. *The Tsar's Bride*, begun in 1867, amounts to little more than sketches. Borodin's operatic reputation rests almost entirely on the magnificent *Prince Igor**, completed by Glazunov and Rimsky-Korsakov. An epic of Russian nationalist opera, it may lack the tragedy and sense of vision of *Boris Godunov*, but it is more lyrical and spectacular, and few operas have made more thrilling use of dance and of the clash of different cultures.

Borromeo

Baritone role in Pfitzner's *Palestrina*. He is the historical Cardinal Charles Borromeo (1538–84).

Borsa, Matteo

Tenor comprimario role in Verdi's *Rigoletto*. He is a courtier.

Bortnyansky, Dimitri (1751–1825)

Russian composer. Like those of most pre-Glinka Russian opera composers, his operas contain no specifically Russian characteristics, but are imitations (skilfully and suavely written) of Italian models, mainly of his teacher Galuppi. His operas, now virtually all forgotten, include *Creonte* (Venice 26 Nov 1776; libr. Marco Coltellini), *Alcide* (Venice 1778; libr. Pietro Metastasio), *Quinto Fabio* (Modena 26 Dec 1778; libr. Apostolo Zeno), *Le Faucon* (St Petersburg 22 Oct 1786; libr. F. H. Lafermière) [R], perhaps his finest work, *La Fête du Seigneur* (Pavlovsk 1787) and *Le Fils Rival* (Pavlovsk 22 Oct 1787; libr. Lafermière) [R Exc].

Bösch, Christian *(b 1941)*
Austrian baritone, an interpreter of Mozart roles, especially Papageno. He possesses a light, melodious and well-schooled voice and is an outstanding singing-actor with a handsome and engaging stage presence. His mother Ruthilde was a successful mezzo.

Boskovsky, Willi *(b 1909)*
Austrian conductor and violinist, particularly associated with the lighter Viennese repertory. Originally a violinist (leader of the Vienna Philharmonic and later the Vienna State Opera Orchestra), he turned increasingly to conducting, becoming one of the finest interpreters of Viennese operetta of the postwar era.

Boston
See Opera Company of Boston

Bottom
Bass role in Britten's *A Midsummer Night's Dream*. A weaver, he is one of the mechanicals.

Boughton, Rutland *(1878–1960)*
British composer. An admirer of Wagner, he attempted to establish a British school of Wagnerian opera with its own Bayreuth, for which purpose he founded the Glastonbury Festival in 1914. Most of his operas were successful and were highly regarded by his contemporaries, including Elgar and Ernest Newman. Whilst hardly on Wagner's level, they are of high quality and great melodic charm, and their current neglect is somewhat surprising. His most ambitious project was an Arthurian cycle, which comprises *The Birth of Arthur* (1920, composed 1909), *The Round Table* (Glastonbury 1916), *The Lily Maid* (Stroud 1934) and the unperformed *Galahad* and *Avalon*. His other operas are his masterpiece *The Immortal Hour**, which enjoyed one of the greatest initial successes of any British opera, the choral drama *Bethlehem* (Somerset 28 Dec 1915; libr. after a Coventry nativity play), the successful *Alkestis* (Glastonbury 1922; libr. after Gilbert Murray's translation of Euripides), *The Queen of Cornwall** and *The Ever Young* (Bath 1935).

Bouillon, de
Roles in Cilea's *Adriana Lecouvreur*: the Prince (bass) and Princess (mezzo), who is having a liason with Maurizio.

Bouilly, Jean Nicolas *(1763–1842)*
French writer and librettist of Jacobin sympathies. He is remembered as the inventor of the 'rescue opera' libretto, especially that for Gaveaux's *Léonore ou L'Amour Conjugal*, which was the basis for Paer's *Leonora*, Mayr's *L'Amore Conjugale* and Beethoven's *Fidelio*. Bouilly claimed that it was based on a true event which he witnessed as a civil administrator in Tours during the Revolution. He also provided texts for Auber (*Le Séjour*

Militaire), Boïeldieu, Cherubini (*Les Deux Journées*), Dalayrac, Isouard and Méhul.

Boulevard Solitude
Opera in one act by Henze. 1st perf. Hanover, 17 Feb 1952; libr. by the composer and Grete Weil after Walter Jockisch's version of the Abbé Antoine-François Prévost's *Histoire du Chevalier des Grieux et de Manon Lescaut*. Principal roles: Manon (sop), des Grieux (ten), Lescaut (bar), Lilaque père et fils (ten and bar). One of the most successful of Henze's earlier operas, it is an updating of the Manon story, set in Paris in the late 1940s, in which des Grieux becomes a drug addict and Manon is jailed after her brother shoots her former protector Lilaque.

Boulez, Pierre *(b 1925)*
French conductor and composer. A leader of the extreme avant-garde in composition, he is also one of the greatest living interpreters of other composers' music, all of which (however complex) he conducts from memory. He holds equivocal views on opera: he once advocated the blowing-up of all opera houses, but this has not stopped him from giving magnificent, if sadly infrequent, performances in them, particularly of Wagner, Schönberg, Debussy and Berg.

Boum, Gen
Bass-baritone role in Offenbach's *La Grande-Duchesse de Gérolstein*. He is the Grand-Duchess's bombastic military commander.

Boult, Sir Adrian *(1889–1983)*
British conductor. One of the greatest British conductors of the 20th century, and a tireless champion of English music, his operatic appearances were extensive in his early days, but

subsequently, and sadly, became very rare. His autobiography, *My Own Trumpet*, was published in 1973.

Bourgeois Gentilhomme, Le
Comedy-ballet by Lully. 1st perf. Château de Chambord, 14 Oct 1670; libr. by Molière. A biting satire on the aping of the aristocracy by the nouveau riche, it is perhaps more of a play with songs and dances than a real opera. A crucial work in the early development of French opera. [R]

Bowman, James *(b 1941)*
British counter-tenor, particularly associated with Handel roles and with Oberon in *A Midsummer Night's Dream*. One of the finest contemporary counter-tenors, with a far more powerful voice than most, he created Astron in *The Ice Break*, the Voice of Apollo in *Death in Venice* and the Priest-Confessor in Maxwell Davies's *Taverner*.

Boyce, William *(1711–79)*
British composer. His many stage works, now largely forgotten, include the masque *Peleus and Thetis* (*c*1740; libr. Lord Lansdowne).

Braithwaite, Warwick *(1898–1971)*
New Zealand conductor, particularly of the Italian and German repertories. He was musical director of the Welsh National Opera (1956–60). His son Nicholas (*b* 1939) is also a conductor who was musical director of Glyndebourne Touring Opera (1977–80).

Brambilla, Marietta *(1807–75)*
Italian contralto. One of the greatest contraltos of the 19th century, with an enormous vocal range, she created

Maffio Orsini in *Lucrezia Borgia*, Pierotto in *Linda di Chamounix* and Paolo in Generali's *Francesca da Rimini*. Her sister Teresa (1813–95) was a successful soprano, who created Gilda in *Rigoletto*. Their niece Teresina (1845–1921) was also a soprano who married Ponchielli.

Brandenburgers in Bohemia, The (*Braniboři v Čechách*)

Opera in three acts by Smetana. 1st perf. Prague, 5 Jan 1866; libr. by Karel Sabina. Principal roles: Olbramovič (bass), Oldřich (bar), Junoš (ten), Ludiše (sop), Jíra (ten), Tausendmark (bar). Smetana's first opera, it is a strongly nationalist work which is virtually unknown outside Czechoslovakia.

Plot: 12th-century Bohemia. Following the death of Přemysl II in battle against the Habsburgs, his widow has requested the aid of the Margrave of Brandenburg against the Habsburgs. Junoš brings news of a revolt in Prague and the knights under Oldřich Rokycarský and the mayor of Prague, Volfram Olbramovič, agree to resist the Brandenburg advance. Tausendmark, rejected in love by Volfram's daughter Ludiše, sides with the Brandenburgers and Ludiše is captured. The crowd choose the runaway serf Jíra as their leader, but his attempt to rescue Ludiše fails and he is jailed on false charges and condemned to death. Junoš, in love with Ludiše, discovers her whereabouts. He engineers Jíra's release and they and the crowd rescue Ludiše, arresting Tausendmark. [R]

Brander

Bass role in Berlioz's *La Damnation de Faust*. He is a student.

Brangäne

Mezzo role in Wagner's *Tristan und Isolde*. She is Isolde's companion.

Brannigan, Owen *(1908–73)*

British bass. One of the best-loved British singers of the postwar era, he combined a large and rich voice with fine acting ability (especially in comedy) and a superb personality. He was especially noted for his Britten and Sullivan interpretations. He created Swallow in *Peter Grimes*, the title-role in *Noye's Fludde*, Collatinus in *The Rape of Lucretia*, Bottom in *A Midsummer Night's Dream* and Dr Hasselbacher in Williamson's *Our Man in Havana*.

Bratislava Opera

(Pressburg or Pozsony when it was part of Austria-Hungary). One of Czechoslovakia's leading companies, it performs at the Slovak National Theatre (cap. 611), which opened in 1919. The company's main founder was Nedbal, and musical directors have included Zdeněk Chalabala, Krešimir Baranović, Zdeněk Košler and Oudrey Lenárd. The company also has an operetta theatre, New Scene (*Nová Scéna*).

Bravura (Italian for 'courage' or 'swagger')

The term is used to describe a performance or a piece of music involving a display of great technical ability and difficulty, as in an Aria di Bravura.

Brazil

See Teatro Amazones, Manaus; Teatro Municipal, Rio de Janeiro

Brazilian opera composers

See Gomes; Villa-Lobos

Other national opera composers include Elías Álvares Lôbo (1834–1901), whose *A Noite de São João* (Rio de Janeiro 14 Dec 1860; libr. José M. de Alençar) was the first Brazilian opera on a native subject, Francisco Braga (1868–1945), Delgado de Carvalho (1872–1921), Itiberê da Cunha (1848–1913), José de Lima Siqueira (*b* 1907), Oscar Lorenzo Fernândez (1897–1948), Manuel Joaquim de Macedo (1847–1925), Francisco Mignone (*b* 1897), Leopoldo Miguez (1850–1902), Alberto Nepomuceno (1864–1920), Henrique Oswald (1854–1931) and Assís Pacheco (1865–1937).

Break

The place in a voice where the tonal quality changes between the chest and head registers.

Brecht, Bertolt *(b Berthold)* *(1898–1956)*

German playwright and librettist. A biting satirist of both Nazi Germany and of capitalism, he is best known for his collaborations with Eisler and with Weill (for whom he wrote *Die Dreigroschenoper, Happy End, Aufstieg und Fall der Stadt Mahogonny, Der Jasager* and *Die Sieben Todsünden*). With Caspar Neher, he also wrote the libretto for Wagner-Régeny's *Der Därmwascher*. His *Puntila* and *Die Verurteilung des Lukullus* were both set by Dessau.

Breeches-role

An alternative British term for trouser-role*.

Bregenz Festival

An annual summer festival in Vorarlberg in Austria which was founded in 1956. Star casts perform at the open-air lakeside theatre (cap. 4, 388) and smaller-scale works are given in the Theater am Kornmarkt. It ranks as one of Europe's leading opera festivals.

Bremen Opera

The original Staatstheater in this German city was destroyed in World War II. Its successor, the Theater am Goetheplatz (cap. 1,100), opened on 27 Aug 1950. With a long tradition of fostering young talent, musical directors have included Heinz Wallberg, Manfred Gurlitt and Anton Seidl.

Brétigny, de

Baritone role in Massenet's *Manon*. He is a tax farmer.

Bretón y Hernández, Tomás *(1850–1923)*

Spanish composer. He wrote six operas, of which *Los Amantes de Teruel* (Madrid 1889), *Garín* (Barcelona 1892) and *La Dolores* (Madrid 1895; libr. after Filiú y Cadina) enjoyed some success in their time. His reputation rests chiefly, however, on his zarzuelas. Of these, *La Verbena de la Paloma** has become perhaps the most popular of all zarzuelas.

Brian, Havergal *(1876–1972)*

British composer. One of the strangest and most isolated figures in British music, he wrote much of his vast output after the age of 80. Best known as a symphonist, he also wrote five operas, only the last of which has ever been performed. They are *The Tigers* (1930; libr. composer), *Turandot* (1950; libr. after Carlo Gozzi), *The Cenci* (1952; libr. after Percy Bysshe Shelley), *Faust* (1956; libr. after Goethe) and *Agamemnon* (London 28 Jan 1971, composed 1957; libr. after

Aeschylus). Despite the ardent and vociferous advocacy of his music by its admirers, Brian remains in musical limbo.

Brigands, Les
Operetta in three acts by Offenbach. 1st perf. Paris, 10 Dec 1869; libr. by Henri Meilhac and Ludovic Halévy. Although never one of the most popular of Offenbach's works, it is still performed from time to time. [R]

Brighella
The traditional Commedia dell'Arte figure appears in a number of operas, including: (1) Tenor role in Strauss' *Ariadne auf Naxos*. (2) Bass role in Wagner's *Das Liebesverbot*. (3) Baritone role in Cowie's *Commedia*.

Brilioth, Helge *(b 1931)*
Swedish tenor. He began as a baritone, turning to tenor roles in 1965 and, although not a true heldentenor, became one of the leading Wagnerian tenors of the 1970s, especially noted for his Siegfried.

Brindisi (from the Italian *far brindisi*, 'to drink one's health')
A drinking song. There are many famous examples in opera, including 'Il segreto per esser felice' in *Lucrezia Borgia* and 'Libiamo, libiamo' in *La Traviata*.

Britain
See Great Britain

British Broadcasting Corporation
The BBC has played a large and invaluable part in Britain's operatic life. The first opera on radio was *Hänsel und Gretel* on 6 Jan 1923 from Covent Garden, which was also the first broadcast from a European opera house. The first studio performance was *Roméo et Juliette* in Oct of the same year. With the advent of the Third Programme (later Radio Three) a vast amount of opera has been broadcast. It has included studio recordings (with many first performances), relays from the Promenade Concerts and from British opera companies, recordings of European performances and studio recordings from other European radio authorities. These broadcasts have included many rare works that could never otherwise have been heard.

In the field of television, the BBC gave the world's first opera performance on TV when it broadcast excerpts from Coates's *Pickwick* in 1936. Only in the last 15 years, however, has opera been a regular feature on BBC television. Performances are now frequently relayed from both Britain and abroad and the BBC have also mounted a number of their own productions, most notably the world première of *Owen Wingrave* (the most important opera specifically commissioned for television) and the award-winning *Der Fliegende Holländer* with Norman Bailey and Gwyneth Jones.

British National Opera Company
Founded in 1922 from the membership of the bankrupt Beecham Opera Company, it performed in London and the provinces under the artistic direction of Percy Pitt and Frederic Austin. It was taken over in 1929 as the Covent Garden English Company, continuing as such until 1931.

British opera composers
See Alwyn; Arne; Arnold; Balfe; Bantock; Barnett; Benedict; Bennett; Berkeley; Berners;

Birtwistle; Bishop; Blake; Bliss; Blow; Boughton; Boyce; Brian; Britten; Bush; Cellier; Chisholm; Coates; Collingwood; Costa; Cowen; Cowie; Crosse; Delius; Dibdin; Elgar; d'Erlanger; Gardner; Gatty; German; Goehr; Goossens; Hamilton; Hoddinott; Holbrooke; Holst; Hopkins; Hughes; Joubert; Knussen; Linley; Litolff; Lloyd; Locke; Lutyens; MacCunn; MacFarren; Maconchy; Maw; Maxwell Davies; Monckton; Musgrave; Oliver; Orr; Osborne; Parry; J. Parry; Pepusch; Purcell; Quilter; Scott; Searle; Shield; Smyth; Stanford; Storace; Sullivan; Tavener; A. G. Thomas; Tippett; Vaughan Williams; Wallace; Walton; Wishart
See also Australian opera composers; Irish opera composers

British royalty in opera

The English and Scottish monarchies, particularly the Tudors, have frequently fascinated opera composers, especially in Italy in the first half of the 19th century. The many British kings and queens who appear as operatic characters include:

(1) *England*: Alfred the Great in Donizetti's *Alfredo il Grande*, Gatty's *King Alfred and the Cakes* and Mayr's *Alfredo il Grande*; Henry II in Donizetti's *Rosmonda d'Inghilterra* and Nicolaï's *Enrico II*; Richard I in Adam's *Richard à Palestine*, Sullivan's *Ivanhoe*, Grétry's *Richard Coeur de Lion* and Handel's *Riccardo Primo*; Richard II in Bush's *Wat Tyler*; Edward III in Donizetti's *L'Assedio di Calais*; Henry V in Hérold's *La Gioventù di Enrico V*, Holst's *At the Boar's Head*, Mercadante's *La Gioventù di Enrico V* and Pacini's *La Gioventù di Enrico V*; Richard III in Meyerbeer's *Margherita d'Anjou*; Henry VIII in Donizetti's *Anna Bolena*, Maxwell Davies's *Taverner* and Saint-Saëns' *Henri VIII*; Mary I in Gomes' *Maria Tudor* and Pacini's *Maria Tudor*; Lady Jane Grey in Vaccai's *Giovanna Grey*; Elizabeth I in Britten's *Gloriana*, Carafa's *Elisabetta in Derbyshire*, Donizetti's *Elisabetta al Castello di Kenilworth*, *Maria Stuarda* and *Roberto Devereux*, Fortner's *Elisabeth Tudor*, German's *Merrie England*, Klenau's *Elisabeth von England*, Mercadante's *Il Conte d'Essex*, Rossini's *Elisabetta Regina d'Inghilterra* and Thomas' *La Songe d'un Nuit d'Eté*; Charles II in MacFarren's *King Charles II*.

(2) *Scotland*: James V in Rossini's *La Donna del Lago*; Mary in Carafa's *Elisabetta in Derbyshire*, Coccia's *Maria Stuarda*, Donizetti's *Maria Stuarda*, Mercadante's *Maria Stuarda* and Musgrave's *Mary Queen of Scots*; Bonnie Prince Charlie in Coccia's *Edoardo in Iscozia*.

Britten, Benjamin (later Lord Britten of Aldeburgh) (1913–76)

British composer and conductor. More than any other musician, Britten may be regarded as the crucial figure in the British musical renaissance of the postwar era and of the international repute in which British music is now held. His music, although rooted in tradition, is strikingly original, and almost no composer since Verdi has possessed such dramatic flair and insight. Two themes which run through many of his operas are the corruption of innocence and the position of the outsider in society. Most of his operas were written for the tenor Sir Peter Pears*, with whom Britten enjoyed a life-long relationship. Their artistic partnership, one of the most remarkable in the history of the arts, resulted not only in some of Britten's greatest music, but also in the establishment of the English Opera Group and the Aldeburgh Festival.

His first stage work was the operetta *Paul Bunyan**, which Britten soon withdrew and which was not heard again until the 1970s. The production of *Peter Grimes**, which marked the reopening of Sadler's Wells after the war, was a milestone in the history of British opera. Regarded by many as his masterpiece, it established Britten overnight in the forefront of European opera composers and was the first British opera to enter the international repertory. He then turned to chamber opera, with *The Rape of Lucretia** and the comedy *Albert Herring**. He next produced a version of *The Beggar's Opera* in 1948 (an edition so radical as to amount virtually to a separate work), the children's opera *The Little Sweep** (the second part of the play *Let's Make an Opera*) and a realisation of *Dido and Aeneas* in 1951. He returned to full-scale opera with the powerful, all-male *Billy Budd** and *Gloriana**, written for the coronation of Queen Elizabeth II. Returning again to chamber opera, he next wrote the deeply disturbing *The Turn of the Screw**, one of his finest and most complex works. It was followed by his first church work *Noye's Fludde**, a setting of a Chester mystery play, and the Shakespearean *A Midsummer Night's Dream**. He then wrote (for very small forces) his *Three Church Parables*: *Curlew River**, *The Burning Fiery Furnace** and *The Prodigal Son**. The television opera, *Owen Wingrave**, gave Britten an opportunity to advocate his life-long pacifism. His last opera was *Death in Venice**, in which he introduced ballet as an integral part of the drama.

As well as directing his own works, Britten was also an outstanding conductor of other composers' music, particularly British composers. His appearances as an operatic conductor were sadly infrequent. He was also a fine pianist.

Brno Opera
Czechoslovakia's second most important company, it performs at the Janáček Opera House (cap. 1,317), which opened in 1965. Its repertory is noted for its advocacy of contemporary works and for its strong Janáček tradition. The annual season runs from September to June. Musical directors have included František Neumann, Milan Sachs, Zdeněk Chalabala, Václav Kašlík, František Jílek and Jiří Pinkas. There is also a chamber house, Miloš Wasserbauer Chamber Opera (*Komorní Opera Miloše Wasserbauera*), which opened in 1957.

Brogni, Cardinal
Bass role in Halévy's *La Juive*. He turns out to be Rachel's father.

Bronze Horse, The
See Cheval de Bronze, Le

Brouwenstijn, Gré *(b 1915)*
Dutch soprano, particularly associated with Wagner and Verdi roles. One of the finest and most musically intelligent sopranos of the immediate postwar era, she had a lovely voice and a fine stage presence.

Bruch, Max *(1838–1920)*
German composer. Best known as an orchestral composer, he also wrote three operas, all now virtually forgotten. They are the Singspiel *Scherz, List und Rache* (Cologne 14 Jan 1858; libr. L. Bischoff, after Goethe), *Die*

Loreley (Mannheim 14 April 1863; libr. Emmanuel Geibl), his best opera, and *Hermione* (Berlin 21 March 1872; libr. E. Hopffer, after Shakespeare's *A Winter's Tale*).

Bruneau, Alfred *(1857–1934)*

French composer. He wrote 12 operas, some of them very successful in their time, in which he attempted a reform of French opera on Wagnerian lines. Strongly influenced by his friend Émile Zola, Bruneau addressed social and political issues in many of his works. His operas include *Le Rêve* (Paris 18 June 1891; libr. Louis Gallet, after Zola), the anti-war *L'Attaque du Moulin**, his most successful work, *Messidor* (Paris 19 Feb 1897; libr. Zola), *L'Ouragan* (*The Hurricane*, Paris 29 April 1901; libr. Zola), the unproduced *Lazare* (1903; libr. Zola), *L'Enfant Roi* (Paris 3 March 1905; libr. Zola) and *Les Quatre Journées* (Paris 25 Dec 1916; libr. composer, after Zola).

Brünnhilde

Soprano role in Wagner's *Die Walküre*, *Siegfried* and *Götterdämmerung*. Daughter of Wotan and Erda, she is the leader of the Valkyries.

Brunswick Staatstheater

The opera house (cap. 1,370) in this German city in Lower Saxony opened in 1948, replacing the previous Landestheater which was destroyed in World War II.

Bruscantini, Sesto *(b 1919)*

Italian baritone, particularly associated with the Italian repertory and with Mozart roles. One of the greatest buffos of the postwar era, especially renowned in Rossini and in *Il Maestro di Cappella*, he enjoyed a remarkably long career and also had success in a number of serious roles, particularly Germont. His somewhat dry voice was good if not outstanding and was allied to fine musicianship, superlative diction and great dramatic ability. Married for a time to the soprano Sena Jurinac*.

Bruson, Renato *(b 1936)*

Italian baritone, especially noted for Verdi and Donizetti roles. One of the greatest baritones of the 20th century, he possesses a glorious voice, rich and even-toned, used with intelligence, a flawless technique and scrupulous good taste. He is a restrained and dignified singing-actor, seen to best advantage as Macbeth.

Brussels

See Théâtre Royal de la Monnaie, Brussels

Bucharest Opera

Romania's principal opera house (cap. 1,000), designed by D. Diocescu, opened in 1953, replacing the previous theatre which had been wrecked by an earthquake in 1940 and, again, by bombs in 1944. The repertory is strong in Italian works and Romanian operas are also championed. The annual season runs from September to June. Musical directors have included Enescu, George Stephănescu, George Georgescu and Jonel Perlea.

Budapest State Opera

Hungary's principal opera company, which currently enjoys a high international reputation, it performs at either the Operaház (cap. 1,261), designed by Milkós Ybl and one of the most beautiful opera houses in the world, or at the Erkel Theatre (cap. 2,450). It follows an enterprising repertory policy, with a strong emphasis on Italian and Hungarian operas. The annual season runs from September to June. Musical directors have included Erkel, Hans Richter, Mahler, Artur Nikisch, Miklós Bánffi, Sergio Failoni, Ferenc Fricsay, János Ferencsik and Ervin Lukács.

Budd, Supt

Bass role in Britten's *Albert Herring*. He is the local police chief.

Buenos Aires

See Teatro Colón, Buenos Aires

Buffo

From the Italian for 'buffoon' or 'comedian', a buffo is a singer of comic roles (as in a basso-buffo), and opera-buffa is comic opera. The French term *bouffe* has the same meaning.

Bühnenfestspiel (German for 'stage festival play')

Wagner used the term to describe *Der Ring des Nibelungen*. He described *Parsifal* as *Bühnenweihfestspiel* (German for 'stage consecration festival play').

Bulgaria

See Sofia National Opera

Bulgarian opera composers

See Atanasov

Other national opera composers include Marin Goleminov (*b* 1908), Parashkev Hadjiev (*b* 1912), Ivan Ivanov (1862–1941), Emanuil Manolov (1860–1902), whose *The Poor Woman* (*Siromakhkinya*, Kazanluk Dec 1900) was the first Bulgarian opera, Lyobomir Pipkov (*b* 1904), Veselin Stoyanov (1902–69) and Pancho Vladige (*b* 1899).

Bülow, Hans von (1830–94)

German conductor and pianist. Often regarded as the first modern-style conductor, he was an ardent champion of Wagner, and conducted the first performances of *Tristan und Isolde* and *Die Meistersinger von Nürnberg*. He was musical director of the Hamburg Opera (1888–91) and the Hanover Opera. He was married to Liszt's daughter Cosima* until she deserted him for Wagner.

Bumbry, Grace (b 1937)

American mezzo and, later, soprano, particularly associated with the Italian and French repertories. She possesses a rich and powerful voice, matched by an exciting stage presence. In 1961, she became the first black singer ever to appear at the Bayreuth Festival.

Buona Figliuola, La (The Good Daughter)

Comic opera in three acts by Piccinni. 1st perf. (as *La Cecchina*) Rome, 6 Feb 1760; libr. by Carlo Goldoni, after Samuel Richardson's *Pamela or Virtue Rewarded*. Principal roles: La Cecchina (sop), Armindoro (ten), Marchese (ten), Lucinda (sop), Sandrina (sop), Paoluccia (sop), Tagliaferro (bar), Mengotto (bar). Piccinni's most successful work, and his only opera which is still performed. He wrote a less successful follow-up, *La Buona Figliuola Maritata* (Bologna, 10 June 1761; libr. by Carlo Goldoni), which is now forgotten.

Plot: The orphan La Cecchina loves, and is loved by, her master the Marchese. This provokes the jealousy of her fellow servants Sandrina and Paoluccia, and of Mengotto who also loves her, and annoys the Marchese's sister Lucinda, who fears that her own marriage prospects will be compromised if her brother marries beneath himself. The German soldier Tagliaferro arrives and reveals that La Cecchina is in fact a baroness, thus allowing all to end happily.

Buona sera, mio signore

Mezzo/tenor/baritone/bass/bass quintet for Rosina, Count Almaviva, Figaro, Dr Bartolo and Don Basilio in Act II of Rossini's *Il Barbiere di Siviglia*.

Burchuladze, Paata *(b 1955)*

Russian (Georgian) bass, particularly associated with the Italian and Russian repertories. Possessing a rich and soaring voice of vast proportions, he is perhaps the finest bass to have emerged in the 1980s.

Burian, František *(1904–59)*

Czech composer and producer, nephew of the tenor Karel Burian*. As a producer he was notable for his work in avant-garde theatre techniques. He wrote eight operas, of which the folk tragedy *Maryša* (Brno 16 April 1940; libr. composer, after A. and V. Mrštík) is still occasionally performed in Czechoslovakia.

Burian, Karel *(1870–1924)*

Czech tenor, often known as Carl Burrian, particularly associated with the Czech and German repertories. One of the greatest singing-actors of his age, he was an outstanding linguist and an artist of remarkable intelligence and musicality. Some contemporary critics rated his voice above Caruso's. He created Herod in *Salome*, an interpretation described by Bax as "horrifying, slobbering with lust and apparently almost decomposing before our eyes". His autobiography, *Z Mých Pamětí*, was published in 1931. His brother Emil (1876–1926) was a successful baritone, and his nephew was the composer František Burian*.

Burletta *(Italian for 'little joke')*

A term used loosely in the 18th century to refer to an intermezzo.

Burmeister, Annelies *(1929–88)*

German mezzo, particularly associated with Wagnerian roles. A dramatic and warm-voiced singer, she created for Dessau the Fishwife in *Veruerteilung des Lukullus* and Laina in *Puntila*.

Burning Fiery Furnace, The

Opera in one act by Britten (Op 77). 1st perf. Orford 9 June 1966; libr. by William Plomer, after the Book of Daniel in the Old Testament. Principal roles: Nebuchadnezzar (ten), Astrologer (bar), Misael (ten), Azarias (bass), Ananias (bar). The second of Britten's *Three Church Parables*, it tells the famous biblical story. [R]

Burrowes, Norma *(b 1944)*

British soprano, particularly associated with Mozart and other soubrette roles. She possesses a lovely voice and a delightful stage presence, especially in comedy. Married first to the conductor Steuart Bedford* and later to the tenor Emile Belcourt.

Burrows, Stuart *(b 1933)*

British tenor, particularly associated with Mozart roles. Possessing a small but very attractive and well-focused voice and phenomenal breath control, he is one of the most elegant and stylish Mozartian vocal interpreters of the postwar era, but is somewhat dull on stage.

Busch, Fritz *(1890–1951)*

German conductor, particularly associated with Mozart operas. He was musical director of the Aachen Opera (1912–19), the Stuttgart Opera (1920–

22), the Dresden State Opera (1922–33) and the Glyndebourne Festival (1934–51), where he built up the infant company. He conducted the first performances of *Doktor Faust*, *Die Ägyptische Helena*, *Intermezzo* and Hindemith's *Cardillac, Mörder, Hoffnung der Frauen* and *Das Nusch-Nuschi*. His autobiography, *Aus den Leben eines Musikers*, was published in 1949.

Bush, Alan *(b 1900)*
British composer. His operas, in a traditional and easily accessible style and with libretti by his wife Nancy, all reflect his left-wing political views, and it is in East Germany that they have met with most success. His stage works include the children's opera *The Press Gang* (1946), *Wat Tyler**, his finest work and a joint winner of the 1951 Festival of Britain competition, the operetta *The Spell Unbound* (1953), *The Men of Blackmoor* (Weimar 1956), *The Sugar Reapers* or *Guyana Johnny* (1966) and *Joe Hill* (1970). His autobiography, *In My Seventh Decade*, was published in 1970.

Busoni, Ferruccio *(1866–1924)*
Italian composer and pianist. His five operas, far more German than Italian in style and outlook, are the unperformed *Sigune* (1889; libr. L. and F. Soyaux, after Rudolf Braumbach), *Die Brautwahl* (Hamburg 12 April 1912; libr. composer, after E. T. A. Hoffmann), *Arlecchino**, *Turandot** and his masterpiece *Doktor Faust**, which was left unfinished at his death

and was completed by his pupil Philipp Jarnach. Although much admired by specialists and musicologists, his operas are only rarely performed.

Bussotti, Sylvano *(b 1931)*
Italian composer. His stage works, in avant-garde style, include *Geographie Française* (Darmstadt 1959), *Memoria* (Palermo 1962), *La Passion Selon Sade* (Palermo 1965; libr. L. Loulié), *Apology* (1972), *Lorenzaccio* (Venice 1972; libr. composer, after Alfred de Musset) and *L'Ispirazione* (Florence May 1988). He has also written three marionette operas: *Nottetempolunapark* (Florence 1954), *Arlechinbatocieria* (Florence 1955) and *Masacre in Gloria* (Aix-en-Provence 1956).

Butt, Dame Clara *(1873–1936)*
British contralto. A greatly loved concert singer, she made only one operatic appearance in her entire career: *Orfeo* in 1920.

Buxton Festival
An annual summer festival in the peak district of northern England, it was founded in 1979. The theme of each festival is a famous writer with operas based on his works as the central items. Performances are given at the Buxton Opera House (cap. 1,000), built in 1903 and designed by Frank Marcham. The musical director is Anthony Hose.

Byron, Lord
See panel on page 90

LORD BYRON

The British romantic poet George Gordon, Lord Byron (1788–1824) is the subject of Banfield's *Lord Byron's Loveletter* and of Thomson's *Lord Byron*. His works have inspired nearly 50 operas. Below are listed, by work, those operas by composers with entries in this dictionary.

The Bride of Abydos

Poniatowski	*La Sposa d'Abido*	1845

Cain

Lattuada	*Caino*	1957

The Corsair

Pacini	*Il Corsaro*	1831
Schumann	*Der Korsar*	1844 (U)
Arditi	*Il Corsaro*	1847
Verdi	*Il Corsaro*	1848

Don Juan

Fibich	*Hedy*	1896

Heaven and Earth

Donizetti	*Il Diluvio Universale*	1830
Glière	*Earth and Sky*	1900

Lara

Maillart	*Lara*	1864

Manfred

Petrella	*Manfredo*	1872

Marino Faliero

Donizetti	*Marino Faliero*	1835

Parisina

Donizetti	*Parisina d'Este*	1833
Mascagni	*Parisina*	1913

Tasso

Donizetti	*Torquato Tasso*	1833

The Two Foscari

Verdi	*I Due Foscari*	1844

C

Cabaletta (from the Italian
cavatinetta, 'short melodic air')
The term has two meanings:

(1) A short aria in simple rhythm
with repeats. These arias are mostly
found in Rossini, who stipulated that
the first statement should be sung as
written and that the second could be
embellished at the singer's discretion.

(2) The second part of a two-part
19th-century Italian aria. Typically
found in Bellini, Donizetti, Pacini and
early Verdi, these are in fast tempo and
are designed to show off the singer's
virtuosity. The slow/fast structure of a
full aria was occasionally reversed:
Donizetti was a master of the slow
cabaletta, writing fine examples in the
final scenes of *Robert Devereux*, *Maria
Stuarda* and *Parisina*.

The cabaletta was a dramatically
suffocating convention; apart from
'Sempre libera' in *La Traviata* and
'Salgo già il trono aurato' in *Nabucco*,
few serve any function other than to
provide the singer with a dazzling
display piece. Verdi eventually
suppressed the cabaletta altogether, and
it has subsequently been used only very
rarely (as, for example, in *The Rake's
Progress*).

Caballé, Montserrat (*b 1933*)
Spanish soprano, particularly associated
with Donizetti, Bellini and Verdi roles.
One of the greatest sopranos of the
20th century, she sang a wide variety
of roles until 1965, when her
sensational success as Lucrezia Borgia
led her to specialise in the bel canto
repertory, of which she was one of the
finest modern exponents. She possessed
a voice of great range and remarkable
beauty which she used with unfailing
musicianship and a flawless technique.
She was at her best in concert, where
her substantial physique was not the
handicap it sometimes proved on stage.
Her husband Bernabé Marti (*b 1934*)
was a successful tenor.

Caccini, Giulio (*c 1545–1618*)
Italian composer. A member of the
Florentine Camerata*, he was largely
responsible for the development of
accompanied recitative, and thus of
opera. His *Dafne** was one of the first
two operas, although it may never have
been performed and its music is lost.
This was followed by *Il Rapimento di
Cefalo* (Florence 9 Oct 1600), written
with three other composers, almost all
of which is lost. He contributed to
Peri's *Euridice** and subsequently made
his own setting of the text, which was
the first opera to be published.

Cadenza (Italian for 'cadence')
An improvised passage in free time
inserted by a singer before the final
cadence of an 18th- or 19th-century
aria. The licence for extravagant vocal
gymnastics which the convention
provided led composers increasingly to
write out the cadenzas themselves,
occasionally intended for specific
singers.

Cadi Dupé, Le (*The Deceived
Cadi*)
Works of this title to the libretto by
Pierre René Lemonnier, after *The
Arabian Nights*, include:

(1) Comic opera in one act by
Monsigny. 1st perf. Paris, 4 Feb 1761.

91

An elegant example of Monsigny's comic style, it was successful in its time but is nowadays forgotten.

(2) Comic opera in one act by Gluck. 1st perf. Vienna, 9 Dec 1761. Principal roles: Cadi (bar), Fatime (sop), Nuradin (ten), Zelmire (sop), Omar (ten), Omega (mezzo). Gluck's last pre-reform opera, it is an entertaining little piece which is still occasionally performed.

Plot: The attentions of the Cadi have turned from his wife Fatime to Zelmire. Despite all his subterfuges, Zelmire rejects his advances as she loves Nuradin. Finally, Zelmire pretends to be Omega, the daughter of Omar the dyer who, according to Omar, is appallingly ugly. The Cadi enters into a marriage contract with the supposed daughter, but when the real Omega arrives she proves to be plain indeed. The Cadi has to pay through the nose to get out of the contract and returns to Fatime, while Zelmire and Nuradin are united. [R]

Caffarelli *(b Gaetano Majorano) (1710–83)*
Italian castrato. One of the most famous of all castrati and mentioned by Dr Bartolo in *Il Barbiere di Siviglia*, he was believed to be the first singer to introduce chromatic scales as vocal decorations in fast sections. He created the title roles in Handel's *Serse* and *Faramondo* and Sextus in Gluck's *La Clemenza di Tito*. Commanding the highest fees ever then paid to a singer, Caffarelli amassed a vast fortune, out of which he purchased two palaces and a dukedom. A highly temperamental man, who had been both jailed and placed under house arrest for his behaviour towards other singers, he wounded the poet Ballot de Sauvot in a duel over the respective merits of Italian and French music.

Cagnoni, Antonio *(1828–96)*
Italian composer. He wrote 19 operas, some of them successful in their time, but all now forgotten. His most important operas are *Don Bucefalo* (Milan 28 June 1847; libr. C. Bassi), *Michele Perrin* (Milan 7 May 1864; libr. M. M. Marcello), *Claudia* (Milan 20 May 1866; libr. Marcello), *Papà Martin* (Genoa 4 March 1871; libr. Antonio Ghislanzoni) and *Francesca da Rimini* (Turin 19 Feb 1878; libr. Ghislanzoni, after Dante's *La Divina Commedia*), his most successful work, which makes considerable use of leitmotivs. His *Re Lear* (1893; libr. Ghislanzoni, after Shakespeare's *King Lear*) was unperformed.

Cain, Henri *(1857–1922)*
French librettist. He provided texts for several composers, including Alfano (*Cyrano de Bergerac*), Blockx (*Thyl Uilenspiegel*), Godard (*La Vivandière*), Honegger and Ibert (*L'Aiglon*), Massenet (*Roma, Cendrillon, Chérubin, Don Quichotte, La Navarraise* and *Sapho*) and Widor (*Les Pêcheurs de Saint-Jean*).

Caius, Dr
Tenor role in Verdi's *Falstaff*. He is the pedant who aspires to marry Nannetta.

Calaf
Tenor role in Puccini's and Busoni's *Turandot*. Timur's son, he is a Tartar prince.

Calchas
The mythological Greek high priest appears in a number of operas, including: (1) Baritone role in Offenbach's *La Belle Hélène*. (2) Bass role in Walton's *Troilus and Cressida*. (3) Bass role in Gluck's *Iphigénie en Aulide*.

Caldara, Antonio *(1670–1736)*

Italian composer. He wrote 60 operas, all of them now forgotten, including *Ifigenia in Aulide* (Vienna 1718; libr. Apostolo Zeno after Euripides), *La Clemenza di Tito* (Vienna 1734; libr. Pietro Metastasio) and *Achille in Sciro* (Vienna 1736; libr. Metastasio).

Caldwell, Sarah *(b 1924)*

American conductor and producer. The first woman American conductor of significance, she founded the Opera Company of Boston in 1957 and has been its director ever since. She also produces most of its performances. In 1973, she became the first woman conductor to appear at the Metropolitan Opera, New York.

Calife de Bagdad, Le

Opera in one act by Boïeldieu. 1st perf. Paris, 16 Sept 1800; libr. by Claude Godard d'Aucour de Saint-Just, after *The Arabian Nights*. Very successful in its time, nowadays only the delightful overture is still remembered.

Calinda, La

Orchestral excerpt in Act II of Delius's *Koanga*. It is a dance that takes its name from an actual Negro dance brought to America by African slaves.

Calisto, La

Opera in three acts by Cavalli. 1st perf. Venice, autumn 1651; libr. by Giovanni Battista Faustini, after Ovid's *Metamorphoses*. Principal roles: Calisto (sop), Diana (mezzo), Jove (bass), Linfea (ten), Endymion (c-ten), Pan (bass), Mercury (bass), Juno (sop). Unperformed for over 300 years, it has recently become Cavalli's most frequently performed work, usually in the version prepared by Raymond Leppard.

Plot: Jove, having decreed that Calisto should become an immortal, comes down to earth to claim her, only to find that she has become one of Diana's nymphs. He disguises himself as Diana so as to win Calisto but Juno turns her into a bear. Meanwhile Endymion, in love with the real Diana, is captured by Pan. Eventually, he is reunited with his goddess, and Jove gives Calisto her immortality by placing her in the heavens as the constellation Ursa Minor. [R]

Callas, Maria *(b Kalogeropoulou)* *(1923–77)*

Greek soprano. The most famous – and the most controversial – opera singer of the 20th century, Callas was one of the finest singing-actresses the operatic stage has ever known. She was mainly associated with the Italian repertory, particularly Tosca, Norma, Anna Bolena and Medea, but also sang the German repertory early in her career. Largely responsible for the modern revival and re-evaluation of the bel canto repertory, she possessed a unique ability to illuminate and communicate the true meaning of a composer's music. Particularly when in partnership with Tito Gobbi, she set entirely new dramatic standards in operatic performance. Her actual singing was variable and her technique imperfect; at its best, her voice was large, agile and very beautiful, but it was not always at its best. She retired from the stage in 1965 and, apart from an ill-advised concert tour with Giuseppe di Stefano in 1972–73, she never sang again in public. She played the title role in Pasolini's film of Euripides' *Medea* in 1970 and made one appearance as a producer, with *Les Vêpres Siciliennes*, in Turin in 1973.

Calunnia, La

Bass aria for Don Basilio in Act I of Rossini's *Il Barbiere di Siviglia*.

Calvé, Emma (b Rosa Calvet de Roquer) (1858–1952)

French soprano, particularly associated with the French and Italian repertories, especially Carmen. One of the finest sopranos of her time, and a tempestuous actress, she created Suzel in *L'Amico Fritz* and, for Massenet, Anita in *La Navarraise* and the title role in *Sapho*. Her autobiography, *Sous les Ciels J'ai Chanté*, was published in 1940.

Calzabigi, Ranieri de' (1714–95)

Italian librettist. After an adventurous time in Paris as an associate of Casanova, during which he edited Pietro Metastasio's works, he settled in Vienna, where he collaborated with Gluck. As well as the later *Paride ed Elena*, he wrote the texts for the two 'reform' operas *Orfeo ed Euridice* and *Alceste*, in which his verses reflect Gluck's desire for dramatic truth and the banishment of artificiality. He also wrote the libretti for Salieri's *Les Danaïdes*, Paisiello's *Elfrida* and *Elvira* and Morandi's *Comala* (1780), which was the first Ossianic* opera.

Cambert, Robert (c 1628–77)

French composer. His *Pomone* (Paris 19 March 1671; libr. Abbé Pierre Perrin) is widely regarded as the first French opera. He also wrote *Les Peines et les Plaisirs d'Amour* (Paris 1671). Only a small portion of the music of either work survives.

Cambiale di Matrimonio, La

(*The Marriage Contract*)

Comic opera in one act by Rossini. 1st perf. Venice, 3 Nov 1810; libr. by Gaetano Rossi after Camillo Federici. Principal roles: Tobias Mill (b-bar), Fanny (sop), Slook (bar), Edoardo (ten). Rossini's first opera to be staged, it is a melodically fresh and entertaining little piece which is still quite often performed.

Plot: The wealthy Canadian merchant Slook offers the English businessman Sir Tobias Mill a large sum of money if he will find him a wife. Mill suggests his daughter Fanny, who is, however, in love with Edoardo Milfort. Slook is impressed by the lovers' determination, sacrifices Fanny and helps them to win Mill's approval for their marriage. [R]

Camden Festival

An annual spring festival in London, founded in 1954 and continuing until 1987, of which opera was the central feature. Called the St Pancras Festival until 1965, it specialised in the revival of long-forgotten operas (some of which subsequently made their way back into the general repertory). Performances were given at St Pancras Town Hall until 1969, and thereafter at the Bloomsbury (formerly Collegiate) Theatre. It was superseded by the Bloomsbury Festival in 1988.

Camerata

See Florentine Camerata

Camille de Rosillon

Tenor role in Lehár's *Die Lustige Witwe*. He is in love with Valencienne.

Cammarano, Salvatore (1801–52)

Italian librettist. Long resident at the Teatro San Carlo, Naples (where he was stage manager), he was one of the better Italian librettists of his day.

Without being inspired, his work is effective and skilfully constructed. He wrote some 50 libretti in all, including texts for Donizetti (*Lucia di Lammermoor, Roberto Devereux, Poliuto, L'Assedio di Calais, Maria di Rohan, Maria de Rudenz, Belisario* and *Pia de' Tolomei*), Mercadante (nine including *La Vestale* and *Il Reggente*), Pacini (six including *Saffo*), Ricci and Verdi (*Alzira, La Battaglia di Legnano, Luisa Miller* and *Il Trovatore*, which last he had not completed at his death).

Campana Sommersa, La (*The Sunken Bell*)

Opera in four acts by Respighi. 1st perf. Hamburg, 18 Nov 1927; libr. by Claudio Gaustalla, after Gerhard Hauptmann's *Die Versunkene Glocke*. Principal roles: Heinrich (ten), Rautendelien (sop), Magda (sop). The second of Respighi's mature operas, it was successful at its appearance but is now virtually forgotten.

Plot: The bell-founder Heinrich is bewitched by the fairy Rautendelein and follows her into the mountains. He returns home on the death of his wife Magda, but is unable to erase the memory of Rautendelein. Later, as he himself lies dying, he calls to her and she returns to him.

Campanello di Notte, Il (*The Night Bell*)

Comic opera in one act by Donizetti. 1st perf. Naples, 1 June 1836; libr. by the composer after Léon Lévy Brunswick, Mathieu-Barthélemy Troin and Victor Lhérie's *La Sonnette de Nuit*. Principal roles: Enrico (bar), Don Annibale Pistacchio (b-bar), Serafina (sop). A delightfully funny little piece, containing some of the longest and fastest patter in all opera, it is still regularly performed.

Plot: The elderly apothecary Don Annibale marries the youthful and pretty Serafina. After they have retired to bed, Serafina's rejected lover, Enrico, interrupts the wedding night by donning a series of disguises in which he repeatedly rings the apothecary's bell and demands ever more complicated and fantastic prescriptions to be dispensed. [R]

Campanini, Cleofonte (*1860–1919*)

Italian conductor, particularly associated with the Italian repertory. One of the finest conductors of his time, he conducted the first performances of *Adriana Lecouvreur*, *Madama Butterfly* and Giordano's *Siberia*. Married to the soprano Eva Tetrazzini*. His brother Italo (1845–96) was a successful tenor.

Campiello, Il (*The Little Square*)

Comic opera in three acts by Wolf-Ferrari. 1st perf. Milan, 12 Feb 1936; libr. by Mario Ghisalberti, after Carlo Goldoni. Wolf-Ferrari's last major success and still occasionally performed, it is set in Venice and tells of four families who live around a little square. It culminates in a street fight between two old women played and sung by tenors.

Campra, André (*1660–1744*)

French composer. The historical link between Lully and Rameau, Campra's operas are a synthesis of what he considered best in the French and Italian schools. His operas include *L'Europe Galante* (Paris 24 Oct 1697; libr. Houdart de la Motte), *Le Carnival de Venise* (Paris 20 Jan 1699; libr. J. F. Regnard), *Tancrède* (Paris 7 Nov 1702; libr. Antoine Danchet, after Torquato Tasso's *Gerusalemme Liberata*), his finest work, *Iphigénie en Tauride* (Paris 6 May 1704; libr. J. F. Duché de

Vancy and Danchet, after Euripides), *Idomenée* (Paris 12 Jan 1712; libr. Danchet), *Les Ages* (Paris 9 Oct 1718; libr. Louis Fuzelier) and *Achille et Deidamie* (Paris 24 Feb 1735; libr. Danchet). Ignored for over 200 years, a few of his works have been revived in the last couple of decades.

Canada

See Canadian Opera Company; Opéra de Montréal, L'; Vancouver Opera Association

Canadian Opera Company

Founded in 1950, it is based at the O'Keefe Center (cap. 3,200) in Toronto and also visits Ottawa and other towns. The annual season is Sept to Oct and Jan to June. Musical directors have included Mario Bernadi.

Canadian opera composers

These include Harry Somers (*b* 1925), Healey Willan (1880–1968) and Charles Wilson (*b* 1931).

Can-Can

A fast and energetic Parisian dance, involving much high kicking, in 2/4 time. It has become almost synonymous with Offenbach, who wrote many. The most famous is the finale to *Orphée aux Enfers*.

Candide

Operetta in three acts by Leonard Bernstein. 1st perf. New York, 1 Dec 1956; libr. by Lillian Hellman, Richard Wilbur, Dorothy Parker and John Latouche after Voltaire's novel. Revised version, 1st perf. New York, 19 Dec 1973; libr. revised by Hugh Wheeler and Stephen Sondheim. Principal roles: Candide (ten), Cunegonde (sop), Maximilian (bass), Paquette (mezzo), Voltaire (speaker). Initially a failure, the revised version has met with considerable success and has been widely performed.

Plot: Dr Pangloss has taught Candide and Cunegonde that this is "the best of all possible worlds", in which belief they go on their travels – and experience exile, war, rape, the Inquisition and frequent betrayals. In the end, they realise that they must come to terms with reality and "make their gardens grow". [R]

Caniglia, Maria *(1905–79)*

Italian soprano, particularly associated with the roles of Tosca, Adriana Lecouvreur and Aida. Possessing a powerful if sometimes squally voice, she created Roxane in Alfano's *Cyrano de Bergerac*, the title role in Respighi's *Lucrezia* and Manuela in Montemezzi's *La Notte Zoraima*. Her husband Pino Donati (1907–75) was artistic director of the Verona Arena, the Chicago Lyric Opera and the Teatro Communale, Bologna.

Canio

Tenor role in Leoncavallo's *Pagliacci*. Nedda's husband, he is leader of the theatrical troupe.

Canon

A contrapuntal piece of music, in which the melody sung by one voice is repeated by others, each of them entering before the previous one has finished. A famous operatic example is the quartet 'S'appressan gl'isante' in Verdi's *Nabucco*.

Cantabile (Italian for 'singable')

The term has two meanings: (1) In general musical usage it means a flowing style of performance. (2) In opera it can also mean the first (slow) movement of an 18th- or 19th-century double aria in an Italian opera.

Cantata
An extended choral work, often featuring soloists and nearly always with orchestra. Composers have occasionally used the term to describe stage works which are really fully operatic. For example, Sullivan's *Trial by Jury* is described as a 'dramatic cantata'.

Cantatrici Villane, Le *(The Boorish Singers)*
Comic opera by Fioravanti. 1st perf. Naples, 1799; libr. by Giovanni Palomba. One of Fioravanti's most successful works, it is his only opera still to be in any way remembered. [R Exc]

Cantelli, Guido *(1920–56)*
Italian conductor. One of the most brilliant conductors of the 1950s, he turned to opera only in the last year of his life. He was killed in an air crash a few days after the announcement of his appointment as musical director of La Scala, Milan.

Canteloube, Joseph *(1879–1957)*
French composer. Although best known as a composer and arranger of songs (mainly from his native Auvergne), he also wrote two operas: *Le Mas* (Paris 3 April 1929; libr. composer) and *Vercingétorix* (Paris 26 June 1933; libr. E. Clémentel and J.-H. Louwyck).

Canterbury Pilgrims, The
Opera in three acts by Stanford. 1st perf. London, 28 April 1884; libr. by Gilbert Arthur A'Beckett after Geoffrey Chaucer's *The Canterbury Tales*. Reasonably successful at its appearance, it is now as good as forgotten.

Cantilena (Italian for 'sing-song')
The term describes a smoothly flowing vocal line, and is thus also a direction that a passage should be thus sung.

Canto figuraturo (Italian for 'figured singing')
An obsolete term, which was the original description of coloratura*.

Canzona (from the Provençal *canzo*, a type of song)
A song which is outside the general dramatic action. In other words, a song within a sung drama. Examples include the 'Canzone del Salce' (The Willow Song) in Verdi's *Otello*, the Veil Song in Verdi's *Don Carlos* and Cherubino's 'Voi che sapete' in Mozart's *Le Nozze di Figaro*.

Canzonetta
The diminutive of canzona (see above), it describes a short song in simple style.

Capecchi, Renato *(b 1923)*
Italian baritone. Although best known as one of the greatest buffos of the postwar era (and one of the few with a really superb voice), his enormous repertory of some 280 roles included Verdi, bel canto, verismo and many 20th-century works. He created roles in Malipiero's *Allegra Brigata*, Ghedini's *Billy Budd* and *Lord Inferno*, Napoli's *Un Curioso Accidente*, R. Malipiero's *La Donna è Mobile* and Bussotti's *L'Ispirazione*. He was an outstanding singing-actor, a great wit and a fine musician. He has also produced a number of operas.

Capellio
Bass role in Bellini's *I Capuleti e i Montecchi*. He is the leader of the Capulets.

Capobianco, Tito (b 1931)

Argentinian producer. His traditional but strongly staged productions have been seen mainly in the United States, particularly at the New York City Opera. He was artistic director of the Cincinnati Opera Association (1962–65) and the San Diego Opera (1977–).

Cappello di Paglia di Firenze, Il (usually known in English as *The Italian Straw Hat*)

Comic opera in four acts by Rota. 1st perf. Palermo, April 1955; libr. by the composer and Ernesta Rota after Eugène Labiche and Marc-Michel's farce. Principal roles: Fadinard (ten), Hélène (sop), Nonancourt (bass), Beaupertuis (bass), Countess (mezzo), Annaïs (mezzo), Emile (bar), Vézinet (ten), Félix (ten). By far Rota's most successful work, it has been widely performed.

Plot: Fadinard is to wed Hélène, daughter of the bumpkin Nonancourt. His horse eats an expensive Florentine straw hat belonging to Annaïs who pursues him with her lover Emile. Annaïs confesses that the hat was given her by her jealous husband and demands a replacement. Fadinard learns that the only identical hat was sold to the Countess Champigny. Visiting her, he is mistaken for the violinist Minardi, pretends to be a suitor to the Countess and asks for the hat as a memento. The Countess tells him that she has given it to her goddaughter, Madame Beaupertuis. After leaving a trail of chaos at the house of Beaupertuis (who is Annaïs' husband), Fadinard decides to cancel his wedding. However a replacement hat is finally found and all ends happily. [R]

Cappuccilli, Piero (b 1929)

Italian baritone, associated with the Italian repertory, especially Verdi. One of the finest Verdi baritones of the postwar era, if a little dull on stage, he possessed a rich and beautiful voice used with a fine technique and unfailing musicianship and was noted for phenomenal breath control.

Capriccio

Opera in one act by Richard Strauss (Op 85). 1st perf. Munich, 28 Oct 1942; libr. by the composer and Clemens Krauss. Principal roles: Countess Madeleine (sop), Count (bar), Flamand (ten), Olivier (bar), La Roche (bass), Clarion (mezzo), Thaupe (ten), Italian singers (sop and ten). Strauss's last opera, set at the time of Gluck's reforms, it is described as a 'conversation piece with music' and discusses the relative importance of words and music in opera.

Plot: Paris, c 1775. At her château, Countess Madeleine is wooed by the composer Flamand and the poet Olivier. While waiting for her to choose between them, the two men argue over the respective merits of their arts. A decision is taken that they will write a work discussing whether music or poetry comes first in opera, and which will involve Madeleine's brother the Count, the theatre manager La Roche, the actress Clarion and others. At the close, the Countess muses over whether the question has any answer that is of the slightest importance. [R]

Capro e la capretta, Il

Mezzo aria for Marcellina in Act IV of Mozart's *Le Nozze di Figaro*. It is frequently cut.

Capuana, Franco (1894–1969)

Italian conductor and composer, particularly associated with the Italian and German repertories and with contemporary operas. He was musical director of La Scala, Milan (1949–52) and conducted the first performances of Alfano's *L'Ultimo Lord*, Refice's *Margherita da Cortona*, Malipiero's *Sette Canzoni* and Ghedini's *La Pulche d'Oro*. He also composed two operas. He died whilst conducting *Mosè in Egitto* in Naples. His sister Maria (1891–1955) was a Wagnerian mezzo.

Capuleti e i Montecchi, I (*The Capulets and the Montagues*)

Opera in two acts by Bellini. 1st perf. Venice, 11 March 1830; libr. by Felice Romani, after Matteo Bandello's novel, itself based on Shakespeare's *Romeo and Juliet*. Principal roles: Giulietta (sop), Romeo (mezzo), Tebaldo (ten), Capellio (bass), Lorenzo (bass). One of Bellini's finest operas, into which he incorporated much music from the unsuccessful *Zaira**, it was widely performed in the 19th century, when part of the final act of Vaccai's *Giulietta e Romeo* was often substituted for Bellini's. Following a long period of neglect, it has been regularly performed in recent years. The story is roughly the same as Shakespeare's except that in this version Giulietta's kinsman, Tebaldo, combines the functions of Tybalt and Paris. [R]

Carafa, Michele Enrico (*1787–1872*)

Italian composer. He wrote 35 operas, in which can be found the influence of both Cherubini and of his close friend Rossini, who remarked that Carafa "made the mistake of being born my contemporary". His operas, long forgotten although many were successful in their time, are solidly written but exhibit little individuality. He was also unfortunate in often choosing subjects on which other composers soon afterwards based some of their finest works. His most successful operas were *Gabriella di Vergy* (Naples 5 July 1816; libr. Andrea Leone Tottola), *Jeanne d'Arc* (Paris 10 March 1821), *Le Solitaire* (Paris 22 Aug 1822; libr. François-Antoine-Eugène de Planard), *Le Valet de Chambre* (Paris 16 Sept 1823; libr. Eugène Scribe and Anne-Honoré Joseph de Mélesville), *Masaniello* (Paris 27 Dec 1827–two months before Auber's version), *Le Nozze di Lammermoor* (Paris 12 Dec 1829; libr. Luigi Balocchi, after Sir Walter Scott's *The Bride of Lammermoor*), *La Prison d'Edimbourg* (Paris 20 July 1833; libr. Scribe and de Planard, after Scott's *The Heart of Midlothian*) and *Thérèse* (Paris 26 Sept 1838; libr. de Planard and Adolphe de Leuven).

Caramello

Tenor role in J. Strauss's *Eine Nacht in Venedig*. He is the Duke of Urbino's barber.

Caramoor Festival

An annual summer festival, founded in 1946, which is held at a private estate in Katonah (New York). Opera is the central feature, and the repertory is notable for its 17th-century and contemporary works. Musical directors have included Julius Rudel.

Cara selve

Soprano aria for Atalanta in Handel's *Atalanta*.

Cardillac

Opera in three acts by Hindemith (Op 39). 1st perf. Dresden, 9 Nov 1926; libr. by Ferdinand Lion, after E. T. A. Hoffmann's *Das Fraulein von Scuderi*. Revised version, 1st perf. Zürich, 20 June 1952. Principal roles: Cardillac (bar), Daughter (sop), Lady (sop), Officer (ten), Cavalier (ten). Hindemith's first full-length opera, it embodies the 'new objectivist' movement in German art and is his most frequently performed stage work.

Plot: 17th-century Paris. Cardillac, a master jeweller, is so obsessed with his creations that he cannot bear to part with them, believing that the artist and his work should never be separated. Consequently, he murders each of his customers after a sale. Things get out of hand with the involvement of an opera singer whose lover buys a belt from Cardillac, and that of his own daughter's army-officer lover. The jeweller finally loses his reason, confesses to the killings and is murdered by the mob. [R]

Carlo

(1) Baritone role in Verdi's *Ernani*. He is the Emperor Charles V. (2) Tenor role in Verdi's *Don Carlos*. King Philip's son, he is the Infante of Spain. (3) Tenor role in Verdi's *Giovanna d'Arco*. He is King Charles VII of France (1403–61). (4) Baritone role in Verdi's *La Forza del Destino*. Don Carlo de Vargas, he is Leonora's vengeful brother. (5) Tenor role in Verdi's *I Masnadieri*. He is Massamiliano's son. (6) Bass role in Bellini's *Bianca e Fernando*. He is the deposed Duke of Agrigento. (7) Tenor role in Donizetti's *Linda di Chamounix*. The Vicomte de Sirval, he is in love with Linda.

Carl Rosa Opera Company

Founded by the German violinist, Karl August Nicolaus Rose (1842–89), and dedicated to performing opera in English, the company gave its first performance in Sept 1875. The longest-lived British touring opera company, it continued to operate until 1958, when most of its membership was incorporated into Sadler's Wells Opera. Musical directors included Eugène Goossens.

Carmen

Opera in four acts by Bizet. 1st perf. Paris, 3 March 1875; libr. by Henri Meilhac and Ludovic Halévy, after Prosper Mérimée's novel. Principal roles: Carmen (mezzo), Don José (ten), Micaëla (sop), Escamillo (bar), Zuniga (bass), Frasquita (sop), Mercédès (mezzo), Remandado (ten), Dancairo (ten), Morales (bar). A failure at its first performance, it soon came to be appreciated not only as Bizet's masterpiece, but as one of the greatest of all operas, and can lay a strong claim to be the most popular opera ever written. For many years, the spoken dialogue was replaced by recitatives written by Guiraud, but virtually all modern productions revert to the original opéra-comique structure.

Plot: Carmen, a tempestuous, wayward and beautiful gypsy girl, desired by all the men, works in a Seville cigarette factory. Arrested after a fight with one of her colleagues, she is assigned to the custody of Don José, a corporal in the local barracks whose betrothed, Micaëla, has just arrived from their country village to look for him. Thoroughly bewitched by Carmen, he allows her to escape and is himself placed under arrest. Meanwhile, at the tavern of Lillas Pastia, the glamorous toreador, Escamillo, arrives with his entourage and sets his sights on Carmen. Although tempted by him, she decides to wait for José. He arrives at the tavern on his release and becomes involved in a fight with his superior officer, Zuniga. Although reluctant to do so, he is prepared to desert the army and join Carmen and a band of her smuggler companions in the mountains. The fickle gypsy grows bored with José and, when Escamillo seeks her out, she agrees to attend his forthcoming bullfight in Seville. When Micaëla appears, pleading with José to return home with her, Carmen urges him to go. Ignoring the gypsy's change of heart and spurning Micaëla, the unhappy José follows Carmen to Seville and accosts her outside the bull ring, begging her to start a new life with him. She refuses and, at the very moment the crowd erupts in excitement over Escamillo's triumph, José, crazed with grief and jealousy, stabs Carmen to death. [R]

Carnival (from the Latin *carnem levare*, 'to put away meat')
The festive season before the beginning of Lent. Carnival was (and in Italy still is) the period of the main operatic season, starting on 26 Dec and lasting until Shrove Tuesday.

Carolina
(1) Soprano role in Cimarosa's *Il Matrimonio Segreto*. She is Geronimo's daughter. (2) Mezzo role in Henze's *Elegie für Junge Liebende*. She is Mittenhofer's patroness and secretary.

Caro nome
Soprano aria for Gilda in Act I of Verdi's *Rigoletto*.

Carosio, Margherita (*b 1908*)
Italian soprano who specialised in the delicate Italian roles, notably Violetta. One of the leading lyric sopranos of the inter-war period, she had a light and agile voice and was an actress of charm and pathos. She created Egloge in Mascagni's *Nerone*.

Carré, Michel (*1819–72*)
French librettist. One of the most prolific 19th-century French librettists, he provided texts (often in collaboration with Jules Barbier*) for Bizet (*Les Pêcheurs de Perles*), David (*Lalla Roukh, La Captive* and *Le*

Saphir), Gounod (*Faust, Le Médecin Malgré Lui, Mireille, La Colombe, Philémon et Baucis, Polyeucte* and *Roméo et Juliette*), Lecocq (*Nos Bons Chasseurs*), Massé (*Les Noces de Jeanette* and *Galathée*), Messager (*Mirette*), Meyerbeer (*Dinorah*), Offenbach (*Les Contes d'Hoffmann*), Reyer (*La Statue*), Saint-Saëns (*Le Timbre d'Argent*) and Thomas (*Hamlet, Mignon, Psyché* and *Françoise de Rimini*) amongst others. His nephew Albert was director of the Opéra-Comique, Paris, and himself wrote some libretti, including that for Messager's *La Bosoche*.

Carreras, José (*b 1946*)
Spanish tenor, particularly associated with the Italian and French repertories. One of the finest lyric tenors of the postwar era, he possesses a warm and melodious voice used with fine musicianship. Outstanding in Donizetti and the lighter Verdian roles, he subsequently (and perhaps a little unwisely) undertook a number of heavier roles. His career was interrupted in the late 1980s by his long fight against leukemia.

Carte, Richard d'Oyly (*1844–1901*)
British impresario and administrator. The builder of both the Savoy Theatre and the Royal English Opera House (now the Palace Theatre), he was responsible for bringing about the Gilbert and Sullivan partnership and for founding the D'Oyly Carte Opera Company to perform their works. After his death, the company was run by his wife Helen and then by his son Rupert and his granddaughter Dame Bridget.

Caruso, Enrico (*1873–1921*)
Italian tenor. Generally regarded as the greatest tenor of all time, his most

famous roles were Nemorino, the Duke of Mantua, and Eléazer in *La Juive* (the last role he undertook). His glorious, rich voice had a dark and powerful lower register, and his phrasing, diction and technique remain an object lesson to all singers. He created Maurizio in *Adriana Lecouvreur*, Federico in *L'Arlesiana*, Dick Johnson in *La Fanciulla del West*, Loris in *Fedora* and Loewe in Franchetti's *Germania*. The film made of his life, *The Great Caruso* starring Mario Lanza, is a typical Hollywood biopic, crammed with inaccuracies and sheer invention.

Carvalho, Léon *(b Carvaille)* *(1825–97)*

French administrator. The leading 19th-century French impresario, he was director of the Théâtre Lyrique, Paris (1856–58), the Cairo Opera House (1868–72), and the Opéra-Comique, Paris (1876–87), where he was responsible for introducing many major new French operas. In 1887 he was fined and jailed for negligence after 131 people were killed in a fire which destroyed the Opéra-Comique, but he was reinstated after an appeal in 1891. Married to the soprano Marie Miolan-Carvalho*.

Casa, Lisa della *(b 1919)*

Swiss soprano, and a distinguished interpreter of Richard Strauss and Mozart. One of the loveliest singers of the immediate postwar era, she possessed a rich, creamy voice – heard to perfection as Arabella –which she used with unfailing style and good taste. She created three roles in Einem's *Der Prozess*.

Casella, Alfredo *(1883–1947)*

Italian composer. One of the most influential Italian musicians of the inter-war period, his three operas met with some success in Italy but are unknown elsewhere. They are *La Donna Serpente* (Rome 17 March 1932; libr. C. V. Lodovici after Carlo Gozzi), the chamber opera *La Favola d'Orfeo* (Venice 6 Sept 1932; libr. C. Pavolini after A. Poliziano) and *Il Deserto Tentato* (*The Desert Challenged*, Florence 19 May 1937; libr. Pavolini), which idealised Mussolini's conquest of Ethiopia.

Caspar

Bass role in Weber's *Der Freischütz*. He is an evil huntsman.

Cassandra

Soprano role in Berlioz's *Les Troyens*. She is a Trojan prophetess loved by Chorebus. The role is sometimes sung by a mezzo.

Cassel

See Kassel Staatstheater

Cassilly, Richard *(b 1927)*

American tenor, particularly associated with heroic roles, for which his powerful physique suited him. He possessed a strong if not intrinsically beautiful voice and was a committed singing-actor. He created Troilus in the revised version of *Troilus and Cressida*.

Cassio

Tenor role in Verdi's *Otello*. He is Otello's lieutenant.

Casta diva

Soprano aria for Norma in Act I of Bellini's *Norma*.

Castlenuovo-Tedesco, Mario *(1895–1968)*

Italian composer. He wrote eight operas including the marionette opera *Aucassin et Nicolette* (Florence 1952), *Giglietta di Narbona* (1959; libr. after Shakespeare's *All's Well That Ends Well*), *Il Mercante di Venezia* (1961; libr. after Shakespeare's *The Merchant of Venice*) and a setting of Oscar Wilde's *The Importance of Being Ernest* (1962).

Castor et Pollux

Opera in prologue and five acts by Rameau. 1st perf. Paris, 24 Oct 1737; libr. by Pierre Joseph Bernard. Revised version, 1st perf. Paris, 1754. Principal roles: Pollux (bar), Castor (ten), Thélaïre (sop), Jupiter (bass), Cléone (sop). Sometimes regarded as Rameau's finest work, it is still quite often performed.

Plot: The Heavenly Twins Castor and Pollux both love Thélaïre. Castor is killed and Thélaïre begs Pollux to ask Jupiter to restore him to life. Jupiter agrees on the condition that Pollux renounces immortality and that he and Thélaïre take Castor's place. Pollux agrees but Castor, returning for a day, refuses. Despite Thélaïre's pleas, he insists on returning to the underworld. In the face of such fraternal devotion, Jupiter relents and restores Castor without condition. [R]

Castrato

See panel on page 104

Castro, Juan José *(1895–1968)*

Argentinian composer and conductor. He wrote four operas: *La Zapatiera Prodigosa* (1943; libr. after Federico García Lorca), *Proserpina y el Extranjero* (Milan 1952), *Bodas de Sangre* (*Blood Wedding*, 1956; libr. after Lorca) and the unfinished and unperformed *Cosecha Negra* (1961), which was orchestrated by Eduardo Ogando.

Catalani, Alfredo *(1854–93)*

Italian composer, whose early death cut short a career of great promise. An admirer of Wagner and a friend of Boito, his operas are romantic in style but have an orchestral prominence unusual in Italian opera. His first opera *La Falce* (Milan 19 July 1875; libr. Arrigo Boito) was followed by *Elda* (1876), later revised as *Loreley**, *Dejanice* (Milan 17 March 1883; libr. Antonio Zanardini), *Edmea* (Milan 27 Feb 1886; libr. Antonio Ghislanzoni), which was successful in its time, and *La Wally**, by far his finest and most enduring work.

Cataline Conspiracy, The

Opera in two acts by Hamilton. 1st perf. Stirling, 16 March 1974; libr. by the composer. Principal roles: Cataline (bar), Cicero (ten), Fulvia (sop), Quintus (ten), Sempronia (mezzo), Crassus (bass), Aurelia (mezzo). Hamilton's first major opera to be performed, it is written in serial style but employs traditional operatic devices.

Plot: Rome, 64 BC. The unscrupulous Cataline gains patrician support for his election as consul as a step towards overthrowing the republic and establishing a personal dictatorship. He is defeated in the election, however, by the democrat Cicero, on whom he vows to take revenge. He forms a secret conspiracy which is betrayed by Quintus by way of Fulvia, and is expelled after Cicero exposes him in the senate. He leads a rebel army against Rome but is killed in battle. The republic is thus preserved.

Catalogue Aria

Bass-baritone aria ('Madamina') for Leporello in Act I of Mozart's *Don Giovanni*.

See also Aria di Catalogo

CASTRATO

The castrato was a eunuch male singer, whose sexual organs were 'modified' before puberty to preserve and develop a soprano or contralto vocal range: hence the terms 'male soprano' and 'male alto'. The word is derived from the Italian *castrare*, 'to castrate'. An alternative term occasionally encountered is *evirato*, from the Italian *evirare*, 'to emasculate'.

The voice first appeared in the 17th century in church choirs, when boys were regularly castrated to preserve their voices. The Roman Catholic Church condoned the practice on the grounds that St Paul in one of his epistles had enjoined that women should remain silent in church. Castrati soon made their appearance in opera, and in the late Baroque they were perhaps the most important singers: their voices were more powerful, rich and flexible than women's and the sheer unnaturalness of them epitomised the artificiality of opera at the time. By the early 19th century, a more humane age had come to appreciate the barbarity of the practice, and it was finally made illegal – Rossini only just escaped the indignity. The last major composers to write roles for castrati were Rossini himself and Meyerbeer in the early 1820s, by which time the voice was already considered strange and somehow unpleasant. The very last professional castrato was Alessandro Moreschi (1858–1922), whose voice is preserved on records, but he never appeared in opera.

In later years, roles which had been written for castrati were either transposed for tenors or were taken by sopranos or mezzos *in travesti*. More recently, many of these roles have been sung by counter-tenors, who produce a similar (if far less powerful) sound without recourse to the surgeon's knife.

The following six castrati, all Italian, have entries in this dictionary:

Caffarelli	Guadagni, Gaetano	Senesino
Farinelli	Nicolini	Velutti, Giovanni Battista

Catania

See Teatro Massimo Bellini, Catania

Caterina Cornaro

Opera in prologue and two acts by Donizetti. 1st perf. Naples, 12 Jan 1844; libr. by Giacomo Sacchero, after Jules-Henri Vernoy de Saint-Geroges' libretto for Halévy's *La Reine de Chypre*. Principal roles: Caterina (sop), Gerardo (ten), Lusignano (bar), Mocenigo (bass), Andreas (bass). Donizetti's last opera, it contains some fine music but is infrequently performed.

Plot: Caterina, daughter of Andreas, is to marry the young Frenchman Gerardo, but the marriage is postponed when Mocenigo reports that Lusignano, King of Cyprus, wishes to marry Caterina. After a great deal of intrigue, which includes the slow poisoning of Lusignano by Mocenigo, Gerardo joins the Knights of the Cross to help Lusignano defend Cyprus against Venice. Lusignano is fatally wounded and dies commending the Cypriots to Caterina's care whilst Gerardo returns to Rhodes.

Cauldron of Annwn, The

Operatic trilogy by Holbrooke (Op 53, 56 and 75). A setting of Lord Howard de Walden's dramatic poem based on the *Mabinogion*, the three operas are *The Children of Don* (London 1912), *Dylan, Son of the Wave* (London 1913) and *Bronwen* (1929). A vast Wagnerian-style work based on Celtic mythology, it is a cycle of considerable imaginative power and does not deserve the total obscurity into which it has fallen.

Cavalieri, Emilio de' *(c 1550–1602)*

Italian composer. A member of the Florentine Camerata*, his *La Rappresentazione di Anima e di Corpo** is a sacred stage oratorio and perhaps the most important 'proto-opera'.

Cavalieri, Lina *(b Natalina) (1874–1944)*

Italian soprano, particularly associated with Italian and French lyric roles. Said to have been one of the most beautiful women ever to appear in opera, her colourful life moved from childhood deprivation, through a liaison with a Russian prince, to operatic failure and then triumph, four marriages, tokens of royal esteem (many of them running to several carats), and starring in films (including *Manon Lescaut*) to her death in an air raid. She created L'Ensoleillad in Massenet's *Chérubin*. Her autobiography, *Le Mie Verità*, was published in 1936, and she was the subject of a film biography, *La Donna più Bella del Mondo* starring Gina Lollobrigida, which was made in 1957.

Cavalieri di Ekebù, I

Opera in four acts by Zandonai. 1st perf. Milan, 7 March 1925; libr. by Arturo Rossato, after Selma Lagerlöf's *Gösta Berlings Saga*. Principal roles: Berling (ten), Comandante (mezzo), Anna (sop), Cristiano (bar). One of Zandonai's best works, it was

successful in its time but is today rarely performed.

Cavalleria Rusticana *(Rustic Chivalry)*

Opera in one act by Mascagni. 1st perf. Rome, 17 May 1890; libr. by Giovanni Targioni-Tozzetti and Guido Menasci, after Giovanni Verga's play. Principal roles: Santuzza (sop), Turiddù (ten), Alfio (bar), Lola (mezzo), Mamma Lucia (mezzo). By far Mascagni's best known work, it was the winner of a competition organised by the publishers, Sonzogno, for a one-act opera. An instant success, it has remained ever since one of the most popular of all operas. Marking the advent of the verismo style in Italian opera, it is almost invariably coupled with Leoncavallo's *Pagliacci*: affectionately known as 'Cav' and 'Pag', the two are also sometimes referred to as the 'heavenly twins'.

Plot: Sicily. The soldier Turiddù has returned from war to find that his love Lola has married the village carter Alfio. After a brief fling with Santuzza, who is expecting his child, he restarts his affair with Lola. Santuzza begs him not to abandon her, but when he scornfully rejects her she reveals the entire story to Alfio. Alfio challenges Turiddù to a duel by the Sicilian custom of biting his ear. Turiddù bids goodbye to his mother Mamma Lucia and goes to face Alfio, who kills him, leaving Santuzza wracked with grief. [R]

Cavalli, Pier Francesco *(b Caletti-Bruni) (1602–76)*

Italian composer. He wrote over 40 operas, of which 28 are still extant. For nearly 300 years, Cavalli was little more than a name in the history books, but with the recent revival of interest in early music many of his operas have been staged in recent years, some of them frequently. His operas lack the dramatic power and insight of Monteverdi, but contain much beautiful and charming music. Most modern performances are given in realisations by Raymond Leppard or Jane Glover, the latter being the more scrupulous observer of Cavalli's intentions. His first opera was *Le Nozze di Teti e di Peleo* (Venice 24 Jan 1639; libr. O. Persiani). Of its successors, the most important are *L'Egisto**, *L'Ormindo**, *Giasone* (Venice 5 Jan 1649; libr. Giacinto Andrea Cicognini) [R], the most successful of his operas in his lifetime, *Rosinda* (Venice 1651; libr. Giovanni Battista Faustini), *La Calisto**, *Eritrea* (Venice 1652; libr. Faustini), *Serse**, *L'Erismena**, *Ercole Amante** and *Scipione Affricano* (Venice 9 Feb 1664; libr. Nicolò Minato).

Cavaradossi, Mario

Tenor role in Puccini's *Tosca*. He is a Republican painter in love with Tosca.

Cavatina (diminutive of the Italian *cavata*, meaning 'extraction')

In 18th-century opera, a cavata was a short arioso at the end of a recitative, the melody being 'carved out' of the preceding music. The diminutive form describes an 18th- or 19th-century single-part aria in relatively simple style.

Cebotari, Maria *(1910–49)*

Russian soprano, particularly associated with Mozart and Strauss roles. Her attractive voice was matched by a delightful stage presence, and her tragically early death robbed the immediate postwar era of one of its finest light lyric sopranos. She created Aminta in *Die Schweigsame Frau*, Julia in Sutermeister's *Romeo und Julia*, Lucille in Einem's *Dantons Tod* and Iseut in Martin's *Le Vin Herbé*.

Cecil

The English statesman Sir Robert Cecil (1563–1612) appears as a baritone role in: (1) Donizetti's *Maria Stuarda*. (2) Britten's *Gloriana*.

Cecilia

Opera in three acts by Refice. 1st perf. Rome, 15 Feb 1934; libr. by E. Mucci. Refice's finest opera, described as an *azione sacra*, it tells of the legend of St Cecilia (the patron saint of music) and Valerian, and of the former's martyrdom.

Celeste Aida

Tenor aria for Radamès in Act I of Verdi's *Aida*.

Cellier, Alfred *(1844–91)*

British composer and conductor. He wrote many operettas, some of which enjoyed considerable success in their day. They include *Nell Gwynne* (Manchester 16 Oct 1876; libr. H. B. Farnie), later revised as the highly successful *Dorothy**, *The Spectre Knight* (London 9 Feb 1878; libr. James Albery) and *The Mountebanks* (London 4 Jan 1892; libr. W. S. Gilbert), which was produced posthumously. As a conductor, he prepared many of the Savoy Operas for their first performances and arranged several of the overtures. His brother François (*d* 1914) was also a conductor, closely associated with Sullivan's stage works.

Cena delle Beffe, La (*The Jesters' Supper*)

Opera in four acts by Giordano. 1st perf. Milan, 20 Dec 1924; libr. by Sem Benelli, after his play. Principal roles: Ginevra (sop), Gabriello (ten), Neri (bar), Giannetto (ten). One of the most unpleasant and sadistic of all verismo pieces, it enjoyed some success at its appearance but is now very rarely performed.

Plot: 15th-century Florence. Giannetto is brutally treated by the brothers Neri and Gabriello because he is in love with Neri's mistress Ginevra. Giannetto manoeuvres Neri into killing his own brother, who is revealed as another of Ginevra's lovers.

Cendrillon (Cinderella)

Opera in four acts by Massenet. 1st perf. Paris, 24 May 1899; libr. by Henri Cain after Charles Perrault's version of the fairy-tale. Principal roles: Cendrillon (mezzo), Prince (sop), La Fée (sop), Pandolfe (bar), Haltière (mezzo), Noémie (sop), Dorothée (mezzo), King (ten). After a long period of neglect, Massenet's charming if somewhat stickily romantic setting of the story is now regularly performed. [R]

Cenerentola, La (Cinderella) or La Bontà in Trionfo

(Goodness Triumphant)

Comic opera in two acts by Rossini. 1st perf. Rome, 25 Jan 1817; libr. by Jacopo Ferretti, after Charles-Guillaume Étienne's libretto for Isouard's Cendrillon, itself based on Charles Perrault's version of the fairy-tale. Principal roles: Cenerentola (mezzo), Don Ramiro (ten), Don Magnifico (bass), Dandini (bar), Alidoro (bass), Tisbe (sop), Clorinda (mezzo). Purged of the supernatural which Rossini so disliked, it is one of the greatest of all opera buffas, and is Rossini's only comedy to contain moments of genuine pathos.

Plot: Angelina, known as Cenerentola, is maltreated by her stepfather, Don Magnifico, and her nasty stepsisters, Tisbe and Clorinda. The family is awaiting the arrival of the prince Don Ramiro, who is searching

for a bride. Ramiro arrives, disguised as his own valet Dandini, meets Cenerentola and falls in love with her. Dandini, disguised as his master, is fawned over by the rest of the family. Ramiro's tutor, the philosopher Alidoro, knows of Cenerentola's goodness and arranges for her to attend a ball where she dazzles everybody. Before she leaves she gives Ramiro one of the pair of bracelets which Alidoro has given her. The next day, Ramiro finds her at her home, recognises her although she is in rags, matches the bracelet and insists on marrying her. She ascends the throne, a Princess, and forgives the cruelty of her family. [R]

Ceprano, Count

Bass comprimario role in Verdi's Rigoletto. He is a courtier.

Cerquetti, Anita (b 1931)

Italian soprano who enjoyed a short but brilliant career playing leading dramatic roles, such as Gioconda, in the Italian repertory.

Cervantes, Miguel

See panel on page 108

Cesti, Pietro Antonio (1623–69)

Italian composer. With Cavalli, he ranks as the most important of Monteverdi's successors and, like Cavalli, his music was long forgotten, but a number of his works have been revived in recent years. His 11 operas are Orontea*, Cesare Amante (Venice 1651; libr. D. Varotari), Alessandro il Vincitor (Venice 1651; libr. Francesco Sbarra), L'Argia (Innsbruck 1655; libr. G. F. Apolloni), La Magnanimità d'Alessandro (Innsbruck 1662; libr. Sbarra), Il Tito (Venice 1666; libr. N. Beregan), Nettuno e Flora (Vienna July 1666; libr. Sbarra), the spectacular Il Pomo d'Oro*, La Disgrazie d'Amore

MIGUEL CERVANTES

The Spanish writer Miguel de Cervantes Saavedra (1547–1616) himself appears as a character in a number of works, including J. Strauss's *Das Spitzenbuch der Königin*. His works, especially *Don Quixote*, have inspired over 100 operas and zarzuelas. Below are listed, by work, those operas by composers with entries in this dictionary.

La Cueva de Salamanca

Winter	*Der Bettelstudent*	1785

Don Quixote

Caldara	*Sancio Panza*	1733
Piccinni	*Il Curioso*	1756
Telemann	*Don Quichotte der Löwenritter*	1761
Philidor	*Sancho Pança Dans Son Isle*	1762
Paisiello	*Don Quixote*	1769
Salieri	*Don Chisciotte alle Nozze di Gamace*	1770
Dittersdorf	*Don Quixote der Zweyte*	1779
Mendelssohn	*Die Hochzeit des Camacho*	1827
Mercadante	*Don Chisciotte*	1829
MacFarren	*An Adventure of Don Quixote*	1846
Hervé	*Don Quichotte et Sancho Pança*	1848
Kienzl	*Don Quixote*	1898
Chapí	*La Venta di Don Quijote*	1902
Heuberger	*Don Quixote*	1910
Massenet	*Don Quichotte*	1910
Ábrányi	*Don Quixote*	1917
de Falla	*El Retablo de Maese Pedro*	1923
Frazzi	*Don Chisciotte*	1952

La Fuerza de la Sangre

Auber	*Léocadie*	1824

La Gitanilla

Balfe	*The Bohemian Girl*	1843

Los Habladores

Offenbach	*Les Bavards*	1862

La Numancia

Barraud	*Numance*	1955

El Viejo Celoso

Petrassi	*Il Cordovano*	1949

(Vienna 19 Feb 1667; libr. Sbarra) and *Semirami* (Vienna 9 July 1667; libr. G. A. Moniglia).

C'est une chanson d'amour
Soprano/tenor duet for Antonia and Hoffmann in the Antonia Act of Offenbach's *Les Contes d'Hoffmann*.

Chabrier, Emmanuel *(1841–94)*
French composer and pianist. He wrote a number of stage works, but completed only four of them. Composed in various styles, his operas are notable for their sparkling melodies, brilliant orchestration and sharp sense of characterisation. His first two stage works were unfinished operettas, both with libretti by his friend Paul Verlaine: *Fisch-Ton-Kan* (Paris 22 April 1941, composed 1863) and *Vaucochard et Fils Premier* (Paris 22 April 1941, composed 1864). Next came an unfinished opera *Jean Hunyade* (1867; libr. H. Fouquier), much of which he re-used in later works. His first completed operas were the comedies *L'Etoile** and *Une Education Manquée**. Coming under the spell of Wagner, he then wrote the heroic *Gwendoline**. It was followed by the comedy *Le Roi Malgré Lui**, perhaps his most successful work. He completed only one act of his last opera *Briséis* (Paris 8 May 1899; libr. Catulle Mendès and Georges Ephraim Michel, after Goethe's *Die Braut von Corinth*).

A man of wide artistic tastes, he was one of the first to appreciate the Impressionist school of painting; he was a personal friend of Manet and possessed one of the finest private collections of Impressionist paintings.

Chaconne (once called Chacony in Britain)
A piece of music, either vocal or instrumental and originally for dancing, in slow three-beat time in which a single theme is repeated again and again in the bass. An operatic example is 'When I am laid in earth' in Purcell's *Dido and Aeneas*.

Chacun le sait
Soprano aria for Marie in Act I of Donizetti's *La Fille du Régiment*.

Chagall, Marc *(1887–1985)*
Russian painter and designer. One of the greatest 20th-century artists, he undertook a number of operatic designs, most notably for *Die Zauberflöte* at the Metropolitan Opera, New York in 1967. He also designed the murals for the ceiling of the Paris Opéra and for the foyer of the new Metropolitan Opera at Lincoln Center.

Chailly, Luciano *(b 1920)*
Italian composer. His operas have met with some success in Italy but have not been performed elsewhere. They are: *Ferrovia Sopra e Levata* (Bergamo 1955; libr. Dino Buzzati), *Una Domanda di Matrimonio* (Milan 1957; libr. C. Fino and S. Bertone after Anton Chekhov's *The Proposal*), *Il Canto del Cigno* (Bologna 1957; libr. composer after Chekhov's *Swan Song*), *La Riva delle Sirti* (Monte Carlo 1959; libr. R. Prinzhofer after Gracq), *Procedura Penale* (Como 1959; libr. Buzzati), *Il Mantello* (Florence 1960; libr. Buzzati), *Era Proibito* (Milan 1963; libr. Buzzati), *Vassiliev* (Genoa 1967; libr. composer, after Chekhov's *The Crisis*), *Markheim* (Spoleto 1967; libr. Prinzhofer after Robert Louis Stevenson), *L'Idiota* (Rome 1970; libr. G. Loverso, after Fyodor Dostoyevsky's *The Idiot*), *Sogno, Ma Forse No* (Trieste 1974) and *Il Libro dei Reclami* (1975). He was artistic director of La Scala, Milan (1968–71) and the Teatro

Regio, Turin (1972). His son is the conductor Riccardo Chailly*.

Chailly, Riccardo (b 1953)

Italian conductor. Son of the composer Luciano Chailly*, he is one of the leading Italian conductors of the younger generation, and is particularly associated with the operas of Verdi and Rossini. Musical director of the Teatro Communale, Bologna (1986–).

Chalabala, Zdeněk (1899–1962)

Czech conductor, particularly connected with the Czech and Russian repertories. One of the finest postwar Czech conductors, he was musical director of the Ostrava Opera (1945–47), the Brno Opera (1949–52), the Bratislava Opera (1952–53) and the Prague National Theatre (1953–62). His wife Běla Ruzumová (b 1903) was a successful coloratura soprano.

Chaliapin, Fyodor (1873–1938)

Russian bass, and a major exponent of the Russian repertory. Sometimes regarded as the greatest of all basses, he had a magisterial voice of great power and range, and was a well-nigh unrivalled singing-actor. His portrayals, especially of Boris, exerted a strong influence on subsequent generations of singers. He created the title role in Massenet's Don Quichotte and Salieri in Rimsky-Korsakov's Mozart and Salieri, and also made two films: Tsar Ivan the Terrible (1915) and Don Quixote (1933). His two volumes of autobiography, Pages From My Life and Man and Mask, were published in 1927 and 1932 and he also wrote a biography of Maxim Gorky.

Chamber opera

A loose term signifying an opera written for small forces for performance in small theatres. The 18th-century intermezzi fall into this category, and many chamber operas have been written in the 20th century by composers such as Britten and Holst.

Champagne Aria

Baritone aria ('Finch' han dal vino') for the Don in Act I of Mozart's Don Giovanni. The name has no relevance whatsoever to the subject matter of the aria, but for some reason it has become the standard way of referring to it.

Chanson de la Puce (Song of the Flea)

Bass aria for Méphistophélès in Part II of Berlioz's La Damnation de Faust.

Chapí y Lorente, Ruperto (1851–1909)

Spanish composer. He wrote eight operas, including Las Naves de Cortés (Madrid 19 April 1874), Roger de Flor (Madrid 25 Jan 1878) and La Bruja (Madrid 10 Dec 1887), which show the influence of Massenet. His reputation rests chiefly, however, on his 155 zarzuelas, many of which remain popular in Spain. The most successful include El Milagro de la Virgen (1884; libr. M. Pina Domínguez), Las Hijas del Zebedo (Madrid 1889; libr. J. Estremera), Las Bravías (Madrid 12 Dec 1896; libr. Carlos Fernández Shaw and J. López Silva, after Shakespeare's The Taming of the Shrew), La Revoltosa (Madrid 25 Nov 1897; libr. Fernández Shaw and López Silva) [R], his most popular work, La Chavala (Madrid 23 Oct 1898) and La Patria Chica (Nov 1907).

Charlotte

Mezzo role in Massenet's Werther. She is Albert's fiancée and the Bailie's eldest daughter.

Charpentier, Gustave (1860–1956)

French composer who brought elements of verismo into French opera and whose works show his socialist leanings. His first opera *Didon* (1887; libr. A. de Lassus) was followed by *Le Couronnement de la Muse* (Paris 1898) and the sensationally successful *Louise**, on which his reputation rests. *Julien**, a follow-up to the story, was a complete failure.

Charpentier, Marc-Antoine (1636–1704)

French composer. He wrote 17 operas, many of which enjoyed great success. Subsequently, they lay long forgotten, but there has recently been a considerable revival of interest in his stage works. His operas include *Le Malade Imaginaire* (1673; libr. Molière), *Les Amours d'Acis et de Galatée* (1678), *Endimion* (1681), *Andromède* (1682; libr. Pierre Corneille), *Actéon* (1683) [R], the magnificent *David et Jonathas** and his masterpiece *Médée**.

Chausson, Ernest (1855–99)

French composer. Best known as an orchestral composer, he also wrote three operas. They are *Les Caprices de Marianne* (1882; libr. after Alfred de Musset), *Hélène* (1884; libr. after Leconte de Lisle) – neither of which has ever been performed – and *Le Roi Arthus**. He also helped to complete Franck's unfinished *Ghisèle*.

Che farò senza Euridice

Mezzo aria for Orfeo in Act III of Gluck's *Orfeo ed Euridice*.

Che gelida manina

Tenor aria for Rodolfo in Act I of Puccini's *La Bohème*.

Ch'ella mi creda

Tenor aria for Dick Johnson in Act III of Puccini's *La Fanciulla del West*.

Chelsea Opera Group

Founded in 1950 by Sir Colin Davis and others, it gives concert performances, mainly in London and the home counties, with amateur orchestra and chorus and professional soloists.

Che puro ciel

Mezzo aria for Orfeo in Act II of Gluck's *Orfeo ed Euridice*.

Chéreau, Patrice (b 1944)

French producer. His highly controversial and radically 'deconstructionist' productions are epitomised by the Bayreuth centenary *Ring* of 1976. He directed the première of the three-act version of *Lulu* in Paris in 1979.

Chère enfant que j'appelle

Soprano/mezzo/bass trio for Antonia, the spirit of the Mother and Dr Miracle in the Antonia Act of Offenbach's *Les Contes d'Hoffmann*.

Cherry Duet

Soprano/tenor duet ('Suzel, buon dì') for Suzel and Fritz in Act II of Mascagni's *L'Amico Fritz*.

Chérubin

Opera in three acts by Massenet. 1st perf. Monte Carlo, 14 Feb 1905; libr. by Henri Cain and Francis de Croisset. Principal roles: Chérubin (sop), Nina (mezzo), L'Ensoleillad (sop), Philosopher (bar). Telling of the subsequent doings of Beaumarchais' Cherubino, it has never been one of

Massenet's more popular operas and is rarely performed.

Cherubini, Luigi *(1760–1842)*

Italian composer. He wrote 25 operas, beginning with *Il Quinto Fabio* (Alessandria 1779; libr. Apostolo Zeno). His next 12 works were unremarkable opera serias, mainly to Metastasian texts, his mature style developing when he moved to Paris in 1788. His later operas, beginning with *Démophon* (Paris 2 Dec 1788; libr. Jean-François Marmontel) mark the foundation both of French grand opera and of romantic opera in general. His mature works are noted for their complex ensembles, rich orchestration, dramatic effects and for the nobility and beauty of the vocal writing. The unfinished *Marguerite d'Anjou* (1790) was followed by his first major work *Lodoïska**, the once popular *Eliza* (Paris 13 Dec 1794; libr. J. A. de Reveroni Saint-Cyr) and his masterpiece *Médée**. There followed *L'Hôtellerie Portugaise* (Paris 25 July 1898; libr. E. Aignan), *Le Punition* (Paris 23 Feb 1799; libr. J. L. B. Desfaucherets), *La Prisonnière* (Paris 12 Sept 1799; libr. Victor Joseph Étienne de Jouy, Charles de Longchamps and Claude Godard d'Aucour de Saint-Just), which was written in collaboration with Boïeldieu, *Les Deux Journées**, *Epicure* (Paris 14 March 1800; libr. C. A. Demoustier), *Anacréon**, *Faniska* (Vienna 25 Feb 1806; libr. Josef Sonnleithner), *Pimalione* (Paris 30 Nov 1809; libr. S. Vestris, after Jean-Jacques Rousseau), *Le Crescendo* (Paris 30 Sept 1810; libr. C. A. Sewrin), *Les Abencérages** and *Ali Baba* (Paris 22 July 1833; libr. Eugène Scribe and Anne-Honoré Joseph de Mélesville after *The Arabian Nights*).

Cherubini's influence on the subsequent development of opera was enormous. Beethoven regarded him more highly than any other composer, and he had a strong influence on Weber, Wagner, Spontini and many French composers including Auber. He was an austere and somewhat pedantic director of the Paris Conservatory (1821–41).

Cherubino

Soprano trouser-role in Mozart's *Le Nozze di Figaro*. He is an amorous pageboy in the Almaviva household. The role is frequently sung by a mezzo. His subsequent career is the subject of Massenet's *Chérubin*.

Chest voice

The lowest of the three vocal registers, below 'middle' and 'head' and the richest in tone. It is often overindulged, particularly by dramatic mezzos.

Cheti, cheti

Baritone/bass duet for Dr Malatesta and Pasquale in Act III of Donizetti's *Don Pasquale*. Perhaps the greatest of all buffo duets.

Cheval de Bronze, Le *(The Bronze Horse)*

Opera in three acts by Auber. 1st perf. Paris, 23 March 1835; libr. by Eugène Scribe. Principal roles: Yang (ten), Tsing Sing (bass), Peki (sop), Stella (sop). Very successful in its time, nowadays only the famous overture is remembered. The score is notable for Auber's 'oriental' touches.

Plot: China. The mandarin Tsing Sing is turned to stone by one of his wives. Another wife, Peki, flies on the magical bronze horse to seek the help of the fairy princess Stella. Stella gives Peki a magic bracelet with which to break the spell. She does so on condition that the mandarin divorces her, thus freeing her to marry her true love, the farmer Yang.

Chevrotement
A French term for Goat's Trill or Bleat*.

Chiara, Maria *(b 1939)*
Italian soprano, particularly associated with Verdi and Puccini roles. One of the leading Italian sopranos of the 1970s, she possessed an attractively smooth voice used with fine musicianship.

Chicago Lyric Opera
One of the leading American opera companies, it was founded in 1954 by Carol Fox, who was its administrator until her death in 1981. The repertory tends to be traditional, with an emphasis on Italian works. The annual season runs from Sept to Feb, and performances are given at the Civic Opera House (cap. 3,636). Musical directors have included Bruno Bartoletti.

Children's operas
Although there were companies of child performers in the 18th century, especially in Austria, it is really only in the 20th century that operas have been specifically written for casts of children. Britten, Williamson, Bennett, Crosse, Menotti, Fortner, Hindemith, Milhaud, Copland and Cui all wrote stage works for children.

Chile
See Teatro Municipal, Santiago

Chilean opera composers
These include Pablo Garrido Vargas (*b* 1905) and Juan Orrego Salas (*b* 1919).

Chimène
Mezzo role in Massenet's *Le Cid*. She is Count Gormas's daughter.

Chi mi frena
Soprano/mezzo/tenor/tenor/baritone/bass sextet for Lucia, Alisa, Edgardo, Arturo, Enrico and Raimondo in Act II of Donizetti's *Lucia di Lammermoor*. One of the greatest ensembles in all opera.

Chisholm, Erik *(1904–65)*
British conductor, composer and musicologist. One of the leading British conductors of the inter-war period, he also wrote ten operas. They include *The Isle of Youth* (1941; libr. composer, after J. Stephens), *Simoon* (1953; libr. after August Strindberg), the trilogy *Murder in Three Keys* (New York 1954), *The Inland Woman* (Cape Town 1954; libr. after M. Lavin) and *The Pardoner's Tale* (1961; libr. after Geoffrey Chaucer's *The Canterbury Tales*). His writings include a book on Janáček.

Chocolate Soldier, The
See Tapfere Soldat, Der

Choëphores, Les
Opera in one act by Milhaud. 1st perf. Paris, 15 June 1919; libr. by Paul Claudel, after Aeschylus's *Oresteia*. Principal roles: Elektra (sop), Orestes (bar), Clytemnestra (sop). The second part of Milhaud's Aeschylean trilogy, it deals with the relationship between Elektra and Orestes. [R]

Chorebus
Baritone role in Berlioz's *Les Troyens*. He is a Trojan commander in love with Cassandra.

Chorley, Henry Fothergill *(1808–72)*
British critic. The leading British critic of his time, his *Thirty Years' Musical*

Recollections (1862) is a prime source of information about operatic life in London at the time. He also wrote the libretti for Sullivan's *The Sapphire Necklace* and Wallace's *The Amber Witch*.

Chorus (from the Greek Χορός, a festive dance, and thus also those who performed it)

In opera, chorus means either a group of singers who perform and sing as a single body, or the music written for it. Integral to French opera from its earliest days, the chorus became important in Italian opera only in the mid-18th century.

Chorus

Roles in Britten's *The Rape of Lucretia*; Male (ten) and Female (sop).

Christie, John *(1882–1962)*

Wealthy British patron of the opera. Married to the soprano Audrey Mildmay*, he founded and built the Glyndebourne Opera House in 1934 at his country seat in Sussex. His son George (*b* 1934) succeeded him as principal administrator.

Christmas Carol, A

Opera in two acts by Musgrave. 1st perf. Norfolk (Virginia), 7 Dec 1979; libr. by the composer after Charles Dickens' novel. Principal roles: Scrooge (bar), Belle (sop), Bob Cratchit (ten), Ben (bar), Mr Fezziwig (bass). One of Musgrave's most successful operas, which has been widely performed, the plot follows Dickens closely. [R]

Christmas Eve *(Notch Pered Rozhdestvom)*

Opera in four acts by Rimsky-Korsakov. 1st perf. St Petersburg, 10 Dec 1895; libr. by the composer, after Nikolai Gogol. Principal roles: Oksana (sop), Vakula (ten), Chub (bass), Solokha (mezzo), Devil (ten), Priest (ten), Panas (bass), Mayor (bar), Patsyuk (bass). Although it contains some delightful music, it has never been one of Rimsky's more popular works and is performed only rarely.

Plot: On Christmas Eve, the Devil and the witch Solokha decide to cause mischief by stealing the moon and whipping up a snow storm. The blacksmith Vakula comes to serenade Oksana, but bumps into the latter's father, Chub, in the storm and mistakes him for a rival. Oksana tells Vakula that she will marry him only if he brings her the empress's slippers as a present. At Solokha's cottage, the Devil, the Mayor, the Priest and Chub all arrive and hide in sacks so as not to be seen. Vakula carries them away and the villagers are highly entertained when they are opened. Vakula, still carrying one sack, visits the dumpling-eating medicine man Patsyuk to ask how to get the Devil's help in his quest. Patsyuk suggests he opens his sack, and Vakula forces the Devil whom he finds in it, to take him to St Petersburg. He acquires the slippers, but in his absence Oksana has decided that she loves him anyway.

Christoff, Boris *(b 1914)*

Bulgarian bass, particularly associated with the Italian and Russian repertories. A notable King Philip and an outstanding Boris Godunov, he was one of the finest singing-actors of the postwar era. His magnificent voice boasted a highly individual timbre, and his dramatic insight was remarkable. One of the truly great operatic artists, despite a temperament which many colleagues found difficult to work with.

Christophe Colomb

Opera in two parts by Milhaud (Op 102). 1st perf. Berlin, 5 May 1930; libr. by Paul Claudel. Principal roles: Columbus (bar), Queen Isabella (sop), King of Spain (bass), Narrator (speaker). The first work of Milhaud's so-called *New World Trilogy*, it is a religious allegory treating the events of Columbus' life in 27 short scenes connected by the use of a narrator, the chorus and film projections. Rarely peformed.

Christopher Columbus

Operetta in four acts by Offenbach. 1st perf. Belfast, 3 July 1976; libr. by Don White. Principal roles: Columbus (ten), Beatriz (sop), Rosa (mezzo), Fleurette (sop), Gretel (sop), Police Chief (bar), Luis de Torres (bar), Queen Isabella (sop), King Ferdinand (bar). A pastiche arranged by Patric Schmid of Opera Rara from 22 of Offenbach's forgotten operettas, it is an outrageous and riotously funny piece telling of Columbus' voyage to the Americas to discover Coca-Cola! [R]

Chrysothemis

Soprano role in Richard Strauss's *Elektra*. She is Elektra's sister.

Chueca, Federico *(1848–1908)*

Spanish composer. He wrote 37 zarzuelas, mostly in *Género chico* form. The most successful was *La Gran Vía* (Madrid 2 July 1886) [R], which was written in collaboration with Valverde and is one of the very few zarzuelas to have been performed in Britain.

Chukhadjian, Tigran *(1837–98)*

Armenian composer. The first Armenian composer to attempt a synthesis of Western musical styles with his national folk heritage, his ardent nationalism has ensured him a place in that tragic people's history. His operas are *Arshak II* (*Arshak Ekrod*, 1945, composed 1868), three comedies *Arif* (Constantinople 1872; libr. H. Atjemian), *The Balding Elder* (*Kyose Kyokhava*, 1873) and *The Chick-Pea Seller* (*Leblebidji*, Constantinople 1876; libr. T. Nalian), the fairy-tale *Zemire* (1880) and *Indiana* (1897).

Church Parable

Britten's term to describe his three short operas written for very small forces and designed for church performance: *Curlew River**, *The Burning Fiery Furnace** and *The Prodigal Son**.

Ciboletta

Soprano role in J. Strauss's *Eine Nacht in Venedig*. She is Pappacoda's fiancée.

Ciboulette

Operetta in three acts by Hahn. 1st perf. Paris, 7 April 1923; libr. by Robert de Flers and Francis de Croisset. Principal roles: Ciboulette (sop), Antonin (ten), Duparquet (bar), Zénobie (mezzo). By far Hahn's most successful work, it is still performed from time to time. [R]

Cid, Le

Opera in four acts by Massenet. 1st perf. Paris, 30 Nov 1885; libr. by Adolphe Philippe d'Ennery, Louis Gallet and Edouard Blau after Pierre Corneille's play. Principal roles: Don Rodrigue (ten), Chimène (mezzo), Don Diègue (bass), Count Gormas (bass). An essay in Meyerbeerian grand opera, it is one of Massenet's most heroic and exciting scores. It was an immediate success, but is nowadays only occasionally performed.

Plot: 12th-century Seville. To avenge the honour of his father Don Diègue,

Rodrigue, known as 'The Cid', reluctantly fights a duel with Count Gormas, the father of his beloved Chimène. Gormas is killed, and Chimène is torn between her love and the honour of her family. Rodrigue fights heroically against the Moors, and when he returns he and Chimène are reconciled. [R]

La Cieca

Mezzo role in Ponchielli's *La Gioconda*. She is Gioconda's blind mother.

Cielo e mar

Tenor aria for Enzo in Act II of Ponchielli's *La Gioconda*.

Cigna, Gina *(b Ginetta Sens) (b 1900)*

Italian soprano. The leading Italian dramatic soprano of the inter-war period, she was especially famous as Turandot and Gioconda. She was forced to retire in 1948 after being seriously injured in a car accident.

Cikker, Ján *(1911–90)*

Czech composer. The leading contemporary Slovak composer, his operas in post-romantic style have met with success in both Czechoslovakia and elsewhere. His operas are the nationalist *Juro Jánošík* (1954), *Mr Scrooge* (1963, composed 1954; libr. after Charles Dickens's *A Christmas Carol*), the nationalist *Prince Bajazid* (*Beg Bajazid*, 1957), *Resurrection* (*Vzkriesenie*, 1962; libr. after Tolstoy), *The Play of Love and Death* (*Hra o Láske a Smrti*, Munich 1969; libr. after Romain Rolland) and *Coriolanus* (1973; libr. after Shakespeare) [R].

Cilea, Francesco *(1866–1950)*

Italian composer. One of the leading verismo composers, his operas are notable for their somewhat cloying charm, but are largely innocent of any dramatic insight. His first opera *Gina* (Naples 9 Feb 1889; libr. Enrico Golisciani) was followed by *La Tilda* (Florence 7 April 1892; libr. Antonio Zanardini), the successful *L'Arlesiana**, *Adriana Lecouvreur**, his finest and most enduring work, *Gloria* (Milan 15 April 1907; libr. Arturo Colautti) and the unperformed *Il Matrimonio Selvaggio* (1909; libr. G. di Bognasco).

Cimarosa, Domenico *(1749–1801)*

Italian composer. He wrote 63 operas, winning especial renown in comedy, in which field he was compared in his day to Mozart. His comedies are notable for their pace and vivacity, their delightful melodies and their deft orchestration. His serious operas, whilst musically solid, are dramatically somewhat cold and formal. The most successful of his works include *Il Fanatico per gli Antichi Romani* (Naples 1777; libr. Giovanni Palomba), *L'Italiana in Londra* (Rome 28 Dec 1778; libr. Giuseppe Petrosellini), *Il Pittor Parigino* (Rome 1781; libr. Petrosellini) [R], *I Due Baroni di Rocca Azzurra* (Rome Feb 1783; libr. Palomba), *L'Olimpiade* (Vicenza 10 July 1784; libr. Pietro Metastasio), *Il Marito Disperato* (Naples 1785; libr. G. Lorenzi), *L'Impresario in Angustie* (Naples 1786; libr. Giuseppe Maria Diodati), the hilarious intermezzo *Il Maestro di Cappella**, his masterpiece *Il Matrimonio Segreto**, *I Traci Amanti* (Naples 19 June 1793; libr. Palomba), *Le Astuzie Femminili**, *Gli Orazi ed i Curiazi* (Venice 26 Dec 1796; libr. Antonio Sografi, after Pierre Corneille's *Horace*), perhaps his finest serious work, and *Artemesia* (Venice 1801; libr. G. B. Colloredo). He appears as a character in Isouard's *Cimarosa*.

Cincinnati Opera Association
The second oldest opera company in the United States, it was founded in 1920. Until 1974, it performed in the open air at the local zoo, and thereafter has been based at the Music Hall (cap. 3,632). It has a long reputation for fostering major talent, and is sometimes known as 'the cradle of American opera singers'. The annual season is held in June and July and the repertory is predominantly French and Italian.

Cinderella
See Cendrillon; Cenerentola, La

Cinq-Mars
Opera in four acts by Gounod. 1st perf. Paris, 5 April 1877; libr. by Paul Poirson and Louis Gallet after Alfred de Vigny's novel. Reasonably successful at its appearance, but now virtually forgotten.

Cinta di fiori
Bass aria for Giorgio in Act II of Bellini's *I Puritani*.

Cio-Cio-San
Soprano role in Puccini's *Madama Butterfly*. It is Butterfly's Japanese name.

Ciro in Babilonia (*Cyrus in Babylon*) or La Caduta di Baldassare
Opera in two acts by Rossini. 1st perf. Ferrara, 14 March 1812; libr. by Francesco Aventi. One of Rossini's earliest serious works, it is nowadays all but forgotten.

Claggart, John
Bass role in Britten's *Billy Budd*. He is the evil master-at-arms of H. M. S. Indomitable.

Claque (French for 'clap' or 'smack')
One of opera's least attractive features, the claque is a group in the audience paid by the management to get the applause going and to stimulate enthusiasm. It is also sometimes paid by singers to cheer them and to hiss their rivals. Its leader is called the *chef de claque* in France and the *capo di claque* in Italy. The phenomenon is virtually as old as opera itself, but it became an established institution only in the early 19th century in France and, very soon afterwards, in Italy. The claque members regard themselves as encouraging talent and high artistic standards: the story is often told of the Parma claque which, hired to cheer a visiting tenor, was so appalled by his singing that it refunded his money and hissed all his subsequent performances. The fun really starts when there are rival claques at the same performance: a clash between pro- and anti-Callas claques once led to a serious riot at the Paris Opéra. The claque is still very much a feature of operatic life in Italy, and also in Vienna. In Britain — whatever Italian singers who have been given a hostile reception may maintain to the contrary — the claque does not really exist.

Clarion
Mezzo role in Richard Strauss's *Capriccio*. She is an actress.

Claudel, Paul (*1868–1965*)
French poet and librettist. Closely linked to the Symbolist school, he provided libretti for Honegger (*Jeanne d'Arc au Bûcher*) and Milhaud (*Christophe Colomb*, *Saint Louis* and the *Orestie* trilogy). Rossellini's *L'Annonce Faite à Marie* is a setting of his verse-play.

Claudine von Villa Bella

Opera in three acts by Schubert (D 239). 1st perf. Vienna, 26 April 1913 (composed 1815); libr. by Goethe. Principal roles: Claudine (sop), Pedro (ten), Lucinda (sop), Carlos (ten), Alonzo (bass), Basco (bass). One of Schubert's early Singspiels, the music of Acts II and III was destroyed in a fire. The overture and Act I are occasionally given in concert.

Claudio

(1) Baritone role in Berlioz's *Béatrice et Bénédict* and tenor role in Stanford's *Much Ado About Nothing*. He is in love with Hero. (2) Tenor role in Wagner's *Das Liebesverbot*. He is Isabella's brother. (3) Bass role in Handel's *Agrippina*. He is the Roman Emperor Claudius.

Clement IX, Pope *(b Giulio Rospigliosi) (1600–69)*

Italian cleric, poet and librettist. A keen patron of letters and music, he provided the texts for Steffano Landi's *Il Santo Alessio* (1632), Abbatini's *Dal Male il Bene* (1653) and Marazzoli's *Chi Soffre, Speri* (Rome 27 Feb 1639), which is thought to be the first comic opera.

Clemenza di Tito, La *(The Clemency of Titus)*

Works about the Roman Emperor Titus (39–81 AD), all with libretti by or after Pietro Metastasio, include:

(1) Opera by Caldara. 1st perf. Vienna, 1734.

(2) Opera by Veracini. 1st perf. London, 12 April 1737; libr. adapted by Corri.

(3) Opera in three acts by Gluck. 1st perf. Naples, 4 Nov 1752.

(4) Opera in three acts by Jommelli. 1st perf. Stuttgart, 30 Aug 1753.

(5) Opera in three acts by Naumann. 1st perf. Dresden, 1 Feb 1769.

(6) Opera in three acts by Anfossi. 1st perf. Rome, 1769.

(7) Opera in two acts by Mozart (K 621). 1st perf. Prague, 6 Sept 1791; libr. adapted by Caterino Mazzolà. Principal roles: Tito (ten), Vitellia (sop), Sesto (mezzo), Annio (mezzo), Publio (bass), Servilia (sop). Mozart's last opera, it was very popular so long as opera seria itself remained so, but thereafter was almost forgotten. In recent years, however, it has once again been widely performed. Despite the stiff formality of its structure, it is a work of great dramatic power.

Plot: Rome, 79–81 AD. Furious that the Emperor Titus has decided to marry Berenice, Vitellia persuades her admirer Sextus to assassinate him, but Titus has a change of plan and decides, instead, to marry Servilia. When he learns that she loves Sextus's friend Annius, he withdraws and determines to marry Vitellia. Vitellia hears of this too late to stop Sextus's plot, but Titus escapes death. Sextus is arrested, tried and condemned to death, and Vitellia eventually confesses her part in the plot. In the end, Titus forgives both of them. [R]

Cleopatra

The Queen of Egypt (69–30 BC) appears in a number of operas, including soprano role in: (1) Handel's *Giulio Cesare*. (2) Barber's *Antony and Cleopatra*.

Cleva, Fausto *(1902–71)*

Italian conductor, working mainly in the United States and particularly associated with the Italian repertory. He was artistic director of the Chicago Opera (1944–46). He died whilst conducting *Orfeo ed Euridice* in Athens.

Cloches de Corneville, Les
(*The Bells of Corneville*)
Operetta in three acts by Planquette. 1st perf. Paris, 19 April 1877; libr. by Charles Gabet and Louis François Clairville. Principal roles: Serpolette (sop), Germaine (mezzo), Marquis (ten), Gaspard (bar), Bailie (ten), Gobo (ten). By far Planquette's most successful work, which enjoyed an initial run of 461 performances, it is still performed. [R]

Clorinda
Mezzo role in Rossini's *La Cenerentola*. She is one of the two ugly sisters.

Cluytens, André *(1905–67)*
Belgian conductor, particularly associated with the French repertory and with Wagner. He was mucial director of the Toulouse Opera (1932–35) and the Opéra-Comique, Paris (1947–49).

Clytemnestra
Agamemnon's husband and joint murderess appears in a number of operas, including: (1) Mezzo role in Richard Strauss's *Elektra*. (2) Mezzo role in Gluck's *Iphigénie en Aulide*. (3) Soprano role in Milhaud's *Les Choëphores*. (4) Mezzo role in Taneyev's *Oresteia*.

Coates, Albert *(1882–1953)*
British conductor and composer. One of the leading operatic conductors of his time, he was musical director of the Elberfeld Opera (1906–08) and the Maryinsky Theatre, St Petersburg (1912–17). He conducted the first performances of Quilter's *Julia* and Lloyd's *The Serf*. His operas include *Samuel Pepys* (Munich 1929), *Pickwick* (London 1936; libr. after Charles Dickens' *The Pickwick Papers*), which was the first opera to be televised, and *Von Hunks and His Devil* (Cape Town 1952).

Coates, Edith *(1908–83)*
British mezzo, long resident at Covent Garden. An impressive singing-actress, she created Auntie in *Peter Grimes*, Bardeau in Bliss' *The Olympians*, and roles in *Gloriana* and Grace Williams' *The Parlour*.

Coccia, Carlo *(1782–1873)*
Italian composer. He wrote many operas, all of them now long forgotten, enjoying his best success with opera semiseria. His most important works are *Il Poeto Fortunato* (Florence 1808), *Clotide* (Venice 8 June 1815), *Maria Stuarda* (London 7 June 1827) and *Caterina di Guisa* (Milan 14 Feb 1833). He was director of the Turin Conservatory (1836–40).

Cocteau, Jean *(1889–1963)*
French playwright and librettist. He wrote libretti for Honegger (*Antigone*), Milhaud (*Le Pauvre Matelot*), Poulenc (*La Voix Humaine*) and Stravinsky (*Oedipus Rex*), in which last he sometimes appeared as the Narrator.

Cola Rienzi, der Letzte der Tribunen
See Rienzi

Colas Breugnon
Sometimes mistakenly used as the title of Kabalevsky's opera (which is actually *The Master of Clamecy**), Colas Breugnon is both the main baritone role and the title of the overture.

Colbran, Isabella *(1785–1845)*
Spanish soprano, particularly associated
with Rossini roles. Regarded as the
finest dramatic coloratura soprano of
the early 19th century, she created, for
Rossini, Desdemona in *Otello*, Elena in
La Donna del Lago, Elcia in *Mosè in
Egitto*, Anna in *Maometto II* and the
title roles in *Elisabetta Regina
d'Inghilterra*, *Zelmira*, *Armida* and
Semiramide. She was the mistress of
both Domenico Barbaia* and the King
of Naples, but left both for Rossini,
whose first wife she became in 1822;
they were separated in 1837.

Colin
Tenor role in Rousseau's *Le Devin du
Village*. The name came to be a generic
term for a sentimental rustic lover in
18th- and 19th-century French opera.

Collatinus
Bass role in Britten's *The Rape of
Lucretia*. He is Lucretia's husband.

Colla voce (Italian for 'with the
voice')
An instruction to an instrument, or an
accompanist, to follow the voice
closely, especially in a passage in free
time.

Collier, Marie *(1926–71)*
Australian soprano, particularly
associated with Puccini and Janáček
roles, notably Tosca and Emilia Marty.
She possessed a vibrant but not flawless
voice and was a powerful – sometimes
almost flamboyant – singing-actress.
She created Hecuba in *King Priam* and
Christine Mannon in Levy's *Mourning
Becomes Electra*.

Colline
Bass role in Puccini's *La Bohème*. He is
the philosopher of the four bohemians.

Collingwood, Lawrence *(1887–
1982)*
British conductor and composer,
particularly associated with Sadler's
Wells Opera, of which he was musical
director (1940–46). He wrote two
operas: *Macbeth* (London 1934; libr.
after Shakespeare) and *The Death of
Tintagiles* (London 1950; libr. after
Maurice Maeterlinck's *La Mort de
Tintagiles*).

Cologne Opera (Köln in German)
The present opera house in this city in
North Rhine Westphalia is the Grosses
Haus (cap. 1,346), designed by Wilhelm
Riphahn and opened in 1957. It
replaced the previous building,
destroyed by bombs in 1943. One of
Germany's leading houses, with a long
tradition of the highest artistic
standards, it has recently been noted
for its Mozart productions. The annual
season runs from Sept to June. Musical
directors have included Emil Ábrányi,
Otto Lohse, Otto Klemperer, Eugene
Szenkar, Otto Ackermann, Wolfgang
Sawallisch, István Kertesz, Sir John
Pritchard and James Conlan.

Colombian opera composers
These include Luis Antonio Escóbar (*b*
1925), José María Ponce de León
(1846–82), whose *Ester* (Bogotá 12
July 1874) was the first Colombian
opera, and Guillermo Uribe-Holguín
(1880–1971).

Coloratura (from the German
Koloratur, 'colouring')
An elaborate and brilliant
ornamentation of the vocal line. The
Italian term *fioritura** means virtually
the same thing. It was originally called
canto figuraturo.

Coloratura mezzo

A mezzo who specialises in florid roles, such as many of those by Rossini. Famous coloratura mezzos have included Conchita Supervia and Marilyn Horne.

Coloratura soprano

A soprano who specialises in florid, highly ornamented singing, and who performs such roles as the Queen of the Night, Olympia, Lucia and Zerbinetta. Famous coloratura sopranos have included Amelita Galli-Curci, Selma Kurtz and Joan Sutherland.

Coltellini, Marco *(1719–77)*

Italian poet and librettist. He succeeded Pietro Metastasio as Court Poet in Vienna and later became official librettist in St Petersburg. He wrote some 20 libretti, many of which were used more than once. His texts were set by Bortnyansky, Galuppi, Gassmann (*La Contessina*), Gluck (*Telemaco*), Hasse, Haydn (*L'Infedeltà Delusa*), Mozart (*La Finta Semplice* and *La Finta Giardiniera*), Paisiello, Piccinni, Salieri (*Armida*), Sarti, D. Scarlatti (*Amleto*), Traetta (*Antigonae*) and Winter amongst others. His daughter, Celeste (1760–1828) was a successful mezzo who created the title role in Paisiello's *Nina*.

Combattimento di Tancredi e Clorinda, Il *(The Duel of Tancred and Clorinda)*

Dramatic cantata by Monteverdi. 1st perf. Venice, 1624. A setting of part of Torquato Tasso's *Gerusalemme Liberata*. Principal roles: Narrator (ten), Clorinda (mezzo), Tancredi (ten). Although not strictly speaking an opera, the work was intended to be performed by costumed singers, and has been regularly staged in recent years. In his preface to it, Monteverdi outlined some of his theories, particularly his innovative use of tremolo and pizzicato to heighten musico-dramatic tension. A seminal work in the development of music-drama.

Plot: During the Crusades, the Christian warrior Tancredi, in love with Clorinda, fights a duel with a Saracen wearing full armour. Only after the Saracen is killed does Tancredi discover that he is in fact Clorinda. [R]

Come dal ciel precipita

Bass aria for Banquo in Act II of Verdi's *Macbeth*.

Com'è gentil

Tenor aria for Ernesto in Act III of Donizetti's *Don Pasquale*.

Come in quest' ora bruna

Soprano aria for Amelia in Act I of Verdi's *Simon Boccanegra*.

Come Paride

Baritone aria for Belcore in Act I of Donizetti's *L'Elisir d'Amore*.

Come per me sereno

Soprano aria for Amina in Act I of Bellini's *La Sonnambula*.

Come scoglio

Soprano aria for Fiordiligi in Act I of Mozart's *Così fan Tutte*.

Come scrito (Italian for 'as written')

An instruction to a singer to perform the music exactly as it is written, without decoration and with no change in tempo.

Come un bel dì di maggio
Tenor aria for Chénier in Act IV of Giordano's *Andrea Chénier*.

Comedy on the Bridge
(*Veselohra na Moste*)
Comic opera in one act by Martinů. 1st perf. Czech radio, 18 March 1937; libr. by Václav Kliment Klicpera. Principal roles: Popelka (sop), Ján (bar), Eva (mezzo), Brewer (bass), Schoolmaster (ten). A brilliant satire on bureaucracy and war, it tells of events on a bridge joining friendly and enemy territory. [R]

Comic opera
A loose term, simply meaning an opera on a comic subject. The first comic opera is believed to have been Marazzoli's *Chi Soffre, Speri* of 1639, which has a libretto by the future Pope Clement IX. Many other terms refer to comic opera, but are more specific as regards style and structure.
See also Ballad opera; Burletta; Dramma giocoso; Farsa; Género chico; Intermezzo; Opéra-bouffe; Opera-buffa; Opéra-comique; Opera semiseria; Operetta; Sainete; Singspiel; Tonadilla; Zarzuela; Zauberoper

Comme autrefois
Soprano aria for Leïla in Act II of Bizet's *Les Pêcheurs de Perles*.

Commedia dell'Arte
A dramatic form of uncertain origin which flourished in Italy in the 16th and 17th centuries. It involved stock characters (Harlequin, Colombine, Pantaloon etc) and stock situations (cunning servants, scheming doctors, duped masters and the like). It had an enormous influence on the development of comic opera (*Il Barbiere di Siviglia* and *Don Pasquale*, for example, are both pure Commedia dell'Arte plots), and its conventions are used to powerful theatrical effect in *Pagliacci*. The early 20th century witnessed a considerable revival of interest in its use, its characters being the basis of *The Love of Three Oranges*, *Ariadne auf Naxos*, Mascagni's *Le Maschere* and Busoni's *Arlecchino* amongst others.

Commendatore
Bass role in Mozart's *Don Giovanni*. He is Donna Anna's father.

Competitions
Competitions have sometimes been held for new operas. They have included that organised by Offenbach in 1857 for a one-act opéra-comique (won jointly by Lecocq's and Bizet's *Le Docteur Miracle*), that of the Italian publishers Sonzogno in 1889 for a one-act opera (won by Mascagni's *Cavalleria Rusticana*), that for the Festival of Britain in 1951 (jointly won by Bush's *Wat Tyler*, Goldschmidt's *Beatrice Cenci*, Benjamin's *A Tale of Two Cities* and Karl Rankl's *Deirdre of the Sorrows*), and that by La Scala for the 1951 Verdi celebrations (jointly won by Napoli's *Masaniello* and Castro's *Proserpina y el Extranjero*).
See also Vocal competitions

Composer
Mezzo trouser-role in Richard Strauss's *Ariadne auf Naxos*.

Composer-librettists
Many composers have prefered to write their own libretti so as to ensure that the text provides them with exactly what they require. The most famous example is Wagner; other composers

who always (or nearly always) wrote their own libretti include Boito, Busoni, Cornelius, Dallapiccola, Floyd, Holst, Janáček, Klebe, Křenek, Leoncavallo, Lortzing, Lualdi, Menotti, Moussorgsky, Pizzetti, Tippett and Viozzi. A number of other composers occasionally provided their own libretti; those who did so successfully include Berlioz, Charpentier, Delius, Donizetti, Hindemith, Martinů, Orff, Prokofiev, Rimsky-Korsakov, Schönberg, R. Strauss and Tchaikovsky. In addition, Blacher, Boito, Egk and Menotti wrote libretti for other composers.

Composers in opera

The lives of a number of composers have been the subject of operatic treatment. Composers who appear as operatic characters include: (1) J. S. Bach in Ábrányi's *A Tamás Templon Karnagya*. (2) Chopin in Orefice's *Chopin*. (3) Cimarosa in Isouard's *Cimarosa*. (4) Haydn in Suppé's *Joseph Haydn*. (5) Lully in Grétry's *Les Trois Ages de l'Opéra* and Isouard's *Lully et Quinault*. (6) Mozart in Flotow's *Die Musikanten*, Rimsky-Korsakov's *Mozart and Salieri*, Hahn's *Mozart* and the Lortzing pastiche *Scenen aus Mozarts Leben*. (7) Paganini in Lehár's *Paganini*. (8) Palestrina in Pfitzner's *Palestrina*. (9) Rousseau in Dalayrac's *L'Enfance de Jean-Jacques Rousseau*. (10) Salieri in Rimsky-Korsakov's *Mozart and Salieri*. (11) Schubert in Suppé's *Franz Schubert*. (12) Stradella in Flotow's *Alessandro Stradella*. (13) Taverner in Maxwell Davies's *Taverner*.

Comprimario (Italian for 'with the principal')

A singer of secondary roles, such as confidantes, messengers, duennas and the like. Performing comprimario roles is not necessarily any less demanding than performing principal ones, and their contribution to an overall performance is crucial. Some famous comprimarios, such as Piero de Palma and Giuseppe Nessi, have been operatic artists of considerable stature.

Comte Ory, Le (*Count Ory*)

Comic opera in two acts by Rossini. 1st perf. Paris, 20 Aug 1828; libr. by Eugène Scribe and Delestre Poirson, after Pierre-Antoine de la Place. Principal roles: Ory (ten), Countess Adèle (sop), Isolier (mezzo), Tutor (bass), Raimbaud (bar), Ragonde (mezzo), Alice (sop). Rossini's last and most sophisticated comic work, it incorporates much music from his earlier *Il Viaggio a Reims**.

Plot: Touraine during the Crusades. Countess Adèle, Ragonde, and their companions have taken a vow of chastity whilst their menfolk are away on the Crusades. The amorous Count Ory, aided and abetted by his Tutor, his page Isolier and his friend Raimbaud, lays siege to the Countess, disguising himself first as a curer of love-sickness and secondly as a journeying nun. The 'nuns' get uproariously drunk and escape only just in time as the ladies' menfolk return. [R]

Concepción

Mezzo role in Ravel's *L'Heure Espagnole*. She is Torquemada's flirtatious wife.

Conductor

See panel on page 124

Confession Scene

The title of Act III, Scene II of Donizetti's *Maria Stuarda*, in which Mary confesses to Talbot before her execution.

CONDUCTOR

The conductor is in overall charge of the musical preparation of an opera production, both orchestrally and vocally, and leads the actual performance from the orchestra pit. It is the conductor who decides how the music will actually sound (in other words, all matters of tempo, balance, style and interpretation), and he is – whatever singers might think – the single most important person in an operatic performance. He thus also tends to be much the most powerful person, which goes some way to explain the dictatorial behaviour of some great conductors, such as Toscanini, Beecham and Karajan.

The modern orchestral conductor as we know him – and occasionally in recent years her – emerged in the 19th century. In the 17th century, the composer would beat time with a long pole, and in the 18th and early 19th centuries, either the first violinist or the harpsichordist would ensure the ensemble. Spohr may perhaps be regarded as the earliest modern-style conductor: he introduced the baton, now used by virtually all conductors. In the second half of the 19th century, the leading conductors tended to be composers: Mahler, Nápravník, Liszt, Messager and Strauss for example. The conductor as a separate species is essentially a 20th-century phenomenon.

The conductor is called *dirigente* in Italy, *chef d'orchestre* in France and *dirigent* in Germany. Conductors are often addressed as and referred to by the courtesy title of *Maestro* (Italian for 'master').

Below are listed the 203 conductors with entries in this dictionary. Their nationalities are given in brackets afterwards.

Abbado, Claudio (It)
Ackermann, Otto (Swit)
Adler, Kurt Herbert (Aus)
Ahronovich, Yuri (Russ)
Albrecht, Gerd (Ger)
Ansermet, Ernest (Swit)
Arditi, Luigi (It)
Armstrong, Richard (Br)
Atherton, David (Br)
Baranović, Krešimir (Yug)
Barbirolli, Sir John (Br)
Barenboim, Daniel (Isr)
Bartoletti, Bruno (It)
Bedford, Steuart (Br)
Beecham, Sir Thomas (Br)
Bellezza, Vincenzo (It)
Bernstein, Leonard (US)
Bertini, Gary (Isr)
Blech, Leo (Ger)
Böhm, Karl (Aus)
Bonynge, Richard (Aust)
Boskovsky, Willi (Aus)
Boulez, Pierre (Fr)
Boult, Sir Adrian (Br)
Braithwaite, Warwick (NZ)

Bülow, Hans von (Ger)
Busch, Fritz (Ger)
Caldwell, Sarah (US)
Campanini, Cleofonte (It)
Cantelli, Guido (It)
Capuana, Franco (It)
Chailly, Riccardo (It)
Chalabala, Zdeněk (Cz)
Cleva, Fausto (It)
Cluytens, André (Belg)
Collingwood, Lawrence (Br)
Conlan, James (US)
Costa, Sir Michael (Br)
Damrosch, Walter (US)
Danon, Oskar (Yug)
Davis, Andrew (Br)
Davis, Sir Colin (Br)
Desmorière, Roger (Fr)
Dobrowen, Issay (Russ)
Dohnányi, Christoph von (Ger)
Doráti, Antal (Hung)
Downes, Edward (Br)
Dutoit, Charles (Swit)

Ehrling, Sixten (Swe)
Elder, Mark (Br)
Elmendorff, Karl (Ger)
Erede, Alberto (It)
Ermler, Mark (Russ)
Fabritiis, Oliviero de (It)
Faccio, Franco (It)
Farncombe, Charles (Br)
Fasano, Renato (It)
Ferencsik, János (Hung)
Ferro, Gabriele (It)
Franci, Carlo (Arg)
Fricsay, Ferenc (Hung)
Frühbeck de Burgos, Rafael (Sp)
Furtwängler, Wilhelm (Ger)
Gardelli, Lamberto (It)
Gardiner, John Eliot (Br)
Gavazzeni, Gianandrea (It)
Gibson, Sir Alexander (Br)
Gielen, Michael (Ger)
Giulini, Carlo Maria (It)
Glover, Jane (Br)
Goodall, Sir Reginald (Br)
Groves, Sir Charles (Br)

Guarnieri, Antonio (It)	Ludwig, Leopold (Aus)	Rescigno, Nicola (US)
Gui, Vittorio (It)	Maag, Peter (Swit)	Richter, Hans (Aus)
Hager, Leopold (Aus)	Maazel, Lorin (US)	Rosbaud, Hans (Aus)
Haitink, Bernard (Neth)	Mackerras, Sir Charles	Rostropovich, Mstislav
Hallé, Sir Charles (Br)	(Aust)	(Russ)
Harnoncourt, Nickolas	Mahler, Gustav (Aus)	Rozhdestvensky, Gennadi
(Aus)	Malgoire, Jean-Claude (Fr)	(Russ)
Heger, Robert (Ger)	Mancinelli, Luigi (It)	Rudel, Julius (Aus)
Inbal, Eliahu (Isr)	Mariani, Angelo (It)	Sabata, Victor de (It)
Janowski, Marek (Pol)	Marinuzzi, Gino (It)	Santi, Nello (It)
Järnefelt, Armas (Fin)	Markevich, Igor (Russ)	Santini, Gabriele (It)
Järvi, Neeme (Est)	Marriner, Sir Neville (Br)	Sanzogno, Nino (It)
Jochum, Eugen (Ger)	Mascheroni, Edoardo (It)	Sargent, Sir Malcolm (Br)
Jullien, Louis (Fr)	Masur, Kurt (Ger)	Sawallisch, Wolfgang (Ger)
Karajan, Herbert von (Aus)	Matačić, Lovro von (Yug)	Schalk, Franz (Aus)
Keilberth, Joseph (Ger)	Mauceri, John (US)	Scherchen, Hermann (Ger)
Kempe, Rudolf (Ger)	Mehta, Zubin (Ind)	Schippers, Thomas (US)
Kertesz, István (Hung)	Messager, André (Fr)	Schmidt-Isserstedt, Hans
Khaikin, Boris (Russ)	Mitropoulos, Dimitri (Gk)	(Ger)
Kleiber, Carlos (Ger)	Molinari-Pradelli,	Scimone, Claudio (It)
Kleiber, Erich (Aus)	Francesco (It)	Seidl, Anton (Hung)
Klemperer, Otto (Ger)	Monteux, Pierre (Fr)	Serafin, Tullio (It)
Knappertsbusch, Hans	Mottl, Felix (Aus)	Simonetto, Alfredo (It)
(Ger)	Muck, Karl (Ger)	Sinopoli, Giuseppe (It)
Kondrashin, Kirill (Russ)	Mugnone, Leopoldo (It)	Solti, Sir Georg (Hung)
Konwitschny, Franz (Ger)	Muti, Riccardo (It)	Stein, Horst (Ger)
Košler, Zdeněk (Cz)	Nápravník, Eduard (Cz)	Stiedry, Fritz (Aus)
Koussevitzky, Serge (Russ)	Neumann, František (Cz)	Stokowski, Leopold (US)
Kovařovic, Karel (Cz)	Neumann, Václav (Cz)	Suitner, Otmar (Aus)
Krauss, Clemens (Aus)	Nikisch, Artur (Hung)	Svetlanov, Yevgeny (Russ)
Krips, Josef (Aus)	Norrington, Roger (Br)	Szell, George (Hung)
Krombholc, Jaroslav (Cz)	Ormandy, Eugene (Hung)	Talich, Václav (Cz)
Kubelík, Rafael (Cz)	Ozawa, Seiji (Jap)	Tate, Jeffrey (Br)
Lamoureux, Charles (Fr)	Panizza, Ettore (Arg)	Temirkanov, Yuri (Russ)
Leibowitz, René (Fr)	Patanè, Giuseppe (It)	Tennstedt, Klaus (Ger)
Leinsdorf, Erich (Aus)	Perlea, Jonel (Rom)	Toscanini, Arturo (It)
Leitner, Ferdinand (Ger)	Plasson, Michel (Fr)	Varviso, Silvio (Swit)
Leppard, Raymond (Br)	Prêtre, Georges (Fr)	Votto, Antonino (It)
Levi, Hermann (Ger)	Previn, André (US)	Wallberg, Heinz (Ger)
Levine, James (US)	Previtali, Fernando (It)	Walter, Bruno (Ger)
Lewis, Sir Anthony (Br)	Pritchard, Sir John (Br)	Weingartner, Felix (Aus)
Lloyd Jones, David (Br)	Quadri, Argeo (It)	Weller, Walter (Aus)
Lockhart, James (Br)	Queler, Eve (US)	Wolff, Albert (Fr)
Lombard, Alain (Fr)	Rankl, Karl (Aus)	Wood, Sir Henry (Br)
López-Cobos, Jesús (Sp)	Rattle, Simon (Br)	Zagrosek, Lothar (Ger)
Loughran, James (Br)	Reiner, Fritz (Hung)	Zedda, Alberto (It)

Confrontation Scene

A title often given to the end of Act II of Donizetti's *Maria Stuarda* when, in a historically fictitious meeting, the queens Mary and Elizabeth roundly insult each other.

Congiura (Italian for 'conspiracy')
A name sometimes given to a
conspiracy scene in an Italian opera,
such as that in Act III of Verdi's
Ernani.

Conlan, James *(b 1950)*
American conductor. One of the finest
of the younger generation of American
conductors, he is particularly associated
with the Italian repertory. Musical
director of the Cologne Opera (1989–).

Connell, Elizabeth *(b 1946)*
South African-born Irish mezzo and
later soprano, particularly associated
with dramatic Italian and German roles,
especially Medea, Lady Macbeth and
Ortrud. She possesses a large and
incisive voice used with intelligence and
musicianship, and is a singing-actress of
considerable dramatic insight.

Constanze
Soprano role in Mozart's *Die
Entführung aus dem Serail*. She is loved
by Belmonte.

Consul, The
Opera in three acts by Menotti. 1st
perf. Philadelphia, 1 March 1950; libr.
by the composer. Principal roles:
Magda Sorel (sop), Secretary (mezzo),
John (bar), Agent (bar), Mother
(mezzo), Magician (ten). Arguably
Menotti's finest full-length work, it is a
verismo piece set in a European police
state, in which the title character never
appears.

Plot: The political dissident John
Sorel is in hiding, waiting for his wife
Magda, his child and his mother to join
him. Magda's attempts to obtain exit
visas are continually hindered by the
red tape of a foreign consulate, where
the Secretary blocks all access to the
Consul. The Sorels' child dies and John
resolves to return, even though Magda
pleads with him not to come, warning
him that she will not be alive. John is
arrested at the consulate and the
Secretary at last promises to help, but
rings Magda too late to prevent her
committing suicide. [R]

Contes d'Hoffmann, Les (*The
Tales of Hoffmann*)
Opera in prologue, three acts and
epilogue by Offenbach. 1st perf. Paris,
10 Feb 1881; libr. by Jules Barbier and
Michel Carré after E. T. A. Hoffmann's
Der Sandmann, *Geschichte vom
Verlorenen Spiegelbilde* and *Rat
Krespel*. Principal roles: Hoffmann
(ten), Antonia/Giulietta/Olympia/Stella
(sop), Dr Miracle/Dapertutto/Coppélius/
Councillor Lindorf (b-bar), Nicklaus
(mezzo), Spalanzani (ten), Crespel
(bass), Frantz (ten), Peter Schlemil (bar).
Offenbach's last and greatest work, it
was not quite completed at his death.
The final scoring was completed by
Guiraud, who also provided recitatives,
although it was intended to have
spoken dialogue. A fascinating and at
times disturbing work, it tells three
inter-connected stories in which
Hoffmann is thwarted in love by his
evil genius. Ideally, the four villains
should be sung by the same man, and
the four heroines by the same woman,
as they are aspects of the same person.
Contrary to most productions, the
Antonia Act should be in the middle.
The work was an immediate success
and has remained ever since one of the
most popular of all operas.

Plot: In Luther's beer cellar in
Nuremburg, the students await the end
of a performance of *Don Giovanni*,
starring Stella, loved by the poet
Hoffmann and also pursued by the

sinister Councillor Lindorf. To pass the time, Hoffman offers to tell the story of his three great loves, in all of which he was aided by his young friend Nicklaus (later revealed as the embodiment of the Muse of Poetry). In Paris, he is sold a magical pair of spectacles by Coppélius and falls in love with Olympia, the 'daughter' of the inventor Spalanzani. She turns out to be a mechanical doll, which Coppélius destroys when he finds that Spalanzani has double-crossed him. In Munich, Hoffmann has fallen in love with the singer Antonia. Her father Crespel has forbidden her to sing, without telling her the reason: she is consumptive as was her dead mother, also a great singer. The evil quack Dr Miracle brings to life the portrait of her mother and urges her to sing ever more ecstatically. The strain is too much and she dies in Hoffmann's arms. In Venice, Hoffmann is having an affair with the courtesan Giulietta, who – at the urging of the magician Dapertutto – steals his reflection. Hoffmann kills Giulietta's former lover Schlemil in a duel and flees for his life, having witnessed Giulietta leaving with another admirer. Back in the beer cellar, it is realised that the three women are aspects of Stella. Hoffmann is now totally drunk, and a triumphant Lindorf escorts Stella away. Nicklaus as Hoffmann's muse urges him to return to poetry. [R]

Continuo

A shortening of *basso continuo*, it is the bass part which accompanies recitative in a 17th- or 18th-century opera. It is played by the harpsichord and sometimes also the cello.

Contralto

Italian for 'against the high', in other words a contrast to a high voice, the term refers to the lowest female vocal range. It is similar to mezzo-soprano (the two terms are often used interchangeably) and is nowadays usually used to describe only a voice (such as that of Dame Clara Butt) or a role (such as Ulrica) of exceptionally dark quality and low range. Only in Germany is it still regarded as a separate range from mezzo. There, where it is called Alt and its singer Altistin, there are two recognised types: (1) *Dramatischer Alt*, such as Erda in *Siegfried*, with a range of f to f''. (2) *Komischer Alt*, such as Widow Browe in *Zar und Zimmermann*, with a range of f to g''.
See also **Mezzo-soprano**

Contro un cor

Mezzo aria for Rosina in Act II of Rossini's *Il Barbiere di Siviglia*. It is Rosina's singing lesson.

Convenienze e Inconvenienze Teatrali, Le

(often given as *Viva la Mamma*) Comic opera in two acts (originally one act) by Donizetti. 1st perf. Naples, 21 Nov 1827; libr. by the composer, after two plays by Antonio Sografi. Revised version, 1st perf. Milan, 1831. An hilarious send-up of opera's backstage intrigues, it contains in Mamma Agata (bar) one of the greatest 'drag' roles in opera. It is still performed from time to time.

Converse, Frederick (1871–1940)

American composer. He wrote four operas, the most successful of which was *The Pipe of Desire* (Boston 31 Jan 1906; libr. George Edward Burton) which, in 1910, became the first American opera to be performed at the Metropolitan Opera, New York. His other operas are *The Sacrifice* (Boston

6 Jan 1911; libr. composer and J. A. Macy), *Sinbad the Sailor* (1913; libr. P. MacKaye) and *The Immigrants* (1914; libr. MacKaye), the last two of which were never performed.

Copenhagen
See Royal Danish Opera

Copland, Aaron *(b 1900)*
American composer. He wrote two operas: the children's opera *The Second Hurricane* (New York 1937; libr. E. Denby) and the successful quasi-folk opera *The Tender Land**.

Copley, John *(b 1933)*
British producer, particularly associated with Mozart operas. He has been especially active at the English National Opera, the Australian Opera and Covent Garden (where he was resident producer). His traditional-style productions are noted for their naturalness and great inventiveness in comedy, as well occasionally for a certain fussiness and campness. As a child actor, he created the Apprentice in *Peter Grimes*.

Coppélius
Bass role in Offenbach's *Les Contes d'Hoffmann*. He is a sinister spectacle-maker in the Olympia Act.

Coq d'Or, Le
See Golden Cockerel, The

Corelli, Franco *(b 1921)*
Italian tenor, particularly associated with heroic Italian roles, especially Manrico. He was perhaps the most thrilling tenore di forza of modern times and was a great favourite with audiences everywhere with his good looks, magnificent voice and ringing high notes. He was, however, hardly

the most subtle of singers: one critic aptly described him as "an adept at tearing a passion to tatters".

Corena, Fernando *(1916–84)*
Swiss bass, particularly associated with the Italian repertory and with Mozart roles, especially Leporello and Dr Bartolo. One of the greatest buffos of the postwar era, he possessed a good voice and was an outstanding comic actor. From 1954, he was largely resident at the Metropolitan Opera, New York. He created a role in Petrassi's *Il Cordovano*.

Corneille, Pierre
See panel on page 129

Cornelius, Peter *(1824–74)*
German composer. A disciple of Liszt and Wagner, he wrote three operas, of which *Der Barbier von Bagdad** was much the most successful. Neither *Der Cid* (Weimar 21 May 1865; libr. composer after Pierre Corneille's *Le Cid*) nor *Gunlöd* (1891, composed *c* 1870; libr. composer) have survived. The latter was unfinished at the composer's death and was completed by Carl Hoffbauer.

Corona *(Italian for 'crown')*
The term used in Italy for fermata*.

Coronation March
March in Act IV of Meyerbeer's *Le Prophète*.

Coronation of Poppea, The
See Incoronazione di Poppea, L'

Coronation Scene
Scene II of the prologue of Moussorgsky's *Boris Godunov*.

PIERRE CORNEILLE

The works of the French playwright Pierre Corneille (1606–84) have had an important influence on opera, both as source material and as the models, with their theme of the conflict between passion and duty, on which Apostolo Zeno and Pietro Metastasio based their libretti. Corneille's plays have inspired some 40 operas. Below are listed, by play, those operas by composers with entries in this dictionary.

Andromède
Lully	*Persée*	1682
Charpentier	*Andromède*	1682

Le Cid
Handel	*Flavio*	1723
Sacchini	*Il Gran Cidde*	1764
Paisiello	*Il Gran Cid*	1775
Cornelius	*Der Cid*	1865
Massenet	*Le Cid*	1885
Debussy	*Rodrigue et Chimène*	1888 (U)

Cinna
Hasse	*Tito Vespasiano*	1735
Graun	*Cinna*	1748
Portugal	*Cinna*	1793
Paer	*Il Cinna*	1795

Horace
Salieri	*Les Horaces*	1786
Zingarelli	*Gli Orazi ed i Curiazi*	1795
Cimarosa	*Gli Orazi ed i Curiazi*	1796
Mercadante	*Orazi e Curiazi*	1846

La Mort de Pompé
Graun	*Cesare e Cleopatra*	1742

Pertharite
Handel	*Rodelinda*	1725

Polyeucte
Donizetti	*Poliuto*	1838
Gounod	*Polyeucte*	1878

Sofonisbe
Caldara	*Sofonisba*	1708
Traetta	*Sofonisba*	1762
Paer	*Sofonisba*	1805

His brother Thomas (1825–1709) was also a playwright, whose *Médée* was the source for M.-A. Charpentier's *Médée* and Cherubini's *Médée*.

Corregidor, Der (*The Magistrate*)
Comic opera in four acts by Wolf. 1st
perf. Mannheim, 7 June 1896; libr. by
Rosa Mayreder, after Pedro de
Alarcón's *El Sombrero de Tres Picos*.
Principal roles: Frasquita (sop), Tio
Lucas (bar), Corregidor (ten), Mercedes
(sop). Wolf's only completed opera, it
contains some delightful music
(including two of his songs
incorporated into the score), but is
hampered by its weak libretto. It is still
occasionally performed.

Plot: Andalusia, 1804. Frasquita,
wife of the miller Tio Lucas, dismisses
her husband's jealousy as without
foundation and uses the advances of
the amorous elderly Corregidor to
obtain a post for her nephew. The
Corregidor, soaking wet from having
fallen into the mill-stream, visits
Frasquita who defends her honour with
a musket, while Tio Lucas is absent,
having been called into town by a false
errand trumped up by the Corregidor.
On his way home, he passes Frasquita
who has gone to look for him, but fails
to notice her in the darkness. Lucas
finds the Corregidor asleep in his bed
and dressed in his clothes. When he
wakes, the Corregidor is beaten by his
own officers from the town and then
refused entry to his own home by his
wife Mercedes, who claims that she has
mistaken Lucas for him. Lucas,
suspected of murdering the Corregidor,
is also soundly beaten. [R]

Corsaro, Il (*The Corsair*)
Opera in three acts by Verdi. 1st perf.
Trieste, 25 Oct 1848, libr. by Francesco
Maria Piave, after Lord Byron's poem.
Principal roles: Corrado (ten), Gulnara
(sop), Pasha Seid (bar), Medora (sop).
One of the least successful of Verdi's
early works, it is only occasionally
performed.

Plot: The pirate captain Corrado
leads an attack against the Turkish
Pasha Seid and is captured and
imprisoned. Seid's favourite slave
Gulnara kills her master, thus rescuing
Corrado and persuading him to take
her with him to his island. Returning,
Corrado finds that his beloved Medora,
believing him dead, has taken poison.
After she dies in his arms, Corrado
hurls himself into the sea. [R]

Cortigiani
Baritone aria for Rigoletto in Act II of
Verdi's *Rigoletto*.

Cosa Rara, Una (*A Rare Thing*)
or **Bellezza ed Onestà** (*Beauty
and Honesty*)
Comic opera in two acts by Martín y
Soler. 1st perf. Vienna, 17 Nov 1786;
libr. by Lorenzo da Ponte, after Luis
Vélez de Guevara's *La Luna della
Sierra*. Principal roles: Isabella (sop),
Lilla (sop), Ghita (sop), Giovanni (ten),
Lubino (bar), Tita (b-bar), Corrado
(ten), Lisargo (bass). By far Martín y
Soler's most successful work, it was
hugely popular for over 50 years but is
nowadays only very occasionally
performed. Mozart quotes from it in
the Supper Scene of *Don Giovanni*.

Plot: The peasant girl Lilla, intended
by her brother Tita as a bride for the
magistrate Don Lisargo, is also pursued
by Prince Giovanni and his chamberlain
Corrado. However, despite all threats
and entreaties, she remains faithful to
her lover Lubino.

Così fan Tutte (*Thus Do They All*)

or **La Scuola degli Amanti** (*The School for Lovers*)
Comic opera in two acts by Mozart (K 588). 1st perf. Vienna, 26 Jan 1790; libr. by Lorenzo da Ponte. Principal roles: Fiordiligi (sop), Ferrando (ten), Dorabella (mezzo), Guglielmo (bar), Don Alfonso (b-bar), Despina (sop). One of the most human and heart-searching music-dramas ever written, it was only infrequently performed in the 19th century (and then only in adaptations) because the story was considered immoral, but is now a regular work in the standard repertory.

Plot: 18th-century Naples. Two officers, Ferrando and Guglielmo, are engaged to the sisters, Dorabella and Fiordiligi. Their cynical bachelor friend, Don Alfonso, takes a wager with them that the fidelity of their fiancées is as shaky as that of all other women. Pretending to be called away on active service, the men disguise themselves as a pair of charming Albanians and each pays court to the other's lover. Alfonso, meanwhile, enlists the aid of the girls' servant Despina, to help in the deception and she disguises herself first as a doctor of mesmerism and later as a notary. The girls do eventually succumb to the persistent ardour of their new 'admirers', Fiordiligi more gradually than Dorabella, and a double wedding is planned. Alfonso has won his bet, the 'Albanians' unmask themselves, and the girls throw themselves on their lovers' mercy. Alfonso reveals the plot and all is eventually sorted out in a spirit of understanding and reconciliation. [R]

Cossotto, Fiorenza (*b 1935*)
Italian mezzo, particularly associated with the Italian repertory. The leading Italian mezzo of recent decades, she possessed a rich and powerful voice and was a compelling singing-actress, especially in roles such as Amneris and Azucena. She created Sister Mathilde in *Dialogues des Carmélites*. Married to the bass Ivo Vinco*.

Cossutta, Carlo (*b 1932*)
Italian-born Argentinian tenor, particularly associated with the Italian repertory. After singing lyric roles, he turned with great success to the dramatic repertoire, particularly Otello. Not only an exciting tenore di forza, he was also a fine musician and a sensitive artist. He created the title role in Ginastera's *Don Rodrigo*.

Costa, Sir Michael (*b Michele Andrea Agniello*) (*1808–84*)
Italian-born British conductor and composer. As musical director of the King's Theatre, London (1833–46), and, later, Covent Garden (1847–69) he was responsible for a vast improvement in the standard of British opera performance. He also composed a number of operas, including *Il Delitto Punito* (1826), *Il Sospetto Funesto* (1827), *Il Carcere d'Ildegonda* (1829), *Malvina* (1829), *Malek Adhel* (Paris 1838; libr. Carlo Pepoli) and *Don Carlo* (London 1844; libr. L. Tarantini, after Friedrich von Schiller).

Cotrubas, Ileana (*b 1939*)
Romanian soprano, particularly associated with Mozart and lighter Italian roles and with Mélisande. She possessed a beautiful voice used with fine musicianship, and had a most affecting stage presence, being equally at home in serious and comic roles. Married to the conductor Manfred Ramin.

Council Chamber Scene
Act I Scene II of Verdi's *Simon Boccanegra*. One of the most powerful

---

COUNTER-TENOR

Counter-tenor was a rare male voice which had a naturally produced tone consisting almost exclusively of head voice. It was relatively common in Britain in the early 18th century, but subsequently all but disappeared. The term has been revived in the postwar era to describe – not entirely accurately – a male alto singing Baroque music originally written for a castrato, whose voice is produced by singing falsetto. The voice's range falls roughly between those of tenor and mezzo-soprano. The first operatic role written specifically for the modern counter-tenor voice was Oberon in *A Midsummer Night's Dream*. Subsequently several contemporary composers have written roles for the voice, notably Maxwell Davies (the Priest-Confessor in *Taverner*), Glass (*Akhnaten*) and Reimann (Edgar in *Lear*).
The three following counter-tenors, all British, have entries in this dictionary:

Bowman, James   Deller, Alfred   Esswood, Paul

---

musico-dramatic scenes in all Italian opera, it was added for the revised version.

Counter-tenor
See panel on this page

Countess Madeleine
Soprano role in Richard Strauss's *Capriccio*. She is loved by Olivier and Flamand.

Countess Maritza
See Gräfin Mariza

Count of Luxemburg, The
See Graf von Luxembourg, Der

Count Ory
See Comte Ory, Le

Coup de glotte (French for 'stroke of the glottis')
A method of vocal 'attack' which consists of the closing and immediate

reopening of the false vocal chords (the two membranes above the real chords).

Couplet
A French term used in the 18th and 19th centuries to denote a song or aria in strophic* form, usually of a comic nature. Mostly found in operetta, an example is 'Ah! que j'aime les militaires' in Offenbach's *La Grande-Duchesse de Gérolstein*.

Covent Garden
See Royal Opera House, Covent Garden

Cover
The term has two meanings in opera: (1) The understudy of a role. (2) Vocal tone that is 'covered' is gentler and more veiled in quality than that produced by open tone. It is produced when the voice is pitched in the soft palate.

Covetous Knight, The (*Skupoy Ritsar*)

Comic opera in one act by Rachmaninov (Op 24). 1st perf. Moscow, 24 Jan 1906; libr. after Alexander Pushkin. Telling of a knight's provocations at the hands of a greedy son and a dishonest usurer, it is hardly ever performed outside Russia. [R]

Cowen, Sir Frederick (*1852–1935*)

British composer. He wrote five stage works, beginning with the operetta *Garibaldi* (1860; libr. composer's sister), written at the age of eight. His four mature operas are *Pauline* (London 22 Nov 1876; libr. H. Hersee, after Edward Bulwer Lytton), *Thorgrim* (London 22 April 1890; libr. J. Bennett), *Signa* (Milan 12 Nov 1893; libr. Gilbert Arthur A'Beckett, H. A. Rudall and G. E. Weatherly, after Ouida) and *Harold* (London 8 June 1895; libr. E. Malet). They are all now forgotten.

Cowie, Edward (*b 1943*)

British composer. He has written one opera, *Commedia* (Kassel 1979).

Cox, Jean (*b 1932*)

American tenor, particularly associated with Wagnerian roles, especially Siegfried. One of the leading heldentenors of the 1970s, he had a strong if not particularly tonally pleasing voice.

Cox, John (*b 1935*)

British producer, particularly associated with Glyndebourne and the English National Opera, where his productions of *Così fan Tutte* and *Patience* displayed his witty sense of characterisation and his eye for detail.

He was director of productions at Glyndebourne (1971–81), general administrator of Scottish Opera (1981–87) and production director at Covent Garden (1988–).

Cox and Box
or The Long-Lost Brothers

Operetta in one act by Sullivan. 1st perf. London, 26 May 1866; libr. by Francis Cowley Burnard, after John Maddison Morton's *Box and Cox*. Principal roles: Box (ten), Cox (bar), Bouncer (b-bar). An amusing little curtain-raiser, it is the only one of Sullivan's non-Gilbertian stage works which is still performed with any regularity.

Plot: The ex-soldier Bouncer is renting one room to two people at once: the journeyman hatter Cox (who works all day) and the journeyman printer Box (who works all night). All goes well until Cox is given the day off, returns home and finds Box in 'his' room. A heated argument ensues and a duel is arranged on the basis that the pistols remain unloaded. All is resolved when the two men realise that they are brothers. [R]

Craig, Charles (*b 1920*)

British tenor who enjoyed a remarkably long career, being particularly associated with the Italian repertory. He was virtually the only postwar British tenor able to sing the heavier Italian roles such as Don Alvaro and Otello.

Credo in un dio crudel

Baritone aria for Iago in Act I of Verdi's *Otello*. It is the one substantial textual addition to Shakespeare in the opera.

Creon

The mythical Greek king appears in

many operas, including (1) Bass role in Cherubini's *Médée*. (2) Baritone role in Honegger's and Orff's *Antigonae*. (3) Bass role in Mayr's *Medea in Corinto*. (4) Baritone role in Stravinsky's *Oedipus Rex*. (5) Bass role in M.-A. Charpentier's *Médée*.

Crescendo (Italian for 'growing', it denotes an increase in loudness)
Luigi Mosca claimed to have first used the device in his *I Pretendi Delusi* of 1811, although it has since been discovered in Terradellas's *Bellerofonte* of 1747. By far the best-known examples are by Rossini, who used the device frequently and was nicknamed 'Signor Crescendo'. The most famous usage is in Don Basilio's 'La calunnia' in *Il Barbiere di Siviglia*.

Crespel
Bass role in Offenbach's *Les Contes d'Hoffmann*. He is Antonia's father.

Crespin, Régine *(b 1927)*
French soprano, particularly associated with the roles of Tosca, the Marschallin and Carmen, and with Wagner and Offenbach roles. One of the finest sopranos of the postwar era, she possessed a warm and powerful voice and exemplary diction. A sensitive and highly intelligent musician, she was also an outstanding comic actress. Later in her career, she turned to mezzo roles, notably the Old Prioress in *Dialogues des Carmélites*.

Crimi, Giulio *(1885–1939)*
Italian tenor, particularly associated with the Italian repertory. One of the leading tenors of the inter-war period, he created Luigi in *Il Tabarro*, Rinuccio in *Gianni Schicchi* and Paolo in Zandonai's *Francesca da Rimini*. He was also a noted teacher, whose pupils included Tito Gobbi.

Crispino e la Comare *(Crispin and the Fairy)*
Comic opera in four acts by L. and F. Ricci. 1st perf. Venice, 28 Feb 1850; libr. by Francesco Maria Piave after S. Fabbrichesi. Principal roles: Crispino (bar), Annetta (sop), Fabrizio (bar), Mirabolano (b-bar), Comare (mezzo), Contino (ten), Asdrubale (bass). A delightful work, it is the most successful of the Ricci brothers' collaborations and is the only Italian comic opera of any importance between *Don Pasquale* and *Falstaff*. It is still occasionally performed.

Plot: With the help of a fairy, Crispino becomes a wealthy physician. However, he grows arrogant and maltreats his wife Annetta. Matters become worse and he almost loses his life before finally repenting his behaviour.

Critic, The or An Opera Rehearsal
Opera in two acts by Stanford (Op 144). 1st perf. London, 14 Jan 1916; libr. by Lewis Cairns James after Richard Brindsley Sheridan's play. Reasonably successful at its appearance, it is nowadays all but forgotten.

Critics
See panel on page 135

Croatian opera composers
See Yugoslavian opera composers

Crociato in Egitto, Il *(The Crusader in Egypt)*
Opera in two acts by Meyerbeer. 1st perf. Venice, 7 March 1824; libr. by Gaetano Rossi. Principal roles: Armando (castrato/mezzo), Palmide (sop), Felicia (mezzo), Adriano (ten),

---

CRITICS

Opera critics are nearly as old as opera itself and have always played an important and occasionally crucial role in its development. The term is perhaps an unfortunate one, as the best critics do a great deal more than simply criticise: they are constructive in nurturing new talent and encouraging high artistic standards. Some, of course, have been merely destructive or reactionary: one critic has gone down in operatic history by saying of *Die Lustige Witwe* "this isn't music"! Both singers and composers have had their tussles with the critics, but the avidity with which they still read them (and usually respect their views) is indication enough of their importance. Several composers have themselves been notable critics, particularly Berlioz, Serov and Thomson.

Below are listed the nine critics with entries in this dictionary. Their nationalities are given in brackets afterwards.

Chorley, Henry F. (Br)	Kerman, Joseph (US)	Porter, Andrew (Br)
Hanslick, Eduard (Ger)	Milnes, Rodney (Br)	Rosenthal, Harold (Br)
Jacobs, Arthur (Br)	Newman, Ernest (Br)	Stasov, Vladimir (Russ)

Aladino (bass). Meyerbeer's first major success, it contains the last significant role ever written for a castrato, although it was later sung by a mezzo. Enormously popular in the 19th century, but now rarely performed.

Plot: During the Sixth Crusade, Armando d'Orville, a knight of Rhodes, has been left for dead in Egypt. Assuming a false name, he becomes an adviser to the Sultan Aladino, whose daughter Palmide he secretly marries and converts to Christianity. His uncle Adriano arrives to seek peace, and Armando's real identity is discovered, leading to a battle and to the Christians being condemned to death. Armando saves the Sultan's life during a coup attempt by the Grand Vizier, after which the Sultan reunites Armando and Palmide and signs a peace treaty.

Cross, Joan *(b 1900)*
British soprano, particularly associated with Sadler's Wells Opera and the English Opera Group, of which she was a founder member. Possessing a lovely voice and a good stage presence, she had a wide repertory but was especially associated with Mozart and Britten roles. For Britten she created Ellen Orford in *Peter Grimes*, the Female Chorus in *The Rape of Lucretia*, Lady Billows in *Albert Herring*, Elizabeth I in *Gloriana* and Mrs Grose in *The Turn of the Screw*. She also produced a number of operas and was administrator of Sadler's Wells Opera.

Crosse, Gordon *(b 1937)*
British composer. He has written four operas. The powerful one-act *Purgatory* (Cheltenham 7 July 1966; libr. after William Butler Yeats) [R] was followed by the comedy *The Grace of Todd* (Aldeburgh 7 June 1969; libr. David Rudkin), *The Story of Vasco* (London 13 March 1974; libr. Ted Hughes after Schehadé) and *Potter Thompson* (London 9 Jan 1975; libr. A. Garner).

135

Crown Diamonds, The
See Diamants de la Couronne, Les

Crozier, Eric *(b 1914)*
British librettist and producer. He wrote the libretti for Britten's *Albert Herring*, *The Little Sweep* and *Billy Budd* (the last with E. M. Forster) and for Berkeley's *Ruth*. He produced a number of Britten operas, including the first performances of *Peter Grimes* and *The Rape of Lucretia*, and was a co-founder of both the Aldeburgh Festival and the English Opera Group.

Crucible, The
Opera in four acts by Ward. 1st perf. New York, 26 Oct 1961; libr. by Bernard Stambler, after Arthur Miller's play. Principal roles: Samuel Parris (ten), John Hale (bar), Thomas Putnam (bass), Betsy (sop), Tituba (mezzo). Ward's finest work, which has been widely performed, it is a conservative but theatrically highly effective setting of Miller's play about the witchcraft trials of 1692 in Salem, Massachusetts.

Cruda funesta
Baritone aria for Enrico in Act I of Donizetti's *Lucia di Lammermoor*.

Cruda sorte
Mezzo aria for Isabella in Act I of Rossini's *L'Italiana in Algieri*.

Crudel, perchè finora
Soprano/baritone duet for Susanna and Count Almaviva in Act III of Mozart's *Le Nozze di Figaro*.

Cruz-Romo, Gilda *(b 1940)*
Mexican soprano, particularly associated with the Italian repertory. A Verdi soprano of great style and refinement with a voice of beauty and considerable power, she also has an appealing stage presence.

Csárdás
A Hungarian dance, divided into slow and fast sections. Much the most famous operatic example is Rosalinde's 'Klänge der Heimat' in J. Strauss's *Die Fledermaus*.

Csárdásfürstin, Die *(The Gypsy Princess)*
Operetta in three acts by Kálmán. 1st perf. Vienna, 13 Nov 1915; libr. by Leo Stein and Béla Jenbach. Principal roles: Sylvia Varescu (sop), Edwin (ten), Boni (ten), Stasi (sop), Feri (ten), Prince (bar). Arguably Kálmán's most successful work, it was an immediate success and is still regularly performed. [R]

Cuban opera composers
These include José Mauri Esteve (1856–1937), Laureano Fuentes y Matons (1825–98), whose *La Hija de Jefté* (Santiago de Cuba 16 May 1875; libr. Antonio Arnao) was the first Cuban opera, Alejandro García-Caturla (1906–40), Amadeo Roldán (1900–39), Eduardo Sánchez de Fuentes (1874–1944), Guillermo Tomás (1868–1933) and Gaspar Villate (1851–91).

Cuénod, Hugues *(b 1902)*
Swiss tenor, specialising in character roles. He enjoyed one of the longest careers in operatic history, singing into his late 80s. Beginning as a night club singer, he possessed a highly individual voice and stage manner and was a singer of great intelligence and musicianship. He created Sellem in *The Rake's Progress*.

Cui, César (1835–1918)

Russian composer (and also a leading expert on military fortifications). A founder, with Balakirev, of the Russian nationalist school known as the Mighty Handful, his importance is now largely historical as none of his operas have remained in the repertory, even in Russia. As well as four children's operas, his stage works include *The Captive of the Caucasus* (St Petersburg 16 Feb 1883, begun 1857; libr. Viktor Krylov after Alexander Pushkin), *The Mandarin's Son* (St. Petersburg 19 Dec 1878, composed 1859; libr. Krylov), *William Ratcliff**, his finest work, his contribution to the collective opera-ballet *Mlada*, *Angelo* (St Petersburg 13 Feb 1876; libr. V. Burenin after Victor Hugo), *Le Filibustier* (Paris 22 Jan 1894; libr. Jean Richepin), *The Saracen* (St Petersburg 14 Nov 1899; libr. after Alexandre Dumas' *Charles VII Chez Ses Grands Vassaux*), *A Feast in Time of Plague* (Moscow 1900; libr. after Pushkin), *Mam'selle Fifi* (Moscow 15 Dec 1903; libr. after Guy de Maupassant), *Matteo Falcone* (Moscow 27 Dec 1907; libr. Vasily Zhukovsky after Prosper Mérimée's *Mosaique*) and *The Captain's Daughter* (St Petersburg 27 Feb 1911; libr. after Pushkin). He also helped to complete Moussorgsky's unfinished *Sorochintsy Fair* and Dargomijsky's *The Stone Guest*.

Cunning Little Vixen, The
(*Přihody Lišky Bystroušky*)

Opera in three acts by Janáček. 1st perf. Brno, 6 Nov 1924; libr. by the composer, after Rudolf Těsnohlídek's verses for drawings by Stanislav Lolek. Principal roles: Vixen (sop), Forester (bar), Fox (sop), Parson (bass), Schoolteacher (ten), Harašta (b-bar), Badger (bass), Forester's Wife (mezzo). One of Janáček's greatest works, its story allowed him to celebrate his love of nature and his fascination with the musical quality of its sounds. The result is enchanting and moving without ever being cloying. Initially slow to make its way, it has been widely performed in recent years and has become one of the most popular of all Czech operas.

Plot: Moravia. The Forester captures the vixen Sharpears and tries to domesticate her. She escapes by fomenting a revolt amongst the hens, takes over the Badger's home and marries the Fox. She is shot by the poacher Harašta. Seeing a vixen cub in the forest, the Forester dreams of the endless renewal of nature. [R]

Cuno

Bass role in Weber's *Der Freischütz*. Agathe's father, he is the head forester.

Cupid

Son of Venus, the Graeco-Roman god of love appears in many operas, including (1) Soprano trouser-role in Monteverdi's *Il Ballo delle Ingrate*. (2) Mezzo trouser-role in Offenbach's *Orphée aux Enfers*. (3) Soprano trouser-role in Rameau's *Anacréon*. (4) Soprano trouser-role in Blow's *Venus and Adonis*.

Curlew River

Opera in one act by Britten (Op 71). 1st perf. Orford, 13 June 1964; libr. by William Plomer, after Juro Motomasa's Japanese Noh play *The Sumida River*. Principal roles: Madwoman (ten), Ferryman (bar), Traveller (bar). The first of Britten's *Three Church Parables*, this is a highly stylised mystery play of great musical concentration, requiring an orchestra of only seven players. The story, transposed from Japan to the English Fenlands and given a Christian interpretation, tells of a Madwoman searching for her lost son. [R]

Curtin, Phyllis (b Smith) (b 1922)

American soprano, particularly associated with Mozart roles and with 20th-century works. A fine singing-actress, she created for Floyd the title-role in *Susannah* and Cathy in *Wuthering Heights*.

Curzio, Don

Tenor comprimario role in Mozart's *Le Nozze di Figaro*. He is a stammering lawyer.

Cuts

The shortening of works by the removal of some of the music is a depressingly frequent practice in major opera houses, those who sanction them presuming to know better than the composer how much is required. In Italian opera, cuts usually take the form of lopping a verse off a cabaletta, but sometimes extend to whole numbers or even entire scenes: almost a quarter of *Lucia di Lammermoor* is cut at Covent Garden. Such disfigurements of major works cannot be in any way condoned.

Cyrano de Bergerac

Works of this title based on Edmond Rostand's play include:

(1) Opera in four acts by Damrosch. 1st perf. New York, 27 Feb 1913; libr. by William James Henderson. Principal roles: Cyrano (bar), Roxane (sop), Christian (ten). Damrosch's most successful work, but now all but forgotten.

(2) Opera in four acts by Alfano. 1st perf. Rome, 22 Jan 1936; libr. by Henri Cain. Principal roles: Cyrano (ten), Roxane (sop). Successful in its time, it is now very rarely performed.

Plot: Paris, c 1640. Cyrano, a noble knight with a large nose, is secretly in love with his cousin Roxane. She, however, loves the soldier Christian. She discovers too late that Christian's passionate love letters to her were actually written by Cyrano.

Czech opera composers

See Benda; Bendl; Blodek; Burian; Cikker; Dvořák; Fibich; Foerster; Gassmann; Hába; Hanuš; Janáček; Jeremiáš; Jirko; Jírovec; Karel; Kovařovic; Krejčí; Kubelík; Martinů; Mysliveček; Nápravník; Nedbal; Novák; Ostrčil; Pauer; Škroup; Smetana; Stamitz; Suchoň; Ullmann; Weinberger

Other national opera composers include Ignaz Brüll (1846–1907), Osvald Chlubna (1895–1971), Ján Fischer (b 1921), Ladislav Holoubek (b 1913), Karel Horký (b 1909), Ilja Hurník (b 1925), Ivo Jirásek (b 1920), Jaroslav Křička (1882–1969) and Zbyněk Vostřák (b 1920).

Czechoslovakia

See Bratislava Opera; Brno Opera; Olomouc Opera; Ostrava Opera; Plzeň Opera; Prague National Theatre

Czerwenka, Oskar (b 1924)

Austrian bass, particularly associated with German comic roles. A rich-voiced singer with a fine stage presence, he was one of the finest Germanic buffos of the postwar period.

Czipra

Mezzo role in J. Strauss's *Der Zigeunerbaron*. She is an old gypsy.

D

D', Da

Names containing these prefixes are listed under the letter of the main surname. For example, Vincent d'Indy is listed under I and Lorenzo da Ponte is listed under P.

Da capo (Italian for 'from the head')

An aria in an 18th-century opera seria, with the structure A – B – A decorated. The second A was often not written out, the singer being given the instruction da capo; in other words, back to the beginning. The best known da capo arias are in Handel's operas. A variant form is the dal segno* aria, in which only a specified part of the first section is repeated.

Dafne

Works of this title, with libretto by Ottavio Rinuccini after Ovid's *Metamorphoses*, include:

(1) Opera in prologue and six scenes by Peri. 1st perf. Florence, 1597. Usually regarded as the first-ever opera, the music is lost.

(2) Opera by Caccini. Composed c1597. Possibly never performed, the music is lost.

(3) Opera-ballet in two parts by Gagliano. 1st perf. Mantua, 1608. Principal roles: Dafne (sop), Apollo (ten), Love (sop), Tirsi (ten), Ovid (ten), Venus (sop). One of the earliest operas to have survived, it is written largely in madrigal style.

Plot: Apollo pursues the Python and shoots it to death with arrows, and is then himself wounded by the arrows of Cupid. He pursues the nymph Dafne,

but she, through the machinations of Cupid, is turned into a laurel tree just before he can catch her. Her loss is lamented by Apollo and Tirsi. [R]

(4) Opera by Schütz. 1st perf. Torgau, 23 April 1627; libr. adapted by Martin Opitz. The earliest German opera, the music is lost.

Dagl' immortali vertici

Baritone aria for Ezio in Act II of Verdi's *Attila*.

Dai campi

Tenor aria for Faust in Act I of Boito's *Mefistofele*.

Dal

Names containing this prefix are listed under the letter of the main surname. For example, Toti dal Monte is listed under M.

Daland

Bass role in Wagner's *Der Fliegende Holländer*. Senta's father, he is a Norwegian sea captain.

Dalayrac, Nicolas *(1753–1809)*

French composer. He wrote 61 stage works, most of them light comedies and all now forgotten. His first opera was *L'Eclipse Totale* (Paris 7 March 1782; libr. Poisson de Lachabeaussière, after Jean de la Fontaine). Its successors included *Nina ou la Folle par Amour* (Paris 15 May 1786; libr. Benoît Joseph Marsollier), his most successful work, and *Tout Pour l'Amour* (Paris 7 July 1796; libr. J. M. Boutet de Monvel after Shakespeare's *Romeo and Juliet*).

Dalibor

Opera in three acts by Smetana. 1st perf. Prague, 16 May 1868; libr. by Josef Wenzig and Ervín Špindler. Principal roles: Dalibor (ten), Milada (sop), King Vladislav (bar), Beneš (bass), Budivoj (bar), Jitka (sop), Vítek (ten). Arguably Smetana's masterpiece, it is one of the finest of all 'rescue operas', and is sometimes referred to as the Czech *Fidelio*. It has always had strong associations with Czech nationalism and aspirations, and its intense nationalism has perhaps been the reason why this magnificent work is seldom performed outside Czechoslovakia.

Plot: 15th-century Prague. The knight Dalibor has killed a Burgrave in revenge for the killing of his friend Zdeněk. The King sentences him to life imprisonment. His main accuser, the Burgrave's daughter Milada, is moved by his noble bearing to pity and then love. She disguises herself as a boy and works as an assistant to the jailer Beneš at Dalibor's prison where they meet, fall in love and plan to escape. They are discovered, however, and after much hesitation the King alters Dalibor's sentence to immediate death. His supporters wait outside to attack. Dalibor brings in Milada, who has been wounded and who dies in his arms, and then stabs himself before the captain of the guard Budivoj arrives with troops. [R]

Dalila

Mezzo role in Saint-Saëns' *Samson et Dalila*. She is a beautiful Philistine who tempts Samson.

Dal labbro

Tenor aria for Fenton in Act III of Verdi's *Falstaff*.

Dallapiccola, Luigi *(1904–75)*

Italian composer and pianist. The leading postwar Italian composer, his music presents a mixture of serial and more traditional and lyrical techniques. His first opera *Volo di Notte** was followed by the powerful *Il Prigioniero**, his finest opera, the dramatic oratorio *Job** and *Ulisse**.

Dallas Civic Opera

Founded in Nov 1957 by Lawrence Kelly, it gives annual seasons in Spring and again in Nov and Dec with top international casts at the Fair Park Music Hall (cap. 3,420). The repertory tends to be conservative and largely Italian. Musical directors have included Nicola Rescigno

Dalla sua pace

Tenor aria for Don Ottavio in Act I of Mozart's *Don Giovanni*.

Dal segno (Italian for 'from the sign')

It is a modification of a da capo aria, in which only a part of the first section (from a point indicated by a sign in the score) is repeated.

Dam, José van *(b 1940)*

Belgian baritone, particularly associated with Mozart, the French repertory and 20th-century works. He is an outstanding musician with an incisive voice of wide range and a fine singing-actor. He created the title role in Messiaen's *St François d'Assise* and a role in Milhaud's *La Mère Coupable*.

Dama Boba, La

Opera in three acts by Wolf-Ferrari. 1st perf. Milan, 1 Feb 1939; libr. by Mario Ghisalberti after Félix Lope de Vega. Successful at its appearance, nowadays only the charming overture is at all remembered.

Dame Blanche, La (The White Lady)

Opera in three acts by Boïeldieu. 1st perf. Paris, 10 Dec 1825; libr. by Eugène Scribe, after Sir Walter Scott's *Guy Mannering* and *Old Morality*. Principal roles: George Brown (ten), Anna (sop), Dickson (ten), Gaveston (b-bar), Jenny (sop). Boïeldieu's finest and most enduring work, which contains some traditional Scottish melodies, it was enormously popular throughout the 19th century: it reached its 1,000th performance, at the Paris Opéra-Comique alone, in 1864. It is still occasionally performed.

Plot: Scotland, 1759. In the castle on the estate of the late Count Avenel is a mysterious White Lady who the farmer, Dickson, has promised to serve. He tells the story to George Brown, a young English officer, who offers to answer a summons from the White Lady in place of Dickson. She turns out to be Anna, ward of the Count's steward, Gaveston, whom she is determined to prevent from acquiring the estate. Relying on money to be provided by the 'ghost' from hidden family treasure, Brown, following the White Lady's instructions outbids Gaveston at the auction for the estate, and Anna reveals both her identity and the fact that Brown is actually the long-lost Avenel heir. [R]

Damnation de Faust, La

Dramatic legend in four parts by Berlioz (Op 24). 1st perf. Paris, 6 Dec 1846. 1st stage perf. Monte Carlo, 18 Feb 1893; libr. by the composer and Almire Gandonnière, after Gérard de Nerval's version of Goethe's *Faust*. Principal roles: Faust (ten), Marguerite (mezzo), Méphistophélès (bass), Brander (bass). Despite its elements of strong theatricality, Berlioz never intended the work to be an opera. It is, however, frequently staged.

Plot: Faust trades his soul with Méphistophélès in exchange for youth, and embarks on a life of debauchery and military glory. He seduces the beautiful Marguerite and then abandons her, and is finally transported to Hell, whilst Marguerite is redeemed. [R]

D'amor sull' ali rosee

Soprano aria for Leonora in Act I of Verdi's *Il Trovatore*.

Damrosch, Walter (1862–1950)

German-born American conductor and composer. A leading interpreter of the German repertory, he introduced many of Wagner's operas to the United States and formed his own company, the Damrosch Opera Company, which performed Wagner with top casts between 1894 and 1899. He also wrote five operas: *The Scarlet Letter* (Boston 11 Feb 1896; libr. G. P. Latrop, after Nathaniel Hawthorne), *The Dove of Peace* (Philadelphia 15 Oct 1912; libr. W. Irwin), *Cyrano de Bergerac**, *The Man Without a Country* (New York 12 May 1937; libr. Arthur Guiterman, after Edward Everett Hale) and *The Opera Cloak* (1942). His autobiography, *My Musical Life*, was published in 1923. His father Leopold (1832–85) was also a leading conductor of the German repertory.

Danaïdes, Les

Opera in three acts by Salieri. 1st perf. Paris, 26 April 1784; libr. by Ranieri de' Calzabigi and Bailli du Roullet. Originally thought to have been written by Gluck, it is one of Salieri's most powerful works, but is nowadays all but forgotten.

Dancairo
Tenor role in Bizet's *Carmen*. He is a smuggler.

Dance
See Ballet

Dance of the Apprentices
Dance in Act III of Wagner's *Die Meistersinger von Nürnberg*.

Dance of the Blessed Spirits
Dance in Act II of Gluck's *Orfeo ed Euridice*.

Dance of the Comedians
Dance in Act III of Smetana's *The Bartered Bride*.

Dance of the Hours
Ballet music in Act III of Ponchielli's *La Gioconda*.

Dance of the Seven Veils
Salome's dance for Herod in Richard Strauss' *Salome*.

Dance of the Tumblers
Dance in Act III of Rimsky-Korsakov's *The Snow Maiden*.

Dance types
See Bolero; Can-Can; Csárdás; Furiant; Gavotte; Gopak; Habañera; Hornpipe; Polka; Polonaise; Tarantella

Danco, Suzanne *(b 1911)*
Belgian soprano, particularly associated with Mozart roles and with 20th-century operas. She had a clear and cool voice, used with fine musicianship and great versatility.

Dandini
Baritone role in Rossini's *La Cenerentola*. He is Don Ramiro's valet.

Danish opera composers
See Enna; Gade; Heise; Klenau; Kuhlau; Nielsen

Other national opera composers include Asger Hamerik (1843–1923), Johann Ernest Hartmann (1726–93), his grandson Johann Peter Emilius Hartmann (1808–1900), Finn Hoffding (*b* 1899), Vagn Holmboe (*b* 1909), Christian Hornemann (1840–1906), Friedrich Ludwig Kunzen (1761–1817), Peter Lange-Müller (1850–1926), Knudaage Riisager (1897–1974) and Christoph Ernst Friedrich Weyse (1774–1842).

Dankevich, Konstantin *(b 1905)*
Ukrainian composer. His *Bogdan Khmelnitsky* (1951) [R] has been one of the most successful modern Ukrainian operas.

Danon, Oskar *(b 1913)*
Yugoslavian conductor, particularly associated with the Russian repertory. He was musical director of the Belgrade Opera (1945–63).

Dansker
Bass role in Britten's *Billy Budd*. He is an old sailor.

Dante
See panel on page 143

Dantons Tod *(Danton's Death)*
Opera in two parts by Einem (Op 6). 1st perf. Salzburg, 6 Aug 1947; libr. by the composer and Boris Blacher, after Georg Büchner's play. Principal roles:

DANTE

The Italian poet Dante Alighieri (1265–1321) himself appears as a character in Rachmaninov's *Francesca da Rimini*, Godard's *Dante et Béatrice* and in operas by four minor composers. His trilogy *La Divina Commedia* has inspired some 25 operas, most of them based on the Francesca da Rimini episode in *L'Inferno*. Below are listed those operas by composers with entries in this dictionary.

Mercadante	*Francesca da Rimini*	1828
Generali	*Francesca da Rimini*	1829
Morlacchi	*Francesca da Rimini*	1836
Götz	*Francesca von Rimini*	1877 (U)
Cagnoni	*Francesca da Rimini*	1878
Thomas	*Françoise de Rimini*	1882
Nápravník	*Francesca da Rimini*	1902
Rachmaninov	*Francesca da Rimini*	1906
Mancinelli	*Paolo e Francesca*	1907
Ábrányi	*Paolo and Francesca*	1912
Puccini	*Gianni Schicchi*	1918

Danton (bar), Robespierre (ten), Camille and Lucille Desmoulins (ten and sop). Dealing with the last days of the French revolutionary leader Georges Jacques Danton (1759–94), it is Einem's first opera and one of his most successful works. It has been widely performed.

Plot: Paris, 1794. Disillusioned with the course taken by the French Revolution, Danton delivers fiery speeches of public denunciation. He is arrested on the orders of Robespierre, tried by a revolutionary tribunal and sentenced to death. At his execution, the mob hails his death with singing and dancing. [R]

Dapertutto

Baritone role in Offenbach's *Les Contes d'Hoffmann*. He is a sinister magician in the Giulietta Act.

Daphne

Opera in one act by Richard Strauss

(Op 82). 1st perf. Dresden, 15 Oct 1938; libr. by Josef Gregor. Principal roles: Daphne (sop), Apollo (ten), Leukippos (ten), Gaia (mezzo), Peneios (bass). Described by Strauss as a 'bucolic comedy', it has never been one of his more popular works, and is only infrequently performed.

Plot: In a village near Mount Olympus, Daphne, daughter of the fisherman Peneios, prefers nature to men. She rejects the shepherd Leukippos, for which her mother Gaia berates her. Enchanted by her beauty, Apollo appears in human form, but his ardour frightens and bewilders her. In jealousy, Apollo kills Leukippos, but when he beholds Daphne's despair, he pleads with Zeus to change her into one of the trees she so loves. Gradually, she is transformed into a laurel tree. [R]

Dara, Enzo *(b 1938)*

Italian bass, particularly associated with Italian comic roles, especially Rossini.

An accomplished buffo, although his voice is far from outstanding.

Darclée, Hariclea (b Hiracly Hartulary) (1860–1939)

Romanian soprano, particularly associated with the Italian and French repertories. Considered by Italians to have had a voice very similar to that of Lilli Lehmann, she created the title roles in *Tosca*, *La Wally* and *Iris*. Her son Ion Hartulary-Darclée (1886–1969) was a conductor who also composed nine operas.

Dardanus

Opera in five acts by Rameau. 1st perf. Paris, 19 Nov 1739; libr. by Leclerc de la Bruyère. Principal roles: Dardanus (ten), Iphise (mezzo), Isménor (bar), Venus (mezzo), Anténor (bar), Teucer (bass). One of Rameau's finest operas, it is still performed from time to time.

Plot: Phrygia. Iphise loves Dardanus, the son of Jupiter. Her father King Teucer wishes her to marry Anténor. After a number of fantastical episodes, including much magic and a monster, Anténor renounces his claim to Iphise and she is united with Dardanus. [R]

Dargomijsky, Alexander (1813–69)

Russian composer. Like many 19th-century Russian composers, he was largely an amateur: Tchaikovsky described him as the "supreme example of the dilettante in music". His first opera *Esmeralda* (Moscow 17 Dec 1847, composed 1840; libr. composer, after Victor Hugo's *Notre-Dame de Paris*) is in French grand opera style and was fairly well received. Its successor, the opera-ballet *The Triumph of Bacchus* (*Torzhestvo Vakha*, 1867, composed 1848; libr. after Alexander Pushkin), was a failure. Of far greater substance was *Rusalka**, which displays considerable wit and powers of characterisation. His last opera was the unfinished *The Stone Guest** (completed by Cui and Rimsky-Korsakov), which is an experimental work employing melodic recitative throughout. It exercised a considerable influence on subsequent Russian composers, particularly Moussorgsky.

Darmstadt Opera

The Grosses Haus (cap. 956) in this town in Hesse-Darmstadt in Germany opened in 1972, replacing the previous theatre which opened in 1819 but which was destroyed by bombs in 1944. Musical directors have included Karl Böhm.

Das

Titles beginning with this form of the German definite article are listed under the letter of the first main word. For example, *Das Rheingold* is listed under R.

Da tempeste

Soprano aria for Cleopatra in Act III of Handel's *Giulio Cesare*.

Daughter of the Regiment, The

See Fille du Régiment, La

Dauvergne, Antoine (1713–97)

French composer. He wrote a number of operas which met with some success in their time but which are largely forgotten today. The most important include *Les Troquers* (Foirc St Laurent 30 July 1753; libr. J.-J. Vade after Jean de la Fontaine), which was the first French opera modelled on the Italian intermezzo style, *La Coquette Trompée* (Fontainebleau 13 Nov 1753; libr. Charles-Simon Favart) [R], *Enée et Lavinie* (Paris 14 Feb 1758; libr. B. L.

de Fontenelle), *Hercule Mourant* (Paris 3 April 1761; libr. Jean-François Marmontel) and *Pyrrhus et Polyxène* (Paris 11 Jan 1763; libr. N.-R. Joliveau).

David

Opera in five acts by Milhaud (Op 320). 1st perf. Jerusalem, 1 June 1954; libr. by Armand Lunel, after the Book of Samuel in the Old Testament. Principal roles: David (bar), Saul (bass), Bathsheba (sop), Jesse (bass), Goliath (bass), Samuel (bass). Written to commemorate the 3,000th anniversary of the founding of Jerusalem, it contains some fine music but is almost never performed.

David

(1) Tenor role in Wagner's *Die Meistersinger von Nürnberg*. He is Hans Sachs' apprentice. (2) Baritone role in Mascagni's *L'Amico Fritz*. He is a rabbi. (3) Tenor role in Nielsen's *Saul and David*. He is Jonathan's friend. (4) Counter-tenor role in Handel's *Saul*.

David, Félicien-César *(1810–76)*

French composer. His travels in the East inspired the oriental subjects of his operas and started the fashion for orientalism in French opera continued by Delibes, Bizet, Rabaud and Gounod. His graceful and melodic operas enjoyed great success in their time but are nowadays largely forgotten. The most important are *La Perle du Brésil* (Paris 22 Nov 1851; libr. J. Gabriel and S. Saint-Etienne), *Herculanum* (Paris 4 March 1859; libr. François Joseph Méry and T. Hadot), *Lalla Roukh* (Paris 12 May 1862; libr. H. Lucas and Michel Carré, after Thomas Moore) and *Le Saphir* (Paris 8 March 1865; libr. Carré, Hadot and Adolphe

de Leuven, after Shakespeare's *All's Well That Ends Well*).

Davide, Giovanni *(1790–1864)*

Italian tenor, son of the tenor Giacomo Davide (1750–1830). Regarded by Stendhal as the finest tenor of his generation, he had an extraordinary range of B♭ to B♭ above high C. For Rossini he created the title role in *Otello*, Don Narciso in *Il Turco in Italia*, Antenore in *Zelmira* and roles in *Ricciardo e Zoraide*, *Ermione* and *La Donna del Lago*. After his voice failed in 1841, he taught in Naples and then became opera manager in St Petersburg. His daughter Giuseppina (1821–1907) was a soprano.

David et Jonathas

Opera in prologue and five acts by M.-A. Charpentier. 1st perf. Paris, 28 Feb 1688; libr. by Père Bretonneau, after the Book of Samuel in the Old Testament. Principal roles: David (c-ten), Jonathan (sop), Saul (bass), Joabel (ten), Achish (bass), Prophetess (c-ten), Ghost of Samuel (bass). Charpentier's penultimate opera, it is a magnificent work containing some fine musical characterisation, and is the finest example of the musico-religious dramas sponsored by the Jesuits. After nearly 300 years of neglect, it has recently been given a number of performances. [R]

Davies, Peter Maxwell

See Maxwell Davies, Sir Peter

Davies, Ryland *(b 1943)*

British tenor, particularly associated with Mozart and lighter Italian and French roles. He possesses a small but pleasant and well-schooled voice and is an accomplished singing-actor. Married

for a time to the mezzo Anne
Howells*.

Davis, Andrew (b 1944)

British conductor, particularly
associated with Strauss and Tippett
operas. One of the finest of the
younger generation of British
conductors, his operatic appearances
were infrequent until recently. Musical
director of the Glyndebourne Festival
(1988–).

Davis, Sir Colin (b 1927)

British conductor, particularly
associated with Mozart, Stravinsky,
postwar British operas and, especially,
Berlioz, of whose music he is often
regarded as the greatest modern
interpreter. One of the leading postwar
British opera conductors, he co-founded
the Chelsea Opera Group and was
musical director of Sadler's Wells Opera
(1961–65) and Covent Garden (1971–
86). He conducted the first
performances of *The Knot Garden*, *The
Ice Break* and Bennett's *The Mines of
Sulphur*, and was the first British
conductor to appear at the Bayreuth
Festival. Married for a time to the
soprano April Cantelo.

De

Names containing this prefix are listed
under the letter of the main surname.
For example, Victoria de los Angeles is
listed under A.

Death

Death appears as a character in a
number of operas, including
(1) Baritone role in Holst's *Sāvitri*.
(2) Contralto role in Stravinsky's *The
Nightingale*. (3) Bass-baritone role in
Ullmann's *Der Kaiser von Atlantis*.
(4) Counter-tenor role in Ridout's *The
Pardoner's Tale*.

Death in Venice

Opera in two acts by Britten (Op 88).
1st perf. Snape, 16 June 1973; libr. by
Myfanwy Piper, after Thomas Mann's
Der Tod in Venedig. Principal roles:
Gustav von Aschenbach (ten), Traveller,
a multiple character of nine roles (bar),
Voice of Apollo (c-ten), Tadzio
(dancer). Britten's last opera, it is
notable for the prominent place
ascribed to dance within the drama.
    Plot: Venice, 1911. The writer
Aschenbach, despairing of his creative
paralysis, finds himself attracted to a
young boy, Tadzio, whom he has seen
with his family on the beach. The two
never actually meet, but Aschenbach
acknowledges to himself with mixed
feelings that he loves the boy.
Subsumed by fantasies about Tadzio's
beauty, he ignores warnings of a
cholera outbreak and falls victim to it.
He dies on the beach while watching
the boy at play. [R]

Debora e Jaële

Opera in three acts by Pizzetti. 1st perf.
Milan, 16 Dec 1922; libr. by the
composer, after the Book of Judges in
the Old Testament. Principal roles:
Debora (mezzo), Jaële (sop), Sisera
(ten), Blind Man (bass). Reasonably
successful at its appearance, it is
nowadays all but forgotten.
    Plot: When the Hebrews accuse Jaële
of friendship with their enemy, Sisera,
Debora promises them victory, and
persuades Jaële to murder Sisera. Jaële
goes to the enemy camp to carry out
the deed but, when it comes to the
point, she is unable to go through with
it. The Hebrews attack their enemy and
win, and Sisera takes refuge with
Debora. She kills him to save him from
torture at the hands of his captors.

Debussy, Claude (1862–1918)

French composer. One of the greatest

and most original composers of his age, his operatic fame rests on *Pelléas et Mélisande**, his only completed opera. Unique in style, its blending of a Wagnerian use of the orchestra with impressionist music and complex symbolism has made it one of the most influential works in the history of opera. Debussy planned a number of other operas, but only two progressed beyond the stage of initial sketches. *Rodrigue et Chimène* (1987, composed 1892; libr. Catulle Mendès after Pierre Corneille's *Le Cid* and G. de Castro's *La Jeunesse du Cid*) contains nearly two hours of music; it was edited for performance with piano by Richard Langham Smith. *La Chûte de la Maison Usher* (New Haven 25 Feb 1977, composed *c* 1915; libr. composer after Edgar Allan Poe's *The Fall of the House of Usher*) [R] contains nearly half an hour of finished material and was edited for performance by W. Harwood.

Decembrists, The (*Dekabristy*)
Opera in four acts by Shaporin. 1st perf. (two scenes only as *Paulina Goebbel*) Leningrad, 1925. 1st complete perf. Moscow, 23 June 1953; libr. by Vsevelod Rozhdestvensky, after A. N. Tolstoy and P. E. Shchogolev. Principal roles: Ryleyev (bar), Bestuzhev (bass), Prince Dmitri (ten), Elena (sop). Perhaps the most important and successful 'orthodox Soviet' opera, it is a patriotic work in a strongly lyrical vein.

Plot: Russia, 1825. Prevented by his mother from marrying Elena, Dmitri leaves the estate, well known for its tyranny over the peasants, and goes to the capital to join Ryleyev, a leader of the revolutionary movement. The Decembrist uprising takes place and, to celebrate its suppression, a courtier gives a masked ball. Elena attends and is pursued by a reveller whom she recognises as the Tsar. She begs to be allowed to share Dmitri's fate and joins the revolutionaries on their way to Siberian exile. The revolution has failed, but Bestuzhev tells the people "from a spark rises a flame". [R]

Decoration
The art of embellishing the vocal line, as in the da capo section of a Handelian aria or in the cabaletta of a 19th-century Italian opera.

Deh! tu di una umile preghiera
Soprano aria for Mary in Act III of Donizetti's *Maria Stuarda*.

Deh vieni
Soprano aria for Susanna in Act IV of Mozart's *Le Nozze di Figaro*.

Deh vieni alla finestra
Baritone aria (the Serenade) for the Don in Act II of Mozart's *Don Giovanni*.

Deidamia
Opera in three acts by Handel. 1st perf. London, 10 Jan 1740; libr. by Paolo Antonio Rolli. Principal roles: Deidamia (sop), Ulisse (mezzo), Achilles (sop), Licomede (bass), Fenice (bar), Nerea (sop). Handel's last Italian opera, it was unsuccessful at its appearance and is nowadays only rarely performed.

Plot: The young Achilles is living disguised as a girl at the palace of Licomede, King of Scyros. He is unmasked by Ulisse and Fenice and summoned to the Trojan War. Before leaving, he marries Licomede's daughter, Deidamia, who has fallen in love with him.

Dein ist mein ganzes Herz
Tenor aria for Prince Sou-chong in Lehár's *Das Land des Lächelns*.

Del
Names containing this prefix are listed under the letter of the main surname. For example, Mario del Monaco is listed under M.

Delibes, Léo *(1836–91)*
French composer. He wrote his first stage work, the operetta *Deux Sous de Charbon* (Paris 9 Feb 1856; libr. J. Moineaux), at the age of 19, going on to write a number of lighter pieces such as *Maître Griffard* (Paris 3 Oct 1857; libr. Mestépès), some of which enjoyed success in their time. After a successful period as a ballet composer, he turned to opera with the comedy *Le Roi l'a Dit**. This was folowed by *Jean de Nivelle* (Paris 8 March 1880; libr. Edmond Gondinet and Philippe Gille) and *Lakmé**, his most successful and enduring opera. His last work, the grand opera *Kassaya* (Paris 24 March 1893; libr. Gille and Henri Meilhac), was left unfinished at his death and was completed by Massenet. His stage works are notable for their graceful and charming melodies and their colourful orchestration, particularly when dealing with the oriental subjects so popular in France at that time.

Delius, Frederick *(1862–1934)*
British composer. His six operas, largely dating from the early period of his career, are notable for their richly orchestrated scores in impressionist late romantic style. *Irmelin** was followed by *The Magic Fountain**, *Koanga**, *A Village Romeo and Juliet**, his most successful work, *Margot la Rouge** and *Fennimore and Gerda**. Despite their beautiful music and the strong advocacy of them by Sir Thomas Beecham and others, none of his operas have won a place in the repertory.

Della
Names containing this prefix are listed under the letter of the main surname. For example, Lisa della Casa is listed under C.

Deller, Alfred *(1912–79)*
British counter-tenor. The first important modern counter-tenor, he was a noted interpreter of Purcell and other Baroque roles. A singer of style and outstanding musicianship, he created Oberon in *A Midsummer Night's Dream* and Death in Alan Ridout's *The Pardoner's Tale*.

Demetrio e Polibio
Opera in two acts by Rossini. 1st perf. Rome, 18 May 1812 (composed 1807); libr. by Vincenza Vigarnò-Mombelli, after Pietro Metastasio's *Demetrio*. Rossini's first opera, it is only very rarely performed.

Demetrius
Baritone role in Britten's *A Midsummer Night's Dream*. He is one of the four lovers.

De' miei bollenti spiriti
Tenor aria for Alfredo in Act II of Verdi's *La Traviata*.

Demon, The
Opera in three acts by Anton Rubinstein. 1st perf. St. Petersburg, 25 Jan 1875; libr. by Pavel Viskovatov, after Mikhail Lermontov's poem. Principal roles: Demon (bass), Tamara (sop), Sinodal (ten), Prince Gudal (bass), Angel (mezzo). Passionate and romantic, it is Rubinstein's finest and

most successful work and his only opera still to be performed in Russia.

Plot: Tamara is betrothed to Prince Sinodal, but is desired by the Demon. The Demon has Sinodal murdered and pursues Tamara into a convent. There, Sinodal – now an angel – mediates to release her from her fate through death. [R]

Denise
Soprano role in Tippett's *The Knot Garden*. She is a political activist.

Denmark
See Royal Danish Opera

Dent, Edward J. *(1876–1957)*
British musicologist and translator. A man of vast learning, his contribution to the improvement of standards of opera in Britain was enormous. Largely responsible for the reappraisal of Mozart in the early years of the century, he was a champion of opera in English and his translations of the Mozart operas set a new standard and remained in use for 50 years. He wrote major books on Mozart, Scarlatti and Busoni.

Denza, Luigi *(1846–1922)*
Italian composer. Although best known for his songs, he also wrote one opera, *Wallenstein* (Naples 1876; libr. after Friedrich von Schiller).

Depuis le jour
Soprano aria for Louise in Act III of Charpentier's *Louise*.

Der
Titles beginning with this form of the German definite article are listed under the letter of the first main word. For example, *Der Freischütz* is listed under F.

Dermota, Anton *(1910–1989)*
Yugoslavian tenor, particularly associated with Mozart roles. One of the most stylish Mozartians of the immediate postwar period, he was also later a distinguished teacher.

Dernesch, Helga *(b 1939)*
Austrian soprano and later mezzo. As a soprano, she was particularly associated with Wagnerian roles, in which her beauty, fine stage presence and warm singing compensated for some lack of the necessary weight. In 1973, she turned successfully to mezzo roles, especially those of Strauss. She created the title role in Fortner's *Elisabeth Tudor* and, for Reimann, Goneril in *Lear* and Hecuba in *Troades*.

Des
Titles beginning with this form of the German definite article are listed under the letter of the first main word. For example, *Des Teufels Lustschloss* is listed under T.

Desdemona
Soprano role in Verdi's and Rossini's *Otello*. She is Otello's wife.

Designers
See Appia, Adolphe; Beaton, Sir Cecil; Benois, Alexandre; Chagall, Marc; Hockney, David; Kokoschka, Oskar; Koltai, Ralph; Lancaster, Sir Osbert; Lazaridis, Stefanos; Messel, Oliver; Neher, Caspar; Piper, John; Quaglio family; Svoboda, Josef

Desmorière, Roger *(1898–1963)*
French conductor, particularly associated with the French repertory and with contemporary works. He was

musical director of the Opéra-Comique, Paris (1944–46), and conducted the first performances of Roussel's *La Testament du Tante Caroline*, Milhaud's *Esther de Carpentras* and Sauget's *La Gaguere Imprévue*.

Despina

Soprano role in Mozart's *Così fan Tutte*. She is maid to Fiordiligi and Dorabella.

Dessau, Paul *(1894–1979)*

German composer and conductor. His first opera was *Giuditta* (1912; libr. M. May), but it was his postwar works which established him as a leading member of the German avant-garde. *Die Verurteilung des Lukullus**, his most successful work, was followed by *Puntila* (Berlin 1966; libr. P. Palitzch and M. Wekwerth after Bertolt Brecht's *Herr Puntila und sein Necht Marti*) [R], *Lanzelot* (Berlin 1969; libr. H. Müller after J. Schwarz's *Der Drache*) and *Einstein* (Berlin 1973; libr. K. Mickel). His wife Ruth Berghaus (*b* 1927) is a noted avant-garde producer, whose extraordinary production of *Don Giovanni* for the Welsh National Opera raised many eyebrows.

Destinn, Emmy *(b Emilie Pavlína Kittlová, then known as Ema Destinnová) (1878–1930)*

Czech soprano, particularly associated with Puccini and Wagner roles. One of the leading dramatic sopranos of her time, she was an outstanding singing-actress with a voice of highly individual timbre. She created Minnie in *La Fanciulla del West*. She also wrote a play, *Rahel*, as well as poems and novels.

Destouches, André *(1672–1749)*

French composer. The historical link between Lully and Rameau, he wrote ten operas, notable for their elegant melodies, many of which enjoyed success but which are all now forgotten. His operas are *Issé* (Fontainebleau 7 Oct 1697; libr. La Motte), *Amadis de Grèce* (Fontainebleau 1699; libr. La Motte), *Marthésie* (Fontainebleau Oct 1699; libr. La Motte), *Omphale* (Paris 10 Nov 1701; libr. La Motte), *Le Carnival et la Folie* (Paris 27 Dec 1703; libr. La Motte), *Callirohé* (Paris 27 Dec 1712; libr. Roy), *Télémaque et Calypso* (Paris 15 Nov 1714; libr. Abbé Simon de Pellegrin), *Sémiramis* (Paris 1718; libr. Roy), *Les Elements* (Paris 22 Dec 1721; libr. Roy) and *Les Stratagèmes de l'Amour* (Paris 19 March 1726; libr. Roy).

Deus ex machina (Latin for 'god from the machine')

A theatrical device, dating back to ancient Greece, in which a god is lowered from above the stage to intervene and resolve the dramatic action. By extension, the term also refers to any arbitrary solution to a tangled plot. The convention was much used in opera seria.

Deutekom, Cristina *(b Stientje Engel) (b 1932)*

Dutch soprano, particularly associated with coloratura roles, especially the Queen of the Night. She had a voice of remarkable agility, used with an outstanding technique, although the sound was sometimes rather white and hard.

Deutsche Oper, Berlin

Previously called the Städtische Oper, the theatre (cap. 1,900) in West Berlin opened on 12 Nov 1912. Destroyed by bombs in 1944, it reopened in 1961. One of Germany's leading houses, it is noted for its adventurous repertory policy. The annual season runs from September to March. Musical directors have included Bruno Walter, Fritz Stiedry, Hans Schmidt-Isserstedt, Leopold Ludwig, Ferenc Fricsay, Lorin Maazel, Jesús López-Cobos and Giuseppe Sinopoli.

Deutsche Oper am Rhein

One of West Germany's leading opera companies, it was formed in 1956 and performs in the North Rhine-Westphalian cities of Düsseldorf and Duisburg. Performances are given at the Düsseldorf Opernhaus (cap. 1,344), opened in 1875 and rebult in 1956, and the Duisburg Stattheater (cap. 1, 200), opened in 1912 and rebuilt in 1950. The repertory is notable for its 20th-century works and for its complete cycles of works by major opera composers. The annual season runs from September to July. Musical directors have included Heinrich Hollreiser, Alberto Erede and Günther Wich.

Deux Aveugles, Les (The Two Blind Men)

Works of this title include:

(1) Opera in one act by Méhul. 1st perf. Paris, 28 Jan 1806; libr. by Benoît Joseph Marsollier. Successful in its time, it is now forgotten.

(2) Operetta in one act by Offenbach. 1st perf. Paris, 5 July 1855; libr. by J. Moinaux. Principal roles: Patachon (ten), Giraffier (bar). Offenbach's first real operetta, it still receives an occasional performance.

Deux Journées, Les (The Two Days)

or **Le Porteur d'Eau** (The Water Carrier, by which title it is usually known in English)

Opera in three acts by Cherubini. 1st perf. Paris, 16 Jan 1800; libr. by Jean Nicolas Bouilly. Principal roles: Count Armand (ten), Mikéli (bass), Constance (sop). One of the most famous 'rescue' operas, it was both successful and influential in its time but is nowadays only rarely performed.

Plot: Paris, 1647. Count Armand has fallen into disfavour with Cardinal Mazarin. He arranges with the water-carrier Mikéli to escape from Paris in a barrel. He and his wife Constance are captured, but Mikéli brings news of their pardon.

Devil

As well as his appearances as Mephistopheles, the Devil appears as a character in a number of operas, including (1) Baritone role in Weinberger's *Shvanda the Bagpiper*. (2) Bass role in Dvořák's *The Devil and Kate*. (3) Bass role in Smetana's *The Devil's Wall*. (4) Baritone role in Massenet's *Grisélidis*. (5) Baritone role in Tchaikovsky's *Vakula the Blacksmith*. (6) Tenor role in Rimsky-Korsakov's *Christmas Eve*. (7) Bass role in Franchetti's *Asrael*.

Devil and Daniel Webster, The

Opera in one act by Moore. 1st perf. New York, 18 May 1939; libr. by the composer, after Stephen Vincent Benét. Principal roles: Daniel Webster (bar), Jabez Stone (ten), Scratch (bass). A work of almost folktale simplicity and strength, it is one of Moore's finest operas.

Plot: A New Hampshire farmer, Jabez Stone, has sold his soul to the Devil in return for ten prosperous years. Disguised as Scratch the lawyer, the Devil comes to collect his debt. Daniel Webster comes to the aid of Stone, demanding a trial and agreeing to a jury of dead men – provided they are American. The jury are all notorious villains from America's past, and Webster secures an acquittal. [R]

Devil and Kate, The (Čert a Káča)

Comic opera in three acts by Dvořák (Op 112). 1st perf. Prague, 23 Nov 1899; libr. by Adolf Wenig, after Božena Němcová's *Fairy Tales*. Principal roles: Káča (mezzo), Jirka (ten), Marbuel (bar), Lucifer (bass), Lady of the Manor (sop). One of Dvořák's most delightful works, it is still very popular in Czechoslovakia but is unaccountably only very rarely performed elsewhere.

Plot: Nobody wants to dance with the unattractive and talkative Káča, so she offers to dance 'with the Devil'. Marbuel appears and takes her down to Hell. The shepherd Jirka volunteers to rescue her, which does not prove difficult as Hell is only too happy to be rid of her garrulity. Jirka's services are also enlisted by the Lady of the Manor on hearing that the Devil is coming for her. In return for her abolishing serfdom, Jirka frightens Marbuel away from the manor by bringing Káča to it. [R]

Devils of Loudun, The (Diably z Loudun)

Opera in three acts by Penderecki. 1st perf. (as *Die Teufels von Loudun*) Hamburg, 20 June 1969; libr. by the composer after Aldous Huxley's novel and John Whiting's *The Devils*. Principal roles: Jeanne des Anges (sop), Urbain Grandier (bar), Fr Barré (bass), Commissioner (ten), Manoury (bar), Adam (ten), Fr Ambrose (bass). Penderecki's first opera, it tells of an historical case of the alleged demonic possession of a group of nuns in 17th-century France. One of the most powerful and disturbing of contemporary operas, it has been widely performed, and is a harrowing indictment of inhumanity and intolerance.

Plot: The prioress Jeanne des Anges and her Ursuline nuns claim to be possessed by the devil. They accuse the worldly priest Urbain Grandier of engendering the possession. Grandier refuses to confess, is tortured and finally burnt at the stake. [R]

Devil's Wall, The (Čertova Stěna)

Opera in three acts by Smetana. 1st perf. Prague, 29 Oct 1882; libr. by Eliška Krásnohorská. Principal roles: Vok (bar), Hedvika (sop), Jarek (ten), Devil/Beneš (bass), Michálek (ten), Záviš (mezzo), Katuška (sop). Smetana's last opera, it is a richly scored romantic comedy, very seldom performed outside Czechoslovakia.

Plot: The Devil overhears Jarek vow that he will not marry Katuška until his master Vok is himself married. Disguising himself as the disreputable hermit Beneš, the Devil causes great confusion and nearly succeeds in preventing Vok's marriage to Hedvika, by damming the River Vltava which threatens to engulf Vok in the abbey in which he has taken refuge. [R]

Devin du Village, Le (The Village Soothsayer)

Opera in one act by Rousseau. 1st perf. Fontainebleau, 18 Oct 1752; libr. by the composer. Principal roles: Colette (sop), Colin (ten), Soothsayer (bar). Rousseau's only work still to be remembered, it was written in emulation of Pergolesi's *La Serva Padrona*, and was part of his contribution to the Guerre des Bouffons*. It had a wide influence and was frequently parodied or adapted, as in Mozart's *Bastien und Bastienne*.

Plot: Colette, having reason to believe that Colin no longer loves her, seeks the aid of the Soothsayer to help win him back. The Soothsayer advises her to feign indifference towards him and, at the same time, tells Colin that Colette is no longer interested. The plan succeeds: Colin woos Colette ardently and all ends happily. [R]

Dexter, John *(1925–90)*

British producer. One of the most brilliant, exciting and controversial British stage directors, he is mainly associated with the Hamburg State Opera and the Metropolitan Opera, New York, where he was director of productions (1974–81). He was responsible for the famous English National Opera production of *The Devils of Loudun* in 1973.

Di

Names containing this prefix are listed under the letter of the main surname. For example, Giuseppe di Stefano is listed under S.

Dì all'azzurro spazio, Un

Tenor aria (the Improvviso) for Chénier in Act I of Giordano's *Andrea Chénier*.

Dialogues des Carmélites

Opera in three acts by Poulenc. 1st perf. Milan, 26 Jan 1957; libr. by Ernest Lavery, after Georges Bernanos' play, itself derived from Gertrude von le Forte's *Die Letzte am Scafott*. Principal roles: Blanche (sop), Madame Lidoine (sop), Old Prioress (mezzo), Marie (mezzo), Chevalier (ten), Marquis (bar). One of the finest postwar operas, it is written in Poulenc's most lyrical and tender vein and has a powerful effect in the theatre.

Plot: Compiègne and Paris, 1789–92. The emotionally fragile Blanche de la Force enters a Carmelite convent in search of tranquillity but is horrified when the simple sister Constance tells

her of her premonition that the two of them will die together. Her fears are aggravated by the anguish of the dying prioress Madame de Croissy. The convent is attacked by the mob, and the sisters, now led by Madame Lidoine, decide to accept martyrdom. Blanche flees but, as the nuns go serenely to the guillotine, she emerges from the crowd and joins them. [R]

Diamants de la Couronne, Les *(The Crown Diamonds)*

Opera in three acts by Auber. 1st perf. Paris, 6 March 1841; libr. by Eugène Scribe and Jules-Henri Vernoy de Saint-Georges. Principal roles: Catarina (sop), Don Henrique (ten), Diana (sop), Rebelledo (bass). Very successful in its time, only the sparkling overture is still remembered.

Plot: The beautiful young queen of Portugal plans to replenish the nation's depleted treasury by selling the crown jewels and replacing them with imitations. To do so, she masquerades as La Caterina, queen of the brigands. The young nobleman Don Henrique falls in love with her and, with the help of his former fiancée Diana, saves her from capture.

Diamond Aria

Baritone aria ('Scintille diamant') for Dapertutto in the Giulietta Act of Offenbach's *Les Contes d'Hoffmann*. It was inserted from one of Offenbach's earlier works.

Diana

The Graeco-Roman goddess of the hunt appears in many operas, including (1) Mezzo role in Cavalli's *La Calisto*. (2) Mezzo role in Offenbach's *Orphée aux Enfers*. (3) Soprano role in Bliss' *The Olympians*. (4) Soprano role in M.-A. Charpentier's *Actéon*. (5) Mezzo role in Gluck's *Iphigénie en Tauride*. (6)

Mezzo role in Haydn's *La Fedeltà Premiata*. (7) Soprano role in Rameau's *Hippolyte et Aricie*.

Díaz, Justino *(b 1940)*
Puerto Rican bass, particularly associated with the Italian and French repertories. A fine singing-actor with a dark and rich voice of remarkable range, he created Antony in Barber's *Antony and Cleopatra* and a role in Ginastera's *Beatrix Cenci*, and played Iago in Zeffirelli's film of *Otello*.

Dibdin, Charles *(1745–1814)*
British composer, writer and theatre manager. He wrote an enormous number of stage works in various forms, of which the most significant is *Lionel and Clarissa* (London 25 Feb 1768; libr. Isaac Bickerstaffe).

Dibuk, Il *(The Dybbuk)*
Opera in prologue and three acts by Rocca. 1st perf. Milan, 24 March 1934; libr. by Renato Simoni, after Shelomoh An-Ski's play. Principal roles: Chanon (ten), Leah (sop), Ezriel (bass). Rocca's most successful opera, it tells of a man's attempts to discover the secrets of the Qabala.

Dich, teure Halle
Soprano aria for Elisabeth in Act II of Wagner's *Tannhäuser*.

Dickens, Charles
See panel on page 155

Dickie, Murray *(b 1924)*
British tenor, particularly associated with German character roles. Mainly resident at the Vienna State Opera, he had a light and pleasant voice and an engaging stage presence which also allowed him to achieve success in operetta. He created the Curé in Bliss'

The Olympians and also produced a number of operas and operettas.

Diction
Referring to the clarity of a singer's enunciation, it is a term which sadly does not feature in the vocabulary of many singers. There is no excuse for bad diction, which is symptomatic of an imperfect technique. Recent singers whose diction has been an object lesson to their colleagues include Alfredo Kraus, Derek Hammond-Stroud, Sesto Bruscantini and Norman Bailey.

Dido
Mezzo role in Berlioz's *Les Troyens*. She is the Queen of Carthage.

Dido and Aeneas
Opera in prologue and three acts by Purcell. 1st perf. Chelsea, 1689; libr. by Nahum Tate, after Virgil's *The Aeneid*. Principal roles: Dido (mezzo), Aeneas (bar), Belinda (sop), Witch (mezzo), Sailor (ten). A masterpiece in miniature, it is Purcell's finest stage work and one of the greatest of all British operas. Unperformed from 1704 to 1895, it is now regularly staged. Many different editions and realisations have been made.

Plot: Carthage. The court and her sister Belinda persuade Queen Dido to admit to her love for Aeneas. The witches plot the downfall of Dido and Carthage, agreeing to raise a storm so that the lovers out hunting will be forced to seek shelter in a cave. There, one of them disguised as Mercury will remind Aeneas of his destiny to go on to Italy. This duly takes place and Aeneas prepares to leave. Dido brushes aside his explanations and makes ready for her death, after which she is mourned by Cupids. [R]

CHARLES DICKENS

The British novelist Charles Dickens (1812–70) himself wrote one opera libretto, that for John Hullah's now long-forgotten *The Village Coquettes* (1836). His novels have inspired some 20 operas. Below are listed, by work, those operas by composers with entries in this dictionary.

A Christmas Carol

Herrmann	*A Christmas Carol*	1954
Cikker	*Mr Scrooge*	1958
Musgrave	*A Christmas Carol*	1979

The Cricket on the Hearth

Goldmark	*Das Heimchen am Herd*	1896
Zandonai	*Il Grillo del Facolare*	1908
Mackenzie	*The Cricket on the Hearth*	1914

The Pickwick Papers

Coates	*Pickwick*	1936

A Tale of Two Cities

Benjamin	*A Tale of Two Cities*	1950

Die
Titles beginning with this form of the German definite article are listed under the letter of the first main word. For example, *Die Fledermaus* is listed under F.

Dies Bildnis ist bezaubernd schön
Tenor aria (the Portrait Aria) for Tamino in Act I of Mozart's *Die Zauberflöte*.

Di felice, Un
Soprano/tenor duet for Violetta and Alfredo in Act I of Verdi's *La Traviata*.

Dikoi
Bass role in Janáček's *Kářa Kabanová*. A wealthy merchant, he is Boris's uncle.

Dimitri
Tenor role in Moussorgsky's *Boris Godunov*. In reality the monk Grigori, he is the false pretender.

Dimitrij
Opera in four acts by Dvořák (Op 64). 1st perf. Prague, 8 Oct 1882; libr. by Marie Červinková-Riegrová after Friedrich von Schiller's *Demetrius* and Ferdinand Mikovec. Revised version, 1st perf. Prague, 1894. Principal roles: Dimitrij (ten), Marfa (sop), Marina

(sop), Xenie (mezzo), Prince Šujský (bar). Dvořák's most heroic opera, containing some powerful choral writing, it is almost never performed outside Czechoslovakia. The story begins at the point at which Moussorgsky's *Boris Godunov* ends.

Plot: Moscow, 1605. Dimitrij and his wife Marina arrive with Polish troops in Moscow. There, Dimitrij wins the hearts of the people and even the endorsement of his supposed mother Marfa, Ivan the Terrible's widow. He foils a plot by Šujský but forgives him after the intercession of Boris' daughter Xenie. The jealousy of Marina (exacerbated by growing Russo-Polish tension) is confirmed when she overhears Dimitrij propose to Xenie. Marina denounces him as a pretender. Marfa is asked to swear that he is not, but when Dimitrij stops her, he is shot dead by Šujský. [R Exc]

Dimitrova, Ghena *(b 1941)*

Bulgarian soprano, particularly associated with dramatic Italian roles, especially Turandot and Lady Macbeth. She possesses a fine voice of great power and range, and has a strong stage presence.

Dinner Engagement, A

Opera in one act by Berkeley (Op 45). 1st perf, Aldeburgh, 17 June 1954; libr. by Paul Dehn. Principal roles: Susan (sop), Philippe (ten), Earl Dunmow (bass), Countess (mezzo), Duchess (mezzo), Kneebone (sop), Boy (ten). Berkeley's most successful opera, it is an entertaining comedy of manners.

Plot: The newly impoverished Lord and Lady Dunmow attempt to marry their daughter Susan to Prince Philippe. The young couple do eventually fall in love, but for reasons other than those foreseen by the Dunmows.

Dinorah
or Le Pardon de Ploërmel

Opera in three acts by Meyerbeer. 1st perf. Paris, 4 April 1859; libr. by Jules Barbier and Michel Carré. Principal roles: Dinorah (sop), Hoël (bar), Corentin (ten). Meyerbeer's slightest work, it is a pastoral piece which was very popular throughout the 19th century but which is nowadays only very rarely performed.

Plot: A magician reveals to the goatherd Hoël the location of a buried treasure trove but warns that the first person to touch it will die. His betrothed Dinorah, believing him to have abandoned her, goes mad. Hoël saves her from drowning, and on seeing him she regains her sanity. Hoël promises to abandon his search for the treasure. [R]

Dio, che nell'alma infondere

Tenor/baritone duet for Carlos and Posa in Act II of Verdi's *Don Carlos*.

Dio di Giuda

Baritone aria for Nabucco in Act IV of Verdi's *Nabucco*.

Dio, mi potevi

Tenor monologue for Otello in Act III of Verdi's *Otello*.

Di Provenza

Baritone aria for Giorgio Germont in Act II of Verdi's *La Traviata*.

Di quella pira

Tenor cabaletta for Manrico in Act III of Verdi's *Il Trovatore*. The notorious high Cs at the end are *not* in the original score.

Di rigori armato il seno

Tenor aria for the Italian Tenor in Act

I of Richard Strauss' *Der Rosenkavalier*.

Dis-moi, Vénus
Soprano aria for Helen in Act II of Offenbach's *La Belle Hélène*.

Di tanti palpiti
Mezzo aria for Tancredi in Act I of Rossini's *Tancredi*.

Dite alla giovine
Soprano/baritone duet for Violetta and Giorgio Germont in Act II of Verdi's *La Traviata*.

Dittersdorf, Karl Ditters von *(1739–99)*
Austrian composer. His 15 Italian opera serias are of little importance. More significant are his 29 Singspiels, whose liveliness and tunefulness helped shape the development of German comic opera. They include *Die Lustigen Weiber von Windsor* (Oels 25 June 1797; libr. composer, after Shakespeare's *The Merry Wives of Windsor*) and *Doktor und Apotheker**, his only work still to be remembered.

Divertissement (French for 'amusement')
A term used in France in the 17th and 18th centuries to describe a danced stage work. It is used of some of the opera-ballets of Lully and Rameau.

Divinités du Styx
Soprano aria for Alceste in Act I of Gluck's *Alceste*.

Divisions
An obsolete term for long vocal runs, as in many Handelian arias.

Djamileh
Comic opera in one act by Bizet. 1st perf. Paris, 22 May 1872; libr. by Louis Gallet, after Alfred de Musset's *Namouna*. Principal roles: Djamileh (sop), Haroun (ten), Speldiano (bar). A failure at its appearance, and still very rarely performed.

Plot: Egypt. Each month, Speldiano buys a new slave girl for his master Haroun. At the end of her month, Djamileh has fallen in love with Haroun and plots with Speldiano to disguise her and re-introduce her. The plan succeeds and Haroun falls in love with her. [R]

Dobbs, Mattiwilda *(b 1925)*
American soprano, particularly associated with coloratura roles. Her pleasant voice was used with an assured technique and she had an appealing stage presence. She was the first black singer to enjoy a major international career in opera.

Dobrowen, Issay *(b Barabeychik)* *(1891–1953)*
Russian conductor and producer. Based in Stockholm from 1941, he was arguably the finest interpreter of the 19th-century Russian repertory in the immediate postwar period.

Dobson, John
British tenor. The leading British comprimario artist of the postwar period, he was long resident at Covent Garden, giving some 1,700 performances there. His voice, although far from outstanding, was intelligently used and he was a fine singing-actor, especially in comic roles such as Sellem and Spalanzani. He created Paris in *King Priam*, Luke in *The Ice Break* and the Cardinal in Maxwell Davies' *Taverner*.

Docteur Miracle, Le

Operetta in one act. Libr by Léon Battu and Ludovic Halévy. Principal roles: Laurette (sop), Pasquin (ten), Mayor (bass), Véronique (mezzo). In 1857, Offenbach organised a competition for a one-act opéra-comique with four characters and lasting three-quarters of an hour. The jury (Auber, Halévy, Thomas, Gounod and Eugène Scribe) awarded joint first prize to the entries of: (1) Lecocq. 1st perf. Paris, 8 April 1857. (2) Bizet. 1st perf. Paris, 9 April 1857 [R].

Plot: Captain Pasquin disguises himself as a charlatan doctor so as to make contact with his beloved Laurette, whose father, the Mayor, has forbidden her to consort with soldiers.

Dohnányi, Christoph von (b 1929)

German conductor, grandson of the composer Ernö von Dohnányi*. Particularly associated with Mozart and Strauss operas and with 20th-century works, he was musical director of the Lübeck Opera (1957–63), the Kassel Staatstheater (1963–66), the Frankfurt Opera (1968–75) and the Hamburg State Opera (1975–84). He conducted the first performances of *Der Junge Lord*, *The Bassarids* and Einem's *Kabale and Liebe*. Married to the soprano Anja Silja*.

Dohnányi, Ernö von (1877–1960)

Hungarian composer and pianist. Although best known as a composer of piano music, he also wrote three operas: *Tante Simona* (Dresden 1912; libr. V. Heindl), *A Vajda Tornya* (Budapest 1932; libr. V. Lanyi, after H. H. Ewers and M. Henry) and the comedy *Der Tenor* (Budapest 1929; libr. E. Goth, after Sternheim's *Bürgerschippel*), his most successful work. His grandson is the conductor Christoph von Dohnányi*.

Doktor Faust

Opera in two prologues, interlude and three scenes by Busoni. 1st perf. Dresden, 21 May 1925; libr. by the composer after Christopher Marlowe's *Dr Faustus*. Principal roles: Faust (bar), Mephistopheles (ten), Duke and Duchess of Parma (ten and sop), Brother (bar), Wagner (bar). Busoni's last opera, it was left unfinished at his death and was completed by his pupil Philipp Jarnach. Recently, a new edition – more complete and more faithful to Busoni's intentions – has been prepared by Anthony Beaumont. Busoni's stage masterpiece, it is an austere and vocally demanding work which has always been much admired by musicians, but which is only infrequently performed.

Plot: Having made his pact with Mephistopheles, Faust seduces the Duchess of Parma soon after her wedding to the Duke and runs away with her. She dies, but pursues him after death and attempts three times to give him the corpse of their child. He finally accepts the corpse and attempts to revive it by magical powers. When he falls dead, a young man arises from the child's corpse who will accomplish all that Faust failed to do. [R]

Doktor und Apotheker (Doctor and Apothecary)

Comic opera in two acts by Dittersdorf. 1st perf. Vienna, 11 July 1786; libr. by Gottlob Stephanie, after Le Comte N.'s *L'Apothicaire de Murcie*. Principal roles: Leonore (sop), Rosalia (sop), Sturnwald (ten), Stossel (bass), Gotthold (ten), Claudia (mezzo), Krautmann (bar). Dittersdorf's finest Singspiel, it is his only work still to be remembered today. [R]

Domgraf-Fassbaender, Willi
(1897–1978)
German baritone, particularly associated
with Mozart roles. One of the leading
lyric baritones of the inter-war period,
he had a beautiful voice used with fine
musicianship and he was an
accomplished singing-actor. He was
resident producer at the Nürnberg
Stadttheater (1953–62). His daughter is
the mezzo Brigitte Fassbaender*.

Domingo, Plácido *(b 1941, or
1934 according to some sources)
Spanish tenor and conductor. Often
regarded as the leading lyrico-dramatic
tenor of the postwar era, he is
especially associated with the Italian
and French repertories, particularly
Otello and Don José (both of which he
has filmed). He has also sung some
German roles and some contemporary
works: he created the title roles in
Torroba's *El Poeta* and Menotti's
Goya. His voice, both beautiful and
heroic, is used with unfailing
musicianship and he is a singing-actor
of some stature. In recent years, he has
also enjoyed success as a conductor.
His autobiography, *My First Forty
Years*, was published in 1983.

Dominik, Count
Baritone role in Strauss's *Arabella*. He
is one of Arabella's suitors.

Domino Noir, Le *(The Black
Domino)*
Opera in three acts by Auber. 1st perf.
Paris, 2 Dec 1837; libr. by Eugène
Scribe. Very successful in its time,
nowadays only the delightful overture is
remembered.

Dom Sébastien de Portugal
Opera in five acts by Donizetti. 1st
perf. Paris, 13 Nov 1843; libr. by

Eugène Scribe after Barbosa Machado's
Memoirs. Principal roles: Sébastien
(ten), Zaïde (mezzo), Camoens (bar),
Jean (bass), Inquisitor (bass). Donizetti's
penultimate opera, written in French
grand opera style, it was only
moderately successful at its appearance
and is nowadays very rarely performed.

Don, Donna
Characters whose names being with this
title are listed under the letter of the
main name. For example, Don Ottavio
is listed under O. Operas, on the other
hand, for example *Don Giovanni* and
Don Carlos, are to be found under D.

Donath, Helen *(b 1940)*
American soprano, particularly
associated with Mozart and lighter
German roles. She possesses a lovely
voice used with outstanding
musicianship and has a delightful stage
presence.

Don Carlos
Opera in four (originally five) acts by
Verdi. 1st perf. Paris, 11 March 1867;
libr. by François Joseph Méry and
Camille du Locle, after Friedrich von
Schiller's play. Revised version, 1st perf.
Milan, 10 Jan 1884. Principal roles:
Don Carlos (ten), Elisabeth de Valois
(sop), King Philip II (bass), Rodrigo,
Marquis of Posa (bar), Eboli (mezzo),
Grand Inquisitor (bass), Monk/Charles
V (bass), Tebaldo (mezzo). Once
described as 'the thinking-man's grand
opera', it is Verdi's longest and most
complex work, dealing with two of his
favourite themes: the way in which
individual destinies can affect those of
millions, and the relationship between
Church and State. One of the
composer's greatest, and nowadays one
of his most popular operas, it contains
not only fine arias and ensembles, but
also much music in his late style: the

confrontation between the King and the Grand Inquisitor is one of the most remarkable musico-dramatic scenes in all opera. A number of different performing editions exist; most productions use the revised four-act version preceded by the original first act. A few modern productions have been given in the original French, and some have restored music that Verdi was forced to cut before the first performance; this includes a duet for Philip and Carlos which Verdi later reworked as the Lachrymosa in his Requiem.

Plot: France and Spain, 1560. To mark the end of the war between France and Spain, the Infante Don Carlos is to marry Elisabeth, daughter of the King of France. They meet and fall in love but it is then announced that King Philip, has decided to marry Elisabeth himself. For the sake of peace, Elisabeth sorrowfully accepts. At the monastery to which the Emperor Charles V retired, Carlos is urged by his friend Rodrigo, the liberal Marquis of Posa, to aid the oppressed people of Flanders. Posa pleads with the King for a less repressive regime and is appointed to Philip's personal service. The King confides to Posa his suspicions of Elisabeth and Carlos. At a masked ball, Elisabeth and Princess Eboli, who loves Carlos, exchange costumes. Carlos, mistaking Eboli for Elisabeth, pours out his love before he realises his mistake. Rejected, Eboli threatens to reveal all to the King but is constrained by Posa. At a grand Auto da Fé, Carlos openly defies the King and is arrested. Alarmed at the growth of liberalism, the Grand Inquisitor demands of Philip the life of Posa and Philip is forced to yield. Philip accuses Elisabeth of adultery, but it is revealed that the false charges were laid by Eboli, herself formerly the King's mistress. Visiting Carlos in prison, Posa is shot by agents of the Inquisition. A popular uprising on behalf of Carlos is quelled by fear at the appearance of the Grand Inquisitor. In the confusion, however, Eboli has helped Carlos escape to the monastery. There he takes leave of Elisabeth, intending to go to Flanders. Philip arrives to arrest him, but the gates of the tomb open and Charles V drags Carlos inside. [R]

Don Giovanni (*Don Juan*) or Il Dissoluto Punito (*The Rake Punished*)

Opera in two acts by Mozart (K 527). 1st perf. Prague, 29 Oct 1787; libr. by Lorenzo da Ponte, partly after Giovanni Bertati's libretto for Gazzaniga's *Don Giovanni Tenorio ossia Il Convitato di Pietra*. Principal roles: Don Giovanni (bar), Leporello (b-bar), Donna Anna (sop), Donna Elvira (sop), Don Ottavio (ten), Zerlina (sop), Masetto (b-bar), Commendatore (bass). Perhaps Mozart's masterpiece and one of the greatest of all music-dramas, it has remained since its appearance one of the most popular of all operas.

Plot: 17th-century Seville. The libertine Don Giovanni, aided by his servant Leporello, attempts to seduce Donna Anna but is disturbed by her father, the Commendatore, whom he kills in a duel. Anna and her fiancé Don Ottavio swear vengeance. Giovanni's attempts to seduce the peasant girl Zerlina, engaged to Masetto, are foiled by Donna Elvira, whom Giovanni has seduced and abandoned. All turn against Giovanni at a party at his villa, but he escapes and finds himself in a churchyard where the statue of the Commendatore speaks. Lightheartedly, Giovanni invites the statue to supper. The statue arrives and drags the unrepentant Giovanni down to hell. [R]

Donizetti, Gaetano *(1797–1848)*
Italian composer. He studied with Mayr at his school in Bergamo, where he created the title role in Mayr's *Il Piccolo Compositore di Musica*. A musician of great talent and facility, he wrote 69 operas. They are notable for their melodic beauty, simple but deft orchestration and their superb vocal lines – few composers ever wrote better (if highly demandingly) for the voice, especially the tenor. Content to work largely within the rigid operatic structure of his day, Donizetti wrote too much too quickly and many of his operas exhibit an over-reliance on formulae. What distinguishes him from his contemporaries Rossini, Bellini, Mercandante and Pacini, is the greater power and considerable, if intermittent, dramatic insight displayed in his best works. His operas went through a long period of neglect and critical disdain, but with the re-emergence of singers capable of doing justice to his music they have been completely re-evaluated in the last 30 years, and a number are now firmly re-established in the repertory. For some of his comedies, Donizetti wrote his own libretti and demonstrated a considerable talent for well-turned doggerel.

The composer's first 32 operas are pleasant but largely unremarkable, being heavily influenced by Rossini. The best of them are comedies, a genre in which he was to become one of the finest-ever Italian exponents. *La Lettera Anonima* (Naples 29 June 1822; libr. G. Genoino), *L'Aio nell'Imbarazzo**, the hilarious *Le Convenienze e Inconvenienze Teatrali** and *Il Giovedi Grasso* (Naples 1828; libr. Domenico Gilardoni) are still performed from time to time. Of his earlier serious works, the most significant are *Emilia di Liverpool* (Naples 28 July 1824; libr. Giuseppe Checcherini, after Scatizzi;

revised version *L'Ermitaggio di Liwerpool*, Naples 1828) [R both versions], *Gabriella di Vergy* (Naples 29 Nov 1869, composed 1826; libr. Andrea Leone Tottola, after Dormont de Belloy; revised version Belfast 9 Nov 1978, composed 1838) [R] and *Elisabetta al Castello di Kenilworth* (Naples 6 July 1829; libr. Tottola, after Sir Walter Scott's *Kenilworth*).

The turning point in his career came in 1830, with the triumphant success of *Anna Bolena**, which placed him at the forefront of European opera composers. The most important of his mature works, some of which had a considerable influence on the young Verdi, are *Ugo Conte di Parigi**, *L'Elisir d'Amore**, *Parisina d'Este**, *Torquato Tasso**, *Lucrezia Borgia**, *Rosmonda d'Inghilterra* (Florence 27 Feb 1834; libr. Felice Romani after *Fair Rosamund*), *Gemma di Vergy**, *Maria Stuarda**, *Marino Faliero**, the sensationally successful *Lucia di Lammermoor**, the archetypal romantic opera and perhaps his most famous work, *Belisario**, *Il Campanello**, *Betly**, *L'Assedio di Calais* (Naples 19 Nov 1836; libr. Salvatore Cammarano after de Belloy's *Le Siège de Calais*) [R], *Pia de' Tolomei**, *Roberto Devereux**, *Maria de Rudenz**, *Poliuto** (later revised as *Les Martyrs*), *La Fille du Régiment**, *La Favorite**, *Rita**, *Maria Padilla* (Milan 26 Dec 1841; libr. Gaetano Rossi after François Ancelot) [R], *Linda di Chamounix**, *Don Pasquale**, one of the greatest of all opera buffas, *Maria di Rohan**, *Dom Sébastien**, *Caterina Cornaro** and the unfinished *Le Duc d'Albe**.

Donna del Lago, La *(The Lady of the Lake)*
Opera in two acts by Rossini. 1st perf. Naples, 24 Sept 1819; libr. by Andrea Leone Tottola after Sir Walter Scott's

poem. Principal roles: Elena (sop), Malcolm (mezzo), Rodrigo (ten), Giacomo (ten), Douglas (bass). Very popular until the mid-19th century, it suffered a long period of neglect, but recently has once again been quite often performed.

Plot: 16th-century Scotland. Elena, the 'lady of the lake', is in love with Malcolm, but has been promised by her father to Rodrigo. She is also loved by 'Uberto', in reality King James V (Giacomo) who, after Rodrigo is killed in a rebellion against him, pardons her banished father, Douglas of Angus, and allows her to marry Malcolm. [R]

Donna Diana

Opera in three acts by Reznicek. 1st perf. Prague, 16 Dec 1894; libr. by the composer after Moreto y Cavaña's *El Lindo Don Diego*. Reznicek's most successful work, the sparkling overture is still popular.

Donna di quindici anni, Una

Soprano aria for Despina in Act II of Mozart's *Così fan Tutte*.

Donna è mobile, La

Tenor aria for the Duke of Mantua in Act III of Verdi's *Rigoletto*. One of the most famous arias in all opera. Also the title of a comic opera by R. Malipiero (1954).

Donna Juanita

Operetta in three acts by Suppé. 1st perf. Vienna, 21 Feb 1880; libr. by F. Zell (Camillo Walzel) and Richard Genée. Set in Spain during the British occupation in 1796, it tells of a French army cadet who disguises himself as a flirtatious girl to help the French capture San Sebastián. It is still sometimes performed in German-speaking countries.

Donna non vidi mai

Tenor aria for Des Grieux in Act I of Puccini's *Manon Lescaut*.

Donne Curiose, Le (*The Inquisitive Women*)

Comic opera in three acts by Wolf-Ferrari. 1st perf. (as *Die Neugierigen Frauen*) Munich, 27 Nov 1903; libr. by Luigi Sugana after Carlo Goldoni's play. A delightful work, it is still occasionally performed.

Plot: 18th-century Venice. Suspicious women decide to spy on their menfolk at their all-male club, where they believe the men indulge in orgies. They contrive a series of subterfuges to gain entry to the club, only to discover that the men are harmlessly enjoying gourmet meals there. The men are initially horrified, but eventually share with the women the secret password: 'here's to friendship'.

Donner

Baritone role in Wagner's *Das Rheingold*. He is the gold of thunder.

Donnerstag aus Licht

See Licht

Don Pasquale

Comic opera in three acts by Donizetti. 1st perf. Paris, 3 Jan 1843; libr. by the composer and Giovanni Ruffini, after Angelo Anelli's libretto for Pavesi's *Ser Marc' Antonio*. Principal roles: Pasquale (b-bar), Norina (sop), Dr Malatesta (bar), Ernesto (ten). An eternally fresh if slightly bitter-sweet comedy, it is one of Donizetti's most technically assured works. An immediate success, it has remained one of the most popular of all opera buffas.

Plot: 19th-century Rome. The wealthy elderly bachelor, Don Pasquale, has decided to marry so as to disinherit his nephew, Ernesto, who refuses to marry the woman his uncle has chosen for him because he is in love with the flighty widow, Norina. The family doctor, Malatesta, aids the young lovers: he arranges a mock marriage between Pasquale and Norina, the latter disguised as Malatesta's demure sister 'Sofronia', a convent girl. No sooner has the ceremony taken place than Norina/Sofronia leads Pasquale such a dance that the old man is utterly miserable and quite put off by the whole idea of marriage. To get rid of 'Sofronia' he readily agrees to Malatesta's suggestion that he allow Ernesto and Norina to wed. [R]

Don Quichotte

Opera in five acts by Massenet. 1st perf. Monte Carlo, 19 Feb 1910; libr. by Henri Cain, after Miguel Cervantes' *Don Quixote* and Jacques le Lorraine's *Le Chevalier de la Longue Figure*. Principal roles: Don Quichotte (bass), Sancho Panza (bar), Dulcinée (mezzo). Massenet's last successful work, it is a gentle, melancholy and autumnal setting, whose title role has attracted many of the greatest basses. The story contains a number of episodes from Cervantes, but Dulcinée is changed into a beautiful courtesan. After a long period of neglect, it has been regularly performed in recent years. [R]

Don Rodrigo

Opera in three acts by Ginastera (Op 31). 1st perf. Buenos Aires, 24 July 1964; libr. by Alejandro Casona. Principal roles: Rodrigo (ten), Florinda (sop), Don Julián (bar), Teudiselo (bass), Fortunata (mezzo). Ginastera's first major success, written in a mixture of atonal and twelve-tone styles, it sets a fine libretto which combines Christian, Arab and Mozarabic traditions of the last Visigoth King of Spain (*d* 711).

Plot: Rodrigo, having defeated his rivals to become King, meets Florinda, daughter of his supporter Don Julián. At his coronation, the crown slips from Florinda's hands. This ill omen is reinforced when Rodrigo opens the iron chest of the Cave of Toledo to discover an Islamic prophecy of doom to the chest's violator. Lusting for Florinda, Rodrigo rapes her. She appeals to her father for vengeance, and he orders the Arab invasion of Spain. Now a wandering beggar, Rodrigo is full of remorse and dies in Florinda's arms.

Don Sanche

or **Le Château** (*The Castle*)

Opera in one act by Liszt. 1st perf. Paris, 17 Oct 1825; libr. by Rancé and E. G. M. Théaulon. Principal roles: Sanche (ten), Elzire (mezzo), Alidor (bar), Page (sop), Zélis (mezzo). Liszt's only opera, written at the age of 13 with the help of his teacher Paer, it is very rarely performed. [R]

Donzelli, Domenico *(1790– 1873)*

Italian tenor, particularly associated with the Italian repertory. Sometimes regarded as the first dramatic tenor, he was famous for being able to sing a high A from the chest. Said to have been a fine singing-actor, he created Pollione in *Norma*, Don Ruiz in *Maria Padilla*, Count Libenskof in *Il Viaggio a Reims* and roles in Rossini's *Torvaldo e Dorliska*, Halévy's *Clari* and Mercandante's *Elisa e Claudio*.

Dorabella

Mezzo role in Mozart's *Così fan Tutte*. Fiordiligi's sister, she is in love with Ferrando.

Doráti, Antal *(1906–88)*
Hungarian conductor and composer,
particularly assoiciated with the German
repertory, especially Haydn, all of
whose mature operas he recorded. Best
known as a symphonic conductor,
however, his operatic appearances were
infrequent in his later years. He was
musical director of the Münster Opera
(1929–33) and also composed an opera
about Elijah. His autobiography, *Notes
of Seven Decades*, was published in
1979.

Dorothy
Operetta by Cellier. 1st perf. (as *Nell
Gwynne*) Manchester, 16 Oct 1876;
libr. by H. B. Farnie. Revised version,
1st perf. London, 25 Sept 1886; libr.
by B. C. Stephenson. Cellier's best
known work, it was sensationally
successful at its appearance but is
nowadays all but forgotten.

Dortmund Stadttheater
The opera house (cap. 1,130) in this
German city in North Westphalia
opened in 1966, replacing the previous
theatre destroyed by bombs in 1943.
Musical directors have included
Wilhelm Schüchter and Marek
Janowski.

Dosifei
Bass role in Moussorgsky's
Khovanschina. He is the leader of the
Old Believers.

Dostoyevsky, Fyodor
See panel on page 165

Dove sei, amato ben?
Soprano aria for Rodelinda in Act I of
Handel's *Rodelinda*.

Dove sono?
Soprano aria for the Countess in Act III
of Mozart's *Le Nozze di Figaro*.

Downes, Edward *(b 1926)*
British conductor, particularly
associated with Verdi and Wagner and
with the Russian repertory (of which he
has made several translations). Closely
associated with Covent Garden, he was
also musical director of the Australian
Opera (1972–76). A champion of
contemporary composers, he conducted
the first performances of Bennett's
Victory, Maxwell Davies' *Taverner*,
Tavener's *Thérèse* and Prokofiev's
Maddalena, which he prepared for
performance.

Down in the Valley
Opera in one act by Weill. 1st perf.
Bloomington, 15 July 1948; libr. by
Arnold Sundgaard. Principal roles:
Brack Weaver (bar), Jennie Parsons
(sop). Based on American folk song, it
tells in a series of flashbacks the story
of a man awaiting execution for having
killed, in self-defence, his rival in love.

**D'Oyly Carte Opera
Company**
A British company founded in 1876 by
Richard d'Oyly Carte to perform the
Gilbert and Sullivan operettas. Long
based at the Savoy Theatre in London,
it also toured extensively in Britain and
North America. It held a monopoly on
professional performances of the Savoy
Operas until the expiry of the copyright
in 1961. Thereafter, comparison with
other productions showed the company
to be increasingly hidebound by
tradition. It ceased operations in 1982,
following the Arts Council's refusal of
financial assistance, but was re-founded
in 1988. Musical directors have

FYODOR DOSTOYEVSKY

The works of the Russian writer Fyodor Dostoyevsky (1821–81) have inspired some 20 operas. Below are listed, by work, those operas by composers with entries in this dictionary.

The Brothers Karamazov

Jeremiáš	*The Brothers Karamazov*	1928
Blacher	*Der Grossinquisitor*	1948
Rossellini	*La Legenda del Ritorno*	1966

Crime and Punishment

Sutermeister	*Raskolnikoff*	1948
Petrovics	*Crime and Punishment*	1969

The Gambler

Prokofiev	*The Gambler*	1929

The Idiot

Chailly	*L'Idiota*	1970

Memoirs From the House of the Dead

Janáček	*From the House of the Dead*	1930

included Isidore Godfrey, James Walker, Royston Nash, Alexander Faris and Bramwell Tovey. The company has been a proving ground for a number of British singers, including Valerie Masterson, Donald Adams and Gillian Knight.

Dragons de Villars, Les
Opera in three acts by Maillart. 1st perf. Paris, 19 Sept 1856; libr. by Joseph Philippe Lockroy and Eugène Cormon. Maillart's most successful work, it was long popular, but nowadays only the charming overture is remembered.

Dramaturg
A German term which has no exact English equivalent. He is a member of the staff of a German or Austrian opera house, whose duties include adapting libretti, editing programmes, handling the press and sometimes also producing or acting.

Dramma giocoso (Italian for 'humorous drama')
A term used in the late 18th century to describe a comic work which also contained serious elements. Much the most famous example is Mozart's *Don Giovanni*.

Dramma per musica (Italian for 'drama through music')

A term used in the 17th century for a dramatic text, intended to be set to music, on a serious subject.

Dreaming About Thérèse

(*Drömmem om Thérèse*)
Chamber opera in two acts by Werle. 1st perf. Stockholm, 26 May 1964; libr. by Lars Runsten, after Emile Zola's *Pour une Nuit d'Amour*. Principal roles: Thérèse (sop), Julien (bar), Colombel (ten). Designed for performance 'in the round' with the orchestra behind the audience, it makes use of both speech and melodrama.

Plot: Thérèse has accidentally killed Colombel. Her price to Julien for a night of love is the disposal of Colombel's body. Julien throws the body into the river and then throws himself in afterwards.

Dreigroschenoper, Die (*The Threepenny Opera*)

Opera in prologue and eight scenes by Weill. 1st perf. Berlin, 31 Aug 1928; libr. by Bertolt Brecht, after John Gay's *The Beggar's Opera*. Adaptation by Blitzstein, 1st perf. Waltham (Mass), 14 June 1952. Principal roles: Polly (sop), Mack the Knife (bar), Jenny (sop), Peachum (bar), Lucy (sop), Tiger Brown (bar). A modern reworking of Gay's play with music in popular style, it was an immediate success and has always remained one of Weill's best known works. Weill's chamber work, *Kleine Dreigroschenmusik*, is drawn from music from the opera.

Plot: 19th-century Soho. Mack the Knife marries Polly, daughter of the underworld leader Peachum. Betrayed by his in-laws and the prostitute Jenny, he escapes from jail, helped by Lucy, daughter of the corrupt police chief Tiger Brown. Recaptured, Mack is about to be hanged when he is pardoned by Queen Victoria on her coronation day. [R]

Drei Pintos, Die (*The Three Pintos*)

Opera in two acts by Weber and Mahler. 1st perf. Leipzig, 20 Jan 1888 (begun 1821); libr. by Theodor Hell, after Carl Ludwig Seidl's *Der Brautkampf*. Principal roles: Don Pinto (bass), Don Gaston (ten), Clarissa (sop), Ambrosio (bar), Don Gomez (ten), Don Pantaleone (bar). Weber abandoned the piece halfway through and it was completed by Mahler, who orchestrated it and filled in the gaps by using other music by Weber. It is given an occasional performance as a musical curiosity.

Plot: Spain. Don Pinto is journeying to marry Clarissa, when a rival for her affections, Ambrosio, makes him drunk, seizes the marriage papers and masquerades as Pinto. Discovering that Clarissa loves Don Gomez he passes the papers to him, and Gomez becomes the third Pinto. After a series of muddles, all ends happily. [R]

Dresden State Opera

The present Schauspielhaus (cap. 1,200) opened in 1948, replacing the Semper Opernhaus, opened in 1841 but destroyed by bombs in February 1945. It has been one of Germany's most important operatic centres from earliest times and has a particularly strong Wagner and Strauss tradition. The annual season runs from September to June. Musical directors have included Weber, Wagner, Ernest von Schuch, Fritz Reiner, Fritz Busch, Karl Böhm, Karl Elmendorff, Joseph Keilberth, Rudolf Kempe, Franz Konwitschny, Lovro von Matačić, Kurt Sanderling and Otmar Suitner.

Dress rehearsal

The final rehearsal of an opera production, consisting of a complete run-through in full costume, hopefully uninterrupted, at which singers normally 'sing out'. At an 'open' dress rehearsal an invited audience is present. It is called *Generalprobe* in Germany, *Répétition Générale* in France and *Prova Generale* in Italy.

Drottningholm Castle Theatre

The opera house (cap. 454) in the Palace of Drottningholm near Stockholm was built by Carl Fredrik Adelcrantz in 1764–66, replacing the previous theatre of 1754, built by Frederick the Great's sister, which was destroyed by fire in 1762. It was restored in 1922 after a long period of neglect, and much of the original wooden scenery and stage machinery is still in use. Since 1948, it has given summer opera seasons with a repertory consisting predominantly of 18th-century works. Musical directors have included Charles Farncombe and Arnold Östman.

Dublin Grand Opera Society

The company was formed in 1941 and gives two seasons a year at the Gaiety Theatre. The repertory is largely Italian and French, and the orchestra is the Radio Telefis Eireann Symphony.

Duc d'Albe, Le (*The Duke of Alba*)

Opera in four acts by Donizetti. 1st perf. Rome, 22 March 1882 (begun 1839); libr. by Eugène Scribe and Charles Duveyrier. Principal roles: Amelia (sop), Alba (bar), Marcello (ten). Left unfinished by Donizetti, it was completed by Matteo Salvi. It is only rarely performed.

Plot: 16th-century Flanders. Egmont's daughter Amelia is in love with Marcello, who turns out to be the missing son of the Duke of Alba, the oppressive Spanish ruler of Flanders. In an attempt to murder the Duke, Amelia accidentally kills Marcello, who intervenes to save his father. Dying, he begs Alba to forgive Amelia.

Due Foscari, I

Opera in three acts by Verdi. 1st perf. Rome, 3 Nov 1844; libr. by Francesco Maria Piave, after Lord Byron's *The Two Foscari*. Principal roles: Francesco Foscari (bar), Lucrezia (sop), Jacopo Foscari (ten), Loredano (bass). Dealing with the historical Doge of Venice, Francesco Foscari (*d* 1457), this is a dark and sombre work containing some striking prefigurations of Verdi's mature style. One of the composer's finest early works, it has been more admired by musicians than audiences and is not performed as frequently as its merits deserve.

Plot: Venice, 1457. The Doge Francesco Foscari accepts with resignation a decision by the Council of Ten to extend the exile of his son Jacopo, falsely accused of murder. The leader of the opposition, Loredano, is unmoved by the pleas of Jacopo's wife Lucrezia, and Jacopo dies of a broken heart as his ship sails for Crete. Loredano persuades the Council to force Francesco to resign. The Doge (who twice in the past had wished to resign but was begged to remain until his death) dies, disgraced, as the bells announce his successor. [R]

Due Illustri Rivali, Le (*The Two Famous Rivals*)

Opera in three acts by Mercadante. 1st perf. Venice, 10 March 1838; libr. by Gaetano Rossi. One of Mercadante's best works, it was very popular in the mid-19th century, but is nowadays very rarely performed.

Duenna, The

Works of this title based on Richard Brindsley Sheridan's play include:

(1) Opera in three acts by Linley (father and son). 1st perf. London, 21 Nov 1775. Perhaps the most successful of all 18th-century British operas, it is nowadays all but forgotten.

(2) Opera in four acts by Prokofiev (Op 86). Also known as *Betrothal in a Monastery* (*Obrucheniye v Monastyre*). 1st perf. Leningrad, 3 Nov 1946 (composed 1940); libr. by the composer and Mira Mendelssohn-Prokofieva. Principal roles: Duenna (mezzo), Jerome (tenor), Louisa (sop), Mendoza (bass), Ferdinand (bar), Clara (mezzo), Antonio (ten), Carlos (bass). Despite its delightful and colourful score, it is infrequently performed.

Plot: Seville. The nobleman Don Jerome wishes his daughter Louisa to marry the elderly Don Mendoza, but she is in love with Antonio. By deceiving her father, Louisa succeeds in marrying Antonio, whilst Mendoza is tricked into marrying the Duenna. [R]

(3) Opera in three acts by Gerhard. 1st perf. BBC radio, 1949; libr. by the composer and Christopher Hassall. Gerhard's only opera, it is a brilliant setting which is unaccountably almost never performed.

Duet

In opera, a musical number for two solo singers, in which the musical content is divided equally.

Duettino

A short duet in simple style.

Dugazon, Louise (b Lefèvre) (1755–1821)

French soprano. One of the most popular singers of her age, she excelled in opéra-comique. She created over 60 roles (including Zemaide in *Le Calife de Bagdad* and Marguerite in *Richard Coeur de Lion*) in works by Grétry, Isouard, Boïeldieu, Dalayrac and others. She gave her name to a type of French soprano voice, which is divided into four subcategories: *jeune Dugazon*, *première Dugazon*, *forte première Dugazon* and *mère Dugazon*. Her son Gustave (1782–1826) was a composer who wrote five operas.

Duisburg

See Deutsche Oper am Rhein

Dukas, Paul (1865–1935)

French composer. He wrote only one opera, the ambitious *Ariane et Barbe-Bleue**. He also helped to complete Guiraud's unfinished *Frédégonde* and edited a number of Rameau's operas.

Duke Bluebeard's Castle (A Kékszakállú Herceg Vára)

Opera in one act by Bartók (Op 16). 1st perf. Budapest, 24 May 1918 (composed 1911); libr. by Béla Balázs. Principal roles: Bluebeard (b-bar), Judith (sop). Bartók's only opera, it is a darkly symbolic work in which the rich, sensuous and superlatively orchestrated score is tightly constructed to lead up to and then down from the climactic opening of the fifth door. Although never especially popular with audiences, it is regularly performed and ranks as one of the greatest 20th-century operas.

Plot: Bluebeard brings his new wife, Judith, home to his castle, which has seven doors and no windows. Wishing to dispel the darkness, Judith demands the keys to the doors. Behind them she discovers a torture chamber, an armoury, a treasury, a rose garden, a vision of Bluebeard's domains and a lake of tears. All are defiled with blood. Behind the seventh door, Judith finds Bluebeard's previous wives who were similarly curious. Judith must join them, leaving Bluebeard once more in darkness and solitude. [R]

Duke of Mantua
Tenor role in Verdi's *Rigoletto*. He is Rigoletto's libertine employer.

Dulcamara, Dr
Bass-baritone role in Donizetti's *L'Elisir d'Amore*. He is an itinerant quack.

Dumas, Alexandre
See panel on page 170

Duni, Egidio *(1709–75)*
Italian composer. Largely resident in France, he was a principal founder of opéra-comique. He wrote some 30 operas, many of which enjoyed great success in their day but are now all forgotten. His most important works include *Ninette à la Cour* (Parma 1755; libr. Charles-Simon Favart, after Carlo Goldoni's *Bertoldo*), *La Buona Figliuola* (Parma 26 Dec 1756; libr. Goldoni after Samuel Richardson's *Pamela*), *La Fille Mal Gardée* (Paris 14 March 1758; libr. Favart), *La Fée Urgèle* (Fontainebleau 26 Oct 1765; libr. Favart, after Voltaire's *Ce Qui Plaît aux Dames*), *La Clochette* (Paris 24 July 1766; libr. Louis Anseaume), *Les Moissonneurs* (Paris 27 Jan 1768; libr. Favart after the Book of Ruth in the Old Testament) and *Les Sabots* (Paris 26 Oct 1768; libr. Jean-Marie Sedaine).

Dunque io son
Mezzo/baritone duet for Rosina and Figaro in Act I of Rossini's *Il Barbiere di Siviglia*.

Duphol, Baron
Baritone comprimario role in Verdi's *La Traviata*. He is Violetta's protector.

Duprez, Gilbert *(1806–96)*
French tenor and composer. One of the leading tenors of the first half of the 19th century, he created the title role in *Benvenuto Cellini* and, for Donizetti, Edgardo in *Lucia di Lammermoor*, Ugo in *Parisina*, Polyeucte in *Les Martyrs* and Fernand in *La Favorite*. He also composed eight operas and was a noted teacher, whose pupils included Emma Albani and Marie Miolan-Carvalho. His autobiography, *Souvenirs d'un Chanteur*, was published in 1880.

Durch die Wälder
Tenor aria for Max in Act I of Weber's *Der Freischütz*.

Durchkomponiert (German for 'continuously composed')
The term is used in Germany to describe an opera with no spoken dialogue and in which the musical numbers merge without a break.

Düsseldorf
See Deutsche Oper am Rhein

Dutch opera composers
See Pijper
Other national opera composers include Hendrik Franciscus Andriessen (*b* 1892), Henk Badings (*b* 1907), Cornelis Dopper (1870–1939), Willem Landré (1874–1948), his son Guillaume (1905–68), S. van Milligen (1849–1929) and Johan Wagenaar (1862–1941).

Dutoit, Charles *(b 1936)*
Swiss conductor, particularly associated

ALEXANDRE DUMAS

The French novelist Alexandre Dumas (1802–70) was himself co-author of two opera libretti, those for Monpou's *Piquillo* and Thomas' *Le Roman d'Elvire*. He also appears as a character in Giordano's *Andrea Chénier*. Some 30 operas have been based on his novels. Below are listed, by work, those operas by composers with entries in this dictionary.

Ascanio
Saint-Saëns	*Ascanio*	1890

Charles VII Chez ses Grands Vassaux
Donizetti	*Gemma di Vergy*	1834
Cui	*The Saracen*	1899

Le Chevalier d'Harmental
Messager	*Le Chevalier d'Harmental*	1896

Les Demoiselles de St Cyr
Humperdinck	*Die Heirat Wider Willen*	1905

Don Juan de Mañara
Pacini	*Carmelita*	1863

Henri III
Flotow	*Le Comte de St Mégrin*	1838

Joseph Balsamo
Litolff	*La Mandragore*	1876

The Man in the Iron Mask
Thomas	*Raymond*	1851

Le Tulipe Noir
Flotow	*Il Fiore di Harlem*	1876

His son Alexandre Dumas (1824–95) was also a writer, whose *La Dame aux Camélias* was the source for Verdi's *La Traviata*.

with the French repertory and with 20th-century works. Best known as a symphonic conductor, his operatic appearances are infrequent.

Duval, Denise *(b 1921)*
French soprano, particularly associated with the French repertory, especially Poulenc. She was a fine singing-actress of great charm and personal beauty with a voice of highly individual timbre. She created Thérèse in *Les Mamelles de Tirésias*, Elle in *La Voix Humaine* and a role in Hahn's *Le Oui des Jeunes Filles*.

Dvořák, Antonín *(1841–1904)*
Czech composer. He wrote ten operas, notable for their fine orchestration, abundant melody and often sharp sense of characterisation. Many are still very popular in Czechoslovakia but are unaccountably seldom heard elsewhere. His operas are: *Alfred* (Olomouc 10 Dec 1938, composed 1870; libr. K. T. Körner), *King and Collier* (*Král a Uhlíř*, Prague 24 Nov 1874; libr. Bernard Guldener), *The Pigheaded Peasants* (*Tvrdé Palice*, Prague 2 Oct 1881, composed 1874; libr. I. Josef Štolba), the historical *Vanda**, *The Cunning Peasant* (*Šelma Sedlak*, Prague 27 Jan 1878; libr. Josef Otakar Veselý), the heroic *Dimitrij**, *Jakobín**, the delightful comedy *The Devil and Kate**, *Rusalka**, his finest opera and his only one to be well-known outside Czechoslovakia, and *Armida**.

Dvořáková, Ludmila *(b 1923)*
Czech soprano, particularly associated with Wagnerian roles and with the

Czech repertory. A fine singing-actress with an exciting if not technically perfect voice, she was one of the leading Wagnerian sopranos of the 1960s.

Dvorský, Peter *(b 1951)*
Czech tenor, particularly associated with the Italian and Czech repertories. The leading contemporary Czech tenor, he has a fine and intelligently used voice, but is a little dull on stage.

Dyck, Ernest van *(1861–1923)*
Belgian tenor. One of the leading heldentenors of the late 19th century, he was especially famous as Lohengrin and Parsifal. He created the title role in *Werther*.

Dyer's Wife
Soprano role in Strauss' *Die Frau ohne Schatten*. She is Barak's wife.

Dzerzhinsky, Ivan *(1909–78)*
Russian composer. His operas, harmonically simple, lyrical and easily accessible are representative of 'orthodox Soviet' music. His first opera *Quiet Flows the Don** was highly successful and was hailed by Stalin as a model of 'socialist realism'. None of his 11 other operas recaptured this initial success. His later works include *Virgin Soil Upturned* (1937; libr. after Mikhial Sholokhov), *Winter Night* (1946; libr. after Alexander Pushkin's *The Snowstorm*), *The Fate of a Man* (1961; libr. after Shokholov), *Grigori Melekhov* (1967) and *Hostile Whirlwinds* (1969).

E

Eames, Emma *(1865–1962)*

American soprano, particularly associated with the French repertory. One of the most popular sopranos of her time and famed for her personal beauty, she created Colombe in Saint-Saëns' *Ascanio*. Her autobiography, *Some Memories and Reflections*, was published in 1927.

Easter Hymn

Chorus ('Regina coeli') in Mascagni's *Cavalleria Rusticana*.

East Germany

See Germany

Easton, Florence *(1884–1955)*

British soprano, long resident at the Metroplitan Opera, New York. One of the most versatile sopranos of the interwar period, her large repertory ranged from Brünnhilde to Cio-Cio-San, and she was able to learn a new role within 12 hours. She created Lauretta in *Gianni Schicchi*, Aelfrida in Taylor's *The King's Henchman* and Mother Tyl in Wolff's *L'Oiseau Bleu*.

Ebert, Carl *(1887–1980)*

German producer and administrator. One of the most influential opera producers of the mid-20th century, particularly successful with Mozart and Verdi, he was general director of the Darmstadt Opera and the Berlin State Opera. He was also a co-founder of the Glyndebourne Festival and organised the Turkish National Theatre and

Opera. His son Peter (*b* 1918) is also a producer and administrator. He was director of productions for Scottish Opera, the Augsburg Stattheater and the Wiesbaden Opera and was general administrator of Scottish Opera (1977–80).

Eboli

Mezzo role in Verdi's *Don Carlos*. She is King Philip's ex-mistress.

Ecco il mondo

Bass aria for Mefistofele in Act II of Boito's *Mefistofele*.

Ecco l'orrido campo

Soprano aria for Amelia in Act II of Verdi's *Un Ballo in Maschera*.

Ecco ridente

Tenor aria for Count Almaviva in Act I of Rossini's *Il Barbiere di Siviglia*.

Echo et Narcisse

Opera in five acts by Gluck. 1st perf. Paris, 24 Sept 1779; libr. by Baron Tschudi, after Ovid's *Metamorphoses*. Revised version, 1st perf. 8 Aug 1780. Principal roles: Echo (sop), Narcisse (ten). Gluck's last opera, it was a failure despite its delicate and charming music. It is nowadays only very rarely performed. [R]

Ecuadorean opera composers

These include Luis H. Salgado (*b* 1903).

Eda-Pierre, Christiane *(b 1932)*

Martiniquan soprano, particularly associated with Mozart roles and with the French repertory. Possessing a rich, beautiful and agile voice, she created the Angel in Messiaen's *St François d'Assise*.

Edelmann, Otto *(b 1917)*

Austrian bass. One of the leading basses of the immediate postwar period, he was particularly associated with Mozart and Wagner roles and with Baron Ochs.

Edgar

Opera in three (originally four) acts by Puccini. 1st perf. Milan, 21 April 1889; libr. by Ferdinando Fontana after Alfred de Musset's *La Coupe et les Lèvres*. Revised version, 1st perf. Ferrara, 28 Feb 1892. Principal roles: Edgar (ten), Fidelia (sop), Tigrana (mezzo), Frank (bar). Puccini's second opera, it is his least successful work and very rarely performed.

Plot: Flanders, 1302. Edgar deserts his love, Fidelia, for the seductive Moorish girl, Tigrana. His brother Frank, who also loves Tigrana, challenges him to a duel and is wounded. In remorse, Edgar leaves Tigrana and joins the army where he and Frank are reconciled. Later, Edgar is believed to have died and, at a requiem for him, a monk recites his crimes and then reveals himself as Edgar. Fidelia rushes to his arms, but is murdered by Tigrana. [R]

Edgardo

Tenor role in Donizetti's *Lucia di Lammermoor*. The dispossessed master of Ravenswood, he is in love with Lucia.

Edinburgh Festival

An annual arts festival in Scotland, of which opera is a central feature, which was founded in 1947 by Audrey Mildmay and Sir Rudolf Bing. In the early days, opera was provided by Glyndebourne, but since 1956 it has been provided by visiting companies from around the world. Ranking as one of the most important European summer festivals, artistic directors have been Bing, Ian Hunter, the Earl of Harewood, Peter Diamand, John Drummond and Frank Dunlop.

Education Manquée, Une

Comic opera in one act by Chabrier. 1st perf. Paris, 1 May 1879; libr. by Eugène Leterrier and Albert Vanloo. Principal roles: Gontran (sop), Hélène (mezzo), Pausanias (bass). A delightful little piece, it is still occasionally performed. [R]

Egisto, L'

Opera in three acts by Cavalli. 1st perf. Venice, 1643; libr. by Giovanni Battista Faustini. Principal roles: Egisto (ten), Clori (sop), Climene (mezzo), Hipparco (ten). After nearly 300 years of neglect, it has had a number of performances in recent years. [R]

Egk, Werner *(1901–83)*

German composer and conductor. Influenced by Stravinsky, he wrote eight operas, whose theatrical flair and readily accessible melodies have won him considerable popularity in Germany and Austria. Elsewhere, his works are very seldom performed. His operas are *Columbus* (Munich Radio 1933; libr. composer), *Die Zaubergeige**, *Peer Gynt**, *Circe* (Berlin 1948; libr. composer, after Pedro Calderón's *El Mayor Encanto Amor*), *Irische Legende**, *Der Revisor**, *Die Verlobung* in *San Domingo** and *17 Tage und 4 Minuten* (Stuttgart 1966). He also wrote the libretto for Blacher's *Abstrakt Oper No 1*.

Eglantine
Soprano role in Weber's *Euryanthe*. She is in love with Adolar.

Ehrling, Sixten *(b 1918)*
Swedish conductor, particularly associated with the German repertory. He was musical director of the Royal Opera, Stockholm (1953–60) and conducted the first performance of Blomdahl's *Aniara*.

Ein, Eine
Titles beginning with the German indefinite article are listed under the letter of the first main word. For example, *Ein Walzertraum* is listed under W.

Einem, Gottfried von *(b 1918)*
Austrian composer. One of the most successful contemporary opera composers, his stage works are highly effective theatrically and eclectic in musical style. His operas include *Dantons Tod**, *Der Prozess**, *Der Zerrissene* (*The Confused*, Hamburg 17 Sept 1964; libr. Boris Blacher, after Johann Nepomuk Nestroy), the highly successful *Der Besuch der Alten Dame** and *Kabale und Liebe* (Vienna 17 Dec 1976; libr. Blacher and L. Ingrisch after Friedrich von Schiller).

Einsam in trüben Tagen
Soprano aria for Elsa in Act I of Wagner's *Lohengrin*. It is usually referred to as Elsa's Dream.

Eire
See Dublin Grand Opera Society; Wexford Festival

Eisenstein, Gabriel von
Tenor role in J. Strauss' *Die Fledermaus*. He is Rosalinde's husband. The role is often sung by a baritone.

Eisler, Hanns *(1898–1962)*
German composer. He wrote a considerable number of operas, many in collaboration with Bertolt Brecht, which reflect his strong Marxist views. The most important is *Die Mutter* (*The Mother*, Berlin 1931; libr. Brecht, after Maxim Gorky).

Eisslinger, Ulrich
Tenor comprimario role in Wagner's *Die Meistersinger von Nürnberg*. A grocer, he is one of the masters.

È la solita storia
Tenor aria for Federico in Cilea's *L'Arlesiana*.

Elder, Mark *(b 1947)*
British conductor, particularly associated with the Italian and Czech repertories. One of the most talented of the younger generation of British conductors, he conducted the first performance of Blake's *Toussaint*. Musical director of the English National Opera (1980–).

Eléazer
Tenor role in Halévy's *La Juive*. He is a Jewish goldsmith.

Electra
Soprano role in Mozart's *Idomeneo*. She is in love with Idamante.

Elegie für Junge Liebende
(*Elegy for Young Lovers*)
Opera in three acts by Henze. 1st perf. Schwetzingen, 20 May 1961; libr. by W. H. Auden and Chester Kallman.

Principal roles: Gregor Mittenhofer (bar), Hilda Mack (sop), Toni and Dr Reischmann (ten and bass), Elisabeth Zimmer (sop), Carolina (mezzo). One of Henze's finest operas, it has been widely performed.

Plot: Austrian Alps. The egocentric and narcissistic poet Mittenhoffer goes to the Alps annually to seek inspiration for his work from the hallucinations of Hilda Mack, permanently waiting for the return of her husband who disappeared on their honeymoon 40 years earlier. When Mack's body is recovered from a glacier, Mittenhofer has to find inspiration elsewhere and fastens upon the young lovers, Toni and Elisabeth. He sends them out on to the Hammerhorn to collect edelweiss and allows them to die there. This inspires his greatest poem 'Elegy for Young Lovers'. [R Exc]

Elektra

Opera in one act by Richard Strauss (Op 58). 1st perf. Dresden, 25 Jan 1909; libr. by Hugo von Hofmannsthal, after Sophocles' play. Principal roles: Elektra (sop), Chrysothemis (sop), Clytemnestra (mezzo), Orestes (bar), Aegisthus (ten). The first fruit of the Strauss/Hofmannsthal partnership and regarded by some as Strauss's greatest opera, it is a powerful, harsh and frenzied setting of Sophocles' great tragedy. The title role is one of the most vocally demanding in all opera.

Plot: Mycenae. Elektra, daughter of Clytemnestra and the murdered Agamemnon, lives in degradation at the palace, dreaming of the return of her brother Orestes to avenge the crime committed by Clytemnestra who is wracked with remorse and guilt. Strangers arrive with news that Orestes is dead and Elektra unsuccessfully tries to persuade her gentle sister, Chrysothemis, to help her. She starts to dig up the axe that killed Agamemnon

but is interrupted by one of the strangers who, she gradually realises, is Orestes. He enters the palace and kills Clytemnestra. When Clytemnestra's lover Aegisthus returns, Elektra, now half-crazed, joyously lights his way inside to his own death. The achievement of her long-dreamt vengeance is too much for Elektra: while dancing in demented triumph, she falls dead. [R]

Elemer, Count

Tenor role in Strauss's *Arabella*. He is one of Arabella's suitors.

Elena

Soprano role in: (1) Boito's *Mefistofele*. She is Helen of Troy. (2) Rossini's *La Donna del Lago*. Douglas's daughter, she is in love with Malcolm. (3) Shaporin's *The Decembrists*. She is in love with Dmitri. (4) Donizetti's *Marino Faliero*.

Elgar, Sir Edward *(1857–1934)*

British composer. Best known as an orchestral composer, he began one opera *The Spanish Lady* (c 1930; libr. composer and B. Jackson, after Ben Jonson's *The Devil is an Ass*), which did not progress beyond sketches. An orchestral suite was arranged from the music by P. M. Young.

Elias, Rosalind *(b 1931)*

American mezzo, particularly associated with the Italian and French repertories. A rich-voiced singer of fine musicianship, she created, for Barber, Erika in *Vanessa* and Charmian in *Antony and Cleopatra*.

Elisabeth

Soprano role in: (1) Wagner's *Tannhäuser*. She is the Landgrave's daughter. (2) Verdi's *Don Carlos*.

Daughter of the King of France, she is married to Philip II of Spain.
(3) Henze's *Elegie für Junge Liebende*. She is in love with Toni Reischmann.

Elisabetta Regina d'Inghilterra *(Elizabeth, Queen of England)*

Opera in two acts by Rossini. 1st perf. Naples, 4 Oct 1815; libr. by Giovanni Schmidt, after Carlo Federici's play, itself based on Sophie Lee's *The Recess*. Principal roles: Elizabeth I (sop), Leicester (ten), Mathilde (sop), Duke of Norfolk (ten). An important opera historically in that, for the first time, Rossini wrote out the vocal decorations himself, and also for the first time provided orchestral accompaniment for the recitatives. For it Rossini reused the overture and finale from his earlier *Aureliano in Palmira*. The overture turns up again in *Il Barbiere di Siviglia*, where Rosina's first aria is not entirely dissimilar from Elizabeth's. Successful in its time, it is nowadays only occasionally performed.

Plot: 16th-century England. Elizabeth I is furious to discover from the Duke of Norfolk that her favourite, the Earl of Leicester, has secretly married Mathilde. Leicester refuses to give up Mathilde, so Elizabeth has him imprisoned under sentence of death. Norfolk's machinations are eventually unmasked, and Elizabeth forgives Leicester and Mathilde. [R]

Elisetta

Soprano role in Cimarosa's *Il Matrimonio Segreto*. She is Geronimo's daughter.

Elisir d'Amore, L' *(The Love Potion)*

Comic opera in two acts by Donizetti. 1st perf. Milan, 12 May 1832; libr. by Felice Romani, after Eugène Scribe's libretto for Auber's *Le Philtre*. Principal roles: Nemorino (ten), Adina (sop), Dr Dulcamara (b-bar), Belcore (bar), Gianetta (sop). One of Donizetti's best loved works, it is almost an opera semiseria rather than an opera buffa, as it contains both moments of real pathos and – in Dulcamara – one of the greatest of all buffo roles.

Plot: Nemorino is distracted by his inability to win the heart of the capricious landowner Adina, and is further put out when she agrees (partly to spite him) to marry the bumptious sergeant, Belcore. The ambulent quack Dulcamara arrives proclaiming his miraculous nostrums and, in desperation, Nemorino asks him for a love potion. Dulcamara sells him a bottle of Bordeaux with a hastily affixed label. His subsequent inebriated behaviour annoys Adina, who agrees to marry Belcore forthwith. Nemorino is desperate for a second bottle to provide an immediate effect but, having no money, enlists with Belcore and buys another bottle with his pay. Meanwhile, Gianetta and the other girls have learnt that Nemorino's uncle has died and left him a fortune. They suddenly discover how handsome he is. Nemorino, ignorant of his uncle's death, puts their attentions down to the effect of the potion. Adina, miffed by his new indifference, purchases his release from the army and finally admits that she loves him. The two are united and Dulcamara, claiming all the credit, does a brisk trade in love potions. [R]

Ella giammai m'amo

Bass monologue for King Philip in Act IV of Verdi's *Don Carlos*.

Elle a fui

Soprano aria for Antonia in the Antonia Act of Offenbach's *Les Contes d'Hoffmann*.

Ellen Orford

Soprano role in Britten's *Peter Grimes*. She is the village schoolmistress.

Elmendorff, Karl *(1891–1962)*

German conductor, particularly associated with Wagner operas. He was musical director of the Wiesbaden Opera (1932–36 and 1952–56), the Mannheim Opera (1936–42), the Dresden State Opera (1942–45) and the Kassel Staatstheater (1948–51). He conducted the first performance of Haas' *Die Hochzeit des Jobs*.

Elsa

Soprano role in Wagner's *Lohengrin*. She is the falsely accused daughter of the Duke of Brabant.

Elsner, Józef *(1769–1854)*

Polish composer. The first Polish opera composer of significance, he wrote 32 stage works of various kinds, all of them now largely forgotten, even in Poland. The most successful were *Andromeda* (Warsaw 14 Jan 1807; libr. L. Osiński), *The Echo in the Wood* (*Echo w Lesie*, Warsaw 22 April 1807; libr. W. Pekalski) [R], *Leszek the White* (*Leszek Bialy*, Warsaw 2 Dec 1809; libr. Dmuszewski) and *King Lokietek* (*Król Lokietek*, Warsaw 3 April 1818; libr. Dmuszewski) [R]. He was also a noted teacher, whose pupils included Chopin.

È lucevan le stelle

Tenor aria for Cavaradossi in Act III of Puccini's *Tosca*.

Elvino

Tenor role in Bellini's *La Sonnambula*. He is a young Swiss farmer.

Elvira

Soprano role in: (1) Mozart's *Don Giovanni*. She is a lady of Burgos, deserted by the Don. (2) Verdi's *Ernani*. She is in love with Ernani. (3) Bellini's *I Puritani*. She is Gualtiero Walton's daughter. (4) Rossini's *L'Italiana in Algieri*. She is the Bey's wife.

Emerald Isle, The

or The Caves of Carig-Cleena

Operetta in two acts by Sullivan, 1st perf. London, 27 April 1901; libr. by Basil Hood. Principal roles: Lady Rosie Pippin (sop), Molly O'Grady (mezzo), Terence O'Brian (ten), Pat Murphy (bar). Sullivan's last stage work, it was left unfinished at his death and was completed by German. Reasonably successful at its appearance, it is now all but forgotten.

Emilia

Mezzo role in Verdi's and Rossini's *Otello*. Iago's wife, she is Desdemona's companion.

Emperor

(1) Tenor role in Richard Strauss' *Die Frau Ohne Schatten*. (2) Baritone role in Stravinsky's *The Nightingale*. (3) Mezzo trouser-role in Henze's *We Come to the River*.

Emperor Jones, The

Opera in two acts by Gruenberg (Op 36). 1st perf. New York, 7 Jan 1933; libr. by Kathleen de Jaffa, after Eugene O'Neill's play. Principal roles: Brutus Jones (bar), Henry Smithers (ten), Old Nature Witch (sop). Gruenberg's finest work, it met with considerable success at its appearance, but is now almost never performed.

Plot: A Caribbean island. Brutus Jones, an ex-porter, crap shooter and murderer, has fled from justice to a Caribbean island which he rules as a royal despot. Warned by Smithers that his subjects are about to rise against him, he flees through the jungle, tormented by his victims who come to him in hallucinations. Finally, Jones kills himself with a silver bullet – his last.

Emperor of Atlantis, The
See Kaiser von Atlantis, Der

Empress
Soprano role in Richard Strauss's *Die Frau ohne Schatten*. She is the childless woman without a shadow.

Enchantress, The (*Charoydeka*)
Opera in four acts by Tchaikovsky. 1st perf. St Petersburg, 1 Nov 1887; libr. by I. Shpazhinsky. Principal roles: Kuma (sop), Yuri (ten), Mamirov (bass). The least successful of Tchaikovsky's mature operas, it is very rarely performed, even in Russia. [R]

Encore (French for 'again')
A word shouted by British audiences to demand a repeat, and thus also the repeat itself. In Italy and France *bis* is shouted. Originating in the 17th century, encores are a controversial business. Standard in operetta (particularly Gilbert and Sullivan), they are frowned upon in opera except in Italy – where Toscanini had frequent rows with audiences for refusing to allow them. They are virtually unknown in Britain; the only encores in Covent Garden's postwar history were given by Callas and Stignani in *Norma* and Evans and Bruscantini in *Don Pasquale*. The longest encore in operatic history was the premier of *Il Matrimonio Segreto*: Emperor Leopold II was so delighted that he ordered supper to be served to the company and then the entire opera to be repeated.

Enescu, George (*1881–1955*)
Romanian composer and violinist. Best known as an orchestral composer, he also wrote one opera, the unjustly neglected *Oedipe* (Paris 13 March 1936; libr. Edmund Fleg, after Sophocles).

Enfant et les Sortilèges, L'
(*The Child and the Toys*)
Opera in two parts by Ravel. 1st perf. Monte Carlo, 21 March 1925; libr. by Colette. Principal roles: Child (mezzo), Mother (cont), Fire (sop), Arithmetic (ten), Tree (bass), Grandfather Clock (bar), Squirrel (mezzo). A delightful work of great orchestral virtuosity, it was an immediate success and has remained popular.

Plot: Bored with his homework and tired of good behaviour, the Child sticks his tongue out at his mother and is sent to his room. In a fit of temper, he does all the damage he can; abusing and destroying objects, after which he sticks his pen into his pet squirrel and pulls the cat's tail. These objects and all the animals come to upbraid him and, when he calls out for his mother, they attack him. In the fracas, a little squirrel is hurt. The Child tends its injuries, thereby winning the forgiveness of the animals. [R]

England
See Great Britain

English Bach Festival
An annual British music festival, largely based in London, founded in 1963 by the harpsichordist Lina Lalandi. It has given a number of performances of Baroque operas, especially Rameau, in

productions recreating the costumes and performance style of the period.

English Music Theatre

Founded in 1975 as a reorganisation of the English Opera Group*, it toured Britain with a repertory of small- and medium-scale works in productions which laid strong emphasis on the dramatic side. The musical director was Steuart Bedford. A reduction in government subsidy led to its closure in 1979.

English National Opera

Founded by Lilian Baylis as Sadler's Wells Opera, the company began operations in January 1931 and was based at Sadler's Wells Theatre in north London and also toured extensively. In 1958, the company incorporated most of the membership of the Carl Rosa Opera Company, enabling it to undertake larger-scale works. In August 1968, the company moved to the London Coliseum (cap. 2,358), adopting its present name from 3 August 1974. The annual season runs from September to July.

Perhaps the most exciting and innovative of British opera companies, the ENO performs in English with predominantly British and Commonwealth singers. Since its move to the Coliseum, it has developed one of the most enterprising repertories of any major opera company, and a production style that places great emphasis on the dramatic aspect of the works. Productions, whilst sometimes controversial, are always thought-provoking. In recent years, the company has been especially noted for its Janáček and Wagner productions, particularly the English-language *Ring*. Administrators have included Joan Cross, Norman Tucker, Stephen Arlen, the Earl of Harewood and Peter Jonas,

and the postwar musical directors have been Lawrance Collingwood, James Robertson, Sir Alexander Gibson, Sir Colin Davis, Sir Charles Mackerras, Sir Charles Groves and Mark Elder.

English Opera Group

A chamber opera company founded in 1946 by Britten, Eric Crozier and John Piper, for the performance of new operas. Based at Aldeburgh, the company also toured widely in Britain and abroad. Always maintaining high artistic standards, it gave the first performances of many important postwar British operas as well as reviving earlier British works. In 1975, it was reorganised as the English Music Theatre*.

Enna, August *(1860–1939)*

Danish composer. He wrote some 15 operas in late romantic style, all of them now largely forgotten. His first work *Agleia* (Copenhagen 1884) was followed by *The Witch* (*Heksen*, Copenhagen 24 June 1892), by far his most successful work. His later operas include *Kleopatra* (1894; libr. after H. Rider Haggard), *Aucassin og Nicolette* (Copenhagen 2 Feb 1896), *The Little Match-Girl* (*Pigen Med Svovlstikkerne*, Copenhagen 13 Nov 1897; libr. composer, after Hans Christian Andersen), *Lamia* (Antwerp 3 Oct 1899), *Young Love* (*Ung Elskov*, Weimar 1904), *The Princess and the Pea* (*Prinsessen paa Aerten*, Århus 15 Sept 1901; libr. after Andersen), *The Nightingale* (*Nattergalen*, Copenhagen 10 Nov 1912; libr. after Andersen), *Gloria Arséna* (Copenhagen 15 April 1917) and *The Comedians* (*Komedianter*, 1920; libr. after Victor Hugo's *L'Homme Qui Rit*).

Enrichetta

Mezzo role in Bellini's *I Puritani*. She is

179

Queen Henrietta Maria (1609–69), widow of Charles I.

Enrico

(1) Baritone role in Donizetti's *Lucia di Lammermoor*. He is Lucia's brother. (2) Bass role in Donizetti's *Anna Bolena*. He is King Henry VIII. (3) Tenor role in Donizetti's *Rosmonda d'Inghilterra*. He is King Henry II. (4) Baritone role in Donizetti's *Il Campanello*. He is in love with Serafina. (5) Tenor role in Donizetti's *Maria de Rudenz*. (6) Baritone role in Donizetti's *Maria di Rohan*. He is secretly married to Maria. (7) Baritone role in Haydn's *L'Isola Disabitata*. He is loved by Silvia. (8) Tenor role in Donizetti's *L'Aio nell'Imbarazzo*. Giulio's son, he is married to Gilda. (9) Tenor comprimario role in Verdi's *Aroldo*. He is Mina's cousin.

Ensemble (French for 'together')

The term has two meanings in opera:
(1) A group or company of performers, and thus also their musical unanimity.
(2) A concerted operatic number for several soloists, with or without chorus.

Entführung aus dem Serail, Die (*The Abduction from the Seraglio*)

Opera in three acts by Mozart (K 384). 1st perf. Vienna, 16 July 1782; libr. by Gottlieb Stephanie after Christoph Friedrich Bretzner's libretto for André's *Belmont und Constanze*. Principal roles: Constanze (sop), Belmonte (ten), Osmin (bass), Blönchen (or Blonde) (sop), Pedrillo (ten), Pasha Selim (speaker role). Mozart's first major success, it contains some of his finest arias, much music in the then-popular *alla turca* style and, in Osmin, one of the greatest comic roles in opera.

Plot: 16th-century Turkey. Belmonte, a Spanish nobleman, comes to the palace of Pasha Selim, where his betrothed, Constanze, her English maid Blönchen and his valet Pedrillo, in love with Blönchen, have been enslaved since their capture by pirates. Constanze has refused the advances of the Pasha, as has Blönchen those (less politely offered) of the harem-keeper Osmin. Engaged by the Pasha as an architect, Belmonte and Pedrillo plan an escape, but are caught by Osmin. The Pasha learns that Belmonte is the son of his greatest enemy, but as an act of magnanimity allows all his prisoners to go free. [R]

Entr'acte (French for 'between act')

A short orchestral piece played between two acts or scenes of an opera.

Entrée (French for 'entry')

The term has two meanings in opera:
(1) A term used to describe the individual acts of an 18th-century French opera in which each act has a separate and unrelated plot, as in Rameau's *Les Indes Galantes*. (2) A short, march-like orchestral piece played for the entry of an important character in a late 17th-century French opera.

Enzo

Tenor role in Ponchielli's *La Gioconda*. A Genoese nobleman, he is in love with Laura.

Epouse que brave fille

Baritone aria for Lescaut in Act III of Massenet's *Manon*.

Equivoci, Gli (*The Doubles*)

Comic opera in two acts by Storace. 1st perf. Vienna, 27 Dec 1786; libr. by Lorenzo da Ponte, after Shakespeare's *The Comedy of Errors*. Possibly Storace's finest work, parts of which he later reused in other operas, it enjoyed great success in its day but is now very rarely performed.

Era la notte

Baritone aria for Iago in Act II of Verdi's *Otello*.

Erb, Karl *(1877–1958)*

German tenor, particularly associated with Mozart roles. One of the leading lyric tenors of the inter-war period, he created the title-role in *Palestrina*. He is the inspiration for the character Erbe in Thomas Mann's *Dr Faustus*. Married for a time to the soprano Maria Ivogün*.

Ercole Amante *(Hercules in Love)*

Opera in five acts by Cavalli. 1st perf. Paris, 7 Feb 1662; libr. by F. Buti. Principal roles: Ercole (bass), Jole (sop), Hyllus (ten), Dejanira (mezzo), Juno (mezzo), Venus (sop). After nearly 300 years of neglect, it has had a number of performances in recent years. [R]

Erda

Contralto role in Wagner's *Das Rheingold* and *Siegfried*. She is the primaeval Earth Mother.

Erede, Alberto *(b 1909)*

Italian conductor, particularly associated with the Italian repertory and with Wagner. He was musical director of the Deutsche Oper am Rhein (1958–62) and conducted the first performance of Menotti's *The Old Maid and the Thief*.

Erik

Tenor role in: (1) Wagner's *Der Fliegende Holländer*. He is a huntsman in love with Senta. (2) Delius' *Fennimore and Gerda*. A painter, he is engaged to Fennimore.

Erismena, L'

Opera in prologue and three acts by Cavalli. 1st perf. Venice, 26 Dec 1665; libr. by Aurelio Aureli. Revised version, 1st perf. 1670. After nearly 300 years of neglect, it has received a number of performances in recent years.

Eri tu

Baritone aria for Renato in Act III of Verdi's *Un Ballo in Maschera*.

Erkel, Ferenc *(1810–93)*

Hungarian composer and conductor. The founder of the nationalist school of Hungarian opera, his stage works make considerable use of traditional Hungarian material. The first of his eight operas was the successful *Bátori Mária* (Budapest 8 Aug 1840; libr. Béni Egressy, after A. Dugonics). It was followed by *László Hunyadi** and *Bánk Bán**, his two best known works. Their successors were *Sarolta* (Budapest 26 Jan 1862; libr. J. Czanyuga), *Dózsa György* (Budapest 6 April 1867; libr. E. Szigligeti after Maurus Jókai), the nationalist *Brankovics György* (Budapest 20 May 1874; libr. L. Odri and F. Ormai), *Unknown Heroes* (*Névtelen Hosök*, Budapest 30 Nov 1880) and *King Stephen* (*István Király*, Budapest 14 March 1885; libr. A. Váradi after L. Dobra), most of which is by his son Gyula. Erkel also developed a Hungarian equivalent of the English ballad opera known as *népszínmü*, which incorporates both original songs and traditional ballads. The most successful example was *Two Pistols* (*Két Pisztoly*, 1844; libr. Szigligeti). He was musical director of the Budapest State Opera (1838–74).

Erlanger, Baron Frédéric, d' *(1868–1943)*

French-born British composer and

banker. A long-time director and patron of Covent Garden, he wrote two operas. They are *Inès Mendo* (London 1897; libr. after Prosper Mérimée) and *Tess* (Naples 1909; libr. Luigi Illica after Thomas Hardy's *Tess of the d'Urbervilles*), which enjoyed some success in its time but which is now forgotten.

Ermione

Opera in two acts by Rossini. 1st perf. Naples, 27 March 1819; libr. by Andrea Leone Tottola, after Racine's *Andromaque*. Principal roles: Ermione (sop), Andromaca (mezzo), Pirro (ten), Oreste (ten), Fenicio (bass), Pilade (ten). Never one of Rossini's more successful works, it is very rarely performed. [R]

Ermler, Mark *(b 1932)*

Russian conductor, particularly associated with the Russian and Italian repertories. One of the leading contemporary Soviet opera conductors, he was musical director of the Bolshoi Opera.

Ernani

Opera in four acts by Verdi. 1st perf. Venice, 9 March 1844; libr. by Francesco Maria Piave, after Victor Hugo's *Hernani*. Principal roles: Ernani (ten), Elvira (sop), Carlo (bar), da Silva (bass). Verdi's fifth opera, it was the work which established his European reputation. It is notable for its full-blooded melodies as well as for being the first work in which Verdi fully exploited the potential of the baritone voice.

Plot: 16th-century Spain. Elvira is betrothed to the grandee Silva, but is in love with a banished nobleman-turned-outlaw known as Ernani. She is also loved by Carlo, the King of Spain. Carlo takes Elvira away, ostensibly for her safety, and Ernani is challenged to

a duel by Silva. Allowing Silva's right to seek vengeance, Ernani asks that it be postponed so that he may first avenge himself on Carlo. He gives Silva a horn and promises that if he hears Silva use it he will take his life. A group of conspirators including Ernani and Silva plot to assassinate Carlo, but news is brought of Carlo's election as Emperor. At Elvira's request, he forgives the conspirators, restores Ernani's estates and blesses his marriage with Elvira. After a ball to celebrate the wedding, the horn is heard. Silva offers Ernani the choice of poison or the dagger and Ernani stabs himself. [R]

Ernani involami

Soprano aria for Elvira in Act I of Verdi's *Ernani*.

Ernest II *(Duke of Saxe-Coburg-Gotha) (1818–93)*

German statesman and composer, brother of Queen Victoria's husband Prince Albert. Perhaps the most talented of the many royal musical dilettantes, his opera *Diana von Solange* (Coburg 5 Dec 1858; libr. Otto Prechtler) achieved a production at the Metropolitan Opera, New York in 1891.

Ernesto

(1) Tenor role in Donizetti's *Don Pasquale*. Pasquale's nephew, he is in love with Norina. (2) Baritone role in Bellini's *Il Pirata*. He is Imogene's husband. (3) Mezzo trouser-role in Haydn's *Il Mondo della Luna*. He is loved by Flaminia. (4) Soprano trouser-role in Bononcini's *Griselda*.

Ero the Joker *(Ero s Onoga Svijeta*; the Serbian title means *Ero from the Other World)*

Opera in three acts by Gotovac. 1st perf. Zagreb, 2 Nov 1935; libr. by Milan Begović, after a Dalmatian fairy story. Gotovac's most successful opera, it has been widely performed and is arguably the most popular of all Yugoslavian operas, as well as the only one to have enjoyed success elsewhere. It is a folk-inspired work written in predominantly Italian style. [R]

Erwartung (*Expectation*)

Opera in one act by Schönberg (Op 17). 1st perf. Prague, 6 June 1924; libr. by Marie Pappenheim. Principal role: Woman (sop). A powerful monodrama of great expressionist intensity, it tells of a woman awaiting her lover at night in the woods, and then stumbling upon his corpse. [R]

Escamillo

Baritone role in Bizet's *Carmen*. He is a toreador.

Esclarmonde

Opera in prologue, four acts and epilogue by Massenet. 1st perf. Paris, 14 May 1889; libr. by Alfred Blau and Louis de Gramont. Principal roles: Esclarmonde (sop), Roland de Blois (ten), Parséïs (mezzo), Bishop of Blois (bar), Phorcas (bass), Enéas (ten). This is an exotic and richly scored work in which there is some evidence of Wagner's influence in Massenet's use of leitmotivs.

Plot: The sorceress Esclarmonde wins the knight Roland de Blois through her powers of enchantment, but is subsequently forced to give him up in order to retain her kingdom and her magical powers. Later, in a tournament, Roland wins the hand of a veiled princess, who turns out to be Esclarmonde. [R]

È sogno?

Baritone aria (the Jealousy Monologue) for Ford in Act II of Verdi's *Falstaff* in which Verdi parodies his own style.

Essen Opera

Opera in this German town in North Rhine-Westphalia is given at the Städtische Bühnen (cap. 800) which opened in 1892. Damaged in World War II, it was rebuilt in 1950. It has an adventurous repertory policy and stages many 20th-century works. Musical directors have included Heinz Wallberg.

Essex, Earl of

The favourite of Queen Elizabeth I appears in a number of operas, including: (1) Tenor role in Donizetti's *Roberto Devereux*. (2) Tenor role in Britten's *Gloriana*. (3) Baritone role in German's *Merrie England*.

Esswood, Paul (*b* 1942)

British counter-tenor, associated with Handel and other Baroque operas. One of the most stylish and musicianly of contemporary counter-tenors, he created the title role in *Akhnaten*.

Esterháza

A castle near Süttör in Hungary where the Prince Esterházy maintained an opera house in the 18th century. Haydn was musical director for a lengthy period and all of his mature operas were first performed there.

Estes, Simon (*b* 1938)

American bass, particularly associated with Wagnerian roles, especially the Dutchman. One of the few male black singers to have enjoyed a major international career, he possesses a dark, rich and powerful voice and has a remarkable upper register which also allows him to sing high baritone roles such as Macbeth. He created Uncle Albert in Schuller's *The Visitation*.

Estonian opera composers

These include Evald Aav (1900–39), whose *The Vikings* (*Vikerlased*, 1928) was the first real Estonian opera, Gustav Ernesaks (*b* 1908), Eugen Kapp (*b* 1908), his cousin Wilhelm (1913–64), Artur Lemba (1885–1963), Leo Normet (*b* 1922), Eino Tambert (*b* 1930), Velyo Tormis (*b* 1930), Eduard Tubin (1905–82) and Adolf Vedro (*b* 1890).

Esultate!

Otello's first line in Act I of Verdi's *Otello*. Perhaps the most musically thrilling entry of any operatic character.

Etoile, L' (*The Star*)

Comic opera in three acts by Chabrier. 1st perf. Paris, 28 Nov 1877; libr. by Eugene Leterrier and Albert Vanloo. Principal roles: Lazuli (mezzo), Pufft (bar), Laolo (sop), Fretful (bar), Simoon (ten). Chabrier's first completed stage work and still quite often performed, it is a delightful and amusing small work, well enough summed up by Stravinsky who called it "a little masterpiece". [R]

Etoile du Nord, L' (*The Star of the North*)

Opera in three acts by Meyerbeer. 1st perf. (as *Ein Feldlager in Schlesien*) Berlin, 7 Dec 1844; libr. by L. Rellstab. Revised version, 1st perf. (as *Vielka*) Vienna, 18 Feb 1847. Final version, 1st perf. Paris, 16 Feb 1854; libr. revised by Eugène Scribe. Principal roles: Catherine (sop), Peters (bass), Danilowitz (ten), Prascovia (sop), Gritzenko (bar), Georges (ten), Ismailoff (ten), Nathalie (sop). Based on an incident in the life of Frederick the Great, but with the action transferred to Russia, it was enormously successful throughout the 19th century but is nowadays only very rarely performed.

Plot: Peter, the Tsar of Russia, disguised as a carpenter, woos Catherine. Catherine takes the place of her brother Georges in the Russian army. She is mistaken for a conspirator, ordered to be executed and is wounded while escaping. Having lost her mind, she is brought to the Tsar's palace. She regains her sanity on seeing Peter and becomes Tsarina.

Eugene Onegin (*Yevgeny Onyegin*)

Opera in three acts by Tchaikovsky (Op 24). 1st perf. Moscow, 29 March 1879; libr. by the composer and Konstantin Shilovsky after Alexander Pushkin's poem. Principal roles: Onegin (bar), Tatyana (sop), Lensky (ten), Prince Gremin (bass), Olga (mezzo), Filipyevna (cont), Madame Larina (mezzo), M. Triquet (ten), Zaretsky (bass). Described as 'lyric scenes', it is Tchaikovsky's most popular opera and is usually regarded as his masterpiece.

Plot: Russia, late 18th century. The blasé and sophisticated aristocrat, Onegin, is visiting his friend, the poet Lensky, in the country. He accompanies Lensky to pay a call at the house of Madame Larina, whose elder daughter, Olga, is the poet's betrothed. There, Onegin meets Tatyana, Olga's younger sister and an intense and bookish romantic, who falls in love with him at first sight. When Tatyana pours out her passionate yearnings in a letter to Onegin, he responds by saying he can offer her only friendship, and advises her to exercise more self-restraint in the future. At the name-day party for the now humiliated and withdrawn Tatyana, Onegin, bored to tears with his country sojourn, amuses himself by flirting with Olga and thus outrages the jealous Lensky who challenges him to a duel. Both men, in the event, are reluctant to fight, but neither withdraws, and Lensky is killed. Some years later, returned from travelling the world in boredom, loneliness and disillusion, Onegin encounters Tatyana at a fashionable ball and learns that she has married his elderly relative, Prince Gremin, who adores her. He arranges a rendezvous with Tatyana and, expressing remorse for his past behaviour, makes a declaration of love and begs her to leave her husband. The unhappy woman confesses to still loving Onegin but is adamant in rejecting his proposal: honour will not permit her to desert Gremin and Onegin is left alone. [R]

Euridice

Works of this title, recounting the Orpheus myth to the libretto by Ottavio Rinuccini, include:

(1) Opera in prologue and six scenes by Peri (with contributions by Caccini). 1st perf. Florence, 6 Oct 1600. Principal roles: Euridice (sop), Orfeo (ten), Arcetro (bass), Dafne (mezzo), Persephone (mezzo). It is the earliest opera of which the music has survived. [R]

(2) Opera in prologue and six scenes by Caccini. 1st perf. Florence, 5 Dec 1602. Principal roles: Euridice (mezzo), Orfeo (ten), Dafne (sop), Tragedy (mezzo), Charon (bass). It was the first opera to be published.

Euripides

See panel on page 186

Euryanthe

Opera in three acts by Weber (J 291). 1st perf. Vienna, 25 Oct 1823; libr. by Helmina von Chézy after a 13th-century French romance. Principal roles: Euryanthe (sop), Adolar (ten), Eglantine (sop), Lysiart (bar), King Louis VI (bass). The ludicrous and undramatic libretto has prevented the piece from receiving anything more than an occasional performance, despite the fact that the score contains some of the finest music in any German romantic opera.

Plot: 12th-century France. Lysiart takes a wager with Adolar that he can seduce Euryanthe, whom Adolar loves. Euryanthe confides to Eglantine, who also loves Adolar, the secret of the suicide of Adolar's sister. Eglantine passes the information on to Lysiart, who uses it to proclaim falsely Euryanthe's infidelity. Adolar takes Euryanthe into the desert, intending to kill her, but when she saves him from a serpent, he abandons her. She is rescued by King Louis, who is convinced of her innocence. Eglantine, who is about to marry Lysiart, reveals her treachery, Lysiart is arrested, and the lovers are reunited. [R]

Eurydice

The wife of Orpheus appears in innumerable operas, including: (1) Soprano role in Gluck's *Orfeo ed Euridice*. (2) Soprano role in Milhaud's *Les Malheurs d'Orphée*. (3) Mezzo role in Birtwistle's *The Mask of Orpheus*. (4) Soprano role in Monteverdi's *La Favola d'Orfeo*. (5) Mezzo role in Orff's *Antigonae*. (6) Soprano role in Offenbach's *Orphée aux Enfers*.

Eva

Opera in three acts by Foerster (Op 50). 1st perf. Prague, 1 Jan 1899; libr. by the composer, after Gabriela Preissová's *Gazdina Roba*. Principal roles: Eva (sop), Mánek (ten), Mešjanovka (sop), Samko (bar), Zuzka (mezzo). Foerster's most successful work, it is almost never performed outside Czechoslovakia. [R]

Eva

Soprano role in Wagner's *Die*

EURIPIDES

The tragedies of the Greek dramatist Euripides (480–c 406 BC) have inspired some 50 operas. Below are listed, by play, those operas by composers with entries in this dictionary.

Alkestis

Lully	*Alceste*	1674
Gluck	*Alceste*	1767
Portugal	*Alceste*	1798
Boughton	*Alkestis*	1922
Wellesz	*Alkestis*	1924

The Bacchae

Wellesz	*Die Bakchantinnen*	1931
Ghedini	*I Baccanti*	1948
Henze	*The Bassarids*	1966

Hecuba

Malipiero	*Ecuba*	1941

Helen in Egypt

Strauss	*Die Ägyptische Helena*	1928

Hippolytus

Rameau	*Hippolyte et Aricie*	1733
Traetta	*Ippolito ed Aricia*	1759
Pizzetti	*Fedra*	1915

Iphigenia in Aulis

D. Scarlatti	*Ifigenia in Aulide*	1713
Caldara	*Ifigenia in Aulide*	1718
Graun	*Iphigenia in Aulide*	1748
Jommelli	*Ifigenia in Aulide*	1751
Gluck	*Iphigénie en Aulide*	1774
Zingarelli	*Ifigenia in Aulide*	1787
Cherubini	*Iphigenia in Aulide*	1788

Iphigenia in Tauris

Campra	*Iphigénie en Tauride*	1704
D. Scarlatti	*Ifigenia in Tauri*	1713
Traetta	*Ifigenia in Tauride*	1763
Jommelli	*Ifigenia in Tauride*	1771
Gluck	*Iphigénie en Tauride*	1779
Piccinni	*Iphigénie en Tauride*	1781

Medea

Milhaud	*Médée*	1939

Orestes		
Křenek	*Leben des Orest*	1930
The Trojan Women		
Reimann	*Troades*	1985

Meistersinger von Nürnberg. She is Pogner's daughter.

Evangeliman, Der (*The Evangelist*)
Opera in two acts by Kienzl (Op 45). 1st perf. Berlin, 4 May 1895; libr. by the composer after Leopold Florian Meissner. Principal roles: Mathias (ten), Martha (sop), Magdalene (mezzo), Johannes (bar), Engel (bass). Kienzl's most successful work, it applies Wagnerian techniques to a verismo style. Enormously popular at its appearance (with over 5,000 performances in 40 years), it is still occasionally performed in German-speaking countries.

Plot: St Othmar, Austria 1820–50. Johannes is wracked with jealousy over Martha's love for his own brother Mathias, a monk. He has Mathias expelled from the monastery and arrested on a trumped-up arson charge. After many long years in prison, Mathias is released, becomes a street preacher and forgives Johannes. [R]

Evans, Sir Geraint (*b 1922*)
British baritone, particularly associated with Mozart and Britten roles and with Falstaff, Beckmesser and Wozzeck. One of the finest British singers of the postwar era, and the first to enjoy an international career, he had a fine voice and excellent diction and was an outstanding singing-actor, especially in comedy. He created Mr Flint in *Billy Budd*, Lord Mountjoy in *Gloriana*, Antenor in *Troilus and Cressida* and, for Hoddinott, Trader Case in *The Beach at Falesá* and the title role in *Murder the Magician*. He has also produced a number of operas. His autobiography, *A Knight at the Opera*, was published in 1985.

Everding, August (*b 1928*)
German producer and administrator. One of the leading contemporary German producers, particularly noted for his Wagner productions, he was administrator of the Munich Chamber Opera (1963–73), the Hamburg State Opera (1972–77) and the Bavarian State Opera (1976–).

Evirato (from the Italian *evirare*, 'to emasculate')
An alternative term used occasionally for castrato.

Ewing, Maria (*b 1950*)
American mezzo who also sings some soprano roles. Particularly associated with dramatic roles such as Carmen and Salome, she is an intense and compelling singing-actress with a voice of highly individual timbre. Married for a time to the producer Sir Peter Hall*.

Excursions of Mr Brouček, The (*Výlety Pana Broučka*)
Opera in two parts by Janáček. 1st perf. Prague, 23 April 1920; libr. by the composer, Viktor Dyk and

František Procházka, after Svatopluk Čech's novels. The two parts (originally conceived separately) are *Mr Brouček's Excursion to the Moon* (*Výlet Pana Broučka do Měsíce*), composed 1915, and *Mr Brouček's Excursion to the 15th Century* (*Výlet Pana Broučka do XV Stol*), composed 1917. Principal roles: Brouček (ten), Mazal (ten), Málinka (sop), Mr Würfl (bar), Sacristan (bar), Poet (bar), Painter (ten), Svatopluk Čech (ten), Composer (ten), Pot Boy (sop). The two journeys of the bourgeois Mr Brouček provided Janáček with an opportunity to parody artistic pretentiousness and bogus patriotism. A delightful work of sardonic wit and great musical brilliance, it is only infrequently performed outside Czechoslovakia.

Plot: The Prague landlord Mr Brouček has two dreams. Firstly, he is transported to the Moon, where he encounters an outlandish world inhabited by an over-refined artistic community. Secondly, he goes back in time to the 15th century and behaves in a cowardly fashion during the Hussite revolt, before returning to the present. [R]

Ezio

Opera in three acts by Handel. 1st perf. London, 26 Jan 1732; libr. by Pietro Metastasio. Principal roles: Ezio (mezzo), Fulvia (sop), Massimo (ten), Varo (bass), Onoria (mezzo), Valentiniano (mezzo). Never one of Handel's more popular works, it is only infrequently performed despite containing some magnificent music.

Ezio

Baritone role in Verdi's *Attila*. He is a Roman general.

F

Faber
Baritone role in Tippett's *The Knot Garden*. He is Thea's husband.

Fabritiis, Oliviero de *(1902–82)*
Italian conductor, particularly associated with the Italian repertory. He instigated the presentation of opera at the Caracalla Baths in Rome, and conducted the first performances of operas by Mascagni, Pizzetti, Rossellini and Zafred.

Faccio, Franco *(1840–91)*
Italian conductor and composer. A close friend of Boito and one of the greatest conductors of his day, he was musical director of La Scala, Milan (1871–90). He conducted the first performances of *Otello*, *La Gioconda*, *Edgar*, Catalani's *Dejanice* and the revised versions of *Don Carlos* and *Simon Boccanegra*, as well as introducing Wagner's later works to Italy. He composed two operas, both now forgotten: *I Profughi Fiamminghi* (Milan 11 Nov 1863; libr. Emilio Praga) and *Amleto* (Genoa 30 May 1865; libr. Arrigo Boito, after Shakespeare's *Hamlet*). He was also a noted teacher, whose pupils included Smareglia.

Fach (German for 'speciality')
In opera, the term describes the vocal category into which a singer falls, such as basso-buffo, coloratura mezzo, Verdi baritone or heldentenor.

Faery Queen, The
Opera in prologue and five acts by Purcell. 1st perf. London, April 1692; libr. by Elkanah Settle, after Shakespeare's *A Midsummer Night's Dream*. Perhaps more accurately described as incidental music or a series of masques, rather than a true opera, the score was lost by 1701 and was not rediscovered until 1901. Since then it has been regularly performed. [R]

Fafner
Bass role in Wagner's *Das Rheingold* and *Siegfried*. One of the two giants, he is transformed into a dragon in *Siegfried*.

Fair Maid of Perth, The
See Jolie Fille de Perth, La

Falcon, Marie Cornélie *(1812–97)*
French soprano. Her career lasted only six years, but she was regarded as one of the leading dramatic sopranos of her time. She created Valentine in *Les Huguenots*, Rachel in *La Juive* and Madame Arvidson in Auber's *Gustave III*. She gave her name to a type of French soprano voice, with a range of roughly B♭ to C♯ ′′′.

Falke, Dr
Baritone role in J. Strauss' *Die Fledermaus*. A friend of von Eisenstein, he arranges the 'revenge of the bat'.

Fall, Leo *(1873–1925)*
Austrian composer. After unsuccessful attempts at opera, he turned to operetta, in which field he enjoyed enormous success. His many Viennese operettas include *Der Fidele Bauer*

(Mannheim 25 July 1907; libr. Viktor Léon), *Die Dollarprinzessin* (Vienna 2 Nov 1907; libr. Alfred Maria Willner and F. Grunbaum), *Die Geschiedene Frau* (Vienna 23 Dec 1908; libr. Léon), *Eternal Waltz* (London 22 Dec 1911; libr. A. Hurgon), *Der Liebe Augustin* (Berlin 3 Feb 1912; a revision of *Der Rebel* of 1905), *Die Rose von Stamboul* (Vienna 2 Dec 1916; libr. Julius Brammer and Alfred Grünwald), *Madame Pompadour**, his most enduring work, and *Jugend im Mai* (1926).

Falla, Manuel de *(1876–1946)*
Spanish composer. Arguably his country's greatest composer, his stage works make extensive use of traditional Spanish material. In his youth, he composed five zarzuelas, of which only *Los Amores de la Inés* (Madrid 12 April 1902; libr. E. Duggi) has ever been performed. His first opera, *La Vida Breve**, was the winner of a Madrid competition, and has become the most popular of all Spanish operas. His next work was a comedy based on the music of Chopin, *Fuego Fátuo* (*Will o' the Wisp*, 1918; libr. G. Martínez Sierra), which has never been published. Its successor, the marionette opera *El Retablo de Maese Pedro**, is a refined example of his mature style. His last stage work, the ambitious scenic oratorio *L'Atlántida**, was left unfinished at his death and was completed by Ernesto Halffter.

Falsetto (the diminutive of the Italian *falso*, meaning 'false')
It indicates a male voice singing in a register higher than the voice's natural range. It is the type of vocal production employed by modern counter-tenors, and is also used occasionally by baritones or basses for comic effect.

Falstaff
Works of this title, based on Shakespeare's *The Merry Wives of Windsor*, include:

(1) Opera in two acts by Salieri. 1st perf. Vienna, 3 Jan 1799; libr. by C. P. Defrancheschi. Principal roles: Falstaff (bass), Mistress Ford (sop), Ford (ten), Slender (bar). Demonstrating Salieri's considerable gift for comedy, it was successful in its time, but is nowadays very rarely performed. [R]

(2) Opera in two acts by Balfe. 1st perf. London, 19 July 1838; libr. by S. Maggione.

(3) Opera in one act by Adam. 1st perf. Paris, 18 Jan 1856; libr. by Adolphe de Leuven and Jules-Henri Vernoy de Saint-Georges.

(4) Opera in three acts by Verdi. 1st perf. Milan, 9 Feb 1893; libr. (which also draws from *King Henry IV*) by Arrigo Boito. Principal roles: Falstaff (bar), Ford (bar), Alice (sop), Mistress Quickly (mezzo), Nannetta (sop), Fenton (ten), Meg Page (mezzo), Dr Caius (ten), Pistol (bass), Bardolph (ten). Verdi's last and greatest masterpiece, and his first comedy for 50 years, it remains one of the miracles of operatic music. Boito's brilliant text is arguably the finest libretto which any composer has been given. Technically, the music is far more advanced even than *Otello*, with the orchestra almost the principal character. The wit, warmth and wisdom of the score mark the natural culmination of Verdi's long creative career, and that a man of almost 80 could have produced a work of such youthfulness and such breathtaking pace is not the least of the opera's glories.

Plot: 15th-century Windsor. The fat and bibulous Sir John Falstaff sends identical amorous letters to Alice, wife of the wealthy merchant Ford, and to Meg Page. These two, with Mistress

Quickly and Alice's daughter Nannetta, decide to accept Falstaff's advances and teach him a lesson. Ford finds out about Falstaff's plans from the latter's henchmen, Pistol and Bardolph, and from Dr Caius, to whom he has promised Nannetta, who loves the young Fenton. Ford also decides to teach Falstaff a lesson and calls on him with a plan for the seduction of Alice. Falstaff's assignation with Alice is interrupted by Ford's appearance and, hidden in a laundry basket, he is pitched into the Thames. Nontheless, the old reprobate accepts a second invitation to meet Alice at Herne's Oak in Windsor Forest. There, he is given a sound thrashing by the merry wives disguised as goblins and fairies. When the disguises are removed Ford finds that he has accidentally given Nannetta to Fenton in marriage, whilst Caius has been married to Bardolph! He accepts with good grace and Falstaff points out that all the world is a joke. [R]

See also **At the Boar's Head; Lustigen Weiber von Windsor, Die; Sir John in Love**

Falstaff, Sir John

The fat knight of Shakespeare's *The Merry Wives of Windsor* and *King Henry IV* appears in several operas, including: (1) Bass role in Nicolaï's *Die Lustigen Weiber von Windsor*. (2) Baritone role in Verdi's *Falstaff*. (3) Baritone role in Vaughan Williams' *Sir John in Love*. (4) Bass role in Salieri's *Falstaff*. (5) Bass role in Holst's *At the Boar's Head*. (6) Role in Thomas' *La Songe d'un Nuit d'Eté*.

Fanciulla del West, La (known in English as *The Girl of the Golden West*)

Opera in three acts by Puccini. 1st perf. New York, 10 Dec 1910; libr. by Carlo Zangarini and Guelfo Civinini after David Belasco's play. Principal roles: Minnie (sop), Dick Johnson (ten), Jack Rance (bar), Jake Wallace (bass), Ashby (bass). One of Puccini's most modernistic scores, displaying the strong influence of Debussy.

Plot: California, 1850. Minnie, keeper of the Polka Saloon and friend and confidante to the gold miners, falls in love with the stranger Dick Johnson, whom she discovers is the wanted bandit Ramírez. When Dick is wounded by the guns of a posse, she hides him at her cabin, but the sheriff, Jack Rance, who loves Minnie, discovers him there. Minnie and Rance agree to a game of poker to decide Johnson's fate, which she wins by cheating. Rance leaves, but Johnson is captured by the miners and is about to be hanged. Minnie begs them to spare the man she loves and they release him. The lovers ride off to begin a new life. [R]

Fanget an!

Tenor aria for Walther von Stolzing in Act I of Wagner's *Die Meistersinger von Nürnberg*. It is Walther's trial song.

Faninal

Baritone role in Richard Strauss' *Der Rosenkavalier*. He is Sophie's recently ennobled father.

Faramondo

Opera in three acts by Handel. 1st perf. London, 7 Jan 1738; libr. adapted from Apostolo Zeno. Unsuccessful at its appearance, it is nowadays very rarely performed.

Farinelli (b Carlo Broschi) (1705–82)

Italian castrato. Sometimes regarded as the greatest of all the castrati, he possessed a voice of extraordinary agility with a range up to high D. His London appearances caused women to faint, and in 1737 he was hired by Philip V of Spain to assuage his melancholia. He is reputed to have achieved this by singing the same four songs every night for ten years! He is the subject of Barnett's *Farinelli* and Auber's *La Part du Diable*.

Farncombe, Charles *(b 1919)*

British conductor (and also a qualified civil engineer), particularly associated with Handel and other Baroque operas. He was musical director of the Drottningholm Castle Theatre (1972–79) and of the Handel Opera Society for the duration of its existence.

Farrar, Geraldine *(1882–1967)*

American soprano, particularly associated with the Italian and French repertories. Based at the Metropolitan Opera, New York, she combined a glorious voice with fine musicianship and great personal beauty. Her popularity was enhanced by appearances in some dozen films, and her young female admirers acquired the nickname of 'Gerry-flappers'. She created the Goosegirl in *Die Königskinder*, Louise in Charpentier's *Julien* and the title roles in *Suor Angelica*, Giordano's *Madame Sans-Gêne* and Mascagni's *Amica*. Her autobiography, *Such Sweet Compulsion*, was published in 1938.

Farrell, Eileen *(b 1920)*

American soprano with a large and powerful voice and a keen dramatic sense, she was particularly associated with dramatic Italian roles. She also sang much Wagner in the concert hall, but never on the stage.

Farsa *(Italian for 'farce')*

A term describing an early 19th-century Italian comic opera in light style and usually in one act. An example is Rossini's *Il Signor Bruschino*.

Fasano, Renato *(1902–79)*

Italian conductor and musicologist, particularly associated with 18th-century Italian works. As founder of the chamber orchestra, I Virtuosi di Roma, in 1947, and of the Piccolo Teatro Musicale Italiano in 1957, he was responsible for important revivals of many works in performances throughout Europe.

Fasolt

Bass role in Wagner's *Das Rheingold*. He is one of the two giants who build Valhalla for Wotan.

Fassbaender, Brigitte *(b 1939)*

German mezzo, daughter of the baritone Willi Domgraf-Fassbaender*. Particularly associated with Mozart, Strauss and Wagner roles, she is a rich-voiced singer of outstanding musicianship. A fine singing-actress, she has had especial success in trouser-roles, notably Octavian.

Fatal mia donna

Soprano/baritone duet for Lady Macbeth and Macbeth in Act I of Verdi's *Macbeth*.

Fata Morgana

Soprano role in Prokofiev's *The Love of Three Oranges*. She is a witch.

Fate *(Osud)*

Opera in three acts by Janáček. 1st perf. Brno Radio, 18 Sept 1934 (composed 1904); libr. by the composer and Fedora Bartošová. Principal roles: Živný (ten), Míla (sop), Míla's Mother (mezzo), Dr Suda (ten), Lhotský (bar). Much the least known of Janáček's mature works, it has been slow to make its way, even in Czechoslovakia, despite containing magnificent music. A semi-autobiographical work, it was long thought to be unstageable, a myth exploded by the English National Opera's award-winning production in 1983.

Plot: Luhačovice (Moravia), c. 1890. Under pressure from her mother, Míla has been obliged to stop meeting the composer Živný. They meet again and decide to live together. During a furious altercation, Míla's mother throws herself from a high staircase, also dragging Míla (who tries to save her) to her death. On the eve of its performance, students parody Živný's new opera. Živný explains it to them, and they realise that it is Živný's confession and autobiography. [R]

Fatinitza

Operetta in three acts by Suppé. 1st perf. Vienna, 5 Jan 1876; libr. by F. Zell (Camillo Walzel) and Richard Genée after Eugène Scribe's libretto for Auber's La Circassienne. Suppé's first full-length work, it met with great initial success and is still occasionally performed in German-speaking countries.

Fauré, Gabriel (1845–1924)

French composer. He wrote two operas, both heavily influenced by Wagner. Prométhée (Béziers Arena 24 Aug 1900; libr. Jean Lorrain and André-Ferdinand Hérold after Aeschylus's Prometheus) is a vast work, designed for open-air performance, which is now forgotten. Far more successful was Pénélope*, which contains some of his finest music.

Faure, Jean-Baptiste (1830–1914)

French baritone, particularly associated with the French repertory and long resident at the Opéra-Comique, Paris. He created Nélusko in L'Africaine, Hoël in Dinorah, Posa in Don Carlos and the title role in Hamlet. He was also a noted teacher, publishing two books on singing. His wife Caroline Lefèbvre (1828–1905) was a successful soprano.

Faust

Works of this title based on the German Faust legend include:

(1) Opera in two acts by Spohr (Op 60). 1st perf. Dresden, 1 Sept 1816; libr. by Joseph Karl Bernard, after Maximilian von Klinger's Fausts Leben, Thaten und Höllenfahrt. Principal roles: Faust (bar), Mephistopheles (bass), Cunigund (sop), Count Hugo (ten). One of Spohr's finest works, it was very successful in its time but is now very rarely performed.

(2) Opera in five acts by Gounod. 1st perf. Paris, 19 March 1859; libr. by Jules Barbier and Michel Carré, after Goethe's play. Principal roles: Faust (ten), Marguerite (sop), Méphistophélès (bass), Valentin (bar), Siebel (mezzo), Dame Marthe (mezzo). Gounod's greatest success, it was perhaps the most popular of all operas in the second half of the 19th century, and it is still regularly performed. In Germany, where it is not unjustifiably viewed as a travesty of Goethe, it is usually given as Marguerite.

Plot: 16th-century Germany. The ageing philosopher Faust sells his soul to Méphistophélès in return for renewed youth and the love of Marguerite. Méphistophélès frustrates the attentions of Siebel, Marguerite's faithful admirer charged with protecting her by her brother, Valentin, and introduces her to Faust, with whom she falls in love. Valentin returns from the wars to find her compromised, and challenges Faust to a duel. Valentin is killed and Faust abandons Marguerite.

She bears Faust's child and is condemned to death for killing it in shame. The repentant Faust tries to rescue her from prison where she is now deranged, but she recognises him as evil and dies renouncing her love for him. Méphistophélès declares her condemned, but angels announce her salvation and raise her to Heaven, while Méphistophélès forces Faust down to Hell. [R]

See also Damnation de Faust, La; Doktor Faust; Mefistofele

Faust

A German itinerant conjuror (*c* 1488–1541) who, in legend, is said to have sold his soul to the Devil in return for a period of renewed youth. He appears in several operas, including: (1) Baritone role in Spohr's *Faust*. (2) Tenor role in Berlioz's *La Damnation de Faust*. (3) Tenor role in Gounod's *Faust*. (4) Tenor role in Boito's *Mefistofele*. (5) Baritone role in Busoni's *Doktor Faust*. (6) Bass role in Prokofiev's *The Fiery Angel*.

Favart, Charles-Simon *(1710–92)*

French librettist. The finest comic librettist of his time, he wrote the texts of over 150 operas. His libretti were set by Dauvergne, Duni, Gluck, Grétry, Monsigny, Philidor, Uttini and many others. His wife Marie (1727–72) was a successful soprano.

Favero, Mafalda *(1903–81)*

Italian soprano, particularly associated with the Italian repertory. Largely based at La Scala, Milan, she created Gasparina in *Il Campiello*, Finea in *La Dama Boba*, Laura in Zandonai's *La Farsa Amorosa*, Madelon in Lattuada's *Le Preziose Ridicole* and the title role in Mascagni's *Pinotta*. Her husband Alessandro Ziliani (1907–77) was a successful tenor, who created roles in *Pinotta* and Wolf-Ferrari's *La Vedova Scaltra*.

Favola d'Orfeo, La *(The Fable of Orpheus)*

Opera in prologue and five acts by Monteverdi. 1st perf. Mantua, Feb 1607; libr. by Alessandro Striggio. Principal roles: Orfeo (ten), Messenger (mezzo), Euridice (sop), Charon (bass), Pluto (bass), Proserpina (sop), Apollo (bass). Unperformed from its première until the early 20th century, it is now established as the first great operatic masterpiece, and is the earliest opera which is nowadays regularly performed.

Plot: The Messenger interrupts the celebrations of the forthcoming marriage between the singer, Orfeo, and Euridice with the news of Euridice's death. Orfeo determines to look for her in Hades and persuades Charon to ferry him over the River Styx. Pluto and his wife Proserpina agree to his request to take Euridice back to earth on condition that he does not look at her until he has completed the journey. Just as they are in sight of their journey's end, however, he can no longer resist, and looks at her. Euridice at once sinks back into Hades, leaving Orfeo grief-stricken. Apollo comforts him with the promise that in eternity he will be able to gaze on Euridice for ever. [R]

Favola per musica *(Italian for 'fable with music')*

A term used in the early 17th century to describe a musical setting of a mythological or legendary subject, such as the Orpheus myth.

Favorite, La

Opera in four acts by Donizetti. 1st perf. Paris, 2 Dec 1840; libr. by Alphonse Royer and Gustave Vaëz, after F. T. de Baculard d'Arnaud's *Le Comte de Comminges*. Principal roles: Léonore (mezzo), Fernand (ten), Alfonso (bar), Baldassare (bass), Inès (sop). Incorporating much music from his unfinished *L'Ange de Nisida*, it is one of Donizetti's finest works, still regularly performed, and arguably his most 'Verdian' in musico-dramatic style. It is nearly always given in an Italian translation.

Plot: Castile, 1340. Léonore returns the love of the novice Fernand, but conceals her identity because she is the illicit mistress of King Alfonso. She uses her influence to secure Fernand a military appointment and he saves the King's life in battle. He asks for Léonore's hand as a reward. Under threat of excommunication because of his adulterous relationship with Léonore, Alfonso agrees, but Léonore is unable to tell Fernand the truth before the wedding takes place. When he discovers that Léonore has been Alfonso's mistress, Fernand returns to the monastery. Before he takes his final vows, Léonore comes to beg his forgiveness. His passion is reawakened, but she collapses and dies in his arms. [R]

Fedeltà Premiata, La (*Fidelity Rewarded*)

Opera in three acts by Haydn. 1st perf. Esterháza, 25 Feb 1781; libr. after Giovanni Battista Lorenzi's *L'Infedelità Fedele*. Principal roles: Celia (sop), Fileno (ten), Amaranta (mezzo), Count Perrucchetto (bar), Melibeo (bass), Nerina (sop), Lindoro (ten), Diana (sop).

Plot: The temple of Diana of Cumae, run by the priest Melibeo, is cursed: a pair of faithful lovers must be sacrificed to a monster until 'an heroic soul shall offer his own life'. Around the love of Fileno and Celia revolve the intrigues and amorous complications of Amaranta, her brother Lindoro, his abandoned love Nerina and Count Perrucchetto. Despairing, because of the intrigues, of ever being united with Celia, Fileno offers to make the sacrifice. However, Diana intervenes to declare the curse lifted and the lovers are united. [R]

Federica

Mezzo role in Verdi's *Luisa Miller*. The Duchess of Ostheim, she is Count Walther's niece.

Federico

(1) Bass role in Verdi's *La Battaglia di Legnano*. He is the historical Frederick Barbarossa (*c* 1122–90). (2) Tenor role in Cilea's *L'Arlesiana*. He loves the girl from Arles. (3) Tenor role in Donizetti's *Emilia di Liverpool*. (4) Tenor comprimario role in Verdi's *Stiffelio*. He is Lina's cousin.

Fedora

Opera in three acts by Giordano. 1st perf. Milan, 17 Nov 1898; libr. by Arturo Colautti, after Victorien Sardou's *Fédora*. Principal roles: Fedora (sop), Loris (ten), des Sirieux (bar), Olga (mezzo). A vulgar piece of verismo, it is Giordano's only work, apart from *Andrea Chénier*, to have survived.

Plot: The Russian nihilist, Loris Ipanov, kills the intended husband of Fedora Romanov, because his wife had an affair with the victim. Fedora sets out to extract vengeance, but falls in love with Loris when she discovers the reason for his crime. Members of Loris's family suffer and he vows revenge, knowing only that an unknown woman is responsible. Fedora, knowing that the truth will soon come out, poisons herself, leaving Loris to understand only when it is too late. [R]

Fedra

Works of this title based on Euripides' *Hippolytus* include:

(1) Opera in three acts by Pizzetti. 1st perf. Milan, 20 March 1915; libr. by Gabriele d'Annunzio. Principal roles: Fedra (sop), Ippolito (ten), Teseo (bass). Successful at its appearance, it is nowadays only very rarely heard. Pizzetti's first opera to be performed, it is an austere setting of the well-known myth.

Plot: Phaedra, the wife of Theseus, conceives an uncontrollable passion for her stepson Hippolytus. When he spurns her advances, she hangs herself, leaving behind a letter which falsely accuses him of having dishonoured her.

(2) Opera in one act by Romano Romani. 1st perf. Rome, 3 April 1915; libr. by Alfredo Lenozoni.

Feen, Die *(The Fairies)*

Opera in three acts by Wagner. 1st perf. Munich, 29 June 1888 (composed 1834); libr. by the composer, after Carlo Gozzi's *La Donna Serpente*. Principal roles: Ada (sop), Arindel (ten), Günther (ten), Gernot (bass). Wagner's first completed opera, which bears little resemblance to his mature works, it is only very occasionally performed.

Plot: King Arindel of Tramond has married the fairy Ada, whom he is fated to lose if he should ever curse her under the strain of some misfortune of which she appears to be the cause. This, unfortunately, he does, and Ada is turned to stone. However, his grief is so great that the spell is broken, and he is allowed to enter fairyland as Ada's husband. [R]

Feldlager in Schlesien, Ein

See Etoile du Nord, L'

Felsenstein, Walter *(1901–75)*

Austrian producer. One of the most brilliant postwar opera directors, his period as Intendant of the Komische Oper in East Berlin (1947–75) established that theatre's reputation for innovative, dramatically consistent and often controversial productions. His most famous productions there included *The Cunning Little Vixen*, *Les Contes d'Hoffmann* and *Carmen*.

Femmine d'Italia, Le

Bass aria for Ali in Act II of Rossini's *L'Italiana in Algieri*.

Fenella

Mute role in Auber's *La Muette de Portici*. She is the dumb girl of the opera's title.

Fenena

Mezzo role in Verdi's *Nabucco*. Nabucco's younger but legitimate daughter, she loves the Hebrew Ishmael. The role is sometimes sung by a soprano.

Fennimore and Gerda

Opera in 11 scenes by Delius. 1st perf. Frankfurt, 21 Oct 1919 (composed 1910); libr. by the composer, after Jens Peter Jacobsen's *Niels Lyhne*. Principal roles: Fennimore (sop), Niels (bar), Erik (ten), Gerda (sop). One of Delius' less successful works, it is only very rarely performed, despite containing much beautiful music, particularly in the interludes which connect the scenes.

Plot: Fennimore is engaged to the painter Erik, whose friend Niels also loves her. Niels leaves for Erik's sake, but the marriage is unsuccessful. Erik spends all his time with friends and Fennimore, feeling neglected, asks Niels to help. Niels suggests that Erik travel to reawaken his inspiration, and Erik goes to a fair. Niels swears eternal fidelity to Fennimore, and their old love reawakens. Whilst awaiting Niels, Fennimore receives a telegram saying that Erik has been killed in an accident. Full of remorse, she blames herself and Niels. Niels finally settles down with the pretty young Gerda. [R]

Fenton

The character in Shakespeare's *The Merry Wives of Windsor* appears as tenor role in: (1) Verdi's *Falstaff*. (2) Nicolai's *Die Lustigen Weiber von Windsor*. (3) Vaughan Williams' *Sir John in Love*.

Feo, Francesco *(c 1685–1761)*

Italian composer. One of the leading early composers of Neapolitan opera of which he wrote many. A number of them were very successful in their day but are all now forgotten. They include *Siface* (Naples 13 May 1723; libr. Pietro Metastasio, after D. David's *La Forza della Virtù*) and *Ipermestra* (Rome Jan 1728; libr. Antonio Salvi).

Ferencsik, János *(1907–84)*

Hungarian conductor, particularly associated with the German and Hungarian repertories. He was musical director of the Budapest State Opera (1950–84).

Fermata (Italian for 'stop') (musical symbol: ⌒)

A term describing a pause on a held note. In Italy, the term *corona* is used.

Fernand Cortez
or La Conquête de Mexique

(*The Conquest of Mexico*)
Opera in three acts by Spontini. 1st perf. Paris, 28 Nov 1809; libr. by Victor Joseph Etienne de Jouy and Joseph Alphonse Esménard, after Alexis

Piron's play. Revised version, 1st perf. Paris, 28 May 1817. Principal roles: Cortez (ten), Amazily (sop), Montezuma (bass), Telasco (bar), Alvaro (ten). One of Spontini's finest and most spectacular operas (the original version included a cavalry charge), it was enormously successful at its appearance and is still occasionally performed.

Plot: Mexico. The conquistador Cortez loves Amazily, daughter of the Aztec King Montezuma, and hopes by their marriage to bring about peace. After putting down a mutiny by his troops, he burns his boats and with the help of Amazily (now a Christian) he rescues his brother Alvaro from being sacrificed to the Aztec gods. Montezuma finally agrees to his marriage with Amazily.

Fernández Caballero, Manuel *(1835–1906)*

Spanish composer. One of the most successful and prolific composers of zarzuela, he wrote some 220 stage works. The most popular include *Los Sobrinos del Capitán Grant* (Madrid 25 Aug 1877; libr. M. Ramos Carrión after Jules Verne), *El Salto del Pasiego* (Madrid 17 March 1878; libr. L. Equílez), *Château Margaux* (Madrid 5 Oct 1887; libr. J. Jackson Veyan), *El Dúo de la Africana* (Madrid 13 May 1893; libr. M. Echegaray) [R], *La Viejecita* (Madrid 29 April 1897; libr. Echegaray) [R], *El Señor Joaquín* (Madrid 18 Feb 1898; libr. J. Romea) and *Gigantes y Cabezudos* (Madrid 29 Nov 1898; libr. Echegaray) [R].

Fernando

Opera in one act by Schubert (D 220). 1st perf. Magdeburg, 18 Aug 1918 (composed 1815). libr. by Albert Stadler. Principal roles: Fernando (ten), Elenore (sop), Philipp (sop), Jäger (bass). One of Schubert's earliest

Singspiels, it is almost never performed.
[R]

Ferne Klang, Der (*The Distant Sound*)

Opera in three acts by Schreker. 1st
perf. Frankfurt, 18 Aug 1912
(composed 1909); libr. by the
composer. Principal roles: Fritz (ten),
Grete (sop). Schreker's most successful
work, still occasionally performed in
Germany, it is a lush impressionist
piece in late romantic style.

Plot: Fritz, a composer, leaves his
beloved, Grete, to go in search of a
'lost chord'. He meets Grete again in a
Venetian brothel and eventually dies in
her arms.

Ferrando

(1) Tenor role in Mozart's *Cosi fan
Tutte*. He is an officer in love with
Dorabella. (2) Bass role in Verdi's *Il
Trovatore*. He is the captain of di
Luna's guard.

Ferrari-Trecate, Luigi (*1884–1964*)

Italian composer. He wrote 12 operas,
some of which met with some success
in Italy but which are unknown
elsewhere. They include *Regina Ester*
(Faenza 1900), the marionette opera
Ciotollino (Rome 1922; libr.
Giovacchino Forzano), *La Bella e il
Mostro* (Milan 1926; libr. F. Salvatori),
L'Austuzie di Bertoldo (Genoa 1934;
libr. Carlo Zangarini and O. Lucarini),
Ghirlino (Milan 1940; libr. E.
Anceschi), *L'Orso Rè* (Milan 1950;
libr. Anceschi and M. Cerradi-Cervi)
and *La Campana del Zio Tom* (Parma
1953; libr. Anceschi, after Harriet
Beecher Stowe's *Uncle Tom's Cabin*).

Ferretti, Jacopo (*1784–1852*)

Italian librettist. A cut above most of
his contemporary Italian colleagues, he
was particularly noted for his comic
texts with their elegance and subtle
social comment. Writing his first
libretto in 1810, he went on to provide
over 60 more for, among others,
Carafa, Coccia, Donizetti (*L'Aio
nell'Imbarazzo, Torquato Tasso, Olivio
e Pasquale* and *Il Furioso*), Fioravanti
(*Didone Abbandonata*), Mayr,
Mercadante, Morlacchi, Pacini (*Il
Corsaro*), Portugal, L. and F. Ricci,
Rossi, Rossini (*La Cenerentola* and
Mathilde di Shabran), and Zingarelli
(*Baldovino* and *Berenice*).

Ferrier, Kathleen (*1912–53*)

British contralto. One of the best-loved
British singers of the 20th century and
sometimes regarded as the greatest
voice which Britain has ever produced,
her tragically early death from cancer
robbed music of a voice of exceptional
beauty, richness, nobility and
compassion, unparalleled in modern
times. Well-established as a concert
artist, she turned to opera in 1946,
singing only two roles: the title role in
The Rape of Lucretia (which she
created) and Gluck's *Orfeo*, with which
role her name is indissolubly linked.
The Kathleen Ferrier Memorial Prize,
Britain's most prestigious vocal
competition, was established in her
memory.

Ferro, Gabriele

Italian conductor, particularly
associated with Rossini operas and with
revivals of neglected 19th-century
Italian works. One of the finest
contemporary Rossini interpretors.

Fervaal

Opera in prologue and three acts by
d'Indy (Op 40). 1st perf. Brussels, 12
March 1897; libr. by the composer.
Principal roles: Fervaal (ten), Guilhen
(sop), Arfagard (bar). The most

important of d'Indy's operas, heavily influenced by Wagner, it is nowadays all but forgotten.

Plot: France during the Saracen invasions. Wounded in battle, the Celtic chief Fervaal is nursed back to health by the Saracen sorceress Guilhen. They fall in love. Deceived by the Druid Arfagard into believing Fervaal unfaithful, Guilhen destroys the Celts.

Festa teatrale (Italian for 'theatrical festival')

A name used in the late 17th and 18th centuries for the sumptuous operatic works provided for public and state occasions, such as royal weddings. An example is Handel's *Atalanta*.

Festival of Two Worlds, Spoleto

An annual festival in Umbria (Italy), founded by Menotti in 1958. Using young American and European artists, the festival specialises in contemporary works and in revivals of 19th-century Italian bel canto operas. Performances are given at the Teatro Nuovo (cap. 900), which opened in 1864. Musical directors have included Thomas Schippers, Christopher Keene and Christian Badea.

Festivals

Although a few annual opera festivals (such as Bayreuth, Glyndebourne and Salzburg) date back further, the summer opera festival, sometimes in the open air, is essentially a postwar phenomenon. Some, such as Bayreuth and Halle, are devoted to the works of one composer; others, such as Salzburg and Bregenz, present the standard repertory with star-studded casts. Perhaps the most rewarding are those such as Wexford which specialise in the revival of long-neglected operas.

See Aix-en-Provence Festival; Aldeburgh Festival; Bayreuth Festival; Bregenz Festival; Buxton Festival; Camden Festival; Caramoor Festival; Edinburgh Festival; English Bach Festival; Festival of Two Worlds, Spoleto; Glyndebourne Festival; Göttingen Festival; Handel Festival, Halle; Maggio Musicale Fiorentino; Orange Festival; Pesaro Festival; Salzburg Festival; Savonlinna Festival; Verona Arena; Wexford Festival

Feuersnot (*Fire Famine*)

Opera in one act by Richard Strauss (Op 50). 1st perf. Dresden, 21 Nov 1901; libr. by Ernst von Wolzogen after *The Quenched Fires of Oudenaarde* in J. W. Wolf's *Sagas of the Netherlands*. Principal roles: Kunrad (bar), Diemut (sop). Strauss' second opera, only infrequently performed, it is a thinly-veiled satirical attack on those who rejected first Wagner and then his disciple, Strauss himself.

Plot: 12th-century Munich. On St John's Eve, Kunrad causes all the fires in the city to go out. He allows them to burn again only when Diemut, whom he loves and who has publicly humiliated him for his passion, admits that she reciprocates his feelings. [R]

Février, Henri (*1875–1957*)

French composer. He wrote three operettas and six operas. The latter are *Le Roi Aveugle* (Paris 1906; libr. H. le Roux), *Monna Vanna**, by far his most successful work, *Carmosine* (1913), *Gismonda* (Paris 1918; libr. after Victorien Sardou), *La Damnation de Blanche-Fleur* (Monte Carlo 1920) and *La Femme Nue* (Monte Carlo 1929). He also wrote a biography of his friend and teacher, Messager.

Fiakermilli
Soprano role in Richard Strauss'
Arabella. She is the regimental mascot.

Fiamma, La (*The Flame*)
Opera in three acts by Respighi. 1st
perf. Rome, 23 Jan 1934; libr. by
Claudio Gaustalla after Hans Wiessner
Jenssen's *The Witch*. Principal roles:
Silvana (sop), Donello (ten), Basilio
(bar), Eudossia (mezzo). Respighi's
penultimate and most successful opera.

Plot: 17th-century Ravenna. The
witch Agnese di Cervia is lynched and
her daughter Silvana (second wife of
Basilio, Exharch of Ravenna) is unable
to prevent it. Agnese curses Basilio's
family, including Silvana, for whom she
predicts a fate similar to her own.
Silvana falls in love with her stepson
Donello and confesses her adultery to
the ailing Basilio who falls dead at the
news. Silvana is accused of having
killed Basilio by witchcraft, arraigned
before the bishop and, failing to defend
herself, is condemned. [R]

Fibich, Zdeněk (*1850–1910*)
Czech composer. Influenced by
Schumann and, more especially,
Wagner, he wrote seven operas, some
of which deserve to have had more
success outside Czechoslovakia than has
come their way. His first two operas,
Bukovín (Prague 16 April 1874; libr.
Karel Sabina) and *Blaník* (Prague 25
Nov 1881; libr. Eliśka Krásnohorská),
are immature, but his powerful musical
imagination is fully apparent in *The
Bride of Messina* (*Nevěsta Mesinská*,
Prague 28 March 1884; libr. Otakar
Hostinský, after Friedrich von Schiller)
[R Exc] and *The Tempest* (*Bouře*,
Prague 1 March 1895; libr. Jaroslav
Vrchlický, after Shakespeare). At this
point Fibich formed a liason with the
poetess Anežka Schulzová, for whom he
left his family. She wrote the libretti for

his last three operas, all of which are
marked by considerable erotic fervour
in the music. *Hedy* (Prague 12 Feb
1896; libr. after Lord Byron's *Don
Juan*) was followed by *Šárka**, his
masterpiece, and the ambitious *The Fall
of Arkun* (*Pád Arkuna*, Prague 9 Nov
1900).

In addition to his operas, Fibich also
wrote the melodrama trilogy
Hippodamie. It comprises *The Wooing
of Pelops* (*Námluvy Pelopovy*, 1889),
The Atonement of Tantalus (*Smir
Tantalův*, 1890) and *The Death of
Hippodamia* (*Smrt Hippodamie*, 1891).

Fidalma
Mezzo role in Cimarosa's *Il
Matrimonio Segreto*. She is Carolina's
aunt.

Fidelio
or Die Eheliche Liebe (*Wedded
Love*)
Opera in two (originally three) acts by
Beethoven (Op 72). 1st perf. (as
Leonore) Vienna, 20 Nov 1805; libr.
by Josef Sonnleithner, after Jean-Nicolas
Bouilly's libretto for Gaveaux's *Léonore
ou l'Amour Conjugal*. Revised version,
1st perf. Vienna, 29 March 1806; libr.
revised by Stefan von Breuning. Final
version, 1st perf. Vienna, 23 May
1814; libr. revised by Georg Friedrich
Treitschke. Principal roles: Leonore
(sop), Florestan (ten), Rocco (bass),
Don Pizzaro (bar), Marzelline (sop),
Jacquino (ten), Don Fernando (b-bar).
Beethoven's only opera, it is the most
famous of all 'rescue operas'. Suffused
with Beethoven's deep humanity and
burning passion for human freedom,
the music totally transcends the
Singspiel structure in which the opera is
written. One of the greatest of all
operatic works, it occupies a unique
position in the repertory. There are
four overtures to the opera: *Leonora*

No 1 (composed for a projected Prague performance), *Leonora No 2* (the first written and played at the première), the magnificent *Leonora No 3* (which is sometimes inserted between the final two scenes) and *Fidelio* (which now begins the work). The original version of the opera is still sometimes performed.

Plot: 18th-century Seville. The noble Florestan has been imprisoned for political reasons. His wife, Leonore, has disguised herself as the boy Fidelio and entered the service of the jailer Rocco. Rocco's daughter Marzelline has fallen in love with Fidelio, to the displeasure of her admirer Jacquino, the gatekeeper. Leonore discovers that Florestan is in the deepest dungeon and that the evil governor Don Pizzaro plans to kill him before an imminent ministerial inspection takes place. Rocco and Fidelio dig his grave in the dungeon and Pizzaro attempts to murder Florestan but is prevented from doing so by Leonore who reveals herself as Florestan's wife. The arrival of the minister, Don Fernando, puts paid to the murder attempt. Pizzaro is arrested, and Fernando allows Leonore herself to remove her husband's chains. [R both versions]

Fidès

Mezzo role in Meyerbeer's *Le Prophète*. She is Jean de Leyden's mother.

Fieramosca

Baritone role in Berlioz's *Benvenuto Cellini*. He is a sculptor in love with Teresa.

Fierrabras

Opera in three acts by Schubert (D 796). 1st perf. Vienna, 9 Feb 1858 (composed 1823); libr. by Josef Kupelwieser, after *Eginhard und Emma*. Principal roles: Fierrabras (ten),

Florinda (sop), Roland (bar), King Karl (bass), Emma (sop), Maragond (mezzo), Eginhard (ten), Boland (bar). Schubert's most structurally advanced opera, it contains some of his most dramatically effective music but is unaccountably only very rarely performed. Set in the time of Charlemagne, it is a story of love and chivalry during the Moorish wars.

Fiery Angel, The *(Ognenny Angel)*

Opera in five acts by Prokofiev (Op 37). 1st perf. Paris, 25 Nov 1954 (composed 1927); libr. by the composer, after Valery Bryusov's novel. Principal roles: Renata (sop), Ruprecht (bar), Heinrich (mute), Inquisitor (bass). A terrifying story of sorcery and demonic possession, it is one of Prokofiev's greatest works but is unaccountably only infrequently performed. It remained unperformed in his lifetime and Prokofiev used some of the music in his third symphony.

Plot: 16th-century Germany. The knight Ruprecht meets Renata, who believes that Count Heinrich is the incarnation of an angel which visited her when she was a child. She at first mistakes him for Heinrich, and he, having fallen in love with her, accompanies her to Cologne to help her search for Heinrich. When they finally find him, and he rejects her, she persuades Ruprecht to duel with him and the knight is hurt, but wins Renata's affections. Later, in an increasing state of madness, she accuses him of being possessed by the Devil and threatens to leave. Eventually, Renata enters a convent where she seems to unleash evil spirits, and is ordered by the Inquisition to be tortured and burnt. [R]

Fiesco, Jacopo

Bass role in Verdi's *Simon Boccanegra*.

He is a stoical old patrician who has brought up Amelia.

Figaro

The barber of Beaumarchais' plays appears as: (1) Baritone role in Paisiello's and Rossini's *Il Barbiere di Siviglia*. (2) Bass-baritone role in Mozart's *Le Nozze di Figaro*.

Figlia di Iorio, La *(Jorio's Daughter)*

Works of this title based on Gabriele d'Annunzio's play include:

(1) Opera in three acts by Franchetti. 1st perf. Milan, 29 March 1906. Principal roles: Mila (sop), Aligi (ten), Lazzaro (bar). Arguably the finest of Franchetti's verismo pieces, it is nowadays all but forgotten.

(2) Opera in three acts by Pizzetti. 1st perf. Naples, 4 Dec 1954. Principal roles: Mila (sop), Aligi (ten), Lazzaro (bar). A word-for-word setting of the play, it is one of Pizzetti's finest works but is only very rarely performed.

Plot: Abruzzi, Italy. Pursued by peasants who believe her to be a witch, Mila is saved by Aligi, who falls in love with her even though he is already engaged. They are discovered in a mountain cave by Aligi's father Lazzaro, who has his son beaten and tied up. Aligi escapes and kills his father who is about to rape Mila. Mila accuses herself of Lazzaro's murder and the mob have her burned.

Figner, Medea *(b Mei) (1858–1952)*

Italian-born Russian mezzo and later soprano, particularly associated with the Russian and French repertories. Possessing a beautiful voice and superb technique, she created Lisa in *The Queen of Spades* and the title roles in *Iolanta* and Nápravník's *Francesca da Rimini*. Her autobiography, *My Memoirs*, was published in 1912. Her husband Nikolai (1857–1918) was a successful tenor, who created Hermann in *The Queen of Spades*, Vaudemont in *Iolanta* and Vladimir in Nápravník's *Dubrovsky*.

Fila di voce *(Italian for 'a spinning of the voice')*

It is the instruction to a singer to hold a soft, sustained note without either expanding or diminishing the tone. An example is the final note of Violetta's 'Addio del passato' in Verdi's *La Traviata*.

Fille de Madame Angot, La *(Mrs Angot's Daughter)*

Operetta in three acts by Lecocq. 1st perf. Brussels, 4 Dec 1872; libr. by Paul Siraudin, Louis François Clairville and Victor Koning, after A. F. Eve Maillot's *Madame Angot ou la Poissarde Parvenue*. Principal roles: Clairette (sop), Ange Pitout (ten), Pomponnet (bar). By far Lecocq's most successful work, it enjoyed an initial run of 500 performances, and is still regularly performed. The ballet *Mam'zelle Angot* is derived from music from the operetta.

Plot: 19th-century Paris. Clairette, daughter of the late Madame Angot, is engaged to the hairdresser Pomponnet but loves the satirist Ange Pitout. She tries to release herself from the engagement but ends up still planning to marry Pomponnet. [R]

Fille du Régiment, La *(The Daughter of the Regiment)*

Comic opera in two acts by Donizetti. 1st perf. Paris, 11 Feb 1840; libr. by Jules-Henri Vernoy de Saint-Georges and Jean François Alfred Bayard. Principal roles: Marie (sop), Tonie (ten), Sulpice (bass), Marquise de Berkenfeld (mezzo). Donizetti's first

French opera and one of his most delightful comedies (which Mendelssohn said that he wished he'd written), it was an instant success and has remained popular ever since. It is written in opéra-comique style, but in Italy, where it is given as *La Figlia del Reggimento*, recitatives replace the spoken dialogue.

Plot: Swiss Tyrol, *c* 1815. The orphan girl Marie has been raised as a 'daughter' by the 21st Regiment, a section of which is led by Sulpice. She loves the young Tyrolean Tonie who had saved her life. Tonie enlists in the regiment in order to marry her, but she is claimed as a long-lost niece by the Marquise. At her château, the Marquise, aided and abetted by Sulpice, attempts to teach Marie the social graces. She is bored, however, and the arrival of Tonie and the regiment rescues her from an arranged marriage. The Marquise confesses that Marie is actually her illegitimate daughter and gives her blessing to the girl's marriage to Tonie. [R]

Fille du Tambour-Major, La

(*The Drum-Major's Daughter*)
Operetta in three acts by Offenbach. 1st perf. Paris, 13 Dec 1879; libr. by Henri Charles Chivot and Alfred Duru. Offenbach's last substantial operetta, it has never ranked as one of his most popular works but is still performed from time to time. [R Exc]

Films

See Operatic films

Filosofo di Campagna, Il (*The Country Philosopher*)

Opera in three acts by Galuppi. 1st perf. Venice, 26 Oct 1764; libr. by Carlo Goldoni. Principal roles: Don Tritemio (bar), Eugenia (sop), Lesbina (sop), Nardo (bar), Rinaldo (ten). Galuppi's most enduring work, and one of the finest of all 18th-century Italian opera buffas, it is still occasionally performed.

Plot: Don Tritemio, who lives in the country with his daughter Eugenia, is in love with her companion Lesbina. The Don wishes Eugenia to marry the rich farmer Nardo, but she is in love with Rinaldo. To assist Eugenia, Lesbina disguises herself as Eugenia and succeeds in arousing Rinaldo's jealousy, but he then falls in love with Lesbina. [R]

Finale (Italian for 'end')

The final part of an operatic act. In the 18th and early 19th centuries, this usually consisted of an extended ensemble.

Finch' han dal vino

Baritone aria (the so-called Champagne Aria) for the Don in Act I of Mozart's *Don Giovanni*.

Finland

See Finnish National Opera; Savonlinna Festival

Finnish National Opera

(*Suomalainen Ooppera* in Finnish)
The company was formed in 1914 by Aïno Ackté and others and in recent years has won international acclaim for its performances, especially of contemporary Finnish operas. Musical directors have included Armas Järnefelt, Jussi Jalas and Leif Segerstam. There is also a chamber company (*Suomen Kansallisooppera*) which performs at the Russky Theatre (cap. 669). A new opera house in Helsinki is currently under construction.

Finnish opera composers

See: Kokkonen; A. Merikanto; O. Merikanto; Sallinen; Sibelius

Other national opera composers include Paavo Heininan (*b* 1938), Leevi Madetoja (1887–1947), Erkki Merlartin (1875–1937), Fredrik Pacius (1809–91) and Tauno Pylkkänen (*b* 1918).

Finta Giardiniera, La *(The Pretended Garden-Girl;* sometimes given in English as *Sandrina's Secret)*

Opera in three acts by Mozart (K 196). 1st perf. Munich, 13 Jan 1775; libr. by Marco Coltellini after Ranieri de' Calzabigi's libretto for Anfossi. Principal roles: Sandrina (sop), Arminda (sop), Ramiro (mezzo), Count Belfiore (ten), Nardo (bar), Serpetta (sop), Don Anchise (ten). An assured and attractive work, it is the earliest of Mozart's operas which is still regularly performed.

Plot: Countess Violante is believed to have died as a result of a violent quarrel with her lover, Belfiore, who has disappeared. Disguised as a gardener, Sandrina, the Countess searches for Belfiore, who she has forgiven. She is employed by the mayor Anchise, whose daughter, Arminda, Belfiore is courting and who sets his own sights on 'Sandrina'. After much amorous intrigue and a string of complications, everything is satisfactorily sorted out and everyone except the mayor gets married. [R]

Finta Semplice, La *(The Pretended Simpleton)*

Comic opera in three acts by Mozart (K 51). 1st perf. Salzburg, 1 May 1769; libr. by Marco Coltellini, after Carlo Goldoni. Principal roles: Rosina (sop), Giacinta (sop), Ninetta (sop), Fracasso (ten), Polidoro (ten), Cassandro (bass), Simone (bass). Mozart's first publicly performed opera, it is still occasionally performed.

Plot: The Hungarian baroness Rosina exercises her charms on two infatuated brothers, Cassandro and Polidoro, so that they will allow her own brother Fracasso to marry their sister Giacinta. [R]

Finto Stanislao, Il

See Giorno di Regno, Un; Jírovec

Fiora

Soprano role in Montemezzi's *L'Amore dei Tre Re*. Married to Manfredo, she is in love with Avito.

Fioravanti, Valentino *(1764–1837)*

Italian composer, excelling in opera buffa. He wrote 77 operas, including *I Virtuosi Ambulante* (Paris 1807; libr. Luigi Balocchi) and *Ogni Eccesso è Vizioso* (1824), but only *Le Cantatrici Villane** is at all remembered. His son Vincenzo (1799–1877) was also a composer of opera buffas, some of which met with success in Naples. Of his 35 operas, the most important is *Il Ritorno di Pulcinella dagli Studi di Padova* (Naples 1837).

Fiordiligi

Soprano role in Mozart's *Così fan Tutte*. Dorabella's sister, she is in love with Guglielmo.

Fiorilla

Soprano role in Rossini's *Il Turco in Italia*. She is married to Don Geronio.

Fioritura *(Italian for 'flowering')*

A florid decoration of the vocal line. It is also known, not quite accurately, as coloratura.

Firenze è come un albero fiorito

Tenor aria for Rinuccio in Puccini's *Gianni Schicchi*.

Fischer-Dieskau, Dietrich *(b 1925)*

German baritone, particularly associated with Mozart, Strauss, Wagner and Verdi roles and with contemporary operas. One of the greatest singers of the 20th century, he was equally renowned for his lieder singing as for his opera interpretations. A fine singing-actor of outstanding intelligence and musicianship and a champion of modern composers, he created Mittenhofer in *Elegie für Junge Liebende* and the title role in Reimann's *Lear*. One of the most recorded singers in history, he has also appeared as a conductor, and his writings include *Wagner und Nietzsche: der Mystagoge und sein Abtrunniger* and a biography of Schubert. Married to the soprano Julia Varady*.

Fisher, Sylvia *(b 1910)*

Australian soprano, particularly associated with Wagner and Britten roles. A fine dramatic soprano with a strong stage presence, she created Miss Wingrave in *Owen Wingrave*.

Flagello, Ezio *(b 1931)*

American bass, particularly associated with the Italian repertory and with Mozart roles, especially Leporello. He possessed a dark and very rich voice with a remarkable upper register extending to high A, and was a fine singing-actor. He created Enobarbus in Barber's *Antony and Cleopatra*.

Flagstad, Kirsten *(1895–1962)*

Norwegian soprano, particularly associated with Wagnerian roles, especially Isolde. One of the greatest 20th-century dramatic sopranos, she possessed a radiant voice of remarkable power which was used with unfailing musicianship. She faced some hostility after the war because of her husband's association with the Quislings, but this was soon overcome and she remained a great favourite with audiences until her retirement in 1954. She was director of the Norwegian Opera (1959–60). Her autobiography, *The Flagstad Manuscript* (written with Louis Biancolli), was published in 1965.

Flamand

Tenor role in Richard Strauss' *Capriccio*. He is a musician in love with Countess Madeleine.

Flat *(musical symbol:♭)*

A reduction in the pitch by a semitone (or by a full tone if marked double flat). The term is also used to describe an unintentional and indeterminate lowering of the pitch. This second meaning is used to describe the all-too-prevalent tendency of singers to sing under the note. Its opposite is sharp.

Flavio, Rè di Longobardi

Opera in three acts by Handel. 1st perf. London, 14 May 1723; libr. by Nicola Francesco Haym, after Pierre Corneille's *Le Cid* and Ghigi's libretto for Pollarolo's *Flavio Pertarido*. It is nowadays only very rarely performed.

Fledermaus, Die *(The Bat)*

Operetta in three acts by J. Strauss II. 1st perf. Vienna, 5 April 1874; libr. by Carl Haffner and Richard Genée after Henri Meilhac and Ludovic Halévy's *Le Reveillon*, itself based on Roderick Benedix's *Das Gefängnis*. Principal roles: Rosalinde (sop), Gabriel von Eisenstein (ten), Adele (sop), Alfred (ten), Dr Falke (bar), Col Frank (b-bar),

Prince Orlofsky (mezzo), Frosch (speaker), Dr Blind (ten). The quintessential Viennese operetta, and one of the greatest of all musical comedies, it is the only operetta to have established itself in the repertory of all major opera houses. There is a long tradition, especially in Vienna, of performing the work on New Year's Eve with guest stars appearing in Act II to give their party pieces.

Plot: Vienna. Dr Falke plans to take revenge on his friend Eisenstein for a humiliating practical joke of which he was the butt. Before leaving to serve a brief prison sentence for a minor offence, Eisenstein accepts Falke's invitation to a party. His wife Rosalinde is expecting a visit from an old flame Alfred, an opera singer. She gives her maid Adele the night off and she and Alfred sit down to a domestic evening. The prison governor, Col Frank, on his way to a party, comes to escort Eisenstein to prison and Alfred, in Eisenstein's dressing gown, allows himself to be arrested rather than compromise Rosalinde. At Prince Orlofsky's party all the characters play the parts assigned to them in Falke's plot: Eisenstein, disguised as the Marquis de Renard, flirts with a disguised Adele, makes friends with Frank (disguised as the Chevalier Chagrin) and then provides evidence of infidelity to his own wife, Rosalinde, whom he woos in her disguise as a Hungarian countess. Even the blasé Orlofsky is amused. At the prison, Frosch presides boozily until the arrival of Frank, distinctly the worse for wear. Eisenstein, arriving for his prison term, discovers who was arrested in his stead (and why) but Rosalinde has evidence of his own peccadillos. Falke irons everything out and claims his revenge, and all agree to blame everything on the champagne. [R]

Flemish opera composers
See Blockx

Other Flemish opera composers include Pierre Benoît (1834–1901), whose *The Village in the Mountains* (*Het Dorp in 't Gebergte*, 1856) was the first opera written to a Flemish libretto, August de Boeck (1865–1937), Paul Gilson (1865–1942) and Joseph Mertens (1834–1901).

See also Belgian opera composers

Fleur que tu m'avais jetée, La

Tenor aria (the Flower Song) for Don José in Act II of Bizet's *Carmen*.

Fliegende Holländer, Der (*The Flying Dutchman*)

Opera in three acts (originally one act) by Wagner. 1st perf. Dresden, 2 Jan 1843; libr. by the composer after Heinrich Heine's *Aus den Memorien des Herren von Schnabelewopski*. Principal roles: Dutchman (b-bar), Senta (sop), Daland (bass), Erik (ten), Mary (mezzo), Steersman (ten). Wagner's first 'canonical' opera, it is a powerful and highly atmospheric setting notable for its remarkable characterisation of the doomed sea captain. Most modern productions revert to Wagner's original one-act structure.

Plot: 18th-century Norway. The Dutchman, as punishment for having uttered a blasphemy, has been condemned to sail the seas for ever, unless redeemed by the love of a woman faithful unto death. Allowed to come ashore once every seven years in search of such a woman, he lands in Norway and meets Daland, an old sea captain who, seduced by the Dutchman's wealth, suggests marriage to his daughter Senta. Senta, loved by the simple huntsman Erik, has long been obsessed with the legend of the Dutchman, and falls in love with him immediately. The Dutchman overhears her begging Erik to understand her feelings, mistakenly thinks her unfaithful and, distraught, immediately sails away. Senta throws herself off a cliff, calling to him that she has been faithful unto death. Her death is his redemption: the Dutchman's ship sinks, and he and Senta are seen ascending to heaven. [R]

Flight of the Bumble Bee, The

Orchestral excerpt, very popular in the concert hall, from Rimsky-Korsakov's *The Tale of Tsar Sultan*. It describes Gvidon's journey, transformed into a bee, to find the Tsar.

Flint, Mr

Bass role in Britten's *Billy Budd*. He is an officer of H.M.S. Indomitable.

Flora

(1) Soprano role in Britten's *The Turn of the Screw*. She is one of the two children in the Governess' charge. (2) Soprano role in Tippett's *The Knot Garden*. She is the ward of Faber and Thea. (3) Mezzo role in Menotti's *The Medium*. She is the medium of the opera's title. (4) Mezzo role in Verdi's *La Traviata*. Flora Bervoix, she is a friend of Violetta's.

Florence

See Florentine Camerata; Maggio Musicale Fiorentino; Teatro Communale, Florence

Florence Pike

Mezzo role in Britten's *Albert Herring*. She is Lady Billows' housekeeper.

Florentine Camerata

An academy of musicians and writers founded in Florence in the late 16th century, whose aim was the recreation of the ideals of classical Greek tragedy and who took as their point of departure Aristotle's description of drama as "words sweetened by music". They developed a declamatory style of singing called *recitar cantando* which was applied to dramatic texts. They may thus be viewed as the inventors of opera. The leading members included Ottavio Rinuccini*, the poet who wrote the earliest opera libretti, Count Giovanni Bardi (1534–*c* 1614), at whose home the academy met, and the composers Caccini*, de Cavalieri*, Vincenzo Galilei (*c* 1520–91), the father of the astronomer, and Peri*.

Florentinische Tragödie, Eine

(*A Florentine Tragedy*)
Opera in one act by Zemlinsky (Op 16). 1st perf. Stuttgart, 30 Jan 1917; libr. by Max Meyerfeld, after Oscar Wilde's play. Principal roles: Simone (bar), Bianca (mezzo), Guido (ten). A lush work in late romantic style, it suffered a long period of neglect but has recently had a number of performances.

Plot: Renaissance Florence. Through the arousal of his jealousy, the merchant Simone abandons his role of passive cuckold and murders his wife Bianca's lover, Giudo Bardi. [R]

Florestan

Tenor role in Beethoven's *Fidelio*. Leonore's husband, he is a political prisoner.

Florid

A style of singing in which the vocal line is heavily ornamented, as for example in many arias by Handel or Rossini.

Floridante

Opera in three acts by Handel. 1st. perf London, 9 Dec 1721; libr. by Paolo Antonio Rolli, after Silvani's *La Costanza in Trionfo*. It is nowadays only very infrequently performed.

Flosshilde

Mezzo role in Wagner's *Das Rheingold* and *Götterdämmerung*. She is one of the three Rhinemaidens.

Flotow, Friedrich von *(1812–83)*

German composer. He wrote 18 operas in a light and sentimental style, which mixed German Singspiel and French opéra-comique elements with Italian lyricism. His works are tuneful and engaging but are largely innocent of any dramatic or musical originality. Nowadays, only *Martha**, by far his most successful work, and *Alessandro Stradella** are still remembered. Of his other operas, *Le Naufrage de la Méduse* (Paris 31 May 1839; libr. H. and T. Cogniard), *La Veuve Grapin* (Paris 21 Sept 1859; libr. P. A. A. Pittaud de Forges), *Zilda* (Paris 28 May 1866; libr. Jules-Henri Vernoy de Saint-Georges, Henri Charles Chivot and Alfred Duru) and *L'Ombre* (Paris 7 July 1870; libr. Saint-Georges and Adolphe de Leuven) achieved some success in their time.

Flower Duet

Soprano/mezzo duet ('Scuoti quella fronda di ciliego') for Cio-Cio-San and Suzuki in Act II of Puccini's *Madama Butterfly*.

Flowermaidens

The seductive inhabitants of Klingsor's magic garden in Act II of Wagner's *Parsifal*.

Flower Song

Tenor aria ('La fleur que tu m'avais jetée') for Don José in Act II of Bizet's *Carmen*.

Floyd, Carlisle *(b 1926)*

American composer. One of the leading contemporary American opera composers, he has written seven operas (for all of which he wrote his own libretti), most of which have met with considerable success. *Susannah** established his reputation, which was upheld by *Wuthering Heights** and *The Passion of Jonathan Wade* (New York 12 Nov 1962). His subsequent works are *Markheim* (1966), *Of Mice and Men* (Seattle 20 Jan 1970; libr. after John Steinbeck), *Bilby's Doll* (Houston 29 Feb 1976) and *Willie Stark* (1981).

Flute

Tenor role in Britten's *A Midsummer Night's Dream*. A bellows mender, he is one of the mechanicals.

Fluth

Roles in Nicolaï's *Die Lustigen Weiber von Windsor*: Herr Fluth (bar) and his wife Frau Fluth (sop).

Flying Dutchman, The

See Fliegende Holländer, Der

Foco insolito, Un

Bass aria for Pasquale in Act I of Donizetti's *Don Pasquale*.

Foerster, Josef Bohuslav *(1859–1951)*

Czech composer. He wrote six operas, the first three of which are in traditional Czech style. *Debora* (Prague

27 Jan 1893; libr. Mosenthal and J. Kvapil) was unsuccessful, but its successor *Eva** remains his most popular work. It was followed by *Jessika* (Prague 16 April 1905; later called *Kupec Benátský*; libr. Jaroslav Vrchlický, after Shakespeare's *The Merchant of Venice*). In his final three operas, for each of which he wrote his own libretto, his interests become increasingly spiritual and symbolic. They are *The Invincibles* (*Nepřemožení*, Prague 19 Dec 1919), *The Heart* (*Srdce*, Prague 15 Nov 1923) and *The Simpleton* (*Bloud*, Prague 28 Feb 1936; libr. after Tolstoy) and were largely unsuccessful. His wife Berta Foerstrová-Lauetererová (1869–1936) was a successful soprano, who created, for Dvořák, Julia in *Jakobín* and Xenie in *Dimitrij*.

Foltz, Hans
Bass comprimario role in Wagner's *Die Meistersinger von Nürnberg*. A coppersmith, he is one of the masters.

Fontainebleau!
Tenor aria for Carlos in Act I of Verdi's *Don Carlos*.

Foppa, Giuseppe Maria
(1760–1845)
Italian librettist. He wrote over 80 libretti, the best being comedies. He provided texts for Coccia, Fioravanti, Generali, Mayr (11 operas), Paer (*Sargino*), Portugal, Rossini (*L'Inganno Felice, La Scala di Seta, Sigismondo* and *Il Signor Bruschino*), Spontini, Zingarelli (*La Notte dell'Amicizia* and *Giulietta e Romeo*) and others.

Force of Destiny, The
See Forza del Destino, La

Ford
The wealthy merchant in Shakespeare's *The Merry Wives of Windsor* appears as: (1) Baritone role in Verdi's *Falstaff*. (2) Bass role in Vaughan Williams' *Sir John in Love*. (3) Tenor role in Salieri's *Falstaff*.

Forester
Baritone role in Janáček's *The Cunning Little Vixen*. He is the vixen's captor.

Forest Murmurs
Orchestral excerpt in Act II of Wagner's *Siegfried*.

Foresto
Tenor role in Verdi's *Attila*. He is an Aquilean knight.

Forrester, Maureen *(b 1930)*
Canadian mezzo, particularly associated with Wagner and Handel roles. She possessed a rich voice of great range which she used with unfailing musicianship, and she was also an accomplished comic actress.

Forsell, John *(b Carl Johan Jacob)* *(1868–1941)*
Swedish baritone, particularly associated with Mozart roles, especially Don Giovanni. He was administrator of the Royal Opera, Stockholm (1923–39) and was also a noted teacher, whose pupils included Jussi Björling and Set Svanholm.

Fortner, Wolfgang *(1907–87)*
German composer. He wrote seven operas, whose musical style attempts to reconcile diatonic and serial systems, some of which have met with success in Germany. *Cress Ertrinkt* (1930; libr. A. Zeitler) was written for performance by schools, and was followed by the one-

act pantomime *Die Witwe von Ephesus* (1953; libr. Grete Weill, after Petronius) and the television opera *Der Wald* (*The Forest*, 1953; staged Essen 1954). His reputation was established with *Bluthochzeit* (*Blood Wedding*, Cologne 8 June 1957; libr. Enrique Beck, after Federico García Lorca's *Bodas de Sangre*). His other operas are the comedy *Corinna* (1958; libr after Gérard de Nerval), *In Seinem Garten Liebt Don Perlimplin Belisa* (Schwetzingen 1962; libr. after Lorca's *Amor de Don Perlimplín con Belisa en su Jardín*) and *Elisabeth Tudor* (1972; libr. M. Braun).

Fortunio

Operetta in three acts by Messager. 1st perf. Paris, 5 June 1907; libr. by G. A. de Caillavet and Roger de Flers, after Alfred de Musset's *Le Chandelier*. Principal roles: Fortunio (ten), Jacqueline (mezzo), Clavaroche (bass), Maître André (bar). One of Messager's most successful works, it is still occasionally performed. [R]

Forza del Destino, La (*The Force of Destiny*)

Opera in four acts by Verdi. 1st perf. St Petersburg, 10 Nov 1862; libr. by Francesco Maria Piave, after Angel de Saavedra Ramírez de Baquedano, Duke of Rivas's *Don Alvaro ó la Fuerza del Sino* and a scene from Friedrich von Schiller's *Wallensteins Lager*. Revised version, 1st perf. Milan, 27 Feb 1869; libr. revised by Antonio Ghislanzoni. Principal roles: Don Alvaro (ten), Leonora (sop), Don Carlo (bar), Padre Guardiano (bass), Preziosilla (mezzo), Fra Melitone (bar), Marquis of Calatrava (bass), Trabuco (ten). One of Verdi's richest 'middle period' scores, with one of the finest of all operatic overtures, it was for long either heavily cut or grossly reorganised on account

of its sprawling plot. Recently it has been realised that the piece is most effective as Verdi wrote it: the 'genre' scenes are as integral to the drama as the private tragedy of the Calatrava family. The opera is also notable for containing, in Melitone, Verdi's only wholly comic character before *Falstaff*.

Plot: 18th-century Spain and Italy. Don Alvaro and his beloved, Leonora, are about to elope when they are disturbed by her father, the Marquis of Calatrava. In the ensuing confrontation, Alvaro accidentally kills the Marquis, and the lovers flee. Circumstances separate them and Leonora seeks refuge with Padre Guardiano, who allows her to become a religious hermit by way of penance. Alvaro joins a regiment under an assumed name and saves the life of a comrade whom he has befriended but, wounded in battle, entrusts his friend with the destruction of a box containing private documents. Unbeknownst to him, his friend is Leonora's brother, Carlo, also serving under another name, who has sworn to avenge his father's death and his sister's honour. His suspicions aroused, Carlo opens the box to discover Leonora's portrait and realises that his friend is his enemy. He seeks out Alvaro and challenges him to a duel which is interrupted, and Alvaro seeks refuge at the monastery. Carlo tracks him down, resumes the fight, and is mortally wounded. Alvaro seeks absolution for him from the Hermit, who is revealed to be Leonora, and the dying Carlo stabs his sister to death. (In the original version, Alvaro throws himself from a cliff, uttering a curse against Destiny.) [R]

Forzano, Giovacchino (1883–1970)

Italian librettist and producer. After a short period as a baritone, he turned to writing and production. He wrote many libretti, including texts for Ferrari-Trecate (*Ciotollino*), Franchetti (*Notte di Legenda* and *Glauco*), Giordano (*Il Rè*), Leoncavallo (*La Reginetta delle Rose*, *La Candidata* and *Edipo Rè*), Mascagni (*Lodoletta* and *Il Piccolo Marat*), Puccini (*Suor Angelica* and *Gianni Schicchi*), Vittadini (*Fiametta e l'Avaro*) and Wolf-Ferrari (*Gli Amanti Sposi* and *Sly*). He produced the first performances of *Turandot*, *Nerone*, Giordano's *La Cena delle Beffe* and Zandonai's *I Cavalieri di Ekebù*.

Foss, Lukas *(b Fuchs)* *(b 1922)*
German-born American composer. He has written three operas, which have met with some success in the United States. They are *The Jumping Frog of Calaveras County* (Bloomington 18 May 1950; libr. Jean Karsavina after Mark Twain), the television opera *Griffelkin* (6 Nov 1955; staged Karlsruhe 1973; libr. Alastair Reid) and the nine-minute mini-opera *Introductions and Goodbyes* (Spoleto 1960; libr. Gian-Carlo Menotti).

Four Saints in Three Acts
Opera in four acts by Thomson. 1st perf. Ann Arbor, 20 May 1933; libr. by Gertrude Stein. Principal roles: St Teresa I (sop), St Teresa II (mezzo), St Ignatius (bar). One of the finest and most successful American operas, it is an allegory in which two saints and their followers help one another to achieve salvation. Thomson's lyrical score contrasts with the surreal and almost plotless libretto. Thomson hoped for (and productions have often had) an all-black cast. [R]

Fox, Carol *(1926–81)*
American administrator. She was a co-founder of the Chicago Lyric Opera in 1952 and was later its general manager (1956–80).

Fra Diavolo
or **L'Hôtellerie de Terracine**
Opera in three acts by Auber. 1st perf. Paris, 28 Jan 1830; libr. by Eugène Scribe. Principal roles: Fra Diavolo (ten), Zerlina (sop), Lord Cockburn (bar), Lady Pamela (mezzo), Lorenzo (ten), Mathés (bass). Auber's only opera still to be regularly performed, it is one of the finest opéra-comiques and is based on the historical Fra Diavolo (*d* 1806), who was an Italian brigand and renegade monk.

Plot: 18th-century Naples. The notorious bandit, Fra Diavolo, disguised as a Marquis, institutes a series of elaborate plans to relieve the travelling Englishman Lord Cockburn and his wife, Pamela, of their gold. In the course of his machinations he compromises the honour of Zerlina, the innkeeper Mathés' daughter, loved by the soldier Lorenzo, and of Lady Pamela. His schemes are to no avail, however, and he is eventually trapped and caught by Lorenzo. The honour of the innocent ladies is restored, Lorenzo gets the reward offered by Lord Cockburn for the capture of Diavolo, and all ends happily. [R]

Fra Gherardo
Opera in three acts by Pizzetti. 1st perf. Milan, 16 May 1928; libr. by the composer after the 13th-century *Chronicles of Salimbene da Parma*. Principal roles: Gherardo (ten), Mariola (sop). Pizzetti's fifth opera, written in arioso style, it was successful at its appearance but is now infrequently performed.

Plot: 12th-century Parma. The wealthy weaver Gherardo leaves the city after an affair with the orphan girl Mariola, and joins a religious order of friars. He returns to lead a peasant uprising against the corrupt authorities, is charged with heresy and burnt at the stake. Mariola, meanwhile, meets her death at the hands of a mad woman.

Françaix, Jean *(b 1912)*

French composer. He has written five operas, some of which have met with a modicum of success in France. They are *Le Diable Boîteux* (*The Limping Devil*, Paris 1937; libr. composer after Alain René le Sage) [R], the comedy *L'Apostrophe* (1942; libr. after Anne-Honoré de Balzac), *Le Main de Gloire* (Bordeaux 1950; libr. after Gérard de Nerval), *Paris à Nous Deux* (1954; libr. composer and F. Roche) and *La Princesse de Clèves* (1965; libr. composer and M. Lanjean after Madame de la Fayette).

France

See Aix-en-Provence Festival; Arts Florissants, Les; Grand Théâtre, Marseilles; Grand Théâtre Graslin, Nantes; Grand Théâtre Municipal, Bordeaux; Monte Carlo Opera; Opéra Bastille, Paris; Opéra-Comique, Paris; Opéra de Lyon; Opéra du Rhin; Orange Festival; Paris Opéra; Salle de l'Opéra, Versailles; Théâtre Bouffes-Parisiens; Théâtre de l'Opéra, Nice; Théâtre des Champs-Elysées, Paris; Théâtre Municipal, Nancy; Toulouse Capitole

Francesca da Rimini

Works of this title, all essentially derived from Dante's *La Divina Commedia*, include:

(1) Opera in three acts by Mercadante. 1st perf. Madrid, 1830; libr. by Felice Romani.

(2) Opera in four acts by Cagnoni.

1st perf. Turin, 19 Feb 1878; libr. by Antonio Ghislanzoni.

(3) Opera by Nápravník (Op 17). 1st perf. St Petersburg, 9 Dec 1902; libr. by O. O. Palacek and E. P. Ponomarev.

(4) Opera in prologue, two scenes and epilogue by Rachmaninov (Op 25). 1st perf. Moscow, 24 Jan 1906; libr. by Modest Tchaikovsky. Principal roles: Lanzeotto (b-bar), Francesca (sop), Paolo (ten), Virgil (bass), Dante (ten). Containing some of Rachmaninov's most powerful music, it is still occasionally performed but is hampered by its weak libretto.

Plot: The Ghost of Virgil tells Dante that the souls in the Inferno are those who have overindulged sexually and cites the story of Paolo and Francesca. Lanzeotto Malatesta suspects his wife, Francesca, of loving his younger brother Paolo, who conducted Lanzeotto's courtship by proxy and led Francesca to believe that she was to marry him. Francesca asks to enter a convent whilst Lanzeotto is at the wars, but he appoints Paolo to look after her. Francesca gives in to Paolo's passionate urgings and Lanzeotto, returning, kills them both. [R]

(5) Opera in four acts by Zandonai. 1st perf. Turin, 19 Feb 1914; libr. by Tito Ricordi, after Gabriele d'Annunzio's play. Principal roles: Francesca (sop), Paolo (ten), Gianciotto (bar), Malatestino (ten). Zandonai's most successful and enduring work, it is still quite often performed.

Plot: Ravenna and Rimini in the 13th century. The hideous Gianciotto, wishing to marry Francesca, tricks her into a betrothal by sending his handsome young brother, Paolo, to escort her to him. Paolo and Francesca fall instantly in love, and matters are complicated further when a third brother, Malatestino, becomes violently infatuated with her. When Francesca rejects Malatestino, he betrays her and Paolo to Gianciotto, who is thus provoked into murdering them. [R]

Francesco

(1) Baritone role in Verdi's *I Due Foscari*. He is the historical Francesco Foscari (*d* 1457), Doge of Venice. (2) Baritone role in Verdi's *I Masnadieri*. He is Massamiliano's evil son. (3) Tenor comprimario role in Auber's *Fra Diavolo*. (4) Tenor comprimario role in Berlioz' *Benvenuto Cellini*.

Franchetti, Alberto *(1860–1942)*

Italian composer. His considerable personal wealth allowed him to ensure the best performances for his works and to indulge his taste for the spectacular. In style, his operas are a kind of verismo Meyerbeer. There are nine of them, a number of which enjoyed considerable success in their time: *Asrael* (Reggio Emilia 11 Feb 1888; libr. Ferdinando Fontana after Thomas Moore's *Loves of the Angels*), *Cristoforo Colombo* (Genoa 6 Oct 1892; libr. Luigi Illica), *Fior d'Alpe* (Milan 1894; libr. L. di Castelnuovo), *Il Signor di Pourceaugnac* (Milan 1897; libr. Fontana after Molière's *Monsieur de Pourceaugnac*), the highly successful *Germania* (Milan 11 March 1902; libr. Illica), *La Figlia di Iorio**, perhaps his finest work, *Notte di Legenda* (Milan 1915; libr. Giovacchino Forzano), *Giove di Pompei* (Rome 5 July 1921; libr. Illica and E. Romagnoli), written in collaboration with Giordano, and *Glauco* (Naples 1922; libr. Forzano).

Franci, Carlo *(b 1927)*

Argentinian conductor and composer, particularly associated with Rossini operas and with contemporary works. He conducted the first performances of operas by Henze, Lualdi, Rota and Tosatti. He has composed one opera,

L'Imperatore (Bergamo 1958). His father Benvenuto (1891–1985) was a successful baritone, who created Neri in Giordano's *La Cena delle Beffe*, Cristiano in Zandonai's *I Cavalieri di Ekebù* and a role in Mascagni's *Il Piccolo Marat*.

Franck, César *(1822–90)*

Belgian composer. He wrote three operas, none of them remembered today. They are the opéra-comique *Valet de Ferme* (1852; libr. Gustave Vaëz and Alphonse Reyer), which has never been performed, *Hulda* (Monte Carlo 8 March 1894; composed 1885; libr. Charles Grandmougnin, after Bjørnstjerne Bjørnson) and the unfinished *Ghisèle* (Monte Carlo 5 April 1896; libr. Gilbert-Augustin Thierry), which was completed by five of his pupils including Chausson and d'Indy.

Frank, Col

Bass-baritone role in J. Strauss' *Die Fledermaus*. He is the prison governor.

Frankfurt Opera

One of Germany's leading houses, the theatre was originally opened in 1880 but was destroyed by bombs in 1943. The rebuilt Schauspielhaus (cap. 1,430) reopened in 1951. The annual season runs from October to June. Musical directors have included Clemens Krauss, Wilhelm Steinberg, Franz Konwitschny, Sir Georg Solti, Lovro von Matačić, Christoph von Dohnányi, Michael Gielen and Gary Bertini.

Franklin, David *(1908–73)*

British bass. A fine singing-actor, he was particularly associated with Mozart roles and with Rocco in *Fidelio*. He created Mars in Bliss' *The Olympians*. An operation for throat cancer ended his singing career in 1951, but he later enjoyed great success as a radio and television personality. He wrote the libretto for Phyllis Tate's *The Lodger*, and published his autobiography, *Basso Cantante*, in 1969.

Frantz, Ferdinand *(1906–59)*

German bass-baritone, particularly associated with Wagnerian roles, especially Wotan and Hans Sachs. Apart from Hans Hotter, he was the finest Wagnerian baritone of the immediate postwar period. His wife Helena Braun (*b* 1903) was a successful soprano.

Franz

Tenor role in Offenbach's *Les Contes d'Hoffmann*. He is Crespel's deaf servant.

Fra poco a me

Tenor aria for Edgardo in Act III of Donizetti's *Lucia di Lammermoor*. Its cabaletta, 'Tu che a Dio' is the final scene of the opera.

Fraschini, Gaetano *(1816–87)*

Italian tenor. One of the leading lyric tenors of the mid-19th century, he created Gerardo in *Caterina Cornaro*, six roles for Pacini including Faone in *Saffo*, and, for Verdi, Foresto in *Attila*, Zamoro in *Alzira*, Corrado in *Il Corsaro*, Arrigo in *La Battaglia di Legnano*, the title role in *Stiffelio* and Gustavus in *Un Ballo in Maschera*. The Teatro Fraschini in Pavia is named after him.

Frasquita

Operetta in three acts by Lehár. 1st perf. Vienna, 12 May 1922; libr. by Heinrich Reichert and Alfred Maria Willner. Although never one of Lehár's most successful works, it is still occasionally performed in German-speaking countries.

Frasquita

Soprano role in: (1) Bizet's *Carmen*. She is a gypsy friend of Carmen's. (2) Wolf's *Der Corregidor*. She is the miller's wife.

Frau ohne Schatten, Die *(The Woman Without a Shadow)*

Opera in three acts by Richard Strauss (Op 65). 1st perf. Vienna, 10 Oct 1919; libr. by Hugo von Hofmannsthal after his own story. Principal roles: Empress (sop), Dyer's Wife (sop), Emperor (ten), Barak (bar), Nurse (mezzo), Spirit Messenger (b-bar), Barak's brothers (ten, bar and bass). The most ambitious (and, some would say, the most pretentious) work of the Strauss/Hofmannsthal partnership, it is a symbolic fairy-tale. Despite Strauss' description of it as his *Zauberflöte*, it is heavily Wagnerian.

Plot: The Emperor is married to a supernatural being, whose father has stipulated that if their marriage remains childless (a condition symbolised by the inability of the Empress to cast a shadow), she must return whence she came while her husband will be turned to stone. With her Nurse, the Empress goes in search of a shadow and comes to the hut of Barak, a humble dyer. Barak's complaining wife has no children, but she does have a shadow, and agrees to sell her prospects of motherhood for the riches which the Nurse offers her. Seeing Barak's anguish when his wife tells him of the plan, the Empress refuses to take the shadow. Later, she sees Barak and his wife undergoing supernatural punishment, and then witnesses her own husband nearly turned to stone, but still refuses to accept a shadow at someone else's expense. In this moment of supreme unselfishness, she is granted a shadow, thus releasing everybody from their sufferings. [R]

Frazzi, Vito *(1888–1975)*
Italian composer. His operas, most of them on an ambitious scale, include *Re Lear* (Florence 1939; libr. G. Papini, after Shakespeare's *King Lear*), *L'Ottava Moglie di Barbablu* (Florence 1940), *Don Chisciotte* (Florence 1952; libr. composer after Miguel Cervantes' *Don Quixote*) and the unperformed *Il Giardino Chiuso*. He was also a noted editor of early Italian operas.

Fredda ed immobile
The ensemble which ends Act I of Rossini's *Il Barbiere di Siviglia*.

Freia
Soprano role in Wagner's *Das Rheingold*. She is the goddess of youth.

Freiburg Opera
Opera in this German town in Baden-Württemberg is given at the Grosses Haus, which opened in 1910. Destroyed in 1944, it reopened (cap. 1, 133) in 1949. Musical directors have included Franz Konwitschny, Marek Janowski and Ádám Fischer.

Freischütz, Der *(The Free-Shooter)*
Opera in three acts by Weber (J 277). 1st perf. Berlin, 18 June 1821; libr. by Johann Friedrich Kind, after Johann Apel and Friedrich Laun's *Gespensterbuch*. Principal roles: Agathe (sop), Max (ten), Caspar (bass), Ännchen (sop), Prince Ottakar (bar), Cuno (bass), Hermit (bass), Kilian (bar), Samiel (speaker). Weber's finest and most enduring work, it tells the legend of the free-firing bullets: six will unerringly reach their target but the seventh belongs to the Devil. The first performance was one of the most sensationally successful in operatic history, and the work has had a vast influence on the subsequent development of opera. The famous Wolf's Glen Scene has probably never been surpassed as a musical depiction of the macabre.

Plot: 17th-century Bohemia. The head forester, Cuno, intends to hold a shooting contest to decide the hand of his daughter Agathe. Max, who loves her, is off-form and in desperation accepts the offer of Caspar, who has sold his soul to the devil, to obtain the free-firing bullets for him. In spite of warnings by Agathe and her cousin Ännchen, Max goes to the haunted Wolf's Glen, where Caspar invokes Samiel and casts the bullets. At the contest before Prince Ottakar, five bullets have been used and Caspar secretly fires the sixth; the seventh is thus at Samiel's disposal. Max fires and both Agathe and Caspar fall. A holy Hermit restores Agathe to life whilst Samiel claims Caspar. Max is set to undergo a year's probation to prove himself worthy of Agathe. [R]

Fremstad, Olive *(b Olivia Rundquist) (1871–1951)*
Swedish-born American soprano. Beginning as a mezzo, she turned to soprano roles in 1903 and became one of the greatest Wagnerian sopranos of the early 20th century. She had a rich, sumptuous voice and a powerful dramatic sense. She is the inspiration for the principal character in Willa Cather's novel *The Song of the Lark*.

French opera composers
See Adam; Auber; Audran; Auric; Barraud; Bécaud; Berlioz; Bizet; Blavet; Boïeldieu; Bondeville; Bruneau; Cambert; Campra;

Canteloube; Chabrier;
Charpentier; M.-A. Charpentier;
Chausson; Dalayrac; Dauvergne;
David; Debussy; Delibes;
Destouches; Dukas; Fauré;
Février; Françaix; Ganné;
Gaveaux; Godard; Gounod;
Guiraud; Halévy; Hérold; Hervé;
Ibert; d'Indy; Jolivet; R.
Kreutzer; Lalo; Landowski;
Lappara; Leclair; Lecocq;
Leroux; Lesueur; Lesur; Lully;
Magnard; Maillart; Massé;
Massenet; Méhul; Messager;
Messiaen; Meyerbeer; Milhaud;
Monpou; Monsigny; Offenbach;
Philidor; Pierné; Planquette;
Poulenc; Rabaud; Rameau;
Ravel; Rebel; Reyer; Roussel;
Saint-Saëns; Satie; Sauget;
Thomas; Tomasi; Varney;
Viardot-García; Widor

Freni, Mirella *(b Fregni) (b 1935)*
Italian soprano, particularly associated
with the Italian and French repertories.
Combining a glorious, lyrical voice with
a charming stage presence, she began as
a soubrette but subsequently turned
successfully to more dramatic roles.
Married to the bass Nicolai Ghiaurov*.

Freunde von Salamanka, Die
(*The Friend from Salamanca*)
Opera in two acts by Schubert (D 326).
1st perf. Vienna, 19 Dec 1875
(composed 1815); libr. by Johann
Mayrhofer. Like all of Schubert's early
Singspiels, it contains some delightful
music, but is almost never performed.
[R]

Frezzolini, Erminia *(1818–84)*
Italian soprano. One of the leading
lyric sopranos of the mid-19th century,
she created Giselda in *I Lombardi*, the
title role in *Giovanna d'Arco* and
Camilla in Mercadante's *Orazi e
Curiazi*. Her father Giuseppe (1789–
1861) was a successful buffo who
created Dulcamara in *L'Elisir d'Amore*,
and her husband Antonio Poggi (1806–
75) a tenor, who created Carlo in
Giovanna d'Arco.

Frick, Gottlob *(b 1906)*
German bass, particularly associated
with Wagnerian roles and with Rocco
and Osmin. One of the finest
Wagnerian basses of the postwar era,
with a black and powerful voice, he
enjoyed a remarkably long career,
singing into his 70s. He created Caliban
in Sutermeister's *Die Zauberinsel* and
the Carpenter in Haas' *Die Hochzeit
des Jobs*.

Fricka
Mezzo role in Wagner's *Das Rheingold*
and *Die Walküre*. She is Wotan's wife.

Fricsay, Ferenc *(1914–63)*
Hungarian conductor, particularly
associated with Mozart operas. One of
the finest opera conductors of the
immediate postwar period, he was
musical director of the Budapest State
Opera (1939–45), the Berlin State
Opera (1951–52) and the Bavarian
State Opera (1956–58). He conducted
the first performances of Martin's *Le
Vin Herbé*, Orff's *Antigonae* and
Einem's *Dantons Tod*.

Friedenstag (*Peace Day*)
Opera in one act by Richard Strauss
(Op 81). 1st. perf Munich, 24 July
1938; libr. by Josef Gregor after Pedro
Calderón's *La Rendención de Breda*.
Principal roles: Maria (sop),
Commandant (bar). An anti-militarist
tract and a plea for peace, it is one of

Strauss' least successful works, and is only very rarely performed.

Plot: A Catholic town, 24 Oct 1648. On the last day of the Thirty Years' War, the Catholic Commandant of the town plans to blow up the citadel rather than surrender to the Lutheran commander. However, his wife Maria persuades him to accept the Peace of Westphalia.

Friederike

Operetta in three acts by Lehár. 1st perf. Berlin, 4 Oct 1928; libr. by Ludwig Herzer and Fritz Löhner. Principal roles: Friederike (sop), Goethe (ten), Paula (sop), Weyland (bar), Lenz (bar), Cristel (mezzo). Dealing with the Friederike Brion episode in the life of Goethe, it was successful at its appearance and is still occasionally performed. [R]

Friedrich, Götz (b 1930)

German producer. A brilliant but controversial producer of left-wing political views, he was closely associated with the Komische Oper in East Berlin, and Covent Garden where he was director of productions (1976–81). Administrator of the Deutsche Oper, Berlin (1981–). He wrote a biography of his teacher, Walter Felsenstein.

Friml, Rudolf (1879–1972)

Czech-born American composer. A highly successful operetta composer, the most enduring of his 24 stage works are The Firefly (New York 2 Dec 1912; libr. Otto Harbach), High Jinks (New York 10 Dec 1913), Rose Marie (New York 2 Sept 1924; libr. Harbach and Oscar Hammerstein II) and The Vagabond King (New York 21 Sept 1925; libr. W. H. Post and Brian Hooker, after Justin Huntly McCarthy's If I Were King).

Frist ist um, Die

Bass-baritone monologue for the Dutchman in Act I of Wagner's Der Fliegende Holländer.

Fritz

Tenor role in: (1) Offenbach's La Grande-Duchesse de Gérolstein. He is a soldier in love with Wanda. (2) Mascagni's L'Amico Fritz. He is a confirmed bachelor. (3) Schreker's Der Ferne Klang. He is a young composer.

Froh

Tenor role in Wagner's Das Rheingold. He is the God of Spring.

From the House of the Dead
(Z Mrtvého Domu)

Opera in three acts by Janáček. 1st perf. Brno, 12 April 1930; libr. by the composer, after Fyodor Dostoyevsky's Memoirs From the House of the Dead. Principal roles: Shiskov (bar), Skuratov (ten), Luka (ten), Petrovič (bar), Aljeja (sop), Shapkin (ten), Chekunov (bar), Commandant (b-bar). Janáček's last and most overwhelmingly powerful work, it is a harrowing but ultimately hopeful piece, which Janáček had not entirely completed at his death. It was prepared for performance by Břetislav Bakala and Osvald Chlubna. Initially slow to make its way, it has been widely performed in the last 20 years.

Plot: A Siberian prison camp. The arrival and release of the political prisoner Petrovič frame scenes from prison life where the inmates relate their past histories, go about daily prison life and enact two plays. [R]

Frosch

Speaking role in J. Strauss' Die Fledermaus. He is the tipsy jailer who presides over the proceedings in Act III. The role is often played by a star actor;

recent British Froschs have included Frankie Howerd, Bernard Breslaw and Clive Dunn.

Frühbeck de Burgos, Rafael
(b 1933)
Spanish conductor. Best known as a choral and symphonic conductor, his operatic appearances have been infrequent.

Frumerie, Gunnar de *(b 1908)*
Swedish composer and pianist. He wrote one opera, the successful *Singoalla* (1940; libr. E. Byström-Baeckström, after Victor Rydberg) [R].

Fugère, Lucien *(1848–1935)*
French baritone. Based largely at the Opéra-Comique in Paris, he enjoyed an exceptionally long career, singing into his early 80s. An outstanding singing-actor, he was particularly associated with the French repertory and with Mozart. He created over 30 roles, including the Father in *Louise*, Henri de Valois in *Le Roi Malgré Lui*, Pandolfe in *Cendrillon*, the Devil in Massenet's *Grisélidis*, des Grieux in *Le Portrait de Manon*, and, for Messager, Maître André in *Fortunio* and a role in *La Basoche*.

Fugue
A contrapuntal piece of music for a given number of voices, in which the voices enter successively in imitation of each other. The most famous operatic example is the great comic fugue 'Tutto nel mondo è burla' which ends Verdi's *Falstaff*.

Full score *(or orchestral score)*
The complete music of an opera, showing all the vocal and orchestral parts.

Fundación para Arte Lirica, Lima
Peru's opera company, founded in 1981 by Luigi Alva who is its artistic director, it gives a short annual season at the Teatro Municipal.

Fuor del mar
Tenor aria for Idomeneo in Act II of Mozart's *Idomeneo*. The most fearsomely demanding of Mozart's heroic tenor arias, there is an alternative, less demanding version.

Furiant
A fast Czech dance with rapidly changing rhythms. There is a famous operatic example in Smetana's *The Bartered Bride*.

Furtiva lagrima, Una
Tenor aria for Nemorino in Act II of Donizetti's *L'Elisir d'Amore*. One of the best-loved of all tenor arias.

Furtwängler, Wilhelm *(1886–1954)*
German conductor, particularly associated with Wagner operas and *Fidelio*. One of the greatest 20th-century interpreters of the German repertory, he was musical director of the Lübeck Opera (1911–15), the Mannheim Opera (1915–20) and the Berlin State Opera. His equivocal relationship with the Nazis caused him difficulties after the war, and he was not allowed to conduct in the United States.

Fux, Johann Joseph *(1660–1741)*
Austrian composer. Best known as a composer of church music and as the author of a famous treatise on counterpoint, he also wrote 19 operas.

The most successful included *Angelica Vincatrice di Alcina* (Vienna 14 Sept 1716; libr. Pietro Pariati, after Lodovico Ariosto's *Orlando Furioso*), *Elisa* (Laxenburg 28 Aug 1719; libr. Pariati) and *Costanza e Fortezza* (Prague 28 April 1723; libr. Pariati), his finest work.

Fyodor

Mezzo trouser-role in Moussorgsky's *Boris Godunov*. He is the Tsarevich. The role is occasionally sung by a treble.

Gabriele
Soprano role in: (1) Offenbach's *La Vie Parisienne*. She is a glove maker. (2) J. Strauss' *Wiener Blut*. She is Count Zedlau's wife.

Gabriele Adorno
Tenor role in Verdi's *Simon Boccanegra*. He is a patrician in love with Amelia.

Gade, Niels *(1817–90)*
Danish composer. His stage works include the Singspiel *Mariotta* (1850; libr. C. Borgaard, after Eugène Scribe) and the opera-ballet *Fairy Spell*.

Gagliano, Marco da *(1582–1643)*
Italian composer. One of the earliest opera composers, he was –like Gluck 150 years later – a reformer anxious to banish the excesses of singers and to achieve dramatic naturalness. These aims he expressed in the preface to his *La Dafne**. He wrote two other operas, both in collaboration with Peri: *Il Medoro* (1616), which is lost, and *La Flora* (Florence 1628; libr. Andrea Salvadori).

Gaito, Constantino *(1878–1945)*
Argentinian composer. Perhaps the most important Argentinian nationalist composer, his 11 operas include *Shafras* (Buenos Aires 1907), the unperformed *I Doria* (1914), *Caio Petronio* (Buenos Aires 1919), *Fior de Neve* (Buenos Aires 1922), *Ollantay* (Buenos Aires 1926), *Lázaro* (Buenos Aires 1929), which marked the first appearance in opera of the tango, and his most successful work *La Sangre de las Guitarras* (Buenos Aires 1932), which incorporates regional gaucho dances.

Galeffi, Carlo *(1882–1961)*
Italian baritone, particularly associated with the Italian repertory, especially Verdi. One of the finest Italian baritones of the inter-war period, he created Manfredo in *L'Amore dei Tre Re*, Fanuèl in *Nerone* and, for Mascagni, Raimondo in *Isabeau* and roles in *Parisina* and *Amica*.

Galitsin, Prince
Tenor role in Moussorgsky's *Khovanschina*. He is loved by the regent Sophia.

Galitsky, Prince
Bass role in Borodin's *Prince Igor*. He is Igor's brother-in-law.

Gallet, Louis *(1835–95)*
French librettist. One of the most prolific French librettists of the second half of the 19th century, he provided texts for Bizet (*Djamileh* and the unfinished *La Coupe du Roi de Thulé* and *Don Rodrigue*), Bruneau (*L'Attaque du Moulin* and *La Rêve*), Godard (*Les Guelfes*), Gounod (*Cinq-Mars* and the unfinished *Maître Pierre*), Guiraud (*Frédégonde* and *Le Kobold*), Massenet (*Le Roi de Lahore*, *Le Cid*, *Marie-Magdeleine* and *Thaïs*) and Saint-Saëns (*La Princesse Jaune*, *Etienne*

Marcel, Ascanio, Proserpine and *Déjanire*).

Galli, Filippo *(1783–1853)*

Italian tenor, later a bass. After ten years as a successful tenor, an illness changed his voice and he became one of the greatest basses of the early 19th century. He created Henry VIII in *Anna Bolena* and, for Rossini, Mustafà in *L'Italiana in Algieri*, Fernando in *La Gazza Ladra*, the title role in *Maometto II*, Macrobio in *La Pietra del Paragone*, Assur in *Semiramide*, Selim in *Il Turco in Italia* and Batone in *L'Inganno Felice*. His brother Vincenzo (1798–1858) was a successful buffo.

Galli-Curci, Amelita *(1882–1963)*

Italian soprano, particularly associated with lighter Italian roles. The leading coloratura soprano of the early 20th century, she possessed a voice of extraordinary agility, but tended always to sing slightly sharp.

Galli-Marié, Celestine *(b Marié de l'Isle) (1840–1905)*

French mezzo, particularly associated with the French repertory. An outstanding singing-actress, with excellent diction and a fine voice, she created the title roles in *Carmen* and *Mignon*, Man Friday in Offenbach's *Robinson Crusoé* and Lazarillo in Massenet's *Don César de Bazan*, as well as roles in operas by Guiraud, Maillart and Massé. Of her Carmen, Tchaikovsky said that she "managed to combine with the display of unbridled passion an element of mystical fatalism".

Galuppi, Baldassare *(1706–85)*

Italian composer. He wrote 91 operas, enjoying particular success in comedy, especially with the 13 works written in collaboration with Carlo Goldoni. His comedies include *L'Arcadia in Brenta* (Venice 14 May 1749; libr. Goldoni), *Il Mondo della Luna* (Venice 29 Jan 1750; libr. Goldoni), *Il Mondo alla Roversa* (Venice 14 Nov 1750; libr. Goldoni), *Le Virtuose Ridicole* (Venice 1752; libr. Goldoni after Molière's *Les Précieuses Ridicules*) and *Il Filosofo di Campagna**, his only work which is still remembered. In operatic history, he enjoys an important place as a pioneer of the ensemble-type finale.

Gambler, The *(Igrok)*

Opera in four acts by Prokofiev (Op 24). 1st perf. Brussels, 29 April 1929; libr. by the composer, after Fyodor Dostoyevsky. Principal roles: Alexei (ten), Pauline (sop), General (bass), Grandmother (mezzo), Marquis (ten), Blanche (mezzo), Mr Astley (bar). Written in Prokofiev's most aggressively expressionistic style, it is a powerful depiction of greed and obsession. Initially slow to make its way, it is nowadays quite often performed.

Plot: In a German spa town during the 1860s, the General is in love with the penniless coquette Blanche, but has gambled away his money and is in debt to the Marquis. He anxiously awaits the death of his wealthy old aunt whose fortune he is to inherit, but she arrives at the spa bursting with health and loses every penny at the gaming tables. Meanwhile, Alexei, tutor to the General's children, loves Pauline, his employer's stepdaughter. To prevent Pauline from having to marry the Marquis, Alexei, who has already lost money from Pauline at gambling, tries his luck again. This time he wins but, when he gives the money to Pauline, she throws it back in his face. [R]

Ganné, Louis *(1862–1923)*

French composer. He wrote a number

of operettas, of which the most enduring were *Les Saltimbanques* (Paris 1899) [R] and *Hans le Joueur de Flûte* (Monte Carlo 1906) [R Exc].

García, Manuel (I) *(1775–1832)*
Spanish tenor and composer. One of the leading lyric tenors of the early 19th century, he created Egeo in *Medea in Corinto*, Norfolk in *Elisabetta Regina d'Inghilterra* and Count Almaviva in *Il Barbiere di Siviglia*. He also composed 43 light operas in Italian, Spanish and French which were admired by Rossini, but which are now totally forgotten. In 1825 he founded an opera company in New York, touring the United States and Mexico, where he lost all his money to bandits. His second wife María Joaquina Sithces (1780–1854) was a successful mezzo, who created Ismene in *Medea in Corinto*. Their children included María Malibran*, Manuel García II* and Pauline Viardot-García*. He was also a noted teacher, whose pupils included Adolphe Nourrit, Henriette Méric-Lalande and his own children.

García, Manuel (II) *(1805–1906)*
Spanish baritone and teacher, son of the tenor Manuel García* and brother of María Malibran* and Pauline Viardot-García*. His singing career lasted only five years, after which he retired because of vocal problems and devoted himself to teaching, becoming one of the greatest singing teachers in history. The first person to make a scientific study of vocal production, he invented the laryngoscope in 1855 and was a professor at the Royal Academy of Music (1848–95). His theoretical writings include *Mémoires Sur la Voix Humaine* (1840), *Traîté Complet de l'Art du Chant* (1847) and *Hints on Singing* (1894); the second is often regarded as the finest treatise on

singing ever written and is still in widespread use. His most famous pupils included Jenny Lind, Erminia Frezzolini and Sir Charles Santley. His first wife Eugenia (1815–80) was a successful soprano; their son Gustave (1837–1925) was a baritone.

Gardelli, Lamberto *(b 1915)*
Italian conductor and composer, particularly associated with the Italian repertory, especially Verdi, all of whose early operas he recorded. One of the outstanding Verdi interpreters of recent times, he also composed four operas, including *Alba Novella* (1937) and *Il Sogno* (1942).

Garden, Mary *(1874–1967)*
British soprano, particularly associated with the French repertory. One of the finest lyric sopranos of the early 20th century, she had a fine voice used with great intelligence and was an outstanding singing-actress, especially as Salome. She created Mélisande in *Pelléas et Mélisande*, Queen Orlanda in Leroux's *La Reine Fiammette* and the title roles in Massenet's *Sapho* and *Chérubin* and Saint-Saëns' *Hélène*. Later resident in the United States, she became director of the Chicago Opera (1919–20). Her autobiography, *The Mary Garden Story*, was published in 1951.

Gardiner, John Eliot *(b 1943)*
British conductor, particularly associated with Purcell, Handel and Gluck, and with the French repertory. One of the finest modern exponents of the Baroque repertory, he prepared Rameau's unfinished *Les Boréades* for performance. He was musical director of the Opéra de Lyon (1983–88).

Gardner, John *(b 1917)*
British composer. He has written three

operas: *The Moon and Sixpence* (London 24 May 1957; libr. P. Terry, after W. Somerset Maugham), *The Visitors* (Aldeburgh 1972; libr. O. Greenwood) and the children's opera *Bel and the Dragon* (1973; libr. T. Kraemer).

Gasdia, Cecilia *(b 1960)*
Italian soprano, particularly associated with Rossini, Bellini and Donizetti roles. Possessing a beautiful and agile voice used with a superb technique, she is one of the finest exponents of the bel canto repertory to have emerged in the late 1980s.

Gasparini, Francesco *(1668–1727)*
Italian composer. He wrote 61 operas, all of them now forgotten, of which the most successful was *Ambleto* (Venice 1705; libr. Apostolo Zeno and Pietro Pariati), which is not based on Shakespeare.

Gasparone
Operetta in three acts by Millöcker. 1st perf. Vienna, 26 Jan 1884; libr. by F. Zell (Camillo Walzel) and Richard Genée. Millöcker's last work to enjoy any significant success, it is still performed from time to time in German-speaking countries. [R]

Gassmann, Florian *(1729–74)*
Bohemian composer. He wrote 25 operas, many of which enjoyed considerable success in their time but which are now virtually forgotten. He was especially successful with comedy, in which genre his most important works are *L'Amore Artigiano* (Vienna 26 April 1767; libr. Carlo Goldoni), *La Notte Critica* (Vienna 5 Jan 1768; libr. Goldoni) and *La Contessina* (Mährisch-Neustadt 3 Sept 1770; libr. Marco Coltellini, after Goldoni).

Gatti-Casazza, Giulio *(1869–1940)*
Italian administrator. He was administrator of La Scala, Milan (1898–1908) and of the Metropolitan Opera, New York (1908–35), and was responsible for a vast improvement in the standard and prestige of both houses. Married for a time to the soprano Frances Alda*. His autobiography, *Memories of Opera*, was published in 1941.

Gatty, Nicholas Comyn *(1874–1946)*
British composer. He wrote six operas in a direct and readily accessible style which enjoyed some success in their time but which are all now forgotten. They are *Greysteel* (Sheffield 1906; libr. Reginald Gatty, after the Icelandic saga *Gisli the Outlaw*), *Duke or Devil* (Manchester 16 Dec 1909; libr. Ivor Gatty), *Prince Ferelon* (London 21 May 1921; libr. composer), *The Tempest* (London 17 April 1920; libr. after Shakespeare), *Macbeth* (1920; libr. after Shakespeare) and *King Alfred and the Cakes* (London Dec 1930; libr. R. Gatty).

Gavazzeni, Gianandrea *(b 1909)*
Italian conductor, composer and musicologist. Particularly associated with 19th-century and contemporary Italian operas, he conducted the first performances of Pizzetti's *L'Assassinio nella Cattedrale* and *La Figlia di Iorio*. He wrote books on Donizetti, Moussorgsky, Pizzetti and Wagner, and also composed one opera, *Paolo e Virginia* (1935).

Gaveaux, Pierre *(1761–1825)*
French composer. He wrote some 30 operas, all long forgotten, of which the

most important (for historical rather than musical reasons) is *Léonore**, the first setting of the *Fidelio* story.

Gavotte
An old dance in 4/4 time which begins on the third beat of the bar. There is a famous operatic example in Sullivan's *The Gondoliers*.

Gay, John *(1685–1732)*
British poet, playwright and librettist. He wrote the texts for Pepusch's *The Beggar's Opera* and *Polly* and Handel's *Acis and Galatea* and also built the first theatre at Covent Garden.

Gayarré, Julián *(1844–90)*
Spanish tenor, particularly associated with the Italian and French repertories. During his finest period, from 1876 to 1886, he was regarded by many as the greatest tenor of his age. He created Enzo in *La Gioconda* and the title role in Donizetti's *Le Duc d'Albe*.

Gayer, Catherine *(b 1937)*
American soprano, particularly associated with coloratura roles and with contemporary operas. A fine singing-actress with an agile and intelligently used voice, she created the Companion in Nono's *Intolleranza*, Nausikaa in Dallapiccola's *Ulisse*, the title role in Reimann's *Melusine* and Christina in Orr's *Hermiston*.

Gayle
Soprano role in Tippett's *The Ice Break*. She is Yuri's girl-friend.

Gaztambide y Garbayo, Joaquín *(1792–1870)*
Spanish composer. He wrote 44 zarzuelas, of which the first, *La Mensajera* (Madrid 24 Dec 1849; libr. L. Olona) helped to revive the popularity of the genre after its long period of decline. Of his other works, the most successful was *La Catalina* (Madrid 23 Oct 1854; libr. Olona after Eugène Scribe's libretto for Meyerbeer's *L'Etoile du Nord*).

Gazza Ladra, La *(The Thieving Magpie)*
Opera in two acts by Rossini. 1st perf Milan, 31 May 1817; libr. by Giovanni Gherardini after Jean Marie Théodore Bauduin d'Aubigny and Louis Charles Caigniez's *La Pie Voleuse*. Principal roles: Ninetta (mezzo), Podestà (bass), Giannetto (ten), Fernando (b-bar), Pippo (mezzo), Fabrizio (bar), Lucia (mezzo), Isaac (ten). Beginning with one of the most famous of all operatic overtures, it is one of Rossini's finest works and is an outstanding example of opera semiseria.

Plot: Ninetta is engaged to Giannetto, the son of the farmer Fernando, in whose house she is employed as a maid. She is suspected of having stolen and sold some of her master's silverware and the Podestà presses charges against her because she has rebuffed his advances. She is found guilty and condemned to death but, on her way to her execution, the real thief is discovered – a magpie. [R]

Gazzaniga, Giuseppe *(1743–1818)*
Italian composer. He wrote many operas, all of them nowadays forgotten, achieving particular success in comedy. His most important work is the dramma giocoso *Don Giovanni Tenorio ossia Il Convitato di Pietra* (Venice 5 Feb 1787; libr. Giovanni Bertati), which had some influence on Mozart's *Don Giovanni*.

Gebet
A German term for a *preghiera**.

Geburstag der Infantin, Der
(*The Birthday of the Infanta*)
or **Der Zwerg** (*The Dwarf*)
Opera in one act by Zemlinsky (Op 17). 1st perf. Cologne, 28 May 1922; libr. by Georg Klaren, after Oscar Wilde. Principal roles: Dwarf (ten), Infanta (sop), Ghita (sop), Estóban (bass). Zemlinsky's finest opera, it suffered a long period of neglect, but has recently been widely performed.

Plot: As a birthday present, the spoilt Infanta, Donna Clara, is given an ugly dwarf. The dwarf falls in love with her, even though she treats him like a toy. When, for the first time, the dwarf sees himself in a mirror, he dies of a broken heart. The Infanta is merely annoyed that her toy no longer works. [R]

Gedda, Nicolaï (*b Ustinov*) (*b 1925*)
Swedish tenor, particularly associated with lyrical French, German, Italian and Russian roles and also with Mozart and Viennese operetta. One of the finest tenors of the 20th century, and an outstanding linguist who is fluent in six languages, he possessed a voice of great beauty which he used with style, elegance, good taste and a superb technique. Although not large, the voice's projection was so good that he was able to sing a number of heroic roles. He created the Husband in Orff's *Trionfo d'Afrodite* and Anatol in Barber's *Vanessa*.

Gedge, Mr
Baritone role in Britten's *Albert Herring*. He is the vicar.

Geduldige Socrates, Der (*The Patience of Socrates*)
Opera by Telemann. 1st perf. Hamburg, 1721; libr. by Johann Ulrich von König, after Nicolò Minato's *La Pazienza di Socrate*. An entertaining little piece about the domestic trials of the Greek philosopher Socrates (469–399 BC), it is still occasionally performed. [R]

Gelsenkirchen Stadttheater
The original opera house in this German town in North Rhine Westphalia opened in 1935 but was destroyed by bombs in 1944. The new house (cap. 1,050) opened in 1959. In conjunction with the Bochum Opera, it forms the Musiktheater im Revier. Musical directors have included Ljubomir Romansky.

Gemma di Vergy
Opera in two acts by Donizetti. 1st perf. Milan, 26 Dec 1834; libr. by Emanuele Bidera, after Alexandre Dumas' *Charles VII Chez ses Grands Vassaux*. Principal roles: Gemma (sop), Conte di Vergy (bar), Guido (bass), Tamas (ten), Ida (mezzo). An uneven work containing some fine moments, it suffered a long period of neglect but has recently been given a number of performances.

Plot: 15th-century Paris. The Count of Vergy plans to divorce his barren wife Gemma and has already chosen a successor. Gemma's Arab slave Tamas, who is in love with her, kills the Count's esquire, but is offered a pardon if he will confess to planning to kill the Count. Gemma intervenes on Tamas's behalf and a reconciliation with her husband seems possible until the new wife Ida appears. Gemma, with a knife at Ida's throat, forces the Count to confess his love for Ida, but she is disarmed by Tamas. At the wedding, Gemma begs Tamas to kill her, but instead he stabs the Count before killing himself. [R]

Gencer, Leyla *(b 1924)*

Turkish soprano, particularly associated with Donizetti and Verdi roles and with the revival of a number of long-forgotten Italian bel canto operas. A highly dramatic singing-actress with a fine voice, she created Madame Lidoine in *Dialogues des Carmélites* and the First Woman of Canterbury in Pizzetti's *L'Assassinio nella Cattedrale.*

Gendarmes Duet

Baritone/bass duet in Offenbach's *Geneviève de Brabant.* One of the most famous of all comic duets.

Genée, Richard *(1823–95)*

German librettist and composer. One of the best librettists of the Viennese school of operetta, he provided texts – often in collaboration with F. Zell (Camillo Walzel) – for Millöcker (*Der Bettelstudent* and *Gasparone*), Offenbach (*Der Schwarze Korsar*), J. Strauss (*Die Fledermaus, Cagliostro in Wien, Eine Nacht in Venedig* and *Der Spitzenbuch der Königin*), Suppé (*Fatinitza, Donna Juanita* and *Boccaccio*) and Ziehrer (*Ein Deutschmeister*). He composed several operettas himself, including *Der Geiger aus Tirol* (*The Fiddler from Tyrol*, Danzig 1857), *Der Seekadett* (*The Naval Cadet*, Vienna 24 Oct 1876; libr. F. Zell) and *Nanon* (Vienna 10 March 1877; libr. composer and Zell, after E. G. M. Théaulon and F. V. A. d'Artois).

Generali, Pietro *(b Mercandetti) (1773–1832)*

Italian composer. He wrote many operas which were successful in their day, but he was soon eclipsed by Rossini and nowadays none of his works are remembered. Perhaps his most successful opera was *Pamela Nubile* (Venice 12 April 1804; libr. Gaetano Rossi, after Carlo Goldoni's libretto for Piccinni's *La Buona Figliuola*).

Generalmusikdirektor

The title of the musical director of a German or Austrian opera house.

Generalprobe (German for 'principal rehearsal')

The dress rehearsal of an opera in a German or Austrian opera house. The final preceding rehearsal, and the last at which any adjustments may still be made, is called Hauptprobe.

Género chico (Spanish for 'little type')

A type of zarzuela, also known as zarzuelita, which is in one act and always on a comic subject.

Geneva

See **Grand Théâtre, Geneva**

Geneviève

Mezzo role in Debussy's *Pelléas et Mélisande.* She is the mother of Pelléas and Golaud.

Gennaro

Tenor role in: (1) Donizetti's *Lucrezia Borgia.* Maffio Orsini's friend, he turns out to be Lucrezia's son. (2) Wolf-Ferrari's *I Gioielli della Madonna.* He is a blacksmith.

Genoa

See **Teatro Carlo Felice, Genoa**

Genoveva

Opera in four acts by Schumann (Op 81). 1st perf. Leipzig, 25 June 1850; libr. by the composer and Robert Reinick, after Johann Ludwig Tieck's *Leben und Tod der Heiligen Genoveva* and Christian Friedrich Hebbel's *Genoveva*. Principal roles: Genoveva (sop), Golo (ten), Siegfried (bar), Drago (bass), Margareta (sop). Schumann's only completed opera, it is very rarely performed, although the overture is well-known.

Plot: medieval Trier and Strasbourg. During the absence of her husband Siegfried, who has gone on the Crusades, Genoveva rebuffs advances made to her by Golo. Embittered, Golo has her tried for betraying her husband with the chaplain, Drago. In spite of the evil intriguing of the witch Margareta, the returning Siegfried saves his wife from the executioner. [R]

Gentele, Göran *(1917–72)*

Swedish producer and administrator. His many notable productions, mostly in Sweden, included the controversial *Un Ballo in Maschera* in which Gustavus III was portrayed as a homosexual, as he is in history. He was director of the Royal Opera, Stockholm (1963–71) and was appointed general manager of the Metropolitan Opera, New York but was killed in a car crash a few weeks before taking up the appointment.

Gérald

Tenor role in Delibes' *Lakmé*. He is a British officer.

Gérard, Carlo

Baritone role in Giordano's *Andrea Chénier*. He is a servant in the Coigny household who becomes a revolutionary leader.

Gerechter Gott

Soprano aria for Adriano in Act III of Wagner's *Rienzi*.

Gerhard, Roberto *(1896–1970)*

Spanish composer. His only opera is the brilliant and unjustly neglected *The Duenna**.

Gerhilde

Soprano role in Wagner's *Die Walküre*. She is one of the Valkyries.

German, Sir Edward *(b Jones) (1862–1936)*

British composer. His first stage work, *The Two Poets* (London July 1886; libr. W. H. Scott) is insignificant, but the enormous success of *Merrie England** led to his being hailed as Sullivan's successor. However, although his operettas are tuneful and well-written, they are not on the same level as Sullivan's. His later works are *A Princess of Kensington* (London 22 Jan 1903; libr. Basil Hood), the successful *Tom Jones** and *Fallen Fairies* (London 15 Dec 1909; libr. W. S. Gilbert). He also completed Sullivan's unfinished *The Emerald Isle*.

German opera composers

See d'Albert; J. C. Bach; Beethoven; Blacher; Bruch; Cornelius; Dessau; Egk; Eisler; Ernest II of Saxe-Coburg; Flotow; Fortner; Gerster; Gluck; Goldschmidt; Götz; Graun; Handel; Hartmann; Hasse; Henze; Hiller; Hindemith; Hoffmann; Keiser; Klebe; K. Kreutzer; Loewe; Lortzing; Marschner; Mendelssohn; Naumann; Nessler; Nicolai; Orff; Pfitzner; Poissl; Reimann; Reinecke; Rihm; Riotte; Schillings; Schreker; Schumann; Schütz; Spohr; Stockhausen; R. Strauss; Telemann; Wagner; S.

Wagner; Wagner-Régeny;
Weber; Weill; Winter; Wolf;
Zimmermann; U. Zimmermann

Germany

See Aachen Opera; Augsburg
Stadttheater; Bavarian State
Opera; Bayreuth Festival; Berlin
State Opera; Bielefeld
Stadttheater; Bonn Stadttheater;
Bremen Opera; Brunswick
Staatstheater; Cologne Opera;
Darmstadt Opera; Deutsche
Oper, Berlin; Deutsche Oper am
Rhein; Dortmund Stadttheater;
Dresden State Opera; Essen
Opera; Frankfurt Opera;
Freiburg Opera; Gelsenkirchen
Stadttheater; Göttingen Festival;
Handel Festival, Halle; Hamburg
State Opera; Hanover Opera;
Kaiserslautern Opera; Karlsruhe
Staatstheater; Kassel
Staatstheater; Kiel Opera;
Komische Oper, Berlin; Leipzig
Opera; Lübeck Opera; Mainz
Opera; Mannheim Opera;
Nürnberg Stadttheater;
Saarbrücken Opera; Stuttgart
Opera; Weimar Opera;
Wiesbaden Opera; Wuppertal
Opera

Germont

Roles in Verdi's *La Traviata*: Alfredo
Germont (ten) and his father Giorgio
(bar). The former is generally referred
to as Alfredo (he is Violetta's lover),
the latter as Germont.

Geronimo

Bass-baritone role in Cimarosa's *Il
Matrimonio Segreto*. He is Carolina's
father.

Geronio, Don

Bass role in Rossini's *Il Turco in Italia*.
He is married to Fiorilla.

Gershwin, George *(1898–1937)*

American composer, whose tragically
early death from a brain tumor cut
short a brilliant career. He wrote many
stage works, including 16 musical
comedies, of which two may be
considered operatic. *Blue Monday Blues*
(1923; libr. de Sylva), later called *135th
Street*, was an unsuccessful piece
employing jazz-style recitative as a link
to popular songs. His operatic fame
rests on his masterpiece, the all-black
Porgy and Bess*.

Gerster, Ottmar *(1897–1969)*

German composer. The most successful
of his operas were *Enoch Arden* (1936;
libr. after Alfred Lord Tennyson) and
Die Hexe von Passau (1941).

Geschwitz, Countess

Mezzo role in Berg's *Lulu*. She is Lulu's
lesbian lover.

Gertrude

(1) Soprano role in Humperdinck's
Hänsel und Gretel. She is the children's
mother. (2) Mezzo role in Gounod's
Roméo et Juliette. She is Juliet's nurse.

Gesamtkunstwerk (German for 'unified work of art')

A term much used by Wagner to
describe a form of drama in which all
aspects of the arts (music, poetry,
drama, design etc) combine to form a
single unified work of art.

Gespenstersonate, Die (*The Ghost Sonata*)

Opera in three scenes by Reimann. 1st
perf. Berlin, 1984; libr. by the

composer and Uwe Schendel, after August Strindberg's *Spöksonaten*. Principal roles: Hummel (bar), Arkenholz (ten), the Mummy (mezzo), Girl (sop), Colonel (ten), Bengtsson (bass), Johansson (ten). One of the most successful modern chamber operas, written for an orchestra of 12 players, it has been widely performed.

Plot: The student Arkenholz is befriended by Hummel, an old man in a wheel-chair. Through a window of a house they see a beautiful girl, Hummel's illegitimate daughter, whom Hummel says Arkenholz can meet. In the house, the mistress is the girl's mother, known as the Mummy, who sits in a cupboard and talks like a parrot. Hummel accuses those in the house of various crimes which he threatens to expose, but the Mummy threatens in turn to expose a murder he committed in the past. Hummel crawls into her cupboard and hangs himself. Arkenholz declares his love for the girl, but she is tainted like everybody else in the house and dies.

Gessler

Bass role in Rossini's *Guillaume Tell*. He is the tyrannical governor of Switzerland.

Ghedini, Giorgio *(1892–1965)*

Italian composer. His eight operas have met with some success in Italy but are virtually unknown elsewhere. They include *Maria d'Alessandria* (Bergamo 9 Sept 1937; libr. C. Meano), *Rè Hassan* (Venice 26 Jan 1939; libr. T. Pinelli), *La Pulce d'Oro* (Genoa 15 Feb 1940; libr. Pinelli), *Le Baccanti* (Milan 22 Feb 1948; libr. Pinelli, after Euripides's *The Bacchae*), *Billy Budd* (Venice 8 Sept 1949; libr. Quasimodo, after Herman Melville's *Billy Budd, Sailor*) and *Lord Inferno* (later called *L'Ipocrita Felice*, Italian Radio 22 Oct 1952; libr. Franco

Antonicelli, after Max Beerbohm's *The Happy Hypocrite*).

Ghent

See **Royal Opera, Ghent**

Ghiaurov, Nicolai *(b 1929)*

Bulgarian bass, particularly associated with the Italian and Russian repertories. One of the outstanding basses of the postwar era, he possessed a large, rich and beautiful voice used with fine musicianship. He was an accomplished singing-actor with a commanding stage presence, equally at home in serious or comic roles. Married to the soprano Mirella Freni*.

Ghislanzoni, Antonio *(1824–93)*

Italian librettist and baritone. He wrote some 85 libretti, providing texts for Catalani (*Edmea*), Cagnoni (*Papà Martin*, *Re Lear* and *Francesca da Rimini*), Gomes (*Fosca* and *Salvator Rosa*), Petrella (*I Promessi Sposi*), Ponchielli (*I Lituani*) and Verdi (*Aida* and the revised *La Forza del Destino*) amongst others.

Ghiuselev, Nicola *(b 1936)*

Bulgarian bass, particularly associated with the Russian and Italian repertories. An often underrated singer, he possesses a rich and powerful voice used with considerable intelligence and has a strong stage presence.

Ghosts

See **Supernatural in opera**

Ghost Sonata, The

See **Gespenstersonate, Die**

Giacomini, Giuseppe *(b 1940)*

Italian tenor, particularly associated with the Italian repertory. He possesses a fine, incisive voice, tastefully used, and has a forthright stage presence.

Giacomo

(1) Baritone role in Verdi's *Giovanna d'Arco*. He is Giovanna's father. (2) Tenor role in Rossini's *La Donna del Lago*. He is King James V of Scotland.

Già d'insolito ardore

Bass aria for Mustafà in Act I of Rossini's *L'Italiana in Algieri*.

Già i sacerdoti

Mezzo/tenor duet for Amneris and Radamès in Act IV of Verdi's *Aida*.

Già nella notte

Soprano/tenor duet for Desdemona and Otello in Act I of Verdi's *Otello*.

Giannetto

Tenor role in Rossini's *La Gazza Ladra*. He is Ninetta's fiancé.

Giannini, Vittorio *(1903–66)*

American composer. He wrote six operas: *Lucidia* (Munich 1934), *The Scarlet Letter* (Hamburg 1938; libr. after Nathaniel Hawthorne), *The Taming of the Shrew* (Cincinnati 1953; libr. composer and Dorothy Fee, after Shakespeare), his most successful work, *The Harvest* (Chicago 1961), *Rehearsal Call* (New York 1962) and *The Servant of Two Masters* (New York 1967; libr. after Carlo Goldoni). His father Ferruccio (1868–1948) was a successful tenor, and his sister Dusolina (1900–86) was a dramatic soprano, who created Hester in his *The Scarlet Letter*.

Gianni Schicchi

Comic opera in one act by Puccini. 1st perf. New York, 14 Dec 1918; libr. by Giovacchino Forzano, after Canto XXX of the *Inferno* in Dante's *La Divina Commedia*. Principal roles: Gianni Schicchi (bar), Lauretta (sop), Rinuccio (ten), Simone (bass), Zita (mezzo). The third panel of *Il Trittico*, it is Puccini's only comedy and is an entertaining and technically brilliant work.

Plot: Florence, 1299. The greedy relatives gathered at the deathbed of the deceased Buoso, led by Simone and Zita, are horrified to discover that Buoso has left his entire fortune to a monastery. They ask the wily Gianni Schicchi, whose daughter Lauretta loves Buoso's nephew, Rinuccio, to help them make a new will, giving him detailed instructions as to how everything is to be bestowed. Schicchi dresses up as Buoso and gets into his bed. When the lawyer arrives, Schicchi dictates Buoso's will, and, but for the house which he wills to the lovers, bequeathes everything to his 'good friend Gianni Schicchi'. [R]

Gibson, Sir Alexander *(b 1926)*

British conductor with a wide-ranging repertory. He was musical director of Sadler's Wells Opera (1957–59) and Scottish Opera (1962–87), of which he was the founder. He conducted the first performances of Gardner's *The Moon and Sixpence*, Orr's *Hermiston* and Hamilton's *The Cataline Conspiracy*.

Gielen, Michael *(b 1927)*

German conductor, particularly associated with 20th-century operas, especially Schönberg. He was musical director of the Royal Opera, Stockholm (1960–65), the Netherlands Opera (1972–77) and the Frankfurt Opera (1978–87). He conducted the first performance of Zimmermann's *Die Soldaten*.

Gigli, Beniamino *(1890–1957)*

Italian tenor, particularly associated with the Italian repertory. One of the greatest tenors of the 20th century, despite his paucity of taste and his virtual inability to act, he possessed a beautiful, honeyed voice used with passion and a superb technique. His *Memoirs* were published in 1957. His daughter Rina was a successful soprano.

Gil, Count

Baritone role in Wolf-Ferrari's *Il Segreto di Susanna*. He is Susanna's jealous husband.

Gilbert, Sir William Schwenk
(1836–1911)

British playwright, poet, librettist and producer. His collaboration with Sullivan on the 14 Savoy Operas was one of the most remarkable artistic partnerships in history. Whatever their setting, his texts for Sullivan are parodies of all the institutions and ideals which the British hold most sacred, and are marked by his especial brand of 'topsy-turvy' humour, pithy dialogue and a brilliance of versification (especially in the patter songs) which has seldom if ever been equalled. He also wrote the libretti for Cellier's *The Mountebanks* and German's *Fallen Fairies*. A brilliant wit and a theatrical martinet, he also acted as producer for the Savoy Operas.

Gilbert and Sullivan

See Carte, Richard d'Oyly; D'Oyly Carte Opera Company; Gilbert, W. S.; Savoy Operas; Sullivan, Sir Arthur

Gilda

Soprano role in: (1) Verdi's *Rigoletto*. She is Rigoletto's daughter. (2) Donizetti's *L'Aio nell' Imbarazzo*. She is Enrico's wife.

Giménez y Bellido, Gerónimo
(b Jiménez) (1854–1923)

Spanish composer and conductor. Musical director of the Teatro Apolo and then the Teatro de la Zarzuela in Madrid, he wrote many zarzuelas, mainly in *Género chico* form, which are notable for their use of traditional gypsy music. His most successful works include *Tannhauser el Estanquero* (Madrid 1890), *Trafalgar* (Madrid 1890; libr. J. de Burgos), *La Boda de Luis Alonso* (Madrid 1897; libr. Burgos), which is about the famous popular dancer 'La Tempranica', *El Barbero de Sevilla* (Madrid 1901), *Los Viajes de Gulliver* (Madrid 1911; libr. Paso and Abiati, after Jonathan Swift's *Gulliver's Travels*), which was written in collaboration with Vives, and *Tras Tristán* (Madrid 1918; libr. J. R. Martín).

Ginastera, Alberto *(1916–83)*

Argentinian composer, writing mainly in twelve-tone form. The leading modern Argentinian composer, his observation that "sex, violence and hallucination are three of the basic elements from which grand opera can be constructed" was put into practice in many of his stage works. His four operas, which have been widely performed, are *Don Rodrigo**, *Bomarzo**, *Beatrix Cenci** and *Barabbas* (1977; libr. after Michel de Ghelerode).

Gioconda, La *(The Joyful Girl)*

Opera in four acts by Ponchielli. 1st perf. Milan, 8 April 1876; libr. by Arrigo Boito, after Victor Hugo's *Angelo, Tyran de Padove*. Principal roles: Gioconda (sop), Enzo (ten), Barnaba (bar), Laura (mezzo), Alvise (bass), La Cieca (cont). By far Ponchielli's most successful work and his only opera still to be performed, the ballet music (the *Dance of the Hours*) has become a popular concert item.

Plot: 17th-century Venice. The banished nobleman, Enzo Grimaldo, is in Venice disguised as a sailor. He is loved by the street singer La Gioconda but is himself in love with Laura, wife of the councillor Alvise. The spy Barnaba, who lusts after Gioconda, denounces Enzo to the council. Enzo has a secret meeting with Laura on his ship, where Gioconda comes to confront him. Recognising Laura as the woman who saved her blind mother, La Cieca, from the mob when she had been accused of witchcraft by Barnaba, she warns her that Alvise is coming to arrest Enzo. Laura escapes and Enzo sets fire to his ship and flees with Gioconda. Finding out about her affair with Enzo, Alvise orders Laura to take poison, but Gioconda substitutes a sleeping potion and contrives to have Laura's 'corpse' taken to her house where Enzo will fetch her. To win Enzo's freedom she promises herself to Barnaba, but after Laura and Enzo have been reunited and left she takes Laura's poison herself. As she falls at the furious Barnaba's feet, he tells the dying girl that he has strangled La Cieca. [R]

Gioielli della Madonna, I (*The Jewels of the Madonna*)

Opera in three acts by Wolf-Ferrari. 1st perf. (as *Der Schmuck der Madonna*) Berlin, 23 Dec 1911; libr. by Enrico Golisciani and Carlo Zangarini. Principal roles: Maliella (sop), Raffaele (bar), Gennaro (ten). Wolf-Ferrari's one excursion into the verismo field, it is still occasionally performed, and the orchestral suite arranged from the opera has given the music wider currency.

Plot: Naples. Raffaele, a leader of the Camorra (the Neapolitan Mafia), tells Maliella that he loves her so much

that he would dare to steal the jewels from the statue of the Madonna. The blacksmith Gennaro, himself in love with Maliella, overhears her considering the offer, and commits the theft himself. She accepts Gennaro but then confesses to Raffaele who rejects her. She throws the jewels at Gennaro's feet and drowns herself. Gennaro returns the jewels to the statue and stabs himself in despair.

Giordano, Umberto (*1867–1948*)

Italian composer. He wrote 12 operas in verismo style, notable for their violent passions and their skilful use of the tried and trusted Mascagnian clichés of the genre. Several are theatrically effective but they have only limited musical qualities and are largely innocent of any genuine dramatic insight. His operas are the unperformed *Mariana* (1889; libr. Enrico Golisciani), *Mala Vita* (Rome 21 Feb 1892; libr. Nicola Daspuro; revised version *Il Voto*, Milan 10 Nov 1897), *Regina Diaz* (Naples 5 March 1894; libr. Giovanni Targioni-Tozzetti and Guido Menasci, after Édouard Lockroy's *Un Duel Sous le Cardinal de Richelieu*), *Andrea Chénier**, by far his most enduring work, the successful *Fedora**, *Siberia**, *Marcella* (Milan 9 Nov 1907; libr. L. Stecchetti, after Henri Cain and Jules Adenis), *Mese Mariano* (Palermo 17 March 1910; libr. S. de Giacomo) [R], *Madame Sans-Gêne**, *Giove di Pompei* (Rome 5 July 1921; libr. E. Romagnoli and Luigi Illica), which was written in collaboration with Franchetti, *La Cena delle Beffe** and *Il Rè* (Milan 12 Jan 1929; libr. Giovacchino Forzano).

Giorgetta

Soprano role in Puccini's *Il Tabarro*. Michele's wife, she is loved by Luigi.

Giorgio

Bass role in Bellini's *I Puritani*. The Puritan Lord George Walton, he is Elvira's uncle.

Giorno di Regno, Un (*A One-Day Reign*)
or Il Finto Stanislao (*The False Stanislaus*)

Comic opera in two acts by Verdi. 1st perf. Milan, 5 Sept 1840; libr. by Felice Romani, after Alexandre Vincent Pineu-Duval's *Le Faux Stanislas*. Principal roles: Belfiore (bar), Marchesa del Poggio (sop), Giulietta (mezzo), Edoardo (ten), Baron Kelbar (b-bar), Treasurer (bar). Very loosely based on an incident in the War of the Polish Succession, it is Verdi's only opera buffa. It was a total failure at its appearance and is still only rarely performed despite its enjoyable if not particularly sophisticated melodies.

Plot: Brest, 1733. A Parisian officer, Belfiore, poses as Stanislaus, King of Poland, to act as a decoy whilst the real Stanislaus attempts to secure his throne. In his capacity as 'King', Belfiore visits Baron Kelbar's castle and helps the Baron's daughter, Giulietta, to be united with her true love Edoardo, by removing her unwanted betrothed, the Treasurer, from the proceedings. At the same time, he effects a reconciliation with his own loved one, the Marchesa del Poggio, who thought he had abandoned her. [R]

Giovanna

(1) Mezzo role in Donizetti's *Anna Bolena*. She is the historical Jane Seymour (*c* 1509–37), third wife of Henry VIII. (2) Soprano role in Verdi's *Giovanna d'Arco*. She is Joan of Arc. (3) Mezzo comprimario role in Verdi's *Rigoletto*. She is Gilda's maid. (4)

Mezzo comprimario role in Verdi's *Ernani*. She is Elvira's companion.

Giovanna d'Arco (*Joan of Arc*)

Opera in prologue and three acts by Verdi. 1st perf. Milan, 15 Feb 1845; libr. by Temistocle Solera, after Friedrich von Schiller's *Die Jungfrau von Orleans*. Principal roles: Giovanna (sop), Carlo (ten), Giacomo (bar). Like many of Verdi's early operas, it is an uneven work with some beautiful and original numbers side-by-side with passages of rumbustious clap-trap. After a long period of neglect, it has received a number of performances in recent years.

Plot: France, 1429. King Charles VII of France is considering surrender to the English, but is inspired to fight on by the peasant Joan, who has heard celestial voices urging her to come to the aid of her country. After inspiring the French soldiers to victory, Joan tells Charles that she returns his affection but that she cannot yield to it, because her voices have forbidden her mortal love. Her father Giacomo, fearing that she is a witch, denounces her and she is captured by the English. Learning the truth, Giacomo contrives her escape, but she is mortally wounded while leading the French to another victory. [R]

Gira la cotte

Chorus in Act I of Puccini's *Turandot*.

Girl of the Golden West, The

See Fanciulla del West, La

Giselda

Soprano role in Verdi's *I Lombardi*. She is Arvino's daughter.

Giudici ad Anna

Anna's great phrase at the end of Act I

of Donizetti's *Anna Bolena* when she is told that she is to be tried.

Giuditta (*Judith*)

Opera in three acts by Lehár. 1st perf. Vienna, 20 Jan 1934; libr. by Paul Knepler and Fritz Löhner. Principal roles: Giuditta (sop), Octavio (ten), Manuelle (bar), Antonio (bass), Anita (sop), Pierrino (ten), Sebastiano (ten). Lehár's last stage work and his one successful opera.

Plot: Giuditta deserts her husband and goes to Africa with the army officer, Octavio, who has seduced her. After Octavio's regiment has departed, Giuditta becomes a dancer. Octavio deserts from the army and takes a job as a pianist in a restaurant, where he again meets Giuditta – dining with a new lover. Giuditta leaves with her admirer, and Octavio continues to play as the restaurant lights are turned out. [R]

Giulia

Soprano role in Spontini's *La Vestale*. She is the vestal virgin loved by Licinio.

Giulietta

(1) Soprano role in Offenbach's *Les Contes d'Hoffmann*. A courtesan, she is the third of Hoffmann's loves. (2) Soprano role in Bellini's *I Capuleti e i Montecchi*. She is loved by Romeo. (3) Mezzo role in Verdi's *Un Giorno di Regno*. She is in love with Edoardo.

Giulietta e Romeo

Works of this title, based on Shakespeare's *Romeo and Juliet*, include:

(1) Opera by Zingarelli. 1st perf. Milan, 30 Jan 1796; libr. by Giuseppe Maria Foppa. A chillingly formal treatment, it was one of Zingarelli's most successful works but is nowadays forgotten.

(2) Opera in two acts by Vaccai. 1st perf. Milan, 31 Oct 1825; libr. by Felice Romani. Vaccai's most successful opera, which was long popular, it is nowadays all but forgotten. In the 19th century, part of the final scene was often inserted into Bellini's *I Capuleti e i Montecchi*.

(3) Opera by Zandonai. 1st perf. Rome, 1922; libr. by Arturo Rossato. One of Zandonai's most successful works, it is still occasionally performed. [R]

Giulini, Carlo Maria (*b* 1914)

Italian conductor, particularly associated with Mozart, Rossini and Verdi operas, notably *Don Carlos*. One of the outstanding conductors of the postwar era, he abandoned opera in the late 1960s, returning to it only for a few recordings and for a single production of *Falstaff* in 1982.

Giulio Cesare in Egitto (*Julius Caesar in Egypt*)

Opera in three acts by Handel. 1st perf. London, 20 Feb 1724; libr. by Nicola Francesco Haym, after G. F. Bussani. Principal roles: Caesar (c-ten), Cleopatra (sop), Ptolemy (c-ten), Sextus (mezzo), Cornelia (mezzo), Achillas (bass). One of Handel's greatest and nowadays most frequently performed operas.

Plot: Egypt, 48 BC. Caesar has arrived in Egypt in pursuit of Pompey, who has been murdered by Ptolemy. Hearing of Caesar's wrath, Ptolemy plans to murder him as well and imprisons Pompey's widow Cornelia and her son Sextus. Ptolemy's sister Cleopatra attempts to charm Caesar into helping her against her brother, whilst Ptolemy's attempts on Cornelia's virtue are thwarted by Sextus. Caesar's and Cleopatra's dalliance is interrupted by a mob calling for Caesar's blood.

Although defeated by Ptolemy, Caesar swims to safety, finds a secret way into the palace and kills Ptolemy. He crowns Cleopatra sole ruler of Egypt. [R]

Giunto sul passo estremo

Tenor aria for Faust in the epilogue of Boito's *Mefistofele*.

Giuramento, Il (*The Oath*)

Opera in three acts by Mercadante. 1st perf. Milan, 11 March 1837; libr. by Gaetano Rossi, after Victor Hugo's *Angelo, Tyran de Padove*. Principal roles: Elaisa (sop), Viscardo di Benevento (ten), Manfredo (bar), Bianca (mezzo), Brunoro (bass). Mercadante's finest and most successful opera, it is still occasionally performed.

Plot: 14th-century Syracuse. Viscardo loves Bianca, wife of Manfredo, Count of Syracuse. Elaisa, who also loves Viscardo, has sworn eternal friendship with an unknown benefactress who once saved her father's life and has given her a medallion. The benefactress turns out to be Bianca. Bianca is threatened with death by Manfredo because the traitorous Brunoro has sent him a note making him believe her unfaithful. True to her vow, Elaisa contrives to save her rival's life, but is killed by Viscardo who wrongly believes that she has poisoned Bianca.

Giustino

Opera in three acts by Handel. 1st perf. London, 16 Feb 1737; libr. by Nicolò Beregani. Principal roles: Giustino (c-ten), Anastasio (sop), Vitalino (ten), Arianna (sop), Leocasta (mezzo), Fortune (sop), Polidarte (bass), Amanzio (mezzo). Although never one of Handel's most popular works, it is still occasionally performed.

Glasgow

See Scottish Opera

Glass, Philip (*b 1937*)

American composer. The leading minimalist composer, he has written four full-scale stage works, which have enjoyed a remarkable degree of success. They are *Einstein on the Beach* (Avignon 26 July 1976; libr. Robert Wilson) [R], *Satyagraha* (Rotterdam 5 Sept 1980; libr. Constance de Jong, after the *Baghavad-Gita*) [R], the hugely successful *Akhnaten** and *The Making of the Representative for Planet 8* (Houston 8 July 1988; libr. Doris Lessing, after her novel). He has also written three chamber operas: *The Photographer*, *The Juniper Tree* (1984) and *The Fall of the House of Usher*.

Glauce

Soprano role in Cherubini's *Médée*. She is Creon's daughter.

Glazunov, Alexander (*1865–1936*)

Russian composer. Best known as an orchestral composer, he wrote no operas himself, but helped to complete Borodin's unfinished *Prince Igor*.

Gli

Titles beginning with this plural form of the Italian definite article are listed under the letter of the first main word. For example, *Gli Equivoci* is listed under E.

Glière, Reinhold (*1875–1956*)

Russian composer. He wrote several operas, all now largely forgotten, of which the most successful was *Shah-Senem* (Baku 1934), which is rooted in Azerbaijani folk music.

Glinka, Mikhail *(1804–57)*

Russian composer. The founder of the Russian nationalist school of opera and the first Russian composer to win acceptance elsewhere, he created Russian opera virtually single-handedly. Largely self-taught, his only two completed operas are *A Life for the Tsar** (known in Russia since 1917 as *Ivan Susanin*) and *Ruslan and Ludmila**. His use of folk polyphony, of regional dances and, in *Ruslan*, his choice of a colourful Russian fairy tale all had an incalculable influence on the development of Russian music, especially when combined with his brilliant and colourful orchestration and his fine vocal writing. He occupies a seminal position in the history of music, and the infrequency of performance of his operas in the West is quite inexplicable.

Gloire immortelle

Soldiers' chorus in Act IV of Gounod's *Faust*.

Gloria all'Egitto

Chorus which opens the Triumph Scene in Act II of Verdi's *Aida*.

Gloriana

Opera in three acts by Britten (Op 53). 1st perf. London, 8 June 1953; libr. by William Plomer, after Lytton Strachey's *Elizabeth and Essex*. Principal roles: Elizabeth I (sop), Earl of Essex (ten), Lord Mountjoy (bar), Lady Penelope Rich (sop), Sir Walter Raleigh (bass), Cecil (bar), Henry Cuffe (bar), Frances (mezzo), Spirit of the Masque (ten), Blind Ballad Singer (b-bar), Recorder of Norwich (bass). Commissioned to celebrate the coronation of Queen Elizabeth II, the work was a failure at its appearance but has subsequently been revived with great success and its merits totally re-evaluated. A pageant of Tudor scenes, it concentrates on events in the later part of Elizabeth I's reign, especially the conflicting demands on her of duty and her love for Essex.

Glossop, Peter *(b 1928)*

British baritone, particularly associated with Verdi roles, especially Rigoletto and Iago (which he filmed). One of the finest Verdi baritones of the postwar era, he had a rich and powerful voice and a strong stage presence. His first wife Joyce Blackham (*b* 1935) was a successful mezzo.

Glover, Jane *(b 1949)*

British conductor and musicologist, particularly associated with Cavalli, about whom she wrote the definitive biography as well as preparing critical editions of his operas. The first British woman conductor of importance, she has had particular success with Mozart, and was musical director of Glyndebourne Touring Opera (1981–85).

Gluck, Christoph Willibald von *(1714–87)*

German composer. One of the most important figures in the history of opera, and sometimes regarded as its second founder, he wrote 46 operas. His early works are unremarkable essays in established forms, mainly Metastasian opera seria. Those to texts by Pietro Metastasio include *Artaserse* (Milan 26 Dec 1741), his first opera, *La Clemenza di Tito* (Naples 4 Nov 1752) and *Le Cinesi* (Vienna 24 Sept 1754) [R]. He then composed a series of French opéra-comiques in which his sense of characterisation begins to appear. Of these, *L'Ivrogne Corrigé** and *Le Cadi Dupé** are still occasionally performed.

The turning-point in Gluck's career

came in 1762 with *Orfeo ed Euridice**, his most famous work. Six conventional operas followed, of which only *La Rencontre Imprévue** is of any significance, before he began his great reform of opera in collaboration with the poet Ranieri de' Calzabigi. The appearance of *Alceste** marks the birth of modern music-drama. In his famous preface to the musical score, Gluck set out his reform aims: to strive for simplicity and total clarity, to banish the excesses and abuses of singers, and to "restrict music to its true office by means of expression and by following the situations of the story". In effect, Gluck was returning to the principles of the original founders of opera who had desired to recreate the simplicity and drama of Greek tragedy. This is reflected in his choice of subjects for his later operas, all of which are dervied from Greek mythology. Following *Paride ed Elena**, he moved to Paris, where he produced *Iphigénie en Aulide** as well as major French revisions of *Orfeo* and *Alceste*. These sparked off the famous feud between his supporters and those of Piccinni. *Armide** was followed by *Iphigénie en Tauride**, his masterpiece and one of the greatest of all music-dramas. In his last opera, *Echo et Narcisse**, he returned unsuccessfully to a simpler, pastoral form.

Glückliche Hand, Die (*The Lucky Hand*)
Opera in one act by Schönberg (Op 18). 1st perf. Vienna, 14 Oct 1924 (composed 1917); libr. by the composer. Principal role: Man (bar). Telling of a man's search for artistic fulfilment and for his own identity, it is an attempted synthesis of music, movement and the 'orchestration' or 'colour modulation' of lighting. [R]

Glyndebourne Festival
An annual summer opera festival near Lewes (in Sussex) in southern England which opened on 28 May 1934. The opera house was built in 1934 by John Christie* and his wife Audrey Mildmay* in the grounds of the former's estate. It was enlarged (cap. 830) twice. The annual season runs from May to August, and its aim is the presentation of opera in ideal surroundings in productions of rigorous musical and dramatic preparation. Particularly noted for its Mozart productions, Glyndebourne also has a strong Rossini and Strauss tradition and has played a considerable part in the recent revival of interest in Monteverdi and Cavalli. Performances are given in the original language with international casts, and the Festival has an enviable reputation for presenting the greatest singers before they have become famous. The musical directors have been Fritz Busch, Vittorio Gui, Sir John Pritchard, Bernard Haitink and Andrew Davis. The resident orchestra is the London Philharmonic.

Glyndebourne Touring Opera
A company formed in 1968 to tour Glyndebourne's productions throughout England with young British singers. Musical directors have been Myer Fredman, Kenneth Montgomery, Nicholas Braithwaite, Jane Glover and Graeme Jenkins. The orchestra is the London Sinfonietta.

Gnecchi, Vittorio (*1876–1954*)
Italian composer. A number of his operas enjoyed success in their time, but all of them are now forgotten. The most important include *Cassandra* (Bologna 1905; libr. Luigi Illica, after Homer's *The Iliad*), which Strauss was accused of plagiarising in *Elektra* because of the remarkable similarity of

some of the motifs, and *La Rosiera* (1927; libr. composer and Carlo Zangarini, after Alfred de Musset), which contains one of the earliest uses of quarter-tones.

Goat's Trill

Another name for bleat*. It is called *Chevrotement* in French, *Trillo Caprino* in Italian, *Bockstriller* in German and *Trino de Cabra* in Spanish.

Gobatti, Stefano *(1852–1913)*

Italian composer. His first opera *I Goti* (Bologna 30 Nov 1873; libr. S. Interdonato) was sensationally successful at its appearance and he was hailed as a second Verdi. The popularity soon waned, however, and Verdi himself – not normally given to being rude about other composers – described the opera as "the most monstrous musical abortion ever composed". Its successors, *Luce* (Bologna 25 Nov 1875; libr. Interdonato) and *Cordelia* (Bologna 6 Dec 1881; libr. Carlo d'Ormeville after Shakespeare's *King Lear*) were failures, and *Masias* (1900; libr. E. Sanfelice) was never performed. Accused of having the evil eye, he developed persecution mania and died in a lunatic asylum.

Gobbi, Tito *(1913–84)*

Italian baritone, particularly associated with the Italian repertory, especially Simon Boccanegra, Iago, Falstaff and Scarpia. One of the greatest singing-actors in operatic history, he possessed a fine voice used with great intelligence and extraordinary tonal variety: each of his 100 roles had its own vocal colour. An actor of outstanding ability and insight and a master of make-up, he set – particularly when in partnership with Maria Callas – entirely new standards of dramatic performance in opera. He

created Teperlov in Rocca's *Monte Ivnor*, Ulysses in Malipiero's *Ecuba*, Albafiorita in Persico's *La Locandiera*, Ahmed in Lualdi's *Le Nozze di Huara*, the Storyteller in Napoli's *Il Tesoro* and the title role in Ghedini's *Lord Inferno*. He also appeared in 26 films, notably *Glass Mountain*, and *Pagliacci* with Gina Lollobrigida, and later in his career produced a number of operas. He also established a school for the advanced training of young singers at the Villa Schifanoia in Italy. His autobiography, *My Life*, was published in 1979.

Godard, Benjamin *(1849–95)*

French composer. His eight operas include *Les Guelfes* (Rouen 17 Jan 1902, composed 1882; libr. Louis Gallet), *Pedro de Zalaméa* (Antwerp 31 Jan 1884; libr. L. Détroyat and Armand Silvestre, after Pedro Calderón), the once-popular *Jocelyn**, *Dante et Béatrice* (Paris 31 May 1890; libr. Edouard Blau) and the successful *La Vivandière**. His facile style and early success did not always endear him to his contemporaries: when he said to Chabrier that it was a pity that he had turned to opera so late, the latter retorted "what a pity you started so soon"!

God of battle, The

Bass aria for Hercules in Act I of Handel's *Hercules*.

Goehr, Alexander *(b 1932)*

British composer. He has written three stage works: the black comedy *Arden Must Die**, the 'dramatic madrigal' *Naboth's Vineyard* (London 1968) and *Shadow Play* (London 1970; libr. K. Cavender, after Plato's *Republic*). His father Walter (1903–60) was a German conductor and composer. He wrote the first opera for radio *Malpopita* (1930),

GOETHE

The German playwright and poet Johann Wolfgang von Goethe (1749–1832) was himself interested in opera. He wrote a number of Singspiel texts, and as director of the Weimar Theatre included many operas in the repertory. He also appears as a character in Lehár's *Friederike*. Some 120 operas have been based on his works. Below are listed, by work, those operas by composers with entries in this dictionary.

Die Braut von Corinth

Chabrier	*Briséïs*	1899 (U)

Claudine von Villa Bella

Schubert	*Claudine von Villa Bella*	1815
Coccia	*Claudine in Torino*	1817

Erwin und Elmire

Schoeck	*Erwin und Elmire*	1916

Faust

Berlioz	*La Damnation de Faust*	1846
Gounod	*Faust*	1859
Boito	*Mefistofele*	1868/75
Brian	*Faust*	1956

Der Gott und die Bajadere

Auber	*Le Dieu et la Bayadère*	1830

Götz von Berlichingen

Goldmark	*Götz von Berlichingen*	1902

Jery und Bately

Winter	*Jery und Bately*	1790
K. Kreutzer	*Jery und Bately*	1810
Adam	*Le Chalet*	1834
Donizetti	*Betly*	1836

Die Leiden des Jungen Werthers

R. Kreutzer	*Charlotte et Werther*	1792
Coccia	*Carlotta e Werther*	1814
Massenet	*Werther*	1892

Märchen

Klebe	*Das Märchen von der Schönen Lilie*	1969

Pandora

Gerster	*Das Verzauberte Ich*	1949

Scherz, List und Rache

Winter	*Scherz, List und Rache*	1790
E. T. A. Hoffmann	*Scherz, List und Rache*	1801
Bruch	*Scherz, List und Rache*	1858
Wellesz	*Scherz, List und Rache*	1928

Wilhelm Meisters Lehrjahre

Thomas	*Mignon*	1866

and as a conductor was particularly associated with early and Baroque operas.

Goethe, Johann Wolfgang von
See panel on page 239

Goetz
See Götz

Gogol, Nikolai
See panel on page 241

Golaud
Baritone role in Debussy's *Pelléas et Mélisande*. He is Pelléas' half-brother.

Golden Cockerel, The (*Zolotoy Petuschok*; sometimes incorrectly called *Le Coq d'Or*)
Opera in three acts by Rimsky-Korsakov. 1st perf. Moscow, 7 Oct 1909; libr. by Vladimir Ivanovich Belsky, after Alexander Pushkin's poem. Principal roles: King Dodon (bass), Queen of Shemakha (sop), Astrologer (ten), Prince Gvidon (ten), Prince Afron (bar), Cockerel (sop). Rimsky's last opera and his best known in the West, it is a fairytale work which ran into censorship problems at its appearance because of its alleged satire on Tsar Nicholas II's handling of the Russo-Japanese War. It is notable for its brilliant and colourful orchestration and for containing, in the Astrologer, possibly the highest tenor role ever written. The orchestral suite arranged from the opera has given the music a wider currency.

Plot: The Astrologer gives King Dodon a golden cockerel that will crow if the King is threatened with danger. The delighted monarch offers the Astrologer whatever he desires in exchange for the magic bird, but the Astrologer defers his choice. The cockerel crows and the King goes to war. He meets and marries the beautiful Queen of Shemakha and brings her back to his kingdom where the Astrologer, claiming his payment, asks to be given the Queen. Dodon kills him for his impertinence, whereupon the cockerel pecks Dodon to death and the Queen disappears. [R]

Goldmark, Karl (*b Károly*) (1830–1915)
Hungarian composer. He wrote seven operas in eclectic style, being particularly influenced by Wagner and

NIKOLAI GOGOL

The works of the Russian writer Nikolai Vasilievich Gogol (1809–52) have inspired some 60 operas, mostly Russian. Below are listed, by work, those operas by composers with entries in this dictionary.

Christmas Eve

Tchaikovsky	*Vakula the Blacksmith/The Little Slippers*	1874/85
Lysenko	*Christmas Eve*	1874
Rimsky-Korsakov	*Christmas Eve*	1895

The Diary of a Madman

Searle	*The Diary of a Madman*	1958

The Gamblers

Shostakovich	*The Gamblers*	1941 (U)

The Inspector General

Egk	*Der Revisor*	1957

May Night

Serov	*May Night*	1853
Rimsky-Korsakov	*May Night*	1879
Lysenko	*The Drowned Woman*	1885

The Nose

Shostakovich	*The Nose*	1930

Sorochintsy Fair

Moussorgsky	*Sorochintsy Fair*	1880 (U)

Taras Bulba

Lysenko	*Taras Bulba*	1890
Beruti	*Taras Bulba*	1895

The Wedding

Moussorgsky	*The Marriage*	1868 (U)
Martinů	*The Marriage*	1953

Mendelssohn. His greatest success was his first opera *Die Königin von Saba**, his only stage work which is still remembered. Its successors were *Merlin* (Vienna 19 Nov 1886; libr. Siegfried Lipiner), *Das Heimchen am Herd* (Vienna 21 March 1896; libr. Alfred Maria Willner, after Charles Dickens' *The Cricket on the Hearth*), *Die Kriegsgefangene* (*The Prisoner of War*, Vienna 17 Jan 1899; libr. A. Formey), *Götz von Berlichingen* (Budapest 16 Dec 1902; libr. Willner, after Goethe) and *Ein Wintermärchen* (Vienna 2 Jan

1908; libr. Willner, after Shakespeare's *A Winter's Tale*). His two volumes of autobiography, *Erinnerungen aus meinen Leben*, were published in 1922 and 1929.

Goldoni, Carlo *(1707–93)*

Italian playwright and librettist. His comedies were set by many composers, including Duni, Galuppi (13 including *Il Filosofo di Campagna*), Gassmann (*L'Amore Artigiano*), Paisiello, Piccinni (*La Buona Figliuola*), Sarti, Traetta and Vivaldi. In the 20th century, his plays have inspired operas by Giannini, Malipiero, Martinů and, particularly, Wolf-Ferrari.

Goldschmidt, Berthold *(b 1903)*

German composer and conductor, long resident in Britain. He wrote two operas: *Der Gewaltige Hahnrei* (Mannheim 1932; libr. after Crommelynck's *Le Cocu Magnifique*) and *Beatrice Cenci* (London 16 April 1988, composed 1951; libr. Martin Esslin after Percy Bysshe Shelley's *The Cenci*), which was a joint winner of the Festival of Britain competition.

Goltz, Christel *(b 1912)*

German soprano, particularly associated with R. Strauss roles and with contemporary operas. An intense singing-actress with a clear and powerful voice of great range, she created the title roles in Orff's *Antigonae* and Liebermann's *Penelope*.

Gomes, Carlos *(1836–96)*

Brazilian composer. The only Latin American composer before Ginastera to win international recognition, he wrote nine operas, largely in Italian style, many of which enjoyed great success. They are *A Noite do Castelo* (Rio de Janeiro 4 Sept 1861; libr. A. J. Fernandes dos Reis), *Joanna de Flandres* (Rio de Janeiro 15 Sept 1863; libr. S. de Mendonça), his masterpiece *Il Guarany**, *Fosca* (Milan 16 Feb 1873; libr. Antonio Ghislanzoni), *Salvator Rosa* (Genoa 12 March 1874; libr. Ghislanzoni), *Maria Tudor* (Milan 27 March 1879; libr. Emilio Praga, after Victor Hugo's *Marie Tudor*), the successful *O Escravo* (*The Slave*, Rio de Janeiro 27 Sept 1889; libr. R. Paravicini, after Tauney), which incorporates native Brazilian Indian instruments, *Côndor* (Milan 21 Sept 1891; libr. M. Canti) and *Colombo* (1892). After a long period of neglect outside Brazil, there has recently been a minor revival of interest in his operas.

Gomez, Jill *(b 1942)*

Guyanese-born British soprano, particularly associated with Mozart roles and with the British and Spanish repertories. She possesses a pure, silvery voice used with fine musicianship and has an appealing stage presence. She created Flora in *The Knot Garden* and the Countess in Musgrave's *The Voice of Ariadne*.

Gondoliers, The
or The King of Barataria

Operetta in two acts by Sullivan. 1st perf. London, 7 Dec 1889; libr. by W. S. Gilbert. Principal roles: Don Alhambra del Bolero (b-bar), Duke and Duchess of Plaza-Toro (bar and mezzo), Marco and Giuseppe Palmieri (ten and bar), Gianetta (sop), Tessa (mezzo), Casilda (sop), Luiz (ten or bar), Antonio (bar), Inez (cont). One of the finest and most popular of all the Savoy Operas, it enjoyed an initial run of over 550 performances. It contains some of Sullivan's freshest and most delightful music, which is married to a brilliant text by Gilbert which satirises republican principles.

Plot: Venice and Barataria. To

prevent the spread of Methodism, the Grand Inquisitor Don Alhambra abducted the son of the King of Barataria and entrusted him to the care of a Venetian gondolier. Over the years, the latter grew unable to say who was the prince and who was his own son. The two children have now grown up to be the gondoliers, Marco and Giuseppe, who marry Gianetta and Tessa. The Duke and Duchess of Plaza-Toro arrive and inform their daughter Casilda (who is in love with their attendant Luiz) that she was married in infancy to the prince of Barataria and that as his father has been killed she is now queen. Don Alhambra arranges for Marco and Giuseppe to reign jointly until the real king is discovered and they remodel the monarchy on republican lines with everyone ranking equal. The king's foster-mother Inez, who is Luiz's mother, is found and reveals that when the Inquisition came to take the prince she substituted her own son, and that the real king is Luiz. Luiz and Casilda are thus united. [R]

Gondromark
Roles in Offenbach's *La Vie Parisienne*: the Swedish Baron (bar) and his wife the Baroness (mezzo).

Gonzalve
Tenor role in Ravel's *L'Heure Espagnole*. He is an admirer of Concepción.

Goodall, Sir Reginald *(1901–90)*
British conductor, particularly associated with Wagner operas. After conducting the first performance of *Peter Grimes*, he was a member of the music staff at Covent Garden from 1946, conducting a wide repertory. It was not until he was approaching his 70s that his Wagnerian stature was appreciated, first with the Sadler's Wells

Die Meistersinger in 1968 and even more with the English National Opera's *Ring*, which established him as one of the greatest Wagnerians of the postwar era. His appearances were infrequent, largely because of the extraordinarily long preparation and rehearsal time which he demanded.

Good Friday Music
(Karfreitagzauber)
The music in Act III Scene I of Wagner's *Parsifal* during which Parsifal is annointed before entering the castle of the Grail.

Goossens, Sir Eugène *(1893–1962)*
British composer and conductor. He wrote two operas: *Judith** and *Don Juan de Mañara* (London 1937; libr. Arnold Bennett, after Prosper Mérimée's *Les Âmes du Purgatoire*). He was a distinguished director of the New South Wales Conservatory (1947–56). His autobiography, *Overture and Beginners*, was published in 1951. His brother Leon was a celebrated oboist and his sisters Sidonie and Marie were both harpists. Their father Eugène (1867–1958) was a conductor, who was musical director of the Carl Rosa Opera Company (1899–1915) and who conducted the first performance of Stanford's *The Critic*.

Gopak
A fast Russian folk dance in 2/4 time. There is a famous operatic example in Tchaikovsky's *Mazeppa*.

Gorgheggio (Italian for 'warbling')
A form of decorative vocalisation consisting of rapid and numerous rising and falling notes. It was used by singers in the 18th and 19th centuries to show off their virtuosity.

Goro

Tenor role in Puccini's *Madama Butterfly*. He is a marriage broker.

Gorr, Rita *(b Marguerite Geirnaert) (b 1926)*

Belgian mezzo, particularly associated with the French repertory and with Wagnerian roles. She possessed a large, rich-toned voice and was an intense singing-actress, especially in dramatic roles such as Kundry and Amneris.

Gossec, François *(b Gossé) (1734–1829)*

Belgian composer. An admirer of Gluck, he wrote some 20 operas, all now forgotten, of which the comedies were most successful. His most important works include *Les Pêcheurs* (Paris 23 April 1766; libr. d'Offémont), *Toinon et Toinette* (Paris 20 June 1767; libr. J. A. Julien), the tragédie-lyrique *Sabinus* (Versailles 4 Dec 1773; libr. M. P. G. de Chabanon de Maugris), which contains some anticipations of Spontini's style, and *Thésée* (Paris 1 March 1782; libr. E. Morel de Chéfdeville, after Philippe Quinault's libretto for Lully).

Göteborg Opera

Opera in this town in Sweden is given at the Stora Theatre (cap. 615), which opened in September 1859. Musical directors have included Tullio Voghera, Sixten Ehrling and Gunnar Staern.

Gothenburg

See Göteborg Opera

Gotovac, Jakov *(1895–1982)*

Yugoslavian composer and conductor. His eight stage works are *Morana* (Brno 29 Nov 1930; libr. A. Muratbegović), *Ero the Joker**, his most successful work, *Kamenik* (1946), *Mila Gojsalića* (Zagreb 18 May 1952), *Dalmaro* (Zagreb 20 Dec 1958), *Stanac* (Zagreb 6 Dec 1959), the Singspiel *Derdan* (1955) and the opera-oratorio *Peter Svačić* (1969). A distinguished conductor, he was musical director of the Zagreb Opera (1923–57).

Götterdämmerung *(Twilight of the Gods)*

Opera in three acts by Wagner; part 4 of *Der Ring des Nibelungen**. 1st perf. Bayreuth, 17 Aug 1876; libr. by the composer, after the *Nibelungenlied*. Principal roles: Brünnhilde (sop), Siegfried (ten), Hagen (bass), Günther (bar), Gutrune (sop), Waltraute (mezzo), Alberich (bar), Norns (sop, mezzo and cont), Woglinde (sop), Wellgunde (mezzo), Flosshilde (mezzo). For plot see *Der Ring des Nibelungen*. [R]

Göttingen Festival

An annual festival founded in 1920 in Lower Saxony in Germany, and devoted to Handel's works. The inaugural production of *Rodelinda* under Oskar Hagen may be said to mark the beginning of the modern Handel revival. Performances are given at the Stadttheater (cap. 740), which opened in 1890.

Götz, Hermann *(1840–76)*

German composer. He is chiefly remembered for his *Der Widerspenstigen Zähmung**, whose quasi-Mozartian elegance makes it one of the finest German comic operas of the period. His second opera *Francesca von Rimini* (Mannheim 30 Sept 1877; libr. composer, after Dante's *La Divina Commedia*) was left unfinished at his death and was completed by Ernst Frank.

Gounod, Charles *(1818–93)*

French composer. One of the most successful of all 19th-century opera composers, he wrote 13 stage works. They are notable for their wealth of appealing melodies, their grateful vocal writing and their deft orchestration. It must, however, be admitted that for all the immense popularity of his best works (a popularity that has waned somewhat in recent years), his operas cannot be considered great music-dramas. Rather, they are pleasant and graceful confections which need not be taken too seriously. In addition, the sanctimonious quasi-religious side of his nature, coupled with his taste for the grandiose, often stifle his simple but genuine gifts of musical expression.

Gounod's first opera *Sapho** was a success, but it was followed by a failure, the melodramatic *La Nonne Sanglante* (Paris 18 Oct 1854; libr. Eugène Scribe and Germain Delavigne, after M. G. Lewis's *The Monk*). The composer displayed a considerable gift for comedy in *Le Médecin Malgré Lui**, which was followed by the sensationally successful *Faust**, the work that placed him at the forefront of European composers. The successful *Philémon et Baucis** was followed by *La Colombe* (Baden-Baden 3 Aug 1860; libr. Jules Barbier and Michel Carré, after Jean de la Fontaine's *Le Faucon*), *La Reine de Saba**, the beautiful Provençal *Mireille**, the highly successful *Roméo et Juliette**, *Cinq-Mars**, the unfinished *Maître Pierre* (1877; libr. Louis Gallet), *Polyeucte* (Paris 7 Oct 1878; libr. Barbier and Carré, after Pierre Corneille) and *Le Tribut de Zamora* (Paris 1 April 1881; libr. Adolphe Philippe d'Ennery and Jules Brésil).

Goyescas

Opera in three scenes by Granados. 1st

perf. New York, 28 Jan 1916; libr. by Fernando Periquet y Zuaznabar. Principal roles: Rosario (sop), Fernando (ten), Paquiro (bar), Pepa (mezzo). Inspired by paintings by Goya, it is Granados' only stage work which is still remembered, and was arranged from his earlier piano pieces of the same name.

Plot: The high-born Rosario arouses the jealousy of her lover Fernando by accepting the attentions of the bull-fighter Paquiro, whose own beloved Pepa is also outraged. Fernando escorts Rosario to a ball, where Paquiro challenges him to a duel. After a garden meeting with Rosario, Fernando is killed. [R]

Gozzi, Carlo

See panel on page 246

Grace note

A vocal ornament consisting of one or more notes inserted by a singer as an embellishment or decoration of the vocal line, as in an appoggiatura*.

Graf, Herbert *(1904–73)*

Austrian producer. Son of the Viennese critic Max Graf, he was one of the leading opera producers of the mid-20th century. His productions were traditional in the best sense of the word, and he was dedicated to the encouragement of young talent. He was director of productions at the Metropolitan Opera, New York (1936–60), the Zürich Opernhaus (1960–63) and the Grand Théâtre, Geneva (1965–73). His writings include *Opera for the People* (1951) and *Producing Opera for America* (1961).

Gräfin Mariza *(Countess Maritza)*

Operetta in three acts by Kálmán. 1st

CARLO GOZZI

The works of the Italian comic playwright Carlo Gozzi (1720–1806) have inspired some 20 operas. Below are listed, by play, those operas by composers with entries in this dictionary.

L'Amore delle Tre Melerance

Prokofiev	*The Love of Three Oranges*	1921

La Donna Serpente

Wagner	*Die Feen*	1834
Casella	*La Donna Serpente*	1932

Il Re Cervo

Henze	*König Hirsch*	1956

Turandot

Busoni	*Turandot*	1917
Puccini	*Turandot*	1926 (U)
Brian	*Turandot*	1950

---

perf. Vienna, 28 Feb 1924; libr. by Julius Brammer and Alfred Grünwald. Principal roles: Mariza (sop), Count Tassilo (ten), Zsupán (ten), Lisa (sop), Manja (mezzo), Bozena (mezzo). An immediate success, it has remained one of Kálmán's most popular works. [R]

Graf von Luxembourg, Der
(*The Count of Luxemburg*)
Operetta in three acts by Lehár. 1st perf. Vienna, 12 Nov 1909; libr. by R. Bodanzky and Alfred Maria Willner. Principal roles: René (ten), Angèle (sop), Juliette (sop), Brissard (ten), Basil (bass). One of Lehár's earliest successes, it is still regularly performed. [R]

Graham, Colin (*b* 1931)
British producer. One of the leading postwar British opera producers, his uncontroversial productions are notable for his elucidation of character and for his handling of crowd scenes (particularly so in the English National Opera's *War and Peace*). He was director of productions of the English Opera Group (1963–75), the English Music Theatre (1975–78) and the English National Opera (1978–80). Artistic director of the Opera Theater of St Louis (1978–). He also wrote the libretto for Bennett's *A Penny for a Song*.

Gramophone
See Opera recordings

Gramm, Donald (*b Grambsch*)
(1927–83)
American bass-baritone, particularly associated with Mozart roles and with

20th-century works. He possessed a fine voice used with great intelligence and was an outstanding singing-actor.

Granados y Campiña, Enrique *(1867–1916)*

Spanish composer. His first stage work, the zarzuela *María del Carmen* (Madrid 12 Nov 1898; libr. J. Feliu y Codina), was a success, but its five successors (all zarzuelas with libretti by Apeles Mestre) are forgotten. They are the unperformed *Petrarca*, *Picarol* (Barcelona 25 Feb 1901), *Follet* (Barcelona 4 April 1903), *Gaziel* (Barcelona 27 Oct 1906) and *Liliana* (Barcelona 1911). Success returned, however, with his last work, the opera *Goyescas**, his masterpiece. He died when the ship on which he was returning from America was sunk by a torpedo. His son Edoardo (1894–1928) was also a composer who wrote 13 zarzuelas, the most successful of which were *Bufón y Hostelero* and *La Ciudad Eterna*.

Grand Duke, The or The Statutory Duel

Operetta in two acts by Sullivan. 1st perf. London, 7 March 1896; libr. by W. S. Gilbert. Principal roles: Ludwig (b-bar), Julia Jellicoe (sop), Rudolph (bar), Ernest Dummkopf (ten), Dr Tannhäuser (bar), Baroness von Krakenfeldt (mezzo), Lisa (mezzo), Prince and Princess of Monte Carlo (bass and sop), Herald (bar). The last and least successful of the Savoy Operas. It is a complex and over-laboured work, redeemed in places by flashes of Sullivan's old genius, but is very rarely performed.

Plot: An old law banning duelling states that instead contestants will each draw a card, and the one drawing the lowest will become technically and legally dead. Ludwig, leading actor of Ernest's theatrical troupe, challenges the miserly Grand Duke Rudolph to such a duel and wins. Ludwig takes over the reins of government. There are soon many claimants to Ludwig's hand: his own fiancée, the soubrette, Lisa; the leading lady, Julia Jellicoe; the aging Baroness who had been about to marry Rudolph; and the Princess of Monte Carlo, engaged to the Grand Duke in infancy. Eventually all is resolved when the notary Dr Tannhäuser discovers that the law states that the ace which Ludwig drew in the duel always counts low. So, Ludwig never was Grand Duke, and the couples sort themselves out to their mutual satisfaction. [R]

Grande-Duchesse de Gérolstein, La

Operetta in three acts by Offenbach. 1st perf. Paris, 12 April 1867; libr. by Henri Meilhac and Ludovic Halévy. Principal roles: Grand-Duchess (sop), Fritz (ten), Wanda (sop), Gen Boum (b-bar), Prince Paul (ten), Baron Puck (ten). One of Offenbach's most brilliant musical and political satires, Bismarck said of its portrayal of petty German princedoms "C'est tout à fait ça". An instant and triumphant success, it has remained popular ever since.

Plot: The Prime Minister Baron Puck wishes his amorous Grand Duchess to wed the wimpish Prince Paul, but she has an eye for the military. That eye lights on Fritz, whose sweetheart Wanda is desired by the Duchess's bombastic military commander Gen Boum. She promotes Fritz through the ranks from private to commander-in-chief in the space of five minutes to the fury of everyone else. Fritz wins a bloodless battle but refuses the Duchess's love because of Wanda. The piqued Duchess joins a conspiracy by Boum, Puck and Paul to remove Fritz. Persuaded to marry Paul, the Duchess allows Fritz to be tricked and humiliated and then demotes him with the same rapidity with which she promoted him. Fritz and Wanda are reunited, Boum is reinstated and the Duchess, although lumbered with Paul, soon notes another handsome solider. [R]

Grandi, Margherita *(b Marguerite Garde) (b 1894)*
Australian soprano, particularly associated with dramatic Italian roles. She possessed a powerful voice and was a forceful singing-actress in the grand manner. She created the title role in Massenet's *Amadis* and Diana in Bliss' *The Olympians*.

Grand Inquisitor
Bass role in Verdi's *Don Carlos*. He is the blind, 90-year-old Antonio Valdés, Cardinal-Archbishop of Seville.

Grand opera
A vague term, which can have a number of meanings, including: (1) In Britain, an opera on a serious subject with no spoken dialogue. Sullivan's *Ivanhoe*, for example, is described as a grand opera. (2) Very loosely, a large-scale spectacular opera, such as *Aida*. (3) Most accurately, the type of opera (often with libretti by Eugène Scribe) produced at the Paris Opéra in the first half of the 19th century. These are in four or, more usually, five acts, are on heroic subjects requiring magnificent scenic effects and had to include a ballet. Pioneered by Spontini, they are epitomised by the operas of Meyerbeer. The operas written by Italians for the Opéra fall into this category, for example Rossini's *Guillaume Tell*, Donizetti's *La Favorite* and Verdi's *Les Vêpres Siciliennes* and *Don Carlos*.

Grand Théâtre, Geneva
The opera house (cap. 1,488) in this Swiss city opened in December 1962, replacing the previous theatre of the same name which dated from 1879. It has enjoyed a high reputation in recent times, particularly when Herbert Graf was director of productions, and has an enterprising repertory policy. The annual season runs from September to June. Musical directors have included Ernest Ansermet.

Grand Théâtre, Liège
The theatre (cap. 1,246) in this town in Belgium opened in 1820. The home of the Opéra de Wallonie from 1967 to 1974, it is now the base of the Centre Lyrique de Wallonie.

Grand Théâtre, Marseilles
The opera house (cap. 1,786) opened in 1924. It gives an annual season from October to May with a largely Italian repertory. Musical directors have included Reynaldo Giovanninetti.

Grand Théâtre, Nancy
The opera house (cap. 1,300) in this town in Vosges (France) opened in 1919.

Grand Théâtre Graslin, Nantes
The opera house in this town in Loire-Atlantique (France) opened in 1788. It shares productions with Avignon, Rouen and Tours. Musical directors have included Jésus Etcheverry.

Grand Théâtre Municipal, Bordeaux
The opera house (cap. 1,100) in this city in the Gironde (France) was designed by Victor Louis and opened in 1780. The annual season runs from October to May, and productions are shared with the Toulouse Capitole.

Grane

The name of Brünnhilde's horse in *Der Ring des Nibelungen*.

Graun, Carl Heinrich (c 1704–59)

German composer, largely resident in Berlin. One of the leading exponents of the opera seria style in Germany, he wrote 33 operas, all now largely forgotten, a number of which have libretti by Frederick the Great. His only work still to be at all remembered is *Montezuma**.

Graz Opernhaus

The present theatre (cap. 1,400) in this town in Styria (Austria) opened in 1899. Musical directors have included Franz Schalk and Berislav Klobučar.

Great Britain

See Aldeburgh Festival; Beecham Opera Company; British National Opera Company; Buxton Festival; Camden Festival; Carl Rosa Opera Company; Chelsea Opera Group; D'Oyly Carte Opera Company; Edinburgh Festival; English Bach Festival; English Music Theatre; English National Opera; English Opera Group; Glyndebourne Festival; Glyndebourne Touring Opera; Handel Opera Society; Kent Opera; London Opera Centre; National Opera Studio; New Opera Company; New Sadler's Wells Opera; Opera Factory; Opera North; Opera Northern Ireland; Opera Rara; Royal Opera House, Covent Garden; Scottish Opera; Welsh National Opera

Greece

See Greek National Opera

Greek drama

The originators of opera in the late 16th century developed the form as an attempt to recreate classical Greek tragedy, taking as their cue Aristotle's description of drama as 'words sweetened by music'. Classical Athenian drama was indeed chanted to an orchestral accompaniment and involved both dance and choral singing. The earliest operas all took their subject matter from Graeco-Roman mythology, which has continued to be important operatic source material ever since, especially in the 20th century. At least 200 operas have been based directly on the plays of the Athenian tragedians (see panels for Aeschylus, Euripides and Sophocles).

In addition, Schubert and Petrovics wrote comedies based on Aristophanes' *Lysistrata*.

Greek National Opera (*Ethniki Lyriki Skini* in Greek)

The company was founded in 1939 and achieved its present form in 1944. Based at the Olympia Theatre (cap. 1,000) in Athens, it also visits Salonika and sometimes gives open-air performances in the classical amphitheatre in Epidauros. The annual season runs from November to May. Artistic directors have included Kostas Paskalis.

Greek opera composers

See Kalomiris; Xyndas

Other national opera composers include Dionysios Lavrangas (1864–

1951), Spiros Samaras (1863–1917) and Marios Varvoglis (1885–1967).

Greek Passion, The

Opera in four acts by Martinů. 1st perf. Zürich, 9 June 1961; libr. by the composer, after Nikos Kazantzakis' *Christ Recrucified*. Principal roles: Grigoris (bass), Michelis (ten), Kostandis (bar), Yannakos (ten), Catherine (sop), Manolios (ten), Panait (ten), Lenio (sop), Fotis (b-bar). One of Martinů's finest operas, sadly only infrequently performed, it is notable for its superb choral scenes, based on the composer's study of Orthodox church music.

Plot: a Greek village. The inhabitants are to put on a Passion play and the various local actors begin to take on the characteristics of the individuals they are to portray. The rich farmer's son Manolis, who is to play Jesus, begs for compassion for a group of refugees and is supported by the local whore Catherine, who is to play Mary Magdalene, and by three apostles (Michelis, Kostandis and Yannakos). The priest Grigoris denies shelter to the refugees and excommunicates Manolis who he feels is undermining his authority. Manolis is then killed by Panait, who is to play Judas. [R]

Gregor, Albert

Tenor role in Janáček's *The Macropolus Case*. He is a disputant in the Gregor v Prus case.

Greindl, Josef *(b 1912)*

German bass, particularly associated with Wagnerian roles. One of the finest German basses of the immediate postwar era, he had a rich voice used with outstanding artistry.

Gremin, Prince

Bass role in Tchaikovsky's *Eugene Onegin*. He is Tatyana's elderly husband.

Gretel

Soprano role in Humperdinck's *Hänsel und Gretel*. She is Hänsel's sister.

Grétry, André *(1741–1813)*

Belgian composer. He wrote over 50 operas, achieving his greatest success in opéra-comique style. His operas are notable for their grace, elegance and charming melodies, but his self-confessed paucity in harmony tends after a while to lead to a sense of sameness. The most important of his operas are *Le Huron* (Paris 20 Aug 1768; libr. Jean-François Marmontel after Voltaire's *L'Ingénu*), his first major success and an early operatic example of the theme of Rousseau's 'noble savage', *Lucile* (Paris 5 Jan 1769; libr. Marmontel) [R], *Le Tableau Parlant* (Paris 20 Sept 1769; libr. Louis Anseaume), *Zémire et Azor**, his most successful and enduring work, *Le Magnifique* (Paris 4 March 1773; libr. Jean-Marie Sedaine after Jean de la Fontaine), *Le Jugement de Midas* (Paris 28 March 1778; libr. Thomas d'Hèle) [R Exc], *L'Amant Jaloux* (Versailles 20 Nov 1778; libr. d'Hèle, after S. Centlivre's *The Wonder: a Woman Keeps a Secret*) [R], *Richard Coeur de Lion**, his most ambitious work, and *Guillaume Tell**.

Grieg, Edvard *(1843–1907)*

Norwegian composer. Best known as a composer of piano music, he also wrote one opera, the unfinished *Olav Trygvason**.

Grieux, Chevalier des

The chevalier in love with Manon

appears as tenor role in: (1) Massenet's *Manon*. (2) Puccini's and Auber's *Manon Lescaut*. (3) Henze's *Boulevard Solitude*.

Grieux, Comte des
Bass role in Massenet's *Manon*. He is Chevalier des Grieux's father.

Grigori
(1) Tenor role in Moussorgsky's *Boris Godunov*. A young monk, he becomes the false pretender Dimitri. (2) Baritone role in Rimsky-Korsakov's *The Tsar's Bride*. He is in love with Marfa.

Grimgerde
Mezzo role in Wagner's *Die Walküre*. She is one of the Valkyries.

Griselda
Opera in three acts by Bononcini. 1st perf. London, 22 Feb 1722; libr. by Paolo Antonio Rolli after Apostolo Zeno. Principal roles: Griselda (mezzo), Ernesto (sop), Gualtiero (mezzo), Almirena (mezzo), Rambaldo (bass). One of Bononcini's most successful works, it is nowadays all but forgotten. [R Exc]

Grisélidis
Opera in prologue and two acts by Massenet. 1st perf. Paris, 20 Nov 1901; libr. by Armand Silvestre and Eugène Morand, after Giovanni Boccaccio. Principal roles: Grisélidis (sop), Devil (bar), Alain (ten), Marquis (bass). Reasonably successful at its appearance, it is nowadays all but forgotten.

Plot: (the same as 'the pleasant comedy of patient Griselidis' in Geoffrey Chaucer's *The Canterbury Tales*). Grisélidis, wife of the Marquis, is loved by Alain. The Devil attempts to persuade her to accept Alain, maintaining that the Marquis is unfaithful. She refuses, and the Devil abducts her child, which the Marquis succeeds in rescuing.

Grisi, Giuditta *(1805–40)*
Italian mezzo. One of the outstanding mezzos of the first half of the 19th century, she created Romeo in *I Capuleti e i Montecchi* and the title role in L. Ricci's *Chiara di Rosembergh*. She tended to be overshadowed by her younger sister Guilia Grisi* and by her cousin the great ballerina Carlotta Grisi.

Grisi, Giulia *(1811–69)*
Italian soprano, sister of Giuditta Grisi* and cousin of the ballerina Carlotta Grisi. Regarded as one of the greatest of all 19th-century sopranos, she possessed a rich and flexible voice, suitable for both dramatic and lyrical roles. She created Adalgisa in *Norma*, Elvira in *I Puritani*, and, for Donizetti, Adelia in *Ugo Conte di Parigi*, Norina in *Don Pasquale* and Elena in *Marino Faliero*. She retired in 1861 and her attempted come-back in 1866 as Lucrezia Borgia was a disaster. She lived with the tenor Giovanni Mario* for many years.

Grist, Reri *(b 1932)*
American soprano, particularly associated with Mozart roles and with coloratura roles such as Zerbinetta and Oscar. She possessed a sweet and agile voice and had a most enchanting stage presence.

Grossmächtige Prinzessin
Soprano aria for Zerbinetta in Richard Strauss' *Ariadne auf Naxos*. Described by Strauss as "the grand coloratura aria with all the tricks".

Groves, Sir Charles (b 1915)

British conductor, particularly associated with the Italian and British repertories. One of the most popular contemporary British conductors, he was musical director of the Welsh National Opera (1961–63) and the English National Opera (1977–79). He conducted the first performance of Crosse's *The Story of Vasco*.

Gruberová, Edita (b 1946)

Czech soprano, particularly associated with Mozart and with coloratura roles, especially Zerbinetta and Lucia. She possesses a voice of considerable size and remarkable agility, which is used with musicianship and an excellent technique.

Gruenberg, Louis Theodore (1884–1964)

Polish-born American composer. His operas include the jazz-inspired *Daniel Jazz* (1923), *The Emperor Jones**, his most successful work, *Jack and the Beanstalk* (New York 31 Nov 1930; libr. J. Erskine) and the radio opera *Green Mansions* (CBS 1937; libr. after W. H. Hudson).

Grümmer, Elisabeth (1911–86)

German soprano, particularly associated with Mozart and Strauss roles. She possessed a beautiful voice used with a fine technique and was an accomplished singing-actress.

Guadagni, Gaetano (c 1725–92)

Italian castrato. Possessor of a superb voice and said to have been unrivalled as an operatic actor (he studied with David Garrick), he created, for Gluck, the title roles in *Orfeo* and *Telemaco*.

Guarany, II

Opera in four acts by Gomes. 1st perf. Milan, 19 March 1870; libr. by Tomaso Scalvini and Carlo d'Ormeville, after José Martiniano de Alençar's novel. Principal roles: Pery (ten), Cecilia (sop), Don Antonio de Mariz (bass), Don Alvaro (ten), Gonzales (bar), Ruy-Bento (ten), Alonso (bass), Pedro (bass). Gomes' masterpiece, it was enormously successful at its appearance and is still occasionally performed. The *Symphonia do Guarany*, added in 1872, has become an unofficial Brazilian national anthem.

Plot: The Guarani prince Pery rescues his beloved Cecilia from the Spaniards Alonso, Ruy-Bento and Gonzales, who had planned to hand her over to the enemy Aymara tribe. Cecilia's father Antonio rescues them from hostile Indians. Pery and Cecilia reach safety and freedom, but Antonio is killed when a dynamite charge explodes in his castle, also killing the Spanish villains.

Guarnieri, Antonio (1880–1952)

Italian conductor, mainly associated with La Scala, Milan. An outstanding interpreter of the Italian repertory, he conducted the first performances of Respighi's *Belfagor*, Casella's *Il Deserto Tentato* and Bloch's *Macbeth*. His sons Arrigo (1910–75) and Ferdinando (b 1936) were also both conductors.

Guatemalan opera composers

These include José Escolástico Andrino and Jesús Castillo (1877–1946).

Gueden, Hilde (1917–88)

Austrian soprano, particularly associated with Mozart and Strauss roles. She had a beautiful, silvery voice which was able to encompass lyrical, soubrette and coloratura roles. She also enjoyed considerable success in Viennese operetta.

Guelfi, Giangiacomo (b 1924)

Italian baritone, particularly associated with Verdi and Puccini roles. He had a large, powerful and exciting voice and was an extrovert performer. He created Lazzaro in Pizzetti's *La Figlia di Iorio*.

Guerre des Bouffons (French for 'war of the comic actors'; also known as *Querelle des Bouffons*)

The name given to one of the most remarkable episodes in operatic history, when all of Paris was divided from 1752 to 1754 between the supporters of traditional French serious opera as exemplified by Lully and Rameau, and those of the new Italian opera buffa as exemplified by Pergolesi's *La Serva Padrona*. The traditionalists included Louis XV, Madame de Pompadour, the court and the aristocracy; on the other hand, the Queen and the intellectuals (particularly Diderot, Rousseau and d'Alembert) supported the Italians for having breathed new life into a moribund and stiflingly conventional form. Rousseau's contribution (in addition to composing operas in the Italian style) was his famous *Lettre Sur la Musique Française* of 1753.

Guerrero y Torres, Jacinto (1895–1951)

Spanish composer. He wrote some 50 zarzuelas, of which the most successful include *La Alsaciana* (1921) [R] and *Los Gavilanes* (1923) [R].

Guglielmi, Pietro Alessandro (1728–1804)

Italian composer. He wrote 103 operas, all of them now forgotten, achieving his greatest success with comedy, where his innovations were admired by Rossini.

In his serious operas, such as *Tito Manlio* (Rome 8 Jan 1763; libr. G. Roccaforte) he considerably expanded the role of the chorus. His son Pietro Carlo (c 1763–1817) was also a composer, whose most successful opera was *Paolo e Virginia* (Naples 1816).

Guglielmo

Baritone role in Mozart's *Così fan Tutte*. He is an officer in love with Fiordiligi.

Guglielmo Ratcliff

Opera in four acts by Mascagni. 1st perf. Milan, 16 Feb 1895; libr. by Count Andrea Maffei, after Heinrich Heine's *Wilhelm Ratcliff*. Principal roles: Guglielmo (ten), Maria (sop), Count Douglas (bar), MacGregor (bass), Margherita (mezzo). Reasonably successful at its appearance, it is nowadays all but forgotten.

Plot: Scotland. Ratcliff falls in love with Maria and vows to kill anyone who tries to marry her. Count Douglas becomes engaged to Maria and Ratcliff challenges him to a duel, where Douglas spares his life. Maria learns from her nurse Margherita that Ratcliff's father and her mother had once hoped to marry but were prevented from doing so, that her mother married her father MacGregor instead, and that MacGregor had killed Ratcliff's father. The injured Ratcliff bursts in, kills Maria and dies. On discovering the two corpses, Douglas commits suicide.

Gui, Vittorio (1885–1975)

Italian conductor and composer, particularly associated with Rossini and Mozart operas. One of the outstanding conductors of the inter-war period, he was a co-founder of the Maggio Musicale Fiorentino in 1933 and was musical director of the Glyndebourne

Festival (1952–63). He composed several operas, including *Fata Malerba* (Turin 1927).

Guillard, Nicolas François
(1752–1814)

French librettist. Less prolific but producing work of a far higher standard than most of his contemporaries, he wrote some dozen libretti, including texts for Grétry, Lesueur (*La Mort d'Adam*), Paisiello, Sacchini (three including *Oedipe à Colone*), Salieri (*Les Horaces*) and, especially, Gluck (*Iphigénie en Tauride*). This last was described by Alfred Einstein as "the best book that ever came into Gluck's hands".

Guillaume Tell (*William Tell*)
Works of this title about the legendary Swiss patriot include:

(1) Opera in three acts by Grétry. 1st perf. Paris, 9 April 1791; libr. by Jean-Marie Sedaine, after A. M. Lemierre. Successful in its time, it is now forgotten. Tchaikovsky quotes it in *The Queen of Spades*.

(2) Opera in five acts by Rossini. 1st perf. Paris, 3 Aug 1829; libr. by Victor Joseph Etienne de Jouy, Florent Bis and Armand Marast, after Friedrich von Schiller's *Wilhelm Tell*. Principal roles: Tell (bar), Arnold (ten), Mathilde (sop), Melchtal (bass), Gessler (bass), Jemmy (sop), Walther (bass), Edwige (mezzo). Rossini's last, longest, most ambitious and most serious opera, it is hampered by its appalling libretto and has suffered from disfiguring cuts almost from its inception. It is an uneven work, but in the scenes which fired his imagination Rossini wrote some of his greatest and noblest music, as well as providing the work with perhaps the most famous of all operatic overtures. It is still quite often performed, but not as frequently as its merits deserve.

Plot: 13th-century Switzerland. The Swiss patriot Tell helps a fugitive to escape from the occupying Austrians. The Austrians arrest Melchtal, father of Arnold, who loves the Hapsburg princess, Mathilde. She wishes Arnold to join the Austrians and marry her, but hearing of his father's execution, he joins the patriots. Tell and his young son Jemmy refuse to pay homage to the Austrian tyrant Gessler and Tell is forced to shoot an apple placed on Jemmy's head. Stating that if he had failed he would have shot a second arrow at Gessler, he is arrested, but Mathilde – after rescuing Jemmy – gives herself as a hostage for Tell to the patriots. Jemmy sets fire to Tell's house as the signal for the revolt planned by Arnold. During a storm, Tell escapes from the boat taking him to captivity, kills Gessler and joins the patriots in a victory over the Austrians. [R]

Guillot de Morfontaine
Tenor role in Massenet's *Manon*. He is an ageing roué.

Guiraud, Ernest *(1837–92)*
French composer. He wrote eight operas, all of them now forgotten, including *Le Kobold* (Paris 2 July 1870; libr. Charles Nuittier and Louis Gallet), *Madame Turlupin* (1872), *Piccolino* (Paris 11 April 1876; libr. Nuittier, after Victorien Sardou) and *Frédégonde* (Paris 18 Dec 1895; libr. Gallet), which was left unfinished at his death and was completed by Saint-Saëns and Dukas. Nowadays he is solely remembered for his completion of Offenbach's *Les Contes d'Hoffmann* and for having provided recitatives for *Carmen*. He was also a noted teacher, whose pupils included Debussy, and his *Traité d'Instrumentation* (1895) was one of the earliest analyses of Wagner.

Günther
Baritone role in Wagner's
Götterdämmerung. Gutrune's brother,
he is the leader of the Gibichungs.

Guntram
Opera in three acts by Richard Strauss.
(Op 25). 1st perf. Weimar, 10 May
1894; libr. by the composer. Principal
roles: Guntram (ten), Freihild (sop),
Friedhold (bass), Duke Robert (bar),
Jester (ten). Strauss' first opera, it was
dedicated to Verdi, but is written in
imitation of Wagner. A failure at its
appearance, it is almost never
performed.
    Plot: 13th-century Germany. Wishing
to free the people from Duke Robert's
tyrannical rule, Guntram kills Robert in
a duel. Subsequently, because he feels
guilty at having loved Robert's wife
Freihild, he gives her up to embark on
a life of solitude. [R]

Guridi y Bidaolo, Jesús *(1886–1961)*
Spanish composer. One of the leading
20th-century Basque composers, his
stage works include the operas
Mirentxu (Madrid 1915; libr. A.
Echave) and *Amaya* (Bilbao 1920; libr.
J. M. Arroita Jáuregui) and a number
of zarzuelas, of which *El Caserío*
(Madrid 1926; libr. F. Romero and
Carlos Fernández Shaw) [R] was very
successful.

Gurnemanz
Bass role in Wagner's *Parsifal*. He is an
old knight of the Grail.

Gustavo
Tenor role in Verdi's *Un Ballo in
Maschera*. He is King Gustavus III of
Sweden.

Guthrie, Sir Tyrone *(1900–71)*
British producer, particularly associated
with Sadler's Wells Opera. One of the
leading British theatre producers of the
immediate postwar era, his productions
were noted for their dramatic
naturalness and for their vivid handling
of the chorus.

Gutrune
Soprano role in Wagner's
Götterdämmerung. She is Günther's
sister.

Gwendoline
Opera in two acts by Chabrier. 1st
perf. Brussels, 10 April 1886; libr. by
Catulle Mendès. Principal roles:
Gwendoline (sop), Armel (ten), Harald
(bar). Chabrier's only completed serious
opera, it is heavily influenced by
Wagner. It is nowadays almost never
performed, although the overture is still
quite well-known. Set in 8th-century
Britain, it tells of a Viking king who
falls in love with the daughter of his
Saxon prisoner.

Gypsy Baron, The
See Zigeunerbaron, Der

Gypsy Princess, The
See Csárdásfürstin, Die

Gyrowetz, Adalbert
See Jírovec, Vojtěch

Hába, Alois *(1893–1973)*

Czech composer. The leading exponent of microtonal music, his first opera *The Mother** is the most important quarter-tone opera. His second opera *New Earth* (*Nová Země*, 1936; libr. F. Gladkov and F. Pujman) is in the traditional semitonal system, but his last work, the unperformed *Thy Kingdom Come* (*Přijd Království Tvé*, 1942; libr. composer), employs sixth-tones. Hába's interest in quarter-tone music derived from its use by Moravian folk singers, who employ microtonal inflections to darken or brighten the mood of the music they are singing. Despite the respect and interest which his operas aroused, they have been little performed, partly no doubt because of the obvious practical difficulty for singers to pitch microtones accurately. His brother Karel (*b* 1898) was also a composer. His three operas are *Jánošík* (Prague 23 Feb 1934; libr. A. Klášterský), *Ancient History* (*Stará Historie*, 1940) and the children's opera *Smolíček* (1950; libr. V. Čtvrtek).

Habañera

A Spanish song and dance in 2/4 time. Its origins are Cuban, deriving from the dancing of the *ñañigos*, the black inhabitants of a district of Havana (Habana in Spanish). The best-known operatic example is 'L'amour est un oiseau rebelle' in Bizet's *Carmen*, which is adapted from the song *El Arregilito* by the Spanish composer Sebastián Yradier (1809–65).

Hab' mir gelobt

Soprano/soprano/mezzo trio for the Marschallin, Sophie and Octavian in Act III of Richard Strauss' *Der Rosenkavalier*.

Haddon Hall

Operetta in two acts by Sullivan. 1st perf. London, 24 Sept 1892; libr. by Sydney Grundy. Principal roles: Dorcas (mezzo), Dorothy (sop), Sir George (b-bar), Lady Vernon (mezzo), Oswald (ten), Rupert (bass). The best of Sullivan's non-Gilbertian works, it was successful at its appearance but is nowadays only very rarely performed.

Hadjibeyov, Uzeir *(1885–1948)*

Azerbaijani composer. Founder of the first Azerbaijani school of music in 1922, he wrote seven operas in addition to a number of successful musical comedies. His operas are *Leila and Medjun* (Baku 25 Jan 1908; libr. composer, after Mohammed Fizuli), *Sheikh Senan* (Baku 1909; libr. composer), *Rustam and Sohrab* (Baku 1910; libr. composer), *Asli and Kerem* (Baku 1912; libr. composer), *Shah Abbas and Hurshidbanu* (Baku 1912; libr. composer), the unperformed *Harun and Leila* (1915) and the epic *Kyor-Ogly* (Baku 1937; libr. M. Ordabadi), his most successful work.

Hadley, Henry *(1871–1937)*

American composer. He wrote six operas, some of which enjoyed success in their time but which are all nowadays forgotten. They are *Safié*

(Mainz 1909), *Azora, Daughter of Montezuma* (Chicago 26 Dec 1917; libr. David Stevens), *Bianca* (1918), *Cleopatra's Night* (New York 31 Jan 1920; libr. Alice Leal Pollock, after Théophile Gautier's *Une Nuit de Cléopâtre*), the radio opera *A Night in Old Paris* (1933) and *Nancy Brown*.

Häfliger, Ernst *(b 1919)*

Swiss tenor, particularly associated with Mozart roles and with 20th-century works. A stylish singer of fine musicianship, he created Tiresias in Orff's *Antigonae* and roles in operas by Martin.

Hagegård, Håkan *(b 1945)*

Swedish baritone, particularly associated with Mozart roles, notably Papageno (which he played in the Bergman film). He has a warm and easily-produced voice and a most engaging stage personality.

Hagen

Bass role in Wagner's *Götterdämmerung*. Alberich's son, he is Günther's half-brother.

Hager, Leopold *(b 1935)*

Austrian conductor, particularly associated with Mozart, all of whose early operas he has recorded with the Salzburg Mozarteum.

Hahn, Reynaldo *(1875–1947)*

Venezuelan composer, largely resident in France. He wrote many stage works, both opera and operetta, much the most successful being *Ciboulette**. His other works include *Mozart* (Paris 1925; libr. Guitry) and *Le Marchand de Venise* (Paris 1935; libr. M. Zamacoïs after Shakespeare's *The Merchant of Venice*). He was director of the Paris Opéra (1945–46).

Haitink, Bernard *(b 1929)*

Dutch conductor, particularly associated with Mozart, Strauss, Wagner and Verdi operas. Quickly establishing himself as one of the outstanding postwar symphonic conductors, his operatic appearances were rare until 1976. He was musical director of the Glyndebourne Festival (1978–88) and then of Covent Garden (1988–).

Haken, Eduard *(b 1910)*

Czech bass, particularly associated with the Czech repertory, especially the Watersprite in *Rusalka*. He had a rich and powerful voice and was a fine singing-actor, equally at home in serious or comic roles.

Halévy, Fromental *(b Elias Lévy)* *(1799–1862)*

French composer. He wrote 37 operas and, with Meyerbeer, may be regarded as the archetypal composer of the mid-19th century French grand opera tradition. His most successful works include *Clari* (Paris 9 Dec 1829; libr. P. Giannone), *La Juive**, his masterpiece and his only work which is still remembered, the comedy *L'Eclair* (Paris 16 Dec 1835; libr. Jules-Henri Vernoy de Saint-Georges and François-Antoine-Eugène de Planard), *La Reine de Chypre* (Paris 22 Dec 1841; libr. Saint-Georges), *La Tempesta* (London 8 June 1850; libr. Eugène Scribe and Giannone, after Shakespeare's *The Tempest*), *La Dame de Pique* (Paris 28 Dec 1850; libr. Scribe, after Prosper Mérimée's translation of Alexander Pushkin's *The Queen of Spades*) and *Noé* (Karlsruhe 5 April 1885; libr. Saint-Georges), which was left unfinished and was completed by his son-in-law, Bizet. He also completed Hérold's unfinished *Ludovic*. He was a noted teacher, whose pupils included

Gounod, Massé and Bizet. His nephew was the librettist Ludovic Halévy*.

Halévy, Ludovic *(1834–1908)*

French playwright and librettist, nephew of the composer. One of the finest of all French librettists, he is best known for his texts (often in collaboration with Henri Meilhac*) for Offenbach, with their biting satire on Third Empire Society. He provided libretti for Bizet (*Carmen* and *Le Docteur Miracle*), Delibes, Flotow (*Naida*), Lecocq (six including *Le Docteur Miracle* and *Le Petit Duc*) and Offenbach (*Barbe-Bleue*, *La Belle Hélène*, *Les Brigands*, *La Grande-Duchesse de Gérolstein*, *Orphée aux Enfers*, *La Périchole* and *La Vie Parisienne*). His play *Le Réveillon* is the source for *Die Fledermaus*.

Halka *(Helen)*

Opera in four (originally two) acts by Moniuszko. 1st perf. Wilno, 11 Jan 1848; libr. by Wlodzimierz Wolski, after Kazimierz Wladyslaw Wójcicki's *Góralka*. Revised version, 1st perf. Wilno, 28 Feb 1854. Principal roles: Halka (sop), Jontek (ten), Stolnik (bass), Janusz (bar), Zofia (mezzo). Moniuszko's most successful work and perhaps the most popular of all Polish operas.

Plot: Carpathia, *c* 1840. Halka loves Janusz, who himself is in love with Zofia. Janusz seduces Halka but then abandons her. Halka kills herself whilst Janusz and Zofia are being married. [R]

Hall, Sir Peter *(b 1930)*

British producer. Director of the National Theatre (1973–87), he has had a long association with opera, which he treats as total music theatre. He worked first at Covent Garden, most notably with *Moses und Aron* and *Tristan und Isolde*, but did not take up his post as co-director in 1971 because of artistic disagreements. Since then he has worked largely at Glyndebourne, winning particular acclaim for his Mozart productions. He also produced the *Ring* at Bayreuth in 1983. Married for a time to the mezzo Maria Ewing*.

Halle

See Handel Festival, Halle

Hallé, Sir Charles *(b Carl Halle)* *(1819–95)*

German-born British conductor. Although best known as a symphonic conductor and as the founder of the Manchester orchestra which bears his name, he also conducted a number of operas in the early part of his career.

Hallström, Ivar *(1826–1901)*

Swedish composer. He wrote a large number of operas and operettas, many inspired by Swedish folk legend. Several enjoyed considerable success in their time but are now largely forgotten. His most successful works include *The White Lady of Drottningholm* (*Hvita Frun på Drottningholm*, Stockholm 1847), the operetta *The Enchanted Cat* (*Den Förtrollade Katten*, Stockholm 1869), *The Miller-Wolf* (*Mjölnarvargen*, Stockholm 1871; libr. after Michel Carré and Eugène Cormon's *Le Diable au Moulin*), *The Bewitched* (*Den Bergtagna*, Stockholm 24 May 1874; libr. Hedburg), his finest work which is still occasionally revived, *The Vikings* (*Vikingarne*, Stockholm 1877; libr. Hedburg), *The Silver Ring* (*Silverringen*, Stockholm 1880; libr. after Jules Barbier and Léon Battu), the operetta *Neaga* (Stockholm 1885; libr. Queen Carmen Sylva of Romania) and *The Devil's Snares* (*Den Ondes Snaror*, Göteborg 1900; libr. Christienson).

Hamburg State Opera

The present opera house (cap. 1,675) was designed by Gerhard Weber and opened in 1955. One of Germany's leading houses, it has had a strong tradition of presenting 20th-century works, particularly when Rolf Liebermann was administrator (1959–72). The annual season runs from August to June. Musical directors have included Hans von Bülow, Mahler, Felix Weingartner, Egon Pollack, Karl Böhm, Eugene Jochum, Leopold Ludwig, Horst Stein, Christoph von Dohnányi and Gerd Albrecht.

Hamilton, Iain *(b 1922)*

British composer, writing first in serial style and later in a more tonal form. His stage works, some of which have met with success in Britain, include the unperformed *Agamemnon* (1969; libr. composer, after Aeschylus), *The Cataline Conspiracy**, *The Royal Hunt of the Sun**, *Tamburline* (1977; libr. after Christopher Marlowe), *Anna Karenina* (London 1981; libr. after Tolstoy) and *Lancelot* (1985).

Hamlet

Works of this title based on Shakespeare's play include:

(1) Opera in five acts by Thomas. 1st perf. Paris, 9 March 1868; libr. by Jules Barbier and Michel Carré. Principal roles: Hamlet (bar), Ophélie (sop), Laerte (ten), Gertrude (mezzo), Claudius (bass). Thomas' only opera apart from *Mignon* to have survived, it was enormously popular in the 19th century, but is nowadays only infrequently performed. The plot follows Shakespeare fairly closely until the end, when Hamlet ascends the throne. [R]

(2) Opera in three acts by Searle (Op 48). 1st perf. Hamburg, 6 March 1968; libr. by the composer. Principal roles: Hamlet (bar), Ophelia (mezzo), Claudius (ten), Gertrude (mezzo), Polonius (bass), Laertes (ten), Player King and Queen (bass and sop). Searle's most successful opera, it has received a number of productions.

(3) Opera in three acts by Szokolay (Op 25). 1st perf. Budapest, 1968.

Hammond, Dame Joan *(b 1912)*

New Zealand soprano, particularly associated with the Italian repertory, especially Puccini. A greatly loved singer, she had a rich and beautiful lyric soprano which was, sadly, heard only infrequently in the opera house. Her autobiography, *A Voice, A Life*, was published in 1970.

Hammond-Stroud, Derek *(b 1929)*

British baritone, particularly associated with the roles of Alberich, Bunthorne, Faninal and Beckmesser. Possessor of a fine voice and phenomenal diction, he was an outstanding singing-actor, equally at home in serious or comic roles.

Handel, Georg Friedrich *(1685–1759)*

German composer, largely resident in England. Apart from the masque *Acis and Galatea**, his stage works fall into two categories: firstly, Italian opera serias written between 1705 and 1741, and secondly dramatic oratorios, both sacred and secular, written from 1743. Into the stiflingly formal structure of opera seria Handel poured magnificent and often highly dramatic music and may be regarded as much the greatest exponent of the genre. His early works enjoyed great success, but owing to changes in public taste (epitomised by the success of *The Beggar's Opera* and its satire on the excesses of opera seria) they met with increasing disfavour. Turning to dramatic oratorios, a form which allowed him to use a chorus, Handel once more achieved great success.

His first opera *Almira** was followed by *Nero* (Hamburg 25 Feb 1705; libr. Friedrich C. Feustking), the music of which is lost, *Rodrigo**, *Agrippina** and *Rinaldo**, his first opera for London. The remainder of his operas are *Il Pastor Fido**, *Teseo**, *Silla* (London 2 June 1714; libr. Giacomo Rossi), *Amadigi di Gaula* (London 25 May 1715; libr. Nicola Francesco Haym after Houdart de la Motte's *Amadis de Grèce*), *Radamisto**, *Muzio Scevola* (London 15 April 1721; libr. Paolo Antonio Rolli, after S. Stampiglia), which has an act each by Amadei, Handel and his great rival Bononcini, *Floridante**, *Ottone**, *Flavio**, *Giulio Cesare**, *Tamerlano**, *Rodelinda**, *Scipione**, *Alessandro**, *Admeto**, *Riccardo Primo**, *Siroe**, *Tolomeo**, *Lotario**, *Partenope**, *Poro**, *Ezio**, *Sosarme**, *Orlando**, *Arianna**, *Ariodante**, *Alcina**, *Atlanta**, *Arminio**, *Giustino**, *Berenice**, *Faramondo**, *Serse**, *Imeneo** and *Deidamia**. His first dramatic oratorio was *Samson**. Originally performed in concert, they nonetheless conform to nearly all accepted notions of what constitutes an opera and they have been frequently staged in the 20th century. The most successful include *Semele**, *Hercules**, *Saul**, *Athalia** and *Belshazzar**.

By the late 18th century, Handel's operas had fallen into complete neglect. The 20th-century revival of interest in his works began in Germany in the 1920s. Since World War II, the revival has spread to Britain (particularly through the work of the Handel Opera Society) and to the United States.

Handel Festival, Halle
An annual festival in Saxony devoted to the operas of Handel, it was founded in 1953. Performances are given at the Theater des Friedens (cap. 1,035), which originally opened in 1886.

Handel Opera Society
A British company founded in 1955 at the instigation of Edward J. Dent to revive public interest in Handel's stage works. Until its demise in 1985, it staged over 30 of Handel's operas and oratorios. The musical director was Charles Farncombe. There is also a Handel Opera Society in the United States.

A Hand of Bridge
Mini-opera by Barber (Op 35). 1st perf. Spoleto, 17 June 1959; libr. by Gian-Carlo Menotti. [R]

Hannah
Mezzo role in Tippett's *The Ice Break*. She is Gayle's black friend.

Hanover Opera
The present theatre (cap. 1,554) in this city in Lower Saxony opened in 1950, replacing the previous Royal Opera House which was opened in September 1852 but was destroyed in World War II. Musical directors have included Marschner, Ludwig Fischer, Hans von Bülow, Arno Grau, Emil Ábrányi, Rudolf Krasselt, Franz Konwitschny, Johannes Schüler, Günther Wich and Georg Alexander Albrecht.

Hänsel und Gretel
Opera in three acts by Humperdinck. 1st perf. Weimar, 23 Dec 1893; libr. by Adelheid Wette, after the Grimm brothers' *Fairy Tales*. Principal roles: Gretel (sop), Hänsel (mezzo), Peter

(bar), Witch (mezzo), Gertrude (sop), Sandman (sop), Dew Fairy (sop). Humperdinck's greatest success and one of the most popular of all operas, it is an expansion in Wagnerian style of his earlier nursery music written for a children's play by his sister.

Plot: Harz Mountains. Gertrude scolds her children Hänsel and Gretel for playing instead of doing the household chores and sends them off to the woods to pick strawberries. When their father, Peter, comes home, he is alarmed for the children's safety: a Witch lives in the woods who bakes children in her oven. The children have lost their way in the wood and the Sandman sends them sleep and 14 angels to guard them. Roused by the Dew Fairy, they find a house made of sweets surrounded by gingerbread children. Starting to eat, they are captured by the Witch. However, the children outwit the Witch, push her into the oven and break her spell. Gretel releases the gingerbread children and when their parents, who have been searching for them, arrive, all join in a hymn of thanks. [R]

Hans Heiling

Opera in prologue and three acts by Marschner (Op 80). 1st perf. Berlin, 24 May 1833; libr. by Eduard Devrient, after Karl Theodor Körner. Principal roles: Heiling (bar), Anna (sop), Spirit Queen (sop). Marschner's finest and most successful opera, it is still performed from time to time.

Plot: Harz Mountains, 16th century. Hans Heiling, the son of the Spirit Queen and a mortal father, assumes human shape and falls in love with Anna. She rejects him when she discovers who he really is.

Hanslick, Eduard (1825–1904)

Austrian critic. An advocate of non-representational music, a theory he expounded in *Vom Musikalisch-Schönen* (1854), he came into conflict with the new ideas of Liszt and, even more so, Wagner. Largely because of Wagner's merciless caricature of him as Beckmesser in *Die Meistersinger von Nürnberg*, he has gone down in history as the archetypal rigid, conservative and reactionary critic. In fact, he was far more generous, cultured and intelligent than his detractors would admit.

Hanson, Howard (1896–1982)

American composer. Best known as a symphonic composer, he also wrote one opera: *Merry Mount* (New York 10 Feb 1934; libr. Richard Stokes after Nathaniel Hawthorne's *The May-Pole Lovers of Merry Mount*).

Hanuš, Jan (b 1913)

Czech composer. He wrote four operas: *The Flames* (*Plameny*, 1956; libr. J. Pokorný), *The Servant of Two Masters* (*Sluha Dvou Pánů*, 1959; libr. Pokorný, after Carlo Goldoni), *The Torch of Prometheus* (*Podhoden Prometheova*, 1963; libr. Pokorný, after Aeschylus) and *The Tale of One Night* (*Pohádka Jedne Noci*, 1968; libr. Pokorný, after *The Thousand and One Nights*). The last two have not been performed.

Harašta

Bass-baritone role in Janáček's *The Cunning Little Vixen*. He is a poacher.

Harewood, Earl of (b George Henry Hubert Lascelles) (b 1923)

British critic and administrator, he is a first cousin to Queen Elizabeth II. He was controller of opera planning at Covent Garden (1953–60), artistic director of the Leeds Festival (1958–74) and of the Edinburgh Festival (1961–65) and managing director of the

English National Opera (1972–86). He
founded *Opera* magazine in 1950 and
was its editor until 1953, and he edited
and contributed to the revised *Kobbé's
Complete Opera Book*.

Harlequin
The traditional Commedia dell'Arte
figure appears in a number of operas,
including: (1) Baritone role in Richard
Strauss' *Ariadne auf Naxos*. (2)
Speaking role in Busoni's *Arlecchino*.
(3) Tenor role in Cowie's *Commedia*.

Harmonie der Welt, Die *(The Harmony of the World)*
Opera in five scenes by Hindemith. 1st
perf. Munich, 11 Aug 1957; libr. by
the composer. Principal roles: Kepler
(bar), Wallenstein (ten). Set during the
Thirty Years' War, it deals with the life
of the astronomer Johannes Kepler
(1571–1630) and his musical theories
of planetary motion, and is a study of
the relationship between the artist and
the social and political currents of his
time. The music, in Hindemith's fully
tonal late style, is best known through
the symphony which he prepared from
the opera.

Harnoncourt, Nikolaus *(b 1929)*
Austrian conductor and cellist,
particularly associated with Mozart
operas and the Baroque repertory. He
has directed many outstanding operatic
performances on original instruments,
mainly with the Vienna Concentus
Musicus, which he founded in 1953.

Harper, Heather *(b 1930)*
British soprano, particularly associated
with Mozart, Strauss and Wagner roles
and with postwar British works. She
had a beautiful voice used with great
intelligence and a sympathetic stage
presence. She created Mrs Coyle in

Owen Wingrave, Nadia in *The Ice
Break* and Luisita in Benjamin's
Mañana.

Harriet, Lady
Soprano role in Flotow's *Martha*. She is
Maid of Honour to Queen Anne.

Harris, Sir Augustus *(1852–96)*
British administrator. As administrator
of Covent Garden (1888–96), he
presided over one of its most brilliant
periods. He insisted on operas being
performed in their original language,
built up a company of many of the
world's greatest singers, and introduced
Wagner's later works and the early
verismo operas to London. His father,
also Augustus, was stage manager at
Covent Garden for 27 years, and was
co-author of the libretti for Balfe's *The
Rose of Castille* and *Satanella* and
Wallace's *The Desert Flower*.

Hartmann, Karl Amadeus *(1905–63)*
German composer. His chamber opera
Der Simplicius Simplicissimus Jugend
(Cologne 10 Oct 1949, composed
1935; revised version Mannheim 1956)
met with considerable success in
Germany.

Hartmann, Rudolf *(1900–88)*
German producer, particularly
associated with Wagner and Richard
Strauss, for whom he staged the first
performances of *Friedenstag*, *Der Liebe
der Danae* and *Capriccio*. A producer
in the traditional mould, he was
administrator of the Bavarian State
Opera (1953–67).

Harwood, Elizabeth *(b 1938)*
British soprano, particularly associated
with Mozart roles. She had a beautiful
silvery voice and her lovely appearance

and fine stage presence made her a most appealing singing-actress. Sadly, her voice deteriorated severely at an early age.

Háry János

Opera in prologue, five parts and epilogue by Kodály (Op 15). 1st perf. Budapest, 16 Oct 1926; libr. by Béla Paulini and Zsolt Harsányi, after János Garay's poem. Principal roles: Háry (bass), Örzse (mezzo), Marie-Louise (sop), Empress (sop), Bombazine (bass), Marczi (bar). Kodály's best-known opera, which contains long stretches of spoken dialogue, it tells of the great liar of Hungarian folklore and his love for Napoleon's second wife. The music is best known from the orchestral suite, which comprises six numbers from the opera. [R]

Hasse, Johann (1699–1783)

German composer. He wrote some 100 operas and may be regarded as the archetypal German composer of opera seria. He set virtually every one of Pietro Metastasio's texts (56 operas and 13 intermezzi) with music which at its best is rich and elegant but which was already outdated by the end of his own life. The most successful of his operas include *Il Sesostrate* (Naples 13 May 1726; libr. A. Carasale, after Apostolo Zeno and Pietro Pariati), *Artaserse* (Venice Feb 1730; libr. D. Lalli, after Metastasio), *Cleofide* (Dresden 13 Sept 1731; libr. Michelangelo Boccardo, after Metastasio) [R] and *Attilio Regolo* (Dresden 12 Jan 1750; libr. Metastasio). His wife Faustina Bordoni (1700–81) was one of the leading sopranos of her age. She created Rosanne in Handel's *Alessandro*, and her rivalry with Francesca Cuzzoni (c 1700–70) led to the famous incident during Bononcini's *Astianatte* when the two divas ended up pulling each other's

hair. The incident is the basis for some of the satire in *The Beggar's Opera*, and she is the subject of a minor opera.

Háta

Mezzo role in Smetana's *The Bartered Bride*. She is Tobias Mícha's wife.

Hat man nicht

Bass aria (the Gold Aria) for Rocco in Act I of Beethoven's *Fidelio*.

Haugland, Aage (b 1944)

Danish bass, particularly associated with Wagnerian roles. He has a dark and powerful (if not always well-focused) voice, and a strong stage presence which is aided by his powerful physique.

Hauk, Minnie (b Mignon Hauck) (1851–1929)

American soprano, particularly associated with the French repertory, especially Carmen which she sang over 600 times. She made her debut at the age of 14 and enjoyed a brilliant career, including forming her own company, but unexpectedly retired at the height of her powers. Her autobiography, *Memoires of a Singer*, was published in 1925.

Haunted Manor, The (Straszny Dwor)

Opera in four acts by Moniuszko. 1st perf. Warsaw, 28 Sept 1865; libr. by Jan Checiński. Principal roles: Hanna (sop), Jadwiga (mezzo), Damazy (ten), Stefan (ten), Miecznik (bar). One of Moniuszko's finest works, it is still popular in Poland but is rarely performed elsewhere. [R]

Hauptprobe (German for 'chief rehearsal')

The last rehearsal of an opera

production before the dress rehearsal in a German or Austrian opera house, and the last at which any changes may still be made.

Häusliche Krieg, Der
See **Verschworenen, Die**

Haute-contre (French for 'high counter')
The term was used in 18th-century France to describe a high tenor (*not* singing falsetto). The voice's range was roughly d to b'.

Ha! welch' ein Augenblick'
Baritone aria for Don Pizzaro in Act I of Beethoven's *Fidelio*.

Ha wie will ich triumphieren
Bass aria for Osmin in Act III of Mozart's *Die Entführung aus dem Serail*.

Haydn, Joseph (1732–1809)
Austrian composer. In addition to five marionette operas, of which only *Philemon und Baucis* (Esterháza 2 Sept 1773; libr. G. K. Pfeffel) survives, he wrote 20 operas, both serious and comic. His mature operas, all but the last written for the Esterháza ensemble, are notable for their fine orchestration, their blending of serious and comic elements in the same work, their fine ensemble writing and their freeing of the formal aria structure. His first opera was *Der Krumme Teufel* (*The Limping Devil*, Vienna 29 May 1753; libr. J. Kurz after Alain René le Sage). Its music is lost, as is that for his next four operas. His first surviving work is *Acide e Galatea* (Esterháza 11 Jan 1763; libr. Giannambrogio Migliavacca, after Ovid's *Metamorphoses*). Its successors were *La Cantarina* (Esterháza July 1767), *Lo Speziale**, *Le Pescatrici* (Esterháza 16 Sept 1770; libr. Carlo Goldoni), *L'Infedeltà Delusa**, *L'Incontro Improvviso**, *Il Mondo della Luna**, his most frequently performed work in recent years, *La Vera Costanza**, *L'Isola Disabitata**, *La Fedeltà Premiata**, *Orlando Paladino**, *Armida** and *L'Anima del Filosofo*, usually known as *Orfeo ed Euridice**.

Although Haydn did not possess the dramatic insight of either Gluck or Mozart, the musical qualities of his operas are such that the oblivion into which they fell was wholly unjustified. In the last 15 years, there has been a major revival of interest in his operas: nearly all have been recorded and performances are becoming quite frequent. His younger brother was the composer Michael Haydn*, and Suppé's *Joseph Haydn* (1887) is based on his life.

Haydn, Michael (1737–1806)
Austrian composer, brother of Joseph Haydn. He wrote a number of operas, including *Andromeda e Perseo* (14 Mar 1787), and Singspiels, all of which are now forgotten.

Head voice (often referred to by its Italian, *Voce di testa*)
The highest register of the voice, so named because it gives the singer the sensation of vibration in the top of his head. It is the brightest and most brilliant in tone.

Hebrew National Opera
Founded by the soprano Edis de Philippe, the company gave its first performance on 29 Nov 1947. Performances, mostly sung in Hebrew, are given in Tel-Aviv, Haifa and Jerusalem. The operas of Wagner and Strauss are banned because of their alleged Nazi associations.

Hector

The Trojan hero appears in a number of operas, including: (1) Baritone role in Tippett's *King Priam*. (2) Bass role in Berlioz's *Les Troyens*, in which he is a ghost.

Heger, Robert *(1886–1978)*

German conductor and composer, particularly associated with the German repertory. He was musical director of the Ulm Stadttheater (1908–09), the Kassel Staatstheater (1935–44) and the Berlin State Opera (1944–50) and conducted the first performances of Haas' *Tobias Wunderlich* and Klenau's *Elisabeth von England*. He also composed five operas.

Heinrich

(1) Bass role in Wagner's *Lohengrin*. He is Henry the Fowler, King of Saxony. (2) Tenor role in Wagner's *Tannhäuser*. He is a minstrel knight.

Heise, Peter *(1830–79)*

Danish composer. His two operas are *The Pasha's Daughter* (*Paschaens Datter*, Copenhagen 1869; libr. H. Hertz) and *King and Marshal**, which is one of the most popular of all Danish operas.

Heldenbariton

See Baritone

Heldentenor (German for 'heroic tenor')

A tenor with the power and stamina required to sing the heavier roles in the German repertory, particularly those of Wagner. It is the German equivalent of the Italian *tenore di forza*.

Hélène

(1) Soprano role in Verdi's *Les Vêpres*

Siciliennes. She is the sister of Duke Frederick of Austria. (2) Mezzo role in Prokofiev's *War and Peace*. She is Prince Anatol's sister. (3) Soprano role in Rota's *Il Capello di Paglia di Firenze*. She is Fadinard's fiancée. (4) Mezzo role in Chabrier's *Une Éducation Manquée*. (5) Mezzo role in Offenbach's *La Belle Hélène*. She is Helen of Troy.

Helen of Troy

The wife of Menelaus appears in many operas, including: (1) Soprano role in Richard Strauss' *Die Ägyptische Helena*. (2) Mezzo role in Tippett's *King Priam*. (3) Mezzo role in Offenbach's *La Belle Hélène*. (4) Soprano role in Boito's *Mefistofele*.

Helmwige

Soprano role in Wagner's *Die Walküre*. She is one of the Valkyries.

Helsinki

See Finnish National Opera

Hempel, Frieda *(1885–1955)*

German soprano. One of the finst sopranos of the early 20th century, she possessed a technically impeccable voice and a fine stage presence. Her versatility was such that she could sing the Queen of the Night and Rosina as well as Eva and the Marschallin. Her autobiography, *Mein Leben dem Gesang*, was published in 1955.

Hemsley, Thomas *(b 1927)*

British baritone, particularly associated with Beckmesser and with contemporary roles. His rather dry-toned voice was not outstanding, but was used with great intelligence and musicianship and he was an accomplished singing-actor. He created Demetrius in *A Midsummer Night's*

Dream, Mangus in *The Knot Garden* and Caesar in Hamilton's *The Cataline Conspiracy*.

Hendricks, Barbara *(b 1948)*
American soprano, particularly associated with Mozart roles. She possesses one of the loveliest voices to have emerged in recent years, which she uses with musicianship and great intelligence. She also has a most affecting stage presence. She played Mimì in Luigi Comencini's film of *La Bohème*.

Henri VIII
Opera in four acts by Saint-Saëns. 1st perf. Paris, 5 March 1883; libr. by Léonce Détroyat and Armand Silvestre. Principal roles: Henri (bar), Anne (sop), Gomez (ten). Saint-Saëns' most successful work apart from *Samson et Dalila*, it is nowadays all but forgotten. It tells of Henry VIII's love for Anne Boleyn despite her love for the Spanish Ambassador Gomez.

Henze, Hans Werner *(b 1926)*
German composer. One of the most prolific and successful contemporary opera composers, his operas are written in a variety of forms and styles, but all tend to reflect his left-wing political views and his interest in the artist as an individual and in his relationship with society. His first opera *Das Wundertheater* (Heidelberg 7 May 1949; libr. after Miguel Cervantes) was followed by the radio opera *Ein Landarzt* (Hamburg 19 Nov 1951; libr. after Franz Kafka) and *Boulevard Solitude*, his first major work. The radio opera *Das Ende einer Welt* (Hamburg 4 Dec 1953; libr. W. Hildesheimer) was followed by the controversial *König Hirsch*, in which his penchant for lyrical fantasy is first apparent. His other operas are *Der Prinz von Homberg*, the highly successful *Elegie für Junge Liebende*, the satirical *Der Junge Lord*, the powerful *The Bassarids*, perhaps his finest opera, *Der Floss der Medusa* (Nürnberg 1972), *Rachel la Cubana* (New York 4 March 1974; libr. Enzensberger, after M. Barnet), the vast and pretentious *We Come to the River* and *The English Cat* (1984). He has also made realisations, so drastic as to amount virtually to new works, of Paisiello's *Don Quixote* (Montepulciano Aug 1976) and Monteverdi's *Il Ritorno d'Ulisse in Patria* (Salzburg 1987).

Herbert, Victor *(1859–1924)*
Irish-born American composer. He is best known as a composer of operettas, of which he wrote 35. The most successful were *Naughty Marietta* (New York 1910; libr. Young) and *Eileen* (1917). He also wrote two operas: *Natoma* (New York 1911) and *Madeleine* (New York 24 Jan 1914; libr. Grant Stewart).

Hercules
Secular oratorio in three acts by Handel. 1st perf. London, 5 Jan 1745; libr. by T. Boughton, after Sophocles' play. Principal roles: Hercules (bass), Dejanira (mezzo), Iole (sop), Hyllus (ten), Lichas (sop). Although not strictly speaking an opera, it is frequently staged. [R]

Herincx, Raimund *(b 1927)*
British baritone, particularly associated with 20th-century operas. His enormous repertory also included Wagner and many Italian and French roles. A fine singing-actor with a powerful if not intrinsically beautiful voice, he created Faber in *The Knot Garden*, the White Abbot in Maxwell Davies' *Taverner*, Segura in Williamson's *Our Man in*

Havana and the Governor in Henze's *We Come to the River.*

Hermia

Mezzo role in Britten's *A Midsummer Night's Dream.* She is one of the four lovers.

Héro

Soprano role in Berlioz's *Béatrice et Bénédict.* She is in love with Claudio.

Herod

The tetrarch of Judea (*c* 74–4 BC) appears as: (1) Tenor role in Richard Strauss' *Salome.* (2) Baritone role in Massenet's *Hérodiade.*

Hérodiade

Opera in four acts by Massenet. 1st perf. Brussels, 19 Dec 1881; libr. by Paul Milliet and Georges Hartmann, after Gustave Flaubert's *Hérodias.* Principal roles: Salome (sop), Herod (bar), Hérodiade (mezzo), John the Baptist (ten), Phanuel (bass), Vitellius (bar). One of Massenet's richest and most powerful scores, it is still performed quite often. In this version of the biblical story, John the Baptist admits to loving Salome, who stabs herself after Herod has had John killed. [R Exc]

Herodias

Mezzo role in Strauss' *Salome.* Salome's mother, she is married to Herod.

Hermann

Tenor role in Tchaikovsky's *The Queen of Spades.* He is a young officer in love with Lisa.

Hérold, Ferdinand *(1791–1833)*

French composer, whose early death cut short a career of great promise. His first opera *La Gioventù di Enrico V* (Naples 5 Jan 1815; libr. Landriani, after Shakespeare's *King Henry IV*) was a success, and was followed by *Charles de France* (Paris 18 June 1816), written in collaboration with Boïeldieu, and *Les Rosières* (Paris 27 Jan 1817; libr. E. G. M. Théaulon), his first major work. There followed 14 other operas (including one written in collaboration with Auber) before *Zampa**, his masterpiece, and *Le Pré aux Clercs**. His last opera *Ludovic* was unfinished and was completed by Halévy. His operas are notable for their delightful melodies, fine orchestration and sometimes ambitious structure.

Herrmann, Bernard *(1911–75)*

American composer. Best known as a highly successful composer of film music, he also wrote one opera, *Wuthering Heights**.

Hervé *(b Florimond Ronger) (1825–92)*

French composer. He wrote over 100 operettas, for many of which he provided his own libretti. The most successful included *Chilpéric* (Paris 24 Oct 1868; libr. composer), *Le Petit Faust* (Paris 28 April 1869; libr. Jaime and Héctor Crémieux) and *Mam'zelle Nitouche**, his most enduring work.

Herz, Joachim *(b 1924)*

German producer and administrator. A disciple of Walter Felsenstein, his powerful productions are conceived as total music-theatre. He was director of the Leipzig Opera (1957–77) and the Komische Oper, Berlin (1977–81). He has worked in Britain with the English National Opera (*Salome* and *Fidelio*) and the Welsh National Opera (*Madama Butterfly*).

Herzeleide

Soprano monologue for Kundry in Act II of Wagner's *Parsifal*.

Heuberger, Richard *(1850–1914)*

Austrian composer. He wrote four operas, including *Manuel Venegas* (1889; libr. after Pedro Alarcón's *El Niño de la Bola*), but is best known for his operettas. The most successful of his six works in this genre were *Der Opernball** and *Don Quixote* (1910; libr. after Miguel Cervantes).

Heure Espagnole, L' *(Spanish Time)*

Opera in one act by Ravel. 1st perf. Paris, 19 May 1911; libr. by Franc-Nohain (Maurice Legrand), after his play. Principal roles: Concepción (mezzo), Ramiro (bar), Gonzalve (ten), Don Iñigo Gómez (bass), Torquemada (ten). A witty, elegant and brilliantly orchestrated work, it was an immediate success and has remained popular ever since.

Plot: 18th-century Toledo. Torquemada the clockmaker has to spend a day away servicing the town's public clocks. This leaves the coast clear for his wife, Concepción, to pursue her love affairs, but he makes problems by allowing his customer, the muleteer Ramiro, to wait in his shop until he returns. Concepción's admirers, Gonzalve and Don Iñigo, arrive and successively hide inside clocks. After a deal of complication and clock-changing, Concepción gives her favours to Ramiro. [R]

Hidalgo, Elvira de *(1892–1980)*

Spanish soprano, particularly associated with Italian coloratura roles. One of the leading lyric sopranos of the early 20th century, she was also a noted teacher whose pupils included Maria Callas.

Hiller, Johann Adam *(b Hüller) (1728–1804)*

German composer. Usually regarded as the founder of Singspiel, he wrote 12 works in the genre, all first performed in Leipzig. The most important are *Der Teufel ist Los* (1766; libr. Christian Felix Weise, after Charles Coffey and John Mottley's *The Devil To Pay*), *Lottchen auf Hofe* (24 April 1767; libr. Weise, after Carlo Goldoni's *Bertoldo*), the enormously successful *Die Jagd** and *Der Dorfbarbier* (*The Village Barber*, 1771; libr. Weise, after Jean-Marie Sedaine's *Blaise le Savetier*).

Hindemith, Paul *(1895–1963)*

German composer, resident in the United States after he was banned by the Nazis as 'musically degenerate'. One of the most influential 20th-century German composers, he was the inventor of what came to be known as *Gebrauchsmusik* ('utility music'). His early stage works verge on atonality, but he later reverted to an advanced tonal idiom which he explained in much theoretical writing.

His first three operas are largely forgotten. They are *Mörder, Hoffnung der Frauen* (*Murder, Hope of Women*, Stuttgart 4 June 1921; libr. Oskar Kokoschka), the marionette opera *Das Nusch-Nuschi* (Stuttgart 4 June 1921), which is based on a Burmese story, and *Sancta Susanna* (Frankfurt 26 March 1922; libr. Stramm). His next opera, *Cardillac**, remains his best-known stage work. It was followed by *Hin und Zurück**, the satirical *Neues vom Tage**, the children's opera *Wir Bauen eine Stadt* (1931), *Mathis der Maler**, which was banned by the Nazis, *Die Harmonie der Welt** and *Das Lange Weihnachtsmahl* (Mannheim 17 Dec

1961; libr. after Thornton Wilder's *The Long Christmas Dinner*).

Hines, Jerome *(b Heinz)* *(b 1921)*
American bass (and mathematician), particularly associated with Verdi and Wagner roles. He was a fine singing-actor with a good (if not exceptional) voice of huge size. He also composed an opera, *I Am the Way*, about the life of Jesus. His writings include a book of interviews with 40 leading singers about the art of singing and his autobiography, *This is My Story, This is My Song*, which was published in 1968.

Hin und Zurück *(There and Back)*
Opera in one act by Hindemith (Op 45a). 1st perf. Baden-Baden, 17 July 1927; libr. by Marcellus Schiffer, after an English revue sketch. Principal roles: Robert (ten), Helene (sop). A clever little comedy, it was reasonably successful at its appearance, but is nowadays only very rarely performed.

Plot: Helene is unfaithful to her husband Robert. The action reaches a climax with a pistol shot, after which supernatural forces intervene to re-enact the story in reverse until the point at which it started is reached.

Hippolyte et Aricie
Opera in prologue and five acts by Rameau. 1st perf. Paris, 1 Oct 1733; libr. by Abbé Simon Joseph de Pellegrin, after Euripides' *Hippolytus* and Jean-Baptiste Racine's *Phèdre*. Principal roles: Phedra (mezzo), Theseus (bar), Hippolytus (ten), Aricia (sop), Pluto (bass), Diana (mezzo), Love (sop), High Priestess (sop). Rameau's first full-length opera, it is his best-known work and has been regularly performed in recent years. Dealing with the classical Greek myth, the plot concentrates on the love of Phedra for her stepson

Hippolytus, the illegitimate son of Theseus. [R]

Hislop, Joseph *(1884–1977)*
British tenor, largely resident in Sweden. Particularly associated with the French repertory and with Verdi and Puccini roles, he had a strong voice, which he used with style and musicianship. He was also a noted teacher, whose pupils included Jussi Björling, Birgit Nilsson and Peter Glossop.

History of Dioclesian, The
See Prophetess, The

H.M.S. Pinafore
or The Lass That Loved a Sailor
Operetta in two acts by Sullivan. 1st perf. London, 25 May 1878; libr. by W. S. Gilbert. Principal roles: Sir Joseph Porter (bar), Josephine (sop), Capt Corcoran (bar), Ralph Rackstraw (ten), Little Buttercup (mezzo), Dick Deadeye (bass), Bill Bobstay (b-bar), Hebe (mezzo). One of the most enduringly popular of all the Savoy Operas, which enjoyed an initial run of over 700 performances, it is a satire on class levels and on the traditions of the Royal Navy.

Plot: The former office boy and now First Lord of the Admiralty, Sir Joseph Porter, seeks the hand of Capt Corcoran's daughter Josephine. She loves a common sailor, Ralph Rackstraw, but cannot bring herself to admit it to him because of their social disparity. Sir Joseph, thinking her dazzled by his rank, propounds the theory that love is a platform upon which all ranks meet – thus neatly pleading Ralph's cause. The bumboat woman, Little Buttercup, reveals that when younger she was a baby-farmer and mixed up two children: Ralph and the Captain. So the Captain is really Ralph and Ralph is really the Captain and can wed Josephine. [R]

Hobson
Bass role in Britten's *Peter Grimes*. He is the town carter.

Hockney, David *(b 1937)*
British painter and designer. One of the most successful contemporary British artists, his operatic designs have included *The Rake's Progress* and *Die Zauberflöte* at Glyndebourne, *L'Enfant et les Sortilèges* and *The Nightingale* at Covent Garden and *Tristan und Isolde* in Los Angeles.

Hoddinott, Alun *(b 1929)*
British composer. He has written four operas: *The Beach at Falesá* (Cardiff 26 March 1974; libr. G. Jones, after Robert Louis Stevenson), *Murder the Magician* (Welsh TV 11 Feb 1976; libr. J. Morgan), *What the Old Man Does is Always Right* (Fishguard 27 July 1977; libr. Myfanwy Piper, after Hans Christian Andersen) and *The Rajah's Diamond* (Welsh TV 24 Nov 1979; libr. Piper).

Hodgson, Alfreda *(b 1940)*
British mezzo with a rich and beautiful voice used with intelligence and outstanding musicianship. Best known as a concert singer, her operatic appearances have been sadly infrequent.

Höffgen, Marga *(b 1921)*
German mezzo, particularly associated with Wagnerian roles, notably Erda. Best known as an oratorio artist, her operatic appearances were infrequent.

Hoffman, Grace *(b Goldie) (b 1925)*
American mezzo, particularly associated

with Verdi and Wagner roles. She possessed a rich and beautiful voice used with great musicianship, and had a fine stage presence.

Hoffmann, E. T. A.
See panel on page 271

Hofmann, Peter *(b 1944)*
German tenor, particularly associated with Wagnerian roles, especially Siegmund and Parsifal. One of the leading contemporary Wagnerian singers, although not a true heldentenor.

Hoffmannsthal, Hugo von *(1874–1929)*
Austrian poet, playwright and librettist. One of the greatest of all operatic librettists, his collaboration with Richard Strauss produced *Elektra, Der Rosenkavalier, Ariadne auf Naxos, Die Frau ohne Schatten, Die Ägyptische Helena* and *Arabella*. The workings of their partnership may be studied in their joint correspondence, first published in English in 1961. He also wrote the libretto for Wellesz's *Alkestis*.

Hofoper *(German for 'court opera')*
The title in the 18th and 19th centuries of a German or Austrian opera house which was under the direct control of an imperial or princely court.

Ho! Jolly Jenkins
Baritone aria for Friar Tuck in Act II of Sullivan's *Ivanhoe*.

Ho-Jo-to-ho!
Brünnhilde's war cry in Act II of Wagner's *Die Walküre*.

Holbrooke, Josef *(1878–1958)*
British composer. He wrote five operas, much the most important being the

E. T. A. HOFFMANN

The German writer, composer, critic and conductor Ernst Theodor Amadeus Hoffmann (1776–1822) occupies an important place in operatic history, both as a composer and as the literary source of several later operas. One of the most influential figures in the German romantic movement, he directed theatre companies in Bamberg, Leipzig and Dresden and composed 11 Singspiels in addition to his writings. His operas are *Die Maske* (1799; libr. composer), *Scherz, List und Rache* (Posen 1801; libr. composer, after Goethe), *Der Renegat* (1804), *Faustina* (1804), *Die Lustigen Musikanten* (Warsaw 6 April 1805; libr. Brentano), the lost *Der Kanonikus von Mailand* (1805; libr. Rohrmann, after Alexandre Duval's *Le Souper Imprévu*), *Liebe und Eifersucht* (1808; libr. composer, after Pedro Calderón), *Der Trank der Unsterblichkeit* (1808; libr. J. von Soden), *Dirna* (Bamberg 11 Oct 1809; libr. Soden), *Saul* (Bamberg 29 June 1811; libr. J. Seyfried, after L. C. Caigniez's *Le Triomphe de David*) and *Undine**, his finest work, parts of which anticipate the later German romantic operas of Weber, Marschner and Lortzing.

Hoffmann appears as a character in Offenbach's *Les Contes d'Hoffmann* and in three other operas by minor composers. Some 30 operas have been based on his works. Below are listed, by work, those operas by composers with entries in this dictionary.

Die Bergwerke von Falun

Wagner-Régeny	*Das Bergwerk zu Falun*	1961

Die Brautwahl

Busoni	*Die Brautwahl*	1912

Fantasiestücke

Malipiero	*I Capricci di Callot*	1942

Das Fräulein von Scuderi

Offenbach	*Der Goldschmied von Toledo* (pastiche)	1919
Hindemith	*Cardillac*	1926/52

Geschichte vom Verlorenen Spiegelbilde

Offenbach	*Les Contes d'Hoffmann* (Giulietta Act)	1881

Die Königsbraut

Offenbach	*Le Roi Carotte*	1872

Meister Martin

Blockx	*Maître Martin*	1892

Rat Krespel

Offenbach	*Les Contes d'Hoffmann* (Antonia Act)	1881

Der Sandmann

Adam	La Poupée de Nuremberg	1852
Offenbach	Les Contes d'Hoffmann (Olympia Act)	1881
Audran	La Poupée	1896

Wagnerian trilogy *The Cauldron of Annwn**. His other works are *Pierrot and Pierrette* (London 1910; libr. Walter E. Grogan; revised version *The Stranger*, 1924), the opera-ballet *The Enchanter* (Chicago 1915; libr. composer) and the comedy *The Snob* (libr. G. K. Chesterton, C. McEvoy and H. H. Ryan).

Holland
See Netherlands Opera

Hölle Rache, Die
Soprano aria for the Queen of the Night in Act II of Mozart's *Die Zauberflöte*.

Holm, Richard *(1912–88)*
German tenor, particularly associated with Mozart roles. He had a small but well-schooled voice, used with fine musicianship, and a good stage presence. He created Kent in Reimann's *Lear*.

Holst, Gustav *(1874–1934)*
British composer. His first four operas, *Landsdown Castle* (1893), *The Revoke* (1895; libr. F. Hart), *The Idea* (1898; libr. Hart) and *The Youth's Choice* (1902; libr. composer) are pale imitations of Sullivan and are forgotten, as also is his next opera *Sita* (1906; libr. composer, after the *Ramayana*), which Holst later dismissed as "good old Wagnerian bawling". His operatic maturity dates from the Sanskrit *Sāvitri**, possibly the finest British opera since *Dido and Aeneas*, and the founding work of modern British chamber opera. It was followed by *The Perfect Fool**, the Shakespearean *At the Boar's Head** and *The Wandering Scholar**. His daughter Imogen (1907–84) is a conductor, composer and musicologist who wrote the standard work on her father's music.

Holzbauer, Ignaz *(1711–83)*
Austrian composer. His most successful opera *Günther von Schwarzburg* (Mannheim 5 Jan 1777; libr. A. Klein), which was much admired by Mozart, is historically important in that it was the first full-length opera on a German subject with recitative replacing the dialogue of Singspiel.

Homer, Louise *(b Louise Dilworth Beatty) (1871–1947)*
American mezzo, particularly associated with Wagnerian roles. One of the finest mezzos of the early 20th century, she created the Witch in *Die Königskinder* and roles in Converse's *The Pipe of Desire* and Parker's *Mona*. Her nephew is the composer Samuel Barber*.

Home, Sweet Home
Aria from Bishop's *Clari*. As well as being a great concert favourite in the 19th century (Adelina Patti sometimes sang it in the lesson scene in *Il Barbiere di Siviglia*), it has also been used in altered form by a number of other composers, most notably by Donizetti in 'Al dolce guidami' in *Anna Bolena*, which led Bishop to bring an action for 'piracy and breach of copyright'.

Honegger, Arthur *(1892–1955)*
Swiss composer. A member of the group 'Les Six', he wrote 13 stage works in a variety of forms. His first work, the dramatic psalm *Le Roi David**, immediately placed him in the forefront of contemporary composers. It was followed by *Antigone**, *Judith**, the operetta *Les Aventures du Roi Pausole* (Paris 12 Dec 1930; libr. A. Willemetz, after Louÿs), the melodrama *Amphion* (Paris 23 June 1931) and the dramatic oratorio *Jeanne d'Arc au Bûcher**, perhaps his best known work. His later operas are *L'Aiglon** and *Gonzague* (Paris 1930; libr. R. Kerdick, after P. Veber), both written in collaboration with Ibert, *Les Milles et Une Nuit* (Paris 1937), the operetta *Les Petites Cardinal* (Paris 1937; libr. Willemetz and P. Brach, after Ludovic Halévy), also written with Ibert, the dramatic legend *Nicolas de Flue* (Neuchâtel 1941; libr. D. de Rougemont) and *Charles le Téméraire* (Mézières May 1944; libr. René Morax).

Höngen, Elisabeth *(b 1906)*
German mezzo, particularly associated with Wagner and Strauss roles and with Lady Macbeth. She had a fine, rich and powerful voice and was an impressive singing-actress.

Honour and arms
Bass aria for Harapha in Act I of Handel's *Samson*.

Honour Monologue
Baritone aria ('L'onore! Ladri!') for Falstaff in Act I of Verdi's *Falstaff*.

Hopf, Hans *(b 1916)*
German tenor, particularly associated with dramatic German roles. One of the leading dramatic tenors of the immediate postwar period.

Hopkins, Antony *(b Reynolds) (b 1921)*
British composer and conductor. His stage works include *Lady Rohesia* (London 1948), *The Man From Tuscany* (1951) and *Three's Company* (Crewe 1953; libr. Michael Flanders) [R]. He was musical director of Intimate Opera (1952–63) and has also enjoyed a highly successful broadcasting career as a commentator on music.

Horche, die Lerche singt
Tenor aria for Fenton in Act II of Nicolaï's *Die Lustigen Weiber von Windsor*.

Horn, Count
Bass role in Verdi's *Un Ballo in Maschera*. Tom in the Boston setting, he is one of the two conspirators.

Horne, Marilyn *(b 1929)*
American mezzo, particularly associated with Rossini and other coloratura roles. One of the greatest singers of the 20th century, she first came to prominence dubbing the singing for Dorothy Dandridge in the film *Carmen Jones* in 1954. She possesses a large, rich and dark voice of extraordinary agility and with a phenomenal range of over three octaves, which is used with outstanding musicianship and a matchless technique. Although best known as one of the greatest exponents of the bel canto repertory, she has also sung Wagner, Verdi, Berg, Handel and the French repertory with equal success. Married for a time to the conductor Henry Lewis.

Hornpipe
A lively British sailor's dance originally

with three, but more recently with two, beats in the bar. It is so named because it was originally accompanied by a pipe made from animal horn. The best known operatic example is in Sullivan's *Ruddigore*.

Horseman, The (*Ratsumies*)

Opera in three acts by Sallinen. 1st perf. Savonlinna, 17 July 1975; libr. by Paavo Haavikko. Principal roles: Antti (bass), Anna (sop), Merchant of Novgorod and his wife (ten and sop). Sallinen's first opera, it has proved to be one of the most successful of contemporary works and has been widely performed. [R]

Hosenrolle

A German term for trouser-role*.

Hotter, Hans (b 1909)

German bass-baritone, particularly associated with Wagnerian roles, notably Wotan, of which he is often regarded as the greatest 20th-century exponent. He possessed a large, rich and finely-projected voice and was a singing-actor of exceptional intelligence and insight. Also a distinguished interpreter of other German roles, he created Olivier in *Capriccio*, the Commandant in *Friedenstag* and a role in Einem's *Der Besuch der Alten Dame*. He enjoyed an exceptionally long career, singing into his late 70s, and also produced a number of operas, notably the *Ring* at Covent Garden.

Houston Grand Opera Association

Founded in 1956, the company gives an annual season at the John and Alice Wortham Theater (cap. 2,200), which opened in October 1987. Operas are given in both English and the original language, and the company has encouraged American operas and young American artists. Musical directors have included Walter Herbert and John de Main.

Howell, Gwynne (b 1938)

British bass, particularly associated with Verdi and Wagner roles. He possesses a rich and warm voice of great beauty and considerable range, although his acting abilities are rather limited. He created Richard Taverner in Maxwell Davies' *Taverner*.

Howells, Anne (b 1941)

British mezzo, particularly associated with Mozart roles and with contemporary works. A fine singing-actress (especially in comedy) with a well-schooled voice, she created Lena in Bennett's *Victory*, Cathleen in Maw's *The Rising of the Moon* and a role in Liebermann's *La Forêt*. Married first to the tenor Ryland Davies* and later to the bass Stafford Dean.

Hughes, Arwel (1909–88)

British composer and conductor. One of the most important composers to set Welsh texts, his two operas are *Menna* (1953; libr. W. Griffith) and *Love the Doctor* (*Serch yw'r Doctor*, 1960; libr. Saunders Lewis, after Molière's *L'Amour Médecin*). His son Owain Arwel is a conductor.

Hugh the Drover

Opera in two acts by Vaughan Williams. 1st perf. London, 14 July 1924, libr. by Harold Child. Principal roles: Hugh (ten), Mary (sop), John the Butcher (bar). Described as a ballad opera, it incorporates traditional folk material into the operatic structure. Successful at its appearance, it is nowadays only very rarely performed.

Plot: Cotswolds during the Napoleonic Wars. Hugh, having beaten

John the Butcher in a boxing match, is accused by John of spying for the French and is put into the village stocks. Mary, engaged to John against her will, unlocks him and leaves with him when the army clears him of treason. [R]

Hugo, Victor
See panel on page 276

Les Huguenots
Opera in five acts by Meyerbeer. 1st perf. Paris, 29 Feb 1836; libr. by Eugène Scribe and Emile Deschamps. Principal roles: Marguerite (sop), Raoul de Nangis (ten), Valentine (sop), Comte de St Bris (bar), Comte de Nevers (bar), Urbain (mezzo), Marcel (bass). Meyerbeer's best known opera, it is the archetypal 19th-century French grand opera. Dealing with events surrounding the St Bartholemew's Day massacre, it was for nearly a century one of the most popular of all operas. Nowadays, it is only infrequently performed. Performances are sometimes known as 'The Night of the Seven Stars' because of the seven great voices which it requires.

Plot: France, 1572. To mark a truce between the Catholic and Huguenot factions, the Protestant nobleman Raoul is engaged to marry Valentine, daughter of the Catholic Count, St Bris. Raoul and his retainer Marcel dine with the Catholics and Raoul is summoned before Queen Marguerite de Valois who expresses her hopes for religious reconciliation. Raoul meets Valentine and recognises her as someone whose life he had saved and, also, someone he has seen visiting the Catholic de Nevers at night. Unaware that her reason was to break off her previous engagement to Nevers, Raoul believes her unfaithful and cancels the planned marriage. The outraged Catholics plan to kill Raoul,

but Valentine (now married to Nevers) warns him via Marcel. Coming to thank her, Raoul overhears the Catholics planning the massacre of the Huguenots. Valentine confesses her love for him and, when Nevers is killed, they exchange vows of fidelity before they are both killed in the massacre. [R]

Hummel, Johann Nepomuk
(1778–1837)
Austrian composer. Although best known as an orchestral composer, he also wrote a number of operas and Singspiels, of which the most successful was *Mathilde von Guise* (Vienna 26 March 1810; libr. after L. E. F. C. Mercier-Dupray).

Humming
See Bocca chiusa

Humming Chorus
Chorus in Act II of Puccini's *Madama Butterfly*.

Humperdinck, Engelbert
(1854–1921)
German composer. A disciple of Wagner, he assisted in the preparation of *Parsifal*, even composing eight bars of it (which were later removed). His first opera *Hänsel und Gretel** was by far his most successful, and its formula of presenting children's fairy tales with simple melodies woven into a Wagnerian structure was followed in many of his later compositions. His other operas are *Die Sieben Geislein* (Berlin 19 Dec 1895; libr. Adelaide Wette after the brothers Grimm), *Dornröschen* (Frankfurt 12 Nov 1902; libr. E. Ebeling and B. Filhès after Charles Perrault), *Die Heirat Wider Willen* (Berlin 14 April 1905; libr. H.

VICTOR HUGO

The French playwright, novelist and poet Victor Hugo (1802–85) himself wrote one opera libretto, an adaptation of his own *Notre-Dame de Paris* for Bertin's long-forgotten *Esmeralda* (1836). His works have inspired over 70 operas. Below are listed, by work, those operas by composers with entries in this dictionary.

Angelo, Tyran de Padove

Mercadante	*Il Giuramento*	1837
Ponchielli	*La Gioconda*	1876
Cui	*Angelo*	1876

Antoine et Cléopâtre
(translation of Shakespeare's *Antony and Cleopatra*)

Bondeville	*Antoine et Cléopâtre*	1972

Han d'Islande

Moussorgsky	*Han d'Islande*	1856 (U)

Hernani

Bellini	*Ernani*	1830 (U)
Verdi	*Ernani*	1844

L'Homme Qui Rit

Enna	*The Comedians*	1920

La Légende des Siècles

Mancinelli	*Isora di Provenza*	1884

Lucrèce Borgia

Donizetti	*Lucrezia Borgia*	1833

Marie Tudor

Balfe	*The Armourer of Nantes*	1836
Pacini	*Maria Tudor*	1843
Gomes	*Maria Tudor*	1879
Wagner-Régeny	*Der Günstling*	1935

Marion Delorme

Ponchielli	*Marion Delorme*	1885

Notre-Dame de Paris		
Dargomijsky	*Esmeralda*	1847
Poniatowski	*Esmeralda*	1847
A. G. Thomas	*Esmeralda*	1883
Schmidt	*Notre-Dame*	1914

Quatre-Vingt-Treize		
Chapí	*Los Hijos de Batallón*	1898

Le Roi s'Amuse		
Verdi	*Rigoletto*	1851

Ruy Blas		
Poniatowski	*Ruy Blas*	1843
Marchetti	*Ruy Blas*	1869

Torquemada		
Rota	*Torquemada*	1943

Humperdinck after Alexandre Dumas' *Les Demoiselles de St Cyr*), *Die Königskinder**, a revision of an earlier version of 1897 and his only other work to have survived, *Die Marketenderin* (Cologne 10 May 1914; libr. R. Misch) and *Gaudeamus* (Darmstadt 18 March 1919; libr. Misch).

Hunding
Bass role in Wagner's *Die Walküre*. He is Sieglinde's husband.

Hungarian opera composers
See Ábrányi; Balassa; Bartók; Dohnányi; Erkel; Goldmark; Kálmán; Kodály; Lehár; Ligeti; Liszt; Petrovics; Szokolay

Hungary
See Budapest State Opera; Esterháza

Hunter, Rita *(b 1933)*
British soprano, particularly associated with Verdi and Wagner roles. One of the finest lyrico-dramatic British sopranos of the postwar period, she had a strong, pure and surprisingly agile voice, heard at its best as Leonora in *Il Trovatore*. Her technique was such that she was able to sing Brünnhilde and Norma in the same season at the Metropolitan Opera, New York. She had an appealing stage presence, although her substantial physique was a serious handicap. Her autobiography, *Wait Till the Sun Shines, Nellie*, was published in 1986.

Huon, Sir
Tenor role in Weber's *Oberon*. A knight, he is the Duke of Guienne.

Hylas
Tenor role in Berlioz's *Les Troyens*. He is a homesick sailor.

Hymn to the Sun

(1) Soprano aria for the Queen of Shemakha in Act II of Rimsky-Korsakov's *The Golden Cockerel*. (2) Chorus ('Son io! Son io la vita!') in Act I of Mascagni's *Iris*.

Hynninen, Jorma *(b 1941)*

Finnish baritone, particularly associated with Mozart and Verdi roles. A singer of style and musicianship, he has also been noted for his performances in modern Finnish operas, creating Topi in Sallinen's *The Red Line*. Artistic director of the Finnish National Opera (1984–).

I

I

Titles beginning with the plural form of the Italian definite article are listed under the letter of the first main word. For example, *I Masnadieri* is listed under M.

Iago

Otello's ensign, he appears as:
(1) Baritone role in Verdi's *Otello*.
(2) Tenor role in Rossini's *Otello*.

Ibert, Jacques *(1890–1962)*

French composer. He wrote seven operas in a light classical style. *Persée et Andromède* (Paris 15 May 1929, composed 1921; libr. Nino, after Laforge) was followed by *Angélique**, his most successful work, and *Le Roi d'Yvetot* (Paris 15 Jan 1930; libr. Jean Limzon and André de la Tourasse, after Pierre-Jean Béranger). Next came three works written in collaboration with Honegger: *Gonzague* (Paris 1930; libr. R. Kerdick, after P. Veber), *L'Aiglon** and the operetta *Les Petites Cardinal* (Paris 1939; libr. A. Willemetz and P. Brach, after Ludovic Halévy). His last work was *Barbe-Bleue* (1943; libr. W. Aguet).

Ice Break, The

Opera in three acts by Tippett. 1st perf. London, 7 July 1977; libr. by the composer. Principal roles: Lev (bar), Nadia (sop), Yuri (bar), Hannah (mezzo), Gayle (sop), Olympion (ten), Luke (ten). Discussing contemporary issues such as race relations and political imprisonment, it deals with the submerging of personality and the need for rebirth.

Plot: an American airport. Lev arrives in America after 20 years in a prison camp to join his wife Nadia and their son Yuri. Also at the airport is the fan club of the black champion, Olympion, led by Yuri's girlfriend Gayle and her black friend Hannah. Violent tensions develop in the crowd, and between individuals, and a race riot breaks out in which Olympion and Gayle are killed and Yuri is seriously injured. After treatment by the doctor Luke, Yuri, released from his plasters, is reconciled with his father.

Ich baue ganz

Tenor aria for Belmonte in Act III of Mozart's *Die Entführung aus dem Serail*.

Idamante

Soprano trouser-role in Mozart's *Idomeneo*. He is Idomeneo's son. The role is often sung by either a tenor or a mezzo.

Idomeneo, Rè di Creta

(Idomeneus, King of Crete)
Opera in three acts by Mozart (K 366). 1st perf. Munich, 29 Jan 1781; libr. by Giambattista Varesco, after Antoine Danchet's libretto for Campra's *Idomenée*. Principal roles: Idomeneo (ten), Idamante (sop), Ilia (sop), Electra (sop), Arbace (ten), Voice of Neptune (bass), High Priest (bar). Mozart's first undisputed masterpiece, it remained virtually unperformed for many years, but in recent decades has become the earliest of Mozart's operas to win a permanent place in the repertory. Despite its static nature as an opera seria, it is intensely dramatic and

contains some of the composer's greatest music.

Plot: Crete. While returning home from the Trojan War, Idomeneo is threatened by a storm at sea and, in exchange for his safety, has promised Neptune that he will sacrifice the first person he meets on landing. This turns out to be his son Idamante, who is in love with the Trojan captive Ilia. The appalled Idomeneo attempts to circumvent his vow by accepting Arbace's advice that Idamante should take the princess Electra home to Argos. Another storm delays the departure and a sea monster ravages the coasts of Crete. Idamante kills the monster and, learning of his father's vow, offers himself for sacrifice. The Voice of Neptune intervenes, however, decreeing that Idamante shall reign in Idomeneo's stead with Ilia as his bride. Electra, who loves Idamante, collapses distraught. [R]

I dreamt that I dwelt in marble halls
Soprano aria for Arline in Act II of Balfe's *The Bohemian Girl*.

I got plenty o' nuttin'
Bass aria for Porgy in Act I of Gershwin's *Porgy and Bess*.

I have attained the highest power
Bass monologue for Boris in Act II of Moussorgsky's *Boris Godunov*.

Il
Titles beginning with the Italian definite article are listed under the letter of the first main word. For example, *Il Trovatore* is listed under T.

Ilia
Soprano role in Mozart's *Idomeneo*.

The daughter of Priam, she is a Trojan captive loved by Idamante.

Illica, Luigi *(1857–1919)*
Italian playwright and librettist. He wrote, often in collaboration with others, some 80 libretti. He provided texts for Alfano (*La Fonte di Enschir* and *Il Principe Zilah*), Catalani (*La Wally*), d'Erlanger (*Tess*), Franchetti (*Cristoforo Colombo* and *Germania*), Giordano (*Andrea Chénier* and *Siberia*), Gnecchi (*Cassandra* and *Giuditta*), Mascagni (*Le Maschere*, *Iris* and *Isabeau*), Mascheroni (*Lorenza* and *La Perugina*), Montemezzi (*Hellera*), Panizza (*Aurora*), Puccini (*Manon Lescaut, La Bohème, Madama Butterfly* and *Tosca*), Smareglia (*Il Vassallo di Szigeth*) and Vittadini (*Il Mare di Tiberiade*).

Ilosfalvy, Róbert *(b 1927)*
Hungarian tenor. Possessing a well-schooled and intelligently used voice, he was originally associated with Italian lyric roles but later turned successfully to heavier roles such as Walther von Stolzing.

Imeneo
Opera in three acts by Handel. 1st perf. London, 22 Nov 1740; librettist unknown. Principal roles: Imeneo (bar), Tirinto (mezzo), Rosmene (sop), Clomiri (sop), Argenio (bass). Handel's penultimate Italian opera, it was a failure at its appearance and is nowadays only very rarely performed.

Immolation Scene
The final part of Act III of Wagner's *Götterdämmerung*, in which Brünnhilde lights Siegfried's funeral pyre.

Immortal Hour, The
Opera in two acts by Boughton. 1st

perf. Glastonbury, 26 Aug 1914; libr. by Fiona Macleod (William Sharp). Principal roles: Etain (sop), Midir (ten), Eochaidh (bar), Dalua (bass), Manus (bass). Boughton's finest opera, written in Wagnerian style, it was sensationally successful at its appearance but is nowadays only very rarely performed.

Plot: Dalua, the Lord of Shadow, allows the mortal King Eochaidh to marry the fairy princess Etain. A year later, the fairy prince Midir comes to claim Etain and she accompanies him to the Land of Heart's Desire. Eochaidh falls dead at Dalua's touch. [R]

Imogene

Soprano role in Bellini's *Il Pirata*. Married to Ernesto, she loves the pirate Gualtiero.

Impresario

See **Schauspieldirektor, Der**

Inaffia l'ugola

Baritone aria (the Drinking Song) for Iago in Act I of Verdi's *Otello*.

In alt *(Italian for 'in the high')*

A term describing the octave above the top line of the treble stave. The octave higher is *in altissimo*.

In a Well *(V Studni)*

Comic opera in one act by Blodek. 1st perf. Prague, 17 Nov 1867; libr. by Karel Sabina. Principal roles: Veruna (mezzo), Lidunka (sop), Vojtěk (ten), Jánek (bass). The most successful of all Czech comic operas apart from *The Bartered Bride*, it is still very popular in Czechoslovakia but is almost never performed elsewhere.

Plot: The beautiful Lidunka loves Vojtěch, but her mother wants her to wed the rich old farmer Jánek. She consults the local witch, Veruna, who

tells her that she will see the face of her lover in a nearby well on St John's Eve. Jánek overhears and climbs a tree above the well but falls in. During his attempts to get out he startles Lidunka and is disgraced. [R]

Inbal, Eliahu *(b 1936)*

Israeli conductor, particularly associated with the Italian repertory. He has been responsible for the revival of a number of forgotten 19th-century Italian works.

Incontro Improvviso, L' *(The Chance Meeting)*

Opera in three acts by Haydn. 1st perf. Esterháza, 29 Aug 1775; libr. by Karl Friberth. Principal roles: Ali (ten), Rezia (sop), Balkis (sop), Dardane (mezzo), Osmin (bass), Calandro (bar). A typical example of the musical craze of the period for all things Turkish, it is very rarely performed. [R]

Incoronazione di Poppea, L' *(The Coronation of Poppea)*

Opera in prologue and three acts by Monteverdi. 1st perf. Venice, autumn 1642; libr. by Gian Francesco Busenello, after Tacitus's *Annals*. Principal roles: Poppea (mezzo), Nero (ten), Ottavia (mezzo), Ottone (bar), Seneca (bass), Drusilla (sop), Arnalta (mezzo), Valetto (ten). Monteverdi's last, and arguably greatest, stage work, it was the first opera written on an historical rather than a mythological subject. Unperformed for nearly 300 years, it has been regularly performed in recent decades, often in the edition prepared by Raymond Leppard.

Plot: Rome, 62 AD. Returning home to his mistress Poppea, Ottone discovers that she has been appropriated by Nero. Nero's mortified wife, Ottavia, bemoans her fate and is offered solace by the philosopher Seneca. Although the goddess of wisdom has forewarned

Seneca that he may die if he interferes, the philosopher counsels Nero against his plans to divorce Ottavia, and is subsequently ordered by the Emperor to take his own life. When Ottone's attempts at reconciliation with Poppea are rejected, he transfers his attentions to her lady-in-waiting, Drusilla, who is in love with him. Ottavia orders Ottone, under threat of exposure to Nero, to murder Poppea in her sleep. Disguised as Drusilla, he makes the attempt but Poppea wakes up, and Drusilla is charged with the attempted crime. She is condemned to death, whereupon Ottone confesses and they are both exiled. Nero banishes Ottavia and Poppea is crowned empress. [R]

Indes Galantes, Les (The Gallant Indians)

Opera-ballet in prologue and four acts by Rameau. 1st perf. Paris, 23 Aug 1735; libr. by Louis Fuzelier. One of Rameau's greatest successes, still quite often performed, it tells four love stories from different parts of the world. The four self-contained entrées are Le Turc Genereux (The Generous Turk), Les Incas de Pérou (The Incas of Peru), much the finest of the four, Les Fleurs (The Flowers) and Les Sauvages (The Savages), which was added in 1736. [R]

In des Lebens Frühlingstagen

Tenor aria for Florestan in Act II of Beethoven's Fidelio.

Indian Queen, The

Masque in five acts by Purcell. 1st perf. London, 1695; libr. by John Dryden and Robert Howard. Really more of a play with music than a real opera, the music for Act V is by Purcell's brother Daniel. [R]

In diesen heil'gen Hallen

Bass aria for Sarastro in Act II of Mozart's Die Zauberflöte.

Indy, Vincent d' (1851–1931)

French composer. He wrote six stage works, all of them now largely forgotten. They are the opéra-comique Attendez-Moi Sous l'Orme (Wait For Me Under the Oak, Paris 11 Feb 1882; libr. J. Prével and R. de Bonnières after Régnard), the Wagnerian Le Chant de la Cloche (Paris 1886; libr. composer after Friedrich von Schiller's Das Lied von der Glocke), Fervaal*, his most successful work, L'Etranger (Brussels 7 Jan 1903; libr. composer), La Légende de St Christophe (Paris 9 June 1920; libr. composer, after J. de Voragine's Golden Legend) and the operetta La Rêve de Cinyras (Paris 10 June 1927, composed 1923; libr. Xavier de Courville). He also helped to complete the unfinsihed Ghisèle by his teacher Franck.

In einem Waschkert

Baritone/bass duet for Herr Fluth and Falstaff in Act II of Nicolaï's Die Lustigen Weiber von Windsor. One of the finest of all buffo duets.

Infedeltà Delusa, L' (Infidelity Deluded)

Opera in two acts by Haydn. 1st perf. Esterháza, 26 July 1773; libr. by Marco Coltellini. Principal roles: Sandrina (sop), Filippo (ten), Vespina (sop), Nanni (bar), Nencio (ten). After a long period of neglect it has received a number of performances in the last decade.

Plot: Filippo wishes his daughter Sandrina to marry the wealthy young Nencio, but she loves the peasant Nanni, whose sister Vespina loves (and is loved by) Nencio. However, for social advantage, Nencio is prepared to marry Sandrina, and Vespina sets out to prevent this. Disguising herself in turn as a nagging old harridan, a drunken German flunkey, a notary and a nobleman, she causes total confusion and finally manages to transpose the names on the wedding contract so that the true lovers are united. [R]

Infelice, e tu credevi
Bass aria for da Silva in Act I of Verdi's *Ernani*.

In fernem land
Tenor aria for Lohengrin in Act III of Wagner's *Lohengrin*.

Inganno Felice, L' (*The Happy Deceit*)
Comic opera in one act by Rossini. 1st perf. Venice, 8 Jan 1812; libr. by Giuseppe Maria Foppa, after Giovanni Palomba's libretto for Paisiello. Principal roles: Isabella (sop), Batone (bass), Duke Bertrando (ten), Tarabotto (bar). One of Rossini's early little farces, it is still occasionally performed.

Inghilleri, Giovanni (*1894–1959*)
Italian baritone and composer, particularly associated with the Italian repertory. One of the leading Italian baritones of the inter-war period, he created roles in Malipiero's *Giulio Cesare* and Casella's *La Donna Serpente*. He composed one opera, *La Burla*.

Iñigo Gómez, Don
Bass role in Ravel's *L'Heure Espagnole*. He is a banker in love with Concepción.

In mia man
Soprano/tenor duet for Norma and Pollione in Act II of Bellini's *Norma*.

Innsbruck
See Tirolese Landestheater, Innsbruck

In quegli anni
Tenor aria for Don Basilio in Act IV of Mozart's *Le Nozze di Figaro*. It is often cut.

In quelle trine morbide
Soprano aria for Manon in Act II of Puccini's *Manon Lescaut*.

In questa reggia
Soprano aria for Turandot in Act II of Puccini's *Turandot*.

Intendant
The title of the administrator of a German or Austrian opera house.

Interlude
In opera, an orchestral piece between two scenes, such as the Storm Interlude in Britten's *Peter Grimes*.

Intermezzo
The term has two meanings in opera:

(1) A short, self-contained and usually comic work placed between the acts of an 18th-century Italian opera seria. Much the most famous is Pergolesi's *La Serva Padrona*. The form has also been used more recently for specific dramatic purposes, as for example in Henze's *The Bassarids*.

(2) A short orchestral piece played between two scenes. Mascagni wrote famous examples in *Cavalleria Rusticana* and *L'Amico Fritz*.

Intermezzo
Opera in two acts by Richard Strauss (Op 72). 1st perf. Dresden, 4 Nov 1924; libr. by the composer. Principal

roles: Christine (sop), Robert (bar), Baron Lummer (ten), Anna (sop). Based on incidents in his own married life, it has never been one of Strauss' more popular works and is only infrequently performed.

Plot: Vienna and Grundlsee, 1920s. The composer Robert Storch is permanently castigated by his shrewish wife Christine because he is too mild to stand up to her. She flirts with the young Baron Lummer but threatens divorce when she opens a passionate love letter accidentally addressed to her husband. The misunderstanding is cleared up, but Christine is appeased only when Robert is finally driven to upbraid her. [R]

Intolleranza (Intolerance)

Opera in two acts by Nono. 1st perf. (as Intolleranza 1960) Venice, 13 April 1961; libr. by the composer after A. M. Ripellino. Revised version, 1st perf. Florence, 1974; libr. revised by J. Karsunke. Principal roles: Emigrant (ten), Companion (sop), Tortured Man (bass). Nono's first opera, which has exercised considerable influence on the younger generation of Italian composers, it is a condemnation – written from Nono's customary extreme left-wing political stance – of the indifference and intolerance of the modern world. Its stormy première was one of the most notorious in modern operatic history, provoking a major political riot orchestrated by the Neo-Fascist Ordine Nuovo.

Intonation

A term describing whether or not a singer remains at the correct pitch, neither sharp nor flat, in other words, stays in tune.

Intrusive H

A vocal fault mainly found in long runs on one syllable. An effect of 'ha-ha-ha' rather than 'a-a-a' is produced because the singer has started each note with an unvocalised breath.

In uomini

Soprano aria for Despina in Act I of Mozart's Così fan Tutte.

Invano, Alvaro

Tenor/baritone duet for Don Alvaro and Don Carlo in Act IV of Verdi's La Forza del Destino.

Invisible City of Kitezh, The

The opera's full title is The Legend of the Invisible City of Kitezh and the Maiden Fevronia (Skazaniye o Nevidimon Grade Kitezhe i Devie Fevronie). Opera in four acts by Rimsky-Korsakov. 1st perf. St Petersburg, 20 Feb 1907; libr. by Vladimir Ivanovich Belsky, after Alexander Pushkin. Principal roles: Prince Vsevelod (ten), Fevronia (sop), Grishka (ten). One of Rimsky's finest operas, notable for its superb orchestration and for the characterisation of the drunken Grishka, it combines two legends: that of St Fevronia and that of the rescue of Kitezh from the Tartars. Regularly performed in Russia, it is only very rarely heard elsewhere.

Plot: Miraculous invisibility saves Kitezh from the Tartars, but Fevronia, the wife of Prince Vsevelod, is captured. Grishka helps her to escape and she is guided through a magic forest back to Kitezh by the spirit of Vsevelod. [R]

Iolanta

Opera in nine scenes by Tchaikovsky (Op 69). 1st perf. St Petersburg, 18 Dec 1892; libr. by Modest Tchaikovsky, after Henrik Hertz's Kong Renés Datter. Principal roles: Iolanta (sop),

Vaudemont (ten), Robert (bar), King René (bass), Ibn Hakia (bar), Martha (mezzo). Tchaikovsky's last opera, it has never been one of his more popular works and is only infrequently performed outside Russia.

Plot: 15th-century Provence. Iolanta, the daughter of King René, is unaware that she is blind. The doctor Ebn-Hakia tells the King that she can be cured only if she is conscious of her blindness and wants to see, but the king will not have her told. Vaudemont, to whom she was engaged as a child, arrives, falls in love with her, and describes the beauties of the world to her. The King threatens him with death, but her sight is restored and the couple are betrothed. [R]

Iolanthe
or The Peer and the Peri

Operetta in two acts by Sullivan. 1st perf, London, 25 Nov 1882; libr. by W. S. Gilbert. Principal roles: Lord Chancellor (bar), Phyllis (sop), Fairy Queen (cont), Earls Mountarrarat and Tolloller (b-bar and ten), Strephon (bar), Iolanthe (mezzo), Private Willis (bass), Celia (sop), Leila (sop). One of the best-loved of the Savoy Operas, which enjoyed an initial run of nearly 400 performances, it is a satire on the House of Lords and also contains some of Sullivan's finest music.

Plot: Strephon, son of a mortal father and the fairy Iolanthe, loves the shepherdess Phyllis, a ward of court. Iolanthe, exiled for marrying a mortal, is pardoned by the Fairy Queen and the Queen promises Strephon her protection. The entire House of Lords wishes to marry Phyllis, and the Lord Chancellor forbids Strephon to see her. Phyllis overhears Strephon talking to Iolanthe and thinks him unfaithful – nobody believes that the young-looking woman is his mother. Strephon calls on the Fairy Queen for aid and it is

decided that Strephon is to enter Parliament, where the members will vote as he wants on all measures because of his fairy powers, and that the peerage is to be thrown open to competitive examination. Phyllis, having turned to Earls Mountarrarat and Tolloller, is wretched, and forgives Strephon when she discovers the truth that he is only half a mortal. Iolanthe pleads Strephon's case to the Lord Chancellor and when he remains unmoved reveals that she is his wife whom he thought long dead. All objection to Strephon and Phyllis marrying is thus removed and the fairies all marry the peers. [R]

Io morrò
Baritone aria for Rodrigo in Act IV of Verdi's *Don Carlos*.

Iopas
Tenor role in Berlioz's *Les Troyens*. He is Dido's court poet.

Io son l'umile ancella
Soprano aria for Adriana in Act I of Cilea's *Adriana Lecouvrer*.

Io son rico
Soprano/bass duet (the Barcarolle) for Adina and Dr Dulcamara in Act II of Donizetti's *L'Elisir d'Amore*.

Iphigenia in Aulide
Works based on Euripides' play (often by way of Jean-Baptiste Racine's version) include:

(1) *Ifigenia in Aulide*. Opera by D. Scarlatti. 1st perf. Rome, 11 Jan 1713; libr. by C. S. Capece.

(2) *Ifigenia in Aulide*. Opera by Caldara. 1st perf. Vienna, 1718; libr. by Apostolo Zeno.

(3) *Ifigenia in Aulide*. Opera by

Porpora. 1st perf. London, 3 May 1735; libr. by Paolo Antonio Rolli.

(4) *Iphigenia in Aulide*. Opera by Graun. 1st perf. Berlin, 13 Dec 1748; libr. by Frederick the Great and Villati.

(5) *Ifigenia in Aulide*. Opera by Jommelli. 1st perf. Rome, 9 Feb 1751; libr. by M. Verazi.

(6) *Iphigénie en Aulide*. Opera in three acts by Gluck. 1st perf. Paris, 19 April 1774; libr. by Bailli Leblanc du Roullet. Principal roles: Iphigénie (sop), Agamemnon (bar), Achilles (ten), Clytemnestra (mezzo), Calchas (bass). One of Gluck's finest works, even if a little below the level of his other *Iphigénie*, it is still performed quite often, sometimes in the edition prepared by Wagner in 1846.

Plot: Having vowed to sacrifice his daughter Iphigenia in return for a favourable wind to Troy, Agamemnon is beset by remorse. When Iphigenia and her mother Clytemnestra arrive (believing the girl has come to marry Achilles), he attempts to circumvent the sacrifice demanded by the high priest Calchas. Meanwhile Achilles, enraged at the proposed killing of his betrothed, heads an attack on the Greeks, but Calchas announces that the gods have decided to grant a fair wind without the sacrifice. [R]

(7) *Ifigenia in Aulide*. Opera by Zingarelli. 1st perf. Milan, 27 Jan 1787; libr. by F. Moretti.

(8) *Iphigenia in Aulide*. Opera in three acts by Cherubini. 1st perf. Turin, 12 Jan 1788; libr. by F. Moretti.

Iphigenia In Tauride

Works based on Euripides' play include:

(1) *Iphigénie en Tauride*. Opera by Campra. 1st perf. Paris, 6 May 1704; libr. by J. F. Duché de Vancy and Antoine Danchet.

(2) *Ifigenia in Tauri*. Opera by D. Scarlatti. 1st perf. Rome, 15 Feb 1713; libr. by C. S. Capece.

(3) *Ifigenia in Tauride*. Opera in three acts by Traetta. 1st perf. Vienna, 4 Oct 1763; libr. by Marco Coltellini.

(4) *Ifigenia in Tauride*. Opera by Jommelli. 1st perf. Naples, 30 May 1771; libr. by M. Verazi.

(5) *Iphigénie en Tauride*. Opera in four acts by Gluck. 1st perf. Paris, 18 May 1779; libr. by Nicolas François Guillard. Principal roles: Iphigénie (sop), Oreste (bar), Pylade (ten), Thoas (b-bar), Diana (mezzo). Gluck's greatest work and one of the greatest of all operas, it is still quite regularly performed, but not as frequently as its outstanding musico-dramatic merits deserve.

Plot: After the Trojan War, on the islands of Tauris, Iphigenia has become a priestess of Diana and is unaware of her father's murder by her mother and the revenge taken by her brother Oreste. Oreste and his companion, Pylade, arrive incognito and are captured, and the Scythian king, Thoas, orders them to be sacrificed. Oreste gives Iphigenia the news of her parents' death, but also says that Oreste is dead. Iphigenia wishes to save him, but he – pursued by the Furies – persuades her to save Pylade instead. Just as the sacrifice is about to take place, brother and sister recognise each other and Diana appears with a pardon for Oreste. [R]

(6) *Iphigénie en Tauride*. Opera by Piccinni. 1st perf. Paris, 23 Jan 1781; libr. by A. du Congé Dubreuil. Principal roles: Iphigénie (mezzo), Oreste (bass), Pylade (ten). As a result of the famous feud between the supporters of Gluck and Piccinni, an enterprising impresario had them both set the same story. Piccinni's version contains some fine music, but both the contemporary public and history decided in favour of Gluck.

Ippolitov-Ivanov, Mikhail
(1859–1935)

Russian composer and conductor. He wrote seven operas, all of them now forgotten. They include *Ruth* (1887; libr. after the Old Testament), *Azra* (1890), *Asya* (1900; libr. after Ivan Turgenev), *Treachery* (1910; libr. after A. I. Sumbatov), *Ole the Norseman* (1916) and *The Last Barricade* (1933; libr. after N. A. Krasheninikov). He also prepared Moussorgsky's unfinished *The Marriage* for performance and conducted the first performances of Rimsky-Korsakov's *The Tale of Tsar Sultan* and *The Tsar's Bride*.

Ireland

See Dublin Grand Opera Society; Opera Northern Ireland; Wexford Festival

Irene

(1) Soprano role in Wagner's *Rienzi*. She is Rienzi's sister. (2) Mezzo role in Donizetti's *Belisario*. She is Belisario's daughter. (3) Mezzo role in Handel's *Tamerlano*. (4) Mezzo role in Handel's *Atalanta*.

Iris

Opera in three acts by Mascagni. 1st perf. Rome, 22 Nov 1898; libr. by Luigi Illica. Principal roles: Iris (sop), Osaka (ten), Kyoto (bar), Il Cieco (bass). A brutal and unpleasant verismo story, it met with considerable success at its appearance and is still occasionally performed.

Plot: 19th-century Japan. When the pure girl, Iris, whom he loves, cannot be persuaded to reciprocate his feelings, Osaka arranges for the brothel keeper, Kyoto, to abduct her and hold her captive in the brothel. Her blind father, Il Cieco, believing that she has gone there voluntarily, curses her and flings mud at her, driving her to drown herself in a sewer. [R]

Irische Legende *(Irish Legend)*

Opera in five scenes by Egk. 1st perf. Salzburg, 17 Aug 1955; libr. by the composer, after William Butler Yeats's *The Countess Cathleen*. Principal roles: Cathleen (sop), Aleen (bass), Oona (mezzo). It has met with success in German-speaking countries but is little known elsewhere.

Plot: Ireland in the future. The Devil has brought about a famine and people sell their souls to him in exchange for food. The poet Aleen is abducted by demons and his lover, Countess Cathleen, offers to sell her soul to redeem him. However, she is saved and rises to heaven.

Iris hence away

Mezzo aria for Juno in Act II of Handel's *Semele*.

Irish opera composers

See Balfe; Stanford; Wallace

Other national opera composers include Augusta Holmès (1847–1903), Robert O'Dwyer, whose *Eithne* (1910) was the first opera written in Erse, and Geoffrey Palmer.

Irmelin

Opera in three acts by Delius. 1st perf. Oxford, 4 May 1953 (composed 1892); libr. by the composer. Principal roles: Irmelin (sop), Nils (ten). Delius' first opera, it is very rarely performed.

Plot: The Princess Irmelin seeks true love. The Prince Nils, disguised as a swineherd, is in search of the ideal woman and is told that he will find her at the end of the silver stream. He goes there and discovers Irmelin. [R]

Isabeau

Opera in three acts by Mascagni. 1st perf. Buenos Aires, 2 June 1911; libr. by Luigi Illica. Principal roles: Isabeau (sop), Folco (ten), King Raimondo (bar), Giglietta (mezzo). Moderately successful in its time, this version of the Lady Godiva story is nowadays only very rarely performed.

Plot: As a punishment for refusing to choose a husband, King Raimondo orders his daughter Isabeau to ride naked through the streets at noon. The people pass a law that anyone daring to look at her shall be put to death. The law is disobeyed by the young woodsman Folco. Isabeau, now in love with him, vainly tries to prevent his being lynched by the mob and then kills herself over his dying body. [R Exc]

Isabella

(1) Mezzo role in Rossini's *L'Italiana in Algieri*. The Italian girl of the opera's title, she loves Lindoro. (2) Soprano role in Suppé's *Boccaccio*. (3) Soprano role in Martín y Soler's *Una Cosa Rara*. (4) Soprano role in Wagner's *Das Liebesverbot*. She is a novice. (5) Soprano role in Meyerbeer's *Robert le Diable*. She is a Sicilian princess loved by Robert. (6) Soprano role in Rossini's *L'Inganno Felice*. (7) Soprano role in Donizetti's *L'Assedio di Calais*. She is Edward III's wife.

Isabella, Queen

Queen Isabella I of Spain (1451–1504) appears in a number of operas, including soprano role in (1) Milhaud's *Christophe Colomb*. (2) de Falla's *L'Atlántida*. (3) Offenbach's *Christopher Columbus*.

Ishmael

Tenor role in Verdi's *Nabucco*. An Israelite, he loves Nabucco's daughter Fenena.

Isis

Opera in prologue and five acts by Lully. 1st perf. Paris, 5 Jan 1677; libr. by Philippe Quinault. One of Lully's most successful works, it is still occasionally performed. [R Exc]

Isola Disabitata, L' (*The Uninhabited Island*)

Opera in two acts by Haydn. 1st perf. Esterháza, 6 Dec 1770; libr. by Pietro Metastasio. Principal roles: Costanza (mezzo), Gernando (ten), Silvia (sop), Enrico (bar). It is very infrequently performed.

Plot: Gernando, his wife Costanza, and her sister Silvia are shipwrecked on an island and Gernando is captured by pirates. After 13 years Costanza is convinced that Gernando has deserted her and teaches Silvia that all men are hateful. Freed at last, Gernando arrives with his friend Enrico, whom Silvia observes in wonder. Gernando believes Costanza dead and is comforted by Enrico, but Silvia, now in love with Enrico, reports that she is alive. Costanza and Gernando finally meet, and after some suspicions Costanza is assured of his fidelity. [R]

Isolde

Soprano role in Wagner's *Tristan und Isolde*. She is an Irish queen betrothed to King Mark of Cornwall.

Isolier

Mezzo trouser-role in Rossini's *Le Comte Ory*. He is Ory's page.

Isouard, Nicolò (*sometimes known simply as Nicolò*) (1775–1818)

Maltese composer. He wrote some 40 operas, a number of which enjoyed considerable success in their time but which are all now forgotten. The most important include *Artaserse* (Livorno 1794; libr. Pietro Metastasio), *Le Tonnelier* (Paris 17 May 1801; libr. E. J. B. Delrieu and F. A. Quétant), *Cendrillon* (Paris 22 Feb 1810; libr. Charles-Guillaume Etienne, after Charles Perrault), *Joconde* (Paris 28 Feb 1814; libr. Etienne) and *Jeannot et Colin* (Paris 17 Oct 1814; libr. Étienne), perhaps his finest work.

Israel
See Hebrew National Opera

Israeli opera composers
See Tal

Other national opera composers include Menachem Avidom (*b* 1908) and Ami Mayani (*b* 1936).

It ain't necessarily so
Tenor aria for Sportin' Life in Act II of Gershwin's *Porgy and Bess*.

Italiana in Algieri, L' (*The Italian Girl in Algiers*)
Comic opera in two acts by Rossini. 1st perf. Venice, 22 May 1813; libr. by Angelo Anelli. Principal roles: Isabella (mezzo), Lindoro (ten), Mustafà (bass), Taddeo (bar), Ali (bass), Elvira (sop), Zulma (mezzo). Rossini's first great comic success, it remains one of the finest and most popular of all opera buffas, rich in humour, melody and florid arias.

Plot: Algiers. The Bey Mustafà is bored with his wife Elvira and tells Ali, the captain of his corsairs, to find him a European wife. The Italian Isabella, searching for her lover, Lindoro, held captive by the Bey, is shipwrecked along with her ever-hopeful elderly admirer Taddeo, and is brought to Mustafà. He is captivated by her and

Isabella devises a plan to gain everyone's freedom. She flirts with Mustafà, and Lindoro and Taddeo initiate him into the brotherhood of the Pappatachi, who must eat and remain silent. Isabella, Lindoro and all escape in a ship from under the Bey's nose, he believing that this is just a test of his fidelity to his vow. Their departure returns him to the arms of Elvira, and all ends happily. [R]

Italianate
A term used to describe singing which is in the lyrical and full-bodied style usually associated with Italian opera. It is used mainly in reference to non-Italian works and non-Italian singers where such singing is unusual and comes as a welcome surprise. An example is Alberto Remedios' singing of Siegfried.

Italian opera composers
See Albinoni; Alfano; Anfossi; Arditi; Banfield; Bellini; Berio; Boccherini; Boito; Bononcini; Busoni; Busotti; Caccini; Cagnoni; Caldara; Carafa; Casella; Castlenuovo-Tedesco; Catalani; de Cavalieri; Cavalli; Cesti; Chailly; Cherubini; Cilea; Cimarosa; Coccia; Dallapiccola; Denza; Donizetti; Duni; Faccio; Feo; Ferrari-Trecate; Fioravanti; Franchetti; Frazzi; Gagliano; Galuppi; Gasparini; Gazzaniga; Generali; Ghedini; Giordano; Gnecchi; Gobatti; Guglielmi; Jommelli; Lattuada; Leo; Leoncavallo; Leoni; Lualdi; Maderna; Malipiero; Mancinelli; Marchetti; Mascagni; Mayr; Mercadante; Montemezzi; Monteverdi; Morlacchi; Mortari;

Napoli; Nono; Orefice; Pacini;
Paer; Paisiello; Pavesi;
Pergolesi; Peri; Petrassi;
Petrella; Piccinni; Pizzetti;
Ponchielli; Porpora; Puccini;
Refice; Respighi; F. Ricci; L.
Ricci; Rinaldo di Capua; Rocca;
Rossellini; Rossi; Rossini; Rota;
Sacchini; Salieri; Sarti; A.
Scarlatti; D. Scarlatti; Smareglia;
Spontini; Stradella; Tosatti;
Traetta; Uttini; Vaccai; Vecchi;
Veracini; Verdi; Veretti; Viozzi;
Vittadini; Vivaldi; Wolf-Ferrari;
Zafred; Zandonai; Zingarelli

Italian Straw Hat, The
See Cappello di Paglia di
Firenze, Il

Italian Tenor
Tenor role in (1) Richard Strauss' *Der
Rosenkavalier*. (2) Strauss' *Capriccio*.

Italy
See Festival of Two Worlds,
Spoleto; Florentine Camerata;
Maggio Musicale Fiorentino;
Pesaro Festival; La Piccola
Scala, Milan; Teatro alla Scala,
Milan; Teatro Carlo Felice,
Genoa; Teatro Communale,
Bologna; Teatro Communale,
Florence; Teatro Communale
Giuseppe Verdi, Trieste; Teatro
dell'Opera, Rome; Teatro
Donizetti, Bergamo; Teatro la
Fenice, Venice; Teatro Massimo,
Palermo; Teatro Massimo
Bellini, Catania; Teatro
Municipale, Reggio Emilia;
Teatro Petruzzelli, Bari; Teatro
Regio, Parma; Teatro Regio,
Turin; Teatro San Carlo, Naples;
Verona Arena

Ite sul colle
Bass aria for Oroveso in Act I of
Bellini's *Norma*.

Ivan IV
Opera in five acts by Bizet. 1st perf.
Tübingen, 1946 (composed 1862); libr.
by François-Hippolyte Leroy and Henri
Trianon. Principal roles: Ivan (bar),
Marie (sop), Igor (ten), Temrouk (b-
bar), Yorloff (bass), Young Bulgarian
(ten). Bizet's only grand opera and
telling of events in the reign of Ivan the
Terrible (1547–84), it contains much
fine music but is almost never
performed. Bizet incorporated some of
the music into later works. [R Exc]

Ivanhoe
Opera in four acts by Sullivan. 1st perf.
London, 31 Jan 1891; libr. by Julian
Russell Sturgis, after Sir Walter Scott's
novel. Principal roles: Ivanhoe (ten),
Bois-Guilbert (bar), Rowena (sop),
Rebecca (sop), King Richard (bass),
Friar Tuck (bar), Ulrica (cont), Cedric
(bar). Sullivan's only opera, it contains
some fine music and intermittent
moments of dramatic power, but the
overall effect is cold and uninteresting.
Reasonably successful at its appearance
(it enjoyed an initial run of 160
consecutive performances), it is
nowadays almost never performed.

Plot: Ivanhoe and King Richard I
return in disguise from the Third
Crusade to rescue England from
misrule. At a tournament, Ivanhoe
defeats the templar Brian de Bois-
Guilbert. The templar abducts Rowena,
daughter of the Saxon Cedric, and
makes an attempt on the honour of
Rebecca, daughter of Isaac of York.
Rebecca escapes and nurses the
wounded Ivanhoe back to health whilst

Richard leads Friar Tuck and the men of Sherwood against the templar and burns his castle. Richard persuades Cedric to consent to Rowena's marriage to Ivanhoe. Ivanhoe fights the templar for the hand of Rowena (who has been unjustly accused of witchcraft) and kills him.

Ivan Susanin
See Life for the Tsar, A

Ivan the Terrible
See Maid of Pskov, The

Ivogün, Maria *(b Ilse Kempner) (1891–1987)*
Hungarian soprano, particularly associated with coloratura roles, especially Zerbinetta. She created Ighino in *Palestrina* and was later a noted teacher, whose pupils included Elisabeth Schwartzkopf and Rita Streich. Married first to the tenor Karl Erb* and later to the pianist Michael Raucheisen.

Ivrogne Corrigé, L' *(The Reformed Drunkard)*
Comic opera in two acts by Gluck. 1st perf. Vienna, April 1760; libr. by Louis Anseaume after Jean de la Fontaine's *The Drunkard in Hell*. It is the only one of Gluck's early comic operas which is still occasionally performed.

J

Jack
Tenor role in Tippett's *The Midsummer Marriage*. He is in love with Bella.

Jacobs, Arthur *(b 1922)*
British critic and musicologist. One of the most perceptive and scholarly of contemporary British critics, his writings include the Penguin *Dictionary of Music* and a biography of Sullivan. A champion of opera in English, he has made some 20 translations and also wrote the libretto for Maw's *One Man Show*.

Jacquino
Tenor role in Beethoven's *Fidelio*. The porter, he is in love with Marzelline.

Jagd, Die *(The Hunt)*
Opera in three acts by Hiller. 1st perf. Leipzig, 29 Jan 1770; libr. by Christian Felix Weisse, after C. Colle's *La Partie de Chasse de Henri IV* and Jean-Marie Sedaine's *Le Roi et le Fermier*. Hiller's finest work and the archetypal early Singspiel, it was one of the most popular of all operas in Germany in the late 18th and early 19th centuries. It is nowadays forgotten.

J'ai des yeux
Bass aria for Coppélius in the Olympia Act of Offenbach's *Les Contes d'Hoffmann*.

Jakobín *(The Jacobin)*
Opera in three acts by Dvořák (Op 84). 1st perf. Prague, 12 Feb 1889; libr. by Marie Červinková-Riegrová. Principal roles: Jiří (ten), Terinka (sop), Bohuš (bar), Benda (ten), Filip (bass), Julie (mezzo), Count Vilém (bass), Adolf (bar). One of Dvořák's most attractive scores, notable for the delightful characterisation of the schoolmaster Benda, it is only infrequently performed outside Czechoslovakia.

Plot: a Czech village, 1793. Bohuš, the son of Count Vilém, returns from France with his wife Julie and learns that he is about to be replaced as heir by his cousin Adolf. Bohuš is arrested as a Jacobin, but Julie (with the help of the schoolteacher Benda) succeeds in changing the Count's mind. [R]

Janáček, Leos *(1854–1928)*
Czech composer. His nine operas, which inhabit a sound world unlike that of any other composer, contain much of his greatest music. Born in Brno and spending most of his life there, he lived and worked outside the mainstream of European music, whose developments influenced him hardly at all. Long considered a minor provincial composer, he was unknown outside Brno until 1916, when the Prague production of *Jenůfa* made him famous in the country at large; his international fame and status date only from recent decades. His operas are characterised by an intense humanism, a deep feeling for nature and its sounds, an almost total disregard for traditional dramatic values, a vocal line largely dictated by the values of Czech speech rhythms, intense lyricism, and by harmonies and orchestration which might best be described as 'spikey'.

His first opera *Šárka** gives sporadic indications of what was to come, but its successor, *The Beginnings of a Romance**, is in traditional Czech style. It is in *Jenůfa**, the most popular and accessible of his mature operas, that he found his true voice. His later operas, for each of which he wrote his own libretto, are the semi-autobiographical *Fate** (*Osud*), the historico-surrealist comedy *The Excursions of Mr Brouček**, the Ostrovskian *Káťa Kabanová**, the nature-inspired *The Cunning Little Vixen**, and *The Macropolus Case**. His last, overwhelmingly powerful masterpiece, the Dostoyevskian *From the House of the Dead**, was produced posthumously.

For many years, *Jenůfa* was Janáček's only work to be regularly performed internationally, but in the last 25 years all of his mature operas have won a permanent place in the repertory. This has been especially the case in Britain, where he has now become one of the most frequently performed of all opera composers. This has arisen as a result of the single-handed championship of his works by Sir Charles Mackerras, the finest contemporary interpreter of his music.

Jánek

(1) Tenor role in Janáček's *The Macropolus Case*. Jaroslav Prus' son, he is in love with Kristina. (2) Bass role in Blodek's *In a Well*. He is a rich old farmer.

Janků, Hana

See Svobodová-Janků, Hana

Janowitz, Gundula *(b 1937)*

German soprano, particularly associated with Mozart and Strauss roles. She is an intelligent singer with a full, rich voice, but sometimes appears a little cool and distant on stage.

Janowski, Marek *(b 1940)*

Polish conductor, particularly associated with Wagner operas. He was musical director of the Freiburg Opera (1973–74) and the Dortmund Stadttheater (1975–79).

Japan

See Nikikai Opera Company; Tokyo Chamber Opera Group

Japanese opera composers

These include Yasushi Akutagawa (1925–89), Sadao Bekku (*b* 1922), Ikuma Dan (*b* 1924), Kunio Todo (*b* 1915) and Kosaku Yamada (1886–1965).

Järnefelt, Armas *(1869–1958)*

Finnish conductor and composer. Particularly associated with Wagner operas, he was musical director of the Royal Opera, Stockholm and artistic director of the Finnish National Opera (1932–36). His first wife was the soprano Maikki Pakarinen (1871–1929); his second wife Liva Edström (1876–1971) was a successful mezzo.

Järvi, Neeme *(b 1927)*

Estonian conductor, particularly associated with the Russian repertory. He was musical director of the Estonian Opera Theatre from 1963 until he left the USSR. Since then, his operatic appearances have been infrequent.

Jason

The Greek mythological hero appears in a number of operas, including: (1) Tenor role in Cherubini's *Médée*. (2) Tenor role in Mayr's *Medea in Corinto*.

(3) Baritone role in Křenek's *Der Goldene Bock*.

Jealousy Monologue
Baritone aria ('È sogno?') for Ford in Act II of Verdi's *Falstaff*.

Jean
Tenor role in Massenet's *Le Jongleur de Notre-Dame*. He is the juggler of the opera's title. The role is sometimes sung by a soprano.

Jean de Leyden
Tenor role in Meyerbeer's *Le Prophète*. He is the leader of the Anabaptists.

Jean de Paris
Opera in two acts by Boïeldieu. 1st perf. Paris, 4 April 1812; libr. by Claude Godard d'Aucour de Saint-Just. One of Boïeldieu's most successful operas, it is nowadays all but forgotten.

Plot: The widowed Princess of Navarre is betrothed to the French crown prince. Preparations for her arrival at an inn in the Pyrenees are interrupted by the appearance of the Prince, disguised as Jean de Paris, together with his entourage. Despite the protests of the Princess's Seneschal, they take over the inn, but Jean says that the Princess may stay there. The Princess recognises Jean but plays along with his disguise and, during a dance, tells him that she has already chosen her husband. All is revealed and the two are united.

Jeanne d'Arc au Bûcher (*Joan of Arc at the Stake*)
Dramatic oratorio in prologue and ten scenes by Honegger. 1st perf. Basel, 12 May 1938; libr. by Paul Claudel. Principal roles: Joan (speaker), Friar Dominic (speaker), Virgin Mary (sop), Archbishop Cauchon (ten). Described as

a lyric mystery play, it is Honegger's most frequently performed stage work. Tied to the stake, Joan relives her life and trial at the moment of her death. [R]

Je crois entendre encore
Tenor aria for Nadir in Act I of Bizet's *Les Pêcheurs de Perles*.

Je dis que rien
Soprano aria for Micaëla in Act III of Bizet's *Carmen*.

Jemmy
Soprano trouser-role in Rossini's *Guillaume Tell*. He is Tell's son.

Jenifer
Soprano role in Tippett's *The Midsummer Marriage*. King Fisher's daughter, she is in love with Mark.

Jeník
Tenor role in Smetana's *The Bartered Bride*. He is Mícha's son.

Jenůfa
Opera in three acts by Janáček. 1st perf. Brno, 21 Jan 1904; libr. by the composer, after Gabriela Preissová. Principal roles: Jenůfa (sop), Kostelnička (sop), Laca (ten), Števa Burja (ten), Foreman of the Mill (bar), Mayor (bass), Grandmother Burja (mezzo), Karolka (mezzo), Jano (sop). The opera's official title is *Her Foster-Daughter* (*Její Pastorkyňa*), but *Jenůfa* is always used outside Czechoslovakia. Janáček's first major success, it remains his most frequently performed work.

Plot: Jenůfa, pregnant by the drunken layabout Števa, is afraid that he will become a soldier rather than marry her. Števa's stepbrother Laca also loves Jenůfa and is jealous. Jenůfa's formidable foster-mother, the

Kostelnička (or sexton's wife), is unaware of Jenůfa's condition and rules that there can be no wedding until the drunken Števa has stayed sober for a year. Laca makes advances to Jenůfa, who rebuffs him. He scars her face with his knife but is immediately overwhelmed with remorse. Kostelnička hides Jenůfa until after the birth of her baby, but Števa – now engaged to the Mayor's daughter Karolka – promises nothing beyond financial help. Realising that Laca loves Jenůfa but that the baby stands in the way, Kostelnička drugs Jenůfa and throws the baby into the mill-stream, telling Jenůfa that it died whilst she was delirious. Jenůfa agrees to marry Laca, but on their wedding day a child's body is found under the melting ice and Jenůfa recognises it as hers. She is accused of murder but the penitent Kostelnička confesses, and is forgiven by Jenůfa, who also offers Laca his freedom. Loving her truly, he stands by her. [R]

Jeremiáš, Otakar *(1892–1962)*
Czech composer and conductor. His operas, written in post-Janáček style, include *The Brothers Karamazov* (*Bratři Karamazovi*, Prague 8 Oct 1928; libr. composer and J. Maria, after Fyodor Dostoyevsky) and *Owlglass* (*Enšpígl*, Prague 13 May 1949; libr. J. Maranek, after C. de Coster), a setting of the Till Eulenspiegel legend. He was musical director of the Prague National Theatre (1945–47 and 1948–51). His brother Jaroslav (1889–1919) was also a composer, who wrote one opera *The Old King* (*Starý Král*, Prague 13 April 1919; libr. R. de Gourmont).

Jerger, Alfred *(1889–1976)*
Austrian baritone, particularly associated with Mozart and Strauss roles. Based largely in Vienna, he began as a conductor, later becoming one of the finest Mozartians of the inter-war period. He created Mandryka in *Arabella* and the Man in *Die Glückliche Hand*. He later produced a number of operas and was also a noted teacher, whose pupils included Leonie Rysanek.

Jeritza, Maria *(b Mimi Jedlitzková) (1887–1982)*
Czech soprano. One of the finest singing-actresses of the inter-war period, she was particularly associated with Strauss roles and with Tosca, Thaïs and Carmen. She created the Empress in *Die Frau ohne Schatten*, the title role in both versions of *Ariadne auf Naxos* and Marietta in *Die Tote Stadt*. Her autobiography, *Sunlight and Song*, was published in 1924.

Jerum! Jerum!
Baritone aria (the Cobbling Song) for Hans Sachs in Act II of Wagner's *Die Meistersinger von Nürnberg*.

Jérusalem
See Lombardi, I

Jerusalem, Siegfried *(b 1940)*
German tenor, particularly associated with the German repertory. He began by achieving success in lyric roles such as Tamino, but has recently turned to Wagner although he is by no means a natural heldentenor.

Jessel, Miss
Soprano role in Britten's *The Turn of the Screw*. She is the former governess whose ghost attempts to corrupt Flora.

Jessonda
Opera in three acts by Spohr (Op 63). 1st perf. Kassel, 28 July 1823; libr. by Eduard Heinrich Gehe, after Antoine M. Lemierre's *La Veuve de Malabar*.

Principal roles: Jessonda (sop), Nadori (ten), Amazili (sop), Tristan d'Acunha (bar). Spohr's most successful opera, it is nowadays only very rarely performed.

Plot: India. Custom decrees that Jessonda, the Rajah's widow, must die on her husband's funeral pyre. The young Brahmin priest, Nadori, who must tell her this, falls in love with her sister Amazili and agrees to help save Jessonda. Meanwhile, Jessonda is recognised by her former lover, the Portuguese general d'Acunha, who is besieging Goa. He is unable to attack and rescue her because of a truce, but when he learns that the priest Daudon has broken the truce, he enters the temple by a secret passage and Jessonda is saved.

Je suis Brésilien
Tenor aria for the Brazilian in Act I of Offenbach's *La Vie Parisienne*. It contains some of the composer's fastest patter.

Je vais mourir
Mezzo aria for Dido in Act V of Berlioz's *Les Troyens*.

Je veux vivre
Soprano aria for Juliet in Act I of Gounod's *Roméo et Juliette*.

Jewels of the Madonna, The
See Gioielli della Madonna, I

Jewel Song
Soprano aria ('Ah, je ris') for Marguerite in Act III of Gounod's *Faust*.

Ježibaba
Mezzo role in Dvořák's *Rusalka*. She is a witch.

Jiménez, Jerónimo
See Giménez, Gerónimo

Jirko, Ivan *(b 1926)*
Czech composer and critic (and also a practising psychiatrist). He has written a number of operas which have met with some success in Czechoslovakia. They include *Twelfth Night* (*Večer Třikrálový*, 1964; libr. after Shakespeare), *The Strange Adventure of Arthur Rowe* (*Podivné Dobrodružstvi Arthura Rowa*, 1969; libr. composer, after Graham Greene's *The Ministry of Fear*), *The Millionairess* (*Milionářka*, 1972) and *The Strumpet* (*Devka*, 1974).

Jírovec, Vojtěch *(sometimes Germanised as Adalbert Gyrowetz) (1763–1850)*
Bohemian composer. He wrote 30 operas and singspiels, none of which is remembered today. The most important include *Agnes Sorel* (Vienna 4 Dec 1806), his most successful work, *Der Augenarzt* (*The Optician*, Vienna 1 Oct 1811), *Il Finto Stanislao* (Milan 5 July 1818; libr. Felice Romani, after Alexandre Vincent Pineu-Duval's *Le Faux Stanislas*) and *Hans Sachs im Vorgerückten Alter* (Dresden 1834).

Joan of Aro
See Giovanna d'Arco; Jeanne d'Arc au Bûcher; Maid of Orleans, The

Job
Dramatic oratorio by Dallapiccola. 1st perf. Rome, 30 Oct 1950; libr. by the composer after the Old Testament.

Jobin, Raoul *(1906–74)*
Canadian tenor, particularly associated with the French repertory. He created

Luca in Menotti's *The Island God* and Fabrice in Sauget's *Chartreuse de Parme*. His son André (*b* 1933) is also a tenor.

Jocasta
Oedipus' wife and mother appears in a number of operas, including: (1) Mezzo role in Stravinsky's *Oedipus Rex*. (2) Soprano role in Orff's *Oedipus der Tyrann*.

Jocelyn
Opera in four acts by Godard (Op 100). 1st perf. Brussels, 25 Feb 1888; libr. by P. Armand Silvestre and V. Capone, after Alphonse de Lamartine's poem. Godard's most successful opera, telling of a brother at a seminary tempted by earthly love, it is nowadays remembered only for the tenor's *Berceuse*.

Jochum, Eugen *(1902–87)*
German conductor, particularly associated with Wagner operas. One of the finest 20th-century interpreters of the German classical repertory, he was musical director of the Duisburg Opera (1930–32) and the Hamburg State Opera (1934–45). His brother Georg (1909–70) was also a conductor, who was musical director of the Linz Opera (1940–45).

Johnson, Dick
Tenor role in Puccini's *La Fanciulla del West*. He is the wanted bandit, Ramírez.

Johnson, Edward *(1878–1959)*
Canadian tenor and administrator. Particularly associated with heavier Italian and German roles, he created the title role in Taylor's *Peter Ibbetson*, Ippolito in Pizzetti's *Fedra*, Sir Gower in Hanson's *Merry Mount*, Aethelwold

in Taylor's *The King's Henchman* and roles in Alfano's *L'Ombra di Don Giovanni* and Montemezzi's *La Nave*. He was general manager of the Metropolitan Opera, New York (1935–50).

Jo ho hoe
Soprano aria for Senta in Act I of Wagner's *Der Fliegende Holländer*.

Jokanaan
Baritone role in Richard Strauss' *Salome*. He is John the Baptist.

Jolie Fille de Perth, La *(The Fair Maid of Perth)*
Opera in four acts by Bizet. 1st perf. Paris, 26 Dec 1867; libr. by Jules-Henri Vernoy by Saint-Georges and Jules Adenis, after Sir Walter Scott's novel. Principal roles: Catherine (sop), Henry (ten), Ralph (bar), Duke of Rothsay (bar), Mab (mezzo), Simon (b-bar). A work of great melodic charm, it is seldom performed although the orchestral suite has given the music a wider currency.

Plot: Perth. The armourer Henry Smith loves Catherine Glover. He gives shelter to the gypsy Mab and is then visited by Catherine, her father Simon, and Ralph, who also loves Catherine. The Duke of Rothsay invites Catherine to his castle and asks Mab, his former mistress, to help abduct her. Mab pretends to agree but foils the Duke's machinations and engineers a reconciliation between Catherine and Henry. [R]

Jolivet, André *(1905–74)*
French composer. A member of the 'Jeune France' group, he wrote one opera, the comedy *Dolorès ou Le Miracle de la Femme Laide* (French Radio 1947, composed 1942; libr. H. Ghéon).

Jommelli, Niccolò *(1714–74)*

Italian composer. He wrote 82 operas, of which 29 are lost. They include *L'Errore Amoroso* (Naples 1737; libr. A. Palombo), *Ricimero* (Rome 16 Jan 1740; libr. Apostolo Zeno and Pietro Pariati), *Astianatte* (Rome 4 Feb 1741; libr. Antonio Salvi), *Ezio* (Bologna 29 April 1741; libr. Pietro Metastasio), *Merope* (Venice 26 Dec 1741; libr. Zeno), *Semiramide* (Venice 26 Dec 1742; libr. F. Silvani) and *La Clemenza di Tito* (Stuttgart 30 Aug 1753; libr. Metastasio). None of his operas is remembered today.

Jonathan

The biblical friend of King David appears in a number of operas, including: (1) Tenor role in Handel's *Saul*. (2) Tenor role in Nielsen's *Saul and David*. (3) Soprano trouser-role in M.-A. Charpentier's *David et Jonathas*.

Jones, Della

British mezzo, particularly associated with Rossini, Handel and Mozart roles. The finest Rossini mezzo to have emerged in Britain, she possesses a rich voice of considerable range and remarkable agility and she has a fine stage presence, especially in comedy. She created Dolly in Hamilton's *Anna Karenina*.

Jones, Dame Gwyneth *(b 1936)*

British soprano, particularly associated with Wagner and Strauss roles and, earlier in her career, with Verdi. The finest British dramatic soprano of the postwar era, she has a radiant and powerful voice of seemingly limitless resources. Her voice was afflicted with a serious beat in her middle career, but this has been eradicated. She is a deeply committed singing-actress of great personal beauty.

Jongleur de Notre-Dame, Le *(Our Lady's Juggler)*

Opera in three acts by Massenet. 1st perf. Monte Carlo, 18 Feb 1902; libr. by Maurice Léna, after Anatole France's *L'Étui de Nacre*. Principal roles: Jean (ten), Boniface (b-bar), Prior (bass). Very successful at its appearance, it is nowadays only infrequently performed.

Plot: 14th-century Cluny. The juggler Jean is a novice in an order of monks who utilise their various talents in praise of the Virgin Mary. Jean pays his homage to her in the only way he can: he puts on his costume and does his juggling routine. Apart from the kindly Boniface, the brothers are scandalised, but the statue of the Virgin smiles and blesses him, accepting his offering. [R]

Jonny Spielt Auf *(Johnny Strikes Up)*

Opera in two parts by Křenek (Op 45). 1st perf. Leipzig, 10 Feb 1927; libr. by the composer. Principal roles: Jonny (bar), Anita (sop), Max (ten), Daniello (bass), Yvonne (sop). A jazz-inspired piece, it is Křenek's most successful and enduring work.

Plot: The lives of four musicians intertwine: the opera singer Anita, the jazz-band leader Jonny, the composer Max and the violin virtuoso Daniello. Jonny steals Daniello's violin and becomes the world's greatest living player, setting all the world dancing the Charleston with his performance from the North Pole. [R]

Joplin, Scott *(1868–1917)*

American composer. He wrote two rag-time operas: *A Guest of Honour* (composed *c* 1905; libr. composer) and

Treemonisha (Houston May 1975, composed 1911; libr. composer) [R].

José, Don
(1) Tenor role in Bizet's *Carmen*. He is a soldier in love with Carmen. (2) Bass role in Delius' *Koanga*. He is a plantation owner. (3) Baritone role in Goossens' *Don Juan de Mañara*.

Joseph
Opera in three acts by Méhul. 1st perf. Paris, 17 Feb 1807; libr. by Alexandre Duval, after the Old Testament. Principal roles: Joseph (ten), Jacob (bar). Méhul's finest and most successful opera, it is nowadays almost never performed.

Plot: Joseph, under the assumed name of Cleophas, has saved Egypt from famine. His brothers and his blind father Jacob arrive in Memphis seeking food, but do not recognise Joseph. Joseph reveals his identity, pardons his brothers and begs his father to do the same.

Joubert, John *(b 1927)*
South African composer. He has written six operas: the radio opera *Antigone* (BBC 1954; libr. R. Trickett, after Sophocles), *In the Drought* (Johannesburg 1956; libr. A. Wood), *Silas Marner* (Cape Town 1961; libr. Trickett, after George Eliot), the children's opera *The Quarry* (London 1965; libr. D. Holbrook), *Under Western Eyes* (London 1969; libr. Cedric Cliffe, after Josef Conrad) and the children's opera *The Prisoner* (Barnet 1973; libr. S. Tunnicliffe, after Tolstoy).

Jour et nuit
Tenor aria for Franz in the Antonia Act of Offenbach's *Les Contes d'Hoffmann*.

Journet, Marcel *(1867–1933)*
French bass with a remarkable range which also enabled him to sing high baritone roles. One of the finest basses of the inter-war period, he was particularly associated with the roles of Hans Sachs and Méphistophélès. He created Simon Mago in *Nerone*.

Jouy, Victor Joseph Étienne de *(1764–1846)*
French playwright and librettist. As resident librettist at the Paris Opéra, he specialised in 'spectacular' subjects and situations, sometimes providing verses of considerable quality. His most fruitful collaboration was with Spontini, for whom he wrote the libretti for *Milton, Fernand Cortez* and *La Vestale*. He also provided texts for Boïeldieu, Cherubini (*Les Abencérages*), Dalayrac, Méhul and Rossini (*Guillaume Tell* and *Moïse et Pharaon*).

Judgement Scene
A name often given to Act IV Scene I of Verdi's *Aida* in which Radamès silently faces his judges off-stage whilst Amneris curses the priests' lust for blood. One of opera's most powerful scenes.

Judith
Works of this title based on the book in the Apocrypha include:

(1) Opera by Serov. 1st perf. St Petersburg, 28 May 1863; libr. by A. Maykov and others.

(2) Opera in three acts by Honegger. 1st perf. Monte Carlo, 13 Feb 1926; libr. by René Morax.

(3) Opera in one act by Goossens (Op 46). 1st perf. London, 25 June 1929; libr. by Arnold Bennett. [R]

Judith
Mezzo role in Bartók's *Duke*

Bluebeard's Castle. She is Bluebeard's new wife. The role is sometimes sung by a soprano.

Jugoslavia

See Yugoslavia

Juha

Opera in three acts by A. Merikanto. 1st perf. Helsinki Radio, Dec 1958 (composed 1922); libr. by Aïno Ackté, after J. Aho. Principal roles: Juha (b-bar), Marja (sop), Shemeikka (ten), Anja (sop). One of the finest of all Finnish operas, but little known outside Finland. [R]

Juive, La (*The Jewess*)

Opera in five acts by Halévy. 1st perf. Paris, 23 Feb 1835; libr. by Eugène Scribe. Principal roles: Eléazer (ten), Rachel (sop), Prince Léopold (ten), Eudoxie (sop), Cardinal Brogni (bass). Halévy's masterpiece and his only opera still to be performed.

Plot: 15th-century Constance. Rachel, daughter of the Jewish goldsmith Eléazer, discovers that her lover, whom she knows as Samuel, is actually Prince Léopold, and married to Princess Eudoxie. Rachel exposes the relationship to the court and Cardinal Brogni condemns her, Léopold and Eléazer to death. Léopold's sentence is commuted to banishment, and Brogni offers to spare Rachel if Eléazer will accept Christianity. When he refuses, Rachel is thrown into a vat of boiling oil, while Eléazer reveals that she was Brogni's own long-lost daughter. [R Exc]

Julien

or **La Vie du Poète** (*The Poet's Life*)

Opera in prologue and four acts by Charpentier. 1st perf. Paris, 4 June 1913; libr. by the composer. Principal roles: Julien (ten), Ghost of Louise (sop). Incorporating music from his earlier dramatic symphony *La Vie du Poète*, it is Charpentier's unsuccessful attempt to provide a follow-up to *Louise*. It is nowadays forgotten.

Julien

Tenor role in Charpentier's *Louise*. He is a poet in love with Louise.

Julietta

or **The Dream Book** (*Snář*)

Opera in three acts by Martinů. 1st perf. Prague, 16 March 1938; libr. by the composer, after Georges Neveux's *Juliette ou La Clé des Songes*. Principal roles: Michel (ten), Julietta (sop). Martinů's most frequently performed opera, it is a surrealist dream fantasy.

Plot: Michel, a travelling bookseller, has returned to a small coastal town haunted by the memory of a girl singing at a window. The inhabitants have all lost their memories. Michel, ignorant of this fact, finds their behaviour inexplicable and comes to question his own reality and finds his meetings with Julietta unsatisfactory. Michel is unable to return to Paris because the railway station has disappeared. He finds himself in a 'Dream Office' where he thinks he hears Julietta calling to him, but – as he is shown – there is nobody at all there. [R]

Julius Caesar

See Giulio Cesare

Jullien, Louis (*1812–60*)

French conductor and composer, largely resident in London. A flamboyant personality in mid-19th-century music, he was an operatic conductor of some ability and composed one opera, the unsuccessful *Pietro il Grande* (London Aug 1852), which he financed himself.

Junge Lord, Der (*The Young Lord*)

Comic opera in two acts by Henze. 1st perf. Berlin, 7 Aug 1965; libr. by Ingeborg Bachmann after Wilhelm Hauff's *Der Sheik von Alexandria*. Principal roles: Lord Barrat (ten), Secretary (bar), Luise (sop), Wilhelm (ten), Baroness Grünwiesel (mezzo), Sir Edgar (mime). One of Henze's most successful works, it is a biting satire on bourgeois manners and has been widely performed.

Plot: Hülsdorf-Gotha, 1830. The rich Englishman Sir Edgar, who has rented a house on the town square, antagonises the local notables by his superior and distant manner. When, however, he introduces his nephew, Lord Barrat, to the community, they sycophantically condone his eccentric and outrageous behaviour until it is revealed that he is a circus ape dressed in human clothes. [R]

Jungwirth, Manfred (*b 1919*)

Austrian bass, particularly associated with Richard Strauss roles, especially Baron Ochs. He had a dark, rich voice and was a highly accomplished singing-actor, excelling in comic performances.

Junius

Baritone role in Britten's *The Rape of Lucretia*. He is a Roman general.

Juno

The wife of Jupiter, the Graeco-Roman goddess appears in a number of operas, including: (1) Mezzo role in Handel's *Semele*. (2) Soprano role in Cavalli's *La Calisto*. (3) Mezzo role in Offenbach's *Orphée aux Enfers*. (4) Mezzo role in Cavalli's *Ercole Amante*.

Jupiter

The Graeco-Roman high god appears in many operas, including: (1) Tenor role in Handel's *Semele*. (2) Bass role in Cavalli's *La Calisto*. (3) Tenor role in Monteverdi's *Il Ritorno d'Ulisse in Patria*. (4) Baritone role in Rameau's *Platée*. (5) Baritone role in Rameau's *Naïs*. (6) Bass-baritone role in Offenbach's *Orphée aux Enfers*. (7) Baritone role in Richard Strauss' *Die Liebe der Danae*. (8) Bass role in Klebe's *Alkmene*. (9) Baritone role in Bliss' *The Olympians*. (10) Bass role in Gounod's *Philémon et Baucis*.

Jurinac, Sena (*b Srebrenka*) (*b 1921*)

Yugoslavian soprano, particularly associated with Mozart and Strauss roles, notably Ilia and Octavian. She possessed one of the loveliest voices of the immediate postwar period, used with outstanding artistry and intelligence, and was an affecting singing-actress. Married for a time to the baritone Sesto Bruscantini*.

K

Kabaiwanska, Raina *(b 1934)*
Bulgarian soprano, particularly
associated with Verdi and Puccini roles
and with the verismo repertory. She
possesses a beautiful, creamy voice used
with intelligence and musicianship and
is a singing-actress of considerable
ability.

Kabalevsky, Dimitri *(1904–87)*
Russian composer. He wrote five
operas, of which much the best known
is *The Master of Clamecy** (sometimes
incorrectly called *Colas Breugnon* after
its famous overture). His other operas
are *Under Fire* (*Vogne*, 1943; libr.
Solodar), *The Family of Taras* (*Semya
Tarasa*, 1950; libr. S. Tsenin, after B.
Gorbatov), *Nikita Vershinin* (1955; libr.
Tsenin, after V. Ivanov) and the
operetta *The Sisters* (1967).

Kabanicha
Mezzo role in Janáček's *Káťa
Kabanová*. A merchant's widow, she is
the formidable head of the Kabanov
household.

Kaiserslautern Opera
The first opera house in this German
town in the Rhineland-Palatinate
opened in 1862, but burnt down five
years later. A second theatre, opened in
1897, was destroyed in 1944. The
present house (cap. 750) opened in
1950. Musical directors have included
Rudolf Moralt, Herbert Albert, Otmar
Suitner, Erich Riede and Wilfried
Emmert.

Kaiser von Atlantis, Der (*The
Emperor of Atlantis*)
or **Die Tod Dank Ab** (*Death
Abdicates*)
Opera in four scenes by Ullmann. 1st
perf. Amsterdam, 16 Dec 1975
(composed 1944 in Theresienstadt
concentration camp); libr. by Peter
Kien. Principal roles: Emperor Überall
(bar), Death (bass), Pierrot (ten),
Drummer (mezzo), Soldier (ten), Girl
(sop). Written in a mixture of musical
styles, it is a powerful defiance of the
Nazi system by both composer and
librettist – both of whom were
murdered in Auschwitz. Prepared for
performance by the conductor Kerry
Woodward, it has been widely
performed in the last decade and is a
powerful work rendered even more
compelling and harrowing by the
appalling circumstances of its
composition.

Kálmán, Emmerich *(b Imre)*
(1882–1953)
Hungarian composer. His first stage
work was *The Gay Hussars* (*Tártájárás*,
Budapest 1908; libr. K. von Bakonyi).
Of his many Viennese operettas, the
most enduring have proved to be *Die
Csárdásfürstin**, *Gräfin Mariza** and
Die Zirkusprinzessin*. His last work,
Arizona Lady (Berne 1954; libr. Alfred
Grünwald and G. Beer), was completed
by his son Charles.

Kalomiris, Manolis *(1883–1962)*
Greek composer. He wrote five operas:
The Master Mason (*O Protomastoros*,

1916; libr. after Nikos Kazantzakis), *The Mother's Ring* (*To Dakhtilidi tis Manas*, 1917; revised version 1939) [R], his most successful work, *Sunrise* (*Anatoli*, 1945; libr. Kambyssis), *The Shadowy Waters* (*Ta Xotika Nera*, 1951; libr. after William Butler Yeats) and *Constantinos o Palaeologos* (1961; libr. after Kazantzakis).

Kammersänger (German for 'chamber singer')

A distinguished honorary title bestowed on individual singers by the Austrian and West German governments.

Kanawa, Dame Kiri Te *(b 1944)*

New Zealand soprano, particularly associated with Mozart and Strauss roles, especially Countess Almaviva, Donna Elvira and Arabella. Her rich, alluring and creamy voice, combined with her beautiful stage appearance, has made her one of the best-loved singers of modern times. She can be a most affecting actress, but needs a strong producer.

Kansas City Lyric Theater

Founded by Russell Patterson and Morton Walker, the company gave its first performance in September 1958. It presents opera in English and uses young American artists. Its repertory is notable for its large number of American operas.

Kapellmeister

See Maestro di cappella

Karajan, Herbert von *(1908–89)*

Austrian conductor and producer. One of the most famous conductors of the 20th century, if sometimes dictatorial and controversial in his attitude to music making, he was particularly

associated with Wagner, Verdi, Mozart and Strauss operas. He was musical director of the Ulm Stadttheater (1928–34), the Aachen Opera (1934–38), the Vienna State Opera (1958–64) and the Salzburg Festival (1958–60 and 1964–88), where he founded the Salzburg Easter Festival in 1967. At Salzburg, he nearly always acted as his own producer, being especially interested in the technical side. He conducted and directed a film of *Otello* and conducted the first performance of Orff's *Trionfo d'Afrodite*.

Karel, Rudolf *(1890–1945)*

Czech composer. He completed one opera and began two others. *Godmother Death* (*Smrt Kmotřička*, 1933) is a fairy-tale work which is still occasionally performed in Czechoslovakia. Work on *The Taming of the Shrew* (*Zkrocení zlé Ženy*; libr. after Shakespeare) was interrupted by his arrest by the Nazis. *Three Hairs of an Old Wise Man* (*Tři Vlasy děda Vševěda*, 1948) was sketched in prison and was completed by his pupil Zbyněk Vostřák. He died in Terezín concentration camp.

Karlsruhe Staatstheater

Opera in this German town in Baden-Württemberg is given at the house built in 1851, destroyed during World War II, and rebuilt in 1954 (cap. 1,055). Musical directors have included Hermann Levi, Felix Mottl, Joseph Krips, Joseph Keilberth, Alexander Krannhals and Günter Neuhold.

Karolka

Mezzo role in Janáček's *Jenůfa*. She is Števa's fiancée.

Kašlík, Václav *(1917–89)*

Czech producer, conductor and composer. One of the leading – and most controversial – postwar producers, he was noted for his application of experimental visual techniques to opera, often working in collaboration with the designer Josef Svoboda*. He described his rule for production as being "to present contemporary problems and feelings amusingly, even in a form which is so often so stiff as opera". He was musical director of the Brno Opera (1943–45) and wrote four operas, including *Krakatit* (1961; libr. after Karel Čapek), which employs jazz and popular elements.

Kassel Staatstheater

The Hoftheater in this German city in Hesse was opened in February 1814 but was destroyed in 1943. The present theatre (cap. 1,010) opened in September 1959. Musical directors have included Spohr, Mahler, Robert Heger, Karl Elmendorff, Christoph von Dohnányi, Gerd Albrecht, James Lockhart and Ádám Fischer.

Káťa Kabanová

Opera in three acts by Janáček. 1st perf. Brno, 23 Nov 1921; libr. by the composer, after Alexander Nikolayevich Ostrovsky's *The Storm*. Principal roles: Káťa (sop), Kabanicha (mezzo), Boris (ten), Tichon (ten), Dikoi (bass), Varvara (mezzo), Vanya Kudriash (ten), Kuligin (bar). One of Janáček's most successful works, it has been widely performed in the last 20 years.

Plot: Kalinov on the Volga, 1860s. Káťa lives with her husband Tichon and her intimidating mother-in-law Kabanicha, who loathes her. Unable to suppress her secret passion for Boris, Káťa yields to temptation and meets him during Tichon's absence on business. At the height of a violent thunderstorm, she confesses the situation to Tichon and Kabanicha and runs away. She meets Boris one last time, then drowns herself in the river. [R]

Kate and the Devil
See Devil and Kate, The

Katerina Ismailova
See Lady Macbeth of the Mtsensk District

Kauer, Ferdinand (1751–1831)
Austrian composer. He wrote a large number of stage works in various styles, a number of which enjoyed great success in their time. His most important work is *Das Donauweibchen* (*The Danube Spirit*, Vienna 11 Jan 1798; libr. K. F. Hensler), which was one of the most popular of all operas in Central Europe in the early 19th century.

Kecal
Bass role in Smetana's *The Bartered Bride*. He is a marriage broker.

Keene, Ned
Baritone role in Britten's *Peter Grimes*. He is an apothecary.

Keilberth, Joseph (1908–68)
German conductor, particularly associated with Strauss and Wagner operas. He was musical director of the Karlsruhe Staatstheater (1933–40) and the Bavarian State Opera (1959–68). He died whilst conducting *Tristan und Isolde* at Bayreuth.

Keiser, Reinhard (1674–1739)
German composer. Based predominantly in Hamburg, he wrote over 100 operas, some with polyglot libretti, many of which were successful in their time but which are all now forgotten. His most important works were *Störtebecker und*

Goedje Michel (1701), *Die Edelmuthige Octavia* (5 Aug 1705), *Masagnello Furioso* (June 1706) and *Der Lächerliche Prinz Jodelet* (1726).

Kéléman, Zoltán *(1926–79)*
Hungarian baritone, particularly associated with Wagnerian roles. The outstanding Alberich of the 1970s, he had a powerful and incisive voice and was a fine singing-actor.

Kellog, Clara Louise *(1842–1916)*
American soprano, particularly associated with the French and Italian repertories. One of the earliest American singers to win fame in Europe, in 1872 she formed the Lucca-Kellog Company in partnership with the soprano Pauline Lucca (1841–1908), which toured the USA until 1874. She then formed her own English Opera Company, supervising every aspect of performance. Her autobiography, *Memoirs of an American Prima Donna*, was published in 1913.

Kelly, Michael *(1762–1826)*
Irish tenor and composer. One of the leading singing-actors of his time, he enjoyed a long career in Italy, Vienna and England. A friend of Mozart, he created Don Basilio and Don Curzio in *Le Nozze di Figaro*. His two-volume autobiography, *Reminiscences of Michael Kelly of the King's Theatre*, was published in 1826 and is a principal source for details of operatic life at that time. He also composed a number of light operas, including *The Bard of Erin*.

Kempe, Rudolf *(1910–76)*
German conductor, particularly associated with Wagner and Strauss operas. One of the finest and best-loved 20th-century interpreters of the German repertory, he was musical director of the Dresden State Opera (1949–52) and the Bavarian State Opera (1952–54). Married to the soprano Elisabeth Lindermeier.

Kent Opera
Founded in 1969 by Norman Platt, it is based in Canterbury and Tunbridge Wells and visits most towns in southern England. It quickly developed remarkably high artistic standards, with many fine productions by Jonathan Miller, and has been particularly noted for its Monteverdi and Mozart performances. All operas are sung in English. Musical directors have been Roger Norrington and Iván Fischer.

Kerman, Joseph *(b 1924)*
American musicologist. His *Opera as Drama* (1956) is one of the most influential, as well as controversial, operatic books of the postwar period. His thesis is that only Mozart and Verdi achieved true music-drama, whilst Wagner, Monteverdi, Gluck, Beethoven, Debussy and Berg fell only just short. The book is famous for its diatribes against Richard Strauss and Puccini, particularly the description of *Tosca* as "that shabby little shocker".

Kertesz, István *(1929–73)*
Hungarian conductor, particularly associated with Mozart operas. He was musical director of the Augsburg Stadttheater (1958–63) and the Cologne Opera (1964–73). His tragic death in a boating accident cut short a brilliant career.

Khaikin, Boris *(1904–78)*
Russian conductor, particularly associated with the Russian repertory. He was musical director of the Kirov Opera (1936–54) and conducted the

first performances of *The Duenna, The Story of a Real Man* and *The Master of Clamecy.*

Khovanschina

Opera in five acts by Moussorgsky. 1st perf. St Petersburg, 21 Feb 1886; libr. by the composer and Vladimir Stasov. Principal roles: Dosifei (bass), Ivan Khovanksy (bass), Marfa (mezzo), Prince Galitsin (ten), Shaklovity (b-bar), Andrei (ten), Scribe (ten), Emma (sop). A gloomy but powerful musico-dramatic work, which incorporates the one completed scene from Moussorgsky's earlier *The Landless Peasant*, it was left unfinished and was completed and orchestrated by Rimsky-Korsakov.

Plot: Moscow, 1682–89. It is a time of strife between various factions when Peter the Great ascends the throne of Russia. The party led by Prince Ivan Khovansky finds common cause with the Old Believers, led by Dosifei, against Peter's adherents, led by Prince Galitsin. Ivan's son, Andrei, is reunited with his former love Marfa, an Old Believer and prophetess. Peter and his followers emerge triumphant, and Ivan is murdered by the treacherous boyar Shaklovity. Rather than submit to religious reform, the Old Believers, with Marfa and Andrei, immolate themselves in their forest refuge. [R]

Khrennikov, Tichon *(b 1913)*

Russian composer. He has written three operas in 'orthodox Soviet' style which have not been performed outside Russia. They are *Into the Storm* (*V Burya*, 1939; libr. A. Faiko, after N. Virta), *Frol Skobeyev* (1950; libr. S. Tsenin) and *The Mother* (1957; libr. Faiko, after Maxim Gorky).

Kiel Opera

The present theatre (cap. 918) in this German city in Schleswig-Holstein opened in 1953, replacing the previous theatre of 1841 which was destroyed in 1944. Musical directors have included Georg Winkler, Peter Ronnefeld and Hans Zender.

Kienzl, Wilhelm *(1857–1941)*

Austrian composer. He wrote ten operas in Wagnerian style, including *Urvasi* (Dresden 1886; libr. A. Godel, after Kalidasa), *Heilmar der Narr* (Munich 1892; libr. composer's father), *Der Evangeliman**, by far his most successful work, and *Der Kuhreigen* (Vienna 1911; libr. R. Batka, after R. H. Bartsch).

King, James *(b 1925)*

American tenor, particularly associated with heavier German roles, especially Florestan and Siegmund. Beginning as a baritone, he turned to tenor roles in 1961 and enjoyed a remarkably long career. His voice was powerful and incisive, if not intrinsically beautiful, and he had a good stage presence.

King and Marshal *(Drot og Marsk)*

Opera in four acts by Heise. 1st perf. Copenhagen, 1878; libr. by C. Richardt. Principal roles: King Erik (ten), Lord Marshal (b-bar), Ingeborg (mezzo), Aase (sop), Rane (ten). One of the most popular of all Danish operas, it is almost unknown anywhere else. [R]

King Arthur
or The British Worthy

Opera in prologue, five acts and epilogue by Purcell. 1st perf. London, June 1691; libr. by John Dryden. Perhaps more of a play with music than a true opera. [R]

King Fisher

Baritone role in Tippett's *The Midsummer Marriage*. Jenifer's father, he is a business tycoon.

King Goes Forth to France, The

Opera in three acts by Sallinen. 1st perf. Savonlinna, 7 July 1984; libr. by Paavo Haavikko. Principal roles: King (bar), Prime Minister (bass), Nice Caroline (sop), Caroline with the Mane (mezzo), Anne who Steals (sop), Anne who Strips (mezzo), English Archer (bar), Guide (ten), Froissart (speaker). Sallinen's third opera, it has been widely performed and confirms his position as one of the finest of contemporary opera composers.

Plot: At a time in the future, England is being overwhelmed by a new Ice Age. The Prime Minister urges the young King to marry, introducing the two Carolines and the two Annes. However, the King resolves to assume power, abandon England, and lead his people across the Channel to France. The Prime Minister, fearful of the King's adventurist policies, observes that their route is following that of Edward III. The Hundred Years' War is re-enacted, including the Battle of Crécy and the incident of the six Burghers at the siege of Calais, and the King marches on Paris.

King Priam

Opera in three acts by Tippett. 1st perf. Coventry, 29 May 1962; libr. by the composer, after Homer's *The Iliad*. Principal roles: Priam (bass), Paris (ten), Achilles (ten), Hector (bar), Helen (mezzo), Andromache (mezzo), Hecuba (sop), Old Man (bass), Hermes (ten), Young Guard (ten), Nurse (mezzo), Patroclus (bar). One of the finest 20th-century British operas, it views the events of the Trojan War from the Trojan standpoint and deals with what Tippett describes as "the mysterious nature of human choice".

Plot: Troy. The main characters each make choices and suffer the consequences: Priam in supposedly killing the infant Paris and later restoring his son's patrimony; Paris himself in having abducted Helen; Hector in killing Patroclus and Achilles in killing Hector in revenge; and, finally, Priam's choice of death as the price of dishonour when he realises that he has no choices left. [R]

King Roger (*Król Roger*)

Opera in three acts by Szymanowski (Op 46). 1st perf. Warsaw, 19 June 1926; libr. by the composer and Jaroslaw Iwaszkiewicz. Principal roles: King Roger (bar), Roxane (sop), Shepherd (ten), Edrisi (ten), Archbishop of Palermo (bass), Abbess (mezzo). Szymanowski's masterpiece and virtually the only Polish opera to be performed elsewhere, it deals with supposed events in the reign of Roger II of Sicily (*c* 1095–1154).

Plot: 12th-century Sicily. A shepherd prophet from India arrives at the court of King Roger, whose wife Roxane falls in love with him. He is denounced as a heretic by the Archbishop, but eventually he converts Roger from Christianity to his own Dionysian cult and a bacchanal is celebrated in a Greek temple. [R]

King's Henchman, The

Opera in three acts by Taylor (Op 19). 1st perf. New York, 17 Feb 1927; libr. by Edna St Vincent Millay. Principal roles: Eadgar (bar), Aethelwold (ten), Aelfrida (sop), Ase (mezzo). Taylor's finest opera, it was very successful at its appearance but is nowadays almost never performed.

Plot: 10th-century Britain. King Eadgar has heard rumour of the beauty of the Princess Aelfrida of Devon. He sends his closest associate, Aethelwold, to Devon to woo her on his behalf, but Aethelwold and Aelfrida fall in love. Aethelwold marries the Princess, sending word to Eadgar that Aelfrida is ugly and unworthy of his attention, but Eadgar himself arrives, discovers the falsehood and kills Aethelwold.

Kipnis, Alexander (1891–1978)

Ukrainian bass, particularly associated with the German repertory and with Boris Godunov. One of the greatest basses of the inter-war period, he had a rich, majestic and smoothly produced voice, a fine technique and outstanding interpretative abilities. His son is the harpsichordist Igor Kipnis.

Kirsten, Dorothy (b 1917)

American soprano, particularly associated with the French and Italian repertories. An accomplished singing-actress of great personal beauty, she had a fine lyric soprano voice and appeared in a number of films, including The Great Caruso.

Kirov Opera

Originally called the Maryinsky Theatre, this opera house (cap. 1,780) in Leningrad (formerly St Petersburg) was built by Alberto Cavos and opened in 1860. It became the State Academic Theatre in 1919 and acquired its present name in 1935, being named after the Politbureau member, Sergei Kirov, who was assassinated in the city in December 1934. For long Russia's principal opera house, it now ranks second behind the Bolshoi. Its repertory and stagings tend to be conservative, but its musical standards are very high. Musical directors have included Eduard Nápravník, Albert Coates, Boris

Khaikin, Yuri Temirkanov and Valery Gergiev.

Kiss, The (Hubička)

Comic opera in three acts by Smetana. 1st perf. Prague, 7 Nov 1876; libr. by Eliška Krásnohorská, after Joanna Mužáková. Principal roles: Vendulka (sop), Lukáš (ten), Martinka (mezzo), Poloucký (bass), Matouš (bass). A slight but delightful love story, it is still very popular in Czechoslovakia but is only rarely performed elsewhere. It was the first work which Smetana composed after becoming deaf.

Plot: The widower Lukáš wishes to marry his old love Vendulka. She is delighted but – believing the superstition that a kiss given to a widower before his remarriage causes grief to the deceased wife –refuses to let him kiss her. This causes a lover's tiff and Vendulka flees to the mountains with her aunt Martinka, who engages in border smuggling. Lukáš follows her, begs forgiveness, and reconciliation follows. [R]

Klänge der Heimat

Soprano aria (the Csárdás) for Rosalinde in Act II of J. Strauss' Die Fledermaus.

Klebe, Giselhr Wolfgang (b 1925)

German composer. He has written ten operas, a number of which have met with success in Germany. They are Die Räuber (Düsseldorf 1957; libr. after Friedrich von Schiller), Die Ermörderung Caesar (Essen 1959; libr. after Shakespeare's Julius Caesar), Die Tödlichen Wunsche (The Deathly Wishes, Düsseldorf 1959; libr. after Honoré de Balzac), Alkmene*, his most successful work, Figaro Lässt sich Scheinen (Figaro Seeks a Divorce, Hamburg 1963; libr. composer, after

Ödön von Horváth), *Jakobowsky und der Oberst* (Hamburg 1969; libr. composer, after Franz Werfel), *Das Märchen von der Schönen Lilie* (Schwetzingen 1969; libr. composer, after Goethe's *Märchen*), *Ein Wahrer Held* (*A True Hero*, Zürich 1975; libr. after J. M. Synge's *The Playboy of the Western World*), *Das Mädchen von Domrémy* (Stuttgart 1976; libr. composer, after Schiller) and *Das Rendez-vous* (Hanover 1977).

Kleiber, Carlos *(b 1930)*
German conductor, son of the conductor Erich Kleiber*. Particularly associated with German works, and with *Otello*, he is a perfectionist who demands very long rehearsal periods and whose repertory is small.

Kleiber, Erich *(1890–1956)*
Austrian conductor, particularly associated with Mozart operas and with the German repertory. One of the greatest operatic conductors of the 20th century, he was musical director of the Mannheim Opera (1922–23) and the Berlin State Opera (1923–34). He conducted the first performances of *Wozzeck*, Schreker's *Der Singende Teufel* and Milhaud's *Christophe Colomb*. His son is the conductor Carlos Kleiber*.

Klemperer, Otto *(1885–1973)*
German conductor and composer. Regarded as one of the greatest conductors of the 20th century, he was particularly associated with Mozart and Wagner operas and with *Fidelio* (which he also produced at Covent Garden). He was musical director of the Strasbourg Opera (1914–17), the Cologne Opera (1917–24), the Wiesbaden Opera (1924–27) and the Berlin State Opera (1927–33). He conducted the first performances of *Die*

Tote Stadt, Hindemith's *Neues vom Tage* and Zemlinsky's *Der Geburstag der Infantin*. He also composed an opera, the unperformed *Das Ziel* (1915). His autobiography, *Minor Recollections*, was published in 1964.

Klenau, Paul von *(1883–1946)*
Danish composer and conductor. He wrote seven operas, of which the most important are *Kjartan und Gudrun* (Mannheim 1918; libr. composer; revised 1924 as *Gudrun auf Island*), *Michael Kohlhaas* (Stuttgart 1933; libr. composer, after Heinrich Wilhelm von Kleist) and *Rembrandt van Rijn* (Berlin 1937; libr. composer).

Klingsor
Bass-baritone role in Wagner's *Parsifal*. He is an evil sorcerer expelled from the brotherhood of the Grail.

Klose, Margarete *(1902–68)*
German mezzo, particularly associated with Wagner and Verdi roles. One of the finest German mezzos of the inter-war period, she was a versatile singer with a fine voice and a good stage presence. She created Oona in Egk's *Irische Legende*.

Kluge, Die *(The Clever Girl)*
Comic opera in six scenes by Orff. 1st perf. Frankfurt, 20 Feb 1943; libr. by the composer, after the Grimm brothers' *Fairy Tales*. Principal roles: Girl (sop), King (bar), Peasant (bass), Donkey Man (ten), Muleteer (bass). Orff's best-known and most accessible stage work, which has often been performed with marionettes, it remains regularly performed.
Plot: The King is bored with the wise sayings and cleverness of the Girl he married after she had answered his riddles. He sends her packing and says that she may have anything in the

palace that she wants as a parting gift. When she tells him that it is the king himself she wants, he relents on the condition that she stops being clever. [R]

Knappertsbusch, Hans *(1888–1965)*

German conductor, particularly associated with Wagner and Strauss operas. One of the finest 20th-century Wagnerian interpreters, he was musical director of the Dessau Opera (1920–22) and the Bavarian State Opera (1922–35). He conducted the first performances of Coates' *Samuel Pepys* and Pfitzner's *Das Herz*.

Kniplová, Naděžda *(b Pokorná)* *(b 1932)*

Czech soprano, particularly associated with the Czech repertory and with Wagner roles. One of the finest modern Czech dramatic sopranos, she has a powerful voice and a keen dramatic sense.

Knot Garden, The

Opera in three acts by Tippett. 1st perf. London, 2 Dec 1970; libr. by the composer. Principal roles: Faber (bar), Thea (mezzo), Denise (sop), Flora (sop), Mel (bar), Dov (ten), Mangus (bar). A complex metaphysical drama with human relationships discussed through a comparison with characters in Shakespeare's *The Tempest*, its structure is defined by the titles of its three acts: Confrontation, Labyrinth and Charade. The tenor song cycle *Songs for Dov* is drawn from music from the opera.

Plot: The psychoanalyst Mangus and the physically scarred revolutionary activist Denise act as catalysts to explore the emotional tangles of two couples: Faber, whose marriage to Thea has grown stale and who lusts for his

ward Flora, and the musician Dov and his lover, the black poet Mel. [R]

Knussen, Oliver *(b 1952)*

British composer and conductor. His stage works include *Where the Wild Things Are* (Brussels 28 Nov 1980; libr. by Maurice Sendak) [R] and *Higgledy-Piggledy Pop* (Glyndebourne 1984).

Koanga

Opera in prologue, three acts and epilogue by Delius. 1st perf. Elberfeld, 30 March 1904; libr. by Charles Francis Keary, after George Washington Cable's *The Grandissimes*. Principal roles: Koanga (bar), Palmyra (sop), Don José (bass), Simón Pérez (ten), Clotida (mezzo), Uncle Joe (bass). One of Delius' finest works, it is, unaccountably, very rarely performed.

Plot: Mississippi. The mulatto Palmyra repulses the plantation overseer Pérez and falls in love with a newly arrived slave, the former African chieftain Koanga. The plantation owner Don José agrees to their marriage, but Pérez abducts Palmyra at the wedding. Koanga escapes into the forest and causes a plague by means of voodoo. Koanga kills Pérez but is himself captured and killed and Palmyra stabs herself. [R]

Kobbé, Gustav *(1857–1918)*

American musicologist and critic. His *Complete Opera Book* (1919) is one of the classic operatic reference works. It was revised and updated by the Earl of Harewood in 1976.

Kodály, Zoltán *(1882–1967)*

Hungarian composer. He wrote three operas, all of which contain long passages of spoken dialogue, on nationalist themes. They are the successful *Háry János**, *The Spinning*

Room* and *Czinka Panna* (Budapest 15 March 1948; libr. Balázs).

Kokkonen, Joonas *(b 1921)*

Finnish composer. His one opera, *The Last Temptations**, has proved to be one of the most successful modern operas.

Kokoschka, Oskar *(1886–1980)*

German painter and designer, famous for his use of greens. He undertook a number of operatic designs, most notably *Die Zauberflöte* in Geneva in 1965. He also wrote the libretti for Hindemith's *Mörder, Hoffnung der Frauen* and Křenek's *Orpheus und Eurydike*.

Kolenatý, Dr

Baritone role in Janáček's *The Macropolus Case*. He is a lawyer.

Kollo, René *(b Kollodzievski) (b 1937)*

German tenor, grandson of the operetta composer Walter Kollo. Particularly associated with Wagnerian roles, he was the leading Wagner tenor of the 1970s and early 1980s but was not a true heldentenor. He also achieved success in operetta.

Köln

See Cologne Opera

Koltai, Ralph *(b 1924)*

Hungarian-born British designer. Often working in collaboration with the producer Michael Geliot (*b* 1933), his modernistic sets make extensive use of scaffolding and tubular effects. He has worked extensively for Scottish Opera, and for the English National Opera where he designed the famous English-language *Ring*.

Komische Oper, Berlin

Formerly the Metropol-Theater, this house (cap. 1,120) in East Berlin opened on 23 Dec 1947. Under the administration of Walter Felsenstein it soon became one of the most innovative, controversial and stimulating houses in Europe. The annual season runs from September to July. Musical directors have included Kurt Masur, Zdeněk Košler, and Rolf Reuter.

Konchak

Bass role in Borodin's *Prince Igor*. He is the Polovtsian Khan.

Konchakovna

Mezzo role in Borodin's *Prince Igor*. She is Konchak's daughter.

Kondrashin, Kirill *(1914–81)*

Russian conductor, particularly associated with the Russian repertory. Best known as a symphonic conductor, his operatic appearances were rare. He defected from the USSR in 1978.

Konetzni, Hilde *(1905–80)*

Austrian soprano, particularly associated with Wagnerian roles, especially Sieglinde. Based largely at the Vienna State Opera, she possessed a voice of great beauty used with fine style. Her sister Anny (1902–68) was also a soprano, specialising in Wagner and Strauss roles.

König Hirsch *(King Stag)*

Opera in three acts by Henze. 1st perf. Berlin, 23 Sept 1956; libr. by Heinz von Cramer, after Carlo Gozzi's *Re Cervo*. Revised version *Il Re Cervo*, 1st perf. Kassel, 1963. Principal roles: King Leandro (ten), Costanza (sop), Tartaglia (b-bar), Checco (ten), Coltellino (ten),

Scollatella (sop). One of Henze's most successful works, it is a melodic, almost neoclassical fairy tale.

Plot: King Leandro, abandoned in the forest as a child by the evil governor Tartaglia, has been nurtured by wild animals. He returns to claim his crown and to choose his bride, but the machinations of Tartaglia lead to his renouncing the throne and returning to the forest. He enters the body of a stag, whilst Tartaglia assumes his form and initiates a cruel dictatorship in the city. Unable to sublimate his human longings, the King once more returns to the city, where Tartaglia is murdered by his own assassins and the King recovers his human form.

Königin von Saba, Die (The Queen of Sheba)

Opera in four acts by Goldmark (Op 27). 1st perf. Vienna, 10 March 1875; libr. by Salomon Hermann Mosenthal. Principal roles: Assad (ten), Solomon (bar), Sulamith (sop), Queen of Sheba (mezzo), High Priest (bass). By far Goldmark's most successful opera, it is an exotic work of great lyrical beauty.

Plot: Although engaged to Sulamith, daughter of the High Priest, Solomon's favourite Assad has fallen in love with the Queen of Sheba. Solomon insists that the marriage must take place. Assad commits a sacrilege and is imprisoned. When he is freed, he searches for Sulamith in the desert, finds her, but dies in her arms. [R]

Königskinder, Die (The Royal Children)

Opera in three acts by Humperdinck. 1st perf. New York, 28 Dec 1910 (composed 1897 and later revised); libr. by Else Bernestein-Porges under the pen name Ernst Rosmer. Principal roles: Prince (ten), Goose-girl (sop), Witch (mezzo), Fiddler (bar). Humperdinck's only work apart from Hänsel und Gretel to have survived, it was originally written as speech over music, the first appearance in opera of sprechstimme*.

Plot: The Goose-girl, who is in reality a princess placed under a spell by the Witch, falls in love with the Prince. With the aid of the Fiddler, she takes flight and joins the Prince. However, the people reject her, and she and the Prince, poisoned by the Witch, die together in the snow. [R]

Konwitschny, Franz (1901–62)

German conductor, particularly associated with Wagner operas. He was musical director of the Freiburg Opera (1933–37), the Frankfurt Opera (1937–45), the Hanover State Opera (1945–49) and the Berlin State Opera (1955–62).

Kónya, Sándor (b 1923)

Hungarian tenor, particularly associated with heavier German and Italian roles such as Lohengrin and Calaf. He created the title role in Henze's König Hirsch.

Korngold, Erich (1897–1957)

Austrian composer. His five operas are Der Ring des Polykrates (Munich 28 March 1916; libr. after Heinrich Teweles), Violanta*, Die Tote Stadt*, his most successful work, Das Wunder der Heliane (Hamburg 10 Oct 1927; libr. Hans Müller, after H. Kaltneker) and Die Kathrin (Stockholm 7 Oct 1939; libr. composer). He also enjoyed a highly successful career writing film scores, one of which, Give Us This Night (1936), contains a mini-opera Romeo and Juliet.

Korrepetitor

The répétiteur* in a German or Austrian opera house.

Košler, Zdeněk *(b 1928)*
Czech conductor, particularly associated
with the Czech repertory, contemporary
works and with Prokofiev operas. He
was musical director of the Olomouc
Opera (1958–62), the Ostrava Opera
(1962–66), the Komische Oper, Berlin
(1966–68), the Bratislava Opera and
the Prague National Theatre (1989–).

Kostelnička
Soprano role in Janáček's *Jenůfa*. She is
Jenůfa's formidable foster-mother. The
role is sometimes sung by a mezzo.

Köth, Erika *(1927–89)*
German soprano, particularly associated
with coloratura roles, especially
Zerbinetta and Lucia. She had a
smallish voice, but of great agility with
a range extending remarkably high.

Köthner, Fritz
Baritone role in Wagner's *Die
Meistersinger von Nürnberg*. A baker,
he is one of the masters.

Koussevitsky, Serge *(1874–
1951)*
Russian conductor, particularly
associated with the Russian repertory.
Best known as a symphonic conductor,
his operatic appearances were rare. In
1942, he founded the Koussevitsky
Music Foundation (since 1950
permanently endowed as the Serge
Koussevitsky Music Foundation in the
Library of Congress), which has
commissioned many important new
works, including *Peter Grimes*. He
founded the Berkshire Festival in 1937.

Kovalyov, Maj
Baritone role in Shostakovich's *The
Nose*. He is the unfortunate owner of
the nose which detaches itself and
begins to lead an independent life.

Kovařovic, Karel *(1862–1920)*
Czech composer and conductor. The
most successful of his five operas was
The Dogheads (*Psohlavci*, Prague 1898;
libr. Sípek, after A. Jirásek) [R Exc],
which is still occasionally performed in
Czechoslovakia. He was musical
director of the Prague National Theatre
(1900–20) and conducted the first
performances of *Rusalka* and operas by
Ostrčil, Foerster and Novák.

Kozlovsky, Ivan *(b 1900)*
Russian tenor, particularly associated
with the Russian repertory. One of the
leading Russian lyric tenors of the
inter-war period, he founded an opera
company of his own which functioned
from 1938 to 1941, for which he also
acted as producer.

Krásnohorská, Eliška *(1847–
1926)*
Czech poetess and librettist. She
provided texts for Bendl (*Lejla*,
Brětislav, *Karel Škréta* and *The Child
of Tabor*), Fibich (*Blaník*) and Smetana
(*The Kiss*, *The Secret*, *The Devil's Wall*
and the unfinished *Viola*).

Kraus, Alfredo *(b 1927)*
Spanish tenor, particularly associated
with the roles of Werther, the Duke of
Mantua, Ferrando and Edgardo. His
ravishing lyric tenor, innate
musicianship, flawless technique,
impeccable diction and scrupulous good
taste combined to make him one of the
greatest 20th-century exponents of
Bellini, Donizetti and lighter French
roles. He was also a successful
exponent of zarzuela.

Kraus, Otakar *(1909–80)*
Czech baritone, long resident at Covent
Garden. A fine singing-actor, he was
particularly associated with the role of
Alberich. He created Tarquinius in *The

Rape of Lucretia, Nick Shadow in *The Rake's Progress*, Diomede in *Troilus and Cressida* and King Fisher in *The Midsummer Marriage*. He was also a noted teacher, whose pupils included Robert Lloyd, Elizabeth Connell and Gwynne Howell.

Krause, Tom *(b 1934)*

Finnish baritone, particularly associated with Mozart roles. He had a very attractive lyrical voice, used with style and fine musicianship, and a good stage presence. He created Jason in Křenek's *Der Goldene Bock* and the title role in Searle's *Hamlet*.

Krauss, Clemens *(1893–1954)*

Austrian conductor, particularly associated with Strauss operas. He was musical director of the Bavarian State Opera (1937–44) and conducted the first performances of *Arabella*, *Friedenstag*, *Capriccio* (of which he co-authored the libretto), *Die Liebe der Danae* and *Die Kluge*. Married to the soprano Viorica Ursuleac*.

Krejčí, Iša *(1904–68)*

Czech composer and conductor. His most important opera is the neo-classical *The Tumult at Ephesus* (*Pozdvižení v Efesu*, 1946; libr. after Shakespeare's *The Comedy of Errors*), which has had considerable success in Czechoslovakia. He was musical director of the Olomouc Opera (1945–58).

Křenek, Ernst *(b 1900)*

Austrian composer, who has written in traditional, jazz and serial styles. His 16 stage works are *Die Zwingburg* (Berlin 21 Oct 1924; libr. Franz Werfel), *Der Sprung über den Schatten* (*The Jump Over the Shadow*, Frankfurt 9 June 1924; libr. composer), *Orpheus und Eurydike* (Kassel 27 Nov 1926;

libr. Oskar Kokoschka), the jazz-inspired *Jonny Spielt Auf**, his most successful work, the three *Zeitopern*, *Der Diktator*, *Das Geheime Königreich* and *Schwergewicht* (Weisbaden 6 May 1928; libr. composer), *Leben des Orest* (Leipzig 19 Jan 1930; libr. composer, after Euripides' *Orestes*), *Cefalo e Procri* (Venice 1934; libr. R. Küfferle), *Karl V* (Prague 22 June 1938, composed 1934 but banned by the Nazis; libr. composer), *Tarquin* (Cologne 1950, composed 1940; libr. E. Lauery), *What Price Confidence?* (Saarbrücken 1946; libr. composer), *Pallas Athene Weint* (Hamburg 1955; libr. composer), *Der Goldene Bock* (Hamburg 1964; libr. composer), the television opera *Der Zauberspiegel* (*The Magic Mirror*, Munich 1966; libr. composer) and *Das Kommt Davon* (1970). His autobiography, *Horizons Circled*, was published in 1974.

Kreutzer, Konrad *(1780–1849)*

German composer. His first work was an operetta *Die Lächerliche Werbung* (*The Ridiculous Wooing*, Freiburg 1800). His subsequent operas include *Konradin von Schwaben* (Stuttgart 30 March 1812; libr. K. R. Weitzmann), *Feodora* (Stuttgart 1812; libr. Kotzebue), *Libusse* (Vienna 4 Dec 1822; libr. J. K. Bernard) and *Das Nachtlager von Granada**, by far his most successful work.

Kreutzer, Rodolphe *(1766–1831)*

French violinist, composer and conductor. Best known as the dedicatee of Beethoven's 'Kreutzer' violin sonata, he was also a successful opera composer. His 40 operas, all now forgotten, include *Paul et Virginie* (Paris 15 Jan 1791; libr. E. G. F. de Favières), *Lodoïska* (Paris 1 Aug 1791; libr. Dejaure), *Imogène* (Paris 27 April 1796; libr. Dejaure, after Shakespeare's

Cymbeline), *Astyanax* (Paris 12 April 1801; libr. Dejaure), *Aristippe* (Paris 24 May 1808; libr. P. F. Giraud and M. T. Leclercq) and *Abel* (Paris 23 March 1810; libr. François Benoît Hoffman). His last opera *Matilde* (1827) was not performed. He conducted the first performance of Spontini's *Olympie*.

Krips, Josef *(1902–74)*
Austrian conductor, particularly associated with Mozart operas. One of the finest opera conductors of the 20th century, he was musical director of the Karlsruhe Staatstheater (1926–33) and the Vienna State Opera (1945–50). His brother Henry (*b* 1912) was a successful operetta conductor.

Kristina
Soprano role in Janáček's *The Macropolus Case*. Vítek's daughter, she is a young singer.

Krombholc, Jaroslav *(1918–83)*
Czech conductor, particularly associated with the Czech repertory. He was musical director of the Prague National Theatre (1963–83). His wife Marie Tauberová (*b* 1911) was a successful soprano.

Kubelík, Rafael *(b 1914)*
Czech conductor and composer, son of the composer Jan Kubelík. Particularly associated with the Czech and German repertories, he was musical director of the Brno Opera (1931–41), Covent Garden (1955–58) and the Metropolitan Opera, New York (1973–74). He has written five operas, of which the most important is *Cornelia Faroli* (Augsburg 1972). Married to the soprano Elsie Morison*.

Kubiak, Teresa *(b 1937)*
Polish soprano, particularly associated with the Italian and Russian repertories. A lyrico-dramatic soprano with a voice of considerable power and beauty, she also had an appealing stage presence.

Kuhlau, Friedrich *(1786–1832)*
Danish composer and flautist. He wrote a number of operas, some successful in their time but all now forgotten, of which the most important is *The Elf's Hill* (*Elverhoj*, Copenhagen 6 Nov 1828; libr. J. L. Heiberg).

Kundry
Soprano role in Wagner's *Parsifal*. She is the enchantress enslaved by Klingsor. The role is often sung by a mezzo.

Kunz, Erich *(b 1909)*
Austrian bass-baritone, particularly associated with the roles of Papageno and Beckmesser. A fine singing-actor with a superb (indeed, almost irrepressible) sense of comedy, he also enjoyed great success as an operetta artist.

Kupper, Annelies *(1906–88)*
German soprano, particularly associated with Mozart roles, especially Countess Almaviva. A warm-voiced singer, she created the title-role in *Die Liebe der Danae*.

Kurka, Robert *(1921–57)*
American composer, whose early death from leukemia robbed music of a considerable talent. Influenced by Weill and by jazz, he wrote one opera, *The Good Soldier Schweik* (New York 23 April 1958; libr. Lewis Allen, after Jaroslav Hašek), which had considerable success, especially the orchestral suite arranged by the composer.

Kurwenal

Baritone role in Wagner's *Tristan und Isolde*. He is Tristan's retainer.

Kurz, Selma *(1874–1933)*

Austrian soprano, renowned for her phenomenal trill. Particularly associated with French and Italian coloratura roles, she was perhaps the finest coloratura of the inter-war period and was also an affecting actress. She created Zerbinetta in *Ariadne auf Naxos*.

Kusche, Benno *(b 1916)*

German bass-baritone, particularly associated with German character roles. A fine singing-actor, equally at home in opera and operetta, he created a role in Orff's *Antigonae*. Married to the soprano Christine Görner.

Kutuzov, Marshal

Bass-baritone role in Prokofiev's *War and Peace*. He is the historical Russian commander during the Napoleonic invasion.

Kuznetsova, Maria *(1880–1966)*

Russian soprano, particularly associated with the Russian and French repertories. Daughter of the painter Nikolai Kuznetsov, she escaped from Russia in 1918 disguised as a boy and hidden in a trunk on a Swedish ship. The finest Russian soprano of the immediate pre-revolutionary period, she created Fevronia in *The Invisible City of Kitezh*. Later, influenced by Isadora Duncan, she gave dance recitals and appeared in the première of Strauss' ballet *Josephslegende*. She also directed her own touring opera company in the 1920s and 1930s.

Kyoto

Baritone role in Mascagni's *Iris*. He is a brothel keeper.

La

Titles beginning with the feminine form of the French, Italian and Spanish definite article are listed under the letter of the first main word. For example, *La Vida Breve* is listed under V.

Lablache, Luigi *(1794–1858)*

Italian bass. A fine singing-actor with a huge physique, he was one of the greatest basses of the first half of the 19th century. He created Massamiliano in *I Masnadieri*, Filippo in *Bianca e Fernando*, Giorgio in *I Puritani*, eight roles for Donizetti including the title roles in *Marino Faliero* and *Don Pasquale*, and Caliban in Halévy's *La Tempesta*. He was also a noted teacher, whose pupils included Queen Victoria.

Laca Klemeň

Tenor role in Janáček's *Jenůfa*. He is Števa's stepbrother.

Lacerato spirito, Il

Bass aria for Jacopo Fiesco in the prologue of Verdi's *Simon Boccanegra*.

Là ci darem la mano

Soprano/baritone duet for Zerlina and the Don in Act I of Mozart's *Don Giovanni*.

Lady Macbeth

Soprano role in Verdi's and Bloch's *Macbeth*. The Verdi is sometimes sung by a mezzo.

Lady Macbeth of the Mtsensk District, The

Opera in four acts by Shostakovich (Op 29). 1st perf. Leningrad, 22 Jan 1934; libr. by the composer and A. Preis after Nikolai Leskov. Revised version *Katerina Ismailova*, 1st perf. Moscow, 26 Dec 1962. Principal roles: Katerina (sop), Sergei (ten), Boris (bass), Zinovy (ten), Sonyetka (mezzo), Aksinya (sop). One of the greatest 20th-century Russian operas, it was successful at its première but provoked the famous anti-formalism attack in *Pravda* of 28 Jan 1936, entitled 'Chaos instead of music'. The opera then disappeared in Russia until the production of the toned-down revised version. This second version initially made the work known in the West, but nowadays the original version is usually preferred.

Plot: Russia, 1865. Katerina is bored and frustrated by life with her husband, the merchant Zinovy Ismailov. She falls in love with Sergei, a new and attractive employee on the family farm and, during Zinovy's absence on business, commences an illicit affair with him. When Katerina's autocratic and unpleasant father-in-law, Boris, realises the situation, she feeds him mushrooms laced with rat poison and he dies a horrible death. On her husband's return, and with Sergei's help, she strangles him and hides his body in the cellar. During the celebrations of the subsequent wedding of Katerina and Sergei, the police arrive, find the corpse and arrest the couple. Exiled to Siberia, they are on a long march through the snow when Sergei, grown tired of Katerina, takes up with another prisoner, Sonyetka, publicly humiliating his wife. As the convicts cross a bridge, Katerina seizes Sonyetka and jumps with her into the icy river below. [R both versions]

Lakmé

Opera in three acts by Delibes. 1st perf. Paris, 14 April 1883; libr. by Philippe Gille and Edmond Gondinet, after the latter's *Le Mariage de Loti*. Principal roles: Lakmé (sop), Gérald (ten), Nilakantha (bar), Mallika (mezzo), Frédéric (bass). By far Delibes' most successful work, it is still regularly performed.

Plot: mid-19th-century India. Gérald, a British officer, loves and is loved by Lakmé, daughter of the Brahmin priest, Nilakantha. Swearing to take revenge on the violator of his temple, Nilakantha forces Lakmé to sing at the bazaar so as to identify him and, when Gérald appears, Lakmé faints, thus giving him away. Nilakantha stabs Gérald but Lakmé nurses him back to health at a secret hideout in the forest where he is eventually found by his brother officer, Frédéric, who persuades him to return to his duty as a soldier. When Lakmé returns, she senses the change in her lover and kills herself by eating the poisonous datura leaf. [R]

Lalo, Edouard *(1823–92)*

French composer. His first opera *Fiesque* (libr. C. Beauquier, after Friedrich von Schiller's *Fiesco*) made little impression: composed in 1866, only a section has ever been performed (Paris 1873). This failure discouraged Lalo and it was 20 years before he returned to opera again with the highly successful *Le Roi d'Ys**. His last opera was the unfinished *La Jacquerie* (Monte Carlo 8 March 1895; libr. Edouard Blau and S. Arnaud), of which he completed only one act; the remaining four acts were written by Arthur Coquard.

Lamento *(Italian for 'lament')*

A tragic aria, often placed just before the climax of the plot in an early 17th-century Italian opera. The most famous example is 'Lasciatemi morire' in Monteverdi's *Arianna*.

Lamoral, Count

Baritone role in Richard Strauss' *Arabella*. He is one of Arabella's suitors.

Lamoureux, Charles *(1834–99)*

French conductor and violinist, in 1881 he founded the Paris orchestra which bore his name. The leading French conductor of his time, he was one of the earliest champions of Wagner.

Lancaster, Sir Osbert *(1908–86)*

British cartoonist and designer. A famous lampooner of the foibles of the British upper classes, he turned to opera design in 1952, and was closely associated with Glyndebourne. Always wittily executed and with a superb eye for ludicrous detail, his most notable designs included those for *The Rake's Progress* and *L'Heure Espagnole* at Glyndebourne and *The Sorcerer* for the D'Oyly Carte Opera Company.

Land des Lächelns, Das *(The Land of Smiles)*

Operetta in three acts by Lehár. 1st perf. Berlin, 10 Oct 1929; libr. by Ludwig Herzer and Fritz Löhner. Principal roles: Prince Sou-chong (ten), Lisa (sop), Mi (sop), Gustl (bar). A revision of the unsuccessful *Die Gelbe Jacke* of 1923, it was an immediate success and has remained ever since one of Lehár's most popular works. [R]

Landgrave

Bass role in Wagner's *Tannhäuser*. He is Hermann, Landgrave of Thuringia.

Landowski, Marcel *(b 1915)*
French composer. His operas include *Le Ventriloque* (Le Mans 1956; libr. composer and P. Arnold) [R], *Le Fou* (Nancy 1956; libr. composer) [R], *Les Adieux* (1960; libr. composer), *L'Opéra de Poussière* (Avignon 1962; libr. composer and Caillet), *Le Fantôme de l'Opéra* and *Montségur* (Toulouse 1985).

Langdon, Michael *(b 1920)*
British bass. A fine singing-actor, particularly in comic roles, he was especially associated with the role of Baron Ochs. One of the leading postwar British basses in Mozart and the German and British repertories, he created the He-Ancient in *The Midsummer Marriage*, Mr Ratcliffe in *Billy Budd*, the Recorder of Norwich in *Gloriana*, the Doctor in Henze's *We Come to the River* and the title role in Orr's *Hermiston*. He was the first director of the National Opera Studio (1978–85). His autobiography, *Notes From a Low Singer*, was published in 1982.

Langridge, Philip *(b 1939)*
British tenor, particularly associated with Britten, Mozart and Janáček roles, especially Idomeneo and Živný in *Fate*. A singer of outstanding intelligence and musicianship, with a voice of highly individual timbre, he is also an accomplished singing-actor. He created the title role in Birtwistle's *Punch and Judy* and roles in Penderecki's *Paradise Lost* and Thomas Wilson's *Confessions of a Justified Sinner*. Married to the mezzo Ann Murray*.

Laparra, Raoul *(1876–1943)*
French composer, whose music makes considerable use of Basque and Spanish traditional music. He wrote a number of operas, of which the most successful was *La Habañera* (Paris 26 Feb 1908; libr. composer). He was killed in an air raid.

Largo (Italian for 'broad')
A musical notation meaning slow. In opera, the term is best known as the name often given to 'Ombra mai fù' in Handel's *Serse*.

Largo al factotum
Baritone aria for Figaro in Act I of Rossini's *Il Barbiere di Siviglia*.

Là rivedrà nell'estasi
Tenor aria for Gustavus in Act I of Verdi's *Un Ballo in Maschera*.

Lascia ch'io pianga
Mezzo aria for Rinaldo in Act II of Handel's *Rinaldo*.

Lasciatemi morire
The lament from Monteverdi's *Arianna*. It is the only substantial piece of music from the opera which survives.

Last rose of summer, The
A traditional Irish air (originally called *The Groves of Blarney*) for which new words were written by Thomas Moore. It was used in this form by Flotow for Lady Harriet's 'Die letzte Rose' in Act II of *Martha*.

Last Savage, The
Opera in three acts by Menotti. 1st perf. (as *L'Ultimo Selvaggio*) Paris, 21 Oct 1963; libr. by the composer. Principal roles: Kodanda (ten), Kitty (sop), Abdul (bar), Sardula (sop). One of the more successful of Menotti's more recent works, it satirises modern civilisation.

Plot: India and Chicago. Wanting to marry off his daughter, the American

college girl Kitty, to the Indian prince
Kodanda, her father devises a
complicated scheme to prepare her for
this. He arranges for her to capture and
tame a 'prehistoric man', Abdul (hired
to play the part), but his plans
miscarry: Kitty falls in love with Abdul
and Kodanda marries Sardula, the
servant girl.

Last Temptations, The

(*Viimeiset Kiusaukset*)
Opera in two acts by Kokkonen. 1st
perf. 1975; libr. by Lauri Kokkonen.
Principal roles: Paavo (bass), Riita
(sop), Juhana (ten), Blacksmith (bar).
One of the most successful and
dramatically effective contemporary
operas, it has been widely performed,
and tells of the historical religious
revivalist, Paavo Routsalinen (1777–
1852). [R]

László, Magda *(b 1919)*

Hungarian soprano, particularly
associated with 20th-century operas. A
fine singing-actress, she created Cressida
in *Troilus and Cressida* and the Mother
in Dallapiccola's *Il Prigioniero*.

László Hunyadi

Opera in four acts by Erkel. 1st perf.
Budapest, 27 Jan 1844; libr. by Béni
Egressy, after Lörnic Tóth. Principal
roles: László (ten), King (bar), Mária
(sop). One of Erkel's finest works, and
the piece which may be said to mark
the foundation of Hungarian opera, it
is strongly nationalist and employs
traditional Hungarian material. Still
very popular in Hungary, it is only very
rarely performed elsewhere. [R]

Latin America

See Fundación para Arte Lirica,
Lima; Palacio de las Bellas
Artes, Mexico City; Teatro
Amazones, Manaus; Teatro
Colón, Buenos Aires; Teatro
Municipal, Rio de Janeiro;
Teatro Municipal, Santiago

Latin American opera composers

See Beruti; Castro; Gaito;
Ginastera; Gomes; Hahn;
Panizza; Villa-Lobos; and entries
for national composers from
Argentina, Brazil, Chile,
Colombia, Cuba, Ecuador,
Guatemala, Mexico, Peru,
Uruguay and Venezuela

Lattuada, Felice *(1882–1962)*

Italian composer. He wrote six operas,
mainly in verismo style. They are *La
Tempesta* (Milan 1922; libr. Arturo
Rossato, after Shakespeare's *The
Tempest*), *Sandha* (Genoa 1924; libr.
Ferdinando Fontana), *Le Preziose
Ridicole* (Milan 9 Feb 1929; libr.
Rossato, after Molière's *Les Précieuses
Ridicules*), *Don Giovanni* (Naples
1929; libr. Rossato, after J. Zorilla), *La
Caverna di Salamanca* (Genoa 1938;
libr. V. Piccoli, after Miguel Cervantes)
and *Caino* (Milan 1957; libr. F. L. and
G. Zambianchi, after Lord Byron's
Cain). His autobiography, *La Passione
Dominante*, was published in 1951.

Latvian opera composers

These include Alfreds Kalniņš (1879–
1951), Jānis Mediņš (1890–1966), his
brother Jāzeps Mediņš (1877–1947)
and Margers Zariņš (*b* 1910).

Laughing Song

Soprano aria ('Mein Herr Marquis') for
Adele in Act II of J. Strauss' *Die
Fledermaus*.

Laura

(1) Mezzo role in Ponchielli's *La Gioconda*. Alvise's wife, she loves Enzo. (2) Soprano role in Weber's *Die Drei Pintos*. (3) Soprano role in Millöcker's *Der Bettelstudent*. She is in love with Simon. (4) Mezzo role in Dargomijsky's *The Stone Guest*. (5) Mezzo comprimario role in Verdi's *Luisa Miller*. She is a village girl.

Lauretta

Soprano role in Puccini's *Gianni Schicchi*. Schicchi's daughter, she loves Rinuccio.

Lauri-Volpi, Giacomo *(1892–1979)*

Italian tenor, particularly associated with the Italian repertory. One of the greatest tenors of the inter-war period, his ringing voice and outstanding technique made him especially famous in dramatic roles such as Calaf, although he had equal success in lyrical roles. He enjoyed an exceptionally long career, singing into his early 70s. Married to the soprano Maria Ros.

Lawrence, Marjorie *(1909–79)*

Australian soprano (who also sang some mezzo roles), particularly associated with the German and French repertories. A distinguished Wagnerian, she was striken by poliomyelitis in 1941 but managed to continue her career even though she was never again able to walk unaided. She created Keltis in Canteloube's *Vercingétorix*. Her autobiography, *Interrupted Melody*, was published in 1949.

Lazaridis, Stefanos *(b 1945)*

British designer, principally associated with the English National Opera, where his most notable designs have included *Hänsel und Gretel*, *Il Trovatore*, *The Mikado* and *Lady Macbeth of Mtsensk*.

Lazzari, Virgilio *(1887–1953)*

Italian bass, largely resident at the Metropolitan Opera, New York from 1933. A fine singing-actor, he was particularly associated with the Italian repertory, especially Archibaldo in *L'Amore dei Tre Re*.

Le

Titles beginning with the masculine singular form of the French definite article are listed under the letter of the first main word. For example, *Le Roi d'Ys* is listed under R.

Lear

Opera in two parts by Reimann. 1st perf. Munich, 9 July 1978; libr. by Claus H. Henneberg, after Shakespeare's *King Lear*. Principal roles: Lear (bar), Cordelia (sop), Goneril (sop), Regan (sop), Edgar (c-ten), Gloucester (b-bar), Kent (ten), Edmund (ten), Fool (bar), French King (bass). Reimann's best-known opera and one of the most widely performed contemporary operas, it is a powerful and often violent setting which follows Shakespeare closely. [R]

Lear, Evelyn *(b Schulman) (b 1928)*

American soprano, particularly associated with Strauss, Mozart and Berg roles. A singer of outstanding intelligence and artistry, she created the title role in Klebe's *Alkmene*, Jeanne in Egk's *Die Verlobung in San Domingo*, Lavinia in Levy's *Mourning Becomes Electra* and Arkadina in Pasatieri's *The Seagull*. Married to the baritone Thomas Stewart*.

Leave me loathsome light
Bass aria for Somnus in Act III of
Handel's *Semele*.

Leclair, Jean-Marie *(1697–1764)*
French composer. Best known for his
chamber music, he wrote one opera
Scylla et Glaucus (Paris 4 Oct 1746;
libr. d'Alberet) [R]. He was perhaps the
only composer to be murdered.

Lecocq, Charles *(1832–1918)*
French composer. He wrote over 50
operettas, many of which found great
favour. His most successful works
include *Le Docteur Miracle**, *Fleure-de-
Thé* (Paris 11 April 1868; libr. Henri
Charles Chivot and Alfred Duru), *Les
Cent Vièrges* (Brussels 16 March 1872;
libr. Chivot, Duru and Louis François
Clairville), *La Fille de Madame Angot**,
his most enduring work, *Giroflé-Girofla*
(Brussels 21 March 1874; libr. Letterier
and Albert Vanloo), *La Petite Mariée*
(Paris 21 Dec 1875; libr. Letterier and
Vanloo), *Le Petit Duc**, *Le Coeur et le
Main* (Paris 19 Oct 1883; libr. Nuittier
and Beaumont), *Ali-Baba* (Brussels 11
Nov 1888; libr. Vanloo and Busnach)
and *La Belle au Bois Dormant* (Paris
19 Feb 1900; libr. Vanloo and G.
Duval). His only more serious work,
Plutus (Paris 31 May 1886; libr.
Millaud and Jollivet), was a failure.

Legato (Italian for 'bound together')
It denotes singing smoothly. Its
opposite is staccato*.

Légende de Kleinzach, La
Tenor aria for Hoffmann in the
prologue to Offenbach's *Les Contes
d'Hoffmann*.

Legend of the Invisible City of Kitezh and the Maiden Fevronia, The

See Invisible City of Kitezh, The

Leggero (originally spelt *leggiero*)
(Italian for 'light')
In opera, the term describes a type of
soprano suited to lighter lyric roles
such as Gilda.

Lehár, Franz *(b Ferenc) (1870–1948)*
Hungarian composer. His first stage
work was an unsuccessful opera,
Kukuška (Leipzig 27 Nov 1896; libr. F.
Falzari), but it was as an operetta
composer that he achieved outstanding
success. His first work in this genre
was *Wiener Frauen* (Vienna 21 Nov
1902; libr. O. Tann-Bergler and E.
Norini). It was followed by *Tatyana*
(Brünn 21 Feb 1905; libr. M. Kalbeck),
a revision of *Kukuška*, and *Die Lustige
Witwe**, his masterpiece which
immediately made him world famous.
There followed *Der Mann Mit den Drei
Frauen* (Vienna 21 Jan 1908; libr. J.
Bauer), *Der Graf von Luxembourg**,
Das Fürstenkind (Vienna 7 Oct 1909;
libr. Viktor Léon), *Zigeunerliebe**, *Eva*
(Vienna 24 Nov 1911; libr. Robert
Bodanzky, Alfred Maria Willner and E.
Spero), *Endlich Allein* (Vienna 10 Feb
1914; libr. Willner and Bodanzky), *Der
Sterngucker* (*The Astronomer*, Vienna
14 Jan 1916; libr. Willner and Fritz
Löhner), *Wo die Lerche Singt* (Budapest
1 Jan 1918; libr. Willner and Heinrich
Reichert, after F. Martos), *Die Blaue
Mazur* (Vienna 28 May 1920; libr. Leo
Stein and Bela Jénbach), *Frasquita**,
Die Gelbe Jacke (Vienna 9 Feb 1923;
libr. Léon) and *Clo-Clo* (Vienna 8
March 1924; libr. Jenbach). Many of
the later works were unsuccessful but,
partly because of their championship by
Richard Tauber, his next works re-
established his popularity. *Paganini**
was followed by *Der Zarewitsch**,
Friederike*, the highly successful *Das*

*Land des Lächelns** (a revision of *Die Gelbe Jacke*) and *Schön ist die Welt* (Berlin 3 Dec 1930; libr. Löhner and Ludwig Herzer), a revision of *Endlich Allein*. For his last work he returned, this time successfully, to opera with *Giuditta**.

Lehmann, Lilli *(1848–1929)*
German soprano, particularly associated with Mozart and Wagner roles. One of the most famous singers of the 19th century, she had an enormous repertory of 170 roles. She was artistic director of the Salzburg Festival, as well as a noted teacher, whose pupils included Geraldine Farrar and Olive Fremstad. Her autobiography, *Mein Weg*, was published in 1913, and she translated Victor Maurel's autobiography into German. Her sister Marie (1851–1931) was also a successful soprano, and her husband Paul Kalisch (1855–1946) a noted heroic tenor.

Lehmann, Lotte *(1888–1976)*
German soprano. One of the greatest and best-loved singers of the 20th century, she was particularly associated with Strauss roles, especially the Marschallin. She created the Composer in *Ariadne auf Naxos*, the Dyer's Wife in *Die Frau ohne Schatten* and Christine in *Intermezzo*. Her glorious voice, superlative artistry and aristocratic stage presence made her one of the finest opera singers ever. She wrote novels, poetry and her autobiography, *On Wings of Song*, which was published in 1937. She was also a distinguished teacher, whose pupils included Mattiwilda Dobbs, Grace Bumbry and Judith Beckmann.

Leibowitz, René *(1913–72)*
Polish-born French conductor and composer. He was a noted interpreter of the French and Russian repertories

and also composed five operas, of which the most significant is *Les Espagnols à Venise* (Grenoble 1970).

Leicester, Earl of
The historical Robert Dudley, Earl of Leicester, appears in a number of operas, including tenor role in: (1) Donizetti's *Maria Stuarda*. (2) Rossini's *Elisabetta Regina d'Inghilterra*. (3) Donizetti's *Elisabetta al Castello di Kenilworth*. (4) Auber's *Leicester*.

Leider, Frida *(1888–1975)*
German soprano, particularly associated with Wagnerian roles. Her rich voice and powerful dramatic sense made her arguably the finest of all inter-war Wagnerian sopranos. Her autobiography, *Das War Mein Teil*, was published in 1959.

Leiferkus, Sergei *(b 1946)*
Russian baritone, particularly associated with the Italian and Russian repertories. One of the finest of contemporary baritones, he possesses a bright, beautiful and smoothly-produced voice used with outstanding musicianship and is an accomplished singing-actor. He was the first Soviet singer to appear with a regional British opera company.

Leïla
Soprano role in Bizet's *Les Pêcheurs de Perles*. She is a Brahmin priestess loved by Zurga and Nadir.

Leinsdorf, Erich *(b Landauer)* *(b 1912)*
Austrian conductor, particularly associated with Wagner, Verdi and Puccini operas. Resident in the United States since 1937, he was musical director of the New York City Opera (1956–57) but was principally associated with the Metropolitan

Opera. His autobiography, *Cadenza: a Musical Career*, was published in 1976.

Leipzig Opera

The present house (cap. 1,682) opened on 8 October 1960, replacing the previous theatre which had been destroyed by bombs in 1943. Currently one of East Germany's leading houses, its orchestra is the famous Leipzig Gewandhaus. Musical directors have included Artur Nikisch, Gustav Brecher, Helmut Seidelmann, Paul Schmitz, Václav Neumann and Rolf Reuter.

Leise, leise

Soprano aria for Agathe in Act II of Weber's *Der Freischütz*.

Leitmetzerin, Marianne

Soprano role in Richard Strauss' *Der Rosenkavalier*. She is Sophie's duenna.

Leitmotiv (German for 'leading motif')

A musical fragment (melodic, harmonic or rhythmic) associated with a particular character, object or idea which serves as a musical identification tag. Although it had previously been used embryonically (most notably in Grétry's *Richard Coeur de Lion*), it was with Wagner that the concept reached its fullest development, especially in *Der Ring des Nibelungen*, with motifs combining and metamorphosing as an integral part of the symphonic structure.

Leitner, Ferdinand (b 1912)

German conductor, particularly associated with the German repertory. He was musical director of the Munich Opera (1946–47), the Stuttgart Opera (1947–69) and the Zürich Opernhaus (1969–84). He conducted the first

performance of Klebe's *Ein Wahrer Held*.

Lemeshev, Sergei (1902–77)

Russian tenor, particularly associated with French, Russian and Italian lyric roles. Possessor of a beautiful, luscious voice used with fine musicianship and a superb technique, he was also a noted teacher and producer.

Lemnitz, Tiana (b 1897)

German soprano, particularly associated with the German and Italian repertories, especially Octavian and Pamina. A versatile singer with a very lovely voice, she was one of the finest German lyric sopranos of the inter-war period.

Leningrad

See Kirov Opera

Lensky

Tenor role in Tchaikovsky's *Eugene Onegin*. He is a poet engaged to Olga.

Lenya, Lotte (b Karoline Wilhelmine Blamauer) (1898–1981)

Austrian singer and actress. Following her marriage to Kurt Weill in 1926, she became one of the leading exponents of his music, creating Jenny in *Die Dreigroschenoper* and Anna in *Die Sieben Todsünden*.

Leo, Leonardo (1694–1744)

Italian composer. He wrote over 70 operas, all now long forgotten, but a number of which (particularly the comedies) were successful in their time. He was the first composer to introduce the chorus into Neapolitan opera. He was also a noted teacher, whose pupils included Jommelli and Piccinni.

Leoncavallo, Ruggero *(1857– 1919)*

Italian composer. Although his name is inevitably coupled with that of Mascagni, he was a far more talented and sophisticated artist. His choice of subjects and styles (from vast Wagnerian music-drama to fatuous operettas) often led to failure, but in the field of moderate verismo he was a composer of considerable dramatic effectiveness. His stage works, for many of which he wrote his own libretti, are *I Medici* (Milan 9 Nov 1893; composed 1889), the first part of a projected Wagnerian trilogy dealing with Renaissance Italy, *Pagliacci**, which made him world famous and on which his reputation chiefly rests, *Chatterton* (Rome 10 March 1896; libr. after Alfred de Vigny), the unjustly neglected *La Bohème**, the successful *Zazà**, *Der Roland* (Berlin 13 Dec 1904; libr. after W. Alexis), *Maia* (Rome 15 Jan 1910; libr. A. Nessi, after P. de Choudens), *Melbruck* (Rome 19 Jan 1910; libr. Nessi), *Zingari* (London 16 Sept 1912; libr. E. Cavacchioli and G. Emanuel, after Alexander Pushkin's *The Gypsies*), *La Reginetta delle Rose* (Rome 24 June 1912; libr. Giovacchino Forzano), *Are You There?* (London 1 Nov 1913; libr. E. Wallace and A. de Courville), *La Candidata* (Rome 6 Feb 1915; libr. Forzano), *Goffredo Mameli* (Genoa 27 April 1916; libr. Belvederi), *Prestammi Tua Moglie* (Montecatini 2 Sept 1916; libr. E. Corradi), the operetta *A Chi la Giarettiera?* (Rome 16 Oct 1919), the ambitious *Edipo Rè* (Chicago 13 Dec 1920; libr. Forzano, after Sophocles), the operetta *Il Primo Bacio* (Montecatini 29 April 1923; libr. L. Bonelli) and the unfinished *La Maschera Nuda* (Naples 26 June 1925; libr. Bonelli and F. Paolieri), which was completed by S. Allegri.

Leoni, Franco *(1864–1949)*

Italian composer. Among his nine verismo operas, all the palest of pale imitations of Puccini and Mascagni, are *Raggio di Luna* (Milan 1890), *Rip van Winkle* (London 1897), *Ib and Little Christina* (London 1901; libr. after Hans Christian Andersen), the once-popular *L'Oracolo**, *Tzigana* (Genoa 1910), *Francesca da Rimini* (Paris 1914; libr. M. Crawford) and *La Terra del Sogno* (Milan 1920).

Leonora

Opera in two acts by Paer. 1st perf. Dresden, 3 Oct 1804; libr. by Giovanni Schmidt, after Jean Nicolas Bouilly's libretto for Gaveaux's *Léonore*. Principal roles: Leonora (sop), Florestano (ten), Don Pizzaro (ten), Rocco (bass), Giacchino (bar), Marcellina (sop). Although it contains some fine music, it is nowadays all but forgotten. [R]

Leonora

(1) Soprano role in Verdi's *La Forza del Destino*. Carlo's sister, she loves Don Alvaro. (2) Soprano role in Verdi's *Il Trovatore*. A lady-in-waiting to the queen, she loves Manrico. (3) Soprano role in Verdi's *Oberto*. She is Oberto's daughter. (4) Soprano role in Paer's *Leonora*. She is Florestano's wife. (5) Mezzo role in Cimarosa's *Le Astuzie Femminili*. She is Dr Romualdo's fiancée. (6) Soprano role in Nielsen's *Maskarade*. She is Leonard's daughter. (7) Soprano role in Donizetti's *Rosmonda d'Inghilterra*.

Leonore

See Fidelio

Leonore

(1) Soprano role in Beethoven's *Fidelio*. She is Florestan's wife. (2) Mezzo role

in Donizetti's *La Favorite*. She is the King of Castile's mistress. (3) Soprano role in Dittersdorf's *Doktor und Apotheker*. (4) Soprano role in Flotow's *Alessandro Stradella*. She is Bassi's ward.

Léonore
or **L'Amour Conjugal** (*Wedded Love*)
Opera in two acts by Gaveaux. 1st perf. Paris, 19 Feb 1798; libr. by Jean Nicolas Bouilly. The opera from which Beethoven derived the story of *Fidelio*.

Leonore 40/45
Opera in two acts by Liebermann. 1st perf. Basel, 26 March 1952; libr. by Heinrich Strobel. Principal roles: Huguette (sop), Alfred (ten), Emile (bar). Leibermann's most successful work.

Plot: Paris, 1940s. The French girl Huguette meets the German soldier Alfred at a concert during the Nazi occupation. Alfred deserts and is held as a prisoner of war, but the two are reunited after the war through the intervention of Huguette's guardian angel, Emile.

Léonore viens
Baritone aria for Alfonso in Act II of Donizetti's *La Favorite*.

Léopold, Prince
Tenor role in Halévy's *La Juive*. Eudoxie's husband, he loves Rachel.

Leporello
Don Juan's servant, he appears as: (1) Bass-baritone role in Mozart's *Don Giovanni*. (2) Bass role in Dargomijsky's *The Stone Guest*.

Leppard, Raymond (*b* 1927)
British conductor and musicologist. A specialist in 17th-century opera, he has made a number of controversial realisations of operas by Monteverdi and Cavalli. He conducted the first performance of Maw's *The Rising of the Moon*.

Leroux, Xavier (*1863–1919*)
French composer. He wrote a number of operas in the style of his teacher Massenet, all of which are now forgotten. They include *Astarte* (Paris 15 Feb 1901; libr. Louis de Gramont), *La Reine Fiammette* (Paris 23 Dec 1903; libr. Catulle Mendès), *Le Chemineau* (Paris 6 Nov 1907; libr. Jean Richepin) and *Le Carillonneur* (Paris 20 March 1913; libr. Richepin, after G. Rodenbach).

Les
Titles beginning with the plural form of the French definite article are listed under the letter of the first main word. For example, *Les Huguenots* is listed under H.

Lescaut
Manon's brother appears as baritone role in: (1) Puccini's *Manon Lescaut*. (2) Massenet's *Manon*. (3) Henze's *Boulevard Solitude*.

Lesson scenes
A popular device in 18th- and 19th-century comic operas. The two most famous examples are singing lessons: for Rosina in Rossini's *Il Barbiere di Siviglia* and for Marie in Donizetti's *La Fille du Régiment*.

Lesueur, Jean-François (*1760–1837*)
French composer. An important forerunner of French grand opera and of continuous non-number operas, he ranked during the Napoleonic period as

one of the three leading opera composers with Cherubini and Méhul. His works, nowadays all largely forgotten, are *La Caverne* (Paris 15 Feb 1793; libr. Palat-Dercy, after Alain René le Sage's *Gil Blas*), *Paul et Virginie* (Paris 13 Jan 1794; libr. A. Dubreuil), *Télémaque* (Paris 11 May 1796; libr. Palat-Dercy), *Ossian* (Paris 10 July 1804; libr. Palat-Dercy and Jacques Marie Deschamps), his most successful work, *Le Triomphe de Trajan* (Paris 23 Oct 1807; libr. J. A. Esménard), *La Mort d'Adam* (Paris 21 March 1809; libr. Nicolas François Guillard) and the unperformed *Alexandre à Babylon* (1815; libr. Baour-Lormain). He was also a noted teacher, whose pupils included Berlioz, Thomas and Gounod.

Lesur, Daniel *(b 1908)*
French composer. A member of the 'Jeune France' group, his stage works are *Andrea del Sarto* (Marseilles 1969; libr. composer, after Alfred de Musset) [R] and *Ondine* (1982).

Let's Make an Opera
See Little Sweep, The

Letter Duet
Soprano/soprano duet ('Sull'aria') for Susanna and Countess Almaviva in Act III of Mozart's *Le Nozze di Figaro*.

Letter scene
A popular device in 17th-, 18th- and early 19th-century operas, in which a character reads (not sings) a letter brought to him. Nowadays, however, the name is usually used to refer to Tatyana's scene in Act I of Tchaikovsky's *Eugene Onegin*.

Let the bright seraphim
Soprano aria for the Israelite Woman in Act III of Handel's *Samson*.

Letzte Rose, Die
See Last rose of summer, The

Lev
Baritone role in Tippett's *The Ice Break*. Nadia's husband, he is a released political prisoner.

Levi, Hermann *(1839–1900)*
German conductor, particularly associated with Wagner operas. One of the first great Wagnerian interpreters, he was musical director of the Karlsruhe Staatstheater (1867–72) and the Munich Opera (1872–96) and conducted the first performance of *Parsifal*.

Levine, James *(b 1943)*
American conductor, particularly associated with the Italian and German repertories. His interpretations, especially of Verdi and Wagner, are carefully prepared and finely balanced and nuanced, if occasionally rather hard-driven. Musical director of the Metropolitan Opera, New York from 1975 and artistic director since 1986. He is also an accomplished pianist.

Levy, Martin David *(b 1932)*
American composer. His operas, in mildly dissonant style, include *The Tower* (1957), *Escorial* (1958), *Mourning Becomes Electra* (New York 16 March 1967; libr. Henry Butler, after Eugene O'Neill), his finest work, and *The Balcony* (1978).

Lewis, Sir Anthony *(1915–83)*
British conductor and musicologist, particularly associated with Handel and other Baroque composers. A distinguished principal of the Royal Academy of Music, his operatic appearances were infrequent.

Lewis, Richard (b 1914)

British tenor, particularly associated with Mozart and 20th-century roles, especially Idomeneo and Achilles. A versatile artist of outstanding musicianship, he enjoyed a remarkably long career, singing into his late 60s. He created Troilus in *Troilus and Cressida*, Mark in *The Midsummer Marriage*, Achilles in *King Priam* and Amphitryon in Klebe's *Alkemene*.

Libiamo, libiamo

Soprano/tenor duet (the Brindisi) for Violetta and Alfredo in Act I of Verdi's *La Traviata*.

Librettists

See panel on page 329

Libretto (Italian for 'little book')

The term now almost universally used to describe the words of an opera or operetta. It is called *livret* in France.

Libuše

Opera in three acts by Smetana. 1st perf. Prague, 11 June 1881; libr. by Josef Wenzig and Ervín Špindler. Principal roles: Libuše (sop), Přemysl (bar), Chrudoš (bass), Šťáhlav (ten), Krasava (sop). An intensely nationalist work, written for the inauguration of the Prague National Theatre, its ending with Libuše's prophecy of the history of the Czech nation has ensured that it is always the work played on special national occasions. It is only very rarely performed outside Czechoslovakia.

Plot: The Czech ruler, princess Libuše, mediates in a dispute over patrimony between the brothers Chrudoš and Šťáhlav. When Chrudoš denigrates her suitability and integrity as a ruler, Libuše chooses the wise and strong peasant Přemysl as her husband and abdicates her power to him. He becomes the founder of the Přemyslide dynasty. [R]

Licht (Light)

Operatic cycle by Stockhausen. Projected to comprise seven works (one for each day of the week), two have so far been performed: *Donnerstag* (*Thursday*) 1st perf. Milan, 15 March 1981 [R], and *Samstag* (*Saturday*) 1st perf. Milan, 25 May 1984. [R]

Liebe der Danae, Die (The Love of Danae)

Opera in three acts by Richard Strauss (Op 83). 1st perf. Salzburg, 14 Aug 1952 (composed 1940); libr. by Josef Gregor. Principal roles: Danae (sop), Midas (ten), Jupiter (bar). A semi-comic mixture of classical legends, it has never been one of Strauss' more popular works and is infrequently performed.

Plot: Jupiter is in love with Danae and assumes the form of Midas, who also loves her, in order to win her. Danae prefers Midas and Jupiter deprives him of his divinity and his golden touch. Midas and Danae live an ordinary mortal existence and when Jupiter again offers Danae wealth and position and she again refuses, Jupiter is impressed by such loyalty and gives the couple his blessing. [R]

Liebermann, Rolf (b 1910)

Swiss composer and administrator. He has written four operas, all of which have met with a degree of success, in styles ranging from jazz to twelve-tone. *Leonore 40/45** was followed by *Penelope**, *Die Schule der Frauen* (Louiseville 1955; libr. Elisabeth Montagu, after Molière's *L'Ecole des Femmes*; revised version, Salzburg 1957; libr. revised Heinrich Strobel) and *La Fôret* (Geneva 1986). He was administrator of the Hamburg Opera

LIBRETTISTS

Sadly, few major writers have turned their hands to the fashioning of opera libretti, perhaps because the librettist is always overshadowed by the composer, however good the libretto might be. There have, of course, been some important exceptions: Maurice Maeterlinck wrote the libretto for Dukas' *Ariane et Barbe-Bleue*, Arnold Bennett that for Goossens' *Judith*, E. M. Forster that for Britten's *Billy Budd*, W. H. Auden those for Henze's *Elegie für Junge Liebende* and *The Bassarids*, Collette for Ravel's *L'Enfant et les sortilèges*. J. B. Priestley for Bliss' *The Olympians*, and in earlier times both Voltaire and Carlo Goldoni wrote operatic libretti. By and large, however, the purveyors of libretti (particularly in 19th-century Italy and France) were all too often minor playwrights such as Eugène Scribe, journalists, or plain literary hacks such as Andrea Leone Tottola, accustomed to turning out words at a moment's notice. A few, such as Felice Romani, were of a considerably higher calibre, but they were exceptional. The overall literary quality of operatic libretti is thus poor; few composers enjoyed the good fortune of Verdi, Mozart, Strauss and Sullivan of collaborating regularly with artists of the stature of Boito, da Ponte, Hofmannsthal and Gilbert.

Unusual or surprising operatic librettists have included Catherine the Great of Russia (three operas by Pashkevich), Frederick the Great of Prussia (several operas by Graun), the director Franco Zeffirelli (Barber's *Antony and Cleopatra*), the poet Ted Hughes (Crosse's *The Story of Vasco*), Hans Christian Andersen (four Danish operas), the comedian Michael Flanders (Hopkins' *Three's Company*), the painter Oskar Kokoschka (Hindemith's *Mörder, Hoffnung der Frauen* and Křenek's *Orpheus und Eurydike*), Charles Dickens (Hullah's *The Village Coquettes*), the conductor Clemens Krauss (Strauss' *Capriccio*) and the singers David Franklin (Phyllis Tate's *The Lodger*) and Aïno Ackté (Merikanto's *Juha*).

Several composers (particularly Berlioz, Janáček, Leoncavallo, Lortzing, Moussorgsky, Pizzetti, Tippett and Wagner) preferred to write their own libretti, and some (Blacher, Boito, Egk and Menotti) have provided libretti for other composers.

See also **Composer-librettists; Libretto; Writers; Writers as librettists**
Below are listed the 54 librettists with entries in this dictionary. Their nationalities are given in brackets afterwards.

Adami, Giuseppe (It)	Favart, Charles Simon (Fr)	Krásnohorská, Eliška (Cz)
Anelli, Angelo (It)	Ferretti, Jacopo (It)	Marmontel, Jean-François (Fr)
Auden, W. H. (Br)	Foppa, Giuseppe Maria (It)	Meilhac, Henri (Fr)
Barbier, Jules (Fr)	Forzano, Giovacchino (It)	Mélesville, Anne-Honoré Joseph de (Fr)
Bertati, Giovanni (It)	Gallet, Louis (Fr)	Mendès, Catulle (Fr)
Boito, Arrigo (It)	Gay, John (Br)	Merelli, Bartolomeo (It)
Bouilly, Jean Nicolas (Fr)	Genée, Richard (Ger)	Metastasio, Pietro (It)
Brecht, Bertolt (Ger)	Ghislanzoni, Antonio (It)	Neher, Caspar (Ger)
Cain, Henri (Fr)	Gilbert, W. S. (Br)	Piave, Francesco Maria (It)
Calzabigi, Ranieri de' (It)	Guillard, Nicolas François (Fr)	Ponte, Lorenzo da (It)
Cammarano, Salvatore (It)	Halévy, Ludovic (Fr)	Quinault, Philippe (Fr)
Carré, Michel (Fr)	Hofmannsthal, Hugo von (Aus)	Rinuccini, Ottavio (It)
Claudel, Paul (Fr)	Illica, Luigi (It)	Romani, Felice (It)
Clement IX, Pope (It)	Jouy, Victor Joseph Étienne de (Fr)	Rossato, Arturo (It)
Cocteau, Jean (Fr)		Rossi, Gaetano (It)
Coltellini, Marco (It)		
Crozier, Eric (Br)		

Sabina, Karel (Cz)	Scribe, Eugène (Fr)	Willner, Alfred Maria
Saint-Georges, Jules-Henri	Tchaikovsky, Modest	(Aus)
Vernoy de (Fr)	(Russ)	Zeno, Apostolo (It)
Schikaneder, Emanuel	Tottola, Andrea Leone (It)	
(Aus)		

(1959–73) and of the Paris Opéra (1973–80), where he re-established the house's international position. His autobiography, *Actes et Entractes*, was published in 1976.

Liebestod (German for 'love-death') The name always given to Isolde's final monologue 'Mild und leise' in Act III of Wagner's *Tristan und Isolde*. Wagner himself used the term to describe the love duet in Act II.

Liebesverbot, Das (*The Ban on Love*)
or Die Novize von Palermo
(*The Novice of Palermo*).
Opera in two acts by Wagner. 1st perf. Magdeburg, 29 March 1836; libr. by the composer after Shakespeare's *Measure for Measure*. Principal roles: Friedrich (bass), Luzio (ten), Isabella (sop), Brighella (bass), Mariana (sop), Dorella (sop), Claudio (ten). Wagner's second completed opera, and his first to be staged, it bears little resemblance to his mature works and is almost never performed.

Plot: 16th-century Palermo. The hypocritical Governor of Sicily, Friedrich, has issued a ban on love-making under penalty of death. Claudio is falsely condemned and is interceded for by his sister, the novice Isabella. Friedrich agrees to reprieve Claudio in return for Isabella's favours. Isabella sends Friedrich's estranged wife Mariana to the rendezvous in disguise. Friedrich is humiliated and forced to revoke his decree, whilst Isabella marries Claudio's friend Luzio.

Lied (German for 'song')
A term used in 19th-century German opera to describe a solo number in a simpler style than a formal aria.

Liederspiel (German for 'song play')
A German dramatic form, consisting of dialogue interspersed with songs, which developed from Singspiel. Few important composers have used the form, an example of which is Mendelssohn's *Die Heimkehr aus der Fremde*.

Liège
See **Grand Théâtre, Liège**

Life For the Tsar, A (*Zhizn'za Tsarya*)
Opera in four acts by Glinka. 1st perf. St Petersburg, 9 Dec 1836; libr. by Baron Gyorgy Fyodorovich Rosen. Principal roles: Ivan Susanin (bass), Sobinin (ten), Antonida (sop), Vanya (mezzo). Glinka's first opera, it may be said to mark the foundation of the Russian nationalist opera school and is a work of crucial historical importance. It is still regularly performed in Russia and Eastern Europe, but only infrequently in the West. Originally entitled *Ivan Susanin*, the title was changed before the first performance; the original title has been used in Russia since the Revolution.

Plot: Russia, 1613. An invading Polish army is attempting to capture the recently-elected Tsar, who is a student at a monastery. Ivan Susanin, a patriotic Russian peasant, accepts a Polish bribe to lead them to their quarry but, in reality, he leads them astray in the forest while his son-in-law Sobinin takes a group of men to warn the Tsar. When the Poles discover what Ivan has done, they kill him, but the Tsar is safe. [R]

Ligendza, Caterina *(b 1937)*

Swedish soprano, particularly associated with Wagnerian roles. She had a beautiful even-toned voice with a gleaming upper register, and a fine stage presence.

Ligeti, György *(b 1923)*

Hungarian composer. His one opera *Le Grand Macabre* (Stockholm 12 April 1978; libr. composer and Michael Meschke, after Michel de Ghelerode's *La Ballade du Gran Macabre*) [R Exc] has met with considerable success and has been widely performed.

Lighthouse, The

Opera in prologue and one act by Maxwell Davies. 1st perf. Edinburgh, 2 Sept 1980; libr. by the composer. Principal roles: Sandy (ten), Blazes (bar), Arthur (bar). Arguably Maxwell Davies' finest opera, it has been widely performed, and is a powerful and claustrophobic work based on the true disappearance of three lighthouse keepers.

Plot: a Hebridean lighthouse, 1900. The characters of the three lighthouse keepers Arthur, Blazes and Sandy are explored, along with their interrelationships. Tension between them mounts until (along with the audience) they are blinded by mysterious lights. The ending is deliberately ambiguous as to their fate: either they were mad, or they were ghosts, or they were destroyed by a sea beast.

Lily of Killarney, The

Opera in three acts by Benedict. 1st perf. London, 10 Feb 1862; libr. by John Oxenford and Dion Boucicault, after the latter's *Colleen Bawn*. Principal roles: Hardress Cregan (ten), Eily O'Connor (sop), Danny (bar). Benedict's most successful work, it is a story of suspicious happenings in rural Ireland. Enormously popular in the second half of the 19th century, it is nowadays almost never performed.

Lima

See Fundación para Arte Lirica, Lima

Lincoln Center for the Performing Arts

An arts complex in New York which houses, amongst other bodies, the New York City Opera, the Metropolitan Opera and the Juilliard School of Music.

Lind, Jenny *(b Johanna) (1820–87)*

Swedish soprano, particularly associated with Italian and French coloratura roles. Known as the 'Swedish Nightingale', she was one of the greatest singers of the 19th century, possessing a well-focused, limpid and agile voice of great purity. She created Amalia in *I Masnadieri*.

Linda di Chamounix

Opera in three acts by Donizetti. 1st perf. Vienna, 19 May 1842; libr. by Gaetano Rossi, after Adolphe Philippe d'Ennery and Gustave Lemoine's *La Grâce de Dieu*. Principal roles: Linda (sop), Carlo (ten), Antonio (bar), Pierotto (mezzo), Preffeto (b-bar), Marchese (bass). Once described as

"*Lucia di Lammermoor* with a happy ending", it is one of the finest examples of opera semiseria. Enormously popular throughout the 19th century, it is still quite often performed.

Plot: Haute-Savoie and Paris, *c* 1760. To save their daughter Linda from the attentions of the Marchese de Boisfleury, Antonio and Maddalena send her to Paris. There she falls in love with Carlo, who she knows as a poor painter but who is, in reality, the Marchese's nephew. Although her honour is not compromised, Linda lives in an apartment owned by Carlo and, believing her to be Carlo's mistress, her father curses her. Hearing that Carlo is to marry someone else, Linda loses her reason. Returning home, her senses are restored when she discovers that Carlo has refused the marriage planned by his mother. The two are united. [R]

Lindholm, Berit *(b Jonsson)* *(b 1934)*

Swedish soprano, particularly associated with Wagner and Strauss roles. Possessing a vibrant and incisive voice and a good stage presence, she was one of the leading Wagnerian sopranos of the 1970s.

Lindorf

Bass role in Offenbach's *Les Contes d'Hoffmann*. Hoffmann's evil genius, he appears in the three tales as Coppélius, Dr Miracle and Dapertutto.

Lindoro

Tenor role in: (1) Rossini's *L'Italiana in Algieri*. He is in love with Isabella. (2) Haydn's *La Fedeltà Premiata*. He is Amaranta's brother.

Linley, Thomas *(1733–95)*

British composer. He wrote many stage works, of which only *The Duenna* (London 21 Nov 1775; a setting of his son-in-law Sheridan's play) is still in any way remembered. It was written in collaboration with his son Thomas (1756–78) who was also a composer.

Linz Landestheater

The opera house in this Austrian city opened in 1958. Musical directors have included Theodor Gaschbauer.

Lionel

(1) Tenor role in Flotow's *Martha*. He loves Lady Harriet. (2) Baritone role in Tchaikovsky's *The Maid of Orleans*. He is a Burgundian allied to the English.

Lisa

Soprano role in: (1) Tchaikovsky's *The Queen of Spades*. She is Prince Yeletsky's fiancée. (2) Kálmán's *Gräfin Mariza*. (3) Bellini's *La Sonnambula*. She is the inn-keeper. (4) Lehár's *Das Land des Lächelns*.

Lisbon

See Teatro São Carlos, Lisbon

Lisette

Soprano role in Puccini's *La Rondine*. She is Magda's maid.

Lisitsian, Pavel *(b 1911)*

Russian baritone, particularly associated with the Russian and Italian repertories. The leading Russian baritone of the immediate postwar era, in 1960 he became the first Soviet singer to appear at the Metropolitan Opera, New York. He created Napoleon in *War and Peace*.

Liszt, Franz *(b Ferenc)* *(1811–86)*

Hungarian composer, pianist and conductor. Although he wrote only one opera, the youthful *Don Sanche**, he made a considerable contribution to opera, largely through his friendship with and championship of Wagner, whose father-in-law he eventually became. He was musical director of the Weimar Opera (1848–59), where he conducted the first performances of *Der Barbier von Bagdad*, *Lohengrin* and Schubert's *Alfonso und Estrella*. He also produced many transcriptions of operatic melodies for the piano, mainly of the Italian and German repertories.

Lithuanian opera composers

These include Vitolis Baumilas (*b* 1928), Balis Dvarionas (*b* 1904), Beniaminos Gorbulskis (*b* 1925), Julius Juzeliunas (*b* 1916), Georgy Karnavičius (1884–1931), Abel Klenickis (*b* 1904), Vytautas Klova (*b* 1926), Vytautas Laurušas (*b* 1930), Mikas Petrauskas (1873–1937), whose *Birute* (Vilnius 1906) was the first Lithuanian opera, Anastas Račiūnas (*b* 1905) and Stasys Šimkus (1887–1943).

Litolff, Henry Charles *(1818–91)*

British composer. Although best known as an orchestral composer, he also wrote a number of operas, none of which are remembered today. They include *La Mandragore* (1876; libr. after Alexandre Dumas' *Joseph Balsamo*) and *Les Templiers* (Brussels 25 Jan 1886; libr. Jules Adenis, Armand Silvestre and L. Bonnemère).

Little Slippers, The

See Vakula the Blacksmith

Little Sweep, The

Children's opera in one act by Britten (Op 45). 1st perf. Aldeburgh, 14 June 1949; libr. by Eric Crozier, forming the second half of his play *Let's Make an Opera*. Principal roles: Sammy (treble),

Black Bob (bass), Clem (ten), Mrs Baggot (mezzo), Rowan (sop). A charming and educational introduction to opera for younger children, the audience itself takes part in four numbers. In the first half, preparations for the opera are discussed, and in the opera itself the story of a family's rescue of a little sweep's boy is enacted. [R]

Litvinne, Félia *(b Françoise-Jeanne Schütz) (1860–1936)*

Russian-born French soprano, particularly associated with Wagnerian roles and with Alceste. She possessed a brilliant, flexible and resonant voice and had a powerful stage presence. Her autobiography, *Ma Vie et Mon Art*, was published in 1933.

Liù

Soprano role in Puccini's *Turandot*. She is a slave girl serving Timur.

Lloyd, George *(b 1913)*

British composer. He has written three operas: *Iernin* (Penzance 1934; libr. William Lloyd), *The Serf* (London 1938; libr. W. Lloyd) and *John Socman* (1951; libr. W. Lloyd).

Lloyd, Robert *(b 1940)*

British bass, particularly associated with Mozart and Wagner roles and with the Italian repertory. Perhaps the finest British bass of the post-war era, he possesses a voice of great beauty and richness, as well as considerable power, and has a good stage presence.

Lloyd Jones, David *(b 1934)*

British conductor and musicologist, particularly associated with the Russian repertory. He produced the criticial edition, now in almost universal use, of the original version of *Boris Godunov*, and has been musical director of Opera North since its foundation. He conducted the first performance of Hamilton's *The Royal Hunt of the Sun*.

Lo

Titles beginnning with this form of the Italian definite article are listed under the letter of the first main word. For example, *Lo Speziale* is listed under S.

Locke, Matthew (c 1630–77)

British composer. His stage works include the masque *Cupid and Death* (26 March 1653), written in collaboration with Christopher Gibbons, and (with other composers) the opera *The Siege of Rhodes* (London 1656).

Lockhart, James (b 1930)

British conductor with a wide-ranging repertory. He was musical director of the Welsh National Opera (1968–72), the Kassel Staatstheater (1972–80) – the first British conductor to be musical director of a German opera house – and the Koblenz Opera (1981–). He conducted the first performances of Walton's *The Bear* and Edlin's *The Fisherman*.

Lockit

Bass role in Pepusch's *The Beggar's Opera*. He is the jailer.

Lodoïska

Opera in three acts by Cherubini. 1st perf. Paris, 18 July 1791; libr. by Claude François Fillette-Loraux. Principal roles: Lodoïska (sop), Dourlinski (bar), Floreski (ten), Titzikan (bar). An important early example of a rescue opera, it was both popular and influential in its time but is nowadays all but forgotten.

Plot: Dourlinski wants to marry Lodoïska and keeps her incarcerated in his castle on the Polish border. She, however, loves Floreski, who is able to rescue her when the castle is attacked and destroyed by the Tartars led by Titzikan.

Lodoletta

Opera in three acts by Mascagni. 1st perf. Rome, 30 April 1917; libr. by Giovacchino Forzano, after Ouida's *Two Little Wooden Shoes*. Principal roles: Lodoletta (sop), Flammen (ten), Antonio (bass). Reasonably successful at its appearance, it is nowadays almost never performed.

Plot: 19th-century Holland and Paris. Antonio loves Lodoletta and gives her a pair of red shoes. After his death Lodoletta falls in love with Flammen, an artist, and goes to Paris to seek him. Afraid to enter his house because there is a party in progress, she waits outside and dies in the snow where Flammen finds her.

Lodovico

Bass role in Verdi's *Otello*. He is the Venetian envoy.

Loewe, Carl Gottfried (1796–1869)

German composer. Although best known as a song composer, he also wrote a number of operas, none of which are remembered today. They include *Malekadhel* (1832; libr. C. Pichler, after Sir Walter Scott's *The Talisman*) and *Emmy* (1842; libr. Melzer and Hauser, after Scott's *Kenilworth*).

Loge

Tenor role in Wagner's *Das Rheingold*. He is the god of fire.

Lohengrin

Opera in three acts by Wagner. 1st
perf. Weimar, 28 Aug 1850; libr. by
the composer, after an anonymous
German epic. Principal roles: Lohengrin
(ten), Elsa von Brabant (sop), Ortrud
(sop), Telramund (bar), Heinrich (bass),
Herald (bar). Wagner's last opera in
'traditional' style, it has always been
one of his most popular works.

Plot: 10th-century Antwerp. King
Henry the Fowler of Germany, visiting
Antwerp, finds there is a dispute in
progress concerning the succession to
the Dukedom of Brabant. Friedrich of
Telramund claims the title, accusing
Elsa of having murdered the true heir,
her brother Gottfried. The King decrees
single combat between Telramund and
Elsa's champion to decide the issue.
The Herald calls for Elsa's champion
but nobody comes forward, and she
describes her dream of a shining knight.
Lohengrin, drawn by a swan, then
appears and agrees to champion and
marry her provided she never asks his
name or origin. Lohengrin defeats
Telramund, who is outlawed as a
traitor. Telramund conspires with his
wife Ortrud to undermine Elsa's faith
in Lohengrin. During the wedding
ceremony they accuse Lohengrin in
public of using sorcery. Later, the now-
troubled Elsa is unable to restrain
herself and asks Lohengrin's identity.
Telramund breaks in but is killed by
Lohengrin, who tells everyone the
answer to Elsa's question: he is
Lohengrin, a knight of the Holy Grail,
permitted to live amongst men only so
long as his identity is unknown. He
bids farewell to Elsa, and his swan is
revealed as the bewitched Gottfried, the
rightful heir, now returned to human
form. [R]

Lola

Mezzo role in Mascagni's *Cavalleria*
Rusticana. She is Alfio's wife and
Turiddù's mistress.

Lombard, Alain *(b 1940)*

French conductor, particularly
associated with the French repertory. A
sensitive and often exciting interpreter
of his native repertory, who began his
career as a child prodigy, he was
musical director of the Opéra du Rhin
(1974–80).

Lombardi alla Prima Crociata, I *(The Lombards at the First Crusade)*

Opera in four acts by Verdi. 1st perf.
Milan, 11 Feb 1843; libr. by
Temistocle Solera, after Tomasso
Grossi's poem. Revised version
Jérusalem 1st perf. Paris, 26 Nov 1847;
libr. revised by Alphonse Reyer and
Gustave Vaëz. Principal roles (with *I
Lombardi* first): Giselda/Hélène (sop),
Pagano/Roger (bass), Oronte/Gaston
(ten), Arvino/Comte de Toulouse (ten).
Verdi's fourth opera, it is a typical
example of his vigorous early style, and
has been regularly performed in recent
decades. The original version is nearly
always preferred.

Plot: Milan and the Holy Land,
1096–97. Pagano returns from an exile
imposed for trying to kill his brother
Arvino. He bungles his attempt to
repeat the crime, accidentally killing his
father and, exiled again, becomes a
hermit living near Antioch. Arvino's
daughter Giselda is captured by the
Moslems and falls in love with Oronte,
their leader's son. Arvino, leading the
Crusaders, is disowned by his daughter
when Oronte is killed by the Lombard
forces. In sight of Jerusalem the now-
saintly Pagano is mortally wounded and
is granted forgiveness by Arvino and
Giselda. [R]

London
See Great Britain

London, George *(b Burnstein) (b 1919)*
Canadian-born American baritone, producer and administrator. Making his name as a member of the Bel Canto Trio with Mario Lanza and Frances Yeend, he became particularly associated with the Italian and German repertories and with Boris Godunov, in which role he became the first American singer ever to appear at the Bolshoi Opera. A superb singing-actor with a magnificent dark voice, he was one of the finest operatic artists of the postwar era. He was responsible for a number of notable productions in the United States, and was administrator of the Opera Society of Washington (1975–80), the Los Angeles Opera Association and the Kennedy Center, Washington (1968–71).

London Coliseum
See English National Opera

London Opera Centre
Britain's principal school of advanced operatic study until 1977, when it was superseded by the National Opera Studio*. Musical directors included James Robertson.

Loose, Emmy *(1914–87)*
Austrian soprano, particularly associated with Mozart roles. She had an appealingly silvery voice used with a fine technique, and an attractive stage presence.

López-Cobos, Jesús *(b 1940)*
Spanish conductor, particularly associated with the Italian repertory. He was musical director of the Deutsche Oper, Berlin (1978–88).

Loreley
Works of this title about the water siren of German legend include:

(1) Unfinished opera by Mendelssohn (Op 98). Begun 1847; libr. after Emmanuel Geibel.

(2) Opera in three acts by Bruch (Op 16). 1st perf. Mannheim, 14 April 1863; libr. after Emmanuel Geibel. Principal roles: Lenore (sop), Otto (ten), Bertha (sop), Hubert (bar), Reinald (bass). Bruch's best work, it is nowadays all but forgotten.

(3) Opera in three acts by Catalani. 1st perf. (as *Elda*) Turin, 31 Jan 1880; libr. by Carlo d'Ormeville. Revised version, 1st perf. Turin, 16 Feb 1890; libr. revised by Angelo Zanardini. Principal roles: Loreley (sop), Walther (ten), Anna (sop). Catalani's only opera apart from *La Wally* to have survived, it is still occasionally performed in Italy.

Plot: Rhineland, *c* 1500. The orphan girl Loreley is in love with Walther, who rejects her in favour of Anna. Loreley promises herself to Alberich, King of the Rhine, if he will transform her into an irresistible enchantress. At the wedding of Walther and Anna, the Loreley appears in her new guise and Walther falls in love with her, abandoning Anna. However, Loreley now belongs to the river, into which Walther throws himself.

Lorengar, Pilar *(b Lorenza García) (b 1921)*
Spanish soprano, particularly associated with Mozart and lighter Italian roles. She had a beautiful silvery voice and a warmly sympathetic stage presence. Early in her career she was also a successful exponent of zarzuela.

Lorenz, Max *(1901–75)*

German tenor, particularly associated with Wagnerian roles and with Otello. Possibly the finest heldentenor of the inter-war period, he created roles in Einem's *Der Prozess*, Liebermann's *Penelope* and Wagner-Régeny's *Das Bergwerk zu Falun*.

Lorenzo

(1) Bass role in Bellini's *I Capuleti e i Montecchi*. He is the Capulet doctor. (2) Tenor role in Auber's *Fra Diavolo*. He loves Zerlina. (3) Tenor comprimario role in Auber's *La Muette de Portici*.

Loris

Tenor role in Giordano's *Fedora*. He is a Russian nihilist.

Lortzing, Albert *(1801–51)*

German composer. He wrote 12 operas, notable for their sparkling melodies, which developed Singspiel into a more sophisticated form. Many of his operas (for all of which he wrote his own libretti) are still popular in Germany, especially the comedies. His first opera *Ali Pascha von Janina* (Münster 1 Feb 1828, composed 1824) was followed by the comedy *Die Beiden Schützen* (Leipzig 20 Feb 1837; libr. after G. Cords) and *Zar und Zimmermann**, which established his reputation and which remains his most popular work. There followed *Caramo* (Leipzig 20 Sept 1829; libr. after A. Vilein de Saint-Hilaire and P. Duport's *Cosimo*), *Hans Sachs* (Leipzig 23 June 1840; libr. composer and Philipp Reger, after Johann Ludwig Deinhardtstein), *Casanova* (Leipzig 31 Dec 1841; libr. after A. Lebrun), the highly successful *Der Wildschütz**, *Undine**, the still-popular *Der Waffenschmied**, *Zum Grossadmiral* (Leipzig 13 Dec 1847;

libr. after A. W. Ittland's *Heinrich des Fünften Jungenjähre*), the pro-revolutionary *Regina* (Berlin 21 March 1899, composed 1848), which lost him his job, *Rolands Knappen* (Leipzig 25 May 1849) and the comedy *Die Opernprobe**. In addition, the early opera *Die Schätzkammer des Ynka* (1836; libr. R. Blum) is lost and *Szenen aus Mozarts Leben* is a pastiche from his other music.

Los Angeles Music Center Opera

Many opera companies have been formed in Los Angeles, but none lasted more than a few years. The present company was formed in 1986 and gives an annual season from September to March. Performances are given at the Dorothy Chandler Pavilion (cap. 3,197), which opened in 1964.

Lotario

Opera in three acts by Handel. 1st perf. London, 2 Dec 1729; libr. after Antonio Salvi. It is nowadays only very rarely performed.

Lott, Felicity *(b 1947)*

British soprano, particularly associated with Mozart and Strauss roles and with the French repertory. Her beautiful, creamy (although literally bottomless) voice is used with outstanding musicianship and intelligence and she is a singing-actress of considerable accomplishment.

Loughran, James *(b 1931)*

British conductor. Best known as a symphonic conductor, his recent operatic appearances have been rare. He conducted the first performances of Williamson's *Our Man in Havana*, Thomas Wilson's *The Charcoal Burner* and Musgrave's *The Abbot of Drimock*.

Louise

Opera in four acts by Charpentier. 1st perf. Paris, 2 Feb 1900; libr. by the composer. Principal roles: Louise (sop), Julien (ten), Father (b-bar), Mother (mezzo). Charpentier's only work to have survived, it is a verismo piece with socialist overtones. Sensationally successful at its appearance, it clocked up over 1,000 performances in Paris alone during the composer's lifetime. Charpentier's follow-up to the story, *Julien**, was a complete failure.

Plot: Paris, *c* 1900. Not permitted by her parents to marry the painter Julien, Louise, a working-class girl, leaves home and goes to live with her lover in Montmartre. When her mother informs her that her father is seriously ill and wishes to see her, Louise agrees to go home on the condition that she will be free to return to Julien. However, when her father has recovered, her parents will not allow her to leave. Eventually, a violent quarrel erupts and the girl is expelled from the house, leaving her father to curse Paris which has stolen so much from him. [R]

Love of Three Oranges, The

(*Lyubov k Tryom Apelsinam*)
Opera in four acts by Prokofiev (Op 33). 1st perf. Chicago, 30 Dec 1921; libr. by the composer, after Carlo Gozzi's *L'Amore delle Tre Melerance*. Principal roles: Prince (ten), Fata Morgana (sop), Truffaldino (ten), Clarissa (mezzo), King of Clubs (bass), Leander (bass), Pantaloon (bass). Constructed as an opera-within-an-opera, it is a delightful satirical comedy based on the Commedia dell'Arte tradition, and is the most frequently performed of Prokofiev's operas in the

West. The orchestral suite arranged by the composer has given the music wider currency.

Plot: The King of Clubs fears that his ailing son the Prince will die, and is told that only laughter can cure him. Various amusing diversions are attempted, but all are in vain until the witch Fata Morgana accidentally succeeds by falling flat on her back. She prophesies that the Prince will fall in love with three oranges, and he leaves in search of them. He discovers three enormous oranges (all of which contain a princess) and cuts them open in the desert. Two of the princesses die of thirst, but the third survives and eventually goes home with the Prince. [R]

Lualdi, Adriano *(1885–1971)*

Italian composer and conductor. His operas, written in neo-classical style and for all of which he wrote his own libretti, include *Il Cantico* (1915), *Le Furie di Arlecchino* (Milan 1915), *La Morte di Rinaldo* (1920), the marionette opera *Guerrin Meschino* (1920), *La Figlia del Rè* (Turin 1922), *Il Diavolo del Campanile* (Milan 1925; libr. after Edgar Allan Poe's *The Devil in the Belfry*), *La Grançeola* (Venice 1932), *Lumawig e la Saetta* (Rome 1936) and *La Luna dei Caraibi* (Rome 1953; libr. after Eugene O'Neill).

Lübeck Opera

The opera house (cap. 1,012) in this German town in Schleswig-Holstein opened in 1908. Musical directors have included Wilhelm Furtwängler, Berthold Lehmann, Christoph von Dohnányi, Gerd Albrecht and Bernhard Klee.

Luca, Giuseppe de *(1876–1950)*

Italian baritone, particularly associated with the Italian repertory. One of the greatest baritones of the 20th century, possessing a beautiful voice used with a matchless technique, he enjoyed a remarkably long career, singing into his 70s. He created Michonnet in *Adriana Lecouvreur*, Sharpless in *Madama Butterfly*, the title role in *Gianni Schicchi*, Paquiro in *Goyescas* and Gleby in Giordano's *Siberia*.

Luce langue, La
Soprano aria for Lady Macbeth in Act II of Verdi's *Macbeth*. It was newly composed for the 1865 revised version.

Lucerne
See Luzern Stadttheater

Luchetti, Veriano *(b 1939)*
Italian tenor, particularly associated with the Italian repertory. An accomplished and sometimes underrated singer, he has a fine voice used with a good technique but is a little dull on stage.

Lucia
(1) Mezzo role in Mascagni's *Cavalleria Rusticana*. She is Turiddù's mother. (2) Soprano role in Donizetti's *Lucia di Lammermoor*. Enrico's sister, she loves Edgardo. (3) Mezzo role in Rossini's *La Gazza Ladra*. She is Fabrizio's wife. (4) Soprano role in Britten's *The Rape of Lucretia*. She is Lucretia's attendant.

Lucia, Fernando de *(1860– 1925)*
Italian tenor, particularly associated with Verdi and Italian bel canto roles. Possessor of a beautiful voice used with a flawless technique, he created for Mascagni the title role in *L'Amico Fritz*, Osaka in *Iris* and roles in *I Rantzau* and *Silvano*. He was also a distinguished teacher, whose pupils included Georges Thill.

Lucia di Lammermoor
Opera in three acts by Donizetti. 1st perf. Naples, 26 Sept 1835; libr. by Salvatore Cammarano, after Sir Walter Scott's *The Bride of Lammermoor*. Principal roles: Lucia (sop), Edgardo (ten), Enrico (bar), Raimondo (bass), Arturo (ten), Alisa (mezzo). The quintessential romantic opera, it was sensationally successful at its appearance and remains Donizetti's most popular serious work. Whilst the famous Mad Scene provides a spectacular vehicle for a singing-actress, the work's greatest dramatic strengths are to be found in the tenor's final scene and in the sextet, the epitome of operatic ensemble writing.

Plot: 17th-century Scotland. Lucia loves Edgardo, the dispossessed master of Ravenswood and an enemy of her family. The couple exchange rings and vows before Edgardo leaves on a mission and Lucia's brother, Enrico, learning of this, is outraged. He wishes her to make a politically advantageous marriage to Lord Arturo Bucklaw and shows her a forged letter supposedly written by Edgardo which seems to prove her lover's infidelity. In the light of this, and persuaded on by the chaplain Raimondo, she unwillingly accepts the marriage. Edgardo returns, breaks in on the wedding celebrations, curses Lucia and flings her ring at her, provoking Enrico to challenge him to a duel in the Ravenswood cemetery. The strain proves too much for Lucia who loses her reason, murders Arturo and hallucinates about a marriage with Edgardo. Arriving for the duel, Edgardo is told by Raimondo that Lucia is dead. In anguish, Edgardo stabs himself. [R]

Lucio Silla
Opera in three acts by Mozart (K 135). 1st perf. Milan, 26 Dec 1772; libr. by Giovanni da Gamerra and Pietro

Metastasio. Principal roles: Lucio (ten), Cecilio (sop), Giunia (sop), Cinna (sop), Celia (sop), Aufidio (ten). An astonishingly assured early work, telling of an incident in the life of the Roman dictator Lucius Sulla (138–78 BC), it is still occasionally performed.

Plot: Rome. Silla wishes to marry Giunia and has her exiled lover Cecilio condemned to death for plotting against him. Giunia retaliates by censuring him before the Senate, an act which moves him to mercy, and she is reunited with Cecilio. [R]

Lucky Peter's Journey

Opera in three acts by Williamson. 1st perf. London, 18 Dec 1969; libr. by Edmund Tracey, after August Strindberg's *Lycko-Pers Resa*. Principal roles: Peter (bar), Lisa (mezzo). It tells of a quest-hero who finds both himself and true love after rejecting the false attractions of worldly success.

Lucrezia Borgia

Opera in prologue and two acts by Donizetti. 1st perf. Milan, 26 Dec 1833; libr. by Felice Romani, after Victor Hugo's *Lucrèce Borgia*. Principal roles: Lucrezia (sop), Gennaro (ten), Alfonso d'Este (bass), Maffio Orsini (mezzo). Telling a partially fictitious story of Pope Alexander VI's daughter Lucrezia Borgia (1480–1519), it was the most frequently performed of all Donizetti's works throughout the 19th century. Arguably Donizetti's finest tragic opera, it marked the appearance in Italian opera of romantic melodrama and had a considerable influence on other composers.

Plot: Early 16th-century Venice and Ferrara. During Carnival in Venice, Gennaro is drawn to an unknown woman, until Maffio Orsini and his other friends reveal her as the infamous Lucrezia Borgia. Lucrezia's husband,

Duke Alfonso d'Este of Ferrara, is jealous of his wife's interest in Gennaro, and Gennaro – to prove that he has no feelings for Lucrezia – defaces the Borgia crest in front of his friends. Lucrezia demands of Alfonso the death penalty for the offender but is horrified to discover that he is Gennaro who, unbeknownst to all but herself, is her son. Alfonso makes her give Gennaro the poisoned Borgia wine, but after his departure, she persuades the young man to drink an antidote. Gennaro joins Maffio and his friends at a banquet, where Lucrezia – in revenge for her treatment in Venice – has poisoned the wine. Appalled to discover Gennaro amongst the guests, Lucrezia reveals that she is his mother and begs him to take the antidote but, shocked to learn his true parentage, Gennaro prefers to die with his friends. [R]

Ludmila

(1) Mezzo role in Smetana's *The Bartered Bride*. She is Krušina's wife. (2) Soprano role in Glinka's *Ruslan and Ludmila*. She is Svyetozar's daughter.

Ludwig, Christa (b 1928)

German mezzo, particularly associated with Mozart, Strauss and Wagner roles. One of the outstanding mezzos of the postwar era, the range, power and technique of her voice were such that she was also able to sing a number of soprano roles, notably Leonore in *Fidelio*. Also a fine singing-actress, she created Claire in Einem's *Der Besuch der Alten Dame*. Married for a time to the baritone Walter Berry*.

Ludwig, Leopold (1908–79)

Austrian conductor, particularly associated with the German repertory. He was musical director of the Hamburg State Opera (1951–71).

Luigi

Tenor role in Puccini's *Il Tabarro*. He is a bargehand in love with Giorgetta.

Luisa Miller

Opera in three acts by Verdi. 1st perf. Naples, 8 Dec 1849; libr. by Salvatore Cammarano, after Friedrich von Schiller's *Kabale und Liebe*. Principal roles: Luisa (sop), Rodolfo (ten), Miller (bar), Count Walther (bass), Wurm (bass), Federica (mezzo). The work which marks the transition between Verdi's early and middle periods (with Act III entirely inhabiting the second), it has won a permanent place in the repertory in recent years.

Plot: early 17th-century Tyrol. Luisa, daughter of the old soldier Miller, loves Rodolfo, who she believes to be a commoner but who is in fact the son of Count Walther. Walther wishes Rodolfo to marry Federica, Duchess of Ostheim, and plots with his evil steward, Wurm, to separate him from Luisa. Walther has Miller arrested and, to obtain his freedom, Luisa is forced by Wurm to write a letter saying that she never loved Rodolfo but actually loves Wurm. Luisa and Miller plan to go into exile together, but Rodolfo arrives and he and Luisa drink wine that he has poisoned. Realising that she is dying, Luisa tells him the truth, and the dying Rodolfo kills Wurm. [R]

Lully, Jean-Baptiste *(b Giovanni Battista Lulli) (1632–87)*

Italian-born French composer. Court composer to Louis XIV, Lully may be regarded – through his collaborations with Molière and Philippe Quinault – as the effective founder of French opera. With Molière he produced a number of comedy-ballets, of which the most successful was *Le Bourgeois Gentilhomme**. His first true opera was *Les Fêtes de l'Amour et de Bacchus* (Paris 15 Nov 1672). It was followed by *Cadmus et Hermione* (Paris 27 April 1673), the first of his tragédie-lyriques written with Philippe Quinault. These are marked by a clarity of declamation and the first appearance in opera of the modern orchestra with its solid string foundation. To our ears and eyes, these works can seem extremely stiff and formal, but nonetheless they often exhibit considerable dramatic power. His other operas are *Alceste**, *Thésée* (St Germain 12 Jan 1675) [R Exc], *Atys* (St Germain 10 Jan 1676) [R], *Isis**, *Psyché* (Paris 19 April 1678), *Bellérophon* (Paris 31 Jan 1679), *Proserpine* (St Germain 3 Feb 1680), *Persée* (Paris 18 April 1682; libr. after Pierre Corneille's *Andromède*), *Phaëton* (Versailles 6 Jan 1683), *Amadis**, *Roland* (Versailles 18 Jan 1685; libr. after Lodovico Ariosto's *Orlando Furioso*), *Armide et Renaud**, *Acis et Galatée* (Anet 6 Sept 1686; libr. Jean-Galbert de Campistron) and *Achille et Polyxène* (Paris 7 Nov 1687; libr. Campistron). There has recently been a considerable revival of interest in Lully's works, and performances are becoming more frequent.

Lully appears as a character in Grétry's *Les Trois Ages de l'Opéra* and in Isouard's *Lully et Quinault*. He may be said to be the only composer whose profession caused his death: he hit his foot with the pole used to beat time and died of gangrene.

Lulu

Opera in three acts by Berg. 1st perf. (Acts 1 and II only) Zürich, 2 June 1937; 1st complete perf. (edited by Friedrich Cerha) Paris, 24 Feb 1979; libr. by the composer, after Frank Wedekind's *Erdgeist* and *Die Büchse der Pandora*. Principal roles: Lulu (sop), Alwa (ten), Dr Schön (bar), Schigolch (b-bar), Countess Geschwitz (mezzo), Painter (ten), Acrobat (bass),

Schoolboy (mezzo), Marquis (ten), Animal Tamer (bar), Banker (bass), Prince (ten). One of the finest and most compelling of 20th-century operas, the world had to wait for over 40 years after Berg's death to hear it complete because of his widow's refusal to release the Act III material.

Plot: Germany, Paris and London, late 19th century. The Animal Tamer introduces his menagerie, the star turn of which is the femme fatale Lulu, mistress of the newspaper editor Dr Schön. She destroys all her admirers and lovers, and finally kills Schön whom she has manipulated into marrying her. She escapes from prison with the aid of her lesbian lover, Countess Geschwitz. She visits Paris and then settles in London where she supports herself, Geschwitz, Schön's son Alwa and the old swindler Schigolch (who might have been her father) by prostitution. She and the Countess are killed by her last customer, Jack the Ripper. [R]

Luna, Conte di

Baritone role in Verdi's *Il Trovatore*. In reality Manrico's brother, he loves Leonora.

Luna y Carné, Pablo *(1880– 1942)*

Spanish composer. He wrote many successful zarzuelas, of which the most enduring are *Los Molinos de Viento* (*The Windmills*, Seville 1910) [R], *Los Cadetes de la Reina* (Madrid 1913) [R], *El Niño Judío* (Madrid 1918) and *La Pícera Molinera* (Madrid 1928).

Lustigen Weiber von Windsor, Die *(The Merry Wives of Windsor)*

Works of this title based on Shakespeare's play include:

(1) Opera in two acts by Dittersdorf.

1st perf. Oels, 25 June 1796; libr. by the composer.

(2) Opera in three acts by Nicolaï. 1st perf. Berlin, 9 March 1849; libr. by Salomon Hermann Mosenthal. Principal roles: Falstaff (bass), Frau Fluth (sop), Herr Fluth (bar), Anne Reich (sop), Fenton (ten), Herr Reich (bass), Frau Reich (mezzo). Arguably the greatest of all German comic operas, it is Nicolaï's only work to have survived. An instant success, it remains enormously popular in German-speaking countries but, unaccountably, is seldom performed elsewhere, although the sparkling overture is well known.

Plot: 15th-century Windsor. Falstaff sends love letters to Frau Fluth and Frau Reich who determine to teach him a lesson. Herr Fluth wishes his daughter Anne to marry Slender and repels her admirer Fenton. Falstaff, arriving for his assignation, is dumped into the Thames in a laundry basket. The disguised Fluth visits Falstaff at the Garter Inn whilst Anne is serenaded in her garden by her admirers. Fluth institutes a search for his wife's supposed lover and Falstaff is smuggled out disguised as a deaf old woman. In Windsor Forest, Falstaff is discomfited by the merry wives disguised as fairies, but all ends happily without malice. [R]

Lustige Witwe, Die *(The Merry Widow)*

Operetta in three acts by Lehár. 1st perf. Vienna, 30 Dec 1905; libr. by Viktor Léon and Leo Stein, after Henri Meilhac's *L'Attaché d'Ambassade*. Principal roles: Hanna Glawari (sop), Count Danilo (ten), Valencienne (sop), Camille de Rossilon (ten), Baron Mirko Zita (bar), Cascada (ten), St Brioche (bar). The work which established Lehár's reputation, it was sensationally successful at its appearance, remaining ever since one of the most popular of all operettas.

Plot: Paris. Hanna, widow of the banker Glawari, has been left a fortune. It is essential to the finances of Pontevedro that she marries a Pontevedrian rather than a foreigner. The Pontevedrian Ambassador Baron Zeta – whose 'highly respectable wife' Valencienne is pursued by Camille de Rossilon – orders his high-living attaché Count Danilo to serve his fatherland for a change and marry Hanna. The two had been in love in the past, but Danilo has vowed that he will never say 'I love you' to Hanna. It takes much intrigue and all Hanna's wiles to get him to give in so that all can end happily and Pontevedro be saved from bankruptcy. [R]

Lutyens, Elizabeth (b 1906)
British composer. Her operas, written in twelve-tone style, are *Infidelio* (1954; libr. composer), *The Numbered* (1967; libr. M. Volonakis, after Canetti's *Die Befristeten*) and *Time Off? Not a Ghost of a Chance* (London 1972; libr. composer).

Luxon, Benjamin (b 1937)
British baritone, particularly associated with Mozart and Britten roles and with Eugene Onegin. A warm-voiced singer and a fine singing-actor, he created the title role in *Owen Wingrave* and the Jester in Maxwell Davies' *Taverner*.

Luzern Stadttheater
The opera house in this town in Switzerland was designed by Luis Pfuffler von Wyer and opened on 17 November 1839. It burnt down in 1924, was rebuilt to the same design in 1926 and was enlarged (cap. 564) in 1929. Musical directors have included Ernest Hans Baar, Ulrich Mayer and Roderick Brydon.

Lyon
See Opéra de Lyon

Lyric
Strictly meaning a vocal performance accompanied by the lyre, the term has come to mean anything which is sung. Hence the frequent description of opera as lyric drama and of its stage as the lyric theatre.

Lysander
Tenor role in Britten's *A Midsummer Night's Dream*. He is one of the four lovers.

Lysenko, Mykola (1842–1912)
Ukrainian composer. He wrote a number of operas and operettas, many of them successful in the Ukraine, but his aversion to having his works translated into Russian has prevented them from becoming better known. His most successful works include *Christmas Eve* (Kharkov 1883, composed 1873; libr. Starytsky, after Nikolai Gogol), *Natalka Poltavka* (1889; libr. Starytsky, after Koltayrevsky) [R] and *Taras Bulba* (Kiev Dec 1903, composed 1890; libr. Starytsky, after Gogol) [R].

Lysiart
Baritone role in Weber's *Euryanthe*. The Count of Forest, he is the knight who wagers that he can prove Euryanthe unfaithful.

Maag, Peter *(b 1919)*

Swiss conductor, particularly associated
with Mozart operas. He has been
responsible for the revival of neglected
18th- and 19th-century works and
often acts as producer as well as
conductor. He was musical director of
the Bonn Stadttheater (1954–59), the
Teatro Regio, Parma (1972) and the
Teatro Regio, Turin (1974–76).

Maazel, Lorin *(b 1930)*

American conductor, particularly
associated with Wagner and Puccini
operas. One of the leading
contemporary American conductors,
who first appeared as a child prodigy,
he was musical director of the Deutsche
Oper, Berlin (1965–71) and the Vienna
State Opera (1982–84) and was the
first American conductor to appear at
the Bayreuth Festival. He conducted the
first performances of Dallapiccola's
Ulisse and Berio's *Un Rè in Ascolto*.
He is also an accomplished violinist.

Macbeth

Works of this title based on
Shakespeare's play include:

(1) Opera in four acts by Verdi. 1st
perf. Florence, 14 March 1847; libr. by
the composer and Francesco Maria
Piave. Revised version, 1st perf. Paris,
21 April 1865; libr. revised by Count
Andrea Maffei. Principal roles: Macbeth
(bar), Lady Macbeth (sop), Banquo
(bass), Macduff (ten), Malcolm (ten).
Verdi's first Shakespearean opera, and
arguably his finest early period work, it
suffered a long spell of neglect but is
now firmly re-established in the
repertory. Despite occasional
unevenness, it is a sombre and powerful
setting, following the play closely but
with Lady Macbeth becoming even
more the dominant partner. The revised
version is nearly always preferred.

Plot: Scotland. The generals Macbeth
and Banquo are met by the witches
who foretell that Macbeth will reign
but that Banquo's issue will reign after.
Macbeth's ambitious wife Lady
Macbeth persuades him to murder King
Duncan during the King's visit to their
castle. Macbeth gains the crown and
has Banquo killed. The pair's
consciences give them no rest: the
witches reiterate to Macbeth that
Banquo's line will rule and Lady
Macbeth, walking in her sleep, is
obsessed by the image of Duncan's
blood and eventually dies. Rebels led
by Macduff invade from England and
Macbeth is defeated and killed.
Duncan's son Malcolm is proclaimed
king. [R]

(2) Opera in three acts by Bloch. 1st
perf. Paris, 30 Nov 1910; libr. by
Edmond Fleg. Principal roles: Macbeth
(bar), Lady Macbeth (sop), Macduff
(bass), Banquo (ten), Three Witches
(sop, mezzo and cont), Duncan (ten).
Block's only opera, it is a powerful and
imaginative setting, whose almost total
neglect is unaccountable.

Macchia, Una

Soprano aria (the Sleepwalking Scene)
for Lady Macbeth in Act III of Verdi's
Macbeth.

McCormack, Count John
(1884–1945)
Irish tenor, particularly associated with the Italian repertory. His operatic career was short: he retired because of his self-confessed lack of acting ability. He had a beautiful, limpid voice and outstanding diction, and his elegant phrasing and remarkable breath control remain an object lesson to all singers. He created Paul Merrill in Herbert's *Natoma*. His autobiography, *John McCormack: His Life Story*, was published in 1918.

McCracken, James *(1926–88)*
American tenor, particularly associated with dramatic roles, especially Otello. An exciting heroic tenor, whose powerful physique and thrilling stage presence distracted attention from some quite serious vocal shortcomings. Married to the mezzo Sandra Warfield. Their joint autobiography, *A Star in the Family*, was published in 1971.

MacCunn, Hamish *(1868–1916)*
British composer and conductor. Influenced by Wagner, he was a leading advocate of a native Scottish musical school. The most successful of his operas was *Jeanie Deans* (Edinburgh 15 Nov 1894; libr. J. Bennett, after Sir Walter Scott's *The Heart of Midlothian*). Of his other works, only *Diarmid* (London 23 Oct 1897; libr. Duke of Argyle) met with success.

Macduff
A Scottish noble, he appears as: (1) Tenor role in Verdi's *Macbeth*. (2) Bass role in Bloch's *Macbeth*.

MacFarren, Sir George *(1813–87)*
British composer. He wrote seven operas, all now forgotten, including *The Devil's Opera* (London 13 Aug 1838; libr. composer), *An Adventure of Don Quixote* (London 3 Feb 1846; libr. composer, after Miguel Cervantes), *King Charles II* (London 24 Oct 1849; libr. D. Ryan), *Robin Hood* (London 2 Nov 1863; libr. John Oxenford) and *Helvellyn* (London 3 Nov 1864; libr. Oxenford). His wife Natalia (1827–1916) was a contralto who also made many fine opera translations for the music publishers, Novello.

MacHeath
Baritone role in Pepusch's *The Beggar's Opera*. He is a highwayman.

McIntyre, Donald *(b 1934)*
New Zealand baritone, particularly associated with Wagnerian roles, especially Wotan. One of the leading heldenbaritons of the 1970s, he had a powerful voice and a strong if somewhat generalised stage presence. He created Heyst in Bennett's *Victory*.

Mackerras, Sir Charles *(b 1925)*
Australian conductor, particularly associated with Handel, Gluck, Mozart, Sullivan and Verdi operas and, especially, with the Czech repertory: he is widely regarded as the greatest living interpreter of Janáček, and the immense current popularity of Janáček in Britain is due almost exclusively to his advocacy. His wide tastes, exciting and dynamic style and his outstanding scholarship and musicianship have combined to make him one of the foremost contemporary opera conductors. He was musical director of the English National Opera (1970–77) and the Welsh National Opera (1987–). He conducted the first performance of *Noye's Fludde* and also arranged the popular ballets *Pineapple Poll* and *The*

Lady and the Fool from the operatic music of Sullivan and early Verdi.

MacNeil, Cornell *(b 1922)*

American baritone, particularly associated with Verdi roles, especially Rigoletto. One of the finest Verdi baritones of the 1960s, even if, at times, a little uncommitted on stage. He created John Sorel in *The Consul*. His son Walter is a tenor.

Maconchy, Elizabeth *(b 1907)*

British composer. She has written five operas: *The Sofa* (London 1959; libr. Ursula Vaughan Williams, after Claude Prosper Jolyot de Crébillon), *The Departure* (London 1963; libr. Anne Ridler), *The Birds* (1967; libr. composer, after Aristophanes), *The Three Strangers* (Bishop's Stortford 1968; libr. after Thomas Hardy) and *The Jesse Tree* (Dorchester 1970; libr. Ridler).

The Macropolus Case *(Věc Makropulos)*

Opera in three acts by Janáček. 1st perf. Brno, 18 Dec 1926; libr. by the composer after Karel Čapek's play. Principal roles: Emilia Marty (sop), Jaroslav Prus (bar), Albert Gregor (ten), Dr Kolenatý (bar), Vítek (ten), Kristina (sop), Jánek (ten), Hauk Šendorf (ten). One of Janáček's greatest works, the central figure of the 300-year-old woman provides a magnificent challenge to a great singing-actress. Initially slow to make its way, the opera has been widely performed in recent years.

Plot: Prague, 1920s. As a result of having been forced to test an elixir of life invented by her alchemist father, Elena Macropolus has lived in various guises for over 300 years. She is currently assuming the name of Emilia Marty, a famous opera singer. Afraid that the strength of the elixir is fading, she goes to great lengths to procure the original formula which is amongst the papers which form part of an estate which has been the subject of a long-running lawsuit between the families of Albert Gregor and Jaroslav Prus. After giving herself to Prus, who declares her totally cold, she gains the formula but realises that she is tired of life, incapable of emotion and wishes to die. Expiring, she gives the formula to the young singer Kristina, who loves Prus' son Jánek, who immediately burns it. [R]

Madama Butterfly

Opera in three (originally two) acts by Puccini. 1st perf. Milan, 17 Feb 1904; libr. by Giuseppe Giacosa and Luigi Illica after David Belasco's play, itself based on John Luther Long's story. Revised version, 1st perf. Brescia, 28 May 1904. Principal roles: Cio-Cio-San (sop), Lt Pinkerton (ten), Sharpless (bar), Suzuki (mezzo), Goro (ten), Bonze (bass), Prince Yamadori (bar), Kate Pinkerton (mezzo). Although it was a fiasco at its première, it soon established itself as one of the best-loved of all operas.

Plot: Nagasaki, early 1900s. The American naval officer Pinkerton has arranged, through the marriage broker Goro, to wed the young and pretty Cio-Cio-San – an arrangement which he does not take seriously. Despite the warnings of her uncle the Bonze, the girl renounces her family and her religion and marries Pinkerton, to whom she gives her heart and soul. He returns to America and, although three years pass with no word from him, she remains faithful to him, living with her devoted companion Suzuki, and her adored child that she has borne to her husband in his absence, and rejecting Yamadori and other suitors. The American consul, Sharpless, breaks the news to her, as gently as he can, that Pinkerton is returning with an American wife. She refuses to listen, however, and undertakes an all-night vigil with Suzuki, eagerly waiting for his arrival. The next day when Pinkerton arrives with his wife Kate, Butterfly (as she is called), has to face reality. Giving her child an American flag to play with, she commits hari-kari. [R]

Madame Pompadour

Operetta in three acts by Fall. 1st perf. Berlin, 9 Sept 1922; libr. by R. Schanzer and E. Welisch. An immediate success, it has always been one of Fall's most popular works and is still regularly performed.

Madame Sans-Gêne (*Madam Free-and-Easy*)

Opera in three acts by Giordano. 1st perf. New York, 25 Jan 1915; libr. by Renato Simoni, after Emile Moreau and Victorien Sardou's play. Principal roles: Madame Sans-Gêne (sop), Napoleon (bar), Lefèbvre (ten). A romantic comedy and rather different from Giordano's normal verismo style, it was reasonably successful at its appearance, but is nowadays all but forgotten.

Plot: Paris and Compiègne, 1792 and 1811. The laundress Catherine Huebscher, who later become the Duchess of Danzig, twice during the revolutionary period saves the life of Lefèbvre, Count of Neipperg. As Duchess, she presents the Emperor Napoleon with an unpaid laundry bill dating from the time when he was a young army lieutenant.

Madamina

Bass-baritone aria (the Catalogue Aria) for Leporello in Act I of Mozart's *Don Giovanni*.

Mädchen oder Weibchen, Ein

Baritone aria for Papageno in Act II of Mozart's *Die Zauberflöte*.

Maddalena

Mezzo role in Verdi's *Rigoletto*. She is Sparafucile's sister.

Madeleine

Soprano role in Giordano's *Andrea Chénier*. The Countess of Coigny's daughter, she loves Chénier.

Maderna, Bruno (1920–73)

Italian composer and conductor. His operas, some of which employ electronic music, include *Don Perlimplin* (Italian Radio 1962; libr. composer, after Federico García Lorca), *Hyperion* (Venice 1964; libr. Virginia Puechner, after Friedrich Hölderlin), *Von A Bis Z* (Darmstadt 1969) and *Satyricon* (Scheveningen 1973; libr. composer and I. Strasfogel, after Petronius). As a conductor, he specialised in early and modern operas and conducted the first performance of Nono's *Intolleranza*.

Madre, pietosa vergine

Soprano aria for Leonora in Act II of Verdi's *La Forza del Destino*.

Madrid

See Teatro de la Zarzuela, Madrid

Madrigal

A contrapuntal composition for several voices which originated in Italy in the 16th century and soon afterwards became very popular in England. The madrigals in 19th-century British stage works, such as 'Sing a merry madrigal' in Sullivan's *The Mikado*, are not true madrigals in the original sense in that they have independent instrumental parts which the 16th-century madrigal did not. Menotti's *The Unicorn, the Gorgon and the Manticore* is a 20th-century usage of the form.

Mad scenes

An enormously popular device in 19th-century Italian and French romantic opera, it provided an opportunity for exciting and demanding vocal writing for great singers. Much the most famous example is in *Lucia di Lammermoor*, but there are also fine arias in *Anna Bolena*, *I Puritani* and Thomas' *Hamlet*. They are nearly always for soprano, although Donizetti wrote mad scenes for tenor (in *Maria Padilla*) and baritone (in *Torquato Tasso* and *Il Furioso*). Modern 20th-century sophisticates tend to laugh at the convention, but it should be remembered that in the early 19th century madness was widely regarded as a romantic rather than a clinical state of mind. The convention is gloriously parodied by Gilbert and Sullivan with Mad Margaret in *Ruddigore*.

Maestro (Italian for 'master')

A courtesy title by which composers and conductors are often referred to and addressed as.

Maestro di cappella (Italian for 'chapel master')

A term used to describe the 18th-century official who was in charge of the music of a court, as for example Haydn was at Esterháza. He was called *Kapellmeister* in Germany and *Maître de Chapelle* in France.

Maestro di Cappella, Il (often given in English as *The Music Master*)

Intermezzo in one act by Cimarosa. 1st perf. *c* 1790. A highly amusing little monodrama for a bass-baritone, it concerns a pompous maestro rehearsing an orchestra and often imitating the sounds of the instruments. Always popular with great buffos, it is still regularly performed. [R]

Maeterlinck, Maurice (1862–1949)

Belgian symbolist playwright. He wrote the libretto for Dukas' *Ariane et Barbe-Bleue*, and Dubussy's *Pelléas et Mélisande* is a word-for-word setting of his play. His *Monna Vanna* was set by Février, Ábrányi and Rachmaninov, his *Soeur Béatrice* and *L'Oiseau Bleu* by Wolff, and his *La Mort de Tintagiles* by Collingwood.

Magda

Soprano role in: (1) Puccini's *La Rondine*. She is Rambaldo's mistress. (2) Menotti's *The Consul*. She is John Sorel's wife.

Magdalene

Mezzo role in: (1) Wagner's *Die Meistersinger von Nürnberg*. She is Eva's nurse. (2) Keinzl's *Der Evangeliman*.

Maggio Musicale Fiorentino

(Italian for Florence May Festival) The Festival was founded by Vittorio Gui in 1933. Originally biannual, it became an annual event in 1938. Performances are given at the Teatro Communale*, the Teatro Pergola (cap. 1,000) and the Boboli Gardens. The repertory is mainly Italian, with an emphasis on Verdi, early 19th-century works and contemporary operas. Artistic directors have included Igor Markevich, Riccardo Muti and Luciano Berio.

Magic Fire Music
The ending of Act III of Wagner's *Die Walküre* as Wotan calls on Loge to surround Brünnhilde's rock with flames.

Magic Flute, The
See Zauberflöte, Die

Magic Fountain, The
Opera in three acts by Delius. 1st perf. BBC Radio, 20 Nov 1977 (composed 1893); libr. by the composer. Principal roles: Solana (ten), Watawa (mezzo), Wapanacki (bar), Talum Hadjo (bass). Delius' second opera, it is virtually never performed. [R]

Magnard, Albéric *(1865–1914)*
French composer. He composed three operas, for all of which he wrote his own libretti, in a dramatic but austere style. They are *Yolande* (Brussels 27 Dec 1892), *Guercoeur* (Paris 24 April 1931, composed 1900) [R] and *Bérénice* (Paris 15 Dec 1911; libr. after Jean-Baptiste Racine). He was killed whilst defying German soldiers who were advancing across his land.

Magnifico, Don
Bass role in Rossini's *La Cenerentola*. He is Cenerentola's stepfather.

Mahagonny Singspiel
Opera in one act by Weill. 1st perf. Baden-Baden, 1927; libr. by Bertolt Brecht. Principal roles: Jessie (sop), Billy (ten), Johnnie (ten), Jimmy (bass). The short work from which Brecht and Weill developed *Aufstieg und Fall der Stadt Mahagonny**. [R]

Mahler, Gustav *(1860–1911)*
Austrian composer and conductor. He wrote three youthful operas: *Herzog Ernst von Schwaben* (c 1878), which he destroyed, *Die Argonauten* (c 1880), also destroyed, and *Rübezahl* (c 1882; libr. composer), which is lost. He also completed Weber's unfinished *Die Drei Pintos**.

Mahler's operatic importance rests on his reputation as one of the greatest conductors of his age. He was musical director of the Kassel Staatstheater (1884), the Budapest State Opera (1888–91), the Hamburg State Opera (1891–97) and the Vienna State Opera (1897–1907), where his performances became legendary, both for their musical and dramatic qualities.

Maiden in the Tower, The
(Jungfruburen)
Opera in one act by Sibelius. 1st perf. Helsinki, 7 Nov 1896; libr. (in Swedish) by Hertzberg. Sibelius' only opera, it is almost never performed. [R]

Maid of Orleans, The
(Orleanskaya Deva)
Opera in four acts by Tchaikovsky. 1st perf. St Petersburg, 25 Feb 1881; libr. by the composer, after Vasily Zhuhovsky's translation of Friedrich von Schiller's *Die Jungfrau von Orleans*. Principal roles: Johanna (sop), Charles (ten), Lionel (bar), Thibault (bass), Dunois (bar), Raimond (ten), Archbishop (bass). Telling of Joan of Arc, it is written in French grand opera style and is only infrequently performed outside Russia despite its fine music. It deals with Joan's life from the time of her decision to take up arms to her execution. [R]

Maid of Pskov, The
(Pskovityanka)
Opera in four acts by Rimsky-Korsakov. 1st perf. St Petersburg, 13 Jan 1873; libr. by the composer, after Lev Alexandrovich Mey's play. Revised version composed 1877 but never

performed; its prologue was later revised as the one-act opera *Boyarynya Vera Sheloga* (Moscow 27 Dec 1898). Final version *Ivan the Terrible*, 1st perf. St Petersburg, 18 April 1895. Principal roles: Ivan (bass), Olga (sop), Mikhail Tucha (ten), Prince Yuri (bass), Nikita Matuta (ten). Rimsky's first opera, it is only infrequently performed.

Plot: 16th-century Russia. Ivan IV has destroyed Novgorod and is approaching Pskov. There, Princess Olga loves Tucha, but has been promised by her presumed father Prince Yuri Tokmakov to Matuta. Ivan enters Pskov and meets Olga. He grants clemency to the city and takes Olga with him, later revealing that she is his own daughter. Tucha attempts to rescue Olga, but she is accidentally shot dead.

Maillart, Aimé *(1817–71)*
French composer. He wrote six operas: *Gastibelza* (Paris 15 Nov 1847), *Les Moulins de Tilleuls* (Paris 1849), *La Croix de Marie* (Paris 1852), *Les Dragons de Villars**, by far his most successful work, *Les Pêcheurs de Catane* (Paris 1860) and *Lara* (Paris 1864; libr. after Lord Byron).

Mainz Opera
The present opera house (cap. 1,100) in this German city in the Rhineland-Palatinate opened in 1951, replacing the previous theatre of 1813 which was destroyed in 1942. Musical directors have included Karl Maria Zwisler and Helmut Wessell-Therhorn.

Maître de Chapelle, Le (often given in English as *The Music Master*)
Comic opera in two acts by Paer. 1st perf. Paris, 29 March 1821; libr. by Sophie Gay, after Alexandre Duval's *Le Souper Imprévu*. Principal roles: Bernabé (bar), Célénie (sop), Gertrude (sop), Benetto (ten). Paer's most successful work and still occasionally performed, it tells of a fashionable opera composer's attempts to be up-to-date and contains some digs at opera's then rising star, Rossini. [R]

Makropolos Affair, The
See Macropolus Case, The

Malatesta, Dr
Baritone role in Donizetti's *Don Pasquale*. He is Ernesto's friend and Pasquale's physician. The name means 'Dr Headache'.

Malgoire, Jean-Claude *(b 1940)*
French conductor and oboist, associated with Baroque operas, especially Rameau and Lully. With his orchestra La Grande Ecurie et la Chambre du Roy he has been responsible for performances and recordings of many long-neglected works.

Malheurs d'Orphée, Les (*The Sorrows of Orpheus*)
Opera in three acts by Milhaud (Op 85). 1st perf. Brussels, 7 May 1926; libr. by Armand Lunel. Principal roles: Orpheus (bar), Eurydice (mezzo), Blacksmith (ten), Wheelwright (bass), Weaver (bass). A retelling of the Orpheus myth in a contemporary setting, it is arguably Milhaud's most successful opera and is still quite often performed. In this version, neither the humanly produced magic of the chemist Orpheus nor the sympathy of the animals which he treats is able to save the life of his gypsy lover Eurydice. [R]

Mallbran, María *(b García) (1808–36)*
Spanish mezzo, daughter of Manuel

García I* and sister of Pauline Viardot-Garcia* and Manuel García II*. One of the most famous singers of the first half of the 19th century, she was essentially a contralto with a soprano register added; the dead patch in between she was apparently able to conceal with great skill. Said to have possessed an exciting stage presence, she created the title roles in *Maria Stuarda* and Balfe's *The Maid of Artois*. She died as a result of injuries sustained in a riding accident. Alfred de Musset's *Stances* is a tribute to her, and she is the subject of an opera by a minor composer, Robert R. Bennett.

Malipiero, Gian Francesco
(1882–1973)

Italian composer. He wrote over 30 operas in contemporary style but strongly influenced by his love and knowledge of early music. His operas, almost all of them to his own libretti, include the triptych *L'Orfeide**, *Giulio Cesare* (Genoa 8 Feb 1936; libr. after Shakespeare's *Julius Caesar*), *Antonio e Cleopatra* (Florence 4 June 1938; libr. after Shakespeare), *Ecuba* (Rome 11 Jan 1941; libr. after Euripides), *I Capricci di Callot* (Rome 24 Oct 1942; libr. after E. T. A. Hoffmann's *Fantasiestücke*), *Il Figliuolo Prodigo* (Italian Radio 25 Jan 1953; libr. P. Castellano Castellani) and *Venere Prigioniera* (Florence 14 May 1957; libr. after E. Gonzales).

He also helped to produce complete critical editions of the works of Monteverdi and Vivaldi. His nephew Riccardo (*b* 1914) is also a composer, who has written three operas: the twelve-tone *Minnie la Candida* (Parma 1942; libr. M. Bontempelli), the comedy *La Donna è Mobile* (Milan 1957; libr. G. Zucconi) and the television opera *Battone alle Porta* (1962; libr. Dino Buzzati).

Mal per me
Baritone aria for Macbeth in Act IV of the original 1847 version of Verdi's *Macbeth*. Macbeth's death aria, it was cut in the revised version, but some modern productions have reinstated it.

Maltese opera composers
See Isouard
Other national opera composers include Carmelo Pace.

Mamelles de Tirésias, Les
(The Breasts of Tirésias)
Comic opera in two acts by Poulenc. 1st perf. Paris, 3 June 1947; libr. by Guillaume Apollinaire. Principal roles: Thérèse (sop), Husband (ten), Gendarme (bar), Director (bar), Lacouf (ten), Presto (bass), Reporter (ten). An outrageously funny surrealist comedy, it was an immediate success and is still regularly performed.

Plot: Zanzibar (an imaginary town on the French Riviera), 1910. Thérèse is converted to feminism and to demonstrate her emancipation she undoes her blouse so as to lose her sinful breasts (symbolically shown as balloons which she explodes). Now to be called Tirésias, she defies her husband, informing him that from now on he must undertake all the duties of a housewife, including bearing children. This last he does in spectacular fashion, producing 40,000 in a single day. After appearing as a fortune teller to recommend frequent procreation, Thérèse eventually resumes her normal role and rejoins her relieved and happy husband. [R]

Mamma morta, La
Soprano aria for Madeleine de Coigny in Act III of Giordano's *Andrea Chénier*.

Mam'zelle Nitouche

Operetta in three acts by Hervé. 1st perf. Paris, 26 Jan 1883; libr. by Henri Meilhac, Albert Millaud and Ernest Blum. Hervé's most successful work, it is still occasionally performed.

Manaus

See Teatro Amazones, Manaus

Manca un foglio

Bass aria for Dr Bartolo in Act I of Rossini's *Il Barbiere di Siviglia*. A less demanding alternative to the aria 'A un dottor', it was composed by Pietro Romani (1791–1877).

Mancinelli, Luigi *(1848–1921)*

Italian composer and conductor. He wrote four operas, all of them now forgotten. They are *Isora di Provenza* (Bologna 2 Oct 1884; libr. Angelo Zanardini, after Victor Hugo's *La Légende des Siècles*), *Ero e Leandro* (Norwich 8 Oct 1896; libr. Arrigo Boito), *Paolo e Francesca* (Bologna 11 Nov 1897; libr. Arturo Colautti, after Dante's *La Divina Commedia*) and the unperformed *Il Sogno di una Notte d'Estato* (1917; libr. F. Salvatori, after Shakespeare's *A Midsummer Night's Dream*). One of the leading conductors of his time, he was musical director of the Teatro Real, Madrid (1888–95) and was also closely associated with Covent Garden, the Teatro Communale, Bologna and the Metropolitan Opera, New York. He conducted the first performance of Stanford's *Much Ado About Nothing*.

Mandryka

Baritone role in Strauss' *Arabella*. He is a rich landowner who is a suitor of Arabella's.

Manfredo

Baritone role in: (1) Montemezzi's *L'Amore dei Tre Re*. Archibaldo's son, he is married to Fiora. (2) Mercadante's *Il Giuramento*. The Count of Syracuse, he is Bianca's husband.

Mangus

Baritone role in Tippett's *The Knot Garden*. He is a psychoanalyst.

Manners, Charles *(b Southcote Mansergh) (1857–1935)*

Irish bass and administrator. A popular British singer of the late 19th century, he created Private Willis in *Iolanthe*. His wife Fanny Moody (1866–1945) was a successful soprano. In 1898, they jointly formed the Moody-Manners Opera Company, which toured Britain until May 1916.

Mannheim Opera

Opera in this German city in Baden-Württemberg is given at the Nationaltheater (cap. 1,200), which opened in January 1957, replacing the previous theatre of the same name which was destroyed by bombs in 1943. Musical directors have included Rezniček, Vincenz Lachner, Felix Weingartner, Artur Bodansky, Wilhelm Furtwängler, Erich Kleiber, Karl Elmendorff, Horst Stein and Hans Wallat.

Manon

Opera in five acts by Massenet. 1st perf. Paris, 19 Jan 1884; libr. by Henri Meilhac and Philippe Gille, after the Abbé Antoine-François Prévost's *L'Histoire du Chevalier des Grieux et de Manon Lescaut*. Principal roles: Manon (sop), des Grieux (ten), Lescaut (bar), Comte des Grieux (bass), Guillot (ten), de Brétigny (bar). An immediate success, it has always been one of the most popular of French operas, although Sir Thomas Beecham's famous remark that he would give all six of Bach's Brandenburg Concerti for it would seem to be pushing its merits a little far. Massenet's follow-up to the story, *Le Portrait de Manon* (Paris 8 May 1894; libr. Georges Boyer), was unsuccessful.

Plot: France, 1721. The high-spirited Manon arrives at an inn to meet her cousin, Lescaut, charged with escorting her to a convent. There, she encounters the Chevalier des Grieux with whom she falls in love and they run away to Paris. Lescaut disapproves of the liaison and des Grieux assures him of his honorable intentions, but his father, Comte des Grieux, also disapproves and has his son abducted. Manon allows herself to be tempted by a life of luxury with the wealthy de Brétigny, but when she learns that des Grieux has entered a seminary she rushes to him and wins him back. Des Grieux is accused of cheating in a gaming-house row, and the two are arrested. Des Grieux is released after his father's intercession, but Manon is condemned to deportation as a prostitute. On the road to Le Havre, her lover attempts to rescue her, but her strength fails and she dies in his arms. [R]

Manon Lescaut

Works of this title based on the Abbé Antoine-François Prévost's *L'Histoire de Chevalier des Grieux et de Manon Lescaut* include:

(1) Opera in three acts by Auber. 1st perf. Paris, 23 Feb 1856; libr. by Eugène Scribe. One of Auber's best works, it was very successful in its day but is now almost forgotten. [R]

(2) Opera in four acts by Puccini. 1st perf. Turin, 1 Feb 1893; libr. by Luigi Illica, Giuseppe Giacosa, Giulio Ricordi, Marco Praga and Domenico Oliva. Principal roles: Manon (sop), des

Grieux (ten), Lescaut (bar), Geronte (bass), Edmondo (ten). Puccini's third opera and the work which established his reputation, it is still regularly performed.

Plot: 18th-century France and America. Manon, accompanied by her brother Lescaut, is on her way to a convent. She meets and falls in love with the Chevalier des Grieux and, taking the coach of the elderly Geronte (who had himself hoped to use it to abduct Manon), the couple go to Paris. After a while, Manon is seduced by the wealth offered by Geronte and leaves des Grieux. They are later reunited and decide to go away together but, before leaving, Manon stops to pick up her jewellery, the gift of Geronte. This delay leads to their arrest by agents hired by Geronte, and Manon is sentenced to deportation to New Orleans. Des Grieux gains permission to accompany her, helps her escape in America, and they go in search of an English colony. However, the now ailing Manon loses all strength and dies in the wilderness. [R]

Manrico

Tenor role in Verdi's *Il Trovatore*. The troubador of the opera's title, he is believed to be Azucena's son.

Manru

Opera in three acts by Paderewski (Op 20). 1st perf. Dresden, 29 May 1901; libr. by Alfred Nossig, after Josef Ignacy Krazewski's *The Cabin Behind the Wood*. Principal roles: Manru (ten), Ulana (sop), Asa (sop), Oros (bar). Paderewski's only opera, it met with considerable success at its appearance but is now all but forgotten.

Plot: Galicia. Ulana has married the gypsy Manru against her mother's wishes, but he proves inconstant. Ulana rekindles his passion with the aid of a love potion, but he is drawn back to his own people by the gypsy girl Asa. Ulana drowns herself in despair and Manru, now the leader of the gypsy tribe, is killed by Oros, who also loves Asa, and who Manru deposed for the leadership.

Manuguerra, Matteo *(b c 1925)*
Tunisian-born French baritone, particularly associated with the French and Italian repertories, especially Verdi. Possessing a rich and firm voice of considerable power, he did not begin singing until the age of 35, but became one of the leading Verdi baritones of the 1970s.

Maometto II

Opera in two acts by Rossini. 1st perf. Naples, 3 Dec 1820; libr. by Cesare della Valle, after his *Anna Erizo* and Voltaire's *Mahomet*. Principal roles: Maometto (bass), Anna (sop), Erisso (ten), Calbo (mezzo). Revised version *Le Siège de Corinthe**. After a long period of neglect, this original version has received a number of performances in the last few years. Set in the 15th century, the opera deals with the story of Anna, daughter of the governor of a Venetian colony in Greece, who falls in love with the Turkish monarch Maometto, but places duty before love. [R]

M'appari

See Ach so fromm

Marcellina

Mezzo role in Mozart's *Le Nozze di Figaro*. She is Dr Bartolo's housekeeper.

Marcello

A Parisian painter in love with Musetta, he appears as: (1) Baritone role in Puccini's *La Bohème*. (2) Tenor role in Leoncavallo's *La Bohème*.

Marchesi de Castrone, Mathilde *(b Graumann) (1821– 1913)*

German teacher and mezzo. One of the most famous singing teachers of the 19th century, her pupils included Emma Calvé, Emma Eames, Mary Garden, Sybil Sanderson and Nellie Melba. She wrote a method of singing and her autobiography, *Marchesi and Music*, which was published in 1897. Her husband Salvatore (Cavaliere de Castrone, Marchese della Raiata) (1822–1908) was a successful baritone who also translated French and German operas into Italian. Their daughter Blanche (1863–1940) was a Wagnerian soprano and later a teacher. Her autobiography, *Singer's Pilgrimage*, was published in 1923.

Marchetti, Filippo *(1831–1902)*

Italian composer. He wrote seven operas, all of which are now forgotten. They are *Gentile de Varano* (Turin Feb 1856; libr. R. Marchetti), *La Demente* (Turin 29 Nov 1856; libr. G. Checchetelli), the unperformed *Il Paria* (1859; libr. Checchetelli), *Romeo e Giulietta* (Trieste 25 Oct 1865; libr. M. Marcello after Shakespeare), *Ruy Blas* (Milan 3 April 1869; libr. Carlo d'Ormeville after Victor Hugo), by far his most successful work which was widely performed, *Gustavo Wasa* (Milan 7 Feb 1875; libr. d'Ormeville) and *Don Giovanni d'Austria* (Turin 11 March 1880; libr. d'Ormeville).

Marcoux, Vanni *(b Jean Emile Diogène) (1877–1962)*

French bass-baritone, particularly associated with the French and Italian repertories. His huge repertory of 240 roles ranged from Scarpia to Arkel. He created Uin-Sci in Leoni's *L'Oracolo*, Colonno in Février's *Monna Vanna*, the title role in Massenet's *Panurge* and a role in Honegger and Ibert's *L'Aiglon*. He was director of the Grand Théâtre, Bordeaux (1948–51).

Mařenka

Soprano role in Smetana's *The Bartered Bride*. She loves Jeník.

Marfa

Mezzo role in Moussorgsky's *Khovanschina*. She is Prince Andrei's former lover.

Margot la Rouge

Opera in one act by Delius. 1st perf. BBC Radio, 9 Oct 1981 (composed 1902); libr. Rosenval. Principal roles: Margot (mezzo), Thibault (ten), Artist (b-bar), Lili (sop), Poigne (bar), Patronne (mezzo). A taut, quasi-verismo work, it is almost never performed. [R]

Marguerite

(1) Soprano role in Gounod's *Faust* and mezzo role in Berlioz's *La Damnation de Faust*. She is the girl seduced by Faust. (2) Soprano role in Mayerbeer's *Les Huguenots*. She is the Queen of France. (3) Soprano role in Grétry's *Richard Coeur de Lion*.

Maria

(1) Mezzo role in Gershwin's *Porgy and Bess*. (2) Soprano role in Tchaikovsky's *Mazeppa*. She is Kochubei's daughter. (3) Soprano role in Mascagni's *Guglielmo Ratcliff*. MacGregor's daughter, she is loved by Ratcliff. (4) Mezzo role in Prokofiev's *War and Peace*. (5) Soprano role in Strauss' *Friedenstag*. She is the Commandant's wife. (6) Soprano role in Erkel's *László Hunyadi*.

Maria de Rudenz

Opera in three acts by Donizetti. 1st perf. Venice, 30 Jan 1838; libr. by Salvatore Cammarano. Principal roles: Maria (sop), Corrado (bar), Enrico (ten), Matilde de Wolff (mezzo), Rambaldo (bass). After a long period of neglect, it has received a number of performances in recent years. [R]

Maria di Rohan

Opera in three acts by Donizetti. 1st perf. Vienna, 5 June 1943; libr. by Salvatore Cammarano, after Edouard Lockroy's *Un Duel Sous le Cardinal de Richelieu*. Principal roles: Maria (sop), Riccardo (ten), Enrico (bar), Armando (mezzo), Fiesque (bass). Successful at its appearance, it is still occasionally performed.

Plot: France. Enrico, secretly married to Maria, has been arrested for killing Cardinal Richelieu's nephew. Maria falls in love with Riccardo, Comte de Chalais, with whom she intercedes on behalf of Enrico. Enrico challenges Riccardo to a duel and kills him. Maria herself wishes to die, but Enrico insists that she suffers a life of disgrace.

Maria Egiziaca

Opera in one act by Respighi. 1st perf. New York, 16 March 1932; libr. by Claudio Gaustalla. Reasonably successful at its appearance, it is nowadays all but forgotten.

Maria Golovin

Opera in three acts by Menotti. 1st perf. Brussels, 20 Aug 1958; libr. by the composer. Revised version 1st perf. Washington, 22 Jan 1965. Principal roles: Donato (bar), Maria (sop), Mother (mezzo), Agata (sop), Prisoner (bar), Zuckertanz (ten). Telling of a woman awaiting the return of her husband from a prisoner-of-war camp after World War I who becomes the mistress of a jealous young blind man, it has proved one of the most successful of Menotti's full-scale works.

Mariani, Angelo *(1821–73)*
Italian conductor, particularly associated with Verdi operas. The first of the great modern-style Italian conductors, he was musical director of the Teatro Carlo Felice, Genoa (1852–73) and the Teatro Communale, Bologna (1860–73). His performances of Verdi's patriotic works were so exciting that he was threatened with imprisonment for inciting revolution. He conducted the first performance of Verdi's *Aroldo* and was the first Italian conductor to champion Wagner's works.

Maria Stuarda *(Mary Stuart)*
Opera in three acts by Donizetti. 1st perf. (as *Buondelmonte*) Naples, 18 Oct 1834; 1st perf. in original form Milan, 30 Dec 1835; libr. by Giuseppe Bardari, after Friedrich von Schiller's *Maria Stuart*. Principal roles: Mary (sop), Elizabeth I (sop), Leicester (ten), Talbot (bass), Cecil (bar). Censorship problems caused the music to be hastily adapted to a new libretto by Salatino. Unsuccessful at its appearance, it remained totally unperformed for over 100 years, but in the last 15 years it has firmly established itself in the repertory. One of Donizetti's finest works, it is notable for the richly-wrought Confession Scene and for the tremendous (albeit fictitious) confrontation between the two queens.

Plot: London and Fotheringhay, 1567. Queen Elizabeth I loves the Earl of Leicester, but he loves the imprisoned Mary Queen of Scots. He promises Mary's sympathetic jailer Talbot that he will do all in his power to secure Mary's release, and persuades Elizabeth – against her better judgement – to meet Mary. On Leicester's advice, Mary humbles herself before Elizabeth and begs for mercy. Elizabeth so taunts her that Mary's patience finally snaps and she roundly insults Elizabeth, calling her 'vile bastard'. Despite Leicester's pleas, Elizabeth – urged on by Cecil – signs Mary's death warrant and names Leicester as witness to the execution. Mary confesses to Talbot (revealed as a secret Catholic priest) and prays with the crowd for peace in England. Forgiving Elizabeth, she is led to execution. [R]

Marino Faliero
Opera in three acts by Donizetti. 1st perf. Paris, 12 March 1835; libr. by Emanuele Bidera, after Casimir Delavigne's play and Lord Byron. Principal roles: Marino (bass), Elena (sop), Israele (bar). Successful at its appearance, it is now rarely performed.

Marie
Soprano role in: (1) Donizetti's *La Fille du Régiment*. She is the regimental 'daughter' loved by Tonie. (2) Berg's *Wozzeck*. She is Wozzeck's mistress. (3) Poulenc's *Dialogues des Carmélites*. She is a nun. (4) Bizet's *Ivan IV*. (5) Korngold's *Die Tote Stadt*. She is Paul's dead wife. (6) Lortzing's *Der Waffenschmeid*. She is Stadinger's daughter. (7) Lortzing's *Zar und Zimmermann*. She is the Burgomaster's daughter loved by Peter Ivanov.

Marina Mniszek
Mezzo role in Moussorgsky's *Boris Godunov*. She is a Polish princess.

Marinuzzi, Gino *(b Giuseppe)* *(1882–1945)*
Italian conductor and composer, particularly associated with Wagner operas and with 20th-century Italian

works. He was musical director of the Chicago Opera (1919–21) and the Rome Opera (1928–34). He conducted the first performances of *La Rondine* and Pizzetti's *Fedra*. He also composed three operas: *Barbarina* (Palermo 1903), *Jacquerie* (Buenos Aires 1918) and *Palla de' Mozzi* (Milan 1932).

Mario, Giovanni *(b Giovanni Matteo, Cavaliere di Candia) (1810–83)*
Italian tenor, particularly associated with Donizetti roles. Regarded as one of the greatest lyric tenors of the first half of the 19th century, he combined a beautiful and stylish voice with acting ability and a handsome appearance. He created Ernesto in *Don Pasquale*. He lived with the soprano Giulia Grisi*.

Marionette operas
The earliest known opera written for performance with marionettes is Francesco Pistocchi's *Leandro* (Venice 1679). In the 18th century, a puppet theatre was maintained at Esterháza, for which Haydn wrote five marionette operas, including *Philemon und Baucis*. 20th-century marionette operas include de Falla's *El Retablo de Maese Pedro*, Castelnuovo-Tedesco's *Aucassin et Nicolette*, Hindemith's *Das Nusch-Nuschi* and several by Lualdi. The two main European marionette companies are the Teatro dei Piccoli in Rome and the Salzburg Marionettentheater, which specialises in Mozart operas.

Maritana
Opera in three acts by Wallace. 1st perf. London, 15 Nov 1845; libr. by Edward Fitzball, after Adolphe Philippe d'Ennery and Philippe François Dumanoir's *Don César de Bazan*. Principal roles: Maritana (sop), Don José (bar), King (bar). Built around a character from Victor Hugo's *Ruy Blas*, it tells of a gypsy singer seduced by the King of Spain. By far Wallace's most successful opera, it was enormously popular until the end of the 19th century, but is nowadays virtually never performed.

Mark
Tenor role in Tippett's *The Midsummer Marriage*. He loves Jenifer.

Mark, King
Bass role in Wagner's *Tristan und Isolde*. The King of Cornwall, he is betrothed to Isolde.

Markevich, Igor *(1912–83)*
Russian conductor and composer, particularly associated with the French and Russian repertories. Best known as a symphonic conductor, his operatic appearances were infrequent. He was musical director of the Maggio Musicale Fiorentino (1944).

Marmontel, Jean-François *(1723–99)*
French playwright and librettist. Author of the entry on opera in the *Grande Encyclopédie* and a supporter of Piccinni in the famous controversy with Gluck, he wrote a large number of libretti. He provided texts for Cherubini (*Démophoön*), Dauvergne, Grétry (*Le Huron, Lucile* and *Zémire et Azor*), Philidor (*Persée*), Piccinni (*Atys* and *Roland*), Rameau (*Acante et Céphise*) and Zingarelli (*Antigone*) amongst others. His play *Bélisaire* is the source for Donizetti's *Belisario*.

Mârouf, Savetier du Caire *(Mârouf, Cobbler of Cairo)*
Opera in four acts by Rabaud. 1st perf. Paris, 15 May 1914; libr. by Lucien Népoty, after *The Thousand and One Nights*. Principal roles: Mârouf (ten), Sultan (bass), Sultan's daughter (sop).

By far Rabaud's most successful work, it is still performed quite often in France and Belgium.

Plot: The cobbler Mârouf goes to sea to escape his cruel wife. After being shipwrecked, he is introduced to the Sultan as a wealthy merchant, and marries the potentate's daughter. He plunders the royal treasury, eternally promising that his caravans of valuable goods are on their way, but eventually tells his wife the truth. She continues to love him despite his chicanery, and, together they decamp. A magic ring provides Mârouf with money and a palace and, when the furious Sultan catches up with him, the evidence of his son-in-law's wealth earns the Sultan's forgiveness. [R]

Marquise de Berkenfeld
Mezzo role in Donizetti's *La Fille du Régiment*. She turns out to be Marie's mother.

Marquise de Brinvilliers, La
Opera in three acts by Auber, Batton, Henri-Montan Berton, Blangini, Boïeldieu, Carafa, Cherubini, Hérold and Paer. 1st perf. Paris, 31 Oct 1831; libr. by Eugène Scribe and Castil-Blaze. The most successful of the many collectively-written operas popular in Paris in the mid-19th century, it is now forgotten.

Marriner, Sir Neville *(b 1924)*
British conductor, particularly associated with Mozart and the Baroque repertory. Founder of the Academy of Saint Martin-in-the-Fields, his operatic appearances (mainly Mozart and Rossini) have been very rare.

Marschallin (or Feldmarschallin)
Soprano role in Richard Strauss' *Der Rosenkavalier*. She is the Princess von Werdenberg, in love with Octavian.

Marriage, The
Works of this title based on Nikolai Gogol's comedy include:

(1) Unfinished opera in four acts by Moussorgsky. Also known as *The Matchmaker (Zhenitba)*. 1st perf. (Act I only) St Petersburg, 1 April 1909 (composed 1864). Principal roles: Podkolesin (bar), Fyokla (mezzo), Kochkaryov (ten), Stepan (bass). Moussorgsky completed only the first act and the work is usually performed as a torso. There is, however, a completed version, with the remaining three acts written by Ippolitov-Ivanov (1931). It is an historically important work in that it applies Dargomijsky's ideas of melodic recitative to a prose text, and also marks the first use in Russian opera of leitmotiv.

Plot: The clerk Podkolesin is undecided about marrying a merchant's daughter but is urged by the marriage broker Fyokla not to delay. Kochkaryov, whose own marriage was arranged by Fyokla and turned out to be a disaster, extols the blessings of married life. [R]

(2) Opera in one act by Martinů. 1st perf. NBC TV, 7 Feb 1953; libr. by the composer. One of the earliest operas specifically written for television, it is nowadays all but forgotten.

Marriage of Figaro, The
See Nozze di Figaro, Le

Marschner, Heinrich *(1795–1861)*
German composer. One of the most important figures in German romantic opera, and often regarded as the link between Weber and Wagner, his best works are notable for their complex harmonies, their rich orchestration and

their delineation of character, especially figures containing both good and evil elements. He was musical director of the Dresden Opera (1824–26), the Leipzig Opera (1827–31) and the Hanover Opera. His operas are *Saidir und Zulima* (Bratislava 26 Nov 1818), *Der Holzdieb* (Dresden 22 Feb 1825; libr. Friedrich Kind), *Lucretia* (Danzig 17 Jan 1827; libr. A. Eckschlager), *Der Vampyr**, his first major success, *Der Templer und die Jüdin**, *Das Falkners Braut* (Leipzig 10 March 1832; libr. Wilhelm August Wöhlbruck, after K. Spindler), *Hans Heiling**, his finest and most enduring work, *Das Schloss am Ätna* (Leipzig 29 Jan 1836; libr. E. A. F. Klingermann), *Der Bäbu* (Hanover 19 Feb 1838; libr. Wöhlbruck), his only comedy, *Kaiser Adolf von Nassau* (Dresden 5 Jan 1845; libr. H. Rau), *Austin* (Hanover 25 Jan 1852; libr. M. Marschner) and *Sangeskönig Hiarne* (Frankfurt 13 Sept 1863; libr. W. Grote). A currently much underrated composer, a few of his works are still occasionally performed in Germany, but elsewhere they are now largely unknown.

Marseilles
See Grand Théâtre, Marseilles

Marten aller Arten
Soprano aria for Constanze in Act II of Mozart's *Die Entführung aus dem Serail*.

Martha
or Der Markt von Richmond
Opera in four acts by Flotow. 1st perf. Vienna, 25 Nov 1847; libr. by Friedrich Wilhelm Riese, after Jules-Henri Vernoy de Saint-Georges' ballet-pantomime *Lady Henriette ou La Servante de Greenwich*. Principal roles: Lady Harriet (sop), Lionel (ten), Nancy (mezzo), Plunkett (b-bar), Sir Tristram

(b-bar). By far Flotow's most successful work, it is still regularly performed.

Plot: Richmond, *c* 1710. As a diversion, Lady Harriet, a lady-in-waiting to Queen Anne, and her maid Nancy disguise themselves as peasant girls, and go to Richmond Fair, and hire themselves out as domestic servants to the young farmers Plunkett and Lionel. Despite the women's inability to cook or sew, the two farmers fall in love with them. The women depart and Lionel is left heartbroken. Returned to court, Harriet becomes aware that she loves Lionel and, when he discovers that he is the lost heir to the earldom of Derby, the couple are reunited. [R]

Marthe, Dame
Mezzo role in Gounod's *Faust*. She is Marguerite's companion.

Martin, Frank *(1890–1974)*
Swiss composer. He wrote four stage works, which have not received the recognition their merits deserve. The dramatic oratorio *Le Vin Herbé** was followed by the opera *Der Sturm**, the scenic oratorio *Le Mystère de la Nativité* (Geneva 23 Dec 1959) and the comedy *Monsieur de Pourceaugnac* (Geneva 23 April 1963; libr. composer, after Molière).

Martin, Janis *(b 1939)*
American soprano, particularly associated with Wagnerian roles and with 20th-century works, especially Marie in *Wozzeck*. Beginning as a mezzo, she turned to soprano roles in 1971. She has a powerful and incisive voice and is an outstanding singing-actress.

Martin, Jean-Blaise *(c 1768–1837)*
French baritone, long resident at the Opéra-Comique, Paris, where he created

14 roles in operas by Boïeldieu, Dalayrac, Isouard and Méhul. Specialising in comic servant roles, he possessed a voice of extraordinary range and has given his name to a type of very high French baritone who sings roles such as Pelléas.

Martinelli, Giovanni *(1885–1969)*

Italian tenor, particularly associated with the Italian repertory. One of the most famous tenors of the 20th century, he had a bright, silvery voice used with style and an impeccable technique. Although the voice was not large, his projection was so good that he was able to sing heroic roles such as Calaf and Tristan. He created Fernando in *Goyescas*, Pantagruel in Massenet's *Panurge* and Lefèbvre in Giordano's *Madame Sans-Gêne*. He enjoyed a remarkably long career, giving his final performance (as Emperor Altoum) at the age of 82.

Martinů, Bohuslav *(1890–1959)*

Czech composer who wrote in a variety of styles. His stage works are the comedy *The Soldier and the Dancer* (*Voják a Tanečnice*, Brno 5 May 1928; libr. J. L. Budín, after Plautus), the jazz-inspired *Les Larmes du Couteau* (Brno 1968, composed 1928; libr. G. Ribemont-Dessaignes), the Dadaist *Trois Souhaits* (Brno 1971, composed 1929; libr. Ribemont-Dessaignes), the unfinished operatic film *La Semaine de Bonté* (1929; libr. Ribemont-Dessaignes), the mystery cycle *The Miracle of Our Lady**, the radio opera *The Voice of the Forest* (*Hlas Lesa*, Czech Radio 6 Oct 1935; libr. V. Nezval), *The Suburban Theatre* (*Divadlo za Bránou*, Brno 20 Sept 1936; libr. composer), the comedy *Alexandre Bis* (Mannheim, 1964, composed 1937; libr. A. Wurmser) [R], the surrealist *Julietta**, his most

successful work, the brilliant radio opera *Comedy on the Bridge**, the two television operas *What Men Live By* (*Čím Člověk Žije*, New York 1953; libr. composer, after Tolstoy's *How Men Live*) and *The Marriage**, the unfinished *La Plaint Contre Inconnu* (1953; libr. composer, after Georges Neveux), the comedy *Mirandolina* (Prague 17 May 1959; libr. composer, after Carlo Goldoni's *La Locandiera*), the powerful *The Greek Passion** and *Ariadne* (Gelsenkirchen 1961; libr. composer, after Neveux), which was inspired by Maria Callas.

Martín y Soler, Vicente *(1754–1806)*

Spanish composer. His vivacious and tuneful comedies met with great success in their day, first in Vienna (where he collaborated with Lorenzo da Ponte) and later in St Petersburg, where two of his operas had libretti by Catherine the Great. His only opera still to be at all remembered is *Una Cosa Rara**.

Marton, Éva *(b Heinrich) (b 1943)*

Hungarian soprano, particularly associated with dramatic roles such as Tosca, Turandot and Brünnhilde. She possesses a powerful and exciting voice and has a strong and voluptuous stage presence.

Marty, Emilia

Soprano role in Janáček's *The Macropolus Case*. She is the woman who has lived for over 300 years.

Martyrs, Les

See Poliuto

Marullo

Baritone comprimario role in Verdi's *Rigoletto*. He is a courtier.

Mary

Mezzo role in Wagner's *Der Fliegende Holländer*. She is Senta's companion.

Maryinsky Theatre

See Kirov Opera

Mary Queen of Scots

Opera in three acts by Musgrave. 1st perf. Edinburgh, 6 Sept 1977; libr. by the composer, after Amelia Elguera's play. Principal roles: Mary (sop), James (bar), Lord Darnley (ten), Earl of Bothwell (ten), Riccio (bass), Ruthven (ten), Merton (bar). Telling of events during Mary's time in Scotland, it has proved to be one of the most successful modern British operas and has been widely performed. [R]

Mary Stuart

See Maria Stuarda

Marzelline

Soprano role in Beethoven's *Fidelio*. She is Rocco's daughter, in love with Fidelio.

Masaniello

Tenor role in Auber's *La Muette de Portici*. He is the historical Thomas Aniello, who led the Neapolitan revolt against Spanish rule in 1647. The opera itself is sometimes referred to by this name.

Mascagni, Pietro *(1863–1945)*

Italian composer. He wrote 16 operas, his fame resting largely on the first: *Cavalleria Rusticana**, winner of a competition for a one-act opera, which introduced the vogue for verismo into Italian opera. His subsequent operas are the pastoral *L'Amico Fritz**, the heavily melodramatic *I Rantzau* (Florence 10 Nov 1892; libr. Giovanni Targioni-Tozzetti and Guido Menasci), *Guglielmo Ratcliff**, *Silvano* (Milan 25 March 1895; libr. Targioni-Tozzetti), *Zanetto**, the successful *Iris**, the Commedia dell'Arte *Le Maschere**, *Amica* (Monte Carlo 16 March 1905; libr. P. Berel), *Isabeau**, *Parisina* (Milan 15 Dec 1913; libr. Gabriele d'Annunzio, after Lord Byron), *Lodoletta**, the operetta *Sì* (Rome 13 Dec 1919; libr. Carlo Lombardo and A. Franci), the unjustly neglected *Il Piccolo Marat**, possibly his finest work, *Pinotta* (San Remo 23 March 1932; libr. Targioni-Tozzetti) and the pretentious *Nerone**, written in praise of Mussolini. The use made of him by the Fascists as their musical mouthpiece led to a boycott of his work by most Italian musicians and he spent his last years in virtual disgrace. Musically coarse, vulgar and bombastic and displaying almost no dramatic insight, Mascagni is perhaps the most overrated of all opera composers.

Maschere, Le *(The Masks)*

Opera in prologue and three acts by Mascagni. 1st perf. Milan, Rome, Venice, Turin, Verona and Genoa simultaneously, 17 Jan 1901; libr. by Luigi Illica. Its première was one of the most famous fiascos in operatic history: only in Rome, where Mascagni conducted, did it have any success; elsewhere it was roundly hissed and the Genoese audience did not even allow it to be finished. A Commedia dell'Arte story, nowadays only its overture is in any way remembered.

Mascheroni, Edoardo *(1852–1941)*

Italian conductor and composer. One of the leading Verdi and Wagner interpreters of his day, he conducted the first performances of *Falstaff* and Catalani's *La Wally* and *Loreley*. He also composed two operas: *Lorenza* (Rome 1901; libr. Luigi Illica) and *La Perugina* (Naples 1909; libr. Illica). His brother Angelo (1855–95) was also a conductor.

Mascotte, La

Operetta in three acts by Audran. 1st perf. Paris, 28 Dec 1880; libr. by Alfred Duru and Henri Charles Chivot. Principal roles: Bettina, Pippo, Prince Laurent, Rocco, Fiametta. By far Audran's most successful and enduring work, it was an instant success and had clocked up over 1,700 performances in Paris alone within 20 years. It is still quite often performed in France.

Plot: The farmer Rocco is plagued by ill-luck, and his brother sends him as a mascot the goose-girl Bettina, loved by Rocco's shepherd Pippo. The unlucky Prince Laurent persuades Bettina to come to his castle. Knowing that her power as a mascot depends on her continued virginity, Laurent keeps Pippo away from her by pretending to be about to marry her himself. Pippo turns to Laurent's sister Fiametta, but his love returns to Bettina before the wedding and the two escape together. After a war in which Laurent is defeated and Pippo covers himself in glory, all is sorted out and forgiven. Pippo and Bettina marry, hoping that her good luck will prove hereditary. [R]

Ma se m'è forza perderti

Tenor aria for Gustavus in Act III of Verdi's *Un Ballo in Maschera*.

Masetto

Bass-baritone role in Mozart's *Don Giovanni*. He is a peasant engaged to Zerlina.

Maskarade

Comic opera in three acts by Nielsen (Op 39). 1st perf. Copenhagen, 11 Nov 1906; libr. by Vilhelm Andersen, after Ludwig Holberg's play. Principal roles: Leander (ten), Leonora (sop), Jeronimus (bass), Arv (ten), Magdelone (mezzo), Henrik (bar). A delightful work, which is still very popular in Denmark (where it is the national opera), it is, inexplicably, almost unknown elsewhere.

Plot: Copenhagen, 1723. Jeronimus wishes his son Leander to marry the daughter of his friend Leonard, but the young man resists the idea of marrying a girl he has never met. Leonard's daughter, Leonora, is equally opposed to the scheme. She wishes instead to marry the young man with whom she fell in love at a masked ball. After much intrigue and complication, and to the joy of both parties, it transpires that the young man at the ball was Leander. [R]

Masked Ball, A

See Ballo in Maschera, Un

Masnadieri, I (*The Robbers*)

Opera in four acts by Verdi. 1st perf. London, 22 July 1847; libr. by Count Andrea Maffei, after Friedrich von Schiller's *Die Räuber*. Principal roles: Carlo (ten), Amalia (sop), Francesco (bar), Massamiliano (bass), Arminio (ten), Pastor Moser (bass). One of the finest of Verdi's early period works but performed comparatively infrequently in recent years, it is notable for containing, in Francesco, Verdi's first serious study in evil.

Plot: early 18th-century Germany. Carlo has been banished from the home of his father Massamiliano through the intrigues of his jealous younger brother Francesco who wishes to usurp his position, and is driven to become the leader of a robber band. Francesco brings false evidence of Carlo's death, but Carlo's beloved Amalia still repulses his advances. After Carlo has burnt down a city to rescue a captured comrade, he is reunited with Amalia and rescues his father whom Francesco has imprisoned and who is starving to death. He contrives Francesco's death but his men refuse to release him from his oath of loyalty to them. He kills Amalia in their presence. [R]

Masque

A 16th- and 17th-century court entertainment which originated in Italy and France and soon reached Britain. Usually treating mythological subjects, it combined music, poetry, elaborate costumes and dancing. It was superseded by opera proper, but for a while the two forms existed together, and it is almost impossible to draw a strict distinction between them in certain works such as Purcell's *The Faery Queen*, Blow's *Venus and Adonis* and Arne's *Comus*.

Massamila Doni

Opera by Schoeck (Op 50). 1st perf. Dresden, 2 March 1937; libr. by Armin Rüger, after Honoré de Balzac. Principal roles: Massamila (sop), Emilio (ten), Duke Cattaneo (ten), Tinti (sop), Prince Vendramin (bar), Capraja (bass). One of Schoeck's finest works, it is very rarely performed. [R]

Massamiliano

Bass role in Verdi's *I Masnadieri*. Count Moor, he is the father of Carlo and Francesco.

Massana, Antonio *(1890–1966)*

Spanish composer. His two operas, admired in Spain but unknown elsewhere, are *Nuredduna* and *Canigó* [R].

Massard, Robert *(b 1925)*

French baritone, particularly associated with the French repertory. One of the very few really outstanding French singers of the postwar era, his rich and beautiful voice was used with fine musicianship, and he had a good stage presence.

Massé, Victor *(b Félix Marie)* *(1822–84)*

French composer. He wrote over 20 operettas, of which the most successful included *Les Noces de Jeanette**, his best known work, *La Reine Topaz* (Paris 27 Dec 1856; libr. J. P. Lockroy and Léon Battu) and *Paul et Virginie* (Paris 15 Nov 1876; libr. Jules Barbier and Michel Carré, after B. de Saint-Pierre). He was chorus master of the Paris Opéra (1860–76).

Massenet, Jules *(1842–1912)*

French composer. His 28 operas begin with: *La Grande-Tante* (Paris 3 April 1867; libr. Jules Adénis and Charles Granvallet), *Don César de Bazan* (Paris 30 Nov 1872; libr. Adolphe Philippe d'Ennery, Philippe Dumanoir and Jules Chantepie), and the operetta *L'Adorable Bel-Boule* (1874), which Massenet later destroyed, as also he did *Bérengère et Anatole* (Paris 1876; libr. Henri Meilhac and Paul Poirson). *Le Roi de Lahore** was his first major success. It was followed by *Hérodiade**, *Manon**, perhaps his most popular opera, *Le Cid**, *Esclarmonde**, *Le Mage* (1891), *Werther**, *Thaïs**, *Le Portrait de Manon* (Paris 8 May 1894; libr. Georges Boyer), an unsuccessful follow-up to *Manon*, the verismo *La Navarraise**, *Sapho**, *Cendrillon**, *Grisélidis**, *Le Jongleur de Notre-Dame**, *Amadis* (Monte Carlo 1 April 1922, composed 1902; libr. Jules Clarétie), *Marie-Magdeleine* (Nice 9 Feb 1903; libr. Louis Gallet), a revision of his oratorio of 1873, *Chérubin**, *Ariane* (Paris 31 Oct 1906; libr. Catulle Mendès), *Thérèse**, *Bacchus* (Paris 5 May 1909; libr. Mendès), *Don Quichotte**, *Roma* (Monte Carlo 17 Feb 1912; libr. Henri Cain, after Alexandre Parodi), *Panurge* (Paris 25 April 1913; libr. Georges Spitmüller, after François Rabelais' *Pantagruel*) and *Cléopâtre* (Monte Carlo 23 Feb 1914; libr Louis Payren).

Massenet's operas are notable for their grace and charm, their fine sense of theatre and their elegant orchestration. What d'Indy described as the "discreet and semi-religious eroticism" of his music, particularly in works such as *Thaïs*, can both attract and repel; in Britain the second has often been the case. After a period of neglect and denigration, his stage works have returned to favour in recent years and performances are far more frequent. Massenet also completed Delibes' unfinished *Kassya* and was a distinguished teacher. His pupils included Bruneau, Charpentier, Leroux and Rabaud.

Master of Clamecy, The (also known as *Colas Breugnon* which, strictly, is the name of the hero and the title of the overture)

Opera in three acts by Kabalevsky (Op 24). 1st perf. Leningrad, 22 Feb 1938; libr. by the composer and V. G. Bragin, after Romain Rolland's *Colas Breugnon*. Revised version, 1st perf. Moscow, 20 March 1971. Principal roles: Colas (bar), Selina (mezzo), Duke (ten), Jacqueline (sop), Gifflard (bass), Curé (bass), de Termes (sop). Kabalevsky's most successful opera, it is hardly ever performed outside Russia, although the exciting overture is well-known.

Plot: 16th-century Burgundy. The sculptor Colas loves Selina, but Gifflard, who also loves her, spreads a rumour that his rival loves Mlle de Termes, a guest whom the tyrannical Duke has brought from Paris. Blind with jealousy, Selina tells the drunken Curé to marry her to Gifflard. Thirty years later, during which Colas has lived with his old love Jacqueline, the Duke takes Colas' sculpture of Selina to his castle. His soldiers bring a plague to the town, in which Jacqueline dies. Colas and Selina meet and are reunited. Gifflard tells the Duke that Colas is a rebel and the Duke destroys the statue of Selina. Colas, furious at the wanton destruction of art, vows revenge. Pretending to be repentant, he offers to make a sculpture of the Duke. At its unveiling, the sculpture shows the Duke sitting back-to-front on a donkey. Publicly ridiculed and humiliated, the Duke retreats in shame to his castle. [R]

Master Peter's Puppet Show
See Retablo de Maese Pedro, El

Mastersingers of Nuremburg, The
See Meistersinger von Nürnberg, Die

Masterson, Valerie (b 1937)
British soprano, particularly associated with Mozart, Sullivan and Handel roles and, especially, the French repertory, of which she is one of the leading contemporary exponents. Her beautiful and agile voice and exemplary diction, combined with her most affecting stage presence, have made her one of the most popular British artists of recent years. She created Wife of Soldier 2 in Henze's *We Come to the River*.

Mastilović, Danica (b 1933)
Yugoslavian soprano, particularly associated with Strauss, Wagner, and

the heavier Verdi roles. Hers was a large and bright-toned, if sometimes unwieldy, voice which she used to exciting effect, and she had a strong stage presence.

Masur, Kurt (b 1927)
German conductor, particularly associated with the German repertory. One of the finest contemporary interpreters of 19th-century German music, he is best known as a symphonic conductor. His recent operatic appearances have been infrequent. He was musical director of the Mecklenburg Staatstheater (1958–60) and the Komische Oper, Berlin (1960–64).

Matačić, Lovro von (1899–1985)
Yugoslavian conductor, particularly associated with the German repertory. He was musical director of the Belgrade Opera (1926–32), the Zagreb Opera (1932–38), the Dresden State Opera (1956–58) and the Frankfurt Opera (1961–66). He also produced a number of operas.

Mathis, Edith (b 1938)
Swiss soprano, particularly associated with Mozart roles. A highly intelligent and musical singer with a beautiful voice and a delightful stage presence, she created Luise in Henze's *Der Junge Lord* and Kathi in Einem's *Der Zerrissene*. Married to the conductor Bernhard Klee.

Mathis der Maler (*Matthias the Painter*)
Opera in seven scenes by Hindemith. 1st perf. Zürich, 28 May 1938; libr. by the composer. Principal roles: Mathis (bar), Archbishop Albrecht (ten), Ursula (mezzo), Regina (sop), Riedinger (bass), Schwalb (ten). Telling of the painter Matthias Grünwald (c 1480–1528),

creator of the Isenheim altarpiece, and his involvement in the Peasants' War of 1524, its 1934 première in Berlin was banned by the Nazis. It is still occasionally performed, but the music is best known through the symphony which Hindemith arranged from music from the opera.

Plot: Mainz, 1524. Through their leader Schwalb and his daughter Regina, the painter Mathias becomes involved in the Peasants' War. His patron, Archbishop Albrecht, decides to renounce the world and become a hermit. Mathias is tempted to give up painting and espouse the peasants' cause, but in a dream sequence (recreating two of his paintings) he comes to see that his best way of serving mankind is through his art. Regina dies and Mathias returns to his painting with fresh inspiration. [R]

Mathilde
Soprano role in Rossini's *Guillaume Tell*. She is a Hapsburg princess in love with Arnold.

Mathilde de Shabran
or **Bellezza, e Cuor di Ferro** (*Beauty and Heart of Iron*)
Opera in two acts by Rossini. 1st perf. Rome, 24 Feb 1821; libr. by Jacopo Ferretti after J. M. Boutet de Monvel's *Mathilde* and François Benoît Hoffman's libretto for Méhul's *Euphrosine*. Never one of Rossini's more successful works, it is nowadays almost never performed.

Matrimonio Segreto, Il (*The Secret Marriage*)
Comic opera in two acts by Cimarosa. 1st perf. Vienna, 7 Feb 1792; libr. Giovanni Bertati after George Colman and David Garrick's *The Clandestine Marriage*. Principal roles: Geronimo (bass), Elisetta (sop), Carolina (sop),

Count Robinson (bar), Paolino (ten), Fidalma (mezzo). Cimarosa's only work still to be regularly performed, it is arguably the greatest 18th-century opera buffa apart from those by Mozart. Its première was the occasion of the longest encore in operatic history: Emperor Leopold II was so delighted that he ordered supper served to the company and the entire opera repeated immediately.

Plot: 18th-century Bologna. Paolino has secretly married Geronimo's daughter Carolina. Their situation is complicated by Carolina's aunt Fidalma, who loves Paolino, and by the arrival of the Englishman Count Robinson who, although betrothed to Geronimo's other daughter Elisetta, falls in love with Carolina. After much scheming and amorous intrigue, the truth about the marriage is revealed and all ends happily. [R]

Matteo

Tenor role in Richard Strauss' *Arabella*. He is Arabella's former suitor, loved by Zdenka.

Mauceri, John *(b 1945)*

American conductor, particularly associated with Bernstein and Weill works and with the Italian repertory, especially Verdi and Puccini. Musical director of Scottish Opera (1987–).

Maurel, Victor *(1848–1923)*

French baritone, particularly associated with the Italian repertory, especially Verdi. Although his voice was not outstanding, he was a singing-actor of exceptional ability (he sometimes appeared as a straight actor), and is often regarded as the leading baritone of his generation. He created Tonio in *Pagliacci*, Gonzales in Gomes' *Il Guarany* and, for Verdi, Iago in *Otello* and the title roles in *Falstaff* and the

revised *Simon Boccanegra*. He was also a painter of some ability and designed the Metropolitan Opera's *Mireille* in 1919. He wrote three books on singing and his autobiography, *Dix Ans de Carrière*, which was published in 1897 and which was later translated into German by Lilli Lehmann.

Maurizio

(1) Tenor role in Cilea's *Adriana Lecouvreur*. The Count of Saxony, he loves Adriana. (2) Bass role in Wolf-Ferrari's *I Quatro Rusteghi*. He is Filipeto's father.

Mavra

Comic opera in one act by Stravinsky. 1st perf. Paris, 3 June 1922; libr. by Boris Kochno, after Alexander Pushkin's *The Little House at Kolomna*. Principal roles: Vasili (ten), Parasha (sop), Mother (mezzo), Sosedka (mezzo). A witty little piece, written in a blend of Russian and Italian styles, it is still quite often performed.

Plot: a 17th-century Russian town. Parasha's mother sends her to look for a replacement for their deceased cook. Parasha dresses her boyfriend, the hussar Vasili, as a woman and introduces him to the house as the maid Mavra. Unfortunately, her mother catches 'Mavra' shaving and he is forced to make a hasty exit out of the window. [R]

Maw, Nicholas *(b 1935)*

British composer. He has written two operas: the comedy *One Man Show* (1964; libr. Arthur Jacobs) and *The Rising of the Moon* (Glyndebourne 1970; libr. Beverley Cross).

Max

Tenor role in: (1) Weber's *Der Freischütz*. He is a forester in love with

Agathe. (2) Křenek's *Jonny Spielt Auf.* He is a composer.

Maximilien

Opera in three acts by Milhaud (Op. 110). 1st perf. Paris, 4 Jan 1932; libr. by Armand Lunel, after Rudolf Stephen Hoffmann's play, itself based on Franz Werfel's *Juarez und Maximilian*. Part of Milhaud's New World Trilogy (along with *Christophe Colomb* and *Bolivar*), it tells of the ill-fated establishment of the Hapsburg Archduke Maximilian as Emperor of Mexico in 1864. Unsuccessful at its appearance, it is nowadays all but forgotten.

Maxwell Davies, Sir Peter *(b 1934)*

British composer. One of the most original and successful contemporary British composers, and founder of both the Fires of London ensemble and the Kirkwall Festival in the Orkney Islands, he has written five operas. The successful *Taverner** was followed by *The Martyrdom of Saint Magnus* (Kirkwall 18 June 1977; libr. composer, after Brown), the children's opera *The Two Fiddlers* (Kirkwall 16 June 1978; libr. composer), the powerful and claustrophobic *The Lighthouse** and *Resurrection* (Darmstadt 18 Sept 1988).

May Night *(Mayskaya Noch)*

Opera in three acts by Rimsky-Korsakov. 1st perf. St Petersburg, 21 Jan 1880; libr. by the composer, after Nikolai Gogol. Principal roles: Levko (ten), Hanna (mezzo), Ponnochka (sop), Headman (bass). The first of Rimsky's fairy-tale operas, it contains some delightful music but is only very rarely performed, even in Russia.

Plot: With the assistance of the water nymph Pannochka, Levko teaches his father the Headsman a lesson for attempting to seduce Hanna. He also manages to obtain permission to marry Hanna. [R]

Mayr, Richard *(1877–1935)*

Austrian bass, particularly associated with Wagner and Strauss roles, especially Baron Ochs, a role of which he is usually regarded as the greatest ever interpreter. A fine singing-actor with a rich and powerful voice, he created Barak in *Die Frau ohne Schatten*.

Mayr, Simone *(b Johannes Simon) (1763–1845)*

German-born Italian composer. A crucial figure in the development of Italian opera, he introduced the full symphony orchestra to Italy from Germany, himself made major advances in orchestration which influenced composers throughout Europe, and developed the range and fluency of both serious and comic Italian opera. His first opera *Saffo* (Venice 17 Feb 1794; libr. Antonio Sografi) was a success and was followed by 61 others. The most important include *Che Originali* (Venice 18 Oct 1798; libr. Gaetano Rossi), which established his European reputation, *Ginevra di Scozia* (Trieste 21 Apr 1801; libr. Rossi), *L'Amore Conjugale* (Padua 26 July 1805; libr. Rossi, after Jean Nicolas Bouilly's libretto for Gaveaux's *Léonore*), *La Rosa Bianca e la Rosa Rossa* (Genoa 21 Feb 1813; libr. Felice Romani), which began the Italian craze for operas on historical British subjects, and the magnificent *Medea in Corinto**, his masterpiece. He founded the Bergamo Conservatory in 1805, where his pupils included Donizetti, who he taught free for ten years. For long Mayr was merely a name in the history books, but recent years have seen a revival of interest in his music.

Mazeppa

Opera in three acts by Tchaikovsky. 1st perf. Moscow, 15 Feb 1884; libr. by the compser and Viktor Burenin, after Alexander Pushkin's *Poltava*. Principal roles: Mazeppa (bar), Vasili Kochubei (bass), Maria (sop), Andrei (ten), Liubov (mezzo), Iskra (ten), Orlik (bar). Tchaikovsky's most 'nationalist' opera in style, it contains some magnificent music but is only infrequently performed outside Russia.

Plot: 18th-century Ukraine. Having been refused the hand of Kochubei's daughter Maria, Mazeppa abducts her. Andrei, who loves Maria, takes revenge by telling the government that Mazeppa is in league with the Swedes. The Tsar believes Mazeppa rather than Andrei, however, and has Kochubei executed. Mazeppa shoots Andrei, and Maria goes insane. [R]

Mazurok, Yuri *(b 1931)*

Russian baritone, particularly associated with Verdi and Tchaikovsky roles. One of the finest Russian baritones of the post-war era, he possessed a beautiful, bright and finely-projected voice which he used with outstanding musicianship. On stage, he sometimes appeared a little uncommitted.

Meco all'altar di Venere

Tenor aria for Pollione in Act I of Bellini's *Norma*.

Medea

See Médée

Medea in Corinto

Opera in two acts by Mayr. 1st perf. Naples, 28 Nov 1813; libr. by Felice Romani, partly after Euripides' *Medea*. Principal roles: Medea (sop), Giasone (ten), Creusa (sop), Egeo (ten), Creonte (bass), Ismene (mezzo). Mayr's finest work, it is an opera of considerable dramatic power and the delineation of the title role presents a wonderful challenge to a great singing-actress. Enormously popular until the mid-19th century, it was long forgotten, but has received a number of performances in recent years. It is a straightforward setting of the story of Jason and Medea with the addition of Egeo, King of Athens, as Creusa's rejected lover. [R]

Médecin Malgré Lui, Le *(The Doctor Despite Himself)*

Comic opera in three acts by Gounod. 1st perf. Paris, 15 Jan 1858; libr. by Jules Barbier and Michel Carré, after Molière's play. Gounod's first major success, it is now very infrequently performed.

Médée *(Medea)*

Works of this title about the sorceress of Greek legend include:

(1) Opera in prologue and four acts by M.-A. Charpentier. 1st perf. Paris, 4 Dec 1693; libr. by Thomas Corneille. Principal roles: Médée (sop), Jason (ten), Créon (bass), Nerine (sop), Oronte (bass), Creuse (sop). Charpentier's last and greatest stage work, it has had a number of performances in recent years. [R]

(2) Opera in three acts by Cherubini. 1st perf. Paris, 13 March 1797; libr. by François Benoît Hoffman, after Thomas Corneille. Principal roles: Médée (sop), Jason (ten), Dircé (sop), Créon (bass), Néris (mezzo). Cherubini's best-known and most enduring work, it has been regularly performed since its revival for Maria Callas in 1953. Most performances are given in Italian, using the recitatives composed by Franz Lachner in 1855.

Plot: Corinth. Medea, abandoned by

Jason, arrives at the court of Creon in a failed attempt to win him back from Dircé. Despite the people's fear of her as an enchantress, she obtains Creon's permission to remain in Corinth for a further day. Taking revenge, she brings about a horrible death for Dircé and, with her own hands, kills the children she bore Jason. [R]

(3) Opera in one act by Milhaud (Op 191). 1st perf. Angers, 1939; libr. by Madeleine Milhaud, after Euripides' *Medea*.

Méditation

Orchestral intermezzo with solo violin in Massenet's *Thaïs*.

Medium, The

Opera in two acts by Menotti. 1st perf. New York, 8 May 1946; libr. by the composer. Principal roles: Madame Flora (mezzo), Monica (sop), Toby (mute), Mr and Mrs Gobineau (bar and mezzo). Arguably Menotti's finest opera and still regularly performed, it is a powerfully atmospheric piece of theatre.

Plot: Assisted by her daughter Monica, and the dumb boy, Toby, who loves Monica, the fake medium, Madame Flora, puts gullible clients in touch with their dead children. During a séance, she has the sensation of a hand around her throat, and confesses her fraudulence to her clients, the Gobineaus. They refuse to believe her, but she dismisses them, and beats and evicts Toby. The boy returns to look for Monica, and hides in a cupboard. Madame Flora takes him for a ghost and shoots him. [R]

Mefistofele

Opera in prologue, four acts and epilogue by Boito. 1st perf. Milan, 5 March 1868; libr. by the composer, after Goethe's *Faust*. Revised version, 1st perf. Bologna, 4 Oct 1875.

Principal roles: Mefistofele (bass), Faust (ten), Margherita (sop), Elena (sop). The work on which Boito's reputation as a composer rests, its disastrous première led to a virtual pitched battle between its admirers and detractors. The revised version was an immediate success and the work has been regularly performed ever since, especially in Italy and the United States. Drawing on both parts of Goethe's work, it has always been a controversial opera, with opinions sharply divided as to its merits. It is certainly the most high-minded Italian opera since those of Gluck, and the title role remains one of the greatest parts ever written for a bass.

Plot: In Heaven, Mefistofele wagers that he can win Faust's soul. Faust accepts his offer of service and renewed youth in return for his soul after death. Faust meets and seduces Margherita but then abandons her. Margherita, having killed the child she bore Faust, dies insane in prison. Mefistofele shows Faust his power at the Witches' Sabbath and then transports him back to ancient Greece, where Faust dallies with Helen of Troy. Finding his youth gone again, the dying Faust repents and the heavenly host announce his salvation; Mefistofele has lost his wager and yells his defiance at Heaven. [R]

Meg Page

Mezzo role in Verdi's *Falstaff*. She is one of the merry wives.

Mehta, Zubin *(b 1936)*

Indian conductor, particularly associated with Verdi, Wagner and Puccini operas. One of the most famous contemporary conductors, more frequently heard in the concert hall than in the opera house, he conducted the first performance of Levy's *Mourning Becomes Electra*.

Méhul, Etienne-Nicolas (1763–1817)

French composer. Inspired by Gluck, his operas are notable for their lofty and austere style, for their originality of orchestration and for their blending of classical and romantic elements. Not only successful but also highly respected in his day, he had a crucial influence on the development of both German romantic opera and of French grand opera. His first performed opera was *Euphrosine* (Paris 4 Sept 1790; libr. François Benoît Hoffman). It was followed by 24 others, of which the most successful included *Ariodant**, *Les Deux Aveugles**, the Ossianic *Uthal** and his masterpiece *Joseph**, which was popular for a century. A fine and historically significant composer who is currently unjustly neglected.

Meier, Waltraud (b 1956)

German mezzo, particularly associated with Wagnerian roles. Possessing a rich voice of great beauty and considerable power, used with fine musicianship, as well as a strong and handsome stage presence, she is one of the finest mezzos to have emerged in the late 1980s.

Meilhac, Henri (1831–97)

French playwright and librettist. One of the finest French librettists of the 19th century and an outstanding satirist, he wrote a large number of libretti, many in collaboration with Ludovic Halévy*. He provided texts for Bizet (*Carmen*), Delibes (*Kassya*), Hervé (*Mam'zelle Nitouche*), Lecocq (four including *Le Petit Duc*), Massenet (*Bérengère et Anatole* and *Manon*), Offenbach (*Barbe-Bleue, La Belle Hélène, Les Brigands, La Grand-Duchesse de Gérolstein, La Périchole, Vert-Vert* and *La Vie Parisienne*) and Planquette (*Rip*). Of his plays, *L'Attaché d'Ambassade* is the source for *Die Lustige Witwe* and *Le Réveillon* for *Die Fledermaus*.

Mein Herr Marquis

Soprano aria (the Laughing Song) for Adele in Act II of J. Strauss' *Die Fledermaus*.

Meistersinger von Nürnberg, Die (The Mastersingers of Nuremburg)

Opera in three acts by Wagner. 1st perf. Munich, 21 June 1868; libr. by the composer. Principal roles: Hans Sachs (bar), Walther von Stolzing (ten), Eva (sop), Veit Pogner (bass), Sixtus Beckmesser (bar), David (ten), Magdalene (mezzo), Fritz Köthner (bar), Nightwatchman (b-bar). Wagner's only mature comedy and his only work dealing with ordinary historical figures, it concerns the cobbler-poet Hans Sachs (1494–1576) and the Guild of Mastersingers.

Plot: 16th-century Nuremburg. The Franconian knight Walther von Stolzing loves Eva, daughter of the wealthy Pogner, who has decided that her hand will be given to the winner of a singing contest. Walther wishes to enter the contest but is ignorant of the strict and complex rules of the guild. With the aid of the cobbler-poet Sachs and in the face of the bitter opposition of the pedantic town clerk Beckmesser, who also aspires to marry Eva, Walther wins the contest with his Prize Song and is given Eva's hand. [R]

Mel

Baritone role in Tippett's *The Knot Garden*. A poet, he is Dov's black lover.

Melba, Dame Nellie (b Helen Porter Mitchell) (1861–1931)

Australian soprano, particularly

associated with the Italian and French repertories. One of the most famous of all sopranos, she began as a high coloratura but later moved to the lyric repertory. She had a fresh, pure and beautiful voice of remarkable agility with a range up to f''', which she used with a matchless technique. Long resident at Covent Garden, where her word was law, she created the title role in Saint-Saëns' *Hélène*. She retired to Australia in 1926 as director of the Melbourne Conservatory. Her autobiography, *Melodies and Memoirs*, was published in 1925. Both the famous toast and an ice-cream were named in her honour, and a film of her life, starring Patrice Munsel, was made in 1953.

Melchior, Lauritz *(1890–1973)*
Danish tenor, particularly associated with Wagnerian roles. One of the greatest of all heldentenors, he began as a baritone, turning to tenor roles in 1918. He had a large, ringing voice which he used to thrilling effect and he seemed apparently tireless. He gave more Wagner performances than possibly any other singer in history, singing Tristan alone over 200 times. He took part in the first-ever operatic radio broadcast in 1920, and also appeared in a number of Hollywood films, including *Luxury Liner* (1947) and *The Stars Are Singing* (1952).

Melchtal
Bass role in Rossini's *Guillaume Tell*. He is Arnold's father.

Mélesville, Anne-Honoré Joseph de *(b Duveyrier) (1787–1865)*
French playwright and librettist. A prolific writer, he provided texts for Adam (*Le Chalet* and *Lambert Simnel*), Auber (*Leicester* and *Les Lacs des*

Fées), Carafa (*Le Valet de Chambre*), Cherubini (*Ali Baba*), Hérold (*Zampa*), Offenbach and others. Many were written in collaboration with Eugène Scribe*.

Mélisande
Soprano role in Debussy's *Pelléas et Mélisande*. She is a girl discovered in the forest by Golaud.

Melismata (from the plural of the Greek *melisma*, 'song')
A group of notes sung to a single syllable. The term is also used loosely to describe any florid passage of cadenza type.

Melitone, Fra
Baritone role in Verdi's *La Forza del Destino*. A grumbling monk, he is Verdi's only wholly comic character before *Falstaff*.

Melodrama
A spoken text accompanied by instrumental music. If it is for a single actor it is sometimes called 'monodrama', if for two 'duodrama'. Developing in the mid-18th century, the first full-scale melodrama was Rousseau's *Pygmalion* and the finest examples were written by Benda. The form has been used more recently by Fibich. A number of early 19th-century operas contain melodrama scenes, the most famous being the Wolf's Glen Scene in Weber's *Der Freischütz* and the grave-digging scene in *Fidelio*. The Italian term *melodramma* simply means a sung drama, in other words an opera.

Melot
Tenor role in Wagner's *Tristan und Isolde*. He is Tristan's jealous friend. The role is sometimes sung by a baritone.

Mendelssohn-Bartholdy, Felix *(1809–47)*

German composer and conductor. He wrote seven operas early in his career, none of which achieved any lasting success. They are *Die Soldatenliebschaft* (Wittenberg 28 April 1962, composed 1820; libr. J. L. Casper), *Die Beiden Pädagogen* (*The Two Teachers*, Berlin 27 May 1962, composed 1821; libr. Casper, after Eugène Scribe) [R], *Die Wandernden Komödianten* (1822), *Der Onkel aus Boston* (Berlin 3 Feb 1824), *Die Hochzeit des Camacho* (Berlin 29 April 1827; libr. Karl Klingemann, after Miguel Cervantes' *Don Quixote*) and *Die Heimkehr aus der Fremde* (*The Return From Abroad*, sometimes known in Britain as *Son and Stranger*, Leipzig 10 April 1851, composed 1829; libr. Klingemann) [R].

The only opera of his maturity is the unfinished *Loreley* (1847; libr. after Emmanuel Geibel).

Mendès, Catulle *(1841–1909)*

French poet and librettist. A member of the *Parnassiens* and a disciple of Wagner (about whom he wrote a book), he wrote a number of opera libretti. He provided texts for Chabrier (*Gwendoline* and *Briséis)*, Debussy (the unfinished *Rodrigue et Chimène*), Hahn (*La Carmélite*), Leroux (*La Reine Fiammette*), Massenet (*Ariane* and *Bacchus*) and Messager (*Isoline*). He was killed in a railway accident.

Menelaus

The husband of Helen of Troy appears as tenor role in: (1) Offenbach's *La Belle Hélène*. (2) Richard Strauss' *Die Ägyptische Helena*.

Menotti, Gian-Carlo *(b 1911)*

Italian-born American composer, librettist and producer. One of the most successful and prolific of contemporary opera composers, he shows immense theatrical flair, although his music, in readily accessible post-Puccinian style, is shallow, inconsequential and devoid of any real dramatic insight. His first surviving opera was the successful satire *Amelia al Ballo**. It was followed by *The Old Maid and the Thief**, *The Island God* (New York 20 Feb 1942), the powerful *The Medium**, the comedy *The Telephone**, the highly successful *The Consul**, the popular *Amahl and the Night Visitors**, the first opera written specifically for television, the verismo *The Saint of Bleecker Street**, the satirical *The Unicorn, the Gorgon and the Manticore* (Washington 21 Oct 1956), which is written in madrigal style, and *Maria Golovin**. His more recent operas, nearly all feeble, are the television opera *Labyrinth* (NBC 3 May 1963), *The Last Savage**, the science-fiction fantasy *Help! Help! the Globolinks!* (Hamburg 18 Dec 1968), described as written for 'children and those who like children', *The Most Important Man in the World* (New York 12 March 1971), *Tamu-Tamu* (Chicago 5 Sept 1973), *The Hero* (Philadelphia 1 June 1976), *La Loca* (San Diego 1979), *The Boy Who Grew Too Fast* (Wilmington 24 Sept 1982) [R] and *Goya* (Washington 1986).

In addition to writing the libretti for all of his own operas, Menotti also wrote those for Barber's *Vanessa*, *A Hand of Bridge* and the revised *Antony and Cleopatra*, and Foss' *Introductions and Goodbyes*. He founded the Festival of Two Worlds, Spoleto in 1958, where he has often acted as producer.

Mephistopheles

The Devil in this guise appears in a number of operas, including: (1) Bass role in Gounod's *Faust*. (2) Bass role in Boito's *Mefistofele*. (3) Tenor role in Busoni's *Doktor Faust*. (4) Bass role in

Berlioz's *La Damnation de Faust*. (5) Bass role in Spohr's *Faust*.

Mercadante, Saverio *(1795–1870)*

Italian composer. One of the most prolific and successful Italian composers of his day, his career spanned Rossini's peak and Verdi's middle period, and he played a crucial role in the development of Italian opera by enriching the orchestration and pioneering a freer dramatic form in a way which influenced Verdi. His first major success was his seventh opera *Elisa e Claudio* (Milan 30 Oct 1821; libr. Luigi Romanelli, after F. Casari's *Rosella*). The most successful of the more than 50 works that followed included *Donna Caritea* (Venice 21 Feb 1826; libr. P. Pola), *Zaira* (Naples 31 Aug 1831; libr. Felice Romani, after Voltaire's *Zaïre*), *I Normanni a Parigi* (Turin 7 Feb 1832; libr. Romani), *I Briganti* (Paris 22 March 1836; libr. J. Crescini, after Friedrich von Schiller's *Die Räuber*), *Il Giuramento**, his finest work, *Le Due Illustri Rivali**, *Il Bravo* (Milan 9 March 1839; libr. Gaetano Rossi and M. Marcello) [R], the once-popular *La Vestale* (Naples 10 March 1840; libr. Salvatore Cammarano), *Il Reggente* (Turin 2 Feb 1843; libr. Cammarano, after Eugène Scribe's libretto for Auber's *Gustave III*), *Orazi e Curiazi* (Naples 10 Nov 1846; libr. Cammarano), which was long popular, and *Virginia* (Naples 7 April 1866, composed 1851; libr. Cammarano, after Alfieri). After a long period of complete neglect, there has recently been a revival of interest in his works and performances are becoming more frequent. He was a respected director of the Naples Conservatory from 1840.

Mercédès

Mezzo role in Bizet's *Carmen*. She is a gypsy friend of Carmen's.

Mercury

The Graeco-Roman messenger of the gods appears in a number of operas, including: (1) Baritone role in Cavalli's *La Calisto*. (2) Tenor role in Offenbach's *Orphée aux Enfers*. (3) Tenor role in Rameau's *Platée*. (4) Baritone role in Oliver's *Tom Jones*. (5) Baritone role in Klebe's *Alkmene*. (6) Bass role in Handel's *Atalanta*. (7) Tenor role in Rameau's *Hippolyte et Aricie*. (8) Bass comprimario role in Berlioz's *Les Troyens*.

Merelli, Bartolomeo *(1794–1879)*

Italian administrator and librettist. One of the great 19th-century Italian impresarios, he was manager of La Scala, Milan (1836–46 and 1861–63) and the Kärntnertortheater in Vienna (1836–48 and 1853–55). One of the first to encourage Verdi, he also wrote a number of libretti, providing texts for his fellow student Donizetti (*Enrico di Borgogna* and *Zoraide di Granata*), Mayr, Morlacchi and Vaccai (*Il Lupo d'Ostenda*).

Méric-Lalande, Henriette *(1798–1867)*

French soprano. One of the leading lyric sopranos of the early 19th century, she created Palmide in Meyerbeer's *Il Crociato in Egitto* and, for Bellini, Bianca in *Bianca e Gernando*, Imogene in *Il Pirata*, Alaide in *La Straniera* and the title role in *Zaira*. When past her prime, she also created (unsuccessfully) the title role in *Lucrezia Borgia*, causing Donizetti much trouble: she refused to make her first entry masked (on the grounds that her adoring public might not recognise her) and stood on her prerogative as prima donna in demanding a brilliant final aria, despite its dramatic unsuitability. Donizetti was forced to give way, but looking at the fearsome difficulties of 'Era desso il figlio mio' it is clear that he exacted a subtle and terrible revenge which contributed to her débâcle.

Merikanto, Aarre *(1893–1958)*

Finnish composer, son of the composer Oskar Merikanto*. His one opera *Juha** is one of the finest of all Finnish operas.

Merikanto, Oskar *(1868–1924)*

Finnish composer. He wrote three operas, all unknown outside Finland. They are *The Maid of the North* (*Pohjan Neiti*, Viipuri 1908, composed 1898), which was the first opera written to a Finnish libretto, *Elinan Surma* (Helsinki 1910) and *Regina von Emmeritz* (Helsinki 1920). His son was the composer Aarre Merikanto*.

Mérimée, Prosper
See panel on page 375

Merli, Francesco *(1887–1976)*

Italian tenor, particularly associated with heavier Italian roles. One of the leading lyrico-dramatic tenors of the inter-war period, he created the title role in Respighi's *Belfagor*.

Merrie England

Operetta in two acts by German. 1st perf. London, 2 April 1902; libr. by Basil Hood. Principal roles: Bessie Throckmorton (sop), Sir Walter Raleigh (ten), Elizabeth I (mezzo), Earl of Essex (bar), Jill-All-Alone (mezzo), Walter Wilkins (bass). German's finest stage work, it was sensationally successful at its appearance and is still occasionally performed.

Plot: late 16th-century England. Sir Walter Raleigh and the Earl of Essex vie for the favours of Queen Elizabeth I. She discovers that Raleigh is secretly in love with Bessie Throckmorton, but her attempts to have Bessie killed are thwarted by a plot of Essex's. [R]

Merrill, Nathaniel *(b 1927)*

American producer, resident at the Metropolitan Opera, New York since 1960. His productions, often in collaboration with the designer Robert O'Hearn (*b* 1921), are in traditional style.

Merrill, Robert *(b 1917)*

American baritone, particularly associated with the Italian repertory, especially Verdi. One of the finest Verdi baritones of the postwar era, he had a rich and beautiful voice used with fine musicianship. He also appeared in a number of films, and his autobiography, *Once More From the Beginning*, was published in 1965. Married for a time to the soprano Roberta Peters*.

Merriman, Nan *(b Katherine-Ann) (b 1920)*

American mezzo, particularly associated with the Italian repertory. She had a rich, warm and characterful voice and was an accomplished actress, especially in comedy.

Merry Widow, The
See Lustige Witwe, Die

Merry Wives of Windsor, The
See Lustigen Weiber von Windsor, Die

Mes amis, écoutez l'histoire

Tenor aria for Chapelou in Act I of Adam's *Le Postillon de Longjumeau*.

PROSPER MÉRIMÉE

The works of the French writer Prosper Mérimée (1803–70) have inspired some 25 operas. Below are listed, by work, those operas by composers with entries in this dictionary.

Les Ames du Purgatoire

Alfano	*Don Juan de Mañara/L'Ombra di Don Giovanni*	1914/41
Goossens	*Don Juan de Mañara*	1937
Tomasi	*Don Juan de Mañara*	1952

Carmen

Bizet	*Carmen*	1875

La Carrosse du Saint-Sacrement

Offenbach	*La Périchole*	1868
Berners	*La Carrosse du Saint-Sacrement*	1924

Chronique du Règne de Charles IX

Hérold	*Le Pré aux Clercs*	1832

Colomba

Pacini	*La Fidanzata Corsa*	1842

La Dame du Pique (translation of Pushkin's *The Queen of Spades*)

Halévy	*La Dame du Pique*	1850

Donna Uraca

Malipiero	*Donna Uraca*	1954

Inès Mendo

d'Erlanger	*Inès Mendo*	1897

Mosaïque

Cui	*Matteo Falcone*	1907

La Vénus d'Ille

Schoeck	*Venus*	1919

Mesplé, Mady *(b 1931)*
French soprano, particularly associated
with the French repertory, both opera
and operetta. She had an appealing
stage presence and her voice, if small
and sometimes a little brittle, was
intelligently used. She created Sardula in
Menotti's *The Last Savage*.

Messa di voce (Italian for
'placing of voice')
The art of increasing and diminishing
the tone on a single note, it is an
important indication of a singer's vocal
technique and control. It is called
Schwellton in Germany and *Son filé* in
France.

Messager, André *(1853–1929)*
French composer and conductor. He
wrote 17 stage works, mostly operettas,
which are notable for their elegance
and delightful melodies, their deft
orchestration and their sure theatrical
sense. His most successful works
include *La Basoche**, *Madame
Chrysanthème* (Paris 26 Jan 1893; libr.
Georges Hartmann and A. Alexandre,
after P. Loti), *Mirette* (London 3 July
1894; libr. Michel Carré), *Les P'tites
Michu* (Paris 16 Nov 1897; libr.
Georges Duval and Albert Vanloo) [R
Exc], *Fortunio**, *Véronique**, his most
enduring work, and *Monsieur
Beaucaire**. One of the finest
conductors of the early 20th century,
he was musical director of the Opéra-
Comique, Paris (1898–1903 and 1919–
20), Covent Garden (1901–07) and the
Paris Opéra (1907–14). A champion of
Wagner and of the French and Russian
repertories, he conducted the first
performances of *Pelléas et Mélisande*,
Louise, Leoni's *L'Oracolo*, Leroux's *La
Reine Fiammette* and Massenet's
Grisélidis.

Messel, Oliver *(1904–78)*
British designer. One of the most
successful and fanciful designers of the
immediate postwar period, he worked
mainly at Glyndebourne (on Mozart
and Rossini), Covent Garden (notably
Die Zauberflöte), and the Metropolitan
Opera, New York (*Le Nozze di Figaro*
and *Ariadne auf Naxos*).

Messiaen, Olivier *(b 1908)*
French composer and organist, notable
for his musical use of bird song. A
member of the 'Jeune France' group, he
wrote one opera, the vast *Saint
François d'Assise**.

Metaphor aria
An aria, very popular in 18th-century
opera seria, in which a character takes
a metaphor or simile to illustrate his or
her dramatic or emotional situation. A
famous example is Fiordiligi's 'Come
scoglio' in Mozart's *Così fan Tutte*.

Metastasio, Pietro *(b Trapassi)*
(1698–1782)
Italian poet and librettist. The leading
librettist of Italian opera seria, most of
his texts were written in Vienna, where
he succeeded Apostolo Zeno* as court
poet in 1729. Aiming to elevate and
purify Italian opera, his dramas (mostly
drawn from Roman history or
mythology) usually involve complex
amorous relationships and a conflict
between love and duty. His verses are
elegant and frequently vivid in their
imagery, but to 20th-century audiences
often seem artificial and dramatically
disjointed. He wrote some 50 texts in
all, including intermezzi and religious
pieces. The 29 opera seria texts are:
Achille in Sciro, *Adriano in Siria*,
Alessandro nell'Indie, *Antigono*,
Artaserse, *Attilio Regolo*, *Catone in
Utica*, *Ciro Riconosciuto*, *La Clemenza*

di Tito, Demetrio, Demofoonte, Didone Abbandonata, L'Eroe Cinesi, Ezio, L'Impresario delle Canarie, Ipermestra, L'Isola Disabitata, Issipile, Nitteti, L'Olimpiade, Il Re Pastore, Romola ed Ersilia, Ruggiero, Semiramide, Siface, Siroe, Temistocle, Il Trionfo di Clelia and *Zenobia*. They were set innumerable times (there are at least 50 settings of *Artaserse*), until well into the 19th century. Amongst the many composers who set his texts are Anfossi, Arne, J. C. Bach, Bononcini, Bortnyansky, Caldara, Cherubini, Cimarosa, Duni, Feo, Gluck, Graun, Handel, Hasse (56 settings), Haydn, Isouard, Jommelli, Mayr, Mercadante, Mozart, Mysliveček, Naumann, Pacini, Paer, Paisiello, Pergolesi, Piccinni, Porpora, Portugal, Sacchini, Salieri, D. Scarlatti, Traetta, Uttini, Vivaldi, Winter and Zingarelli.

Métella

Soprano role in Offenbach's *La Vie Parisienne*. She is loved by Raoul and Bobinet.

Metropolitan Opera, New York

The leading United States opera house, the original theatre in Broadway opened on 22 October 1883. The present house (cap. 4,000) in the Lincoln Center for the Performing Arts, opened on 16 September 1966. In the postwar period, administrators have been Edward Johnson, Sir Rudolf Bing and Anthony Bliss, and musical directors Rafael Kubelík and James Levine. The repertory tends to be highly conservative and productions are traditional. The annual season runs from September to April.

The Metropolitan Opera Guild, founded in 1935 and with a membership of over 200,000, does outstanding work in sponsorship and in encouraging educational activities. The weekly radio programme, Metroplitan Opera Auditions of the Air, begun in 1936, was one of the world's most prestigious vocal competitions and was responsible for discovering most of the leading American singers. Sadly, the broadcasts are now discontinued.

Mexican opera composers

These include Gustavo Campo (1863–1934), Ricardo Castro (1864–1907), Miguel Bernal Jiménez (1910–56), Melesio Morales (1838–1908), Aniceto Ortega (1823–75), Cenobio Paniagua (1821–82) and Manuel de Zumaya (*c* 1678–1756), whose *La Parténope* (Mexico City 1 May 1711; libr. Silvio Stampiglia) is probably the first Latin American opera by a native composer.

Mexico

See Palacio de la Bellas Artes, Mexico City

Meyer, Kerstin *(b 1928)*

Swedish mezzo, particularly associated with Strauss roles and with contemporary works. An outstanding singing-actress of great intelligence and musicianship, she created Agave in *The Bassarids*, Elizabeth in Maw's *The Rising of the Moon*, Mrs Arden in Goehr's *Arden Must Die*, Gertrude in Searle's *Hamlet* and Mrs Clairborne in Schuller's *The Visitation*.

Meyerbeer, Giacomo *(b Jakob Liebmann Beer) (1791–1864)*

German-born French composer. His first two operas *Jephthas Gelübde* (Munich 23 Dec 1812; libr. A. Schreiber) and the comedy *Wird und Gast* (Stuttgart 6 Jan 1813; libr. J. G. Wohlbrück) were failures, and it was only when he moved to Italy and wrote in imitation of Rossini that he met with success. His Italian operas are *Romilda e Costanza* (Padua 19 July 1817; libr. Gaetano Rossi), *Semiramide Riconsosciuta* (Turin March 1819; libr. Rossi, after Pietro Metastasio), *Emma di Resburgo* (Venice 26 June 1819; libr. Rossi), *Margherita d'Anjou* (Milan 14 Nov 1820; libr. Felice Romano, after Pixérécourt), *L'Esule di Granata* (Milan 12 March 1822; libr. Romani) and *Il Crociato in Egitto**, his first major work. It was, however, in France that he achieved his greatest successes, becoming the leading purveyor of French grand opera. The première of *Robert le Diable** was one of the most sensationally successful in operatic history, and *Les Huguenots** placed him at the forefront of European composers. *Ein Feldlager in Schlesien* (Berlin 7 Dec 1844) was less successful, but triumphed in its revised form as *L'Etoile du Nord**. His last three operas, all highly successful, were *Le Prophète**, the more pastoral *Dinorah** and *L'Africaine**, which was produced posthumously.

Few composers have ever had a more inflated reputation. In his lifetime, Meyerbeer stood pre-eminent in his field and, for 50 years, his operas were performed more often than those of almost any other composer. History (and changing tastes) has subsequently come to view him very differently. His vast and spectacular works, with their marches, ballets, scenic splendours and all the other paraphernalia, are now perceived to have cloaked a very limited musical talent. He did have a considerable ability in orchestration, but his melodies are short-winded and show no insight into character or dramatic situation. As one critic has so aptly observed: "the inflated form leads to inflated music". His influence on other composers (notably Donizetti, Verdi, the later French school and the Wagner

of *Rienzi*) has been overestimated: it was one of style and presentation rather than of music.

Mezza voce (Italian for 'half voice')

Singing at half-power, in other words, quietly and unemotionally.

Mezzo-contralto

A term which is occasionally used to denote a mezzo-soprano whose voice is nearer in range and tonal colour to a contralto than to a soprano.

Mezzo-soprano

See panel on page 379

Mia letitzia, La

Tenor aria for Oronte in Act II of Verdi's *I Lombardi*.

Miami

See Opera Guild of Greater Miami

Micaëla

Soprano role in Bizet's *Carmen*. She is a country girl in love with Don José.

Mícha, Tobias

Bass role in Smetana's *The Bartered Bride*. A landowner, he is Vašek's (and Jeník's) father.

Micheau, Janine *(1914–76)*

French soprano, particularly associated with the French repertory. Her voice, if occasionally slightly tremulous, was pleasingly silvery and used with fine musicianship and she had an appealing stage presence. She created, for Milhaud, Manuela in *Bolivar* and Creuse in *Médée*.

MEZZO-SOPRANO

Mezzo-soprano is the middle female vocal range, between soprano and contralto, and is often referred to simply as mezzo. The voice's range, of roughly g to b ''' is similar to that of a soprano minus the very top notes, but the voice is heavier and the tone is darker. There is no hard and fast distinction between mezzo and contralto; nowadays mezzo is usually used to describe virtually all non-sopranos, with contralto reserved for exceptionally low and dark voices such as Clara Butt or Kathleen Ferrier. The term mezzo-contralto is occasionally used to denote a mezzo nearer in range and tonal colour to a contralto than to a soprano. The term coloratura mezzo is also sometimes encountered, mainly in reference to Rossini roles such as Cenerentola.

See also **Alto; Coloratura mezzo; Contralto**

Below are listed the 67 mezzos and contraltos with entries in this dictionary. Their nationalities are given in brackets afterwards.

Alboni, Marietta (It)
Anderson, Marian (US)
Arkhipova, Irina (Russ)
Baker, Dame Janet (Br)
Baltsa, Agnes (Gk)
Barbieri, Fedora (It)
Berbié, Jane (Fr)
Berganza, Teresa (Sp)
Brambilla, Marietta (It)
Bumbry, Grace (US)
Burmeister, Annelies (Ger)
Butt, Dame Clara (Br)
Coates, Edith (Br)
Cossotto, Fiorenza (It)
Dernesch, Helga (Aus)
Elias, Rosalind (US)
Ewing, Maria (US)
Fassbaender, Brigitte (Ger)
Ferrier, Kathleen (Br)
Forrester, Maureen (Can)
Galli-Marié, Celestine (Fr)
Gorr, Rita (Belg)
Grisi, Giuditta (It)
Hodgson, Alfreda (Br)

Höffgen, Marga (Ger)
Hoffman, Grace (US)
Homer, Louise (US)
Höngen, Elisabeth (Ger)
Horne, Marilyn (US)
Howells, Anne (Br)
Jones, Della (Br)
Klose, Margarete (Ger)
Ludwig, Christa (Ger)
Malibran, María (Sp)
Meier, Waltruad (Ger)
Merriman, Nan (US)
Meyer, Kerstin (Swe)
Minton, Yvonne (Aust)
Murray, Ann (Br)
Obraztsova, Elena (Russ)
Parr, Gladys (Br)
Pollak, Anna (Br)
Quivar, Florence (US)
Randová, Eva (Cz)
Resnik, Regina (US)
Schumann-Heink, Ernestine (Cz)

Simionato, Giulietta (It)
Sinclair, Monica (Br)
Stade, Frederica von (US)
Stevens, Risë (US)
Stignani, Ebe (It)
Supervia, Conchita (Sp)
Tassinari, Pia (It)
Thebom, Blanche (US)
Toczyska, Stefania (Pol)
Tourangeau, Huguette (Can)
Tourel, Jennie (Can)
Troyanos, Tatiana (US)
Unger, Caroline (Hung)
Valentini-Terrani, Lucia (It)
Veasey, Josephine (Br)
Verrett, Shirley (US)
Viardot-García, Pauline (Fr)
Walker, Edith (US)
Walker, Sarah (Br)
Watts, Helen (Br)
Zareska, Eugenia (Ukr)

Michele
Baritone role in Puccini's *Il Tabarro*. He is a bargee married to Giorgetta.

Mi chiamono Mimì
Soprano aria for Mimì in Act I of Puccini's *La Bohème*.

Michonnet

Baritone role in Cilea's *Adriana Lecouvreur*. He is stage manager of the Comédie-Française.

Midsummer Marriage, The

Opera in three acts by Tippett. 1st perf. London, 27 Jan 1955; libr. by the composer. Principal roles: Mark (ten), Jenifer (sop), King Fisher (bar), Bella (sop), Jack (ten), He- and She-Ancients (bass and mezzo), Sosostris (cont). Tippett's first (and most frequently staged) opera, it is an orchestrally lush symbolic work telling of two couples' quests for sexual and spiritual fulfilment.

Plot: Midsummer's Day. Mark is engaged to Jenifer, daughter of the business tycoon King Fisher, but she feels the need to seek and find a greater understanding of herself before she can go through with the wedding ceremony. The two enter, separately, a cave in a mysterious clearing in the woods and are followed by King Fisher, his secretary Bella and her boyfriend Jack. After a series of rituals and dances (and the death of King Fisher) the couple emerge, having found new understanding, both of themselves and of each other, and are ready to marry. [R]

Midsummer Night's Dream, A

Opera in three acts by Britten (Op 64). 1st perf. Aldeburgh, 11 June 1960; libr. by the composer and Peter Pears, after Shakespeare's play. Principal roles: Oberon (c-ten), Titania (sop), Bottom (bass), Lysander (ten), Demetrius (bar), Hermia (mezzo), Helena (sop), Puck (speaker), Peter Quince (bass), Flute (ten), Theseus (bass), Hippolyta (mezzo), Snout (ten), Snug (bass), Starveling (bar). One of Britten's finest operas, it is an ingenious setting of the play, and is notable for its brilliant and witty orchestration, for providing, in Oberon, the first operatic role written for a counter-tenor, and for its operatic parody in the Pyramus and Thisbe episode – Flute has a mad scene. The plot follows Shakespeare very closely. [R]

Migenes-Johnson, Julia (b 1945)

American soprano. A powerful and at times flamboyant singing-actress with a voice of highly individual timbre, she came to international prominence in 1984 playing Carmen in Franco Rosi's film. She has also had considerable success as a television personality.

Mighty Handful, The

(or 'The Mighty Five')
A translation of the Russian term *Moguchaya Kuchka*, invented by the critic Vladimir Stasov, and later applied to the five great nationalist Russian composers Balakirev, Borodin, Cui, Moussorgsky and Rimsky-Korsakov.

Mignon

Opera in three acts by Thomas. 1st perf. Paris, 17 Nov 1866; libr. by Jules Barbier and Michel Carré, after Goethe's *Wilhelm Meisters Lehrjahre*. Principal roles: Mignon (mezzo), Wilhelm (ten), Lothario (bass), Philine (sop), Frédéric (mezzo). Thomas' finest and most enduring opera.

Plot: late 18th-century Germany and Italy. Wilhelm Meister purchases Mignon from a gypsy band which had abducted her as a child, in order to save her from the ill-treatment meted out to her. She serves him as his page, grows to love him and is jealous of his feelings for the actress Philine. Mignon has befriended an elderly and deranged minstrel Lothario (in fact her father, who has been searching for her) who overhears her wishing that a castle in which Philine is acting would catch fire. He sets it alight, unaware that Mignon has entered it. Wilhelm rescues her from the fire and realises that he loves her. [R]

Mikado, The
or The Town of Titipu

Operetta in two acts by Sullivan. 1st perf. London, 14 March 1885; libr. by W. S. Gilbert. Principal roles: Ko-Ko (bar), Nanki-Poo (ten), Yum-Yum (sop), Pooh-Bah (b-bar), Katisha (mezzo), Pish-Tush (bar), Mikado (bass), Pitti-Sing (mezzo), Peep-Bo (sop). An instant success, which enjoyed an initial run of 672 performances, it has remained ever since the most enduringly popular of all the Savoy Operas. Despite its Japanese setting, the butts of its satire are, of course, all very English.

Plot: Titipu, Japan. Under the Mikado's law, the cheap tailor Ko-Ko has been condemned to death for flirting but was reprieved at the last moment and appointed Lord High Executioner. He is due to marry Yum-Yum, one of his three wards, but she has fallen in love with the strolling musician Nanki-Poo. He reveals to Yum-Yum that he is in fact the Mikado's son, who fled from court to escape the attentions of the elderly Katisha. The Mikado sends words that he is displeased that no executions have recently taken place in the city and wishes the situation to be rectified within a month. Nanki-Poo, in despair because he cannot have Yum-Yum, agrees to be executed in a month rather than commit suicide provided that he can marry Yum-Yum in the meantime. Ko-Ko agrees, but just after the wedding the Mikado is seen approaching and Ko-Ko cannot bring himself to execute anyone. He makes a false affidavit of execution but Katisha

sees Nanki-Poo's name on it. The Mikado, although 'not a bit angry', condemns Ko-Ko to death for compassing the death of the heir apparent. Ko-Ko persuades Katisha to love him and she pleads for mercy with the Mikado and all is satisfactorily resolved. [R]

Milan

See **Piccola Scala, La**; **Teatro alla Scala, Milan**

Milanov, Zinka *(b Kunc) (1906–89)*

Yugoslavian soprano, particularly associated with heavier Verdi roles, especially Leonora in *Il Trovatore*. Largely resident first at the Zagreb Opera and then from 1938 at the Metropolitan Opera, New York, she was one of the outstanding Verdi sopranos of the immediate postwar period, possessing a voice of great beauty and sensitivity.

Mildmay, Audrey *(1900–53)*

British soprano, particularly associated with Mozart roles. Her marriage to John Christie* inspired the founding of the Glyndebourne Festival, and she was also a co-founder of the Edinburgh Festival.

Mild und Leise

Soprano aria (the *Liebestod*) for Isolde in Act III of Wagner's *Tristan und Isolde*.

Miles

Treble role in Britten's *The Turn of the Screw*. He is the boy corrupted by the ghost of a former manservant.

Milhaud, Darius *(1892–1974)*

French composer. A member of the group 'Les Six' and one of the most prolific modern French composers, he wrote many stage works in a variety of styles and forms. They include *Le Brebis Egarée* (Paris 1915; libr. Jammes), *Esther de Carpentras* (Paris Radio 1937, composed 1925; libr. Armand Lunel) *Les Malheurs d'Orphée**, perhaps his most successful opera, *Le Pauvre Matelot**, *Christophe Colomb**, *Maximilien**, *Médée**, *Bolivar**, *Les Choëphores**, *David**, *La Mère Coupable* (Geneva 1965; libr. Madeleine Milhaud, after Pierre Augustin Caron de Beaumarchais) and *Saint Louis* (Italian Radio 1972; libr. Paul Claudel). He also wrote three children's operas.

Miller

Baritone role in Verdi's *Luisa Miller*. An old soldier, he is Luisa's father.

Miller, Dr Jonathan *(b 1934)*

British producer (and also a qualified doctor), associated first with Kent Opera and then with the English National Opera. His productions are notable for their striking innovativeness and originality of setting, as shown in his 'Mafia' *Rigoletto* (set in New York in the 1950s) and in his 1920s *The Mikado*.

Millöcker, Karl *(1842–99)*

Austrian composer. He wrote many Viennese operettas, of which the most successful were *Gräfin Dubarry* (Vienna 31 Oct 1879; libr. F. Zell and Richard Genée), *Der Bettelstudent** his most famous work, *Gasparone** and *Der Arme Jonathan* (Vienna 4 Jan 1890; libr. H. Wittmann and J. Bauer). *Die Dubarry* (1931) is a pastiche of his music arranged by Theo Mackeben.

Milnes, Rodney *(b 1936)*

British critic. One of the most discerning, lively, constructive and witty of contemporary British opera critics, he wrote for *The Spectator* and became editor of *Opera* in 1986. He has also made some successful opera translations.

Milnes, Sherrill *(b 1935)*

American baritone, particularly associated with the Italian repertory, especially Verdi. His incisive voice has a firm line and thrilling high notes, but he is not really a true Verdi baritone. He has a strong if somewhat generalised stage presence. He created Adam Brandt in Levy's *Mourning Becomes Electra*. Married to the soprano Nancy Stokes.

Milton

Opera in one act by Spontini. 1st perf. Paris, 27 Nov 1804; libr. by Victor Joseph Etienne de Jouy. Based on the life of the English poet John Milton (1608–74), it was Spontini's first major success. A fine work, it is nowadays all but forgotten.

Mime

Tenor role in Wagner's *Das Rheingold* and *Siegfried*. A Nibelung dwarf, he is Alberich's brother (pronounced as Meemer).

Mimì

Soprano role in Puccini's and Leoncavallo's *La Bohème*. She is a poor seamstress.

Mines of Sulphur, The

Opera in three acts by Bennett. 1st perf. London, 24 Feb 1965; libr. by Beverley Cross. Principal roles: Jenny (sop), Boconnion (ten), Rosalind (mezzo), Tovey (bar), Braxton (bar), Leda (mezzo), Sherrin (bass). Bennett's most successful opera, it is written in serial style, but much of the vocal writing is nonetheless lyrical and easily accessible. It tells of the murder by a deserter and his gypsy girlfriend of the owner of an 18th-century English manor house, for which the arrival of a group of strolling players acts as catalyst.

Minimalism

A form of musical composition pioneered by Glass, in which the same musical figure is repeated many times before changing to another figure only very slightly different. This figure is in turn repeated many times and so on *ad infinitum*.

Minnie

Soprano role in Puccini's *La Fanciulla del West*. She is the miners' Bible-teacher.

Minnie della mia casa

Baritone aria for Jack Rance in Act I of Puccini's *La Fanciulla del West*.

Minton, Yvonne (b 1938)

Australian mezzo, particularly associated with Mozart, Strauss, Wagner and Berlioz roles. One of the leading mezzos of the 1970s, she possessed a rich and beautiful voice used with unfailing musicianship, and she had a strong stage presence. She created Thea in *The Knot Garden* and Maggie Dempster in Maw's *One Man Show*.

Miolan-Carvalho, Marie (b Caroline Félix) (1827–95)

French soprano, particularly associated with the French repertory. The leading French lyric soprano of the mid-19th century, she created, for Gounod, Marguerite in *Faust*, Baucis in *Philémon et Baucis*, Juliette in *Roméo et Juliette* and the title role in *Mireille*.

Married to the administrator Léon Carvalho*.

Mio tesoro, Il

Tenor aria for Don Ottavio in Act II of Mozart's *Don Giovanni*.

Mira, o Norma

Soprano/soprano duet for Norma and Adalgisa in Act II of Bellini's *Norma*.

Miracle, Dr

Bass role in Offenbach's *Les Contes d'Hoffmann*. He is a sinister quack who treats Antonia by remote control.

Miracle of Our Lady, The (Hry o Marii)

Opera in four parts by Martinů. 1st perf. Brno, 23 Feb 1935; libr. by the composer, after H. Ghéon. It is a cycle of four mystery plays: *Wise Virgins and Foolish Virgins*, *Mariken of Nimègue*, *The Nativity* and *Sister Paskalina*. Although it contains some beautiful music, it is only rarely performed. [R]

Mireille

Opera in three (originally five) acts by Gounod. 1st perf. Paris, 19 March 1864; libr. by Michel Carré, after Frédéric Mistral's *Mireio*. Revised version, 1st perf. Paris, 15 Dec 1864. Principal roles: Mireille (sop), Vincent (ten), Ourrias (bar), Taven (mezzo), Maître Ramon (bass). Containing some of Gounod's most beautiful music, it is still quite often performed.

Plot: 19th-century Arles. Mireille loves Vincent, but her father Maître Ramon wishes her to marry another suitor, the bull-tender Ourrias. Mireille and Vincent agree to meet at a certain place of sanctuary if they are in trouble. Ourrias attempts to kill Vincent but fails. The lovers meet at their sanctuary and Maître Ramon blesses their union. (In the original version Vincent is killed by Ourrias who then drowns, and Mireille dies of exhaustion attempting to reach the meeting place.) [R]

Mir ist die Ehre Widerfahren

The Presentation of the Rose in Act II of Richard Strauss' *Der Rosenkavalier*.

Mir ist so wunderbar

Soprano/soprano/tenor/bass quartet for Marzelline, Leonore, Jacquino and Rocco in Act I of Beethoven's *Fidelio*.

Misail

Tenor role in Moussorgsky's *Boris Godunov*. He is an itinerant monk.

Miserere

Soprano aria for Leonora in Act IV of Verdi's *Il Trovatore*. The words are the opening of Psalm 51.

Miserly Knight, The

See Covetous Knight, The

Mitchell, Leona *(b 1949)*

American soprano, particularly associated with the Italian and French repertories. She possesses a rich and creamy voice used with fine musicianship and has an affecting stage presence.

Mitchinson, John *(b 1932)*

British tenor, particularly associated with heroic roles. Long established as a concert artist, he turned to opera only much later in his career, successfully undertaking roles such as Tristan and Dalibor. A much underrated singer, he displayed great musicianship and sensitivity and was possibly the finest lyrico-heroic British tenor of the

postwar era. He created Solano in Delius' *The Magic Fountain*.

Mitridate, Rè di Ponto

(*Mithridates, King of Pontus*)
Opera in three acts by Mozart (K 87). 1st perf. Milan, 26 Dec 1770; libr. by Vittorio Amadeo Cigna-Santi, after Jean-Baptiste Racine's *Mithridate*. Principal roles: Mitridate (ten), Sifarce (sop), Aspasia (sop), Isamene (sop), Farnace (mezzo), Arbate (mezzo), Marzio (ten). Telling of Mithridates (*c* 132–63 BC), it is Mozart's first full-length serious work, written at the age of 14, and is musically astonishingly assured and fluent. It is still occasionally performed.

Plot: Nymphaeum. Mitridate and his two sons Farnace and Sifarce – each of a different and former marriage – vie for the affections of Aspasia. Farnace, betrothed to Isamene, is also in alliance with Mitridate's enemies, the Romans. He redeems his honour by avenging his father's deafeat by the Romans, and the dying Mitridate, having taken poison, gives him his blessing. [R]

Mitropoulos, Dmitri *(1896–1960)*

Greek conductor and composer. One of the outstanding conductors of the mid-20th century, at his best in complex works such as *Wozzeck*, his operatic appearances were sadly infrequent. He conducted the first performance of Barber's *Vanessa*, and himself wrote one opera, *Soeur Béatrice* (Athens 1920; libr. after Maurice Maeterlinck). The Dmitri Mitropoulos Prize, established in his memory in 1961, is one of the most prestigious conducting competitions.

Mittenhofer, Gregor

Baritone role in Henze's *Elegie für Junge Liebende*. He is an egotistical poet.

Miura, Tamaki *(1884–1946)*
Japanese soprano, particularly associated with the French and Italian repertories, especially Cio-Cio-San. The first oriental artist to enjoy a major career in Western music, she created the title role in Messager's *Madame Chrysanthème*.

Mlada
Opera in four acts by Rimsky-Korsakov. 1st perf. St Petersburg, 1 Nov 1892; libr. by the composer, after Victor Krylov's libretto for the unfinished opera-ballet commissioned in 1872 from Borodin, Cui, Rimsky and Moussorgsky. Principal roles: Voislava (sop), Jaromir (ten), Mstivoi (bass), Lumir (mezzo), Morena (mezzo), High Priest (bar). Set in 10th-century Pomerania, it is only very rarely performed, even in Russia.

Mödl, Martha *(b 1912)*
German soprano and later mezzo, particularly associated with Wagnerian roles. Beginning as a mezzo, she turned to dramatic soprano roles, becoming one of the leading Brünnhildes of the 1950s. A dramatic singer of great intelligence with a warm voice, she returned to the mezzo repertoire in the 1960s. She created roles in Einem's *Kabale und Liebe* and Reimann's *Die Gespenstersonate*, and continued singing into her mid-70s.

Moffo, Anna *(b 1935)*
American soprano, particularly associated with lighter Italian and French roles. She had a seductive and agile voice and was an appealing singing-actress of great personal beauty. Her charms – both vocal and physical – were not always wisely deployed, however, and her voice deteriorated early.

Moïse et Pharaon
See Mosè in Egitto

Molière
See panel on page 386

Molinari-Pradelli, Francesco *(b 1911)*
Italian conductor, particularly associated with the Italian repertory. Appearing frequently at La Scala, Milan and the Metropolitan Opera, New York, he was rock-solid and reliable if not always inspiring.

Moll, Kurt *(b 1938)*
German bass, particularly associated with Wagner, Mozart and Strauss roles. One of the finest contemporary Germanic basses, he possesses a large, rich and beautiful voice which he uses with fine musicianship. He is an accomplished singing-actor, equally at home in serious or comic roles.

Monaco
See Monte Carlo Opera

Monaco, Mario del *(1915–82)*
Italian tenor, particularly associated with heroic Italian roles, especially Otello. The leading tenore di forza of the 1950s and one of the greatest postwar Otellos, he possessed a thrilling voice of considerable range and great power which he used to strong dramatic effect. His son Giancarlo is a producer.

Mona Lisa
Opera in prologue, two acts and epilogue by Schillings. 1st perf. Stuttgart, 26 Sept 1915; libr. by Beatrice Dovsky. Principal roles: Wife/Mona Lisa (sop), Lay Brother/Giovanni

MOLIÈRE

The French playwright and actor Molière (*b* Jean-Baptiste Poquelin) (1622–73) himself assisted in laying the foundations of French opera through his collaborations with Lully and M.-A. Charpentier. They produced a number of comedy-ballets, of which the most famous is *Le Bougeois Gentilhomme*. His works have inspired some 80 operas. Below are listed, by play, those operas by composers with entries in this dictionary.

L'Amour Médecin

Lully	*L'Amour Médecin*	1665
Wolf-Ferrari	*L'Amore Medico*	1913
Hughes	*Love the Doctor*	1960

L'Avare

Pashkevich	*The Miser*	1782

Le Bourgeois Gentilhomme

Lully	*Le Bourgeois Gentilhomme*	1670
Hasse	*Larinda e Vanesio*	1726
Strauss	*Ariadne auf Naxos*	1916

L'Ecole des Femmes

Liebermann	*The School for Wives*	1955
Mortari	*La Scuola delle Mogli*	1959

L'Ecole des Maris

Bondeville	*L'École des Maris*	1936

Georges Dandin

Lully	*Georges Dandin*	1668

Le Malade Imaginaire

Charpentier	*Le Malade Imaginaire*	1673
Napoli	*Il Malato Immaginario*	1939
Pauer	*Zdravý Nemocný*	1970

Le Marriage Forcé

Lully	*Le Marriage Forcé*	1664

Le Médecin Malgré Lui

Gounod	*Le Médecin Malgré Lui*	1858
Veretti	*Il Medico Volante*	1927

Monsieur de Pourceaugnac		
Lully	Monsieur de Pourceaugnac	1669
Franchetti	Il Signor di Pourceaugnac	1897
Martin	Monsieur de Pourseaugnac	1963

Les Précieuses Ridicules		
Galuppi	Le Virtuose Ridicole	1752
Lattuada	Le Preziose Ridicole	1929
Bush	If the Cap Fits	1956

La Princesse d'Elide		
Galuppi	Alcimena	1749

Psyché		
Uttini	Psyché	1766

Sganarelle		
Pasatieri	Il Signor Deluso	1974

Le Sicilien		
Lully	Le Sicilien	1667

Tartuffe		
Benjamin	Tartuffe	1964

(ten), Husband/Giocondo (bar). Schillings' most successful opera and still occasionally performed, it is a gruesome piece of verismo.

Plot: Florence. In the prologue, a honeymooning couple visit a Carthusian monastery, where a lay brother recounts the tale of Mona Lisa, whose elderly husband, Giocondo, shut her lover Giovanni into a cupboard to suffocate. When Giocondo opened the cupboard, Mona Lisa pushed him in and locked it. In the epilogue, the three characters are shown to be the modern counterparts of those in the story.

Monckton, Lionel *(1861–1924)*
British composer and critic. He wrote a number of operettas and musical comedies. Nowadays he is almost solely remembered for his collaboration with Talbot on *The Arcadians**.

Mon coeur s'ouvre à ta voix
(often known in English as 'Softly awakes my heart')
Mezzo aria for Dalila in Act II of Saint-Saëns' *Samson et Dalila*.

Mond, Der: ein Kleines Welttheater (*The Moon: a Little World Theatre*)
Opera in three acts by Orff. 1st perf. Munich, 5 Feb 1939; libr. by the composer, after Grimm's *Fairy Tales*. Principal roles: Narrator (ten), four Boys (ten, bar, bar and bass), St Peter (b-bar). One of Orff's most successful operas, it is still quite often performed.

Plot: Four boys steal the Moon,

387

each taking a quarter of it to their graves. As the world darkens, the boys put the pieces back together and raise the Moon up as a lamp. This causes all the dead to awaken with such an uproar that St Peter hears it in Heaven, descends to the nether regions, takes the Moon and puts it in the heavens as a star. [R]

Mondo della Luna, Il (*The World on the Moon*)

Opera in three acts by Haydn. 1st perf. Esterháza, 3 Aug 1777; libr. by P. F. Pastor, after Carlo Goldoni. Principal roles: Ecclitico (ten), Buonafede (bar), Lisetta (mezzo), Clarice (sop), Flaminia (sop), Ernesto (mezzo), Cecco (ten). Haydn's most frequently performed opera.

Plot: The wealthy merchant Buonafede opposes his daughter's wish to marry Ernesto. The pseudo-astrologer, Ecclitico, who loves Buonafede's other daughter Clarice, deceives the merchant into believing he can travel through the heavens. Ecclitico gives Buonafede a drugged potion and disguises his garden as a moonscape. There, Buonafede is tricked into allowing the lovers to marry the mates of their choice. When the deception is revealed, he eventually forgives everyone. [R]

Moniuszko, Stanislaw (*1819–72*)

Polish composer. Poland's most importat opera composer, and a crucial figure in the development of Polish national music, he began as an operetta composer. His first opera *Halka** was an immediate success and remains his most popular work. His others include *The Raftsman* (*Flis*, Warsaw 24 Sept 1858; libr. W. Boguslawski [R], *The Countess* (*Hrabina*, Warsaw 7 Feb 1860; libr. W. Wolski) [R Exc], *Verum Nobile* (Warsaw 1 Jan 1861; libr. Jan Checiński) [R], the highly successful *The Haunted Manor** and *Paria* (Warsaw 11 Dec 1869; libr. Checiński, after Casimir Delavigne). He was musical director of the Warsaw National Opera.

Monna Vanna

Opera in four acts by Février. 1st perf. Paris, 10 Jan 1909. A word-for-word setting of Maurice Maeterlinck's play. Principal roles: Monna Vanna (sop), Prinzivalle (ten), Guido Colonno (bar). Février's most successful opera, it is nowadays all but forgotten.

Plot: Italy. Florentine forces are besieging Pisa. Their commander Prinzivalle offers to lift the siege if Monna Vanna, married to the Pisan leader Colonno, will come to him. Colonno refuses the offer, but Monna is prepared to make the sacrifice to save her city. Prinzivalle recognises her as a childhood friend and respects her honour, whilst also lifting the siege. Colonno refuses to believe that his wife has not been compromised and has Prinzivalle jailed. This causes Monna to turn against her husband: she obtains the prison key, tells Prinzivalle that she loves him, and the two escape together.

Monodrama

The term has two meanings in opera: (1) Strictly speaking, a melodrama* with one actor. (2) More generally, the term is used of any work with a single character, such as Schönberg's *Erwartung* or Poulenc's *La Voix Humaine*.

Monostatos

Tenor role in Mozart's *Die Zauberflöte*. He is Sarastro's Moorish slave.

Monpou, Hippolyte (*1804–41*)

French composer. He wrote a number

of comic operas which enjoyed some success in their day but which are all now forgotten. They include *Les Deux Reines* (Paris 6 Aug 1835; libr. Arnould and F. Soulié), *Le Luthier de Vienne* (Paris 30 June 1836; libr. Adolphe de Leuven and Jules-Henri Vernoy de Saint-Georges), *Le Piquillo* (Paris 31 Oct 1837; libr. Alexandre Dumas père), *Le Planteur* (Paris 1 March 1839; libr. Saint-Georges) and the unfinished *Lambert Simnel* (Paris 14 Sept 1843; libr. Eugène Scribe and Anne-Honoré Joseph de Mélesville), which was completed by Adam.

Monsieur Beaucaire

Operetta in prologue and three acts by Messager. 1st perf. Birmingham, 7 April 1919; libr. by Frederick Lonsdale and Adrian Ross, after Booth Tarkington's novel. Principal roles: Mary (sop), Beaucaire (bar), Lucy (mezzo), Molyneux (ten). One of Messager's most successful works, it is a tale of mistaken identities set in Bath at the time of Beau Nash. [R Exc]

Monsigny, Pierre Alexandre (1729–1817)

French composer. He was a prolific composer of opéra-comiques, whose form he was responsible for deepening and enriching. The most important of his operas, which are notable for their great melodic charm, are *Le Cadi Dupé**, *Le Roi et le Fermier* (Paris 22 Nov 1762; libr. Jean-Marie Sedaine, after Robert Dodsley's *The King and the Miller of Mansfield*), *Rose et Colas* (Paris 8 March 1764; libr. Sedaine), *Aline Reine de Golconde* (Paris 15 April 1766; libr. Sedaine), *Le Déserteur* (Paris 6 March 1769; libr. Sedaine), his finest opera, *La Belle Arsène* (Fontainebleau 6 Nov 1773; libr. Charles-Simon Favart) and *Félix* (Fontainebleau 10 Nov 1777; libr. Sedaine).

Montano

Bass comprimario role in Verdi's *Otello*. He is Otello's predecessor as governor of Cyprus.

Montarsolo, Paolo *(b 1925)*

Italian bass, particularly associated with buffo roles, especially Rossini. One of the leading buffos of the postwar era, he enjoyed a remarkably long career and was a fine comic actor with a good if not outstanding voice.

Monte, Toti dal *(b Antonietta Meneghel) (1893–1975)*

Italian soprano. The outstanding soprano leggiero of the inter-war period, her voice, although small and sometimes inclined to whiteness, was pure and extraordinarily agile. Her autobiography, *Una Voce nel Mondo*, was published in 1962.

Monte Carlo Opera

The Grand Théâtre (cap. 500), designed by Jean-Louis-Charles Garnier, opened on 25 Jan 1879. Its greatest period was under the management of Raoul Gunsbourg (1859–1955) from 1892 to 1951, especially the first 20 years of this century, when many works by leading French and Italian composers received their premières. For a time, admission was free, as it was subsidised by the casino. The annual season runs from January to April and the repertory tends to be conservative. Artistic directors have included Henri Tomasi and Renzo Rossellini.

Montemezzi, Italo *(1875–1952)*

Italian composer. Largely self-taught and writing in an electic late-romantic style, his operas stand outside the mainstream of Italian music of his time. His first opera, the unperformed *Bianca* (libr. Z. Strani), was followed by *Giovanni Gallurese* (Turin 28 Jan 1905; libr. Francesco d'Angelantonio), *Hellera* (Turin 1909; libr. Luigi Illica) and the magnificent *L'Amore dei Tre Re**, his masterpiece. Its successors were the once-popular *La Nave* (Milan 3 Nov 1918; libr. Tito Ricordi, after Gabriele d'Annunzio), *La Notte di Zoraima* (Milan 31 Jan 1931; libr. Mario Ghisalberti) and the radio opera *L'Incantesino* (NBC 1943; libr. Sem Benelli).

Monterone, Count

Bass-baritone role in Verdi's *Rigoletto*. He is an old man whose daughter has been seduced by the Duke.

Monteux, Pierre *(1876–1964)*

French conductor, particularly associated with the French repertory. Although best known as a symphonic conductor, he also gave many fine opera performances in France and the United States. A consummate musician, he was a greatly loved artist with a delightful sense of humour: when he took over the London Symphony Orchestra at the age of 86, he insisted on a 25-year contract! He conducted the first performance of Stravinsky's *The Nightingale*.

Monteverdi, Claudio *(1567–1643)*

Italian composer. The first major figure in the history of opera, and one of the greatest of all opera composers, only a wretched portion of his stage works has survived. His first work for the stage, which combines the existing vocal and orchestral traditions with the new dramatic ideas of the Florentine Camerata*, is *La Favola d'Orfeo**. He wrote some works for a festival in Mantua in 1608, of which the opera-ballet *Il Ballo delle Ingrate** survives, as do fragments of the opera *Arianna**. Of the works he wrote for Venice, Parma and Mantua in the 1620s only *Il Combattimento di Tancredi e Clorinda** survives; at least 12 others are lost, including a comedy *La Finta Pazza* (1627; libr. Giulio Strozzi). In old age, he returned to opera with three final works: *Le Nozze d'Enea con Lavinia* (Venice 1641), which is lost, *Il Ritorno d'Ulisse in Patria** and his masterpiece *L'Incoronazione di Poppea**.

He was the first composer to grasp the essentials of music-drama and to execute them in music of beauty, subtlety and fluidity which illuminates and heightens emotional and dramatic situations. The first great musical delineator of character, both serious and comic, he was also the first (and still one of the very few) to achieve true music-drama. For nearly 300 years Monteverdi was little more than a name in the history books; now he is acknowledged as the first opera composer of genius, and his works are firmly established in the repertory.

Montezuma

Works of this title about Montezuma II (1466–1520), the last Aztec ruler of Mexico, include:

(1) Opera in three acts by Graun. 1st perf. Berlin, 6 Jan 1755; libr. by Frederick the Great. Principal roles: Montezuma (mezzo), Eupaforice (sop), Tezeuco (ten), Pilpatoè (sop), Erissena (sop), Ferdinando Cortes (mezzo). One of Graun's finest works, it is nowadays all but forgotten. [R Exc]

(2) Opera in three acts by Sessions. 1st perf. Berlin 19 April 1964; libr. by Giuseppe Antonio Borgese, after Bernal Díaz del Castillo. Principal roles: Montezuma (ten), Díaz (bar), Malinche (sop), Córtez (bar). Sessions' finest work, it is a lush historical pageant.

Plot: 16th-century Mexico. Through the eyes of the chronicler, Bernal Díaz, we are shown the Spanish landings of 1519, the love of Fernand Córtez for Malinche, the controversy amongst the Spanish over how to treat the Aztecs, and the killing of Montezuma by his own people.

Montfort, Guy de

Baritone role in Verdi's *Les Vêpres Siciliennes*. He is the French governor of Sicily.

Montreal

See Opéra de Montréal

Moore, Douglas *(1893–1969)*

American composer. Written in romantic style, his stage works are easily accessible, with a strong foundation in American folk music, and have met with considerable success in the United States. His operas include the chamber work *White Wings* (Hartford 9 Feb 1949; libr. P. Barry), *The Devil and Daniel Webster**, *Giants in the Earth* (New York 28 March 1951; libr. A. Sundgaard, after Rolvaag), *The Ballad of Baby Doe**, his most successful work, and *Carry Nation* (Kansas City 28 April 1966; libr. William North Jayme) [R].

Moore, Grace *(1901–47)*

American soprano, largely resident at the Metropolitan Opera, New York. After singing in musical comedy, she turned to opera, becoming particularly associated with the Italian and French repertories, especially Louise (which she filmed). A fine actress, she was a great favourite with audiences, even if some maintained that her talents were plastic rather than vocal. She also enjoyed great success in the cinema, with films such as *New Moon*, *Love Me For Ever*

and *One Night of Love*. Her autobiography, *You're Only Human Once*, was published in 1944. She was killed in an air crash.

Moreno Torroba, Federico

See Torroba, Federico Moreno

Morgenlich leuchtend

Tenor aria (the Prize Song) for Walther von Stolzing in Act III of Wagner's *Die Meistersinger von Nürnberg*.

Morison, Elsie *(b 1924)*

Australian soprano, particularly associated with Mozart roles. She created the title role in Hughes' *Menna*. Married to the conductor Rafael Kubelík*.

Morlacchi, Francesco *(1784–1841)*

Italian composer. He wrote many operas which, although notable for their abundant melody, fine vocal writing and adventurous orchestration, are all now forgotten. His most successful operas include *Il Corradino* (Parma 25 Feb 1808; libr. Antonio Sografi), *Le Danaidi* (Rome 11 Feb 1810; libr. S. Scatizzi, after Pietro Metastasio's *Ipermestra*) and *Tebaldo ed Isolina* (Dresden 1822; libr. Gaetano Rossi). He was Kapellmeister in Dresden (1810–32), where he had a bitter rivalry with Weber, who said of him "the fellow has little musical knowledge, but he has talent, a flow of ideas, and especially a fund of good comic stuff in him".

Morris, James *(b 1947)*

American bass-baritone, particularly associated first with Italian roles and more recently with Wagnerian roles, especially Wotan. Often regarded as the finest contemporary Wotan, he has a rich and beautiful voice used with intelligence and fine musicianship.

Morrò, ma prima in grazia

Soprano aria for Amelia in Act III of Verdi's *Un Ballo in Maschera*.

Mortari, Virgilio *(b 1902)*

Italian composer. His operas, in neo-classical style, include *La Scuola delle Mogli* (1930; libr. C. V. Ludovici, after Molière's *L'Ecole des Femmes*), *L'Allegra Piazetta* (1945), *La Figlia del Diavolo* (Milan 1954; libr. C. Pavolini) and *Il Contratto* (Italian Radio 1962; libr. G. Marotta and B. Randone). He was also a noted editor of the music of 17th- and 18th-century Italian composers.

Moscow

See Bolshoi Opera

Mosè in Egitto *(Moses in Egypt)*

Opera in three acts by Rossini. 1st perf. Naples, 5 March 1818; libr. by Andrea Leone Tottola, after Francesco Ringhieri's *Sara in Egitto*. Revised version, *Moïse et Pharaon* 1st perf. Paris, 26 March 1827; libr. revised by Luigi Balocchi and Victor-Joseph Etienne de Jouy. Principal roles: Moses (bass), Elcia (sop), Osiride (ten), Pharaoh (bar), Aronne (ten), Amaltea (mezzo), Amenosi (mezzo). One of the finest of Rossini's serious works, it is still quite often performed. It is notable for the grave and noble delineation of Moses and for its fine choruses. A love story, concerning Moses's sister Elcia and Pharaoh's son Osiride, has been grafted on to the Old Testament story of the deliverance of the Hebrews from Egypt. [R]

Moser, Augustin

Tenor comprimario role in Wagner's *Die Meistersinger von Nürnberg*. A tailor, he is one of the masters.

Moses und Aron

Unfinished opera in three acts by Schönberg. 1st perf. Hamburg Radio, 12 March 1954 (composed 1932). 1st stage perf. Zürich, 6 June 1957; libr. by the composer, after the Book of Exodus in the Old Testament. Principal roles: Aron (ten), Moses (speaker), Ephraimite (bar). Schönberg's last and greatest opera, the final act remained unset at his death. The work is usually performed in two acts, although some productions include Act III with the words spoken.

Plot: The inspired but inarticulate Moses cannot communicate to the Hebrews his revelation of God's word. He therefore allows his brother Aron to explain by miracles and other familiar images. Descending from Mount Sinai, Moses discovers the people worshipping the Golden Calf. He shatters the idol, but despairs of being able to put across his message without the help of a distorting intermediary such as Aron. [R]

Moshinsky, Elijah *(b 1946)*

Australian producer. One of the leading contemporary British theatre directors, his opera productions are notable for their delineation of character and for their fine handling of crowd scenes, and are traditional in the best sense of the word. He has had particular success with low-budget productions, notably with *Peter Grimes* and *Lohengrin* at Covent Garden. Associate producer at Covent Garden (1988–).

Mother, The *(Matka)*

Opera in ten scenes by Hába (Op 35). 1st perf. Munich, 19 May 1931; libr. by the composer. Principal roles: Křen (ten), Maruša (sop). Hába's best known work, it was the first (and remains the most important) quarter-tone opera. It is only infrequently performed, partly because of its great technical difficulties. [R]

Mother of Us All, The

Opera in three acts by Thomson. 1st perf. New York, 7 May 1947; libr. by Gertrude Stein. Principal roles: Susan Anthony (mezzo), Jo the Loiterer (ten), Anne (sop), Daniel Webster (bar). One of the finest American operas, it tells of the 19th-century American feminist leader Susan Brownell Anthony (1820–1906). [R]

Motif

See Leitmotiv

Mottl, Felix (1856–1911)

Austrian conductor and composer, particularly associated with Wagner operas, all of whose vocal scores he edited. He was musical director of the Karlsruhe Staatstheater (1880–1904) and conducted the first performances of Part I of Les Troyens and Wolf-Ferrari's Il Segreto di Susanna and I Quatro Rusteghi. He also composed three operas. He died whilst conducting Tristan und Isolde in Munich. His wife Zdenka Fassbender (1879–1954) was a successful dramatic soprano.

Mousquetaires au Couvent, Les (The Musketeers at the Convent)

Operetta in three acts by Varney. 1st perf. Paris, 16 March 1880; libr. by P. Ferrier and J. Prével. Principal roles: Marie (sop), Gontran (ten), Louise (sop), Brissac (bar), Simone (mezzo), Bridaine (bass). Varney's most successful work, it is a delightful and amusing piece which is still occasionally performed in France. [R]

Moussorgsky, Modest (1839–81)

Russian composer. A member of the 'Mighty Handful', he was largely without formal musical training. He completed only one opera, but nonetheless ranks as one of the greatest of all opera composers. His first three operatic projects amounted to little more than sketches: Han d'Islande (1856; libr. after Victor Hugo), Oedipus in Athens (1858; libr. after Ozerov), which was incorporated into later works, and St John's Eve (1858; libr. after Nikolai Gogol). Much more was written of his next opera Salammbô*, but he completed only one act of his next project The Marriage*. Next came his one completed work, his masterpiece Boris Godunov*, not only a seminal work in the development of Russian music, but one of the finest of all operas. Only one scene of The Landless Peasant (1870; libr. after Spielhagen's Hans und Grete) was completed, and the collective opera-ballet Mlada (1872; libr. Victor Krylov), with Borodin, Cui and Rimsky-Korsakov, was abandoned. Much nearer to completion was the dark and magnificent Khovanschina*, which was followed by the unfinished comedy Sorochintsy Fair*. His last project Pugachevshchina (1877; libr. after Alexander Pushkin) amounts to little more than sketches.

Moussorgsky's genius and startling originality lie in his musical use of the inflections and speech rhythms of the Russian language, his unerring dramatic insight, his musical delineation of both comic and serious characters, his brilliant if highly unorthodox orchestration and his nationalism and identification with the Russian people. His influence on the subsequent history of music, not just in Russia, has been enormous.

Mozart, Wolfgang Amadeus
(1756–91)
Austrian composer who, with Verdi and Wagner, ranks as one of the three greatest of all opera composers. A child prodigy, his first stage work, the sacred play *Die Schuldigkeit des Ersten Gebotes* (Salzburg 1767; libr. L. A. Weiser) [R] was written at the age of 11. His early operas, all of which display astonishing musical assurance, are the Latin comedy *Apollo et Hyacinthus**, *La Finta Semplice**, the Singspiel *Bastien und Bastienne**, *Mitridate, Rè di Ponto**, *Ascanio in Alba**, *Il Sogno di Scipione**, *Lucio Silla** and *La Finta Giardiniera**, his first work of real significance. It was followed by the pastoral *Il Re Pastore**, the unfinished Singspiel *Zaïde** and his first masterpiece *Idomeneo**. The enormously successful *Die Entführung aus dem Serail** was followed by the two unfinished comedies *L'Oca del Cairo** and *Lo Sposo Deluso** and the theatrical satire *Der Schauspieldirektor** before the full glories of his last five operas: *Le Nozze di Figaro**, *Don Giovanni**, *Così fan Tutte**, *Die Zauberflöte** and *La Clemenza di Tito**.

In his three great Italian works, written in collaboration with Lorenzo da Ponte, Mozart breaks through the rigid structures of opera, presenting music-drama of great fluidity and remarkable human insight. His mastery of extended ensemble, his blending of serious and comic elements, his dramatic insight and his loosening of the musico-dramatic structures all had an incalculable influence on the subsequent development of opera. Mozart appears as a character in Hahn's *Mozart*, Flotow's *Die Musikanten*, Rimsky-Korsakov's *Mozart and Salieri* and the Lortzing pastiche *Szenen aus Mozarts Leben*.

Mozart and Salieri
Opera in two acts by Rimsky-Korsakov (Op 48). 1st perf. Moscow, 7 Dec 1898. A setting of Alexander Pushkin's play. Principal roles: Mozart (ten), Salieri (b-bar). Dealing with the jealousy of mere talent for the unpredictability of genius, it perpetuates the myth that Salieri poisoned Mozart. [R]

Much Ado About Nothing
Opera in four acts by Stanford (Op 76a). 1st perf. London, 30 May 1901; libr. by Julian Russell Sturgis, after Shakespeare's play. Reasonably successful at its appearance, it is now all but forgotten.

Muck, Karl *(1859–1940)*
German conductor, particularly associated with the German repertory. Widely regarded as the finest Wagnerian conductor of his time, he was musical director of the Berlin State Opera (1908–12). He conducted the first performance of Smyth's *The Forest*.

Muette de Portici, La *(The Dumb Girl of Portici)* (also known as *Masaniello*)
Opera in five acts by Auber. 1st perf. Paris, 29 Feb 1828; libr. by Eugène Scribe and Germain Delavigne. Principal roles: Masaniello (ten), Elvire (sop), Alfonso (ten), Pietro (bar), Fenella (mute). Arguably Auber's greatest work but currently unjustly neglected, it is in effect the first French grand opera. A performance of the work in Brussels on 25 Aug 1830 sparked off the revolution which led to Belgian independence.

Plot: Naples, 1647. Masaniello is moved by the oppression of his people by the Spanish. When the viceroy Alfonso betrays his dumb sister Fenella, he leads a revolt against the Spanish. The revolt is initially successful but is then crushed. Masaniello is killed and Fenella commits suicide by jumping into the erupting mouth of Mount Vesuvius. [R]

Mugnone, Leopoldo (1858–1941)

Italian conductor and composer, particularly associated with the Italian repertory. One of the most admired operatic conductors of his time, he conducted the first performances of *Cavalleria Rusticana*, *Tosca*, Franchetti's *La Figlia di Iorio* and Giordano's *Mese Mariano*. He also composed five operas.

Müller, Wenzel (b Václav) (1767–1835)

Austrian composer. One of the most successful and prolific Singspiel composers, he wrote over 200 stage works, all of them now forgotten. The most successful included *Kaspar der Fagottist* (Vienna 8 June 1791; libr. J. Perinet), *Das Neue Sonntagskind* (Vienna 1793; libr. Perinet, after Hafner) and *Die Teufelsmuhle am Wienerberg* (Vienna 12 Nov 1799; libr. Hensler).

Mullings, Frank (1881–1953)

British tenor, particularly associated with Wagnerian roles and with Otello. The only true British heldentenor, he had a powerful voice and physique and was an imposing singing-actor. He created Apollo in Boughton's *Alkestis* and a role in Stanford's *The Critic*.

Munich

See Bavarian State Opera

Murray, Ann (b 1949)

British mezzo, particularly associated with Mozart, Rossini and Strauss roles and with the French repertory. An outstanding singing-actress, she possesses a beautiful voice of considerable range and agility which is used with unfailing musicianship. Married to the tenor Philip Langridge*.

Musetta

Marcello's old flame, she appears as: (1) Soprano role in Puccini's *La Bohème*. (2) Mezzo role in Leoncavallo's *La Bohème*.

Musgrave, Thea (b 1928)

British composer. One of the most successful contemporary British opera composers, she has an assured sense of theatre and has written seven operas in lyrical serial style. They are: *The Abbot of Drimock* (London 19 Dec 1962; composed 1955; libr. Maurice Lindsay), *The Decision* (London 30 Nov 1967; libr. Lindsay), *The Voice of Ariadne*, *Mary Queen of Scots*, *A Christmas Carol*, *Harriet, the Woman Called Moses* (Norfolk 1985) and *An Occurence at Owl Creek Bridge* (June 1988; libr. after Ambrose Bierce).

Music drama

A term used to describe an opera in which the musical and dramatic elements are meant to be totally fused. The term first came into prominence with Wagner.

Musorgsky, Modeste

See Moussorgsky, Modest

Mustafà

Bass role in Rossini's *L'Italiana in Algieri*. He is the Bey of Algiers.

Muti, Riccardo (b 1941)

Italian conductor, particularly associated with the Italian repertory and with Mozart. One of the most brilliant and exciting of the younger generation of conductors, his performances are noted for their intensity, thorough preparation and scrupulous regard for the composer's intentions. He was musical director of the Maggio Musicale Fiorentino (1977–80) and La Scala, Milan (1987–).

Muzio, Claudia *(1889–1936)*
Italian soprano, particularly associated with the Italian repertory. One of the leading lyric sopranos of the inter-war period, she possessed a beautiful voice and a warm stage presence. She created Giorgetta in *Il Tabarro*, Mariela in Smareglia's *L'Abiso* and the title roles in Zandonai's *Melonis* and Refice's *Cecilia*.

Mysliveček, Joseph *(1737–81)*
Bohemian composer, largely resident in Italy, where he was known as *il divino Boemo*. His first opera *Medea* (Parma 1764; libr. F. W. Gotter) was successful and was followed by over 30 more opera serias, many to Metastasian texts. Widely praised in his day, his operas are now as good as forgotten.

Nabokov, Nicolas *(b Nikolai)*
(1903–78)
Russian-born American composer. He
wrote two operas, both of which met
with some success. They are *The Holy
Devil* (Louisville 16 April 1958; libr.
Spender; revised version *Der Tod des
Grigori Rasputin* Cologne 27 Nov
1959) and *Love's Labours Lost*
(Brussels 7 Feb 1973; libr. W. H.
Auden and Chester Kallman, after
Shakespeare). He was secretary-general
of the anti-communist Congress for
Cultural Freedom.

Nabucco, *officially called*
Nabucodnosor *(Nebuchadnezzar)*
Opera in four acts by Verdi. 1st perf.
Milan, 9 March 1842; libr. by
Temistocle Solera, after Eugène Anicet-
Bourgeois and Francis Cornue's play.
Principal roles: Nabucco (bar), Abigaille
(sop), Zaccaria (bass), Ishmael (ten),
Fenena (mezzo), High Priest of Bel
(bass). Verdi's third opera, it was an
immediate and triumphant success and
was the work which established his
reputation. One of the most popular of
the composer's early works, it is
notable for its fine choruses and for the
powerful characterisation of the
vengeful Abigaille.

Plot: Jerusalem and Babylon, 587 BC.
The prophet Zaccaria comforts the
Hebrews as the attacking Assyrian
forces close in. The Hebrew Ishmael
loves Fenena, the Assyrian king
Nabucco's younger daughter, and
rejects the love of Abigaille, Nabucco's
elder but illegitimate child. Nabucco
arrives in triumph and Zaccaria
threatens to kill Fenena if the Temple is
profaned. To the horror of his
compatriots (who are unaware that
Fenena is a secret convert), Ishmael
releases Fenena and Nabucco orders the
destruction of Jerusalem. In Nabucco's
absence, Abigaille discovers the
document proving her illegitimacy, and
when the High Priest tells her than
Fenena is releasing the Hebrews, she
vows to seize the throne. Nabucco
returns and quells the revolt. He
proclaims himself god, whereupon a
lightning bolt strikes him down and he
loses his reason. Abigaille seizes the
crown that falls from his head.
Abigaille tricks Nabucco into signing
the death warrant of all the Hebrews
(and of Fenena). However, Nabucco's
senses are restored after he prays to the
god of the Hebrews and he regains
control. The dying Abigaille repents
and Zaccaria crowns Nabucco King of
Kings. [R]

Nachtigal, Konrad
Baritone comprimario role in Wagner's
Die Meistersinger von Nürnberg. A
tinsmith, he is one of the masters.

Nacht in Venedig, Eine (*A
Night in Venice*)
Operetta in three acts by Johann
Strauss II. 1st perf. Berlin, 3 Oct 1883;
libr. by F. Zell (Camillo Walzel) and
Richard Genée. Principal roles: Duke of
Urbino (ten), Annina (sop), Caramello
(ten), Ciboletta (mezzo), Pappacoda
(bar), Delaqua (bar), Agricola (mezzo).
One of Strauss' most successful works,
it is still regularly performed, often in
the version prepared by Korngold and
Hubert Marischka (Vienna, 21 June
1923).

Plot: 18th-century Venice. During Carnival, the libidinous Duke of Urbino is entertaining the senators. Amongst them, Delaqua has a young and pretty wife and is concerned about the Duke's intentions. He sends her away and plans to take his cook Ciboletta to the ball instead. His plans are overheard by the Duke's barber Caramello, who takes the place of the gondolier for the journey to the Duke's palace, but does not know that Delaqua's wife has arranged for a friend to take her place. Caramello discovers that the girl he has brought to the Duke is his own sweetheart Annina. After much amorous intrigue and misunderstanding, everyone is finally restored to their rightful lover and all join in the fun of Carnival. [R]

Nachtlager von Granada, Das

(*The Night Camp in Granada*) Opera in two acts by K. Kreutzer. 1st perf. Vienna, 13 Jan 1834; libr. by Karl Johann Braun von Braunthal after Friedrich Kind's play. Principal roles: Infante (ten), Gabriela (sop), Gómez (bar). By far Kreutzer's most successful work, it is still occasionally performed in German-speaking countries.

Plot: The Infante of Spain is disguised as a huntsman and seeks shelter for the night from a group of shepherds. They agree, but when they catch him flirting with Gabriela, who is loved by Gómez, they decide to kill him and relieve him of his possessions. Gabriela, who returns Gómez's love, is also pursued by Vasco, and she asks the huntsman for help. The latter promises to intercede on her behalf with the Infante. Meeting the Infante's followers, Gabriela and Gómez learn the huntsman's true identity, and reveal the plans against his life. The Infante ensures their betrothal. [R]

Nadia

Soprano role in Tippett's *The Ice Break*. She is Lev's wife.

Nadir

Tenor role in Bizet's *Les Pêcheurs de Perles*. A fisherman, he is Zurga's friend and rival for Leïla's love.

Nancy

Mezzo role in: (1) Flotow's *Martha*. She is Lady Harriet's maid. (2) Britten's *Albert Herring*. She is Sid's girlfriend.

Nancy

See Théâtre Municipal, Nancy

Nannetta

Soprano role in Verdi's *Falstaff*. Ford's daughter, she is in love with Fenton.

Nantes

See Grand Théâtre Graslin, Nantes

Naples

See Teatro San Carlo, Naples

Napoleon

The French general and emperor appears in a number of operas, including: (1) Baritone role in Prokofiev's *War and Peace*. (2) Baritone role in Giordano's *Madame Sans-Gêne*. (3) Bass role in Kodály's *Háry János*. (4) Baritone role in Blake's *Toussaint*.

Napoli, Jacopo (b 1911)

Italian composer. His comic operas, often incorporating Neapolitan songs, have met with some success in Italy, but are unknown elsewhere. His operas include *Il Malato Immaginario* (Naples

1939; libr. Mario Ghisalberti, after Molière's *Le Malade Imaginaire*), *Miseria e Nobilità* (Naples 1946; libr. V. Viviani, after E. Scarpetta), *Un Curioso Accidente* (Bergamo 1950; libr. Ghisalberti), *Masaniello* (Milan 1953; libr. Viviani), *I Pescatori* (Naples 1954; libr. Viviani), *Il Tesoro* (Rome 1958; libr. Viviani), *Il Rosario* (Brescia 1962; libr. Viviani), *Il Povero Diavolo* (Trieste 1963; libr. Viviani), *Il Barone Avaro* (Naples 1970; libr. M. Paci) and *Dubrovski II* (Naples 1973; libr. after Alexander Pushkin).

Nápravník, Eduard *(1839–1916)*

Czech composer and conductor, long resident in Russia. He wrote four operas which met with some success in their time but which are all now forgotten. They are *Nizhegorodtsy* (St Petersburg 8 Jan 1868; libr. P. I. Kalashnikov), *Harold* (St Petersburg 23 Nov 1886; libr. P. P. Weinburg, after E. von Wildenbruch), *Dubrovsky* (St Petersburg 15 Jan 1895; libr. Modest Tchaikovsky, after Alexander Pushkin) [R] and *Francesca da Rimini* (St Petersburg 9 Dec 1902; libr. O. O. Palecek and E. P. Ponomarev, after Dante's *La Divina Commedia*). As musical director of the Maryinsky Theatre (now the Kirov Opera) from 1869, he was a tireless champion both of higher standards and of young Russian composers. He conducted the first performances of over 80 operas, including the revised *Boris Godunov*, *The Demon*, *The Oprichnik*, *Vakula the Blacksmith*, *The Maid of Orleans*, *The Queen of Spades*, *Iolanta*, *The Stone Guest*, *May Night*, *The Maid of Pskov*, *The Snow Maiden* and Cui's *William Ratcliff*.

Narbal

Bass role in Berlioz's *Les Troyens*. He is Dido's minister.

Narciso, Don

Tenor role in Rossini's *Il Turco in Italia*. He is Fiorilla's lover.

Narraboth

Tenor role in Richard Strauss' *Salome*. He is captain of the palace guard.

Nash, Heddle *(1894–1961)*

British tenor, particularly associated with Mozart roles and with David in *Die Meistersinger*. A stylish and elegant singer, he created Dr Manette in Benjamin's *A Tale of Two Cities*. His son John Heddle-Nash (*b* 1928) was a baritone.

Natasha

Soprano role in Prokofiev's *War and Peace*. Count Rostov's daughter, she loves Prince Andrei.

National Opera Studio

The British centre for advanced operatic training, it opened in 1978 as the successor to the London Opera Centre*. Situated in London, its directors have been Michael Langdon and Richard van Allan.

Naumann, Johann Gottlieb *(1741–1801)*

German composer. He wrote some 25 operas, all of them now forgotten, for Italy, Germany, Sweden and Denmark, where his *Orpheus og Euridice* (Copenhagen 31 Jan 1786; libr. C. D. Biehl after Ranieri de' Calzabigi) was the first major opera written to a Danish libretto. His most successful work was the comedy *La Dama Soldata* (Dresden 30 March 1791; libr. Claudio Mazzolà).

Navarini, Francesco *(1853–1923)*

Italian bass, particularly associated with the Italian and French repertories. One of the leading basses of the late 19th century, he had a powerful voice and a strong stage presence which was aided by his enormous height. He created Lodovico in *Otello*.

Navarraise, La *(The Girl From Navarre)*

Opera in two acts by Massenet. 1st perf. London, 20 June 1894; libr. by Jules Clarétie and Henri Cain, after the former's *La Cigarette*. Principal roles: Anita (sop), Araquil (ten), Garrido (bar), Remigio (bass). Massenet's one excursion into the verismo field, it was successful at its appearance and is still occasionally performed.

Plot: near Bilbao, 1870s. The orphan girl Anita loves the sergeant Araquil, whose father Remigio opposes the match because she lacks a dowry. Learning that General Garrido is offering a large reward for the death of a rebel, Anita decides to do the deed. She crosses enemy lines and is followed by Araquil who wishes to discover if she is a spy as rumour reports. Anita kills the rebel and is given the reward by Garrido, but Araquil has been mortally wounded and accuses her of selling herself to Garrido. Anita loses her reason and thinking that distant bells signal her wedding with Araquil falls dead on top of his corpse. [R]

Neapolitan opera

A loose term which describes the 18th-century school of Italian opera composers, many of whom (but by no means all) were based in Naples. The leading figures were Cimarosa, Jommelli, Paisiello, Pergolesi, Piccinni, Sacchini, A. Scarlatti and Traetta. Although the term is usually used to describe a style of opera seria, many Neapolitan composers were also masters of opera buffa, which in this school is marked by great vivacity.

Neblett, Carol *(b 1946)*

American soprano, particularly associated with Puccini roles, notably Minnie in *La Fanciulla del West*. She possesses a rich if not absolutely outstanding voice and is a compelling singing-actress.

Nedbal, Oskar *(1874–1930)*

Czech composer and conductor. With the exception of *Jacob the Farmer* (*Sedlák Jakub*, Brno 13 Oct 1922; libr. L. Novák, after Félix Lope de Vega), all of his stage works are operettas, some of which are still occasionally performed. They include *Die Keusche Barbora* (Vienna 7 Oct 1911), *Polenblut* (Vienna 25 Oct 1913), *Die Winzerbraut* (Vienna 11 Feb 1916), *Die Schöne Saskia* (Vienna 1917), *Mamzel Napoleon* (1918) and *Donna Gloria* (1925). He was musical director of the Bratislava Opera from 1923, and played a crucial role in the promotion of Slovak music.

Nedda

Soprano role in Leoncavallo's *Pagliacci*. She is Canio's wife.

Neher, Caspar *(1897–1962)*

German designer and librettist. One of the leading operatic designers of the inter-war period, he also wrote a number of libretti, providing texts for Einem (*Agamemnon*), Wagner-Régeny (*Persische Episode, Der Günstling, Die Bürger von Calais* and *Johanna Balk*) and Weill (*Die Bürgschaft*).

Neidlinger, Gustav *(b 1912)*

German baritone, particularly associated

with Wagnerian roles, especially Alberich. A fine singing-actor with a powerful and incisive voice, he was the leading Alberich of the 1950s and 1960s.

Nel cor più
Originally a duet in Paisiello's *La Molinara*, in an altered form it has become one of the most popular of all arie antiche.

Nel giardin del bello
Mezzo aria (the Veil Song) for Eboli in Act II of Verdi's *Don Carlos*.

Nélusko
Baritone role in Meyerbeer's *L'Africaine*. He is a captured slave.

Nè mai dunque
Soprano aria for Wally in Act III of Catalani's *La Wally*.

Németh, Mária *(1897–1967)*
Hungarian soprano, particularly associated with the Italian repertory. One of the leading dramatic sopranos of the inter-war period, her remarkable technique enabled her to sing roles as diverse as the Queen of the Night and Turandot.

Nemico della patria
Baritone aria for Gérard in Act III of Giordano's *Andrea Chénier*.

Nemirovich-Danchenko, Vladimir *(1858–1943)*
Russian producer. A co-founder with Konstantin Stanislavsky in 1898 of the Moscow Arts Theatre, his revolutionary stage methods had a vast influence on opera performance both in Russia and elsewhere. He founded a Musical Studio in 1919, which in 1926 became the Nemirovich-Danchenko Musical Theatre and merged with the Stanislavsky Opera Theatre in 1941. He rejected conventional stagings in favour of abstract and stylised productions and freely altered libretti, as in his famous Bizet staging, *Carmencita and the Soldier* (1924). He enjoyed a close artistic relationship with Khrennikov and also wrote the libretto for Rachmaninov's *Aleko*.

Nemorino
Tenor role in Donizetti's *L'Elisir d'Amore*. He is a country lad in love with Adina.

Neri, Giulio *(1909–58)*
Italian bass, particularly associated with the Italian repertory, especially Don Basilio, the Grand Inquisitor and Mefistofele. He had a dark, powerful, cavernous voice and a strong stage presence.

Néris
Mezzo role in Cherubini's *Médée*. She is Medea's servant.

Nero
The Roman emperor (37–68 AD) appears in a number of operas, including: (1) Tenor role in Monteverdi's *L'Incoronazione di Poppea*. (2) Tenor role in Boito's and Mascagni's *Nerone*. (3) Soprano trouser-role in Handel's *Agrippina*.

Nerone *(Nero)*
Works of this title about the Emperor Nero include:

(1) Opera in four acts by Boito. 1st perf. Milan, 1 May 1924; libr. by the composer. Principal roles: Nero (ten), Simon Mago (b-bar), Fanuèl (bar), Asteria (sop), Rubria (mezzo), Tigellino (bass), Gobrias (ten). Boito's second

opera, on which he worked intermittently for some 40 years, it was left unfinished at his death and was prepared for performance by Toscanini and Vincenzo Tommasini. A fifth act was written but never composed. Dealing with the confrontation between the decadent Roman Empire and the new Christianity, it was greeted at its appearance with respect rather than enthusiasm, and is nowadays only very rarely performed.

Plot: Rome, *c* 60 AD. Simon Mago, who has been unmasked by Nero as a fake magician, betrays the Christians to the Emperor who condemns them to die in the circus. Simon and his followers set Rome on fire. Many of Nero's intended victims escape, but Rubria is mortally wounded and dies in the arms of the Christian leader Fanuèl. [R]

(2) Opera in three acts by Mascagni. 1st perf. Milan, 16 Jan 1935; libr. by Giovanni Targioni-Tozzetti, after Pietro Cossa. Principal roles: Nerone (ten), Atte (sop), Egloge (sop), Menecrate (bar), Rufo (bass). Mascagni's last opera, written in honour of Mussolini, it is a pretentious piece which is now justifiably forgotten.

Nessi, Giuseppe *(1887–1961)*

Italian tenor, particularly associated with the Italian repertory. The leading Italian comprimario artist of the inter-war period, he was a master of make-up and was an accomplished comic actor. He created Pang in *Turandot*, Gobrias in *Nerone* and Donna Pasqua in Wolf-Ferrari's *Il Campiello*.

Nessler, Victor *(1841–90)*

German composer and conductor. He wrote ten operas, of which the most successful were *Der Rattenfänger von Hameln* (*The Ratcatcher of Hameln*, Leipzig 19 March 1879) and *Der*

Trompeter von Säckingen*, his only work which is still remembered.

Nessun dorma

Tenor aria for Calaf in Act III of Puccini's *Turandot*.

Nesterenko, Yevgeny *(b 1938)*

Russian bass, particularly associated with the Russian and Italian repertories. One of the outstanding basses of the postwar era, he possesses a magnificent and powerful voice used with unfailing musicianship and is an accomplished singing-actor, equally at home in serious or comic roles.

Netherlands Opera *(De Nederlandsche Opera* in Dutch)

Holland's principal opera company, which is based at the Town Hall Music Theatre (cap. 1,594) in Amsterdam, it was founded in 1946. It became the *Nieuwe Nederlandsche Opera* in 1965 on its reorganisation, and an associated Opera Studio (for chamber works) was founded in 1974. Musical directors have included Michael Gielen and Edo de Waart.

Neues vom Tage *(News of the Day)*

Opera in three acts by Hindemith. 1st perf. Berlin, 8 June 1929; libr. by Marcellus Schiffer. Principal roles: Press Chief (bass), Married Couple (sop and bar), Agency Employees (mezzo and ten). A comedy, with serious undertones, about the way in which the gutter press goes about getting its stories, it is still occasionally performed in Germany. Like many of Hindemith's operas, it fell foul of the Nazis: Dr Goebbels objected to the scene in which the young wife lies in the bath and extols the joys of constant hot water.

Neumann, František *(1874–1929)*

Czech conductor and composer. Particularly associated with the Czech repertory, he was musical director of the Brno Opera (1919–29), where he conducted the first performances of Janáček's *Káťa Kabanová*, *Šárka*, *The Cunning Little Vixen* and *The Macropolus Case*, as well as operas by Novák and Ostrčil. He also composed eight operas.

Neumann, Václav *(b 1920)*

Czech conductor, particularly associated with the Czech and German repertories. He was musical director of the Leipzig Opera, the Stuttgart Opera (1970–73) and the Prague National Theatre, and conducted the first performance of Cikker's *The Play of Love and Death*.

Nevers, Comte de

Baritone role in Meyerbeer's *Les Huguenots*. He is betrothed to Valentine.

Neway, Patricia *(b 1919)*

American soprano, particularly associated with 20th-century operas. An intense singing-actress, with a powerful and steely voice, she created Magda Sorel in *The Consul*, the Mother in Menotti's *Maria Golovin* and Leah in David Tamkin's *The Dybbuk*.

Newman, Ernest *(b William Roberts) (1868–1959)*

British critic. One of the most influential 20th-century British critics, he is principally remembered for his analyses of Wagner. His *Wagner Nights*, *Wagner as Man and Artist* and the four-volume *Life of Richard Wagner* remain seminal studies.

New Opera Company

A British company founded in 1957 to promote 20th-century operas. In the past often working in collaboration with Sadler's Wells Opera, the company has given eight world premières as well as some 20 British premières. The musical director is Leon Lovett.

New Opera South Australia

Based in Adelaide, the company was formed in 1974, and performs at either the Festival Theatre (cap. 2,000), which opened in 1973, or the Victorian Opera Theatre (cap. 1,000). Musical directors have included Myer Fredman and Andrew Green.

New Orleans Opera House Association

New Orleans has a long operatic tradition, and – partly because of Louisiana's historical background as a French colony – has always been particularly associated with the French repertory. The present company was formed in 1943 and performs at the New Orleans Theater of the Performing Arts (cap. 2,300), which opened in 1973. The annual season runs from October to March. Musical directors have included Walter Herbert, Renato Cellini and Knud Anderson.

New Sadler's Wells Opera

Based at Sadler's Wells Theatre (cap. 1,499) in London and also touring Britain, the company was formed in 1980 and its repertory consisted largely of operetta. Financial difficulties forced it into liquidation in early 1989. The musical director was Barry Wordsworth.

New World Trilogy

A title often given to Milhaud's three otherwise unconnected operas on Latin

American subjects: *Christophe Colomb**, *Maximilien** and *Bolivar**.

New Year

Opera by Tippett. 1st perf. Houston, 27 Oct 1989; libr. by the composer. Tippett's latest opera, it deals with the dreams and fantasies of two sets of characters (three from Somewhere Today and three from Nowhere Tomorrow). Its orchestration includes electric guitars, saxophones and specially created electronic ingredients.

New York

See American Opera Society; Lincoln Center for the Performing Arts; Metropolitan Opera, New York; New York City Opera

New York City Opera

Standing in a relationship to the Metropolitan Opera somewhat similar to that of the English National Opera to Covent Garden, the company was formed in February 1944. Since 22 February 1966, it has been based at the New York State Theater (cap. 2,779) in the Lincoln Center for the Performing Arts. One of the most exciting opera companies in the USA, it pursues a highly adventurous repertory policy, encourages American opera and has nurtured many of the finest modern American singers. Musical directors have been László Halász, Joseph Rosenstock, Erich Leinsdorf, Julius Rudel, Christopher Keene and Sergiu Comissiona. General directors have included Beverly Sills.

New Zealand Opera Company

The company was founded in 1954 by the singer Donald Munrow, and gives an annual season at venues throughout the country. The repertory is conservative. Musical directors have included László Heltay.

Nice

See Théâtre de l'Opéra, Nice

Nice dilemma, A

Soprano/tenor/baritone/baritone quartet for the Plaintiff, the Defendant, Counsel for Plaintiff and the Judge in Sullivan's *Trial By Jury*. One of Sullivan's finest pieces of musical satire, it is based on the quintet 'D'un pensiero' in Act I of Bellini's *La Sonnambula*.

Nicklaus

Mezzo trouser-role in Offenbach's *Les Contes d'Hoffmann*. Hoffmann's young companion, he is the physical embodiment of the Muse of Poetry.

Nicolaï, Otto *(1810–49)*

German composer and conductor. His first opera *Enrico II* (Trieste 26 Nov 1839; libr. Felice Romani) was a failure, but its successor *Il Templario* (Turin 11 Feb 1840; libr. G. M. Marini, after Sir Walter Scott's *Ivanhoe*) established his reputation. *Gildippe ed Odoardo* (Genoa 26 Dec 1840; libr. Temistocle Solera) and *Il Proscritto* (Milan 13 March 1841; libr. Gaetano Rossi) were unsuccessful, but his last opera *Die Lustigen Weiber von Windsor** remains one of the greatest and most popular of all German comic operas. A distinguished conductor, he was musical director of the Berlin Opera and was the effective founder of the Vienna Philharmonic Orchestra.

Nicolini *(b Nicolò Grimaldi) (1673–1732)*

Italian castrato. One of the most famous singers of the 18th century, also highly regarded as an actor, he sang in

Italy and then in London, where he created the title roles in Handel's *Rinaldo* and *Amadigi di Gaula*. The critic Addison described him as "the greatest performer in dramatic music that is now living, or that ever appeared upon a stage".

Nicolò
See Isouard, Nicolò

Nielsen, Carl *(1865–1931)*
Danish composer. His two operas, the powerful *Saul and David** and the comedy *Maskarade** (which is the Danish national opera), both remain very popular in Denmark, but for quite unaccountable reasons have failed to establish themselves in the international repertory.

Nightingale, The *(Solovey;* sometimes incorrectly called *Le Rossignol)*
Opera in three acts by Stravinsky. 1st perf. Paris, 26 May 1914; libr. by the composer and Stepan Nikolayevich Mitusov, after Hans Christian Andersen. Principal roles: Nightingale (sop), Emperor (bar), Fisherman (ten), Cook (mezzo), Bonze (bass), Chamberlain (bass), Death (cont). Written over two different periods, the music is stylistically disjointed but nevertheless offers a delightful setting of Andersen's Chinese fairy tale. The symphonic poem *Le Chant du Rossignol* is drawn from music from the opera.

Plot: Ancient China. The Nightingale sings in the forest for the Fisherman. Although she knows that her voice will be less sweet there, she agrees to sing at the palace, where the Emperor is moved to tears by the beauty of her song. Three Japanese envoys arrive bearing a mechanical nightingale as a gift for the Emperor. The real bird

leaves sadly which causes offence to the Emperor who banishes it. However, when Death stands at the Emperor's bedside, the real bird returns to restore the monarch's life with her song. [R]

Night in Venice, A
See Nacht in Venedig, Eine

Nikikai Opera Company
Japan's leading opera company, it was founded in 1952 by Mutsumu Shibata. It gives an annual season at the Nissei Theatre (cap. 1,350) in Tokyo, which opened in 1964.

Nikisch, Artur *(1855–1922)*
Hungarian conductor, particularly associated with the German repertory. One of the leading conductors of his age, he was musical director of the Leipzig Opera (1879–99) and the Budapest State Opera (1893–95). He conducted the first performances of Nessler's *Der Trompeter von Säckingen*, Holbrooke's *Dylan* and Smyth's *The Wreckers*.

Nilakantha
Baritone role in Delibes' *Lakmé*. Lakmé's father, he is a Brahmin priest.

Nile Scene
A title often given to Act III of Verdi's *Aida*.

Nilsson, Birgit *(b 1918)*
Swedish soprano, particularly associated with Wagner, Strauss and heavier Verdi roles and with Turandot. One of the greatest dramatic sopranos of all time, she possessed an enormous, steely voice of truly awesome power which she used with unfailing musicianship and dramatic insight. Her Isolde and Elektra are unlikely ever to be equalled, let alone surpassed.

Nilsson, Christine (b Törnerhjelm) (1843–1921)

Swedish soprano, particularly associated with the French and Italian repertories. One of the leading lyric sopranos of the mid-19th century, she created Ophélie in Thomas' *Hamlet* and Edith in Balfe's *Il Talismano*.

Nimsgern, Siegmund (b 1940)

German baritone, particularly associated with the German repertory, especially Strauss and Wagner and 20th-century works. One of the leading contemporary German baritones, he has a rich voice of considerable power which is used with great intelligence and musicianship, and he has a good stage presence.

Ninetta

Mezzo role in Rossini's *La Gazza Ladra*. She is the girl falsely accused of stealing.

Nissen, Hans Hermann (1893–1980)

German bass-baritone, particularly associated with Wagnerian roles. Possessing a rich and sonorous voice and a good stage presence, he was a leading Wotan and Hans Sachs of the inter-war period.

Nuin mi tema

Otello's final monologue in Act IV of Verdi's *Otello*.

Noble, Dennis (1899–1966)

British baritone, particularly associated with the Italian repertory. The leading British baritone of the inter-war period, he created Sam Weller in Coates' *Pickwick*, a role in Lloyd's *The Serf* and, for Goossens, Achior in *Judith* and Don José in *Don Juan de Mañara*.

Noble, John

British baritone. One of the most underrated British singers of the postwar era, he possessed a beautiful voice used with outstanding musicianship and intelligence. Best known as a concert singer, his operatic appearances were infrequent, but he was especially associated with the title role in Vaughan Williams' *The Pilgrim's Progress*.

Nobles seigneurs

Soprano aria for Urbain in Act I of Meyerbeer's *Les Huguenots*.

Noces de Jeanette, Les (*Jeanette's Wedding*)

Operetta in one act by Massé. 1st perf. Paris, 4 Feb 1853; libr. by Jules Barbier and Michel Carré. Massé's most successful work, it is still regularly performed in France.

Nonet

In opera, a musical number for nine solo singers, with or without chorus. There is a fine example in Act I Scene II of Verdi's *Falstaff*.

Noni, Alda (b 1916)

Italian soprano. One of the leading soubrettes of the immediate postwar period, she was an accomplished actress with a tremendous sense of humour and was particularly associated with the roles of Norina, Despina and Zerbinetta.

Non mi dir

Soprano aria for Donna Anna in Act II of Mozart's *Don Giovanni*.

Nono, Luigi (1924–90)

Italian composer. A leading exponent of the extreme avant-garde in Italy, his intensely left-wing political views — always paraded in his music — have tended to obscure his considerable musical abilities. His first opera *Intolleranza** is one of the most controversial postwar operas and provoked a serious political riot at its première. His other operas are *Al Gran Sale Carico d'Amore* (Milan 4 April 1975; libr. composer) and *Prometeo* (1984).

Non pianger
Soprano aria for Elisabetta in Act II of Verdi's *Don Carlos*.

Non più andrai
Bass-baritone aria for Figaro in Act I of Mozart's *Le Nozze di Figaro*. Mozart quotes it in the Supper Scene of *Don Giovanni*.

Non più di fiori
Soprano aria for Vitellia in Act II of Mozart's *La Clemenza di Tito*.

Non più mesta
Mezzo aria for Cenerentola in Act II of Rossini's *La Cenerentola*. The final scene of the opera.

Non so più
Soprano aria for Cherubino in Act I of Mozart's *Le Nozze di Figaro*.

Non temer, amato bene
Soprano aria for Idamante in Act II of Mozart's *Idomeneo*.

No! pazzo son!
Tenor aria for des Grieux in Act III of Puccini's *Manon Lescaut*.

Nordica, Lillian *(b Norton) (1857–1914)*
American soprano. Originally noted for her performances in the French and Italian repertories, she later turned to Wagner with equal success. Her technique was so assured that she was able to sing Brünnhilde and Violetta on consecutive nights. She created Zelika in Stanford's *The Veiled Prophet*.

Norina
Soprano role in Donizetti's *Don Pasquale*. She is a flighty young widow loved by Ernesto.

Norma
Opera in two acts by Bellini. 1st perf. Milan, 26 Dec 1831; libr. by Felice Romani, after Louis Alexandre Soumet's play. Principal roles: Norma (sop), Adalgisa (sop), Pollione (ten), Oroveso (bass). Bellini's masterpiece and one of the finest of all bel canto operas, the title role is one of the most musico-dramatically demanding in the entire repertory.

Plot: 1st century Gaul. Norma is the daughter of Oroveso, high priest of the Druids and herself their high priestess. Her father desires war against the Romans but Norma, leading the rituals in the temple, seeks to avoid it because she loves the Roman Proconsul, Pollione, to whom she has secretly borne two children. Pollione, however, has left her for another woman whose identity she does not know, and she prays for his return. Her rival is, in fact, her best friend, the young priestess, Adalgisa, who agrees to join Pollione in Rome, and comes to Norma to confess her betrayal of her chastity and her religion. During their meeting, Pollione appears, and the women learn the truth that he is the lover of both of them. Norma resolves to renounce Pollione in favour of Adalgisa, on the understanding that the latter will care for her children, but Adalgisa is incapable of such betrayal and pleads with her lover to return to Norma and his children. He refuses, inflaming Norma to call for war just as Pollione is arrested for breaking into the sacred temple in an attempt to abduct Adalgisa. His deed carries the death penalty but Norma, realising she still loves him, offers her tribe a substitute – a defiled virgin of the priesthood. It is herself. She confesses her sins, gives her children to her father, and mounts the flaming pyre that has been prepared for her. Pollione, moved to renewed love by her self-sacrifice and courage, joins her in the flames. [R]

Norman, Jessye *(b 1945)*

American soprano who also sings some mezzo roles. One of the best-loved singers of modern times and possessor of one of the richest and loveliest voices of the 20th century, she is particularly associated with Wagner and Strauss roles and with the French repertory. An artist of outstanding sensitivity and musicianship, her operatic appearances have sadly been intermittent and her substantial physique means that her roles have to be selected with care.

Norns

Soprano, mezzo and contralto roles in Wagner's *Götterdämmerung*. Daughters of Erda, they are the three fates.

Norrington, Roger *(b 1934)*

British conductor, particularly associated with Mozart, early and Baroque operas and with the French repertory. Originally a tenor, he was musical director of Kent Opera (1969–85) and has prepared many scholarly editions of early operas.

Norwegian Opera

Norway's first full-time opera company (*Norsk Operaselskap*) was founded in 1951. It acquired its present form (as *Den Norske Opera*) in November 1957, with Kirsten Flagstad as administrator. Based in Oslo, it also visits other towns. The annual season runs from August to June. Musical directors have included Oivin Fjelstad and Martin Turrovsky.

Norwegian opera composers

See Grieg; Sinding

Other national opera composers include Sigvardt Apestrand (1856–1941), Bjarne Brustad (*b* 1895), Arne Eggen (1881–1955), Catharinus Elling (1858–1942), Johannes Haarklou (1847–1925), Ludvig Paul Irgens Jenssen (1894–1969), Ole Olsen (1850–1927), Gerhard Schjelderup (1859–1933) and Waldemar Thrane (1790–1828), whose *A Mountain Adventure* (*Fjeldeventyret*, Oslo 9 Feb 1825; libr. H. A. Bjerregaard) was the first opera written to a Norwegian libretto.

Nose, The *(Nos)*

Comic opera in three acts by Shostakovich (Op 15). 1st perf. Leningrad, 12 Jan 1930; libr. by the composer, A. Preis, A. Zamyatin and G. Yonin after Nikolai Gogol's story. Principal roles: Maj Kovalyov (bar), Nose (ten), Police Inspector (ten). A merciless skit on philistinism and Soviet officialdom, it is one of Shostakovich's most complex scores. Not surprisingly, it was unacceptable to the 'anti-formalist' Stalin period, but more recently it has been successfully reintroduced in Russia. It has also met with success elsewhere – officialdom, after all, being much the same the world over. It contains in the Police Inspector possibly the highest tenor role ever written.

Plot: The civil servant Kovalyov wakes up one morning to discover that his nose is missing. Having detatched itself, the nose leads an independent life, turning up in bizarre places. Kovalyov tries to place an advertisement in the 'missing' columns of the press, but the newspapers refuse to accept the advert. Finally, it is returned to him by the Police Inspector but has to be surgically replaced. The operation fails, but eventually the nose returns to Kovalyov of its own free will. [R]

Notary

Notaries are stock figures in comic opera, and in a tradition going back at least as far as Pergolesi, they often stammer – as do, for example, Dr Blind in *Die Fledermaus* and Don Curzio in *Le Nozze di Figaro*.

Nothung! Nothung!

Tenor aria (the Forging Song) for Siegfried in Act I of Wagner's *Siegfried*. 'Nothung' (meaning needful) is the name of the magic sword.

Notte e giorno

Leporello's words at the opening of Act I of Mozart's *Don Giovanni*. They are quoted by Nicklaus in the prologue of Offenbach's *Les Contes d'Hoffmann*.

Nourabad

Bass role in Bizet's *Les Pêcheurs de Perles*. He is the high priest.

Nourrit, Adolphe *(1802–39)*

French tenor. One of the outstanding tenors of the first half of the 19th century, he was principally associated with the Paris Opéra. His replacement there in 1837 by Gilbert Duprez* caused him to suffer from severe melancholia which led to his committing suicide. He created the title role in *Robert le Diable*, Raoul in *Les Huguenots*, Eléazer in *La Juive*, Masaniello in *La Muette de Portici* and, for Rossini, Néocles in *Le Siège de Corinth*, the title role in *Le Comte Ory*, Aménophis in *Moïse et Pharaon* and Arnold in *Guillaume Tell*.

Novák, Vitězslav *(1870–1949)*

Czech composer. His four operas, all on nationalist subjects, have had considerable success in Czechoslovakia but have made little headway elsewhere. The comedy *The Imp of Zvíkov* (*Zvíkovský Rarášek*, 1915; libr. L. Stroupežnický) was followed by the patriotic *Karlštejn* (1916; libr. O. Fischer), *The Lantern* (*Lucerna*, 1923; libr. H. Jelínek) [R], his most successful opera, and *The Grandfather's Heritage* (*Dědův Odkaz*, 1926; libr. A. Klášterský).

Novotná, Jarmila *(b 1907)*

Czech soprano, particularly associated with Mozart and Strauss roles and with the Czech repertory. One of the most stylish and aristocratic sopranos of the inter-war period, she was also a fine singing-actress. She created the title role in Lehár's *Giuditta*.

Now the Great Bear

Tenor aria for Grimes in Act I of Britten's *Peter Grimes*.

Noye's Fludde

Church opera in one act by Britten (Op 59). 1st perf. Orford, 18 June 1958. A setting of part of a Chester miracle play. Principal roles: Noye (bass), Mrs Noye (mezzo), Voice of God (speaker). Telling the biblical story of the Flood, the score calls for a children's orchestra and for audience participation in hymn singing. [R]

Nozze di Figaro, Le (*The Marriage of Figaro*)

Opera in four acts by Mozart (K 492). 1st perf. Vienna, 1 May 1786; libr. by Lorenzo da Ponte, after Pierre Augustin Caron de Beaumarchais' *La Folle Journée ou Le Marriage de Figaro*. Principal roles: Figaro (b-bar), Susanna (sop), Count and Countess Almaviva (bar and sop), Cherubino (sop), Dr Bartolo (bass), Don Basilio (ten), Marcellina (mezzo), Barbarina (sop), Antonio (bass), Don Curzio (ten). One of the greatest, most human and most popular of all operas, it is the earliest of Mozart's Italian masterpieces, and is notable for its extraordinary depth of characterisation and for the plasticity of its kaleidoscopic ensembles.

Plot: 18th-century Spain. Count Almaviva's valet Figaro is to be married to the Countess's maid Susanna, and the Count is regretting having abolished the old custom of first rights to the lord of the manor. The Count keeps attempting to thwart or postpone the marriage – and the activities of the love-sick adolescent page-boy Cherubino nearly give him grounds by seeming to compromise the Countess and Susanna – but is always outwitted by his servants with the aid of the Countess. After much intrigue and disguise, and many complications, everything is sorted out. The wedding can now take place and a chastened Count begs the Countess's forgiveness. [R]

Nucci, Leo (*b 1942*)

Italian baritone, particularly associated with the Italian repertory, especially Verdi. A true Verdi baritone, he possesses a rich and bright-toned voice with a thrilling upper register and has a good stage presence.

Nuit d'ivresse

Mezzo/tenor duet for Dido and Aeneas in Act IV of Berlioz's *Les Troyens*.

Number opera

A loose term meaning an opera in which the scenes are composed of self-contained individual musical numbers (arias, duets, trios, etc), rather than an opera in which each scene is a single, unbroken piece of music.

Nürnberg Stadttheater

The present opera house (cap. 1,456) in this German city in Bavaria opened in 1905. Musical directors have included Robert Heger, Hans Gierster and Christian Thielemann.

Nurse

Mezzo role in: (1) Strauss' *Die Frau ohne Schatten*. (2) Moussorgsky's *Boris Godunov*. (3) Tippett's *King Priam*. (4) Sutermeister's *Romeo und Julia*. (5) Dukas' *Ariane et Barbe-Bleue*.

Obbligato (Italian for 'obligatory')
Strictly speaking, it refers to a part for a solo instrument that cannot be omitted. Confusingly, however, it is also occasionally used to mean a part that may be omitted. In opera, it is easiest to regard it as a term referring to a major instrumental solo in an aria or ensemble, as for example the flute in the Mad Scene in *Lucia di Lammermoor* or the basset horn in 'Parto, parto' in *La Clemenza di Tito*.

O beau pays de la Touraine
Soprano aria for Marguerite in Act II of Meyerbeer's *Les Huguenots*.

Oberon
or The Elf-King's Oath
Opera in three acts by Weber (J 306). 1st perf. London, 12 April 1826; libr. by James Robinson Planché, after William Sotheby's translation of Wieland's poem, itself based on *Huon de Bordeaux* in the 13th-century *La Bibliothèque Bleue*. Principal roles: Reiza (sop), Sir Huon (ten), Sherasmin (bar), Fatima (mezzo), Oberon (ten), Puck (sop). Weber's last opera, it contains some of his greatest music. The ludicrous libretto has prevented it taking the regular place in the repertory which its musical qualities merit. Many attempts have been made to revise or 'improve' the libretto, but these have nearly always succeeded only in making matters worse.
    Plot: Oberon has quarrelled with his wife and decides not to see her again until a pair of faithful lovers can be found. He chooses Sir Huon (aided by his esquire Sherasmin) to rescue Reiza

and her attendant Fatima, who are in trouble in Baghdad. Through the connivance of Oberon and Puck, the foursome undergoes shipwreck, capture by pirates, slavery and sentence of death, before Oberon intervenes to save them and transport them to the court of Charlemagne, having accepted them as examples of fidelity. [R]

Oberon
Counter-tenor role in Britten's *A Midsummer Night's Dream*. Titania's husband, he is the king of the fairies. It was the first role written specifically for a modern counter-tenor.

Oberspielleiter (German for 'senior producer')
The title of the principal resident producer in a German or Austrian opera house.

Oberto, Conte di San Bonifacio
Opera in two acts by Verdi. 1st perf. Milan, 17 Nov 1839; libr. by Antonio Piazza and Temistocle Solera. Principal roles: Oberto (bass), Leonora (sop), Riccardo (ten), Cuniza (sop). Verdi's first opera, it is still occasionally performed.
    Plot: Bassano, 1228. Riccardo, Count of Salinguerra has seduced Leonora, the daughter of Oberto, but now intends to marry Cuniza. With the aid of Cuniza, Leonora and her father challenge Riccardo with his faithlessness and he agrees to return to Leonora. Even so, the outraged Oberto challenges Riccardo to a duel and loses his life. [R]

Obraztsova, Elena (b 1939)
Russian mezzo, particularly associated
with the Italian and Russian repertories.
An exciting dramatic mezzo in the
grand tradition, she possesses a rich
and powerful voice (if not always fully
knit together) and has a strong stage
presence.

Oca del Cairo, L' (The Goose of
Cairo)
Unfinished comic opera in two acts by
Mozart (K 422). 1st perf. Paris, 6 June
1867 (composed 1783); libr. by
Giovanni Battista Varesco. Principal
roles: Don Pippo (bar), Celidora (sop),
Lavina (sop), Brondello (ten),
Calandrino (ten), Auretta (sop),
Chichibio (ten). A story of complex
amorous intrigues, it contains seven
musical numbers in various states of
completion.

Ocean thou mighty monster
See Ozean, zu Ungeheuer!

Ochs von Lerchenau, Baron
Bass role in Richard Strauss' Der
Rosenkavalier. He is the Marschallin's
boorish country cousin.

Octavian
Mezzo trouser-role in Strauss' Der
Rosenkavalier. The young Count
Rofrano, he is the Rose Cavalier of the
opera's title.

Octet
In opera, a musical number for eight
solo singers, with or without chorus.
There is a fine example in Strauss'
Capriccio.

Odabella
Soprano role in Verdi's Attila. She is
the daughter of the Lord of Aquileia.

O don fatale
Mezzo aria for Eboli in Act IV of
Verdi's Don Carlos.

O du mein holder
Abendstern (often known in
English as 'Star of eve')
Baritone aria for Wolfram in Act III of
Wagner's Tannhäuser.

Oedipus
The mythical Greek king of Thebes
who kills his father and marries his
mother is the subject of many operas
derived from Sophocles' two
masterpieces Oedipus the King and
Oedipus at Colonus. The most
important are Sacchini's Oedipe à
Colone, Leoncavallo's Edipo Rè,
Stravinsky's Oedipus Rex*, Enescu's
Oedipe and Orff's Oedipus der
Tyrann*.

Oedipus der Tyrann (Oedipus
the King)
Opera in three acts by Orff. 1st perf.
Stuttgart, 11 Dec 1959. Principal roles:
Oedipus (ten), Jokasta (sop), Kreon
(bass), Tiresias (ten), Priest (bar). An
austere and powerful setting of
Friedrich Hölderlin's translation of
Sophocles' play, it is only infrequently
performed. [R]

Oedipus Rex
Opera-oratorio in two acts by
Stravinsky. 1st perf. Paris, 30 May
1927; libr. by Jean Cocteau, after
Sophocles' Oedipus the King, translated
into Latin by Jean Daniélou. Principal
roles: Oedipus (ten), Jocasta (mezzo),
Creon (bar), Messenger (bar), Tiresias
(bass), Shepherd (ten), Narrator
(speaker). Deliberately written in a dead
language to lend a timeless quality to
the drama (though a narrator describes
events in contemporary language), the

action is restricted to a minimum: the characters are masked, and move only their heads and arms, so as to give "the impression of living statues". One of Stravinsky's greatest works, it is still regularly performed, more often in the concert hall than the opera house.

Plot: Ancient Thebes. Creon, sent by Oedipus to Delphi to discover why Thebes has been visited by plague, returns with the message that the murderer of Oedipus' father is living in the city and must be punished. Oedipus forces the seer Tiresias to reveal that the murderer is a king. Queen Jocasta is adamant that oracles should be disregarded – had they not wrongly foretold that the former King, her husband, would be killed by his own son, whereas he had been killed by robbers at a crossroad? The truth begins to emerge: Oedipus knows that he himself killed an old man at a crossroad, and Ieanus the shepherd reveals that the parents who raised him had, in fact, adopted him. Jocasta, realising she has married her son, hangs herself and Oedipus puts out his own eyes. [R]

Oestvig, Karl *(1889–1968)*
Norwegian tenor, particularly associated with heroic German roles. One of the leading heldentenors of the inter-war period, he created the Emperor in *Die Frau ohne Schatten* and Giovanni in Schillings' *Mona Lisa*. Married to the soprano Maria Rajdl.

Offenbach, Jacques *(b Jakob Eberst) (1819–80)*
German-born French composer and cellist who, with Sullivan and Johann Strauss II, ranks as one of the three greatest operetta composers. His operettas, particularly those written in collaboration with Henri Meilhac* and Ludovic Halévy*, are merciless satires

on the society and morals of the Second Empire and often simultaneously debunk famous mythological stories. Offenbach also satirised famous composers, often by quoting their music in absurd situations or by setting it to ludicrous words. His own music is unfailingly tuneful, with tangy and sparkling orchestration, and is often marked by his exuberant high spirits. After the Franco-Prussian War and the fall of the Second Empire, the mood of Paris was less receptive to Offenbach's outrageous frivolity, and his later works are often of a more lyrical and sentimental character.

Beginning with *Les Deux Aveugles** in 1855, he wrote nearly 100 stage works, first for his Théâtre Bouffes-Parisiens* and later for larger theatres. The most successful include *Le Marriage aux Lanternes* (Paris 10 Oct 1857; libr. Léon Battu and Michel Carré), the immortal *Orphée aux Enfers*, Mesdames de la Halle* (Paris 3 March 1858; libr. A. Lapointe) [R], *Geneviève de Brabant* (Paris 19 Nov 1859; libr. A. Jaime and E. Tréfeu), *La Chanson de Fortunio* (Paris 5 Jan 1861), *Monsieur Choufleuri Restera Chez-Lui* (Paris 1861; libr. Héctor Crémieux and Ludovic Halévy) [R], the ever-popular *La Belle Hélène*, Barbe-Bleue*, La Vie Parisienne*, the sensationally successful *La Grande-Duchesse de Gérolstein*, Robinson Crusoé*, the more sentimental *La Périchole*, Les Brigands*, Pomme d'Api* (Paris 4 Sept 1873; libr. Halévy and W. Busnach) [R], *Madame Favart* (Paris 28 Dec 1878; libr. Henri Charles Chivot and Alfred Duru) and *La Fille du Tambour-Major**. In a very different vein are his two operas: the unsuccessful *Das Rheinnixen* (Vienna 14 Feb 1864; libr. August von Wolzogen, after Tréfeu and Charles Nuittier) and his masterpiece *Les Contes d'Hoffmann**, which was not quite completed at his death. The popular ballet *Gaité Parisienne* was arranged by Manuel Rosenthal in 1938 from music from his operettas, and the operetta *Christopher Columbus** is the finest of a number of pastiches ' arranged from his forgotten works.

Oiseaux dans la charmille, Les

Soprano aria (the Doll's Song) for Olympia in Act I of Offenbach's *Les Contes d'Hoffmann*.

O Isis und Osiris

Bass aria for Sarastro in Act II of Mozart's *Die Zauberflöte*.

Olav Trygvason

Unfinished opera by Grieg (Op 50). Libr. by Bjørnstjerne Bjørnson. Begun in 1873, Grieg completed only three scenes of his sole operatic project. The scenes are sometimes performed in concert as a cantata. [R]

Old Maid and the Thief, The

Opera in one act by Menotti. 1st perf. NBC Radio, 22 April 1939; 1st stage perf. Philadelphia, 11 Feb 1941; libr. by the composer. Principal roles: Bob (bar), Miss Todd (mezzo), Laetitia (sop), Miss Pinkerton (sop). A verismo piece, it tells of a young man who steals everything from the three women who befriend him. It is still occasionally performed.

O légère hirondelle

Soprano aria for Mireille in Act I of Gounod's *Mireille*.

Olga

(1) Mezzo role in Tchaikovsky's *Eugene Onegin*. Tatyana's sister, she is engaged to Lensky. (2) Soprano role in Prokofiev's *The Story of a Real Man*.

She loves Alexei. (3) Mezzo role in Giordano's *Fedora*. (4) Soprano role in Rimsky-Korsakov's *The Maid of Pskov*. She is Ivan the Terrible's daughter.

Oliver, Stephen *(b 1948)*

British composer. He has written a number of stage works, including *The Duchess of Malfi* (Oxford 1971), *The Donkey* (1973), *Tom Jones* (1976; libr. after Henry Fielding), *The Garden* (1977) and the duodrama *A Man of Feeling* (1982).

Olivero, Magda *(b 1914)*

Italian soprano, particularly associated with the Italian repertory, especially Tosca and Adriana Lecouvreur. An oustanding singing actress, she enjoyed two careers: she retired in 1941, but returned to the stage in 1951, and continued to sing into her late 60s.

Olivier

Baritone role in Richard Strauss' *Capriccio*. He is a poet in love with the Countess.

Olomouc Opera (Olmütz when it was part of Austria-Hungary)

Opera at this town in Czechoslovakia is given at the Oldřich Stibor Theatre (cap. 750). Musical directors have included Iša Krejčí and Zdeněk Košler.

O luce di quest' anima

Soprano aria for Linda in Act I of Donizetti's *Linda di Chamounix*.

Olympia

Soprano role in Offenbach's *Les Contes d'Hoffmann*. The first of Hoffmann's loves, she is a mechanical doll created by Spalanzani.

Olympians, The

Opera in three acts by Bliss. 1st perf.

London, 29 Sept 1949; libr. by J. B. Priestley. Principal roles: Diana (sop), Madeleine (sop), Bardeau (mezzo), Jupiter (bar), Bacchus (ten), Mars (bass), Curé (ten), Lavette (bass). The first of Bliss' two operas, it tells of the ancient gods who are now reduced to becoming a troupe of strolling players but who regain their former power and glory on one night each year. It is almost never performed.

Olympie

Opera in three acts by Spontini. 1st perf. Paris, 22 Dec 1819; libr. by Michel Dieulafoy and Charles Brifaut, after Voltaire's play. Principal roles: Olympie (sop), Statire (mezzo), Cassandre (ten), Antigone (bass). One of Spontini's finest works, it is only very rarely performed.

Plot: Alexander the Great's successors Cassandre and Antigone vie for the hand of his daughter Olympie. Olympie prefers Cassandre, but the choice is opposed by Alexander's widow Statire (disguised as a priestess), who believes that Cassandre poisoned her husband. Antigone is mortally wounded in battle with Cassandre's forces and confesses to the poisoning. The way is thus clear for the lovers to wed and Statire is installed as supreme ruler. [R]

Olympion

Tenor role in Tippett's *The Ice Break*. He is a black 'champion'.

Ombra mai fù

Mezzo aria for Xerxes in Act I of Handel's *Serse*. It is nearly always referred to as 'Handel's Largo', even though it is marked larghetto in the score.

Ombre légère

Soprano aria (the Shadow Song) for Dinorah in Meyerbeer's *Dinorah*.

O mio babbino caro

Soprano aria for Lauretta in Puccini's *Gianni Schicchi*.

O mon Fernand

Mezzo aria for Léonore in Act III of Donizetti's *La Favorite*.

O monumento

Baritone aria for Barnaba in Act I of Ponchielli's *La Gioconda*.

O namenlose Freude

Soprano/tenor duet for Leonore and Florestan in Act II of Beethoven's *Fidelio*.

O Nature

Tenor aria for Werther in Act I of Massenet's *Werther*.

Oncina, Juan *(b 1925)*

Spanish tenor, particularly associated with Rossini and lighter Donizetti roles. One of the leading tenore di grazias of the 1950s, he later – unwisely and unsuccessfully – undertook heavier roles. Married to the soprano Tatiana Menotti.

O'Neill, Dennis *(b 1948)*

British tenor, particularly associated with the Italian repertory, especially Verdi. One of the few British tenors of the postwar period to produce a real Italianate sound, he has a fine and intelligently used voice and a good stage presence.

Onore! ladri! L'
Baritone aria (the Honour Monologue) for Falstaff in Act I of Verdi's *Falstaff*.

O nube
Soprano aria for Mary in Act II of Donizetti's *Maria Stuarda*.

O Paradis
Tenor aria for Vasco da Gama in Act IV of Meyerbeer's *L'Africaine*.

O patria mia
Soprano aria for Aida in Act III of Verdi's *Aida*.

Open-air performances
The earliest open-air opera performances were probably those of a number of Lully's works in the gardens of Versailles. Nowadays, open-air performances are a frequent feature of the European summer festival scene. The most notable are at Bregenz in Austria, Aix-en-Provence and Orange in France, Savonlinna in Finland and Verona in Italy.

Opera (Italian for 'work')
A shortening of the term *opera in musica*, it means a dramatic text which is sung by one or more singers to an instrumental accompaniment. It originated in Italy in the last decade of the 16th century with the endeavours of the Florentine Camerata* to recreate the conditions of Greek drama. A large number of varieties of opera have subsequently evolved, which are described in this dictionary under their various titles.
See Ballad opera; Burletta; Cantata; Chamber opera; Comic opera; Divertissement; Dramma giocoso; Dramma per musica; Farsa; Favola per musica; Festa teatrali; Género chico; Grand opera; Intermezzo; Liederspiel; Marionette operas; Masque; Melodrama; Monodrama; Music-drama; Neapolitan opera; Number opera; Opera-ballet; Opéra-bouffe; Opera-buffa; Opéra-comique; Opéra-lyrique; Opera-oratorio; Opera semiseria; Opera seria; Operetta; Quartertone operas; Rescue opera; Sainete; Secular oratorio; Singspiel; Spieloper; Tonadilla; Tragédie-lyrique; Twelve-tone operas; Verismo; Zarzuela; Zauberoper

Opera
A monthly British magazine, founded by the Earl of Harewood in 1950, it deals with both the national and international opera scenes. Its editors have been Lord Harewood, Harold Rosenthal and Rodney Milnes.

Opéra, Paris
See Paris Opéra.

Opera-ballet
A theatrical form which flourished in France in the late 17th century and which refers to a work which combines dance with a sung dramatic text. Many of Lully's stage works fall into this category, and Rameau used the term to describe several of his works, such as *Les Fêtes d'Hébé* and *Les Indes Galantes*.

Opéra-Bastille, Paris
Designed by Carlos Ott, the theatre (cap. 2,700) opened on 13 July 1989. Daniel Barenboim was appointed its first musical director, but was dismissed

in January 1989 over artistic and financial differences and the whole project has been left in total disarray despite the appointment of Myung Whun Chung as musical director.

Opéra-bouffe (French for 'comic opera')

The term derives from the Italian opera-buffa, although its meaning is not quite the same. It describes a comic work (either opera or operetta) with spoken dialogue. It is the term used by Offenbach to describe most of his stage works.

Opera-buffa (Italian for 'comic work')

An Italian opera on a comic subject. It developed as a form in its own right from the early 18th-century intermezzi.

Opéra-comique (French for 'comic opera')

A slightly vague term, whose name is misleading. It refers to a French opera which contains spoken dialogue. The term was used from c 1790–1880 to refer to any piece, whether serious or comic, which was not through-composed. It describes works as diverse as *Carmen*, *Fra Diavolo* and *Les Contes d'Hoffmann*.

Opéra-Comique, Paris

Often referred to as the Salle Favart after its location in the Rue Favart, the present theatre (cap. 1,331) opened on 7 December 1898, replacing the previous theatre of the same name which opened in 1783 but which was destroyed by fire in 1887. Paris' second house, it was originally the home of those works named after it which could not be produced at the Opéra because of the latter's ban on spoken dialogue.

The annual season runs from September to July. Musical directors have included Messager, Jean Fournet, André Cluytens and Roger Desmorière.

Opera Company of Boston

Founded in 1957 by the conductor Sarah Caldwell, who is its artistic and musical director, it pursues an enterprising repertory policy, having given many US premières. The annual season runs from December to May. Since 1979, performances have been given at the Opera House (formerly the Keith Memorial Theater) (cap. 2,500).

Opéra de Lyon

The opera company in this city in the Rhône (France) performs at the Grand Théâtre (cap. 3,000), which opened in 1831 and was enlarged in 1842. The annual season runs from October to June, and in recent years the company has been noted for its adventurous repertory, particularly of 20th-century works. Musical directors have included Theodor Guschlbauer, John Eliot Gardiner and Kent Nagano.

Opéra de Montréal

Founded in 1980 to replace the defunct Opéra du Québec, which had operated from 1971 to 1975, this Canadian company gives four productions a year at the Salle Wilfrid Pelletier (cap. 3,000), which opened in 1967. The artistic director is Jean-Paul Jeannotte.

Opéra du Rhin

Formed in 1972, the company is based at the opera house (cap. 1,000) in Strasbourg, but also gives performances in Colmar and Mulhouse. The annual season runs from September to July. Musical directors have included Alain Lombard and Theodor Guschlbauer.

Opera Factory

A chamber company formed by the producer David Freeman in Sydney in 1973, in Zürich in 1976 and in London in 1981. It gives small-scale and often highly controversial modern-style productions. The orchestra is the London Sinfonietta, and the musical director is Paul Daniel.

Opera films

Operatic films are nearly as old as the cinema itself, many being made even in the silent days; the first was *Faust* in 1903. The first sound film of an opera was an Italian *Pagliacci*, since when a large number have been made, especially in Italy and Russia. Some have been content to reproduce a theatrical performance on the large screen, whilst others have adopted a large-scale, often open-air approach, removing the work entirely from its theatrical setting. Amongst the most successful of earlier operatic films were *Louise* with Grace Moore and Georges Thill, *Pagliacci* with Tito Gobbi and Gina Lollobrigida, the Thomas Beecham/Robert Helpmann *The Tales of Hoffmann* and Stroyeva's *Boris Godunov*. More recently, Zeffirelli's *La Traviata* and Josef Losey's *Don Giovanni* have met with great success, as has Ingmar Bergman's *The Magic Flute* and Franco Rosi's *Carmen*. No operas have been written specifically for the cinema, but mention may be made of Korngold's *Romeo and Juliet*, a mini-opera written for the film *Give Us This Night* (1936).

Opera Guild of Greater Miami

Founded in 1941 by the tenor Arturo di Filippi, it gives performances at the Miami Beach Auditorium (cap. 3,700) and at the Dade County Auditorium (cap. 2,550). The repertory is largely traditional. The musical director is Emerson Buckley.

Opéra-lyrique (French for 'lyric opera')

The term was used in France in the second half of the 19th century to describe an opera somewhat lighter and less formal in style than grand opera but more serious than opéra-comique. It was used to define many of the works of Gounod, Thomas and Massenet.

Opera North

Originally called English National Opera North, the company began operations on 15 November 1978 as an off-shoot of the English National Opera. The company is now completely autonomous. Based at the Grand Theatre, Leeds (cap. 1,534), the musical director is David Lloyd Jones.

Opera Northern Ireland

The company gives short international seasons at the Frank Matcham-designed Grand Opera House in Belfast. The orchestra is the Ulster Orchestra, and musical directors have included Alun Francis and Kenneth Montgomery.

Opera-oratorio

A term describing a work which partakes of the qualities of both opera and oratorio, being of a largely static nature but setting a dramatic text and intended to be staged. Much the best known example is Stravinsky's *Oedipus Rex*.

Opera Rara

A British company founded to promote the revival of long-forgotten operas, mainly of the early 19th century. Originally devoted to giving staged or concert performances, it has recently concentrated on recordings, particularly of Donizetti. The artistic director is Patric Schmid.

Opera recordings

The gramophone has, from its earliest days, played an important part in operatic life, as indeed opera and opera singers have played an important part in the gramophone's life: it was well observed that "Caruso made the gramophone and the gramophone made Caruso". The earliest operatic recordings were of extracts made on cylinders in the mid-1890s, but these were soon superseded by those made on Emile Berliner's shellac plate, the familiar flat disc. The first 'complete' opera recording was a heavily abridged *Il Trovatore* made between 1903 and 1906; very soon afterwards Leoncavallo conducted an almost uncut recording of *Pagliacci*. The advent of electrical, as opposed to the earlier acoustic, recordings in the 1920s marked a great improvement in sound quality, but the gramophone did not fully come into its own until the appearance of the long-playing record in 1950 made complete opera recordings a far more practical proposition – now even more so with the advent of the Compact Disc. Since then, the gramophone has made a vast contribution to the widening of the repertory – some 760 different operas have been commercially recorded – and to making opera more widely accessible.

Against the great benefits to opera brought by the gramophone must be set some drawbacks and dangers. The major record companies are now so important and powerful that their plans are sometimes allowed to dictate both repertory and casting to opera houses; they have been largely responsible for the evils of the 'star system', which has come near to destroying the ideal of ensemble performance. Also, modern technology is now so advanced that the finished product can often sound clinical, artificial and devoid of any drama or spontaneity. In addition, recording techniques are such that singers can be (and often are) made to sound a great deal better than they actually are.

See Appendix 2 for a listing of all commercially recorded operas.

Opera semiseria (Italian for 'half-serious work')

The term originated in the mid-18th century with Piccinni's *La Buona Figliuola* to describe a work of a largely light character but which also contains some serious elements. Famous 19th-century examples include *La Gazza Ladra* and *Linda di Chamounix*.

Opera seria (Italian for 'serious work')

The principal operatic form of the 18th century, it described an opera on a serious subject with certain fixed conventions, such as formalised emotions, elaborate da capo arias and plots involving characters from mythology or ancient history. The drama usually revolved around a conflict between love and duty, as epitomised by the texts of Apostolo Zeno* and Pietro Metastasio*. The form soon developed a rigid formality which was both dramatically suffocating and highly artificial. In reaction against this the Singspiel developed in Germany and opera-buffa in Italy.

Opera Society of Washington

Founded in 1956, it now performs at the Kennedy Center for the Performing Arts (cap. 2,200), which opened in September 1971. It pursues one of the most enterprising repertory policies of any American company. Artistic directors have included George London, and musical directors Paul Calloway.

Operatic deaths

Many operatic characters meet their ends – invariably untimely ones – during the course of the story. Some of these come by their deaths in the most bizarre and extraordinary fashion. Below are listed some of the more recherché deaths to be found in operatic plots.

- Fenella in Auber's *La Muette de Portici* jumps from the royal palace of Naples into the erupting mouth of Mount Vesuvius.
- Rachel in Halévy's *La Juive* is thrown into a vat of boiling oil (on the orders of her father).
- Iris in Mascagni's *Iris* throws herself into a sewer.
- Adriana in Cilea's *Adriana Lecouvreur* dies from smelling a bunch of poisoned violets.
- Sélika in Meyerbeer's *L'Africaine* dies from inhaling the poisonous scent of the Manchineel tree.
- Lakmé in Delibes' *Lakmé* dies from eating the poisonous Datura leaf.
- Manfredo and Avito in Montemezzi's *L'Amore dei Tre Re* die from kissing the poison-smeared lips of a dead woman.
- Wally and Hagenbach in Catalani's *La Wally* are killed in an avalanche.
- Owen in Britten's *Owen Wingrave* dies from sleeping in a haunted room.
- Antonia in Offenbach's *Les Contes d'Hoffmann* sings herself to death.
- Zampa in Hérold's *Zampa* is drowned by the hand of a statue.
- Cio-Cio-San in Puccini's *Madama Butterfly* commits hara-kiri (mercifully off-stage).
- Boris in Shostakovich's *Lady Macbeth of Mtsensk* dies from rat poison administered by his daughter-in-law in a dish of mushrooms
- Aida and Radamès in Verdi's *Aiда* are buried alive.
- Baron Scarpia in Puccini's *Tosca* is stabbed by an opera singer.
- Vrenchen and Sali in Delius' *A Village Romeo and Juliet* commit suicide by drowning in a barge floating down the river.
- Billy in Britten's *Billy Budd* is hung from the yard-arm.
- Marietta in Korngold's *Die Tote Stadt* is strangled with her own hair.
- Guenievre in Chausson's *Le Roi Arthus* strangles herself with her own hair.
- Chim-Fen in Leoni's *L'Oracolo* is strangled with his own pig-tail.
- Gherardo in Pizzetti's *Fra Gherardo* is burnt at the stake.
- Robbins in Gershwin's *Porgy and Bess* is killed with a cotton-hook.
- Leonora in Verdi's *Il Trovatore* dies from poison sucked from a ring.
- Pentheus in Henze's *The Bassarids* is torn to pieces by a group of women (including his mother).
- Magda Sorel in Menotti's *The Consul* commits suicide by gassing herself.
- King Dodon in Rimsky-Korsakov's *The Golden Cockerel* dies from being pecked on the head by a cockerel.
- Most of the cast in Poulenc's *Dialogues des Carmélites* are guillotined.

Operetta (Italian for 'little work') There is no exact definition of the term operetta. It describes a musical stage work in lighter operatic style, usually with spoken dialogue and nearly always of a comic nature. A great deal of musical snobbery exists on the subject of operetta: many people (but seldom professional musicians) fall into the error of equating lightness of style and subject with lightness of quality. By any criteria, the four major exponents of the genre (Offenbach, Sullivan, Johann Strauss II and Lehár) were master composers, and the finest operettas are of vastly superior musical quality to, for example, the garbage produced by the minor Italian verismo composers.

Although virtually every country (except perhaps Italy) has its own operetta tradition, there are four principal schools. Viennese operetta is exemplified by Lehár, J. Strauss, Millöcker, Kálmán and Zeller; French operetta is dominated by Offenbach, the considerable contribution of Lecocq, Planquette and especially Messager often being overlooked. English operetta is synonymous with Sullivan; virtually no other composers' works have survived. In Spain, zarzuela* has had many fine exponents, particularly Bretón and Vives. Most opera companies carry a few operettas in their repertories and some (such as the Vienna Volksoper, the D'Oyly Carte Opera Company and New Sadler's Wells Opera) have specialised in it.

See also **Opéra-bouffe; Tonadilla; Zarzuela**

Opernball, Der (*The Opera Ball*)
Operetta in three acts by Heuberger. 1st perf. Vienna, 5 Jan 1898; libr. by Waldeberg and Viktor Léon, after Delacour and Hennequin's *Les Dominos Roses*. By far Heuberger's most successful work, it is still regularly performed in German-speaking countries.

Opernprobe, Die (*The Opera Rehearsal*)
or **Die Vornehmen Dilettanten**
Comic opera in one act by Lortzing. 1st perf. Frankfurt, 20 Jan 1851; libr. by the composer, after J. F. Jünger's *Die Komödie aus dem Stegreif*. Lortzing's last opera, it is an amusing little piece which is still sometimes performed in Germany. [R]

O Prêtes de Baal
Mezzo aria for Fidès in Act V of Meyerbeer's *Le Prophète*.

Oprichnik, The
Opera in two acts by Tchaikovsky. 1st perf. St Petersburg, 24 April 1874; libr. by the composer, after Ivan Ivanovich Lazhechnikov. Tchaikovsky's first opera to be publicly performed, it incorporates music from the discarded *The Voyevoda*. It is nowadays only very rarely performed, even in Russia. [R]

O quante volte
Soprano aria for Giulietta in Act I of Bellini's *I Capuleti e i Montecchi*. Bellini borrowed the music from his earlier *Adelson e Salvini*.

Oracolo, L' (*The Oracle*)
Opera in one act by Leoni. 1st perf. London, 28 June 1905; libr. by Camille Zanoni, after Chester Bailey Fernald's *The Cat and the Cherub*. Principal roles: Uin-Sci (bass), Ah-Yoe (sop), Chim-Fen (bar), San-Lui (ten), Hu-Tsin (bass), Hua-Qui (mezzo). Leoni's only work still to be at all remembered, its lurid story of murder, madness and mayhem in San Francisco's Chinatown ensured it an initial success and disguised its banal musical qualities. Nowadays it is hardly ever performed.

Plot: San Francisco, 19th century. The evil opium dealer Chim-Fen abducts the child of the rich merchant Hu-Tsin and offers to 'find' the child in return for marriage to Ah-Yoe. Chim-Fen murders Ah-Yoe's beloved San-Lui, causing her to go insane. San-Lui's father Uin-Sci (the oracle of the opera's title) kills Chim-Fen by strangling him with his own pig-tail. [R]

Ora di morte

Soprano/baritone duet for Lady Macbeth and Macbeth in Act III of Verdi's *Macbeth*. Written for the revised version, it replaced Macbeth's cabaletta, 'Vada in fiamme'.

Ora e per sempre addio

Tenor monologue for Otello in Act II of Verdi's *Otello*.

Orange Festival

An annual open-air summer opera festival in Provence (France), which was founded in 1971 by Jacques Bourgeois and Jean Darnel. Performances –usually of 'spectacular' works such as *Aida* – are given at the Roman amphitheatre (cap. 13,000). Top international casts are engaged and the setting is majestic, although the Mistral presents an occasional acoustical hazard.

Orchestration

The art of writing for the orchestra. The fathers of modern operatic orchestration are usually regarded as Mayr and Berlioz. Subsequent masters of orchestration have included Richard Strauss, Rimsky-Korsakov, late Verdi and Ravel.

Or co' dadi

Soldiers' chorus in Act III of Verdi's *Il Trovatore*.

Orefice, Giacomo *(1865–1922)*

Italian composer. He wrote a number of operas in verismo style, of which the most successful included *Chopin* (Milan 1901; libr. A. Orvieto) and *Il Mosè* (Genoa 1905; libr. Orvieto). He was also a leading advocate and editor of early music.

Oresteia

Operatic trilogy by Taneyev. 1st perf. St Petersburg, 29 Oct 1895; libr. by Venkstern, after Aeschylus' Oresteian Trilogy. Principal roles: Agamemnon (bass), Clytemnestra (mezzo), Aegisthus (bar), Cassandra (sop), Elektra (sop), Orestes (ten), Apollo (bar), Pallas Athene (sop). Taneyev's only operatic work, it is more a three-act opera than a trilogy. Although it contains some fine music, it is almost never performed. [R]

Orestes

The son of Agamemnon and Clytemnestra appears in many operas, including:
(1) Baritone role in Richard Strauss' *Elektra*.
(2) Baritone role in Gluck's *Iphigénie en Tauride*.
(3) Mezzo trouser-role in Offenbach's *La Belle Hélène*.
(4) Baritone role in Milhaud's *Les Choëphores*.
(5) Tenor role in Taneyev's *Oresteia*.

Orfeide, L'

Operatic triptych by Malipiero, comprising *La Morte delle Maschere*, *Sette Canzoni* and *Orfeo, ovvero L'Ottava Canzone*. 1st perf. (Part II only) Paris, 10 July 1920. 1st complete perf. Düsseldorf, 31 Oct 1925; libr. by the composer. Malipiero's finest stage work.

Orfeo, L'

See Favola d'Orfeo, La

Orfeo ed Euridice *(Orpheus and Eurydice)*

Works of this title include:
(1) Opera in three acts by Gluck. 1st perf. Vienna, 5 Oct 1762; libr. by Ranieri de' Calzabigi. Revised version,

Orphée et Eurydice 1st perf. Paris, 2 Aug 1774; libr. revised by Pierre-Louis Moline. Principal roles: Orfeo (mezzo/ten), Amor (sop), Euridice (sop). Gluck's most famous work and his first reform opera.

Plot: The musician Orfeo mourns the death of his beloved wife, Euridice. Amor tells him that Zeus will allow him to go to the underworld to plead for her return, but if she is released he must not look back on her until they have returned to the living world. Orfeo charms the Furies with the beauty of his singing and finds Euridice amongst the blessed spirits. He leads her away, but his seeming indifference in not looking at her makes Euridice threaten to go back to Hades. Her distress moves him to look at her and she sinks back into the shadows. Orfeo laments his loss and Amor, taking pity on him, once again brings Euridice back to life. [R]

(2) Opera in four acts by Haydn. Also known as *L'Anima del Filosofo* (*The Spirit of the Philosopher*). 1st perf. 1951 (composed 1791); libr. by C. F. Badini. Principal roles: Orfeo (ten), Euridice (sop), Creonte (bass), Genio (sop). Haydn's last opera, intended for performance in London, it contains some of his greatest stage music but is unaccountably almost never performed.

Orff, Carl *(1895–1982)*
German composer. His stage works were intended to free opera from what he regarded as late 19th-century excesses, and are heavily dependent on simple rhythms and on traditional folk melodies. His operas are *Der Mond**, *Die Kluge**, his most successful work, *Die Bernauerin**, *Antigonae**, *Trionfo d'Aphrodite**, *Oedipus der Tyrann**, *Ludus de Nato Infante Mirificus* (Stuttgart 1960; libr. composer), *Prometheus* (Stuttgart 1966; libr. after

Aeschylus) and *De Temporum Fine Comoedia* (Salzburg 1973) [R].

Orlando
Opera in three acts by Handel. 1st perf. London, 23 Jan 1733; libr. by Grazio Braccioli, after Lodovico Ariosto's *Orlando Furioso*. Principal roles: Orlando (c-ten), Angelica (sop), Dorinda (sop), Zoroastro (bass), Medoro (ten). Telling of Orlando's struggle against love and insanity and his realisation that his destiny is to fight in defence of Christendom, it has received a number of performances in recent years. [R]

Orlando Furioso
Opera in three acts by Vivaldi. 1st perf. Venice, autumn 1727; libr. by Grazio Braccioli, after Lodovico Ariosto. Principal roles: Orlando (mezzo), Angelica (sop), Alcina (mezzo), Ruggiero (b-bar), Bradamante (mezzo), Medoro (ten), Astolfo (bass). Vivaldi's second setting of the Orlando story, it contains some magnificent music, but is almost never performed. [R]

Orlando Paladino
Opera in three acts by Haydn. 1st perf. Esterháza, 6 Dec 1782; libr. by Nunziato Porta, after Lodovico Ariosto's *Orlando Furioso*. Principal roles: Orlando (ten), Angelica (sop), Alcina (mezzo), Medoro (ten), Pasquale (bar), Rodomonte (bar), Eurilla (sop), Charon (bass). Described as a *dramma eroïcomico*, it combines serious and comic elements and is one of Haydn's best operas. After a long period of neglect, it has received a number of performances in the last decade.

Plot: Rodomonte, King of Barbary, seeking the deranged Orlando, learns that Angelica, Queen of Cathay, and her lover Medoro are in a nearby castle. Angelica fears that Orlando will kill Medoro and seeks the aid of the sorceress Alcina. Rodomonte challenges Orlando but they are told by the shepherdess Eurilla that Angelica and Medoro are attempting to escape by sea. Orlando thwarts their escape and is taken by Alcina to the River Lethe to cure his madness. At Alcina's command, Charon's spell of madness is lifted and Orlando and Rodomonte are reconciled. Angelica and Medoro can now marry, and Eurilla marries Orlando's squire Pasquale. [R]

Orlofsky, Prince

Mezzo trouser-role in Johann Strauss' *Die Fledermaus*. He is an easily-bored young Russian prince. The role is occasionally sung by a tenor.

Ormandy, Eugene *(b Jenö Blau)* *(1899–1985)*

Hungarian conductor and violinist, long resident in the United States. Best known as a symphonic conductor, his operatic appearances were very rare.

Ormindo, L'

Opera in three acts by Cavalli. 1st perf. Venice, 1644; libr. by Giovanni Faustini. Principal roles: Ormindo (ten), Erisbe (mezzo), Ariadeno (bass), Osmano (bass), Erice (ten), Sicle (sop). After more than 300 years of complete neglect, it has been regularly performed in recent years, usually in the edition prepared by Raymond Leppard.

Plot: North Africa. Erisbe, Queen of Morocco and Fez, elopes with the Tunisian prince Ormindo. Erisbe's husband Ariadeno orders the pair to be poisoned, but his captain, Osmano, substitutes a sleeping draft. When the lovers waken, the repentant Ariadeno gives up both his throne and his wife to Ormindo. [R]

Ornamentation

The art of embellishing the vocal line. *See* Appoggiatura; Coloratura; Fioritura

Oronte

Tenor role in Verdi's *I Lombardi*. He is the son of the tyrant of Antioch.

Orontea

Opera in three acts by Cesti. 1st perf. Venice, 1649; libr. by Cinto Andrea Cicognini. Principal roles: Orontea (mezzo), Alidoro (bar), Salindra (sop), Corindo (c-ten), Giacinta (mezzo), Aristea (mezzo), Tibrino (sop), Creonte (bass). One of Cesti's most successful works, it is still occasionally performed. [R]

Oroveso

Bass role in Bellini's *Norma*. Norma's father, he is the Druid high priest.

Orphée aux Enfers *(Orpheus in the Underworld)*

Operetta in four (originally two) acts by Offenbach. 1st perf. Paris, 21 Oct 1858; libr. by Héctor Crémieux and Ludovic Halévy. Revised version, 1st perf. Paris, 7 Feb 1874. Principal roles: Eurydice (sop), Orpheus (ten), Pluto (ten), Jupiter (bar), Public Opinion/ Calliope (mezzo), John Styx (ten), Diana (mezzo), Cupid (sop), Venus (sop), Juno (mezzo), Mars (bass). Perhaps the most enduringly popular of all French operettas, it is an hilarious burlesque of Greek mythology as well as a satire on Second Empire society.

Plot: Eurydice is bored to death with her husband Orpheus and his everlasting fiddle playing and has been having an affair with the shepherd Aristeus. She is bitten by a snake and when Aristeus reveals himself as Pluto she is delighted to accompany him to the underworld. Orpheus, in any event in love with a shepherdess, is only too happy to see the back of her, but Public Opinion insists that he try to claim her back. Jupiter's attempts to instil good behaviour into the other deities are thwarted first by their reminding him of his own innumerable amorous adventures and then by the arrival of Orpheus, who pleads (unwillingly) to have Eurydice back. Jupiter decides to investigate the affair personally and descends to the underworld with the rest of the gods. Eurydice, kept in seclusion and guarded by the dim-witted former King of Boeotia John Styx, is bored and accepts the advances of Jupiter, who disguises himself as a fly to get into her room. Orpheus arrives and Jupiter allows him to have Eurydice back provided he does not turn and look at her. Then, to make sure that he does, he hurls a thunderbolt at Orpheus' feet. Eurydice decides to become a Bacchante, and all join in the famous Can-Can. [R]

Orr, Robin *(b Robert Kemsley) (b 1909)*
British composer. He wrote two operas: *Full Circle* (Perth 1968; libr. S. G. Smith) and *Hermiston* (Edinburgh 1975; libr. B. Bryden, after Robert Louis Stevenson's *Weir of Hermiston*).

Or sai chi l'onore
Soprano aria for Donna Anna in Act I of Mozart's *Don Giovanni*.

Orsini, Maffio
Mezzo trouser-role in Donizetti's *Lucrezia Borgia*. He is Genaro's companion.

Ortel, Hermann
Baritone comprimario role in Wagner's *Die Meistersinger von Nürnberg*. A soap boiler, he is one of the masters.

Ortlinde
Soprano role in Wagner's *Die Walküre*. She is one of the Valkyries.

Ortrud
Mezzo role in Wagner's *Lohengrin*. She is Telramund's wife.

Osborne, Nigel *(b 1948)*
British composer. His stage works include *Hell's Angels* (London 1986) and *The Electrification of the Soviet Union* (Glyndebourne 1987; libr. Craig Raine after Boris Pasternak's *The Last Summer*).

Oscar
Soprano trouser-role in Verdi's *Un Ballo in Maschera*. He is Gustavus' page.

O silver moon
Soprano aria for Rusalka in Act I of Dvořák's *Rusalka*.

Oslo
See Norwegian Opera

Osmin
Bass role in: (1) Mozart's *Die Entführung aus dem Serail*. He is the harem keeper. (2) Mozart's *Zaïde*. He is captain of the Sultan's guard. (3) Haydn's *L'Incontro Improvviso*.

O soave fanciulla
Soprano/tenor duet for Mimì and Rodolfo in Act I of Puccini's *La Bohème*.

O souverain
Tenor aria for Rodrigo in Act II of Massenet's *Le Cid*.

Ossian

A probably mythical third-century Gaelic bard. The 'rediscovery' of his works in the 1760s caused a sensation, which their exposure as the work of James Macpherson did little to abate. They began the fashion for romantic subjects set in Scotland and had a considerable influence on the romantic movement as a whole. The most important Ossianic operas are Lesueur's *Ossian* and Méhul's *Uthal**.

Ostrava Opera (Ostrau when it was part of Austria-Hungary)

Opera in this town in Czechoslovakia is given at the Zdeněk Nejedlý State Theatre, which opened in 1908 and was rebuilt in 1948. Musical directors have included Jaroslav Vogel, Zdeněk Chalabala, Bohumil Gregor and Zdeněk Košler.

Ostrčil, Otakar *(1879–1935)*

Czech composer and conductor. He wrote eight operas, influenced by the styles of Fibich and Mahler. They are the unfinished *The Fishermen* (*Rybáři*, 1894), *Jan Zhořelecký* (1898), the unfinished *Cymbelin* (1899; libr. after Shakespeare), *The Death of Vlasta* (*Vlasty Skon*, Prague 14 Dec 1904; libr. K. Pippich), *Kunál's Eyes* (*Kunálovy Oči*, Prague 25 Nov 1908; libr. K. Mašek, after Julius Zeyer), *The Bud* (*Poupě*, Prague 25 Jan 1912; libr. F. X. Svoboda), *The Legend of Erin* (*Legenda z Erinu*, Brno 16 June 1921; libr. Zeyer) and *Johnny's Kingdom* (*Honzovo Království*, Brno 26 May 1934; libr. J. Maránek, after Tolstoy's *The Tale of Ivan the Jester*), by far his most successful work. He was musical director of the Prague National Theatre (1920–35) and conducted the first performances of *The Excursions of Mr Brouček* and *Shvanda the Bagpiper*.

Osud

See Fate

Otello

Works of this title based on Shakespeare's *Othello* include:

(1) Opera in three acts by Rossini. Subtitled *Il Moro di Venezia* (*The Moor of Venice*). 1st perf. Naples, 4 Dec 1816; libr. by Marchese Francesco Beria di Salsa. Principal roles: Otello (ten), Desdemona (sop), Iago (ten), Rodrigo (ten), Elmiro (bass), Emilia (mezzo). Although it is a travesty of Shakespeare, it contains some of Rossini's finest and most beautiful serious music, particularly in the last act. Enormously popular throughout the 19th century, it is rarely performed today.

Plot: Otello is in love with Desdemona, but she has been promised to Rodrigo. Otello interrupts the wedding ceremony, and Desdemona is locked away by her father Elmiro. Iago contrives to persuade Otello that Desdemona is unfaithful to him with Rodrigo, and Otello challenges Rodrigo to a duel. Otello is banished but secretly returns and kills Desdemona. He and Iago both kill themselves in remorse. [R]

(2) Opera in four acts by Verdi. 1st perf. Milan, 5 Feb 1887; libr. by Arrigo Boito. Principal roles: Otello (ten), Desdemona (sop), Iago (bar), Emilia (mezzo), Cassio (ten), Lodovico (bass). Verdi's last and finest tragic opera, it has been acknowledged from its appearance as one of the greatest of all music-dramas. It is faithful to Shakespeare's plot, except that the Venetian act is omitted and Iago is largely stripped of all motivation, acting solely because it is his nature to be evil.

Plot: 15th-century Cyprus. Otello, the Moorish governor of Cyprus, returns through a storm, having

conquered the Turkish infidels. His evil
ensign Iago is jealous of the planned
promotion of Cassio, and through a
series of cunning manoeuvers makes it
appear to Otello that Cassio is having
an affair with his wife Desdemona.
Iago's insidious and poisonous
innuendos arouse Otello's jealousy and
when he is recalled to Venice, he
strangles Desdemona in her bed. Iago's
wife Emilia reveals her husband's
treachery and Otello kills himself. [R]

O terra addio
Soprano/tenor duet for Aida and
Radamès in Act IV of Verdi's *Aida*.
The final scene of the opera.

O toi Palerme
Bass aria for Procida in Act I of Verdi's
Les Vêpres Siciliennes.

Ottakar
(1) Baritone role in Weber's *Der
Freischütz*. He is the local prince. (2)
Tenor role in J. Strauss' *Der
Zigeunerbaron*. He is Mirabella's son.

Ottavia
Mezzo role in Monteverdi's
L'Incoronazione di Poppea. She is
Nero's wife.

Ottavio, Don
Tenor role in Mozart's *Don Giovanni*.
He is Donna Anna's fiancé.

Ottone
Baritone role in Monteverdi's
L'Incoronazione di Poppea. He is in
love with Poppea.

Ottone, Rè di Germania (*Otto, King of Germany*)
Opera in three acts by Handel. 1st perf.
London, 12 Jan 1723; libr. by Nicola

Francesco Haym, after S. B.
Pallavicino's libretto for Lotti's *Teofane*.
Very rarely performed.

O tu che in seno
Tenor aria for Don Alvaro in Act III of
Verdi's *La Forza del Destino*.

Our Man in Havana
Opera in three acts by Williamson. 1st
perf. London, 2 July 1963; libr. by
Sidney Gilliat, after Graham Greene's
novel. Principal roles: Bramble (ten),
Milly (sop), Beatrice (sop), Segura (bar),
Dr Hasselbacher (bass). Williamson's
first major opera, it is a melodrama
with satirical overtones. Williamson
arranged an orchestral suite from the
opera's music in 1966.

Où va la jeune Hindoue?
Soprano aria (the Bell Song) for Lakmé
in Act II of Delibes' *Lakmé*.

Overture (derived from the French *ouverture*, 'opening')
The instrumental music which is played
before the start of an opera. It was
originally simply a short prelude, but
was developed by Lully into a longer
piece with a slow section in dotted
rhythm followed by a faster section.
The Italian overture, developed by A.
Scarlatti, was in three sections: fast-
slow-fast. In the 19th century, the
overture became more complex, often
being developed symphonically and
usually employing thematic material
from the opera itself. A number of
famous overtures such as *Ruslan and
Ludmila*, *Zampa*, *La Forza del Destino*
and many by Rossini are regularly
played in the concert hall, and some
composers – such as Auber – are
nowadays remembered almost solely for
their overtures. The overture is usually
called *sinfonia* in Italy.

O welche Lust

Chorus of prisoners in Act I of
Beethoven's *Fidelio*.

Owen Wingrave

Opera in two acts by Britten (Op 85).
1st perf. BBC TV, 24 May 1971. 1st
stage perf. London, 10 May 1973; libr.
by Myfanwy Piper after Henry James.
Principal roles: Owen (bar), Kate Julian
(mezzo), Coyle (bar), Mrs Coyle (sop),
Miss Wingrave (sop), Mrs Julian (sop),
Lechmere (ten), Sir Philip Wingrave
(ten). Perhaps the most important opera
written specifically for television, it gave
Britten the opportunity to preach his
life-long pacifism.

Plot: 19th-century England. Owen
and Lechmere study with the military
cram Coyle, but Owen is pacifist and
wants nothing to do with war. He
returns to his country seat, where his
family, with their long military
tradition, are horrified when he tells
them of his refusal to join the army,
and he is disinherited. His fiancée,
Kate, accuses him of cowardice and
dares him to sleep in the haunted
room. He does so and is found dead in
the morning. [R]

Ozawa, Seiji *(b 1935)*

Japanese conductor. Best known as a
symphonic conductor, his operatic
appearances have been infrequent. He
conducted the first performance of
Messiaen's *St François d'Assise*.

Ozean, zu Ungeheuer! (often

known by its English translation as
'Ocean thou mighty monster')
Soprano aria for Reiza in Act II of
Weber's *Oberon*.

O zittre nicht

Soprano aria for the Queen of the
Night in Act I of Mozart's *Die
Zauberflöte*.

P

Pace, pace

Soprano aria for Leonora in Act IV of Verdi's *La Forza del Destino*.

Pacini, Giovanni *(1796–1867)*

Italian composer. One of the most prolific and successful Italian composers of his day, he wrote over 70 operas, virtually all of them now forgotten. Known as '*il maestro della cabaletta*', his melodies are strong and eminently singable and he made considerable advances in harmony and orchestration. However, his operas lack real dramatic insight and are not on the same level as those of Donizetti, Bellini and Mercadante. The most successful of them include *Adelaide e Comingio* (Milan 30 Dec 1817; libr. Gaetano Rossi), *Alessandro nell'Indie* (Naples 29 Sept 1824; libr. Andrea Leone Tottola, after Pietro Metastasio), *L'Ultimo Giorno di Pompei* (Naples 19 Nov 1825; libr. Tottola), *Niobe* (Naples 19 Nov 1826; libr. Tottola), *Il Talismano* (Milan 10 June 1829; libr. G. Barbieri, after Sir Walter Scott's *The Talisman*), *Ivanhoe* (Venice 19 March 1832; libr. Rossi, after Scott), *Saffo**, his finest work, *La Fidanzata Corsa* (Naples 10 Dec 1842; libr. Salvatore Cammarano, after Prosper Mérimée's *Colomba*), *Maria Tudor* (Palermo 11 Feb 1843; libr. L. Tarantini, after Victor Hugo's *Marie Tudor*), *Medea* (Palermo 28 Nov 1843; libr. B. Castiglia) and *Lorenzo de' Medici* (Venice 4 March 1845; libr. Francesco Maria Piave). His autobiography, *Le Mie Memorie Artistiche*, was published in 1865.

Paderewski, Ignacy *(1860–1941)*

Polish pianist, composer and statesman. One of the greatest pianists of his age (and the first Prime Minister of the recreated state of Poland in 1919), he also wrote one opera, the successful *Manru**.

Padmâvatî

Opera-ballet in two acts by Roussel (Op 18). 1st perf. Paris, 1 June 1923; libr. by Louis Laloy. Principal roles: Padmâvatî (mezzo), Alaouddin (bar), Ratan-sen (ten), Brahmin (ten). Roussel's most successful stage work, it is notable for the prominent place given to dance.

Plot: Tchitor (India), 1303. Ratan-sen, King of Tchitor, is offered an alliance by the Mogul sultan Alaouddin, who demands Ratan-sen's wife Padmâvatî as a pledge. Ratan-sen reluctantly agrees, but when a Brahmin arrives to ask that she be handed over, the mob riots and he is torn to pieces. Ratan-sen's troops are defeated by Alaouddin, but rather than have the betrayal of her on Ratan-sen's conscience, she stabs him. By custom, she must therefore die on his funeral pyre. [R]

Padre Guardiano

Bass role in Verdi's *La Forza del Destino*. He is the abbot of the monastery.

Paer, Ferdinando *(1771–1839)*

Italian composer, resident in Paris from 1807. He wrote some 40 operas, achieving his greatest successes in opera semiseria. His most successful works include *Griselda* (Parma Jan 1798; libr. Angelo Anelli), *Camilla* (Vienna 28 Feb 1799; libr. G. Carpani), *Achille* (Vienna 6 June 1801; libr. Giovanni da Gamerra), *Sargino* (Dresden 26 May 1803; libr. Giuseppe Maria Foppa), *Leonora**, *Agnese di Fitzhenry* (Parma Oct 1809; libr. L. Buonavoglia) and *Le Maître de Chapelle**, his most enduring work. He was also a distinguished teacher, whose pupils included Liszt, whose youthful *Don Sanche** he helped to complete.

Paganini

Operetta in three acts by Lehár. 1st perf. Vienna, 30 Oct 1925; libr. by Paul Knepler and Béla Jenbach. Principal roles: Paganini (ten), Maria Anna (sop), Prince Felice (ten), Bella (mezzo), Beppo (bar). Loosely based on the life of the violinist and composer Niccolò Paganini (1782–1840), it is still regularly performed in German-speaking countries. [R]

Pagano

Bass role in Verdi's *I Lombardi*. He is Arvino's brother.

Pagliacci (*Clowns*)

Opera in prologue and two acts by Leoncavallo. 1st perf. Milan, 21 May 1892; libr. by the composer. Principal roles: Canio (ten), Nedda (sop), Tonio (bar), Silvio (bar), Beppe (ten). Leoncavallo's masterpiece, it is based on a genuine incident which the composer learnt of from his magistrate father. Almost invariably coupled with Mascagni's *Cavalleria Rusticana*, it is one of the finest of all verismo operas, and the 'play within a play' is handled with great theatrical skill.

Plot: Calabria, late 1860s. Tonio tells the audience that they are to witness a piece of true life. A theatrical troupe led by Canio arrives in the village, and the hunchbacked clown Tonio makes advances to Canio's wife Nedda, who repulses him with a whip. Tonio overhears Nedda planning to elope with her lover the farmer Silvio and informs Canio. During the evening's Commedia dell'Arte performance, Canio is struck by the similarities of the play and his own situation. He demands the name of Nedda's lover and stabs her when she refuses to tell him. Silvio hastens to her aid and is also stabbed by Canio. [R]

Pagliughi, Lina *(1907–80)*

Italian soprano, particularly associated with lighter Italian roles, especially Gilda. She possessed a beautiful, limpid voice which she used with an outstanding technique. Her husband Primo Montanari (1895–1972) was a successful tenor.

Paisiello, Giovanni *(1740–1816)*

Italian composer. The finest Italian composer of the late 18th century, he wrote at least 83 operas in various styles, achieving his greatest successes in comedy. His operas are notable for their elegant and charming melodies, their deft orchestration and their sharp and sometimes sensitive delineation of character. His most important works include *L'Idolo Cinese* (Naples 1767; libr. Giovanni Battista Lorenzi), the enormously successful *Il Barbiere di Siviglia**, *Il Re Teodoro di Venezia**, *La Molinara* (Naples 1788; libr. Giovanni Palomba) and *Nina* (Naples 25 June 1789; libr. Lorenzi and Giuseppe Carpani, after Benoît Joseph Marsollier's libretto for Dalayrac) [R].

Palacio de las Bellas Artes, Mexico City

The theatre opened in 1934, and is the home of Mexico's Opera Nacional, which was founded in 1943 by the mezzo Fanny Anitúa (1887–1968). The annual season runs from September to June.

Palacios, Ernesto

Peruvian tenor, particularly associated with Rossini and Mozart roles. He possesses a small but well-projected voice of considerable range and remarkable agility and accuracy, which is used with an outstanding technique. One of the finest contemporary tenore di grazias.

Palermo

See Teatro Massimo, Palermo

Palestrina

Opera in three acts by Pfitzner. 1st perf. Munich, 12 June 1917; libr. by the composer. Principal roles: Palestrina (ten), Borromeo (bar), Ighino (sop), Silla (mezzo), Cardinal Morone (bar), Cardinal Navagerio (ten), Cardinal Madruscht (bass), Count Luna (bar), Pope Pius IV (bass). Pfitzner's masterpiece, it tells of the Italian composer Giovanni Pierluigi da Palestrina (1525–94) and his saving of the art of contrapuntal music at the time of the Counter-Reformation through the composition of his *Missa Papae Marcelli*. Notable for its detailed depiction of the Council of Trent and for its remarkable portrayal of Cardinal Borromeo, its infrequency of performance is totally inexplicable.

Plot: 1563. The Council of Trent is preparing to ban polyphonic music. The retired composer Palestrina resists the blandishments of Cardinal Borromeo to compose an exemplary new-style mass. The spirits of past masters encourage the tired and uncertain Palestrina and eventually his great mass is completed and acclaimed. His son Ighino,

however, is drawn to the new music and joins the Florentine Camerata. [R]

Paliashvili, Zakhary *(1871–1933)*

Russian (Georgian) composer. Perhaps the most important Georgian composer, his three operas are *Absolom and Etery* (*Abesalom da Eteri*, Tbilsi 1919; libr. P. Mirianashvili, after *Eteriani*) [R], which incorporates traditional Georgian music, *Twilight** and *Latavra* (Tbilsi 1928).

Palma, Piero de

Italian tenor, particularly associated with Italian character roles. Perhaps the finest and most famous of all postwar comprimario artists, he had a fine voice and an excellent stage presence.

Pamina

Soprano role in Mozart's *Die Zauberflöte*. She is the daughter of the Queen of the Night.

Panerai, Rolando *(b 1924)*

Italian baritone, particularly associated with the Italian repertory and with Mozart roles. A fine singing-actor with a beautiful voice, he enjoyed a remarkably long career, firstly as a Verdi baritone (excelling as Ford) and subsequently as a buffo. He created the title tole in Turchi's *Il Buon Soldato Svejk*.

Pang

Tenor role in Puccini's *Turandot*. He is one of the three courtiers.

Panizza, Ettore *(b Héctor) (1875–1967)*

Argentinian composer and conductor. He wrote four operas: *Il Fidanzato del Mare* (Buenos Aires 1897), *Medioevo Latino* (Genoa 1900), *Aurora* (Buenos

Aires 1908; libr. Luigi Illica), his most successful work, and *Bisanzio* (Genoa 1939). One of the leading conductors of the early 20th century, he was closely associated with La Scala, Milan, Covent Garden, the Metropolitan Opera, New York and the Teatro Colón, Buenos Aires. He conducted the first performances of Zandonai's *Conchita* and *Francesca da Rimini*, Wolf-Ferrari's *Sly* and Menotti's *The Island God*. His autobiography, *Medio Siglo de Vida Musical*, was published in 1952.

Pantomime (from the Greek
παντόμιμος, 'imitation of everything') A dramatic form in which the artists express themselves in dumb show. Many operas, particularly 18th-century intermezzi, include a pantomime character, for example Vespone in *La Serva Padrona*.

Paolino
Tenor role in Cimarosa's *Il Matrimonio Segreto*. A young lawyer, he is secretly married to Carolina.

Paolis, Alessio de *(1893–1964)*
Italian tenor, particularly associated with Italian character roles. He abandoned principal roles in 1932 and became one of the outstanding comprimario artists of the 20th century. Resident at the Metropolitan Opera, New York from 1938, he sang there until his death.

Paolo
(1) Baritone role in Verdi's *Simon Boccanegra*. He is the goldsmith Paolo Albiani. (2) Bass role in Wagner's *Rienzi*. He is the conspirator Paolo Orsini. (3) Tenor role in Rachmaninov's and Zandonai's *Francesca da Rimini*. He is Francesca's lover.

Papagena
Soprano role in Mozart's *Die Zauberflöte*. She is the girl reserved by Sarastro to be Papageno's wife.

Papageno
Baritone role in Mozart's *Die Zauberflöte*. He is a bird-catcher.

Paradise Lost
Opera by Penderecki. 1st perf. Chicago, 29 Nov 1978; libr. by Christopher Fry, after John Milton's poem. Penderecki's second opera.

Paride ed Elena (*Paris and Helen*)
Opera in five acts by Gluck. 1st perf. Vienna, 3 Nov 1770; libr. by Ranieri de' Calzabigi, after Ovid. Principal roles: Elena (sop), Paride (ten), Erasto (sop), Athene (sop). Never one of the more successful of Gluck's operas, it is more soft and tender than his other mature works, and lacks their dramatic power. Gluck incorporated parts of it into several later works. It is nowadays hardly ever performed.

Plot: Paris arrives in Greece to collect his reward of the most beautiful woman in the world, promised him for having picked Venus in the famous Judgement of Paris. His wooing of Helen is initially unsuccessful and he is ordered to depart. As he leaves, Helen confesses that she loves him and they flee together. They are pursued by the wrath of Athene but are succoured by Erasto (Cupid in disguise). [R]

Parigi o cara
Soprano/tenor duet for Violetta and Alfredo Germont in Act III of Verdi's *La Traviata*.

Paris

See Opéra Bastille, Paris; Opéra-Comique, Paris; Paris Opéra; Théâtre Bouffes-Parisiens; Théâtre des Champs-Elysée, Paris

Paris

The Trojan prince who steals Helen of Troy appears in a number of operas, including tenor roles in: (1) Offenbach's *La Belle Hélène*. (2) Tippett's *King Priam*. (3) Gluck's *Paride ed Elena*.

Pari siamo

Baritone monologue for Rigoletto in Act I of Verdi's *Rigoletto*.

Parisina

Works of this title based on Lord Byron's poem include:

(1) Opera in three acts by Donizetti. 1st perf. Florence, 17 March 1833; libr. by Felice Romani. Principal roles: Parisina (sop), Ugo (ten), Nicolò d'Este (bar), Stella de Tolomei (mezzo). Very successful at its appearance, it is still occasionally performed and is notable for its richly wrought final scene.

Plot: Nicolò d'Este deserts his mistress Stella de Tolomei (and mother of his son Ugo) to marry Parisina Malatesta. Ugo lives with them, and he and Parisina fall in love. After a year's secret affair, they are discovered and Nicolò has them sentenced to death. The imprisoned Ugo refuses to see his mother, and after his execution, Nicolò sends his still-warm heart to Parisina.

(2) Opera in three (originally four) acts by Mascagni. 1st perf. Milan, 15 Dec 1913; libr. by Gabriele d'Annunzio. Principal roles: Parisina (sop), Ugo (ten), Nicolò d'Este (bar), Stella (mezzo). It is nowadays forgotten.

Paris Opéra

The present opera house (cap. 2,131), which has the largest stage in the world, opened on 5 January 1875, replacing the previous theatre which opened in 1822 and was burnt down in 1873. It is often referred to as the Salle Garnier after its designer Jean-Louis-Charles Garnier (1825–98). Its greatest period was in the mid-19th century, where grand opera as epitomised by Meyerbeer reigned supreme. It drew all the great composers like a magnet, even those who despised its conventions, such as Wagner and Verdi, who called it 'la grande boutique'. In the postwar era, its artistic standards fell alarmingly until they were dramatically revived during Rolf Liebermann's administration (1971–80). Musical directors have included Messager, Silvio Varviso and Lothar Zagrosek.

Parlando (Italian for 'speaking')

An instruction to allow the vocal tone to approximate to that of ordinary speech.

Parma

See Teatro Regio, Parma

Parmi veder le lagrime

Tenor aria for the Duke of Mantua in Act II of Verdi's *Rigoletto*.

Parr, Gladys (1892–1988)

British mezzo, particularly associated with Wagner and Britten roles. The leading British mezzo of the inter-war period, she possessed a finely projected if not over-large voice, had excellent diction and was a good singing-actress. She created, for Britten, Florence Pike in *Albert Herring*, Miss Baggott in *The Little Sweep* and Mrs Noye in *Noye's Fludde*. Later in her career she turned to straight acting.

Parry, Sir Hubert *(1848–1918)*

British composer. Although best known as a choral composer, he also wrote one opera, *Guinevere* (1886; libr. U. Taylor).

Parry, Joseph *(1841–1903)*

British composer. He wrote six operas, of which *Blodwen* (Aberdare 1878; libr. R. Davies) [R Exc] was the first opera written to a Welsh libretto. His son Joseph Haydn (1864–94) was also a composer, who wrote three operas.

Parsifal

Opera in three acts by Wagner. 1st perf. Bayreuth, 26 July 1882; libr. by the composer after Wolfram von Eschenbach's *Parzival*. Principal roles: Parsifal (ten), Kundry (sop), Gurnemanz (bass), Amfortas (bar), Klingsor (b-bar), Titurel (bass). Wagner's last opera, he described it as *Buhnenweihfestspiel* (German for 'stage consecration festival play'). Its copyright forbade performances outside Bayreuth until the end of 1913, although this was occasionally infringed.

Plot: Many years previously, the vessel of the Holy Grail was given into the keeping of Titurel and his Christian knights, as was the Sacred Spear. These relics have been guarded in a fortified castle at Montsalvat, a beacon of Christianity in pagan Spain. Nearby lives the evil sorcerer Klingsor and the beautiful enchantress Kundry, enemies of the Christian knights. When Titurel grew old, he handed over the kingdom of the Grail to his son Amfortas who, determined to kill Klingsor, entered his enemy's magic garden. There, he fell prey to Kundry's charms and lost the Sacred Spear to Klingsor. Badly wounded by the spear, he continues to suffer – only the touch of the Sacred Spear will close the gash it made. A prophecy from the sanctuary of the Grail has told Amfortas that only a 'holy fool', unaware of sin, will be able to resist Kundry and regain the Sacred Spear. The plot of the opera deals with the fulfilment of this prophecy as a guileless youth, Parsifal, is brought to the venerable knight Gurnemanz, charged with killing a holy swan. When it becomes clear that the boy is innocent of the crime, and entirely ignorant of the world, he is selected to rescue the Sacred Spear. He triumphs, heals Amfortas, and is anointed King of the Grail by Gurnemanz. As Amfortas and the knights kneel to Parsifal, he baptises Kundry who finds at last the redemption of peaceful death. [R]

Partagez mes fleurs

Soprano aria (the Mad Scene) for Ophélie in Thomas' *Hamlet*.

Partenope

Opera in three acts by Handel. 1st perf. London, 24 Feb 1730; libr. by Silvio Stampiglia. Principal roles: Partenope (sop), Rosmira (mezzo), Emilio (ten), Arsace (c-ten), Armindo (sop), Ormonte (bass). Although never one of Handel's most successful operas, it is still performed from time to time. [R]

Parto, parto

Mezzo aria for Sextus in Act I of Mozart's *La Clemenza di Tito*. The solo obbligato instrument is a basset horn.

Pasatieri, Thomas *(b 1946)*

American composer. His 11 operas, which have met with some success in the United States, include *Calvary* (Washington 1971; libr. after William Butler Yeats), *The Trial of May Lincoln* (New York TV 14 Feb 1972; libr. A. H. Bailey), *Black Widow* (Seattle 2 March 1972; libr. composer, after M. de Unamuno's *Dos Madres*), *The*

Seagull (Houston 5 March 1974; libr. Kenward Elmslie, after Anton Chekhov), his finest work, *Ines de Castro* (Baltimore 1 April 1976; libr. Bernard Stambler) and *Washington Square* (Detroit 1 Oct 1976; libr. Elmslie, after Henry James).

Pasero, Tancredi *(1893–1983)*
Italian bass, particularly associated with the Italian repertory. Largely resident at La Scala, Milan, he was one of the finest basses of the inter-war period. He created the title role in Pizzetti's *Orsèolo*, the Miller in Giordano's *Il Rè* and Babilio in Mascagni's *Nerone*.

Pashkevich, Vasily *(1742–97)*
Russian composer. One of the most significant forerunners of the Russian nationalist school, his operas employ traditional folk material and make use of natural speech rhythms. The most important of his works include *Misfortune From a Carriage* (*Neschastye ot Karoty*, St Petersburg 1779; libr. J. B. Kryazhnin), *The Miser* (*Skupoy*, St Petersburg 1782; libr. Kryazhnin, after Molière's *L'Avare*) [R], *Fevey* (1786; libr. Catherine the Great) and *Fedul and His Children* (*Fedul s Det'mi*, 1791; libr. Catherine the Great and A. V. Khrapovitsky), which was written in collaboration with Martín y Soler.

Paskalis, Kostas *(b 1929)*
Greek baritone, particularly associated with Verdi roles, especially Macbeth. An intense singing-actor with a rich and powerful voice, he created Pentheus in *The Bassarids*. Director of the Greek National Opera (1988–).

Pasta, Giuditta *(b Negri) (1797–1865)*
Italian soprano. One of the greatest singers of the first half of the 19th century, she had a voice of great range with a powerful lower register, even if it was not always of even quality. Her real greatness lay in her reputation as the outstanding singing-actress of her time. She created Amina in *La Sonnambula*, Bianca in Donizetti's *Ugo Conte di Parigi*, the title roles in *Anna Bolena*, *Norma*, *Beatrice di Tenda* and Pacini's *Niobe*, and a role in Rossini's *Il Viaggio a Reims*.

Pasticcio (Italian for 'pie')
Known in Britain by its French translation, pastiche, it is an opera or operetta put together from parts of already written works by one or more composers. Very popular in the 18th-century, they have more recently been largely restricted to operetta: two Offenbach examples are *Christopher Columbus** and *Der Goldschmied von Toledo* (Mannheim 7 Feb 1919; libr. Zwerenz, after E. T. A. Hoffmann's *Das Fräulein von Scuderi*), which was arranged by Zamara and Stern.

Pastor Fido, Il *(The Faithful Shepherd)*
Opera in three acts by Handel. 1st perf. London, 22 Nov 1712; libr. by Giacomo Rossi, after Giovanni Battista Guarini's play. Revised version, 1st perf. London, Nov 1734. Principal roles: Mirtillo (sop), Amarilli (sop), Silvio (mezzo), Dorinda (sop), Eurilla (sop). Handel's second opera written for London, it is still occasionally performed.
  Plot: Arcadia. Amarilli loves Mirtillo but is betrothed against her will to Silvio. Silvio, loved by Dorinda, cares only for hunting. Eurilla, who is also in love with Mirtillo, traps Amarilli in a compromising situation for which the punishment is death. Whilst hunting, Silvio shoots Dorinda in mistake for an animal and falls in love with her. By

the orders of the goddess Diana, Amarilli is reprieved and united with Mirtillo and Silvio is united with Dorinda. [R]

Patanè, Giuseppe *(1932–89)*

Italian conductor, particularly associated with the Italian repertory. Always conducting from memory, he was a fine and often underrated interpreter of Verdi and Puccini. His father Franco (1908–68) was also a successful conductor.

Patience
or Bunthorne's Bride

Operetta in two acts by Sullivan. 1st perf. London, 25 April 1881; libr. by W. S. Gilbert, after *The Rival Curates* in his *Bab Ballads*. Principal roles: Reginald Bunthorne (bar), Patience (sop), Archibald Grosvenor (bar), Col Calverley (b-bar), Lady Jane (mezzo), Duke of Dunstable (ten), Lady Angela (mezzo), Major Murgatroyd (bar), Lady Saphir (mezzo), Lady Ella (sop). A brilliant satire on the aesthetic movement, with send-ups of Oscar Wilde and Whistler, it was an immediate success which enjoyed an initial run of over 550 performances.

Plot: A year ago the rapturous maidens had been engaged to officers in the Dragoon Guards, but since then have become aesthetic under the influence of the fleshly poet Bunthorne, with whom they are all in love. Bunthorne loves the village milkmaid Patience. When her childhood sweetheart Grosvenor, now an idyllic poet, arrives, she feels unable to respond to his advances, much as she loves him, because Lady Angela has explained to her that true love must be entirely unselfish. She therefore offers herself to Bunthorne, and all the other ladies (except the middle-aged Lady Jane) immediately transfer their affections to Grosvenor. Grosvenor hates their attentions and Bunthorne cannot live without admiration, so they come to an arrangement: Grosvenor agrees to become an ordinary young man, which allows Patience to love him. Bunthorne's hopes of a bride are frustrated, however: at great personal inconvenience the Dragoons have adopted aestheticism to show how much they love the ladies, and the ladies are won over, while the Duke decides to marry Lady Jane. [R]

Patineurs, Les

Ballet music (the Skaters' Waltz) in Act III of Meyerbeer's *Le Prophète*.

Patter

Music in which an enormous number of words are fitted into the shortest possible period of time. Developed in Italian opera in the mid-18th century, it has since had an important place in both opera-buffa and operetta. Its finest exponents have been Mozart, Rossini, Donizetti, Offenbach and Sullivan. It is usually found in a song or aria (see Aria di Catalogo), but is sometimes for more than one voice, as in the trio 'My eyes are fully open' in Sullivan's *Ruddigore*.

Patti, Adelina *(1843–1919)*

Italian soprano, particularly associated with Italian and French lyric roles. Largely based at Covent Garden, she was the reigning coloratura soprano of the second half of the 19th century. She had a voice of great range and remarkable agility, said to have been outstandingly pure and beautiful. The highest-paid singer of her day, she insisted on contracts excusing her from rehearsal, and dictated the size in which her name was to appear on posters. She purchased a castle at Craig-y-Nos in South Wales and in 1891 built a beautiful private opera house there. The second of her three husbands, Ernest Nicolini (1834–98), was a successful tenor.

Patzak, Julius *(1898–1974)*
Austrian tenor, particularly associated with heavier roles, especially Florestan and Palestrina. Although his voice was not outstanding, he was one of the finest tenors of the 20th century on account of his great intelligence and musicianship, his fine diction and his almost total identification with the role he was performing. He created roles in Orff's *Der Mond*, Einem's *Dantons Tod*, Martin's *Le Vin Herbé* and Pfitzner's *Das Herz*.

Pauer, Jiří *(b 1919)*
Czech composer. One of the most successful contemporary Czech composers, his operas include *The Garrolous Slug* (*Žvanivý Slimejš*, 1950; libr. M. Mellanová, after J. Hloucha), *Zuzana Vojířová* (Prague 1958; libr. after J. Bor) [R], his most successful work, *Little Red Riding Hood* (*Červená Karkulka*, 1960; libr. Mellanová), the comedy *Matrimonial Counterpoints* (*Manželské Kontrpunkty*, 1961) and *Zdravý Nemocný* (1968; libr. after Molière's *Le Malade Imaginaire*) [R Exc].

Paul Bunyan
Operetta in prologue and two acts by Britten (Op 17). 1st perf. New York, 5 May 1941; libr. by W. H. Auden. Revised version, 1st perf. BBC Radio, 1 Feb 1976. Principal roles: Narrator (bar), Tiny (sop), Johnny Inkslinger (ten), Hot Biscuit Slim (ten), Sam Sharkey (ten), Ben Benny (bass). Britten's first stage work, it is based on American folk legend. Soon withdrawn, the piece did not reappear until the composer revised it. Since then, it has enjoyed a number of successful productions. [R]

Pauly, Rosa *(b Rose Pollak)* *(1894–1975)*
Hungarian soprano, particularly associated with Strauss roles, especially Elektra. One of the leading dramatic sopranos of the inter-war period, she was an outstanding singing-actress.

Pauvre Matelot, Le *(The Poor Sailor)*
Opera in three acts by Milhaud (Op 92). 1st perf. Paris, 16 Dec 1927; libr. by Jean Cocteau. Principal roles: Sailor (ten), Wife (sop), Friend (bar), Father (bass). A strange story, although based on an actual event, Milhaud sets it with deliberately light and banal music.

Plot: The Sailor has been away at sea for 15 years. His wife remains faithful, ignoring the Father's suggestions that she should find another man and repulsing the advances of the Friend. The Sailor returns home, telling his wife (who does not recognise him) that he is a rich friend of her husband's, and attempts to seduce her. She kills him and steals his money to help her husband return. [R]

Pavarotti, Luciano *(b 1935)*
Italian tenor, particularly associated with the Italian repertory. One of the most popular of contemporary opera singers, he has a voice of great beauty and richness, with thrilling high notes, which he uses with a fine technique. However his very substantial physique sometimes makes it impossible to take him seriously on stage. He starred in the film *Yes Giorgio*, and his autobiography, *My Own Story*, was published in 1981.

Pavesi, Stefano *(1779–1850)*
Italian composer. One of the most

prolific Italian composers, he wrote some 70 operas, all of them now long forgotten. The most successful included *La Fiera* (1804), *La Festa della Rosa* (1808), *Ser Marcantonio* (Milan 26 Dec 1810; libr. Angelo Anelli) and *Fenella* (Venice 5 Feb 1831; libr. Gaetano Rossi, after Eugène Scribe's libretto for Auber's *La Muette de Portici*).

Peachum

Roles in Pepusch's *The Beggar's Opera*: Peachum (bass), a receiver, his wife Mrs Peachum (mezzo) and their daughter Polly (sop).

Pearl Fishers, The

See Pêcheurs de Perles, Les

Pears, Sir Peter *(1910–86)*

British tenor, particularly associated with Britten and other English roles. One of the oustanding postwar British operatic artists, he was a musician of great intelligence and artistry with a beautiful voice of highly individual timbre and had excellent diction. A singing-actor of subtlety and insight, he was Britten's constant companion, and with him founded both the English Opera Group and the Aldeburgh Festival. Much of Britten's music was written specifically for him, and he created the title roles in *Peter Grimes* and *Albert Herring*, the Male Chorus in *The Rape of Lucretia*, Capt Vere in *Billy Budd*, the Earl of Essex in *Gloriana*, Peter Quint in *The Turn of the Screw*, Flute in *A Midsummer Night's Dream*, the Madwoman in *Curlew River*, Nebuchadnezzar in *The Burning Fiery Furnace*, the Temper in *The Prodigal Son*, Sir Philip in *Owen Wingrave* and Aschenbach in *Death in Venice*. He also created Pandarus in *Troilus and Cressida* and, for Berkeley, the title role in *Nelson* and Boaz in *Ruth*.

Pêcheurs de Perles, Les *(The Pearl Fishers)*

Opera in three acts by Bizet. 1st perf. Paris, 30 Sept 1863; libr. by Eugène Cormon and Michel Carré. Principal roles: Leïla (sop), Zurga (bar), Nadir (ten), Nourabad (bass). Bizet's most successful opera apart from *Carmen*, it is notable for its colourful and exotic orchestration and for the great friendship duet, one of the most famous numbers in all opera.

Plot: Ceylon. The local fishermen elect Zurga as their leader. Nadir returns to the village and he and Zurga recall how their friendship was once threatened when they both fell in love with an unknown priestess. They swear eternal friendship. The priestess Leïla arrives for a vigil of prayer for the safety of the fishermen, and Nadir recognises her as the woman he and Zurga had loved. He goes to her and they acknowledge their love, but are caught by the high priest Nourabad. For breaking her vow of chastity, she and Nadir are condemned to death. Zurga discovers that in the past Leïla had saved his life, and sets fire to the village to allow the lovers to escape. [R]

Pedrell, Felipe *(1841–1922)*

Spanish composer. A champion of Spanish national music, he is regarded as the father of Spanish music-drama and is sometimes called the 'Spanish Wagner'. After some youthful zarzuelas, he turned to opera, taking his inspiration from folk music. His operas include *L'Ultimo Abenzerragio* (Barcelona 14 April 1874; libr. J. B. Altés and F. Fors), *Quasimodo* (Barcelona 20 April 1875), *Cleopatra* (Madrid 1875), *Tasse à Ferrare* (Madrid 1881) and *Los Pirineos* (Barcelona 4 Jan 1902; libr. V. Baleguer). Whilst they contain some fine music, his operas are considered too academic and studious to have won popular acceptance. He exercised most influence as a teacher, whose pupils included Albéniz, de Falla, Gerhard and Granados.

Pedrillo
Tenor role in Mozart's *Die Entführung aus dem Serail*. He is Belmonte's servant.

Pedro
(1) Tenor role in d'Albert's *Tiefland*. He is a shepherd married to Marta. (2) Bass role in Meyerbeer's *L'Africaine*. He is married to Inès. (3) Bass role in Berlioz's *Béatrice et Bénédict*. (4) Baritone role in Donizetti's *Maria Padilla*. He is Pedro the Cruel, King of Castile. (5) Baritone role in Offenbach's *La Périchole*.

Peerce, Jan *(b Jacob Pincus Perlemuth) (1904–84)*
American tenor, particularly associated with the Italian and French repertories. An artistic and musical singer with a fine technique, he enjoyed a remarkably long career, singing into his early 70s. In 1956, he became the first American tenor to appear at the Bolshoi Opera after World War II. He also appeared in a number of films.

Peer Gynt
Opera in three acts by Egk. 1st perf. Berlin, 1938; libr. by the composer, after Henrik Ibsen's play. Principal roles: Peer Gynt (bar), Solveig (sop), Aase (mezzo), Ingrid (sop), Mads (ten), Old Man (ten). One of Egk's most successful works, it is still sometimes performed in Germany. [R]

Pelléas et Mélisande
Opera in five acts by Debussy. 1st perf. Paris, 30 April 1902. A virtual word-for-word setting of Maurice Maeterlinck's play. Principal roles: Pelléas (ten), Mélisande (sop), Golaud (bar), Arkel (bass), Geneviève (mezzo), Yniold (sop). Debussy's only completed opera, it is a symbolic work of haunting beauty and expressiveness. Unique in style, it is one of the seminal works of 20th-century music.

Plot: Allemonde. Golaud discovers the distraught Mélisande in the forest, persuades her to follow him and later marries her. He brings her to the home of his grandfather King Arkel, where she meets Golaud's mother Geneviève and his young half-brother Pelléas, to whom she is attracted. Her loss of her wedding ring awakens Golaud's suspicions, and he sets his little son Yniold to spy on the pair. The two finally admit their love for each other, and Golaud murders Pelléas. Mélisande flees, is discovered and brought back to the castle, and dies telling Golaud that she has done nothing to be ashamed of. [R]

Penderecki, Krzysztof *(b 1933)*
Polish composer. One of the most important contemporary composers, he has written three operas, all of which demonstrate considerable theatrical flair. They are the powerful *The Devils of Loudun**, *Paradise Lost** and *Die Schwarze Maske* (Salzburg 1986; libr. after Hauptmann).

Penelope
Opera in two parts by Liebermann. 1st perf. Salzburg, 17 Aug 1954; libr. by Heinrich Strobel. An updating of the classical legend of Penelope and Odysseus, it is based on an actual incident in World War II. It is still occasionally performed.

Pénélope
Opera in three acts by Fauré. 1st perf. Monte Carlo, 4 March 1913; libr. by

René Fauchois, after Homer's *The Odyssey*. Principal roles: Pénélope (sop), Ulysse (ten), Eurimaque (bar), Eumée (bar), Euryclée (mezzo), Alkandre (mezzo), Phylo (sop). Telling of Ulysses' return to his faithful wife, Pénélope, it contains some of Fauré's most refined and beautiful music, but is only very infrequently performed. [R]

Pensa alla patria
Mezzo aria for Isabella in Act II of Rossini's *L'Italiana in Algieri*.

Penthesilea
Opera in two acts by Schoeck (Op 39). 1st perf. Dresden, 8 Jan 1927; libr. by the composer, after Heinrich Wilhelm von Kleist. Principal roles: Penthesilea (mezzo), Achilles (bar), Prothoe (sop), Diomedes (ten), High Priestess (mezzo). Often regarded as Schoeck's finest opera, it is very infrequently performed. [R]

Pepusch, John Christopher
(b Johann Christoph) (1667–1752)
German-born British composer. He composed a number of masques, but is best known for his arrangements of other composers' music in the ballad operas *The Beggar's Opera** and *Polly**. His wife Margherita de l'Epine (*d* 1746) was a successful soprano.

Perche non ho
Soprano aria for Rosmonda in Act I of Donizetti's *Rosmonda d'Inghilterra*. In the 19th century, it was often substituted for 'Regnava nel silenzio' in *Lucia di Lammermoor*.

Percy, Riccardo
Tenor role in Donizetti's *Anna Bolena*. He is Anna's former lover.

Perfect Fool, The
Comic opera in one act by Holst (Op 39). 1st perf. London, 14 May 1923; libr. by the composer. Principal roles: Princess (sop), Troubador (ten), Traveller (bass), Fool (speaker). An allegory in Elizabethan style, which contains parodies of Verdi and Wagner, it was successful at its appearance but is nowadays almost never performed, although the ballet music is occasionally given in the concert hall. It tells of a Princess wooed by a Wagnerian Traveller and a Verdian Troubador, who is finally won by the Fool who is not interested in her.

Pergolesi, Giovanni Battista
(1710–36)
Italian composer, whose early death cut short a brilliant talent. Sometimes regarded as the father of comic opera, his works are notable for their sharp rhythms, their delightful melodies and their witty and characterful vocal writing. His first opera *Salustia* (Naples Jan 1732; libr. after Apostolo Zeno's *Alessandro Severo*) was a failure and the music is lost, but the full-length comedy *Lo Frate 'Nnamorato* (Naples 27 Sept 1732; libr. G. Federico) was a success. The opera seria *Il Prigionier Superbo* (Naples 5 Sept 1733) is notable largely for having the most famous of all intermezzi: *La Serva Padrona**, and the same may be said for *Adriano in Siria* (Naples 25 Oct 1734; libr. Pietro Metastasio) with its successful intermezzo *La Contadina Astuta* (libr. T. Mariani) [R]. *L'Olimpiade* (Rome 8 Jan 1735; libr. Metastasio) was a failure, but his last opera *Il Flaminio* (Naples 1735; libr. Federico) was his most successful serious work and is still occasionally revived. After his death he was claimed to be the author of several other intermezzi, notably *Il Maestro di*

Musica (Paris 19 Sept 1752)[R] and *Il Geloso Schernito* [R], but it is now almost certain that he did not write them.

Peri, Jacopo *(1561–1633)*

Italian composer. A leading member of the Florentine Camerata*, his *Dafne** of 1597 is usually regarded as the first opera, and his *Euridice** is the earliest opera of which the music survives. His other operas include *Tetide* (1608; libr. F. Cini), the lost *Il Medoro* (Florence 25 Sept 1619; libr. Andrea Salvadori), written in collaboration with Gagliano, *Adone* (1620; libr. J. Cicognini) and *La Flora* (Florence 14 Oct 1628; libr. Salvadori), also written in collaboration with Gagliano.

Périchole, La

Operetta in three acts by Offenbach. 1st perf. Paris, 6 Oct 1868; libr. by Henri Meilhac and Ludovic Halévy, after Prosper Mérimée's *La Carrosse du Saint Sacrement*. Principal roles: Périchole (sop), Piquillo (ten), Don Andrès (bar), Pédro (bar). One of Offenbach's most popular works, it is in a more lyrical and romantic style than most of his other operettas, and tells of the historical Peruvian street singer, whose house may still be seen in Lima.

Plot: mid-18th century Peru. The impoverished street singers Périchole and her lover Piquillo cannot even afford a wedding service. The Viceroy Don Andrès, during an incognito tour of Lima, falls for Périchole and offers her a position at court, which she accepts, leaving a remorseful letter for Piquillo. Etiquette does not allow unmarried women to live within the palace, so a husband has to be found for Périchole. By chance, Don Andrès' men choose Piquillo, getting him too drunk to recognise the bride. When he

appreciates what has happened, he denounces Périchole and is imprisoned. The two finally escape, happily reconciled, and Don Andrès forgives them. [R]

Perlea, Jonel *(b Ionel) (1900–70)*

Romanian conductor, particularly associated with the Italian and German repertories. A fine and often underrated musician, he was musical director of the Bucharest Opera (1929–36). Following a heart attack and a stroke in 1957, he learned to conduct with his left arm only.

Per pietà

Soprano aria for Fiordiligi in Act II of Mozart's *Così fan Tutte*.

Persiani, Fanny *(b Tacchinardi) (1812–67)*

Italian soprano. One of the leading lyric sopranos of the early 19th century, she was said to have possessed a small but extraordinarily agile voice of great range. She created, for Donizetti, the title roles in *Lucia di Lammermoor*, *Rosmonda d'Inghilterra* and *Pia de' Tolomei*. Her father Niccolò Tacchinardi (1772–1850) was a successful tenor, despite being a virtual hunchback. Her husband Giuseppe Persiani (c 1800–69) was a composer, the most successful of whose operas was *Inès de Castro* (Naples 1835; libr. Salvatore Cammarano).

Pertichino *(Italian for 'understudy')*

A name given in the 18th and 19th centuries to a character who listens to another singer's narration during an aria.

Pertile, Aureliano *(1885–1952)*

Italian tenor, particularly associated with the Italian repertory. Although his voice was not especially beautiful, he was an intense and highly intelligent singing-actor with a bright-toned voice able to encompass roles as diverse as Edgardo and Otello. Toscanini's favourite tenor, and one of the finest Italian artists of the inter-war period, he created the title roles in Wolf-Ferrari's *Sly* and both Boito's and Mascagni's *Nerone*.

Peru

See Fundación para Arte Lirica, Lima

Peruvian opera composers

These include César Bolaños (*b* 1931), Reynaldo la Rosa (*c* 1852–1954) and José María del Valle Riestra (1859–1925), whose *Ollanta* (Lima 14 Feb 1919), based on the Quechuan poem *Ollantai*, is the principal Peruvian opera on a national subject.

Pesaro Festival

An Italian summer festival founded in 1980 and devoted to the operas of Rossini. Performances are given at the Teatro Communale Gioacchino Rossini (cap. 914), which opened (as the Teatro Nuovo) in June 1818.

Peter

Baritone role in: (1) Humperdinck's *Hänsel und Gretel*. He is the children's father. (2) Lortzing's *Zar und Zimmermann*. He is Peter the Great of Russia.

Peter Grimes

Opera in three acts by Britten (Op 33). 1st perf. London, 7 June 1945; libr. by Montagu Slater, after George Crabbe's *The Borough*. Principal roles: Peter Grimes (ten), Ellen Orford (sop), Balstrode (bar), Ned Keene (bar), Swallow (bass), Auntie (mezzo), Bob

Boles (ten), Mrs Sedley (mezzo), Hobson (bass), Rector (ten). Britten's first opera and often regarded as his masterpiece, it deals with his favourite theme: the position of the outsider in society. Its première was one of the most important events in British musical history, as it marked not only the appearance of a composer of genius but also heralded the postwar British operatic renaissance.

Plot: a Suffolk town, *c* 1830. Although the locals distrust his isolation and his temper, the fisherman Grimes is cleared of responsibility in the mysterious death of his young apprentice. Grimes is befriended by the widowed schoolteacher Ellen Orford, whom he hopes to marry, and who assists and supports him in finding him a new apprentice. The boy meets with a fatal accident and the frightened Grimes puts to sea just before a deputation of suspicious townsfolk led by the lawyer Swallow and the bigoted Methodist preacher Bob Boles arrives at his hut. Grimes returns to shore in the fog, almost deranged by his experiences, and the retired sea captain, Balstrode, advises him to avoid the consequences of the boy's death by taking his boat out to sea and sinking it. [R]

Peter Ibbetson

Opera in three acts by Taylor (Op 20). 1st perf. New York, 7 Feb 1931; libr. by the composer and Constance Collier, after George du Maurier's novel. Principal roles: Peter (ten), Col Ibbetson (bar), Mary (sop), Mrs Deane (mezzo). One of the most successful of all American operas at its appearance, it is nowadays only rarely performed.

Plot: England and France, 1855–87. Peter, tyrannised by his cruel uncle Colonel Ibbetson, finds escape in dreams about his childhood. He returns to his birthplace and meets his childhood playmate Mary. He kills his uncle and is sentenced to life imprisonment. For over 40 years, he finds solace in dreams as Mary visits him. When he learns of her death he joins her.

Peters, Roberta *(b 1930)*
American soprano, particularly associated with Italian coloratura roles. One of the leading coloraturas of the 1950s, she possessed a bright-toned voice of great agility if a little lacking in individuality. Married for a time to the baritone Robert Merrill*.

Peter the Miner *(Piér li Houïeu)*
Opera in one act by Ysaÿe. 1st perf. Liège, 4 March 1931; libr. (in Walloon) by the composer. Ysaÿe's only opera, it was successful at its appearance but is nowadays all but forgotten.

Petit Duc, Le *(The Little Duke)*
Operetta in three acts by Lecocq. 1st perf. Paris, 25 Jan 1878; libr. by Henri Meilhac and Ludovic Halévy. One of Lecocq's most successful works, it is still performed from time to time. [R Exc]

Petrassi, Goffredo *(b 1904)*
Italian composer. He wrote two operas: *Il Cordovano* (Milan 12 May 1949; libr. after Miguel Cervantes' *El Viejo Celoso*) and *Morte dell' Aria* (Rome 24 Oct 1950; libr. T. Scialoja). He was artistic director of the Teatro la Fenice, Venice (1937–40).

Petrella, Clara *(b 1914)*
Italian soprano, particularly associated with the Italian repertory. An outstanding singing-actress, nicknamed the 'Duse of Singers', she created Anna in Rossellini's *Il Vortice*, Mila in Pizzetti's *La Figlia di Iorio*, Beatrice in Rossellini's *Uno Sguardo dal Ponte*, the

title role in Pannain's *Madame Bovary* and a role in Pizzetti's *Cagliostro*.

Petrella, Errico *(1813–77)*
Italian composer. He wrote his first opera *Il Diavolo Color di Rosa* (Naples July 1829; libr. Andrea Leone Tottola) at the age of 15 and went on to write many more, a number of which enjoyed considerable success in their time but which are all now forgotten. The most important include *Le Precauzioni* (Naples 20 May 1851; libr. M. d'Arienzo), *Marco Visconti* (Naples 9 Feb 1954; libr. D. Bolognese) and *I Promessi Sposi* (Lecco 20 Oct 1869; libr. Antonio Ghislanzoni, after Alessandro Manzoni).

Petrov, Ivan *(b Krause) (b 1920)*
Russian bass, particularly associated with the Russian and Italian repertories. The leading Russian bass of the 1950s, he possessed a magnificent, rich and beautiful voice of considerable range and power which he used with outstanding artistry. He created a role in Shaporin's *The Decembrists*.

Petrov, Osip *(1806–78)*
Russian bass, particularly associated with the Russian repertory. One of the greatest of all Russian singers, he had a magnificent voice of great range (B to f♯) and was an outstanding singing-actor fully in tune with the aims of the emerging nationalist school, whose finest interpreter he became. He created Varlaam in *Boris Godunov*, Ivan in *A Life for the Tsar*, Ruslan in *Ruslan and Ludmila*, Ivan in Rimsky-Korsakov's *The Maid of Pskov*, the Mayor in Tchaikovsky's *Vakula the Blacksmith*, Prince Gudal in Rubenstein's *The Demon*, for Dargomijsky, Leporello in *The Stone Guest* and the Miller in *Rusalka* and, for Serov, Oziya in *Judith* and Vladimir in *Rogneda*. His wife

Anna Yakovlevna Vorobyova (1816–1901) was a successful mezzo, who created Vanya in *A Life for the Tsar*.

Petrovics, Emil *(b 1930)*

Hungarian composer. His three operas, written in atonal style, have met with considerable success. They are *C'Est la Guerre* (Budapest 1962; libr. M. Hubay) [R], *Lysistrate* (Budapest 1962; libr. after Aristophanes) [R] and *Crime and Punishment* (*Bün és Bünhödés*, Helsinki 1970; libr. G. Maar, after Fyodor Dostoyevsky) [R]. He is artistic director of the Budapest State Opera.

Pfitzner, Hans *(1869–1949)*

German composer and conductor. An ardent admirer of Wagner, his operas are traditional in style, in line with his dislike of modernism in music. His five operas are *Der Arme Heinrich**, *Die Rose von Liebesgarten* (Elberfeld 9 Nov 1901; libr. James Grun), *Christelflein* (Munich 11 Dec 1906; libr. composer and I. von Stach; revised version 1917), his masterpiece *Palestrina** and *Das Herz* (Munich 12 Nov 1931; libr. H. Hahner-Mons). Although it has many ardent advocates, his music remains little performed. He was musical director of the Strasbourg Opera (1910–16).

Philadelphia Opera Company

Formed in March 1975 by a merger of the Philadelphia Lyric Opera Company (founded in 1923) and the Philadelphia Grand Opera Company (founded in 1927), it is the latest of many companies which have existed in Philadelphia. The annual season runs from October to May, and performances are given at the Academy of Music (cap. 2,800).

Philémon et Baucis

Opera in three acts by Gounod. 1st perf. Paris, 18 Feb 1860; libr. by Jules Barbier and Michel Carré, after Ovid's *Metamorphoses*. Principal roles: Philémon (ten), Baucis (sop), Jupiter (bass), Vulcain (bar). Successful in its time, it is nowadays only very rarely performed.

Plot: Jupiter and Vulcan are travelling in disguise and are shown great hospitality by the poor elderly couple Philemon and Baucis. As a reward for their kindness, the couple's youth is restored, whereupon Jupiter promptly falls in love with the now pretty and young Baucis.

Philidor, François André *(b Danican) (1726–95)*

French composer. One of the most important early composers of opéra-comique, he wrote over 30 works, notable for their imaginative orchestration and for their melodic and harmonic richness. His most successful operas include *Blaise le Savetier* (Paris 9 March 1759; libr. Jean-Marie Sedaine, after Jean de la Fontaine), *Le Sorcier* (Paris 2 Jan 1764; libr. A. A. H. Poinsinet), *Tom Jones**, arguably his finest work, and *Le Bon Fils* (Paris 11 Jan 1773; libr. F. A. Devaux). He was also an outstanding chess player, publishing a notable study of the game.

Philip II

Bass role in Verdi's *Don Carlos*. Carlos' father, he is the King of Spain.

Phrasing

A phrase is a group of notes which constitute a melodic unit. Phrasing is thus a singer's ability correctly to observe a melody's division into these units. It can often give an indication of a singer's breath control: whether, for example, a baritone can produce the final section of Ford's Jealousy

Monologue in Verdi's *Falstaff* without breaking the phrase.

Pia de' Tolomei

Opera in two acts by Donizetti. 1st perf. Venice, 18 Feb 1837; libr. by Salvatore Cammarano, after Sestini. Principal roles: Pia (sop), Nello della Pietra (bar), Ghino (ten), Rodrigo (mezzo), Lamberto (bass). Very successful at its appearance, it is nowadays only very rarely performed.

Piangea cantando

Soprano aria (the Willow Song) for Desdemona in Act IV of Verdi's *Otello*.

Piave, Francesco Maria
(1810–76)

Italian librettist. He wrote some 70 libretti in all, providing texts for Balfe, Mercadante, Pacini (*Lorenzo de' Medici*), and F. and L. Ricci (*Crispino e la Comare*) amongst others, but is best known for his texts for Verdi (*I Due Foscari, Ernani, Il Corsaro, Macbeth, Stiffelio, Rigoletto, La Traviata, Simon Boccanegra, Aroldo* and *La Forza del Destino*). His complaisance and willingness to take orders made him the type of librettist Verdi liked best: the kind he could bully. This has perhaps led to his work being rather underrated; some of his texts are a distinct cut above the contemporary average, and that for *Rigoletto* is theatrically superb. He was resident stage manager at the Teatro la Fenice, Venice (1843–67).

Piccaver, Alfred *(b Peckover)* *(1884–1958)*

British tenor, particularly associated with the Italian repertory. Largely resident at the Vienna State Opera, he possessed a beautiful, velvety lyric tenor, used with elegance and an outstanding technique.

Picchi, Mirto *(1915–80)*

Italian tenor, particularly associated with the Italian repertory and with 20th-century works. One of the leading tenors of the immediate postwar period, he had a fine voice and was an admired singing-actor. He created roles in Pizzetti's *Cagliostro* and *La Figlia di Iorio* and Castro's *Proserpina y el Extranjero*. His autobiography, *Un Trono Vicino al Sol*, was published in 1978.

Piccinni, Niccolò *(1728–1800)*

Italian composer. His first opera was *Le Donne Dispettose* (Naples 1754; libr. A. Palomba), which was followed by over 100 others. One of the last masters of the Neapolitan school, the greatest successes of his first (Italian) period were in comedy, particularly *La Buona Figliuola**, his only work still to be remembered. His opera serias, such as *L'Olimpiade* (Rome 1768; libr. Pietro Metastasio) were successful in their time but were soon forgotten. He moved to Paris in 1776, where he became involved in the famous controversy with Gluck. This was a quarrel between their respective supporters, not between the two composers, between whom there was no ill-feeling. His *Roland* (Paris 27 Jan 1778; libr. Jean-François Marmontel, after Philippe Quinault) was a success which fuelled the controversy, which came to a head when an enterprising impresario had both composers set *Iphigénie en Tauride**. The popular verdict (and that of history) went in favour of Gluck, but even so, Piccinni's works continued to be performed in Paris long after his death, especially *Didon* (Fontainebleau 16 Oct 1783; libr. Marmontel). His son Luigi (1766–1827) was also a composer, who wrote several operas.

Piccola Scala, La

A chamber theatre (cap. 600) within the building of the Teatro alla Scala in Milan, it opened in December 1955. It presents smaller-scale 18th- and 19th-century works as well as contemporary operas.

Piccolo Marat, Il

Opera in three acts by Mascagni. 1st perf. Rome, 2 May 1921; libr. by Giovacchino Forzano and Giovanni Targioni-Tozzetti, after Victor Martin's *Sous la Terreur*. Principal roles: Jean-Charles de Fleury (ten), Mariella (sop), L'Orco (bass), Carpenter (bar), Soldier (bar). Telling of the Terror in Paris which followed the murder of the revolutionary leader Jean-Paul Marat in 1793, it was successful at its appearance and is sometimes regarded as Mascagni's finest opera. Its almost total disappearance in recent years is unjustified.

Plot: Paris, 1793. The young Prince de Fleury insinuates himself into the favour of the President of the Council (L'Orco) to secure the release of his mother who has been condemned to death by the Jacobins. His seeming revolutionary zeal earns him the soubriquet of 'the little Marat'. With the aid of his loved one, Mariella, and the Carpenter, he captures L'Orco in a drunken sleep and forces him to sign his mother's release warrant. He is wounded, but all escape to freedom.

Pierné, Gabriel *(1863–1937)*

French composer and organist. He wrote eight operas, of which the most successful were *La Coupe Enchantée* (1895), *On Ne Badine Pas Avec l'Amour* (1910; libr. after Alfred de Musset) and *Sophie Arnould* (1927), which is based on the life of the 18th-century soprano.

Pietà, rispetto, amore

Baritone aria for Macbeth in Act IV of Verdi's *Macbeth*.

Pietra del Paragone, La *(The Touchstone)*

Comic opera in two acts by Rossini. 1st perf. Milan, 26 Sept 1812; libr. by Luigi Romanelli. Principal roles: Asdrubale (bar), Clarice (mezzo), Pacuvio (bar), Macrobio (bass), Giocondo (ten), Fulvia (sop). One of Rossini's earliest major successes, it is still performed quite often.

Plot: So as to test the genuineness of his friends' affections, Count Asdrubale pretends to have been stripped of his riches by an African prince, whom he then proceeds to impersonate. All of his friends fail the test dismally, except for Giocondo and Clarice, with whom Asdrubale is in love. [R]

Pietro

Bass role in Verdi's *Simon Boccanegra*. He is Paolo's henchman.

Piff, paff

Bass aria for Marcel in Act I of Meyerbeer's *Les Huguenots*.

Pijper, Willem *(1894–1937)*

Dutch composer. His one completed opera *Halloween* (*Halewijn*, 1933) met with considerable success in Holland. His second opera *Merlijn* was left unfinished.

Pilarczyk, Helga *(b 1925)*

German soprano, particularly associated with 20th-century operas, especially *Erwartung*. A singer of great intelligence and an outstanding singing-actress, she created roles in Henze's *König Hirsch* and Křenek's *Pallas Athene Weint* and *Der Goldene Bock*.

Pilgrims' Chorus

Chorus in Acts I and III of Wagner's *Tannhäuser*.

Pilgrim's Progress, The

Opera in four acts by Vaughan Williams. 1st perf. London, 26 April 1951; libr. by the composer, after John Bunyan. Principal roles: Pilgrim (bar), Watchful (bar), Evangelist (bar), Lord Hate-Good (b-bar), Herald (bar), Apollyon (bass), Bunyan (bar), Mr By-Ends (ten). Described as a 'morality', it is Vaughan Williams' last opera and incorporates his earlier Bunyan setting *The Shepherds of the Delectable Mountains* of 1922. Although its structure may not be conventionally operatic, it contains some of the finest music of any British opera (some of which found its way into Williams' 5th symphony). Its failure deeply hurt the composer, and the work's relegation to virtual neglect is both unaccountable and quite unjust. [R]

Pimpinone

Works of this title, telling the same story as Pergolesi's *La Serva Padrona*, include:

(1) Intermezzo by Albinoni. 1st perf. 1708; libr. by Pietro Pariati. Principal roles: Pimpinone (b-bar), Vespetta (mezzo). [R]

(2) Intermezzo in two parts by Telemann. Subtitled *Die Ungleiche Heyrath* (*The Unequal Marriage*). 1st perf. Hamburg, 27 Sept 1725; libr. by Johann Peter Praetorius, after Pietro Pariati. Principal roles: Pimpinone (bar), Vespetta (sop). Telemann's best-known stage work, it is still quite often performed. [R]

Pimyen

Bass role in Moussorgsky's *Boris Godunov*. He is an old monkish chronicler.

Ping

Baritone role in Puccini's *Turandot*. He is one of the three courtiers.

Pini-Corsi, Antonio *(1858–1918)*

Italian baritone, particularly associated with comic Italian roles. An outstanding buffo, he created Ford in *Falstaff*, Schaunard in *La Bohème*, Happy in *La Fanciulla del West*, the Innkeeper in *Die Königskinder* and roles in Giordano's *Siberia* and Franchetti's *La Figlia di Iorio*. His brother Gaetano was a leading comprimario tenor, who created Goro in *Madama Butterfly*.

Pinkerton, Lt B. F.

Tenor role in Puccini's *Madama Butterfly*. He is the American naval officer who marries, then abandons, Butterfly.

Pinza, Ezio *(b Fortunio) (1892–1957)*

Italian bass, particularly associated with the Italian and Russian repertories. Long resident at the Metropolitan Opera, New York, he was perhaps the greatest bass of the inter-war period. He had a large and beautiful voice used with nobility and fine musicianship, and he was an outstanding singing-actor. He created Tigellino in *Nerone* and the Blind Man in Pizzetti's *Debora e Jaële*. He appeared in a number of films, notably *South Pacific* (1949), and his autobiography was published in 1958.

Piper, John *(b 1903)*

British painter and designer. A founder member of the English Opera Group, his stage designs have followed the

447

same shaded and atmospheric style as his paintings. His most notable designs were for Britten premières: *The Rape of Lucretia, Albert Herring, Billy Budd, Gloriana, The Turn of the Screw, Owen Wingrave* and, particularly, *A Midsummer Night's Dream* and *Death in Venice*. His wife Myfanwy is a librettist, who wrote for Britten (*The Turn of the Screw, Owen Wingrave* and *Death in Venice*) and Hoddinott (*What the Old Man Does is Always Right* and *The Rajah's Diamond*).

Pique Dame
See Queen of Spades, The

Piquillo
Tenor role in Offenbach's *La Périchole*. He is a street singer in love with Périchole.

Pirata, Il (*The Pirate*)
Opera in two acts by Bellini. 1st perf. Milan, 27 Oct 1827; libr. by Felice Romani, after Charles Maturin's *Bertram or the Castle of St Aldobrand*. Principal roles: Imogene (sop), Gualtiero (ten), Ernesto (bar), Goffredo (bass), Adele (mezzo). Bellini's third opera, and the work which established his reputation, it suffered a long period of neglect, but in recent years has once more been regularly performed.

Plot: 13th-century Sicily. After the Battle of Benevento, Gualtiero has been deprived of his estates and has turned to piracy. He returns to discover that his beloved Imogene has married his enemy Ernesto. Ernesto catches Imogene at a secret meeting with Gualtiero and challenges the latter to a duel. Ernesto is killed, Gualtiero is arrested and Imogene goes out of her mind. [R]

Pirates of Penzance, The
or The Slave of Duty
Operetta in two acts by Sullivan. 1st perf. Paignton and New York (virtually simultaneously), 30/31 Dec 1879; libr. by W. S. Gilbert. Principal roles: Frederic (ten), Mabel (sop), Pirate King (b-bar), Maj-Gen Stanley (bar), Ruth (mezzo), Sgt of Police (bass), Edith (mezzo), Samuel (bar). An immediate success, which enjoyed an initial run of nearly 400 performances, it is a satire on the army and police, and has always been one of the most popular of the Savoy Operas.

Plot: 19th-century Cornwall. Because of an error by his nurse Ruth, Frederic has been apprenticed to the Pirate King and is out of his indentures having reached his 21st birthday. He falls in love with Mabel, daughter of Maj-Gen Stanley, and decides that for the sake of society his former associates must be exterminated. As the police expedition against the pirates is about to set out, the Pirate King informs Frederic that he was born in leap year on 29th February and that his contract states that he is apprenticed until his 21st birthday, not his 21st year.

He feels honour-bound to rejoin the pirates. The pirates defeat the policemen, but submit when called upon to do so in Queen Victoria's name. Ruth reveals that the pirates are all noblemen who have 'gone wrong' and the snobbish Gen Stanley orders them to be released and to resume their former positions. The pirates marry his daughters and Mabel and Frederic are united. [R]

Pistol
Falstaff's associate appears in a number of operas, including: (1) Bass role in Verdi's *Falstaff*. (2) Baritone role in Holst's *At the Boar's Head*. (3) Bass role in Vaughan Williams' *Sir John in Love*.

Pizarro, Don
Baritone role in Beethoven's *Fidelio* and

tenor role in Paer's *Leonora*. He is the evil prison governor.

Pizzetti, Ildebrando *(1880–1968)*

Italian composer. Perhaps the most important post-Puccinian Italian opera composer, he wrote three youthful one-act operas, including *Il Cid* (1902), and began work on several other projects, none of which he finished. The first of his 13 mature operas, mostly written in arioso style and for nearly all of which he wrote his own libretti, was *Fedra**. It was followed by the unpublished *Gigliola* (1915; libr. Gabriele d'Annunzio), *Debora e Jaële**, *Fra Gherardo**, *Lo Straniero* (Rome 29 April 1930), *Orsèolo* (Florence 4 May 1935), *L'Oro* (Milan 2 Jan 1947; composed 1941), *Vanna Lupa**, the radio operas *Ifigenia* (RAI 3 Oct 1950; libr. composer and A. Perrini) and *Cagliostro* (RAI 5 Nov 1952), *La Figlia di Iorio**, the highly successful *L'Assassinio nella Cattedrale**, *Il Calzare d'Argento* (Milan 23 March 1961; libr. Riccardo Bacchelli) and *Clittenestra* (Milan 1 March 1965).

Plançon, Pol *(1854–1914)*

French bass, particularly associated with the French repertory, especially Méphistophélès. A fine singing-actor, he possessed a beautiful, smooth voice of enormous range and remarkable flexibility. He created Don Gormas in *Le Cid*, Garrido in *La Navarraise*, Francis in Saint-Saëns' *Ascanio* and Friar Francis in Stanford's *Much Ado About Nothing*.

Planquette, Robert *(1848–1903)*

French composer. He wrote some 20 operettas, of which *Les Cloches de Corneville** was much the most successful. Of the others, *Rip van Winkle* (London 14 Oct 1882; libr. H.

B. Farnie) [R Exc], *Nell Gwynne* (London 7 Feb 1884; libr. Farnie) and *Mam'zelle Quat'sous* (Paris 5 Nov 1897; libr. A. Mars and M. Desvallières) made the most impression.

Plasson, Michel *(b 1933)*

French conductor, particularly associated with the French repertory, especially Massenet and Offenbach. A persuasive interpreter of 19th-century French music, he was musical director of the Metz Opera (1965–71) and the Toulouse Capitole (1972–).

Platée

Opera-ballet in prologue and three acts by Rameau. 1st perf. Versailles, 31 March 1745; libr. by Jacques Autreau and Adrien-Joseph le Valois d'Orville. Principal roles: Platée (ten), Cithéron (bar), Jupiter (bar), Mercury (ten), Folly (sop), Momus (ten), Thespis (ten), Thalie (sop). One of the very earliest comic operas, it tells a rather bitter and unpleasant story of the mock marriage of an ugly woman with a god. It is still performed from time to time. [R]

Plebe! Patrizi!

Baritone aria for Boccanegra in the Council Chamber Scene of Verdi's *Simon Boccanegra*.

Pleurez, o mes yeux

Mezzo aria for Chimène in Act III of Massenet's *Le Cid*.

Plishka, Paul *(b 1941)*

American bass, particularly associated with the Italian and French repertories. One of the finest contemporary American basses, he has a rich and smooth voice used with fine musicianship and has a good stage presence.

Plowright, Rosalind (b 1949)

British soprano, particularly associated with the Italian repertory, especially Verdi. An exciting and rich-voiced singer with a good stage presence, she has a voice of highly individual timbre which does not always hit the ear too easily.

Plunkett

Bass-baritone role in Flotow's *Martha*. He is a farmer.

Pluto

The Graeco-Roman god of the underworld appears in many operas, including: (1) Bass role in Rameau's *Hippolyte et Aricie*. (2) Bass role in Monteverdi's *Il Ballo delle Ingrate*. (3) Tenor role in Offenbach's *Orphée aux Enfers*. (4) Bass role in Rameau's *Naïs*. (5) Bass role in Monteverdi's *La Favola d'Orfeo*.

Plzeň Opera (Pilsen when it was part of Austria-Hungary)

Opera in this town in Czechoslovakia is given at the J. K. Tyl Theatre (cap. 1,000), which opened in 1902.

Poe, Edgar Allan

See panel on page 451

Pogner, Veit

Bass role in Wagner's *Die Meistersinger von Nürnberg*. A goldsmith, he is Eva's father.

Poisoned Kiss, The
or The Empress and the Necromancer

Opera in three acts by Vaughan Williams. 1st perf. Cambridge, 12 May 1936; libr. by Evelyn Sharp (later revised by Ursula Vaughan Williams), after Richard Garnett's *The Poison Maid*. Principal roles: Tormentilla (sop), Amaryllus (ten), Dispascus (bass). A ludicrous story of rival magicians and their poisons and antidotes, it contains some fine music, but the dreadful libretto has ensured that the piece is almost never performed.

Poissl, Johann Nepomuk von (1783–1865)

German composer. An important historical figure, he was the transitional German composer between Mozart and Weber (who admired his works). His operas show a move away from French and Italian models towards through-composed German opera. The most important of his works, for many of which he wrote his own libretti, include *Antigonus* (Munich 12 Feb 1808; libr. composer), *Athalia* (Munich 3 June 1814; libr. G. Wöhlbruck, after Jean Baptiste Racine's *Athalie*), *Der Wettkampf zu Olympia* (Munich 21 April 1815; libr. composer, after Pietro Metastasio), *Nittetis* (Darmstadt 29 June 1817; libr. composer, after Metastasio) and *Der Untersberg* (Munich 30 Oct 1829; libr. E. von Schenk). None of his operas are remembered today.

Poland

See Poznań Opera; Warsaw National Opera

Polish opera composers

See Elsner; Moniuszko; Paderewski; Penderecki; Poniatowski; Rudziński; Szymanowski; Zeleński

Other national opera composers include Maciej Kamieński (1734–1821), whose *Sorrow Turned to Joy* (*Nedza Uszcześliwiona*, Warsaw 1778; libr. Wojciech Boguslawski) was the first Polish opera, Karol Kurpiński (1785–

EDGAR ALLAN POE

The works of the American writer and poet Edgar Allan Poe (1809–49) have inspired many composers, although the most important works (such as Rachmaninov's *The Bells*) are non-operatic. Poe's influence on opera was more general than simply providing source material: in his position as the leading exponent of the Gothic movement, he exerted a strong influence in Europe, especially in France on composers such as Debussy. Below are listed, by story, those operas based on his works by composers with entries in this dictionary.

The Devil in the Belfry
Lualdi · *Il Diavolo nel Campanile* · 1925

The Fall of the House of Usher
Debussy · *La Chûte de la Maison Usher* · 1915 (U)

The Purloined Letter
Blacher · *Das Geheimnis des Entwendeten Briefes* · 1975

Some Words With a Mummy
Viozzi · *Allamistakeo* · 1954

The System of Dr Tarr and Prof Fether
Tosatti · *Il Sistema della Dolcezza* · 1950

1857) and Adam Wieniawski (1876–1950).

Poliuto

Opera in three acts by Donizetti. 1st perf. Naples, 30 Nov 1848 (composed 1838); libr. by Salvatore Cammarano, after Pierre Corneille's *Polyeucte*. Revised version, *Les Martyrs* 1st perf. Paris, 10 April 1840; libr. by Eugène Scribe. Principal roles (with *Les Martyrs* second): Poliuto/Polyeucte (ten), Paolina/Pauline (sop), Severo/Sévère (bar), Callistene/Callysthènes (bass), Nearco/Néarche (ten). One of Donizetti's finest operas (with some unusual features such as an overture with chorus), it is still quite often performed, usually in the original version.

Plot: Armenia, 257 AD. Poliuto, a secret convert to Christianity, is arrested and condemned to death. His wife Paolina, although still partly in love with her former betrothed the Roman pro-consul Severo, decides to share her husband's martyrdom.

451

Polka

A Bohemian dance in 2/4 time which originated in the early 19th century. There is a famous operatic example in Weinberger's *Shvanda the Bagpiper*.

Pollak, Anna *(b 1912)*

Austrian-born British mezzo, long resident at Sadler's Wells Opera. A fine singing-actress, she created Bianca in *The Rape of Lucretia*, Mrs Strickland in Gardner's *The Moon and Sixpence*, several roles in Williamson's *English Eccentrics* and, for Berkeley, Lady Nelson in *Nelson* and the title role in *Ruth*. She was a distinguished Carmen and a memorable Prince Orlofsky.

Pollione

Tenor role in Bellini's *Norma*. A Roman pro-consul, he is Norma's former lover.

Polly

Ballad opera in three acts by Pepusch and Samuel Arnold. 1st perf. London, 19 June 1777 (composed 1729); libr. by John Gay. A less successful follow-up to *The Beggar's Opera*, it was banned by the Lord Chamberlain and did not reach the stage for nearly 50 years, when Arnold's songs were added. It is only very rarely performed.

Polonaise *(French for 'Polish')*

A Polish ceremonial dance in 3/4 time. There are many examples in opera, including *Eugene Onegin* and *Boris Godunov*. It is called *polacca* in Italy.

Polovtsian Dances

Choral dances in Act II of Borodin's *Prince Igor*.

Pomo d'Oro, Il *(The Golden Apple)*

Opera in prologue and five acts by

Cesti. 1st perf. Vienna, 13 July 1667; libr. by Francesco Sbarra. Written to celebrate the wedding of Emperor Leopold I, its première was probably the most splendid and elaborate operatic performance in history, involving a specially built theatre and 21 separate stage sets. Based on the Greek legend of the Judgement of Paris, the music for Act V is lost.

Ponchielli, Amilcare *(1834–86)*

Italian composer. The last Italian romantic composer, he wrote nine operas. They are *I Promessi Sposi* (Cremona 30 Aug 1856; libr. after Alessandro Manzoni; revised version Milan 4 Dec 1872; libr. Emilio Praga), the unperformed *Bertrand dal Bormio* (1858), *La Savoiarda* (Cremona 19 Jan 1861; libr. F. Guidi; revised version, *Lina* Milan 17 Nov 1877; libr. Carlo d'Ormeville), *Roderico* (Piacenza 26 Dec 1863; libr. Guidi, after R. Southey's *Roderick*), *I Lituani* (Milan 6 March 1874; libr. Antonio Ghislanzoni, after Mickiewicz's *Konrad Wallenrod*; revised version, *Aldona* St Petersburg 1884), *La Gioconda**, his masterpiece and his only work still to be performed, *Il Figliuol Prodigo* (Milan 26 Dec 1880; libr. Angelo Zanardini) and *Marion Delorme* (Milan 17 March 1885; libr. Enrico Golisciani, after Victor Hugo). The unfinished *I Mori di Valenza* (Monte Carlo 17 March 1914, begun 1874; libr. Ghislanzoni, after Eugène Scribe's *Piquillo Alliaga*) was completed by Arturo Cadore. He was also a noted teacher, whose pupils included Puccini and Mascagni. Married to the soprano Teresina Brambilla*.

Pong

Tenor role in Puccini's *Turandot*. He is one of the three courtiers.

Poniatowski, Józef *(Prince of Monte Rotondo) (1816–73)*
Polish composer and tenor. He wrote 13 operas, all now largely forgotten, including *Giovanni di Procida* (Florence 25 Nov 1839; libr. composer, after G. N. Niccolini), *Ruy Blas* (Lucca 2 Sept 1843; libr. after Victor Hugo), *La Sposa d'Abido* (Venice Feb 1845; libr. G. Peruzzini, after Lord Byron's *The Bride of Abydos*), *Pierre de Médicis* (Paris 9 March 1860; libr. Jules-Henri Vernoy de Saint-Georges), *L'Aventurier* (Paris 26 Jan 1865; libr. Saint-Georges) and *Gelmina* (London 4 June 1872; libr. F. Rizzelli).

Ponnelle, Jean-Pierre *(1932–88)*
French producer and designer. An original and brilliantly inventive producer, especially in comedy (although he made his debut with *Tristan und Isolde*) and a designer of great talent, his productions were notable for their sharp precision and sense of ensemble and, occasionally, for their excess of detail and stage business. His most notable work included Cologne's Mozart cycle, Rossini operas at La Scala, *Don Pasquale* at Covent Garden and Zürich's Monteverdi cycle.

Pons, Lily *(b Alice Joséphine) (1898–1976)*
French-born American soprano, particularly associated with Italian and French coloratura roles. One of the few outstanding coloraturas of the inter-war period, she had a light, agile voice and a charming stage presence. She also appeared in a number of films. Married for a time to the conductor André Kostelanetz.

Ponselle, Rosa *(b Ponzillo) (1897–1981)*
American soprano, particularly associated with the Italian repertory. Largely resident at the Metropolitan Opera, New York, she was possibly the finest lyrico-dramatic soprano of the inter-war period. She combined a gloriously rich and beautiful voice with great intelligence and considerable acting ability. She was artistic director of the Baltimore Civic Opera from 1954, and was also a distinguished teacher, whose pupils included Sherrill Milnes and James Morris. Her sister Carmela (1888–1977) was a successful mezzo.

Ponte, Lorenzo da *(b Emmanuele Conegliano) (1749–1838)*
Italian poet and librettist. He wrote 36 opera libretti, including texts for Martín y Soler (*Una Cosa Rara*), Paer (*Il Nuovo Figaro*), Salieri (*Il Ricco d'un Giorno, Il Talismano, Il Pastor Fido, Axur, Rè d'Ormus* and *La Cifra*), Storace (*Gli Equivoci*) and Winter, but is best known for his collaboration with Mozart, for whom he wrote *Le Nozze di Figaro, Così fan Tutte, Don Giovanni* and the unfinished *Lo Sposo Deluso*. He was later Professor of Italian at Columbia University and helped to establish opera in the United States. His libertine life may be studied in his four-volume *Memorie*, which was published between 1823 and 1827.

Popes
A number of pontiffs appear as operatic characters, including: (1) Leo I in Verdi's *Attila*. (2) Alexander VI in Osborne's *Hell's Angels*. (3) Pious IV in Pfitzner's *Palestrina*. (4) Clement VII in Berlioz's *Benvenuto Cellini*. (5) St Peter (traditionally the first pope) in Orff's *Der Mond*.
See also **Clement IX, Pope**

Popp, Lucia *(b 1939)*
Czech soprano, particularly associated

with Mozart roles. Beginning as a soubrette, she subsequently turned with equal success to rather heavier German and Italian roles. She has a beautiful, silvery voice, used with great intelligence and musicianship, and is a fine singing-actress with a delightful stage presence. Married first to the conductor György Fischer and later to the tenor Peter Seiffert.

Porgi amor

Soprano aria for Countess Almaviva in Act II of Mozart's *Le Nozze di Figaro*.

Porgy and Bess

Opera in three acts by Gershwin. 1st perf. Boston, 30 Sept 1935; libr. by Ira Gershwin and Du Bose Heyward, after Dorothy and Du Bose Heyward's *Porgy*. Principal roles: Porgy (bass), Bess (sop), Sportin' Life (ten), Crown (bar), Serena (mezzo), Jake (bass), Clara (sop), Maria (mezzo), Robbins (ten). Gershwin's masterpiece, it is notable both for its incorporation of Broadway musical idioms into opera and for its highly successful use of traditional Negro music such as spirituals. Gershwin's will requires that all stage performances must be given with an all-black cast.

   Plot: Catfish Row, 1920s. The pugnacious stevedore Crown and the crippled Porgy vie for the affections of Bess. Bess moves from Crown to Porgy, who eventually kills Crown. Lured by the gambler, Sportin' Life, Bess leaves for New York and Porgy decides to follow her. [R]

Poro, Rè dell'Indie

Opera in three acts by Handel. 1st perf. London, 2 Feb 1731; libr. by Samuel Humphries, after Pietro Metastasio's *Alessandro nell'Indie*. Never one of Handel's more successful operas, it is nowadays only very rarely performed. [R]

Porpora, Nicola *(1686–1768)*

Italian composer and teacher. He wrote some 50 operas, mainly opera serias to Metastasian texts, many of which enjoyed considerable success in their day but which are all now long forgotten. They include *Siface* (Milan 26 Dec 1725; libr. Pietro Metastasio), *Ezio* (Venice 1728; libr. Metastasio) and *Mitridate* (London 24 Jan 1736; libr. C. Cibber). He was also one of the most famous singing teachers of his age, whose pupils included Caffarelli and Farinelli.

Portamento (Italian for 'carrying')

The vocal technique of bridging the interval between two notes with no break in the sound and with a very slight anticipation of the second note.

Porterlied

Bass-baritone aria (the drinking song) for Plunkett in Act III of Flotow's *Martha*.

Porter, Andrew *(b 1928)*

British critic and translator. One of the most perceptive, intelligent and constructive of contemporary British critics, he wrote largely for the *Financial Times* and later for *The New Yorker*. He won great acclaim for his magnificent translation of the *Ring* for the English National Opera, for whom he also made fine translations of *Rigoletto* and *Don Carlos* (the full original score of which he rediscovered in Paris).

Portugal

See Teatro São Carlos, Lisbon

Portugal, Marcos Antônio da Fonseca *(b Ascenção; also known as Portogallo) (1762–1830)*

Portuguese composer. He wrote 21 light comedies in Portuguese, including the popular *A Castanheira* (Lisbon 1787), and 35 Italian operas. Many of the latter enjoyed great success in their day but are all now forgotten. They include *Alceste* (Lisbon 1798), *Gli Orazi e Curiazi* (Ferrara 1798; libr. Antonio Sografi) and *Fernando nel Messico* (Venice 1799; libr. F. Tarducci), usually regarded as his finest work.

Portuguese opera composers

See Almeida; Portugal; Silva

Other national opera composers include José de Arneiro (1838–1903), Rui Coelho (*b* 1892), Alfredo Keil (1850–1907), Antônio Leal Moreira (*d* 1819) and Francisco da Sá Noronha (1820–81).

Posa, Marquis of

Baritone role in Verdi's *Don Carlos*. He is Rodrigo, the liberal friend of Carlos.

Postillon de Longjumeau, Le

Opera in three acts by Adam. 1st perf. Paris, 13 Oct 1836; libr. by Adolphe de Leuven and Léon Lévy Brunswick. Principal roles: Chapelou (ten), Madame de Latour (sop), de Courcy (bar). Adam's most successful opera and his only work which is still performed.

Plot: France. The postillion Chapelou leaves his bride Madeleine on their wedding night intending to become a great opera singer. Possessing a fine voice, he is engaged by de Courcy, the manager of the royal amusements, to sing at Fontainebleau, where he becomes a great star. He proposes to the wealthy Madame de Latour, who turns out to be none other than Madeleine. All thus ends happily. [R]

Postlude

The opposite of prelude, it means a final piece of music. In opera, it usually refers to a short orchestral piece after an aria. A famous example is that to Fiesco's 'Il lacerato spirito' in Verdi's *Simon Boccanegra*.

Poulenc, Francis *(1899–1963)*

French composer. A member of the group 'Les Six', he wrote four stage works. They are the operetta *Le Gendarme Incompris* (Paris May 1921; libr. Jean Cocteau), the surrealist comedy *Les Mamelles de Tirésias**, the religious *Dialogues des Carmélites** and the monodrama *La Voix Humaine**.

Pountney, David *(b 1947)*

British producer. One of the outstanding British opera producers of the younger generation, his productions are sometimes highly controversial, but are always powerfully theatrical and always thought-provoking. He has had particular success with the Welsh National Opera and Scottish Opera Janáček cycle and with *Hänsel und Gretel, Fate, Doktor Faust* and *Christmas Eve* for the English National Opera. He was director of productions for Scottish Opera (1976–80) and for the English National Opera (1982–).

Poveri fiori

Soprano aria for Adriana in Act IV of Cilea's *Adriana Lecouvreur*.

Poznań Opera (Posen when it was part of Prussia)

The opera house (cap. 950) in this Polish city opened on 2 June 1945, and in 1949 was named the Stanislaw

Moniuszko Opera House. The repertory is notable for its large number of Polish works, and its artistic standards have always been high. Musical directors have included Walerian Bierdiajew and Robert Satanowski.

Prague National Theatre

The present opera house (cap. 1,598) opened on 18 Nov 1883, replacing the previous theatre of the same name which opened on 11 June 1881 but which burnt down less than two months later. Czechoslovakia's leading opera house, which maintains very high artistic standards, musical directors have included Adolf Čech, Karel Kovařovic, Otakar Ostrčil, Václav Talich, Otakar Jeremiáš, Zdeněk Chalabala, Jaroslav Krombholc, Václav Neumann and Zdeněk Košler. Also associated with the National Theatre complex are the Tyl Theatre (cap. 1,129), which opened on 21 April 1783 and was enlarged in 1834, and the Smetana Theatre (originally called the Neues Deutches Theater) (cap. 1,044), which opened in 1887 and whose musical directors included Angelo Neumann, Zemlinsky and George Szell.

Pré aux Clercs, Le (The Clerks' Meadow)

Opera in three acts by Hérold. 1st perf. Paris, 15 Dec 1832; libr. by François-Antoine-Eugène de Planard, after Prosper Mérimée's Chronique du Règne de Charles IX. Principal roles: Marguerite de Valois (mezzo), Isabelle de Béarn (sop), Baron de Mergy (ten), Comte de Comminges (bar). Sct at the time of the St Bartholomew Massacre, it is Hérold's last completed opera. It was enormously successful at its appearance, clocking up 1,000 performances in Paris alone within 40 years, but is nowadays all but forgotten.

Plot: Paris. The Baron de Mergy and the Comte de Comminges are rivals for the love of Isabelle de Béarn, the ward of Marguerite de Valois. The two men fight a duel at the field known as Pré aux Clercs and Comminges is killed. Isabelle and the Baron are united.

Preghiera (Italian for 'prayer')

An aria or chorus in which the characters pray for divine assistance, it was a highly popular ingredient of early 19th-century Italian opera. There are famous examples in Mosè in Egitto and Maria Stuarda.

Prelude (from the Latin praeludium, something played before another work)

An orchestral introduction to the act of an opera, such as the openings to the third acts of Parsifal and La Traviata. Usually shorter than an overture, it lacks the latter's formal structure.

Près des remparts de Séville

Mezzo aria (the Seguidilla) for Carmen in Act I of Bizet's Carmen.

Prêtre, Georges (b 1924)

French conductor, particularly associated with the French and Italian repertories. One of the leading postwar interpreters of French opera, even if sometimes rather idiosyncratic, he conducted the first performance of La Voix Humaine.

Previn, André (b Andreas Priwin) (b 1929)

American conductor and composer, long resident in Britain. Best known as a symphonic conductor, his operatic appearances have been very rare indeed.

Previtali, Fernando (1907–85)

Italian conductor, particularly associated with the Italian repertory, especially Verdi and 20th-century works. He was musical director of the Radio Italiana Orchestra (1936–53), with which he conducted the 1951 Verdi cycle, and was artistic director of the Teatro Regio, Turin and the Teatro Communale, Genoa. He conducted the first performances of Dallapiccola's *Volo di Notte* and Ghedini's *Rè Hassan* and *Le Baccanti*.

Prey, Hermann (b 1929)

German baritone, particularly associated with Mozart and Schubert roles and with Viennese operetta. One of the outstanding operatic artists (and Lieder singers) of the postwar era, he has a warm and beautiful voice used with great intelligence and musicianship, and is a fine singing-actor with an engaging stage personality. He created Meton in Křenek's *Pallas Athene Weint*. His autobiography, *First Night Fever*, was published in 1986.

Preziosilla

Mezzo role in Verdi's *La Forza del Destino*. She is a gypsy camp-follower.

Přibyl, Vilém (b 1925)

Czech tenor, particularly associated with heavier German, Italian and Czech roles, especially Florestan and Dalibor. Possibly the finest Czech tenor of the postwar era, he had a fine and remarkably well-placed voice which he used with musicianship and great intelligence.

Price, Leontyne (b 1927)

American soprano, particularly associated with Verdi and Puccini roles, especially Aida. One of the outstanding lyrico-dramatic sopranos of the postwar era, she had a rich, warm and luscious voice which she used with unfailing musicianship. Her fine stage presence was enhanced by her great personal beauty. She created Cleopatra in Barber's *Antony and Cleopatra*. Married for a time to the baritone William Warfield (b 1920).

Price, Margaret (b 1941)

British soprano, particularly associated with Mozart and Verdi roles, especially Donna Anna and Desdemona. One of the outstanding contemporary Mozartians, she has a rich and creamy voice, with considerable reserves of power, which she uses with fine musicianship and an assured technique.

Prigioniero, Il (*The Prisoner*)

Opera in prologue and one act by Dallapiccola. 1st perf. Turin Radio, 30 Nov 1949; 1st stage perf. Florence, 20 May 1950; libr. by the composer, after Villiers de l'Isle Adam's *La Torture par l'Espérance* and Charles Coster's *La Légende d'Ulenspiegel*. Principal roles: Prisoner (bar), Mother (sop), Jailer/ Grand Inquisitor (ten). Dallapiccola's masterpiece and arguably the finest postwar Italian opera, it is an intensely powerful work, notable for its impressive choral writing.

Plot: late 16th-century Saragossa. A prisoner of the Inquisition finds new hope when his jailer calls him 'friend'. He finds his prison door ajar, and makes his way past monks who appear not to notice him into a spring garden. There, however, he is enfolded in the arms of the jailer, now revealed as the Grand Inquisitor. The prisoner realises that he has succumbed to the worst torture of all: that of hope. [R]

Prima, Primo (Italian for 'first')

A title given to the leading singer, as in Prima donna, Primo uomo, Primo tenore etc. A reigning diva is sometimes called Prima donna assoluta.

Prima Donna

Comic opera in one act by Benjamin.
1st perf. London, 23 Feb 1949
(composed 1933); libr. by Cedric Cliffe.
Set in 18th-century Venice, it is a satire
on the rivalries of two jealous singers.
Successful at its appearance, it is
nowadays all but forgotten.

Prima la Musica e Poi le
Parole (First the Music and Then the Words)

Comic opera in one act by Salieri. 1st
perf. Vienna, 7 Feb 1786; libr. by
Giovanni Battista Casti. Principal roles:
Maestro (bass), Poet (bar), Eleonora
(sop), Tonina (mezzo). Salieri's best-
known opera, it was first performed
together with Mozart's Der
Schauspieldirektor as a kind of
unofficial competition between the two
composers. It is a discussion between a
poet and a composer about the relative
importance of their respective
contributions to opera. It is still
occasionally performed. [R]

Prince Igor (Knyaz Igor)

Opera in prologue and four acts by
Borodin. 1st perf. St Petersburg, 4 Nov
1890 (composed 1869); libr. by the
composer, after a scenario by Vladimir
Stasov. Principal roles: Igor (bar),
Konchak (bass), Vladimir (ten),
Yaroslavna (sop), Konchakovna
(mezzo), Prince Galitsky (bass).
Borodin's masterpiece, it was left
unfinished at his death and was
completed by Rimsky-Korsakov and
Glazunov. A vast nationalist epic, it
incorporates much traditional material,
and few operas have depicted so
successfully (or so excitingly) the clash
of different cultures.

Plot: Russia, 1185. Igor departs to
wage battle against the Tartar Polovtski
tribe. In his absence, his wife

Yaroslavna forces the governor Prince
Galitsky (Igor's brother) to curb his
feverish supporters. Igor is defeated and
he and his son Vladimir are captured.
Vladimir falls in love with
Konchakovna, the daughter of
Konchak, the Polovtsian Khan.
Konchak offers Igor his freedom if he
will cease hostilities against him, but
the Prince refuses and escapes. Holding
Vladimir as a hostage and allowing him
to marry Konchakovna so as to
discourage escape attempts, Konchak
decides to march on Russia. Igor
returns home to a warm welcome and
resolves to raise new troops to meet the
Polovtsian threat. [R]

Princess

Mezzo role in Puccini's Suor Angelica.
She is Angelica's aunt.

Princess Ida
or Castle Adamant

Operetta in three acts by Sullivan. 1st
perf. London, 5 Jan 1884; libr. by W.
S. Gilbert, partly after Alfred Lord
Tennyson's The Princess. Principal
roles: Ida (sop), Hilarion (ten), Cyril
(ten), Florian (bar), King Gama (bar),
King Hildebrand (b-bar), Arac (bass),
Lady Blanche (mezzo), Lady Psyche
(sop), Melissa (sop). Musically one of
the finest of all the Savoy Operas (and
the only one to be in three acts and to
have dialogue in blank verse), it is a
satire on women's emancipation and on
the Darwinian theory of evolution.

Plot: King Gama's daughter Ida,
married as a baby to King Hildebrand's
son Hilarion, believes that man (being
descended from apes) is an inferior
species to woman. She has shut herself
away in a university with her followers
and has resolved to have nothing
further to do with men. Hilarion and
his friends Cyril and Florian secretly
enter Ida's castle disguised as women

undergraduates, but are discovered when Cyril gets drunk. Hilarion is condemned to death and Hildebrand's forces besiege the castle. Ida finally relents and accepts Hilarion when it is pointed out to her that without men there will be no posterity to praise her noble ideals. [R]

Prinz von Homberg, Der

Opera in three acts by Henze. 1st perf. Hamburg, 22 May 1960; libr. by Ingeborg Backmann, after Heinrich Wilhelm von Kleist's play. Principal roles: Prince Friedrich (bar), Natalie (sop), Elector of Brandenburg (ten).

Plot: The military exploits of Prince Friedrich have been responsible for Brandenburg's military victory. Nonetheless, the Elector condemns him to death for military disobedience. Friedrich accepts the sentence, but is then pardoned and united with his beloved Natalie.

Prise de Troie, La (The Capture of Troy)

Part I (Acts I and II) of Berlioz's Les Troyens*.

Pritchard, Sir John (b 1921)

British conductor, particularly associated with Mozart operas and with the Italian repertory. One of the leading British opera conductors of the postwar era, he was musical director of the Glyndebourne Festival (1969–78), the Cologne Opera (1978–88), the Théâtre Royal de la Monnaie, Brussels (1981–86) and the San Francisco Opera Association (1986–). He conducted the first performances of Gloriana, King Priam and The Midsummer Marriage.

Procida

Bass role in Verdi's Les Vêpres Siciliennes. He is a Sicilian physician and patriot.

Prodigal Son, The

Opera in one act by Britten (Op 81). 1st perf. Orford, 10 June 1968; libr. by William Plomer, after St Luke's Gospel. Principal roles: Abbot/Tempter (ten), Younger Son (ten), Elder Son (bar), Father (bass). The third of Britten's Three Church Parables, it is a taut and economical setting of the famous biblical story. [R]

Producer

See panel on page 460

Prokofiev, Sergei (1891–1953)

Russian composer. He wrote three youthful operas which he later destroyed, including The Giant (Velikan, 1900), written at the age of nine. His eight mature operas are Maddalena (BBC Radio 25 March 1979; composed 1911) [R], which was prepared for performance by Edward Downes, The Gambler*, his first major success, The Love of Three Oranges*, his best-known opera in the West, the powerful The Fiery Angel*, Semyon Kotko*, the comedy The Duenna*, the vast and magnificent War and Peace*, and The Story of a Real Man*, which was written as a kind of apologia after his condemnation for 'formalism' by the Stalinists in 1948. His pungent, witty and sometimes grotesque and iconoclastic early style gave way in his later works (partly as a result of political circumstances) to a more lyrical and patriotic vein.

Prompter

He sits in a small box (called buca in Italy) and feeds the singers the words of nearly every line, and in Italy also relays the conductor's beat. The system, one of opera's worst features, is hardly conducive to a musico-dramatic

PRODUCER

The operatic producer (sometimes also called director) is essentially a 20th-century phenomenon. In the 17th century, the ballet master was in charge of stage movement, and in the 18th century either the stage manager or (in comedy) the principal basso-buffo was responsible. In the mid-19th century, composers began to realise the importance of the overall mis-en-scène, and a number – such as Weber, Verdi and Spohr – took an active part in production. The modern concept of the producer derives (as do virtually all developments in operatic performance) from Wagner, with his insistence on *Gesamtkunstwerk* ('unified work of art'). His ideas were quickly adopted by musicians elsewhere (especially by Mahler and Toscanini), and it was soon realised that they were best executed by producers from the theatre. The results of this last development have contributed greatly to the raising of dramatic standards in opera performances, but they have not always been happy. Some producers (especially in the postwar period) have used opera as a means of promoting their personal political views, often wilfully twisting the composer's intentions in the process. The producer is called *Régisseur* in France, *Spielleiter* in Germany, *Regista* in Italy and General Stage Director in the United States.

In recent years, a number of conductors have acted as their own producers, such as Herbert von Karajan, Otto Klemperer, Yuri Temirkanov and Peter Maag. Many singers have also acted as producers, the most successful including Tito Gobbi, Sir Geraint Evans, Graziella Sciutti, George London, Ragnar Ulfung, Hans Hotter and Regina Resnik.

Below are listed the 31 operatic producers with entries in this dictionary. Their nationalities are given in brackets afterwards.

Arundell, Dennis (Br)	Graham, Colin (Br)	Ponelle, Jean-Pierre (Fr)
Capobianco, Tito (Arg)	Guthrie, Sir Tyrone (Br)	Pountney, David (Br)
Chéreau, Patrice (Fr)	Hall, Sir Peter (Br)	Rennert, Günther (Ger)
Copley, John (Br)	Hartmann, Rudolf (Ger)	Strehler, Giorgio (It)
Cox, John (Br)	Herz, Joachim (Ger)	Ustinov, Peter (Br)
Dexter, John (Br)	Kašlík, Václav (Cz)	Visconti, Luchino (It)
Ebert, Carl (Ger)	Merrill, Nathaniel (US)	Wagner, Wieland (Ger)
Everding, August (Ger)	Miller, Dr Jonathan (Br)	Wallmann, Margherita
Felsenstein, Walter (Aus)	Moshinsky, Elijah (Aust)	(Aus)
Friedrich, Götz (Ger)	Nemirovich-Danchenko,	Zeffirelli, Franco (It)
Gentele, Göran (Swe)	Vladimir (Russ)	
Graf, Herbert (Aus)		

performance – particularly when some prompters are so loud that an aria becomes a duet. Some companies, such as the English National Opera, have mercifully banished the prompt box from most performances. The prompter is called *Maestro suggeritore* in Italy and *Souffleur* in France and Germany.

Prophète, Le

Opera in five acts by Meyerbeer. 1st perf. Paris, 16 April 1849; libr. by Eugène Scribe. Principal roles: Jean de Leyden (ten), Berthe (sop), Fidès (mezzo), Count Oberthal (bar), Zacharias (bass). Based on an historical incident during the 16th-century

Anabaptist uprising when Jan Neuckelzoon (1509–36) had himself crowned in Münster, it was enormously popular in the 19th century but is nowadays only infrequently performed.

Plot: Dordrecht and Münster, early 16th century. The wedding of Jean de Leyden and Berthe is frustrated by Count Oberthal, who desires Berthe himself and orders her to his castle. To take revenge against Oberthal, Jean joins the rebellious Anabaptists, whose prophet he becomes, leading them in the capture of Münster. His arbitrary power goes to his head and he develops a taste for cruelty, degrading his mother Fidès and precipitating Berthe to commit suicide. At last appreciating the extent of his depravity, he readily joins his revelling followers in a building which he knows will explode. Fidès joins him in the inferno. [R]

Prophetess, The
or The History of Dioclesian
Opera by Purcell. 1st perf. London, 1690; libr. by Thomas Betterton, after Sir Francis Beaumont and John Fletcher's play. Perhaps more of a play with music than a real opera, it is rarely performed. [R Exc]

Prosdocimo
Baritone role in Rossini's *Il Turco in Italia*. He is a poet.

Protagonist, Der
Opera in one act by Weill (Op 14). 1st perf. Dresden, 27 March 1926; libr. by Georg Kaiser, after his play. Principal roles: Girl (mezzo), Husband (ten), Wife (bar), Monk (bass). Weill's first opera, it is occasionally performed. [R]

Prova generale (Italian for 'general trial')
The dress rehearsal in an Italian opera house.

Prozess, Der (The Trial)
Opera in two acts by Einem (Op 14). 1st perf. Salzburg, 17 Aug 1953; libr. by Boris Blacher and Heinz von Kramer, after Franz Kafka's novel. One of Einem's best works, it has met with considerable success in Germany.

Prus, Jaroslav
Baritone role in Janáček's *The Macropolus Case*. Jánek's father, he is a disputant in the Gregor v Prus case.

Publius
Bass role in Mozart's *La Clemenza di Tito*. He is a Roman centurion.

Puccini, Giacomo (1858–1924)
Italian composer. Usually regarded as the master verismo composer, few of his operas are in fact truly verismo works in the mould set by Mascagni. More lyrical and eclectic in style than his contemporaries, he was influenced by Verdi and later by Wagner, Debussy and even Lehár and Stravinsky. His first opera *Le Villi** was followed by the unsuccessful *Edgar**. Its successor *Manon Lescaut** was his first mature work and placed him at the forefront of contemporary opera composers. It was followed by *La Bohème**, *Tosca**, the initially unsuccessful *Madama Butterfly**, *La Fanciulla del West**, the quasi-operetta *La Rondine**, *Il Trittico* (*Il Tabarro**, *Suor Angelica** and *Gianni Schicchi**, his only comedy) and the unfinished *Turandot**.

George Bernard Shaw was quick off the mark to hail Puccini as Verdi's successor, but this is to push Puccini's merits too far. He was an accomplished musical craftsman, whose technique became ever more impressive, he had a happy gift for comedy and he possessed a sure theatrical sense. However, his music – for all its emotionalism and rich lyricism – is largely innocent of the true dramatic insight possessed by Verdi.

Punch and Judy

Opera in one act by Birtwistle. 1st perf. Aldeburgh, 8 June 1968; libr. by Stephen Pruslin. Principal roles: Punch (bar), Choregos (bar), Judy (mezzo), Lawyer (ten), Doctor (bass), Pretty Polly (sop). Birtwistle's first opera, dealing with the subject of violence, it has met with considerable success. [R]

Puppet operas

See Marionette operas

Purcell, Henry *(c 1659–95)*

British composer. He wrote only one true opera, *Dido and Aeneas**, a masterpiece in miniature which ranks him as the greatest British opera composer before Britten. He wrote many other stage works, mainly incidental music to plays. Of these, *The Faery Queen**, *King Arthur**, *The Prophetess** and *The Indian Queen** are quasi-operatic and are sometimes staged as operas. His brother Daniel (*c* 1663–1717) was also a composer who wrote many stage works, including the masque *The Judgement of Paris* (1701; libr. William Congreve) and the last act of his brother's *The Indian Queen*.

Puritani di Scozia, I *(The Puritans of Scotland)*

Opera in three acts by Bellini. 1st perf. Paris, 25 Jan 1835; libr. by Carlo Pepoli, after Jacques Ancelot and Xavier Boniface Saintine's *Têtes Rondes et Cavaliers*, itself based on Sir Walter Scott's *Old Morality*. Principal roles: Elvira (sop), Arturo (ten), Riccardo (bar), Giorgio (bass), Enrichetta

(mezzo), Gualtiero (bass). Bellini's last opera and one of his finest works.

Plot: mid-17th century Plymouth. The Puritan governor Gualtiero Walton has promised the hand of his daughter Elvira to Sir Richard Forth. However, Elvira loves the royalist Lord Arthur Talbot and Gualtiero consents to the match. On the wedding day, Arthur is given a pass to leave the castle with his bride. He discovers that Charles I's widow Henrietta is held captive in the castle and uses his pass to let her escape, wearing Elvira's bridal dress as a disguise. Sir Richard sees Arthur leaving with another woman, and the knowledge causes Elvira to go out of her mind. Returning later to see Elvira, Arthur is arrested and sentenced to death. However, news is brought of a Puritan victory and a general amnesty for all prisoners. Elvira regains her reason and is united with Arthur. [R]

Pushkin, Alexander

See panel on page 463

Pygmalion

Opera-ballet in one act by Rameau. 1st perf. Paris, 27 Aug 1748; libr. by Ballot de Savot, after Houdart de la Motte's *Le Triomphe des Arts*. Principal roles: Pygmalion (ten), Céphise (sop), Love (sop), Statue (sop). It is still occasionally performed.

Plot: the sculptor Pygmalion has fallen in love with a female statue which he has created. He rejects the love of Céphise, and Love brings the statue to life. Pygmalion takes her hand and she falls in love with him. Love summons the Graces, who instruct the statue in dancing. [R]

Pylade

Tenor role in Gluck's *Iphigénie en Tauride*. He is Orestes' companion.

ALEXANDER PUSHKIN

The works of the Russian writer and poet Alexander Sergeyevich Pushkin (1799–1837) have inspired some 110 operas, far more than any other Russian writer. He is also the subject of operas by two minor composers. Below are listed, by work, those operas based on his writings by composers with entries in this dictionary.

Boris Godunov
Moussorgsky	*Boris Godunov*	1869

The Captain's Daughter
Cui	*The Captain's Daughter*	1911

The Captive of the Caucasus
Cui	*The Captive of the Caucasus*	1883

The Covetous Knight
Rachmaninov	*The Covetous Knight*	1906

Dubrovsky
Nápravník	*Dubrovsky*	1895
Napoli	*Dubrovski II*	1973

Eugene Onegin
Tchaikovsky	*Eugene Onegin*	1879

A Feast in Time of Plague
Cui	*A Feast in Time of Plague*	1901

The Golden Cockerel
Rimsky-Korsakov	*The Golden Cockerel*	1909

The Gypsies
Rachmaninov	*Aleko*	1893
Leoncavallo	*Zingari*	1912

The Little House at Kolomna
Stravinsky	*Mavra*	1922

Mistress into Maid
Zajc	*Lizinka*	1878

Mozart and Salieri

Rimsky-Korsakov	*Mozart and Salieri*	1898

Poltava

Tchaikovsky	*Mazeppa*	1884

The Queen of Spades

Halévy	*La Dame du Pique*	1850
Suppé	*Pique Dame*	1865
Tchaikovsky	*The Queen of Spades*	1890

Rusalka

Dargomijsky	*Rusalka*	1856

Ruslan and Ludmila

Glinka	*Ruslan and Ludmila*	1842

The Snowstorm

Dzerzhinsky	*Winter Night*	1946

The Stone Guest

Dargomijsky	*The Stone Guest*	1872 (U)

The Tale of Tsar Sultan

Rimsky-Korsakov	*The Tale of Tsar Sultan*	1900

The Triumph of Bacchus

Dargomijsky	*The Triumph of Bacchus*	1848

Quadri, Argeo *(b 1911)*
Italian conductor, particularly
associated with the Italian and French
repertories. Largely resident at the
Vienna Volksoper from 1957, he was a
reliable and rock-solid Italian maestro
of the old school.

Quaglio family
A family of German designers of Italian
extraction, descended from the fresco
painter Giulio Quaglio (1610–*c* 69). At
least 15 members of the family worked
in opera. The most important included:
(1) Giulio Quaglio (*c* 1700–65), who
worked in Vienna and designed the
original *Orfeo ed Euridice*.
(2) Lorenzo Quaglio (1730–1804), who
worked mainly in Mannheim and
Munich and who designed the original
Idomeneo.
(3) Simon Quaglio (1795–1878), who
worked in Munich and who was one of
the first designers to use built scenery.
He designed over 100 productions,
including a notable *Die Zauberflöte* in
1818.
(4) Angelo Quaglio (1829–90), who
worked in Munich and designed in an
illusionistic historical style. He assisted
Wagner on the first performances of
*Tristan und Isolde, Die Meistersinger
von Nürnberg, Das Rheingold* and *Die
Walküre*.
(5) Eugen Quaglio (1857–1942), who
worked mainly in Berlin and Prague.

Quand'ero paggio
Baritone arietta for Falstaff in Act II of
Verdi's *Falstaff*.

Quand j'étais roi de Béotie
Tenor aria for John Styx in Act III of
Offenbach's *Orphée aux Enfers*.

Quand l'Helvétie
Tenor/baritone/bass trio for Arnold,
Tell and Walther in Act III of Rossini's
Guillaume Tell. It is mercilessly
parodied by Offenbach in the Patriotic
Trio in Act III of *La Belle Hélène*.

Quando le sere al placido
Tenor aria for Rodolfo in Act II of
Verdi's *Luisa Miller*.

Quanto è bella
Tenor aria for Nemorino in Act I of
Donizetti's *L'Elisir d'Amore*.

Quarter-tone operas
A quarter-tone is half of a semitone: a
musical interval which was not found
in Western music until the 20th
century, when its use still remained
exceptional. Very few quarter-tone
operas have been written, partly
because of the obvious difficulty for
singers to pitch a quarter-tone
accurately. The most important quarter-
tone opera is Hába's *The Mother**.

Quartet
In opera, a musical number for four
solo singers, with or without chorus.
There are particularly fine examples in
Fidelio and *Rigoletto*.

Quatre Saisons, Les (*The Four Seasons*)

Ballet music in Act III of Verdi's *Les Vêpres Siciliennes*.

Quatro Rusteghi, I (*The Four Curmudgeons*; usually given in Britain as *The School for Fathers*)

Comic opera in three acts by Wolf-Ferrari. 1st perf. (as *Die Vier Grobiane*) Munich, 19 March 1906; libr. (in Venetian dialect) by Giuseppe Pizzolato, after Carlo Goldoni's *I Rusteghi*. Principal roles: Lunado (bass), Margarita (mezzo), Lucieta (sop), Simone (b-bar), Marina (sop), Maurizio (bass), Filipeto (ten), Cancion (bass), Felice (sop), Riccardo (ten). Wolf-Ferrari's most successful full-length work, it is still regularly performed.

Plot: 18th-century Venice. Four curmudgeonly husbands vainly attempt to keep their women in order. The woman decide to teach their menfolk a lesson by allowing Lunado's daughter Lucieta to see Filipeto, the son of Maurizio, before their pre-arranged wedding, even though the men have forbidden this. [R]

Queen of Cornwall, The

Opera by Boughton. 1st perf. Glastonbury, Aug 1924; libr. after Thomas Hardy's play. Boughton's last opera and one of his finest works, it is a setting of the Tristan legend. Reasonably successful at its appearance, it is nowadays forgotten.

Queen of Golconda, The (*Drottningen av Golconda*)

Comic opera in three acts by Berwald. 1st perf. Stockholm, 3 April 1968 (composed 1864); libr. by the composer, after J. B. C. Vial and E. G. F. de Favières. Arguably Berwald's finest stage work, only the delightful overture is at all well-known.

Queen of Sheba, The

See Königin von Saba, Die; Reine de Saba, La

Queen of Shemakha

Soprano role in Rimsky-Korsakov's *The Golden Cockerel*. She is married to King Dodon.

Queen of Spades, The (*Pikovaya Dama*; sometimes incorrectly called *Pique Dame*)

Opera in three acts by Tchaikovsky (Op 68). 1st perf. St. Petersburg, 19 Dec 1890; libr. by the composer and Modest Tchaikovsky, after Alexander Pushkin. Principal roles: Hermann (ten), Lisa (sop), Countess (mezzo), Count Tomsky (bar), Prince Yeletsky (bar), Pauline (mezzo), Surin (bass). One of Tchaikovsky's finest and most powerful works.

Plot: late 18th-century St Petersburg. The poor soldier Hermann has fallen in love with a girl whom his friend Count Tomsky tells him is engaged to Prince Yeletsky. She is Lisa, granddaughter of the Countess who was once known as the Queen of Spades because she possessed the secret of the "three cards". Lisa returns Hermann's love and he becomes obsessed with learning the secret of winning at gambling so as to win money to marry Lisa. He demands the secret from the Countess, but she dies of fright without telling him. Lisa asks Hermann to meet her by the river, where the ghost of the Countess reveals the secret to Hermann and tells him to marry Lisa. When they meet, Hermann confirms Lisa's fears that he now cares more about gambling than about her by rushing off to a gaming house. In despair Lisa drowns herself in the river. Hermann wins on the first two cards and stakes his all on the third, but loses to Yeletsky, who draws the Queen of Spades. Hermann curses the Countess, whose ghost appears to him, then kills himself. [R]

Queen of the Night
Soprano role in Mozart's *Die Zauberflöte*. She is Pamina's mother.

Queler, Eve *(b 1936)*
American conductor, particularly associated with revivals of long-neglected operas, for the performance of which she founded the Opera Orchestra of New York in 1968.

Quel sangue versato
Soprano cabaletta for Elizabeth I in Act III of Donizetti's *Roberto Devereux*. The final scene of the opera and one of Donizetti's finest slow cabalettas, it is unusual in form in that the two verses have different words.

Querelle de Bouffons
See Guerre des Bouffons

Questa o quella
Tenor aria for the Duke of Mantua in Act I of Verdi's *Rigoletto*.

Questo è il bacio di Tosca
(*This is the kiss of Tosca*)
Tosca's famous cry as she stabs Baron Scarpia in Act II of Puccini's *Tosca*.

Quickly, Mistress
The gossip in Shakespeare's *Merry Wives of Windsor* and *King Henry IV* appears as: (1) Mezzo role in Verdi's *Falstaff*. (2) Soprano role in Holst's *At the Boar's Head*. (3) Mezzo role in Vaughan Williams' *Sir John in Love*.

Quiet Flows the Don (*Tikhiy Don*)
Opera in four acts by Dzerzhinsky. 1st perf. Leningrad, 22 Oct 1935; libr. by Leonid Dzerzhinsky, after Mikhail Sholokhov's novel. Principal roles: Grigory Melekhov (ten), Natalya (sop), Aksinya (mezzo), Yevgeny Listinsky (bar). Much the most successful of Dzerzhinsky's operas, it was hailed by Stalin as a model of 'socialist realism', and was a landmark in the development of 'orthodox Soviet' music. It has met with no success outside Russia.

Plot: Russia, 1914–17. Grigory's parents are forcing him into a marriage with Natalya. His beloved Aksinya appears at the wedding and the two elope together. Grigory goes to war and Aksinya works as a cook in the household of General Listinsky. She hears (incorrectly) that Grigory has been killed and is seduced by the general's son Yevgeny. On the Austrian front, Grigory foretells that the Tsar will be overthrown and the war concluded. Discovering Aksinya's infidelity, he kills Yevgeny before marching off with the revolutionary forces.

Quiet Place, A
Opera in three acts by Bernstein. 1st perf. Houston, 17 June 1983; libr. by Stephen Wadsworth. Principal roles: Sam (bar), Sam Junior (bar), Dede (sop), François (ten). Bernstein's only full-length opera, it was originally written as a sequel to his *Trouble in Tahiti**, but the earlier opera was subsequently incorporated as two flashbacks. [R]

Qui la voce
Soprano aria (the Mad Scene) for Elvira in Act III of Bellini's *I Puritani*.

Quilico, Louis *(b 1929)*

Canadian baritone, particularly associated with the Italian and French repertories. He possessed a rich, warm and bright-toned voice with an exciting upper register and had a good stage presence. He created a role in Milhaud's *La Mère Coupable*. His son Gino is also a successful baritone.

Quilter, Roger *(1877–1953)*

British composer. Best known as a song composer, he also wrote one opera, the unsuccessful *Julia* (London 3 Dec 1936).

Quinault, Philippe *(1635–88)*

French playwright and librettist. His long collaboration with Lully included *Cadmus et Hermione*, *Alceste*, *Thésée*, *Atys*, *Isis*, *Proserpine*, *Persée*, *Phaéton*, *Amadis*, *Roland* and *Armide et Renaud*, and their partnership laid the foundations of French opera. A number of his texts were subsequently set by other composers, including Gluck, Piccinni and Uttini. He appears as a character in Isouard's *Lully et Quinault*.

Quince, Peter

Bass role in Britten's *A Midsummer Night's Dream*. He is the leader of the mechanicals.

Quint, Peter

Tenor role in Britten's *The Turn of the Screw*. He is the dead manservant whose ghost attempts to corrupt Miles.

Quintet

In opera, a musical number for five solo singers, with or without chorus. There is a famous example in Wagner's *Die Meistersinger von Nürnberg*.

Quivar, Florence *(b 1944)*

American mezzo, particularly associated with the Italian and French repertories. She possesses a rich and beautiful voice used with fine musicianship. Best known as a concert singer, her operatic appearances to date have been sporadic.

Quixote, Don

The hero of Miguel Cervantes' novel appears in many operas, including: (1) Bass role in Massenet's *Don Quichotte*. (2) Baritone role in de Falla's *El Retablo de Maese Pedro*.

Quotations

Composers have often quoted other composers' music in their works. This takes three forms. There is plagiarism or straight theft; for example, the introduction to the Ulrica scene in Verdi's *Un Ballo in Maschera* is lifted from the beginning of the Tower Scene in Donizetti's *Roberto Devereux*. In operetta there is quotation for satirical purposes: the sending-up of a famous operatic number. Examples of this include the Patriotic Trio in *La Belle Hélène* (based on *Guillaume Tell*), the conspiracy scene in *La Grande-Duchesse de Gérolstein* (based on *Les Huguenots*) and 'A nice dilemma' in *Trial by Jury* (based on *La Sonnambula*). Finally, there is direct quotation for a specific purpose. Examples of operatic melodies deliberately quoted elsewhere include:

- Gluck's *Orfeo ed Euridice* in Offenbach's *Orphée aux Enfers*.
- Grétry's *Guillaume Tell* in Tchaikovsky's *The Queen of Spades*.
- Martín y Soler's *Una Cosa Rara* in Mozart's *Don Giovanni*.
- Mozart's *Don Giovanni* in Offenbach's *Les Contes d'Hoffmann*.
- Mozart's *Le Nozze di Figaro* in Mozart's *Don Giovanni*.

- Rossini's *Guillaume Tell* in Shostakovich's Symphony No 15.
- Rossini's *Otello* in Donizetti's *Il Campanello*.

- Sarti's *Fra Due Litiganti* in Mozart's *Don Giovanni*.
- Sullivan's *H.M.S. Pinafore* in Sullivan's *Utopia Limited*.

Rabaud, Henri *(1873–1949)*
French composer and conductor. He
wrote six operas: *La Fille de Roland*
(1904; libr. P. Ferrari, after H. de
Bornier), *Mârouf**, by far his most
successful work, *L'Appel de la Mer*
(1924; libr. composer, after John
Millington Synge's *Riders to the Sea*),
Roland et le Mauvais Garçon (1934;
libr. Lucien Népoty), *Martine* (1947;
libr. J. J. Bernard) and the unfinished
Les Jeux de l'Amour et du Hasard
(1954; libr. Marivaux), which was
completed by Busser and d'Ollone. He
was director of the Paris Opéra (1914–
18) and of the Paris Conservatory
(1920–40).

Rachel
Soprano role in Halévy's *La Juive*. She
is Cardinal Brogni's daughter.

Rachel, quand du Seigneur
Tenor aria for Eléazer in Act IV of
Halévy's *La Juive*.

Rachmaninov, Sergei *(1873–
1943)*
Russian composer, conductor and
pianist. He wrote four operas: the
student graduation work *Aleko**, the
comedy *The Covetous Knight**,
Francesca da Rimini* and the
unfinished *Monna Vanna* (1906; libr.
M. Slonov, after Maurice Maeterlinck).

Racine, Jean Baptiste
See panel on page 471

Radamès
Tenor role in Verdi's *Aida*. He is an
Egyptian general loved by Amneris and
in love with Aida.

Radamisto
Opera in three acts by Handel. 1st perf.
London, 27 April 1720; libr. by Nicola
Francesco Haym, after Domenico Lalli's
L'Amor Tirannico. Principal roles:
Radamisto (mezzo), Polissena (sop),
Zenobia (mezzo), Tigrana (sop),
Tiridate (ten), Farasmene (bass). It is
still performed from time to time.

Radio
See British Broadcasting
Corporation

Ragonde
Mezzo role in Rossini's *Le Comte Ory*.
She is Countess Adèle's companion.

Raimbaud
Baritone role in Rossini's *Le Comte
Ory*. He is Ory's friend.

Raimondi, Gianni *(b 1923)*
Italian tenor, particularly associated
with Verdi and Donizetti roles. He had
a pure, warm-timbred voice with a
brilliant upper register which he used
with style and great elegance of
phrasing.

Raimondi, Ruggero *(b 1941)*
Italian bass, particularly associated with
the Italian repertory and with Don
Giovanni (which he played in Joseph

JEAN BAPTISTE RACINE

Along with Philippe Quinault and Pierre Corneille, the French poet and playwright Jean Baptiste Racine (1639–99) exercised a considerable influence on opera in that his tragedies, with their theme of the conflict between love and duty and their concept of the benevolent despot, were the models on which Pietro Metastasio and Apostolo Zeno based many of their opera seria libretti. Some 20 operas have been based directly on his plays. Below are listed, by play, those operas by composers with entries in this dictionary.

Andromaque
| Rossini | *Ermione* | 1814 |

Athalie
| Handel | *Athalia* | 1733 |
| Poissl | *Athalia* | 1814 |

Bajazet
| Hervé | *Les Turcs* | 1869 |

Bérénice
| Magnard | *Bérénice* | 1911 |

Iphigénie en Aulide
| Graun | *Iphigenia in Aulide* | 1748 |
| Gluck | *Iphigénie en Aulide* | 1774 |

Mithridate
| Graun | *Mitridate* | 1750 |
| Mozart | *Mitridate, Rè di Ponto* | 1770 |

Phèdre
| Rameau | *Hippolyte et Aricie* | 1733 |

Losey's film). The leading contemporary Italian bass, he possesses a warm, light-toned and beautiful basso cantante, which is used with fine musicianship and intelligence. He is an outstanding singing-actor, equally at home in serious or comic roles.

Raimondo
Bass role in Donizetti's *Lucia di Lammermoor*. He is the Ravenswood chaplain.

Rake's Progress, The
Opera in three acts and epilogue by Stravinsky. 1st perf. Venice, 11 Sept 1951; libr. by W. H. Auden and Chester Kallman after engravings by Hogarth. Principal roles: Tom Rakewell (ten), Anne Truelove (sop), Nick Shadow (bar), Baba the Turk (mezzo), Mother Goose (mezzo), Truelove (bass), Sellem (ten). The culmination of Stravinsky's neo-classical period, it

ranks as one of the greatest of all postwar operas.

Plot: 18th-century England. Tom Rakewell is engaged to Truelove's daughter Anne. The sinister Nick Shadow arrives to tell Tom that he has inherited a fortune from an unknown relation, and lures him to London and a life of vice and dubious business ventures. There Shadow becomes his servant and Tom, rejecting the faithful Anne, marries the bearded Baba the Turk at Nick's suggestion. Nick then persuades him to invest all his money in an invention supposed to turn stones into bread and Tom is ruined. The auctioneer Sellem disposes of his possessions. After a year, Shadow reveals himself to be the Devil, and offers Tom a game of cards with the young man's life as the stake. Tom wins, but Shadow drives him insane. Confined to the lunatic asylum of Bedlam, Tom believes himself to be Adonis and thinks that the visiting Anne is Venus. When she leaves he dies of grief. [R]

Rakhmaninoff, Sergey

See Rachmaninov, Sergei

Rákoczy March

March in Part I of Berlioz's *La Damnation de Faust*.

Raleigh, Sir Walter

The British explorer and statesman Sir Walter Raleigh (*c* 1552–1618) appears in a number of operas, including: (1) Bass role in Britten's *Gloriana*. (2) Tenor role in German's *Merrie England*. (3) Bass comprimario role in Donizetti's *Roberto Devereux*.

Ralf, Torsten *(1901–54)*

Swedish tenor, particularly associated with Strauss and Wagner roles. One of the leading dramatic tenors of the inter-war period, he created Apollo in *Daphne* and a role in Sutermeister's *Die Zauberinsel*. His brother Oscar (1881–1964) was also a successful heroic tenor, who also translated some 40 operas into Swedish. His autobiography, *The Tenor Goes Into the Ring*, was published in 1953.

Rameau, Jean-Philippe *(1683– 1764)*

French composer. His first real opera was *Samson* (1733; libr. Voltaire). It was followed, amongst others, by *Hippolyte et Aricie**, possibly his best-known work, *Les Indes Galantes**, *Castor et Pollux**, *Dardanus**, the opera-ballet *Les Fêtes d'Hébé* (Paris 21 May 1739; libr. A. G. de Montdorge) [R Exc], *La Temple de la Gloire* (Versailles 27 Nov 1745; libr. Voltaire), *La Princesse de Navarre* (1745; libr. Voltaire) [R Exc], the comedy *Platée**, *Zoroastre**, *Naïs* (Paris 22 April 1749; libr. Louis de Cahusac) [R], *Acante et Céphise* (Paris 18 Nov 1751; libr. Jean-François Marmontel), *Anacréon**, *Pygmalion**, *Les Paladins* (Paris 12 Feb 1760; libr. D. de Monticourt) [R Exc] and the unfinished *Les Boréades**.

Building on Lully's groundwork, Rameau was one of the fathers of French opera. Whilst retaining Lully's classical formality, Rameau brought far greater flexibility and power to his work, and laid greater emphasis on the drama, both musically and structurally. He expanded the role of the orchestra whilst simultaneously curbing the excesses of singers, in a way which looks forward to (and indeed influenced) Gluck, who said of one of his operas "it stinks of music". The leading representative of the French tradition in the Guerre des Bouffons*, Rameau was highly regarded by his contemporaries: Campra said of *Hippolyte et Aricie* that it had "enough music for ten operas" and went on to predict – correctly – "this man will drive us all from the stage". Rameau's full stature and historical importance have only recently been fully appreciated. His works suffered a long period of neglect, but in the last decade there has been a major revival of interest in his operas (especially in Britain and France) and performances are now quite frequent.

Ramey, Samuel *(b 1942)*
American bass, particularly associated with the French and Italian repertories, especially Rossini. One of the outstanding operatic artists of the younger generation, he possesses a magnificent voice of considerable agility which he uses with fine musicianship and an assured technique. He is also an impressive singing-actor.

Ramiro
(1) Tenor role in Rossini's *La Cenerentola*. He is the prince in search of a bride. (2) Baritone role in Ravel's *L'Heure Espagnole*. He is a muleteer. (3) Mezzo trouser-role in Mozart's *La Finta Giardiniera*.

Ramphis
Bass role in Verdi's *Aida*. He is the high priest.

Rance, Jack
Baritone role in Puccini's *La Fanciulla del West*. He is the sheriff.

Randle, Thomas *(b 1958)*
American tenor, particularly associated with Mozart roles and with 20th-century works. He possesses a beautiful dark-toned voice of considerable range, used with musicianship and good taste, and has exemplary phrasing and diction. An impressive singing-actor

with a handsome stage appearance, he is one of the most talented and versatile young artists to have emerged in the late 1980s.

Randová, Eva *(b 1936)*
Czech mezzo, particularly associated with the Czech and German repertories. An intense and powerful singing-actress with a magnificent, rich and intelligently used voice, she is a dramatic mezzo in the grand tradition.

Rangoni
Baritone role in Moussorgsky's *Boris Godunov*. He is a Jesuit priest.

Rangström, Türe *(1884–1947)*
Swedish composer. He wrote three operas which met with some success in Sweden: *The Crown Bride* (*Kronbruden*, Stuttgart 1919, composed 1915), *In the Middle Ages* (*Middelalderlig*, 1918) and the unfinished *Gilgamesj* (1944; libr. after *The Epic of Gilgamesh*), which was completed by J. Fernström.

Rankl, Karl *(1898–1968)*
Austrian conductor and composer, particularly associated with the German repertory. He was musical director of Covent Garden (1946–51), where he helped to build up the new company, and of the Australian Opera (1958–60). He conducted the first performance of Křenek's *Karl V*. He also composed one opera, the unperformed *Deidre of the Sorrows* (1951; libr. after John Millington Synge), which was a joint winner of the Festival of Britain competition.

Raoul
Tenor role in: (1) Meyerbeer's *Les Huguenots*. He is a Huguenot soldier.

(2) Offenbach's *La Vie Parisienne*. He is a rake in love with Métella.

Rape of Lucretia, The

Opera in two acts by Britten (Op 37). 1st perf. Glyndebourne, 12 July 1946; libr. by Ronald Duncan, after André Obey's *Le Viol de Lucrèce*, itself based on Livy and Shakespeare's *The Rape of Lucrece*. Principal roles: Lucretia (mezzo), Tarquinius (bar), Male and Female Chorus (ten and sop), Bianca (mezzo), Junius (bar), Collatinus (bass), Lucia (sop). Britten's second opera, it is a taut and powerful chamber work, written for an orchestra of 12, which interprets the classical story from a Christian standpoint.

Plot: Rome, 500 BC. Collatinus' wife Lucretia is the only wife proved to have been faithful to her absent officer husband, when the men unexpectedly return home. Her fidelity inflames and challenges the proud Tarquinius, who rides from Rome and rapes her. She kills herself in shame. [R]

Rappresentazione di Anima e di Corpo, La (*The Representation of the Soul and the Body*)

Sacred dramatic oratorio by de Cavalieri. 1st perf. Rome, Feb 1600; libr. by Agostino Manni. An allegorical work, which marks one of the earliest uses of the monodic style in sacred music, the characters represent various human attributes as well as the soul and the body. Perhaps the most important 'proto-opera'. [R]

Rataplan

A word used to describe the sound of a drum, and so often used in vocal music with a military flavour. There are operatic examples in *Les Huguenots*, *La Fille du Régiment* and *La Forza del Destino*, and Sullivan sends it up in *Cox and Box*.

Rattle, Simon (*b* 1955)

British conductor, particularly associated with Mozart and Janáček operas. Perhaps the most talented and exciting of the younger generation of British conductors, his operatic performances, mainly at Glyndebourne, have to date been sadly sporadic. He is married to the soprano Elise Ross.

Ravel, Maurice (*1875–1937*)

French composer, notable for his witty and brilliantly orchestrated music. He wrote two highly successful one-act operas: *L'Heure Espagnole** and *L'Enfant et les Sortilèges**.

Reardon, John (*1930–88*)

American baritone, particularly associated with Italian and 20th-century operas. A fine singing-actor with a large and wide-ranging repertory, he was also a successful film and television artist. He created roles in Moore's *Wings of the Dove* and *Carrie Nation*, Pasatieri's *The Seagull* and Levy's *Mourning Becomes Electra*.

Rebel, Jean-Fery (*1666–1747*)

French composer. Best known as an orchestral composer, he also wrote one opera, *Ulisse* (Paris 23 Jan 1703; libr. H. Guichard).

Re Cervo, Il

See König Hirsch

Recitative

Musical declamation, written in ordinary notation but in which some freedom of rhythm is allowed, and which follows the pattern of ordinary speech rhythms. There are two types: (1) *Secco*. Italian for 'dry'.

Accompanied by the harpsichord (and sometimes also by a string bass), it is used for the rapid dialogue which carries forward the plot, particularly in comic operas. It had ceased to be used by the mid-19th century. (2) *Accompagnato*. Italian for 'accompanied', also known as *Stromentato*. Possibly first employed in 1663 by the composer Rovettino, it is a more elaborate accompaniment of the vocal line using the normal orchestra. It was used to accompany more emphatic phrases, such as the declamatory introduction to an aria. The dividing line between accompanied recitative and aria became increasingly blurred as the 19th century progressed.

Recondita armonia
Tenor aria for Cavaradossi in Act I of Puccini's *Tosca*.

Recorded opera
See Opera recordings; Video recordings

A check-list of all operas which have been commercially recorded will be found in Appendix 2.

Redburn, Mr
Baritone role in Britten's *Billy Budd*. He is the first lieutenant aboard H.M.S. Indomitable.

Rè dell'abisso
Mezzo aria for Ulrica in Act I of Verdi's *Un Ballo in Maschera*.

Red Line, The
Opera in two acts by Sallinen. 1st perf. Helsinki, 30 Nov 1978; libr. by the composer after Ilmari Kianto. Principal roles: Topi (bar), Riika (sop), Puntarpaa (bar), Simana (bass), Kaisa (mezzo). Sallinen's second opera, it has been widely performed. [R]

Red Whiskers
Tenor role in Britten's *Billy Budd*. He is an indentured sailor.

Reeves, Sims *(b John) (1818–1900)*
British tenor, particularly associated with the Italian and French repertories. The leading British tenor of the mid-19th century, he created Lyonnel in Balfe's *The Maid of Honour*. The latter part of his career was devoted solely to oratorio. His autobiography, *Life and Recollections*, was published in 1881.

Refice, Licinio *(1883–1954)*
Italian composer and priest. Most of his music was written for the church, but he also wrote two operas: the successful 'azione sacra' *Cecilia** and *Margherita da Cortona* (Milan 1938; libr. E. Mucci). He died whilst conducting a performance of the former.

Reggio Emilia
See Teatro Municipale, Reggio Emilia

Regina coeli
Chorus (the Easter Hymn) in Mascagni's *Cavalleria Rusticana*.

Régisseur
The term used in France for an opera producer.

Register
A part of the compass of the voice, which imparts its own distinctive sensation to the singer. The three registers are chest, middle and head.

Regnava nel silenzio

Soprano aria for Lucia in Act I of Donizetti's *Lucia di Lammermoor*. In the 19th century, it was often replaced by 'Perche non ho' from *Rosmonda d'Inghilterra*.

Reich, Günter *(1921–89)*

German baritone, particularly associated with 20th-century German roles, especially Schönberg, and Dr Schön in *Lulu*. An outstanding interpreter of 20th-century music, his powerful and incisive voice was used with great intelligence, and he had a strong stage presence. He created roles in Zimmermann's *Die Soldaten* and Blacher's *Zweihunderttausend Taler*.

Reimann, Aribert *(b 1936)*

German composer and pianist. One of the most successful contemporary German opera composers, with a powerful theatrical sense, he has written five operas. *Ein Traumspiel* (Kiel 1965; libr. C. Henius, after August Strindberg's *A Dream Play*) was followed by *Melusine* (Schwetzingen 1971; libr. Claus H. Henneberg, after Iwan Goll), the powerful Shakespearean *Lear**, the chamber opera *Die Gespenstersonate** and *Troades* (Munich 1985; libr. after Euripides' *The Trojan Women*) [R].

Reinecke, Carl *(1824–1910)*

German composer. Best known as a composer of piano music, he also wrote six operas (all now forgotten) in Wagnerian style. They are *Der Vierjährige Posten* (1855; libr. after Theodor Körner), *König Manfred* (Weisbaden 1867; libr. F. Röber), *Ein Abenteuer Handels* (Schwerin 1874; libr. W. le Grove), *Glückskind und Pechvaga* (1883), *Auf Hohen Befehl* (Hamburg 1886) and *Der Gouverneur*

von Tours (Schwerin 1891; libr. E. Bormann). A distinguished teacher, he was director of the Leipzig Conservatory from 1897.

Reine de Saba, La *(The Queen of Sheba)*

Opera in four acts by Gounod. 1st perf. Paris, 28 Feb 1862; libr. by Jules Barbier and Michel Carré after Gérard de Nerval's poem. Principal roles: Balkis (sop), Adoniram (ten), Solomon (bass). Telling of the love between the Hebrew sculptor, Adoniram, and Balkis the Queen of Sheba, ending in his death, it was successful in its time, but is nowadays almost never performed.

Reiner, Fritz *(1888–1963)*

Hungarian conductor, long resident in the United States and particularly associated with Wagner and Strauss operas. He was musical director of the Dresden State Opera (1914–21).

Reinmar

Bass role in Wagner's *Tannhäuser*. He is a minstrel-knight.

Reiza

Soprano role in Weber's *Oberon*. She is Haroun de Raschid's daughter.

Reizen, Mark *(b 1895)*

Russian bass, particularly associated with the Russian repertory. One of the finest Russian basses of the inter-war period, he enjoyed an extraordinarily long career, singing Prince Gremin at the Bolshoi on his 90th birthday.

Remedios, Alberto *(b 1935)*

British tenor, particularly associated with Wagnerian roles, especially Siegfried and Walther von Stolzing. A lyric tenor (who has had success in the French repertory) rather than a heldentenor, he is one of the very few postwar Siegfrieds to have truly sung the role rather than shouted it. His voice was warm, Italianate and seemingly tireless. His brother Ramon (*b* 1940) is also a tenor.

Remendado

Tenor role in Bizet's *Carmen*. He is a smuggler.

Renard

Burlesque in two parts by Stravinsky. 1st perf. Paris, 18 May 1922; libr. by the composer and Charles Ferdinand Ramuz, after Russian folk tales. Described as *histoire burlesque chantée et jouée*, it is played by dancers or acrobats whilst the soloists (two tenors and two basses) are placed in the orchestra pit.

Plot: By preaching to it, the fox persuades the cock down from its perch, but the bird is rescued by the tomcat and the ram. The fox tries again and very nearly succeeds, the cock being saved this time by suggestions to the fox that his wife is being unfaithful. Eventually, the ram and the tomcat strangle the fox. [R]

Renato

Baritone role in Verdi's *Un Ballo in Maschera*. Ankerström in the Swedish setting, he is Amelia's husband.

Rencontre Imprévu, Le (*The Unexpected Meeting*)

Comic opera in three acts by Gluck. 1st perf. Vienna, 7 Jan 1764; libr. by L. H. Dancourt, after d'Orneval and Alain René le Sage's *Les Pèlerins de la Mecque*. Gluck's last comic work, it was long popular but is nowadays only very rarely performed.

Rennert, Günther (*1911–78*)

German producer and administrator. One of the leading postwar German producers, his stagings were notable for their handling of crowd scenes and for their deep insight into character motivation. He was administrator of the Hamburg Opera (1946–56), turning it into one of Germany's finest companies, and the Bavarian State Opera (1967–76). His brother Wolfgang (*b* 1922) is a successful conductor.

Re Pastore, Il (*The Shepherd King*)

Opera in two acts by Mozart (K 208). 1st perf. Salzburg, 23 April 1775; libr. by Pietro Metastasio. Principal roles: Amintas (sop), Alessandro (ten), Elisa (sop), Tamiris (sop), Agenore (ten). A pastoral work of great charm, dealing with a supposed event in the life of Alexander the Great, it is still quite often performed.

Plot: Alessandro, having conquered Sidon, discovers that the poor shepherd Amintas is in fact the rightful heir to the throne. Alessandro reinstates him and wishes him to marry Tamiris, the daughter of the late usurper, unaware that Tamiris is in love with his own counsellor Agenore. Rather than be separated from his beloved, the shepherdess Elisa, Amintas renounces the throne. Alessandro gives in, appointing Amintas 'shepherd-king' with Elisa as his consort. [R]

Répétiteur (French for 'rehearser')

The title in France and Britain of that member of an opera house's music staff who coaches the singers in their roles. He is called *Korrepetitor* in Germany and *Maestro collaboratore* in Italy.

Répétition générale (French for 'general repetition')
The final dress rehearsal in a French or Belgian opera house.

Rescigno, Nicola
American conductor, particularly associated with the Italian repertory. He was musical director of the Chicago Lyric Opera (1954–56) – of which he was a co-founder – and the Dallas Civic Opera (1957–).

Rescue opera
A term which describes an opera in which the central feature of the plot is the rescue of one of the principal characters from a dangerous situation. The genre became very popular in France at the time of the Revolution, when the plot often involved the rescue of an illegally held political prisoner. It was exemplified by Jean Nicolas Bouilly's libretto for Gaveaux's *Léonore ou l'Amour Conjugal*, which provided Beethoven with the story for *Fidelio*. Other influential early examples were Cherubini's *Lodoïska* and *Les Deux Journées*, and a fine example from the later 19th century is Smetana's *Dalibor*.

Resnik, Regina *(b 1922)*
American soprano and later mezzo, particularly associated with Carmen, and with Strauss roles, notably Clytemnestra. An outstanding singing-actress with a rich and powerful voice, she created the Baroness in Barber's *Vanessa* and Delilah in Bernard Rogers' *The Warrior*. From 1971, she turned successfully to opera production.

Respighi, Ottorino *(1879–1936)*
Italian composer. He wrote nine operas in late romantic style. The comedy *Re Enzo* (Bologna 1905; libr. A. Donini) was followed by the unperformed

Marie-Victoire (1909; libr. E. Guiraud), *Semirâma* (Bologna 1910; libr. A. Cenè), *La Bella Addormentata nel Bosco* (Rome 1922; libr. G. Bistolfi), the comedy *Belfagor* (Milan 1923; libr. E. L. Morselli and Claudio Gaustalla), *La Campana Sommersa**, *Maria Egiziaca**, *La Fiamma**, his most successful work, and *Lucrezia* (Milan 1937; libr. Gaustalla), which employs 17th-century dramatic recitative. A leading advocate of early Italian music, he prepared an edition of Monteverdi's *La Favola d'Orfeo* in 1935.

Reszke, Edouard de *(b Edward)* *(1853–1917)*
Polish bass, brother of the tenor Jean de Reszke*, particularly associated with Verdi and Wagner roles and with the French repertory, especially Méphistophélès. One of the greatest basses in operatic history, he had a rich voice of enormous proportions, an imposing stage presence (aided by his great height), and was an outstanding singing-actor. He created Don Diègue in *Le Cid*, Gilberto in Gomes' *Maria Tudor*, Ruben in Ponchielli's *Il Figliuol Prodigo*, the King in Catalani's *Elda* and Fiesco in the revised *Simon Boccanegra*. He retired to Poland, where, after the outbreak of World War I, he lived in great poverty, first in a cellar and then in a cave.

Reszke, Jean de *(b Jan Mieczyslaw) (1850–1925)*
Polish tenor, brother of the bass Edouard de Reszke*. Often regarded as one of the greatest of all tenors, he sang as a baritone for the first five years of his career. Particularly associated with the French repertory, he had a voice of outstanding beauty used with an impeccable technique and was a fine singing-actor. He created the title-role in *Le Cid*. He was also a

distinguished teacher, whose pupils included Bidú Sayão, Dame Maggie Teyte and Steuart Wilson. His sister Joséphine (*b* Józefina) (1855–91) was a successful soprano, who created Sita in *Le Roi de Lahore*.

Retablo de Maese Pedro, El
(*Master Peter's Puppet Show*)
Marionette opera in one act by De Falla. 1st perf. Seville, 23 March 1923; libr. by the composer, after Miguel Cervantes' *Don Quixote*. Principal roles: Peter (ten), Don Quixote (bar), Narrator (treble or sop). The most famous of all marionette operas, it marks a change in De Falla's style to a more austere and medieval-influenced mode.

Plot: Peter's puppets perform the story of the rescue of Melisendra from the Moors in the stable of an inn to an audience which includes Don Quixote. Quixote views the marionettes as real humans in need of help and leaves his seat to do battle. He beheads 'the Moors' and ruins the performance. [R]

Re Teodoro di Venezia, Il
(*King Theodore of Venice*)
Opera in two acts by Paisiello. 1st perf. Vienna, 23 Aug 1784; libr. by Giovanni Battista Casti. One of Paisiello's most successful works, it is still very occasionally performed.

Rethberg, Elisabeth (*b* Sattler) (1894–1976)
German soprano, particularly associated with the German and Italian repertories, especially Aida. One of the finest lyrico-dramatic sopranos of the inter-war period, with a voice of exceptional beauty, she created the title role in *Die Ägyptische Helena*. Her husband George Cehanovsky (1892–1986) was a distinguished comprimario

baritone, who sang for 40 seasons at the Metropolitan Opera, New York.

Revisor, Der (*The Inspector*)
Opera in five acts by Egk. 1st perf. Schwetzingen, 9 May 1957; libr. by the composer, after Nikolai Gogol's *The Inspector-General*. Principal roles: Chlestakov (ten), Mayor (bass), Mayor's Wife (mezzo), Mayor's Daughter (sop). A comedy telling of a destitute civil servant mistaken for a senior official, it is one of Egk's most successful works and has been widely performed.

Reyer, Ernest (*b* Rey) (1823–1909)
French composer. An admirer of Wagner and Berlioz, both of whom influenced him to some extent, he wrote five operas. The opéra-comique *Maître Wolfram* (Paris 20 May 1954; libr. F. J. Méry and T. Gautier) was followed by the successful *La Statue* (Paris 11 April 1861; libr. Jules Barbier and Michel Carré, after *The Arabian Nights*), *Erostrate* (Baden-Baden 21 Aug 1862; libr. Méry and E. Pacini), *Sigurd**, his masterpiece, and the successful *Salammbô**. His autobiography, *40 Ans de Musique*, was published in 1909.

Rezniček, Emil (1860–1945)
Austrian composer and conductor. His most important operas are *Die Jungfrau von Orleans* (Prague 19 June 1887; libr. composer, after Friedrich von Schiller), *Donna Diana**, by far his best known work, *Till Eulenspiegel* (Karlsruhe 12 Jan 1902; libr. composer) and *Holofernes* (Berlin 27 Oct 1923; libr. composer, after Christian Friedrich Hebbel's *Judith*). He was musical director of the Mannheim Opera (1896–99).

Rheinberger, Josef *(1839–1901)*
Lichtensteinian composer and organist.
Although best known as a composer of
organ music, he also wrote two operas:
Die Sieben Raben (Munich 1869; libr.
F. Bonn and F. von Hoffnaass) and
Türmers Tüchterlein (Munich 1873;
libr. M. Stahl). He also wrote some
children's Singspiels.

Rheingold, Das *(The Rhine Gold)*
Opera in one act by Wagner. 1st perf.
Munich, 22 Sept 1869 (composed
1854); libr. by the composer, after the
Nibelungenlied. The prologue or
preliminary evening of *Der Ring des
Nibelungen**. Principal roles: Alberich
(bar), Wotan (bar), Loge (ten), Fricka
(mezzo), Fasolt (bass), Fafner (bass),
Mime (ten), Donner (bar), Freia (sop),
Erda (cont), Froh (ten), Woglinde (sop),
Wellgunde (mezzo), Flosshilde (mezzo).
For plot see *Der Ring des Nibelungen*.
[R]

Ribbing, Count
Bass role in Verdi's *Un Ballo in
Maschera*. Samuel in the Boston setting,
he is one of the two conspirators.

Riccardo
(1) Tenor role in Verdi's *Un Ballo in
Maschera*. He is Richard Earl of
Warwick, governor of Boston. In the
Swedish setting, he is Gustavus III. (2)
Tenor role in Donizetti's *Anna Bolena*.
He is Anne's old love Richard Percy.
(3) Tenor role in Donizetti's *Maria di
Rohan*. He is the Comte de Chalais. (4)
Tenor role in Wolf-Ferrari's *I Quatro
Rusteghi*. (5) Baritone role in Bellini's *I
Puritani*. He is the Puritan general Sir
Richard Forth. (6) Tenor role in Verdi's
Oberto. He is the Count of Salinguerra.

**Riccardo Primo, Rè
d'Inghilterra** *(Richard I, King of
England)*
Opera in three acts by Handel. 1st perf.
London, 11 Nov 1727; libr. by Paolo
Antonio Rolli, after F. Briani's *Isacio
Tiranno*. Never one of Handel's more
successful operas, it is only rarely
performed.

Ricci, Federico *(1809–77)*
Italian composer, brother of Luigi
Ricci*. He wrote many operas in
Donizettian style, achieving his greatest
successs in comedy. His operas, all now
forgotten, include *La Prigione di
Edimburgo* (Trieste 13 March 1838;
libr. Gaetano Rossi, after Sir Walter
Scott's *The Heart of Midlothian*), *Un
Duello Sotto Richelieu* (Milan 17 Aug
1839; libr. F. dall'Ongaro, after
Edouard Lockroy's *Un Duel Sous le
Cardinal de Richelieu*) and *Une Folie à
Rome* (Paris 30 Jan 1869; libr. V.
Wilder). In collaboration with his
brother he also wrote four further
operas, including *Crispino e la
Comare**, the most successful mid-19th
century Italian comic opera.

Ricci, Luigi *(1805–59)*
Italian composer, brother of Federico
Ricci*. His operas, all now long
forgotten, include *Chiara di Rosemberg*
(Milan 11 Oct 1831; libr. Gaetano
Rossi), *Un Avventura di Scaramuccio*
(Milan 8 March 1834; libr. Felice
Romani), *Le Nozze di Figaro* (Milan 13
Feb 1838; libr. Rossi, after Pierre
Augustin Caron de Beaumarchais' *La
Folle Journée*) and *La Festa di
Pedigrotte* (Naples 23 June 1852; libr.
M. d'Arienzo). He also wrote four
operas in collaboration with his
brother, including *Crispino e la
Comare**. His son Luigino (1852–1906)
was also a composer, whose operas

include *Frosina* (1870), *Cola di Rienzi* (1880) and *Don Chischiotte* (1887).

Ricciarelli, Katia *(b 1946)*
Italian soprano, particularly associated with Bellini, Donizetti and Verdi roles, especially Luisa Miller. The leading contemporary Italian lyric soprano, she has a beautiful, well-schooled and intelligently used voice and an attractive stage personality. She appeared as Desdemona in Zeffirelli's film of *Otello*.

Richard, Coeur de Lion
(Richard Lionheart)
Opera in three acts by Grétry. 1st perf. Paris, 21 Oct 1784; libr. by Jean-Marie Sedaine. Principal roles: Blondel (bar), Richard (ten), Laurette (sop), Marguerite (sop). Grétry's masterpiece, which is still occasionally performed, it is notable for the romance 'Une fièvre brûlante', which appears nine times in the opera in various musical transformations, and is one of the finest early uses of leitmotiv.
  Plot: Disguised as a blind troubador, Blondel, the minstrel of King Richard I of England, travels in search of his imprisoned master. With the aid of Marguerite of Flanders, he contacts Richard through the use of his song, and finally rescues him. [R]

Richter, Hans *(1843–1916)*
Hungarian conductor, particularly associated with Wagner operas. Considered to be the leading interpreter in his time of the German repertory, he conducted the first complete performance of *Der Ring des Nibelungen* and the first performance of Smareglia's *Il Vassallo di Szigeth*. He was musical director of the Vienna State Opera (1893–1900).

Ricordi
An Italian family company of music publishers, specialising in opera. Founded in 1808 by Giovanni Ricordi (1785–1853), it is based in Milan and handles the operas of Bellini, Boito, Catalani, Donizetti, Menotti, Montemezzi, Pizzetti, Poulenc, Puccini, Respighi, Rossini, Verdi and Zandonai.

Ridderbusch, Karl *(b 1932)*
German bass, particularly associated with the German repertory, especially Wagner. One of the leading Wagnerian basses of the 1970s, he had a dark, powerful and incisive voice, intelligently used, and a strong stage presence.

Ride of the Valkyries
The name usually given to the opening of Act III of Wagner's *Die Walküre*.

Riders of the Sea
Opera in one act by Vaughan Williams. 1st perf. London, 30 Nov 1937. A virtual word-for-word setting of John Millington Synge's play. Principal roles: Maurya (mezzo), Bartley (bar), Cathleen (sop), Nora (sop). Vaughan Williams' operatic masterpiece, it is a taut, powerful and intense work that can have an overwhelming impact in the theatre. Its infrequency of performance is totally inexplicable.
  Plot: West coast of Ireland, early 20th century. Maurya has already lost four sons and her husband to the sea. Her daughters Nora and Cathleen identify some clothing that has washed up on the shore as belonging to a fifth son. When her last son, Bartley, is also claimed by the sea as he is taking horses to a fair, Maurya's anguish at last finds peace in resignation. [R]

Riegel, Kenneth *(b 1938)*
American tenor, particularly associated with character roles, especially the Dwarf in *Der Geburstag der Infantin*. An outstanding singing-actor, his voice

– although very far from beautiful – is used with intelligence and musicianship. He created the Leper in Messiaen's *St François d'Assise*.

Rienzi

Full title: **Cola Rienzi, der Letzte der Tribunen** (*Cola Rienzi, the Last of the Tribunes*) Opera in five acts by Wagner. 1st perf. Dresden, 20 Oct 1842; libr. by the composer, after Mary Russell Mitford's play and Edward Bulwer Lytton's novel. Principal roles: Rienzi (ten), Adriano (mezzo), Irene (sop), Paolo Orsini (bar), Stefano Colonna (bass), Cardinal Raimondo (bass). Wagner's third opera and his first major success, it is one of the longest operas ever written. It was composed in the grandest and most spectacular style in an attempt to out-Meyerbeer Meyerbeer. It is still performed from time to time, often in a cut version.

Plot: Mid-14th-century Rome. The patrician, Paolo Orsini, engaged in the abduction of Irene, sister of the Papal notary Rienzi, is disturbed in the act by Stefano Colonna, another patrician from a rival faction. A fight breaks out, attracting the crowd, as well as Adriano, Colonna's son in love with Irene, and the infuriated Rienzi. Spurred on by Cardinal Raimondo, Rienzi urges the crowd to stand up to the excesses of the noblemen and, because of his feelings for Irene, Adriano supports him. The defeated nobles swear loyalty to Rienzi but plot to murder him and are condemned to death. Adriano pleads their cause successfully but, later, when they break their oath of allegiance, the populace is aroused and kills them. However, feelings turn, and Rienzi becomes the object of the people's hostility and the Cardinal's disfavour, and is excommunicated. Adriano, warning Irene that her brother

is in danger, begs her to flee with him, but she refuses him and seeks Rienzi, who is praying in the capitol, and who also advises her to go to safety with Adriano. The outraged mob appears and, ignoring Rienzi's appeals, stone him and set fire to the capitol. As Irene and Rienzi are about to perish, Adriano arrives and rushes headlong to join them in the flames. [R]

Rigoletto

Opera in three acts by Verdi. 1st perf. Venice, 11 March 1851; libr. by Francesco Maria Piave, after Victor Hugo's *Le Roi s'Amuse*. Principal roles: Rigoletto (bar), Gilda (sop), Duke of Mantua (ten), Sparafucile (bass), Maddalena (mezzo), Count Monterone (b-bar). Verdi's first 'middle period' opera, it marks a turning point in the history of Italian opera in that the composer, for the first time, broke right through the restricting operatic conventions of the day. The finest Italian music-drama since those of Monteverdi, its title role is often regarded as the most musico-dramatically demanding ever written for a baritone. An immediate success, it has remained ever since one of the most enduringly popular of all operas.

Plot: 16th-century Mantua. The hunchbacked court jester Rigoletto laughs at the grief and rage of the aged Count Monterone, whose daughter has been seduced by the libertine Duke, and Monterone lays a father's curse on him. The courtiers, who hate Rigoletto, discover that he has a young girl hidden away. Unaware that she is his adored daughter Gilda, whom he has raised in convent-like seclusion, they assume her to be his mistress and abduct her for the Duke's enjoyment, even tricking Rigoletto into helping them. Meanwhile, the Duke is already aware of Gilda: he visits her disguised as a poor student and she falls in love with him. The courtiers show no pity towards Rigoletto even when they discover who Gilda is, and he vows vengeance on the Duke for having dishonoured her. He hires the assassin Sparafucile to kill the Duke, who is lured to a lonely inn by Sparafucile's sister Maddalena. Despite her dishonour, Gilda still loves the Duke and when she realises what is to happen she manoeuvres herself into taking his place, and is fatally stabbed. Rigoletto gloats over the sack delivered to him, containing what he believes to be the Duke's body, only to find it is that of the dying Gilda. As she expires, Rigoletto recalls Monterone's curse and collapses in anguish. [R]

Rihm, Wolfgang (b 1952)

German composer. One of the most successful contemporary German avant-garde composers, his operas include *Deploration* (1974), *Dis-Kontur* (1975), the widely performed *Jakob Lenz* (Karlsruhe 6 March 1980; libr. Michael Fröhling, after Georg Büchner's *Lenz*), *Die Hamletmaschine* (Mannheim 1987) and *Die Eroberung von Mexico* (Hamburg 1990).

Rimsky-Korsakov, Nikolai (1844–1908)

Russian composer (and also a senior naval officer). A member of the 'Mighty Handful', his 15 operas are notable for their use of colourful Russian fairy tales and for their brilliant orchestration and rich and often exotic harmonies. His first opera *The Maid of Pskov** (later revised as *Ivan the Terrible*) was followed by *May Night**, *The Snow Maiden**, the opera-ballet *Mlada**, *Christmas Eve**, the epic *Sadko**, the duodrama *Mozart and Salieri**, *Boyarinya Vera Sheloga* (Moscow 27 Dec 1898; derived from the prologue of the unperformed second

version of *The Maid of Pskov*), *The Tsar's Bride**, *The Tale of Tsar Sultan**, *Serviliya* (St Petersburg 14 Oct 1902; libr. composer, after Lev Alexandrovich Mey), *Kashchey the Immortal* (Moscow 25 Dec 1902; libr. composer, after E. M. Petrovsky) [R], *Pan Voyevoda* (St Petersburg 16 Oct 1904; libr. I. M. Tumenev), *The Invisible City of Kitezh** and *The Golden Cockerel**, his best-known work in the West.

An ardent advocate of the music of his contemporaries, Rimsky completed Dargomijsky's *The Stone Guest*, Moussorgsky's *Khovanschina* and Borodin's *Prince Igor*, as well as preparing a version of *Boris Godunov* which was in almost universal use for some 70 years. He was also a noted teacher whose pupils included Glazunov, Prokofiev, Respighi and Stravinsky. His autobiography, *My Musical Life*, was published in 1909.

Rinaldo

Opera in three acts by Handel. 1st perf. London, 24 Feb 1711; libr. by Giacomo Rossi after Torquato Tasso's *Gerusalemme Liberata*. Principal roles: Rinaldo (mezzo), Goffredo (ten), Almirena (sop), Armida (sop), Argante (bass). Handel's first opera written for London, it was an immediate success and is still quite often performed.

Plot: The crusader Rinaldo, who is in love with Almirena, is fighting against the Saracens under Argante. Argante's mistress Armida uses her magical powers against Rinaldo, but ends up by falling in love with him. Eventually, Argante and Armida are defeated. [R]

Rinaldo di Capua (c 1710–c 72)

Italian composer. Reputed to be the illegitimate son of a nobleman, very little is known about him. He wrote many stage works, beginning with opera serias and later turning with great success to comedy. He is now remembered solely for the delightful intermezzo *La Zingara**. Very little of his work survives: his son sold off most of his collected works as waste paper.

Ring des Nibelungen, Der
See panel on page 485

Rinuccini, Ottavio *(1552–1621)*
Italian poet and librettist. A member of the Florentine Camerata*, he was the first opera librettist. His *Dafne* was set by Peri, Caccini, Gagliano and (in translation) by Schütz, and his *Euridice* by Peri and Caccini. He also wrote the texts for Monteverdi's *Arianna* and *Il Ballo delle Ingrate*.

Rinuccio
Tenor role in Puccini's *Gianni Schicchi*. He is in love with Lauretta.

Rio de Janeiro
See Teatro Municipal, Rio de Janeiro

Riotte, Philipp Jakob *(1776–1856)*
German composer. He wrote a number of operas and Singspiels, all of them now long forgotten, of which the most successful included *Pedro und Elmira* (1805), *Der Berggeist* (1818), *Die Wildschützen* (1820), *Nurredin, Prinz von Persien* (Vienna 1825) and the Weber parody *Staberl als Freischütz* (1826).

Risurrezione *(Resurrection)*
Opera in four acts by Alfano. 1st perf. Turin, 30 Nov 1904; libr. by Cesare Hanau, after Tolstoy's novel. Principal roles: Katusha (sop), Prince Dimitri (ten), Simonson (bar). Written in verismo style, it is one of Alfano's best works. Successful in its time, it is nowadays all but forgotten.

Plot: 19th-century Russia. Prince Dimitri seduces and abandons his childhood friend Katusha. She attempts but fails to meet him at a railway station. She is exiled to Siberia on a false charge, and when Dimitri comes to her there, she proudly rejects him. He visits her a second time, now offering marriage, but although she still loves him, Katusha decides to marry her fellow-prisoner Simonson.

Rita
or **Le Mari Battu** *(The Beaten Husband)*
Comic opera in one act by Donizetti. 1st perf. Paris, 7 May 1860 (composed 1841); libr. by Gustave Vaëz. Principal roles: Rita (sop), Gasparo (bar), Beppe (ten). A delightful little piece, it is still quite often performed.

Plot: Switzerland. Rita, the proprietress of an inn, hen-pecks her husband Gasparo. Gasparo meets Rita's former husband Beppe (who had been believed dead), and the two gamble for the privilege of losing her. Beppe loses, but Rita promises to mend her ways. [R]

Ritorna vincitor
Soprano aria for Aida in Act I of Verdi's *Aida*.

Ritornello *(Italian for 'little return')*
An orchestral section added to an aria in a 17th- or early 18th-century opera to summarise and encapsulate the emotional content of the piece.

Ritorno d'Ulisse in Patria, Il
(The Return of Ulysses to His Country)
Opera in prologue and five acts by Monteverdi. 1st perf. Venice, Feb 1641;

DER RING DES NIBELUNGEN
(*The Ring of the Nibelung*)

Operatic tetralogy by Wagner (described as 'a stage festival play for three days and a preliminary evening'). 1st complete perf. Bayreuth, 13, 14, 16 and 17 August 1876; libr. by the composer, after the *Nibelungenlied*. An allegory of humanity and its search for power, it is the largest and most complex work in the history of opera, and is the music-drama which accords most closely with Wagner's artistic theories as propounded in his writings. Originally conceived as a single opera, *Siegfrieds Tod* (*The Death of Siegfried*), Wagner was irresistibly drawn towards the earlier mythological aspects of the legend, and the figure of the suffering god Wotan came to dominate the final conception. The work's composition spanned over 20 years, as Wagner laid the project aside for a long period after completing the second act of *Siegfried*. The tetralogy comprises:

(1) *Das Rheingold* (*The Rhine Gold*). Opera in one act. 1st perf. Munich, 22 Sept 1869 (composed 1854). Principal roles: Alberich (bar), Wotan (bar), Loge (ten), Fricka (mezzo), Fasolt (bass), Fafner (bass), Mime (ten), Erda (cont), Donner (bar), Freia (sop), Froh (ten), Woglinde (sop), Wellgunde (mezzo), Flosshilde (mezzo).

Plot: The three Rhinemaidens guard a lump of magic gold; anyone who renounces love and fashions a ring from it will become the master of the world. This they explain to Alberich, the leader of the Nibelung dwarfs, as they reject his advances. Alberich curses love and steals the gold. On Valhalla, the chief god Wotan has had his fortress built by the giants Fasolt and Fafner, the price for which has been agreed as Freia, the goddess whose golden apples keep the gods young and vigorous. Hearing of the vast wealth acquired by Alberich through the power of the Ring, the giants agree to accept gold as payment instead of Freia. With the aid of Loge, the God of Fire, Wotan takes from Alberich both the Ring and the Tarnhelm, a magic helmet made by Alberich's brother Mime which can transform its wearer into any shape. He ignores Alberich's curse of death, placed on all who possess the Ring. Freia must be hidden by gold before the giants will release her, and only the Ring will fill the final chink. After the earth-mother Erda has urged him to shun the Ring, Wotan reluctantly yields it to the giants. Fafner kills Fasolt and takes both Ring and Tarnhelm. The gods enter Valhalla. [R]

(2) *Die Walküre* (*The Valkyrie*). Opera in three acts. 1st perf. Munich, 26 June 1870 (composed 1856). Principal roles: Wotan (bar), Brünnhilde (sop), Siegmund (ten), Sieglinde (sop), Fricka (mezzo), Hunding (bass).

Plot: In search of wisdom, Wotan has visited Erda who has borne him nine daughters, the warrior-maidens the Valkyries. Knowing that his treaties forbid him to take action himself to recover the Ring, Wotan is attempting to bring forward a free agent who can do what he is powerless to accomplish. With a mortal woman he has begotten two children, Siegmund and Sieglinde. The two were separated at birth and Sieglinde is unhappily married to Hunding. Exhausted after fighting, Siegmund arrives at Hunding's home, and he and Sieglinde are immediately attracted to each other. Drugging Hunding, they realise their kinship, declare their love and elope together. Wotan's wife Fricka is outraged at the love of a brother and sister, and Wotan is forced to agree that Siegmund must die. He explains his dilemma to Brünnhilde, the leader of the Valkyries, telling her that she must shield Hunding in the fight. Knowing that this goes against Wotan's innermost wishes, she rebels against him and shields Siegmund. However, Wotan intervenes and both contestants are killed. Brünnhilde realises that Sieglinde is pregnant and is bearing the future hero who will redeem the gods. She aids her escape and gives her the shards of Siegmund's sword which had been made by Wotan. The furious Wotan deprives Brünnhilde of her godhead and puts her into a deep sleep on a rock surrounded by fire. He decrees that the man who braves the power of his spear can claim her as his bride. [R]

(3) *Siegfried*. Opera in three acts. 1st perf. Bayreuth, 16 Aug 1876 (composed 1869). Principal roles: Siegfried (ten), Wotan/Wanderer (bar), Brünnhilde (sop), Mime (ten), Alberich (bar), Fafner (bass), Erda (cont), Woodbird (sop).

Plot: Sieglinde has died during the birth of her son Siegfried. He has been raised by Alberich's brother Mime, who plans to use the boy to gain the Ring for himself. He knows that only the shards of Siegmund's sword will suffice to kill Fafner, but he is unable to reforge them. Wotan (disguised as the Wanderer) tells him that they will be forged only by one who has never learnt fear. The fearless Siegfried duly reforges the sword but, wishing to learn fear, allows Mime to lead him to the lair of Fafner, transformed by the Tarnhelm into a mighty dragon. He kills Fafner and the dragon's blood which he tastes allows him to understand the song of the Woodbird, which warns him of Mime's plans, tells him of Brünnhilde's rock and advises him to take the Ring and the Tarnhelm. Siegfried kills the treacherous Mime. In conversation with Erda, Wotan resolves that the younger generation must inherit his lordship, but the arrogant behaviour of Siegfried on his arrival forces him to bar the boy's way with his spear. Siegfried shatters the spear with his sword, and Wotan allows him to pass through the flames unhindered. He discovers Brünnhilde, wakes her with a kiss, and the two fall in love. [R]

(4) *Götterdämmerung* (*Twilight of the Gods*). Opera in three acts. 1st perf. Bayreuth, 17 Aug 1876 (composed 1874). Principal roles: Brünnhilde (sop), Siegfried (ten), Hagen (bass), Günther (bar), Gutrune (sop), Waltraute (mezzo), Alberich (bar), Norns (sop, mezzo and cont), Woglinde (sop), Wellgunde (mezzo), Flosshilde (mezzo).

Plot: Pledging his love to Brünnhilde, Siegfried travels down the Rhine and arrives at the hall of the Gibichungs, led by Günther and his half-brother Hagen (who is Alberich's son). Siegfried is given a drugged drink which makes him forget Brünnhilde and fall in love with Günther's sister Gutrune. In the meantime, her sister Waltraute visits Brünnhilde and tells her of Wotan's anguish and fear and of the necessity for the Ring to be returned to the Rhine. Brünnhilde, to whom Siegfried has given the Ring, refuses. Disguised as Günther by the power of the Tarnhelm, Siegfried drags Brünnhilde from her rock and delivers her as an unwilling wife for Günther, taking the Ring from her hand. Seeing the Ring on the drugged Siegfried's finger, she believes him unfaithful and plots with Hagen against him. Hagen stabs Siegfried in the back and in a dispute over the Ring kills Günther. When Hagen goes to take the Ring, the dead Siegfried's hand rises against him. Brünnhilde orders a vast funeral pyre to be built, which she lights and mounts. The flames destroy the hall and eventually also Valhalla and the entire old order. The Rhine overflows its banks, and the Rhinemaidens take back their gold. [R]

libr. by Giacomo Badoara, after Homer's *The Odyssey*. Principal roles: Ulisse (ten), Penelope (mezzo), Minerva (sop), Melanto (mezzo), Ericlea (mezzo) Jove (ten), Eumaeus (ten), Time (bass). Unperformed for nearly 300 years, it has been widely heard in recent years, often in the edition prepared by Raymond Leppard.

Plot: Ulisse's faithful wife Penelope, surrounded by suitors, laments her husband's continued absence at the Trojan War. Ulisse comes to Ithaca and Minerva urges him to return to his home, which he does disguised as a beggar. Penelope announces that she will marry the suitor who is able to draw Ulisse's bow. None of them are able to do so, but the 'beggar' succeeds with ease. Ulisse kills the suitors and is reunited with Penelope. [R]

Ritual Dances
Choral dances in Act II of Tippett's *The Midsummer Marriage*.

Rizza, Gilda dalla *(1892–1975)*
Italian soprano, particularly associated with Italian verismo roles. She created Magda in *La Rondine*, Giulietta in Zandonai's *Giulietta e Romeo*, Mariella in Mascagni's *Il Piccolo Marat* and roles in Vittadini's *Anima Allegra* and Marinuzzi's *Palla de' Mozzi*.

Roar, Leif
Danish baritone, particularly associated with Wagnerian roles, especially Wotan. One of the leading heldenbaritons of the 1970s, he created a role in Klebe's *Märchen von der Schönen Lilie*.

Robert le Diable (*Robert the Devil*)
Opera in five acts by Meyerbeer. 1st perf. Paris, 21 Nov 1831; libr. by Eugène Scribe and Germain Delavigne. Principal roles: Robert (ten), Bertram (bass), Isabella (sop), Alice (sop). The work which established Meyerbeer's reputation in France, its première was one of the most sensationally successful in operatic history. It was very popular throughout the 19th century, but is nowadays only infrequently performed.

Plot: 13th-century Sicily. Duke Robert of Normandy is the son of a mortal woman and the Devil, masquerading as Bertram. In exchange for his soul, Bertram offers Robert the love of Isabella, but Robert is dissuaded by his foster-sister Alice. Now redeemed, Robert marries Isabella, and Bertram returns to Hell.

Roberto Devereux, Conte d'Essex
Opera in three acts by Donizetti. 1st perf. Naples, 29 Oct 1837; libr. by Salvatore Cammarano, after François Ancelot's *Elisabeth d'Angleterre*. Principal roles: Elizabeth (sop), Robert (ten), Duke of Nottingham (bar), Sarah (mezzo). An embroidered version of the love of Elizabeth I and the Earl of Essex (1567–1601), it is an uneven work, but in its best passages achieves an almost Verdian power and sweep. The overture contains an historical anachronism in that it employs 'God Save the King', which was not written until long after Elizabeth's time. After a century's neglect, the opera has been regularly performed in recent years, and provides a magnificent vehicle for a singing-actress.

Plot: England, 1598. Elizabeth loves Robert, the Earl of Essex, who is secretly in love with Sarah, the wife of his staunch friend the Duke of Nottingham. Elizabeth has given Robert a ring, promising her help at any time it is presented to her. Robert gives the ring to Sarah, who gives him a scarf embroidered with her initials. The Council sentences Robert to death for treason, and when he is searched the scarf is found: Nottingham realises that his wife has been unfaithful with his best friend and a furious Elizabeth signs Robert's death warrant. Robert writes to Sarah asking her to deliver the ring to Elizabeth, but Nottingham intercepts the letter and deliberately holds up the ring's delivery until after Robert has been executed. The heartbroken Elizabeth has Nottingham arrested and makes ready to abdicate. [R]

Robin, Mado *(1918–60)*
French soprano, particularly associated with French and Italian coloratura roles. She possessed a voice of great agility and range, and is said to have sung the highest note ever emitted by a singer: c above high c.

Robinson, Count

Baritone role in Cimarosa's *Il Matrimonio Segreto*. He is an English 'Milord'.

Robinson, Forbes *(1926–87)*

British bass, particularly associated with Mozart, Verdi and Britten roles, especially Claggart and Don Giovanni. He possessed a superbly rich and powerful voice, and was an outstanding singing-actor, whose interpretations ranged from a terrifyingly malevolent Claggart to an outrageously funny Dulcamara. He created the title role in *King Priam*.

Robinson Crusoé

Operetta in three acts by Offenbach. 1st perf. Paris, 23 Nov 1867; libr. by Eugène Cormon and Héctor Crémieux, after Daniel Defoe. Principal roles: Crusoe (ten), Edwige (sop), Man Friday (mezzo), Suzanne (sop), Toby (ten), Jim Cocks (bar), Sir William Crusoe (bass), Deborah (mezzo). It contains some of Offenbach's most charming and entertaining music, but has been hampered by its weak libretto. Modern British performances have used an entirely new libretto written for Opera Rara by Don White. [R]

Rocca, Lodovico *(b 1895)*

Italian composer. His operas, written in late verismo style, met with some success in Italy but have been little performed elsewhere. They include *La Morte di Frine* (Milan 1937, composed 1920; libr. C. Meano), *In Terra di Leggenda* (Bergamo 1936, composed 1923; libr. Meano), *Il Dibuk**, his most successful work, *Monte Ivnor* (Rome 1939; libr. Meano, after Werfel's *Die 40 Tage de Musa Dagh*) and *L'Uragano* (Milan 1952; libr. E.

Possenti, after Alexander Nikolayevich Ostrovsky's *The Storm*).

Rocco

Bass role in Beethoven's *Fidelio* and Paer's *Leonora*. Marzelline's father, he is the jailer.

Rodelinda, Regina de' Longobardi

Opera in three acts by Handel. 1st perf. London, 13 Feb 1725; libr. by Antonio Salvi and Nicola Francesco Haym after Pierre Corneille's *Pertharite*. Principal roles: Rodelinda (sop), Grimoaldo (ten), Bertarido (mezzo), Edwige (mezzo), Garibaldo (bass). One of the most successful of all Handel's operas, it is still regularly performed.

Plot: Milan. Bertarido, the rightful King of Lombardy, is believed to be dead. He returns home in secret to discover that Grimoaldo has usurped the throne and is trying to force his wife Rodelinda to marry him. Bertarido is arrested and imprisoned. He escapes and prevents Grimoaldo from being murdered by his own evil henchman, Garibaldo. In gratitude, Grimoaldo gives up the throne and pays homage to Bertarido as his rightful ruler. [R]

Rodolfo

(1) Tenor role in Puccini's and baritone role in Leoncavallo's *La Bohème*. He is a poor poet. (2) Tenor role in Verdi's *Luisa Miller*. He is Count Walther's son. (3) Bass role in Bellini's *La Sonnambula*. He is a count recently returned to the village.

Rodrigo

Opera in three acts by Handel. 1st perf. Florence, 1707; librettist unknown, after F. Silvani's *Il Duello d'Amore e di Vendetta*. Principal roles: Rodrigo (sop), Esilena (sop), Florinda (sop), Giuliano (ten), Evanco (sop), Fernando (c-ten). One of Handel's earliest stage works, it is very rarely performed.

Rodrigo

(1) Baritone role in Verdi's *Don Carlos*. He is the liberal Marquis of Posa. (2) Tenor role in Rossini's *La Donna del Lago*. He is a rebel chief married to Elena. (3) Tenor role in Massenet's *Le Cid*. He is the Cid of the opera's title.

Rodríguez de Hita, Antonio
(1724–87)

Spanish composer. The most important early zarzuela composer, his collaboration with the dramatist Ramón de la Cruz (1731–94) had an enormous influence on the subsequent development of the genre. His most important zarzuelas are the heroic *Briseida* (Madrid 10 July 1768), *Las Segadoras de Vallecas* (Madrid 13 Sept 1768), an impressive depiction of peasant life, and *Las Labradoras de Murcia* (Madrid 16 Sept 1769), which is almost a slice of verismo a century before its time.

Roi Arthus, Le *(King Arthur)*

Opera in three acts by Chausson (Op 23). 1st perf. Brussels, 30 Nov 1903 (composed 1895); libr. by the composer. Principal roles: Arthus (bar), Guenièvre (sop), Lancelot (ten), Mordred (bar), Merlin (bass). The only one of Chausson's operas ever to have been staged, it is a heavily Wagnerian setting of parts of the Arthurian cycle. It is only very rarely performed.

Plot: Arthur, victorious over the Saxons, praises Lancelot. The jealous Mordred surprises Lancelot at a tryst with Arthur's Queen Guinevere. Lancelot injures Mordred and flees. Mordred informs Arthur, who, relucant to believe the pair's guilt, summons Lancelot to court. Unwilling to perjure himself, Lancelot refuses the summons and elopes with Guinevere. Merlin's prediction that the kingdom will fall spurs Arthur to pursue Lancelot, who flees from Arthur's sword Excalibur. Guinevere upbraids Lancelot, who returns to fight, and then strangles herself in shame with her own hair. Arthur wounds Lancelot and then forgives him. A heavenly chariot descends to convey Arthur to a better world. [R]

Roi David, Le *(King David)*

Dramatic psalm in two parts by Honegger. 1st perf. Mézières, 11 June 1921; libr. by René Morax, after the Book of Samuel in the Old Testament. Principal roles: David (ten), Young David (mezzo), Michal (sop), Angel (sop). The work which established Honegger's reputation, it is still performed from time to time. [R]

Roi de Lahore, Le *(The King of Lahore)*

Opera in five acts by Massenet. 1st perf. Paris, 27 April 1877; libr. by Louis Gallet, after the *Mahabharata*. Principal roles: Sita (sop), Alim (ten), Scindia (bar), Indra (bass), Kaled (mezzo), Timour (b-bar). Massenet's first major success, it is still performed from time to time.

Plot: 11th-century India. The priestess Sita is loved by King Alim of Lahore and by his minister Scindia. Scindia kills Alim, but the Hindu god Indra permits Alim to return to earth as a beggar. Sita kills herself so as to be with Alim in paradise. [R]

Roi d'Ys, Le *(The King of Ys)*

Opera in three acts by Lalo. 1st perf. Paris, 7 May 1888; libr. by Edouard Blau, after a Breton legend. Principal roles: Mylio (ten), Rozenn (sop), Margared (mezzo), Karmac (bar), King (bass). By far Lalo's most successful work, it is quite often performed.

Plot: Brittany. The princess Margared loves the warrior Mylio, but he is engaged to Margared's sister Rozenn. On the night of the wedding, the jealous Margared opens the floodgates and allows the sea to drown the city of Ys. Only after Margared has confessed and thrown herself into the sea, does the city's patron saint cause the waters to recede. [R]

Roi l'a Dit, Le (*The King Said So*) Comic opera in three acts by Delibes. 1st perf. Paris, 24 May 1873; libr. by Edmond Gondinet. A delightful little piece, it is Delibes' only work apart from *Lakmé* still to be at all remembered.

Plot: Having falsely maintained that he has fathered a son, the Marquis de Montecontour is forced by circumstances to enrol a peasant lad to play the part. The boy immediately takes advantage of the situation, causing the Marquis acute embarrassment. The Marquis is forced to get rid of him and allow him to marry his sweetheart, but he is compensated for the loss of his 'son' with a dukedom.

Roi Malgré Lui, Le (*The King Despite Himself*) Comic opera in three acts by Chabrier. 1st perf. Paris, 18 May 1887; libr. by Emile de Najac and Paul Burani (revised by Jean Richepin), after François Ancelot's play. Principal roles: Henri de Valois (bar), Minka (sop), de Nangis (ten), Alexina (sop). One of Chabrier's most sparkling and entertaining scores, it is still performed from time to time, but not as often as its charm and merit deserve.

Plot: France, 1574. Henri de Valois is about to be crowned King of France and is unwilling to accept his simultaneous election as King of Poland. He learns from his fiancée Minka that there is a plot afoot to assassinate him. Disguising himself as his friend De Nangis, Henri joins the conspirators. Nangis himself arrives at the conspirators' camp and is mistaken for Henri. The plot is foiled and both Henri and De Nangis escape unharmed. Henri agrees to accept the crowns of both France and Poland. [R]

Rolfe-Johnson, Anthony (*b 1940*)
British tenor, particularly associated with Mozart, Handel and Britten roles. Possessing a beautiful voice used with intelligence and outstanding musicianship, he is one of the most stylish contemporary Mozartians. He has a dignified stage presence.

Romani, Felice (*1788–1865*)
Italian librettist. By far the most accomplished Italian librettist of his day, he wrote over 100 texts, notable for their elegant verses and for their illumination of a character's inner feelings. He provided libretti for Bellini (*Il Pirata, La Straniera, Zaira, I Capuleti e i Montecchi, La Sonnambula, Norma, Beatrice di Tenda* and the revised *Bianca e Fernando*), Donizetti (ten, including *Anna Bolena, L'Elisir d'Amore, Ugo Conte di Parigi, Parisina, Lucrezia Borgia* and *Rosmonda d'Inghilterra*), Jírovec (*Il Finto Stanislao*), Mayr (*Rosa Bianca e Rosa Rossa* and *Medea in Corinto*), Mercadante (16 texts), Meyerbeer (*L'Esule di Granata* and *Margherita d'Anjou*), Morlacchi, Nicolaï (*Enrico II*), L. Ricci, Rossi, Rossini (*Aureliano in Palmira, Bianca e Faliero* and *Il Turco in Italia*), Vaccai (*Giulietta e Romeo*), Verdi (*Un Giorno di Regno*) and Winter (*Maometto II*).

Romania
See Bucharest Opera

Romanian opera composers
See Enescu

Other national opera composers include Tiberiu Brediceano (1877–1968), Eduard Caudella (1841–1923), Paul Constantinescu (1908–63), Gheorghe Dima (1847–1925), Sabin Dragoiu (1894–1968) and Ciprian Porumbescu (1855–83).

Romanza (Italian for 'romance')
The term has two meanings in opera: (1) A slow single-movement aria in a 19th-century Italian opera, such as 'Una furtiva lagrima' in Donizetti's *L'Elisir d'Amore*. (2) More generally, any song or aria of a lyrical and intimate nature.

Romberg, Sigmund *(1877–1951)*
Hungarian-born American composer. He wrote some 50 operettas and musical comedies, of which the most successful included *Blossom Time* (29 Sept 1921; libr. D. Donnelley), *The Student Prince**, *The Desert Song* (30 Nov 1926; libr. Otto Harbach and Oscar Hammerstein II) and *The New Moon* (11 Sept 1928; libr. Hammerstein and L. Schwab).

Rome
See Teatro dell'Opera, Rome

Romeo and Juliet
See Capuleti e i Montecchi, I; Giulietta e Romeo; Roméo et Juliette; Romeo und Julia

Roméo et Juliette
Opera in five acts by Gounod. 1st perf. Paris, 27 April 1867; libr. by Jules Barbier and Michel Carré after Shakespeare's *Romeo and Juliet*. Principal roles: Juliette (sop), Roméo (ten), Frère Laurent (bass), Mercutio (bar), Thybalt (ten), Capulet (bar), Gertrude (mezzo), Stephano (sop). One of Gounod's most successful works, still regularly performed, it contains some of his most beautiful and melodious music, even if the work as a whole is a travesty of Shakespeare's original play.

Plot: Renaissance Verona. Juliette meets and falls in love with Roméo at a masked ball given by her father Capulet, unaware that he is a member of the rival Montagu family. Roméo escapes when recognised by Juliette's cousin Thybalt, but returns to serenade her under her balcony. The next day Frère Laurent, hoping for peace between the warring families, secretly marries them. Thybalt kills Roméo's friend Mercutio in a street brawl and Roméo kills Thybalt in revenge, for which he is banished. The lovers say farewell, and to avoid a marriage which Capulet has arranged for his daugher, Frère Laurent gives her a sleeping draught which simulates death. Roméo, unaware of this plan, returns to find Juliette apparently dead and poisons himself in her tomb. When she wakes and the dying Roméo tells her that he has taken poison, she stabs herself and the lovers die in each other's arms. [R]

Romeo und Julia
Opera in two acts by Sutermeister. 1st perf. Dresden, 13 April 1940; libr. by the composer, after Shakespeare's *Romeo and Juliet*. Principal roles: Romeo (ten), Julia (sop), Friar Lawrence (bass), Nurse (mezzo), Capulet (bar), Lady Capulet (mezzo). Sutermeister's most successful opera, it is a concise treatment, written in a readily accessible lyrical vein, which concentrates almost exclusively on the two lovers.

Romerzählung

Tenor monologue for Tannhäuser in Act III of Wagner's *Tannhäuser*.

Ronconi, Giorgio *(1810–90)*

Italian baritone. One of the greatest baritones of the 19th century (more highly regarded than any other by Donizetti), he was also considered an outstanding actor. He created the title role in *Nabucco* and, for Donizetti, Cardenio in *Il Furioso*, the title role in *Torquato Tasso*, Nello della Pietra in *Pia de' Tolomei*, Enrico in *Il Campanello*, Corrado in *Maria de Rudenz*, Don Pedro in *Maria Padilla* and Enrico in *Maria di Rohan*. His father Domenico (1772–1839) was a successful tenor and also a noted teacher.

Rondine, La *(The Swallow)*

Opera in three acts by Puccini. 1st perf. Monte Carlo, 27 March 1917; libr. by Giuseppe Adami, after Alfred Maria Willner and Heinrich Reichert. Principal roles: Magda (sop), Ruggero (ten), Prunier (ten), Lisette (sop), Rambaldo (bar). Originally planned as a Viennese operetta, it is Puccini's lightest work in style. Although never one of his more popular works, it is still performed quite often.

Plot: mid-19th century Paris and Nice. Magda is the mistress of the wealthy businessman Rambaldo. At one of their parties, she falls in love with the young Ruggero. She meets him in disguise at a café and they decide to elope together. They live together in Nice and Ruggero wishes them to marry. However, rather than make Ruggero suffer his family's disapproval, she renounces him and returns to Rambaldo. [R]

Rosa, Carl

See Carl Rosa Opera Company

Rosalinde

Soprano role in Johann Strauss' *Die Fledermaus*. She is married to Von Eisenstein.

Rosbaud, Hans *(1895–1962)*

Austrian conductor, particularly associated with 20th-century operas, especially those of Schönberg. He was musical director of the Münster Opera (1937–41), the Strasbourg Opera (1941–44) and the Aix-en-Provence Festival (1947–59). He conducted the first performance of *Moses und Aron*.

Rosenberg, Hilding *(1892–1985)*

Swedish composer and conductor. His operas have met with some success in Sweden but are unknown elsewhere. They include *Journey to America* (*Resan till Amerika*, Stockholm 24 Nov 1932; libr. A. Henriksson), *Marionetter* (Stockholm 14 Feb 1939; libr. J. Benavente), *The Island of Happiness* (*Lychsalighetens Ö*, Stockholm 1 Feb 1945; libr. P. D. A. Atterbom), the four-part opera-oratorio *Joseph and his Brothers* (*Josef och hans Bröder*, Swedish Radio 1946–48; libr. after Thomas Mann) and *The House With Two Entrances* (*Hus Med Dubbel Ingång*, Stockholm 24 May 1970; libr. after Pedro Calderón).

Rosenkavalier, Der *(The Rose Cavalier)*

Opera in three acts by Richard Strauss (Op 59). 1st perf. Dresden, 26 Jan 1911; libr. by Hugo von Hofmannsthal. Principal roles: Marschallin (sop), Octavian (mezzo), Baron Ochs (bass), Sophie (sop), Faninal (bar), Valzacchi (ten), Annina (mezzo), Italian Tenor (ten), Marianne (sop). Arguably Strauss' most popular opera, it is his first work in neo-classical style.

Plot: Vienna, 1740s. The middle-aged Marschallin is having an affair with the young nobleman Octavian. Her boorish country cousin Baron Ochs is engaged to Sophie, daughter of the recently ennobled businessman Faninal. He asks the Marschallin to recommend a suitable young man to make the traditional presentation of the Silver Rose to the intended bride, and Octavian is selected for the task. Octavian and Sophie are immediately attracted to each other, whilst Ochs' vulgarity revolts Sophie. Eventually, Ochs is discomfited, Sophie and Octavian are united and the Marschallin resigns herself with dignity to the loss of her lover to a girl of his own age. [R]

Rosenthal, Harold *(1917–86)*

British critic. One of the most influential postwar British opera critics, he edited *Opera* and was ardent in encouraging and championing British artists, although this led him occasionally to overrate them. His autobiography, *My Mad World of Opera*, was published in 1982.

Rose of Persia, The

Operetta in two acts by Sullivan. 1st perf. London, 29 Nov 1899; libr. by Basil Hood. Principal roles: Sultan Mahmoud (bar), Hassan (bar), Yussuf (ten), Zubeydeh (sop). Reasonably successful at its appearance, it is nowadays all but forgotten.

Plot: The wealthy merchant Abu el Hassan enjoys entertaining the city's beggars. The Sultana has been visiting his house disguised as a dancing girl, but is unmasked when Sultan Mahmoud sends the police to bring some of Hassan's guests to the palace for inspection. Mahmoud orders everyone involved to be put to death, but is dissuaded by a favourite slave Yussuf. Instead, Mahmoud orders Hassan to tell a story by instalments with the penalty of death if the ending is sad. By persuading the Sultan that the ending could not possibly be happy if he were executed, he gains the Sultan's pardon.

Rosina

Mezzo role in Rossini's and soprano role in Paisiello's *Il Barbiere di Siviglia*. She is Dr Bartolo's ward.

Rosina

Opera in two acts by Shield. 1st perf. London, 31 Dec 1782; libr. by Frances Brooke. Principal roles: Rosina (sop), Phoebe (sop), William (mezzo), Mr Belville (ten), Capt Belville (ten). One of the most successful 18th-century British operas, it is still very occasionally performed. [R]

Rospigliosi, Giulio

See Clement IX, Pope

Rossato, Arturo

Italian librettist. He provided texts for Alfano (*L'Ultimo Lord* and *Madonna Imperia*), Lattuada (*La Tempesta, Don Giovanni* and *Le Preziose Ridicole*), Vittadini (*Caracciolo*) and Zandonai (*I Cavalieri di Ekebù, Giulietta e Romeo, Giuliano, Una Partita, La Farsa Amorosa* and *Il Bacio*).

Rossellini, Renzo *(1908–82)*

Italian composer. His operas, some of which met with considerable success in Italy, are written in late romantic style. They are *La Guerra* (Naples 1958; libr. composer), *Il Vortice* (Naples 1958; libr. composer), *La Piovra* (Naples 1958; libr. composer), the television opera *La Campane* (1959; libr.

composer), *Uno Sguardo dal Ponte* (Rome 1961; libr. after Arthur Miller's *A View From the Bridge*), *Il Linguaggio dei Fiori* (Milan 1963; libr. composer, after Federico García Lorca), *La Leggenda del Ritorno* (Milan 1966; libr. D. Fabbri, after Fyodor Dostoyevsky's *The Brothers Karamazov*), *L'Avventuriero* (Monte Carlo 1968), the successful *L'Annonce Faite à Marie* (Paris 1970; libr. after Paul Claudel) and *La Reine Morte* (Monte Carlo 1973). He was artistic director of the Monte Carlo Opera from 1973. His brother Roberto (1906–77) was a successful producer, also famous as a film director and one-time husband of Ingrid Bergman.

Rossi, Gaetano *(1774–1855)*

Italian librettist. Official playwright at the Teatro la Fenice, Venice, he wrote over 120 libretti, providing texts for Carafa, Coccia, Donizetti (*Linda di Chamounix* and *Maria Padilla*), Generali, Mayr, Mercadante (including *Le Due Illustri Rivali*, *Il Bravo* and *Il Giuramento*), Meyerbeer (*Il Crociato in Egitto*), Morlacchi, Nicolaï (*Il Proscritto*), Pacini, Paer, Pavesi, Portugal, F. and L. Ricci, Rossini (*La Cambiale di Matrimonio*, *La Scala di Seta*, *Tancredi* and *Semiramide*), Vaccai (*Giovanna d'Arco*) and Winter, amongst others.

Rossi, Lauro *(1812–85)*

Italian composer. He wrote many operas, all now long forgotten, achieving considerable success in comedy, in which field he was widely regarded in his time as Donizetti's successor. His operas include *La Contessa Villane* (Naples 1829; libr. A. Passaro), *La Casa Disabitata* (Milan 11 Aug 1834; libr. Jacopo Ferretti), his most successful work, *Giovanna Shore* (Mexico 1836; libr. Felice Romani) and

Biorn (London 17 Jan 1877; libr. F. Marshall, after Shakespeare's *Macbeth*).

Rossignol, Le
See Nightingale, The

Rossi-Lemeni, Nicola *(b 1920)*

Italian bass, particularly associated with the Italian repertory (both classical and modern) and with Boris Godunov and Méphistophélès. One of the leading basses of the 1950s, his powerful voice was not perfectly knit together, but this was amply compensated for by his outstanding dramatic abilities. He created Thomas à Beckett in Pizzetti's *L'Assassinio nella Cattedrale* and roles in Zafred's *Wallenstein* and Rossellini's *Uno Sguardo dal Ponte* and *La Reine Morte*. He also produced a number of operas. Married to the soprano Virginia Zeani*.

Rossini, Gioacchino *(1792–1868)*

Italian composer. One of the greatest of all composers of comic opera, and the founder of Italian romantic opera, his first opera *Demetrio e Polibio** was written at the age of 14. His first commissioned work, *La Cambiale di Matrimonio**, was followed by *L'Equivoco Stravagante* (Bologna 26 Oct 1811; libr. G. Gasparri), *L'Inganno Felice**, *Ciro in Babilonia**, *La Scala di Seta**, *La Pietra del Paragone** and *Il Signor Bruschino**. The triumphs of *Tancredi** and *L'Italiana in Algieri** placed him at the forefront of Italian composers. There followed *Aureliano in Palmira**, *Il Turco in Italia**, the unsuccessful *Sigismondo* (Venice 26 Dec 1814; libr. Giuseppe Maria Foppa) and the works written during his period as musical director in Naples (1815–23): *Elisabetta Regina d'Inghilterra**, *Torvaldo e Dorliska**, the immortal *Il Barbiere di Siviglia**, *La Gazetta*

(Naples 26 Sept 1816; libr. Giovanni Palomba, after Carlo Goldoni's *Il Matrimonio per Concorso*), *Otello**, the highly successful *La Cenerentola**, *La Gazza Ladra**, *Armida**, *Adelaide di Borgogna**, *Mosè in Egitto**, *Adina* (Lisbon 22 June 1826, composed 1818; libr. G. Bevilaqua-Aldobrandini), *Riccardo e Zoraide* (Naples 3 Dec 1818; libr. F. Berio di Salsa), *Ermione**, *Edoardo e Cristina* (Venice 24 April 1819; libr. Giovanni Schmidt and Andrea Leone Tottola), *La Donna del Lago**, *Bianca e Faliero* (Milan 26 Dec 1819; libr. Felice Romani, after A. van Arnhault's *Blanche et Montcassini*), *Maometto II**, *Mathilde di Shabran**, *Zelmira** and *Semiramide**. He moved to Paris in 1824 as musical director of the Théâtre des Italiens, and there wrote *Il Viaggio a Reims**, *Le Siège de Corinthe** (a revision of *Maometto II*), *Moïse et Pharaon* (a revision of *Mosè in Egitto*), *Le Comte Ory** and *Guillaume Tell**, his finest serious work.

Rossini retired in 1830, writing virtually nothing for the rest of his life apart from the little vocal and instrumental pieces *The Sins of My Old Age*. His historical importance and influence can hardly be overstated; his works were the models for every subsequent Italian and many French composers. His brilliant orchestration, his introduction of accompanied recitative, his powers of comic characterisation and his introduction of elements from opera buffa into serious works all began the process of freeing Italian opera from its suffocating conventions which led through Donizetti to Verdi. His operas are regarded as some of the most florid ever written, but it is important to remember that Rossini was the first composer to write out his own decorations in an attempt to curb the extravagant excesses of singers. A

legendary wit and notoriously indolent (he was the worst self-borrower in musical history), his first wife was the soprano Isabella Colbran*. He later married Olimpe Pélissier, previously the mistress of the painter Horace Vernet.

Rostropovich, Mstislav *(b 1927)*

Russian conductor and cellist, particularly associated with the Russian repertory. An outstanding interpreter of Russian music, his operatic appearances have sadly been intermittent. Married to the soprano Galina Vishnevskaya*, he left the USSR in 1974, and was stripped of his Soviet citizenship. Artistic director of the Aldeburgh Festival.

Roswaenge, Helge *(b Rosenvig le-Hansen) (1897–1972)*

Danish tenor, particularly associated with heroic German and Italian roles. Widely regarded as the finest lyrico-dramatic tenor of the inter-war period, he had a thrilling voice of bite and brilliance. His autobiography, *Mach' es besser, mein Sohn*, was published in 1963.

Rota, Nino *(1911–79)*

Italian composer. His operas, written in a tuneful and readily accessible style, are: the student work *Il Principe Porcaro* (1925; libr. composer, after Hans Christian Andersen's *The Prince and the Swineherd*), *Ariodante* (Parma 1942; libr. E. Trucchi, after Lodovico Ariosto's *Orlando Furioso*), *Torquemada* (Parma 1943; libr. Trucchi, after Victor Hugo), the radio opera *I Due Timidi* (1950; libr. S. Cecchi d'Amico), *Il Cappello di Paglia di Firenze**, by far his most successful work, *Lo Scoiattolo in Gamba* (Venice 1959; libr. E. de Filippo), the radio opera *La Notte di un Nevrastenico*

(1959; libr. R. Bacchelli), *La Scuola di Guida* (Spoleto 1959), *Aladino e la Lampada Magica* (Naples 1968; libr. V. Verginelli), *La Visita Meravigliosa* (Palermo 1970; libr. composer, after H. G. Wells) and *Napoli Milionaria* (Spoleto 1978; libr. de Filippo). He also achieved international fame as a composer of film music, especially for Fellini.

Rothenberger, Anneliese *(b 1924)*

German soprano, particularly associated with lighter German roles, Viennese operetta and some modern dramatic roles such as Lulu. She had a light and beautiful voice, used with intelligence and musicianship, and a charming stage presence. She created Telemachus in Liebermann's *Penelope* and the title role in Sutermeister's *Madame Bovary*.

Rothmüller, Marko *(b 1908)*

Yugoslavian baritone, particularly associated with Verdi roles and with Wozzeck. One of the finest baritones of the immediate postwar period, he had a beautiful voice used with great intelligence and was a characterful actor. He created Truchsess in *Mathis der Maler*. His writings include *Die Musik der Juden* (1951).

Rouleau, Joseph *(b 1929)*

Canadian bass, particularly associated with the Italian and French repertories. He possessed a large, dark voice (occasionally inclined to woolliness) and had an impressive stage presence. He created Bishop Tâché in Somers' *Louis Reil* and Pranzini in Tavener's *Thérèse*.

Rousseau, Jean-Jacques *(1712–78)*

Swiss philosopher, composer and writer. His music is charming if simple, but lacks any great technical skill. His first opera *Les Muses Galantes* (Paris 1742) was followed by the highly successful *Le Devin du Village**, *Pygmalion* (Lyon 1770), written in collaboration with Horace Coignet, which is an early operatic example of melodrama*, and the unfinished *Daphnis et Chloé*. He appears as a character in Dalayrac's *L'Enfance de Jean-Jacques Rousseau*.

Rousseau's operatic importance lies in his writings. Siding with the Italians, he was a central figure in the Guerre des Bouffons*, advocating melody as a form of heightened speech and the use of emotion and personal sensibility as a guide, an advocacy which exercised a powerful influence on the early romantic composers. These beliefs were propounded in his famous *Lettre Sur la Musique Française* (1753) and expanded in his *Dictionnaire de Musique* (1768) and in his contributions on music to the *Grande Encyclopédie*.

Roussel, Albert *(1869–1937)*

French composer. He was deeply inspired by Indian music, which provided the inspiration for his first and finest opera *Padmâvatî**. His two other operas are *La Naissance de la Lyre* (Paris 11 July 1925; libr. T. Reinach, after Sophocles) and the comedy *La Testament du Tante Caroline* (Olomouc 14 Nov 1936; libr. Nino).

Royal Danish Opera

The Theatre Royal (cap. 1,100) in Copenhagen opened in 1874, and a second house, New Stage (cap. 1,091) opened in 1931. The annual season runs from September to June. Musical directors have included Johan Svendsen, Nielsen, Georg Hoeberg, Johan Hye-Knudsen, Egisto Tango, John Frandsen and Michael Schønwandt.

Royal Flemish Opera

(*Koninklijke Vlaamse Opera* in Flemish) Formed in 1893 by the bass Hendrik Fontaine, the company performs at the Royal Opera House (cap. 1,050) in Antwerp. The adventurous repertory has included several operas by Flemish composers. All performances are sung in Flemish, and musical directors have included Fritz Célis. The Flemish Chamber Opera (*Vlaamse Kameropera*), based at the Ring Theatre in Antwerp, was formed in 1971 from an amalgamation of the Dutch Chamber Opera and the Antwerp Chamber Opera, which had been founded in 1960.

Royal Hunt of the Sun, The

Opera in two acts by Hamilton. 1st perf. London, 2 Feb 1977 (composed 1969); libr. by the composer, after Peter Shaffer's play. Principal roles: Pizarro (bar), Atahualpa (bar), Young Martin (ten), Villac Umu (bass), Old Martin (bass), Valverde (bass), Hernando de Soto (ten), Don Diego (ten). Set in 16th-century Peru, it is a powerfully theatrical work telling of the clash of cultures during the Spanish conquest of the Inca Empire.

Royal Opera, Ghent

Originally named the Théâtre Lyrique and acquiring its present name in 1921, the theatre opened in August 1840. It pursues the most adventurous repertory police in Belgium.

Royal Opera House, Covent Garden

London's principal opera house, the present theatre (cap. 2,250) is the third on the site. The first theatre was opened by John Ritch on 7 December 1732 and was destroyed by fire on 19 September 1808. It was rebuilt in 1809 but burnt down in 1856. The present house opened on 15 May 1858. Named the Royal Opera in 1892, it became the home of the present company in 1946. The annual international season, given in tandem with that of the Royal Ballet, runs from mid-September to mid-July. Postwar general administrators have been Sir David Webster, Sir John Tooley and Jeremy Isaacs, and the musical directors have been Karl Rankl, Rafael Kubelík, Sir Georg Solti, Sir Colin Davis and Bernard Haitink. The wide-ranging repertory has been particularly notable for its Wagner, Strauss, Mozart, Berlioz and Tippett productions.

Rozhdestvensky, Gennady (b 1931)

Russian conductor, particularly associated with the Russian repertory. One of the most brilliant and exciting contemporary Soviet conductors, he was musical director of the Bolshoi Opera (1964–70). Married to the pianist Viktoria Postnikova.

Rubato (Italian for 'robbed')

Short for *tempo rubato*, it means performing with a degree of freedom as regards time, so as to give expression to the music. Usually used with reference to pianists, it can also apply to singing.

Rubini, Giovanni Battista (1794–1854)

Italian tenor. One of the outstanding lyric tenors of the early 19th century, although said to have been a poor actor, he created, for Bellini, Fernando in *Bianca e Fernando*, Gualtiero in *Il Pirata*, Elvino in *La Sonnambula* and Arturo in *I Puritani*, and eight roles for Donizetti, including Percy in *Anna Bolena*. He was married to the soprano Adelaide Chaumel.

Rubinstein, Anton *(1830–94)*

Russian composer and pianist. His 15 operas and three opera-oratorios, all but one now forgotten, were modelled on contemporary European composers and show only flashes of the nationalist influence which so absorbed his fellow Russian composers. His operas include *Feramors* (Dresden 1863; libr. J. Rodenberg, after Thomas Moore), *The Demon**, by far his most successful work, *Paradise Lost* (1875; libr. after John Milton), the more nationalist *Kalashnikov the Merchant* (St Petersburg 1880; libr. N. Kulikov, after Mikhail Lermentov) and *Sulamith* (Hamburg 1883; libr. Rodenberg).

Rudel, Julius *(b 1921)*

Austrian conductor, long resident in the United States. Particularly associated with the Italian and French repertories, he was musical director of the New York City Opera (1957–79), the Caramoor Festival (1963–76) and the Kennedy Center, Washington (1971–74). He conducted the first performances of Ginastera's *Bomarzo* and Kurka's *The Good Soldier Schweik*.

Ruddigore
or **The Witch's Curse**

Operetta in two acts by Sullivan. 1st perf. (as *Ruddygore*) London, 22 Jan 1887; libr. by W. S. Gilbert. Principal roles: Robin Oakapple/Sir Ruthven (bar), Rose Maybud (sop), Richard Dauntless (ten), Sir Despard (b-bar), Mad Margaret (mezzo), Dame Hannah (mezzo), Sir Roderick (bass), Old Adam Goodheart (bass), Zorah (sop). A satire on the Victorian passion for Gothic melodrama, it contains some of Sullivan's finest music, particularly in the ghosts' scene.

Plot: Cornwall, *c* 1750. The Murgatroyd family, baronets of Ruddigore, are accursed: each baronet must commit a serious crime every day or perish in agony. To avoid inheriting the title, the meek and mild Ruthven has disguised himself as a farmer called Robin Oakapple and is in love with Rose Maybud, but is too diffident to propose to her. His bumptious foster-brother, the sailor Dick Dauntless, offers to help him, but falls in love with Rose himself. Rose, however, decides that she prefers Robin and the disappointed Dick reveals Robin's true identity to the present baronet Sir Despard. Robin is forced to accept his inheritance and Despard returns to ordinary life, marrying Mad Margaret, one of his earlier victims. Robin's ancestors, led by Sir Roderick, are contemptuous of Robin's pathetic little crimes and order him to do something desperate or perish. He has his servant Old Adam carry off Rose's aunt Dame Hannah, who turns out to be Sir Roderick's former sweetheart. Robin realises that refusal to commit a daily crime amounts to suicide, which is in itself a crime, and that Sir Roderick should thus never have died. Roderick feels at liberty to resume life and marry Dame Hannah, whilst Robin is now free to marry Rose. [R]

Rudziński, Witold *(b 1913)*

Polish composer. His six operas in late romantic style have met with considerable success in Poland, particularly *The Dismissal of the Greek Envoys* (*Odprawa Posłów Greckich*, 1962; libr. B. Ostromecki, after J. Kochanowski) [R].

Ruffo, Titta *(b Ruffo Cafiero Titta)* *(1877–1953)*

Italian baritone, particularly associated with the Italian repertory, especially Verdi. One of the greatest baritones of the 20th century, he possessed a voice of great richness, beauty and remarkable power, described by Giuseppe de Luca as "not a voice, but a miracle". He created the title role in Leoncavallo's *Edipo Rè*. His autobiography, *La Mia Parabola*, was published in 1937.

Ruggero
Tenor role in Puccini's *La Rondine*. He is a young aristocrat in love with Magda.

Rumania
See Romania

Rusalka
Works of this title about the water nymph of Eastern European legend include:

(1) Opera in four acts by Dargomijsky. 1st perf. St Petersburg, 16 May 1856; libr. by the composer, after Alexander Pushkin's dramatic poem. Principal roles: Natasha (sop), Prince (ten), Miller (bass). A delightful work, showing considerable powers of characterisation, it is still quite often performed in Russia but almost never elsewhere.

Plot: The Prince seduces the Miller's daughter Natasha, gets her pregnant and then abandons her. She becomes the water nymph Rusalka. The Miller goes mad with grief and finally throws the Prince into the river. [R]

(2) Opera in three acts by Dvořák (Op 114). 1st perf. Prague, 31 March 1901; libr. by Jaroslav Kvapil, after Friedrich de la Motte Fouqué's *Ondine* and also drawing on Hans Christian Andersen's *The Little Mermaid* and Gerhard Hauptmann's *Die Versunkene Glocke*. Principal roles: Rusalka (sop), Prince (ten), Watersprite (bass), Ježibaba (mezzo), Foreign Princess (sop), Forester (ten), Kitchen Boy (mezzo). Dvořák's finest and most successful opera, it is his only work to be regularly performed outside Czechoslovakia.

Plot: The Watersprite's daughter Rusalka wishes to become human so as to win the love of the Prince. The witch Ježibaba agrees to arrange this provided that Rusalka remains dumb and the Prince remains faithful; if not, both will be damned. After a while, the Prince tires of the mute Rusalka and turns to the Foreign Princess. Repenting, he frees Rusalka from Ježibaba's curse but dies himself. [R]

Ruslan and Ludmila
Opera in five acts by Glinka. 1st perf. St Petersburg, 9 Dec 1842; libr. by the composer, Valerian Fyodorovich Shirkov, N. V. Kukolnik and others, after Alexander Pushkin's poem. Principal roles: Ruslan (bass), Ludmila (sop), Svetozar (bass), Farlaf (bass), Ratmir (mezzo), Gorislava (sop), Finn (ten), Naina (mezzo). Glinka's second opera, it is a vast, sprawling fairy tale containing much magnificent music. In its subject matter, structure, and harmonic and orchestral aspects, it marks the foundation of the distinctively Russian nationalist school of opera. Quite unaccountably, it is almost never performed outside Russia, although the overture is still very popular.

Plot: Ludmila is wooed by the poet-prince Ratmir, the cowardly warrior Farlaf and the knight Ruslan. She disappears at a feast and is promised to whichever suitor can find her. The wizard Finn tells Ruslan that she has been stolen by an evil dwarf and warns him against Farlaf's helper, the evil fairy Naina. Ruslan encounters a giant head whose breathing causes a storm. He calms it and finds a magical sword beneath it. With the sword he kills the dwarf and rescues Ludmila, awakening her from a magical sleep with a ring given to him by the Finn. [R]

Russia

See Baku Opera and Ballet Theatre; Bolshoi Opera; Kirov Opera; Tiflis Opera and Ballet Theatre

Russian opera composers

See Alyabyev; Arensky; Borodin; Bortnyansky; Cui; Dankevich; Dargomijsky; Dzerzhinsky; Glazunov; Glière; Glinka; Hadjibeyov; Ippolitov-Ivanov; Kabalevsky; Khrennikov; Lysenko; Moussorgsky; Paliashvili; Pashkevich; Prokofiev; Rachmaninov; Rimsky-Korsakov; Rubinstein; Serov; Shaporin; Shchedrin; Shostakovich; Stravinsky; Taneyev; Tchaikovsky; Verstovsky

See also Armenian opera composers; Azerbaijani opera composers; Estonian opera composers; Latvian opera composers; Lithuanian opera composers; Ukrainian opera composers

Rysanek, Leonie *(b 1926)*
Austrian soprano, particularly associated with Wagner and Strauss roles. One of the finest Strauss interpreters of the immediate postwar period, she had a rich and beautiful voice with a strong upper register and was a committed singing-actress. Her sister Lotte (*b* 1928) was a successful lyric soprano.

Saarbrücken Opera

Opera in this German city in the Saar is given at the Gau Theater Saarpfalz (cap. 1,132), which originally opened in 1938 and which was rebuilt in 1947. Musical directors have included Matthias Kuntsch.

Sabata, Victor de *(1892–1967)*

Italian conductor and composer. One of the outstanding operatic conductors of the mid-20th century, particularly admired for his Verdi and Wagner, his fiery and sometimes dynamically idiosyncratic readings were often compared to Toscanini's. He conducted the first performance of *L'Enfant et les Sortilèges*, and was musical director of La Scala, Milan (1953–57). He also composed one opera, *Il Macigno* (Milan 1917).

Sabina, Karel *(1813–87)*

Czech librettist, excelling in comedy. He provided texts for Bendl (*The Old Bridegroom*), Blodek (*In a Well* and *Zítek*), Fibich (*Bukovín*) and Smetana (*The Brandenburgers in Bohemia* and *The Bartered Bride*).

Sacchini, Antonio *(1730–86)*

Italian composer. He wrote many operas, much admired in their day but all now largely forgotten, for Italy, London, Germany and Paris. His most important works are *Armida** and his masterpiece *Oedipe à Colone* (Paris 4 Jan 1786; libr. Nicolas François Guillard, after Sophocles' *Oedipus at Colonus*), which was performed nearly 600 times in 60 years at the Paris Opéra alone.

Sachs, Hans

Baritone role in Wagner's *Die Meistersinger von Nürnberg*. The historical cobbler-poet (1494–1576), he is also the subject of operas by Jírovec and Lortzing.

Sacra la sceltra

Baritone aria for Miller in Act I of Verdi's *Luisa Miller*.

Sadko

Opera in seven scenes (three or five acts) by Rimsky-Korsakov. 1st perf. Moscow, 7 Jan 1898; libr. by the composer and Vladimir Ivanovich Belsky. Principal roles: Sadko (ten), Volkhova (sop), Lyubava (mezzo), Sea King (bass), Viking, Indian and Venetian Merchants (bass, ten and bar). One of the most colourful and successful of Rimsky's fairy-tale operas, it is still regularly performed in Russia and Eastern Europe, but only infrequently elsewhere.

Plot: Novgorod. The local merchants beg Sadko to find wealth for the city. He meets the Sea Princess Volkhova, who falls in love with him and encourages him to catch three golden fish in a lake. This he does and sets sail to bring back treasure. He is becalmed on his return because he has failed to make an offering to the Sea King. The treasure is tipped overboard and Sadko is cast adrift on a plank. He sinks to the bottom of the ocean, where he is offered the hand of Volkhova. The energetic dancing at their wedding causes storms which sink shipping. The Sea King's reign is declared over and Sadko and his bride are carried off in a shell drawn by birds. The next day, Volkhava is transformed into a river and Sadko, having been commended back to land by St Nicholas, is found by his wife Lyubava. [R]

Sadler's Wells

See English National Opera; New Sadler's Wells Opera

Saffi

Soprano role in Johann Strauss' *Der Zigeunerbaron*. A gypsy girl, she is Czipra's foster-daughter.

Saffo

Opera in three acts by Pacini. 1st perf. Naples, 29 Nov 1840; libr. by Salvatore Cammarano partly after Grillparzer's play. Principal roles: Saffo (sop), Faone (ten), Alcandro (bar), Climene (mezzo). Telling of the Greek poetess, it is Pacini's finest and most successful opera, but is very rarely performed.

Plot: Ancient Greece. Alcandro, the High Priest of Apollo, disapproves of the love of Faone and the poetess Saffo. He separates them and marries Faone to his daughter Climene. Saffo learns of the wedding only at the ceremony itself and overturns the altar of Apollo in fury. She is condemned to death for sacrilege. Alcandro learns that Saffo is in fact his other daughter, whom he believed to be dead, but he is unable to have the sentence reversed. Saffo accepts her fate, blesses Climene's marriage to Faone, and takes the Leucadian leap, drowning in the Aegean.

Sainete

A genre of Spanish comic opera which portrayed scenes of everyday life in the form of low comedy. Its principal exponents were Blas Laserna and Antonio Soler.

Saint François d'Assise (*St Francis of Assisi*)

Opera in three acts by Messiaen. 1st perf. Paris, 28 Nov 1983; libr. by the composer, after the 14th-century monkish books *Fioretti* and *Considérations sur les Stigmates*. Principal roles: St François (bar), Angel (sop), Leper (ten), Frère Massé (ten), Frère Léon (bar), Frère Bernard (bass), Frère Elie (ten). Messiaen's only opera, it is a vast work of great orchestral complexity and beauty (built around his notations of bird songs) which charts the progress of grace in St Francis's soul.

Plot: The eight tableaux or 'Franciscan scenes' are: (1) Francis explains the necessity to endure suffering. (2) Francis asks God to make him capable of loving a leper. (3) Francis kisses the Leper, who is cured. (4) The Angel discusses predestination with the monks. (5) The Angel gives Francis a foretaste of heavenly bliss. (6) Francis preaches his sermon to the birds. (7) Francis receives the Stigmata. (8) Francis dies and enters a new life. [R]

Saint-Georges, Jules-Henri Vernoy de (*1799–1875*)

French librettist. One of the most prolific 19th-century French librettists, he wrote (in whole or in part) over 80 texts, the best being comedies. He provided libretti for Adam (*Falstaff*), Auber (*Les Diamants de la Couronne* and *Zanetta*), Bizet (*La Jolie Fille de Perth*), Donizetti (*La Fille du Régiment*), Flotow (*Zilda* and *L'Ombre*), Halévy (*La Reine de Chypre* and the unfinished *Noé*), Hérold and Poniatowski, amongst others.

Saint of Bleecker Street, The

Opera in three acts by Menotti. 1st perf. New York, 27 Dec 1954; libr. by the composer. Principal roles: Annina (sop), Michele (ten), Desideria (mezzo), Maria (sop). A verismo piece, it met with some success at its appearance, but is nowadays seldom performed.

Plot: New York's 'Little Italy'. The religious mystic Annina receives the Stigmata on her palms, arousing great awe amongst her Catholic neighbours. Her brother Michele is devoted to her, although he is an agnostic, but his mistress Desideria is violently antagonistic. Desideria is killed in a quarrel and Michele runs away. He later returns and is captured.

Saint-Saëns, Camille *(1835–1921)*

French composer. His 12 operas, written in a conservative and lyrical style, are notable for their fine craftsmanship and for their sometimes striking orchestration, but show little dramatic flair. His first opera *La Princesse Jaune* (Paris 12 June 1872; libr. Louis Gallet), was followed by *Le Timbre d'Argent* (Paris 23 Feb 1877; libr. Jules Barbier and Michel Carré), *Samson et Dalila**, by far his most successful and enduring opera, *Etienne Marcel* (Lyon 8 Feb 1879; libr. Gallet), the once-popular *Henri VIII**, *Prosperpine* (Paris 14 March 1887; libr. Gallet, after A. Vacquerie), *Ascanio* (Paris 21 March 1890; libr. Gallet, after Alexandre Dumas), *Phryné* (Paris 24 May 1893; libr. L. Augé de Lassus), *Les Barbares* (Paris 23 Oct 1901; libr. P. B. Gheusi and Victorien Sardou), *Hélène* (Monte Carlo 18 Feb 1904; libr. composer), *L'Ancêtre* (Monte Carlo 24 Feb 1906; libr. De Lassus) and *Déjanire* (Monte Carlo 14 March 1911; libr. composer, after Gallet). He

also helped to complete Guiraud's unfinished *Frédégonde*.

Salammbô

Works of this title, based on Gustave Flaubert's novel, include:

(1) Unfinished opera by Moussorgsky. 1st perf. Milan, 10 Nov 1980 (begun in 1863); libr. by the composer. Principal roles: Salammbô (mezzo), Matho (bass), Spendius (bar). Moussorgsky abandoned the work halfway through and later incorporated much of the music into other works, including *Boris Godunov*. It has recently been edited and prepared for performance by the conductor Zoltán Peskó. [R]

(2) Opera in five acts by Reyer. 1st perf. Brussels, 10 Feb 1890; libr. by Camille du Locle. Principal roles: Matho (ten), Salammbô (sop). Set in an austere and static style, it met with considerable success at its appearance but is now all but forgotten.

Plot: Matho, leader of the besiegers of Carthage, loves the Carthaginian priestess Salammbô, daughter of Hamilcar. He steals a sacred veil from the Temple of Tanit and is condemned to die at Salammbô's hand. She kills herself in his place and Matho stabs himself in grief.

Salgo già il trono aurato

Soprano cabaletta for Abigaille in Act II of Verdi's *Nabucco*. One of the most splendid pieces of invective in all opera.

Salieri, Antonio *(1750–1825)*

Italian composer. His first opera *La Vestale* (Vienna 1768) was followed by 34 others, many of which enjoyed great success in their day. His serious works are finely constructed and have a certain grandeur, even if they are somewhat stiff and formal; his comedies show a lively sense of characterisation. His most important operas include *La Fiera di Venezia* (Vienna 29 Jan 1772; libr. Gaston Boccherini), *L'Europa Riconosciuta* (Milan 3 Aug 1778; libr. M. Verazi), written for the opening of La Scala, the comedy *La Grota di Trionfo* (Vienna 12 Oct 1785; libr. Giovanni Battista Casti), *Prima la Musica e Poi le Parole**, his best known work which was first performed together with Mozart's *Der Schauspieldirektor*, *Les Danaïdes** (once thought to have been written by Gluck, and written under the influence of Gluck's reforms), *Les Horaces* (Paris 7 Dec 1786; libr. Nicolas François Guillard, after Voltaire's *Horace*), the sensationally successful *Tarare** and *Falstaff**.

In the early 19th century, a rumour spread that Salieri had poisoned Mozart out of jealousy, and he appears in this guise as a character in Rimsky-Korsakov's *Mozart and Salieri* (based on Alexander Pushkin's play). He has long been acquitted of this charge. He was a noted theorist and respected teacher, whose many pupils included Beethoven and Schubert. Perhaps partly as a result of the success of the play and film *Amadeus*, there has recently been a considerable revival of interest in Salieri's music.

Salle de l'Opéra, Versailles

Designed by Ange-Jacques Gabriel for Louis XV, the beautiful theatre (cap. 600) opened on 16 May 1770. After being the seat of the National Assembly in the 1870s, it fell into disuse until 1952. Since then, it has been used as a venue for special performances.

Sallinen, Aulis *(b 1935)*

Finnish composer. His three operas, written in serial style, but incorporating both tonal and folk-music elements, show a powerful musico-dramatic imagination which ranks him as one of the finest of contemporary opera composers. *The Horseman**, *The Red Line* * and *The King Goes Forth to France** have all been widely performed. A fourth, *Kullervo*, is due to open the new opera house in Helsinki in 1992.

Salminen, Matti *(b 1945)*

Finnish bass, particularly associated with Wagner and Mozart roles. He possesses a dark, rich and powerful voice, used with fine musicianship, and has a strong stage presence which is aided by his powerful physique. He created Antti in Sallinen's *The Horseman*.

Salome

Opera in one act by Richard Strauss (Op 54). 1st perf. Dresden, 9 Dec 1906. A setting of Hedwig Lachmann's translation of Oscar Wilde's play. Principal roles: Salome (sop), Herod (ten), Jokanaan (bar), Herodias (mezzo), Narraboth (ten), Page (mezzo). A work of great orchestral power and brilliance, in which Strauss carried harmonic audacity to new lengths, the unashamedly erotic nature of the music caused it to be condemned as obscene and many early performances were banned. If the work has nowadays lost its capacity to shock, it has lost none of its power to thrill.

Plot: Galilee, *c* 30 AD. Salome, daughter of Herodias and stepdaughter of the tetrarch Herod, is fascinated by the prophetic voice of Jokanaan (John the Baptist), which she hears emerging from the cistern in which Herod has him imprisoned. She demands to see him and becomes infatuated with him physically. He repulses her, but she has become obsessed with him and is quite unmoved when Narraboth, the captain of the guard who loves her, kills himself. The lascivious Herod, who lusts after his stepdaughter, asks Salome to dance for him. She refuses until he promises to grant her anything she should ask. She performs the Dance of the Seven Veils and, as her reward, demands the head of Jokanaan, much to the delight of Herodias against whom Jokanaan has preached. Herod prevaricates but eventually has to agree. Jokanaan's severed head is brought to Salome on a platter and she exults over it, finally kissing the dead lips. Overcome with revulsion, Herod orders her crushed to death by the shields of his guards. [R]

Salud
Soprano role in De Falla's *La Vida Breve*. She is in love with Paco.

Salut à la France
Soprano aria for Marie in Act II of Donizetti's *La Fille du Régiment*.

Salut, demeure
Tenor aria for Faust in Act II of Gounod's *Faust*.

Salzburg Festival
An annual summer festival in Austria, which was founded in 1921. Performances are given at the Grosses Festpielhaus (cap. 2,160), which opened in 1960. One of the most prestigious (and expensive) European festivals, opera is given with top international casts and the repertory consists principally of Mozart, Strauss, Verdi and contemporary works. The Salzburg Easter Festival, mainly devoted to Wagner, was founded in 1967. Artistic directors have included Herbert von Karajan.

Samson
Works of this title about the Old Testament figure include:

(1) Oratorio in three parts by Handel. 1st perf. London, 18 Feb 1743; libr. by Newburgh Hamilton, after John Milton's *Samson Agonistes*. Principal roles: Samson (ten), Dalila (sop), Micah (mezzo), Harapha (bass), Manoah (bass), Israelite Woman (sop). One of Handel's greatest oratorios, it is not strictly speaking an opera, but it is frequently staged. [R]

(2) Opera in two acts by Szokolay (Op 34). 1st perf. Budapest, 1973; libr. after László Németh. [R]

Samson et Dalila
Opera in three acts by Saint-Saëns. 1st perf. Weimar, 2 Dec 1877; libr. by Ferdinand Lemaire, after the Book of Judges in the Old Testament. Principal roles: Samson (ten), Dalila (mezzo), High Priest of Dagon (bar), Old Hebrew (bass), Abimelech (bass). Saint-Saëns' operatic masterpiece, and his only work still to be performed, it is notable for its superb choruses, lavish spectacle, and the sensuous beauty of Dalila's music.

Plot: Gaza. Samson leads a successful Hebrew revolt against their Philistine overlords, in which the satrap Abimelech is killed. Prompted by the High Priest of Dagon, the Philistine seductress Dalila renders Samson powerless by cutting off his hair, from which his strength is derived. Finally, Samson's strength is restored to him through prayer, and he pulls down the Temple of Dagon, killing his enemies and himself. [R]

Sanderson, Sibyl *(1865–1903)*
American soprano, particularly associated with the French repertory. Famed for her personal beauty and for her acting ability as much as for her wide-ranging voice, she created the title roles in *Thaïs*, *Esclarmonde* and Saint-Saëns' *Phryné*.

San Diego Opera Guild

Founded in 1965, the company performs at the Civic Theater (cap. 2,945). The annual season runs from January to April, and the repertory gives mixed standard works with a number of US premières. Musical directors have included Walter Herbert.

San Francisco Opera Association

Founded in 1923, the company performs at the War Memorial Opera House (cap. 3,252), which opened on 15 Oct 1932. The annual season runs from September to December, and the repertory consists largely of standard Italian and German works given with top international casts. Musical directors have been Gaetano Merola, Kurt Herbert Adler and Sir John Pritchard.

Santa Fe Opera

Founded in 1957 by John Crosby, the company gives an annual summer season, notable for its highly adventurous repertory. The original outdoor theatre burnt down in 1967; the present modernistic replacement (cap. 1,773) opened the following year.

Santi, Nello *(b 1931)*

Italian conductor, particularly associated with the Italian repertory. Considered a good 'singer's conductor', his performances can sometimes seem sluggish, but on occasion (such as his recording of *L'Amore dei Tre Re*) can be thrilling.

Santiago

See Teatro Municipal, Santiago

Santini, Gabriele *(1886–1964)*

Italian conductor, particularly associated with the Italian repertory. A rock-solid Italian maestro of the old school, especially fine in Verdi, he was musical director of the Rome Opera (1945–62). He conducted the first performances of Giordano's *Il Rè* and Alfano's *Dottor Antonio*.

Santley, Sir Charles *(1834–1922)*

British baritone. The finest British baritone of the 19th century, his voice – whilst not intrinsically beautiful – was used with expressiveness and fine musicianship, and he was an effective dramatic performer. He sang the Dutchman in the first-ever performance of a Wagner opera in Britain and created Danny Man in *The Lily of Killarney*, the Rhine King in Wallace's *Lurline* and, for Balfe, Clifford in *The Puritan's Daughter* and Fabio in *The Armourer of Nantes*.

Santuzza

Soprano role in Mascagni's *Cavalleria Rusticana*. She is the girl seduced and abandoned by Turiddù. The role is sometimes sung by a mezzo.

Sanzogno, Nino *(1911–83)*

Italian conductor, particularly associated with modern operas and with 18th-century Italian works. Based largely at La Scala, Milan, he conducted the first performances of *Dialogues des Carmélites*, Milhaud's *David*, Malipiero's *L'Allegra Brigata* and Turchi's *Buon Soldato Svejk*.

Sapho

Opera in four (originally three) acts by Gounod. 1st perf. Paris, 16 April 1851; libr. by Emile Augier. Revised version, 1st perf. Paris, 2 April 1884. Telling of the Greek poetess, it contains some fine music but is nowadays only very rarely performed.

Sapho

Opera in five acts by Massenet. 1st perf. Paris, 27 Nov 1897; libr. by Henri Cain and Arthur Bernède, after Alphonse Daudet's novel. Principal roles: Fanny Legrand (sop), Jean (ten). One of Massenet's most erotically-scented operas, nowadays very rarely performed, it tells of the seduction of an unsophisticated country youth by a former artist's model who is attempting to rise above her past. [R]

Sarah

Mezzo role in Donizetti's *Roberto Devereux*. The Duke of Nottingham's wife, she is in love with Robert.

Sarastro

Bass role in Mozart's *Die Zauberflöte*. He is the priest of Isis.

Sardou, Victorien

See panel on page 508

Sargent, Sir Malcolm *(1895–1967)*

British conductor, particularly associated with the British repertory, especially Sullivan. He conducted much opera in the early part of his career (including the first performances of *At the Boar's Head*, *Troilus and Cressida* and Vaughan Williams' *Sir John in Love*, *Hugh the Drover* and *Riders to the Sea*), but later devoted himself largely to the concert hall. A great showman who always wore a carnation in his buttonhole – he was nicknamed 'Flash Harry' – he did invaluable work in making music more readily accessible to ordinary people.

Šárka

Works of this title about the legendary Czech heroine include:

(1) Opera in three acts by Janáček. 1st perf. Brno, 11 Nov 1925 (composed 1887 and revised 1888 and 1918); libr. by Julius Zeyer, after his play. Principal roles: Šárka (sop), Ctirad (ten), Přemysl (bass). Janáček's first opera, only very rarely performed, it is written in Czech romantic style but gives some indication of his future development.

Plot: When his wife, Queen Libuše, has died, Přemysl resolves to disband her council of women. Under the leadership of Šárka, the women revolt. Šárka falls in love with the warrior-hero Ctirad, but nonetheless causes his death. She throws herself on to his funeral pyre.

(2) Opera in three acts by Fibich (Op 51). 1st perf. Prague, 28 Dec 1897; libr. by Anežka Schulzová. Principal roles: Šárka (sop), Ctirad (ten), Přemysl (bar), Vlasta (mezzo). Fibich's finest and most successful work, it is still regularly performed in Czechoslovakia, but is little known elsewhere.

Plot: At the court of the Czech ruler Přemysl, the women have lost their influence following the death of his wife Libuše. Šárka challenges Ctirad, the leading opponent of the women, to a duel, which he contemptuously refuses. In the fighting which follows, Šárka tricks Ctirad into 'rescuing' her when he discovers her tied to a tree. However, instead of calling her troops, Šárka falls in love with him and warns him of the ambush. Ctirad, returning Šárka's love, refuses to escape and summons the women's troops himself. The women take him away injured, but Šárka tells Přemysl where he is being held and the men rescue him. The women are killed, and Šárka leaps to her death. [R]

Sarti, Giuseppe *(1729–1802)*

Italian composer. He wrote some 75 operas, mostly for Denmark, Russia

VICTORIEN SARDOU

The French playwright Victorien Sardou (1831–1908) himself wrote a number of operatic libretti, including Offenbach's *Le Roi Carotte* and *Fantasio*, Lecocq's *Les Prés Saint-Gervais*, Saint-Saëns' *Les Barbares* and Bizet's unfinished *Grisélidis*. Some 25 operas have been based on his works. Below are listed, by play, those operas by composers with entries in this dictionary.

Fédora
Giordano	*Fedora*	1898

Gismonda
Février	*Gismonda*	1919

Madame Sans-Gêne
Giordano	*Madame Sans-Gêne*	1915

Les Noces de Fernande
Millöcker	*Der Bettelstudent*	1882

Patrie!
Rossi	*La Contessa di Mons*	1874

Piccolino
J. Strauss	*Ein Karneval in Rom*	1873
Guiraud	*Piccolino*	1876

La Tosca
Puccini	*Tosca*	1900

and Italy, some of which enjoyed great success in their day but which are all now forgotten. They include *Fra Due Litiganti* (Milan 14 Sept 1782; libr. after Carlo Goldoni's *Le Nozze*), an aria from which is quoted in the Supper Scene of Mozart's *Don Giovanni*, and *The First Government of Oleg* (St Petersburg 26 Oct 1790; libr. Catherine the Great), written in collaboration with Pashkevich, which is one of the earliest Russian operas.

Sass, Sylvia (b 1951)
Hungarian soprano, particularly associated with Verdi roles. Her exceptional vocal and dramatic talent prompted some to hail her as a second Maria Callas. However – partly as a result of taking on too much too young – her voice has declined early.

Satie, Erik (*b Alfred Eric Leslie*) (*1866–1925*)

French composer. Best known for his witty piano music, he also wrote a number of stage works, including the marionette opera *Geneviève de Brabant* (1899; libr. J. P. Contamine de Latour) and the operettas *Pousse l'Amour* (1905), which is lost, and *Le Piège de Méduse* (1913).

Sauget, Henri (*1901–89*)

French composer, writing mainly in a smart, slick, metropolitan style influenced by the music of the group 'Les Six'. His seven operas are *Le Plumet du Colonel* (1924; libr. composer), *La Contrebasse* (1930; libr. H. Troyat, after Anton Chekhov), *La Voyante* (1932), which is a monodrama for soprano, *La Chartreuse de Parme* (Paris 1939; libr. Armand Lunel, after Stendahl), by far his most substantial work, *La Gaguere Imprévue* (Paris 1944; libr. P. Bertin, after Jean-Marie Sedaine), *Les Caprices de Marianne* (Aix-en-Provence 1954; libr. J. P. Grédy, after Alfred de Musset) and *Le Pain des Autres* (1974; libr. E. Kinds, after Ivan Turgenev).

Saul

Oratorio in three parts by Handel. 1st perf. London, 16 Jan 1739; libr. by Charles Jennens, after A. Cowley's *Davideis* and the Book of Samuel in the Old Testament. Principal roles: Saul (bass), David (c-ten), Jonathan (ten), Merab (sop), Michal (sop), Abner (bass). One of the greatest of all Handel's oratorios, it is not strictly speaking an opera, but is quite often staged. [R]

Saul and David

Opera in four acts by Nielsen. (Op 25). 1st perf. Copenhagen, 28 Nov 1902; libr. by Einar Christiansen, after the Book of Samuel in the Old Testament. Principal roles: Saul (bass), David (ten), Mikal (sop), Jonathan (ten), Samuel (bass), Abner (bass), Witch of Endor (mezzo). One of the greatest works of Scandinavian music, it is notable for its magnificent choruses, its vividly contrasting vocal writing and its compelling dramatic sweep, which presents Saul as a tragic man of some complexity. The work's failure to have entered the international repertory is utterly inexplicable.

Plot: The elements of the biblical story covered in the opera are the summoning of the ghost of Samuel by the Witch of Endor, David's love for Saul's daughter Mikal, Jonathan's return with news of the victory over the Philistines, Saul's jealousy of David and David's accession to the throne after the death of Saul. [R]

Sāvitri

Opera in one act by Holst. (Op 25). 1st perf. London, 5 Dec 1916; libr. by the composer, after the *Mahabharata*. Principal roles: Sāvitri (mezzo), Satyavan (ten), Death (bass). Perhaps the finest British opera since Purcell's *Dido and Aeneas*, it is a highly stylised work drawn from Indian mythology, whose refined and beautiful music is achieved with a remarkable economy of means.

Plot: India. Sāvitri hears the voice of Death. It has come for her husband Satyavan, who is approaching. Sāvitri promises Death anything which it demands except for Satyavan's life. Satyavan dies, although he has told Sāvitri that he is under the spell of Maya (illusion). So great is Sāvitri's

love that Satyavan is restored to life.
[R]

Savonlinna Festival

Originally founded in 1912, this annual
summer festival in Finland –held in July
in the courtyard of the medieval castle
(cap. 2,157) – was established on a
regular basis in 1967. Its wide-ranging
repertory has included notable
productions of modern Finnish operas,
and its very high artistic standards have
established it as one of Europe's major
summer festivals; a visiting critic was
recently prompted to observe that
"opera is alive and well and living in
Finland". Artistic directors have
included Martti Talvela.

Savoy Operas

A collective title often given to the 14
Gilbert and Sullivan operattas, all but
the first six of which were first
performed at London's Savoy Theatre
(cap. 1,122), built by Richard d'Oyly
Carte and for long the London base of
the D'Oyly Carte Opera Company.

Sawallisch, Wolfgang *(b 1923)*

German conductor, particularly
associated with the German repertory,
especially Strauss. One of the leading
contemporary interpreters of 19th-and
20th-century German opera, he was
musical director of the Aachen Opera
(1953–58), the Wiesbaden Opera
(1958–60), the Cologne Opera (1960–
63) and the Bavarian State Opera
(1971–). He conducted the first
performance of Einem's *Der Zerrissene*.
His autobiography, *Im Interesse der
Deutlichkeit*, was published in 1988.

Sayão, Bidú *(b Balduina de Oliveira) (b 1902)*

Brazilian soprano, particularly
associated with lighter French and
Italian roles. She had a light, silvery

and flexible voice used with taste and
style. As an actress, she was both a
skilled comedienne and affectingly
pathetic in tragic roles. Her second
husband Giuseppe Danise (1883–1963)
was a successful baritone.

Scala, La

See Teatro alla Scala, Milan

Scala di Seta, La *(The Silken Ladder)*

Opera in one act by Rossini. 1st perf.
Venice, 9 May 1812; libr. by Giuseppe
Maria Foppa, after François-Antoine-
Eugène de Planard's *L'Echelle de Soie*.
Principal roles: Giulia (sop), Dorvil
(ten), Dormont (bass), Blansac (bar),
Lucilla (mezzo), Germano (bass). One
of Rossini's early farces, it is still very
occasionally performed, but is
nowadays largely remembered for its
famous overture.

Plot: Dorvil, secretly married to
Giulia, climbs the silken ladder every
night to reach her bedroom. She devises
various schemes to keep her marriage a
secret from her guardian Dormont, who
is arranging a marriage for her, and to
ward off the attentions of the servant
Germano and of Dorvil's friend
Blansac. When the secret marriage is
revealed, all is satisfactorily resolved.
[R]

Scaramuccio

Tenor role in Richard Strauss' *Ariadne
auf Naxos*. He is a member of the
Commedia dell'Arte troupe.

Scarlatti, Alessandro *(1660–1725)*

Italian composer. One of the most
important figures in the history of
opera, he wrote 115 operas, of which
some 70 have survived. Regarded as the
founder of classical opera, he gave to

opera seria its established format: the so-called 'Italian' overture, the da capo aria, the use of recitativo secco and also of accompanied recitative (which he used to powerful dramatic effect). The first great master of the Neapolitan school, his operas are nowadays only rarely revived and he is more widely regarded by musicologists than by operagoers. His most important operas include *Il Pompeo* (Rome 25 Jan 1683; libr. Niccolò Minato), *Gli Equivoci in Amore* (Rome Dec 1690; libr. Giovanni Battista Lucini), *Il Mitridate Eupatore* (Venice 1707; libr. G. Frigimelica Roberti), his masterpiece, and *Il Trionfo dell'Onore**, his one wholly comic work. His son was the composer Domenico Scarlatti*.

Scarlatti, Domenico *(1685–1757)*

Italian composer, son of Alessandro Scarlatti*. Although best known as a keyboard composer, he also wrote seven operas, of which the most successful was *Ambleto* (Rome 1715; libr. Apostolo Zeno and Pietro Pariati).

Scarpia, Baron Vitellio

Baritone role in Puccini's *Tosca*. He is the sadistic chief of police.

Scena *(Italian for 'scene')*

It is derived from the Greek σκηνη, meaning 'stage'. The term has two applications to opera: (1) A musical piece of predominantly dramatic purpose, usually for a solo singer, which is less formally constructed and less lyrical than an aria. A famous example is Leonore's 'Abscheulicher!' in Beethoven's *Fidelio*. (2) A part of an operatic act in which the scenery and/or the number of characters on the stage remains the same.

Scenario *(Italian for 'scenery')*

An outline libretto, giving indications of the plot, the characters and the number and type of scenes. The German term *scenarium* refers to a complete libretto, including detailed indications of staging.

Schalk, Franz *(1863–1931)*

Austrian conductor, particularly associated with the German repertory, especially Wagner. A co-founder of the Salzburg Festival, he was musical director of the Vienna State Opera (1924–29) and conducted the first performance of *Die Frau ohne Schatten*.

Schaunard

Baritone role in Puccini's and Leoncavallo's *La Bohème*. A musician, he is one of the four bohemians.

Schauspieldirektor, Der *(The Impresario)*

Comic opera in one act by Mozart (K 486). 1st perf. Vienna, 7 Feb 1786; libr. by Gottlieb Stephanie. Principal roles: Madame Silberklang (sop), Madame Herz (sop), Vogelsang (ten), Bu (speaker). First given on the same evening as Salieri's *Prima la Musica e Poi le Parole*, it is often given with an altered libretto, sometimes making Mozart himself the impresario.

Plot: The put-upon impresario has to cope with the rivalry between two prima donnas, Mesdames Herz and Silberklang. Each offers an example of their vocal accomplishment, and quarrel over which of them should be paid more until, finally, they attempt to out-sing each other in a trio with the tenor Vogelsang. [R]

Scherasmin

Baritone role in Weber's *Oberon*. He is Sir Huon's esquire.

511

Scherchen, Hermann *(1891– 1966)*

German conductor, particularly associated with 20th-century operas. A tireless champion of contemporary composers, he conducted the first performances of Dallapiccola's *Il Prigioniero*, Hába's *The Mother*, Henze's *König Hirsch* and Dessau's *Verurteilung des Lukullus*.

Schigolch

Baritone role in Berg's *Lulu*. He is an asthmatic old man who might be Lulu's father.

Schikaneder, Emanuel *(b Johann) (1751–1812)*

Austrian actor, playwright, impresario and librettist. As manager of the Theater an der Weiden in Vienna, he presented seasons of zauberoper*, and commissioned *Die Zauberflöte* from Mozart, writing the libretto and creating Papageno. In 1800, he opened the Theater an der Wien, which he managed until 1806. He also provided libretti for Beethoven (the sketched-only *Vestas Feuer*), Paisiello, Seyfried, Süssmayr (*Der Spiegel von Arkadien*) and Winter (*Das Labyrith*, a follow-up to *Die Zauberflöte*).

Schiller, Friedrich von

See panel on page 513

Schillings, Max von *(1868– 1933)*

German composer and conductor. He wrote three operas: *Ingwelde* (Karlsruhe 1894; libr. Ferdinand von Sporck) and *Moloch* (Dresden 1906; libr. E. Gerhäuser) were written under the influence of Wagner, but *Mona Lisa**, by far his most successful work, is an essay in verismo. He was musical

director of the Stuttgart Opera (1911– 18) and administrator of the Berlin State Opera (1919–25). His wife Barbara Kemp (1881–1951) was a successful Wagnerian soprano.

Schipa, Tito *(b Raffaele Attilio Amadeo) (1889–1965)*

Italian tenor, particularly associated with lighter Italian and French roles. One of the finest lyric tenors of the inter-war period, he had a small but elegant and beautiful voice used with a matchless technique, aristocratic phrasing and impeccable diction. Beniamino Gigli said of him: "When Schipa sang we all had to bow down to his greatness." He created Ruggero in *La Rondine*. His autobiography, *Si Confessa*, was published in 1961.

Schippers, Thomas *(1930–77)*

American conductor, whose tragically early death from cancer cut short a brilliant career. He was particularly associated with the German and Italian repertories, especially Verdi, for which his vigorous and dynamic style well suited him. Also a champion of modern composers (especially American), he conducted the first performances of *The Tender Land*, de Falla's *L'Atlántida*, Barber's *Antony and Cleopatra* and Mcnotti's *The Saint of Bleecker Street*. He was musical director of the Festival of Two Worlds, Spoleto (1958–75).

Schlusnus, Heinrich *(1888– 1952)*

German baritone, particularly associated with Verdi and Wagner roles. One of the finest German baritones of the inter-war period, he played an important part in the Verdi revival which began in Germany at that period.

FRIEDRICH VON SCHILLER

The works of the German poet and playwright Friedrich von Schiller (1759–1805) have inspired some 50 operas. Below are listed, by play, those operas by composers with entries in this dictionary.

Die Braut von Messina

Vaccai	*La Sposa di Messina*	1839
Fibich	*The Bride From Messina*	1884

Die Bürgschaft

Schubert	*Die Bürgschaft*	1816 (U)

Demetrius

Dvořák	*Dimitrij*	1882

Don Carlos

Costa	*Don Carlo*	1844
Verdi	*Don Carlos*	1867

Fiesco

Lalo	*Fiesque*	1866

Der Gang nach dem Eisenhammer

K. Kreutzer	*Fridolin*	1837

Die Jungfrau von Orleans

Vaccai	*Giovanna d'Arco*	1827
Balfe	*Joan of Arc*	1837
Verdi	*Giovanna d'Arco*	1845
Tchaikovsky	*The Maid of Orleans*	1881
Reznicek	*Die Jungfrau von Orleans*	1887

Kabale und Liebe

Verdi	*Luisa Miller*	1849
Einem	*Kabale und Liebe*	1976

Das Lied von der Glocke

d'Indy	*Le Chant de la Cloche*	1912

Das Mädchen von Domrémy

Klebe	*Das Mädchen von Domrémy*	1976

Maria Stuart

Donizetti	*Maria Stuarda*	1834

Die Räuber

Mercadante	*I Briganti*	1836
Verdi	*I Masnadieri*	1847
Zajc	*Amelia*	1860
Klebe	*Die Räuber*	1957

Wallenstein

Verdi	*La Forza del Destino*	1865
Denza	*Wallenstein*	1876
Weinberger	*Wallenstein*	1937
Zafred	*Wallenstein*	1965

Wilhelm Tell

Rossini	*Guillaume Tell*	1829

Schmidt, Franz *(1874–1939)*
Austrian composer, writing in late romantic style. The more important of his two operas is *Notre Dame* (Vienna 1914; libr. composer, after Victor Hugo's *Notre Dame de Paris*) [R]. Its successor *Fredigundis* (1921; libr. after F. Dahn) was a failure.

Schmidt-Isserstedt, Hans *(1900–73)*
German conductor and composer. An outstanding Mozart interpreter, he was musical director of the Deutsche Oper, Berlin from 1944. He also composed one opera, *Hassan Gewinnt* (Rostock 1928).

Schneider, Hortense *(1833–1920)*
French soprano, particularly associated with Offenbach roles. The greatest operetta star of the 19th century, she combined a fine voice with outstanding acting ability and an inimitable sense of comedy. For Offenbach, she created Boulotte in *Barbe-Bleue* and the title roles in *La Belle Hélène*, *La Périchole* and *La Grande-Duchesse de Gérolstein*. Her bewitching performance in the last was the talk of Europe and made her sought after by most of its crowned heads. On arriving at the Paris International Exhibition at the entrance reserved for royalty, she announced "I am the Grand-Duchess of Gerolstein" and was immediately admitted!

Schock, Rudolf *(1915–86)*
German tenor, particularly associated with the German and Italian repertories. The leading German lyric tenor of the immediate postwar period, he had a warm, smoothly-produced voice of sufficient power to enable him to sing some heavier roles such as Walther von Stozzling. He created a role in Liebermann's *Penelope*.

Schoeck, Othmar *(1886–1957)*
Swiss composer. His stage works include the comedy *Don Ranudo de Colibrados* (Zürich 16 April 1919; libr. Armin Rüger, after Ludvig af Holberg), *Venus* (Zürich 10 May 1922; libr. Rüger, after Prosper Mérimée's *La Vénus d'Ille*), *Penthesilea**, his finest work, *Von Fischer und Syner Fru**, *Massamila Doni** and *Das Schloss Dürande* (Berlin 1 April 1943; libr. H. Burte, after Eichendorff). For long his works made little headway outside Switzerland, but recently there has been some increase of interest in his music.

Schöffler, Paul *(1897–1977)*
German baritone, particularly associated with Wagner and Strauss roles. Beginning as a lyric baritone, he later successfully undertook heavier roles, notably Hans Sachs. A fine singing-actor, he created Jupiter in *Die Liebe der Danae* and the title role in Einem's *Dantons Tod*. He enjoyed a remarkably long career, singing well into his 70s.

Schön, Dr
Baritone role in Berg's *Lulu*. Alwa's father, he is Lulu's admirer.

Schönberg, Arnold *(1874–1951)*
Austrian composer, writer and painter. One of the most influential figures in 20th-century music, he began composing in late romantic style, but then abandoned tonality and developed the twelve-tone* or serial system. His four remarkable stage works are the atonal monodrama *Erwartung**, the expressionistic *Die Glückliche Hand**, the comedy *Von Heute auf Morgen**, the first twelve-tone opera, and his unfinished masterpiece *Moses und Aron**. He was also a distinguished teacher, whose pupils included Berg, Ullmann and Webern.

Schöne Galatea, Die *(Beautiful Galatea)*
Operetta in one act by Suppé. 1st perf. Berlin, 30 June 1865; libr. by Leopold K. Dittmar Kohl von Kohlenegg. Principal roles: Galatea (sop), Pygmalion (ten), Gannymede (mezzo), Midas (ten). One of Suppé's, most successful works, it is still regularly performed in German-speaking countries. [R]

School for Fathers, The
See Quatro Rusteghi, I

Schorr, Friedrich *(1888–1953)*
Hungarian bass-baritone, particularly associated with Wagnerian roles, especially Wotan and Hans Sachs. Regarded as the outstanding heldenbariton of the inter-war period, he had a warm and noble voice of considerable power, capable of great beauty in quiet passages, and his diction was exemplary.

Schreier, Peter *(b 1935)*
German tenor, particularly associated with Mozart and lyrical German roles. One of the most stylish Mozartians of the postwar era, his beautiful voice is used with innate style and outstanding musicianship. An accomplished singing-actor and a renowned Lieder singer he has, since 1970, also achieved considerable success as a conductor.

Schreker, Franz *(1878–1934)*
Austrian composer. He wrote seven operas, first in late romantic, then in avant-garde and, lastly, in neo-classical style. *Der Ferne Klang**, his most successful work, was followed by *Das Spielwerk und die Prinzessin* (Frankfurt 15 March 1913; libr. composer), *Die Gezeichneten* (Frankfurt 25 April 1918; libr. composer), *Der Schatzgräber*

(Frankfurt 21 Jan 1920; libr. composer), *Irrelohe* (Cologne 27 March 1924; libr. composer), the unperformed *Christophorus* (1927; libr. composer), *Der Singende Teufel* (Berlin 10 Dec 1928; libr. composer) and *Der Schmied von Gent* (Berlin 29 Oct 1932; libr. composer, after de Coster).

Schröder-Devrient, Wilhelmine *(1804–60)*

German soprano. Daughter of the bass Friedrich Schröder (1744–1816), she was the first great singing-actress in the modern sense. The outstanding dramatic soprano of her day, especially renowned as Leonore in *Fidelio*, her actual vocal technique was deficient, but the power of her acting overcame these defects, and her abilities opened up new musico-dramatic possibilities to composers. She was highly regarded by contemporary composers such as Weber and, particularly, Wagner. She created Adriano in *Rienzi*, Senta in *Der Fliegende Holländer*, Venus in *Tannhäuser* and the title role in Spohr's *Jessonda*. Wagner's *Über Schauspieler und Sänger* includes a detailed tribute to her and is dedicated to her memory.

Schubert, Franz *(1797–1828)*

Austrian composer. One of the greatest vocal composers in history, he was also one of history's most ill-fated opera composers. Only three of his 14 operas were performed in his lifetime and many are seriously weakened by poor libretti. Their structural and dramatic weaknesses have sadly ensured that they are now only very rarely heard, despite the magnificent music which many of them contain. His stage works are the unfinished *Der Spiegelritter* (Swiss Radio 11 Dec 1949, composed 1812; libr. August von Kotzebue) [R], *Des Teufels Lustschloss**, *Der Vierjährige Posten**, *Fernando**, *Claudine von Villa Bella**, of which two acts are lost, *Die Freunde von Salamanka**, the unfinished *Die Bürgschaft* (Vienna 7 March 1908, composed 1816; libr. after Friedrich von Schiller), *Die Zwillingsbruder**, the unfinished *Die Zauberharfe**, the unfinished *Sakuntala* (Vienna 12 June 1971, composed 1820; libr. Johann Philip Neumann, after Kalidasa), *Alfonso und Estrella**, perhaps his finest opera, *Fierrabras**, his structurally most advanced stage work, *Die Verschworenen**, and the unfinished *Der Graf von Gleichen* (1827; libr. Eduard von Bauernfeld).

Schuller, Gunther *(b 1925)*

American composer and conductor (and originally a horn player). He has written two operas which have met with some success in the United States: *The Visitation* (Hamburg 12 Oct 1966; libr. composer, after Franz Kafka's *Der Prozess*) and the children's opera *The Fisherman and His Wife* (Boston 8 May 1970; libr. after the brothers Grimm). An advocate of 'third stream' music, his works fuse traditional and jazz styles.

Schumann, Elisabeth *(1885–1952)*

German soprano, particularly associated with Mozart and Strauss roles, especially Sophie. She had a light, silvery voice of great beauty, used with superlative musicianship and allied to a stage personality of great warmth and charm. One of the greatest singers of the inter-war period, she was also an outstanding lieder singer and later a distinguished teacher. The second of her three husbands, Karl Alwin (1891–1945), was a conductor.

Schumann, Robert *(1810–56)*

German composer. His one completed opera *Genoveva** contains some fine music, but betrays Schumann's basic lack of any dramatic talent. He toyed with a number of other operatic projects, of which fragments of the unfinished *Der Korsar* (1844; libr. O. Marbach, after Lord Byron's *The Corsair*) have survived. He married the pianist Clara Schumann.

Schumann-Heink, Ernestine

(b Rössler) (1861–1936)
Czech contralto, particularly associated with Wagnerian roles. One of the greatest contraltos of all time, her enormous repertory of some 150 roles ranged from Amneris to Katisha in *The Mikado*. She had a rich and opulent voice of extraordinary flexibility and vast range (virtually three octaves), which she used with total technical assurance and innate musicianship. Her recording of the Brindisi from *Lucrezia Borgia* remains one of the most astonishing pieces of vocalisation ever committed to disc. She created Clytemnestra in *Elektra*.

Schütz, Heinrich *(1585–1672)*

German composer. The leading 17th-century German composer of sacred music, he also wrote two stage works: *Dafne**, which is the first German opera, and the opera-ballet *Orpheus und Eurydice* (1638). The music for both works is lost.

Schwarz, Hans

Bass comparimario role in Wagner's *Die Meistersinger von Nürnberg*. A stocking weaver, he is one of the masters.

Schwarzkopf, Elisabeth *(b 1915)*

German soprano, particularly associated with Mozart roles and with the Marschallin, although her wide repertoire also embraced Verdi and Puccini. One of the greatest singers of the postwar era, she began as a coloratura, but soon moved to more lyrical roles. As well as possessing an exquisitely modulated voice, she was an artist of outstanding intelligence and musicianship, whose aristocracy of tone and style, combined with great personal beauty, made her one of the best-loved singers of her age. Also an outstanding Lieder singer, the exceptional refinement of her vocal technique occasionally lent a suggestion of artificiality and self-consciousness, but this seldom detracted from her great interpretative powers. She created Anne Truelove in *The Rake's Progress*. Her husband, Walter Legge (d 1979), was artistic director of the Philharmonia Orchestra and a recording producer responsible for many famous operatic recordings for EMI. Schwarzkopf's memoirs of him, *On and Off the Record*, was published in 1982.

Schweigsame Frau, Die *(The Silent Woman)*

Opera in three acts by Richard Strauss. (Op 80). 1st perf. Dresden, 24 June 1935; libr. by Stefan Zweig, after Ben Jonson's *Epicoene*. Principal roles: Sir Morosus (bass), Aminta (sop), Henry (ten), Housekeeper (mezzo), Barber (bar). An extravagent and inventively written comedy, whose plot is almost identical to that of *Don Pasquale*, it has never been one of the composer's more popular works, and is infrequently performed.

Plot: London, c1780. The bad-tempered former admiral, Sir Morosus, is unable to tolerate noise. His Barber suggests that he might achieve domestic harmony by marrying a silent woman and undertakes to find him such a bride. Meanwhile Morosus, furious to learn that his nephew Henry, who has joined a touring opera company, has married the singer Aminta, disinherits the young man. The Barber and Henry retaliate by duping Sir Morosus into a supposed marriage with 'Timida', a silent woman, who is none other than Aminta in disguise. Immediately after the ceremony, 'Timida' becomes extremely noisy until Morosus will go to any lengths to get out of his marriage. The deception is revealed and Morosus, relieved to be rid of his 'wife', forgives all concerned. [R]

Schwertleite

Mezzo role in Wagner's *Die Walküre*. She is one of the Valkyries.

Scimone, Claudio *(b 1934)*

Italian conductor and musicologist, particularly associated with Rossini and with 18th-century Italian works. He has been responsible for notable performances and recordings in scholarly editions, many with the chamber orchestra I Solisti Veneti, which he founded in 1959.

Scintille diamant

Baritone aria (the Diamond Aria) for Dapertutto in the Giulietta Act of Offenbach's *Les Contes d'Hoffmann*. Offenbach incorporated it from one of his earlier works.

Scipione

Opera in three acts by Handel. 1st perf. London, 12 March 1726; libr. by Paolo Antonio Rolli, after Apostolo Zeno's *Scipione nelle Spagne*. Principal roles: Scipione (c-ten), Berenice (sop), Lucejo (c-ten), Armira (mezzo), Lelio (ten), Ernando (bass). It is still performed from time to time.

Sciutti, Graziella *(b 1927)*

Italian soprano, particularly associated with Mozart and lighter Italian roles. One of the finest soubrettes of the postwar era, her elegantly pointed singing, her fine diction and her charming and vivacious stage presence led to her being dubbed 'the Callas of the Piccola Scala'. She created the title role in Sauget's *Les Caprices de Marianne*, and has also had considerable success as a producer.

Score

A term used to describe the written and ordered form of the various orchestral and vocal ingredients of a piece of music. Opera employs two types: (1) Vocal score: all the vocal parts (solo and chorus) with a piano reduction. (2) Orchestral (or Full) score: all the vocal parts with the complete orchestral parts.

Scotland

See Scottish Opera

Scott, Cyril *(1879–1970)*

British composer. Best known as an orchestral composer, he also wrote three operas, all to his own libretti. They are *The Alchemist* (1917), *The Saint of the Mountain* (1925) and *Maureen O'Mara* (1946).

Scott, Sir Walter

See panel on page 519

Scotti, Antonio *(1866–1936)*

Italian baritone, particularly associated with the Italian repertory, especially Verdi and the role of Scarpia. His voice, although not large, was used with outstanding artistry and he was one of the finest singing-actors of his day. He created Chim-Fen in Leoni's *L'Oracolo*. He formed the financially disastrous Scotti Grand Opera Company, which toured the USA and Canada from 1919 to 1922.

SIR WALTER SCOTT

The works of the Scottish poet and novelist Sir Walter Scott (1771–1832) have inspired some 60 operas, most of them written in the first half of the 19th century at the height of the romantic movement. Below are listed, by work, those operas by composers with entries in this dictionary.

The Bride of Lammermoor

Carafa	Le Nozze di Lammermoor	1829
Donizetti	Lucia di Lammermoor	1835

The Fair Maid of Perth

Bizet	La Jolie Fille de Perth	1867

Guy Mannering

Boïeldieu	La Dame Blanche	1825

The Heart of Midlothian

Carafa	La Prison d'Edimbourg	1833
F. Ricci	La Prigione d'Edimburgo	1838
MacCunn	Jeanie Deans	1894

Ivanhoe

Marschner	Der Templer und die Jüdin	1829
Pacini	Ivanhoe	1832
Nicolaï	Il Templario	1840
Sullivan	Ivanhoe	1891

Kenilworth

Auber	Leicester	1823
Donizetti	Elisabetta al Castello di Kenilworth	1829
Loewe	Emmy	1842

The Lady of the Lake

Rossini	La Donna del Lago	1819

Rob Roy

Flotow	Rob Roy	1836

The Talisman

Pacini	Il Talismano	1829
Loewe	Malekadhel	1832
Adam	Richard en Palestine	1844
Balfe	Il Talismano	1874

Woodstock

Flotow	Alice	1837

Scottish Opera

Founded by Sir Alexander Gibson in 1962, the company is based at the Theatre Royal, Glasgow (cap. 1,560) and tours throughout Scotland and northern and central England. The annual season runs from September to June. The company soon established high artistic standards, and has been particularly noted for its Wagner and Britten productions. Musical directors have been Gibson and John Mauceri.

Scotto, Renata *(b 1933)*

Italian soprano, particularly associated with the Italian repertory. A singer of fine intelligence and artistry, she began in light lyrical roles and was an especially successful Bellini interpreter. Later in her career she turned to Puccini and still heavier roles such as Lady Macbeth and Gioconda, which were exciting but showed signs of vocal strain. Her autobiography, *More Than a Diva*, was published in 1984.

Scribe, Eugène *(1791–1861)*

French playwright and librettist. Author of over 300 plays and libretti (his collected works run to 76 volumes), he was the most prolific and successful French librettist of the 19th century. The dominant writer at the Paris Opéra, his libretti epitomise the spectacular, theatrical but often dramatically empty structure of French grand opera. His prodigious output, which led to snide references to the 'Scribe factory', included libretti for virtually every major composer of the period. He provided texts for Adam (seven including *Giralda*), Auber (38, including *La Muette de Portici*, *Fra Diavolo*, *Le Cheval de Bronze*, *Le Domino Noir*, *Les Diamants de la Couronne* and *Manon Lescaut*), Audran, Boïeldieu (four including *La Dame Blanche*), Carafa, Cherubini (*Ali Baba*), Donizetti (*Le Duc d'Albe*, *Dom Sébastien* and *Les Martyrs*), Gounod (*La Nonne Sanglante*), Halévy (six including *La Juive*), Hérold, Meyerbeer (*Robert le Diable*, *Les Huguenots*, *L'Etoile du Nord*, *Le Prophète* and *L'Africaine*), Monpou, Offenbach, Rossini (*Le Comte Ory*), Thomas and Verdi (*Les Vêpres Siciliennes*), amongst others. His libretti for Auber's *Le Philtre* and *Gustave III* were the sources for *L'Elisir d'Amore* and *Un Ballo in Maschera*, and his play *Adrienne Lecouvreur* was the source for Cilea's *Adriana Lecouvreur*.

Scuoti o venti

Baritone aria for Rodolfo in Act IV of Leoncavallo's *La Bohème*.

Searle, Humphrey *(1915–82)*

British composer. His three operas are *The Diary of a Madman* (Berlin 1958; libr. composer, after Nikolai Gogol), *The Photo of the Colonel* (Frankfurt 1964; libr. composer, after Eugène Ionesco) and *Hamlet**.

Seattle Opera Association

Founded in 1965, the company gives an annual season from September to May at the Opera House (cap. 3,100), which was built for the 1962 World Fair. Performances are given with international casts, and the repertory policy is adventurous. In addition, the company has since 1972 given two *Ring* cycles each summer, one in English and one in German.

Secco (Italian for 'dry')
A form of recitative, accompanied by the harpsichord, which is little more than pitched speech and which is used in comic opera to carry forward the action between the formal musical numbers.

Secret, The (*Tajemství*)
Opera in three acts by Smetana. 1st perf. Prague, 18 Aug 1878; libr. by Eliška Krásnohorská. Principal roles: Malina (bass), Roza (mezzo), Kalina (bar), Bonifác (bass), Blaženka (sop), Vítek (ten). Notable for its fine ensemble writing and for its light and subtle characterisation, it is still very popular in Czechoslovakia, but is rarely performed elsewhere.

Plot: 18th-century Bohemia. The rivalry between Kalina and Malina has prevented their children Vítek and Blaženka from marrying, and has also stopped Malina's sister Roza from wedding the once-poor Kalina. The deceased friar Barnabáš had promised Kalina a secret which would enable him to marry Roza. This turns out to be the directions to a tunnel to her house, where both pairs of lovers are finally united. [R]

Secular oratorio
An 18th-century English stage form, which consisted of an oratorio on a non-religious topic. It was little different from opera, except that it employed a chorus. Much the best-known examples are by Handel, such as *Semele*, *Samson* and *Hercules*.

Seefried, Irmgard (*1919–88*)
German soprano, particularly associated with Mozart, especially Susanna, and Strauss roles. Largely based at the Vienna State Opera, she possessed a voice of great beauty, used with

outstanding artistry, and was one of the finest Mozart singers of the postwar era. She was married to the violinist Wolfgang Schneiderhahn.

Segreto di Susanna, Il
(*Susanna's Secret*)
Comic opera in one act by Wolf-Ferrari. 1st perf. (as *Susannas Geheimnis*) Munich, 4 Dec 1909; libr. by Enrico Golisciani. Principal roles: Susanna (sop), Count Gil (bar). Arguably Wolf-Ferrari's finest opera, it is based on the two-character 18th-century intermezzo. An immediate success, it has remained popular ever since, especially its sparkling overture.

Plot: Piedmont, 1840. Susanna's husband Count Gil, who strongly disapproves of smoking, returns home one day to the smell of tobacco. He works himself up into a rage, certain that the smoke indicates that his wife has been entertaining a lover. Susanna has to admit to her secret: she is herself a smoker. Gil confesses that actually he too enjoys it, and the couple are happily reconciled. [R]

Segreto per esser felice, Il
Mezzo aria (the Brindisi) for Maffio Orsini in Act II of Donizetti's *Lucrezia Borgia*.

Seidl, Anton (*1850–98*)
Hungarian conductor, particularly associated with Wagner operas. One of the finest early Wagnerian interpreters, he was musical director of the Bremen Opera (1883–85) and from 1885 was based largely at the Metropolitan Opera, New York. He married the soprano Augusta Krauss.

Selig, wie die Schöne
Soprano/mezzo/tenor/baritone/bass quintet for Eva, Magdalene, Walther von Stolzing, Hans Sachs and Veit

Pogner in Act III of Wagner's *Die Meistersinger von Nürnberg*.

Sélika

Mezzo role in Meyerbeer's *L'Africaine*. She is an African queen loved by Vasco da Gama.

Selim

Bass role in Rossini's *Il Turco in Italia*. He is the Turk of the opera's title.

Sellem

Tenor role in Stravinsky's *The Rake's Progress*. He is an auctioneer.

Sembrich, Marcella *(b Prakseda Marcellina Kochańska) (1858–1935)*

Polish soprano, particularly associated with Italian and French coloratura roles. Long based at the Metropolitan Opera, New York, she had a beautiful, brilliant and expressive voice with a range of c' to f''', which she used with an outstanding technique. She was also an accomplished violinist.

Semele

Secular oratorio in three acts by Handel. 1st perf. London, 10 Feb 1744; libr. by William Congreve. Principal roles: Semele (sop), Jupiter (ten), Juno (mezzo), Iris (sop), Somnus (bass), Athamus (c-ten), Ino (mezzo), Cadmus (bass), Apollo (ten). Although not strictly speaking an opera, it is the most popular and most frequently staged of all Handel's dramatic oratorios. Its glorious, sensuous music and its sharp sense of characterisation make it one of the finest of all English musical stage works.

Plot: Jupiter loves the beautiful but vain mortal, Semele, much to the fury of his wife Juno. The disguised Juno persuades Semele to ask Jupiter to show himself to her in his full glory.

This Jupiter does, burning Semele to a cinder in the process. [R]

Semeon Kotko

Opera in five acts by Prokofiev (Op 81). 1st perf. Moscow, 23 June 1940; libr. by the composer, after Valentin Katayev's *I, Son of the Working People*. A patriotic work, with which Prokofiev found renewed favour with the Soviet authorities, it is set in the Ukraine in 1918 against the background of the Revolution. It is very rarely performed outside Russia. [R]

Semiramide

Opera in two acts by Rossini. 1st perf. Venice, 3 Feb 1823; libr. by Gaetano Rossi, after Voltaire's *Sémiramis*. Principal roles: Semiramide (sop), Arsace (mezzo), Assur (bass), Idreno (ten), Oroe (bass), Ghost of Nino (bass), Azema (sop). Rossini's last opera written for Italy, it contains some of his finest (and most demanding) music in serious vein. An immediate success, it is still regularly performed.

Plot: Babylon. With the aid of her lover Assur, Queen Semiramide has murdered her husband Nino. Assur wishes to marry her, but she is attracted to the young soldier Arsace, ignorant of the fact that he is actually her son. Arsace, who loves the princess Azema, is informed of his relationship to Semiramide by the priest, Oroe. Semiramide announces that she plans to marry Arsace, whereupon Nino's ghost appears and announces that Arsace will indeed be king, but only after crimes have been punished. Assur follows Arsace to Nino's tomb, intending to kill him, but Semiramide – now aware of Arsace's parentage – also goes, in order to protect him. Arsace kills Semiramide with a stroke intended for Assur. Nino's murder is thus expiated and

Arsace ascends the throne and marries Azema. [R]

Sempre libera

Soprano cabaletta for Violetta in Act I of Verdi's *La Traviata*.

Seneca

Bass role in Monteverdi's *L'Incoronazione di Poppea*. He is the historical stoic philosopher.

Sénéchal, Michel *(b 1927)*

French tenor, particularly associated with French and Italian character roles. The leading French character singer of the postwar era, he has a fine voice and stage presence, and a repertory which ranges from Baroque to contemporary. He created Frère Elie in Messiaen's *St François d'Assise*.

Senesino *(b Francesco Bernardi) (c 1680–c 1750)*

Italian castrato. Assumed by some to have been the greatest of all castrati, his voice – of great beauty – was of contralto range, and was described by a contemporary as "clear, penetrating and flexible, with faultless intonation and a perfect shake". Notoriously temperamental, he enjoyed his greatest successes in London with Handel, with whom he worked from 1721–28 and from 1730–33, after which they quarrelled, and for whom he created roles in *Ottone*, *Flavio*, *Giulio Cesare*, *Tamerlano*, *Scipione*, *Rodelinda*, *Alessandro*, *Admeto*, *Riccardo Primo*, *Siroe*, *Tolomeo*, *Poro*, *Ezio*, *Sosarme* and *Orlando*. He should not be confused with the castrati Giusto Fernandindo Tenducci *(c 1736–90)* and Andrea Martini *(1761–1819)*, both of whom were also known as Senesino.

Senta

Soprano role in Wagner's *Der Fliegende Holländer*. She is Daland's daughter and the Dutchman's redemption.

Sento avvampar feroce

Tenor aria for Gabriele Adorno in Act II of Verdi's *Simon Boccanegra*.

Senza Mamma

Soprano aria for Angelica in Puccini's *Suor Angelica*.

Septet

In opera, a musical number for seven solo singers, with or without a chorus.

Serafin, Tullio *(1878–1968)*

Italian conductor, particularly associated with the Italian repertory. Largely based at La Scala, Milan, the Rome Opera, where he was artistic director (1934–43), and the Metropolitan Opera, New York, he was often regarded as the finest Italian conductor of his time and he was also an astute coach who encouraged young singers. He conducted the first performances of Gruenberg's *The Emperor Jones*, Taylor's *The King's Henchman* and *Peter Ibbetson*, Montemezzi's *L'Amore dei Tre Re* and *La Nave* and Hanson's *Merry Mount*. His wife Elena Rakowska (1878–1964) was a successful Wagnerian soprano.

Seraglio, The

See Entführung aus dem Serail, Die

Serbian opera composers

See under Yugoslavian opera composers

Serena

Mezzo role in Gershwin's *Porgy and Bess*. She is Robbins' widow.

Serenade (From the Italian *serenata*, 'evening song')

A type of song, the opposite of an aubade, which is a song for the morning, traditionally sung by a lover beneath his lady's window. The most famous operatic examples are Don Giovanni's 'Deh, vieni' and Almaviva's 'Ecco ridente' in *Il Barbiere di Siviglia*.

Serenata (Italian for 'evening song')

The term has two meanings in opera: (1) A serenade (see above). (2) A term occasionally used in the 18th century to describe a short operatic work given to celebrate a royal or social event. Much the most famous example is Handel's *Acis and Galatea*.

Sereni, Mario *(b 1928)*

Italian baritone, particularly associated with the Italian repertory. Resident at the Metropolitan Opera, New York from 1957, he was a true Verdi baritone with a rich and beautiful voice, marred only by his frequent tendency to sing flat.

Sergei

Tenor role in Shostakovich's *Lady Macbeth of Mtsensk*. He is the labourer with whom Katerina falls in love.

Serial composition

See Twelve-tone operas

Serov, Alexander *(1820–71)*

Russian composer and critic. Influenced by Verdi and the French school, and an opponent of the new Russian nationalist school, his three operas met with great success in Russia, but are unknown elsewhere. *Judith* (St Petersburg 28 May 1863; libr. A. Mayakov and others, after the Apocrypha) was followed by *Rogneda* (St Petersburg 8 Nov 1865; libr. composer and D. V. Averkiyev) [R Exc] and the unfinished *The Power of Evil* (*Vrazhya Sila*, St Petersburg 1 May 1871; libr. composer and Alexander Nikolayevich Ostrovksy), which was completed by Nikolai Solovyov. A difficult man, Serov was an acerbic but perceptive critic who supported the Liszt-Wagner school, although he himself was not influenced by Wagner. His wife Valentina Bergmann was a pianist and composer who wrote one opera, *Uriel Acosta* (Moscow 1885).

Serpina

Soprano role in Pergolesi's *La Serva Padrona*. She is the chambermaid who tricks her master into marrying her.

Serrano, José *(1873–1941)*

Spanish composer. He wrote over 50 zarzuelas, of which the most successful included *La Canción del Olvido* (Valencia 17 Nov 1916; libr. F. Romero and Carlos Fernández Shaw) [R], *Los de Aragon* (Madrid 16 April 1927; libr. J. J. Lorente) [R] and *La Dolorosa* (Madrid 24 Oct 1930; libr. Lorente).

Serse (*Xerxes*)

Works of this title about the Persian Emperor include:

(1) Opera in three acts by Cavalli. 1st perf. Venice, 12 Jan 1654; libr. by Niccolò Minato. Principal roles: Serse (c-ten), Amastre (sop), Arsamene (c-ten), Romilda (sop), Adelanta (sop), Ariodate (ten), Eumene (ten). After nearly 300 years of neglect, it has received an occasional performance in the last decade. [R]

(2) Opera in three acts by Handel.

1st perf. London, 15 April 1738; libr. adapted from Niccolò Minato's text for Cavalli. Principal roles: Serse (mezzo), Romilda (sop), Arsamene (c-ten), Amastre (mezzo), Atalanta (sop), Ariodate (bass), Elvino (bar). Always one of Handel's most popular operas, it is notable for its inclusion of some London street songs, for containing the only wholly comic character in a Handel opera, and for the aria famously known as 'Handel's Largo'.

Plot: Babylon. Serse is engaged to Amastre, but falls in love with his brother Arsamene's fiancée Romilda after hearing her sing. This generates much misunderstanding and jealousy, further complicated by the incompetent behaviour of Arsamene's servant Elvino. Amastre views the proceedings in male disguise, finally revealing herself so as to bring Serse back to her. [R]

Serva Padrona, La (The Maid-Mistress)

Intermezzo in two parts by Pergolesi. 1st perf. Naples, 28 Aug 1733; libr. by Gennaro Antonio Federico. Principal roles: Serpina (sop), Uberto (b-bar), Vespone (mute). The most famous of all intermezzi and the work which precipitated the Guerre de Bouffons* in Paris, it was originally given between the acts of the opera seria Il Prigionier Superbo.

Plot: Serpina, employed as a maid by Uberto, tricks her master into marrying her by pretending to leave with a ferocious soldier – in fact the mute servant, Vespone, in disguise. [R]

Servilia

Soprano role in Mozart's La Clemenza di Tito. She is Sextus' sister.

Sessions, Roger (1896–1985)

American composer, whose style developed from neo-classicism through extended tonality to serialism. He wrote two operas: The Trial of Lucullus (1947; libr. after Bertolt Brecht) and Montezuma*.

Se vuol ballare

Bass-baritone aria for Figaro in Act I of Mozart's Le Nozze di Figaro.

Sextet

In opera, a musical number for six solo singers, with or without chorus. Much the most famous example is 'Chi mi frena' in Donizetti's Lucia di Lammermoor.

Sextus

Mezzo trouser-role in: (1) Mozart's La Clemenza di Tito. He is Servilia's brother. (2) Handel's Giulio Cesare. He is Pompey's son.

Seyfried, Ignaz (1776–1841)

Austrian composer. He wrote many stage works in a variety of styles, including Singspiels for Emanuel Schikaneder, parodies and biblical dramas, including Saul (1810) and Die Makabäer (1818). All of his works have been long forgotten.

Shadow, Nick

Baritone role in Stravinsky's The Rake's Progress. He is the sinister figure who leads Tom to destruction.

Shadow Song

Soprano aria ('Ombre legère') for Dinorah in Meyerbeer's Dinorah.

Shakespearean operas

See panel on page 526

Shamus O'Brien

Opera in two acts by Stanford.

SHAKESPEAREAN OPERAS

The works of the English poet and playwright William Shakespeare (1564–1616) have inspired more operas than those of any other writer: nearly 200 operas have been based solely or in part on his works. He also appears as a character in a number of operas, including Thomas' *La Songe d'un Nuit d'Eté*. Below are listed, by play, the Shakespearean operas by composers with entries in this dictionary.

All's Well That Ends Well

David	*Le Saphir*	1865
Audran	*Gilette de Narbonne*	1882
Castelnuovo-Tedesco	*Giglietta di Narbona*	1959

Antony and Cleopatra

Malipiero	*Antonio e Cleopatra*	1938
Barber	*Antony and Cleopatra*	1966
Bondeville	*Antoine et Cléopâtre*	1973

As You Like It

Veracini	*Rosalinda*	1744

The Comedy of Errors

Storace	*Gli Equivoci*	1786
Krejčí	*The Tumult at Ephesus*	1946

Cymbeline

R. Kreutzer	*Imogène*	1796
Ostrčil	*Cymbelin*	1899 (U)

Hamlet

Mercadante	*Amleto*	1822
Faccio	*Amleto*	1865
Thomas	*Hamlet*	1868
Zafred	*Amleto*	1961
Searle	*Hamlet*	1968
Szokolay	*Hamlet*	1969

Julius Caesar

Malipiero	*Giulio Cesare*	1936
Klebe	*Die Ermörderung Caesar*	1959

King Henry IV

Hérold	*Il Gioventù di Enrico V*	1815
Pacini	*Il Gioventù di Enrico V*	1820
Morlacchi	*Il Gioventù di Enrico V*	1823
Mercadante	*Il Gioventù di Enrico V*	1834
Holst	*At the Boar's Head*	1925

King Lear

Gobatti	Cordelia	1881
Cagnoni	Re Lear	1890
Frazzi	Re Lear	1939
Reimann	Lear	1978

Love's Labours Lost

| Nabokov | Love's Labours Lost | 1973 |

Macbeth

Verdi	Macbeth	1847/65
Rossi	Biorn	1877
Bloch	Macbeth	1910
Gatty	Macbeth	1920
Collingwood	Macbeth	1934

Measure for Measure

| Wagner | Das Liebesverbot | 1836 |

The Merchant of Venice

Foerster	Jessika	1905
Alpaerts	Shylock	1913
Hahn	Le Marchand de Venise	1935
Castelnuovo-Tedesco	Il Mercante di Venezia	1961

The Merry Wives of Windsor

Philidor	Herne le Chasseur	1773
Dittersdorf	Die Lustigen Weiber von Windsor	1796
Salieri	Falstaff	1799
Balfe	Falstaff	1838
Nicolaï	Die Lustigen Weiber von Windsor	1849
Adam	Falstaff	1856
Verdi	Falstaff	1893
Vaughan Williams	Sir John in Love	1929

A Midsummer Night's Dream

Purcell	The Faery Queen	1692
Alyabyev	The Enchanted Night	1839
Mancinelli	Un Sogno di una Notte d'Estato	1917
Arundell	A Midsummer Night's Dream	1930
Britten	A Midsummer Night's Dream	1960

Much Ado About Nothing

Berlioz	*Béatrice et Bénédict*	1862
Stanford	*Much Ado About Nothing*	1901
Hahn	*Beaucoup de Bruit Pour Rien*	1936

Othello

Rossini	*Otello*	1816
Verdi	*Otello*	1887

Romeo and Juliet

Benda	*Romeo und Julie*	1776
Dalayrac	*Tout Pour l'Amour*	1792
Zingarelli	*Giulietta e Romeo*	1796
Vaccai	*Giulietta e Romeo*	1825
Bellini	*I Capuleti e i Montecchi*	1830
Marchetti	*Romeo e Giulietta*	1865
Gounod	*Roméo et Juliette*	1867
Zandonai	*Giulietta e Romeo*	1922
Sutermeister	*Romeo und Julia*	1940
Blacher	*Romeo und Julia*	1950

The Taming of the Shrew

Götz	*Der Widerspenstigen Zähmung*	1874
Chapí	*Las Bravías*	1896
Wolf-Ferrari	*Sly*	1927
Persico	*La Bisbetica Dominata*	1931
Karel	*The Taming of the Shrew*	1939 (U)
Giannini	*The Taming of the Shrew*	1953

The Tempest

Locke and others	*The Tempest*	1674
Purcell	*The Tempest*	1695
Winter	*Der Sturm*	1798
Müller	*Der Sturm*	1798
Alyabyev	*The Tempest*	1835
Halévy	*La Tempesta*	1850
Fibich	*The Tempest*	1895
Gatty	*The Tempest*	1920
Lattuada	*La Tempesta*	1922
Sutermeister	*Der Zauberinsel*	1942
Atterberg	*Stormen*	1949
Martin	*Der Sturm*	1956

Twelfth Night

Smetana	*Viola*	1875 (U)
Jirko	*Twelfth Night*	1964

A Winter's Tale

Bruch	*Hermione*	1872
Goldmark	*Ein Wintermärchen*	1908

(Op 61). 1st perf. London, 2 March 1896; libr. by George H. Jessop, after Sheridan le Fanu. Reasonably successful at its appearance, it is now virtually forgotten.

Shaporin, Yuri *(1889–1966)*

Russian composer. His one opera, the vast *The Decembrists**, has proved to be the finest stage work written in 'orthodox Soviet' style and has been widely performed.

Sharp (Musical symbol: ♯). A

raising in pitch, either – intentionally – by a semitone, or – unintentionally – by an indeterminate amount, as when a singer accidentally sings above the written note. Its opposite is 'flat'.

Sharpless

Baritone role in Puccini's *Madama Butterfly*. He is the American Consul in Nagasaki.

Shchedrin, Rodion *(b 1932)*

Russian composer. Writing in 'orthodox Soviet' style, his operas have met with some success in Russia, particularly *Not Love Alone* (1961).

Shicoff, Neil *(b 1949)*

American tenor, particularly associated with Italian and French lyric roles. Possessing a clean and well-focused voice and a good stage presence, he is one of the most accomplished lyric tenors of the younger generation, although his performances are occasionally marred by a certain gracelessness and seeming off-handedness.

Shield, William *(1748–1829)*

British composer and violinist. He wrote over 50 light operas, including *The Flitch of Bacon* (London 17 Aug 1778), *Rosina**, his only work still to be remembered, and *Robin Hood* (London 17 April 1784; libr. MacNally).

Shilling, Eric *(b 1920)*

British baritone, particularly associated with buffo roles, especially Sullivan and Offenbach, and Col Frank in *Die Fledermaus*, which last was one of the classic buffo interpretations of modern times. Possessing good diction, great comic talent and a far better voice than most buffos, he enjoyed a remarkably long career, mainly with the English National Opera. He created Hawthorne in Williamson's *Our Man in Havana* and Major Braun in Crosse's *The Story of Vasco*.

Shirley, George *(b 1934)*

American tenor, particularly associated with Mozart roles, especially Idomeneo, and with Pelléas and Loge. He was the first male black singer to win a major international reputation in opera. His dark-toned but lyrical voice and his sense of classical phrasing, combined with his intelligence and keen dramatic sense, made him one of the most sensitive and compelling artists of the 1960s.

Shirley-Quirk, John *(b 1931)*

British baritone, particularly associated with Mozart roles and with the English repertory, especially Britten. A firm-voiced singer of great intelligence and musicianship, his stage performances were notable for their intensity and dramatic commitment. He created Lev in *The Ice Break*, Coyle in *Owen*

Wingrave, the Traveller in *Death in Venice*, Shadrach in *The Burning Fiery Furance*, the Ferryman in *Curlew River* and the Father in *The Prodigal Son*.

Shostakovich, Dimitri *(1906–75)*

Russian composer. His first opera, the satirical *The Nose**, was written in the eccentric and experimental style common in Russia after the Revolution. His operatic reputation rests chiefly on *Lady Macbeth of the Mtsensk District**. Perhaps the finest Russian opera of the 20th century, it provoked the Stalin-inspired attack on 'formalism' with the famous *Pravda* article of 28 Jan 1936 entitled 'Chaos Instead of Music'. The toned-down revised version of the opera, *Katerina Ismailova*, finally won acceptance in Russia, but the original version is much the greater opera. His other stage works are the unfinished *The Gamblers* (1941; libr. after Nikolai Gogol) [R] and the operetta *Moscow, Cheremushky* (Moscow 24 Jan 1959), which is a satire on the housing question. He also edited a new version of *Boris Godunov*. His son Maxim (*b* 1938) is a successful conductor.

Shuard, Amy *(1924–75)*

British soprano. Beginning as a lyric soprano, she later undertook heavier roles, and developed into the finest British dramatic soprano of the 1960s. Her keen dramatic sense enabled her to excel in roles such as Aida, Lady Macbeth and, particularly, Turandot.

Shuisky, Prinoe

Tenor role in Moussorgsky's *Boris Godunov* and baritone role in Dvořák's *Dimitrij*. He is a scheming boyar.

Shvanda the Bagpiper *(Švanda Dudák)*

Opera in two acts by Weinberger. 1st perf. Prague, 27 April 1927; libr. by Miloš Kareš and Max Brod, after J. K. Tyl. Principal roles: Shvanda (bar), Dorotka (sop), Queen Ice Heart (mezzo), Devil (bass), Babinsky (ten). Weinberger's first opera, and by far his most successful work, it is a folk opera of great charm which was widely performed in the inter-war period. Nowadays it is best remembered through concert performances of the famous polka and fugue.

Plot: The bagpiper Shvanda falls in with the robber Babinsky, under whose influence he has a series of not altogether pleasant adventures. He travels to the realm of Queen Ice Heart and then to Hell, from which Babinsky rescues him by winning a game of cards with the bored Devil. Eventually, Shvanda is reunited with his sweetheart Dorotka. [R]

Sibelius, Jean *(1865–1957)*

Finnish composer. Best known as one of the greatest of all symphonic composers, he also wrote one opera, *The Maiden in the Tower**.

Siberia

Opera in three acts by Giordano. 1st perf. Milan, 19 Dec 1903; libr. by Luigi Illica. Principal roles: Vassili (ten), Stephana (sop), Gleby (bar). A rough piece of verismo, it met with some success at its appearance but is now as good as forgotten.

Plot: Russia. In a duel, Vassili injures Prince Alexis, whose mistress Stephana he loves. Exiled to Siberia, Vassili is joined by Stephana but, when they attempt to escape, she is fatally wounded by the guards. Before she dies she succeeds in persuading the camp commander Gleby to release her lover.

Sicilian Vespers, The
See Vêpres Siciliennes, Les

Sid
Baritone role in Britten's *Albert Herring*. He is Nancy's boyfriend.

Siebel
Mezzo trouser-role in Gounod's *Faust*. He is a youth in love with Marguerite.

Siège de Corinthe, Le
Opera in three acts by Rossini. 1st perf. Paris, 9 Oct 1826; libr. by Luigi Balocchi and Alexandre Soumet. Rossini's first opera written for Paris, it is a revision of his earlier *Maometto II**. Modern performances have tended to use a conflation of both versions. [R]

Siegfried
Opera in three acts by Wagner. 1st perf. Bayreuth, 16 Aug 1876 (composed 1869); libr. by the composer, after the *Nibelungenlied*. It is Part Three of *Der Ring des Nibelungen**. Principal roles: Siegfried (ten), Wotan/Wanderer (bar), Brünnhilde (sop), Mime (ten), Alberich (bar), Fafner (bass), Erda (cont), Woodbird (sop). For plot see *Der Ring des Nibelungen*. [R]

Sieglinde
Soprano role in Wagner's *Die Walküre*. Married to Hunding, she is Siegmund's sister and eventual lover.

Siegmund
Tenor role in Wagner's *Die Walküre*. He is Sieglinde's brother and lover.

Siepi, Cesare *(b 1923)*
Italian bass, who enjoyed a remarkably long career based mainly at La Scala, Milan and, from 1950, at the Metropolitan Opera, New York. Particularly associated with Mozart roles and with the Italian repertory, especially Don Giovanni and Mefistofele, he was one of the greatest basses of the postwar era. His rich and even-toned voice was of great beauty and was used with matchless style and musicianship and phenomenal breath control. His sharp dramatic sense and his intelligence made him an accomplished singing-actor. He created Nonno Innocenzo in Pizzetti's *L'Oro*.

Signor Bruschino, Il
or **Il Figlio per Azzardo** (*The Son By Accident*)
Comic opera in one act by Rossini. 1st perf. Venice, Jan 1813; libr. by Giuseppe Maria Foppa, after Alisan de Chazet and Maurice Ourry's play. Principal roles: Guadenzio (bar), Sofia (sop), Florville (ten), Bruschino (b-bar), Filiberto (bass). The last of Rossini's early one-act farces, it is still performed quite often and its overture is famous for Rossini's instruction to the violinists to strike the strings with the wood of the bow.

Plot: 18th-century Italy. In order to marry Sofia, Florville impersonates the young man, the son of Bruschino, to whom she has been betrothed by her guardian, Guadenzio, but has never seen. When Bruschino arrives he aids the lovers for his own reasons, and they manage to wed before the confusion is sorted out. [R]

Sigrune
Mezzo role in Wagner's *Die Walküre*. She is one of the Valkyries.

Sigurd

Opera in five acts by Reyer. 1st perf. Brussels, 7 Jan 1884; libr. by Camille du Locle and Alfred Blau, after the Younger Edda. Principal roles: Sigurd (ten), Gunther (bar), Brunehild (sop), Hilda (sop). Reyer's most successful work, it is a lyrical treatment of the Siegfried episode in the Nibelung story. It enjoyed great popularity in France at the height of the post-Wagnerian vogue for operas based on Nordic mythology, but it is nowadays only very rarely performed.

Si J'Etais Roi (If I Were King)

Opera in three acts by Adam. 1st perf. Paris, 4 Sept 1852; libr. by Adolphe Philippe d'Ennery and Jules Brésil. One of Adam's most successful works, nowadays only the delightful overture is at all remembered.

Silja, Anja (b 1940)

German soprano, particularly associated with Wagnerian roles and with 20th-century works, especially Berg. One of the finest operatic artists of the postwar era, she possesses a strong and firmly-placed voice and is a singing-actress of remarkable power and insight. Many of her finest performances were given in productions by Wieland Wagner, with whom she enjoyed a close artistic relationship. Married to the conductor Christoph von Dohnányi*.

Silken Ladder, The

See Scala di Seta, La

Sills, Beverly (b Belle Silverman) (b 1929)

American soprano, particularly associated with Italian and French coloratura roles. Long resident at the New York City Opera, she had a small voice of exceptional agility, but the tone was often white and brittle and was aptly described by one critic as "all icing sugar and no cake". An outstanding singing-actress, she achieved greatest acclaim for her portrayal of Donizetti's three Tudor queens in Anna Bolena, Maria Stuarda and, particularly, Roberto Devereux. She was director of the New York City Opera (1979–88). Possibly the most popular American singer since Grace Moore, her autobiography, Bubbles, was published in 1976.

Silva, Don Ruy Gómez de

Bass role in Verdi's Ernani. He is a Spanish grandee in love with Elvira.

Silva, José da (1705–39)

Portuguese composer. He wrote five long-forgotten operas which were, in part, parodies of the Jesuit tragi-comedies so popular at that time. For his pains, he was burnt at the stake for heresy by order of the Inquisition.

Silveri, Paolo (b 1913)

Italian baritone, particularly associated with the Italian repertory, especially Verdi. Beginning as a bass, he enjoyed a short but brilliant career as one of the finest Verdi baritones of his time. In 1959, he made one excursion into the tenor repertory, singing Otello in Dublin.

Silvio

Baritone role in Leoncavallo's Pagliacci. He is a farmer in love with Nedda.

Simionato, Giulietta (b 1910)

Italian mezzo, particularly associated with the Italian repertory. Perhaps the finest Italian mezzo of the postwar era, her rich, creamy voice was used with a technique and musicianship which enabled her to encompass both dramatic Verdi roles and Rossini coloratura roles. A fine singing-actress, she was ebullient in comedy and intense and commanding in tragedy. She created the Young Mother in Pizzetti's *L'Orsèolo*.

Simon Boccanegra

Opera in prologue and three acts by Verdi. 1st perf. Venice, 12 March 1857; libr. by Francesco Maria Piave, after Antonio García Gutiérrez's play. Revised version, 1st perf. Milan, 24 March 1881; libr. revised by Arrigo Boito. Principal roles: Simon Boccanegra (bar), Jacopo Fiesco (bass), Amelia (sop), Gabriele Adorno (ten), Paolo Albiani (bar), Pietro (bass). Musically and dramatically uneven in its original form, Verdi revised it drastically at the height of his powers, adding the great Council Chamber Scene and building the role of the Doge into one of the most musico-dramatically demanding ever written for a baritone. The composer's darkest and most sombre work, for a century it was only very rarely performed, but in recent years its qualities have been appreciated and it is nowadays very popular.

Plot: 14th-century Genoa. The corsair Boccanegra has had a daughter, whose whereabouts are now unknown, by the daughter of the patrician leader Fiesco, who refuses to make peace with Boccanegra until the girl is found. The plebeians under the leadership of the goldsmith Paolo engineer the election of Boccanegra as Doge, to the fury of Fiesco. Twenty years later, Boccanegra encounters the orphan Amelia, who has been brought up by Fiesco and who loves the patrician Gabriele Adorno. He discovers that she is in fact his long-lost daughter. Paolo asks Boccanegra's permission to marry Amelia, but is rebuffed. He has her abducted, but she escapes and Boccanegra, realising

Paolo's treachery, forces him to pronounce a curse on himself in front of the Council. Paolo poisons Boccanegra's drink and before he dies the Doge is reconciled with Fiesco, blesses Amelia's union with Gabriele, and names the latter as his successor. Fiesco proclaims Gabriele as the new Doge. [R]

Simoneau, Léopold *(b 1918)*

Canadian tenor, particularly associated with Mozart roles and with the French repertory. A singer of outstanding style and refinement, he was arguably the finest interpreter of the French lyric repertory during the 1950s and early 1960s. He was artistic director of the Opéra de Québec for a brief period from 1971. His wife, Pierette Alarie (*b* 1921), was a successful coloratura soprano.

Sinclair, Monica *(b 1926)*

British mezzo, particularly associated with Handel roles and with the British repertory. Possessing a rich and agile voice, she was also an accomplished singing-actress, being particularly successful in comedy. She created Madame Popova in Walton's *The Bear*.

Sinding, Christian *(1856–1941)*

Norwegian composer. Although best known for his piano music, he also wrote two operas: *Der Heilige Berg* (Dessau 1914; libr. D. Duncker) and the unperformed *Titandrod* (libr. O. Sinding).

Sinfonia

The term usually used by Italian composers to describe the overture to an opera.

Singher, Martial *(1904–90)*

French baritone, particularly associated

with the French repertory. An elegant-voiced singer, he was from 1943 largely resident at the Metropolitan Opera, New York. He created Bassanio in Hahn's *Le Marchand de Venise*. He was also a distinguished teacher, whose pupils included Jeannine Altmeyer, Judith Blegen, Donald Gramm, James King, Louis Quilico, John Reardon and Benita Valente.

Singing-actor

A term which has been much used in the postwar era to describe a singer whose operatic performances place as much emphasis on dramatic interpretation as on pure singing. Tito Gobbi and Maria Callas remain the most renowned examples.

Singspiel (German for 'song-play')

A form of opera which evolved in Germany and Austria in the 18th century as an equivalent of the French opéra-comique, and which consisted of self-contained musical numbers connected by spoken dialogue. Important early exponents of the genre were Hiller, Benda and Dittersdorf, and the form reached its apotheosis with Mozart's *Die Zauberflöte* and Beethoven's *Fidelio*.
See also Liederspiel; Spieloper; Zauberoper

Sinopoli, Giuseppe *(b 1946)*

Italian conductor and composer, particularly associated with the Italian repertory, especially Verdi and Puccini. One of the most successful Italian conductors of the younger generation, his interpretations are always exciting if sometimes hard-driven, highly idiosyncratic and far from everyone's taste, thereby causing much critical controversy. He has also composed one opera, *Lou Salomé* (Munich May 1981) in post-expressionistic style.

Sì pel ciel

Tenor/baritone duet (the Oath Duet) for Otello and Iago in Act II of Verdi's *Otello*.

Sì può?

Baritone aria (the Prologue) for Tonio in Leoncavallo's *Pagliacci*, which is sung in front of the curtain.

Sir John in Love

Opera in four acts by Vaughan Williams. 1st perf. London, 21 March 1929; libr. by the composer, after Shakespeare's *The Merry Wives of Windsor* and other sources. Principal roles: Falstaff (bar), Mistress Page (sop), Ann Page (sop), Page (bar), Mistress Ford (mezzo), Ford (bass), Fenton (ten), Mistress Quickly (mezzo), Pistol (bass). One of Vaughan Williams' finest works and, unaccountably, very rarely performed, it combines folk-song idioms and some ardent love music in a work of great charm and high spirits. [R]

Siroe, Rè di Persia

Opera in three acts by Handel. 1st perf. London, 17 Feb 1728; libr. by Nicola Francesco Haym, after Pietro Metastasio. Never one of Handel's more successful works, it is now only rarely performed.

Sitzprobe (German for 'sitting rehearsal')

The term used in Germany, Austria and Britain to describe the first complete rehearsal of an opera production in which the soloists and chorus join the orchestra. It is called *prova all'Italiana* in Italy.

Sì vendetta

Soprano/baritone duet for Gilda and

Rigoletto in Act II of Verdi's *Rigoletto*. One of opera's most powerful vengeance duets.

Škroup, František *(1801–62)*
Bohemian composer, conductor and singer. A crucial figure in the development of Czech opera (and composer of the Czech national anthem), he was early drawn into the movement for Czech national music. His first opera *The Tinker* (*Dráteník*, Prague 2 Feb 1826; libr. Josef Chmelenský), in which he himself sang the title role, was the first opera written to a Czech libretto. His later works, all Singspiels, were unsuccessful. They comprise seven works in German and a further two in Czech: *Oldřich and Božena* (Prague 14 Dec 1828; libr. Chmelenský) and *Libuše's Marriage* (*Libušin Sňatek*, Prague 11 April 1835; libr. Chmelenský).

Sleepwalking Scene
Soprano scene: (1) for Lady Macbeth ('Una maccia') in Act IV of Verdi's *Macbeth*. (2) for Amina ('Ah! non credea mirarti') in Act II of Bellini's *La Sonnambula*.

Slezak, Leo *(1873–1946)*
Austrian tenor, particularly associated with heroic German and Italian roles, notably Otello. A singer of huge voice and physique, his vocal production was sometimes uneven, but this was more than compensated for by his magnificent phrasing, excellent diction and warm stage personality. After leaving the stage, he enjoyed a second career as a comedian in several Austrian films. His sense of humour was legendary: he once so dissolved the chorus at the Metropolitan Opera, New York during a performance of *Aida* that they were all fined by the management – the fine was paid by

Slezak. His autobiography, *Song of Motley: Being the Reminiscences of a Hungry Tenor*, was published in 1938. His daughter Margarete (1901–53) was a successful soprano.

Slobodskaya, Oda *(1888–1970)*
Russian soprano, particularly associated with the Russian repertory. Resident from 1922 in Paris, where she created Parasha in Stravinsky's *Mavra*, and subsequently in London, she also enjoyed great success as an operetta artist.

Slovenian opera composers
See under Yugoslavian opera composers

Sly
Opera in three acts by Wolf-Ferrari. 1st perf. Milan, 29 Dec 1927; libr. by Giovacchino Forzano, partly after Shakespeare's *The Taming of the Shrew*. One of Wolf-Ferrari's most stylish and ambitious works, it is nowadays only very rarely performed.

Smareglia, Antonio *(1854–1929)*
Italian composer. He wrote nine operas in a quasi-verismo style which was also influenced by Wagner. Several enjoyed great success in their time, especially in Germany, but they are nowadays largely forgotten. His first opera was the successful *Preziosa* (Milan 20 Nov 1879; libr. after Henry Longfellow's *The Spanish Student*). It was followed by *Bianca di Cervia* (Milan 7 Feb 1882; libr. F. Pozza), *Rè Nala* (Venice 8 Feb 1887; libr. V. Valle), a failure which he later destroyed, *Il Vassallo di Szigeth* (Vienna 18 June 1889; libr. Pozza and Luigi Illica), *Cornil Schut* (Dresden 6 June 1893), the highly successful *Nozze Istriane* (Trieste 28 March 1895; libr. Illica), *La Falena*

(Venice 6 Sept 1897; libr. Silvio Benco), *Oceàna* (Milan 20 Jan 1903; libr. Benco), perhaps his finest work, and *Abisso* (Milan 10 Feb 1914; libr. Benco). Totally blind by 1900, he was forced to dictate his last two operas.

Smetana, Bedřich *(1824–84)*

Czech composer. Regarded as the 'father of modern Czech music', his eight completed operas established a definitive groundwork of national music-dramas on which other composers built, but which they seldom surpassed. Notable for their prodigality of delightful melodies, their remarkable ensembles, their fine orchestration and their often deep psychological insight into character, his operas have (with one exception) been performed only infrequently outside Czechoslovakia, a neglect which is both unjust and inexplicable. The patriotic *The Brandenburgers in Bohemia** was followed by his masterpiece, the ever-popular and ever-fresh *The Bartered Bride** and the lofty and heroic *Dalibor**, his finest serious work. After the historical *Libuše** (which is the Czech national opera and which was written for the opening of the Prague National Theatre), he produced the light comedy *The Two Widows**, *The Kiss**, *The Secret**, and *The Devil's Wall**. The Shakespearean *Viola** was left incomplete.

Smeton

Mezzo trouser-role in Donizetti's *Anna Bolena*. He is a page in love with Anna.

Smyth, Dame Ethel *(1858–1944)*

British composer. The first woman composer of importance, she encountered a great deal of chauvinistic hostility and played an important part in the campaign for women's suffrage. Her pure professionalism and her power-driver personality cut through all obstacles, and she achieved the near-impossible feat of getting all of her operas performed in major houses during her own lifetime. She composed six of them, whose style mixes late German romanticism with a breezy and irresistible Englishness. *Fantasio* (Weimar 1898; libr. composer, after Alfred de Musset) was followed by *The Forest* (Berlin 9 April 1902; libr. composer), the highly successful *The Wreckers**, *The Boatswain's Mate**, perhaps her finest work, *Fête Galante* (Manchester 1923; libr. Edward Shanks, after Maurice Baring) and *Entente Cordiale* (London 1925). Her nine books include two volumes of autobiography, *Impressions That Remained* and *Streaks of Life*, which were published in 1919 and 1921.

Snow Maiden, The

(Snegourchka)

Opera in prologue and four acts by Rimsky-Korsakov. 1st perf. St Petersburg, 10 Feb 1882; libr. by the composer, after Alexander Nikolayevich Ostrovksy's play. Principal roles: Snow Maiden (sop), Bobyl (ten), Lel (mezzo), Mizgir (bar), Spring (mezzo), King Frost (bass), Tsar Berendey (ten), Bobylikha (mezzo), Kupava (sop). One of Rimsky's most successful fairy-tale works, it combines the human and fantastic worlds in a charming manner, and boasts a score of delicacy and great orchestral brilliance. Still very popular in Russia and Eastern Europe, it is only infrequently performed elsewhere.

Plot: The Snow Maiden begs Spring to be allowed to remain, even though winter is ending. Mizgir falls in love with her and his former love Kupava's complaints to the Tsar achieve nothing, as the Tsar is captivated by her beauty. Terrified by Mizgir's passion, the Snow

Maiden asks Spring to give her warmth of heart. This Spring agrees to, but warns her that she must keep it a secret from the sun. The sun finds out, however, and its rays melt the Snow Maiden. Mizgir drowns himself in despair. [R]

Sobinin
Tenor role in Glinka's *A Life for the Tsar*. He is Ivan's son-in-law.

Sobinov, Leonid *(1872–1934)*
Russian tenor, particularly associated with the Russian and Italian repertories, especially Lensky. The finest Russian tenor of the early 20th century, he was director of the Bolshoi Opera (1917–18 and 1921).

Söderström, Elisabeth *(b 1927)*
Swedish soprano, particularly associated with Mozart, Strauss and Janáček roles. One of the most versatile operatic artists of the postwar era, she possessed a beautiful voice used with outstanding artistry and sensitivity, and was a singing-actress of uncommon insight and intensity, equally at home in serious and comic roles. Her remarkable versatility was amply demonstrated in 1959, when she sang the Marschallin, Sophie and Octavian in *Der Rosenkavalier* within a year. She created the title role in Berwald's *The Queen of Golconda*. Her autobiography, *In My Own Key*, was published in 1979.

Sofia National Opera
Bulgaria's principal opera house (cap. 1,200) replaced the previous theatre which had been destroyed in World War II. The annual season runs from September to June, and the repertory is strong in Russian and Italian works as well as native Bulgarian operas. Artistic directors have included the tenor

Dimiter Uzunov and the bass Dimiter Petkov.

Sogno di Scipione, Il *(Scipio's Dream)*
Opera in one act by Mozart (K 126). 1st perf. Salzburg, 29 April 1772; libr. by Pietro Metastasio. One of Mozart's earliest works, described as a dramatic serenade, it is only very rarely performed. [R]

Sois immobile
Baritone aria for Tell in Act III of Rossini's *Guillaume Tell*.

Soldaten, Die *(The Soldiers)*
Opera in four acts by Zimmermann. 1st perf. Cologne, 15 Feb 1965; libr. by the composer, after Jakob Michael Lenz's play. Principal roles: Marie (sop), Stolzius (bar), Baron Desportes (ten), Charlotte (mezzo), Countess de la Roche (mezzo), Wesener (bass). Zimmermann's only completed opera, it is written in serial style and employs jazz, film, dance, circus and electronic music, and several scenes take place simultaneously. One of the most controversial of all modern operas, it has been widely performed. The composer arranged a symphony from the music.

Plot: Marie is engaged to Stolzius, but allows herself to be seduced by Baron Desportes. She subsequently takes a number of other lovers, and ends up as a soldiers' prostitute. [R]

Soldiers' Chorus
(1) 'Gloire immortelle' in Act IV of Gounod's *Faust*. (2) 'Or co' dadi' in Act III of Verdi's *Il Trovatore*.

Solenne in quest' ora
Tenor/baritone duet for Don Alvaro

and Don Carlo in Act III of Verdi's *La Forza del Destino*.

Solti, Sir Georg *(b 1912)*

Hungarian conductor and pianist (currently a British citizen). Particularly associated with Strauss, Wagner and Verdi operas, he is one of the outstanding operatic conductors of the postwar era. His performances are notable for their precision, great orchestral brilliance and their almost electric intensity and excitement. He was musical director of the Bavarian State Opera (1947–52), the Frankfurt Opera (1952–61) and Covent Garden (1961–71).

Sombre forêt

Soprano aria for Mathilde in Act II of Rossini's *Guillaume Tell*.

Song of the Flea

Bass aria ('Chanson de la Puce') for Méphistophélès in Part II of Berlioz's *La Damnation de Faust*.

Song of the Viking Guest

Bass aria for the Viking Merchant in Rimsky-Korsakov's *Sadko*.

Son io dinanzi al Rè?

Bass/bass scene for King Philip and the Grand Inquisitor in Act IV of Verdi's *Don Carlos*. One of the most tremendous musico-dramatic scenes in all opera.

Son lo spirito che nega

Bass aria for Mefistofele in Act I of Boito's *Mefistofele*.

Sonnambula, La *(The Sleepwalking Girl)*

Opera in two acts by Bellini. 1st perf. Milan 6 March 1831; libr. by Felice Romani, after Eugène Scribe's ballet-pantomime *La Sonnambule*. Principal roles: Amina (sop), Elvino (ten), Count Rodolfo (bass), Lisa (sop), Teresa (mezzo). Bellini's most pastoral work, it was an immediate success and is still regularly performed.

Plot: 19th-century Switzerland. Elvino becomes engaged to Amina, foster-daughter of Teresa. She is complimented by a stranger who is in fact the lord of the manor Count Rodolfo, returning after a long absence. The innkeeper Lisa, who also loves Elvino, visits the Count in his room, running away and dropping a handkerchief when she hears a noise. Amina, sleepwalking, enters the bedroom of the Count, who tactfully leaves, and lies down to sleep. When she is found the next day in the Count's room, Elvino refuses to believe the Count's explanation. He breaks off his engagement to Amina and decides to wed Lisa, but also breaks off that liaison when her handkerchief is found. Amina is later seen by all sleepwalking on the roof of the mill. When she has reached safety, Elvino wakes her and the two are reunited. [R]

Sophie

Soprano role in Richard Strauss' *Der Rosenkavalier*. She is Faninal's daughter, betrothed to Baron Ochs.

Sophocles

See panel on page 539

Soprano

See panel on page 540
See also Coloratura soprano; Dugazon; Falcon; Soubrette

Sorcerer, The

Operetta in two acts by Sullivan. 1st perf. London, 17 Nov 1877; libr. by W. S. Gilbert. Principal roles: John

SOPHOCLES

The tragedies of the Greek dramatist Sophocles (495–406 BC) have inspired some 50 operas. Below are listed, by play, those operas by composers with entries in this dictionary.

Antigonae

Traetta	Antigonae	1772
Honegger	Antigonae	1927
Krejčí	Antigona	1934
Orff	Antigonae	1949
Joubert	Antigone	1954

Elektra

Strauss	Elektra	1909

Herakles

Handel	Hercules	1745

Oedipus the King

Leoncavallo	Edipo Rè	1920
Stravinsky	Oedipus Rex	1927
Enescu	Oedipe	1936
Orff	Oedipus der Tyrann	1959

Oedipus at Colonus

Sacchini	Oedipe à Colone	1786
Zingarelli	Edipo a Colono	1802

Wellington Wells (bar), Aline (sop), Alexis (ten), Dr Daly (bar), Constance (sop), Lady Sangazure (mezzo), Sir Marmaduke Pointdextre (bass), Mrs Partlet (mezzo), Notary (bass). The first surviving full-length work of the Gilbert and Sullivan partnership, it is a satire on Victorian social conventions.

Plot: Alexis is engaged to Aline, while their respective parents, Sir Marmaduke Pointdextre and Lady Sangazure are also attracted to each other. Mrs Partlet's daughter Constance loves the curate Dr Daly but dares not express her feelings. In furtherance of his campaign to break down social barriers, Alexis hires the family sorcerer J. W. Wells to distribute a love potion to the village which will cause the drinker (if unmarried) to love the first person he sees. The potion is administered, with the lovers themselves drinking it, and everybody falls in love with the socially wrong people: Sir Marmaduke with Mrs Partlet, Aline with Dr Daly, Constance with the aged Notary and Lady Sangazure with Wells. Eventually, Wells offers himself up to the dark forces to break the spell and everybody returns to their rightful partners. [R]

SOPRANO

Soprano is the highest female voice. The word derives from the Italian *sopra* ('above'). The term is also used to describe the highest artificial male voice (male soprano; see castrato). Many different subdivisions of the soprano voice have evolved, particularly in France, Germany and Italy. They sometimes overlap and do not correspond precisely from one country to another. They are seldom used by composers, but are useful as an indication of the character of a role, if less so for its exact tessitura. The main French, German and Italian categories of soprano are as follows:

	Name	Range	Example
France	soprano dramatique	g to c'''	Valentine in *Les Huguenots*
	soprano lyrique	b♭ to c♯'''	Title role in *Lakmé*
	soubrette	b♭ to c'''	Zerlina in *Fra Diavolo*
	soprano demicaractère	a to c '''	Title role in *Manon*
	Falcon	b to c♯'''	Alice in *Robert le Diable*
Germany	dramatischer Sopran	g to c'''	Brünnhilde in *Götterdämmerung*
	lyrischer Sopran	b♭ to c♯'''	Title role in *Arabella*
	hoher Sopran or koloratur Sopran	g to f'''	Zerbinetta in *Ariadne auf Naxos*
	soubrette	b♭ to c'''	Ännchen in *Der Freischütz*
Italy	soprano drammatico	g to c'''	Title role in *Aida*
	soprano lirico	b♭ to c'''	Mimì in *La Bohème*
	soprano lirico spinto	a to c♯'''	Leonora in *Il Trovatore*
	soprano leggiero	g to f'''	Title role in *Linda di Chamounix*

Below are listed the 225 sopranos with entries in this dictionary. Their nationalities are given in brackets afterwards.

Ackté, Aïno (Fin)
Albanese, Licia (It)
Albani, Dame Emma (Can)
Alda, Frances (NZ)
Amara, Lucine (US)
Ameling, Elly (Neth)
Anderson, June (US)

Angeles, Victoria de los (Sp)
Arnould, Sophie (Fr)
Arroyo, Martina (US)
Augér, Arleen (US)
Austral, Florence (Aust)
Baillie, Dame Isobel (Br)

Bampton, Rose (US)
Barstow, Josephine (Br)
Battle, Kathleen (US)
Begnis, Giuseppina Ronzi de (It)
Behrens, Hildegard (Ger)
Bellincioni, Gemma (It)

Beňačková, Gabriela (Cz)
Berger, Erna (Ger)
Bjoner, Ingrid (Nor)
Blegen, Judith (US)
Bori, Lucrezia (Sp)
Borkh, Inge (Swit)
Brouwenstijn, Gré (Neth)
Bumbry, Grace (US)
Burrowes, Norma (Br)
Caballé, Montserrat (Sp)
Callas, Maria (Gk)
Calvé, Emma (Fr)
Caniglia, Maria (It)
Carosio, Margherita (It)
Casa, Lisa della (Swit)
Cavalieri, Lina (It)
Cebotari, Maria (Russ)
Cerquetti, Anita (It)
Chiara, Maria (It)
Cigna, Gina (It)
Colbran, Isabella (Sp)
Collier, Marie (Aust)
Connell, Elizabeth (Ire)
Cotrubas, Ileana (Rom)
Crespin, Régine (Fr)
Cross, Joan (Br)
Cruz-Romo, Gilda (Mex)
Curtin, Phyllis (US)
Danco, Suzanne (Belg)
Darclée, Hariclea (Rom)
Dernesch, Helga (Aus)
Destinnová, Emmy (Cz)
Deutekom, Cristina (Neth)
Dimitrova, Ghena (Bulg)
Dobbs, Mattiwilda (US)
Donath, Helen (US)
Dugazon, Louise (Fr)
Duval, Denise (Fr)
Dvořáková, Ludmila (Cz)
Eames, Emma (US)
Easton, Florence (Br)
Eda-Pierre, Christiane
 (Mart)
Falcon, Marie (Fr)
Farrar, Geraldine (US)
Farrell, Eileen (US)
Favero, Mafalda (It)
Figner, Medea (Russ)
Fisher, Sylvia (Aust)
Flagstad, Kerstin (Nor)
Fremstad, Olive (US)
Freni, Mirella (It)
Frezzolini, Erminia (It)

Galli-Curci, Amelita (It)
Garden, Mary (Br)
Gasdia, Cecilia (It)
Gayer, Catherine (US)
Gencer, Leyla (Turk)
Goltz, Christel (Ger)
Gomez, Jill (Br)
Grandi, Margherita (Aust)
Grisi, Giulia (It)
Grist, Reri (US)
Gruberová, Edita (Cz)
Grümmer, Elisabeth (Ger)
Gueden, Hilde (Aus)
Hammond, Dame Joan
 (NZ)
Harper, Heather (Br)
Harwood, Elizabeth (Br)
Hauk, Minnie (US)
Hempel, Frieda (Ger)
Hendricks, Barbara (US)
Hidalgo, Elvira de (Sp)
Hunter, Rita (Br)
Ivogün, Maria (Hung)
Janowitz, Gundula (Ger)
Jeritza, Maria (Cz)
Jones, Dame Gwyneth (Br)
Jurinac, Sena (Yug)
Kabaiwanska, Raina (Bulg)
Kanawa, Dame Kiri Te
 (NZ)
Kellogg, Clara Louise (US)
Kirsten, Dorothy (US)
Kniplová, Naděžda (Cz)
Konetzni, Hilde (Aus)
Köth, Erika (Ger)
Kubiak, Teresa (Pol)
Kupper, Annelies (Ger)
Kurz, Selma (Aus)
Kuznetsova, Maria (Russ)
László, Magda (Hung)
Lawrence, Marjorie (Aust)
Lear, Evelyn (US)
Lehmann, Lilli (Ger)
Lehmann, Lotte (Ger)
Leider, Frida (Ger)
Lemnitz, Tiana (Ger)
Lenya, Lotte (Aus)
Ligendza, Caterina (Swe)
Lind, Jenny (Swe)
Lindholm, Berit (Swe)
Litvinne, Félia (Fr)
Loose, Emmy (Aus)
Lorengar, Pilar (Sp)

Lott, Felicity (Br)
Martin, Janis (US)
Marton, Éva (Hung)
Masterson, Valerie (Br)
Mastilović, Danica (Yug)
Mathis, Edith (Swit)
Melba, Dame Nellie (Aust)
Méric-Lalande, Henriette
 (Fr)
Mesplé, Mady (Fr)
Micheau, Janine (Fr)
Migenes, Julia (US)
Milanov, Zinka (Yug)
Mildmay, Audrey (Br)
Miolan-Carvalho, Marie
 (Fr)
Mitchell, Leona (US)
Miura, Tamaki (Jap)
Mödl, Martha (Ger)
Moffo, Anna (US)
Monte, Toti dal (It)
Moore, Grace (US)
Morison, Elsie (Aust)
Muzio, Claudia (It)
Neblett, Carol (US)
Németh, Mária (Hung)
Neway, Patricia (US)
Nilsson, Birgit (Swe)
Nilsson, Christine (Swe)
Noni, Alda (It)
Nordica, Lillian (US)
Norman, Jessye (US)
Novotná, Jarmila (Cz)
Olivero, Magda (It)
Pagliughi, Lina (It)
Pasta, Giuditta (It)
Patti, Adelina (It)
Pauly, Rosa (Hung)
Persiani, Fanny (It)
Peters, Roberta (US)
Petrella, Clara (It)
Pilarczyk, Helga (Ger)
Plowright, Rosalind (Br)
Pons, Lily (US)
Ponselle, Rosa (US)
Popp, Lucia (Cz)
Price, Leontyne (US)
Price, Margaret (Br)
Rethberg, Elisabeth (Ger)
Ricciarelli, Katia (It)
Rizza, Gilda dalla (It)
Robin, Mado (Fr)

Rothenberger, Anneliese (Ger)	Söderström, Elisabeth (Swe)	Tietjens, Teresa (Ger)
Rysanek, Leonie (Aus)	Souliotis, Elena (Gk)	Tinsley, Pauline (Br)
Sanderson, Sybil (US)	Steber, Eleanor (US)	Tomowa-Sintow, Anna (Bulg)
Sass, Sylvia (Hung)	Stella, Antonietta (It)	Traubel, Helen (US)
Sayão, Bidú (Braz)	Stich-Randall, Teresa (US)	Turner, Dame Eva (Br)
Schneider, Hortense (Fr)	Storchio, Rosina (It)	Ursuleac, Viorica (Rom)
Schröder-Devrient, Wilhelmine (Ger)	Stratas, Teresa (Can)	Vallin, Ninon (Fr)
Schumann, Elisabeth (Ger)	Streich, Rita (Ger)	Vaness, Carol (US)
Schwarzkopf, Elisabeth (Ger)	Strepponi, Giuseppina (It)	Varady, Julia (Rom)
Sciutti, Graziella (It)	Sutherland, Dame Joan (Aust)	Vaughan, Elizabeth (Br)
Scotto, Renata (It)	Svobodová-Janků, Hana (Cz)	Vishnevskaya, Galina (Russ)
Seefried, Irmgard (Ger)	Tadolini, Eugenia (It)	Vyvyan, Jennifer (Br)
Sembrich, Marcella (Pol)	Tebaldi, Renata (It)	Watson, Claire (US)
Shuard, Amy (Br)	Ternina, Milka (Yug)	Watson, Lillian (Br)
Silja, Anja (Ger)	Teschemacher, Marguerite (Ger)	Welitsch, Ljuba (Bulg)
Sills, Beverly (US)	Tetrazzini, Luisa (It)	Zampieri, Mara (It)
Slobodskaya, Oda (Russ)	Teyte, Dame Maggie (Br)	Zeani, Virginia (Rom)
		Zylis-Gara, Teresa (Pol)

Sorceress, The
See Enchantress, The

Sorochintsy Fair (*Sorochinskaya Yarmarka*)
Unfinished opera in three acts by Moussorgsky. 1st perf. (in edition by Anataloy Liadov and Vyacheslav Karatygin) Moscow, 21 Oct 1913 (composed 1874); libr. by the composer after Nikolai Gogol. New realisation by Cui, 1st perf. Petrograd, 26 Oct 1917. Further version (that now in usual usage) by Cherepnin 1st perf. Monte Carlo, 17 March 1923. Principal roles: Chervik (bass), Khivrya (mezzo), Parasya (sop), Gritzko (ten). A comedy which makes extensive use of Ukrainian folk melodies, Moussorgsky only completed about a third of the work before abandoning it.

Plot: Parasya's disapproving stepmother Khivrya refuses her permission to marry Gritzko. However, the discovery that Khivrya is having an adulterous affair with Chervik diminishes her authority, and the lovers are united. [R]

Sorozábal, Pablo (*b* 1897)
Spanish composer. A prolific creator of zarzuelas, his most successful works include *La Tabernera del Puerto*, *Katiuska*, *Adiós a la Bohemia*, *Las de Cain* and *La Eterna Canción*.

Sosarme, Rè di Media
Opera in three acts by Handel. 1st perf. London, 15 Feb 1732; libr. by Antonio Salvi, after Matteo Noris' libretto for Pollarolo's *Alfonso Primo*. Principal roles: Sosarme (c-ten), Haliates (ten), Argones (bass), Altomarus (bass), Elmira (sop), Melus (mezzo). Containing some of Handel's finest operatic music, the muddled libretto has denied it the frequency of performance it might otherwise have enjoyed.

Plot: Lydia. Haliates and his son Argones are disputing the throne. The Median King Sosarme, who is engaged to Argones's sister Elmira, unsuccessfully attempts to mediate in the dispute. The official, Altomarus, further exacerbates the situation by attempting to secure the throne for his grandson Melus, who is Haliates' illegitimate son. [R]

Sosostris

Mezzo role in Tippett's *The Midsummer Marriage*. She is a seer.

Sotin, Hans *(b 1939)*

German bass, particularly associated with the German repertory, especially Wagner. One of the finest contemporary German basses, he has a rich and powerful voice, used with fine musicianship, and is an accomplished singer-actor, equally at home in serious or comic roles. He created a role in *The Devils of Loudun*.

Sotto voce (Italian for 'below the voice')

A direction to a singer to sing a phrase or passage quietly.

Soubrette (from the archaic French word *soubret*, 'cunning')

Originally used to describe pert and scheming servant roles (such as Despina and Serpina), the term subsequently came to be used more generally to describe any light soprano comedy role. It is called *servetta* in Italy.

Souliotis, Elena *(b 1943)*

Greek soprano, particularly associated with dramatic Italian roles, especially Abigaille. At her appearance she possessed one of the most abundant vocal and dramatic talents to have emerged for years, but within a very short time, her recklessly undisciplined singing and her undertaking of such heavy roles so young, caused her voice to have deteriorated totally by the age of 30. Her dark, thrilling and resinous singing, of great power, was strangely akin to that of Callas and she had a strong and committed stage presence. What might have been can be judged from her recording of Abigaille's cabaletta, 'Salgo già il trono aurato' which, for all its technical faults, remains one of the most viscerally exciting pieces of dramatic singing ever committed to disc.

Sousa, John Philip *(1854–1933)*

American composer. Best known as a composer of military-style marches, he also wrote a number of operettas, of which the most successful was *El Capitán*. (Boston 13 April 1896).

Souzay, Gérard *(b Tisserand) (b 1920)*

French baritone, particularly associated with the French repertory. One of the most stylish, intelligent and musicianly French singers of the postwar era, he was best known as an outstanding Lieder singer. His operatic appearances were infrequent.

Sovrintendente (Italian for 'superintendent')

The title of the administrator of an Italian opera house.

Soyer, Roger *(b 1939)*

French bass-baritone, particularly associated with the French repertory and with Mozart roles, especially Don Giovanni. His smoothly-produced and beautiful voice is used with considerable intelligence, and he has a strong stage presence.

Spain
See Teatro de la Zarzuela, Madrid; Teatro Liceo, Barcelona

Spalanzani
Tenor role in Offenbach's *Les Contes d'Hoffmann*. An inventor, he is Olympia's 'father'.

Spanish opera composers
See Albéniz; Arriaga; Arrieta; Barbieri; Bretón; Chapí; Chueca; De Falla; Fernández; Gaztambide; Gerhard; Giménez; Granados; Guerrero; Guridi; Luna; Martín y Soler; Massana; Pedrell; Rodríguez de Hita; Serrano; Sorozábal; Torroba; Turina; Usandizaga; Valverde; Vives

Sparafucile
Bass role in Verdi's *Rigoletto*. Maddalena's brother, he is a hired assassin.

Speziale, Lo (*The Apothecary*)
Comic opera in three acts by Haydn. 1st perf. Esterháza, autumn 1768; libr. by Carlo Goldoni. Principal roles: Sempronio (ten), Griletta (sop), Mengone (ten), Volpino (sop). An entertaining little piece, it is still performed very occasionally although most of the music of Act III is lost. [R]

Spieloper (German for 'opera-play')
A form of 19th-century German light opera, very similar to Singspiel, which consisted of an opera on a comic subject and contained spoken dialogue. A number of Lortzing's works fall into this category.

Spinning Chorus
Chorus in Act II of Wagner's *Der Fliegende Holländer*.

Spinning Room, The
(*Székelyfonó*)
Opera in one act by Kodály. 1st perf. Budapest, 24 April 1932. Described as 'lyric scenes with folk songs from Transylvania', it can barely be described as an opera, the dramatic action being very tenuous. It is virtually unknown outside Hungary, but is notable for its fine choral writing. [R]

Spinto (Italian for 'pushed')
A description given to a voice or a role containing vigour or attack. Usually used only in reference to sopranos or tenors, it can be modified, as in soprano lirico spinto, which would describe Leonora in *Il Trovatore*.

Spirto gentil
See Ange si pure

Spohr, Louis (*1784–1859*)
German composer, violinist and conductor. His music marks the link between the older classical composers and the new German romantic school, of which he is in effect the first exemplar. His first opera *Die Prüfung* (Gotha 1806) made little impression. His first major success was his fourth opera *Faust**, which was followed by *Zemir und Azor**, *Jessonda**, his finest work, *Der Berggeist* (1823), *Pietro von Albano* (1827), *Der Alchymist* (1830) and *Die Kreuzfahrer* (1845). He was musical director of the Kassel Staatstheater from 1847 and was perhaps the first modern-style conductor, introducing the use of the baton. He was also one of the earliest champions of Wagner.

Spoleto
See Festival of Two Worlds, Spoleto

Spoletta
Tenor comprimario role in Puccini's *Tosca*. He is one of Scarpia's agents.

Spontini, Gasparo *(1774–1851)*
Italian composer, often referred to as 'the father of grand opera'. His first nine operas, beginning with *I Puntigli delle Donne* (Rome 1795), are unremarkable essays in existing Italian styles. His success dated from his move to Paris in 1803, where he established his reputation with *Milton**, his first major work. Adopting, and intensifying, the classical features of Gluck, Méhul and Cherubini, he applied them to grandiose subjects with striking stage effects, vast choruses and much pageantry. The hugely successful *La Vestale**, his best-known work, was followed by the equally successful *Fernand Cortez**, *Olympie**, *Nurmahal* (1822), *Alcidor* (1825) and *Agnes von Hohenstaufen**. His influence on the development of opera was enormous: Wagner regarded him highly, and he set the guide-lines to which the whole subsequent French grand opera school of Meyerbeer and the rest conformed.

Sportin' Life
Tenor role in Gershwin's *Porgy and Bess*. He is Catfish Row's supplier of 'happy dust'.

Sposo Deluso, Lo *(The Deluded Husband)* or **La Rivalità di Tre Donne per un Solo Amante** *(The Rivalry of Three Women for a Single Lover)*
Unfinished comic opera in two acts by Mozart (K 430). Begun 1783; libr. possibly by Lorenzo da Ponte. Principal roles: Bettina (sop), Pulchiero (ten), Bocconio (bass), Eugenia (sop), Don Asdrubale (ten). Only five numbers exist, three complete and two only sketched.

Plot: Leghorn. The rich old bachelor Bocconio is awaiting his bride, the Roman noblewoman Eugenia. He is chided by his niece Bettina and her sweetheart Asdrubale, and his misogynist friend Pulchiero is scornful. Eugenia arrives but threatens to leave as she feels that she was not received with sufficient ceremony. She recognises Asdrubale as her former lover and faints. While Bocconio goes for medicine, Asdrubale upbraids her for infidelity. [R]

Sprechgesang (German for 'speech-song')
A type of vocal utterance originated by Schönberg, which is midway between singing and ordinary speech. The voice touches the note (which is usually marked in a special way in the score) but does not sustain it. It is employed in many twelve-tone operas such as *Wozzeck*.

Sprechstimme (German for 'speaking voice')
A similar but earlier-derived type of vocal production to Sprechgesang (see above), it was first used by Humperdinck in his 1897 version of *Die Königskinder*, but was omitted in the revised 1910 version.

Squeak
Tenor role in Britten's *Billy Budd*. He is Claggart's below-decks informer.

Stabile, Mariano *(1888–1968)*
Italian baritone, particularly associated
with the Italian repertory, especially
Falstaff which he sang over 1,000
times. His voice was good if never
particularly beautiful, and it was used
with style and intelligence. He had
excellent diction and was an
outstanding singing-actor, especially in
comedy. He created the title role in
Respighi's *Belfagor*, and enjoyed a
remarkably long career.

Staccato (Italian for 'detatched')
A method of singing (an instruction for
which is marked by a dot over the note
in the score) whereby a note is
shortened, and thus detached from the
following note, by being held for rather
less than its full value.

Stade, Frederica von *(b 1945)*
American mezzo, particularly associated
with Mozart roles and with the French
repertory. One of the most
accomplished contemporary lyric
mezzos, she has a beautiful and
smoothly-produced voice, used with
intelligence and musicianship and a fine
technique. She is an accomplished
singing-actress, equally at home in
serious or comic roles. She created
Nina in Pasaticri's *The Seagull*.

Stagione (Italian for 'season')
The term has two meanings in opera:
(1) The *stagione lirica* is the opera
season in an Italian theatre. (2) The
stagione system is the mounting of
several performances of a production
within a fairly short period and
maintaining the same cast. Its opposite
is the repertory system.

Stamitz, Carl *(b Karel Stamic)*
(1745–1801)
Bohemian composer, son of the

composer Johann Stamitz. Although
best known for his orchestral pieces, he
also wrote two stage works: the
Singspiel *Der Verliebte Vormund*
(*c* 1786) and the opera *Dardanens Sieg*
(*c* 1800). The music for both works is
lost.

Stanford, Sir Charles Villiers
(1852–1924)
Irish composer. He wrote ten operas, a
number of which enjoyed very
considerable success in their time. He
had marked theatrical flair, and the
virtual oblivion into which his stage
works have fallen seems somewhat
unjustified. His operas are *The Veiled
Prophet of Khorassan* (Hanover 6 Feb
1881; libr. W. B. Squire, after Thomas
Moore's *Lalla Rookh*), *Savonarola*
(Hamburg 18 April 1884; libr. Gilbert
Arthur A'Beckett), *The Canterbury
Pilgrims**, the unperformed *Lorenza*
(1894), the once-popular *Shamus
O'Brien**, the unperformed *Christopher
Patch* (1897; libr. B. C. Stephenson and
George H. Jessop), the Shakespearean
*Much Ado About Nothing**, the
comedy *The Critic**, the successful *The
Travelling Companion** and the
unfinished *The Miner of Falun* (libr.
Squire and H. F. Wilson).

Stasov, Vladimir *(1824–1906)*
Russian critic. One of the most
important critics in musical history. His
friendship with and encouragement of
the composers of the 'Mighty Handful'
(a phrase which he coined) exerted an
enormous influence on the development
of the Russian nationalist school. He
provided the scenario for *Prince Igor*
and co-authored the libretto for
Khovanschina, as well as writing
important studies of Borodin, Cui,
Glinka, Moussorgsky and Rimsky-
Korsakov.

Steber, Eleanor *(b 1916)*
American soprano, particularly
associated with Verdi, Mozart and
Puccini roles. Largely based at the
Metropolitan Opera, New York from
1940, she had a rich and firm voice of
great beauty, which she used with fine
musicianship. She created the title role
in Barber's *Vanessa*.

Stein, Horst *(b 1928)*
German conductor, particularly
associated with Wagner operas. A fine
and often underrated Wagnerian
interpreter, he was musical director of
the Mannheim Opera (1963–70) and
the Hamburg Opera (1972–77).

Stefano Giuseppe di *(b 1921)*
Italian tenor, particularly associated
with the Italian repertory. Possessor of
one of the smoothest, most beautiful
and liquid tenor voices of the postwar
era, he began by singing lighter lyric
roles. He subsequently (and unwisely)
turned to heavier roles, which caused
his voice to spread and coarsen. Despite
the great natural beauty of his vocal
instrument, he was an unsubtle and at
times vulgar interpreter, and had little
dramatic ability. He created Giuliano in
Pizzetti's *Il Calzare d'Argento*.

Stella, Antonietta *(b 1929)*
Italian soprano, particularly associated
with the Italian repertory. One of the
finest Italian sopranos of the 1950s, she
had a voice of great beauty and
considerable agility. Her fine technique
allowed her to sing roles as diverse as
Linda and Aida.

Stenhammar, Wilhelm *(1871–
1927)*
Swedish composer and conductor.
Although best known as an orchestral
composer, he also wrote two operas:

Gildar på Solhaug (1893; libr. after
Heinrik Ibsen) and *Tirfing* (Stuttgart
1899; libr. A. Boberg).

Števa Burja
Tenor role in Janáček's *Jenůfa*. He is
Laca's stepbrother.

Stevens, Risë *(b Steenberg)*
(b 1913)
American mezzo, particularly associated
with the French repertory, especially
Carmen. Her warm and beautiful voice
was allied to fine musicianship,
outstanding dramatic talent and great
personal beauty. She created Erodiade
in Mortari's *La Figlia del Diavolo*, and
also appeared in a number of films,
including *Going My Way* and *The
Chocolate Soldier*. She was general
manager of the Metropolitan National
Touring Company (1965–67).

Stewart, Thomas *(b 1928)*
American baritone, particularly
associated with Wagnerian roles,
especially Wotan. Although not a true
heroic baritone, his voice was well-
schooled and of considerable power
and range, and he was a fine singing-
actor. Married to the soprano Evelyn
Lear*.

Stich-Randall, Teresa *(b 1927)*
American soprano, particularly
associated with Mozart and lighter
Verdi roles. She had an attractive,
creamy voice and demonstrated great
elegance of line and phrasing. The first
American singer to be named an
Austrian Kammersänger, she created
Henrietta M. in Thomson's *The Mother
of Us All* and a role in Luening's
Evangeline.

Stiedry, Fritz *(1883–1968)*
Austrian conductor, particularly

547

associated with Wagner and Verdi operas. He was a musical director of the Vienna Volksoper (1924–28) and the Berlin State Opera (1929–33). After he was forced to leave Germany by the Nazis he became head of the German wing at the Metropolitan Opera, New York. He conducted the first performances of Weill's *Die Bürgschaft* and Schönberg's *Die Glückliche Hand*.

Stiffelio

Opera in three acts by Verdi. 1st perf. Trieste, 16 Nov 1850; libr. by Francesco Maria Piave, after Emile Souvestre and Eugène Bourgeois' *Le Pasteur ou L'Evangile et le Foyer*. Revised version, *Aroldo** 1st perf. Rimini, 16 Aug 1857. Principal roles: Stiffelio (ten), Lina (sop), Count Stankar (bar), Jorg (bass), Raffaele (ten). The last and one of the finest of Verdi's early period operas, it met with little success at its appearance, partly because audiences found the idea of an adulterous priest's wife shocking. Long believed lost, the orchestral score was rediscovered in 1968 and since then *Stiffelio* has nearly always been preferred to the revised *Aroldo**. A work of considerable dramatic power and insight, it is as yet still only infrequently performed.

Plot: Early 19th-century Germany. The evangelical Protestant minister Stiffelio returns home to discover that his wife Lina has been unfaithful. Her father, Stankar, tries to prevent him from learning the identity of Raffaele, but provokes a duel with the said seducer. Stiffelio stops the fight, but learns the truth and offers Lina a divorce. Stankar kills Raffaele, and Stiffelio forgives Lina from the pulpit. [R]

Stignani, Ebe *(1903–74)*

Italian mezzo, particularly associated with the Italian repertory. The leading Italian mezzo of the inter-war period, she had a rich and powerful voice of remarkable range (f to c′′′), which allowed her to sing some dramatic soprano roles. Her regal, opulent and committed singing distracted attention from the fact that her technique was not perfect and that her acting abilities were limited. She created the Voice in Respighi's *Lucrezia*.

Stile rappresentativo (Italian for 'representational style')

The term was used by the first opera composers of the Florentine Camerata* to describe the style of sung recitative which they introduced in 'representation' of speech.

Still, William Grant *(1895–1978)*

American composer, who employed Negro and American folk idioms in his music. The first black composer to win serious recognition in opera, he wrote first in avant-garde style and later in a neo-romantic vein. His operas are the unperformed *Blue Steel* (1934), *A Bayou Legend* (Jackson 1974, composed 1941; libr. V. Arvey), *Troubled Island* (New York 1949, composed 1928; libr. Arvey and L. Hughes), three unperformed operas *Costaso* (1950; libr. Arvey), *Mota* (1951; libr. Arvey) and *The Pillar* (1956; libr. Arvey), *Minette Fontaine* (1984, composed 1958; libr. Arvey) and *Highway No 1 USA* (1962; libr. Arvey).

Stockhausen, Karlheinz *(b 1928)*

German composer. A leader of the extreme avant-garde, his one operatic work is the cycle *Licht**, projected to comprise seven works, one for each day of the week.

548

Stockholm Opera

The present Royal Opera House (cap. 1,264) opened in 1898, replacing the previous theatre built by Gustavus III (and in which he was assassinated) which had opened in 1782. One of Europe's leading houses, with a long Wagner tradition, the annual season runs from September to June. Artistic directors have included Armas Järnefelt, John Forsell, Harald André, Joel Berglund, Set Svanholm and Göran Gentele.

Stokowski, Leopold (b Antoni Stanislaw Boleslawowich) (1882–1977)

British-born American conductor. Best known as a symphonic conductor, his operatic appearances were extremely rare, but included *Turandot* at the Metropolitan Opera, New York, and the American première of *Wozzeck*.

Stolz, Robert (1880–1975)

Austrian composer and conductor. He wrote some 65 operettas, of which the most successful were *Der Tanz ins Glück* (Vienna 18 Nov 1921; libr. R. Bodanzky and B. Hardt-Warden) and *Zwei Herzen in Drei-vierteltakt* (1933). His great-aunt Teresa (b Terezie Stolzová) (1834–1902) was a successful soprano, regarded by Verdi as one of the ideal interpreters of his later soprano roles.

Stolze, Gerhard (1926–79)

German tenor, particularly associated with German character roles, especially Mime and Herod; his psychopathic portrayal of the second was one of the most extraordinary operatic interpretations of modern times. One of the finest singing-actors of the postwar era (he had begun as a straight actor), his highly individual voice was far from beautiful but was used with musicianship and great intelligence, and its range was such that he was able to sing Oberon in *A Midsummer Night's Dream*. He created the title role in Orff's *Oedipus der Tyrann*, Forstmeister in Erbse's *Julietta* and Satan in Martin's *La Mystère de la Nativité*.

Stone Guest, The (Kamenny Gost)

Opera in three acts by Dargomijsky. 1st perf. St Petersburg, 28 Feb 1872. A setting of Alexander Pushkin's poem. Principal roles: Don Juan (ten), Leporello (bass), Donna Anna (sop), Laura (mezzo), Carlos (bar), Monk (b-bar). An historically important work, it employs dramatic recitative throughout and is the first opera of importance to set a literary text as it stands. It had a considerable influence on subsequent Russian composers, particularly Moussorgsky. Not quite finished at Dargomijsky's death, it was completed by Cui and orchestrated by Rimsky-Korsakov.

Plot: Spain. Don Juan, returned from exile with his servant Leporello, determines to seduce Donna Anna, widow of the Commander whom he has killed. Don Juan flippantly invites the Commander's statue to dine at Donna Anna's house. The statue accepts the invitation and drags Don Juan down to hell. [R]

Storace, Stephen (1762–96)

British composer. He wrote a number of stage works, many of which enjoyed great success in their time. They include *Gli Sposi Malcontenti* (Vienna 1 June 1785; libr. Brunati), *Gli Equivoci**, his only work still to be at all remembered, *La Cameriera Astuta* (Vienna 4 March 1788), *Dido* (London 23 May 1792; libr. Hoare, after Pietro Metastasio's *Didone*) and *The Cherokee* (London 20 Dec 1794; libr. Cobb). His sister Ann (*b* Nancy) (1765–1816) was a successful soprano, especially renowned as a comedienne, who created Susanna in *Le Nozze di Figaro*.

Storchio, Rosina *(1876–1945)*

Italian soprano, particularly associated with Italian and French lyric roles. She had a beautiful voice of considerable agility and a fragile and affecting stage presence. She created Cio-Cio-San in *Madama Butterfly*, the title roles in *Zazà* and Mascagni's *Lodoletta*, Stefana in Giordano's *Siberia* and Musetta in Leoncavallo's *La Bohème*.

Story of a Real Man, The

(*Povest o Nastoyashchem Cheloveke*) Opera in three acts by Prokofiev (Op 117). 1st perf. (privately) Leningrad, 3 Dec 1948; 1st public perf. Moscow, 7 Oct 1960; libr. by the composer and Mira Mendelson-Prokofieva, after Boris Polevoy. Principal roles: Alexei (bar), Olga (sop), Andrei (bass), Commissar (bass). Prokofiev's last opera, it was the piece which he hoped (mistakenly) would bring him back to favour with the Stalinist authorities. It is only infrequently performed.

Plot: Russia, 1942. The aviator Alexei is shot down, into deep forest where he wanders for 18 days before being found. He is taken to hospital, where both his feet are amputated, and where he lies in delirium, horrified to think he will never fly again. The Commandant tells him of an aviator who flew again after similar injury and Alexei resolves to do the same. After initially refusing, the medical team is impressed by his determination and allows him to fly again. Finally, he is reunited with his fiancée Olga. [R]

Stracciari, Riccardo *(1875–1955)*

Italian baritone, particularly associated with the Italian repertory, especially Rossini's Figaro (which he sang over 900 times). One of the finest baritones of the inter-war period, he possessed an imposing voice which he used with style and a fine technique. He was later a distinguished teacher, whose pupils included Alexander Sved, Boris Christoff and Paolo Silveri.

Stradella, Alessandro *(1642–82)*

Italian composer. He wrote a number of operas and intermezzi which influenced the later Neapolitan school, but which are all now forgotten. They include *Il Trespolo Tutore* (Genoa *c* 1677; libr. G. Villifranchi) and *Il Moro per Amore* (Rome 1695; libr. F. Orsini). He led a colourful and adventurous life (he was murdered over an affair to which his mistress's brothers took exception), parts of which form the basis of Flotow's *Alessandro Stradella**.

Straniera, La *(The Foreign Woman)*

Opera in two acts by Bellini. 1st perf. Milan, 14 Feb 1829; libr. by Felice Romani, after Victor-Prévost, Vicomte d'Arlincourt's *L'Etrangère*. Principal roles: Alaide (sop), Arturo (ten), Valdeburgo (bar), Isoletta (mezzo), Prior (bass). One of the least successful of Bellini's mature operas, it is seldom performed.

Plot: 14th-century Brittany. Arturo is engaged to Isoletta, but falls in love with the stranger Alaide, whom some believe to be a witch. Seeing her at a secret meeting with Valdeburgo (who is in fact her brother), Arturo challenges Valdeburgo to a duel during which the latter appears to slip, and drown in a lake. Although Arturo attempts to take the blame, Alaide is accused of murder. However, Valdeburgo turns out to be alive and, at his insistence, Arturo agrees to go ahead with the marriage to Isoletta. However, when he finds out that Alaide is the unlawfully wedded wife of the French king, he kills himself.

Strasbourg

See Opéra du Rhin

Stratas, Teresa (b Anastasia Strataki) (b 1938)

Canadian soprano, with a wide-ranging repertory encompassing coloratura, lyrical and modern dramatic roles. Essentially a lyric soprano (with a highly individual timbre), she sings with great intelligence and musicianship and is one of the finest contemporary singing-actresses. She sang Lulu in the first complete performance of Berg's opera and also created Queen Isabella in De Falla's L'Atlántida and Sardulla in Menotti's The Last Savage. She played Violetta in Zeffirelli's film of La Traviata.

Straus, Oscar (1870–1954)

Austrian composer. He wrote over 40 Viennese operettas, of which much the most successful were Ein Walzertraum* and Der Tapfere Soldat*.

Strauss, Johann (II) (1825–99)

Austrian composer, son of Johann Strauss I. Popularly known as the 'Waltz King', he wrote 16 operettas, establishing the classic form of the Viennese school of the genre. His first work, Indigo und die Vierzig Räuber (Vienna 10 Feb 1871; libr. Maximilian Steiner) was reasonably successful, but its successor Der Karneval in Rom (Vienna 1 March 1873; libr. Josef Braun, after Victorien Sardou's Piccolino) was a failure. His third work was the immortal Die Fledermaus*, the

quintessential Viennese operetta and arguably the most enduringly popular of all light operas. His subsequent works included Cagliostro in Wien (Vienna 27 Feb 1875; libr. F. Zell and Richard Genée), Prinz Methusalem (Vienna 3 Jan 1877; libr. Carl Treumann), Blinde Kuh (Vienna 18 Dec 1878; libr. Rudolf Kneisel), Der Spitzenbuch der Königin (Vienna 1 Oct 1880; libr. Genée and Heinrich Bohrmann-Riegen), Eine Nacht in Venedig*, the highly successful Der Zigeunerbaron*, the more serious Ritter Pázmán (Vienna 1 Jan 1892; libr. Lajos Dóczy) and Der Waldmeister (Vienna 4 Dec 1895; libr. Gustav Davis). The successful Wiener Blut* is a pastiche arranged from his other works.

Strauss, Richard (1864–1949)

German composer and conductor. A disciple of Wagner, he was an infant prodigy, and his early orchestral tone poems established him as a leading modernist as regards harmonic audacity and orchestration, in which latter field he became one of the most brilliant exponents in musical history. His first two operas, Guntram* and Feuersnot*, both heavily influenced by Wagner, met with little success, but the sensational Salome* established him at the forefront of contemporary opera composers. It was followed by the violent Elektra*, arguably his greatest opera, which marked the beginning of his partnership with Hugo von Hofmannsthal*. He then turned to a more lyrical and neo-classical style, inspired by his love of Mozart, with Der Rosenkavalier*, his most popular work. There followed Ariadne auf Naxos*, the vast Die Frau ohne Schatten*, the autobiographical Intermezzo*, Die Ägyptische Helena*, the highly successful Arabella*, Die Schweigsame Frau*, Friedenstag*, the 'bucolic comedy' Daphne*, Die Liebe *der Danae** and the brilliant conversation piece *Capriccio**.

Strauss was also regarded as one of the finest opera conductors of his age, particularly in the German repertory. Working mainly in Munich, Weimar, and at the Berlin State Opera (where he conducted nearly 1,200 performances), he conducted the first performances of *Hänsel und Gretel* as well as those of several of his own operas.

Stravinsky, Igor *(1882–1971)*

Russian composer, resident in Europe after the Russian Revolution. One of the greatest and most influential composers of the 20th century, his music (in a wide variety of styles) is notable for its rhythmic drive and variety and for its remarkable orchestral colours. His six operatic stage works are the beautiful fairy tale *The Nightingale**, the burlesque *Renard**, the conventional comedy *Mavra**, the opera-oratorio *Oedipus Rex**, the neo-classical *The Rake's Progress**, one of the greatest of postwar operas, and the unsuccessful television opera *The Flood* (1962), which is a setting in serial style of part of a York mystery play. His father Fyodor (1843–1902) was a leading bass who created King Frost in *The Snow Maiden* and, for Tchaikovsky, Orlik in *Mazeppa*, the Royal Highness in *Vakula the Blacksmith*, Dunois in *The Maid of Orleans* and Mamirov in *The Enchantress*.

Street Scene

Opera in two acts by Weill. 1st perf. Philadelphia, 16 Dec 1946; libr. by Langston Hughes, after Elmer Rice's play. Principal roles: Anna Maurrant (sop), Frank Maurrant (bass), Olga Olsen (mezzo), Daniel Buchanan (ten), Sam Kaplan (ten). One of the most successful of Weill's later American works, it is written in Broadway musical idiom, but is musically continuous as in traditional opera. It tells of everyday life in a New York tenement, culminating in murder and the heroine's decision to seek a better life elsewhere.

Strehler, Giorgio *(b 1921)*

Italian producer. Beginning as an actor, he turned to opera production in 1947 and has been closely associated with La Scala, Milan, where he has made many notable productions, especially *Simon Boccanegra* and *Don Giovanni*.

Streich, Rita *(1920–87)*

German soprano, particularly associated with Mozart and other German soubrette roles. One of the finest postwar lighter German lyric sopranos, her agile voice was used with musicianship and an assured technique, and she had a good stage presence.

Strepponi, Giuseppina *(1815–97)*

Italian soprano. She enjoyed a short but brilliant career in the 1830s and early 1840s as one of the leading lyrico-dramatic sopranos of her time. She created Federico in F. Ricci's *Luigi Rolla e Michelangelo*, the title role in Donizetti's *Adelia* and Abigaille in *Nabucco*. She became Verdi's companion in 1847, and the two were married in 1859.

Stretta (Italian for 'narrow')

A term used, especially in the 19th century, to describe the last, climactic section of an aria, duet or ensemble written in fast tempo to ensure a rousing finale.

Stride la vampa
Mezzo aria for Azucena in Act II of
Verdi's *Il Trovatore*.

Strophic
A term which describes a song or aria
in which the same music is repeated
exactly (or nearly so) for each verse or
stanza. It is the opposite of a song
which is through-composed*. Thus, to
take two examples from Offenbach's
Les Contes d'Hoffmann, the Doll's
Song is strophic, whilst the Diamond
Aria is through-composed.

Student Prince, The
Operetta by Romberg. 1st perf. New
York, 2 Dec 1924; libr. by Dorothy
Donnelly. Romberg's most successful
work, given wide currency by the film
starring Mario Lanza. [R]

Sturm, Der *(The Tempest)*
Opera in three acts by Martin. 1st perf.
Vienna, 18 June 1956. A virtual word-
for-word setting of August von
Schlegel's translation of Shakespeare's
play. It is written in declamatory vocal
style and incorporates jazz elements to
portray the court society.

Stuttgart Opera
Opera in this German city in Baden-
Württemberg is given at the
Württembergisches Staatstheater (cap.
1,400), which opened in 1912. The
company has a strong Strauss and
Wagner tradition, and the annual
season runs from September to June.
Musical directors have included
Schillings, Fritz Busch, Carl Leonardt,
Herbert Albert, Ferdinand Leitner,
Václav Neumann, Silvio Varviso and
Dennis Russell Davies.

Styx, John
Tenor role in Offenbach's *Orphée aux
Enfers*. He is the slow-witted former
King of Boeotia.

Suchoň, Eugen *(b 1908)*
Czech composer. The first Slovak
composer to win international
recognition, he wrote two operas: the
nationalist *The Whirlpool* (*Krútňava*,
1949; libr. composer and S. Hoza after
M. Urban) [R] and the twelve-tone
Svätopluk (1959; libr. composer,
I. Stodola and J. Krčméry) [R].

Suicidio!
Soprano aria for Gioconda in Act IV of
Ponchielli's *La Gioconda*.

Suitner, Otmar *(b 1922)*
Austrian conductor, particularly
associated with Mozart, Wagner and
Strauss operas. He was musical director
of the Kaiserslautern Opera (1957–60),
the Dresden State Opera (1960–64) and
the Berlin State Opera (1964–).

Suliotis, Elena
See Souliotis, Elena

Sullivan, Sir Arthur *(1842–1900)*
British composer. Despite his desire to
be known as a composer of 'serious'
music (which in operatic terms is
exemplified by his one opera *Ivanhoe**),
he is largely remembered as one of the
greatest of all operetta composers,
particularly through the 14 Savoy
Operas written in collaboration with
W. S. Gilbert. These works are notable
for their sparkling melodies, their subtle
and often brilliant orchestration
(especially for the woodwind), their
clever touches of musical satire and
their superb use of patter. His operettas
are: *The Sapphire Necklace* (London 13

April 1867; libr. Henry Fothergill Chorley), most of which is lost, *Cox and Box**, *The Contrabandista* (London 18 Dec 1867; libr. Francis Cowley Burnand; revised version *The Chieftain*, London 12 Dec 1894), the lost *Thespis**, his first collaboration with Gilbert, the brilliant *Trial By Jury**, *The Zoo**, *The Sorcerer**, *H.M.S. Pinafore**, *The Pirates of Penzance**, *Patience**, *Iolanthe**, *Princess Ida**, the immortal *The Mikado**, *Ruddigore**, *The Yeomen of the Guard**, *The Gondoliers**, *Haddon Hall**, *Utopia Limited**, *The Grand Duke**, *The Beauty Stone* (London 28 May 1898; libr. J. Comyns Carr and A. W. Pinero), *The Rose of Persia** and the unfinished *The Emerald Isle**.

Sulpice
Bass role in Donizetti's *La Fille du Régiment*. He is the regimental sergeant.

Summertime
Soprano aria for Clara in Act I of Gershwin's *Porgy and Bess*.

Suoni la tromba
Baritone/bass duet for Riccardo and Giorgio in Act II of Bellini's *I Puritani*.

Suor Angelica (*Sister Angelica*)
Opera in one act by Puccini. 1st perf. New York, 14 Dec 1918; libr. by Giovacchino Forzano. Principal roles: Angelica (sop), Princess (mezzo). Part Two of *Il Trittico*, it is notable for its all-female cast and for containing Puccini's only major role for a mezzo.

Plot: A convent near Siena, 17th century. Angelica has entered the convent after bearing an illegitimate child. Her aunt, the Princess, visits her and asks her to renounce her share of the family estate and, when Angelica asks about her child, brutally tells her that it is dead. Angelica takes poison and, as she dies, receives a vision of the Virgin bringing the child to her. [R]

Supernatural in opera
Apart from plots involving the supernatural which are drawn from classical mythology, few composers have tackled supernatural subjects. Those who did are largely from the German romantic school. Much the most important work is Weber's *Der Freischütz*; the Wolf's Glen scene remains unsurpassed as a musical depiction of the macabre. Other works of this period include Marschner's *Der Vampyr* and Schubert's *Des Teufels Lustschloss*. Edgar Allan Poe has attracted many composers, but no major operas have been based on his horror stories: Debussy's unfinished *La Chûte de la Maison Usher* is the great might-have-been. More recently, Britten turned twice to Henry James ghost stories: to terrifying effect with *The Turn of the Screw*, rather less successfully with *Owen Wingrave*. The only important comic treatment of the supernatural is Sullivan's *Ruddigore*.

Among the ghosts which appear in opera, the following spectral manifestations may be noted:
- The dead Louise in Charpentier's *Julien*.
- A dead wife in Korngold's *Die Tote Stadt*.
- Two former servants in Britten's *The Turn of the Screw*.
- A statue in Mozart's *Don Giovanni*, Dargomijsky's *The Stone Guest*, and Hérold's *Zampa*.
- A dead opera singer in Offenbach's *Les Contes d'Hoffmann*.
- A jilted lover in Puccini's *Le Villi*.
- A murdered husband in Rossini's *Semiramide*.
- A murdered father-in-law in Shostakovich's *Lady Macbeth of Mtsensk*.

● The dead Oronte in Verdi's
I Lombardi.
A card-playing Countess in
Tchaikovsky's *The Queen of Spades*.
An entire portrait gallery in Sullivan's
Ruddigore.

Supervia, Conchita *(b Concepción Supervia Pascual) (1895–1936)*

Spanish mezzo, particularly associated
with Rossini roles and with Carmen.
The first modern-style coloratura
mezzo, she had a warm and brilliant
voice used with a fine technique, which
was marred only by her pronounced
vibrato which at times approached a
rattle. She had a delightful and
mischievous stage personality.

Suppé, Franz von *(b Francesco Ezechiele Ermenegildo Suppe Demelli) (1819–95)*

Austrian composer. One of the earliest
composers of Viennese operetta, his
most successful works include *Das
Mädchen von Lande* (1847), *Die
Schöne Galatea**, *Fatinitza**, the highly
successful *Boccaccio** and *Donna
Juanita**.

Surtitles

A projected translation in the language
of the audience which appears on a
screen at the top of the proscenium
arch. Introduced in many houses in the
late 1980s, they have assisted audiences
unfamiliar with the language of the
opera, but have aroused controversy
because they can be very distracting.

Susanna

Soprano role in: (1) Mozart's *Le Nozze
di Figaro*. The Countess' maid, she is
engaged to Figaro. (2) Wolf-Ferrari's *Il
Segreto di Susanna*. She is Count Gil's
wife. (3) Moussorgsky's *Khovanschina*.
She is an Old Believer.

Susannah

Opera in two acts by Floyd. 1st perf.
Tallahassee (Florida), 24 Feb 1955;
libr. by the composer, after the
Apocrypha. Principal roles: Susannah
(sop), Sam (ten), Olin Blitch (bass).
Arguably Floyd's finest opera, it
translates the biblical story to rural
Tennessee and employs folk-like
modality and simple vocal lines.

Plot: Tennessee. The local elders
consider Susannah wanton for bathing
in public. The itinerant evangelist Blitch
fails to convert her but succeeds in
falling in love with her. He confesses
his love, and is killed by Susannah's
brother Sam. She is left alone in
bitterness.

Susanna's Secret

See Segreto di Susanna, Il

Süssmayr, Franz Xaver *(1766–1803)*

Austrian composer. Best known for his
completion of his teacher Mozart's
Requiem, he also wrote nearly 30
Singspiels and opera buffas, all now
long forgotten. The most successful was
Der Spiegel von Arkadien (Vienna 14
Nov 1794; libr. Emanuel Schikaneder).

Sutermeister, Heinrich *(b 1910)*

Swiss composer. He has written nine
operas in a direct and readily accessible
style, a number of which have met with
success. They are: *Romeo und Julia**,
Die Zauberinsel (1942; libr. composer,
after Shakespeare's *The Tempest*),
Niobe (1946; libr. Peter Sutermeister),
Raskolnikoff (Stockholm 14 Oct 1948;
libr. P. Sutermeister, after Dostoyevsky's
Crime and Punishment), *Der Rote
Stiefel* (1951; libr. composer, after W.
Hauff), *Titus Feuerfuchs* (Basel 1958;

libr. composer, after Johann Nestroy's *Der Talisman*), *Das Einsiedler Grosse Welttheater* (1960; libr. Eichendorff, after Pedro Calderón de la Barca), *Seraphine* (1961; libr. composer, after François Rabelais) and *Madame Bovary* (1967; libr. composer, after Gustave Flaubert).

Suthaus, Ludwig *(1906–71)*
German tenor, particularly associated with Wagnerian roles, especially Siegmund and Tristan. One of the leading heldentenors of the immediate postwar era.

Sutherland, Dame Joan *(b 1926)*
Australian soprano, particularly associated with Italian and French coloratura roles, especially Lucia. One of the greatest singers of the 20th century (dubbed 'La Stupenda' by the Italians), she possessed a voice of great beauty and far greater power than most coloraturas, combining extraordinary agility with flawless intonation and a phenomenal trill. Her total command of Bellinian and Donizettian style was marred only by poor diction. On stage, she was a superb comedienne but sometimes rather less compelling an actress in serious roles. She created Jenifer in *The Midsummer Marriage*. Married to the conductor Richard Bonynge*.

Suzel
Soprano role in Mascagni's *L'Amico Fritz*. She is the daughter of one of Fritz's tenants.

Suzel, buon dì
Soprano/tenor duet (the Cherry Duet) for Suzel and Fritz in Act II of Mascagni's *L'Amico Fritz*.

Suzuki
Mezzo role in Puccini's *Madama Butterfly*. She is Cio-Cio-San's maid.

Svanholm, Set *(1904–64)*
Swedish tenor, particularly associated with Wagnerian roles. Beginning as a baritone, he turned to tenor roles in 1936, and was one of the finest Wagnerian tenors of the immediate postwar period. His voice, if a little dry of tone, was used with great musicianship and intelligence, and he sang with much dramatic intensity. He was artistic director of the Royal Opera, Stockholm (1956–63).

Svetlanov, Yevgeny *(b 1928)*
Russian conductor and composer, particularly associated with the Russian repertory. Best known in the West as a symphonic conductor of great brilliance and excitement, he has also conducted much opera in Russia, and was principal conductor of the Bolshoi Opera (1962–64).

Svoboda, Josef *(b 1920)*
Czech designer. A qualified architect, he has been chief designer at the Prague National Theatre since 1948. His designs (often for productions by Václav Kašlík*) make extensive use of gauzes, staircases and large blocks which change smoothly into new shapes. He introduced into opera the 'Laterna Magica', which uses cinematographic projection on multiple screens. He has worked widely outside Prague, notably at Covent Garden (including a *Ring* cycle) and at the Metropolitan Opera, New York.

Svobodová-Janků, Hana *(b 1940)*
Czech soprano, particularly associated with heavier Italian and Czech roles.

She possesses a rich and powerful
lyrico-dramatic voice with a strong and
vibrant lower register, and has a good
stage presence.

Swallow
Bass role in Britten's *Peter Grimes*. He
is a lawyer.

Sweden
See Drottningholm Castle
Theatre; Göteborg Opera;
Stockholm Opera

Swedish opera composers
See Atterberg; Berwald;
Blomdahl; Frumerie; Hallström;
Rangström; Rosenberg;
Stenhammar; Werle
   Other national opera composers
include Sven-Erik Bäck (*b* 1919),
Nathaniel Berg (1879–1957), Johan
Andreas Hallén (1842–1925) and
Wilhelm Peterson-Berger (1867–1942).

Swiss opera composers
See Bloch; Honegger;
Liebermann; Martin; Rousseau;
Schoeck; Sutermeister
   Other national opera composers
include Volkmar Andreae (1879–1962),
Willy Burkhard (1900–55), Rudolf
Kelterborn (*b* 1931), Meyer von
Schauensee (1720–89) and Roger
Vuataz (*b* 1898).

Switzerland
See Basel Stadttheater; Berne
Stadttheater; Grand Théâtre,
Geneva; Luzern Stadttheater;
Zürich Opernhaus

Sydney Opera House
The home of the Australian Opera*,

the theatre (cap. 1,984) was designed
by Jorn Utzon and opened on 20
October 1973. The long delays in its
building and its vastly greater cost than
originally thought, caused it to be
regarded as something of a white
elephant. Since its opening, however, its
majestic if radical design and its
breathtaking setting have led to its
being viewed as one of the world's
most beautiful modern buildings.

Szell, Georg *(b György) (1897–1970)*
Hungarian conductor, particularly
associated with the German repertory.
Noted for his painstaking preparation,
his sense of discipline and his accuracy
of orchestral detail, he was musical
director of the Deutsches Theater,
Prague (1929–37) and was resident in
the United States from 1942. He
conducted the first performances of
Liebermann's *Penelope* and *The School
for Wives* and Egk's *Irische Legende*.

Szokolay, Sándor *(b 1931)*
Hungarian composer. One of the most
successful contemporary opera
composers, his four operas are the
powerful *Blood Wedding**, *Hamlet*
(1968), *Samson** and the radio opera
Deluded Peter (*Csalóka Peter*, 1978;
libr. S. Weöres).

Szymanowski, Karol *(1882–1937)*
Polish composer. The leading 20th-
century Polish composer, he wrote three
stage works. The unperformed operetta
The Lottery for Men (*Loteria na
Mezów*, 1909; libr. J. Krzewiński-
Maszyński) was followed by the
successful *Hagith* (Warsaw 13 May
1922, composed 1913; libr. after Felix
Dörmann) and his masterpiece *King
Roger**.

Tabarro, Il (*The Cloak*)

Opera in one act by Puccini. 1st perf. New York, 14 Dec 1918; libr. by Giuseppe Adami, after Didier Gold's *La Houppelande*. Principal roles: Giorgetta (sop), Michele (bar), Luigi (ten), La Frugola (mezzo), Il Tinca (ten), Il Talpa (bass). The first panel of *Il Trittico*, it is the most truly verismo of Puccini's operas in style.

Plot: The Seine, late 19th century. The Parisian bargee Michele discovers that his wife Giorgetta is having an affair with the young stevedore Luigi. He kills Luigi as he is about to keep a rendezvous with Giorgetta, and presents her with the body wrapped in his cloak. [R]

Tacea la notte

Soprano aria for Leonora in Act I of Verdi's *Il Trovatore*.

Taddei, Giuseppe *(b 1916)*

Italian baritone, particularly associated with Mozart, Verdi and Donizetti roles, especially Falstaff. An outstanding singing-actor, equally at home in serious and comic roles, he had a fine voice of considerable power and range which he used with great intelligence. He enjoyed a remarkably long career, singing well into his 70s.

Taddeo

Baritone role in Rossini's *L'Italiana in Algieri*. He is Isabella's ever-hopeful admirer.

Tadolini, Eugenia *(1809–)*

Italian soprano. One of the leading Italian lyric sopranos of the mid-19th century, she created the title roles in *Linda di Chamounix*, *Maria di Rohan* and *Alzira*. Verdi rejected her as the first Lady Macbeth because he said that she sang too beautifully.

Tagliabue, Carlo *(1898–1978)*

Italian baritone, particularly associated with the Italian repertory, especially Verdi. One of the leading Italian baritones of the inter-war period, he had a warm and beautiful voice used with a fine technique, but was rather dull on stage. He created Basilio in Respighi's *La Fiamma*.

Tagliavini, Ferruccio *(b 1913)*

Italian tenor, particularly associated with lighter Italian and French roles, especially Nemorino, the Duke of Mantua and Werther. He was the leading Italian tenore di grazia of the immediate postwar period. Married to the mezzo Pia Tassinari*.

Taille

A term used in late 17th- and early 18th-century French opera to describe the tenor voice. There were two types, *haute-taille* and *basse-taille*. The latter would nowadays be called baritone.

Tajo, Italo *(b 1915)*

Italian bass, particularly associated with the Italian repertory. An outstanding singing-actor, particularly in comedy, he enjoyed a remarkably long career, singing into his mid-70s, latterly specialising in comprimario roles. He created Samuel in Milhaud's *David* and roles in operas by Berio, Lualdi, Malipiero, Nono and Tosatti, and also appeared in Broadway musicals and in three films.

Tal, Josef *(b Grünthal) (b 1919)*
Polish-born Israeli composer. His five operas, which have met with considerable success in Israel, are *Saul at Endor* (Tel Aviv 1957), *Amnon and Tamar* (Wiesbaden 1951; libr. R. Frier), *Ashmadei* (Hamburg Oct 1971; libr. I. Eliraz), *Masada 967* (Jerusalem July 1973; libr. Eliraz) and *Die Versuchung* (Munich 1976; libr. Eliraz).

Talbot
(1) Bass-baritone role in Donizetti's *Maria Stuarda*. He is the historical George Talbot, Earl of Shrewsbury and Mary's jailer. (2) Bass comprimario role in Verdi's *Giovanna d'Arco*. He is the English commander.

Talbot, Howard *(b Richard Lansdale Munkittrick) (1865–1928)*
American composer (subsequently a British citizen). He wrote, in whole or in part, a large number of operettas and musical comedies. Nowadays he is largely remembered for his collaboration with Monckton on *The Arcadians**.

Tale of Tsar Sultan, The
(Skazka o Tsarie Sultanie)
Opera in prologue and four acts by Rimsky-Korsakov. 1st perf. Moscow, 3 Nov 1900; libr. by Vladimir Ivanovich Belsky, after Alexander Pushkin. Principal roles: Tsar Sultan (bass), Milistrisa (sop), Prince Gvidon (ten), Swan Princess (sop). Containing the famous 'Flight of the Bumblebee', it is one of Rimsky's most delightful and orchestrally brilliant fairy-tale works. Still popular in Russia, it is only very infrequently performed elsewhere.

Plot: As a result of the machinations of her jealous sisters, the Tsarina Milistrisa is set adrift in a cask with her son Gvidon. They are cast ashore on Buyan Island, where Gvidon rescues the Swan Princess. She turns him into a bee, and when Milistrisa's sisters try to stop the Tsar visiting the island, he stings them. Gvidon turns the swan back into a princess, and she returns Milistrisa to her husband. [R]

Tale of Two Cities, A
Opera in prologue and three acts by Benjamin. 1st perf. BBC Radio, 1953; 1st stage perf. London, 23 July 1957; libr. by Cedric Cliffe, after Charles Dickens' novel. Principal roles: Charles Darnay (ten), Dr Manette (ten). Benjamin's finest opera (a joint winner of the Festival of Britain Competition), it was successful at its appearance, but is nowadays all but forgotten.

Tales of Hoffmann, The
See **Contes d'Hoffmann, Les**

Talich, Václav *(1883–1961)*
Czech conductor, particularly associated with his country's repertory. The finest Czech conductor of his time, he was musical director of the Prague National Theatre (1935–47) and conducted the first performance of Martinů's *Julietta*. He was also a distinguished teacher, whose pupils included Sir Charles Mackerras.

Talvela, Martti *(1935–89)*
Finnish bass, particularly associated with Wagner, Mozart and Verdi roles, and with Boris Godunov. His large and beautiful voice, his outstanding musicianship, his keen dramatic sense

and his commanding stage presence (aided by an enormous physique) have all combined to make him one of the greatest basses of the 20th century. He created Paavo Routsalainen in Kokkonen's *The Last Temptations*, and was artistic director of the Savonlinna Festival (1972–80).

Tamagno, Francesco *(1850–1905)*

Italian tenor with an extremely powerful (if not always particularly accurate or subtle) voice, he is often regarded as the greatest tenore di forza of all time, thanks to his great dramatic intensity. In addition, his trumpet-like vocal quality was allied to an imposing presence. He created the title role in *Otello*, Gabriele Adorno in the revised *Simon Boccanegra*, Fabiano in Gomes' *Maria Tudor*, a role in Leoncavallo's *I Medici* and, for Ponchielli, Azael in *Il Figliuol Prodigo* and Didier in *Marion Delorme*.

Tamberlik, Enrico *(1820–89)*

Italian tenor, noted for his powerful declamation. Able to produce a high C♯ from the chest, he was the first singer to introduce the notorious high C at the end of 'Di quella pira' in *Il Trovatore*. He created Don Alvaro in *La Forza del Destino* and the title role in Jullien's *Pietro il Grande*.

Tamburini, Antonio *(1800–76)*

Italian baritone. One of the finest baritones of the first half of the 19th century, he created, for Bellini, Ernesto in *Il Pirata*, Valdeburgo in *La Straniera* and Riccardo in *I Puritani*, and eleven roles for Donizetti, including Dr Malatesta in *Don Pasquale* and Israele in *Marino Faliero*.

Tamerlano

Opera in three acts by Handel. 1st perf. London, 31 Oct 1724; libr. by Nicola Francesco Haym, after Agostino Piovene. Principal roles: Tamerlano (c-ten), Bajazet (ten), Asteria (sop), Andronico (c-ten), Irene (mezzo), Leone (bass). It is still performed from time to time.

Plot: Bithinia, 1402. The Tartar ruler Tamerlano has defeated and captured the Turkish Emperor Bajazet. His Greek ally Andronico loves Bajazet's daughter Asteria, whom Tamerlano (although engaged to Irene) also loves. Asteria suprisingly accepts Tamerlano, but when Bajazet threatens suicide, she throws a dagger at Tamerlano's feet, saying that she had planned to kill him during their first embrace. Tamerlano orders Bajazet and Asteria to be executed, but eventually relents because of the love between father and daughter. Finally, Tamerlano commits suicide. [R]

Taming of the Shrew, The

See Giannini; Widerspenstigen Zähmung, Der

Tamino

Tenor role in Mozart's *Die Zauberflöte*. He is an oriental prince charged with rescuing Pamina.

Tancredi

Opera in two acts by Rossini. 1st perf. Venice, 6 Feb 1813; libr. by Gaetano Rossi, after Voltaire's *Tancrède* and Torquato Tasso's *Gerusalemme Liberata*. Principal roles: Tancredi (mezzo), Amenaida (sop), Argirio (ten), Orbazzano (bass), Isaura (mezzo). The work which established Rossini's reputation, it is still quite often performed.

Plot: Syracuse. Tancredi returns home from exile and manages to prevent the marriage of his beloved

Amenaida to his rival Orbazzano. Orbazzano intercepts a letter from Amenaida to Tancredi and presents it as addressed to the enemy Saracens. Amenaida is condemned to death for treason unless a champion will fight for her. Although he believes her guilty, Tancredi fights for her and wins and then goes on to defeat the Saracens. Orbazzano's perfidy is finally unmasked and the lovers are reconciled. [R]

Taneyev, Sergei *(1856–1915)*
Russian composer. His only operatic work is the Aeschylean trilogy *Oresteia**.

Tannhäuser (und der Sängerkrieg auf der Wartburg) *(Tannhäuser and the Singing Contest of the Wartburg)*
Opera in three acts by Wagner. 1st perf. Dresden, 19 Oct 1845; libr. by the composer. Revised version, 1st perf. Paris, 13 March 1861. Principal roles: Tannhäuser (ten), Elisabeth (sop), Wolfram (bar), Venus (mezzo), Landgrave Hermann (bass), Walther (ten), Reinmar (bass), Biterolf (bass), Heinrich (ten). Wagner's second 'canonical' opera, and the most old-fashioned of his mature works, both versions are still performed.

Plot: 13th-century Eisenach. The minstrel-knight Tannhäuser has been seduced by the goddess Venus, but sated with physical pleasure, he calls on the Virgin who releases him from the Venusberg. He returns to his knightly comrades and takes part in the minstrels' contest for the hand of the Landgrave's daughter, Elisabeth, who has long loved him. The words of his song in the contest betray his past carnal knowledge and he is ordered to undertake a pilgrimage to Rome to seek expiation from the Pope. He returns unshriven, but Elisabeth's self-sacrificing love finally redeems him and he joins her in death on her funeral bier. [R]

Tanti affetti
Soprano aria for Elena in Act II of Rossini's *La Donna del Lago*.

Tapfere Soldat, Der *(The Valiant Soldier*; usually given in English as *The Chocolate Soldier)*
Operetta in three acts by O. Straus. 1st perf. Vienna, 14 Nov 1908; libr. by R. Bernauer and Leopold Jacobson, after George Bernard Shaw's *Arms and the Man*. One of Straus' most successful works, it is still regularly performed.

Tarantella
A fast Italian dance in 6/8 time with alternating major and minor sections. The name derives from the Italian town of Taranto, home of the tarantula: the dance was supposed to ward off the spider's poison. There is an operatic example in Sullivan's *Utopia Limited*.

Tarare
Opera in prologue and five acts by Salieri. 1st perf. Paris, 8 June 1787; libr. by Pierre Augustin Caron de Beaumarchais. Revised version, *Axur, Rè d'Ormus*, 1st perf. Vienna, 8 Jan 1788; libr. revised by Lorenzo da Ponte. Often regarded as Salieri's masterpiece, it was sensationally successful at its appearance, but is nowadays virtually forgotten.

Tarquinius
Baritone role in Britten's *The Rape of Lucretia*. He is the proud Prince of Rome.

Tassinari, Pia *(b 1909)*
Italian soprano and later mezzo, particularly associated with the Italian and French repertories. One of the

leading lyric Italian sopranos of the 1930s, her voice later darkened and she became a successful mezzo. Married to the tenor Ferruccio Tagliavini*.

Tate, Jeffrey (b 1943)
British conductor (and also a qualified doctor), particularly associated with Mozart and Strauss operas. One of the finest contemporary Mozartians, he overcame a severe spinal disability to become a conductor, and in 1987 was appointed Covent Garden's first-ever principal conductor. He conducted the first performance of Liebermann's La Forêt.

Tatyana
Soprano role in Tchaikovsky's Eugene Onegin. She is Olga's sister.

Tauber, Richard (b Ernst Seiffert) (1891–1948)
Austrian tenor, particularly associated with Mozart and Lehár roles. One of the finest lyric tenors of the inter-war period, he sang with style, warmth and great elegance. He created a number of roles for Lehár, notably Prince Sou-chong in Das Land des Lächelns and Octavio in Giuditta. He also conducted operetta, composed the operetta Old Chelsea (1942), and appeared in a number of films, including Blossom Time (1934). Married first to the soprano Carlotta Vanconti and later to the actress Diana Napier.

Tavener, John (b 1944)
British composer. He has written one opera, the unsuccessful Thérèse (London 1 Oct 1979; libr. G. McLarnon).

Taverner
Opera in two acts by Maxwell Davies. 1st perf. London, 12 July 1972; libr. by the composer. Principal roles: Taverner (ten), Jester (bar), White Abbot (b-bar), King (bass), Cardinal (ten), Rose Parrow (mezzo), Sir Richard Taverner (bass), Priest-Confessor (c-ten). Maxwell Davies' first major operatic work, it deals with the English composer John Taverner (c 1495–1545) and his involvement in the political issues of his day.

Taylor, Deems (1885–1966)
American composer. He wrote four operas in a readily accessible late romantic style, which met with considerable success in the United States but which are little known elsewhere. The King's Henchman* was followed by Peter Ibbetson*, Ramuntzko (Philadelphia 10 Feb 1942, composed 1937; libr. composer) and The Dragon (New York 6 Feb 1958), which was written for amateur performers.

Tbilsi
See Tiflis Opera and Ballet Theatre

Tchaikovsky, Modest (1850–1916)
Russian librettist, brother of the composer. As well as writing the libretti for his brother's The Queen of Spades and Iolanta, he also provided texts for Arensky (Nal and Damayanti), Nápravník (Dubrovsky) and Rachmaninov (Francesca da Rimini).

Tchaikovsky, Pyotor Ilyich (1840–93)
Russian composer who wrote 11 operas. Following some unfinished juvenilia, his first completed opera was The Voyevoda*, which he subsequently abandoned, retaining the music for later incorporation into other works. His next opera Undine* he also abandoned

after it was rejected for performance. His first opera to reach the stage was *The Oprichnik**, in which his personal style can be discerned in embryo. His style becomes far more apparent in his next work, *Vakula the Blacksmith**. His lyrical love music, his orchestral mastery, his plangent and melancholic vocal lines and his exhilarating dance music all come together in *Eugene Onegin**, which is usually regarded as his operatic masterpiece. Its successor, written in the hope of a Parisian success, was *The Maid of Orleans**, which is cast in the form of French grand opera. For all but the last of his remaining operas, Tchaikovsky returned to Russian subjects, sometimes evincing a more traditionally nationalist style than previously; this is especially the case with *Mazeppa**, which was followed by *The Little Slippers* (a revision of *Vakula the Blacksmith*), the unsuccessful *The Enchantress** and the powerful *The Queen of Spades**. For his last opera he returned to French sources with the medieval *Iolanta**.

Standing somewhat outside the mainstream of Russian nationalist musical development, Tchaikovsky is perhaps the most international of 19th-century Russian composers. All of his mature works are performed internationally, although only *Eugene Onegin* and *The Queen of Spades* have won a permanent place in Western repertories. His brother was the librettist Modest Tchaikovsky*.

Tear, Robert *(b 1939)*
British tenor, particularly associated with character roles, especially David, Loge and Prince Shuisky. A versatile singing-actor of great intelligence and musicianship, he created Misael in *The Burning Fiery Furnace*, the title role in *The Prodigal Son*, Dov in *The Knot Garden*, the Deserter in Henze's *We Come to the River* and Rimbaud in

Tavener's *Thérèse*. He has recently enjoyed some success as a conductor.

Teatro alla Scala, Milan
Possibly the world's most famous opera house, it was designed by Giuseppe Piermarini and opened on 3 August 1778. After its partial destruction in August 1943, it was repaired and reopened in 1946 (cap. 3,600). It is named after Regina della Scala, wife of Bernabò Visconti, Duke of Milan. Musical directors have included Franco Faccio, Arturo Toscanini, Victor de Sabata, Franco Capuana, Claudio Abbado and Riccardo Muti. It has an associated chamber house, La Piccola Scala*.

Teatro Amazones, Manaus
Designed by Bernardo António Oliveira Braga, it opened on 31 December 1896. Built at the height of the Brazilian rubber boom, no expense was spared to make it one of the world's most lavish opera houses. The vast fees offered lured many of the greatest singers of the time to undertake the 26-day trip up the Amazon to perform there. With the end of the rubber boom the house fell into disuse and decay, but it has recently been restored to its former glory.

Teatro Carlo Felice, Genoa
The opera house (cap. 1,500) was designed by Carlo Barabino and opened on 7 April 1828. The annual season runs from January to July. Musical directors have included Angelo Mariani.

Teatro Colón, Buenos Aires
South America's most important opera house and one of the most lavish in the world, the present theatre (cap. 2,478) opened on 25 May 1908. Its artistic standards have varied enormously, usually in direct relation to the degree

of political stability in Argentina. At its best, it ranks as one of the world's greatest opera houses. The annual season runs from May to December.

Teatro Communale, Bologna

The opera house (cap. 1,500) was designed by Antonio Galli Bibiena and opened in 1763. Since the mid-19th century, when it introduced Wagner to Italy, the theatre has been noted for its adventurous repertory policy. Musical directors have included Angelo Mariani, Luigi Mancinelli, Franco Faccio and Riccardo Chailly.

Teatro Communale, Florence

Originally called the Teatro Politeama Fiorentino Vittorio Emmanuele, the theatre opened in 1864. It acquired its present name in 1932 and reopened after modernisation (cap. 1,806) in 1961. As well as hosting performances by the Maggio Musicale Fiorentino*, it gives annual winter and summer seasons.

Teatro Communale Giuseppe Verdi, Trieste

The present opera house, designed by Antonio Selva and Matteo Pertsch, opened on 21 April 1801 as the Teatro Nuovo. It acquired its present name in 1931. Under the artistic direction of Giuseppe Antonicelli (1936–45 and 1951–66) and Raffaelo de Banfield (1972–), it has become one of Italy's leading houses and is noted for its adventurous repertory.

Teatro de la Zarzuela, Madrid

Originally built to house zarzuelas, an annual international opera season from January to July is nowadays also given at this theatre (cap. 1,140), which opened in 1856.

Teatro dell'Opera, Rome

The present opera house (cap. 2,200), designed by Achille Sfondrini, opened on 27 November 1880 as the Teatro Costanzi. After extensive renovation and enlargement, it reopened as the Teatro Real dell'Opera on 28 Feburary 1928; the Real was dropped when Italy became a republic. Its greatest period was in the early 1940s, when it rivalled La Scala. Although it no longer enjoys such eminence, it still ranks as one of Italy's leading houses. Musical directors have included Gino Marinuzzi, Tullio Serafin, Gabriele Santini, Bruno Bartoletti and Gustav Kuhn.

Teatro Donizetti, Bergamo

The opera house in this city in Lombardy was first opened on 24 August 1791 as the Teatro Riccardi; it burnt down in 1797 but was rebuilt two years later. After extensive rebuilding, it reopened (cap. 2,000) in 1897 and was renamed after the city's most famous son. It is noted both for its performances of Donizetti and for its promotion of new works. Its audience has a reputation of being extremely difficult to please.

Teatro la Fenice, Venice

Often regarded as the most beautiful opera house in the world, the theatre was designed by Antonio Selva and opened on 16 May 1792. Burnt down in December 1836, it was rebuilt from Selva's original ground plan and reopened on 26 December 1837. It reached its present form (cap. 1,500) after alterations in 1938. It has recently been noted for important revivals of 19th-century Italian works. The annual season runs from December to May and there is also a summer festival devoted to 20th-century works.

Teatro Liceo, Barcelona (*Gran Teatre del Liceu* in Catalan)

The first theatre of this name opened in 1847, but was destroyed by fire in 1861. The present opera house (cap. 3,000) was designed by José Oriol Mestres and opened on 20 April 1862. Spain's most important opera house, it gives an annual season from November to June, and its charter requires that it give at least one Spanish opera each year. Musical directors have included Michelangelo Veltri.

Teatro Massimo, Palermo

Possessing the third largest operatic stage in Europe, Sicily's principal opera house (cap. 1,800) was designed by G. B. F. Basile and opened in May 1897. It follows one of the most adventurous repertory policies of any Italian house.

Teatro Massimo Bellini, Catania

Named after the city's most famous son, this Sicilian opera house (cap. 1,470) was designed by Carlo Sada and opened on 31 May 1890. It gives annual spring and summer seasons.

Teatro Municipal, Rio de Janeiro

The home of Brazil's national opera company, the theatre (cap. 2,357) opened on 14 July 1909. The annual season runs from March to December.

Teatro Municipal, Santiago

Chile's principal opera house, the theatre (cap. 1,420) opened in 1857. The annual season runs from March to December, and the repertory is predominantly French and Italian.

Teatro Municipale, Reggio Emilia

The opera house (cap. 1,600) in this Italian town in Emilia-Romagna opened in 1857. Designed by Costa, it is widely regarded as one of Italy's most beautiful theatres.

Teatro Petruzzelli, Bari

The opera house (cap. 4,000) in this Italian town in Puglia opened on 14 February 1903, and is one of the world's largest. It is named after the two brothers who planned it.

Teatro Regio, Parma

The opera house (cap. 1,200) was designed by Nicola Bettoli and opened on 16 May 1829. It has been closely associated with Verdi operas and between 1843 and 1951 it gave 1,382 Verdi performances. Its audience has a reputation for being perhaps the most difficult in the world to please and for regarding itself as expert on all matters vocal. The annual season runs from January to April. Musical directors have included Peter Maag.

Teatro Regio, Turin

Designed by Benedetto Alfieri, the opera house opened on 26 December 1740. It was burnt down in February 1936 and did not reopen until 10 April 1973 after a rebuilding (cap. 1,800) by Carlo Mollino and Marcello Zavalani Rossi. In the meantime, opera was given at Turin's second house, the Teatro Carignano (cap. 1,000), also designed by Alfieri and opened in 1753. Musical directors have included Peter Maag.

Teatro San Carlo, Naples

One of the world's largest opera houses (cap. 3,500), it was designed by Antonio Niccolini and opened in 1816, only six months after the previous theatre (dating from Nov 1737) had been destroyed by fire. Its greatest period was between 1809 and 1840 when Domenico Barbaia* was administrator and the theatre witnessed the premières of some of the greatest works of Rossini and Donizetti. Usually regarded as Italy's second most important house after La Scala, its recent fortunes have been variable, largely because of acute financial problems. Its audience has a not entirely undeserved reputation for conservatism, chauvinism, and extremely vocal expression of its disapproval. The theatre has an associated chamber house, the Teatro della Corte.

Teatro São Carlos, Lisbon

Portugal's principal opera house (cap. 1,148), it was designed by José da Costa in imitation of its namesake in Naples and opened on 30 June 1793. The annual season runs from September to July.

Tebaldi, Renata *(b 1922)*

Italian soprano, particularly associated with Verdi and Puccini roles and with Adriana Lecouvreur. The outstanding Italian lyric soprano of the postwar period, she possessed a voice of great beauty and considerable power, which she used with style, elegance and scrupulous good taste. Her radiant voice, warm personality and sympathetic stage presence combined to make her one of the best-loved singers of her time.

Tebaldo

(1) Tenor role in Bellini's *I Capuleti e i Montecchi*. He is Giulietta's kinsman.
(2) Mezzo trouser-role in Verdi's *Don Carlos*. He is Elisabeth's page.

Te Deum

Scene for Baron Scarpia and the chorus at the end of Act I of Puccini's *Tosca*.

Te Kanawa, Kiri

See Kanawa, Dame Kiri Te

Telemann, Georg Philipp
(1681–1767)

German composer. Possibly the most prolific composer in the history of music, his collected output includes over 40 operas, including *Der Neumodische Liebhaber Damon* (1724), *Die Lastregende Liebe* (1728) and *Flavius Bertandus* (1729). Nowadays, his only two operas still to be at all remembered are the comedies *Der Geduldige Socrates** and *Pimpinone**.

Telephone, The

Comic opera in one act by Menotti. 1st perf. New York, 18 Feb 1947; libr. by the composer. Principal roles: Ben (bar), Lucy (sop). One of Menotti's most successful works, it is a descendant of the 18th-century Italian intermezzi, with the telephone taking the place of the traditional mute player.

Plot: Lucy's addiction to talking on the telephone sabotages Ben's intentions to propose marriage to her. Finally, unable to wait around for her calls to finish, he removes himself to a call box in order to propose by telephone. [R]

Television opera

The first televised opera transmission took place in 1936, when the BBC broadcast excerpts from Coates' *Pickwick*. The first broadcast in the United States was an abridged *Pagliacci* from Radio City in March 1941. In recent years, live broadcasts of opera from all over Europe have become frequent. In addition, there have also been many studio productions, of which the most successful has possibly been the BBC's *Der Fliegende Holländer*. Despite the obvious limitations of the small screen and of television's inferior sound quality, the medium has made opera available to millions who could not otherwise see it, and has done much to increase its popularity. The first opera specifically commissioned for television was Menotti's *Amahl and the Night Visitors* (NBC 1951). Other television operas have included Foss' *Griffelkin*, Britten's *Owen Wingrave*, Fortner's *Der Wald*, Crosse's *Purgatory*, Křenek's *Der Zauberspiegel*, Bliss' *Tobias and the Angel*, Rossellini's *La Campane* and Hoddinott's *Murder the Magician*.

Telramund, Friedrich von

Bass-baritone role in Wagner's *Lohengrin*. Ortrud's husband, he is the Count of Brabant.

Temirkanov, Yuri *(b 1938)*

Russian conductor and producer, particularly associated with the Russian repertory. Although best known in the West as a symphonic conductor, he was musical director of the Kirov Opera until 1988, where he regularly acted as producer.

Tempest, The

Opera by Purcell. 1st perf. London, *c* 1695; libr. by Thomas Shadwell and John Dryden, after Shakespeare's play. Perhaps almost more incidental music than a true opera. [R]

Templer und die Jüdin, Der

(*The Templar and the Jewess*) Opera in three acts by Marschner (Op 60). 1st perf. Leipzig, 22 Dec 1829; libr. by Wilhelm August Wöhlbruck, after Sir Walter Scott's *Ivanhoe*. One of Marschner's finest operas, it was extremely popular in the

19th century but is nowadays only very rarely performed.

Tender Land, The

Opera in three (originally two) acts by Copland. 1st perf. New York, 1 April 1954; libr. by Horace Everett. Revised version, 1st perf. Berkshire, 2 Aug 1954. Principal roles: Laurie Moss (sop), Martin (bar), Top (ten). In this romantic pastoral opera, Copland evokes an unpretentious rustic atmosphere with the use of simple 'folksy' material. A beautiful work, it has been very successful in the United States but has been little performed elsewhere.

Plot: American mid-west, early 1930s. Carried away with the celebrations for her high school graduation, Laurie falls in love with the drifting farm hand Martin and plans to run away with him. Martin has second thoughts about it and leaves without her, but the girl nevertheless sets out on her own. [R]

Tennstedt, Klaus *(b 1926)*

German conductor, particularly associated with the German repertory. Best known as one of the outstanding contemporary symphonic conductors, he conducted much opera in the early part of his career, but recently his operatic appearances have sadly been very rare.

Tenor

See panel on page 568
See also Counter-tenor; Haute-contre; Heldentenor; Taille; Tenore di forza; Tenore di grazia; Tenorino; Trial

Tenor all singers above, A

Tenor aria for Captain Fitzbattleaxe in Act II of Sullivan's *Utopia Limited*, in

TENOR

The tenor is the highest natural male voice (both alto and counter-tenor being artificially produced). The tenor's normal vocal range is roughly c to c'', although some Italian bel canto roles go a little higher, and some exceptional Russian roles (such as the Astrologer in *The Golden Cockerel* and the Police Inspector in *The Nose*) require a range up to f''. The word tenor is derived from the period at the end of the Middle Ages when polyphonic music emerged and when that voice's function was to 'hold' (Latin *tenere*) the tune whilst the other voices proceeded in counterpoint to it. Many different subdivisions of the tenor voice have evolved. They often overlap and do not correspond precisely from one country to another. They are seldom used by composers, but they are useful as an indication of the character of a role, if rather less so for its exact tessitura. The main French, German and Italian categories of tenor are as follows:

	Name	Range	Example
France	haute-contre	d to b''	Hippolytus in *Hippolyte et Aricie*
	Trial	c to b''	Franz in *Les Contes d'Hoffmann*
	ténor	c to c''	Title role in *Faust*
	ténor-bouffe	c to c''	Paris in *La Belle Hélène*
Germany	Spieltenor	c to b♭''	Pedrillo in *Die Entführung*
	Wagnerheldentenor	c to b''	Siegfried in *Götterdämmerung*
	hoher Tenor	c to c''	Brighella in *Ariadne auf Naxos*
	lyrischer Tenor	c to c''	Max in *Der Freischütz*
	Heldentenor	c to c''	Sir Huon in *Oberon*
Italy	tenore-buffo	c to b♭''	Bardolph in *Falstaff*
	tenore	c to c''	Gustavus in *Un Ballo in Maschera*
	tenore spinto	c to c''	Radamès in *Aida*
	tenore di forza	c to c''	Title role in *Otello*
	tenore di grazia	c to d''	Elvino in *La Sonnambula*

which the tenor has to crack deliberately on his high notes.

Tenore di forza (sometimes also called *tenore robusto*)
Roughly the Italian equivalent of the German Heldentenor, the term is used to describe a tenor with the sheer lung-power required to raise the roof in such heavy Italian roles as Manrico, Calaf and, particularly, Otello. Epitomised by Francesco Tamagno, recent tenore di forzas have included Franco Corelli, Mario del Monaco and Franco Bonisolli.

Tenore di grazia (Italian for 'tenor of grace')
A term which describes a tenor with the grace, agility and style required for Mozart, Rossini, and lighter Donizetti and Bellini roles. Recent leading tenore di grazias have included Ferruccio Tagliavini, Ugo Benelli and Luigi Alva.

Below are listed the 135 tenors with entries in this dictionary. Their nationalities are given in brackets afterwards.

Alva, Luigi (Per)
Anders, Peter (Ger)
Aragal, Giacomo (Sp)
Araiza, Francisco (Mex)
Atlantov, Vladimir (Russ)
Benelli, Ugo (It)
Bergonzi, Carlo (It)
Björling, Jussi (Swe)
Blachut, Beno (Cz)
Bonci, Alessandro (It)
Bonisolli, Franco (It)
Borgatti, Giuseppe (It)
Borgioli, Dino (It)
Brilioth, Helge (Swe)
Burian, Karel (Cz)
Burrows, Stuart (Br)
Carreras, José (Sp)
Caruso, Enrico (It)
Cassilly, Richard (US)
Corelli, Franco (It)
Cossutta, Carlo (Arg)
Cox, Jean (US)
Craig, Charles (Br)
Crimi, Giulio (It)
Cuénod, Hugues (Swit)
Davide, Giovanni (It)
Davies, Ryland (Br)
Dermota, Anton (Yug)
Dickie, Murray (Br)
Dobson, John (Br)
Domingo, Plácido (Sp)
Donzelli, Domenico (It)
Duprez, Gilbert (Fr)
Dvorský, Peter (Cz)
Dyck, Ernest van (Belg)
Erb, Karl (Ger)
Fraschini, Gaetano (It)
García, Manuel I (Sp)
Gayarré, Julián (Sp)
Gedda, Nicolaï (Swe)
Giacomini, Giuseppe (It)
Gigli, Beniamino (It)
Häfliger, Ernst (Swit)
Hislop, Joseph (Br)
Hofmann, Peter (Ger)
Holm, Richard (Ger)

Hopf, Hans (Ger)
Ilosfalvy, Róbert (Hung)
Jerusalem, Siegfried (Ger)
Jobin, Raoul (Can)
Johnson, Edward (Can)
Kelly, Michael (Ire)
King, James (US)
Kollo, René (Ger)
Kónya, Sándor (Hung)
Kozlovsky, Ivan (Russ)
Kraus, Alfredo (Sp)
Langridge, Philip (Br)
Lauri-Volpi, Giacomo (It)
Lemeshev, Sergei (Russ)
Lewis, Richard (Br)
Lorenz, Max (Ger)
Luchetti, Veriano (It)
Lucia, Fernando de (It)
McCormack, John (Ire)
McCracken, James (US)
Mario, Giovanni (It)
Martinelli, Giovanni (It)
Melchior, Lauritz (Den)
Merli, Francesco (It)
Mitchinson, John (Br)
Monaco, Mario del (It)
Mullings, Frank (Br)
Nash, Heddle (Br)
Nessi, Giuseppe (It)
Nourrit, Adolphe (Fr)
Oestvig, Karl (Nor)
Oncina, Juan (Sp)
O'Neill, Dennis (Br)
Palacios, Ernesto (Per)
Palma, Piero de (It)
Paolis, Alessio de (It)
Patzak, Julius (Aus)
Pavarotti, Luciano (It)
Pears, Sir Peter (Br)
Peerce, Jan (US)
Pertile, Aureliano (It)
Piccaver, Alfred (Br)
Picchi, Mirto (It)
Přibyl, Vilém (Cz)
Raimondi, Gianni (It)
Ralf, Torsten (Swe)

Randle, Thomas (US)
Reeves, Sims (Br)
Remedios, Alberto (Br)
Reszke, Jean de (Pol)
Riegel, Kenneth (US)
Rolfe-Johnson, Anthony (Br)
Roswaenge, Helge (Den)
Rubini, Giovanni Battista (It)
Schipa, Tito (It)
Schock, Rudolph (Ger)
Schreier, Peter (Ger)
Sénéchal, Michel (Fr)
Shicoff, Neil (US)
Shirley, George (US)
Simoneau, Léopold (Can)
Slezak, Leo (Aus)
Sobinov, Leonid (Russ)
Stefano, Giuseppe di (It)
Stolze, Gerhard (Ger)
Suthaus, Ludwig (Ger)
Svanholm, Set (Swe)
Tagliavini, Ferruccio (It)
Tamagno, Francesco (It)
Tamberlik, Enrico (It)
Tauber, Richard (Aus)
Tear, Robert (Br)
Thill, Georges (Fr)
Thomas, Jess (US)
Trial, Antoine (Fr)
Tucker, Richard (US)
Turp, André (Can)
Ulfung, Ragnar (Nor)
Unger, Gerhard (Ger)
Valletti, Cesare (It)
Vanzo, Alain (Fr)
Vickers, Jon (Can)
Vinay, Ramón (Chil)
Windgassen, Wolfgang (Ger)
Wunderlich, Fritz (Ger)
Young, Alexander (Br)
Zanelli, Renato (Chil)
Zenatello, Giovanni (It)
Žídek, Ivo (Cz)

Tenorino (Italian for 'little tenor')
The term is sometimes used, usually rather disparagingly, to describe a tenor – generally a tenore di grazia – with a very small voice.

Tenuto (Italian for 'held')
An instruction to a singer in a vocal score telling him or her to hold a note for a fraction more than its full value. Most singers regard such an instruction as an open invitation to hold a note (especially a high one) for as long as they wish, so as to make their effect.

Teresa
(1) Soprano role in Berlioz's *Benvenuto Cellini*. Balducci's daughter, she is loved by Cellini and Fieramosca. (2) Mezzo role in Bellini's *La Sonnambula*. She is Amina's foster-mother.

Ternina, Milka *(b Trnina) (1863–1941)*
Croatian soprano, particularly associated with Wagnerian roles, with Tosca, and with Leonore in *Fidelio*. One of the outstanding lyrico-dramatic sopranos of her time, she was also a fine singing-actress of great dramatic intensity. Henry James described her performance style as "a devastating experience". She was forced to retire in 1916 as a result of paralysis.

Terzetto
A short trio.

Teschemacher, Marguerite *(1903–59)*
German soprano, particularly associated with the German repertory. Possessing a warm lyrico-dramatic voice and a good stage presence, she created the title role in *Daphne* and Miranda in Sutermeister's *Der Zauberinsel*.

Teseo *(Theseus)*
Opera in five acts by Handel. 1st perf. London, 10 Jan 1713; libr. by Nicola Francesco Haym, after Philippe Quinault's libretto for Lully's *Thésée*. Principal roles: Teseo (mezzo), Medea (mezzo), Agilea (sop), Egeo (c-ten), Arcane (mezzo), Clizia (sop). Never one of Handel's more successful operas, it is very rarely performed.

Tessitura (Italian for 'texture')
A term which describes the range or compass of a role or of a piece of music in relation to the vocal type for which it is written. Thus, for example, Verdi's baritone roles are said to have a particularly high tessitura.

Tetrazzini, Luisa *(1871–1940)*
Italian soprano, particularly associated with coloratura roles, especially Lucia and Violetta. Although her 'acting' was well-nigh non-existent, she was one of the highest paid singers in history, commanding $3,000 per performance in the early 1900s. Although reputed to have earned over $5 million in all, she died in poverty. Her autobiography, *My Life of Song*, was published in 1921. Her sister Eva (1872–1938) was also a successful soprano, and was married to the conductor Cleofonte Campanini*.

Teufels Lustschloss, Des *(The Devil's Pleasuredrome)*
Opera in three acts by Schubert (D 84). 1st perf. Vienna, 12 Dec 1879 (composed 1814); libr. by August von Kotzebue. Schubert's first completed opera, written in Singspiel form, it is almost never performed.

Teyte, Dame Maggie *(b Margaret Tate) (1888–1976)*
British soprano, particularly associated with the roles of Mélisande and Cio-

Cio-San. A singer of outstanding artistry and vocal refinement with an affecting stage presence, she created the Princess in Holst's *The Perfect Fool* and Glycère in Hillemacher's *Circe*. Her autobiography, *A Star on the Door*, was published in 1958.

Thaïs

Opera in three acts by Massenet. 1st perf. Paris, 16 March 1894; libr. by Louis Gallet, after Anatole France's novel. Principal roles: Thaïs (sop), Athanaël (bar), Nicias (ten), Palémon (bass). One of Massenet's finest operas and still regularly performed, it is notable for the religio-erotic fervour of the score and for the famous *Méditation* with solo violin.

Plot: 4th-century Alexandria. The Coenobite monk Athanaël feels called upon to rescue the beautiful courtesan Thaïs from her life of physical pleasure. His friend Nicias, who has purchased her love for a week, introduces him to her at a banquet. He attempts to convert her and she agrees to enter a convent. However, Athanaël discovers to his horror that he has fallen in love with her. He goes to tell her of his love, only to find that she is dying. [R]

The

Titles beginning with the English definite article are listed under the letter of the first main word. For example, *The Mikado* is listed under M.

Thea

Mezzo role in Tippett's *The Knot Garden*. She is Faber's wife.

Theater an der Wien, Vienna

Now the home of the annual Vienna Festival, the theatre (cap. 1,232) was built by Emanuel Schikaneder and opened on 13 June 1801. Vienna's second most important opera house,

and the scene of the first performances of *Fidelio* and *Die Fledermaus*, it was totally renovated following its purchase by the city of Vienna and reopened on 30 May 1962.

Théâtre Bouffes-Parisiens

A theatre (cap. 820) in the Champs-Elysées in Paris which was opened by Offenbach on 5 May 1855. It still retains a strong operetta tradition.

Théâtre de l'Opéra, Nice

The present theatre (cap. 1,230) in this city in Alpes-Maritimes (France) opened in February 1885. Musical directors have included António de Almeida.

Théâtre des Champs-Elysées, Paris

The theatre (cap. 2,000) opened in 1913 and is the usual venue for performances by visiting companies.

Théâtre Municipal, Nancy

The present opera house (cap. 1,310) in this city in Vosges (France) opened in 1919.

Théâtre Royal de la Monnaie, Brussels

Belgium's principal opera house, the present theatre (cap. 1,140) was designed by Joseph Poelaert and opened in 1856, replacing the original theatre built in 1700. It takes its name from an *atelier monnetaire* which existed on the site in the 17th century. The annual season runs from September to July. Musical directors have included André Vandernoot, Sir John Pritchard and Sylvain Cambreling.

Thebom, Blanche *(b 1918)*

American mezzo, particularly associated with Wagnerian roles. Based largely at the Metropolitan Opera, New York from 1944, she was a rich-voiced singer with a good stage presence. In 1968, she became general manager of the short-lived Atlanta Opera Company.

Thérèse

Opera in two acts by Massenet. 1st perf. Monte Carlo, 7 Feb 1907; libr. by Jules Clarétie. Principal roles: Thérèse (mezzo), Armand (ten), André (bar). Never one of Massenet's more successful works, it is nowadays only very rarely performed.

Plot: Versailles and Paris, 1792–93. The aristocratic soldier Armand de Clerval longs for his family home. This is owned by André Thorel, son of the former concierge who bought it after Armand's father fled the Revolution. André hopes to return the château to Armand one day and is unaware that his wife Thérèse is Armand's former love. She is shaken when Armand appears, but although she still loves him she decides to stay with André. Later, André and Thérèse hide Armand from the mob and André gives him his own papers so that he may escape. Thérèse agrees to run away with Armand, but when she hears that André has been arrested and sees him in the cart on his way to the guilloutine, she realises her duty and joins André on the way to execution. [R]

Theseus

The mythical Greek hero appears in many operas, including: (1) Bass-baritone role in Rameau's *Hippolyte et Aricie*. (2) Baritone role in Pizzetti's *Fedra*. (3) Bass role in Handel's *Teseo*.

Thespis
or The Gods Grown Old

Operetta in two acts by Sullivan. 1st perf. London, 26 Dec 1871; libr. by W. S. Gilbert. The first collaboration between Gilbert and Sullivan, all of the music is lost except for the tenor song, 'Little Maid of Arcady' and the chorus 'Climbing over rocky mountain', which Sullivan later reused in *The Pirates of Penzance*. It tells of the mythical Greek actor and his troupe who take over the duties on Mount Olympus so as to allow the gods to have a holiday.

Thieving Magpie, The
See Gazza Ladra, La

Thill, Georges *(1897–1984)*

French tenor, particularly associated with the French repertory, especially Julien in *Louise* (which he filmed). One of the finest lyric tenors of the inter-war period, he combined an Italianate vocal style with an innate feel for the French musical idiom. He created the title role in Canteloube's *Vercingétorix*.

Thomas, Ambroise *(1811–96)*

French composer. His 20 operas varied in style as he responded to the examples set by other more successful (and better) composers. His first opera *La Double Echelle* (Paris 23 Aug 1837; libr. François-Antoine-Eugène de Planard) was followed by 16 more or less successful opéra-comiques, written largely in imitation of Auber. They include *La Perroucquier de la Régine* (Paris 30 March 1838; libr. Planard and P. Dupont), *Angélique et Médor* (Paris 10 May 1843; libr. Thomas Sauvage, after Lodovico Ariosto's *Orlando Furioso*), *Le Caïd* (Paris 3 Jan 1849; libr. Sauvage), the Shakespearean *La Songe d'un Nuit d'Eté* (Paris 20 April 1850; libr. Adolphe de Leuven and J. B. Rosier), *Raymond* (Paris 5 June 1851; libr. De Leuven and Rosier, after Alexandre Dumas' *The Man in the Iron Mask*) and *Le Roman d'Elvire* (Paris 4 Feb 1860; libr. De Leuven and Dumas père). Turning to an imitation of Gounod's style, he produced his most successful works, *Mignon** and *Hamlet**. His last opera, *Françoise de Rimini* (Paris 14 April 1882; libr. Jules Barbier and Michel Carré, after Dante's *La Divina Commedia*) was a failure. Although he was a distinguished director of the Paris Conservatory from 1871, other composers had mixed feelings about him; Berlioz once remarked "there are three kinds of music: good, bad and that by Ambroise Thomas".

Thomas, Arthur Goring (1850–92)

British composer, whose early insanity and death cut short a promising career. His five operas are the unfinished *Don Braggadocio* (libr. C. I. Thomas), *The Light of the Harem* (London 7 Nov 1879; libr. C. Harrison, after Thomas Moore), *Esmeralda* (London 26 March 1883; libr. T. Marzials and A. Randegger, after Victor Hugo's *Notre-Dame de Paris*), *Nadeshda* (London 16 Oct 1885; libr. Julian Russell Sturgis) and the comedy *The Golden Web* (Liverpool 15 Feb 1893; libr. F. Corder and B. C. Stephenson).

Thomas, Jess (b 1927)

American tenor, particularly associated with Wagnerian roles. One of the leading Wagnerian tenors of the 1960s (if not a true heldentenor), he was an artist of fine musicianship and intelligence. He created Octavius Caesar in Barber's *Antony and Cleopatra*.

Thomas and Sally
or The Sailor's Return

Opera in three acts by Arne. 1st perf. London, 28 Nov 1760; libr. by Isaac Bickerstaffe. Principal roles: Sally (sop), Thomas (ten), Squire (ten), Dorcas (mezzo). One of Arne's most successful works, it is still occasionally performed.

Plot: Sally pines for her absent sailor husband Thomas. Dorcas tries unsuccessfully to persuade her to enjoy life and marry the Squire, but Sally rebuffs the Squire's advances, preferring virtue to his wealth. Thomas returns from his voyages just in time to send the Squire packing and praises the faithfulness of the 'British virgin'. [R]

Thomson, Virgil (b 1896)

American composer and critic. His three operas, *Four Saints in Three Acts**, *The Mother of Us All** and *Lord Byron* (New York 20 April 1972; libr. Jack Larson), are amongst the most important American operas. His musical style was heavily influenced by his friendships with Gertrude Stein and Satie. His 15 years with *The New York Herald Tribune* established him as one of the most perceptive and entertaining of American critics. His autobiography, *Virgil Thomson*, was published in 1966.

Three Church Parables

The title given by Britten to his three one-act operas *The Burning Fiery Furnace**, *Curlew River** and *The Prodigal Son**, all of which are written for small forces and intended for such performance.

Threepenny Opera, The

See Dreigroschenoper, Die

Through-composed

The term has three meanings in opera: (1) A song whose melody progresses continuously, as opposed to a strophic* song, in which the same music is repeated exactly (or almost so) for each verse or stanza. Thus, to take two examples from Sullivan's *Princess Ida*, 'O goddess wise' is through-composed and 'If you give me your attention' is strophic. (2) A work with no spoken dialogue in a genre (such as Singspiel, operetta or zarzuela) which normally does contain spoken dialogue. An example is Sullivan's *Trial By Jury*. (3) A work in which each scene is a single, unbroken piece of music, as in Wagner's operas. It is the opposite of number opera*.

Tibbett, Lawrence *(1896–1960)*

American baritone, particularly associated with the Italian repertory, especially Verdi. Arguably the outstanding Verdi baritone of the inter-war period, he was a powerful singing-actor with a truly magnificent voice. He created the title roles in Gruenberg's *The Emperor Jones* and Goossens' *Don Juan de Mañara*, Wrestling Bradford in Hanson's *Merry Mount*, and for Taylor, Eadgar in *The King's Henchman* and Col. Ibbetson in *Peter Ibbetson*. He also appeared in a number of films, including *The Rogue Song* and *The New Moon*. His autobiography, *The Glory Road*, was published in 1933.

Tichon

Tenor role in Janáček's *Káťa Kabanová*. Kabanicha's son, he is Káťa's husband.

Tiefland *(Lowland)*

Opera in prologue and three acts by D'Albert. 1st perf. Prague, 15 Nov 1903; libr. by Rudolf Lothar, after Angel Guimerá's *Terra Baixa*. Principal roles: Martha (sop), Pedro (ten), Sebastiano (bar), Nuri (mezzo), Tommasso (bass). D'Albert's most successful and enduring work, it is written in verismo style.

  Plot: 19th-century Catalonia. The landowner Sebastiano, wishing to be rid of his unwilling mistress, Martha, offers her as a bride to the shepherd Pedro. She distrusts Pedro, who turns on her at the instigation of the villagers, but eventually comes to realise that Pedro loves her. Pedro strangles Sebastiano and they return to the Pyrenees from where Sebastiano had banished them to the lowlands. [R]

Tietjens, Therese *(1831–77)*

German soprano who sang predominantly in England. One of the finest sopranos of the mid-19th century, she possessed a voice of great power and range which enabled her to encompass a wide variety of French and Italian roles. She was particularly associated with the roles of Lucrezia Borgia, Donna Anna and Norma.

Tiflis Opera and Ballet Theatre

The principal opera house in Soviet Georgia, in the city also known as Tbilisi, the theatre (cap. 1,061) opened in 1851, and in the 20th century has promoted the works of many Georgian composers. The annual season runs from September to June.

Timbre

A French term, also used in Britain, for tone-colour*.

Timur

Bass role in Puccini's *Turandot*. The deposed King of Tartary, he is Calaf's father.

Tinsley, Pauline *(b 1928)*

British soprano, particularly associated with dramatic Italian roles, especially Lady Macbeth, Abigaille and Turandot. A thrilling and often sadly underrated singer, she had a steely voice of great power and range which she used with fine musicianship and to exciting dramatic effect.

Tippett, Sir Michael (b 1905)
British composer. Widely regarded as
the greatest living British composer, his
five operas are amongst the most
important of postwar music-dramas.
The Midsummer Marriage*, *King
Priam**, *The Knot Garden**, *The Ice
Break** and *New Year** exhibit great
stylistic differences, but all share
Tippett's strong humanism and almost
mystical use of concepts and illusions.
Less immediately theatrical and
accessible than Britten's operas,
Tippett's works have been slower to
make their way internationally. His
writings, particularly *Moving Into
Aquarius* (1959), have exerted a
considerable influence on contemporary
developments in British music.

Tiresias
The blind seer of Greek mythology
appears in a number of operas,
including: (1) Bass role in Stravinsky's
Oedipus Rex. (2) Tenor role in Henze's
The Bassarids. (3) Bass role in
Honegger's *Antigonae*. (4) Tenor role in
Orff's *Antigonae*. (5) Tenor role in
Dallapiccola's *Ulisse*. (6) Tenor role in
Orff's *Oedipus der Tyrann*.

**Tirolese Landestheater,
Innsbruck**
The present opera house (cap. 793)
opened in December 1967, replacing
the previous theatre originally built in
1653. Musical directors have included
Siegfried Nessler.

Tisbe
Mezzo role in Rossini's *La Cenerentola*.
She is one of the two ugly sisters.

Titurel
Bass role in Wagner's *Parsifal*. He is
Amfortas' father.

Tobias Mill
Baritone role in Rossini's *La Cambiale
di Matrimonio*. He is an English
businessman.

Toczyska, Stefania
Polish mezzo, particularly associated
with the Italian and French repertories.
A dramatic mezzo in the grand
tradition, her voice is large and
powerful with a strong lower register,
and she has a good stage presence.

Todesverkündigung
Brünnhilde's announcement of
Siegmund's death in Act II of Wagner's
Die Walküre.

**Tokyo Chamber Opera
Group**
Founded in 1969 by Ryosuke
Hatanaka, it gives five productions a
year. It has a wide-ranging repertory,
and its artistic standards have been
high.

Tolomeo, Rè d'Egitto (*Ptolemy,
King of Egypt*)
Opera in three acts by Handel. 1st perf.
London, 30 April 1728; libr. by Nicola
Francesco Haym, after C. S. Capece's
Tolomeo e Alessandro. Never one of
Handel's more popular operas, it is
only infrequently performed.

Tolstoy
See panel on page 576

Tom
Bass role in Verdi's *Un Ballo in
Maschera*. Count Horn in the Swedish
setting, he is one of the two
conspirators.

TOLSTOY

The Russian novelist Count Lev Nikolayevich Tolstoy (1828–1910) strongly disliked all opera with the exception of *Don Giovanni* and *Der Freischütz*. He attempted to persuade Tchaikovsky to desist from operatic composition, and he mocked the form in *War and Peace*. Despite this, his works have often inspired composers. Nearly 20 operas have been based on his novels. Below are listed, by work, those operas by composers with entries in this dictionary.

Anna Karenina

Hamilton	*Anna Karenina*	1981

How Men Live

Martinů	*What Men Live By*	1953

Resurrection

Alfano	*Risurrezione*	1904
Cikker	*Resurrection*	1962

The Tale of Ivan the Jester

Ostrčil	*Johnny's Kingdom*	1924

The Two Old Men

Fibich	*Bloud*	1936

War and Peace

Prokofiev	*War and Peace*	1946

Tomasi, Henri *(1901–71)*
French composer and conductor. His operas include *Don Juan de Mañara* (Munich 1958, composed 1952; libr. after Prosper Mérimée's *Les Âmes du Purgatoire*), *L'Atlantide* (Mulhouse 26 Feb 1954; libr. Francis Didelot, after Pierre Benoit), *Sampiero Corso* (Bordeaux 1956), *Le Triomphe de Jeanne* (Rouen 1956), *Princesse Pauline* (Paris 1962), *L'Élixir du Révérend Père Gaucher* (Toulouse 1964) and *Le Silence de la Mer* (Toulouse 1964; libr. after Vercors). He was musical director of the Monte Carlo Opera (1946–50).

Tomlinson, John *(b 1946)*
British bass, particularly associated with Verdi, Mozart and (more recently) Wagnerian roles. Possessing a large and rich voice of considerable power and range, he also has a strong stage presence. He created Villac Umu in Hamilton's *The Royal Hunt of the Sun*.

Tom Jones
Works of this title based on Henry Fielding's novel include:
(1) Opera in three acts by Philidor. 1st perf. Paris, 27 Feb 1765; libr. by Antoine Poinsinet. Sometimes regarded

as Philidor's finest work, it was long popular, but is nowadays all but forgotten.

(2) Operetta in three acts by German. 1st perf. Manchester, 3 April 1907; libr. by A. M. Thompson, Robert Courtenidge and Charles H. Taylor. Principal roles: Tom Jones (bar), Sophia (sop), Honour (mezzo). Enormously successful at its appearance, it is still very occasionally performed.

Tomowa-Sintow, Anna
(b 1941)
Bulgarian soprano, particularly associated with Mozart, Verdi and Strauss roles. Possessing a creamy lyrico-spinto voice, which she uses with style and great intelligence, she is one of the finest contemporary Mozartians and has a good stage presence. She created a role in Orff's *De Temporum Fine Comoedia*.

Tomsky, Count
Baritone role in Tchaikovsky's *The Queen of Spades*. He is a friend of Hermann.

Tonadilla
(Spanish for 'little tune')
A short comic opera, similar to an Italian intermezzo, given between the acts of an opera or play. It developed in Spain in the 18th century as a reaction against the increasing formality of zarzuela. Originally for two, three or four characters and seldom exceeding 20 minutes duration, the genre subsequently developed an independent life as *tonadillas generales*, employing up to ten characters. The leading tonadilla composers are Luis Misón (*d* 1766), Antonio Guerrerro, Pablo Esteve, Ventura Galván, José Palomino and Blas Laserna (1751–1816).

Tone-colour
The sound quality which distinguishes a note sung by one singer from the same note sung by a different one. It is also called timbre in France and Britain.

Tonie
Tenor role in Donizetti's *La Fille du Régiment*. He loves Marie.

Tonio
Baritone role in Leoncavallo's *Pagliacci*. He is the hunchbacked clown in Canio's troupe.

Tooley, Sir John *(b 1924)*
British administrator. He was general administrator of Covent Garden (1970–88), and introduced the popular 'promenade' performances which are occasionally given at low prices to encourage young audiences.

Toreador's Song
Baritone aria ('Votre toast') for Escamillo in Act II of Bizet's *Carmen*.

Torna la pace
Tenor aria for Idomeneo in Act III of Mozart's *Idomeneo*.

Tornami a dir
Soprano/tenor duet for Norina and Ernesto in Act III of Donizetti's *Don Pasquale*.

Toronto
See Canadian Opera Company

Torquato Tasso
Opera in three acts by Donizetti. 1st perf. Rome, 9 Sept 1833; libr. by Jacopo Ferretti, after Giovanni Rosini's *Tasso* and Lord Byron's *Tasso*. Principal roles: Tasso (bar), Eleonora (sop), Roberto (ten), Gherardo (bass), Scandiano (mezzo), Alfonso (bar).

Dealing with events in the life of the Italian poet Torquato Tasso (1544–95), it is one of Donizetti's most adventurous works. As in a Greek drama, the chorus only comments on the action, the villains are a tenor and a basso-buffo, and the enormously demanding title role is for a baritone, prefiguring Verdi. Successful at its appearance, it is still occasionally performed.

Plot: 16th-century Ferrara. The poet Tasso loves Eleanora, sister of the Duke of Ferrara. Don Gherardo believes that Tasso loves his own sweetheart Eleanora di Scandiano, and steals a poem of Tasso's in praise of Eleanora. Gherardo's machinations lead to Tasso being declared insane and confined in an asylum for seven years. When he is released and told that his own Eleanora is dead, he really does go mad. However, he is persuaded to think only of his poetry and returns to writing.

Torquemada
Tenor role in Ravel's *L'Heure Espagnole*. He is a clockmaker married to Concepción.

Torroba, Federico Moreno
(b 1891)
Spanish composer. His many stage works include *Luisa Fernánda* (1932) [R], one of the most successful of all zarzuelas, and the opera *El Poeta* (Madrid 1980).

Torvaldo e Dorliska
Opera in two acts by Rossini. 1st perf. Rome, 26 Dec 1815; libr. by Cesare Sterbini. One of Rossini's least successful works, nowadays only the overture is at all remembered.

Tosatti, Vieri *(b 1920)*
Italian composer. He has written seven operas, which have met with some

success in Italy. They are *Dionisio* (1946), *Il Sistema della Dolcezza* (*Treatment By Kindness*, Bergamo 1951; libr. composer, after Edgar Allan Poe's *The System of Dr Tarr and Prof Fether*), the boxing opera *Partita a Pugni* (*Fist Fight*, Venice 1953), *Il Giudizio Universale* (Milan 1955; libr. C. V. Ludovici, after A. Bonacci), *L'Isola del Tesoro* (Bologna 1958; libr. composer, after Robert Louis Stevenson's *Treasure Island*), *La Fiora delle Meraviglie* (Rome 1963; libr. composer) and *Il Paradiso e il Poeta* (Turin Radio 1971; libr. composer).

Tosca
Opera in three acts by Puccini. 1st perf. Rome, 14 Jan 1900; libr. by Giuseppe Giacosa and Luigi Illica, after Victorien Sardou's *La Tosca*. Principal roles: Floria Tosca (sop), Baron Scarpia (bar), Mario Cavaradossi (ten), Sacristan (b-bar), Cesare Angelotti (bass). An instant success, which has remained one of the most enduringly popular of all operas, Tosca and Scarpia gave to Maria Callas and Tito Gobbi their most thrilling roles, and their performances have become the yardstick by which all others are now measured.

Plot: Rome, June 1800. The artist and republican loyalist Cavaradossi aids the escape of Angelotti, the former consul of the Roman Republic. Baron Scarpia, the chief of police, lusts after Cavaradossi's lover, the singer Tosca, and hopes to recapture Angelotti through her. He has Cavaradossi arrested and tortured until Tosca reveals Angelotti's hiding-place. Scarpia agrees to release Cavaradossi and provide him and Tosca with a safe-conduct after Cavaradossi has been through a mock execution. Scarpia's price is Tosca herself. She agrees, but stabs him with a knife from his own table when he begins to embrace her. Scarpia's 'mock' execution squad proves to have real bullets, and Cavaradossi is killed. By this time, Scarpia's murder has been discovered, and Tosca throws herself off the battlements. [R]

Tosca è un buon falco

Baritone aria for Baron Scarpia in Act II of Puccini's *Tosca*.

Toscanini, Arturo *(1867–1957)*

Italian conductor, particularly associated with Verdi and Puccini operas. He began his career as a cellist (playing in the first performance of *Otello*), making an unexpected conducting debut in Rio de Janeiro in 1886 when he replaced an unpopular colleague. Autocratic, even despotic, and given to severe outbursts of temper, he was nevertheless one of the greatest conductors of the early 20th century. He was musical director of La Scala, Milan for three periods between 1898 and 1929. He conducted the first performances of *La Bohème*, *La Fanciulla del West*, *Turandot*, *Pagliacci*, *Zazà*, Pizzetti's *Debora e Jaèle* and *Fra Gherardo*, Zandonai's *I Cavalieri di Ekebù*, Mascagni's *Le Maschere*, Boito's *Nerone* (which he helped to complete), Giordano's *Madame Sans-Gêne*, Smargelia's *Oceàna* and Franchetti's *Germania*.

Tote Stadt, Die *(The Dead City)*

Opera in three acts by Korngold (Op 12). 1st perf. Hamburg and Cologne simultaneously, 4 Dec 1920; libr. by the composer and his father Julius Korngold under the joint pen-name of Paul Schott, after Georges Rodenbach's *Bruges-la-Morte*. Principal roles: Paul (ten), Marietta (sop), Marie (sop), Frank (bar), Brigitta (mezzo). Korngold's most successful opera, still regularly performed, it is written in lush, late romantic style. The two female roles are traditionally played by the same soprano.

Plot: Bruges, late 19th century. Paul is in mourning for his late wife Marie. He meets the dancer Marietta, in whom he seems to see Marie. In a series of dream visions, he has various experiences with her, ending with her infidelity, which causes him to strangle her with her own hair. [R]

To this we've come

Soprano aria for Magda Sorel in Act II of Menotti's *The Consul*.

Tottola, Andrea Leone *(d 1831)*

Italian librettist. A typical example of the literary hacks who churned out vast numbers of libretti in early 19th-century Italy. Based in Naples, he provided texts for Bellini (*Adelson e Salvini*), Carafa, Donizetti (*La Zingara, Alfredo il Grande, Il Fortunato Inganno, Elisabetta al Castello di Kenilworth, Imelda de' Lambertazzi* and *Gabriella di Vergy*), Fioravanti, Guglielmi, Mayr (*Elena*), Mercadante, Pacini, Petrella, L. Ricci, Rossini (*La Donna del Lago, Mosè in Egitto, Zelmira, Ermione* and *Edoardo e Cristina*) and Vaccai amongst others.

Toulouse Capitole

The present opera house (cap. 1,500) opened in 1923, replacing the previous theatre of the same name which had dated from 1737. The name derives from the twelve consuls (*capitouls*) who ruled the city and who owned the original theatre. Since 1975, the company has shared productions with the Grand Théâtre, Bordeaux. Musical directors have included Louis Izar and Michel Plasson.

Tourangeau, Huguette

Canadian mezzo, particularly associated with Italian bel canto roles and with the French repertory. She possesses a rich, agile and dark-toned voice, used with a fine technique, and has an impressive (if much over-indulged) chest register.

Tourel, Jennie (b Davidson) (1899–1973)

Canadian mezzo, particularly associated with the French repertory. Possessing a voice of remarkable range, which she used with an outstanding technique, she created Baba the Turk in *The Rake's Progress*. She was also a distinguished teacher, whose pupils included Maria Ewing and Barbara Hendricks.

Tous les trois réunis

Soprano/tenor/bass trio for Marie, Tonie and Sulpice in Act II of Donizetti's *La Fille du Régiment*.

Tozzi, Giorgio (b 1923)

American bass, particularly associated with the Italian repertory. Starting as a baritone, he turned to bass roles in 1950, and from 1955 was largely resident at the Metropolitan Opera, New York. A rich-voiced and intelligent singer with an imposing stage presence, he created the Doctor in Barber's *Vanessa*.

Trabuco

Tenor role in Verdi's *La Forza del Destino*. He is a muleteer.

Tradito schernito

Tenor aria for Ferrando in Act II of Mozart's *Così fan Tutte*. It is usually cut because of its formidable difficulty.

Traetta, Tommaso (1727–79)

Italian composer. His first opera *Il Farnace* (Naples 4 Nov 1751; libr. A. M. Luchini, after Apostolo Zeno's *Mitridate*) was a success and he soon became famous, writing operas for Italy, Austria, England and Russia. His most successful works include *Ippolito*

ed Aricia (Parma 9 May 1759; libr. C. I. Fruggoni, after Euripides' *Hippolytus*), *I Tintaridi* (Parma April 1760; libr. Fruggoni, after Pierre Joseph Bernard's *Castor et Pollux*), *Le Servi Rivali* (Venice 1766; libr. P. Chiari) and *Antigonae* (St Petersburg 11 Nov 1772; libr. Marco Coltellini), usually regarded as his finest work. After a long period of neglect, there has recently been a minor revival of interest in his music.

Tragédie-lyrique (French for 'lyric tragedy')

The term used by Lully and Philippe Quinault to describe their stage works, in which epic or mythical subjects were intended to be treated with dramatic naturalness and to exhibit clarity of declamation. First used in 1673 to describe *Cadmus et Hermione*, the term later came into more general use to describe the operas of Lully's successors, such as Rameau and Gluck.

Transcription

The arranging of a piece of music for an instrument for which it was not originally written. In opera, the term is encountered only in reference to Liszt's many arrangements of operatic melodies for the piano.

Transposition

The performance of a piece of music in a key other than that in which it was originally written. Singers will often transpose an aria (usually downwards), either to make specific high notes easier or because the general tessitura of the piece sits uncomfortably with their own vocal range.

Traubel, Helen (1899–1972)

American soprano, particularly identified with Wagnerian roles. Long associated with the Metropolitan

Opera, New York, she left the theatre in 1953 after disagreements with Rudolf Bing over her nightclub appearances. Possessing an enormous, warm-toned voice and superb projection, she created Mary in Damrosch's *The Man Without a Country*. She wrote a number of successful detective stories as well as her autobiography, *St Louis Woman*, which was published in 1959.

Traurigkeit

Soprano aria for Constanze in Act II of Mozart's *Die Entführung aus dem Serail*.

Traveller

(1) Multiple baritone role in Britten's *Death in Venice*. (2) Bass role in Holst's *The Perfect Fool*. (3) Baritone role in Britten's *Curlew River*.

Travelling Companion, The

Opera in four acts by Stanford (Op 146). 1st perf. Bristol, 25 Oct 1926 (composed 1919); libr. by Henry Newbolt, after Hans Christian Andersen. Stanford's last opera, produced posthumously, it was reasonably successful in its time but is nowadays all but forgotten.

Travesti (from the Italian *travestire*, 'to disguise')

A term describing an operatic role which involves the singer dressing as the opposite sex. Although there are a few 'drag' roles for men (there is Mamma Agata in Donizetti's *Le Convenienze*, and Wolf-Ferrari's *Il Campiello* contains a street fight for two old women played by tenors), most are for women playing male characters. In Britain, these are called trouser-roles or breeches-roles.

Traviata, La (*The Fallen Woman*)

Opera in three acts by Verdi. 1st perf. Venice, 6 March 1853; libr. by Francesco Maria Piave, after Alexandre Dumas fils' *La Dame aux Camélias*. Principal roles: Violetta Valéry (sop), Alfredo Germont (ten), Giorgio Germont (bar), Flora Bervoix (mezzo). Although it failed at its première, the opera had established itself within a year and has remained one of the best-loved and most frequently performed, recorded and filmed of all operas.

Plot: Paris, mid-19th century. The beautiful but consumptive demi-monde, Violetta Valéry, gives a lavish party at which Alfredo Germont, a young man of good birth, is present. After the guests have departed Alfredo, who has long loved Violetta from a distance, reveals his feelings and urges her to give up her brittle and shallow life and come to him. Realising this is her first and last chance of true love, Violetta brushes aside her misgivings and she and Alfredo go to live an idyllic life in the country, where Violetta's health seems to improve. Her happiness is shattered when, during Alfredo's absence on an errand, his father, Giorgio, arrives to see her. Germont tells her that her liaison with his son is bringing dishonour to his family and threatening his daughter's marriage prospects, and begs her to give him up. Under the weight of his arguments, the distraught and grief-stricken Violetta complies, and leaves without explanation. In the company of her former protector, Baron Douphol, to whom she has returned, Violetta attends a party given by Flora Bervoix where she encounters Alfredo. In his bitterness, he publicly insults her and she collapses. Violetta is now gravely ill and Germont, suffering remorse for the pain he has caused her, tells Alfredo the truth about her departure and gives his blessing to their relationship. Alfredo rushes to Violetta but, after a joyous embrace, she dies in her lover's arms. [R]

Treble

The unbroken voice of a child. It is most often used with reference to the male voice, and is thus sometimes called 'boy soprano'. Largely because a treble lacks the power and projection of a trained operatic voice, there are few major treble roles in opera; the most important are Miles in *The Turn of the Screw* and Amahl in *Amahl and the Night Visitors*.

Treigle, Norman *(1927–75)*

American bass, particularly associated with the title role in *Mefistofele*. Largely based at the New York City Opera, he was a magnificent singing-actor, both his powerful voice and his stage personality being highly individual. He created roles in *The Tender Land* and Ward's *The Crucible*, and, for Floyd, Olun Blitch in *Susannah* and the title roles in *The Passion of Jonathan Wade* and *Markheim*.

Tremolo (Italian for 'shaking')

In singing, another term for vibrato*.

Trial

A French term, named after the French tenor Antoine Trial (1736–95), which refers to a tenor more highly regarded for his dramatic abilities than for his singing.

Trial By Jury

Dramatic cantata in one act by Sullivan. 1st perf. London, 25 March 1875; libr. by W. S. Gilbert. Principal roles: Learned Judge (bar), Defendant (ten), Plaintiff (sop), Counsel for Plaintiff (bar), Usher (bass). The first surviving work of the Gilbert and Sullivan partnership, it is really a comic opera rather than an operetta as it is entirely through-composed. An instant success, which remains as fresh and delightful as ever, it has sometimes been regarded as Sullivan's masterpiece.

Plot: The Learned Judge hears a case for breach of promise of marriage between the Plaintiff Angelina and the Defendant Edwin. All in court make their partiality towards the Plaintiff abundantly clear, and eventually the Judge decides to marry her himself. [R]

Trieste

See Teatro Communale Giuseppe Verdi, Trieste

Trill

A vocal ornament, also called a 'shake', which consists of the rapid alternation of the written note with its adjacent one (usually the note above). Singers who have been especially renowned for their trill include Joan Sutherland and Selma Kurz.

Trillo

An obsolete vocal ornament, which consisted of a single note repeated with increasing rapidity.

Trimarchi, Domenico

Italian baritone, particularly associated with Italian buffo roles. One of the leading contemporary buffos, he has a good if not outstanding voice, abundant comic talents and phenomenal diction.

Tringles des sistres tintaient, Les

Mezzo aria for Carmen in Act II of Bizet's *Carmen*.

Trinke, Liebchen
Tenor aria for Alfred in Act I of
J. Strauss' *Die Fledermaus*.

Trio
In opera, a musical number for three
solo singers, with or without chorus.

Trionfai
Soprano cabaletta for Lady Macbeth in
Act II of the original 1847 version of
Verdi's *Macbeth*. It was cut in the
revised version and replaced by 'La
luce langue'.

Trionfi
A theatrical tryptych by Orff, which
comprises *Carmina Burana, Trionfo
d'Afrodite** and *Catulli Carmina*. Only
the second can be considered to be in
any way operatic.

Trionfo d'Afrodite (*Triumph of
Aphrodite*)
Scenic concerto by Orff. 1st perf.
Milan, 14 Feb 1953; libr. by the
composer, after Catullus, Euripides and
Sappho. The second panel of Orff's
tryptych *Trionfi*, it comprises various
scenes in praise of love and marriage.
[R]

Trionfo dell'Onore, Il (*The
Triumph of Honour*)
Opera in three acts by A. Scarlatti. 1st
perf. Naples, 26 Nov 1718; libr. by
F. A. Tullio. Scarlatti's only wholly
comic work, and the earliest surviving
Neapolitan comic opera, it is still
performed very occasionally. [R]

Triquet, Monsieur
Tenor role in Tchaikovsky's *Eugene
Onegin*. He is Tatyana's French tutor.

Tristan und Isolde
Opera in three acts by Wagner. 1st

perf. Munich, 10 June 1865; libr. by
the composer. Principal roles: Isolde
(sop), Tristan (ten), Brangäne (mezzo),
Kurwenal (bar), King Mark (bass),
Melot (bar). Wagner's most intense
music-drama, in which he takes
chromatic harmony to new limits, it
occupies a unique position both because
of its overwhelming emotional effect
and because of the enormous influence
which it exerted on the subsequent
development of music.
   Plot: Tristan, nephew to King Mark
of Cornwall, has been despatched to
fetch the Irish princess Isolde and bring
her back as a wife for Mark. Tristan
and Isolde had met previously, when he
slew her intended husband, and she
tended his wounds. Each fell in love
with the other; each kept silent,
believing their feelings unrequited. Now,
aboard the vessel from Ireland, they
resolve to end their separate sufferings
by taking poison. Knowing of this,
Isolde's faithful companion, Brangäne,
substitutes a love potion, and the
couple are overtaken by uncontrollable
passion. Once in Cornwall, the lovers
can only meet under cover of darkness
where, betrayed by the knight Melot,
they are discovered by King Mark.
Tristan is wounded by Melot and taken
home to his own kingdom by his loyal
esquire, Kurwenal. Isolde follows him,
arriving in time to join him in a mutual
embrace of death. [R]

Tristram, Sir
Bass-baritone role in Flotow's *Martha*.
He is Lady Harriet's ageing cousin and
suitor.

Trittico, Il (*The Tryptych*)
The title given by Puccini to his three
contrasting one-act operas *Il Tabarro**,
*Suor Angelica** and *Gianni Schicchi**.

Triumph Scene
The title usually given to the great

public scene (Act II, Scene II) of Verdi's
Aida.

Troilus and Cressida

Opera in three acts by Walton. 1st
perf. London, 3 Dec 1954; libr. by
Christopher Hassall, after Geoffrey
Chaucer. Revised version, 1st perf.
London, 12 Nov 1976. Principal roles:
Cressida (mezzo), Troilus (ten),
Diomede (bar), Pandarus (ten), Calkas
(bass), Evadne (mezzo), Antenor (bar).
Written in Walton's most lyrical and
romantic vein, it contains some of his
finest music, but for some reason is
only infrequently performed.

Plot: The High Priest Calkas wishes
his daughter Cressida to become a
priestess. However, she responds to the
love of Troilus, whose suit is pressed
with the help of her uncle Pandarus.
After Calkas's defection to the Greeks,
Cressida is exchanged for their prisoner
Antenor, and agrees to marriage with
Diomede. Troilus is stabbed in the back
by Calkas whilst he is fighting
Diomede. Cressida is ordered to remain
with the Greeks as a prostitute, but
kills herself over Troilus' body.

Trojans, The

See Troyens, Les

Trompeter von Säckingen, Der

Opera in four acts by Nessler. 1st perf.
Leipzig, 4 May 1884; libr. by Rudolf
Bunge, after von Scheffel. Principal
roles: Werner (ten), Maria (sop),
Damian (bar). Nessler's finest opera, it
was very successful in its time and is
still occasionally performed in
Germany.

Plot: Towards the end of the Thirty
Years' War, the trumpeter Werner falls
in love with the high-born Maria,
whose parents wish her to marry the
simpleton Damian. During an attack on
the city, Damian proves himself a
coward, whilst Werner behaves
heroically. The discovery of a birth-
mark on his arm shows that he is of
noble descent and all objections to his
marrying Maria are removed. [R]

Trouble in Tahiti

Opera in one act by Bernstein. 1st perf.
Waltham (Mass), 1 June 1952; libr. by
the composer. Principal roles: Dinah
(sop), Sam (ten). A satirical domestic
comedy about a bickering suburban
couple, Bernstein later incorporated it
into *A Quiet Place**. [R]

Trouser-role

A term used to describe a soprano or
mezzo singing a male role. Famous
trouser-roles include Cherubino, Oscar,
Octavian and Prince Orlofsky. The term
breeches-role is also used in Britain.

Trovatore, Il (*The Troubador*)

Opera in four acts by Verdi. 1st perf.
Rome, 19 Jan 1853; libr. by Salvatore
Cammarano (completed by Leone
Emanuele Bardare), after Antonio
García Gutiérrez's *El Trovador*.
Principal roles: Manrico (ten), Leonora
(sop), Conte di Luna (bar), Azucena
(mezzo), Ferrando (bass). The
apotheosis and epitome of Italian
romantic and melodramatic opera, it
was an instant success and has
remained one of the most popular of
all operas ever since. The libretto is a
by-word for obscurity and confusion,
but if the listener attends to Ferrando's
narration in the first scene and bears in
mind that the old gypsy Azucena is the
central character, the action becomes
more logical.

Plot: 15th-century Spain. The
troubador Manrico, leader of the rebel
army, is believed to be the son of the
gypsy Azucena. He loves Leonora, who
is also loved by the Conte di Luna,
who leads the King's army. Luna's men

capture Azucena and di Luna's commander Ferrando recognises her as the woman who caused the death of di Luna's brother. She is imprisoned and Manrico is captured during an attempt to rescue her. To secure Manrico's freedom, Leonora offers herself to di Luna, taking a slow poison after he has agreed. Realising that he has been tricked, di Luna has Manrico executed. Azucena reveals that the child who died years ago was her own, and that di Luna has just killed his own brother. [R]

Troyanos, Tatiana (b 1938)

American mezzo. An outstanding artist of great versatility, she possesses a rich, beautiful and flexible voice which she uses with musicianship and great intelligence. She has excelled in a wide range of music and styles, from Handel to Britten and from Bellini to Strauss. A powerful singing-actress, she created Jeanne des Anges in *The Devils of Loudun*.

Troyens, Les (The Trojans)

Opera in two parts (five acts) by Berlioz. Part One, *La Prise de Troie* (*The Capture of Troy*) 1st perf. Karlsruhe, 6 Dec 1890 (composed 1862); Part Two, *Les Troyens à Carthage* (*The Trojans at Carthage*) 1st perf. Paris, 4 Nov 1863. 1st complete uncut perf. in French London, 17 Sept 1969; libr. by the composer, after Virgil's *The Aeneid*. Principal roles: Aeneas (ten), Dido (mezzo), Cassandra (sop), Chorebus (bar), Anna (mezzo), Narbal (bass), Iopas (ten), Pantheus (bass), Ascanius (mezzo), Hylas (ten). Berlioz's masterpiece and one of the greatest of all French operas, it remained virtually unperformed for nearly a century, but has at last entered the repertory of most major opera houses. It is often split over two evenings (although its total length is

less than Wagner's longest works), but Berlioz intended it to be performed on a single evening, and it is that way in which it makes its greatest effect.

Plot: Troy and Carthage. After her lover Chorebus is killed in the sack of Troy, Cassandra leads the women in mass suicide, after foretelling that Aeneas will found a new Trojan kingdom in Italy. Aeneas and his followers are thrown ashore at Carthage, where he falls in love with Dido, to the distress of her sister Anna and her minister Narbal. Aeneas finally responds to the call of destiny and abandons Dido and sets out for Italy. Dido kills herself. [R]

Truelove

Roles in Stravinsky's *The Rake's Progress*: Anne (sop) and her father (bass).

Truffaldino

The Commedia dell'Arte figure appears in a number of operas, including: (1) Bass role in Strauss' *Ariadne auf Naxos*. (2) Tenor role in Prokofiev's *The Love of Three Oranges*. (3) Tenor role in Busoni's *Turandot*.

Tsar's Bride, The (Tsarskaya Nevesta)

Opera in three acts by Rimsky-Korsakov. 1st perf. Moscow, 3 Nov 1899; libr. by the composer and I. F. Tuymenev, after Lev Alexandrovich Mey's play. Principal roles: Marfa (sop), Grigory (bar), Ivan Lykov (ten), Lyubasha (mezzo). Still quite often performed in Russia, it is very little known elsewhere.

Plot: 16th-century Russia. Grigory Gryaznoy employs a love potion in his attempts to win the heart of the boyar Lykov's fiancée Marfa. The potion turns out to be a slow poison arranged by Grigory's former mistress Lyubasha. Ivan the Terrible choses Marfa as his wife, but she dies from the poison soon afterwards. Lyubasha confesses to the murder and is killed by Lykov. [R]

Tsar Sultan
See Tale of Tsar Sultan, The

Tu che la vanità
Soprano aria for Elisabetta in Act V of Verdi's *Don Carlos*.

Tucker, Richard *(b Rubin Ticker)* *(1913–75)*
American tenor, particularly associated with the Italian and French repertories. One of the finest of all American tenors, his full and strongly-projected voice was ideal for lyrico-dramatic roles, and was used with intelligence and unfailing musicianship. As the son of a Romanian Jew, his life's ambition was to sing Eléazer in *La Juive*, an ambition which was finally fulfilled in 1973.

Tudor Ring
A collective title which has occasionally been given in recent years to Donizetti's three operas set in Tudor England, *Anna Bolena*, *Maria Stuarda* and *Roberto Devereux*. They are sometimes given in cycle, but are in no way interconnected.

Tu qui Santuzza
Soprano/tenor duet for Santuzza and Turiddù in Mascagni's *Cavalleria Rusticana*.

Turandot
Works of this title based on Carlo Gozzi's play include:

(1) Opera in two acts by Busoni. 1st perf. Zürich, 11 May 1917; libr. by the composer. Principal roles: Turandot (sop), Calaf (ten), Barak (bar), Adelma (mezzo), Truffaldino (ten). A taut and economical setting, it has been much admired by musicians, but is very rarely performed.

(2) Opera in three acts by Puccini. 1st perf. Milan, 25 April 1926; libr. by Renato Simone and Giuseppe Adami. Principal roles: Turandot (sop), Calaf (ten), Liù (sop), Timur (bass), Ping (bar), Pang (ten), Pong (ten). Puccini's last opera, and usually regarded as his masterpiece, it was left unfinished at his death and was completed by Alfano. It is notable for the exotic richness of its orchestration and for providing one of the most severely demanding of all Italian dramatic soprano roles.

Plot: Legendary China. Turandot, the cruel Princess of Peking, will wed the man who can answer her three riddles; anyone who fails must die. The unknown prince (Calaf), accompanied by his father Timur and the slave-girl Liù who loves him, arrives and accepts the challenge. He guesses the riddles correctly and when Turandot is reluctant to marry him, gives her a day to discover his name whereupon he will sacrifice his life. Turandot threatens to torture the name out of Liù, but she kills herself rather than betray Calaf. Finally, Calaf melts Turandot's resistance with a kiss and tells her his name. Accepting him, she announces that his name is 'love'. [R]

Turco in Italia, Il *(The Turk in Italy)*
Comic opera in two acts by Rossini. 1st perf. Milan, 14 Aug 1814; libr. by Felice Romani, after Caterino Mazzolà's libretto for Süssmayr. Principal roles: Prosdocimo (bar), Fiorilla (sop), Don Narciso (ten), Selim (bass), Zaida (mezzo), Don Geronio (bass), Albazar (ten).

A quasi-Pirandellian story of a poet manipulating stock comic characters, it is a delightful work, which has been regularly performed in the last 20 years.

Plot: 18th-century Naples. The poet Prosdocimo is in search of a plot for an opera. He comes up with a story of intrigue, disguises and misunderstandings involving Fiorilla, her admirer Don Narciso, her boring husband Geronio, Selim, a visiting Turk to whom Fiorilla is attracted, and Selim's old love, Zaida. [R]

Turiddù

Tenor role in Mascagni's *Cavalleria Rusticana*. Mamma Lucia's son, he is a soldier loved by Santuzza.

Turin

See Teatro Regio, Turin

Turina, Joaquín *(1882–1949)*

Spanish composer. He wrote four stage works: the zarzuela *Fea y con Grazia* (1904; libr. S. and J. Álvarez Quintero) and the operas *Margot* (1914; libr. M. Sierra), *La Adúltera Penitente* (1917; libr. Moreto) and *Jardín de Oriente* (1923; libr. Sierra).

Turkish opera composers

These include Kemal Reşit Rey (*b* 1904), Muglis Sabahattin (1890–1947) and Adnan Saygun (*b* 1907). *See also* Armenian opera composers

Turner, Dame Eva *(b 1892)*

British soprano, particularly associated with Wagner and heavier Verdi roles and especially with Turandot. Arguably the greatest dramatic soprano produced by Britain, she possessed a voice of great range and awesome power and had a keen dramatic sense. She was

also a distinguished teacher, whose pupils included Amy Shuard and Rita Hunter.

Turn of the Screw, The

Opera in prologue and two acts by Britten (Op 54). 1st perf. Venice, 14 Sept 1954; libr. by Myfanwy Piper, after Henry James' novella. Principal roles: Governess (sop), Peter Quint (ten), Miles (treble), Flora (sop), Mrs Grose (mezzo), Miss Jessel (sop), Prologue (ten). Britten's tautest opera, it is a work of great musical and structural complexity, achieved with the most economical of means and resources. One of the greatest of all postwar operas, it is a deeply disturbing work (summed up by the interpolated lines "the ceremony of innocence is drowned"), which can have an overwhelming effect in the theatre.

Plot: 19th-century England. The Governess arrives at the country house of Bly to take sole charge of the children Miles and Flora. She becomes convinced that the ghosts of two former servants, Quint and her predecessor and Quint's mistress, Miss Jessel, are attempting to corrupt the children. She determines to do battle with them and save the children's souls. Eventually, Flora is sent away in the care of the housekeeper Mrs Grose, but Miles dies from the strain imposed on him by the conflicting demands of the Governess and Quint. [R]

Turp, André *(b 1925)*

Canadian tenor, particularly associated with the French and Italian repertories. He possessed a warm lyric tenor voice, used with considerable style, and had a good stage presence. A much underrated singer.

Tu sul labbro
Bass aria for Zaccaria in Act II of Verdi's *Nabucco*.

Tutor
Bass role in Rossini's *Le Comte Ory*. He is Ory's long-suffering teacher.

Tutte le feste
Soprano/baritone duet for Gilda and Rigoletto in Act II of Verdi's *Rigoletto*.

Tutto nel mondo è burla
The great comic fugue which ends Act III of Verdi's *Falstaff*.

Twelve-tone operas
Twelve-tone describes a style of composition in which all 12 notes of the octave (on a piano the five black and seven white notes) are treated as equal, in other words they are subjected to an ordered relationship which establishes no 'hierarchy' of notes, unlike the traditional major/minor key system. Originally developed at the beginning of the 20th century by Schönberg as a standardisation of atonal music, the style has since also been employed alongside the traditional key system. Many twelve-tone operas have been written, the first being Schönberg's *Von Heute auf Morgen*. The system is also known as 'serial composition', from the note-row or 'series' in which all 12 notes are placed in a particular predetermined order as the structural basis of the work.

Twilight (*Daisi*)
Opera in three acts by Paliashvili. 1st perf. Tbilsi, 19 Dec 1923; libr. by V. Guniya. Principal roles: Maro (sop), Malkhaz (ten), Nano (mezzo), Kiazo (bar), Tsangala (bass). One of the earliest and finest operas by a Georgian composer, it is unknown outside Russia.

Plot: Maro is engaged to the soldier Kiazo, but is in love with Malkhaz. When Malkhaz returns from abroad, Tsangala informs Kiazo of their relationship. Kiazo vows to be avenged, but is summoned to war to defend his country. He returns, however, and when Maro rejects him, he kills Malkhaz out of jealousy.

Twilight of the Gods
See Götterdämmerung

Two Widows, The (*Dvě Vodvy*)
Comic opera in two acts by Smetana. 1st perf. Prague, 27 March 1874; libr. by Emanuel Züngel, after Félicien Mallefille's *Les Deux Veuves*. Revised version, 1st perf. Prague, 15 March 1878. Principal roles: Karolina (sop), Anežka (sop), Ladislav (ten), Mumlal (bass), Toník (ten), Lidka (sop). Smetana's lightest opera, described as a conversation piece, it is still regularly performed in Czechoslovakia, but is almost unknown elsewhere.

Plot: Ladislav succeeds in meeting his old love Anežka, now a widow, by the expedient of having himself arrested for poaching by the gamekeeper Mumlal on the estate of Anežka's cousin Karolina. Anežka initially rebuffs his advances, but urged on by Karolina they are finally united. [R]

Tytania
Soprano role in Britten's *A Midsummer Night's Dream*. Oberon's wife, she is the queen of the fairies.

Uberto

Bass-baritone role in Pergolesi's *La Serva Padrona*. He is the master of the house, tricked into marrying his servant.

Udite, udite o rustici

Bass aria for Dr Dulcamara in Act I of Donizetti's *L'Elisir d'Amore*.

Ugo Conte di Parigi (*Hugo Count of Paris*)

Opera in two acts by Donizetti. 1st perf. Milan, 13 March 1832; libr. by Felice Romani. Principal roles: Ugo (ten), Bianca (sop), Falco (bar), Emma (sop), Luigi (mezzo). Reasonably successful at its appearance, it is nowadays almost never performed.

Plot: 10th-century Paris. Wishing the French crown to go to his own house of Anjou, Falco plans to provoke rivalry between the famous soldier Ugo and the newly-crowned King Louis V, but Ugo remains loyal to Louis. Louis' betrothed, Bianca, hates her fiancé and secretly loves Ugo, as also does her sister Adelia. Ugo and Adelia become engaged, but the jealous Bianca declares her own love for Ugo. Louis, believing Ugo disloyal, has him arrested. Ugo resists Bianca's request for him to lead a revolt against Louis, but his troops start it without him. Ugo puts down the revolt and Louis is convinced of his loyalty. Ugo and Adelia are married, and the sound of the celebrations drives the outraged Bianca to take poison. [R]

Uhde, Hermann (1914–65)

German bass-baritone, particularly associated with Wagnerian roles, especially the Dutchman. A fine singing-actor with a powerful and incisive voice, he created Creon in Orff's *Antigonae* and Elis in Wagner-Régeny's *Das Bergwerk zu Falun*. He died on stage in Copenhagen during a performance of Bentzon's *Faust III*.

Ukrainian opera composers

See Dankevich; Lysenko

Other national opera composers include Nikolai Arkas (1853–1904), Semyon Gulak-Artemovsky (1813–73), Yuly Meytus (*b* 1903), Pyotr Sokalsky (1832–87) and Natal Vakhnyanin (1841–1908).

Ulfung, Ragnar (*b* 1927)

Norwegian tenor, particularly associated with German character roles. A versatile singing-actor with a wide-ranging repertory, he sang Gustavus III in Göran Gentele's controversial production of *Un Ballo in Maschera* and Monostatos in Bergman's film of *Die Zauberflöte*. He was also especially identified with the roles of Herod and Mime. He created the Blind Man in Blomdahl's *Aniara*, the title role in Maxwell Davies's *Taverner* and Christopher in Werle's *The Journey*. He has also produced a number of operas.

Ulisse (*Ulysses*)

Works of this title about the mythical Greek hero include:

(1) Opera in prologue and five acts by Rebel. 1st perf. Paris, 23 Jan 1703; libr. by H. Guichard.

(2) Opera in prologue, two acts and epilogue by Dallapiccola. 1st perf.

Berlin, 29 Sept 1968; libr. by the composer, after Homer's *The Odyssey*. Principal roles: Ulisse (bar), Nausicaa (sop), Circe/Melanto (mezzo), Telemaco (c-ten or mezzo), Demodoco/Tiresio (ten), Calypso/Penelope (sop), Eumete (ten). Dallapiccola's last and most ambitious opera, it deals with Ulysses' return to Ithaca after the Trojan War with some of his adventures told in flashbacks.

Ullmann, Viktor *(1898–1944)*

Czech composer. A pupil of Schönberg, he is best known for his powerful *Der Kaiser von Atlantis**, written in a Nazi concentration camp. His two other operas are *Peer Gynt* (libr. after Henrik Ibsen) and *Der Sturtz des Antichrists* (1935; libr. Albert Steffens). He was murdered by the Nazis in Auschwitz.

Ulm Stadttheater

The present opera house (cap. 815) in this German town in Baden-Württemberg opened in October 1969, replacing the previous theatre built in 1781 but destroyed by bombs in 1944. Musical directors have included Robert Heger and Herbert von Karajan.

Ulrica

Contralto role in: (1) Verdi's *Un Ballo in Maschera*. Madame Arvidson in the Swedish setting, she is a fortune-teller. (2) Sullivan's *Ivanhoe*.

Un

Titles beginning with this form of the French, Italian and Spanish indefinite article are listed under the letter of the first main word. For example, *Un Ballo in Maschera* is listed under B.

Una

Titles beginning with the feminine form of the Italian and Spanish indefinite

article are listed under the letter of the first main word. For example, *Una Cosa Rara* is listed under C.

Undine

Works of this title, all based on Friedrich de la Motte Fouqué's *Ondine* and dealing with the water-spirit of central European legend, include:

(1) Opera in three acts by E. T. A. Hoffmann. 1st perf. Berlin, 3 Aug 1816; libr. by the composer. Hoffmann's most successful opera, nowadays forgotten, it contains some striking prefigurements of the German romantic school.

(2) Opera in four acts by Lortzing. 1st perf. Magdeburg, 21 April 1845; libr. by the composer. Principal roles: Undine (sop), Hugo (ten), Kühleborn (bar), Veit (ten), Berthalda (sop), Tobias (bass). One of Lortzing's best works, it is still sometimes performed in Germany but is virtually unknown elsewhere.

Plot: Hugo falls in love with the nymph Undine, although his esquire Veit warns her father the water spirit, Kühleborn, that Hugo may desert Undine for Berthalda, who is discovered to be the daughter of Undine's foster-father Tobias. Berthalda seduces Hugo and Undine returns to her own land. Hugo is unable to forget Undine and when Veit opens a sealed well she emerges from it to take Hugo to her own kingdom as her husband. [R]

(3) Opera in three acts by Tchaikovksy. Composed 1869; libr. by V. Sollogub, after Vasily Zhukovsky's translation of Fouqué. Tchaikovsky abandoned the work after it was rejected for performance and only fragments of it survive.

Une

Titles beginning with the feminine form of the French indefinite article are listed

UNFINISHED OPERAS

Many composers have left operas or operettas unfinished, either because of their death or simply because they lost interest in the work. The state of completion of such works varies enormously and often provides musicologists with severe problems. Some, such as Elgar's *The Spanish Lady*, amount to little more than sketches. Others, such as Weber's *Die Drei Pintos* or Mozart's *Zaïde*, contain a considerable amount of finished work. Others again, such as Offenbach's *Les Contes d'Hoffmann* or Puccini's *Turandot*, are all but complete. Below are listed unfinished works by composers with entries in this dictionary; the completor or editor of the work is also given where applicable.

Composer	Work	Completor/Editor
Alfano	*I Cavalieri e la Bella*	
Bellini	*Ernani*	
Benjamin	*Tartuffe*	
Berg	*Lulu*	Friedrich Cerha
Berkeley	*Faldon Park*	
Berlioz	*Les Francs Juges*	
Berwald	*Gustaf Vasa*	
Bizet	*La Coupe du Roi de Thulé*	
	Don Rodrigue	
Blodek	*Zítek*	
Blomdahl	*The Tale of the Big Computer*	
Boito	*Nerone*	Toscanini & Vincenzo Tommasini
Borodin	*Mlada*	
	Prince Igor	Glazunov & Rimsky-Korsakov
	The Tsar's Bride	
Busoni	*Doktor Faust*	Philipp Jarnach
Castro	*Cosecha Negra*	Eduardo Ogando
Chabrier	*Fisch-Ton-Kan*	
	Briséïs	
	Jean Hunyade	
	Vaucochard et Fils Premier	
Cherubini	*Marguerite d'Anjou*	
Cornelius	*Gunlöd*	Carl Hoffbauer

Composer	Work	Completor/Editor
Dargomijsky	*The Stone Guest*	Cui & Rimsky-Korsakov
Debussy	*La Chûte de la Maison Usher*	W. Harwood
	Rodrigue et Chimène	Richard Langham Smith
Delibes	*Kassya*	Massenet
Donizetti	*L'Ange de Nisida*	
	Le Duc d'Albe	Matteo Salvi
	Ne M'Oubliez-Pas	
Elgar	*The Spanish Lady*	
De Falla	*L'Atlántida*	Ernesto Halffter
Franck	*Ghisèle*	Chausson, d'Indy & 3 others
Götz	*Francesca von Rimini*	Ernst Frank
Gounod	*Maître Pierre*	
Grieg	*Olav Trygvason*	
Guiraud	*Frédégonde*	Saint-Saëns & Dukas
Hadjibeyov	*Firuza*	
Halévy	*Noé*	Bizet
Hérold	*Ludovic*	Halévy
Kálmán	*Arizona Lady*	Charles Kálmán
Karel	*The Taming of the Shrew*	
	Three Hairs of an Old Wise Man	Zbyněk Vostřák
Lalo	*La Jacquerie*	Arthur Coquard
Leoncavallo	*La Maschera Nuda*	S. Allegri
Martinů	*La Plainte Contre Inconnu*	
	Le Semaine de Bonté	
Mendelssohn	*Loreley*	
Monpou	*Lambert Simnel*	Adam
Moussorgsky	*Khovanschina*	Rimsky-Korsakov
	The Marriage	Ippolitov-Ivanov
	Salammbô	Zoltán Peskó
	Sorochintsy Fair	Tcherepnin
Mozart	*L'Oca del Cairo*	
	Lo Sposo Deluso	
	Zaïde	Anton André

Composer	Work	Completor/Editor
Offenbach	*Les Contes d'Hoffmann*	Guiraud
Ostrčil	*Cymbelin* *The Fishermen*	
Pijper	*Merlijn*	
Pizzetti	*Gigliola*	
Ponchielli	*I Mori di Venezia*	Arturo Cadore
Prokofiev	*Maddalena*	Edward Downes
Puccini	*Turandot*	Alfano
Rabaud	*Les Jeux de l'Amour et du Hasard*	Busser & d'Ollone
Rachmaninov	*Monna Vanna*	
Rameau	*Les Boréades*	John Eliot Gardiner
Rangström	*Gilgamesj*	J. Fernström
Rousseau	*Daphnis et Chloé*	
Schönberg	*Moses und Aron*	
Schubert	*Die Bürgschaft* *Der Graf von Gleichen* *Der Spiegelritter* *Die Zauberharfe*	
Schumann	*Der Korsar*	
Serov	*The Power of Evil*	Nikolai Solovyov
Shostakovich	*The Gamblers*	
Smetana	*Viola*	
Stanford	*The Miner of Falun*	
Sullivan	*The Emerald Isle*	German
A. G. Thomas	*Don Braggadocio*	
Usandizaga	*La Llama*	Ramón Usandizaga
Weber	*Die Drei Pintos* *Rübezahl*	Mahler
Wolf	*Manuel Venegas*	
Zandonai	*Il Bacio*	
Zimmermann	*Medea*	

under the letter of the first main word. For example, *Une Education Manquée* is listed under E.

Unfinished operas
See panel on page 591

Unger, Caroline *(b Ungher)* *(1803–77)*

Hungarian mezzo with a very wide range which also allowed her to sing soprano. She is famous in musical history for having turned round the deaf Beethoven at the end of the first performance of the Choral Symphony so that he could see the acclaim. One of the greatest singing-actresses of the 19th century, she created Bianca in Mercadante's *Le Due Illustri Rivali*, Isoletta in Bellini's *La Straniera* and, for Donizetti, Marietta in *Il Borgomastro di Saardam*, Antonina in *Belisario* and the title roles in *Maria de Rudenz* and *Parisina*. Rossini described her as possessing "a southern ardour, a northern energy, lungs of bronze, a voice of silver and a talent of gold". Her most famous role was Lucrezia Borgia, described by Chorley as being "of serpentine and deep malevolence, subtly veiled at the moment when its most diabolical works were on foot".

Unger, Gerhard *(b 1916)*

German tenor, particularly associated with German character roles, especially Pedrillo and David. A fine singing-actor, he had a far better voice than most German character tenors, which he used with musicianship and intelligence.

United States of America

See American Opera Society; Baltimore Civic Opera; Caramoor Festival; Chicago Lyric Opera; Cincinnati Opera Association; Dallas Civic Opera; Houston Grand Opera Association; Kansas City Lyric Theater; Lincoln Center for the Performing Arts; Los Angeles Music Center Opera; Metropolitan Opera, New York; New Orleans Opera House Association; New York City Opera; Opera Company of Boston; Opera Guild of Greater Miami; Opera Society of Washington; Philadelphia Opera Company; San Diego Opera Guild; San Francisco Opera Association; Santa Fe Opera; Seattle Opera Association; Virginia Opera Association

Unterbrochene Opferfest, Das *(The Interrupted Sacrifice)*

Opera in two acts by Winter. 1st perf. Vienna, 14 June 1796; libr. by F. Xavier Huber. Winter's most successful work, in German-speaking countries it was one of the most popular of all operas in the early 19th century. It is now forgotten.

Upfold, Mr

Tenor role in Britten's *Albert Herring*. He is the mayor of Loxford.

Uppman, Theodore *(b 1920)*

American baritone, particularly associated with the roles of Pelléas and Papageno. A fine singing-actor with a handsome stage appearance, he created the title role in *Billy Budd* and roles in Floyd's *The Passion of Jonathan Wade*, Villa-Lobos' *Yerma*, Pasatieri's *Black Widow* and Bernstein's *A Quiet Place*.

Urbain

Mezzo trouser-role in Meyerbeer's *Les Huguenots*. He is the Queen's page.

Urna fatale

Baritone aria for Don Carlo in Act III of Verdi's *La Forza del Destino*.

Ursule

Mezzo role in Berlioz's *Béatrice et Bénédict*. She is Héro's companion.

Ursuleac, Viorica *(1894–1985)*

Romanian soprano, particularly associated with Strauss roles, for which Strauss himself considered her lyrico-dramatic voice ideal. She created Maria in *Friedenstag*, the title role in *Arabella*, the Countess in *Capriccio* and roles in Křenek's *Der Diktator* and D'Albert's *Mister Wu*. She was married to the conductor Clemens Krauss*.

Uruguayan opera composers
These include Vicente Ascone (1897–1979), Alfonso Broqua (1867–1946), Eduardo Fabini (1883–1950), Carlos Pedrell (1878–1941), Juarés Lamarque Pons (*b* 1917) and Ramón Rodríguez Socas (1886–1957).

Usandizaga, José María
(1887–1915)
Spanish composer. One of the leading Basque composers, he wrote three operas: *Mendi-Mendiyan* (*High in the Mountains*, Bilbao 1910), *Los Golondrinas* (*The Swallows*, Madrid 1914; libr. G. Martínez Sierra, after his *Teatro del Ensueño*) [R], his most successful work, and *La Llama* (*The Flame*, San Sebastián 1915; libr. Martínez Sierra), which was completed after his death by his brother Ramón.

USSR
See Baku Opera and Ballet Theatre; Bolshoi Opera; Kirov Opera; Tiflis Opera and Ballet Theatre

Ustinov, Peter *(b 1921)*
British actor, writer, producer and designer, great-nephew of the designer Alexandre Benois*. His main contribution to opera has been as a producer; he has directed operas at Covent Garden, the Hamburg State Opera, the Paris Opéra and the Edinburgh Festival. In addition, he is the narrator on Decca's recording of Kodály's *Háry János*.

Uthal
Opera in one act by Méhul. 1st perf. Paris, 17 May 1806; libr. by J. M. B. Bins de Saint-Victor, "in imitation of Ossian*". Successful at its appearance, it is nowadays virtually forgotten, but is notable for Méhul's extraordinary effect of totally omitting violins from the orchestra so as to produce a dark and 'Ossianic' colour.

Utopia Limited
or The Flowers of Progress
Operetta in two acts by Sullivan. 1st perf. London, 7 Oct 1893; libr. by W. S. Gilbert. Principal roles: King Paramount (bar), Princess Zara (sop), Scaphio (bar), Phantis (b-bar), Capt Fitzbattleaxe (ten), Lady Sophy (mezzo), Mr Goldbury (bar), Nekaya (sop), Kalyba (mezzo), Tarara (ten), Lord Drameleigh (bar), Capt Corcoran (bass), Sir Bailey Barre (ten), Mr Blushington (bass). A brilliant satire on British capitalism and imperialism, the score is notable for the famous Christie Minstrels scene in which Sullivan succeeds in making the orchestral strings sound like banjos. Partly because of its large cast and lavish scenes, it is only intermittently performed.

Plot: Utopia (South Pacific). The Anglophile King Paramount is in theory an absolute despot but, in practice, is watched over by the wise men Scaphio and Phantis, who control his actions (even forcing him to write the scandal sheet 'The Palace Peeper') and if he disobeys them will denounce him to the Public Exploder Tarara. His daughter Zara, who has been educated at Girton, returns with six Flowers of Progress, led by Capt Fitzbattleaxe, with whom she is in love, and the company promoter Mr Goldbury. These representatives of England's greatness proceed to remodel Utopia on English principles, but take those principles far further than in England itself. Paramount registers his crown and country under the Limited Liability Act. The King loves Lady Sophy, governess to his younger daughters Nekaya and Kalyba. She rebuffs him because of the scandalous allegations of 'The Palace Peeper', but accepts him when he explains the way he is controlled by the wise men. The English reforms all prove far too successful and Utopia becomes 'swamped by dull prosperity' and rises in revolt at the instigation of Scaphio and Phantis. Zara remembers the one ingredient which she had omitted to introduce: a proper state of political chaos can only be achieved by having government by party. This is adopted, Scaphio and Phantis are foiled, and Utopia becomes a limited monarchy rather than a Monarchy Limited. [R]

Uttini, Francesco *(1723–95)*
Italian composer, largely resident in Sweden. He wrote 17 operas, mostly Metastasian opera serias, beginning with *Alessandro nell'Indie* (Genoa 1743). A number met with considerable success in his day but are all now forgotten. They include *L'Isola Disabitata* (Drottningholm 1755), *Il Re Pastore* (Drottningholm 1755), *Psyché* (Drottningholm 1766; libr. Philippe Quinault, after Molière), *Thetis och Pelée* (Stockholm 18 Jan 1733; libr. J. Wellander, after B. Fontenelle), which was the first major opera written to a Swedish libretto, and *Aline Queen of Golconda* (*Aline, Drottning uti Golconda*, Stockholm 11 Jan 1776; libr. C. B. Zibet, after Jean-Marie Sedaine).

Vaccai, Nicola *(1790–1848)*

Italian composer. His first opera *Il Solitario di Scozia* (Naples 18 Feb 1815; libr. Andrea Leone Tottola, after Giovanni da Gamerra) was followed by 16 others, largely Rossinian in style. They include *Il Lupo d'Ostenda* (Venice 17 June 1818; libr. Bartolomeo Merelli), *Bianca di Messina* (Turin 20 Jan 1826; libr. L. Piossasco), *Giovanna d'Arco* (Venice 17 Feb 1827; libr. Gaetano Rossi, after Friedrich von Schiller's *Die Jungfrau von Orleans*), *Giovanna Grey* (Milan 23 Feb 1834; libr. Carlo Pepoli), *Marco Visconti* (Turin 27 Jan 1838; libr. L. Toccagni) and *Virginia* (Rome 14 Jan 1845; libr. C. Giuliani). Many of his operas were considerable successes in their day, but nowadays only his masterpiece *Giulietta e Romeo** is at all remembered.

Vada in fiamme

Baritone cabaletta for Macbeth in Act III of the original 1847 version of Verdi's *Macbeth*. Verdi's most powerful baritone cabaletta, it was cut in the revised version and replaced by the duet 'Ora di morte'.

V'adoro pupille

Soprano aria for Cleopatra in Act I of Handel's *Giulio Cesare*.

Vainement ma bien-aimée

Tenor aria (the Aubade) for Mylio in Act III of Lalo's *Le Roi d'Ys*.

Vakula the Blacksmith

Opera in four acts by Tchaikovsky (Op 14). 1st perf. St Petersburg, 6 Dec 1876; libr. by Yakov Polonsky, after Nikolai Gogol's *Christmas Eve*. Revised version, *The Little Slippers* (*Cherevichki*) 1st perf. Moscow, 31 Jan 1887. Principal roles: Solokha (mezzo), Devil (bar), Vakula (ten), Oxana (sop), Chub (bass), Panas (ten), Mayor (bass), Schoolteacher (ten). It is only very rarely performed outside Russia. For plot see *Christmas Eve*. [R]

Va! laisse les couleurs

Mezzo aria for Charlotte in Act III of Massenet's *Werther*.

Valdegno, Giuseppe *(b 1914)*

Italian baritone, particularly associated with the Italian repertory, especially Verdi. Toscanini's favourite baritone in his later years, he was a rich-voiced and intelligent singing-actor. He created Alfieri in Rossellini's *Uno Sguardo dal Ponte*. He played Antonio Scotti in the film *The Great Caruso*, and his reminiscence of Toscanini, *Ho Cantato con Toscanini*, was published in 1962.

Valencienne

Soprano role in Lehár's *Die Lustige Witwe*. She is the 'highly respectable wife' of the Pontevedrian Ambassador. The role is sometimes sung by a mezzo.

Valentin

Baritone role in Gounod's *Faust*. He is Marguerite's soldier brother.

Valentine

Soprano role in Meyerbeer's *Les Huguenots*. She is Saint-Bris' daughter.

Valentini-Terrani, Lucia
(b 1948)
Italian mezzo, particularly associated
with the Italian repertory, especially
Rossini. The leading contemporary
Italian coloratura mezzo, she has a rich,
creamy and agile voice used with
musicianship and a fine technique, and
a good stage presence.

Valkyrie, The
See Walküre, Die

Valletti, Cesare *(b 1922)*
Italian tenor, particularly associated
with Mozart, Donizetti and Rossini
roles. A stylish and elegant singer of
scrupulous good taste, he had a
smallish but beautiful voice of
considerable agility and a good stage
presence.

Vallin, Ninon *(1886–1961)*
French soprano, particularly associated
with the French repertory. The leading
French soprano of the inter-war period,
she was a sensitive and versatile singer
with a warm voice of considerable
power and range. She created roles in
operas by d'Erlanger and Leroux.

Vallon sonore
Tenor aria for Hylas in Act V of
Berlioz's *Les Troyens*.

Valverde, Joaquín *(1846–1910)*
Spanish composer. He wrote over 30
zarzuelas, of which the most successful
were *Salón Eslava*, *La Boda de Serafín*
and *La Gran Vía* (Madrid 2 July 1886)
[R], which was written in collaboration
with Chueca. His son Sanjuan (1875–
1918) was also a composer. Perhaps
the most prolific of all zarzuela
composers, he wrote his first work *Con
las de Caín* at the age of 15, and went
on to write a further 250. The most
successful included *El Gran Capitán*
and *El Mirlo Blanco*.

Valzacchi
Tenor role in Richard Strauss' *Der
Rosenkavalier*. Annina's accomplice, he
is an Italian schemer.

Vampyr, Der *(The Vampire)*
Opera in two acts by Marschner (Op
42). 1st perf. Leipzig, 29 March 1828;
libr. by Wilhelm August Wöhlbruck,
after John Polidori's *The Vampyre*.
Principal roles: Sir Ruthven (ten),
Janthe (sop), Emmy (sop), Aubry (bar),
Malvina (sop). One of Marschner's
finest works, even if heavily indebted to
Weber, it was very popular throughout
the 19th century and is still performed
occasionally in Germany.

Plot: The Scottish nobleman Ruthven
has become a vampire. The Devil will
claim his soul unless he sacrifices three
young maidens. His first victim is
Janthe, but he himself is killed. With
the help of Aubry, to whom he reveals
his secret, he is resuscitated in the
moonlight. His second victim is the
vampire-fascinated Emmy. Finally, he
attempts to kill Aubry's fiancée
Malvina, but is denounced by Aubry
just as the clock strikes to mark the
end of his period of respite. He
descends back to Hell.

Van
Names which contain this prefix are
listed under the letter of the main
surname. For example, Richard van
Allan is listed under A.

Vancouver Opera Association
Founded in 1961, it gives an annual
season from October to May at the
Queen Elizabeth Theater (cap. 2,800).

Artistic directors have included Irving Guttman, Anton Guadagno and Richard Bonynge.

Vanda

Opera in five acts by Dvořák (Op 25). 1st perf. Prague, 17 April 1876; libr. by V. B. Šumavský, after J. Šurzycki. Revised 1879 and 1883. Dvořák's first mature opera, it is hardly ever performed, even in Czechoslovakia. [R]

Vaness, Carol (b 1952)

American soprano, particularly associated with Verdi and Mozart roles, especially Vitellia. One of the finest American sopranos of the younger generation, she possesses a rich and beautiful voice used with fine musicianship and has a good stage presence.

Vanessa

Opera in four acts by Barber (Op 32). 1st perf. New York, 15 Jan 1958; libr. by Gian-Carlo Menotti. Principal roles: Vanessa (sop), Anatol (ten), Erika (mezzo), Old Countess (cont), Doctor (bass). Barber's finest opera, it is written in a lush and readily accessible late romantic style.

Plot: Northern Europe, c 1905. Vanessa has waited for 20 years for her lover to return. His son, Anatol, arrives and informs her that her lover is dead. Anatol seduces Vanessa's niece Erika, but eventually marries Vanessa and goes to Paris to live with her. Erika realises that she must now relive Vanessa's long vigil. [R]

Vanna Lupa

Opera in three acts by Pizzetti. 1st perf. Florence, 4 May 1949; libr. by the composer. Principal roles: Vanna Ricci (mezzo), Vieri (ten). A work which contrasts the political ambition and thirst for revenge of a woman (nicknamed Lupa) with her son's passion for freedom, it met with some success at its appearance, but is nowadays all but forgotten.

Vanni-Marcoux

See Marcoux, Vanni

Vanya

(1) Mezzo trouser-role in Glinka's A Life for the Tsar. He is Ivan's foster-son. (2) Tenor role in Janáček's Káťa Kabanová. A student, he is in love with Varvara.

Vanzo, Alain (b 1928)

French tenor, particularly associated with the French repertory. Virtually the only French tenor of international standing of the postwar era, he had a clean lyric voice, which was used with style, intelligence and musicianship.

Va, pensiero

Chorus of Hebrew exiles in Act III of Verdi's Nabucco. Possibly the most famous of all operatic choruses.

Varady, Julia (b 1941)

Romanian soprano, particularly associated with Mozart, Verdi and Strauss roles. An accomplished singing-actress with a rich, beautiful and intelligently used voice, she created Cordelia in Reimann's Lear. Married to the baritone Dietrich Fischer-Dieskau*.

Varesi, Felice (1813–89)

Italian baritone. One of the leading Italian baritones of the mid-19th century, he created Antonio in Linda di Chamounix, the title roles in Macbeth and Rigoletto and Giorgio Germont in La Traviata, which he considered unworthy of him. His daughter Elena Boccabadati (1844–1920) was a successful soprano.

Varlaam

Bass role in Moussorgsky's *Boris Godunov*. He is an itinerant monk.

Várnay, Astrid *(b 1918)*

German soprano and later mezzo, particularly associated with Wagner and Strauss roles, especially Elektra. A powerful and intense singing-actress, who enjoyed a remarkably long career, she had a gleaming voice of great power and range, even if its production was occasionally a little uneven. She turned to mezzo roles in 1962 with equal success. She created Telea in Menotti's *The Island God*, the Grandmother in Banfield's *Lord Byron's Love-Letter* and Jocasta in Orff's *Oedipus der Tyrann*. Married to the conductor Hermann Weigert.

Varney, Louis *(1844–1908)*

French composer. He wrote 37 operettas, of which only the second, *Les Mousquetaires au Couvent**, is still remembered today.

Varvara

Mezzo role in Janáček's *Káťa Kabanová*. She is a foster-child in the Kabanov household.

Varviso, Silvio *(b 1924)*

Swiss conductor, particularly associated with the Italian and German repertories. He was musical director of the Basel Stadttheater (1958–62), the Royal Opera, Stockholm (1965–71), the Stuttgart Opera (1972–79) and the Paris Opéra (1980–81).

Vasco da Gama

Tenor role in Meyerbeer's *L'Africaine*. He is the historical Portuguese explorer (c 1469–1524).

Vašek

Tenor role in Smetana's *The Bartered Bride*. He is Mícha's shy son who eventually joins the circus troupe.

Vasto teatro

Bass aria for Alidoro in Act I of Rossini's *La Cenerentola*.

Vaudeville

A French term which, in opera, refers to a style of finale in which each character sings a verse in turn, followed by a general refrain. The best known examples are the finales of *Die Entführung aus dem Serail* and *Il Barbiere di Siviglia*.

Vaughan, Elizabeth *(b 1936)*

British soprano, particularly associated with Verdi and Puccini roles, especially Cio-Cio-San. One of the finest British lyrico-spinto sopranos of recent years, she had a fine and intelligently used voice and a strong stage presence.

Vaughan Williams, Dr Ralph *(1872–1958)*

British composer. His six operas, although for some strange reason only infrequently performed nowadays, have done much to assist the revival of British opera in the 20th century. *The Shepherds of the Delectable Mountains* (London 11 July 1922; libr. composer, after John Bunyan's *The Pilgrim's Progress*) was followed by the ballad opera *Hugh the Drover**, the Shakespearean *Sir John in Love** and the powerful one-act *Riders to the Sea**, arguably his operatic masterpiece. The comedy *The Poisoned Kiss** was less successful. Vaughan Williams set greatest store by the magnificent if somewhat unoperatic *The Pilgrim's Progress** (into which he incorporated *The Shepherds of the Delectable*

Mountains); its failure to win acceptance was his greatest artistic disappointment.

Va, vecchio John
Baritone arietta for Falstaff in Act II of Verdi's *Falstaff*.

Veasey, Josephine *(b 1930)*
British mezzo, particularly associated with Wagner and Berlioz roles. One of the finest British mezzos of the postwar period with a strong stage presence, she created Helen in *King Priam* and the Emperor in Henze's *We Come to the River*.

Veau d'or, Le
Bass aria for Méphistophélès in Act II of Gounod's *Faust*.

Vecchi, Orazio *(c 1550–1605)*
Italian composer. His *commedia harmonica L'Amfiparnasso**, which has occasionally been staged in recent years, is one of the most important 'proto-operas'.

Vecchia zimarra
Bass aria (the Coat Song) for Colline in Act IV of Puccini's *La Bohème*.

Vecchioto prender moglie, Il
Soprano aria for Berta in Act II of Rossini's *Il Barbiere di Siviglia*. The best-known aria del sorbetto*.

Vedernikov, Alexander *(b 1927)*
Russian bass, particularly associated with the Russian repertory, especially Boris Godunov. A fine singing-actor, he had a dark and rich voice of considerable power and range which he used with unfailing musicianship.

Vedi le foschi
Chorus of gypsies (the Anvil Chorus) in Act II of Verdi's *Il Trovatore*, during which on-stage anvils are struck rhythmically.

Vedova Scaltra, La *(The Deceitful Widow)*
Comic opera by Wolf-Ferrari. 1st perf. Rome, 5 March 1931; libr. by Mario Ghisalberti, after Carlo Goldoni. An elegant example of Wolf-Ferrari's neo-classical style, it was reasonably successful at its appearance but is nowadays only very rarely performed.

Vedrai carino
Soprano aria for Zerlina in Act II of Mozart's *Don Giovanni*.

Vedro mentr'io sospiro
Baritone aria for Count Almaviva in Act III of Mozart's *Le Nozze di Figaro*.

Veil Song
Mezzo aria ('Nel giardin del bello') for Eboli in Act II of Verdi's *Don Carlos*.

Velluti, Giovanni Battista *(1780–1861)*
Italian castrato. The last of the great castrati, he enjoyed great success initially, but later came to be regarded as a somewhat shocking oddity; Mendelssohn heard him and described the sound as 'distasteful'. He created Arsace in Rossini's *Aureliano in Palmira*, the title role in Nicolini's *Coriolano* and Armando in Meyerbeer's *Il Crociato in Egitto*, the last major role written for the castrato voice.

Vendetta, La
Bass aria for Dr Bartolo in Act I of Mozart's *Le Nozze di Figaro*.

Venezuelan opera composers

See Hahn

Other national opera composers include José Angel Montero (1839–81), whose *Virginia* (Caracas 26 April 1873) was the first Venezuelan opera.

Vengeance arias

A type of aria, especially popular in late 18th- and early 19th-century operas, in which a character determines to be avenged. The term refers only to the sentiment of the aria rather than to any formal structure. The most influential early example was 'Oui! Pour mon heureuse adresse' in Act III of Cherubini's *Lodoïska*. Although there are a few vengeance arias for women (of which the most famous is the Queen of the Night's 'Der Hölle Rache' in *Die Zauberflöte*), they are usually for men. Examples include Don Pizarro's 'Ha! Welch' ein Augenblick' in Beethoven's *Fidelio* and Pagano's 'O speranza di vendetta' in Verdi's *I Lombardi*.

Vengeance duets

A popular device, especially favoured by 19th-century Italian composers, to end a scene in rousing style. Verdi wrote particularly fine examples in *Macbeth* ('Ora di morte'), *Rigoletto* ('Si, vendetta') and *Otello* ('Si, pel ciel').

Venice

See Teatro la Fenice, Venice

Venite inginocchiatevi

Soprano aria for Susanna in Act II of Mozart's *Le Nozze di Figaro*.

Venti scudi

Tenor/baritone duet for Nemorino and Belcore in Act II of Donizetti's *L'Elisir d'Amore*.

Venti turbini

Mezzo aria for Rinaldo in Act I of Handel's *Rinaldo*.

Venus

The Graeco-Roman goddess of love appears in innumerable operas, including: (1) Mezzo role in Wagner's *Tannhäuser*. (2) Soprano role in Cavalli's *Ercole Amante*. (3) Soprano role in Blow's *Venus and Adonis*. (4) Soprano role in Rameau's *Dardanus*. (5) Soprano role in Offenbach's *Orphée aux Enfers*. (6) Soprano role in Mozart's *Ascanio in Alba*. (7) Mezzo role in Peri's *Euridice*. (8) Soprano role in Monteverdi's *L'Incoronazione di Poppea*.

Venus and Adonis

Opera in prologue and three acts by Blow. 1st perf. London, 1684; librettist unknown. Principal roles: Venus (sop), Adonis (bar), Cupid (sop). Usually regarded as the earliest British opera, it is still performed from time to time.

Plot: Venus loves the huntsman Adonis and sends him off to demonstrate his skill in the chase. Cupid and the cherubs amuse themselves by tossing the alphabet around the stage. Venus mourns for the dying Adonis and all join in praise of his virtues. [R]

Vêpres Siciliennes, Les (*The Sicilian Vespers*)

Opera in five acts by Verdi. 1st perf. Paris, 13 June 1855; libr. by Eugène Scribe and Charles Duveyrier, after their libretto for Donizetti's *Le Duc d'Albe*. Principal roles: Hélène (sop), Henri (ten), Guy de Montfort (bar), Procida (bass). Verdi's first opera written in French grand opera style, it is the least frequently performed of his mature works. Despite the rigid structure to which he was forced to conform, Verdi gave the work considerable dramatic interest and some splendid music, notably in the overture and in *Les Quatre Saisons*, arguably Verdi's finest ballet music. The story is based on an historical incident, when Sicilian patriots massacred the French in Palermo on 30 March 1282.

Plot: Sicily, 1282. The revolutionary leader Procida, aided by the young Sicilian patriot Henri and by the Duchess Hélène, is planning an uprising with Spanish support. The tyrannical French governor Montfort discovers that Henri is his illegitimate son and tells him so. Although horrified at his parentage, Henri saves his father from an assassination attempt. The arrested conspirators repudiate Henri, but Hélène forgives him when he tells her of his dilemma. Henri persuades Montfort to pardon the conspirators and to agree to his marriage with Hélène. The implacable Procida sees his chance: as the wedding bells sound, the Sicilians massacre the unarmed French. [R]

Veracini, Francesco Maria
(1690–c 1770)
Italian composer and violinist. He composed four operas, all of them now long forgotten. They are *Adriano in Siria* (London 26 Nov 1735; libr. Corri, after Pietro Metastasio), *La Clemenza di Tito* (London 12 April 1737; libr. Corri, after Metastasio), *Partenio* (London 14 March 1738; libr. Paolo Antonio Rolli) and *Rosalinda* (London 31 Jan 1744; libr. Rolli, after Shakespeare's *As You Like It*).

Vera Costanza, La *(True Constancy)*
Opera in three acts by Haydn. 1st perf.

Esterháza, 2 April 1779; libr. by Francesco Puttini. Principal roles: Rosina (sop), Count Errico (ten), Villotto (bass), Lisetta (sop), Irene (sop), Masino (bar), Ernesto (ten). It is only very rarely performed.

Plot: Irene, Ernesto, the fop Villotto and the maid Lisetta are shipwrecked on an island where they encounter Rosina and her brother Masino. Irene recognises Rosina as her nephew Errico's beloved and is unaware that the two are already married. Her attempts to marry off Rosina to Villotto lead to much confusion and amorous intrigue until she finally accepts Rosina as Errico's wife. [R]

Verbena de la Paloma, La
(The Feast of Our Lady of the Dove)
Zarzuela in three scenes by Bretón. 1st perf. Madrid, 19 Feb 1894; libr. by Ricardo de la Vega. One of the most enduringly popular of all zarzuelas. [R]

Verdi, Giuseppe *(1813–1901)*
Italian composer, who, with Mozart and Wagner, ranks as one of the three greatest of all opera composers. Having been rejected by the Milan Conservatory as 'insufficiently talented', he studed privately, and composed his first opera *Rocester* (which is lost) in 1836. His first extant opera *Oberto, Conte di San Bonifacio** was a success, but its successor, *Un Giorno di Regno**, Verdi's only opera buffa, failed after a single performance. Coming at a time when he had lost both his wife and his daughter in quick succession, Verdi vowed to give up composition. He was, however, reluctantly persuaded by La Scala's administrator Bartolomeo Merelli to change his mind. The result was the triumphantly successful *Nabucco**, which placed him at the forefront of Italian composers.

*I Lombardi** confirmed Verdi's

popularity, and *Ernani** established his European reputation. There followed, until 1850, what the composer later referred to as his "years in the galley", during which many operas of varying quality were written in rapid succession. These were *I Due Foscari**, *Giovanna d'Arco**, *Alzira**, *Attila**, *Macbeth**, his finest early work, *I Masnadieri**, *Jérusalem* (a revision of *I Lombardi*), *Il Corsaro**, *La Battaglia di Legnano**, the fine *Luisa Miller** and *Stiffelio**. In recent years, all of Verdi's early works have received performances, and *Nabucco*, *Ernani*, *Macbeth* and *Luisa Miller*, which stand head and shoulders above the others, have won a permanent place in the repertory.

Verdi's 'middle period' began in 1851 with *Rigoletto**, arguably the finest Italian music-drama since those of Monteverdi, and a work which prompted Rossini to observe (somewhat belatedly) "at last I recognise Verdi's genius". From here onwards, each of Verdi's operas shows an increasing emphasis on the drama at the expense of pure vocalism, each has its distinctive 'colour' and shows a growing mastery of orchestration, and each shows an increasing tendency to break up the formal structures of opera to achieve an uninterrupted dramatic flow. The ever-popular *Il Trovatore** and *La Traviata** were followed by the French grand opera *Les Vêpres Siciliennes**, *Aroldo** (a major revision of *Stiffelio*), the dark and sombre *Simon Boccanegra**, *Un Ballo in Maschera**, *La Forza del Destino**, a major revision of *Macbeth*, and his last and greatest middle period works, *Don Carlos** and *Aida**, which mark the transition to the full glories of his later works.

After the composition of his Requiem Mass in 1874, Verdi went into virtual retirement, producing no new music. He enjoyed the life of a country gentleman at his farm at Sant'Agata with the soprano Giuseppina Strepponi*, with whom he lived for many years before marrying her. The availability of Arrigo Boito as a librettist eventually persuaded Verdi to compose again. The results of their remarkable partnership were a major revision of *Simon Boccanegra* and Verdi's last two Shakespearean masterpieces, *Otello** and *Falstaff**, the two greatest Italian operas in which the composer, without any indebtedness to Wagner or his theories, at last achieved true music-drama. Verdi had a deep love and understanding of Shakespeare and served him better than probably any other composer. However, a setting of *King Lear*, a project which obsessed him for 50 years, unfortunately failed to materialise.

Particularly Verdian features which may be found in many of his operas include patriotism, a burning anti-clericalism, a concern with the way in which personal interrelationships can affect the destinies of millions (especially notable in *Don Carlos*), the realisation of the full musico-dramatic potential of the baritone voice, a dark and strikingly individual orchestral sound, and the relationship between father and daughter (a relationship which Verdi himself never experienced). Himself an ardent Italian nationalist, Verdi lent his support to the Risorgimento, giving it its own opera in *La Battaglia di Legnano*. The popular slogan *Viva Verdi* was universally known to stand for *Viva Victor Emmanuele Rè d'Italia*. He was a deputy in the first parliament of united Italy in 1861, and was nominated a senator in 1874. In later life, Verdi engaged in much charitable work, including the endowment in 1899 of the still-functioning Casa di Riposo for retired musicians in Milan.

Verdi baritone

A term used to describe a baritone with the power and extension at the top of the voice necessary to sing Verdi's baritone roles. Most of these roles, especially di Luna in *Il Trovatore*, have a cruelly high tessitura, often a minor third or more above other composers' baritone roles. True Verdi baritones (such as Leonard Warren, Peter Glossop, Robert Merrill or Renato Bruson), who have the upper notes whilst still retaining a dark and rich baritone timbre, are extremely rare.

Vere, Capt

Tenor role in Britten's *Billy Budd*. He is the commander of H.M.S. Indomitable.

Veretti, Antonio *(1900–78)*

Italian composer, who wrote in many styles, including neo-classical, jazz and twelve-tone. His opera include *Il Medico Volante* (1927; libr. after Molière's *Le Médecin Malgré Lui*), *Il Favorito del Re* (Milan 1932; libr. Arturo Rossato) and *Una Favola di Andersen* (1934; libr. after Hans Christian Andersen's *The Match Girl*).

Verismo *(Italian for 'realism')*

A term used to describe a style of Italian opera (largely pioneered by Mascagni), popular in the late 19th and early 20th centuries, which reproduced 'slices of life' rather than the idealised, larger-than-life characters and subjects previously favoured. The most important verismo composers are Cilea, Franchetti, Giordano, Leoncavallo, Mascagni, Orefice, Puccini (only in part a verismo composer) and Zandonai. Some French and German composers imitated the style occasionally; examples include Massenet's *La Navarraise*, D'Albert's *Tiefland* and Schillings' *Mona Lisa*.

Verlobung in San Domingo, Die *(The Betrothal in Santo Domingo)*

Opera in two acts by Egk. 1st perf. Munich, 27 Nov 1963; libr. by the composer, after Heinrich Wilhelm von Kleist. Principal roles: Christoph (ten), Jeanne (sop). One of the most successful of Egk's more recent operas.

Verona Arena

A Roman amphitheatre (cap. 20,000) in Italy, where open-air summer opera seasons have been given since 1913 (except during the two world wars). The repertory consists predominantly of 'spectacular' operas, such as *Aida*, *Nabucco* and *Turandot*. Top international casts are engaged, and the acoustics are superb.

Véronique

Operetta in three acts by Messager. 1st perf. Paris, 10 Feb 1898; libr. by Albert Vanloo and Georges Duval. Principal roles: Florestan (ten), Hélène (sop), Coquenard (bar), Agathe (mezzo). Usually regarded as Messager's finest work, it is still regularly performed in France. [R]

Verrett, Shirley *(b 1931)*

American mezzo, particularly associated with the Italian and French repertories. One of the finest mezzos of the 1970s, who also sang some soprano roles such as Tosca and Lady Macbeth, she had a rich and luscious voice of considerable power which she used with outstanding musicianship. She was an exciting stage performer, aided in roles such as Carmen by her great personal beauty. She was the first black singer ever to appear at the Bolshoi Opera.

Versailles
See Salle de l'Opéra, Versailles

Verschworenen, Die (*The Conspirators*)
also known as **Der Häusliche Krieg** (*Domestic War*)
Opera in one act by Schubert (D 787). 1st perf. Frankfurt, 29 Aug 1861 (composed 1823); libr. by Ignaz F. Castelli, after Aristophanes' *Lysistrata* and *Ecclesiazusae*. A delightful little Singspiel, sadly only very rarely performed, it is set in Crusading times and tells of the women going on sexual strike until their men agree to give up fighting. [R]

Verstovsky, Alexei *(1799–1862)*
Russian composer. His first two operas, the Singspiel *Pan Twardowski* (Moscow 5 June 1828; libr. M. N. Zagoskin) and *Vadim* (Moscow 7 Dec 1832; libr. S. P. Sheviryov, after Vassily Zhukovsky) were unremarkable, but *Askold's Tomb* (Moscow 28 Sept 1835; libr. Zagoskin) was the most successful pre-Glinka Russian opera and had a considerable influence on the general development of Russian opera. His later operas *Longing for the Homeland* (Moscow 2 Sept 1839; libr. Zagoskin), *Chur Valley* (Moscow 28 Aug 1841; libr. A. A. Shakhovsky) and *Gromoboy* (Moscow 5 Feb 1858; libr. D. T. Lensky, after Zhukovsky) were less successful.

Verurteilung (or Verhör) des Lukullus (*The Sentencing*, or *Trial*, of *Lucullus*)
Opera in 12 scenes by Dessau. 1st perf. Berlin, 17 March 1950; libr. by Bertolt Brecht. Revised version, 1st perf. Berlin, 1965. Principal roles: Lukullus (ten), Fishwife (mezzo). Banned by the East German government after its première,

it is an anti-war protest. Dessau's most successful opera, it has been widely performed.

Plot: The dead Lukullus arrives in the underworld and must stand trial before he is permitted to enter the Elysian Fields. He pleads worthiness to enter on the grounds of his great military victories. However, the jury reject his arguments and he is condemned because of the devastation caused by his military activities. [R]

Vespetta
Mezzo role in Albinoni's and soprano role in Telemann's *Pimpinone*. She is a domineering housemaid.

Vespri Siciliani, I
See Vêpres Siciliennes, Les

Vestale, La
Works of this title about the Roman vestal virgin include:

(1) Opera by Salieri. 1st perf. Vienna, 1768; Salieri's first opera, the music is lost.

(2) Opera in three acts by Spontini. 1st perf. Paris, 16 Dec 1807; libr. by Victor Joseph Étienne de Jouy. Principal roles: Giulia (sop), Licinio (ten), High Priestess (mezzo), Cinna (bar), Pontifex Maximus (bass). Spontini's most successful and enduring work, it is still quite often performed.

Plot: Rome. The vestal virgin Giulia loves the general Licinio. He visits her during her vigil in the temple of Vesta, and because of this distraction she allows the sacred flame to go out. She is about to be buried alive for her sacrilege when the flame is rekindled by divine intervention. She is released from her vows and united with Licinio. [R]

(3) Opera in two acts by Pacini. 1st perf. Milan, 6 Feb 1823; libr. by Luigi Romanelli.

(4) Opera in three acts by

Mercadante. 1st perf. Naples, 10 March 1840; libr. by Salvatore Cammarano. Very successful in its time, it is nowadays forgotten.

Vesti la giubba

Tenor aria for Canio (often referred to in English as 'On with the motley') in Act I of Leoncavallo's *Pagliacci*.

V'ho ingannato

Soprano/baritone duet for Gilda and Rigoletto in Act III of Verdi's *Rigoletto*. The final scene of the opera.

Viaggio a Reims, Il (*The Journey to Rheims*)
or L'Albergo del Giglioli d'Oro (*The Golden Lily Inn*)

Comic opera in one act by Rossini. 1st perf. Paris, 19 June 1825; libr. by Luigi Balocchi, partly after Anne-Louise de Staëls's *Corinne ou l'Italie*. Principal roles: Corinna (sop), Madame Cortèse (sop), Melibea (mezzo), Countess Folleville (mezzo), Belfiore (ten), Count Libenskof (ten), Lord Sidney (bass), Don Alvaro (bar), Don Profondo (bass), Baron Tombonok (bass). One of Rossini's finest comic scores, it was written for the coronation of Charles X of France. Requiring ten front-rank singers, it remained virtually unperformed for 150 years, but was revived with huge success at the 1985 Pesaro Festival. Rossini later incorporated much of the music into *Le Comte Ory**.

Plot: Plombières, May 1825. An international group of travellers to the coronation arrive at an inn to find both their journeys and their romantic intrigues interrupted by the lack of coach horses. They pass the time by entertaining one another with stories and songs. [R]

Viardot-García, Pauline (*1821–1910*)

French mezzo and composer, daughter of Manuel García I* and younger sister of María Malibran* and Manuel García II* and also for many years the companion of the novelist Ivan Turgenev. One of the greatest singers of her age, she created Fidès in *Le Prophète* and the title role in Gounod's *Sapho*. She also composed a number of operettas, including *Le Dernier Sorcier* (1867; libr. Turgenev), *Trop de Femmes* (1867; libr. Turgenev), *Cendrillon* (1868) and *L'Ogre* (1868; libr. Turgenev).

Vibrato (Italian for 'vibrated')

A fluctuation in the pitch of the voice in a single note. Sometimes, as in a 'quick vibrato' it is correct and pleasing, but it is more often unpleasant and is a serious vocal problem. In the latter case, it is also called tremolo, knock, beat or – more bluntly – wobble.

Vickers, Jon (*Jonathan Stewart*) (*b 1926*)

Canadian tenor, particularly associated with the roles of Florestan, Aeneas, Otello (which he filmed), Tristan, Radamès, Siegmund and Peter Grimes. One of the greatest heroic tenors of the 20th century, with an incisive voice of highly individual timbre, he was also an intense and compelling singing-actor of remarkable dramatic insight.

Vida Breve, La (*Brief Life*)

Opera in two acts by De Falla. 1st perf. Nice, 1 April 1913 (composed 1905); libr. by Carlos Fernández Shaw. Principal roles: Salud (sop), Paco (ten), Carmela (mezzo), Uncle Salvador (bar), Grandmother (mezzo). De Falla's most successful stage work, and the most important of all Spanish operas, it incorporates much traditional Andalusian music.

Plot: Granada, *c* 1900. The gypsy girl Salud loves Paco, who feigns to return her love but in reality plans to marry Carmela. Salud discovers the truth, denounces Paco at the wedding ceremony then, overcome by grief, falls dead at his feet. [R]

Video recordings

Since video cassettes became widely available in the early 1980s, many opera performances have been filmed, mostly on the VHS system. The majority have been live performances, including many from Covent Garden, the Verona Arena and the Glyndebourne Festival. There have, however, also been some studio recordings, such as the Brent Walker series of the Savoy Operas, and a few famous operatic films of the past (such as Tito Gobbi in *Rigoletto* and *Il Barbiere di Siviglia*) have also been made available.

Viene la sera

Soprano/tenor duet for Cio-Cio-San and Pinkerton in Act I of Puccini's *Madama Butterfly*.

Vieni, la mia vendetta

Bass aria for Don Alfonso in Act I of Donizetti's *Lucrezia Borgia*.

Vieni, t'affreta

Soprano aria for Lady Macbeth in Act I of Verdi's *Macbeth*.

Vienna

See Theater an der Wien, Vienna; Vienna Chamber Opera; Vienna State Opera; Vienna Volksoper

Vienna Chamber Opera

The company was founded in 1953 by Prof Hans Gabor and has always maintained high artistic standards. The repertory consists largely of smaller-scale 18th- and 19th-century works, but also includes a number of contemporary operas.

Vienna State Opera

Called the Hofoper until 1918, the present theatre (cap. 2,200), designed by Eduard van der Null and August Siccard von Siccardsburg, opened on 25 May 1869. Destroyed by bombs in March 1945, it did not reopen until 5 November 1955; in the meantime, the company used the Theater an der Wien*. One of the most prestigious and formal opera houses in the world, the annual season runs from September to June. Musical directors have included Mahler, Hans Richter, Felix Weingartner, Bruno Walter, Karl Böhm, Herbert von Karajan, Lorin Maazel and Claudio Abbado. The orchestra is the Vienna Philharmonic.

Vienna Volksoper

The theatre (cap. 1,473) opened in December 1898 and began giving opera in 1904. The repertory is largely devoted to lighter works and to operetta. The annual season runs from September to June. Musical directors have included Felix Weingartner, Fritz Stiedry and Leo Blech.

Vie Parisienne, La *(Parisian Life)*

Operetta in four acts by Offenbach. 1st perf. Paris, 31 Oct 1868; libr. by Henri Meilhac and Ludovic Halévy. Principal roles: Gabriele (sop), Brazilian (ten), Baron and Baroness Gondromark (bar and mezzo), Raoul (ten), Bobinet (bar), Métella (mezzo), Pauline (sop). One of Offenbach's wittiest and most enduringly popular operettas, it is a satire on Second Empire morals (or lack of them).

Plot: Paris, 1867. The rakes Raoul de Gardefeu and Bobinet both love Métella, but she rebuffs them both. As they are broke, they decide to try and make some money out of the visiting tourists, particularly the fast-living Brazilian millionaire and the Swedish Baron Gondromark, to whose wife Raoul takes a fancy. The Swedes are lodged at Raoul's house, which he tells them is an hotel, and the Baron is kept out of the way at a bibulous party given by Bobinet disguised as a Swiss admiral, with the chambermaid Pauline masquerading as his wife. Total confusion reigns at a masked ball given by the Brazilian, but eventually everything is sorted out and the Brazilian decides to take the glovemaker Gabriele back to Brazil with him. [R]

Vierjährige Posten, Die (The Four-Year-Old Mail)

Opera in one act by Schubert (D 190). 1st perf. Dresden, 23 Sept 1896 (composed 1815); libr. by Theodor Körner. Like the rest of Schubert's early Singspiels, it contains some delightful music but is virtually never performed. [R]

Vieuille, Félix (1872–1953)

French bass, long resident at the Opéra-Comique, Paris. Particularly identified with the French repertory, he had a rich and wide-ranging voice and was a fine singing-actor. He created Arkel in Pelléas et Mélisande, Eumée in Fauré's Pénélope, Bluebeard in Dukas' Ariane et Barbe-Bleue, the Father in Milhaud's Le Pauvre Matelot, the Sultan in Rabaud's Mârouf and Macduff in Bloch's Macbeth. His nephew Jean (1902–64) was a successful bass-baritone.

Vilja-Lied

Soprano aria for Hannah Glawari in Act II of Lehár's Die Lustige Witwe.

Village Romeo and Juliet, A

Opera in prologue and three acts by Delius. 1st perf. Berlin, 21 Feb 1907; libr. by the composer, after the story Romeo und Julia auf dem Dorfe in Gottfried Keller's Die Leute von Seldwyla. Principal roles: Sali (ten), Vrenchen (sop), Dark Fiddler (bar), Manz (bar), Marti (b-bar). Delius' most successful opera, notable for the instrumental 'Walk to the Paradise Garden', is a lushly orchestrated work of great melodic beauty.

Plot: mid-19th-century Switzerland. The farmers Manz and Marti dispute a strip of land which rightfully belongs to the Dark Fiddler. The farmers' children, Vrenchen and Sali, although forbidden by their fathers to meet because of the feud, fall in love. The feud exhausts both fathers' financial resources and Sali attacks Vrenchen's father when the latter discovers the young couple together. The poverty-stricken lovers see no future and commit joint suicide by taking a barge out into the river and sinking it. [R]

Villa-Lobos, Heitor (1887–1959)

Brazilian composer. He wrote nine operas, only three of which have ever been performed. They include Izath (Rio de Janeiro 13 Dec 1958, composed 1918; an expansion of the earlier Eliza of 1915), Jesus (1918), Zoé (1919), Malazarte (1921), Magdalena (Los Angeles 26 July 1948) and Yerma (Santa Fe 12 Aug 1971, composed 1956; libr. after Federico García Lorca).

Villi, Le (The Witches)

Opera in two acts (originally one act)

by Puccini. 1st perf. Milan, 31 May 1884; libr. by Ferdinando Fontana, after Heinrich Heine. Revised version, 1st perf. Turin, 26 Dec 1884. Principal roles: Anna (sop), Roberto (ten), Guglielmo Wulf (bar). Inspired by a folk-legend and, possibly, by Adam's ballet *Giselle* to which the story bears more than a passing resemblance, this was Puccini's first opera. It is still occasionally performed.

Plot: Black Forest. Anna is abandoned by her fiancée Roberto and dies of grief. Her spirit joins the Willis, ghosts who haunt faithless lovers. Urged on by the prayers of her vengeful father Guglielmo, Anna's ghost appears before Roberto and draws him into a frenzied dance of death. [R]

Vinay, Ramón *(b 1912)*

Chilean tenor, particularly associated with the Italian repertory, especially Otello. Beginning as a baritone, he turned to tenor roles in 1943, becoming one of the finest heldentenors of the immediate postwar era, enjoying equal success in Wagner and Verdi. He had a dark-toned voice of ringing power and was a singing-actor of great nobility and insight. He reverted to baritone roles in 1962 and also produced a number of operas.

Vincent

Tenor role in Gounod's *Mireille*. He is in love with Mireille.

Vinco, Ivo *(b 1928)*

Italian bass, particularly associated with the Italian repertory. He had a good if not outstanding voice, and a fine stage presence. Married to the mezzo Fiorenza Cossotto*.

Vin Herbé, Le *(The Drugged Wine)*

Dramatic oratorio by Martin. 1st perf. Zürich, 26 March 1942; a setting of Joseph Bedier's *Tristan et Iseut*. One of Martin's finest works, written for 12 solo voices and seven string instruments, it is only very rarely performed. [R]

Viola

Unfinished opera by Smetana. Composed *c* 1875; libr. by Eliška Krásnohorská, after Shakespeare's *Twelfth Night*. Smetana only completed 365 bars of the music. [R]

Violanta

Opera in one act by Korngold (Op 8). 1st perf. Munich, 28 March 1916; libr. by Hans Müller. Principal roles: Violanta (sop), Alfonso (ten), Trovai (bar), Bracca (ten), Barbara (mezzo). Korngold's first major success, it is still occasionally performed.

Plot: 15th-century Venice. Alfonso has seduced Violanta's sister. She entices him to her home so that her husband Simone Trovai can kill him, but falls in love with him and interposes herself between the two men. She is killed by her husband's dagger. [R]

Violetta Valéry

Soprano role in Verdi's *La Traviata*. Based on the historical Marie Duplessis, with whom Alexandre Dumas fils had an affair, she is the 'Lady of the Camelias', the consumptive demi-monde.

Violins of St Jacques, The

Opera in three acts by Williamson. 1st perf. London, 29 Nov 1966; libr. by William Chappell, after Patrick Leigh Fermor. Principal roles: Berthe (sop), Josephine (mezzo), Marcel (bar), Sosthène (ten). Arguably Williamson's finest stage work, it is set on a Caribbean island shortly before a volcanic eruption and is notable for its exotic orchestration.

Viozzi, Giulio *(b 1912)*

Italian composer. His operas, in late romantic style and for all of which he wrote his own libretti, include the radio opera *Parete Bianca* (1954), *Allamistakeo* (Bergamo 1954; libr. after Edgar Allan Poe's *Some Words With a Mummy*), *Un Intervento Notturno* (Trieste 1957; libr. after R. A. Bowen), *Il Sasso Pagano* (Trieste 1962; libr. after O. von Leitgeb), *La Giacca Dannata* (Trieste 1967; libr. after Dino Buzzati), *Elisabetta* (Trieste 1972; libr. after Guy de Maupassant) and the unperformed *L'Inferno* (libr. after N. Spazzolli).

Vi ravviso

Bass aria for Count Rodolfo in Act I of Bellini's *La Sonnambula*.

Virginia Opera Association

Based in Norfolk, this American company was founded in 1975 and has recently been closely associated with Musgrave operas. The musical director is Peter Mark.

Visconti, Luchino *(1906–76)*

Italian producer and designer. One of the outstanding postwar opera directors, he was particularly associated with La Scala, Milan (where he directed *La Vestale*, *Anna Bolena*, *La Traviata*, *La Sonnambula* and *Iphigénie en Tauride*, all with Maria Callas) and with Covent Garden (where he directed *Don Carlos*, *La Traviata*, *Il Trovatore* and *Der Rosenkavalier*). His designs and stagings were notable for their strong sense of historical style (he occasionally went to the lengths of unearthing 19th-century scenery). He was also co-author of the libretto for

Franco Mannino's *Il Diavolo in Giardino*.

Vishnevskaya, Galina *(b 1926)*

Russian soprano, particularly associated with the Russian and Italian repertories. A powerful dramatic performer (if sometimes in a style which Western audiences found rather old-fashioned), she had a rich voice of considerable power and range which she used with outstanding intelligence and musicianship. Married to the cellist and conductor Mstislav Rostropovich*, she left the USSR in 1974 and she and her husband were stripped of their Soviet citizenship. Her autobiography, *Galina: a Russian Story*, was published in 1984.

Vision fugitive

Baritone aria for Herod in Act II of Massenet's *Hérodiade*.

Vissi d'arte

Soprano aria for Tosca in Act II of Puccini's *Tosca*.

Vítek

Tenor role in: (1) Janáček's *The Macropolus Case*. Kristina's father, he is an old solicitor's clerk. (2) Smetana's *Dalibor*. He is in love with Jitka. (3) Smetana's *The Secret*. He is in love with Blaženka.

Vitellia

Soprano role in Mozart's *La Clemenza di Tito*. She loves the Emperor Titus.

Vittadini, Franco *(1884–1948)*

Italian composer. His operas include the unperformed *Il Mare di Tiberiade* (1914; libr. Luigi Illica), the highly successful *Anima Allegra* (Rome 15 April 1921; libr. Giuseppe Adami, after the Álvarez Quintero brothers' *Genio*

Alegre), *Nazareth* (Pavia 1925; libr. Adami), *La Sagredo* (Milan 1930; libr. Adami), *Caracciolo* (Rome 1938; libr. Arturo Rossato) and *Fiametta e l'Avaro* (Brescia 1951; libr. Adami and Giovacchino Forzano).

Vivaldi, Antonio (c 1678–1741)

Italian composer. He wrote 44 operas, many of them hastily put together from previous works and none of which have won a permanent place in the repertory. His more important operas include *La Senna Festeggiante* (1713; libr. D. Lalli) [R], *L'Incoronazione di Dario* (Venice 1717; libr. A. Morselli) [R], *Tito Manlio* (Mantua 1720; libr. Matteo Noris) [R], *Giustino* (Rome 1724; libr. N. Berengani), *Farnace* (Venice 1726; libr. A. M. Lucchini), *Orlando Furioso**, perhaps his finest opera, *La Fida Ninfa* (Verona 6 Jan 1732; libr. Scipione Mattei) [R], *L'Olimpiade* (Venice 1734; libr. Pietro Metastasio) [R], *La Griselda* (Venice May 1735; libr. Apostolo Zeno) and *Catone in Utica* (Verona May 1737; libr. Metastasio) [R]. There has recently been a revival of interest in his stage works, and a few have been performed after nearly 250 years of neglect.

Viva il vino

Tenor aria for Turiddù in Mascagni's *Cavalleria Rusticana*.

Vivandière, La (*The Canteen Girl*)

Opera in three acts by Godard. 1st perf. Paris, 1 April 1895; libr. by Henri Cain. One of Godard's most successful works, it is nowadays only very rarely performed.

Vivat Bacchus

Tenor/bass duet for Pedrillo and Osmin in Act II of Mozart's *Die Entführung aus dem Serail*.

Vives, Amadeo (1871–1932)

Spanish composer. He began by writing operas, of which *Maruxa* (1914) [R] is still remembered in Spain. He then turned to zarzuela, becoming one of the leading exponents of the genre and writing over 100 of them. The most successful include *Bohemios* (1904) [R], *Los Viajes de Gulliver* (Madrid 1911; libr. Paso and Abiati, after Swift's *Gulliver's Travels*), which was written in collaboration with Giménez, *La Generala* (1912), *Doña Francisquita* (1923) [R] and *La Villana* (1927).

Vivi, ingrato

Soprano aria for Elizabeth I in Act III of Donizetti's *Roberto Devereux*. Its cabaletta, 'Quel sangue versato' is the final scene of the opera.

Vivi tu

Tenor aria for Percy in Act II of Donizetti's *Anna Bolena*.

Vladimir

Tenor role in Borodin's *Prince Igor*. He is Igor's son.

Vocal competitions

Annual vocal competitions for young singers are held in a number of countries. Amongst the most prestigious are the Kathleen Ferrier Memorial Prize in Britain, the Voci Verdiani in Italy, the s'Hertogenbosch in the Netherlands, the Metropolitan Auditions of the Air in New York (now discontinued), the Voice of the World competition in Wales, and those of Moscow, Toulouse and Barcelona.

Vocal ranges

See Baritone; Bass; Castrato; Contralto; Counter-tenor; Mezzo-soprano; Soprano; Tenor

Vocal score
The published music of an opera, showing all the vocal parts with a piano reduction for accompaniment.

Voce di testa
The Italian term for head voice*.

Voce poco fa, Una
Mezzo aria for Rosina in Act I of Rossini's *Il Barbiere di Siviglia*.

Vogelfänger bin ich ja, Der
Baritone aria for Papageno in Act I of Mozart's *Die Zauberflöte*.

Vogelgesang, Kunz
Tenor comprimario role in Wagner's *Die Meistersinger von Nürnberg*. A furrier, he is one of the masters.

Vogelhändler, Der (*The Bird Seller*)
Operetta in three acts by Zeller. 1st perf. Vienna, 10 Jan 1891; libr. by Moritz West and Ludwig Held. Principal roles: Adam (ten), Marie (sop), Count Stanislaus (ten), Briefchristel (sop), Schneck (ten). Zeller's most successful and enduring work, it is still regularly performed in German-speaking countries. [R]

Voice of Ariadne, The
Opera in three acts by Musgrave. 1st perf. Aldeburgh, 11 June 1974; libr. by Amalia Elguera, after Henry James' *The Last of the Valerii*. Principal roles: Countess (sop), Count Valerio (bar), Bianca (sop), Mrs Tracy (mezzo), Baldovino (ten), Mr Lamb (bass). Musgrave's first major success, it is written for an orchestra of 13 players.

Plot: Count Valerio is fascinated by the legend of a statue buried in his garden. Excavation produces a pedestal inscribed 'Ariadne'. He imagines that he hears Ariadne's voice and becomes fixated on a vision of her which estranges him from his wife. Finally he recognises the Countess as the embodiment of his vision and the source of all happiness, which he had been pursuing without realising that he already possessed it.

Voices of the future
Large numbers of young singers are always emerging with abundant vocal and dramatic talent. However, many fail to reach their full potential, often because they become 'sung-out' through undertaking the wrong roles early in their careers. The blame for this can frequently be laid at the door of agents, opera administrators and record companies anxious to cash in on a new talent and giving little thought to nurturing it. In earlier days, young singers learned their craft and tried out their roles in small houses where they did not have to force their voices. Nowadays, except in Germany, this is seldom the case, and the lessons of the early decline of such remarkable voices as those of Elena Souliotis and Sylvia Sass appear to have been ignored.

Among new artists who have appeared on the international scene in the late 1980s, those who have shown exceptional promise for the future include the Romanian baritone Alexandru Agache, the black American baritone Gregg Baker (*b* 1955), the American baritone Thomas Hampson, the Swedish mezzo Anne Sofie von Otter, the Czech-born German tenor Josef Protschka, the Romanian soprano Leontina Vaduva and, particularly, the German baritone Olaf Bär*, the Italian soprano Cecilia Gasdia*, the German mezzo Waltraud Meier* and the American tenor Thomas Randle*.

Voi che fausti

Tenor aria for Alessandro in Act II of Mozart's *Il Re Pastore*.

Voi che sapete

Soprano aria for Cherubino in Act II of Mozart's *Le Nozze di Figaro*.

Voilà donc la terrible cité

Baritone aria for Athanaël in Act II of Massenet's *Thaïs*.

Voi lo sapete o mamma

Soprano aria for Santuzza in Mascagni's *Cavalleria Rusticana*.

Voix Humaine, La (*The Human Voice*)

Opera in one act by Poulenc. 1st perf. Paris, 6 Feb 1959; libr. by Jean Cocteau. One of Poulenc's cleverest works, it is a 45-minute monodrama for soprano, portraying a woman's conversation on the telephone with the lover who has jilted her. [R]

Volo di Notte (*Night Flight*)

Opera in one act by Dallapiccola. 1st perf. Florence, 18 May 1940; libr. by the composer, after Antoine Saint-Exupéry's *Vol de Nuit*. Principal roles: Rivière (b-bar), Fabien's Wife (sop), Radio Telephonist (ten). Dallapiccola's first opera, heavily influenced by Berg, it has been widely performed.

Plot: Buenos Aires, *c* 1930. In the control tower of the airport, the director Rivière plans dangerous night flights despite the loss of an aeroplane. The Radio Telephonist, and Signora Fabien, whose pilot husband is expected on a night flight, gradually come to respect his attitude.

Voltaire

See panel on page 615

Volta la terra

Soprano aria for Oscar in Act I of Verdi's *Un Ballo in Maschera*.

Vom Fischer und syner Fru (*The Fisherman and his Wife*)

Opera by Schoeck (Op 43). 1st perf. Dresden, 3 Oct 1930; libr. (in Low German) by P. O. Runge, after Grimm's *Fairy Tales*. It is very rarely performed. [R]

Von

Names which contain this prefix are listed under the letter of the main surname. For example, Carl Maria von Weber is listed under W.

Von Heute auf Morgen (*From One Day Until Morning*)

Comic opera in one act by Schönberg (Op 32). 1st perf. Frankfurt, 1 Feb 1930; libr. by Schönberg's wife Gertrude under the pen-name of Max Blonda. Principal roles: Wife (sop), Husband (bar), Singer (ten), Friend (sop), Child (sop). The first twelve-tone opera, it is supposedly based on an incident in the life of the composer Schrecker.

Plot: The Wife and her Husband return from a party, where he was attracted to his wife's schoolday Friend and she to the Singer. Stung by the Husband's continual taking of her for granted, the Wife changes into alluring night clothes and announces that she intends to lead a wild life, beginning with the Singer who rings up to suggest continuing the party. Her attitude has the desired effect on the Husband, who confesses the error of his ways, and the two are reconciled. When the Singer and the Friend arrive, they mock the pair's old-fashioned attitude before leaving. Husband and Wife discuss the episode in new-found harmony over

VOLTAIRE

The French philosopher, playwright and novelist Voltaire (*b* François Marie Arouet) (1694–1778) was himself keenly interested in opera. He wrote several opera libretti, including those for Rameau's *Samson*, *La Princesse de Navarre* and *La Temple de la Gloire*. Voltaire appears as a character in Bernstein's *Candide* and in operas by two minor composers. Some 50 operas have been based on his writings. Below are listed, by work, those operas by composers with entries in this dictionary.

Alzire
Zingarelli	*Alzira*	1794
Verdi	*Alzira*	1845

La Bégueule
Monsigny	*La Belle Arsène*	1773

Candide
Bernstein	*Candide*	1958

Ce Qui Plaît aux Dames
Duni	*La Fée Urgèle*	1765

Gertrude
Grétry	*Isabelle et Gertrude*	1766

L'Ingénu
Grétry	*Le Huron*	1768
Leroux	*L'Ingénu*	1931

Mahomet
Winter	*Maometto II*	1817
Rossini	*Maometto II/Le Siège de Corinthe*	1820/26

Mérope
Graun	*Merope*	1756

Olympie
Spontini	*Olympie*	1819
Mercadante	*Statira*	1853

L'Orphelin de la Chine
Winter	*Tamerlan*	1802

Samson
Rameau	*Samson*	1732

Les Scythes		
Mayr	*Gli Sciti*	1800
Mercadante	*Gli Sciti*	1823
Sémiramis		
Rossini	*Semiramide*	1823
Tancrède		
Rossini	*Tancredi*	1813
Zaïre		
Portugal	*Zaira*	1802
Winter	*Zaira*	1805
Bellini	*Zaira*	1829
Mercadante	*Zaira*	1831

breakfast, and the Child asks "what's up-to-date people?". [R]

Von Jugend auf in dem Kampfgefild'
Tenor aria for Sir Huon in Act I of Weber's *Oberon*.

Vorspiel
A German term meaning an orchestral prelude.

Votre toast
Baritone aria (the Toreador's Song) for Escamillo in Act II of Bizet's *Carmen*.

Votto, Antonino *(1896–1985)*
Italian conductor, particularly associated with the Italian repertory. Long resident at La Scala, Milan, he was a rock-solid and often underrated Italian maestro of the old school.

Voyevoda, The
Opera in three acts by Tchaikovsky

(Op 3). 1st perf. Moscow, 11 Feb 1869; libr. by the composer, after Alexander Nikolayevich Ostrovksy's *A Dream on the Volga*. Tchaikovsky's first opera, it was discarded by the composer and parts of it were incorporated into later works. [R Exc]

Vyvyan, Jennifer *(1925–74)*
British soprano, particularly associated with Handel and Britten roles. A warm-voiced singer of fine musicianship, she had an affecting stage presence. She created Lady Penelope Rich in *Gloriana*, Tytania in *A Midsummer Night's Dream*, the Governess in *The Turn of the Screw*, Mrs Julian in *Owen Wingrave* and, for Williamson, Countess Serendin in *The Violins of St Jacques* and several roles in *Lucky Peter's Journey*.

Wach' auf

Chorus in Act III Scene II of Wagner's *Die Meistersinger von Nürnberg*. Sung in honour of Hans Sachs, it is a modernisation of the words with which the historical Sachs greeted Luther and the Reformation.

Wächter, Eberhard *(b 1929)*

Austrian baritone, particularly associated with Wagner and Mozart roles, especially Don Giovanni. An outstanding singing-actor with a fine voice used with style and great intelligence, he created Alfred in Einem's *Der Besuch der Alten Dame*. He is artistic director of the Vienna Volksoper.

Waffenschmied, Der *(The Armourer)*

Opera in three acts by Lortzing. 1st perf. Vienna, 31 May 1846; libr. by the composer, after Ziegler's *Liebhaber und Nebenbuhler in einer Person*. Principal roles: Graf von Liebenau (bar), Marie (sop), Stadinger (bass), Georg (ten). Still popular in Germany, it is almost never performed elsewhere.

Plot: 16th-century Worms. Count Liebenau loves the armourer Stadinger's daughter Marie. He woos her both as himself and in the guise of a young apprentice, Conrad. Marie falls in love with Conrad, but Stadinger wants her to wed the Count's manservant Georg. Georg declines her hand and Stadinger allows her to marry Conrad. The Count reveals that Conrad is actually himself and all ends happily. [R]

Wagner, Cosima *(b Liszt) (1837–1930)*

Daughter of the composer Liszt, she was married first to the conductor Hans von Bülow*, but left him for Wagner, whose second wife she became in 1870. She assisted Wagner in the establishment of the Bayreuth Festival, and was its artistic director (1883–1908).

Wagner, Richard *(1813–83)*

German composer who, with Mozart and Verdi, ranks as one of the three greatest of all opera composers. The single most important and influential figure in the history of opera – indeed of all music – his theories (propounded in both his music-dramas and in his voluminous writings) have had a profound influence on Western culture, affecting not only music, but also philosophy, literature, politics and drama. With the exception of Jesus of Nazareth, he is the most written about individual in human history, and no artist has been more controversial or produced such violent partisanship. The core of Wagner's musico-dramatic theories may be found in his concept of *Gesamtkunstwerk* ('unified work of art'), in which all aspects of the arts – music, poetry, drama and design – combine to form a single work of art. On the purely musical side, this was achieved by a 'symphonic' conception of opera, produced by the development of leitmotiv*. Wagner supervised every aspect of the production of his works and always wrote his own libretti.

His first stage work, *Die Hochzeit* (1832), is lost. Neither of his first two extant operas are of great significance, nor do they give much indication of his future development; *Die Feen** remained unperformed until 1888 and *Das Liebesverbot** met with little success. His first opera of importance, and his first success, was the vast Meyerbeerian *Rienzi**. It was followed by *Der Fliegende Holländer**, nowadays regarded as his first 'canonical' work, *Tannhäuser** and *Lohengrin**, in which his theories first begin to find expression. Realising that his ideas were best expressed through the medium of myth, Wagner turned to the *Nibelungenlied*. What began as a plan for a single opera, *Siegfrieds Tod*, developed into the tetralogy *Der Ring des Nibelungen**, the longest and most complex work in the history of opera. After composing *Das Rheingold*, *Die Walküre* and the first two acts of *Siegfried*, Wagner laid the project aside for nearly 20 years, turning to *Tristan und Isolde** and *Die Meistersinger von Nürnberg**. Returning to the tetralogy, he completed *Siegfried* and composed *Götterdämmerung*. The cycle received its first complete performance in 1876 at the opening of the Bayreuth Festspielhaus, designed by Wagner for the performance of his works. His last opera was the 'stage consecration festival play' *Parsifal**.

Wagner's second wife was Liszt's daughter Cosima*. Their son was the composer Siegfried Wagner* and their grandson the producer Wieland Wagner*. Wagner's adopted niece Johanna (1826–94) was a successful soprano, who created Elisabeth in *Tannhäuser*. She lost her voice in 1861 and became a straight actress, but resumed singing (as a mezzo) in the 1870s and created the first Norn in *Götterdämmerung*.

Wagner, Siegfried *(1869–1930)*
German composer and conductor, son of Richard and Cosima Wagner. He composed 15 operas, none of which achieved any lasting success. The most important were *Der Kobold* (Hamburg 29 Jan 1904; libr. composer), *Der Friedensengel* (Karlsruhe 4 March 1914; libr. composer) and *Der Schmied von Marienburg* (Rostock 16 Dec 1923; libr. composer). He was artistic director of the Bayreuth Festival (1908–30). His sons were the producers Wolfgang and Wieland Wagner*.

Wagner, Wieland *(1917–66)*
German producer and designer, son of Siegfried Wagner* and grandson of Richard and Cosima Wagner. One of the most influential 20th-century German opera producers, his abstract and simplified Wagnerian productions, abandoning naturalism and pageantry, established a style of Wagner production which lasted for 30 years. He described his aims as being to "replace the production ideas of a century ago, now grown sterile, by a creative intellectual approach which goes back to the origins of the work itself. Every new production is a step on the way to an unknown goal." He also created controversial productions of other composers' works, often in collaboration with Anja Silja*, with whom he had a close artistic relationship. With his brother Wolfgang (*b* 1919) he was artistic director of the Bayreuth Festival from 1951.

Wagner-Régeny, Rudolf *(1903–69)*
Hungarian-born German composer. A number of his operas met with some success in Germany, but they are all virtually unknown elsewhere. They include *Der Nackte König* (Gera 1 Dec 1930; libr. V. Braun, after Hans Christian Andersen's *The Emperor's New Clothes*), *Der Günstling* (Dresden

20 Feb 1935; libr. Caspar Neher, after Georg Büchner's version of Victor Hugo's *Marie Tudor*), *Die Bürger von Calais* (Berlin 28 Jan 1939; libr. Neher, after Froissart), *Johanna Balk* (Vienna 4 April 1941; libr. Neher), *Prometheus* (Kassel 12 Sept 1959; libr. composer, after Aeschylus) and *Das Bergwerk zu Falun* (Salzburg 16 Aug 1961; libr. composer, after Hugo von Hofmannsthal).

Wagner tuba

An instrument designed by Wagner for use in *Der Ring des Nibelungen*. More like a modified horn than the usual orchestral tuba, it is in two sizes, tenor and bass. It is mainly associated with Hunding in *Die Walküre*.

Wahn! Wahn!

Baritone monologue for Hans Sachs in Act III of Wagner's *Die Meistersinger von Nürnberg*.

Waldner, Count

Bass role in Richard Strauss' *Arabella*. Married to Adelaide, he is Arabella's and Zdenka's impoverished father.

Wales

See Welsh National Opera

Walker, Edyth *(1867–1950)*

American mezzo, particularly associated with Wagnerian roles. One of the first American singers to enjoy a major operatic career in Europe, she was later also a noted teacher, whose pupils included Irene Dalis and Blanche Thebom.

Walker, Sarah *(b 1945)*

British mezzo, particularly associated with Handel, Monteverdi and Berlioz roles. One of the finest contemporary British operatic artists (and also a noted recitalist), her beautiful voice is used with great intelligence and musicianship and she is an outstanding singing-actress.

Walk to the Paradise Garden

Orchestral excerpt in Scene V of Delius' *A Village Romeo and Juliet*.

Walküre, Die *(The Valkyrie)*

Opera in three acts by Wagner. 1st perf. Munich, 26 June 1870 (composed 1856); libr. by the composer, after the *Nibelungenlied*. Part Two of *Der Ring des Nibelungen**. Principal roles: Wotan (bar), Brünnhilde (sop), Siegmund (ten), Sieglinde (sop), Fricka (mezzo), Hunding (bass). For plot see *Der Ring des Nibelungen*.

Wallace, Ian *(b 1919)*

British bass, particularly associated with Rossini, Mozart and Sullivan roles. One of the finest and most popular postwar British buffos, he had a good if not outstanding voice, allied to fine diction and a superb stage presence.

He has also enjoyed great success as a broadcaster on musical programmes. His autobiography, *Promise Me You'll Sing Mud*, was published in 1975.

Wallace, Jake

Bass role in Puccini's *La Fanciulla del West*. He is an itinerant singer.

Wallace, Vincent *(1812–65)*

Irish composer. After an adventurous life in Australia, India, Chile and Mexico, he settled in London, where his six performed operas established him as one of the most successful 19th-century British composers. His operas, written on an ambitious scale in quasi-Meyerbeerian style, are *Maritana**, by far his most successful work, *Matilda* of *Hungary* (London 28 Feb 1847; libr. Alfred Bunn), *Lurline* (London 23 Feb 1860; libr. Edward Fitzball, after the Loreley legend), which was long popular, *The Amber Witch* (London 28 Feb 1861; libr. Henry Fothergill Chorley), *Love's Triumph* (London 3 Nov 1862; libr. James Robertson Planché) and *The Desert Flower* (London 12 Oct 1864; libr. Augustus Harris and T. J. Williams).

Wallberg, Heinz *(b 1923)*

German conductor, particularly associated with 19th-century German and Italian operas. He was musical director of the Augsburg Stadttheater (1954), the Bremen Opera (1955–61) and the Wiesbaden Opera (1961–74).

Wallmann, Margherita *(b 1904)*

Austrian producer. Originally a dancer and choreographer, she was especially associated with La Scala, Milan, where her productions included many world premières. Her stagings, in traditional style, were noted for their superb handling of crowd scenes and for their fluidity of movement.

Wally, La

Opera in four acts by Catalani. 1st perf. Milan, 20 Jan 1892; libr. by Luigi Illica, after Wilhelmine von Hillern's *Die Geyer-Wally*. Principal roles: Wally (sop), Hagenbach (ten), Gellner (bar), Stromminger (bass), Afra (mezzo), Walter (sop). Catalani's last and finest opera, it is still regularly performed in Italy.

Plot: Tyrol, *c*1800. Hagenbach does not return the love of the hoydenish girl Wally. He humiliates her and she plots to have him killed. Her suitor, Gellner, does this for her by pushing Hagenbach down a ravine. However, Wally is now repentant and rescues him. Hagenbach tells her that he does love her after all, but the two are killed in an avalanche. [R]

Walter, Bruno *(b Schlesinger)* *(1876–1962)*

German conductor, particularly associated with the German repertory. One of the finest operatic conductors of the 20th century, his lyrical and humane interpretations reflected his warm and sympathetic personality. He was musical director of the Munich Opera (1913–22) and the Vienna State Opera (1936–38). He conducted the first performances of Pfitzner's *Palestrina* and *Der Arme Heinrich*, Korngold's *Violanta* and *Der Ring des Polykrates* and Schreker's *Das Spielwerk*. His autobiography, *Theme and Variations*, was published in 1946.

Walther

Tenor role in Wagner's *Tannhäuser*. He is a minstrel knight.

Walther, Count

Bass role in Verdi's *Luisa Miller*. He is Rodolfo's father.

Walther von Stolzing

Tenor role in Wagner's *Die Meistersinger von Nürnberg*. He is a Franconian knight in love with Eva.

Walton, Sir William *(1902–83)*

British composer. His two operas, neither of which are performed as often as their merits deserve, are the neo-classical *Troilus and Cressida** and the witty one-act *The Bear**.

Waltraute

Mezzo role in Wagner's *Die Walküre* and *Götterdämmerung*. She is one of the Valkyries.

Walzertraum, Ein (A Waltz Dream)

Operetta in three acts by O. Straus. 1st perf. Vienna, 2 March 1907; libr. by Felix Dörmann and Leopold Jacobson, after Hans Müller's Das Buch der Abenteuer. Principal roles: Helene (sop), Niki (ten), Montschi (ten), Friederike (mezzo), Wendolin (bar), Franzi (sop). One of Straus' most successful works, it is still regularly performed in German-speaking countries. [R]

Wanda

Soprano role in Offenbach's La Grande-Duchesse de Gérolstein. She is Fritz's sweetheart.

Wanderer

Bass-baritone role in Wagner's Siegfried. He is Wotan in disguise.

Wandering Scholar, The

Opera in one act by Holst. (Op 50). 1st perf. Liverpool, 31 Jan 1934; libr. by Clifford Bax, after Helen Waddell. Principal roles: Pierre (ten), Alison (sop), Fr Philippe (bass), Louis (bar). One of Holst's finest stage works, it is still occasionally performed, usually in the edition prepared in 1968 by Britten and Imogen Holst.

Plot: 13th-century France. Whilst her husband Louis is at the market, Alison receives the lecherous priest Philippe, but they are interrupted by the arrival of the scholar Pierre. They refuse him refreshment and send him away. Pierre returns with Louis and narrates a pointed story which leads to the discovery of Philippe under a pile of straw. [R]

War and Peace (Voyna i Mir)

Opera in two parts (five acts) by Prokofiev. (Op 91). 1st perf. Leningrad, 12 June 1946; libr. by the composer and Mira Mendelson-Prokofieva, after Tolstoy's novel. Revised version, 1st perf. Leningrad, 31 March 1955. Principal roles: Natasha (sop), Prince Andrei (bar), Marshal Kutuzov (b-bar), Pierre (ten), Prince Anatol (ten), Napoleon (bar), Dolokov (bar), Sonya (mezzo), Count Rostov (bar), Akhrosimova (mezzo), Denisov (bar), Hélène (mezzo), Karataev (ten). Arguably Prokofiev's finest opera, its carefully selected scenes from Tolstoy contrast public and private destinies against a backdrop of Russia under threat. The obvious analogy between 1812 and 1944 gave the work a particular relevance and impact at its appearance. Particularly notable for its superb choral writing and for its remarkable portrayal of Kutuzov, it requires vast forces and for that reason is not performed as often as it might be. [R]

Ward, David (1922–83)

British bass, particularly associated with Verdi and Wagner roles, especially Wotan. A singing-actor of great insight and humanity with a warm, rich and beautiful voice, he created Hardy in Berkeley's Nelson.

Ward, Robert (b 1917)

American composer. He has written four operas: He Who Gets Slapped (1957; libr. Bernard Stambler, after Andreyev), the powerful and highly successful The Crucible*, The Lady From Colorado (Central City 1964; libr. Stambler, after Homer Croy) and Claudia Legare (1978; libr. after Heinrik Ibsen).

Warren, Leonard (b Warenoff) (1911–60)

American baritone, particularly associated with the Italian repertory, especially Verdi. One of the greatest of all Verdi baritones, his voice was large, rich, beautiful and powerful with a thrilling upper register. A forthright singing-actor, who also won great popularity as a radio and television singer, he created Ilo in Menotti's *The Island God*. He died on stage during a performance of *La Forza del Destino* at the Metropolitan Opera, New York.

Warsaw National Opera

Poland's principal opera company, it performs at the Teatr Wielki (Grand Theatre), which was designed by Antonio Corazzi and which is the world's largest theatre. Opened in 1833, it was largely destroyed by bombs in 1944; it reopened in November 1965. Musical directors have included Karol Kurpiński, Tomasz Nidecki, Moniuszko, Cesare Tromboni, Emil Mlynarski and Robert Satanowski. The theatre has an associated chamber opera company.

Washington

See Opera Society of Washington

Water Carrier, The

See Deux Journées, Les

Watersprite

Bass role in Dvořák's *Rusalka*. He is Rusalka's father.

Watson, Claire *(b McLamore) (b 1927)*

American soprano, particularly associated with Mozart and Strauss roles. Her beautiful voice was allied to a fine technique, outstanding musicianship and a warm and charming stage personality.

Watson, Lillian

British soprano, particularly associated with Mozart and other soubrette roles. She possesses a bright voice of considerable agility which she uses intelligently, and has a captivating and delightful stage personality.

Watts, Helen *(b 1927)*

British mezzo, particularly associated with Handel and Wagner roles. Possessor of a rich and beautiful voice used with outstanding musicianship and technique, she was best known as a concert singer. Her operatic appearances were sadly infrequent.

Wat Tyler

Opera by Bush. 1st perf. Leipzig, 1953; libr. by Nancy Bush. Principal roles: Wat Tyler (bar), Margaret (sop), John Ball (bass), Richard II (ten), Herdsman (b-bar), Bampton (bar), Minstrel (ten), Queen Mother (mezzo). Bush's finest opera, it tells (from a left-wing viewpoint) of events surrounding the Peasants' Revolt of 1381. It was a joint winner of the Arts Council's 1950 competition for the Festival of Britain.

Weber, Carl Maria von *(1786–1826)*

German composer. His first two operas were written in childhood: the first *Die Macht der Liebe und des Weins* (1798) was destroyed, and the second *Das Waldmädchen* (Freiburg 24 Nov 1800; libr. C. von Steinsberg) was later reworked as *Silvana* (Frankfurt 16 Sept 1810; libr. F. C. Hiemer). Two further works, *Peter Schmoll und seine Nachbarn* (Augsburg March 1803; libr. J. Türk, after C. G. Cramer) and the unfinished *Rübezahl* (1805; libr. J. G. Rhode), followed before the Singspiel *Abu Hassan**, his first major success. In a review written in 1816, Weber referred to "the kind of opera all Germans want – a self-contained work of art in which all elements, contributed by the arts in co-operation, disappear and re-emerge to create a new world". His mature operas attempt to put this striking pre-vision of Wagner's theories into practice, and announce the birth of German romantic opera. The sensational success of *Der Freischütz** marked a turning-point in German musical history. *Euryanthe**, although hampered by its dire libretto, represents a further advance, and *Oberon**, although written in a less complex style, contains some of his finest music. His other mature opera, the comedy *Die Drei Pintos**, was abandoned halfway through and was completed 60 years later by Mahler.

Weber's historical importance can hardly be overstated. His mature works laid the foundations of German national opera, influencing Marschner, Lortzing and, above all, Wagner, who developed Weber's techniques of leitmotiv, of dramatic recitative and of the symphonic use of the orchestra. Weber was musical director at Dresden (1816–26), where he conducted the first performance of Spohr's *Faust*.

Weber, Ludwig *(1899–1974)*

Austrian bass, particularly associated with the German repertory, especially Wagner. Often regarded as the finest Wagnerian bass of the 20th century, he had a rich and warm voice of considerable power and had a sympathetic stage presence, especially as Gurnemanz and Rocco.

Webster, Sir David *(1903–71)*

British administrator. A man of remarkable vision and judgement (with a shrewd nose for talent), he was general administrator of Covent Garden (1945–70). A tremendous showman, he nurtured and built up the infant company from nothing to a position in the late 1960s when many regarded it as the finest company in the world.

We Come to the River

Opera in two acts by Henze. 1st perf. London, 12 July 1976; libr. by Edward Bond. Principal roles: General (bar), Governor (bar), Soldier 2 (ten), Old Woman (mezzo), Young Woman (sop), ADC (bass), Doctor (bass), Emperor (mezzo), Deserter (ten), Wife of Soldier 2 (sop), Rachel (sop). A vast and (in the view of many) pretentious work requiring over 50 soloists, it is an anti-war protest written from Henze's customary left-wing political viewpoint.

Weikl, Bernd *(b 1942)*

Austrian baritone, particularly associated with Mozart and with the German and Italian repertories. He has a rich and warm voice used with fine musicianship and is an accomplished and versatile singing-actor.

Weill, Kurt *(1900–50)*

German composer. Writing in a light and satirical style, and often adopting popular musical forms and advocating left-wing political views, many of his stage works met with great success, particularly those written in collaboration with Bertolt Brecht. His first significant stage work *Der Protagonist** was followed by *Royal Palace* (Berlin 2 March 1927; libr. Iwan Goll), *Der Zar lässt sich Photographieren**, *Mahagonny Singspiel**, *Die Dreigroschenoper**, *Aufstieg und Fall der Stadt Mahagonny**, perhaps his most popular work, *Happy End* (Berlin 2 Sept 1929; libr. Brecht and E. Hauptmann) [R], *Der Jasager* (Berlin Radio 23 June 1930; libr. Brecht, after the Japanese Noh play *Taniko*), *Die Bürgschaft* (Berlin 10 March 1932; libr. Caspar Neher), *Die Silbersee* (Leipzig 18 Feb 1933; libr. Georg Kaiser) [R] and the sung ballet *Die Sieben Todsünden*

(Paris 7 June 1933; libr. Brecht) [R], which is often staged as an opera.

Forced to leave Germany by the Nazis, in 1935 Weill settled in the United States where he wrote a number of further stage works, some in Broadway musical style. They include *Knickerbocker Holiday* (New York 1938; libr. Maxwell Anderson), *Street Scene** and *Down in the Valley**. He was married to the singer Lotte Lenya*.

Weimar Opera

Opera in this German town in Thuringia is given at the Deutsches Nationaltheater (cap. 2,000), which opened in 1907.

Weinberger, Jaromír *(1896– 1967)*

Czech composer. His first opera, written in Czech national style, was the highly successful *Shvanda the Bagpiper**. None of his three other operas even began to approach this initial success. *Die Geliebte Stimme* (Munich 28 Feb 1931; libr. composer), *The Outcasts of Poker Flat* (*Lidé z Pokerflatu*, Brno 19 Nov 1932; libr. M. Kareš, after Bret Harte) and the ambitious *Wallenstein* (*Valdštejn*, Vienna 18 Nov 1937; libr. Kareš, after Friedrich von Schiller) are all now forgotten.

Weingartner, Felix von *(1863– 1942)*

Austrian conductor and composer. One of the finest conductors of the early 20th century, particularly associated with the German repertory, he was musical director of the Mannheim Opera (1888–91), the Berlin State Opera (1891–98), the Vienna State Opera (1908–11 and 1935–36), the Hamburg Opera (1912–14), the Darmstadt Opera (1915–19) and the Vienna Volksoper (1919–24). He composed 12 operas, including *Sakuntala* (Weimar 1884; libr. after Kalidasa).

Welche Wonne, welche Lust

Soprano aria for Blönchen in Act II of Mozart's *Die Entführung aus dem Serail*.

Welitsch, Ljuba *(b Veličhkova) (b 1913)*

Bulgarian soprano, particularly associated with dramatic German and Italian roles, especially Salome. She had a silvery, sensuous voice with a soaring upper register which was combined with a keen dramatic sense. Her prodigal use of her voice, combined with her fiery stage presence, made her one of the most thrilling operatic artists of the immediate postwar era. After 1959, she enjoyed a second career as an actress, appearing in a number of films.

Weller, Walter *(b 1939)*

Austrian conductor and violinist. Leader of the Vienna Philharmonic Orchestra from 1961, he turned to conducting in 1966. Since then, he has given notable performances of the German repertory, mainly at the Vienna State Opera.

Wellesz, Egon *(1885–1974)*

Austrian composer and musicologist, resident in England after World War II. He wrote six operas, largely inspired by myth, in an eclectic style influenced both by Schönberg and by his researches into Baroque opera. His most important operas are *Alkestis* (Mannheim 20 March 1924; libr. Hugo von Hofmannsthal, after Euripides) and *Incognita* (Oxford 5 Dec 1951; libr. E. Mackenzie, after William Congreve).

His writings include *Essays on Opera* (1951).

Wellgunde

Mezzo role in Wagner's *Das Rheingold* and *Götterdämmerung*. She is one of the three Rhinemaidens.

Welsh National Opera

Based at the New Theatre, Cardiff (cap. 1,168) and touring throughout Wales and southern and central England, the company was formed in April 1946 by the baritone John Morgan, the conductor Idloes Owen and the businessman Dr Bill Smith. The company soon established a strong Verdi tradition, partly because of its superb chorus, which remained amateur until 1968. Recently, it has also been noted for its Janáček and Wagner performances, and currently ranks as one of the most exciting and innovative European opera companies. Musical directors have been Idloes Owen, Leo Quayle, Frederick Berend, Vilem Tausky, Warwick Braithwaite, Sir Charles Groves, Bryan Balkwill, James Lockhart, Richard Armstrong and Sir Charles Mackerras.

Werle, Lars Johan *(b 1926)*

Swedish composer. He has written four operas in unconventional theatrical style, which have met with considerable success in Sweden. They are the opera-in-the-round *Dreaming About Thérèse**, *The Journey* (*Resan*, Hamburg 1969; libr. Lars Runsten, after P. C. Jersild's *Till Varmare Länder*), *Tintomara* (Stockholm 1973; libr. E. Söderström, after C. J. L. Almqvist) and *Medusa and the Devil* (*Medusan och Dväjulen*, 1973; libr. E. Grave).

Werther

Opera in four acts by Massenet. 1st perf. Vienna, 16 Feb 1892; libr. by Edouard Blau, Paul Milliet and Georges Hartmann, after Goethe's *Die Leiden des Jungen Werthers*. Principal roles: Werther (ten), Charlotte (mezzo), Sophie (sop), Albert (bar), Bailie (bass), Johann (bass), Schmidt (ten). Arguably Massenet's finest opera, its balance of dramatic urgency and lyrical outpourings well catches the character of Goethe's hero.

Plot: Frankfurt, *c* 1780. The melancholy young poet Werther meets the Bailie's elder daughter Charlotte and falls in love with her. He is distraught to learn that she is engaged to Albert. Obsessed with Charlotte, he decides to travel but keeps writing her impassioned letters while he is gone. Charlotte realises that she feels something for Werther, and when he returns he extracts an admission of love from her before she orders him to leave. Albert suspects what has happened, and when a message arrives from Werther asking for the loan of his pistols, he agrees. Charlotte arrives to find that Werther has shot himself, and he dies in her arms. [R]

West Germany

See Germany

Wexford Festival

Founded by Dr T. J. Walsh (*d* 1988) in 1951, this annual autumn opera festival in the Irish Republic is devoted to the performance of completely forgotten works. One of the most enterprising and popular European opera festivals, it has an enviable reputation for discovering major new vocal talent. The entire local community takes part in the mounting of the festival, which has a charming and welcoming atmosphere like no other. Performances are given at the Theatre Royal (cap. 550) and the orchestra is the Radio Telefis Eireann Symphony.

When I am laid in earth
Mezzo aria for Dido in Act III of
Purcell's *Dido and Aeneas*.

Where e'er you walk
Tenor aria for Jupiter in Act II of
Handel's *Semele*.

White, Willard *(b 1946)*
Jamaican bass, particularly associated
with Mozart and Wagner roles and
with Porgy. He has a dark, rich and
grainy voice of considerable power and
range which is used with fine
musicianship, a commanding stage
presence, and a powerful physique. The
first black singer to have developed a
major career based in Britain, he is a
singing-actor of outstanding ability and
commitment. He has also played
Othello for the Royal Shakespeare
Company.

**Widerspenstigen Zähmung,
Der** *(The Taming of the Shrew)*
Opera in four acts by Götz. 1st perf.
Mannheim, 11 Oct 1874; libr. by
Joseph Viktor Widmann, after
Shakespeare's play. Principal roles:
Katharina (mezzo), Lucentio (ten),
Bianca (sop), Petruchio (bar). Götz's
most successful opera, it is still
performed quite often in German-
speaking countries, but is almost
unknown elsewhere. The libretto
follows Shakespeare closely.

Plot: Padua. Bianca and Lucentio are
in love, but Bianca's termagant elder
sister Katharina is an obstacle to their
marriage. To help the lovers, Petruchio
agrees to marry Katharina, woos her,
and finally tames her. [R]

Widor, Charles Marie *(1844–
1937)*
French composer and organist.
Although best known as a composer of

organ music, he also wrote three
operas: *Maître Ambros* (Paris 6 May
1886; libr. A. Dorchain and Francois
Coppée), *Les Pêcheurs de Saint-Jean*
(Paris 26 Dec 1905; libr. Henri Cain)
and *Nerto* (Paris 27 Oct 1924; libr.
Maurice Léna, after Frédéric Mistral).

Wiener Blut *(Vienna Blood)*
Operetta in three acts by Johann
Strauss II. 1st perf. Vienna, 25 Oct
1899; libr. by Viktor Léon and Leo
Stein. Principal roles: Gabriele (sop),
Pepi (sop), Count Zedlau (ten), Franzi
(sop), Josef (bar), Prime Minister (bar).
A pastiche, it was arranged from other
Strauss pieces by Adolf Müller Jr and
has always been one of the most
popular of Viennese operettas.

Plot: Vienna, 1815. During the
Congress of Vienna, the ambassador
Count Zedlau, although married to
Gabriele, is having affairs with both the
ballerina Franzi and the model Pepi,
who is engaged to his valet Josef. His
attempts to keep all these relationships
going at once causes vast confusion, a
confusion compounded by the
intervention of the aged but amorous
Prime Minister. After much intrigue,
misunderstanding and false identities,
Zedlau realises that he still loves
Gabriele and she forgives his
peccadillos. [R]

Wiesbaden Opera
Opera in this German city in Hesse is
given at the Grosses Haus (cap. 1,325),
which opened in October 1894. Always
noted for its adventurous repertory
policy, musical directors have included
Otto Klemperer, Joseph Rosenstock,
Karl Elmendorff, Wolfgang Sawallisch,
Heinz Wallberg and Siegfried Köhler.
The annual Wiesbaden May Festival
dates originally from 1896; since 1950,
it has been host to visiting companies
from Eastern Europe.

OSCAR WILDE

As well as providing source material for operas, the works of the Irish poet, playwright and novelist Oscar Fingal O'Flahertie Wills Wilde (1856–1900) and the aesthetic movement of which he was the most famous exemplar form the subject of one of operetta's most devastating satires: Sullivan's *Patience*. Nearly 20 operas have been based on his writings. Below are listed, by work, those operas by composers with entries in this dictionary.

The Birthday of the Infanta
Zemlinsky	Der Geburstag der Infantin	1922

The Duchess of Padua
Wagner-Régeny	La Sainte Courtesane	1930

A Florentine Tragedy
Zemlinsky	Eine Florentinische Tragödie	1917

The Happy Prince
Williamson	The Happy Prince	1965

The Importance of Being Ernest
Castelnuovo-Tedesco	The Importance of Being Ernest	1962

Salome
Strauss	Salome	1905

Wilde, Oscar
See panel above

Wildschütz, Der (*The Poacher*) Opera in three acts by Lortzing. 1st perf. Leipzig, 31 Dec 1842; libr. by the composer, after August von Kotzebue's *Der Rehbock*. Principal roles: Baculus (bass), Gretchen (sop), Count Eberbach (bar), Baroness Freimann (sop), Nanette (sop), Baron Kronthal (ten), Countess (mezzo). Lortzing's most successful opera apart from *Zar und Zimmermann*, it remains popular in Germany, but is almost never performed elsewhere.

Plot: The schoolteacher Baculus is caught accidentally poaching on Count Eberbach's estate. The Count's sister Baroness Freimann, disguised as a schoolboy, comes to his aid. She offers to disguise herself as the teacher's fiancée, Gretchen, and intercede with the Count on Baculus's behalf. After a great deal of intrigue, misunderstanding and general complication, Baculus is eventually forgiven. [R]

William Ratcliff

Opera in three acts by Cui. 1st perf. St. Petersburg, 26 Feb 1869; libr. by A. Pleshcheyev, after Heinrich Heine's *Wilhelm Ratcliff*. Cui's most successful opera, it is nowadays all but forgotten, even in Russia. For plot see *Guglielmo Ratcliff*.

Williamson, Malcolm *(b 1931)*

Australian composer. His operas, written in a fluent and readily accessible style, have met with some success in Britain. His stage works are *Our Man in Havana**, *English Eccentrics* (Aldeburgh 11 June 1964; libr. Geoffrey Dunn, after Edith Sitwell). *The Happy Prince* (Farnham 22 May 1965; libr. composer, after Oscar Wilde) [R], the children's opera *Julius Caesar Jones* (London 4 Jan 1966; libr. Dunn) [R], *The Violins of St Jacques**, *Dunstan and the Devil* (Cookham 19 May 1967; libr. Dunn), *The Growing Castle* (Dynevor 13 Aug 1968; libr. composer, after August Strindberg's *A Dream Play*), *Lucky Peter's Journey** and *The Red Sea* (Dartington 14 April 1972; libr. composer).

William Tell

See Guillaume Tell

Willner, Alfred Maria

Austrian librettist. He wrote, in whole or in part, many libretti, both operas and operettas. He provided texts for Fall (*Die Dollarprinzessin*), Goldmark (*Das Heimchen am Herd* and *Ein Wintermärchen*) and Lehár (*Eva, Frasquita, Der Graf von Luxemburg, Wo die Lerche Singt* and *Zigeunerliebe*)

amongst others. Puccini's *La Rondine* is based on one of his plays.

Willow Song

Soprano aria for Desdemona: (1) in Act III of Rossini's *Otello* ('Assisa a pie d'un salice') (2) in Act IV of Verdi's *Otello* ('Piangea cantando').

Windgassen, Wolfgang *(1914–74)*

German tenor, particularly associated with Wagnerian roles, especially Siegfried and Tristan. The leading heldentenor of the postwar era, he was an artist of outstanding intelligence and musicianship, possessing a fine voice and an assured technique. He was director of the Stuttgart Opera (1972–74). His wife Lore Wissmann (*b* 1922) was a successful soprano.

Winter, Peter von *(1754–1825)*

German composer. He wrote 37 operas, for Germany, Italy, Austria, London and Prague. Beginning by writing Singspiels and Zauberopers, he later turned successfully to romantic opera. His most important works include *Das Unterbrochene Opferfest**, at one time one of the most popular of all German operas, *Das Labyrinth* (Vienna 12 June 1798; libr. Emanuel Schikaneder), which is a follow-up to *Die Zauberflöte*, *Zaira* (London 29 Jan 1805; libr. after Voltaire's *Zaïre*), the Ossianic *Colmal* (Munich 15 Sept 1809; libr. M. von Collin) and *Maometto II* (Milan 28 Jan 1817; libr. Felice Romani, after Voltaire's *Mahomet*).

Wishart, Peter *(b 1921)*

British composer. His four operas are *In the Bush* (1956; libr. D. Roberts), *The Captive* (1960; libr. Roberts), *The Clandestine Marriage* (1971; libr. Roberts, after David Garrick and

George Coleman) and *Clytemnestra* (Oxford 1973).

Witches' Sabbath
The title of Act II Scene II of Boito's *Mefistofele*.

Wixell, Ingvar *(b 1931)*
Swedish baritone, particularly associated with Mozart roles, the Italian repertory and with Mandryka. He possesses a bright and incisive voice of considerable power and has excellent diction and a good stage presence. Although he has sung much Verdi, he is not a true Verdi baritone.

Woglinde
Soprano role in Wagner's *Das Rheingold* and *Götterdämmerung*. She is one of the three Rhinemaidens.

Wolf, Hugo *(1860–1903)*
Austrian composer. Although best known as a song composer (and as a vitriolic critic), he also wrote two operas: the successful *Der Corregidor** and the unfinished *Manuel Venegas* (Mannheim 1 March 1903, begun 1897; libr. M. Hoernes, after Pedro Alarcón's *El Niño de la Bola*).

Wolff, Albert *(1884–1970)*
French conductor and composer. One of the finest interpreters of the French repertory in the inter-war period, he was musical director of the Opéra-Comique, Paris (1921–24) and conducted the first performances of *Les Mamelles de Tirésias*, Ibert's *Angélique*, Charpentier's *Julien*, Laparra's *La Jota* and Bondeville's *Madame Bovary*. He also composed three operas: *Soeur Béatrice* (Nice 1948, composed 1911; libr. Maurice Maeterlinck), *Le Marchand des Masques* (Nice 1914; libr. L. Merlet and T. Salignac) and

L'Oiseau Bleu (New York 27 Dec 1919; libr. Maeterlinck).

Wolf-Ferrari, Ermanno *(1876–1948)*
Italian composer. The principal figure of the early 20th century neo-classical school, his operas (nearly all drawn from Goldoni and other 18th-century comic writers) are notable for their grace, rhythmic vitality, charm and sparkling orchestration. His first published opera *La Cenerentola* (Venice 22 Feb 1901; libr. M. Pezzè-Pescolato, after Charles Perrault) was followed by *Le Donne Curiose**, his first success, the popular *I Quatro Rusteghi**, *Il Segreto di Susanna**, perhaps his most enduring success, *I Gioielli della Madonna**, his one excursion into the verismo field, *L'Amore Medico**, *Gli Amanti Sposi* (Venice 19 Feb 1925; libr. G. Pizzolato, Enrico Golisciani and Giovacchino Forzano, after Carlo Goldoni), *Das Himmelskleid* (Munich 21 April 1927; libr. composer, after Perrault), the ambitious *Sly**, *La Vedova Scaltra**, the successful *Il Campiello**, *La Dama Boba** and *Gli Dei a Tebe* (Hanover 4 June 1943; libr. L. Strecker and Mario Ghisalberti).

Wolfram
Baritone role in Wagner's *Tannhäuser*. A minstrel-knight, he is a friend of Tannhäuser's.

Wolf's Glen Scene
The title usually given to Act II, Scene II of Weber's *Der Freischütz*, in which the free-shooting bullets are cast. It remains unsurpassed as a musical depiction of the macabre.

Wood, Sir Henry *(1869–1944)*
British conductor. He conducted a considerable number of operas in the early part of his career, including the

first performance of Stanford's *Shamus O'Brien*, but later devoted himself entirely to the concert hall. The famous annual promenade concerts at London's Royal Albert Hall are his lasting memorial. His autobiography, *My Life of Music*, was published in 1938.

Woodbird
Soprano role in Wagner's *Siegfried*.

Wordsworth, Miss
Soprano role in Britten's *Albert Herring*. She is the schoolmistress.

Workshop
A term which describes an organisation devoted to teaching the techniques of operatic performance to students or amateurs by the preparation of operatic scenes. Opera workshops are most frequently found in the United States.

Wotan
Baritone role in Wagner's *Das Rheingold*, *Die Walküre* and *Siegfried* (in which last he is disguised as the Wanderer). Fricka's husband, he is the ruler of the gods.

Wotan's Farewell
The title usually given to Wotan's final monologue in Act III of Wagner's *Die Walküre* as he takes leave of Brünnhilde.

Wozzeck
Opera in three acts by Berg. 1st perf. Berlin, 14 Dec 1925; libr. by the composer, after Georg Büchner's *Woyzeck*. Principal roles: Wozzeck (bar), Marie (sop), Drum-Major (ten), Doctor (bass), Captain (ten), Margaret (mezzo), Andres (ten), Idiot (ten). Berg's first opera, sometimes regarded as the greatest of all 20th-century operas, it is an intense setting of Büchner's play, combining freely-conceived atonality with a highly complex formal structure. The title character, described by Tito Gobbi as "that tragic torn-off rag of humanity", is one of the most demanding musico-dramatic roles in the repertory.

Plot: To support the son whom he has had by his common-law wife Marie, the poor soldier Wozzeck shaves the Captain and submits to the Doctor's medical experiments. Wozzeck discovers that the frustrated Marie has been having an affair with the Drum-Major. He cuts her throat in the woods and throws the dagger into a pond. Returning to the pond in search of the dagger, he wades in and drowns himself. Marie's body is discovered and the local children tell her uncomprehending child that his mother is dead. [R]

Wreckers, The
Opera in three acts by Smyth. 1st perf. (as *Les Naufrageurs*) Leipzig, 1 Nov 1906; libr. by Harrey Brewster, after his play. Principal roles: Thirza (mezzo), Mark (ten), Pascoe (bass), Avis (sop). Often regarded as Smyth's finest opera, it was successful in its time, but is nowadays all but forgotten.

Plot: 18th-century Cornwall. The local inhabitants pray for ships to be sent to the coast so that they can wreck and despoil them. Their savagery revolts Thirza, wife of the headman Pascoe. With her lover Mark, she lights warning fires on the cliffs. They are discovered, however, and are locked in a cave where they will be drowned by the rising tide.

Writers
See Aeschylus; Andersen; d'Annunzio; Auden; Beaumarchais; Brecht; Byron; Cervantes; Cocteau; Corneille; Dante; Dickens; Dostoyevsky; Dumas; Euripides; Gilbert; Goethe; Gogol; Goldoni; Gozzi;

Hoffmann; Hofmannsthal; Hugo;
Maeterlinck; Mérimée; Molière;
Poe; Pushkin; Racine; Sardou;
Schiller; Scott; Shakespeare;
Sophocles; Tolstoy; Voltaire;
Wilde; Zola

Writers as librettists

Famous writers, poets and playwrights
have turned their attention all too
infrequently to the writing of operatic
libretti. Those who have done so
include:

- Hans Christian Andersen: Gläser's
  The Watersprites and *The Wedding
  on Lake Como*, Weyse's *Kenilworth*
  and Bredal's *The Bride of
  Lammermoor*.
- Gabriele d'Annunzio: Pizzetti's *Fedra*
  and Mascagni's *Parisina*.
- W. H. Auden: Britten's *Paul Bunyan*,
  Henze's *Elegie für Junge Liebende*
  and *The Bassarids*, Nabokov's *Love's
  Labours Lost* and Stravinsky's *The
  Rake's Progress*.
- Pierre-Augustin Beaumarchais:
  Salieri's *Tarare*.
- Arnold Bennet: Goossens' *Judith* and
  Don Juan de Mañara.
- Bjørnstjerne Bjørnson: Grieg's *Olav
  Trygvason*.
- Pedro Calderón: Hidalgo's *La
  Púrpura de la Rosa* and *Celos Aun
  del Aire Matan*.
- G. K. Chesterton: Holbrooke's *The
  Snob*.
- Paul Claudel: Milhaud's *Christophe
  Colomb* and *Les Choëphores* and
  Honegger's *Jeanne d'Arc au Bûcher*.
- Jean Cocteau: Honegger's *Antigonae*,
  Stravinsky's *Oedipus Rex*, Poulenc's
  Le Gendarme Incompris and *La Voix
  Humaine* and Milhaud's *Le Pauvre
  Matelot*.
- Colette: Ravel's *L'Enfant et les
  Sortilèges*.
- Charles Dickens: Hullah's *The Village
  Coquettes*.

- John Dryden: Purcell's *The Indian
  Queen*, *King Arthur* and *The
  Tempest*.
- Alexandre Dumas père: Monpou's
  Piquillo.
- E. M. Forster: Britten's *Billy Budd*.
- Christopher Fry: Penderecki's
  Paradise Lost.
- John Gay: Handel's *Acis and Galatea*
  and Pepusch's *The Beggar's Opera*
  and *Polly*.
- Carlo Goldoni: Galuppi's *Il Filosofo
  di Campagna*, Piccinni's *La Buona
  Figliuola* and many others.
- Ted Hughes: Crosse's *The Story of
  Vasco*.
- Victor Hugo: Bertin's *Esmeralda*.
- Doris Lessing: Glass' *The Making of
  the Representative for Planet 8*.
- Maurice Maeterlinck: Dukas' *Ariane
  et Barbe-Bleue*.
- Dorothy Parker: Bernstein's *Candide*.
- J. B. Priestley: Bliss' *The Olympians*.
- Victorien Sardou: Offenbach's *Le Roi
  Carotte* and *Fantasio*, Saint-Saëns'
  Les Barbares and Bizet's *Grisélidis*.
- Gertrude Stein: Thomson's *Four
  Saints in Three Acts* and *The Mother
  of Us All*.
- Ivan Turgenev: Viardot-García's *Le
  Dernier Sorcier*, *L'Ogre* and *Trop de
  Femmes*.
- Paul Verlaine: Chabrier's *Vaucochard
  et Fils Premier* and *Fisch-Ton-Kan*.
- Voltaire: Rameau's *Samson*, *La
  Princesse de Navarre* and *La Temple
  de la Gloire*.
- Tennessee Williams: Banfield's *Lord
  Byron's Love-Letter*.
- Emile Zola: Bruneau's *La Rêve*,
  Messidor, *L'Ouragan*, *L'Engant-Roi*,
  Naïs Micoulin and *Les Quatre
  Journées*.
- Stefan Zweig: Strauss' *Die
  Schweigsame Frau*.

  See also entries for **Brecht,
  Gilbert, Goethe, Hofmannsthal,
  Molière and Rousseau**

Writers in opera

A number of novelists, poets and playwrights appear as operatic characters, including:

- Giovanni Boccaccio in Suppé's *Boccaccio*.
- John Bunyan in Vaughan Williams' *The Pilgrim's Progress*.
- Lord Byron in Banfield's *Lord Byron's Love-Letter* and Thomson's *Lord Byron*.
- Svatopluk Čech in Janáček's *The Excursions of Mr Brouček*.
- Miguel Cervantes in J. Strauss' *Das Spitzenbuch der Königin*.
- André Chénier in Giordano's *Andrea Chénier*.
- George Crabbe in Britten's *Peter Grimes*.
- Dante Alighieri in Godard's *Dante et Béatrice* and Rachmaninov's *Francesca da Rimini*.
- Alexandre Dumas père in Giordano's *Andrea Chénier*.
- Froissart in Sallinen's *The King Goes Forth to France*.
- Johann Goethe in Lehár's *Friederike*.
- E. T. A. Hoffmann in Offenbach's *Les Contes d'Hoffmann*.
- Jakob Lenz in Rihm's *Jakob Lenz*.
- Lucan in Monteverdi's *L'Incoronazione di Poppea*.
- John Milton in Spontini's *Milton*.
- Ovid in Gagliano's *La Dafne*.
- Philippe Quinault in Isouard's *Lully et Quinault*.
- François Rabelais in Ganné's *Rabelais*.
- Jean-Jacques Rousseau in Dalayrac's *L'Enfance de Jean-Jacques Rousseau*.
- Sappho in Gounod's *Sapho* and Pacini's *Saffo*.
- William Shakespeare in Thomas' *La Songe d'un Nuit d'Eté*.
- Torquato Tasso in Donizetti's *Torquato Tasso*.
- Virgil in Rachmaninov's *Francesca da Rimini*.
- Voltaire in Bernstein's *Candide*.

Wunderlich, Fritz *(1930–66)*

German tenor, particularly associated with Mozart and lighter German roles and with Viennese operetta. The outstanding German lyric tenor of the postwar era, his tragically early death in an accident cut short a brilliant career. He had a suave, beautiful voice used with superb musicianship, and a good stage presence. He created Tiresias in Orff's *Oedipus der Tyrann* and Christoph in Egk's *Die Verlobung in San Domingo*.

Wuppertal Opera

The theatre (cap. 870) in this German town in Rhineland-Westphalia opened in 1956. The company is noted for its progressive repertory policy and for its encouragement of young talent. Musical directors have included Hans-Georg Ratjen, János Kulka and Peter Gülke.

Wurm

Bass role in Verdi's *Luisa Miller*. He is Count Walther's evil retainer.

Wuthering Heights

Works of this title based on Emily Brontë's novel include:

(1) Opera in four acts by Herrmann. Composed 1950; libr. by L. Fletcher. Principal roles: Heathcliff (bar), Nelly (mezzo), Earnshaw (bar), Mr Lockwood (bass), Cathy (sop), Joseph (bass), Edgar and Isabella Linton (ten and mezzo). Herrmann's most ambitious composition, which has never been performed on the stage, it is a straightforward setting of the novel. [R]

(2) Opera in three acts by Floyd. 1st perf. Santa Fe, 16 July 1958; libr. by the composer.

X

Xenia
The daughter of Tsar Boris, she appears as: (1) Soprano role in Moussorgsky's *Boris Godunov*. (2) Mezzo role in Dvořák's *Dimitrij*.

Xerxes
See **Serse**

Xyndas, Spyridon *(c 1812–96)*
Greek composer. He wrote seven operas, of which the most important is the political satire *The Parliamentary Candidate* (*O Ypopifios Vouleftis*, Corfu 1867; libr. I. Rinopoulos), which was the first opera written to a Greek libretto. Most of his music was destroyed in the bombing of Corfu in World War II.

Yamadori, Prince
Baritone role in Puccini's *Madama Butterfly*. He is one of Cio-Cio-San's suitors.

Yaroslavna
Soprano role in Borodin's *Prince Igor*. She is Igor's wife.

Yeltsky, Prince
Baritone role in Tchaikovsky's *The Queen of Spades*. He is Lisa's fiancé.

Yeomen of England, The
Baritone aria for the Earl of Essex in Act I of German's *Merrie England*.

Yeomen of the Guard, The or The Merryman and His Maid
Operetta in two acts by Sullivan. 1st perf. London, 30 Oct 1888; libr. by W. S. Gilbert. Principal roles: Jack Point (bar), Elsie Maynard (sop), Col Fairfax (ten), Phoebe Meryll (mezzo), Wilfred Shadbolt (b-bar), Dame Carruthers (mezzo), Sgt Meryll (bass), Sir Richard Cholmondeley (b-bar), Leonard Meryll (ten), Kate (sop). One of the best-loved and much the most serious of the Savoy Operas, it was an instant success and enjoyed an initial run of over 450 performances. For this work, Sullivan provided perhaps the finest operatic overture by any British composer.

Plot: Tower of London, 16th century. Col Fairfax is condemned to death. He tells Sir Richard, the lieutenant of the Tower, that he wishes to marry before his death in order to thwart the machinations of a relative. Sir Richard encounters the poor strolling players, Jack Point and his sweetheart Elsie Maynard, and persuades Elsie to become a bride for one day. Meanwhile, Sgt Meryll is determined to engineer Fairfax's escape. His daughter Phoebe wheedles the key to Fairfax's cell from her admirer the jailer Shadbolt, and Fairfax is disguised as Meryll's son Leonard, who has been appointed a yeoman but who is not known at the Tower. News arrives that Fairfax had been reprieved but that the warrant had been deliberately held up by his relative. Fairfax reveals himself and claims Elsie as his wife, and the heart-broken Point collapses at her feet. [R]

Yniold
Soprano trouser-role in Debussy's *Pelléas et Mélisande*. He is Golaud's young son. The role is occasionally sung by a treble.

Yodelling (from the German *jodel*)
A method of male vocal production which consists of frequent alterations between the natural voice and falsetto. Used for simple dance-like melodies, it is widely practised in the Austrian Tyrol. Operatic examples of its use may be found in Offenbach's *La Belle Hélène* and *Christopher Columbus*.

Yolanta
See Iolanta

Young, Alexander *(b 1920)*
British tenor, particularly associated
with Handel and Mozart roles and with
Tom Rakewell. One of the most stylish
and musicianly British tenors of the
postwar era, he created Charles Darnay
in Benjamin's *A Tale of Two Cities*,
Philippe in Berkeley's *A Dinner
Engagement* and Popristchin in Searle's
Diary of a Madman.

Ysaÿe, Eugène *(1858–1931)*
Belgian violinist, composer and
conductor. Best known as a composer
of violin music, he also wrote one
opera (to his own libretto in Walloon),
Peter the Miner*.

Yugoslavia
See Belgrade Opera; Zagreb
Opera

**Yugoslavian opera
composers**
See Baranović; Gotovac; Zajc

Other national opera composers
include:
(1) *Croatia*: Blagoje Bersa (1873–1904),
Antun Dubronić (1878–1955), Josip
Hatze (1879–1959) and Vatroslav
Lisinski (1819–54), whose *Love and
Malice* (*Ljubav i Zloba*, 1845) was the
first opera written to a Croatian
libretto.
(2) *Serbia*: Isador Bajic (1878–1915),
Stanislav Binički (1872–1942), Petar
Konjović (1883–1970), Petar Krstić
(1877–1957) and Petar Stojanović
(1883–1957).
(3) *Slovenia*: Gašpar Mašek (1794–
1873), Jurij Mihevec (1805–82), Franz
Pollini (1762–1846), Risto Savin (*b*
Frideric Širca) (1859–1948) and Jacob
Zupan (1734–1810).

Yuri
Baritone role in Tippett's *The Ice
Break*. Lev and Nadia's son, he is
Gayle's boyfriend.

Zaccaria

Bass role in Verdi's *Nabucco*. The prophet of Israel, he is a conflation of the biblical Jeremiah and Ezekiel.

Zaccaria, Nicola *(b 1923)*

Greek bass, particularly associated with the Italian repertory. He possessed a rich and imposing voice of considerable power and had a good stage presence. He created the third Tempter in Pizzetti's *L'Assassinio nella Cattedrale*.

Zafred, Mario *(b 1922)*

Italian composer and critic. His operas, similar in style to 'orthodox Soviet' music and reflecting his left-wing political views, include *Amleto* (Rome 1961; libr. composer and L. Zafred, after Shakespeare's *Hamlet*) and *Wallenstein* (Rome 1965; libr. composer and L. Zafred, after Friedrich von Schiller). He was artistic director of the Teatro Communale Giuseppe Verdi, Trieste (1966) and the Rome Opera (1968–74) and was also music critic of the Rome *Unità* (1949–56).

Zagreb Opera

The Croatian National Opera was organised in its present form by Ivan Zajc* in 1870. Performances are given at the National Theatre (cap. 850), which opened in 1895. Musical directors have included Gotovac, Milan Sachs and Lovro von Matačić.

Zagrosek, Lothar *(b 1942)*

German conductor, particularly associated with Mozart operas and with contemporary works, of which he is one of the leading modern exponents. Musical director of the Paris Opéra. He conducted the first performance of Höller's *Le Maître et Marguerite*.

Zaida

Mezzo role in Rossini's *Il Turco in Italia*. She is Selim's old love.

Zaïde

Unfinished opera in two acts by Mozart (K 344). 1st perf. Frankfurt, 27 Jan 1866 (composed 1779); libr. by Johann Andreas Schachtner, after Joseph von Friebert. Principal roles: Zaïde (sop), Gometz (ten), Allazim (bass), Sultan (ten), Osmin (bar). The performing edition of this Singspiel, elements of which hint at the later *Die Entführung aus dem Serail*, was prepared by Anton André from the 15 musical numbers which survive.

Plot: Turkey. The Sultan's favourite, Zaïde, takes pity on Gometz, the Sultan's European captive, and provides him with money for an escape. Gometz escapes with the aid of the Sultan's renegade servant Allazim, but is recaptured. [R]

Zaira

Works of this title based on Voltaire's *Zaïre* include:

(1) Opera in two acts by Winter. 1st perf. London, 29 Jan 1805.

(2) Opera in two acts by Bellini. 1st perf. Parma, 16 May 1829; libr. by Felice Romani. The least successful of Bellini's mature operas and nowadays

almost never performed, he incorporated much of the music into *I Capuleti e i Montecchi**.

(3) Opera in two acts by Mercadante. 1st perf. Naples, 31 Aug 1831; libr. by Felice Romani.

Zajc, Ivan *(1832–1914)*

Croatian composer. He was the leading figure behind the organisation of the Zagreb Opera in 1870, and one of the first composers to set Croatian libretti. His 21 operas include *Amelia* (Rijeka 24 April 1860; libr. after Friedrich von Schiller's *Die Räuber*), *Nikola Šubić Zrinjski* (Zagreb 4 Nov 1876; libr. Hugo Badalić, after Theodore Körner's *Zriny*), his finest work, *Lizinka* (Zagreb 12 Nov 1878; libr. J. E. Tomić, after Alexander Pushkin's *Mistress Into Maid*) and *Our Father* (*Oče Naš*, Zagreb 16 Dec 1911; libr. J. Benešić, after François Coppée).

Zampa

or **La Fiancée de Marbre** (*The Marble Fiancée*)

Opera in three acts by Hérold. 1st perf. Paris, 3 May 1831; libr. by Anne-Honoré Joseph de Mélesville. Principal roles: Zampa (bar), Camilla (sop), Alfonso (ten), Rita (mezzo), Dandalo (bar), Daniel (bass). By far Hérold's most successful opera, it was enormously popular throughout the 19th century, but is nowadays only infrequently performed. The famous overture is still popular in the concert hall.

Plot: 17th-century Sicily. The pirate chieftain Zampa attempts to abduct Camilla, the fiancée of Alfonso (who is in fact Zampa's brother). He is foiled when a marble statue, inhabited by the spirit of his former wife Alice, whose heart he broke, pulls him away and drowns him.

Zampieri, Mara *(b 1941)*

Italian soprano, particularly associated with the Italian repertory, especially Verdi. One of the finest Italian sopranos of the younger generation, whe possesses an exciting and intelligently used lyrico-spinto voice and has a good stage presence.

Zancanaro, Giorgio

Italian baritone, particularly associated with the Italian repertory, especially Verdi. A true Verdi baritone, he possesses a dark, rich and velvety voice of considerable power and range and has a good stage presence.

Zandonai, Riccardo *(1883–1944)*

Italian composer. One of the leading verismo composers, many of his 12 operas enjoyed considerable success in their day, and a few are still performed. His operas are the unperformed *La Coppa del Re* (1906; libr. G. Chiesa, after Friedrich von Schiller), *Il Grillo del Facolare* (Turin 1908; libr. Cesare Hanau, after Charles Dickens' *The Cricket on the Hearth*), *Conchita* (Milan 1911; libr. M. Vaucaire and Carlo Zangarini, after Louÿs) [R], which established his reputation, *Melenis* (Milan 1912; libr. Zangarini and M. Spirtini, after L. Bouillet), *Francesca da Rimini**, his most successful and enduring work, *La Via della Finestra* (Pesaro 1919; libr. Giuseppe Adami, after Eugène Scribe), the successful *Giulietta e Romeo**, the once-popular *I Cavalieri di Ekebù**, *Giuliano* (Naples 1928; libr. Arturo Rossato, after J. da Varagine), *Una Partita* (Milan 1933; libr. Rossato, after Alexandre Dumas), *La Farsa Amorosa* (Rome 1933; libr. Rossato, after Pedro de Alarcón's *El Sombrero de Tres Picos*) and the unfinished *Il Bacio*

(Rome 1954, composed 1944; libr. Rossato, after Gottfried Keller).

Zanelli, Renato *(b Morales) (1892–1935)*

Chilean baritone and later tenor, particularly associated with dramatic Italian and German roles, especially Otello. Originally a successful baritone, he turned to tenor roles in 1924, and his early death from cancer cut short a brilliant career. He created the title role in Pizzetti's *Lo Straniero*. His brother Carlo Morelli (1897–1970) was a successful baritone.

Zanetto

Opera in one act by Mascagni. 1st perf. Pesaro, 2 March 1896; libr. by Giovanni Targioni-Tozzetti and Guido Menasci, after François Coppée's *Le Passant*. Moderately successful at its appearance, it is nowadays all but forgotten.

Zareska, Eugenia *(1910–79)*

Ukrainian mezzo, long resident at Covent Garden. Particularly associated with the French and Italian repertories, she had a good voice and was a fine singing-actress.

Zarewitsch, Der

Operetta in three acts by Lehár. 1st perf. Berlin, 21 Feb 1927; libr. by Béla Jenbach and Heinrich Reichert, after Gabriela Zapolska-Scharlitt. Principal roles: Zarewitsch (ten), Sonja (sop), Mascha (sop), Iwan (ten). One of the most successful of Lehár's later works, it is still regularly performed in German-speaking countries. [R]

Zar Lässt sich Photographieren, Der *(The Tsar Has His Photograph Taken)*

Opera in one act by Weill (Op 21). 1st perf. Leipzig, 18 Feb 1928; libr. by Georg Kaiser. Principal role: Tsar (bar). A satire on anarchist conspiracy, it tells of the Tsar unwittingly foiling his would-be assassins during a trip to Paris.

Zar und Zimmermann *(Tsar and Carpenter)*
or Die Zwei Peter *(The Two Peters)*

Opera in three acts by Lortzing. 1st perf. Leipzig, 22 Dec 1837; libr. by the composer after Anne-Honoré Joseph de Mélesville, Jean Toussaint Merle and Eugène Centiran de Boirie's *Le Bourgmestre de Sardam*. Principal roles: Peter (bar), Peter Ivanov (ten), Marie (sop), van Bett (bass), Widow Browe (mezzo), Marquis de Chateauneuf (ten). Lortzing's most successful and enduring work, it is still regularly performed in German-speaking countries.

Plot: Saardam (Holland), 1698. Peter the Great of Russia, disguised as Peter Michaelov, is working in the Dutch shipyards in order to learn nautical trades. He befriends the deserter Peter Ivanov, who is in love with the Burgomaster Van Bett's daughter Marie. Asked whether Peter the Great is really in the shipyard, the Burgomaster identifies the wrong Peter. The Russian and English ambassadors are deceived, but the French Ambassador Chateauneuf recognises the real Tsar. Van Bett prepares to send Peter Ivanov home in state, whilst the real Tsar departs quietly for Russia. [R]

Zarzuela
See panel on page 639

Zauberflöte, Die *(The Magic Flute)*

Opera in two acts by Mozart (K 620). 1st perf. Vienna, 30 Sept 1791; libr. by Emanuel Schikaneder (who also created

ZARZUELA

Similar to operetta, zarzuela is a Spanish musical stage work, which often employs traditional Spanish material. It contains spoken dialogue and is usually of a comic nature. The term derives from the Spanish word *zarza* ('bramble'): its origins go back to the 17th century, when *Fiestas de Zarzuela* were given at the Palacio la Zarzuela near Madrid; the palace took its name from the surrounding bramble bushes, and the entertainments performed there were named for the palace. The earliest known zarzuela composer is Juan Hidalgo, whose *Los Celos Hacen Estrellas* was first performed in *c* 1644. Librettists for early zarzuelas included both Pedro Calderón de la Barca and Felix Lope de Vega. During the 18th century, zarzuela became more formal (and much less popular), and the tonadilla* came into being as a reaction against this formality. In the mid-19th century, zarzuela experienced a renaissance when leading Spanish composers turned their attention to the genre, and its popularity became such that both the Teatro de la Zarzuela and the Teatro Apolo in Madrid were built to house it. There are a number of different varieties of zarzuela, of which the two most important are:

(1) *Zarzuelita* or *Género chico* (Spanish for 'little type'), which is in one act and is always on a comic subject.

(2) *Zarzuela Grande*, which is in three acts and often comes close to romantic opera in style and subject matter.

Still enormously popular in Spain, zarzuela has virtually never, however, been successfully exported. Perhaps the most successful of all zarzuelas are Barbieri's *El Barbarillo de Lavapiés*, Bretón's *La Verbena de la Paloma**, Torroba's *Luisa Fernánda* and Vives' *Bohemios*.

See also **Sainete; Tonadilla**

The following 20 zarzuela composers have entries in this dictionary:

Albéniz, Isaac	Fernández Caballero,	Rodríguez de Hita,
Arrieta y Corera, Emilio	Manuel	Antonio
Barbieri, Francisco	Gatztambide, Joaquín	Serrano, José
Bretón y Hernández,	Giménez, Gerónimo	Sorozábal, Pablo
Tomás	Granados, Enrique	Torroba, Federico Moreno
Chapí y Lorente, Ruperto	Guerrero, Jacinto	Valverde, Sanjuan
Chueca, Federico	Guridi, Jesús	Vives, Amadeo
Falla, Manuel de	Luna y Carné, Pablo	

the role of Papageno), partly after Abbé Jean Terrasson's *Sethos*. Principal roles: Tamino (ten), Pamina (sop), Sarastro (bass), Papageno (bar), Queen of the Night (sop), Monostatos (ten), three Ladies (sop, mezzo and mezzo), Speaker of the Temple (b-bar), Papagena (sop). Mozart's penultimate opera, it is a fairy-tale work overlaid with Masonic and humanist symbolism. The best-known example of Zauberoper* and the apotheosis of the singspiel form, it was an immediate success and has remained enduringly popular.

Plot: Three Ladies save the Prince Tamino from a monster and give him a portrait of Pamina, daughter of their mistress the Queen of the Night. He falls in love with Pamina's beauty, and the Queen charges him with rescuing her from the hands of the supposedly evil Sarastro, the priest of Isis. She gives him an enchanted flute to aid him through perils and sends the birdcatcher Papageno with him as a guide. On arrival at the Temple of Isis, Tamino is told by the Speaker that only truth and wisdom reside within and Sarastro bids him enter and learn. Pamina, lusted after by Sarastro's Moorish slave Monostatos, returns Tamino's love, and the two agree to undergo tests to prove their virtue and constancy. Papageno is also tested and even though he makes a poor showing is rewarded with Papagena. With the aid of the flute, Tamino and Pamina pass through the ordeals of fire and water. Sarastro gives Tamino the symbols of rule, and all celebrate the triumph of light over the powers of darkness represented by the defeated Queen of the Night. [R]

Zaubergeige, Die *(The Magic Fiddle)*

Opera in three acts by Egk. 1st perf. Frankfurt, 23 May 1935; libr. by Count Pocci, after Hans Christian Andersen. Principal roles: Kaspar (bar), Gretl (sop), Ninabella (sop), Amandus (ten), Guldensack (bass), Cuperus (bass). Egk's first opera, nowadays only rarely performed, it employs numbers based on popular melodies. [R Exc]

Zauberharfe, Die *(The Magic Harp)*

Unfinished Singspiel in three acts by Schubert (D 644). Composed 1820; libr. by Georg von Hofmann. The overture is well-known, as Schubert reused it in his incidental music to *Rosamunde*.

Zauberoper *(German for 'magic opera')*

A term used in Vienna in the late 18th and early 19th centuries for a form of Singspiel which contained magic, sumptuous scenic effects, music by leading composers and ribald comedy. Fairy-tale themes, such as the Oberon story, were the most popular. Performances were given at the Theater auf der Weiden and later at Emanuel Schikaneder's Theater an der Wien. The best known, and much the greatest, example of the genre is Mozart's *Die Zauberflöte*.

Zazà

Opera in four acts by Leoncavallo. 1st perf. Milan, 10 Nov 1900; libr. by the composer, after Pierre Simon and Charles Berton's play. Principal roles: Zazà (sop), Milio (ten), Cascart (bar). Leoncavallo's most successful opera apart from *Pagliacci*, it is still performed from time to time.

Plot: Paris, 1900. The music-hall singer Zazà falls in love with Milio Dufresne, having won his attentions on a bet.

However, her partner Cascart, who is in love with her, leads her to the discovery that Milio is in fact already married and that he loves his wife. Realising this, Zazà's affections turn to Cascart. [R]

Zazà, piccola zingara

Baritone aria for Cascart in Leoncavallo's *Zazà*.

Zdenka

Soprano trouser-role in Strauss' *Arabella*. The Waldners' younger daughter, she has been brought up as a boy because her parents cannot afford to bring up two girls.

Zeani, Virginia *(b Zehan) (b 1928)*

Romanian soprano, particularly associated with the Italian repertory, especially Violetta. A warm-voiced singer with an affecting stage presence, she won considerable success in bel canto roles before turning to more dramatic roles. She created Blanche in *Dialogues des Carmélites*. Married to the bass Nicola Rossi-Lemeni*.

Zedda, Alberto (b 1928)
Italian conductor and musicologist, particularly associated with Rossini operas. He has produced outstanding critical editions, now in almost universal use, of many of Rossini's major works.

Zeffirelli, Franco (b Gianfranco Corsi) (b 1923)
Italian producer, designer and film-maker. One of the leading postwar opera directors, he has been particularly associated with La Scala, Milan and with Covent Garden, where he directed *Lucia di Lammermoor*, *Cavalleria Rusticana*, *Pagliacci*, *Falstaff* and *Tosca*. He also directed the films of *La Traviata* and the controversial *Otello* (1986) and wrote the libretto for Barber's *Antony and Cleopatra*.

Zeffiretti lusinghieri
Soprano aria for Ilia in Act III of Mozart's *Idomeneo*.

Zeit im Grunde, Die
Soprano monologue for the Marschallin in Act I of Strauss' *Der Rosenkavalier*.

Zeleński, Władysław (1837–1921)
Polish composer. Poland's leading opera composer after Moniuszko, his stage works, all unknown outside Poland, are nationalist in sentiment and make use of traditional Polish folk material. His four operas are *Konrad Wallenrod* (Lwów 26 Feb 1885; libr. after A. Mickiewicz), *Goplana* (Cracow 23 July 1896; libr. L. German, after J. Slowacki), *Janek* (Lwów 4 Oct 1900; libr. German), and *Old Fable* (*Stara Baśń*, Lwów 14 March 1907; libr. A. Bandrowski, after J. I. Kraszewski).

Zeller, Carl (1842–98)
Austrian composer. He wrote one opera, but is best remembered for his many Viennese operettas, of which *Der Vogelhändler** remains widely popular. Of his other works, the most successful were *Der Vagabund* (Vienna 30 Oct 1886; libr. Moritz West and Ludwig Held) and *Der Obersteiger* (*The Master Miner*, Vienna 5 Jan 1894; libr. West and Held).

Zelmira
Opera in two acts by Rossini. 1st perf. Naples, 16 Feb 1822; libr. by Andrea Leone Tottola, after Dormont de Belloy's *Zelmire*. Principal roles: Zelmira (sop), Antenore (ten), Polidoro (bass), Emma (mezzo). Never one of Rossini's more successful works, it is very rarely performed.

Zémire et Azor
Comic opera in four acts by Grétry. 1st perf. Fontainebleau, 9 Nov 1771; libr. by Jean-François Marmontel, after Pierre Claude Nivelle de la Chaussée's *Amour par Amour*. Principal roles: Zémire (sop), Azor (ten), Sander (bar), Ali (ten), Fatme (mezzo), Lisbe (sop). Grétry's most successful and enduring work, it is a version of the Beauty and the Beast story, essentially derived from Charles Perrault's classic tale. [R]

Zemir und Azor
Opera in two acts by Spohr. 1st perf. Frankfurt, 4 April 1819; libr. by Johann Jakob Ihlee, after Jean-François Marmontel's libretto for Grétry (see above). More serious than Grétry's

version, it was successful in its time but is nowadays all but forgotten.

Zemlinsky, Alexander *(1871–1942)*

Austrian composer and conductor. His eight operas are: *Sarema* (Munich 10 Oct 1897; libr. Adolf von Zemlinsky, after R. von Gotschall's *Die Rose von Kaukasus*), *Es War Einmal* (Vienna 22 Jan 1900; libr. Drachmann), *Die Traumgörge* (Nürnberg 1980, composed 1906; libr. M. Feld) [R], *Kleider Machen Leute* (Vienna 2 Oct 1910; libr. Ludwig Held, after Gottfried Keller), *Eine Florentinische Tragödie**, *Der Geburstag der Infantin**, his finest opera, *Der Kreidekreis* (Zürich 14 Oct 1933; libr. after Klabund) and *Der König Kandaules* (1935). There has recently been a considerable revival of interest in his music, and performances are becoming more frequent. He was musical director of the Deutsches Theater, Prague (1911–27), where he conducted the first performance of *Erwartung*. He was also a distinguished teacher, whose pupils included Schönberg (later his brother-in-law) and Korngold.

Zenatello, Giovanni *(1876–1949)*

Italian tenor, particularly associated with heavier Italian roles, notably Otello. Beginning as a baritone, he turned to tenor roles within a year, and his powerful voice with its ringing high notes made him perhaps the finest Italian dramatic tenor of the early 20th century. He created Pinkerton in *Madama Butterfly*, Vassili in Giordano's *Siberia*, Ricci in Cilea's *Gloria* and Aligi in Franchetti's *La Figlia di Iorio*. He instigated the performance of opera at the Verona Arena, and in 1947 he was responsible for launching Maria Callas'

international career. His wife María Gay (1879–1943) was a successful mezzo.

Zeno, Apostolo *(1668–1750)*

Italian poet and librettist, he was Pietro Metastasio's predecessor as court poet in Vienna. His many libretti, often on the theme of the conflict between passion and duty, and frequently written in collaboration with Pietro Pariati (1665–1733), were set by many composers. His libretti were used by Albinoni, Bononcini, Bortnyansky, Caldara, Cherubini, Duni, Fux, Galuppi, Gasparini, Graun, Guglielmi, Handel, Hasse, Mysliveček, Paisiello, Pergolesi, Porpora, Sacchini, D. Scarlatti, Traetta, Vivaldi and Zingarelli amongst others.

Zerbinetta

Soprano role in Strauss' *Ariadne auf Naxos*. She is the star of the Commedia dell'Arte troupe.

Zerlina

Soprano role in: (1) Mozart's *Don Giovanni*. She is a peasant girl engaged to Masetto. (2) Auber's *Fra Diavolo*. She is the innkeeper Mathés' daughter.

Žídek, Ivo *(b 1926)*

Czech tenor, particularly associated with his country's repertory. One of the finest Czech tenors of the postwar period, he possessed a well-placed and firmly-projected voice and had a good stage presence. He created Oleg Koševoj in Mejtus's *Young Guard*.

Ziehrer, Carl Michael *(1843–1922)*

Austrian composer. Several of his many Viennese operettas were successful in their time, but are nowadays only rarely performed. They include *Ein*

Deutschmeister (Vienna 30 Nov 1888; libr. Richard Genée and B. Zappert), *Die Landstreicher* (*The Vagabonds*, Vienna 26 July 1899; libr. L. Krenn and C. Lindau), his most successful work, *Der Fremdenführer* (*The Guide*, Vienna 11 Oct 1902; libr. Krenn and Lindau) and *Der Schätzmeister* (*The Pawnbroker's Valuer*, Vienna 10 Dec 1904; libr. A. Engel and J. Horst).

Zigeunerbaron, Der (*The Gypsy Baron*)

Operetta in three acts by Johann Strauss II. 1st perf. Vienna, 24 Oct 1885; libr. by Ignatz Schitzer, after Maurus Jókai's *Saffi*. Principal roles: Sándor Barinkay (ten), Saffi (sop), Zsupán (bar), Arsena (sop), Czipra (mezzo), Ottokar (ten), Carnero (bar), Mirabella (mezzo). An immediate success, it remains one of the most enduringly popular of all Viennese operettas.

Plot: Banat (Hungary), mid-18th century. Sándor Barinkay returns to claim his ancestral lands and finds that they are occupied by gypsies. The irascible pig-farmer Zsupán hopes that Barinkay will marry his daughter Arsena, although she wishes to marry Ottokar. However, Barinkay falls in love with the gypsy girl Saffi, foster-daughter of the fortune-teller Czipra. She turns out to be a princess and weds Barinkay, leaving Arsena free to marry Ottokar. [R]

Zigeunerliebe (*Gypsy Love*)

Operetta in three acts by Lehár. 1st perf. Vienna, 8 Jan 1910; libr. by Robert Bodanzky and Alfred Maria Willner. Principal roles: Jonel Bolescu (ten), Zorika (sop), Jozsi (ten), Ilona (sop), Peter (ten). Although never one of Lehár's most popular works, it is still occasionally performed in German-speaking countries. [R]

Zimmermann, Bernd-Alois (1918–70)

German composer, who wrote in atonal style. His only completed opera is the controversial and widely performed *Die Soldaten**. A second opera, *Medea*, was left unfinished at the time of his death by suicide.

Zimmermann, Udo (b 1943)

German composer. His operas, written in serial style, have met with considerable success in East Germany, particularly *Die Weisse Rose* (1968; libr. I. Zimmermann) and *Levins Mühle* (1972; libr. I. Zimmermann, after J. Brobowski).

Zingara, La (*The Gypsy Girl*)

Works of this title include:

(1) Intermezzo in one act by Rinaldo di Capua. 1st perf. Paris, *c* 1735; librettist unknown. Principal roles: Nisa (sop), Tagliaborsa (ten), Calcante (bass).

Plot: The gypsy Nisa wishes to marry the rich old miser Calcante. She adopts several stratagems, including disguising her brother Tagliaborsa as a bear. [R]

(2) Opera in two acts by Donizetti. 1st perf. Naples, 12 May 1822; libr. by Andrea Leone Tottola, after Rinaldo di Capua's intermezzo.

Zingarelli, Niccolò Antonio (1752–1837)

Italian composer. His first opera, *I Quattro Pazzi* (Naples 1768) was followed by 33 others, a number of which enjoyed great success in their day but which are all now forgotten. His most important operas include *Montezuma* (Naples 13 Aug 1781), *Gli Orazi e i Curiazi* (Naples 4 Nov 1795; libr. C. Sernicola, after Pierre Corneille's *Horace*), *Giulietta e Romeo**, *Edipo a Colono* (Venice 26

Dec 1802; libr. Antonio Sografi, after Sophocles) and *Berenice* (Rome 12 Nov 1811; libr. Jacopo Ferretti, after Apostolo Zeno's *Lucio Vero*), his finest work. He was also a distinguished teacher, whose pupils include Bellini, Costa, Mercadante, Morlacchi, Petrella and F. Ricci.

Zinovy

Tenor role in Shostakovich's *Lady Macbeth of Mtsensk*. He is Katerina's ineffectual husband.

Zirkusprinzessin, Die (*The Circus Princess*)

Operetta in three acts by Kálmán. 1st perf. Vienna, 1926; libr. by Julius Brammer and Alfred Grünwald. Successful at its appearance, it is still occasionally performed in German-speaking countries. [R Exc]

Zítek, Vilém (*1890–1956*)

Czech bass, particularly associated with the Czech and German repertories. One of the finest basses of the inter-war period, he possessed a rich and dark voice and was an outstanding singing-actor. He created the title role in Blodek's *Zítek*.

Zitti, zitti

(1) Tenor/baritone duet for Don Ramiro and Dandini in Act II of Rossini's *La Cenerentola*. (2) Mezzo/tenor/baritone trio for Rosina, Count Almaviva and Figaro in Act II of Rossini's *Il Barbiere di Siviglia*. (3) Chorus of courtiers in Act I of Verdi's *Rigoletto*.

Živný

Tenor role in Janáček's *Fate*. He is a composer. The role contains autobiographical suggestions on Janáček's part.

Zola, Émile (*1840–1902*)

French novelist and librettist. A close friend of Bruneau, he wrote the libretti for his *La Rêve*, *Messidor*, *L'Ouragan*, *L'Enfant-Roi*, *Naïs Micoulin* and *Les Quatre Journées*. Most of Bruneau's other operas, including *L'Attaque du Moulin*, are based on his works, as also is Werle's *Dreaming About Thérèse*.

Zoo, The

Operetta in one act by Sullivan. 1st perf. London, 5 June 1875; libr. by B. C. Stephenson. Principal roles: Thomas Brown (bar), Aesculapius Carboy (ten), Laetitia (sop), Eliza (sop), Laetitia's father (b-bar). It is only very rarely performed.

Plot: Regent's Park Zoo. Laetitia's father has forbidden his daughter to marry the apothecary Aesculapius, who plans to hang himself near the zoo's refreshment stall. The stall-holder Eliza prevents him, however. Eliza's admirer Thomas Brown is taken ill, and Aesculapius gives her a prescription. Laetitia's father separates the girl from Aesculapius, who heads for the lion's den. However, it is revealed that Brown is in fact the Duke of Islington and he persuades Laetitia's father to relent. [R]

Zorn, Balthazar

Tenor comprimario role in Wagner's *Die Meistersinger von Nürnberg*. A pewterer, he is one of the masters.

Zoroastre

Opera in four acts by Rameau. 1st perf. Paris, 5 Dec 1749; libr. by Louis de Cahusac. Principal roles: Zoroastre (ten), Amélite (sop), Erinice (mezzo), Oromases (bass), Abramène (bass), Céphise (sop). Containing some of Rameau's finest music, much of it incorporated from his earlier *Samson*, it has received a number of performances in recent years. [R]

Zsupán
(1) Baritone role in J. Strauss' *Der Zigeunerbaron*. Arsena's father, he is a miserly pig-farmer. (2) Tenor role in Kálmán's *Gräfin Mariza*.

Zulma
Mezzo role in Rossini's *L'Italiana in Algieri*. She is Elvira's confidante.

Zuniga
Bass role in Bizet's *Carmen*. He is a lieutenant in the army.

Zurga
Baritone role in Bizet's *Les Pêcheurs de Perles*. He is the leader of the pearl fishers.

Zürich Opernhaus
The present theatre (cap. 1,000) was designed by Fellner and Helmer and opened in 1891. One of Switzerland's two leading houses, it has recently been noted for its Mozart and Monteverdi performances. The annual season runs from September to June. Musical directors have included Robert Denzler, Otto Ackermann, Hans Rosbaud, Christian Vöchting and Ferdinand Leitner.

Zweihunderttausand Taler
(*200,000 Thalers*)
Opera in three acts and epilogue by Blacher. 1st perf. Berlin, 25 Sept 1969; libr. after Sholom Aleichem's *The Two Hundred Thousand*. One of Blacher's most successful works, it is an anti-capitalist comedy.

Zwerg, Der
See Geburstag der Infantin, Der

Zwillingsbruder, Die (*The Twin Brothers*)
Opera in one act by Schubert (D 647). 1st perf. Vienna, 14 June 1820; libr. by Georg von Hofmann, after *Les Deux Valentins*. Principal roles: Franz Spiess (bar), Friedrich Spiess (bar), Lieschen (sop), Anton (ten), Mayor (bass). A slight little Singspiel, it is only very rarely performed. Traditionally, the two brothers are played by the same baritone.

Plot: Lieschen is engaged to Anton, but had earlier been promised to Franz Spiess if he returned from the Foreign Legion within a certain time. Franz returns at the last moment and claims Lieschen despite the entreaties of her father. Franz goes to the magistrate to collect the 1,000-thaler dowery and in the meantime his twin Friedrich (long believed dead) arrives and blesses Lieschen's marriage with Anton. Unaware of Friedrich's existence, everyone thinks that Franz is behaving oddly, and he is arrested for schizophrenia. However, Friedrich appears at the court and everything is sorted out. [R]

Zylis-Gara, Teresa (*b 1937*)
Polish soprano, particularly associated with Mozart and Verdi roles. She possesses a beautiful lyric voice, used with intelligence and a fine technique, and has an affecting stage presence.

COMPARATIVE OPERATIC CHRONOLOGY

This chronology covers the 900 operas and operettas with entries in this dictionary. The dates given are the year of first performance or, in a few cases, the year when the opera was written if the work was not performed until many years later.

	ITALY	FRANCE	GERMANY/ AUSTRIA
1597	PERI *Dafne*		
	CACCINI *Dafne*		
1600	PERI *Euridice*		
1602	CACCINI *Euridice*		
1607	MONTEVERDI *La Favola d'Orfeo*		
1608	MONTEVERDI *Arianna*		
	MONTEVERDI *Il Ballo delle Ingrate*		
	GAGLIANO *La Dafne*		
1624	MONTEVERDI *Il Combattimento di Tancredi e Clorinda*		
1627			SCHÜTZ *Dafne*
1641	MONTEVERDI *Il Ritorno d'Ulisse in Patria*		
1642	MONTEVERDI *L'Incoronazione di Poppea*		
1643	CAVALLI *L'Egisto*		
1644	CAVALLI *L'Ormindo*		
1649	CESTI *Orontea*		
1651	CAVALLI *La Calisto*		
1654	CAVALLI *Serse*		
1655	CAVALLI *L'Erismena*		
1662	CAVALLI *Ercole Amante*		
1667	CESTI *Il Pomo d'Oro*		
1670		LULLY *Le Bourgeois Gentilhomme*	
1674		LULLY *Alceste*	
1677		LULLY *Isis*	
1684		LULLY *Amadis*	

BRITAIN	RUSSIA	CZECH	OTHERS
BLOW *Venus and Adonis*			

	ITALY	FRANCE	GERMANY/ AUSTRIA
1686		LULLY *Armide et Renaud*	
1688		CHARPENTIER *David et Jonathas*	
1689			
1690			
1691			
1692			
1693		CHARPENTIER *Médée*	
1695			
1705			HANDEL *Almira*
1707			HANDEL *Rodrigo*
1708	ALBINONI *Pimpinone*		
1709			HANDEL *Agrippina*
1711			HANDEL *Rinaldo*
1712			HANDEL *Il Pastor Fido*
1713			HANDEL *Teseo*
1718	A. SCARLATTI *Il Trionfo dell'Onore*		HANDEL *Acis and Galatea*
1720			HANDEL *Radamisto*
1721			HANDEL *Floridante*
			TELEMANN *Der Geduldige Socrates*
1722	BONONCINI *Griselda*		
1723			HANDEL *Flavio*
			HANDEL *Ottone*
1724			HANDEL *Giulio Cesare*
			HANDEL *Tamerlano*
1725			TELEMANN *Pimpinone*
			HANDEL *Rodelinda*
1726			HANDEL *Alessandro*
			HANDEL *Scipione*
1727	VIVALDI *Orlando Furioso*		HANDEL *Admeto*
			HANDEL *Riccardo Primo*
1728			HANDEL *Tolomeo*
			HANDEL *Siroe*
1729			HANDEL *Lotario*
1730			HANDEL *Partenope*

BRITAIN	RUSSIA	CZECH	OTHERS
PURCELL *Dido and Aeneas*			
PURCELL *The Prophetess*			
PURCELL *King Arthur*			
PURCELL *The Faery Queen*			
PURCELL *The Indian Queen*			
PEPUSCH *The Beggar's Opera*			
PEPUSCH *Polly*			

	ITALY	FRANCE	GERMANY/ AUSTRIA
1731			HANDEL *Poro*
1732			HANDEL *Ezio*
			HANDEL *Sosarme*
1733	PERGOLESI *La Serva Padrona*	RAMEAU *Hippolyte et Aricie*	HANDEL *Athalia*
			HANDEL *Orlando*
1734			HANDEL *Arianna*
1735	RINALDO DI CAPUA *La Zingara*	RAMEAU *Les Indes Galantes*	HANDEL *Alcina*
			HANDEL *Ariodante*
1736			HANDEL *Atalanta*
1737		RAMEAU *Castor et Pollux*	HANDEL *Arminio*
			HANDEL *Berenice*
			HANDEL *Giustino*
1738			HANDEL *Faramondo*
			HANDEL *Saul*
			HANDEL *Serse*
1739		RAMEAU *Dardanus*	
1740			HANDEL *Deidamia*
			HANDEL *Imeneo*
1743			HANDEL *Samson*
1744			HANDEL *Semele*
1745		RAMEAU *Platée*	HANDEL *Belshazzar*
			HANDEL *Hercules*
1748		RAMEAU *Pygmalion*	
1749		RAMEAU *Zoroastre*	
1752		ROUSSEAU *Le Devin du Village*	
1754		RAMEAU *Anacréon*	
1755			GRAUN *Montezuma*
1760	PICCINNI *La Buona Figliuola*		GLUCK *L'Ivrogne Corrigé*
1761		MONSIGNY *Le Cadi Dupé*	GLUCK *Le Cadi Dupé*
1762			GLUCK *Orfeo ed Euridice*
1764	GALUPPI *Il Filosofo di Campagna*	RAMEAU *Les Boréades*	GLUCK *Le Rencontre Imprévu*
1765		PHILIDOR *Tom Jones*	
1767			GLUCK *Alceste*
			MOZART *Apollo et Hyacinthus*

BRITAIN	RUSSIA	CZECH	OTHERS
ARNE *Thomas and Sally*			
ARNE *Artaxerxes*			

	ITALY	FRANCE	GERMANY/ AUSTRIA
1768			MOZART *Bastien und Bastienne*
			HAYDN *Lo Speziale*
1769			MOZART *La Finta Semplice*
1770			HAYDN *L'Isola Disabitata*
			HILLER *Die Jagd*
			MOZART *Mitridate Rè di Ponto*
			GLUCK *Paride ed Elena*
1771		GRÉTRY *Zémire et Azor*	MOZART *Ascanio in Alba*
1772	SACCHINI *Armida*		MOZART *Lucio Silla*
			MOZART *Il Sogno di Scipione*
1773			HAYDN *L'Infedeltà Delusa*
1774			GLUCK *Iphigénie en Aulide*
1775			MOZART *La Finta Giardiniera*
			MOZART *Il Re Pastore*
			HAYDN *L'Incontro Improvviso*
1777			GLUCK *Armide*
			HAYDN *Il Mondo della Luna*
1779			GLUCK *Echo et Narcisse*
			GLUCK *Iphigénie en Tauride*
			HAYDN *La Vera Costanza*
			MOZART *Zaïde*
1781	PICCINNI *Iphigénie en Tauride*		MOZART *Idomeneo*
			HAYDN *La Fedeltà Premiata*
1782	PAISIELLO *Il Barbiere di Siviglia*		MOZART *Die Entführung aus dem Serail*
			HAYDN *Orlando Paladino*
1783			MOZART *L'Oca del Cairo*
			MOZART *Lo Sposo Deluso*
1784	SALIERI *Les Danaïdes*	GRÉTRY *Richard Coeur de Lion*	HAYDN *Armida*
	PAISIELLO *Il Re Teodoro di Venezia*		

BRITAIN	RUSSIA	CZECH	OTHERS
SHIELD *Rosina*			

	ITALY	FRANCE	GERMANY/ AUSTRIA
1786	SALIERI *Prima la Musica e Poi le Parole*		DITTERSDORF *Doktor und Apotheker*
			MOZART *Le Nozze di Figaro*
			MOZART *Der Schauspieldirektor*
1787	SALIERI *Tarare*		MOZART *Don Giovanni*
1790	CIMAROSA *Il Maestro di Cappella*		MOZART *Così fan Tutte*
1791	CHERUBINI *Lodoïska*	GRÉTRY *Guillaume Tell*	MOZART *La Clemenza di Tito*
			MOZART *Die Zauberflöte*
			HAYDN *Orfeo ed Euridice*
1792	CIMAROSA *Il Matrimonio Segreto*		
1794	CIMAROSA *L'Astuzie Femminili*		
1796	ZINGARELLI *Giulietta e Romeo*		WINTER *Das Unterbrochene Opferfest*
1797	CHERUBINI *Médée*		
1798		GAVEAUX *Léonore*	
1799	FIORAVANTI *Le Cantatrici Villane*	MÉHUL *Ariodant*	
	SALIERI *Falstaff*		
1800	CHERUBINI *Les Deux Journées*	BOÏELDIEU *Le Calife de Bagdad*	
1803	CHERUBINI *Anacréon*		
1804	PAER *Leonora*		
	SPONTINI *Milton*		
1805			BEETHOVEN *Leonore*
1806		MÉHUL *Les Deux Aveugles*	
		MÉHUL *Uthal*	
1807	ROSSINI *Demetrio e Polibio*	MÉHUL *Joseph*	
	SPONTINI *La Vestale*		
1809	SPONTINI *Fernand Cortez*		
1810	ROSSINI *La Cambiale di Matrimonio*		
1811			WEBER *Abu Hassan*
1812	ROSSINI *Ciro in Babilonia*	BOÏELDIEU *Jean de Paris*	
	ROSSINI *L'Inganno Felice*		
	ROSSINI *La Pietra del Paragone*		

BRITAIN	RUSSIA	CZECH	OTHERS
STORACE *Gli Equivoci*			MARTÍN Y SOLER *Una Cosa Rara*

	ITALY	FRANCE	GERMANY/ AUSTRIA
1812	ROSSINI *La Scala di Seta*		
1813	CHERUBINI *Les Abencérages*		
	ROSSINI *Aureliano in Palmira*		
	ROSSINI *L'Italiana in Algieri*		
	ROSSINI *Tancredi*		
	ROSSINI *Il Signor Bruschino*		
	MAYR *Medea in Corinto*		
1814	ROSSINI *Il Turco in Italia*		BEETHOVEN *Fidelio*
			SCHUBERT *Des Teufels Lustschloss*
1815	ROSSINI *Elisabetta Regina d'Inghilterra*		SCHUBERT *Claudine von Villa Bella*
	ROSSINI *Torvaldo e Dorliska*		SCHUBERT *Die Vierjährige Posten*
			SCHUBERT *Fernando*
			SCHUBERT *Die Freunde von Salamanka*
1816	ROSSINI *Il Barbiere di Siviglia*		SPOHR *Faust*
	ROSSINI *Otello*		HOFFMANN *Undine*
1817	ROSSINI *Adelaide di Borgogna*		
	ROSSINI *Armida*		
	ROSSINI *La Cenerentola*		
	ROSSINI *La Gazza Ladra*		
1818	ROSSINI *Mosè in Egitto*		
1819	ROSSINI *La Donna del Lago*		SPOHR *Zemir und Azor*
	ROSSINI *Ermione*		
	SPONTINI *Olympie*		
1820	ROSSINI *Maometto II*		SCHUBERT *Die Zwillingsbruder*
			SCHUBERT *Die Zauberhärfe*
1821	PAER *Le Maître de Chapelle*		WEBER *Der Freischütz*
1822	ROSSINI *Zelmira*		SCHUBERT *Alfonso und Estrella*
1823	ROSSINI *Semiramide*		SCHUBERT *Fierrabras*

BRITAIN	RUSSIA	CZECH	OTHERS

	ITALY	FRANCE	GERMANY/ AUSTRIA
1823			SCHUBERT *Die Verschworenen*
			WEBER *Euryanthe*
			SPOHR *Jessonda*
1824	DONIZETTI *L'Aio nell'Imbarazzo*	MEYERBEER *Il Crociato in Egitto*	
1825	BELLINI *Adelson e Salvini*	BOÏELDIEU *La Dame Blanche*	
	VACCAI *Giulietta e Romeo*		
	ROSSINI *Il Viaggio a Reims*		
1826	BELLINI *Bianca e Fernando*		WEBER *Oberon*
	ROSSINI *Le Siège de Corinthe*		
1827	BELLINI *Il Pirata*		
	ROSSINI *Moïse et Pharaon*		
	DONIZETTI *Le Convenienze e Inconvenienze Teatrali*		
1828	ROSSINI *Le Comte Ory*	AUBER *La Muette de Portici*	MARSCHNER *Der Vampyr*
1829	SPONTINI *Agnes von Hohenstaufen*		MARSCHNER *Der Templer und die Jüdin*
	ROSSINI *Guillaume Tell*		
	BELLINI *Zaira*		
	BELLINI *La Straniera*		
1830	DONIZETTI *Anna Bolena*	AUBER *Fra Diavolo*	
	BELLINI *I Capuleti e i Montecchi*		
1831	BELLINI *La Sonnambula*	MEYERBEER *Robert le Diable*	
	BELLINI *Norma*	HÉROLD *Zampa*	
1832	DONIZETTI *L'Elisir d'Amore*	HÉROLD *Le Pré aux Clercs*	
	DONIZETTI *Ugo Conte di Parigi*		
1833	BELLINI *Beatrice di Tenda*		MARSCHNER *Hans Heiling*
	DONIZETTI *Lucrezia Borgia*		
	DONIZETTI *Parisina*		
	DONIZETTI *Torquato Tasso*		

BRITAIN	RUSSIA	CZECH	OTHERS
			LISZT *Don Sanche*

	ITALY	FRANCE	GERMANY/ AUSTRIA
1834	DONIZETTI *Gemma di Vergy*		WAGNER *Die Feen*
	DONIZETTI *Maria Stuarda*		KREUTZER *Das Nachtlager von Granada*
1835	DONIZETTI *Lucia di Lammermoor*	HALÉVY *La Juive*	
	DONIZETTI *Marino Faliero*	AUBER *Le Cheval de Bronze*	
	BELLINI *I Puritani*		
1836	DONIZETTI *Belisario*	MEYERBEER *Les Huguenots*	WAGNER *Das Liebesverbot*
	DONIZETTI *Betly*	ADAM *Le Postillon de Longjumeau*	
	DONIZETTI *Il Campanello*		
1837	MERCADANTE *Il Giuramento*	AUBER *Le Domino Noir*	LORTZING *Zar und Zimmermann*
	DONIZETTI *Pia de' Tolomei*		
	DONIZETTI *Roberto Devereux*		
1838	DONIZETTI *Maria de Rudenz*	BERLIOZ *Benvenuto Cellini*	
	DONIZETTI *Poliuto*		
	MERCADANTE *Le Due Illustri Rivali*		
1839	DONIZETTI *Le Duc d'Albe*		
	VERDI *Oberto*		
1840	DONIZETTI *La Favorite*		
	DONIZETTI *La Fille du Régiment*		
	DONIZETTI *Les Martyrs*		
	VERDI *Un Giorno di Regno*		
	PACINI *Saffo*		
1841	DONIZETTI *Rita*	AUBER *Les Diamants de la Couronne*	
1842	DONIZETTI *Linda di Chamounix*		WAGNER *Rienzi*
	VERDI *Nabucco*		LORTZING *Der Wildschütz*
1843	DONIZETTI *Dom Sébastien*		WAGNER *Der Fliegende Holländer*
	DONIZETTI *Don Pasquale*		

BRITAIN	RUSSIA	CZECH	OTHERS
	GLINKA *A Life for the Tsar*		
	GLINKA *Ruslan and Ludmila*		
BALFE *The Bohemian Girl*			

	ITALY	FRANCE	GERMANY/AUSTRIA
1843	DONIZETTI *Maria di Rohan*		
	VERDI *I Lombardi*		
1844	DONIZETTI *Caterina Cornaro*		FLOTOW *Alessandro Stradella*
	VERDI *Ernani*		
	VERDI *I Due Foscari*		
1845	VERDI *Giovanna d'Arco*		WAGNER *Tannhäuser*
	VERDI *Alzira*		LORTZING *Undine*
1846	VERDI *Attila*	BERLIOZ *La Damnation de Faust*	LORTZING *Der Waffenschmied*
1847	VERDI *Jérusalem*		FLOTOW *Martha*
	VERDI *Macbeth*		
	VERDI *I Masnadieri*		
1848	VERDI *Il Corsaro*		
1849	VERDI *La Battaglia di Legnano*	MEYERBEER *Le Prophète*	NICOLAÏ *Die Lustigen Weiber von Windsor*
	VERDI *Luisa Miller*		
1850	RICCI *Crispino e la Comare*		WAGNER *Lohengrin*
	VERDI *Stiffelio*		SCHUMANN *Genoveva*
1851	VERDI *Rigoletto*	GOUNOD *Sapho*	LORTZING *Die Opernprobe*
1852		ADAM *Si J'Étais Roi*	
1853	VERDI *Il Trovatore*	MASSÉ *Les Noces de Jeanette*	
	VERDI *La Traviata*		
1854		MEYERBEER *L'Etoile du Nord*	WAGNER *Das Rheingold*
1855	VERDI *Les Vêpres Siciliennes*	OFFENBACH *Les Deux Aveugles*	
1856		AUBER *Manon Lescaut*	WAGNER *Die Walküre*
		MAILLART *Les Dragons de Villars*	
1857	VERDI *Aroldo*	LECOCQ *Le Docteur Miracle*	
	VERDI *Simon Boccanegra*	BIZET *Le Docteur Miracle*	
1858		GOUNOD *Le Médecin Malgré Lui*	CORNELIUS *Der Barbier von Bagdad*
		OFFENBACH *Orphée aux Enfers*	
1859	VERDI *Un Ballo in Maschera*	GOUNOD *Faust*	

BRITAIN	RUSSIA	CZECH	OTHERS
			ERKEL *László* *Hunyadi*
WALLACE *Maritana*			
			MONIUSZKO *Halka*
	DARGOMIJSKY *Rusalka*		

	ITALY	FRANCE	GERMANY/ AUSTRIA
1859		MEYERBEER *Dinorah*	
1860		GOUNOD *Philémon et Baucis*	
1861			WAGNER *Tannhäuser* (REVISED)
1862	VERDI *La Forza del Destino*	BERLIOZ *Les Troyens*	
		BERLIOZ *Béatrice et Bénédict*	
		BIZET *Ivan IV*	
		GOUNOD *La Reine de Saba*	
1863		BIZET *Les Pêcheurs de Perles*	BRUCH *Die Loreley*
1864		OFFENBACH *La Belle Hélène*	
		GOUNOD *Mireille*	
1865	VERDI *Macbeth* (revised)	MEYERBEER *L'Africaine*	WAGNER *Tristan und Isolde*
			SUPPÉ *Die Schöne Galatea*
1866		OFFENBACH *Barbe-Bleue*	
		THOMAS *Mignon*	
1867	VERDI *Don Carlos*	OFFENBACH *Robinson Crusoé*	
		OFFENBACH *La Grande-Duchesse de Gérolstein*	
		BIZET *La Jolie Fille de Perth*	
		GOUNOD *Roméo et Juliette*	
1868		OFFENBACH *La Périchole*	WAGNER *Die Meistersinger von Nürnberg*
		OFFENBACH *La Vie Parisienne*	
		THOMAS *Hamlet*	
1869		OFFENBACH *Les Brigands*	WAGNER *Siegfried*

BRITAIN	RUSSIA	CZECH	OTHERS
			ERKEL *Bánk Bán*
BENEDICT *The Lily of Killarney*			
	MOUSSORGSKY *Salammbô*		
	MOUSSORGSKY *The Marriage*		BERWALD *The Queen of Golconda*
			MONIUSZKO *The Haunted Manor*
SULLIVAN *Cox and Box*		SMETANA *The Brandenburgers in Bohemia*	
		SMETANA *The Bartered Bride*	
		BLODEK *In a Well*	
		SMETANA *Dalibor*	
	MOUSSORGSKY *Boris Godunov*		
	TCHAIKOVSKY *Undine*		
	TCHAIKOVSKY *The Voyevoda*		
	BORODIN *Prince Igor*		

	ITALY	FRANCE	GERMANY/ AUSTRIA
1869			
1870			
1871	VERDI *Aida*		
1872		BIZET *Djamileh*	
		LECOCQ *La Fille de Madame Angot*	
1873		DELIBES *Le Roi l'a Dit*	
1874			J. STRAUSS *Die Fledermaus*
			GÖTZ *Der Widerspenstigen Zähmung*
1875	BOITO *Mefistofele*	BIZET *Carmen*	GOLDMARK *Die Königin von Saba*
1876	PONCHIELLI *La Gioconda*		WAGNER *Götterdämmerung*
			SUPPÉ *Fatinitza*
1877		GOUNOD *Cinq-Mars*	
		PLANQUETTE *Les Cloches de Corneville*	
		CHABRIER *L'Etoile*	
		MASSENET *Le Roi de Lahore*	
		SAINT-SAËNS *Samson et Dalila*	
1878		LECOCQ *Le Petit Duc*	
1879		CHABRIER *Une Education Manquée*	SUPPÉ *Boccaccio*
		OFFENBACH *La Fille du Tambour-Major*	
1880		AUDRAN *La Mascotte*	SUPPÉ *Donna Juanita*
		VARNEY *Les Mousquetaires au Couvent*	
1881	VERDI *Simon Boccanegra* (revised)	MASSENET *Hérodiade*	
		OFFENBACH *Les Contes d'Hoffmann*	
1882			MILLÖCKER *Der Bettelstudent*
			WAGNER *Parsifal*

BRITAIN	RUSSIA	CZECH	OTHERS
	CUI *William Ratcliff*		
			GOMES *Il Guarany*
SULLIVAN *Thespis*			
	DARGOMIJSKY *The Stone Guest*		
	RIMSKY-KORSAKOV *The Maid of Pskov*		GRIEG *Olav Trygvason*
	TCHAIKOVSKY *The Oprichnik*	SMETANA *The Two Widows*	
	MOUSSORGSKY *Sorochintsy Fair*		
SULLIVAN *The Zoo*	RUBINSTEIN *The Demon*	SMETANA *Viola*	
SULLIVAN *Trial By Jury*			
	TCHAIKOVSKY *Vakula the Blacksmith*	SMETANA *The Kiss*	
		DVOŘÁK *Vanda*	
SULLIVAN *The Sorcerer*			
SULLIVAN *H.M.S. Pinafore*		SMETANA *The Secret*	HEISE *King and Marshal*
SULLIVAN *The Pirates of Penzance*	TCHAIKOVSKY *Eugene Onegin*		
	RIMSKY-KORSAKOV *May Night*		
SULLIVAN *Patience*	TCHAIKOVSKY *The Maid of Orleans*	SMETANA *Libuše*	
SULLIVAN *Iolanthe*	RIMSKY-KORSAKOV *The Snow Maiden*	DVOŘÁK *Dimitrij*	
		SMETANA *The Devil's Wall*	

	ITALY	FRANCE	GERMANY/ AUSTRIA
1883		SAINT-SAËNS *Henri VIII*	J. STRAUSS *Eine Nacht in Venedig*
		DELIBES *Lakmé*	
		HERVÉ *Mam'zelle Nitouche*	
1884	VERDI *Don Carlos* (revised)	MASSENET *Manon*	MILLÖCKER *Gasparone*
	PUCCINI *Le Villi*	REYER *Sigurd*	NESSLER *Der Trompeter von Säckingen*
1885		MASSENET *Le Cid*	J. STRAUSS *Der Zigeunerbaron*
1886		CHABRIER *Gwendoline*	
1887	VERDI *Otello*	CHABRIER *Le Roi Malgré Lui*	
1888		LALO *Le Roi d'Ys*	WEBER-MAHLER *Die Drei Pintos*
		GODARD *Jocelyn*	
1889	PUCCINI *Edgar*	MASSENET *Esclarmonde*	
1890	MASCAGNI *Cavalleria Rusticana*	MESSAGER *Le Basoche*	
	CATALANI *Loreley*	REYER *Salammbô*	
1891	MASCAGNI *L'Amico Fritz*		ZELLER *Der Vogelhändler*
1892	LEONCAVALLO *Pagliacci*	MASSENET *Werther*	
	CATALANI *La Wally*		
1893	VERDI *Falstaff*	BRUNEAU *L'Attaque du Moulin*	HUMPERDINCK *Hänsel und Gretel*
	PUCCINI *Manon Lescaut*		
1894		MASSENET *La Navarraise*	STRAUSS *Guntram*
		MASSENET *Thaïs*	REZNIČEK *Donna Diana*
1895	MASCAGNI *Guglielmo Ratcliff*	CHAUSSON *Le Roi Arthus*	PFITZNER *Der Arme Heinrich*
		GODARD *La Vivandière*	KIENZL *Der Evangeliman*
1896	GIORDANO *Andrea Chénier*		WOLF *Der Corregidor*

BRITAIN	RUSSIA	CZECH	OTHERS
SULLIVAN *Princess Ida*	TCHAIKOVSKY *Mazeppa*		
STANFORD *The Canterbury Pilgrims*			
SULLIVAN *The Mikado*			
CELLIER *Dorothy*	MOUSSORGSKY *Khovanschina*		
SULLIVAN *Ruddigore*	TCHAIKOVSKY *The Enchantress*	JANÁČEK *Šárka*	
	TCHAIKOVSKY *The Little Slippers*		
SULLIVAN *The Yeomen of the Guard*			
SULLIVAN *The Gondoliers*		DVOŘÁK *Jakobín*	
	TCHAIKOVSKY *The Queen of Spades*		
SULLIVAN *Ivanhoe*		JANÁČEK *The Beginnings of a Romance*	
DELIUS *Irmelin*	TCHAIKOVSKY *Iolanta*		
SULLIVAN *Haddon Hall*	RIMSKY-KORSAKOV *Mlada*		
SULLIVAN *Utopia Limited*	RACHMANINOV *Aleko*		
DELIUS *The Magic Fountain*			
			BRETÓN *La Verbena de la Paloma*
	RIMSKY-KORSAKOV *Christmas Eve*		
	RIMSKY-KORSAKOV *Ivan the Terrible*		
	TANEYEV *Oresteia*		
SULLIVAN *The Grand Duke*			SIBELIUS *The Maiden in the Tower*

		ITALY	FRANCE	GERMANY/ AUSTRIA
1896		PUCCINI *La Bohème*		
		MASCAGNI *Zanetto*		
1897		CILEA *L'Arlesiana*	D'INDY *Fervaal*	
		LEONCAVALLO *La Bohème*	MASSENET *Sapho* 1898	GIORDANO *Fedora*
		MASCAGNI *Iris*		HEUBERGER *Der Opernball*
1899			MASSENET *Cendrillon*	J. STRAUSS *Wiener Blut*
1900		PUCCINI *Tosca*	CHARPENTIER *Louise*	
		LEONCAVALLO *Zazà*		
1901		MASCAGNI *Le Maschere*	MASSENET *Grisélidis*	STRAUSS *Feuersnot*
1902		CILEA *Adriana Lecouvreur*	MASSENET *Le Jongleur de Notre-Dame*	
			DEBUSSY *Pelléas et Mélisande*	
1903		WOLF-FERRARI *Le Donne Curiose*		D'ALBERT *Tiefland*
		GIORDANO *Siberia*		
1904		PUCCINI *Madama Butterfly*		
		ALFANO *Risurrezione*		
1905		LEONI *L'Oracolo*	MASSENET *Chérubin*	LEHÁR *Die Lustige Witwe*
				STRAUSS *Salome*
1906		FRANCHETTI *La Figlia di Iorio*		
		WOLF-FERRARI *I Quatro Rusteghi*		
1907			DUKAS *Ariane et Barbe-Bleue*	O. STRAUS *Ein Walzertraum*
			MESSAGER *Fortunio*	
			MASSENET *Thérèse*	

BRITAIN	RUSSIA	CZECH	OTHERS
STANFORD Shamus O'Brien			
		FIBICH Šárka	
MESSAGER Véronique	D'ALBERT Die Abreise		RIMSKY-KORSAKOV Mozart and Salieri
	RIMSKY-KORSAKOV Sadko		
SULLIVAN The Rose of Persia	RIMSKY-KORSAKOV The Tsar's Bride	DVOŘÁK The Devil and Kate	
		FOERSTER Eva	
	RIMSKY-KORSAKOV The Tale of Tsar Sultan		
SULLIVAN The Emerald Isle		DVOŘÁK Rusalka	PADEREWSKI Manru
STANFORD Much Ado About Nothing			
DELIUS Margot la Rouge			NIELSEN Saul and David
GERMAN Merrie England			
DELIUS Koanga		JANÁČEK Jenůfa	
		JANÁČEK Fate	
		DVOŘÁK Armida	
			DE FALLA La Vida Breve
SMYTH The Wreckers	RACHMANINOV The Covetous Knight		NIELSEN Maskarade
	RACHMANINOV Francesca da Rimini		
GERMAN Tom Jones	RIMSKY-KORSAKOV The Invisible City of Kitezh		
DELIUS A Village Romeo and Juliet			

	ITALY	FRANCE	GERMANY/ AUSTRIA
1908			O. STRAUS *Der Tapfere Soldat*
1909	WOLF-FERRARI *Il Segreto di Susanna*	FÉVRIER *Monna Vanna*	STRAUSS *Elektra*
			SCHREKER *Der Ferne Klang*
			LEHÁR *Der Graf von Luxembourg*
1910	PUCCINI *La Fanciulla del West*	MASSENET *Don Quichotte*	HUMPERDINCK *Die Königskinder*
			LEHÁR *Zigeunerliebe*
1911	WOLF-FERRARI *I Gioielli della Madonna*	RAVEL *L'Heure Espagnole*	STRAUSS *Der Rosenkavalier*
	MASCAGNI *Isabeau*		
1912			
1913	MONTEMEZZI *L'Amore dei Tre Re*	CHARPENTIER *Julien*	
	WOLF-FERRARI *L'Amore Medico*	FAURÉ *Pénélope*	
1914	ZANDONAI *Francesca da Rimini*	RABAUD *Mârouf*	
1915	PIZZETTI *Fedra*		KÁLMÁN *Die Csárdásfürstin*
	GIORDANO *Madame Sans-Gêne*		SCHILLINGS *Mona Lisa*
1916			STRAUSS *Ariadne auf Naxos*
			KORNGOLD *Violanta*
1917	BUSONI *Arlecchino*		ZEMLINSKY *Eine Florentinische Tragödie*
	BUSONI *Turandot*		PFITZNER *Palestrina*
	MASCAGNI *Lodoletta*		SCHÖNBERG *Die Glückliche Hand*
	PUCCINI *La Rondine*		
1918	PUCCINI *Il Tabarro*		
	PUCCINI *Suor Angelica*		
	PUCCINI *Gianni Schicchi*		
1919		MILHAUD *Les Choëphores*	STRAUSS *Die Frau ohne Schatten*
		MESSAGER *Monsieur Beaucaire*	

BRITAIN	RUSSIA	CZECH	OTHERS
MONCKTON & TALBOT *The Arcadians*	RIMSKY-KORSAKOV *The Golden Cockerel*		
DELIUS *Fennimore and Gerda*			BLOCH *Macbeth*
			BARTÓK *Duke Bluebeard's Castle*
HOLBROOKE *The Cauldron of Annwn*			
			DAMROSCH *Cyrano de Bergerac*
BOUGHTON *The Immortal Hour*	STRAVINSKY *The Nightingale*		
SMYTH *The Boatswain's Mate*			GRANADOS *Goyescas*
STANFORD *The Critic*			
HOLST *Sāvitri*			
		JANÁČEK *The Excursions of Mr Brouček*	

	ITALY	FRANCE	GERMANY/ AUSTRIA
1920	MALIPIERO *Orfeide*		KORNGOLD *Die Tote Stadt*
1921	MASCAGNI *Il Piccolo Marat*	HONEGGER *Le Roi David*	
1922	PIZZETTI *Debora e Jaële*		LEHÁR *Frasquita*
	ZANDONAI *Giulietta e Romeo*		ZEMLINSKY *Der Geburtstag der Infantin*
			FALL *Madame Pompadour*
1923		HAHN *Ciboulette*	
		ROUSSEL *Padmâvatî*	
1924	BOITO *Nerone*		SCHÖNBERG *Erwartung*
	GIORDANO *La Cena delle Beffe*		KÁLMÁN *Gräfin Mariza*
			STRAUSS *Intermezzo*
1925	ZANDONAI *I Cavalieri di Ekebù*	RAVEL *L'Enfant et les Sortilèges*	LEHÁR *Paganini*
	BUSONI *Doktor Faust*		BERG *Wozzeck*
1926	PUCCINI *Turandot*	HONEGGER *Judith*	HINDEMITH *Cardillac*
		MILHAUD *Les Malheurs d'Orphée*	WEILL *Der Protagonist*
			KÁLMÁN *Die Zirkusprinzessin*
1927	RESPIGHI *La Campana Sommersa*	IBERT *Angélique*	HINDEMITH *Hin und Züruck*
	WOLF-FERRARI *Sly*	HONEGGER *Antigonae*	KRĚNEK *Jonny Spielt Auf*
		MILHAUD *Le Pauvre Matelot*	WEILL *Mahoganny Singspiel*
			LEHÁR *Der Zarewitsch*
1928	PIZZETTI *Fra Gherardo*		STRAUSS *Die Ägyptische Helena*
			LEHÁR *Friederike*
			WEILL *Die Dreigroschenoper*
			WEILL *Der Zar lässt sich Photographieren*
1929			LEHÁR *Das Land des Lächelns*
			HINDEMITH *Neues vom Tage*

BRITAIN	RUSSIA	CZECH	OTHERS
	PROKOFIEV The Love of Three Oranges	JANÁČEK Káťa Kabanová	
	STRAVINSKY Mavra		MERIKANTO Juha
	STRAVINSKY Renard		
HOLST The Perfect Fool	PALIASHVILI Twilight		DE FALLA El Retablo de Maese Pedro
VAUGHAN WILLIAMS Hugh the Drover		JANÁČEK The Cunning Little Vixen	ROMBERG The Student Prince
BOUGHTON The Queen of Cornwall			
HOLST At the Boar's Head	SHAPORIN The Decembrists		
STANFORD The Travelling Companion			
		JANÁČEK The Macropolus Case	KODÁLY Háry János
			SZYMANOWSKI King Roger
	PROKOFIEV The Fiery Angel	WEINBERGER Shvanda the Bagpiper	TAYLOR The King's Henchman
	STRAVINSKY Oedipus Rex		SCHOECK Penthesilea
GOOSSENS Judith	PROKOFIEV The Gambler		
VAUGHAN WILLIAMS Sir John in Love			

	ITALY	FRANCE	GERMANY/ AUSTRIA
1930		MILHAUD *Christoph Colombe*	WEILL *Aufstieg und Fall der Stadt Mahoganny*
			SCHÖNBERG *Von Heute auf Morgen*
1931	WOLF-FERRARI *La Vedova Scaltra*		
1932	RESPIGHI *Maria Egiziaca*	MILHAUD *Maximilien*	SCHÖNBERG *Moses und Aron*
1933			STRAUSS *Arabella*
1934	REFICE *Cecilia*		LEHÁR *Giuditta*
	ROCCA *Il Dibuk*		
	RESPIGHI *La Fiamma*		
1935	MASCAGNI *Nerone*		EGK *Die Zaubergeige*
			STRAUSS *Die Schweigsame Frau*
1936	WOLF-FERRARI *Il Campiello*		
	ALFANO *Cyrano de Bergerac*		
1937		HONEGGER & IBERT *L'Aiglon*	BERG *Lulu*
1938		HONEGGER *Jeanne d'Arc au Bûcher*	STRAUSS *Daphne*
			STRAUSS *Friedenstag*
			HINDEMITH *Mathis der Maler*
			EGK *Peer Gynt*
1939	WOLF-FERRARI *La Dama Boba*	MILHAUD *Médée*	ORFF *Der Mond*
1940	DALLAPICCOLA *Volo di Notte*		STRAUSS *Die Liebe der Danae*
			SUTERMEISTER *Romeo und Julia*
1941			

BRITAIN	RUSSIA	CZECH	OTHERS
	SHOSTAKOVICH *The Nose*	JANÁČEK *From the House of the Dead*	SCHOECK *Vom Fischer und Syner Fru*
		HÁBA *The Mother*	TAYLOR *Peter Ibbetson*
			YSAŸE *Peter the Miner*
			KODÁLY *The Spinning Room*
BENJAMIN *Prima Donna*			GRUENBERG *The Emperor Jones*
			THOMSON *Four Saints in Three Acts*
HOLST *The Wandering Scholar*	SHOSTAKOVICH *Lady Macbeth of Mtsensk*		
	DZERZHINSKY *Quiet Flows the Don*	MARTINŮ *The Miracle of Our Lady*	GOTOVAC *Ero the Joker*
			GERSHWIN *Porgy and Bess*
VAUGHAN WILLIAMS *The Poisoned Kiss*			
VAUGHAN WILLIAMS *Riders to the Sea*		MARTINŮ *Comedy on the Bridge*	MENOTTI *Amelia al Ballo*
			SCHOECK *Massamila Doni*
	KABALEVSKY *The Master of Clamecy*	MARTINŮ *Julietta*	
			MOORE *The Devil and Daniel Webster*
			MENOTTI *The Old Maid and the Thief*
	PROKOFIEV *Semeon Kotko*		
	PROKOFIEV *The Duenna*		
BRITTEN *Paul Bunyan*			

	ITALY	FRANCE	GERMANY/ AUSTRIA
1942			STRAUSS *Capriccio*
1943		MILHAUD *Bolivar*	ORFF *Die Kluge*
1944			
1945			
1946			WEILL *Street Scene*
1947		POULENC *Les Mamelles de Tirésias*	ORFF *Die Bernauerin*
			EINEM *Dantons Tod*
1948			WEILL *Down in the Valley*
1949	DALLAPICCOLA *Il Prigioniero*		ORFF *Antigonae*
	PIZZETTI *Vanna Lupa*		
1950	DALLAPICCOLA *Job*		DESSAU *Verurteilung des Lukullus*
1951			
1952			HENZE *Boulevard Solitude*
1953			EINEM *Der Prozess*
			ORFF *Trionfo d'Afrodite*
1954	PIZZETTI *La Figlia di Iorio*	MILHAUD *David*	
1955	ROTA *Il Cappello di Paglia di Firenze*		EGK *Irische Legende*
1956			HENZE *König Hirsch*

BRITAIN	RUSSIA	CZECH	OTHERS
			MARTIN *Le Vin Herbé*
		ULLMANN *Der Kaiser von Atlantis*	
BRITTEN *Peter Grimes*			
BRITTEN *The Rape of Lucretia*	PROKOFIEV *War and Peace*		MENOTTI *The Medium*
BRITTEN *Albert Herring*			THOMSON *The Mother of Us All*
			MENOTTI *The Telephone*
	PROKOFIEV *The Story of a Real Man*		
BRITTEN *The Little Sweep*			GERHARD *The Duenna*
BLISS *The Olympians*			
			MENOTTI *The Consul*
			HERRMANN *Wuthering Heights*
BRITTEN *Billy Budd*	STRAVINSKY *The Rake's Progress*		MENOTTI *Amahl and the Night Visitors*
VAUGHAN WILLIAMS *The Pilgrim's Progress*			
			LIEBERMANN *Leonore 40/45*
			BERNSTEIN *Trouble in Tahiti*
BRITTEN *Gloriana*		MARTINŮ *The Marriage*	
BENJAMIN *A Tale of Two Cities*			
BUSH *Wat Tyler*			
BERKELEY *A Dinner Engagement*			LIEBERMANN *Penelope*
WALTON *Troilus and Cressida*			COPLAND *The Tender Land*
BRITTEN *The Turn of the Screw*			MENOTTI *The Saint of Bleecker Street*
TIPPETT *The Midsummer Marriage*			FLOYD *Susannah*
			MOORE *The Ballad of Baby Doe*

	ITALY	FRANCE	GERMANY/ AUSTRIA
1956			
1957		POULENC *Dialogues des Carmélites*	HINDEMITH *Die Harmonie der Welt*
			EGK *Der Revisor*
1958	PIZZETTI *L'Assassinio nella Cattedrale*		
1959		POULENC *La Voix Humaine*	ORFF *Oedipus der Tyrann*
1960			HENZE *Der Prinz von Homberg*
1961	NONO *Intolleranza*		HENZE *Elegie für Junge Liebende*
			KLEBE *Alkmene*
1962			
1963			EGK *Die Verlobung in San Domingo*
1964			
1965			HENZE *Der Junge Lord*
			ZIMMERMANN *Die Soldaten*
1966			HENZE *The Bassarids*
1967			
1968	DALLAPICCOLA *Ulisse*		

BRITAIN	RUSSIA	CZECH	OTHERS
			BERNSTEIN *Candide*
			MARTIN *Der Sturm*
BRITTEN *Noye's Fludde*			MENOTTI *Maria Golovin*
			BARBER *Vanessa*
			FLOYD *Wuthering Heights*
			BLOMDAHL *Aniara*
			BARBER *A Hand of Bridge*
BRITTEN *A Midsummer Night's Dream*			
		MARTINŮ *The Greek Passion*	WARD *The Crucible*
TIPPETT *King Priam*	SHOSTAKOVICH *Katerina Ismailova*		DE FALLA *L'Atlántida*
WILLIAMSON *Our Man in Havana*			MENOTTI *The Last Savage*
BRITTEN *Curlew River*			SZOKOLAY *Blood Wedding*
			GINASTERA *Don Rodrigo*
			SESSIONS *Montezuma*
			WERLE *Dreaming About Thérèse*
BENNETT *The Mines of Sulphur*			
BRITTEN *The Burning Fiery Furnace*			BARBER *Antony and Cleopatra*
WILLIAMSON *The Violins of St Jacques*			
GOEHR *Arden Must Die*			GINASTERA *Bomarzo*
WALTON *The Bear*			
SEARLE *Hamlet*			
BRITTEN *The Prodigal Son*			
BIRTWISTLE *Punch and Judy*			

	ITALY	FRANCE	GERMANY/ AUSTRIA
1969			BLACHER *Zweihunderttausend Taler*
1970			
1971			EINEM *Der Besuch der Alten Dame*
1972			
1973			
1974			
1975			
1976			HENZE *We Come to the River*
1977			
1978			REIMANN *Lear*
1979			
1980			
1983		MESSIAEN *St François d'Assise*	
1984			REIMANN *Die Gespenstersonate*
1989			

BRITAIN	RUSSIA	CZECH	OTHERS
HAMILTON *The Royal Hunt of the Sun*			PENDERECKI *The Devils of Loudun*
WILLIAMSON *Lucky Peter's Journey*			
TIPPETT *The Knot Garden*			
BRITTEN *Owen Wingrave*			
MAXWELL DAVIES *Taverner*			
BRITTEN *Death in Venice*			GINASTERA *Beatrix Cenci*
			SZOKOLAY *Samson*
HAMILTON *The Cataline Conspiracy*			
MUSGRAVE *The Voice of Ariadne*			
			SALLINEN *The Horseman*
			KOKKONEN *The Last Temptations*
MUSGRAVE *Mary Queen of Scots*			
TIPPETT *The Ice Break*			
			SALLINEN *The Red Line*
MUSGRAVE *A Christmas Carol*			
MAXWELL DAVIES *The Lighthouse*			PENDERECKI *Paradise Lost*
			BERNSTEIN *A Quiet Place*
			GLASS *Akhnaten*
			SALLINEN *The King Goes Forth to France*
TIPPETT *New Year*			

APPENDIX 2

OPERA ON RECORD

This appendix provides a check-list, listed by composer, of the *c* 760 operas, operettas and zarzuelas which have been commercially recorded. It should be noted that some have never been released in Britain, and that many others have long been unavailable. This listing does *not* include pirated recordings: although many are easily available, they are officially illegal.

ADAM	*Le Postillon de Longjumeau*	BENNETT	*All the King's Men*
ADAMS	*Nixon in China*	BERG	*Lulu*
D'ALBERT	*Die Abreise*		*Wozzeck*
	Tiefland	BERLIOZ	*Béatrice et Bénédict*
ALBINONI	*Il Nascimento dell'Aurora*		*Benvenuto Cellini*
	Pimpinone		*La Damnation de Faust*
ALWYN	*Miss Julie*		*Les Troyens*
ARNE	*Comus*	BERNSTEIN	*Candide*
	The Cooper		*A Quiet Place*
	Thomas and Sally		*Trouble in Tahiti*
AUBER	*Fra Diavolo*	BIRTWISTLE	*Punch and Judy*
	Manon Lescaut	BIZET	*Carmen*
	La Muette de Portici		*Djamileh*
AUDRAN	*La Mascotte*		*Le Docteur Miracle*
BALASSA	*The Man Outside*		*Ivan IV (Exc)*
BARTÓK	*Duke Bluebeard's Castle*		*La Jolie Fille de Perth*
BARBER	*A Hand of Bridge*		*Les Pêcheurs de Perles*
	Vanessa	BLAVET	*Le Jaloux Corrigé*
BARBIERI	*El Barbarillo de Lavapiés*	BLITZSTEIN	*Regina*
BECAUD	*L'Opéra d'Aran*	BLODEK	*In a Well*
BEESON	*Captain Jinks of the Horse Marines*		*Zítek (Exc)*
	Hello Out There	BLOMDAHL	*Aniara*
	Lizzie Borden	BLOW	*Venus and Adonis*
	The Sweet Bye and Bye	BOÏELDIEU	*La Dame Blanche*
BEETHOVEN	*Fidelio*		*Ma Tante Aurore*
	Leonore	BOITO	*Mefistofele*
BELLINI	*Beatrice di Tenda*		*Nerone*
	I Capuleti e i Montecchi	BONDEVILLE	*L'Ecole des Maris (Exc)*
	Norma	BONONCINI	*Griselda (Exc)*
	Il Pirata	BORODIN	*Prince Igor*
	I Puritani	BORTNYANSKY	*Le Faucon*
	La Sonnambula	BOUGHTON	*The Immortal Hour*
BENATZNY	*White Horse Inn*	BRETÓN	*La Verbena de la Paloma*

684

BRITTEN	Albert Herring	DARGOMIJSKY	Rusalka
	Billy Budd		The Stone Guest
	The Burning Fiery Furnace	DAUVERGNE	La Coquette Trompée
	Curlew River	DEBUSSY	La Chûte de la Maison
	Death in Venice		Usher
	The Little Sweep		Pelléas et Mélisande
	A Midsummer Night's	DELIBES	Lakmé
	Dream	DELIUS	Fennimore and Gerda
	Noye's Fludde		Irmelin
	Owen Wingrave		Koanga
	Paul Bunyan		The Magic Fountain
	Peter Grimes		Margot la Rouge
	The Prodigal Son		A Village Romeo and Juliet
	The Rape of Lucretia	DESSAU	Puntila
	The Turn of the Screw		Verurteilung des Lukullus
BUSONI	Arlecchino	DITTERSDORF	Doktor und Apotheker
	Doktor Faust	DONIZETTI	L'Aio nell'Imbarazzo
CAMPRA	L'Europe Galante		Anna Bolena
CATALANI	La Wally		L'Assedio di Calais
CAVALLI	La Calisto		Il Campanello
	L'Egisto		Don Pasquale
	Ercole Amante		L'Elisir d'Amore
	Giasone		Emilia di Liverpool
	L'Ormindo		La Favorite
	Serse		La Fille du Régiment
			Gabriella di Vergy
CESTI	Orontea		Gemma di Vergy
CHABRIER	Une Education Manquée		Linda di Chamounix
	L'Etoile		Lucia di Lammermoor
	Le Roi Malgré Lui		Lucrezia Borgia
CHAPÍ	El Barquillero		Maria Padilla
	El Punao de Rosas		Maria de Rudenz
	La Revoltosa		Maria Stuarda
	La Tempestad		Ne M'Oubliez-Pas
CHARPENTIER	Louise		Rita
M. CHARPENTIER	Actéon		Roberto Devereux
	David et Jonathas		Ugo Conte di Parigi
	Médée	DUKAS	Ariane et Barbe-Bleue
CHAUSSON	Le Roi Arthus	DVOŘÁK	The Devil and Kate
CHERUBINI	Médée		Dimitrij (Exc)
CHUECCA	Agua		Jakobín
	La Gran Via		Rusalka
CIKKER	Coriolanus		Vanda
CILEA	Adriana Lecouvreur	EGK	Die Zaubergeige (Exc)
	L'Arlesiana	EINEM	Dantons Tod
CIMAROSA	Il Maestro di Cappella	ELSNER	The Echo in the Wood
	Il Matrimonio Segreto		King Loketiek
	Il Pittor Parigino	ERKEL	Bánk Bán
COPLAND	The Tender Land		László Hunyadi
CORNELIUS	Der Barbier von Bagdad	DE FALLA	L'Atlántida
CROSSE	Purgatory		El Retablo de Maese Pedro
DALLAPICCOLA	Il Prigioniero		La Vida Breve
DANKEVICH	Bogdan Kmelnitsky	FAURÉ	Pénélope

FERNÁNDEZ	*El Dúo de la Africana*
	Gigantes y Cabezudos
	La Viejecita
FIBICH	*The Bride From Messina* (Exc)
	Šárka
FIORAVANTI	*Le Cantatrici Villane* (Exc)
FLOTOW	*Martha*
FOERSTER	*Eva*
FRANÇAIX	*Le Diable Boiteux*
FRUMERIE	*Singoalla*
GADE	*Fairy Spell*
GAGLIANO	*La Dafne*
GALUPPI	*Il Filosofo di Campagna*
GANNÉ	*Hans le Joueur de Flûte* (Exc)
	Les Saltimbanques
GERMAN	*Merrie England*
GERSHWIN	*Porgy and Bess*
GIANNINI	*The Taming of the Shrew*
GIORDANO	*Andrea Chénier*
	Fedora
	Mese Mariano
GLASS	*Akhnaten*
GLINKA	*A Life for the Tsar*
	Ruslan and Ludmila
GLUCK	*Alceste*
	Armide
	Le Cadi Dupé
	Le Cinesi
	La Corona
	La Danza
	Echo et Narcisse
	Iphigénie en Aulide
	Iphigénie en Tauride
	Orfeo ed Euridice
	Paride ed Elena
GOLDMARK	*Die Königin von Saba*
GOOSSENS	*Judith*
GOTOVAC	*Ero the Joker*
GÖTZ	*Der Widerspenstigen Zähmung*
GOUNOD	*Faust*
	Mireille
	Roméo et Juliette
GRANADOS	*Goyescas*
GRAUN	*Montezuma* (Exc)
GRÉTRY	*L'Amant Jaloux*
	Le Jugement de Midas (Exc)
	Lucile
	Richard Coeur de Lion
	Zémire et Azor
GRIEG	*Olav Trygvason*
GUERRERO	*La Alsaciana*
	Los Gavilanes
GURIDI	*El Caserío*
HÁBA	*The Mother*
HAHN	*Ciboulette*
HALÉVY	*La Juive* (Exc)
HANDEL	*Acis and Galatea*
	Admeto
	Alcina
	Alessandro
	Ariodante
	Atalanta
	Athalia
	Belshazzar
	Esther
	Giulio Cesare
	Hercules
	Orlando
	Partenope
	Il Pastor Fido
	Poro
	Rinaldo
	Rodelinda
	Samson
	Saul
	Semele
	Serse
	Sosarme
	Tamerlano
HASSE	*Cleofide*
HAYDN	*Armida*
	La Fedeltà Premiata
	L'Incontro Improvviso
	L'Infedeltà Delusa
	L'Isola Disabitata
	Il Mondo della Luna
	Orfeo ed Euridice
	Orlando Paladino
	Lo Speziale
	La Vera Costanza
HEISE	*King and Marshal*
HENZE	*Elegie für Junge Liebende* (Exc)
	Der Junge Lord
HERRMANN	*Wuthering Heights*
HINDEMITH	*Cardillac*
	Mathis der Maler
HOLST	*At the Boar's Head*
	Sāvitri
	The Wandering Scholar
HONEGGER	*Jeanne d'Arc au Bûcher*
	Le Roi David
HOPKINS	*Three's Company*

HUMPERDINCK	Hänsel und Gretel	LULLY	Alceste
	Die Königskinder		Armide et Renaud (Exc)
JANÁČEK	The Cunning Little Vixen		Atys
	The Excursions of Mr		Le Bourgeois Gentilhomme
	Brouček		Isis (Exc)
	Fate		Thésée (Exc)
	From the House of the	LUNA	Los Cadetes de la Reina
	Dead		Los Molinos de Viento
	Jenůfa	LYSENKO	Natalka Poltavka
	Káťa Kabanová		Taras Bulba
	The Macropolus Case	MAGNARD	Guercoeur
JOPLIN	Treemonisha	MARTIN	Le Vin Herbé
KABALEVSKY	The Master of Clamecy	MARTINŮ	Alexandre Bis
KÁLMÁN	Die Csárdásfürstin		Comedy on the Bridge
	Gräfin Mariza		The Greek Passion
	Die Zirkusprinzessin (Exc)		Julietta
KALOMIRIS	The Mother's Ring		The Miracle of Our Lady
KIENZL	Der Evangeliman	MASCAGNI	L'Amico Fritz
KNUSSEN	Where the Wild Things Are		Cavalleria Rusticana
KODÁLY	Háry János		Iris
	The Spinning Room		Isabeau (Exc)
KOKKONEN	The Last Temptations	MASSANA	Canigó
KOVAŘOVIC	The Dogheads (Exc)	MASSENET	Cendrillon
KŘENEK	Jonny Spielt Auf		Don Quichotte
KREUTZER	Das Nachtlager von		Esclarmonde
	Granada		Hérodiade (Exc)
LALO	Le Roi d'Ys		Le Jongleur de Notre-Dame
LANDOWSKI	Le Fou		Manon
	Le Ventriloque		La Navarraise
LECLAIR	Scylla et Glaucus		Le Roi de Lahore
LECOCQ	La Fille de Madame Angot		Sapho
	Le Petit Duc (Exc)		Thaïs
LEHÁR	Friederike		Thérèse
	Giuditta		Werther
	Der Graf von Luxembourg	MAYR	Medea in Corinto
	Das Land des Lächelns	MEALE	Voss
	Die Lustige Witwe	MENDELSSOHN	Die Beiden Pädagogen
	Paganini		Die Heimkehr aus der
	Der Zarewitsch	MENOTTI	Fremde
	Zigeunerliebe		Amahl and the Night
LEONCAVALLO	La Bohème		Visitors
	Pagliacci		Amelia al Ballo
	Zazà		The Boy Who Grew Too
LEONI	L'Oracolo		Fast
LESUR	Andrea del Sarto		The Consul
LIGETI	Le Grand Macabre (Exc)		The Medium
LISZT	Don Sanche		The Saint of Bleecker Street
LORTZING	Die Opernprobe	MERCADANTE	The Telephone
	Undine	MERIKANTO	Il Bravo
	Der Waffenschmied	MESSAGER	Juha
	Der Wildschütz		La Basoche (Exc)
	Zar und Zimmermann		Fortunio
			Monsieur Beaucaire (Exc)

MESSAGER	Les P'tites Michu (Exc)	MOZART	Il Sogno di Scipione
	Véronique		Lo Sposo Deluso
MESSIAEN	St François d'Assise		Zaïde
MEYERBEER	Dinorah		Die Zauberflöte
	Les Huguenots	MUSGRAVE	A Christmas Carol
	Le Prophète		Mary Queen of Scots
MILHAUD	Les Choëphores	NÁPRAVNÍK	Dubrovsky
	Les Malheurs d'Orphée	NICOLAÏ	Die Lustigen Weiber von
	Le Pauvre Matelot		Windsor
MILLÖCKER	Der Bettelstudent	NIELSEN	Maskarade
	Gasparone		Saul and David
MONIUSZKO	Halka	NOVÁK	The Lantern
	The Haunted Manor	OFFENBACH	Barbe-Bleue
	Hrabina (Exc)		Les Bavards
	The Raftsman		La Belle Hélène
	Verum Nobile		Les Brigands
MONCKTON AND	The Arcadians (Exc)		Christopher Columbus
TALBOT			Les Contes d'Hoffmann
MONTEMEZZI	L'Amore dei Tre Re		La Fille du Tambour-Major
MONTEVERDI	Il Ballo delle Ingrate		(Exc)
	Il Combattimento di		La Grande-Duchesse de
	Tancredi e Clorinda		Gérolstein
	La Favola d'Orfeo		Mesdames de la Halle
	L'Incoronazione di Poppea		Monsieur Choufleuri
	Il Ritorno d'Ulisse in Patria		Chez-Lui
MOORE	The Ballad of Baby Doe		Orphée aux Enfers
	Carry Nation		La Périchole
	The Devil and Daniel		Pomme d'Api
	Webster		Robinson Crusoé
MOUSSORGSKY	Boris Godunov		La Vie Parisienne
	Khovanschina	ORFF	Antigonae
	The Marriage		Die Bernauerin
	Salammbô		Die Kluge
	Sorochintsy Fair		Der Mond
MOZART	Apollo et Hyacinthus		Oedipus der Tyrann
	Ascanio in Alba		De Temporum Fine
	Bastien und Bastienne		Comoedia
	La Clemenza di Tito		Trionfo d'Afrodite
	Così fan Tutte	PAER	Leonora
	Don Giovanni		Le Maître de Chapelle
	Die Entführung aus dem	PAISIELLO	Il Barbiere di Siviglia
	Serail		Il Duello
	La Finta Giardiniera		Nina
	La Finta Semplice	PALIASHVILI	Absolom and Etery
	Idomeneo	PARRY	Blodwen (Exc)
	Lucio Silla	PASHKEVICH	The Miser
	Mitridate Rè di Ponto	PAUER	Zdravý Nemocný (Exc)
	Le Nozze di Figaro		Zuzaná Vojířová
	Il Re Pastore	PENDERECKI	The Devils of Loudun
	Der Schauspieldirektor	PEPUSCH	The Beggar's Opera
	Die Schuldigkeit des Ersten	PERGOLESI	La Contadina Astuta
	Gebotes		Il Geloso Schernito

PERGOLESI	Il Maestro di Musica	RAMEAU	La Princesse de Navarre
	La Serva Padrona		(Exc)
PERI	Euridice		Pygmalion
PETROVICS	C'Est la Guerre		Zoroastre
	Crime and Punishment	RAVEL	L'Enfant et les Sortilèges
	Lysistrate		L'Heure Espagnole
PFITZNER	Palestrina	REIMANN	Lear
PLANQUETTE	Les Cloches de Corneville		Troades
	Rip (Exc)	RESPIGHI	La Fiamma
PONCHIELLI	La Gioconda	RIMSKY-KORSAKOV	The Golden Cockerel
POULENC	Dialogues des Carmélites		The Invisible City of Kitezh
	Les Mamelles de Tirésias		Kaschey the Immortal
	La Voix Humaine		May Night
PROKOFIEV	Betrothal in a Monastery		Mozart and Salieri
	The Fiery Angel		Sadko
	The Gambler		The Snow Maiden
	The Love of Three Oranges		The Tale of Tsar Sultan
	Maddalena		The Tsar's Bride
	Semeon Kotko	RINALDO DI CAPUA	La Zingara
	The Story of a Real Man	ROMBERG	The Student Prince
	War and Peace	ROSSINI	Il Barbiere di Siviglia
PUCCINI	La Bohème		La Cambiale di Matrimonio
	Edgar		La Cenerentola
	La Fanciulla del West		Le Comte Ory
	Gianni Schicchi		La Donna del Lago
	Madama Butterfly		Elisabetta Regina
	Manon Lescaut		d'Inghilterra
	La Rondine		Ermione
	Suor Angelica		La Gazza Ladra
	Il Tabarro		Guillaume Tell
	Tosca		L'Italiana in Algieri
	Turandot		Maometto II
	Le Villi		Mosè in Egitto
PURCELL	Dido and Aeneas		Otello
	The Faery Queen		La Pietra del Paragone
	The Indian Queen		La Scala di Seta
	King Arthur		Semiramide
	The Prophetess (Exc)		Le Siège de Corinthe
	The Tempest		Il Signor Bruschino
RABAUD	Mârouf		Tancredi
RACHMANINOV	Aleko		Il Turco in Italia
	The Covetous Knight		Il Viaggio a Reims
	Francesca da Rimini	ROTA	Il Cappello di Paglia di
RAMEAU	Anacréon		Firenze
	Les Boréades	ROUSSEAU	Le Devin du Village
	Castor et Pollux	ROUSSEL	Padmâvatî
	Dardanus	RUBINSTEIN	The Demon
	Les Fêtes d'Hébé (Exc)	RUDZIŃSKI	The Dismissal of the Greek
	Hippolyte et Aricie		Envoys
	Les Indes Galantes	SAINT-SAËNS	Samson et Dalila
	Naïs	SALIERI	Falstaff
	Les Paladins (Exc)		Prima la Musica e Poi le
	Platée		Parole

SALLINEN	The Horseman	STRAUSS	Ariadne auf Naxos
	The Red Line		Capriccio
SATIE	Socrate		Daphne
A. SCARLATTI	Il Trionfo dell'Onore		Elektra
SCHAT	Houdini		Feuersnot
SCHMIDT	Notre Dame		Die Frau ohne Schatten
SCHOECK	Massamila Doni		Guntram
	Penthesilea		Intermezzo
	Vom Fischer und Syner Fru		Die Liebe der Danae
SCHÖNBERG	Erwartung		Der Rosenkavalier
	Die Glückliche Hand		Salome
	Moses und Aron		Die Schweigsame Frau
	Von Heute Auf Morgen	STRAVINSKY	Mavra
SCHUBERT	Alfonso und Estrella		The Nightingale
	Fernando		Oedipus Rex
	Die Freunde von Salamanka		The Rake's Progress
	Der Spiegelritter		Renard
	Die Verschworenen	SUCHOŇ	Krutňavá
	Die Vierjährige Posten		Svätopluk
	Die Zwillingsbruder	SUDER	Kleider Machen Leute
SCHUMANN	Genoveva	SULLIVAN	Cox and Box
SEROV	Rogneda (Exc)		The Gondoliers
SERRANO	La Canción del Olvido		The Grand Duke
	Los de Aragon		H.M.S. Pinafore
	La Reina Mora		Iolanthe
SHAPORIN	The Decembrists		The Mikado
SHCHEDRIN	Dead Souls		Patience
SHIELD	Rosina		The Pirates of Penzance
SHOSTAKOVICH	The Gamblers		Princess Ida
	Lady Macbeth of Mtsensk		Ruddigore
	The Nose		The Sorcerer
SIBELIUS	The Maiden in the Tower		Trial By Jury
SMETANA	The Bartered Bride		Utopia Limited
	The Brandenburgers in		The Yeomen of the Guard
	Bohemia		The Zoo
	Dalibor	SUPPÉ	Boccaccio
	The Devil's Wall		Die Schöne Galatea
	The Kiss	SZOKOLAY	Blood Wedding
	Libuše		Samson
	The Secret	SZYMANOWSKI	King Roger
	The Two Widows	TANEYEV	Oresteia
	Viola	TCHAIKOVSKY	The Enchantress
SOUTULLO	La del Soto del Parral		Eugene Onegin
SPONTINI	Olympie		Iolanta
	La Vestale		The Little Slippers
STOCKHAUSEN	Donnerstag aus Licht		The Maid of Orleans
O. STRAUS	Ein Walzertraum		Mazeppa
J. STRAUSS	Die Fledermaus		The Oprichnik
	Eine Nacht in Venedig		The Queen of Spades
	Wiener Blut		The Voyevoda (Exc)
	Der Zigeunerbaron	TELEMANN	Der Geduldige Socrates
STRAUSS	Die Ägyptische Helena		Pimpinone
	Arabella		

THOMAS	Hamlet	VIVALDI	Orlando Furioso
	Mignon		La Senna Festeggiante
THOMSON	Four Saints in Three Acts		Tito Manlio
	The Mother of Us All	VIVES	Bohemios
TIPPETT	King Priam		Doña Francisquita
	The Knot Garden		Maruxa
	The Midsummer Marriage	WAGNER	Die Feen
TORROBA	Luisa Fernánda		Der Fliegende Holländer
USANDIZAGA	Los Golondrinas		Götterdämmerung
VARNEY	Les Mousquetaires au		Lohengrin
	Couvent		Die Meistersinger von
VAUGHAN			Nürnberg
WILLIAMS	Hugh the Drover		Parsifal
	The Pilgrim's Progress		Das Rheingold
	Riders to the Sea		Rienzi
	Sir John in Love		Siegfried
VERDI	Aida		Tannhäuser
	Alzira		Tristan und Isolde
	Aroldo		Die Walküre
	Attila	WALTON	The Bear
	Un Ballo in Maschera		Troilus and Cressida
	La Battaglia di Legnano	WARD	The Crucible
	Il Corsaro	WEBER	Abu Hassan
	Don Carlos		Die Drei Pintos
	I Due Foscari		Euryanthe
	Ernani		Der Freischütz
	Falstaff		Oberon
	La Forza del Destino	WEILL	Aufstieg und Fall der Stadt
	Un Giorno di Regno		Mahoganny
	Giovanna d'Arco		Die Dreigroschenoper
	I Lombardi		Happy End
	Luisa Miller		Der Protagonist
	Macbeth		Der Silbersee
	I Masnadieri	WEINBERGER	Shvanda the Bagpiper
	Nabucco	WILLIAMSON	All the King's Men
	Oberto		Julius Caesar Jones
	Otello	WOLF	Der Corregidor
	Rigoletto	WOLF-FERRARI	I Quatro Rusteghi
	Simon Boccanegra		Il Segreto di Susanna
	Stiffelio	ZANDONAI	Conchita
	La Traviata		Francesca da Rimini
	Il Trovatore		Giulietta e Romeo
	Les Vêpres Siciliennes	ZELLER	Der Vogelhändler
VIVALDI	Catone in Utica	ZEMLINSKY	Eine Florentinische Tragödie
	La Fida Ninfa		Der Geburtstag der Infantin
	L'Incoronazione di Dario		Die Traumgörge
	L'Olimpiade	ZIMMERMANN	Die Soldaten